RECOMMENDATIONS.

Rev. N. TIBBALS—Dear Brother,

Logan's sermons are among the most elegant in the English language. It was many years after I had seen a copy before I could purchase one. They were out of print. When I obtained one I felt as if I had found a jewel. I read it and re-read it—the more I read it the more I was delighted. His Lectures also are original and full of instruction. I have read many volumes of sermons, but never have derived more pleasure or profit than from the perusal of the eloquent discourses of this distinguished Scotch divine.

Robert Walker's Sermons are much better known to the fathers in the ministry than to their junior brethren. The fathers could obtain them, the latter could not, for they were out of print. The sermons are commended by some of the ablest divines in England and America, and need not my feeble tribute of praise. The lovers of genius and eloquence, the friends of morality and virtue, will thank you for republishing them, and the Christian public will sustain you in your highly approved enterprise.

J. B. WAKELEY,
Pastor of Jane Street M. E. Church.

New-York, *Sept.* 24*th*, 1854.

Pittsfield, *Sept.* 5, 1854.

Rev. N. TIBBALS, *Astoria, L. I.*

My Dear Sir,—I am glad to learn that the Ministers' Association in New York think of republishing some of the genuine old Scotch theologians, particularly the writings of John Logan and Robert Walker. These are wells of pure and cooling waters, refreshing and purifying to those who draw faithfully from them. And a pleasant though [illegible] rely, that as fashions and tastes change, they wheel in a circle, and that the same unsatisfied desires which are setting aside the light, frail, and fragile chairs and tables of our day, and are calling back the strong oaken furniture of past generations, begin also to turn from the light, small-idea books of the present day, and call for the solid oaken thoughts of other days. I hope the willow-age is going by and a more solid one returning. Every such valuable old writer that can be made to live again should be, and thus, in the cycle of ages may it not be that great and good men who are dead will often be reproduced and still prophesy before many people. My best wishes for your success.

Yours truly, JOHN TODD.

Hartford, *Aug.* 31*st*, 1854.

Rev. N. TIBBALS—Dear Sir,

The sermons of Rev. Robert Walker, in two volumes, I regard as among the best in the language. Thoroughly evangelical in doctrine; deeply imbued with the spirit and phraseology of the scriptures; logical in arrangement; perspicuous in style, and faithful in application,—they may be recommended as models of correct sermonizing to young ministers, and to all as replete with Biblical instruction, and of excellent use for general religious reading.

The volume of Logan which it is proposed to publish with those of Walker, differs somewhat from them in character. The author had more genius, and more eloquence; wrote in a vivid style, and abounds more in striking illustrations, but did not perhaps deal so closely with the heart and conscience. Yet many of his sermons are of great excellence,—rich in thought and clear in style and arrangement; and cannot be read or heard without leaving a deep and useful impression on the mind.

J. HAWES.

The sermons of Robert Walker of Edinburgh have long and justly enjoyed a very high reputation, as presenting earnestly the distinctive doctrines of the gospel, in a lucid, manly and forcible style, and with a devout and earnest spirit. Though the colleague of Blair, and personally his friend, he did not belong to that moderate party, as they styled themselves, whom Robertson and Blair headed, whom Witherspoon satirized, and whom Chalmers and the men of the Free Church finally outweighed and outnumbered. WALKER was of the section recognized as the Evangelical, and his sermons have by some theological professors been recommended as among the safest and best models of evangelical preaching. They are not in the least liable to the imputation, which John Foster brought against the once fashionable discourses of Blair, that the author's thoughts seemed to have "*become cooled and stiffened to numbness in waiting so long to be dressed.*" They are grave utterances, in simple, warm and becoming vesture, of words that the Christian would be first to suggest, and which the mere critic could not cavil at. WM. R. WILLIAMS.

NEW YORK, 11*th Oct.* 1854.

I am gratified to learn that a new edition of WALKER's Sermons is nearly ready for the public use. Few preachers combined so many excellences of thought, method, and style; and I have never hesitated to recommend his sermons, as among the very best models for young ministers. They possess, in a high degree, the faultless beauty of his colleague Blair, along with a directness and evangelical fervor, which the published sermons of the latter lack.

ALEXR. T. McGILL,

Professor of Pastoral Theology, Church Government, Composition and Delivery of Sermons.

PRINCETON, *Oct.* 13, 1854.

I have been familiar with the sermons of ROBERT WALKER during the greater part of my life, and have no hesitation in saying that, for perspicuity and purity of style, natural and simple arrangement, evangelical fervor, and an effective exhibition of scriptural truth, I regard them as deserving a place in the very first rank of sermons in the English language.

I have been accustomed from early life to read LOGAN's Sermons, particularly as the effusions of a beautiful and highly gifted mind. They are by no means wanting in evangelical sentiment, or in fervent and impressive appeals; but as specimens of polished and graceful composition, I think the Scotch pulpit has rarely, if ever, furnished any thing superior. H. B. SPRAGUE.

ALBANY, *Sept.* 15, 1854.

NEW HAVEN, *Oct.* 23*d*, 1854.

REV. N. TIBBALS—DEAR BROTHER,

The sermons of Rev. ROBERT WALKER, I have long held in high esteem. While beautifully elucidating the leading doctrines of Christianity, their tendency is highly practical. These sermons are pervaded by a fervor indicating the deep piety of their author and consoling and animating to the heart of the reader. They comprise a series of excellent religious reading, and a most admirable Sabbath companion for any Christian. J. KENNADAY.

SERMONS

ON

PRACTICAL SUBJECTS.

BY

ROBERT WALKER,

LATE ONE OF THE MINISTERS OF THE HIGH CHURCH OF EDINBURGH, SCOTLAND.

WITH AN INTRODUCTION, BY REV. G. B. CHEEVER, D. D.

EDITED BY

"THE MINISTER'S LIBRARY ASSOCIATION."

SECOND AMERICAN EDITION.

THREE VOLS. COMPLETE IN ONE.

NEW YORK:

D. APPLETON AND COMPANY, 346 & 348 BROADWAY.

M.DCCC.LV.

CONTENTS.

INTRODUCTION.

By REV. G. B. CHEEVER, D. D.

The eminent author of the following discourses was at the time of his death, and had been for near thirty years, pastor over the High Church of Edinburgh. For nearly twenty-five years he was colleague with the celebrated Dr. Blair. He died on the 4th of April, 1783, immediately after preaching in the morning, in apparently his usual health. On the occasion of his death, Dr. Blair preached a sermon, in which he described the features of his character such as he had known him almost from childhood, as the friend and companion of his youth, and in the long period of a co-partnership of almost a quarter of a century. Dr. Walker's own father had been a minister of the Canongate, and he himself received his education at the University in Edinburgh, but was first ordained in 1738, at Straiton, in the presbytery of Ayr. In 1746, he was called from that place to South Leith; and from thence, in 1754, to the church in Edinburgh, where he preached the gospel faithfully, even till the day of his translation to the inheritance of the saints in light. Dr. Blair appealed to the hearts and consciences of the congregation as witnesses of his ability, assiduity and fidelity in the ministry of the gospel. "There, indeed, he appeared in his highest character as an eminent and successful laborer in the Lord's vineyard. To this important work his greatest application was bent. With this he allowed nothing else to interfere. His whole ambition centred in acting his part with the dignity and propriety that became the sacred character which he bore. By the elegance, neatness, and chaste simplicity of composition in his sermons, and by the uncommon grace and energy of his delivery, he rose to a high and justly acquired reputation. But mere reputation was not his object. He aimed at testifying the whole counsel of the grace of God; at rightly dividing to every man the word of truth; instructing the ignorant, awakening the careless, reproving the sinner, and comforting the saint."

Dr. Blair here refers his great reputation to the "elegance, neatness, and chaste simplicity of composition in his sermons, and the uncommon grace and energy" with which he delivered them. But if mere elegance, neatness, and chaste simplicity had constituted the grand qualities of his eloquence, and the groundwork for his energy in the pulpit, he could never thus have gained the hold which he possessed upon the minds and hearts of the people, or the permanent reputation that followed him. The richness, completeness and fervor with which the distinguishing doctrines of the gospel are presented in his sermons, accounts both for his popularity and his power. He preached what he had received by the Holy Spirit from the Lord Jesus. His sermons are remarkable for a natural and simple arrangement of the truths contained in the text, developed and illustrated from the Scriptures themselves, and presented and applied with solemn thought and earnest and affectionate feeling. Dr. Blair said truly, that he aimed at testifying the whole counsel of the grace of God, and this sincere and single-hearted purpose rendered him, *by* the grace of God, successful.

He aimed to preach the Word. He aimed at the heart *with* the Word. He did this by the Spirit of God, and not by philosophy. His method is that of the letter by the Spirit; not of the letter merely, which killeth, but of the Spirit, which giveth life. Now, to gain this method of the Spirit, and to preach by the Spirit, required a discipline and learning in the deep things of God, which all the schools could not give; and bestowed also a power, which all the elegance, taste, refinement and philosophy of all ages could not supply. Philosophy may spoil the gospel, but cannot preach the gospel. Our own age, in some directions, is witnessing the process of the gospel being divided, subtilized, and emasculated by philosophy. The Scotch divines have afforded some admirable examples of excellence in the very contrary direction; examples of just and powerful analysis, yet of simple acceptance of the Word of God from God, and of humble and entire reliance upon it as his Word; and a consequent proclamation of its doctrines, not because human philosophy, or the best philosophy, having put them into its crucible, sanctions them, and re-coins them, and so sends them forth under patronage, but because they are from God, and the preaching of them commends itself to every man's *conscience*, and not to his philosophic understanding, or his Kantian Analysis, first or merely, in the sight of God.

We are also witnessing a period of subtle *historical* research and analysis, by which courts of judgment are instituted, to try not merely the claims of particular churches, but the Holy Scriptures themselves and their doctrines, as suspected rogues and criminals, who must be brought to the bar, and if not cleared by historical philosophy, are to be imprisoned or outlawed. The spirit of unbelief applies to these tribunals for an injunction on the work of the Scriptures, which are fast running their highway triumphantly through every man's private grounds, and across every man's authority. The injunction is readily issued, and in every age under new pretences. Wait, it says, till by the demonstration of an organic historic life your scriptural lights can be proved to possess authority. And so from time to time Christianity must suspend its progress, and go back to settle the authenticity of its claims according to the rudiments of the world, after the traditions of men, and not after Christ.

The life of God's Word must be felt, otherwise it cannot be proved, and we know nothing of it. The grand high-priests of truth in all ages have been those who have received the truth from God, and according to his own direction for the prophet Ezekiel, (Ezek. ii. 8,) have *eaten* it. They have fed upon it, as the Bread of Life, and have grown thereby. They have gathered it for themselves, as the Israelites of old had to gather their manna, daily, every morning, for themselves, in their own vessels. *Give us this day our daily bread;* that is the rule of life and knowledge in God's Word. God himself gives it, as directly, as renewedly, as he gave the manna to his people in the wilderness; so must men receive it immediately from God, not man. Every morning the divine miraculous gift of bread lay fresh around the camp, covering the ground like hoar-frost; like masses of pearls, glittering in the sand, new and beautiful. Every morning they gathered it afresh, every day were nourished by it. It was a lively, illustrative, impressive image of the nature of the Word of God as the bread of the soul, and the part each man must play in availing himself of it.

"Thy words were found," says Jeremiah, "and I did eat them; and thy word was unto me the joy and rejoicing of my heart." When it is thus received into the life, it becomes a constraining, overcoming, aggressive life and impulse; it can neither be concealed nor restrained, but must have vent. When Jeremiah found that it exposed him, as the bearer of it, the preacher of it, to mockery and derision, while hardened hearts seemed only to grow harder and more rebellious under it, he thought he would try the experiment of silence. He said within himself, "I will not make mention of the Lord, nor speak any more in his name, because the word of the Lord is made a reproach unto me, and a derision, daily." But this would not do; the burden of revelation, the sense of God's truth, was too mighty for Jeremiah's silence; the rapids of Niagara might as well say, "We will not go over the falls." And Jeremiah describes the result of his experiment: "The Lord's word was in my heart as a burning fire shut up in my bones, and I was weary with forbearing, and I could not stay. And the Lord was with me, as a mighty terrible one." And God himself says: "The prophet that hath a dream, let him tell a dream; and he that hath my word, let him speak my word faithfully. What is the chaff to the wheat, saith the Lord? Is not my word like as a fire, saith the Lord, and like a hammer that breaketh the rock in pieces?"

Baptized with the Holy Ghost and with fire, the early preachers of Christ and him crucified understood the secret of their power, and acted accordingly. "We," said the apostles, "will give ourselves continually to prayer, and to the ministry of the Word." Let a set of ministers be found now to do the same thing, in the same way; let them be wholly given to the Word of God and to prayer, and there cannot be a doubt that the same results would widely follow their ministrations as of old. This *eating of the Word* by prayer, by the Divine Spirit in the heart, is the source of true power. There was never a truer maxim than that of Luther, *Bene orasse est bene studuisse.* He that has prayed well, has studied well; this habit, in and with the Word, is the very spirit of love and of power, and of a sound mind.

Perhaps, therefore, amidst the vast and ever increasing array of the *apparatus* and external paraphernalia of theological study, this sole source of life and power is more and more in danger of being neglected. The temptation of Satan is upon us, under the guise of philosophy and vain deceit; and many other things entering in, choke the Word. They may be good things in their place, but if they take the place of the Word, they become bad things. Saul's armor was a good thing for him; but David's shepherd's sling and five smooth pebbles from the brook were better for him. There be many who work upon the Word of God very much as Saul's armorers or smiths hammered upon his helmet of brass, and his coat of mail; and perhaps not a whit more spiritual in the first work than the last; the Christian armor cannot be so wrought, nor the life, nor the power of the Word so possessed or understood. The Word of God must be *eaten,* must be an inward nourishment and life, must be received from God in prayer. All that have ever done much with the Word, ever proved its overcoming power, have thus learned it. The giants of theology, the princes of epochs, forming, ruling, life-renewing epochs, have been these eaters of the Word. Such men, taught of God, stand high above the herd of students of the mere letter, philologers and philosophers, German or English, and the rabble of undistinguished critics, writers, ministers, who have got their knowledge of religion at second-hand. It is nothing but prayer, and deep spiritual life, that makes men truly original and mighty in the Scriptures. Men may *speculate* with the understanding merely, but they cannot *know.* Yet only thus are they fit to be teachers and laborers for the advancement of the kingdom of the Redeemer. Knowledge *puffeth* up, but love *buildeth* up, says the apostle; a most pithy and striking contrast of the two systems of speculative knowledge by the understanding merely, or human tradition, —and knowledge as life, knowledge original, by the Spirit. An incredible quantity of theological speculation is speculation without life, that like cold ashes, puts out a fire, but cannot kindle.

We are doubtless in danger of giving more heed to books, reviews, philosophies, and the latest methods, or scientific concoctions of fact and thought, than we do to the Word of God and prayer. The intellect has the greater part of our attention, and that, too, in an almost servile dependence upon others; and therefore we are weak. The apostle John said of the young men to whom he wrote, "Ye are strong, and the Word of God abideth in you." That is the true originality and independence. We need to get *what* we get from God, and not man, and to use men's books as a carpenter does his saws. But the stuff we must get out for ourselves. Nay, rather, our work is with living plants, and not dead stuff, cut, squared, and polished to our hand. We are reminded of what Lord Bacon said in his day, that "the delivery of knowledge, as it is now used, is as of fair trees without the roots, good for the carpenter, but not for the planter." But none of our knowledge of divine things ought to be without roots, or cut and dried for us at second-hand by others; it ought to be all a life-knowledge—knowledge rooted in Christ, by ourselves being rooted in him, and receiving knowledge from him in the way of life. That makes all things fresh and original.

"HOLD FAST THE FORM OF SOUND WORDS, WHICH THOU HAST HEARD OF ME, IN FAITH AND LOVE WHICH IS IN CHRIST JESUS. THAT GOOD THING WHICH WAS COMMITTED UNTO THEE, KEEP BY THE HOLY GHOST, WHICH DWELLETH IN US." Grand, profound, comprehensive rule of independence and of life! Not by tradition, nor creeds, nor councils, nor the church, nor history, nor apostolical, nor historical succession, but by the Holy Ghost, nothing else; dependence only on the Holy Ghost, and on the truth, as the Holy Ghost reveals it in God's Word, and keeps it in the heart. *Sanctify them by thy truth; thy word is truth.* Moreover, keep it by the Holy Ghost,—not which dwelleth in the church, but *in us*, as individuals; private judgment of the Scriptures, in entire dependence on the Spirit of God, not on the Church of God. The Holy Ghost must keep the church, or the church cannot keep the truth; and the Holy Ghost can keep the church only by keeping individual believers in Christ Jesus; and can teach the truth to the church, and keep the truth in the church, and sanctify the church by it, only by teaching the truth to individuals, and keeping the truth in individuals, and sanctifying individuals by it. And just so, the Holy Ghost increases and builds up the church, not by successional or organic life in history, but by bringing in continually new living stones into the temple, new regenerated souls into the church, through the door of the church, which is Christ.

The truth is to be kept by the Holy Ghost, and the form of sound words is to be held fast in faith and love, which is in Christ Jesus. Without this, it may be kept in creeds and councils, and denied in spirit; it may be kept as the source of power, and yet withheld and darkened on purpose to maintain exclusive control of the power; it may be kept and affirmed as the key of the kingdom of heaven, only that its keepers may assume authority *over* that kingdom; a fact, in the light of which we should judge the apologies made in certain quarters for the iniquities of the papal church and the popes in consideration of their alleged merits in preserving orthodoxy. They kept it to keep their power *by it*, and corrupted it at their pleasure. They kept it *from* the world to keep their own dominion *over* the world, but not in faith and love in Christ Jesus,—not by the Holy Ghost dwelling in the heart. But it must be held thus, or it is held in unrighteousness; held as a savor of death, not of life; held unto condemnation, not justification. It may be also held and used for selfish and sectarian purposes; a thing which makes the ministers of Christ little better than the sons of Eli, that were sons of Belial, and knew not the Lord. The gospel itself in such hands, and for such purposes, becomes a thing, like those old priest's flesh-hooks, with sectarian teeth; for they struck the flesh-hook with their teeth into the pan, or kettle, or caldron, or pot, and all that the flesh-hook brought up, the priest took for himself. Such is genuine sectarianism, but not such the truth, kept by the Holy Ghost dwelling in the heart, and held fast in faith and love in Christ Jesus.

To be kept by the Holy Spirit, it must be *received* by the Holy Spirit. "Thou hast known the Holy Scriptures, which are able to make thee wise unto salvation, *through faith which is in Christ Jesus.*" The *knowledge* is not enough, unless it be received by faith, and so become wisdom unto salvation; otherwise, it is not life, and cannot give life, any more than a plant could experience or diffuse the virtue of the sunlight by merely reflecting it. If nature should withhold her active co-operation with the sun; if the leaves and flowers, the seeds, germs, and shoots, should only *look*, and not *receive;* should let the light fall on them, and return, unabsorbed, unacted on, not circulated within the veins, nor made part of the life-blood of the vegetable,—in that case, not life, but death would ensue from the very action of the sun; its rays would destroy the plant that might have fed upon them. And just so it is with the light of truth divine, if the heart refuse its co-operation, if it be entertained as a mere speculation. It must be received into a good, honest, believing, loving heart, in order to be understood and experienced as an element of life. Thus only do we purify our souls in obeying the truth through the Spirit, and thus only are we prepared for that for which the keeping of the Word by the Spirit is intended, namely, the preaching of the Word.

This then must be the source of our theology, THE WORD OF GOD, BY

THE SPIRIT OF GOD. Primitive granite, as to the material, cut by ourselves, as much as possible, and not boulders of pudding-stone, big and little, that have been bandied about by floods of philosophy, opinion, dogmatism, and taken where we found them. Divine doctrines themselves, subjected to such attrition in the great caldron of human philosophies, come out at length like blocks whirled in a cataract, all rounded and smoothed, as if turned upon a lathe, but unfit for any thing better than firewood. Blocks of granite itself may be thus rounded, and spoiled for building. The stones must be angular, and well defined, to lie plumb together, and make a strong, durable wall. An angular theology is better than mere pumiced and mortared work of rubble stone, that after a few rains, if a fox run over it, will crumble. "Now Tobiah the Ammonite was by him, and he said, Even that which they build, if a fox go up, he shall even break down their stone wall." The building with human materials, at second hand, a little here, a little there, now English, now German, now French, with mortar ground in mills of excruciating philosophy, under the care of uncircumcised Titans for speculative architects, must lead to such results, that the Sanballats and Tobiahs of a scoffing world may at length have good reason for their infidelity. It is impossible that men who have not themselves learned of God, can teach others; neither can those learned men teach us, whose theology, or history of the church, consists of speculation from a human philosophical standing point; neither is it good to be conversant with men, whose critical acumen is tasked and displayed in mooting objections; for all living theology is a theology of grand positives, that move on to victory by creating life, not analyzing death; rough, majestic, tangible positives, like moving mountains; not refinements, nor subtleties, nor silken theories that rise inflated like balloons.

Neither is it good to take those for teachers, whose views of divine inspiration lead them to trace the different aspects of divine doctrine mainly to different tendencies of mind, philosophy, learning, and preconceived opinion, in the instruments employed of God, instead of attributing all to the providence and grace of one and the self-same Spirit, dividing to each, and on purpose, the measures of wisdom and knowledge according to his will. Against that insidious tendency, after the tradition of men, after the rudiments of the world, and not after Christ, we need to be upon our guard; that root-growth from the stump of a worn-out rationalism, which, under the appearance of subtle investigation and distinction, divides revelation into Petrine, Pauline, Johannean and Jamesian peculiarities, assuming the divers colorings of truth to be of man first, and accidental, and thus lowering the independent authority of the Word of God. That dangerous tendency likewise to mould theology upon ecclesiastical history, instead of bringing ecclesiastical history before the tribunal of New Testament theology; and that wild, unscriptural, dreaming delusion, which sets up one apostle for the development of the Judaic Church, another for the development of the Romish Church, as if God had himself caused that vast corruption, as a providential and essential development of his own Church, giving it a guardian apostolic angel beforehand, and another for the Church of the Reformation, and yet another for the Church of the Future, which is to combine all, by a retro-active, all-digesting, all-assimilating, catholic sweep. All this is no better than philosophy and vain deceit, for we are not complete in Paul, or Peter, or James, or John, but in Christ; and neither one nor the other teach any one-sided or human peculiarity or excrescence, or any exclusive organic church-life, but all lead to one, and centre in one, Christ Jesus, from whom all proceeded, and in whom all are appointed for one and the same church in all ages.

Of national theologies, viewed through the whole two past centuries, the German development is far more one-sided than the English and Scotch; the German development is human-sided, the English, divine-sided; the German development submits to man and philosophy, the English to God and faith; the German development *holds* by philosophy, the English by the Holy Ghost; the German development is that of subtle speculative ingenuity, and opinion-learning, the English that of experimental piety and sound sense; the German development is occupied with the letter of the Word, and searches all things, yea, all *deep* things, *about* the Scriptures, the English with the Scriptures themselves, the pith and marrow of them; the German development fills the field of its operations, as the workmen fill a quarry with blocks and chips, the English raises the stones to a living temple in Christ, a habitation of God through the Spirit.

"Beware lest any man *spoil* you," is the direction of the apostle. There is great profoundness of meaning in the choice of this epithet. Philosophy in such a case does not pretend to reject the truth, but claims to be its exponent, its interpreter, and to add a grace to it, which simple believers in the pure simple word of God cannot possess. Philosophy takes an idea from Revelation, and dresses it up in philosophic garb, and by and by presents it as an original discovery from depths of science or of metaphysics which the Word of God never sounded; and there are not a few fools in every age, who will be caught and dazzled and deluded by such pretences; and some will receive from Pantheism and Atheism itself such plagiarisms, and will tell us of the obligations of Christianity to philosophy. It reminds us of the anecdote told by a traveller in the Oriental world, of a cunning servant, who, when his master had invited some English fellow-traveller on the Nile to dine with him, provided the dinner out of the other's boat, and regaled him with costly delicacies stolen from his own hampers. This is the game that philosophy has often played with Christianity, but always spoils the stolen viands in cooking them. Philosophy is a miserable preacher, always flattering men's own dignity and abstruseness, and cajoling them with high-flown ideas of the profoundness of their own faculties, but in the end setting them with their faces direct *from* Zion, instead of thitherward. Philosophy takes the doctrine of the divine decrees, and the divine all-ruling providence, and dresses it up as a theory of development, and a philosophy of history, apart from God, and then calls us to bow down, and wonder, and adore the march of intellect, and to bring all history, the history of Christianity itself, and even theology, to submit to the canons of this wonderful discovery. There is no end to the Jack-o-lantern pranks it will play, or the marshes across which its wild lights will send you dancing, or the bogs in which it will plunge your unwary steps, if you undertake to follow up its vagaries, or put your mind under its guidance. There are such vain and foolish teachers, vainly puffed up by their fleshly mind, and teaching after the elements of this world, and not after Christ, in regard to whom the only course that we can safely follow is that which our Lord Jesus commands, "Let them alone, they be blind leaders of the blind." *Let them alone ;* have nothing to do with them. From such turn away. From such withdraw thyself. Do not imagine that you must go over into their schools, and learn their tactics, and so be able to contend against them with their own weapons. You can manage them with nothing but the Sword of the Spirit, which is the Word of God. If they challenge you, choose your own weapons, and take simply God's Word. The *Word* of God is suited to a heart inspired and animated by the *Spirit* of God ; but philosophy takes away all a man's ardor, courage, and aggressive spirit, and makes him rely upon external things ; it palsies the power of his soul, and destroys his confidence, and fills him with distrust and skepticism. It keeps him tugging at many a knot, time enough, wisely employed, to have saved a hundred souls, when the only direct and wise way was to cut it, and let it go, and proclaim the truth, as the truth is in Jesus. This is the manner of the sacred writers themselves in dealing with speculative difficulties ; one single *Thus saith the Lord,* settles the whole matter.

The celebrated Whitefield is said to have once declared that the main part of his preparation for the ministry was the reading of the whole Bible, with Henry's Commentary, through upon his knees. It was an admirable discipline of heart and mind, but it would have been of little value without the heart-work of that remarkable man, his work in prayer. He read and studied with his heart all the while directed to the Lord Jesus, and thus, while reading and studying, was all the while himself advancing from power to power, changing from glory to glory. His study of the Word of God was not analytical merely, but experimental, and the knowledge he gained was life-knowledge. That is the only knowledge that invests the soul with power. What can we know of spiritual life without it? A famous military surgeon once got hold of a subject with a wound in his side so extraordinary, that after it was healed by an almost miracle, there remained an opening into the stomach, through which articles of food could be introduced, and the process of digestion by the gastric juice could in some respects be watched as it went on. Did it help him in the least to understand the mystery of life? Or could the sight of another man's digestion, or the scientific study of the phenomena, give the observer any hold upon the living principle, any command over it, or supply the exercise of it in his own vital organs? If this be a somewhat crude and rude illustration, it is nevertheless powerful. No external knowledge will supply the place of inward experience and life. Neither the analysis of the elements of truth, nor the sight of its effect upon others, will ever enable us to understand it as life, without ourselves *eating* it, taking it up into the spiritual circulation, and possessing the life of the Spirit within us. If, as with Paul, it please God "to reveal his Son in us that we might preach him," then we are prepared to preach him, but not otherwise; and this preparation with us must be as entirely and originally by the Spirit of God as it was with Paul, or we are wholly ignorant of the living Word, and of all living theology.

The sermons of Dr. Walker, here presented anew, are living truth. They are much occupied with Christ and his glory; his glory in himself, and the riches of the glory of his inheritance in the saints, and the glory of their inheritance in him. They also search the heart, both of the sinner and the saint, the converted and the unconverted, and they sweetly illustrate and commend the various branches of Christian experience and duty. There is nothing redundant or superfluous, either in style, thought, or imagery, but every thing is appropriate, and every thing tells.

SERMONS.

SERMON I.

Preached in the High Church of Edinburgh, May 5, 1761, at the opening of the Synod of Lothian and Tweeddale.

CHRISTIAN HEROISM.

1 THESSALONIANS III. 8.—"For now we live, if ye stand fast in the Lord."

THE author of this epistle is introduced into the sacred history with other sentiments and views than these words express. He makes his first appearance at a scene of blood, consenting to the death of a holy martyr, and keeping the raiment of them that slew him. Soon after, we hear of him making havoc of the church of Christ in Jerusalem, entering into every house, and dragging both men and women to prison; nay, such was the excess and fury of his zeal, that, breathing out threatenings and slaughter against the disciples of the Lord, he persecuted them even unto strange cities: "I verily thought," said he, in the presence of Agrippa, "that I ought to do many things contrary to the name of Jesus of Nazareth." But here we behold *a new creature* indeed! What things were formerly gain to Paul, these he counts loss for Christ; the once hated name of Jesus is now become dearer to him than life itself; and he who in times past persecuted the saints, now glories in the cross, and preaches the faith he had endeavored to destroy.

In my text, he discovers a temper of most distinguished excellence; a temper, my reverend Fathers and Brethren, which I hope we shall not barely applaud, but earnestly covet and endeavor, by the grace of God, to possess.

To unfold the peculiar excellence of this temper, and to illustrate the importance of it to the ministers of Christ, are the purposes aimed at in the following discourse.

The *first* thing that demands our attention, is the amiable temper expressed in these words: *Now we live, if ye stand fast in the Lord.*

The general meaning of the passage is obvious: It contains an obliging and spirited declaration of the apostle's goodwill to the Christians at Thessalonica. But if we attend to his situation when he wrote this epistle, and place ourselves in the circumstances of those to whom it was addressed, we shall feel an emphasis in the word *now*, that gives a surprising addition both to the tenderness and dignity of his sentiment and expression.

Had the time referred to been a season of prosperity; had Paul, in the height of worldly felicity, meant no more than to assure the Thessalonians, that amidst all his affluence, he kindly remembered them; and though at present beyond the need of wishing any thing for himself, yet that the report of their steadfastness, and the hope of its continuance, had made a considerable addition to his happiness, and heightened his relish for the good things he possessed: even upon this supposition, I apprehend, the particle *now*, would justly be deemed emphatical, and worthy to be accented.

But with what force must it strike us, when we find that it refers to a season of adversity! Paul, at the time of writing this epistle, was a poor, afflicted, solitary man; banished from his friends, living among strangers, laboring with his own hands for a scanty subsistence, and destitute of almost every earthly comfort.

All this the Thessalonians knew full well. With grief they had beheld his sufferings in their own city, when "the unbelieving Jews, moved with envy, took unto them certain lewd fellows of the baser sort," and raised such an uproar, as obliged them to send him away by night into Berea. They further knew, that the same unbelieving and envious Jews, upon hearing that he preached with success at Berea, had followed him thither also, and so inflamed the multitude against him, that he found it necessary to retire as far as Athens, to get beyond the reach of his unrelenting persecutors. Judge then with what emotion they would read this strong, this endearing profession of his concern for their welfare; *they* who, under God, owed their conversion to his ministry, and to whom, as I just now observed, his past sufferings on their own account, and his present distress, were perfectly known.

He had told them a little before, that the bitterest ingredient in all his afflictions, was the apprehension he had, that his sufferings might have a tendency to shake their faith, and to prejudice their minds against the gospel of Christ: "For this cause," says he, "I sent to know your faith, lest, by some means, the tempter have tempted you, and our labor be in vain. But when Timotheus returned, and brought us good tidings of your faith and charity, we were comforted over you, in all our affliction and distress, by your faith." And then he adds, *For now*, even at this present time, distressed and afflicted as we are, yet *now we live, if ye stand fast in the Lord.*

Here then the purest zeal for the honor of his Master, and the most generous love to the souls of men, are happily united, and feelingly expressed in the native language of a warm and upright heart. I say the *purest* zeal and the most *generous* love; for no tincture of selfishness appears in either: if Christ is glorified, if men are saved, Paul obtains his utmost wish; his happiness is independent of every thing else; he enjoys all that in his own estimation is worthy to be accounted life, if his spiritual children stand fast in the Lord.

And is not this a temper of most distinguished excellence? When I called it *amiable*, I only spoke the half of its praise; it hath a *dignity*, as well as a beauty, belonging to it, superior to any thing that is commonly celebrated by that name among men. Would we behold *heroism* in its fairest and most exalted form, instead of looking for it among those whom the world hath styled *heroes*, we shall succeed far better if we turn our eyes to Paul of Tarsus.

Where shall we find such determined courage, such cool intrepidity, and contempt of danger, as in this good and faithful soldier of Christ? "Behold," said he to the elders of the church at Ephesus, "Behold, I go bound in the spirit unto Jerusalem, not knowing the things that shall befall me there; save that the Holy Ghost witnesseth in every city, saying, that bonds and afflictions abide me. But none of these things move me, neither count I my life dear unto myself, so that I may finish my course with joy, and the ministry which I have received of the Lord Jesus, to testify the gospel of the grace of God."—Acts xx. 22.

With what invincible fortitude did he triumph over adversity in every frightful shape! with what noble freedom and independence of spirit, did he exult amidst those sufferings of which human nature hath the greatest abhorrence! "Even unto this hour," says he in his letters to the Corinthians, "we both hunger and thirst, and are buffeted, and have no certain dwelling-place; we are made as the filth of the world, and are the offscouring of all things unto this day. We are troubled on every side, yet not distressed; we are preplexed, but not in despair; persecuted, but not forsaken; cast down, but not destroyed; as deceivers, and yet true; as unknown, and yet well known; as dying, and behold we live; as chastened, and not killed; as sorrowful, yet always rejoicing; as poor, yet making many rich; as having nothing, and yet possessing all things."

And what was it that supported and enlivened his mind under such a load of complicated distress? Hear the account he gave of it to Timothy, which exactly agrees with the declaration in my text: "I endure all things for the elect's sake, that they also may obtain the salvation which is in Christ Jesus, with eternal glory."—2 Tim. ii. 10. Paul denied himself for the good of others, and cheerfully renounced every temporal interest to promote the eternal happiness of men.

With what a graceful mixture of majesty and meekness does he appeal to the Thessalonians in the foregoing part of this epistle! "Our exhortation was not of deceit, nor of uncleanness, nor in guile: but as we are allowed of God to be put in trust with the gospel, even so we speak, not as pleasing men, but God, which trieth our hearts. For neither at any time used we flattering words, as ye know, nor a cloak of covetousness; God is witness: nor of men sought we glory, neither of you, nor yet of others; but we were gentle among you, even as a nurse cherisheth her children: so, being affectionately desirous of you, we were willing to have imparted unto you, not the gospel only, but our own souls also, because ye were dear to us. For what is our hope, our joy, our crown of rejoicing, are not even ye, in the presence of our Lord Jesus Christ at his coming? for ye are our glory and joy."

And what can attract our love, what can merit our esteem, what can excite our admiration, if such a temper doth not? A temper which, to all the magnanimity of the hero, unites all the piety and benevolence of the saint.

But it will not avail us barely to esteem or admire this temper: it is necessary, my Brethren, that we ourselves be possessed of it. I shall therefore proceed, as I proposed, in the

Second place, To illustrate the importance of this excellent temper; the peculiar importance of it to the ministers of Christ. And,

1*st*. It is of importance to guard us against that self-deceit to which, of all men in the world, we are most exposed. The office we hold removes us at a greater distance than other men from any of those temptations to gross and scandalous sins, which wound the conscience, and divulge the secret corruptions of the heart; so that mere decency of conduct may pass with us for real sanctity; and what is purely the effect of restraint from without, may be mistaken by us for the product of a new nature within. Besides, the stated duties that belong to our office frequently contribute to cherish this presumption. God may enable us to deliver his message with becoming warmth and propriety, for the sake of those committed to our care; and his word, though uttered by unhallowed lips, may enter with power and efficacy into the hearts of our hearers. It is an awful truth, that if we measure ourselves either by our manner of performing, or even by the effects that follow our public ministrations, we shall often be liable to err very fatally. Paul thought it possible that one might preach to the saving of others, and after all be a *cast-away;* and I can easily conceive, that the preaching to others may, through want of attention on our part, be in some measure the cause of it. The assistance afforded us in our Master's work, may lead us to form a better opinion of our spiritual condition than is either reasonable or safe; and therefore we have greater need to look frequently and narrowly into our hearts, lest the gifts we receive for the use of the church should pass with us for those peculiar graces of the Spirit, which prove our adoption into the family of God, and manifest our title to the heavenly inheritance.

But did our souls burn with that fervent zeal for the glory of God, and that vehement thirst for salvation of men, which fired the generous breast of this apostle, we should be in no danger of judging too favorably of ourselves. Such high aims would cause our most vigorous efforts to appear so little in our own eyes, that, instead of yielding fuel to our pride, they would rather afford us matter of self-abasement, as bearing no proportion, either to the duty we owe, or the exalted felicity to which we aspire. Conscious of our weakness, how earnestly should we then address God for the influences of his Spirit, to aid us in our work, and to impart virtue and efficacy to the means we employ! And, at the same time, with what holy severity should we examine the most secret recesses of our hearts, lest any root of bitterness should find indulgence there, that might either unfit us for service, or mar our usefulness, by provoking God to withhold that grace upon which both our ability and success depend!

2*dly*. The importance of this temper will further appear from the influence it would have upon our public ministrations.

It would make us better preachers as well as better men.

We should never be at a loss for proper subjects of discourse. This, you must be sensible, is not always the case. Most of us, I suppose, will have the candor to acknowledge, that we have frequently spent more time in seeking a text, than might reasonably have sufficed to compose a sermon; and we shall probably find, upon a fair recollection, that this waste of time has happened most commonly when we set out in preparing for our public work, with no other view than to make a sermon. Fancy is a roving capricious guide; but, when necessity prescribes, it always speaks with precision. We may know with certainty what our people need, when we can only imperfectly guess at what will please them; so that, did the necessities of our hearers get the disposal of our studies, we should seldom hesitate long in the choice of our subjects; and, give me leave to add, we should more frequently preach the same necessary truths, and press them from time to time, with redoubled earnestness, till they appeared to have obtained their full effect upon the hearts of those committed to our care.

Nor is this all. The temper I am recommending would assist us in forming and pronouncing our sermons, no less than in choosing the most profitable subjects. As it would reject all useless, unedifying speculations, so it would effectually banish those gaudy ornaments which too often put the preacher in the place of his text; or, as one hath well expressed it, serve only to evaporate weighty truths, and to make them appear as light as the style. Had we no other aim than to guide our hearers in the way of heaven, perspicuity and persuasion would then become the sole objects of our attention; and these, I apprehend, are more within every man's reach than is commonly imagined. I never knew any person much at a loss, feelingly and intelligibly, to impart to others what he greatly feared, or loved, or hated. Rules of art have their use; but though art hath collected rules, it was Nature that furnished them. Both order and elocution are the offspring of a warm and understanding heart. Let us only feel to purpose, and then we shall speak with propriety and energy. Did we, like Paul, *travail as in birth till Christ were formed in the souls of men*, would not our tongue be as the pen of a ready writer? Did we consider that we speak in the name of God; that we speak to the creatures of God; *to* them, I say, and not merely *before* them; that we publish those truths by which only they can be saved, and proclaim that law by which they shall be judged; did we consider that they and we are fast hastening to judgment, and that neither of us can know how soon the summons of removal may be put into our hands; what shall I say? would not Elihu's situation become ours, when he thus expressed himself, "I am full of matter, the spirit within me constraineth me: behold my belly is as wine that hath no vent; it is ready to burst like new bottles; I will speak that I may be refreshed."—Job xxxii. 18, 19, 20. Nay, my brethren, with such great objects in our eye, we should not only speak, but we should speak as Elihu resolved to do in the following part of the quotation, we should speak with an honest and impartial freedom; for thus he goes on; "Let me not, I pray you, accept any man's person, neither let me give flattering titles unto man; for I know not to give flattering titles; in so doing, my Maker would soon take me away."

3*dly*. This temper would likewise have a happy influence upon all the parts of our external conduct. We should not think it enough to abstain from evil; we should carefully avoid every thing that had the appearance of evil, that our conduct might have nothing in it of a doubtful nature, nothing ambiguous, or that needed to be explained. He lives, alas! at a poor rate, and far below the dignity of his sacred office, who is frequently put to it to vindicate his conduct, and to prove that he hath not exceeded his Christian liberty. A minister of Christ ought to go before his people in every thing that is true, just, pure, lovely, and of good report. His light ought to *shine* in the eyes of men; nay, to shine with such strength, that they may *see* his good works, and be constrained to glorify his Father in heaven.

A holy life is the most persuasive sermon, expressed too in a language which men of all nations equally understand. It even explains what other sermons mean, instead of needing to be explained by them. Men will see more beauty in a truly virtuous action, than in the most rhetorical description we can give of it; and then they lose no time, for they see it at once: whereas, besides the necessary expense of time, much skill and address must likewise be employed, to unfold it in such a manner as to make it thoroughly understood and relished.

In this way, my Brethren, we may preach without ceasing: and if we know any thing of the temper expressed in my text, we shall certainly be ambitious to hold forth the word of life continually; and so to exhibit the religion of Jesus, that, in our practice, all who behold us may have an easy opportunity of reading the laws of Christ every day.

More particularly: Were we possessed of this temper, we should equally disdain to court the great by a fawning servility, or to catch the vulgar by a low popularity.

These are the dangerous extremes, into one or other of which every unprincipled minister is liable to be seduced.

The last of them which is reputed the most base and contemptible, is commonly the resort of those only who, having little to recommend to the wise and good, can find no other way to emerge from obscurity, and to thrust themselves forward into public view; for no man will stoop to this mean compliance who is qualified to act in a higher sphere, if he is not forced to it by hard necessity, either to cover a sore he wishes to conceal, or to bribe men to wink at some criminal indulgence which he cannot hide, and is unwilling to forsake. But though the other extreme is generally supposed to be less ignominious, yet, when weighed in a just balance, I apprehend it will be found at least equally mean, and in some respects far more pernicious.

The popular drudge must always assume the appearance of sanctity: he must declaim strenuously against vice, and study to have his outward behavior decent and irreproachable. Thus far the gratification of his favorite passion will constrain him to plead the cause of religion, and to say and do many things which may have a good effect upon the multitude, whose favorable regard he is anxious to obtain. And though his low ambition may, upon some occasions, prompt him to take advantage of their weakness, by inflaming their zeal about matters of a trivial or indifferent nature; yet, as he can only succeed in this attempt by persuading them that such things are important and necessary, it is obvious, that however he may impose upon their understanding, and give them stones instead of bread, yet he cannot be said to corrupt their integrity, neither doth he weaken the authority of conscience. He may render them ridiculous, but he doth not make them knaves.

Whereas the smiles and rewards of political rulers (for these are the great ones of whom I now speak) are usually courted and obtained by very different means.

As a supple, complying temper, unfettered by conscience, or even a regard to decency, too often proves the best recommendation to their service; hence it is, that many who are candidates for their favor, are so far from assuming an air of sanctity, that they studiously avoid whatever can be deemed the peculiarities of their order, that they may have nothing to distinguish them from the men of the world, or to render them suspected of the remotest disposition, either to canvass the commands of their superiors, or to boggle at any measures they shall please to adopt.

The pernicious tendency of such an infamous plan of conduct is too apparent to need much illustration. Hereby they withhold from their patrons the most convincing and obvious proof of the reality, the excellence, and the efficacy of that religion which the office they hold obliges them to preach. Description and argument, if they are not accompanied with a visible representation of holiness, will make but a feeble impression upon those who are continually beset with the snares of prosperity. Besides, it often happens, that such persons, by means of a liberal education, are in a great measure placed (if I may so speak) beyond the reach of sermons: they have already got a theory of religion into their heads, and are not likely to hear any thing they knew not before; so that they need striking examples more than verbal instructions. These, and these only, are of sufficient force to rouse their attention, and to carry home conviction to their hearts with power.

Did they behold men of moderate, or rather of scanty fortunes, unbiased by worldly hopes or fears, consistent and uniform in their whole behavior, resolute in very part of duty, inflexibly honest, and fortified against all corrupt influence whatsoever; such venerable, though imperfect images of God, would not only penetrate but overawe their souls.

A holy and upright minister of Christ never fails to possess a secret dominion in the hearts of those who are of the most opposite character. Hate him they may, and probably will; but at the same time they are constrained to reverence and esteem him: even "Herod feared John, and observed him, and did many things," because he knew "that he was a just and holy man."

Whereas, on the other hand, when they see those who are clothed with the sacred character, paying no regard at all to propriety of conduct, mixing with the world, and living at large as other men do; when they see them grasping at power, or scrambling for riches; spreading their sails to every wind, and ready to embark in any cause that can recommend them to those who are able to gratify their ambition or covetousness: however they may avail themselves of their treason, yet surely they must despise such traitors in their heart, and look upon them as the dregs and refuse of human kind.

But alas! strange as it may seem, it seldom happens that these perfidious men become so thoroughly contemptible as to be altogether harmless. Even they who despise them most, with a perverse and fatal subtilty, make their example an occasion of hardening their own hearts; fetching arguments from thence to extenuate their guilt, and to cherish their presumptuous hopes of impunity: for it has often been observed, that no twig is so slender that a wicked man will not cling to it, when he feels himself sinking under the rebukes of conscience, and the overwhelming fears of approaching vengeance.

It is surely unnecessary to show, that the temper I have been recommending would effectually guard us against both the pernicious extremes I have been speaking of, and render us equally independent of the *high* and of the *low*. Zeal for the honor of our Lord, and the salvation of precious and immortal souls, would ennoble our minds, and break every slavish yoke in pieces. A true minister of Christ will *call no man master*; like this great apostle, he will endeavor so to speak, and so to act, in every situation, not as pleasing men, but God, who trieth the heart. It will ever appear a small matter to him to be judged of man's judgment: this will be his labor, his only ambition, "that, present or absent, he may be accepted of his Lord." Which leads me to observe, in the

4th and *last* place, That the importance of this temper shall be fully understood and felt by us all at the hour of death, and in the day of judgment.

We must shortly sicken and die: that awful period can be at no great distance from any of us; it may be nearer to some of us than we are aware of. Let us consider it as present; and say, my Fathers and Brethren, were this the last day, the last hour, the last moment of life, what would support us best? what would yield us the most effectual consolation? I need not wait for an answer: every heart must have made it already. The only triumph of a dying minister is that which Paul uttered when the time of his departure was at hand: "I have fought a good fight, I have finished my course, I have kept the faith. Henceforth there is laid up for me a crown of righteousness, which God, the righteous judge, shall give me at that day." He who can say with this holy apostle, "To me to live is Christ," he, and he only, can with him subjoin, "and to die is gain." If *now we live when believers stand fast in the Lord;* if to promote the honor of our Master, and the salvation of our brethren, be the objects of our keenest desires and vigorous pursuit, death can do us no harm: we may cheerfully look beyond the grave to those pure regions of everlasting light, and love, and joy; where "they that be wise, shall shine as the brightness of the firmament, and they that turn many unto righteousness as the stars for ever and ever." Animated by these hopes, let us henceforth go on with fidelity and zeal in performing every part of duty that belongs to us: and, "though Israel be not gathered by our means, yet shall we be glorious in the eyes of the Lord, and our God shall be our strength." He who graciously accepteth according to what a man hath, will not reject "our labor of love;" but will confess us at last before an assembled world; and say, with all the indulgence of a kind and liberal master, "Well done, good and faithful servants, enter ye into the joy of your Lord." *Amen*

SERMON II.

GOD'S OMNISCIENCE.

PROVERBS xv. 3.—"The eyes of the LORD are in every place, beholding the evil and the good."

IN every age of the church the complaint may be repeated, that "all men have not faith." Many who think they have it, are fatally deceived, and shall be found in the issue to have been utterly devoid of this gracious principle. True faith determines the choice, and governs the practice according to the nature of the thing believed. It is called "the evidence," or demonstration, "of things not seen." Let the objects be ever so remote, yet faith brings them near to the mind, and renders them as powerful and operative upon the affections and will as if they were both present and visible. Such is the nature and efficacy of this grace: from whence you may judge whether it be so common as men are apt to imagine.

The subject of my text will afford us a striking illustration of this remark. We have already professed our belief, and we have done it too with some solemnity, that *the eyes of the Lord are in* this *place, beholding the evil and the good.* This we virtually acknowledged when we celebrated his praise: but we did it most explicitly when we offered up our prayers to him; for to what purpose should we pray to an absent or even to an inattentive being? Yet if we examine ourselves impartially, and try our faith by the only proper test, I suspect we shall find too much reason to conclude, either that we do not seriously believe this doctrine, or, at best, that our faith is very weak and imperfect.

Were God visibly present in our assembly; were the great Immanuel, God in our nature, standing in the midst of us; would we praise him so freely, or pray to him so coldly, or speak and hear so unfeelingly as we do? And shall seeing, or not seeing, make such an odds? Did we just now behold the object of our worship, would the mere shutting our eyes render his presence less venerable, or the influence of it less powerful? No, my brethren: our seeing God could only assure us that he is present; and if an equal assurance is obtained by any other means, the influence of his presence will in either case be the same. It is not therefore to the seeing or not seeing God that any difference in our temper or behavior must be imputed; but to the believing, or not believing, the reality of his presence: from which we may justly infer, that every degree of irreverence in our minds, and every undutiful step in our conduct, is a symptom of the weakness and imperfection of our faith; and, consequently, that a course of known sin, or the habitual indulgence of any corrupt affection, affords undoubted evidence, that whatever light we may have in our understanding, yet we do not believe with our heart, that *the eyes of the Lord are in every place, beholding the evil and the good.*

When these things are considered, it will appear that infidelity, in one degree or other, is far more prevalent than we are aware of; and that, notwithstanding our professional assent to the doctrine of my text, yet the best of us have need to get our faith of this interesting truth enlivened and confirmed. I shall therefore proceed to lay the evidence of it before you in as plain and convincing a manner as I can; imploring, in the entrance, that powerful blessing, without which the strongest and most persuasive arguments, like a dart thrown by a weak arm, will either fall short of the heart, or if they reach it, yet strike so feebly as to make no deep or lasting impression.

There are two judges, before one or other of which every question of this kind must necessarily be tried; I mean, *Scripture* and *Reason*. Scripture must determine those who confess its divine original; and they who decline the authority of this judge, can appeal to none other but that Reason with which God hath endowed them; there they must stop, the cause can be carried nowhere else. If therefore it shall appear, that the doctrine of God's universal presence and knowledge is supported both by Scripture and Reason, the question will be finally decided; and unbelief can have no resource but perverse and wilful obstinacy.

First, then, This doctrine is plainly taught and repeatedly asserted in the sacred writings.

The testimony of my text is clear and strong: *The eyes of the Lord are in every place.* They not only "run to and fro throughout the earth," as it is elsewhere expressed, which form of speech might leave room to suppose that God beholds things successively, looking first at one object, afterwards at another, but they are in every place at the same time. How awful are the words of Elihu!—Job xxxiv. 21. "His eyes are upon the ways of man, and he seeth all his goings. There is no darkness, nor shadow of death, where the workers of iniquity may hide themselves."

Nor is his attention confined to "the ways of man," by which is commonly meant his outward behavior; he looks immediately into his heart, and sees the inward frame and tendency of his soul; for "all things are naked and opened to the eyes of him with whom we have to do, even the thoughts and intents of the heart." "Man looketh on the outward appearance," said Samuel, "but the Lord looketh on the heart." He needs no information from our actions; he looketh directly on the heart, out of which are the issues of life. Nay, "Hell and destruction are before the Lord, how much more the hearts of the children of men?" —Prov. xv. 11.

Neither do the Scriptures represent him as a mere spectator, but as a witness and judge, who ponders the thought and action with all their circumstances, and makes a just and righteous estimation of them: "I know, and am a witness, saith the Lord." "The Lord is a God of knowledge, and by him actions are weighed." Nay, he weighs the spirits: "All the ways of a man are clean in his own eyes, but the Lord weigheth the spirits."—Prov. xvi. 2. He, as it were, puts them into a balance, so exactly poised that the smallest grain will turn the scale.

Further, the Scriptures not only ascribe to God the most unlimited and unerring knowledge, but they even render it absurd to suppose the contrary; for how extensive, how spiritual, are his commandments! they reach to every part of our conduct; and not only direct the outward life, but give law to the most retired thought and inward affection. Thus we are told (Prov. xxiv. 9.) that "the thought of foolishness is sin;" and the tenth commandment forbids to covet; hereby giving life and spirit to all the former precepts, and teaching us, as our Saviour afterwards explained them in his sermon upon the mount, that they include the inward disposition, as well as the outward action; and not only prohibit external violence, injustice, falsehood, and sensuality, but heart-hatred, causeless or excessive anger, envy, resentment; in short, the first conception of lust in the soul, as well as the birth of the sinful deed. And can any suppose that God, whose wisdom is perfect, would give laws to his creatures, with the most awful penalties annexed to the transgression of them, if, after all, it behoved Him to be ignorant, in many cases, whether these penalties were incurred or not? No, surely. The spirituality of the law is a full proof by itself, that the knowledge of the Lawgiver must extend to our thoughts, no less than to our words; and that the darkest corners of the heart lie open to his view, as much as the most public actions of the life.

Nay, which completes this part of the evidence, we find God actually judging men's hearts, and rewarding or punishing them according to their secret dispositions. Thus it is written of Amaziah (2 Chron. xxv. 2.) that "he did that which was right in the sight of the Lord, but he did it not with a perfect heart." David is applauded for his good intention to build a house for the Lord, though he was not permitted to execute his design: "Thou didst well," said God, "in that it was in thine heart!" And Abijah, the son of Jeroboam, obtained an honorable exemption from that violent death, and want of burial, to which the rest of that wicked family were doomed; for this express reason, "Because in him there was found some good thing toward the Lord God of Israel."—1 Kings xiv. 13. Upon the whole, then, you see how clearly and explicitly the Scriptures decide in favor of this doctrine, that *the eyes of the Lord are in every place, beholding the evil and the good.* Let us now inquire, in the

Second place, What Reason teacheth us concerning this matter. And here I shall argue from such principles as all men are agreed in, atheists excepted, and these are not parties to the cause in issue. Surely none of us will hesitate to acknowledge, that God is the Creator, the Preserver, the Governor, and the Judge of the world. Now, if in each of these essential characters of the Deity we shall find a separate proof of God's perfect knowledge; how irresistible must the evidence be when they are all united, and with what powerful conviction must it come into our hearts! Let us then consider them apart, and try how far they can lead us in this important inquiry.

In the *first* place, I apprehend, that such knowledge as the Scriptures ascribe to God, will be found inseparably connected with the character of Creator. Is it not reasonable to conclude, that he who made man, and endowed him with the faculty of knowing, possesseth in himself a very perfect knowledge? Nay, must we not conclude, that his knowledge is as far superior to ours as his nature is exalted above ours? Here, then, Reason leads us, by two very easy steps, to attribute to God an infinite knowledge, at least a knowledge that we can no more limit than we can do the Divine nature itself.

The inspired author of the 94th Psalm addressed this argument to the infidels in his day, who scoffingly said, "The Lord shall not see, neither shall the God of Jacob regard it. Understand, ye brutish among the people; and ye fools, when will ye be wise? He that planted the ear, shall he not hear? he that formed the eye, shall he not see? he that teacheth man knowledge, shall he not know?" To the same purpose Isaiah speaks, (Isaiah xxix. 15, 16.) "Woe unto them that seek deep to hide their counsel from the Lord, and their works are in the dark; and they say, Who seeth us, and who knoweth us? Surely your turning of things upside down shall be esteemed as the potter's clay; for shall the work say of him that made it, He made me not? or shall the thing framed say of him that framed it, He had no understanding?" In both these passages, the omniscience of God is rationally deduced from the obvious dictates of natural religion; that we are the creatures of God, and that we derive from him all the faculties we possess: And the conclusion appears so just and necessary, that no objection occurs to me by which the force of it can be evaded. But this argument acquires an additional strength when we consider, in the

2*d*. place, That he is not only our Creator, but likewise our Preserver; for "in him we live and move." The same power that brought us into being is continually exercised in supporting our being; nor can we live independent of God for one moment. Try your strength in the easiest matters; try if you "can make one hair white or black;" and when you have found yourselves unable for that which is least, let this convince you, that you are far less able to do so great a thing as to support and prolong life itself.

Is the ability to move at all, then, constantly derived from God? and can any man dream, that God hath given him power to remove to such a distance, that his own eye cannot reach him? Doth he enable us to think, and shall we exclude him from the knowledge of these thoughts which we have no power to form, but what we receive from him? The absurdity is so glaring, that Reason must at once reject it with disdain.

3*dly*. Unless *the eyes of the Lord* were *in every place*, how could he execute what belongs to the Governor of the world? Can he order things aright which he doth not see? Or must his work lie unfinished in one part of his dominions till he hath gone to perfect it in another? Or shall he carry it on by delegates, as weak and finite creatures are obliged to do? It were blasphemy to think so. With infinite ease doth he govern the world he hath made; and, as he created all things in number, weight, and measure, so he disposeth all things according to the rules of the most perfect wisdom, justice, and goodness. And whatever objections may arise from a partial view of his administration, so that in some cases we may be tempted to say in our hearts, "How doth God know, and is there knowledge in the Most High?" yet Reason teacheth us in general, that the Lord reigneth, who is wise in heart, and mighty in strength; and that, when clouds and darkness are round about him, righteousness and judgment are the habitation of his throne. But this could not be without the most certain and unlimited knowledge of all his creatures, at all times, and in every place and condition. How should he conduct this great family which constantly hangs upon him, without the most intimate acquaintance with every individual? And how strong must our conviction of this truth be, when we consider, that his Providence extends to the minutest things? that "the very hairs of our heads are numbered;" that "a sparrow doth not fall to the ground without him;" and that "when the lot is cast into the lap, the whole disposing thereof is of the Lord."

But the *4th* and most striking argument for the truth of this doctrine arises from this principle, which sober reason hath always admitted, viz., that God is the Judge of the world: for as he is to decide the final state of men, and distribute rewards and punishments according to the strictest equity, so that every mouth shall be stopped, and none shall be able to charge him with rigor or undue severity; the trial must be fair and open, and the proof absolutely clear, upon which a sentence, so essentially connected with the honor of the Judge, is to be founded. But how shall this proof be obtained? shall men be adduced as witnesses against each other? This scheme is encumbered with two objections; neither of which, I think, can be easily removed. If all are guilty, would there not be ground to suspect, that every one's private interest might bring them to a general combination and agreement to conceal each other's faults? Or, if some are innocent, which for once we shall suppose, yet even these may, or rather must, be ignorant of many things: they can attest no more than they have seen; and their testimony, at the utmost, can only relate to outward actions; the temper with which they are done, and the principles from whence they flow, are beyond their knowledge: so that no judgment can pass upon the heart in consequence of any human evidence. Where then shall we go next? Perhaps you will say, that every man's own conscience shall witness against him in that day. But what shall oblige conscience to do this? will mere authority compel a man to become his own accuser, when he knows that no other evidence can be brought against him? This, I think, is harder to be believed than any thing. In short, I see no way by which we can extricate ourselves from these pressing difficulties, but by ascribing to God that perfect and universal knowledge which my text, and sundry other Scriptures attribute to him. Reason must have recourse to this at last, or deny that God shall judge the world. It is his omniscience that supplies the room of foreign witnesses, or makes their testimony valid: it is his omniscience that overawes conscience, and constrains it to be faithful. He alone can tell a man what is in his heart, so that he dare not refuse the charge: and it is this infallible testimony of the Judge himself, who scans all actions, who weighs all thoughts, whose right hand doth ever hold us, and whose eye is constantly upon us, that will stop every mouth in the great day of decision, and convince the whole world that his judgment is true and righteous.

Thus have I endeavored to establish your faith of this important truth, that the *eyes of the Lord are in every place, beholding the evil and the good.* I have argued the cause at the bar of Reason, and have showed you the intimate connection of this doctrine with the most acknowledged dictates of natural religion, to wit, that God is the Creator, the Preserver, the Governor, and the Judge of the world. It is possible that some may ask, Why bestow so much time and labor in proving a point which nobody is disposed to deny? Let this be my apology: I cannot recollect the time when I seriously questioned the truth of this doctrine; but I can well remember a time, when it had no more influence upon my own soul than if I had been sure it was false: and, if your belief be of the same kind, as I fear with too many it is, be assured you have heard no more than was needful: nay, if an infinitely greater Teacher do not preach the subject over again to your hearts with power, your present belief shall only heighten your guilt; and the fewer your doubts are, the greater shall your condemnation be. If your hearts do not feel the constant presence of God, your verbal acknowledgments and speculative belief of it, shall only render your case something worse than the infidel's. Satan can spare this tribute to God: so long as your faith dwells in the brain, or in the tongue, he doth not grudge you the possession of it; and if what you have been hearing sink no deeper, I shall readily admit that you have heard too much. In that case, I have no doubt lost my labor, whether it hath been acceptable to you or not. But I shall not close the subject till I have pointed out the practical use we ought to make of it.

And, 1*st*. Let us take occasion from this doctrine to admire, with humble gratitude, the long-suffering patience, and tender compassions of our God. Is he the immediate witness of all our sins? Doth he see the rebellious thought rising in our minds? And doth he still look on, and spare, till it be fully formed and executed? How incomprehensible then must his patience be! We find it no easy matter to forgive our fellow-men, even when they are penitent; with what difficulty do we suppress our resentment, though the injury hath been committed at a great distance of time, and our offending brother himself was perhaps the first who informed us of it, by a free and sorrowful confession? What then can we think of the divine mercy and forbearance? It were much in God to forgive the transgressions of such creatures as we are, though he had not seen them done, and knew nothing about them, till he heard them from ourselves, in penitent confessions and petitions for pardon; but to bear with us till lust had conceived and brought forth; to see the whole progress of the mind, its plots and contrivances, till the wicked deed be done; to behold the heart full of enmity, without one relenting thought; to spare a creature thus determined to affront him, when by one word he could disarm it of all its power, and render it completely miserable! it is this which sets the patience of God above all human, above all created understanding. O! my brethren, think of this. Should an earthly prince behold one of his subjects, who lived within his palace, and was supported by his bounty, treasonably conspiring against him with his most inveterate enemies; should he, instead of treating him with the severity he deserved, condescend to expostulate with him; and, in the most affectionate manner, entreat him to consult his own safety by returning to his duty, and not to wrest a punishment from him which he was unwilling to inflict; what do you think would be the state of the traitor's mind in such circumstances as these? How would it confound him to know, that his much injured sovereign had all along been privy to his baseness, but, like the most tender father, instead of punishing, had only pitied his folly? We may partly conceive this, but are unable to express it. The most artful description could give but a faint representation of the various feelings of an ingenuous heart, upon such an affecting occasion. And shall not the tender mercy of our God have the same influence upon us? He neither wants power to inflict, nor provocation to justify, the severest punishment our natures are capable of enduring. What shall we say then? He is God, and not man; and therefore it is that we are not consumed. O let his patience, to which we are so infinitely indebted, work upon our ingenuity, that we may not unworthily burden it any more! and particularly let us watch over our hearts at this time, when the subject we are upon necessarily obliges us to set the Lord more immediately before us, as the witness and judge of our present temper and conduct; for surely his *eyes are in* this *place, beholding the evil and the good.*

2*dly*. This doctrine hath an obvious tendency to cherish simplicity and godly sincerity, and to banish all dissimulation and artifice from our hearts. He who realizeth the divine presence will not dare to be a hypocrite; for he knows that his triumphing can be but short, and his joy only for a moment. Man he may deceive, who sees no farther than the outside; but he cannot deceive God, *whose eyes are in every place;* who "searcheth the hearts, and trieth the reins of the children of men." And to what purpose should he labor for the applause of poor dying creatures, if he expose himself to the contempt and abhorrence of that infinite Being, upon whom he necessarily depends for life, and breath, and all things? especially when he considers, that the mask he now wears shall ere long be pulled off, and his real character exposed to the view of an assembled world, in that day "when the hidden works of darkness shall be brought to light, and every one receive according to what he hath done, whether it be good or bad?" This motive to sincerity is plain, and obvious to the weakest understanding. Formality, or mere outward religiousness, must appear a vain, unprofitable thing to the man who believes the doctrine of my text; for what can it avail him to be well thought of by a few, during the short time of his abode on this earth, if at last he shall become the object of everlasting contempt; not to those few only, but to all that ever did or shall exist, till "the mighty angel, setting his right foot upon the sea, and his left foot on the earth, shall lift up his hand to heaven, and swear by him that liveth for ever and ever, That time shall be no more."

3*dly*. This doctrine affords abundant matter of comfort and joy to the truly godly. Omniscience is the attribute of their Father and their friend; his eyes are continually upon them for good; he knows every thing that befalls them, and is perfectly acquainted both with their wants, and with those supplies which are proper and necessary for them. This qualifies him to be the object of their trust and confidence; upon him they may quietly and cheerfully rely, who is never far from any one of them, and "whose eyes run to and fro throughout the whole earth, to show himself strong in behalf of those whose hearts are perfect towards him."

But the omniscience of God is still more comfortable upon other accounts. What a stay and support did it prove to Peter, when our Lord said unto him the third time (John xxi. 17), "Simon, son of Jonas, lovest thou me?" Yes, Lord, said he, I love thee I confess indeed the baseness and treachery of my late conduct; yet still I do, and must protest, that I love thee. It is true that I forsook thee, and impiously denied thee; and wert thou not the all-wise God, as well as my compassionate Saviour, this reiterated question would strike me dumb, and drive me from thy presence; for how could I pretend to love thee, or hope to be credited, after such baseness and perfidy? But this is my refuge: "Thou, Lord, knowest all things." Thou canst look into my heart, and see thyself enthroned there: and therefore, notwithstanding the just cause I have given to all the world besides, to suspect the sincerity of my present profession, yet I humbly dare appeal to thy unlimited knowledge: "Thou, Lord, who knowest all things, knowest that I love thee." This is still the support of upright souls. As perfection is not the attainment of our present state, the dearest of God's children are too often carried away by the force of temptation; insomuch that, had they to do with a man like themselves, they might despair of being able to convince him that they loved him. But the sincere penitent, conscious of that affection which glows within his breast, can with tears make his appeal to God himself, and hope to be believed; because he to whom he appeals, needs no other proof or evidence to convince him than his own immediate and unerring knowledge.

Once more, what hope and joy must spring up in the soul in its secret addresses to God, when it remembers that *his eyes are in every place!* He to whom we pray understandeth our very thoughts afar off. "Lord," said the Psalmist, "all my desire is before thee, and my groaning is not hid from thee." A groan, a sigh, cannot escape his notice; nay, "he puts our tears into a bottle, and a book of remembrance is written before him, for them that think upon his name."

Though words be a tribute due to God, yet he doth not need the information of language: "for when we know not what we should pray for as we ought, the Spirit itself helpeth our infirmities, making intercession for us with groanings which cannot be uttered. And he that searcheth the hearts, knoweth what is the mind of the Spirit, because he maketh intercession for the saints according to the will of God."—Rom. viii. 26, 27. When the humble supplicant, like a diseased Lazarus, can do little more than lay himself down at the door of mercy, unable to pronounce one articulate word; when, like the publican in the parable, he can only smite upon his breast, to point at the place where the distemper lies; the Holy Spirit puts language into these actions, which God perfectly understands, and graciously accepts, because his *eyes are in every place, beholding the evil and the good.*

4thly. This doctrine is no less awful to the wicked than it is comfortable to the sincere and good. Wherever they are, whatever they do, God sees and observes them. Men are frequently induced to commit sin by the hope of concealment: "The eye of the adulterer waiteth for the twilight, saying, No eye shall see me; and disguiseth his face." But this text discovers the folly of such hopes; the Judge himself beholds and knows them; "for there is no darkness nor shadow of death where the workers of iniquity can hide themselves from him." O sinners, think of this; none of your ways are hid from the Lord. He not only knows what you do, but he also knows what opposition and restraint you overcome in doing it. You may fein excuses to your neighbors; you may plead the violence of temptation, the want of recollection, or the strength of passion; and by these alleviations extenuate your guilt, and put some sort of color upon your conduct; but God sees through all these thin disguises; he that heard every whispering of conscience within thee; and the complaints of this oppressed, subdued deputy, are all recorded against thee. Brethren, this is a most alarming consideration; may God impress it upon our hearts, and give it that power and influence which it ought to have! This would humble us to purpose, and make us to loathe ourselves in our own sight because of our abominations.

Surely the heart of man is with good reason said to be "deceitful above all things, and desperately wicked." We are hastening to the tribunal of that Judge, whose eye has been constantly upon us, and from whose sentence there lies no appeal. No craft or policy can evade his justice, neither can any power deliver out of his hands; yet we live as if we had no witness, no judge, nor any cause of importance to be tried. God hath assured us in his word, that "death is the wages of sin;" reason condemns it; conscience either remonstrates against it, or rebukes us for it; yet, in defiance of all these, we hug it in our bosom, and refuse to let it go.

This is such perverse, such unaccountable folly, that were not the whole earth a bedlam, in which all have a tincture of the same disease, it would be regarded with equal surprise and horror. One of the most probable means for restoring men to their right senses, is the serious belief of this important doctrine, that *the eyes of the Lord are in every place, beholding the evil and the good.* Which leads me to observe, in the

5th and *last* place, That an habitual impression of the divine presence would prove at once an effectual restraint from all manner of sin, and the most powerful incitement to every part of our duty.

This would deter us even from the most secret sins, and influence us as much in our closest retirement as when we act in the public view of the world. Had we no other spectators than men, it might be sufficient to maintain a fair outside, because that only falls under their observation; but there is no covering so thick as to hide us from God; the most secret deviation of the heart is subject to his cognizance, as much as the most open transgression of the life; and sins committed in the deepest shades of darkness, are as perfectly known to him as those committed in the clearest noonday. None of the springs from whence they proceed can escape his notice, nor the temper of mind with which they are done; which give the truest light into their nature, and determine the precise degree of their malignity. What reason, then, have we to keep our hearts, as well as our lives, with all diligence; and to dread a sin in privacy no less than when we know that many eyes are upon us?

With respect, again, to the practice of our duty, the influence of a realizing faith of the divine omniscience is so apparent that it needs no illustration. "I have kept thy statutes and thy testimonies," said David; "for all my ways are before thee." Were God habitually present to our minds, we should think nothing too much to be done, or too hard to be endured, in his service. A holy ambition to approve ourselves to him, by whose final sentence we must stand or fall, would render us superior to every trial, and carry us forward in the way of his commandments with increasing vigor and alacrity. We should never "think that we had already attained, either were already perfect; but, forgetting the things which are behind, and reaching forth to those things which are before, we should press towards the mark for the prize of the high calling of God in Christ Jesus."

Upon the whole, then, let us earnestly pray God, that he, by his grace, may strengthen our faith of this important truth, that *the eyes of the Lord are in every place, beholding the evil and the good;* and enable us so to set him before us all the days of our pilgrimage on earth, that hereafter we may be admitted into his presence; where, in the happy society of angels and saints, we shall enjoy the unclouded light of his countenance without interruption and without end. *Amen.*

SERMON III.

PRESUMPTUOUS SINS DEPRECATED.

PSALM xix. 13.—"Keep back thy servant also from presumptuous sins."

MEMORABLE is that saying of the apostle Paul, "I had not known sin but by the law." We can never judge aright of our temper and practice till we prove them by this unerring rule. Many objects appear to have a strong resemblance while we view them apart, and at a distance from each other; which, in almost every feature, are found to disagree when they are brought together and examined with accuracy. Thus there is a seeming conformity to the divine law, an image of sanctity, which very often passeth for real holiness, and leads men "to think of themselves more highly than they ought to think." Paul "was alive without the law once; but when the commandment came, sin revived, and he died." So long as he knew only the letter of the law, and was a stranger to its spiritual meaning, and just extent, he imagined that his prayers, his fastings, and his alms, accompanied with some pieces of bodily exercise, and an abstinence from the grosser acts of sin, were sufficient to recommend him to the friendship of God, and would certainly entitle him to the joys of immortality; but "when the commandment came" in its native purity, and entered into his heart with light and power, he soon discovered his mistake, and was convinced, that his seeming virtues were no more in reality than "dead works;" his pharisaical righteousness a mere painted outside, the delusive picture or "form of godliness."

In like manner, the author of this psalm, after a devout contemplation of the divine law, (which he had magnified in the foregoing verses, by a just and animated detail of its amiable properties and salutary effects) turning his eyes inward, is struck with a sense of his own guilt and pollution: "Who," saith he, "can understand his errors?" Many indeed, too many, alas! I can soon recollect; for every period of my life hath been stained with sin: but besides all these, I now perceive, that in numberless instances, unobserved or forgotten, I must have deviated from so perfect a rule. Upon this he supplicates the mercy of God, and implores the forgiveness of those "errors," or infirmities, which had either escaped his notice or dropped out of his remembrance; "Cleanse thou me from secret faults;" "secret," not only with respect to others, but to myself also; hid from mine own eyes as well as from the eyes of my fellow men. And under this awful impression of the polluting nature even of his unobserved and "secret faults," he views with horror the more aggravated guilt of known and wilful sins; and prays with redoubled earnestness, in the words of my text, that it might please God to restrain or keep him back from these: *Keep back thy servant also from presumptuous sins.*

What these sins are, and how much it concerneth us all to avoid them, I shall endeavor to show in the sequel of this discourse; and, as my text is a prayer, I shall conclude with some directions for the help of those who are willing to make it their own prayer, and wish to offer it up with acceptance and success.

By *presumptuous sins*, we are to understand something different from those unavoidable failings, on account of which it is said, that "there is not a just man upon earth, who doeth good, and sinneth not." Perfection in holiness is not the attainment of our present state; the best offend in many things; and "if we say we have no sin, we deceive ourselves, and the truth is not in us."

There are some sins done through ignorance; and this circumstance, how great soever the offence may be in its own nature, doth certainly render the case of the offender more pitiable. We find "the Apostle and High Priest of our profession, Christ Jesus," pleading this argument for mercy to his murderers; "Father, forgive them, for they know not what they do." St. "Paul obtained mercy, who was before a blasphemer, a persecutor, and injurious, because he did it ignorantly." And the Judge himself hath assured us, (Luke xii. 48.) that "the servant who knew not his Lord's will, and did commit things worth of stripes, shall be beaten with few stripes."

There are other sins into which men are hurried by sudden and violent temptation, which the apostle, writing to the Galatians, calls "being overtaken in a fault," (Gal. vi. 1.,) "outwitted, as it were, and taken by surprise. In this case, he exhorts the brethren to restore such an one in the spirit of meekness;" and the argument he useth is very remarkable; "considering thyself, lest thou also be tempted." It farther dserves our notice, that the persons to whom the exhortation is addressed are supposed to be "spiritual;" yet even to these he recommends compassion and tenderness, because the violence of the temptation might, in like circumstances, have overcome themselves. "Men do not despise a thief," said the wise king of Israel, "if he steal to satisfy his soul when he is hungry." In estimating the different degrees of guilt, regard must always be had to the nature of the temptation; for, according to the strength of that, the pride or perverseness of the sinner is proportionally diminished; especially if it appear that he did not go forth to meet the temptation, but was really *overtaken* by it, in the proper sense of that word, and hurried along with its violence, before his mind could have freedom or leisure to reflect and reason upon the matter.

Having premised these distinctions, we shall now be able to discover, with greater ease and certainty, those peculiar ingredients which render sin presumptuous.

Knowledge is the first. This, as I have already hinted, must lie at the root of every presumptuous sin. He is rather unfortunate than faulty, who, by mistake or accident, hurteth one in the dark; but he who doth it in broad day, and with his eyes open, betrays malevolence, or wicked intention, which doth not admit of any extenuation. It was this that rendered the unbelieving Jews altogether inexcusable, according to the declaration of our Saviour, (John xv. 22.) "If I had not come and spoken unto them, they had not had sin; but now they have no cloak for their sin." Knowledge then being supposed as an essential ingredient.

The sin becomes more presumptuous when it is the fruit of deliberation and contrivance; when the person ruminates and plots, and lays schemes for executing his criminal designs. Such a transgressor is described, (Prov. vi. 14.) "Frowardness is in his heart, he deviseth mischief continually;" and again, (Psalm xxxvi. 4.) "He deviseth mischief upon his bed; he setteth himself in a way that is not good; he abhorreth not evil."

The presumption is farther heightened, when obstinacy is added to knowledge and deliberation; when the transgressor "holdeth fast his iniquity, and will not let it go," but rusheth forward in his wicked course, "even as the horse rusheth into battle." Such was the temper which the Jews expressed in their answer to Jeremiah, (Jerem. xliv. 16.) "As for the word which thou hast spoken to us in the name of the Lord, we will not hearken unto thee, but will certainly do whatsoever thing goeth forth out of our own mouth." And to this obstinacy the epithet of *presumptuous* is directly applied, (Deut. i. 43.) where Moses saith, "I spake unto you, but ye would not hear, but rebelled against the commandment of the Lord, and went presumptuously up into the hill."

Again, if the warnings and reproofs of men be accompanied with the remonstrances of conscience, and enforced by the motions of the Holy Spirit, these give a yet deeper tincture to the sinner's presumption, and render his obstinacy still more criminal. With such guilt were the Jewish rulers directly charged by the first martyr Stephen, (Acts vii. 51.) "Ye stiffnecked, and uncircumcised in heart and in ear, ye do always resist the Holy Ghost; as your fathers did, so do ye."

But the sin becomes presumptuous in the highest degree, when, besides the remonstrances of conscience, and the strivings of the Holy Spirit, God, by some awful dispensations of his Providence, "hedgeth up the sinner's way as with thorns," and yet he will break through. Upon this account a distinguished brand of infamy is set upon Ahaz in the sacred history; of whom it is said, (2 Chron. xxviii. 22.) "In the time of his distress did he trespass yet more against the Lord;" to which it is subjoined, with a peculiar emphasis, "This is that king Ahaz," that obstinate, that incorrigible offender, who stands on record as an awful beacon, for a warning to all succeeding generations. These, I apprehend, are the principal ingredients which render sin presumptuous.

And from this description it will appear, there are some sins which must always be presumptuous, and do not admit of any palliation.

Profane swearing is evidently of this kind. It hath no claim to pleasure, and as little to profit; the swearer seems to be wicked from pure malice, merely for the sake of being wicked. In vain do men plead provocation; for injure them who will, surely God doth them no injury; and if a fellow creature offend them, that can never afford them a reason for affronting their Creator, who is continually doing them good. Besides, it is only one instance of profane swearing for which even this alleviation can be pleaded; let this first act be supposed involuntary, the effect of some sudden disorder in the mind; what becomes of the next? that must necessarily be presumptuous; for the repetition of so unnatural a sin may be easily prevented, if the person hath a real abhorrence of it, and useth any efforts to guard against it. But, alas! how many are there who swear alike, whether they be angry or well pleased; who imprecate damnation upon themselves out of mere wantonness, and make such horrid oaths a principal part of their familiar conversation. If any who hear me are guilty in this manner, let me prevail with them to pause for a little, till they have seriously considered what they are doing. It cost the Redeemer much to purchase salvation for you, not only prayers, but blood too: and dare you pray that your souls may have no share in it? This is the height of madness: Damnation is easily obtained; you need not pray for it; if you apply not the remedy, you perish of course: but it is not so easy to be saved; and must not these imprecations, which you have just cause to fear are recorded against you, increase the difficulty, and remove you farther from the road of mercy? Think of this, O sinners! before it be too late, and speedily forsake this presumptuous sin.

Perjury is still more inexcusable, as it cannot even borrow the pretext of passion or suprise, but is a cool, deliberate act of the most daring impiety. The person who swears in judgment has not only abundance of leisure to consider what he is about to say, but the very manner of administering an oath, in all the courts I know, has something in it peculiarly solemn and awful, on purpose, no doubt, to stir up conscience to perform its office, and to oblige it to be faithful. Nay, the very words of an oath in judgment, express an immediate appeal to the Searcher of hearts, in the tremendous character of final Judge; and conseqently imply, not only the person's consent to accept damnation as the punishment of his falsehood, if he shall conceal or deny what he knows to be the truth, but even a formal and solemn adjuration of God to inflict damnation upon him; which is the highest degree of presumption that can possibly be imagined. But though perjury be a *lie* with peculiar aggravations; yet there can be no *lies* of whatever kind which are not presumptuous in one degree or other, inasmuch as they always require some exercise of invention to make them, and usually a great deal more to support their credit, and to keep them in countenance after they are made.

Theft must in every case be presumptuous; it is a work of time which requires much thought and cunning to adjust the plan of operation, and no less address and conduct in carrying it into execution. Besides, the thief has many restraints to break through, not only the inward conviction of the wrong done to his neighbor, but the fears of a discovery likewise, and that disgrace and punishment with which it will certainly be attended.

The same may be said of "*whoremongers and adulterers, whom God will judge.*" For though such transgressors commonly plead the violence of temptation; yet, as I have already observed, this by itself cannot excuse from presumption unless the temptation be so sudden and surprising, that it gives the person no leisure to exercise his reason; which I am persuaded is seldom or never the case. These works of darkness are usually gone about with greater caution and secrecy than are consistent with mere passion; so that reason hath been employed, though in a wrong way: and this is one of those ingredients that render sin presumptuous.

We may likewise say of *drunkenness*, that in the most cases it is presumptuous. It is an excess which one can scarcely be surprised into, unless the liquor be mixed with some pernicious drug, or hath some peculiar quality with which he is utterly unacquainted. But this, I suppose, is a case that rarely happens. It usually takes some time before a person be intoxicated; and drunkenness comes on by such gradual advances, that one hath sufficient opportunity to observe its approach, and to make his escape, if he is not otherwise determined.

So that all these sins are evidently presumptuous; and as they are too commonly practised among us, I thought it my duty to mention them in particular, for the sake of those who know themselves to be guilty, that they may not waste their precious time in seeking after excuses to defend them against the heavy charge of presumption, but may, without a moment's delay, humble themselves in the presence of that God whom they have so grievously offended, imploring his pardoning mercy for what is past, and his powerful grace to restrain them for the future.

The great importance of his restraint to us all, or how much it concerneth us to be kept back from every presumptuous sin, was the second thing I proposed to illustrate. And this will appear from two considerations.

1*st*. That such sins are most heinous in their nature; and, 2*dly*, most pernicious in their effects and consequences.

1*st*. They are most heinous in their nature. The language of the proud sinner is, Who is Lord over me? He either disowns the authority of God, or bids him defiance, and provokes him to jealousy, as if he were stronger than he. Thus it is written. (Numbers xv. 3.) "The soul that doeth aught presumptuously, reproacheth the Lord;" reproacheth his knowledge, as if God was ignorant of his wickedness; or his justice and truth, as if he would not punish it; or his power, as if he could not. And what horrid impiety is this! O sinners, think of it: your known wilful sins cannot possibly be vindicated from this charge; all I have now said, and a great deal more, shall be made good against you at last, when God shall enter into judgment with your souls. It is vain for you to plead that you do not directly intend these things. I verily believe you think so; for, proud and stubborn as you are, I am confident that you dare not utter such blasphemies before God, nor even avow them to your own hearts. But doth it follow from thence, that you are not chargeable with them? The fallacy of this reasoning can easily be detected. Tell us, do you intend your own damnation? I need not wait for an answer; I am sure you do not. Pray, then, what meaning have you at all? You wilfully transgress the laws of God, but you do not intend to be punished for it: on the contrary, you shudder at the prospect of suffering, and would certainly oppose it with all your might. This is one side. On the other hand, you say, that you have no direct intention to injure or insult the majesty of God; you mean no prejudice to his authority; nor to any of his perfections, his wisdom, holiness, justice, or almighty power. Can any body reconcile these two opposites? You are unwilling to be miserable; and yet you are willing that God should possess those tremendous attributes, by the exercise of which you must be made miserable. This is a flat contradiction. The case is plain, whether you perceive it or not; you would certainly dethrone God if you could; you would reverse his laws, or disarm his power, that you might follow your inclinations without fear or control: And this is the disposition of every presumptuous sinner, though perhaps his heart may be so hard and unfeeling as not to perceive it. These remarks may suffice to show, of what a heinous nature presumptuous sins are. I added, in the

2*d* place, That they are likewise most pernicious in their effects and consequences.

Every wilful sin hardens the heart, and renders it less penetrable than it was before; one conviction overcome, makes way for the conquest of another, and that of a third, and so on; the sinner by degrees waxeth stout against God, till at length every bond that should restrain him is broken asunder, and his heart becomes "fully set in him to do evil." This is the natural effect of presumptuous sinning: conscience being often violated, grows callous and insensible, or, in the language of Scripture, "seared as with a hot iron;" so that it not only loseth its authority, but in great measure its feeling also, and suffers the sinner to rush forward in his wicked course without check or remorse.

But this is not all: These presumptuous sins have not only a hardening influence upon the heart, but they likewise provoke God to inflict a judicial hardness upon it, which of all his judgments is by far the most terrible; for this, as it were, seals up the sinner to final condemnation, and renders his recovery not only difficult, but utterly impossible. "Ephraim is joined to his idols," saith God; "let him alone:" he is obstinately bent upon idolatry, give him no disturbance. By this awful sentence God lays an inhibition, if I may so speak, upon every thing that might either restrain or reclaim the offender; he withdraws his despised grace, and suffers him to wallow in that filthiness he hath chosen, till the fire that is not quenched shall awaken him to a fruitless, despairing conviction of his folly.

But as this judgment is, in a peculiar manner, "God's strange work," to which he never proceeds till all reclaiming methods have been tried and baffled; let us suppose, if you please, that the sinner begins to awaken out of his lethargy; yet how dismal must the effects of his presumptuous sins be, even in this case? Oh! what horror will the remembrance of them raise in his mind? How will they discourage him in his addresses for mercy, to that God whom he hath so imprudently affronted and defied to his face? How will they damp his expectations of pardon, when God sets them all in battle array before him, and conscience takes hold of that dreadful sentence against the presumptuous transgressor, (Numbers xv. 31.) "Because he hath despised the word of the Lord, and hath broken his commandment; that soul shall be utterly cut off; his iniquity shall be upon him?" If so good a man as Heman was obliged to cry out, "While I suffer thy terrors I am distracted;" what must be the condition of the newly awakened, presumptuous sinner?

Nay, let us suppose, that God hath spoken peace to his soul, and given him reason to hope that his iniquities are forgiven; yet these sins of presumption always leave behind them the scars of those gashes which they made upon the heart: and as deep bodily wounds, even after they have been closed, are apt to ache upon a change of weather; so any variation in the person's lot that is capable of being construed into a token of God's anger, will recall to his memory those pardoned iniquities, and make them a fresh occasion of grief and anguish to his doubting, perplexed soul.

Besides, though pardon secures against final condemnation, yet sins of this kind are seldom remitted without some visible testimony of God's displeasure. What calamities befell the author of this psalm, even after the prophet had intimated to him, that "the Lord had put away his sin?" His daughter ravished; the incestuous brother slain; Absalom invades both his throne and his bed; the bulk of his subjects desert him; and he himself, accompanied with a few remaining friends, is driven into the wilderness, and hard put to it to shift for his life. And though David was chargeable with many failings, and some of them gross enough, yet in the character which the inspired historian hath given of him, they are all passed over in silence, except his complicated guilt in the matter of Uriah; but that is expressly mentioned, and left as a blot upon the name of this great and good man, to deter others from such deliberate and presumptuous sins; for thus it is written (1 Kings xv. 5.) "David did that which was right in the eyes of the Lord, and turned not aside from any thing that he commanded him all the days of his life, *save only in the matter of Uriah the Hittite.*" Nay, David with his own hand hath recorded his guilt in the 51st Psalm, where to this day he professes his shame and sorrow, and will continue to do so as long as God shall have a church upon earth. When these things are attended to, the importance of being kept back from presumptuous sins must appear to us in the strongest and most affecting light.

Let me now address those whose consciences bear witness, that they have often transgressed in this manner, and are living perhaps at this very time in the habitual indulgence of some presumptuous sin. Have you seriously considered the danger you are exposed to? David's case, which I just now mentioned, suggests to me one argument that may possibly have weight with you. Some of you, perhaps, are sly offenders; so cunning in your way, that the world hath not found you out. But, say, would it not give you pain to think, that one day you should be discovered? Now, what assurance have you that this shall never happen? David, I suppose, conducted his criminal pursuit with as much address and secrecy as you can do; and after it had lain buried for the space of nine months, I am persuaded he was as fearless of a discovery as you presently are: yet God detected him in an extraordinary manner, and not only made his sin visible in his punishment, but even obliged him, as you have heard, by a solemn exercise of repentance, which is left upon record for the use of the church, to publish his confession of it to all succeeding generations. Have you no apprehension that something of a similar kind may befall yourselves? Cannot God disclose your secret sins if he pleaseth? And have you not cause to fear that he will do it, from what he said to David: "Thou didst it secretly; but I will do this thing before all Israel, and before the sun?" Will God show greater tenderness to your reputation than to that of the man according to his own heart? May he not, in his righteous displeasure, permit that lust, which you presumptuously cherish in your bosom, to grow so strong, that all your cunning shall not be able to keep it within bounds? and then it will fly abroad, and become public of course. I beg you may attend to this: I confess it is a motive of the lowest kind; but low as it is, you ought at least to take its aid, till you get a relish for others of a more ingenuous and spiritual nature.

Consider, farther, what inward torment you must one day feel: at present, perhaps, conscience is asleep; but it shall not always sleep: affliction may awaken it; the approach of death most probably will; and then "shall your fear come as desolation, and your destruction as a whirlwind: distress and anguish shall then come upon you;" for in that awful season, "the Lord shall give thee a trembling heart, and failing of eyes, and sorrow of mind. And thy life shall hang in doubt before thee, and thou shalt fear day and night, and shalt have none assurance of thy life. In the morning thou shalt say, Would God it were even; and at even thou shalt say, Would God it were morning, for the fear of thine heart wherewith thou shalt fear, and for the sight of thine eyes which thou shalt see." Or if this seem not misery enough, look forward a little farther to the tremendous issue: "Who can dwell with devouring flames? who can lie down in everlasting burnings?" Yet this, O sinners, must be your portion, if you live and die in rebellion against God. The sweetness of sin passeth quickly away, but the sting of it is perpetual:

the gnawing worm shall never die, the fire of God's wrath shall never be extinguished.

It is really astonishing, that creatures endowed with reason, and capable of exercising reflection and foresight, should, in such a situation, enjoy any sort of peace for a moment. What is it that supports you? Do you imagine that God will overlook your rebellion, and never call you to an account for your conduct? Hear his own words by the mouth of his prophets: "I will search Jerusalem with candles, and punish the men that are settled on their lees; that say in their heart, the Lord will not do good, neither will he do evil."—Zephaniah i. 12. And again, "Woe unto them that draw iniquity with cords of vanity, and sin as it were with a cart-rope: that say, Let him make speed, and hasten his work, that we may see it; and let the counsel of the Holy One of Israel draw nigh and come, that we may know it."—Isaiah v. 18. Has he not already, in the course of his providence, given sufficient evidence of his hatred of sin; and by many awful tokens of his righteous displeasure, extorted a confession from the most obstinate sinners, "that verily there is a God that judgeth in the earth?"—But you have a proof of this in your own bosom. What means the voice of conscience within you? Whence that fear and horror which sometimes seize upon you? Surely these painful feelings are involuntary; for no man chooseth to be his own tormentor. Well, then, this internal sense is in place of a thousand witnesses, to prove, that God is marking your steps in the mean time, and that ere long he will punish you for all your iniquities; "for, according to this fear, so is the wrath of God," which is the object of it.

Do you presume upon the mercy of God? Listen to that awful declaration in the book of Deuteronomy, (chap. xxix. 19, 20.) "If it come to pass, when he heareth the words of this curse, that he bless himself in his heart, and say, I shall have peace, though I walk in the imagination of my heart; the Lord will not spare him, but the anger of the Lord, and his jealousy, shall smoke against that man, and all the curses that are written in the book of the law shall be upon him." True, God is merciful, but is it not equally true that he is holy and righteous? Can you devise a more lofty description of the divine goodness than that which was published by God himself, when, descending in a cloud upon mount Sinai, he passed by before Moses, and proclaimed his name, "The Lord, the Lord God, merciful and gracious, long-suffering, and abundant in goodness and truth, keeping mercy for thousands, forgiving iniquity, and transgression and sin;" (but observe what follows) "and that will by no means clear the guilty?" Exodus xxxiv. 6, 7. Nay, the most amazing instance of divine love, to wit, God sending his Son into the world to die for sinners, is, at the same time, the most awful proof of his inflexible justice, and of his irreconcilable hatred of sin; seeing no less a sacrifice could expiate the guilt of it, than the blood of him by whom all things were made. Neither shall this costly sacrifice avail us, if we still continue to hold fast our iniquities; for "the Son of God was manifested for this very purpose, that he may destroy the works of the devil." And in vain do we plead the merit of his death, unless we follow the example of his life, and submit to the government of his laws and Spirit; for "he is the author of eternal salvation only to them that obey him."

But, it may be, you hope to make all up by repentance; and though at present there are some sins you are unwilling to part with, yet you propose to do it afterwards, with a resolution never to return any more to folly. Well, sinners, this at least is a plain confession that you are self-condemned creatures in the mean time. You admit that repentance is necessary, and that you are undone without it. And now let me display to you the folly of your conduct. Should you die this night, what would become of you? and what assurance have you that you shall be alive to-morrow? Were not Zimri and Cosbi cut off in the act of sin? And have not many others been carried off by a sudden death, without leisure afforded them to cry for mercy? Your sin, and consequently your misery, is present and certain: your repentance only future, and therefore altogether uncertain; for who knoweth what a day may bring forth? Besides, is it not egregious folly to do that deliberately which needeth repentance? Would he not justly be accounted mad, who should drink a deadly poison, merely to try the strength of an antidote? Though you could repent at pleasure, and had a lease of life to any term of your own choosing, which you well know you have not; yet, even upon this supposition, your conduct would be foolish and irrational. But I have something to add that is still more alarming. Repentance is the gift of God; it is a grace that can only be produced in your hearts by that divine Spirit, whom now you grieve. And is grieving him the way to obtain his assistance? Must God wait your time, and patiently endure all your affronts, and then bestow upon you a pure favor, to which you can plead no title, whenever you shall deign to ask it? No, sinners: there are such awful words in your Bibles as these: "My Spirit shall not always strive with man;" and, "Because when I called, ye refused; when I stretched out my hand, ye did not regard me; therefore will I laugh at your calamity, and mock when your fear cometh." Go, think upon these, and get you to your knees, and beg of God, for Christ's sake, that he may pardon what is past, and restrain you from such presumptuous sins for the future. This brings me to the

Last thing I proposed; which was, to direct you how to put up this prayer to God, *Keep back thy servant from presumptuous sins.*

In the 1*st* place, You must do it sincerely, with an unfeigned and earnest desire that God may hear and grant your request. We are very apt to impose upon ourselves in this matter. Conscience being galled and irritated by presumptuous sins, may grow so turbulent and clamorous, that something must be done to still and pacify it. By this means, we may be forced into the closet, and obliged to use the words of my text, nay, to apply them to those particular sins for which conscience upbraideth us. But, alas! our prayers are ofttimes false and hypocritical; we hate not the sin, but the remorse that follows it; and we wish not so much to be delivered from the sin, as from the fierce challenges of the awful reprover within us. Have you not discovered something of this hypocrisy in the time of praying? Have you not felt a secret love for the sin you professed to renounce; nay, some degree of fear lest God should take you at your word, and render that sin bitter and unpleasant to you? Need I tell you, that such prayers are an abomination to the Lord, and, instead of diminishing, aggravate your guilt? To pray, is not to offer up words, but desires, to God: I therefore said, that in using this petition, you must do it with a sincere and earnest desire that God may hear and grant your request. It was for this purpose I set before you the heinous nature and fatal effects of presumptuous sins, that you might view them as deadly foes, and long to be rescued from their tyranny; for till your hearts are brought to this, in vain do you utter the words of David; your prayers are hollow and insincere, whatever dress you put them into; and are themselves more presumptuous than any of those sins against which you pretend to use them.

2*dly.* We must put up this request from a humble sense of our own weakness, with a lively hope of the mercy of God, and a steadfast reliance upon the efficacy of his grace. These qualifications are absolutely necessary: for till we feel our inability to overcome our impetuous and headstrong passions, we shall not be very importunate with God to restrain them; and we shall soon grow weary in our addresses to him for aid, if we either call in question his good will to bestow it, or doubt of its sufficiency to answer our necessities. We must neither pray proudly nor despairingly; we affront God equally both ways. If we go to him merely in a complimental way, as if we did him honor by asking some slender assistance only to render the conquest more easy; this may provoke him to leave us in the hands of our enemies, till, by some fatal overthrow, we are brought to a thorough conviction of our impotence; for "he resisteth the proud, and giveth grace only to the humble; the hungry are filled with good things, but the rich are sent empty away."

On the other hand, should we either question his willingness or ability to help us; would not this be to cast upon him vile dishonor, after all the illustrious proofs he hath given us, both of his love and saving power? "He that spared not his own Son, but delivered him up for us all; how shall he not with him also freely give us all things?"

Let us therefore, under a deep sense of our depravity and weakness, humbly and importunately cry to God, that he may deliver us from the oppression of our tyrannical lusts; and these cries of the oppressed shall "enter into the ears of the Lord of Sabaoth." At the same time, let us harbor no dishonorable suspicions either of his mercy or of his power; "We have a great High-Priest, who has passed into the heavens, Jesus the Son of God, who now appears in the presence of God for us. Having therefore boldness to enter into the holiest by the blood of Jesus, by a new and living way, which he hath consecrated for us through the vail, that is to say, his flesh; and having a High-Priest who is touched with the feeling of our infirmities, and was in all points tempted like as we are; let us come boldly to the throne of grace, that we may obtain mercy, and find grace to help in time of need."

If we thus ask, we shall certainly receive: the great Captain of our salvation, whose grace is sufficient for all his people, will not only keep us back from presumptuous sins, but in due time he will bruise Satan underneath our feet, and "grant unto us to sit with him on his throne, even as he also overcame, and is set down with his Father on his throne."—Let me only add, in the

Third and *last* place, that our prayers to God for restraining grace, must be accompanied with our own most vigorous efforts to resist all temptations to presumptuous sins, otherwise they shall not be accepted.

God will so do his work, as that we shall do ours likewise; for "God's working in us to will and do," instead of superseding the necessity of our own endeavors, is urged in Scripture as a motive and encouragement to make us "work out our own salvation with fear and trembling." Prayer is not only an acknowledgment of our dependence upon God foı the things we ask, but it likewise imports a resolution on our part to use all proper means for obtaining them; and the vigor of our endeavors is the best proof of our sincerity. Should a person who is just now praying, "Lead me not into temptation," rise immediately from his knees, and go forth to invite or even to meet temptation, who could believe that such a man was in earnest? Let us be doing, and then we may, with greater confidence, both ask the divine aid, and hope to obtain it. If. in a humble dependence upon God, we faithfully employ the strength we have, more shall be added to us as our necessities require: "For to him that hath shall be given. They that wait upon the Lord shall renew their strength; they shall mount up with wings as eagles, they shall run and not be weary, they shall walk and not faint. Wait therefore on the Lord: be of good courage, and he shall strengthen thine heart: wait, I say, on the Lord." *Amen.*

SERMON IV.

FORM AND POWER OF GODLINESS.

2 Timothy iii. 5.—"Having a form of Godliness, but denying the power thereof."

"The sacrifice of the wicked is an abomination to the Lord; but the prayer of the upright is his delight." It is the heart of the worshipper which God principally regards; if that be wrong, external homage is only "vain oblation," which can never ascend to his throne with acceptance. Happy, were it for us, had we a just impression of this interesting truth; but many, alas! are too apt to impose upon themselves. Instead of aspiring to that inward purity which is necessary to qualify them for a communion with God, they seem to have no higher aim, than to lull conscience asleep by the practice of some cheap and common duties, lest its galling reproofs should alarm their fears, and anticipate the horrors of approaching judgment. Thus they dream of safety, when destruction is fast coming upon them; and, with "untempered mortar," rear up for themselves "a refuge of lies," which, ere long, shall be tumbled down, and bury them in its ruins.—For awakening such persons from their fatal security, I have chosen this passage of Holy Scripture, wherein the apostle gives us a part of the character of deceiving hypocrites, or rather, indeed, a comprehensive description of them in a few words: they *have a form of godliness, but deny the power thereof.* Their religion is a mere carcass, a body without the soul, a lifeless picture or image of godliness: they assume the garb and air of sanctity, but are strangers, nay enemies, to the thing itself. That the following discourse may be "profitable for doctrine, for reproof, for correction, and for instruction in righteousness," I shall, in the

First place, Endeavor to open the nature of true *godliness*, and to show wherein the life and *power* of it consists.

Secondly, I shall inquire, whence it is, that any who *deny the power of godliness* should submit to the drudgery of practising the *forms* of it? and then point out the improvement which both saints and sinners ought to make of this subject.

Godliness, in general, is the subjection or devotedness of the soul to God himself. It is the practical acknowledgment of his unlimited sovereignty, and the unreserved dedication of the whole man to his service; or, to speak in the emphatical language of this Apostle, it is "Christ formed" in the heart by the powerful energy of the Holy Spirit: in consequence whereof, the person becomes "a new creature," both with regard to his temper and practice; "he partakes of the divine nature;" and "those members" which were formerly the "servants of sin," are now employed as "instruments of righteousness unto God."

It is not a cold assent to the truths of religion; it is not a natural softness and benevolence of temper; it is not the abstaining from gross sins, or the giving to God a corner of our hearts, and some vacant portions of our time, while the bulk of both is alienated from him, that will entitle us to the character of godly men. As he *only* is God, who is universal Lord, supreme in wisdom, in power, and in goodness; so that *only* is godliness which reveres and honors God, in a way suited to that high and incommunicable character. Genuine piety expresseth itself thus: "Whom have I in heaven but thee, O Lord? and there is none upon earth that I desire besides thee." We are not *godly*, whatever we profess or seem, if in our most deliberate and affectionate choice, we do not prefer the one true God, and the enjoyment of his favor, to all that can be found throughout the wide extent of his works; if we make not his will the measure of ours, his law the sovereign guide of our conduct, and and his glory the ultimate end of our obedience. But more particularly, in the

First place, *Godliness* includes a supreme love to God himself, and a constant prevailing desire to please him, mixed with a holy reverential awe, or fear of offending him. I have joined these together, because they appear to be of equal necessity and use, to constitute that frame and temper of mind wherein the essence of piety or true *godliness* doth consist. Fear is necessary to keep God in our eye: it is the office of love to enthrone him in our heart. Fear cautiously avoids whatever may offend: love yields a prompt and liberal service. Fear regards God as a witness and judge; love cleaves to him as a friend, nay a father. Fear maketh us watchful and circumspect: love renders us active and resolute. In short, they go hand in hand, and mutually assist each other: love keeps fear from being servile and distrustful; and fear keeps love from being forward and secure; and both spring from one root, namely, Faith in God, as a being possessed of infinite perfection, and related to us as our Creator and Governor, our Redeemer and our Judge.

This distinguisheth true *godliness* from every counterfeit, or false appearance of it. The seeming righteousness of the *formalist*, is either assumed to impose upon the world, without any regard to God at all, or else it flows entirely from a tormenting fear of future wrath: in his heart there is an aversion from God and his service, at the very time he is professing to honor him with his body; reluctant and hesitating at every step, he proceeds no farther in the road of duty than he thinks may suffice to escape damnation: he doth more than he would do, were he not forced by necessity; and if left to his own choice, he would rather live at large like the beasts that perish, and render no homage to God at all.

Secondly. The power of godliness consists in the conquest of our corrupt and rebellious passions. These indeed still live and fight within us, and will continue to do so in one degree or other, till death pull down these earthly tabernacles: but if we are truly sanctified, their strength shall gradually languish and decay: victory is sown in that new nature we have got; for "whatsoever is born of God overcometh the world:" Jesus our Lord shall ere long "deliver us from the body of this death, and the God of peace shall in due time bruise Satan underneath our feet."—Whereas the formalist is altogether carnal; corruption prevails against reason and conscience; the flesh gives law; and every faculty of the mind, every member of the body, is a willing slave to its usurped authority. Perhaps he has cunning enough "to wash the outside;" to refrain from those sins which would stain his reputation, and render him contemptible in the opinion of the world; but all the while he feels no hatred of sin in his heart; his conformity to the law doth not flow from an inward principle of holiness, but is purely an artificial thing, calculated to please others; and he cares for no more of it than is absolutely necessary for attaining that end.

Thirdly. The power of godliness ennobles the soul with a holy indifference to all earthly things. The godly man is one whose treasure is in heaven. He hath seen through the deceit and vanity of this world, and therefore esteems it but dross and dung in comparison of God and things eternal; he is hastening to the promised land of rest, and will not eagerly contend for an inheritance in this wilderness, nor be greatly dejected when it is either withheld or taken from him. Faith hath so far annihilated this world, that it is become as nothing in his eye, and hath no bribe to offer that is sufficient to seduce him from the service of his God, or the care of his precious and immortal soul. This holy indifference to earthly things, this divine elevation of sentiment and affection, is an eminent part of the godly man's character, and one of the most striking effects of the power of religion in his heart. The *formalist* may, no doubt, put on the appearance of this; he, too, may talk of his contempt of this world; but when a trying time comes, his hypocrisy and earthly-mindedness will soon discover themselves: "Demas hath forsaken me (said Paul), having loved this present world." Affliction and especially persecution for the sake of Christ, makes a wide and visible distinction betwixt the truth of grace and all the counterfeits of it. This is a test which the formalist cannot stand; the predominant interest must then appear, and can no longer be concealed. In that day, all mere speculations about religion vanish; nor can any thing support the sufferer but what he firmly believes and feels in his heart. The unsound professor may look big for awhile, and part with many lesser things; but when matters are brought to this crisis, "Sell all that thou hast, and take up the cross;" renounce every present sensible enjoyment for the sake of distant invisible blessings; then he must throw aside the mask, and confess that the world is supreme in his heart, and that heaven was never valued by him but as a secondary good, which he wished to have in reversion, when he could keep his hold of this earth no longer.

Fourthly. The soul that is under the power of godliness hath a vehement thirst after the enjoyment of God himself. It is God in Christ whom the godly man seeketh in the ordinances of religion; either to know more of his will, or to have nearer communion with him, or to receive from him fresh supplies of grace, for cleansing and quickening, and comforting his soul. These are to him like the tree unto which Zaccheus climbed up that he might see Jesus: and he useth them only for that end. Doth he go to the sanctuary? it is, "that he may behold the beauty of the Lord, and inquire in his temple." Doth he approach the altar? it is, that he may meet with "God his exceeding joy." As the "hart panteth for the brooks of water, so pants his thirsty, longing soul for God, even the living God;" and he always prefers "the light of his countenance" to the greatest increase "of corn and of wine," or whatever else this earth can afford. Now the formalist is an utter stranger to these exercises of the heart: he feels no anxiety after communion with God: he prays, but never troubles himself with inquiring if his prayer is accepted: he goes to church, not that he may wait upon God, or receive spiritual nourishment from the word preached; but merely to gratify his curiosity, and to get some addition to his stock of notional religion; he grows weary of the necessary bread of life: he loathes that dry manna, and reckons every Sabbath and sermon lost in which he is not amused with variety and change. In short, he looks upon the duties of religious worship merely as a task imposed on him by an arbitrary master, who is too strong for him to contend with; and therefore he performs them for his own safety, and is always glad when they are over, and thinks that God hath nothing more to require at his hand.

Once more, in the *fifth* place, The power of godliness is manifested by a steadfast course of holy living, by an uniform and unreserved obedience to all God's commandments. I observed, in the entrance, that godliness is the subjection or devotedness of the soul to God himself: and in vain do we pretend to this, if we object against any of his laws; for the Apostle James hath assured us, that "whosoever shall keep the whole law, and yet offend in one point, he is guilty of all." "It is not the calling Christ Lord, Lord, but the doing the things which he says," that proveth us to be Christians indeed: "Yea, in this the children of God are manifest, and the children of the devil. He that doeth not righteousnes is not of God." The formalist, as I have already admitted, may go a considerable length in an outward reformation of manners; he may abstain from pollutions of the grosser kind, and even do many things that are materially good: but still he hath his exceptions: some sins are so dear to him, that he will by no means consent to part with them; and some duties are so displeasing to the flesh, that he cannot be reconciled to them at any rate; he therefore endeavors, either to suit his opinion to his inclination, by persuading himself that they are no duties; or, if the evidence of their authority is too strong to be evaded, he may attempt to do something like them in a cold and superficial manner; but the things themselves he will not do. Whereas the godly man "esteems all God's commandments concerning all things to be right, and hates, with a perfect hatred, every false and wicked way." This is the habitual language of his soul: "O that my ways were directed to keep thy statutes! Show me thy way, O Lord, teach me thy path, lead me in thy truth, and teach me; for thou art the God of my salvation; on thee do I wait all the day. What I know not, teach thou me: If I have done iniquity, I will do so no more. Let the words of my mouth, and the meditations of my heart, be acceptable in thy sight, O Lord, my strength and my Redeemer." "His delight is in the law of his God;" and instead of complaining, that the duties required of him are many or burdensome, he rather rejoices, that he is furnished with such a variety of means and occasions of testifying his gratitude to that amiable sovereign, to whom he hath devoted himself, and his all. Love makes the Redeemer's yoke to feel easy, and his burden light; and nothing grieves him so much, as that he cannot do all that he would, in acknowledgment of those manifold, inestimable favors he hath already received, or hopes to enjoy.

Such is the *godly man;* and after this manner doth *godliness* exert its *power*, "casting down imaginations, and every high thing that exalteth itself against the knowledge of God, and bringing every thought," word, and action, into full "captivity to the obedience of Christ."

Here, then, let me entreat you, in the serious review of what hath been delivered upon this branch of the subject, to make a fair and impartial trial of yourselves. God, who knoweth all things, is already acquainted with you: each of you must very soon be acquainted with himself, and all the world shall know you too: death is at hand to open your own eyes, and the last judgment shall publish your real character, and expose it to the view of angels and men; so that, upon all accounts, it is necessary that you be early and thoroughly assured of your condition. If, when weighed in the balance, you are found wanting, you shall have this advantage by the discovery, that it will rouse you from that lethargy, out of which the unquenchable fire would at length awaken you; and powerfully incite you to do something for your safety ere it be too late; "God's arm is not shortened that it cannot save, neither is his ear heavy that it cannot hear." The Lord Jesus is still as "mighty as ever, to save to the uttermost all who will come unto God by him;" and there is nothing that puts you so far out of the road of his mercy as self-deceit and presumption do. Let your case be ever so bad; yet if you are sensible of it, and apply to him for relief, you shall find him, at all times, ready with open arms to receive you; nay, he invites you to come to him in the mildest terms of condescension and grace; "Come unto me, all ye that labor and are heavy laden, and I will give you rest." So that the most compassionate and friendly office that a minister of the gospel can perform, is to call upon sinners loudly and repeatedly, "to examine and prove their own-selves," that, from an alarming sense of danger, they may be compelled, by a happy necessity, to flee for refuge to that almighty Saviour who alone can deliver them from the wrath to come. This indeed is the principal aim of my discourse; I have furnished you with several characters of true godliness, by the help of which you may discover whether you are possessed of it or not. These I now leave with you, that every man's conscience may apply them to himself in particular, and pronounce sentence according to the evidence it may find; and shall proceed to inquire, very briefly, in the

Second place, Whence it is that any who deny the power of godliness, should submit to the drudgery of maintaining the form of it?

With respect to many, it may be said, that they appear in the form of godliness by mere accident; because it happens to be in repute among those with whom they converse. They go to church purely because others do it; they observe an outward decorum of manners to avoid singularity; and walk the customary round of duties from a natural timidity, or perhaps civility of temper, which will not suffer them to do any thing that may be shocking or offensive to their friends or neighbors. Of this sort numbers are to be found in every Christian society; they want boldness, or perhaps invention, to become originals, by striking out a new path for themselves; and therefore they go along with the multitude, comply with the prevailing custom, and have no other rule of life but this short convenient one, to be always in fashion, and to do what others are doing around them.

Ambition may be considered as another source of formality. Men have sagacity enough to discover that reputation is power; and that the more a person is esteemed, the greater authority and influence he will have; and therefore, when religion is in credit, the greatest enemies to the power of godliness often betake themselves to its outward form; which they employ as a ladder to help them to climb in to a higher place, where, with greater ease, they may possess the means of gratifying their pride and lust of domination.

It sometimes happens, too, that covetousness, or the love of money, hath no inconsiderable hand in making men assume the form of godliness. This was the just reproach of the Pharisees, those noted formalists in the Jewish church; they fasted often, they prayed long, they abounded in washings, and in many bodily austerities; but our Saviour hath assured us that they did all "to be seen of men." They were mere pretenders to devotion; *they lived by that craft*, and used the forms of religion merely as an engine for drawing the estates of widows and orphans into their own hands, that, under the trust of managing them for their behoof, they might the more securely and successfully enrich themselves at their cost.

The two last are designing formalists, who know, or at least who may know, that they are hypocrites; strangers, nay, enemies to the power of that godliness which they outwardly profess to esteem and honor.

But there are others who practise the forms of religion to quiet and pacify a natural conscience; and do so many things, that, in appearance at least, *they are not far from the kingdom of God;* but still they resist the Spirit of grace, and will not submit to the *power of godliness.* Reason teacheth them, that as their being is derived from God, so their well-being must wholly depend upon his favor; and revelation proclaims, in the strongest terms, that *without holiness no man shall see God.* Hence they see, that a grossly wicked and profligate course of life would at once cut them off from all hope of happiness; and as they cannot bear the thoughts of being eternally miserable, therefore something must be done in the mean time to keep the garrison in peace. Were they presently to conclude themselves in a state of condemnation, their sensual enjoyments would immediately lose their relish, and the prospect of future approaching vengeance would embitter and poison every comfort they possess. To remedy this, they advance a few steps in the ways of godliness, and frame a religion for themselves, composed of as much truth and duty as may consist with their worldly prosperity and pleasures; which, while it leaves them sufficient room to prosecute their carnal aims, doth at the same time serve for a sheath to conscience, to keep it from wounding them when they are busied in the brutish service of their lusts. Present ease is what they chiefly covet; and they choose no more of religion than serves that purpose.

Thus have I endeavored to show whence it is that men who deny the power of godliness submit to the drudgery of maintaining the form thereof. Some do it to impose upon the world, that they may gratify their ambitious or covetous desires; and others do it to impose upon themselves, that they may not be "tormented before the time."

And now, let me address my discourse to those who, from what they have heard, are in some measure convinced that they are the persons described in this passage. "How long, O ye sons of men, will ye love vanity? How long will ye spend your money for that which is not bread, and your labor for that which will not profit you? How long will you court the deceiving shadow of godliness, and fly from the substance, which would certainly enrich and save you? The prodigal's punishment is your choice; you feed upon husks, when there is bread enough in your Father's house, and to spare; you take all the trouble of appearing religious, and taste none of the comforts that religion affords; you endure all the fatigue of acting a constrained, artificial part before men, when, by yielding to the power of godliness, you might, with less labor, and infinite delight, become the very persons you feign yourselves to be. When you reject the truth and reality of *godliness,* how can you painfully adhere to the *form* of it? Or, when you go to the length of being very punctual in the externals of religion, why do you not go a little farther, and study to be really and inwardly what you outwardly profess, and would seem to be?

Is it the praise of man that you covet? This at best is but an empty, fading thing; neither can you be sure of obtaining it. At any rate, the foundation of it shall be taken away at the final judgment, when every disguise shall be stripped off, and the hidden works of darkness shall be brought to light. Nay, God may detect your base hypocrisy, even before you leave this world; so that, as it is written, (Job xxvii. 23.) "Men shall clap their hands at you, and hiss you out of your place." Is it riches you seek by your seeming religiousness? In this likewise you may be disappointed, according to that other threatening denounced against the hypocrite, (Job xxvii. 16.) "Though he heap up silver as the dust, and prepare raiment as the clay; he may prepare it, but the just shall put it on, and the innocent shall divide the silver." Besides, "riches profit not in the day of God's wrath." And after all, "what is the hope of the hypocrite, though he hath gained, when the Lord taketh away his soul?"—"Can the rush grow up without mire? Can the flag grow without water? While it is yet in its greenness, and not cut down, it withereth before any other herb. So are the paths of all that forget God, and the hypocrite's hope shall perish: whose hope shall be cut off, and whose trust shall be a spider's web. He shall lean upon his house, but it shall not stand; he shall hold it fast, but it shall not endure." And oh! how vain is that hope which shall "perish" at the very time when enjoyment is expected! Be awakened then, ye self-deceivers, and know that your formality, like the harlot's paint, is only a false and borrowed beauty, which shall melt away when you draw near the fire; and however you may now hope, while under the threatenings of God, be assured that you shall not be able to hope when under the execution of them; despair shall then become essential to your misery. My brethren, a dream so transient, so momentary, is not worth the having. For the Lord's sake, then, awake in time, repent unfeignedly of your past hypocrisy, and "give no sleep to your eyes, nor slumber to your eyelids," till your souls be acquainted with the power of godliness, that you may have something better to lean upon than delusive forms, when all earthly props shall slide from beneath you. "O seek the Lord while he is yet to be found, and call upon him while he is near."

But there are sinners of another kind, to whom this subject leads me to speak; those I mean who have not so much as the *form of godliness.* You, I doubt not, have got a great deal to say against hypocrites; perhaps, too, you are very well pleased that so much has been said to expose them in the course of this sermon; and now you exult in the thought, that such a hateful denomination cannot be applied to you; if you are not godly, yet surely you are honest, for you do not pretend to be godly. We shall by and by examine your boasted honesty; in the mean time, it deserves your serious consideration, that, by your own confession, you are in a great measure useless in the world; as you contribute nothing, either to the glory of God, or to the spiritual improvement of your brethren around you. Now, here the formalist hath plainly the advantage of you; for though he neglects and destroys his own soul, yet, by his fair outside, and perhaps by the exercise of his gifts he may recommend religion to the esteem and choice of others; like the sign-post which, though it hath its station without, doth nevertheless mark the door to strangers, and invite them into the house; whereas you neither enter in yourselves nor give any assistance to others; but, on the contrary, do much to discourage and hinder them. But honesty, you say, is the qualification you chiefly value, and you are confident that your claim to that is unquestionable. Not so unquestionable as you imagine. As you do not profess atheism, you must be understood to acknowledge the being of a God; and as you have not publicly renounced your baptism, you certainly mean to pass for Christians. None of you, I suppose, are willing to be reputed the enemies of God and of Christ; on the contrary, would you not exclaim against that man as a censorious, malevolent hypocrite, who should venture to hint the remotest suspicion of this kind? And now, wherein doth your honesty lie? You would be thought to love God, yet you live in open contempt of his authority, while you withhold that worship and homage which are due to him. Is this honesty? You call yourselves Christians, yet you practically reject the institutions of Christ, and cast his most sacred commandments behind your back. Is that to be honest, to profess one thing and to do the contrary? This, I apprehend, is the very essence of hypocrisy; so that, if you hate hypocrites, you are bound in justice to hate yourselves; for even you are hypocrites no less than the formalists, though you are not commonly branded with that opprobrious title. The difference betwixt you lies chiefly in this;—the *formalist* is a sort of bashful hypocrite, who, because he cannot deny the debt, makes a show of paying part, and would be thought to pay the whole; whereas the *profane sinner*, who retains the appellation of *Christian*, though he pays no part of what he acknowledges to be due, would nevertheless be reputed an honest man; and therefore he too is a hypocrite as well as the other, with as little sense, and with much less modesty.

I shall conclude this discourse with a few advices, for the help of those who are aiming at real *godliness*, and would not be deceived with names and counterfeits.

Let your religion, then, my dear friends, be principally seated in the heart; and never reckon that you are possessed of it so long as it lodges merely in the understanding. Knowledge and faith are in order to practice; and we neither know nor believe to any good purpose, unless our knowledge and faith influence our practice, and make us truly better men. Be sure to live upon the great fundamentals of religion, and let not your attention to these be diverted by an intemperate zeal about lesser things. Place not your religion in disputable points and ineffectual opinions, but in those weightier matters of the law and gospel, which are of undoubted importance, and in which holy men, among the different denominations of Christians, are better agreed than is commonly apprehended. Choose God for your portion and felicity; beware of thinking that any thing besides himself is necessary to make you happy; and live daily upon Christ Jesus, as the only Mediator by whom you can either have access to God, or acceptance with him. Indulge no sin; plead for no infirmity; but make it the daily business of your lives to "mortify the deeds of the body," and "to crucify the flesh with its affections and lusts." Walk continually as in the sight of a holy, just, and heart-searching God; and study to be the same in secret that you wish to appear in public. Rest not in a low degree of holiness, but love, and long, and strive for the highest. And, for these purposes, pray without ceasing for those promised influences of divine grace, which alone can heal your diseased natures, and carry you forward from one degree of holiness to another, till, being ripened for glory, an entrance shall in due time be administered unto you abundantly into the everlasting kingdom of our Lord and Saviour Jesus Christ. To whom, with the Father, and the Holy Spirit, be glory and honor, dominion and thanksgiving, for ever and ever. *Amen.*

SERMON V.

CHRIST DESPISED AND REJECTED.

ISAIAH LIII. 3.—"He is despised and rejected of men: He was despised, and we esteemed him not."

THAT the whole of this chapter relates to the Messiah is so universally acknowledged, that I need not spend time in proving it; and whosoever hath read the history of our Saviour's life with a proper degree of attention, cannot fail to have remarked the exact accomplishment of that part of the prophecy which I have chosen for the subject of the following discourse; "Christ came unto his own, but his own received him not." The learned, the rich, and the mighty among the Jews, were almost universally combined against him; the most opposite parties, the Pharisees and the Sadducees, united their endeavors to discredit his doctrine and mission: he was condemned by the supreme council of the nation as an impostor and blasphemer; nay, the whole body of the people disowned him in the most public and contemptuous manner before Pontius Pilate, the Roman governor, crying out as with one voice, "Away with him, away with him! crucify him, crucify him!" Thus was he *despised and rejected of men*, in the days of his humiliation, to which the prophet more immediately refers.

But as the Jews are not the only people chargeable with this crime, as Christ hath been, and still is, *despised and rejected* by many, even by many of those who were baptized into his church, and are called by his name; we may be allowed to consider the prediction in my text as reaching beyond the time of our Saviour's abode on this earth, and looking forward to all that injurious contempt which, in after ages, should be cast upon the blessed Jesus by pretended friends, as well as by open and professed enemies.

In this large extent I shall at present take the liberty to discourse upon these words. And my design is, *first*, to show in what respects it may still be said that men *despise and reject* the Saviour; and, *secondly*, to inquire whence it is that they do this?—After which, I shall lay before you the heinous nature of their guilt, and direct you to the proper improvement of the whole.

I begin with showing in what respects it may still be said that *Christ is despised and rejected of men.*

True it is, that his glorious person is no more exposed to the outrage of men. That body which was "scourged," "buffetted," "spit upon," and "crucified," is now far beyond the reach of any such abusive treatment. He is now exalted to his Father's right hand, where he is adored and worshipped with the most lowly reverence by all the heavenly host. But yet there are some other, and no less criminal respects, in which he is still *despised and rejected* of many. I speak not here of those baptized infidels, who openly deny the Lord "that bought them," and traduce the whole of his religion as a mere human contrivance; neither shall I take much notice of those who, while they profess a general regard to Christ, do, at the same time, entertain and publish opinions evidently inconsistent with a real esteem of him, though it cannot be wholly overlooked, that such there are in the Christian world; some denying his divinity, and others his satisfaction; some disowning the necessity, and others the virtue and efficacy of his grace: all which are so many different ways of vilifying the great Redeemer, and detracting from his true honor and dignity. But, passing these, my design is to show, that even among such as you, my brethren, who I trust are not tainted with these doctrinal errors, it is possible to find some who ungratefully *despise and reject* the Saviour. May God open their hearts to receive conviction, that they may no longer delude themselves with "a name to live," while they are spiritually "dead," and liable to everlasting destruction.

In general, then, all who are grossly ignorant of the religion of Jesus, must necessarily be reputed despisers of him; for as the means of acquiring knowledge are so easy, and the opportunities of receiving instruction so frequent, it must be owing to some culpable neglect of their own, if any who are capable of learning other things be unacquainted with the great doctrines of Christianity; and this neglect too plainly betrays a contemptuous disregard of Christ himself.

More particularly, men may be said to *despise* Christ, when they do not receive him as their alone Saviour, as the true, the living, nay, the only way to the Father. He is set forth in Scripture as the sole mediator between God and man; who, by his atoning sacrifice, hath satisfied divine justice, and purchased the Holy Spirit to heal our diseased natures, and thereby render us meet for the perfection of our happiness, in the enjoyment of that God who cannot behold iniquity: so that we do not properly express our esteem of him, unless we acknowledge him in that important character, and pay to him those practical regards which it claims. To honor him, is to acquiesce thankfully in this ordinance of God for redeeming his fallen creatures; it is to renounce all hope of being justified or saved by any other means, and to rely wholly upon the sacrifice and intercession of this High Priest for the pardon of our sins, and the acceptance of our persons with God; it is to apply that blood to ourselves which "cleanseth from all sin," and to receive his Spirit to dwell within us, and to sway the sceptre over all the powers and faculties of our souls. A lawyer is honored when men employ him, and commit their cause to his management; a physician is honored when men apply to him for advice, and use his prescriptions for their cure:—In like manner, the great Advocate with the Father, and the Sovereign Physician of souls, is honored, not when men talk well of him, and verbally profess an esteem of him, but when they actually commit their cause to him, and place their entire dependence upon him for pardon and grace and complete salvation; and they that come short of this are in reality no other than despisers of Christ; and, as such, shall be disowned by him at his second coming.

Again, Christ is *despised and rejected of men* when they practically deny his authority by breaking his commandments. We are expressly told, "that all power is committed to him in heaven and on earth; for God hath put all things under his feet, and given him to be head over all things for the church." Now, to honor him in this character, is to yield a cheerful and unreserved obedience to his laws; it is to acknowledge his sovereignty over us, and his property in us, not only as our Creator, but likewise as our Redeemer, who hath bought us with his blood; and in consequence thereof, to glorify him both with our bodies and our spirits, which are his. Therefore, all they who make their own will the rule of their conduct, who do not resign themselves entirely to the disposal and government of this King of Zion, whatever their profession be, they certainly despise and reject him; and, though not in words, perhaps, yet by their deeds they say with the rebellious Jews, "*We will not have this man to reign over us.*" "Why call ye me Lord, Lord," said our Saviour, "and do not the things which I say?" plainly intimating, that all outward expressions of esteem are mere hypocrisy and empty grimace, without a sincere and unlimited subjection to his laws.

Further, men *despise* Christ when they do not give him the chief room in their hearts, nor prefer him in their choice to every thing else. The language of a true disciple is, "Whom have I in heaven but thee? and there is none upon earth whom I desire besides thee." If Christ be not esteemed and loved above every thing, he is not truly esteemed or loved at all; and this I take to be the meaning of these strong expressions, (Luke xiv. 26.) "If any man come to me, and hate not his father and mother, and wife and children, and brethren and sisters, yea, and his own life also, he cannot be my disciple." They who are not willing to part with ease and pleasures, with riches, and honors, and friends, with whatever is dear to them in a present world, nay, with life itself, for Christ's sake, plainly discover that they have no just sense of his worth and excellence. They who do not prefer him to the whole world, and cannot rest in his love as a sufficient portion, without any thing else, pretend what they will, they do not truly esteem him. And, to conclude this head,

They too must be numbered among the *despisers* of Christ, who do not publicly confess him before men, or who wilfully neglect any of those ordinances he hath instituted, as the methods of testifying our subjection to him, and the means of receiving benefits from him. I really do not see how any man can be said to esteem Christ, who doth not embrace every proper opportunity of conversing with him, or of hearing tidings concerning him; and, in particular, the habitual neglect of social worship, either in the family or in the church, hath such a strong appearance of estrangement and disregard, that it is hard for me to conceive how any person can persist in it, who doth not in his heart despise the Saviour.

Thus have I endeavored to show in what respects it may be said, even at this present time, that Christ *is despised and rejected of men.*

The causes of this contempt are the *second* thing to be inquired into. And I apprehend the *first* and main cause of this contempt of Christ, among the hearers of the gospel, is a secret unbelief which they are not aware of. For did they truly believe the doctrine concerning the Saviour; that he only "is the way, the truth, and the life; and that no man cometh," or can come, "to the Father, but by him;"—that he is God's beloved Son, in whom he is well pleased;—and that without an interest in him, and entire subjection to him, they cannot be saved; it would be impossible to despise him in any of these ways I have mentioned: for *to them who* thus *believe, Christ is*, and must be *precious.* But men deceive themselves: they have a vague, confused, and indeterminate opinion, and are accustomed to say in the general, that the Scriptures are the word of God; but they never saw the evidence of their truth in such a light as to be thoroughly persuaded of it. They think the doctrines contained in the Christian revelation *may* be true; but here they stop; and because they are not downright infidels, they fancy themselves believers, when in truth they are not.

2dly. The love of this world is another cause of men's contempt of Christ, and of his gospel. They can afford him honorable titles, and external homage; but to follow him fully will not consist with their worldly desires and aims. Such was the young ruler, who addressed that important question to our Saviour, "Good Master, what shall I do to inherit eternal life?"—Luke xviii. 18. He appeared thoughtful and serious, beyond what might have been expected from his age and rank, and had gone an uncommon length in an outward conformity to the law; but when our Lord commanded him "to sell all, and give to the poor, he was sad at that saying, and went away sorrowful, because he had large possessions." Of this we have a striking illustration in the parable of the marriage-supper, which is recorded in the 22d chapter of Matthew's gospel. The invitation is very warm and pressing at the 4th verse: "Behold I have prepared my dinner: my oxen and my fatlings are killed, and all things are ready: come to the marriage." But it follows immediately, "They made light of it, and went their ways, one to his farm, another to his merchandise." This, my brethren, still continues to be a very common cause of men's despising and rejecting Christ. They see the world, but they see not the celestial glory; the one is present, the other only future, and therefore too remote to work upon their affections. If both could be obtained, they would no doubt be very well satisfied; and if religion and their worldly interest take one road, they will be ready enough to pay the compliment to our Lord, and say that they follow him: but when these separate, then their contempt discovers itself; they cleave to the world, and forsake Christ.—"Demas hath forsaken me," said Paul, "having loved this present world."—So true is that saying of the apostle John (1 Epist. ii. 15), "If any man love the world, the love of the Father," and with equal reason we may add, the love of the Redeemer," is not in him."

A *third* cause of this contempt is men's ignorance of their own condition; like the church of the Laodiceans, they "boast that they are rich, and increased with goods, and standing in need of nothing; and know not that they are wretched, and miserable, and poor, and blind, and naked." Some have so high an opinion of their own understanding, that they see no need of a prophet to instruct them. Others have such low thoughts of the evil of sin, and such a conceit of their own righteousness and worth, that they see as little need of a priest to expiate their guilt, and reconcile them to God. A third sort lay so much stress on their unassisted powers, and the efficacy of their own resolutions and endeavors, that a king to subdue them by his grace and spirit appears altogether superfluous. Thus Christ is despised through men's ignorance and pride; unacquainted with their state of darkness, guilt, and corruption, they reject him who cometh in the name of the Lord to save them; they feel not their diseases, and therefore treat the physician with contempt and scorn. Once more, in the

4th place. Not a few pour contempt upon Christ, and reject his offers from day to day, from an opinion that they may obtain his aid at what time soever they shall choose to ask it. They say not indeed with the Atheist, "Let us eat and drink, for to-morrow we die;" neither do they say with the gross Antinomian, Let us sin without fear, seeing Christ hath died for us, and is therefore determined to save us at any rate. But they say what is equally absurd, Let us take a full draught of the sweet poison of sin, seeing the remedy is so near at hand that we may apply it when we please. O that this were not too common! I am afraid it will appear, upon inquiry, that there is too, too much of this vile presumption in our hearts. But can there be a greater dishonor done to Christ? Must his bloody sufferings, and unparalleled love, support our rebellion, and embolden us to sin? Can any thing be more criminal? But this I shall have occasion to speak of immediately; and shall only say at present, that thousands, and ten thousands, have perished, who once had the remedy as near them as you have, and who also, perhaps, dreamed of the same facility in applying it. To which I may add, that out of your own mouths you shall be condemned at last, and shall find nothing to plead in arrest of judgment, when God shall say to you, Why did you not repent, and believe in the Saviour, seeing you thought it so easy, that you could do it when you pleased?

O that men were wise! that they understood these things, and would consider, in this day of their merciful visitation, the things that belong to their peace, before they be for ever hid from their eyes! I cannot allow myself to think, that any of you are already acquainted with all the deformity of the sin I have been speaking of; and that, after viewing it in its full dimensions, you are perfectly reconciled to it, and resolved to persist in it. I would gladly hope that this is not the case; but rather that the great enemy of your happiness has hitherto kept you in the dark, and in great measure concealed from you both your guilt and your danger. Perhaps, to this moment, you have never seriously thought upon your ways, but blindly followed the fashion of the world, and suffered yourselves to be carried along with the crowd, without any suspicion that you are chargeable with crimes of such a hellish nature as are included in *despising and rejecting* the Saviour. I shall therefore proceed, in the

Third place, To give a short representation of the malignity of this sin; which, if duly attended to, may be of use to dissolve the enchantment, by which the god of this world hath so long blinded your eyes, and rendered you insensible to the misery of your condition.

Consider, then, that to *despise and reject* such a Saviour, is the blackest ingratitude that can possibly be imagined. It was a cutting question that Christ put to the Jews when they went about to kill him: "Many good works have I shewed you from my Father, for which of these works do ye stone me?" To render evil for good, hatred for love, is accounted monstrous among men; and the person who behaves in such a manner towards his fellow-creature, is justly condemned and abhorred by all: and yet the most heinous and detestable instance of ingratitude among men is as nothing when compared with your ingratitude towards God. Did he, without any solicitation from you, and not only without, but even contrary to, your desert, send his own Son into the world to save you? Did the Lord Jesus Christ, "the brightness of the Father's glory, and the express image of his person," assume your nature, become a man of sorrows, and acquainted with griefs; lead a poor, afflicted, persecuted life, and at last die a shameful, painful, and accursed death, to satisfy offended justice, and to render your happiness consistent with the honor of the divine government? And is this your requital?

I beseech you, my brethren, to bestow some attention upon this; and if your hearts have any softness at all, such unparalleled baseness cannot fail to make the deepest impression upon them. Does this astonishing, undeserved goodness merit no regard? Doth God's unspeakable gift to men deserve no returns of gratitude and praise? Shall the blood of Christ be shed in vain, nay, trampled under foot, as an unholy thing? Will you "crucify the Son of God afresh," and say, by your neglect of his great salvation, "Away with him! away with him!"—"We have loved strangers, and after them we will go?" Surely you cannot, you will not, pretend to justify this conduct; there is something in it so disingenuous and perverse, so shocking and unnatural, that I am persuaded, when you attend to it, you must loathe and abhor yourselves on account of it.

But this is not the whole of your guilt: Your ingratitude is heightened by the most insolent contempt both of the wisdom and goodness of God. You charge God with folly, when you reject the terms of the gospel-covenant; for your behavior plainly implies one of the following accusations; either that this method of salvation is unnecessary, and that God from all eternity hath employed his counsels about a needless affair; or else that it is ineffectual, and that the person whom God hath chosen to execute this design is not worthy to be depended upon; or that the terms proposed are so rigorous and severe, that a wise man would rather choose to perish than submit to them. Thus dost thou arraign thy God, O sinner! And art thou able to make good thy charge? Dost thou hope to prevail in the day when God shall plead with thee?

Nay, further, by *despising and rejecting* Christ, you openly proclaim war against the Most High, and bid him defiance. He hath "set his King upon his holy hill of Zion," and "put all things under his feet:" he hath ordained, by an irreversible decree, that "all men should honor the Son, even as they honor the Father:" he hath published to the world that there is no other name given among men, by which they can be saved, but the name of Jesus; that this glorious Mediator is constituted the final Judge of mankind; and that they who do not bow to the sceptre of his grace, shall be dashed in pieces with his rod of iron, in that day when he shall be revealed from heaven, with his mighty angels, in flaming fire, to take vengeance upon those who knew not God, and obeyed not this gospel which we now preach to you: And yet, in the face of all these declarations, you proudly say by your conduct, "We will not have this man to reign over us;" we neither fear his power nor court his grace, but are determined to stand on our own defence."

Such, my brethren, is the malignity of your sin: it includes the blackest ingratitude, heightened by the most insolent contempt, nay, an open defiance of the omnipotent God; rejecting his offered mercy, and daring him to execute all the rigor of his justice. I do not mean that you are at present conscious of this complicated impiety; I rather suppose that you are startled when you hear it mentioned, and are ready to reply, as Hazael did to Elisha, "Is thy servant a dog, that he should do these things?" But be assured, all I have now said shall be made good against you at last, if you continue to despise and reject the Saviour: and the greatest mercy that can befall you in the mean time, is, to get those eyes opened which Satan hath so long closed, that you may see and abhor your guilt in this matter. O be exhorted then, deliberately to weigh the representation I have given you! and think what must become of you, if you go out of this world with such a dreadful load of guilt as I have endeavored to describe.

By this time you must all see your concern in this subject. I have told you that it is possible, even among such as you, who attend upon ordinances, and profess a general esteem of Christ, to find *despisers and rejecters of him:* I have mentioned sundry instances of contempt, which persons, who are neither Jews nor infidels, but who call, and even think themselves the disciples of Jesus, may be guilty of; and you have just now heard the heinous nature and the high aggravations of this sin: so that you see they are no trivial matters I have been talking of, but matters which infinitely concern the whole Christian world, and yourselves in particular. I now come to point out the improvement, which I humbly wish, and fervently pray, that every one of you, my dear friends and brethren, would make of this subject.

I would have you, then, as the best and most necessary improvement of all that you have heard, to enter immediately into your own hearts, and make an impartial inquiry into your esteem of Christ, according to the marks I formerly gave you. O beware of self-deceit in this trial! You may weep at the history of his sufferings, when you read or hear how barbarously he was treated by the Jews; and yet you may *reject* him. You may feel some emotions of gratitude and joy, when you hear of the greatness of his love, and the value of his purchase, and yet perish for *despising* him. You may, under alarms of conscience, feel strong desires after him to save you from the wrath of God, and after all, be heart enemies to him. Nay, you may be zealous reprovers of others for despising Christ, and paint the deformity of this sin in stronger colors than I have been able to do; but, alas! if you have no better evidence for proving your esteem of him, your present trust is no better than "the spider's web," and your hope, in the time of your greatest need, shall be as "the giving up of the ghost." In short, your esteem of Christ must be greater than your esteem of all the profits, and pleasures, and honors, of this world; and you must manifest this esteem by a cordial acceptance of him, and an entire subjection to him; otherwise you shall be condemned at last, as persons who have *despised and rejected* this great Redeemer.

Thus, my brethren, have I held up the glass, in which, if you are not wilfully blind, you may behold your true picture: and if you have attended, and suffered conscience to do its office, some of you, I am persuaded, must be convinced that you are the persons who have hitherto *despised and rejected* the Saviour; and therefore it is time for me to ask, What is your present resolution? Is this a state to be continued in? Would any of you, if left to your own choice, be willing to be found in this condition at last? Brethren, this is a serious question, and ought not to be slightly passed over: The Lord Jesus now waiteth upon you for an answer; but remember, that ere long you must wait upon him for a doom. As therefore you would be found of him in peace, come now to a speedy and firm determination. You have despised him too long already; O do not add this farther instance of contempt, to hesitate, while I now plead with you, whether or no you should this moment renounce all competitors, and give him the chief room of your hearts. May I hope you are resolved? Happy you, thrice happy, if you be so! Now you begin to live, your former unworthy behavior shall all be forgiven; and that compassionate Redeemer, who procured sparing mercy for you even when you despised him, and, by his gracious interposition, hath kept you alive till this hour, will not reject your penitent, believing souls, but will accept your esteem and love, though late; and, in return, will bestow upon you all the enriching benefits of his purchase. But if any of you shall justify your former contempt, and resolve to persist in it, I must declare the righteous sentence of God; and I shall do it in the words of John the Baptist (John iii. 36.) "He that believeth not the Son, shall not see life; but the wrath of God abideth on him." Let my counsel therefore be acceptable unto you. "Seek the Lord while he is yet to be found, and call upon him while he is near. Kiss the Son, lest he be angry, and ye perish from the way; for if once his wrath be kindled but a little, then shall it be found that they," and they only, "are blessed who put their trust in him."

SERMON VI.

THH LAW'S SUBJECTS.

Romans iii. 19.—Now we know, that what things soever the law saith, it saith to them who are under the law; that every mouth may be stopped, and all the world may become guilty before God.

The great design of this epistle is to lead men to Christ, as the only refuge for perishing sinners: and because none will value a remedy but they who feel their disease, and wish for health, the apostle therefore, in the two foregoing chapters, examines the condition both of *Gentiles* and *Jews;* under which denominations, the whole posterity of Adam are included; and proves by plain, undeniable facts, that all, without exception, are guilty before God, and consequently, that all stand in need of a Saviour. In the verses immediately preceding my text, he brings several quotations from the Old Testament writings, which give a very strong and melancholy representation of the corruption and depravity of the human kind. But lest the Jews should allege that these, and other passages of the like nature, were only descriptive of the Gentile nations, and could not justly be extended to them, whom God had chosen from the rest of the world, and set apart for himself as his peculiar inheritance; he judged it proper to remind them, that the sacred books, from which he had taken the above description, were primarily addressed to the Jews, and designed for their instruction and use; *We know*, says he, *that what things soever the law saith, it saith to them who are under the law;* consequently these quotations, which are all expressly contained in the law, may and ought to be considered as a just representation of the state of those to whom that law or revelation was given. And he further adds, that they were inserted in Scripture for this very purpose, that the plea of innocence being taken away from the Jews as well as from the Gentiles, *every mouth might be stopped, and* thus *all the world might become guilty before God.* From which words, as they stand connected with the apostle's reasoning, we learn, in the

First place, That it is extremely difficult to bring men to a proper sense and acknowledgment of their guilt and misery.

I hope none will be so unreasonable as to require a labored proof of this observation; for you will easily perceive that I can have no other witnesses to produce but yourselves. I affirm that it is so upon the authority of Scripture; and can only appeal to your own hearts for the truth of it. Besides, none will deny this who are already convinced of their guilt and misery; for this is an essential property of real conviction, that the deeper it is, it renders the person still more sensible of the natural hardness of his heart; so that nothing grieves him so much, as that he cannot grieve more for sinning against God: And they who are of an opposite character, who boast, "That they are rich, and increased with goods, and standing in need of nothing;" such persons, I say, prove the truth of this observation, by demanding a proof of it, and are themselves examples of the thing they deny.

I know it is an easy matter to bring men to a general acknowledgment that they are sinners. Many are ready enough to confess this much, who, at the same time, have a very good opinion of their state: for though they cannot lay claim to perfect innocence, yet they look upon their guilt as a very trivial thing, and imagine that their vices are more than overbalanced by the virtues they are possessed of; and thus, "being ignorant of God's righteousness," or of that righteousness which is necessary to justify a sinner in the sight of God, "they go about to establish their own righteousness, and will not submit themselves unto the righteousness of God."

Pride is the hereditary disease of our natures: we derive it from our first parents; and though it is subdued in all who are sanctified, yet still it lives within them, and is always the last part of the old man that dies. Nay, it is apt to grow upon the ruin of other sins, as we see in that noted instance of the Pharisee, who, under the specious pretext of thanking God for his grace, went up into the temple merely to give vent to his self-admiration: "God," said he, "I thank thee that I am not as other men are, extortioners, unjust, adulterers; I fast twice a week, I pay tithes of all that I possess." What he said might be true; nay, our Lord seems plainly to admit that it was so: yet he tells us, that this vainglorious creature carried nothing away with him but his self-conceit: he returned to his own house without the blessing of God; "For every one that exalteth himself shall be abased; whereas he that humbleth himself shall be exalted."

This, my brethren, is one main cause why the preaching of the gospel hath so little effect. Could we bring men to a sense of their guilt and misery, they would gladly listen to the tidings of a Saviour. But this is difficult work indeed. We can scarcely persuade the most profligate wretch to think himself in danger, till God lay his hand upon him, and set death before his eyes. Judge, then, how hard a task it must be, to convince the more close and reserved sinner! who probably has got beneath him some empty forms of duty, upon which he leans, and confidently presumes that all shall be well with him.

I have frequently observed, that no sermons are so tasteless to many hearers as those which treat of the Saviour: they can listen to other subjects; but when we talk of Jesus Christ, and of that great salvation "which angels desire to look into," they dismiss their attention, and perhaps make a shift to sleep in their seats; when, God knows, were they aware of the thousandth part of their danger, they would find it difficult enough to sleep on their beds. Did we really see ourselves in a just light, could we divest ourselves, for a little, of our pride and prejudice, till we got one serious and impartial view of our natural condition, this would render a Saviour so necessary, that we should never be at rest till we had secured his friendship: But as our Lord himself hath told us "they that are whole have no need of the physician, but they that are sick." I shall therefore proceed to show, in the

Second place, That all men, without exception, are guilty before God; and that whoever attends to the Scriptures of truth, or gives ear to the testimony of his own conscience, may soon discover such plain convincing evidence of guilt, as is sufficient to stop his mouth, and to render him speechless and self-condemned in the presence of a just and holy God. This proposition is perfectly consistent with the former; for the difficulty of bringing men to a right sense and acknowledgment of their guilt and misery, doth not arise from any want of evidence, but is purely owing to their own inattention and pride. The sad truth is clear as noonday; but they shut their eyes, and will not see it.

As the testimony of Scripture is full and explicit, so the short abstract contained in the foregoing verses speaks upon this head with the utmost possible precision. "There is none righteous, no, not one. There is none that understandeth, there is none that seeketh after God. They are all gone out of the way, they are together become unprofitable, there is none that doeth good, no, not one. Their throat is an open sepulchre; with their tongues they have used deceit; the poison of asps is under their lips: whose mouth is full of cursing and bitterness. Their feet are swift to shed blood. Dertsuction and misery are in their ways; and the way of peace have they not known. There is no fear of God before their eyes." And these things, the apostle informs us, were written not merely to stop the mouths of some notorious offenders, who proclaim their sins as Sodom, and hide them not: but *that every mouth might be stopped, and all the world become guilty before God.* Accordingly, at the 23d verse of this chapter, he concludes upon the whole evidence in the following words: "For all have sinned, and come short of the glory of God."

This truth hath been attested by the most eminent saints that ever lived upon earth. "Behold I was shapen in iniquity," said David, "and in sin did my mother conceive me;" and therefore he pleads in another place, "Enter not into judgment with thy servant, O Lord; for in thy sight shall no man living be justified." "We are all as an unclean thing," said the prophet Isaiah, "and all our righteousnesses are as filthy rags; and we all do fade as a leaf. and our iniquities, like the wind, have carried us away." Neither have the saints under the New Testament dispensation been any whit behind them in penitent acknowledgments of their guilt. Paul styles himself "the chief of sinners;" and the beloved disciple declares, in express terms, that all pretensions to innocence are not only false but blasphemous: "If we say that we have no sin, we deceive ourselves, and the truth is not in us." Nay, "if we say that we have not sinned, we make God a liar, and his word is not in us."—1 John i. 8, 9.

This further appears from the various kinds of misery which abound in the world, especially death, from which none of Adam's posterity are exempted. These do necessarily suppose guilt; for it is not agreeable to the justice of God to afflict and punish innocent creatures. Now, this mean of conviction is so plain and obvious, that a man must do great violence to his reason before he can resist the evidence it affords. Goodness and justice are attributes which are universally considered as most essential to the Supreme Being; and yet it is impossible to account for the present calamitous state of mankind, in a consistency with these perfections, upon any other supposition than this, that "all have sinned," and thereby incurred his righteous displeasure. So that you see there is no penury of witnesses upon this head. The Scriptures expressly declare that all are sinners; the most eminent saints under both dispensations have attested the truth of this assertion; and the many awful tokens of the divine displeasure, which we daily behold and feel, render it absurd to suppose the contrary.

But there is yet another witness behind, whose testimony can be liable to no objection; a witness which every man will find within his own breast; I mean *Conscience*, to which I now appeal for the truth of this matter. And here I shall renew the question which Solomon proposed many ages ago: "Who can say, I have made my heart clean, I am pure from my sins?" Can you discover nothing amiss in your temper and practice? Do they in all points agree with the rule of God's word? Dare any of you appeal to the justice of God for acquittal? and claim happiness as the due reward of your obedience? Say, O man! has thou no need at all of pardoning mercy? Wilt thou give it under thy hand, that thou shalt never plead the merits of a Saviour for thy justification? that at the hour of death, or in the day of judgment, thou shalt never once implore his help, nor cry for mercy, but stand upon the foundation of thy personal righteousness before his impartial tribunal? Or rather, my brethren, are you not conscious of innumerable instances of guilt, wherein you have acted in direct opposition, not only to the written law, but to the inward sense and authority of your own minds; doing what ye knew was displeasing to God; and that, not by the mere force of sudden temptation, but coolly and deliberately, in the face of those arguments which ought, in all reason, to have restrained you from them? I think I may venture to affirm, that there is not one person here present who is not able to recollect several instances of this kind; and if our own blind and partial hearts do now condemn us, alas! how shall we justify ourselves at the bar of that God "who is greater than our hearts, and knoweth all things?" This leads me to observe, in the

Third place, That one great end of the law is, to humble the pride of men; that, from a conviction of their guilty and miserable estate by nature, they may, as it were, be compelled, by a happy necessity, to flee for relief to the gospel method of salvation through Christ.

This important truth is directly asserted by the apostle, in my text, and frequently repeated in other parts of his writings. Nay, the principal scope of this epistle is, to call off the Jews from any dependence upon their own righteousness, by giving them a fair representation of the spirituality, extent, and rigor of the law; that, finding themselves unable either to answer its demands, or to endure its curse, they might thankfully embrace the Lord Jesus Christ, who is indeed "the end of the law for righteousness to every one that believeth." And the subserviency of the law to the gospel, or the use of the law to lead men to the Saviour, will evidently appear, if we consider,

That the law demands nothing less than a perfect, unsinning obedience to all its precepts. It makes no manner of allowance for the infirmities of men; for "whosoever shall keep the whole law, and yet offend in one point," in the eye of the Lawgiver, "is guilty of all." It declares what is due to God by his creatures, and insists upon the payment of it even to the uttermost farthing. In the law, strictly considered, there is no provision or promise of pardon to the guilty; on the contrary, it denounces condemnation and wrath against all transgressors of what kind soever; for thus it is written, "Cursed is every one who continueth not in all things which are written in the book of the law to do them." It is not enough to do *some* things which are commanded; we must do them *all:* nor is it even sufficient that we do all things for a season; we must also *continue* in them, otherwise we forfeit the divine friendship, and become liable to the wrath of an infinitely just and omnipotent God. This is the genuine voice of the law, "*Do and live;*" "but the soul that sinneth shall surely die." It knoweth no middle sentence between these two; it doth not whisper one word of mercy; but the smallest deviation subjects the transgressor to the justice of God, and to all the fatal effects of his indignation, both in this life and in that which is to come.

Now, this being the case, it is easy to discern the subserviency of the law to the gospel; or, in other words, the use of the law to lead men to the Saviour. The law discovers sin, and at the same time demands an unsinning obdience. None of us can plead innocence, and the law admits of no excuse for guilt; nay, it is not only silent as to the doctrine of forgiveess, which might leave some room for conjecture and hope, but in plain and awful words pronounces the sentence of death, and dooms to irremediable punishment all the workers of iniquity without exception. Thus the sinner is "bound hand and foot," as it were, "and cast into prison;" *his mouth is stopped*, and nothing remains for him but either to continue in misery, and bear the curse of God for ever; or else to appeal from the law to the gospel, and to claim the benefit of that indemnity which Christ hath purchased with his blood, and freely offers to all who, condemning themselves, and renouncing their own righteousness, flee to him as their hope and city of refuge. From all which we may conclude, in the

Fourth and *last* place, That every apologizing sinner who opens his mouth in his own vindication, doth impiously give God the lie, and exclude himself from the offers of his mercy and grace; whereas the humble, self-condemning sinner lies, so to speak, in the very road of mercy, and shall, through faith in Christ Jesus, obtain salvation with eternal glory.

This inference is so just and obvious, that it scarcely needs any illustration. For if "all are sinners," and if this be one great end of the law, to bring men to a sense and acknowledgment of their guilt, that they may be compelled to flee to Christ Jesus for relief; what foolish, self-destroying creatures must those be, who, in despite of the clearest evidence, and in flat contradiction to the only method of deliverance and hope, will offer to babble in their own defence? What can you propose by this conduct, O sinners! God puts it to your choice, as it were, at what court you would be tried, whether you will plead at the tribunal of justice or of mercy? If you penitently acknowledge your guilt, and cry for mercy through the great Mediator, he is infinitely more willing to bestow it upon you, than you can be to ask it of him; but if you proudly insist in your own vindication; if you extenuate your guilt, or depend upon any thing in yourselves for pardon and acceptance, you thereby incur the rigor of the law; you "shall have judgment without mercy," and "Jesus Christ can profit you nothing."

Be persuaded, then, my dear friends, as the proper improvement of all that has been said, "to humble yourselves presently under the mighty hand of God, that you may be exalted in due time." See and acknowledge your guilt and unworthiness, that you may not be finally *condemned with the world;* and beg of God that he may search and try you, and make you thoroughly acquainted with your real condition; that, finding yourselves "wretched, and miserable, and poor, and blind, and naked," you may repair, without delay, to that all-sufficient Saviour, "whose blood cleanseth from all sin," and "who is made of God, unto all who believe on him, wisdom and righteousness, and sanctification, and redemption."

As for you upon whom the law hath already had its effect, who are weary and heavy laden with the burden of sin, be not discouraged; the seeds of consolation are sown in your griefs; this weeping night shall ere long be succeeded by a joyful morning; and "upon you who" thus "fear his name, shall the Sun of righteousness" shortly "arise with healing in his wings;" for this gracious temper is the peculiar work of the Spirit of God; it is he who brings the light into the soul, whereby its natural deformity is seen; it is he who casts down those proud imaginations which exalt themselves against God, and hide from the sinner his poverty and wretchedness: and it is this divine Spirit, who, by the ministry of the law, removes those false grounds of hope upon which the sinner was accustomed to lean, and obligeth him to ask that interesting question, "What shall I do to be saved?" As John Baptist prepared the way for Christ's public appearance, by rousing the world with the doctrine of repentance; in like manner, the Holy Spirit prepares the heart for the reception of the same glorious Redeemer, by such painful and humbling convictions, as to render him both necessary and desirable to the soul: And therefore it ought to be matter of joy and thankfulness to the sinner, when God smites his heart with a sense of sin; of such sickness, it may be truly said, "This sickness is not unto death, but for the glory of God." Hereby, as it were, he dislodges his enemies, and empties the soul of every other guest, that he may come and fill it with his own gracious presence.

Lift up your heads, then, O trembling sinners! look forward but a very little way, and you may see to the end of that dark valley through which you are now passing. This road became necessary after man's apostasy; and it is the kindness, not the anger, of your heavenly Father, that hath brought you into it. Had your destruction been pleasing to him, he would have suffered you to walk, without disturbance, in the broad way that leads to destruction: but by alarming your fears, he plainly intends to prevent your ruin; and the present taste he hath given you of the bitterness of sin, is graciously meant to divorce your hearts from the love of it, and to render the remedy which he offers, more welcome and precious in your esteem. —For, let it be observed, as a further ground of encouragement, that the gospel-call is particularly addressed to persons of this character: "Come unto me," says the blessed Jesus, "all ye that labor and are heavy laden, and I will give you rest." And herein he exactly fulfils the appointment of his Father, and acts in the most perfect conformity to the commission he received from him; of which we have a fair copy, (Isaiah lxi. at the beginning:) "The Spirit of the Lord God is upon me, because the Lord hath anointed me to preach good tidings to the meek; he hath sent me to bind up the broken-hearted, to proclaim liberty to the captives, and the opening of the prison to them that are bound." From this passage it plainly appears, that humble, convinced souls are his peculiar charge: he is the physician, not of the whole, but of the sick; not of those that justify themselves, but of those who are perishing in their own apprehension, who feel their need of him, and know something of the worth of the salvation which he brings.

Let every humble sinner, then, take comfort from these considerations. God knoweth the penitent relentings of your hearts: Behold, he stands, like the father in the parable, stretching forth his arms to every prodigal son! he registers all your groans, "he putteth your tears into his bottle," and, ere long, "he will give you the oil of joy for mourning, and the garment of praise for your present spirit of heaviness." In the mean time, let me recommend to you the following directions, with which I shall conclude.

Beware of smothering or quenching your convictions. I admit they are bitter, but they are also medicinal; and, by the blessing of God, shall issue in that repentance unto salvation, which is not to be repented of: whereas, if you stifle them at present, your hearts may contract a hardness and insensibility, which, if ever it be cured at all, shall cost you more pain and anguish than you presently feel, or indeed easily imagine.

At the same time, beware of drawing desperate conclusions against yourselves from the discoveries you have got of your guilt and danger. I may justly say to you, what the apostle said in another case, —"Mourn not like those who have no hope." Your case, bad as it may seem, is certainly better than once it was. Formerly you were out of the way of mercy, now you have got into that very path where mercy meets the elect of God: It was then your sin to presume beyond any promise; beware now of despairing against many commands; but amidst all your fears and anxieties, still endeavor to keep hope alive in your hearts.

Especially hasten to the Saviour, who alone can give you rest. This is the great errand upon which convictions are sent; for, as I have already observed, "the law is our schoolmaster to bring us to Christ, —who is the end of the law for righteousness to every one that believeth."—Doth the Lord Jesus appear precious to your souls? do you see your absolute need of him, and his perfect suitableness to your circumstances? O, then, speedily have recourse to him, and receive him thankfully as the "unspeakable gift of God to men!" Embrace him cordially in all the important characters he sustains, as the Prophet, the Priest, and the King, of his Church; and then shall you find, to your present comfort, and your everlasting joy, that he is both "able and willing to save to the uttermost, all who come unto God by him." *Amen.*

SERMON VII.

This, and the four Sermons that immediately follow, were preached at the celebration of our Lord's Supper.

THE FRIEND OF THE WEARY.

MATTHEW XI. 28.—"Come unto me, all ye that labor and are heavy laden, and I will give you rest."

IT was prophesied of our Lord, long before his manifestation in the flesh, that he should "proclaim liberty to the captives, and the opening of the prison to them that are bound:" And lo! here he doth it in the kindest and most endearing manner, offering *rest*, or spiritual relief, to every *laboring and heavy laden sinner. Come unto me, all ye that labor and are heavy laden, and I will give you rest.*

In discoursing from which words, I propose, in dependence upon divine aid,

First. To open the character of those to whom the invitation is addressed:

Secondly. To explain the invitation itself, and show what is included in *coming* to Christ: After which, I shall endeavor, in the

Third place, To illustrate the gracious condescending promise with which our Lord enforces the call: *I will give you rest.*

I BEGIN with the character of those to whom the invitation is addressed. They are such, you see, as *labor and are heavy laden;* that is, who feel the insupportable load of guilt, and the galling fetters of corrupt affections, and earnestly long to be delivered from both; for these were the persons whom our Saviour always regarded as the peculiar objects of his attention and care. By our fatal apostasy, we forfeited at once our innocence and happiness; we became doubly miserable, liable to the justice of God, and slaves to Satan and our own corruptions. But few, comparatively speaking, are sensible of this misery. The bulk of mankind are so hot in the pursuit of perishing trifles, that they can find no leisure seriously to examine their spiritual condition. These indeed have a load upon them, of weight more than sufficient to sink them into perdition; but they are not *heavy laden* in the sense of my text. Our Saviour plainly speaks to those who feel their burden, and are groaning under it; otherwise the promise of rest, or deliverance, could be no inducement to bring them to him. And the call is particularly addressed to such, for two obvious reasons:

First. Because our Lord knew well that none else would comply with it. "The full soul loathes the honey-comb." Such is the pride of our hearts, that each of us would wish to be a saviour to himself, and to purchase heaven by his own personal merit. This was the "rock of offence" upon which the Jews stumbled and fell: they could not bear the thought of being indebted to the righteousness of another for pardon and acceptance with God; for so the Apostle testifies concerning them (Rom. x. 3), "Being ignorant of God's righteousness, they went about to establish their own righteousness, and did not submit themselves unto the righteousness of God." And still this method of justifying sinners is opposed and rejected by every "natural man." He feels not his disease, and therefore treats the physician with contempt and scorn; whereas the soul that is enlightened by the Spirit of God, and awakened to a sense of its guilt and pollution, lies prostrate before the mercy-seat, crying out with Paul when struck to the ground, "Lord, what wilt thou have me do?" It was therefore with peculiar significancy, that our Lord introduced his sermon upon the mount, by adjudging the kingdom of heaven to the "poor in spirit," placing humility in the front of all the other graces, as being the entrance into a religious temper, the beginning of the divine life, the first step of the soul in its return to God.

2dly. The *laboring and heavy laden* are particularly distinguished; because otherwise, persons in that situation, hopeless of relief, might be in danger of excluding themselves from the offer of mercy. If there was only a general call to come to the Saviour, the humble convinced soul, pressed down with a sense of its guilt and depravity, might be ready to object, surely it cannot be such a worthless and wicked creature as I am, to whom the Lord directs his invitation. And therefore, he "who will not break the bruised reed, nor quench the smoking flax," doth kindly encourage them, by this special address, that the very thing which to themselves would appear the greatest obstacle in the way of mercy, might become the means of assuring them, that they are the very persons for whom mercy is prepared.

Let this then encourage every weary, self-condemned sinner: the greater your guilt appears in your own eye, the greater ground you have to expect relief if you apply for it. Mercy looks for nothing but an affecting sense of the need of mercy. Say not, if my burden were of a lesser weight, I might hope to be delivered from it; for no burden is too heavy for Omnipotence: he who is "mighty to save," can easily remove the most oppressive load; "his blood cleanseth from all sin," and "by him all who believe are justified from all things." This great physician did not come to heal some slight distempers, but to cure those inveterate plagues, which none besides himself was able to cure. Whatever your disease be, it shall neither reproach his skill nor his power; and all that he requires on your part, is a submissive temper to use the means he prescribes, with a firm reliance upon their virtue and efficacy. If you are truly convinced that your guilt is so great, and your corruptions so strong, that none in heaven or on earth can save you from them but Christ alone; if you are groaning under the burden of sin, and can find no rest till pardoning mercy and sanctifying grace bring you relief; then are you in the very posture which my text describes; and I may warrantably say unto you what Martha said to Mary, "Arise quickly, the Master is come, and calleth for thee." And this is his call, *Come unto me.* Which is the

Second thing I propose to explain. Now, for understanding this, it will be necessary to remind you of the different characters which our Lord sustains; or, in other words, the important offices which he executes as our Redeemer. These, you know, are three, to wit, the offices of a Prophet, of a Priest, and of a King; in each of which the Lord Jesus must be distinctly regarded by every soul that comes to him. Accordingly, you may observe, that in this gracious invitation, he exhibits himself to our view in all these characters; for to the condescending offer of removing our guilt, he immediately annexes the command, "Take my yoke upon you, and learn of me."

Such is our misery by the fall, that we are not only become the objects of God's righteous displeasure, and liable to that awful punishment which was the penalty of the first covenant, but our nature is wholly diseased and corrupted; so that in us, in our flesh, "dwelleth no good thing." Our understanding is darkened, filled with prejudices against the truth, and incapable of discerning spiritual objects: "For the natural man receiveth not the things of the Spirit of God, they are foolishness to him; neither can he know them, because they are spiritually discerned." Our will is stubborn and rebellious, like "an iron sinew," which no force can bend; so inflexible in its opposition to the divine law, that it is called in Scripture "enmity against God:" and all our affections are wild and ungovernable, deaf to the voice of reason and conscience, in perpetual discord among themselves, and wholly alienated from God, in whom alone they should unite and centre. Such a Saviour, therefore, was necessary for our relief, as could effectually remedy all those evils, and not only redeem us from wrath, but likewise prepare us for happiness, by restoring our nature to that original perfection from which it had fallen.

For this end, our Lord Jesus Christ, that he might be in all respects furnished for this great undertaking, was solemnly invested by his heavenly Father with each of the important offices I have named; that our understanding being enlightened by his divine teaching, and our will subdued by his regal power, we might be capable of enjoying the fruits of that pardon, which, as our great High Priest, he hath purchased with his blood. Now, in all these characters, the Scriptures propose him to our faith; and we do not comply with the invitation in my text, unless we come to him for the proper work of each office, and embrace him in the full extent of his commission; that "of God he may be made unto us, wisdom, and righteousness, and sanctification, and redemption."

It is true, indeed, that the soul, in its first approach to Christ, doth principally regard him as a priest or a sacrifice; and therefore faith, as it is employed for justification, or pardon, is emphatically styled *Faith in his blood.* To this God looks when he justifies a sinner; he views him as sprinkled with the blood of atonement; and therefore, to the same blood the sinner must necessarily look upon his first application to Christ. When the criminal under the law fled to the horns of the altar, he considered the temple rather as a place of protection than of worship. The authority of a teacher, and the majesty of a king, are objects of terror to a self-condemning sinner, and by no means suit his present necessity. Christ as suffering, and "bearing our sins in his own body on the tree," is the only object that can yield him relief and comfort; for where shall he find the rest of his soul, but where God found the satisfaction of his justice?

Nevertheless, though Christ upon the cross be the first and most immediate object of faith, yet the believer doth not stop there; but having discovered a sufficient atonement for his guilt, he proceeds to contemplate the other characters of his Redeemer, and heartily approves of them all as perfectly adapted to all his necessities. He hearkens to his instruction, and cheerfully submits to his yoke, and covets nothing so much as to be taught and governed by him. The ingenuity of faith speaketh after this manner: Seeing Christ is my Priest to expiate my guilt, it is but just and reasonable that he should be my Prophet to teach me, and my King to rule over me; that as I live by his merits, I should also walk by his law.

O blessed Jesus! saith the soul that comes to him, thou true and living way to the Father! I adore thy condescending grace, in becoming a sacrifice and sin-offering for me: and now, encouraged by thy kind invitation, I flee to thee as my only city of refuge; I come to thee "wretched, and miserable, and poor, and blind, and naked;" I have no price to offer thee, no goodness at all to recommend me to thy favor: *laboring and heavy laden*, I cast myself at thy feet, and look to thy free mercy alone for the removal of this burden, which, without thy interposition, must sink me down to the lowest hell. Abhorring myself in every view I can take, I embrace thee for my righteousness; sprinkled with thine atoning blood, I shall not fear the destroying angel: Justice hath already had its triumph on thy cross; and therefore I take thy cross for my sanctuary. This is my rest; and here will I stay, for I like it well.

Nor is this my only errand to thee, O thou complete Saviour! I bring to thee a dark benighted mind to be illuminated with saving knowledge. "Thou hast the words of eternal life;" "in thee are hid all the treasures of wisdom:" I therefore resign my understanding to thy teaching; for no man knoweth the Father but the Son, and those to whom the Son shall reveal him."

I likewise choose thee for my Lord and my King; for thou "art altogether lovely," and in every character necessary to my soul. Here are enemies whom none can vanquish but thyself; here are corruptions, which nothing less than all conquering grace can subdue: I therefore implore thine almighty aid. Do thou possess the throne in my heart, and cast out of it whatever opposeth or offendeth thee. It is thine already by purchase; O make it thine also by conquest! and perform the whole work of a Saviour upon it.

After this manner doth the believer address himself to Christ; and thus doth he answer the call to *come unto him*. From all which we may learn our duty in this matter. Let every *laboring and heavy laden* sinner, who hears me this day, speedily betake himself to the same happy course; plead his own call, and humbly claim his gracious protection; flee without delay to his atoning blood, and cleave to him as the Lord your "righteousness and your strength." I shall afterwards represent to you those sure grounds of hope which may encourage you to do this: In the mean time, let us consider

The gracious promise with which our Lord enforces the invitation: *I will give you rest*. This was the

Third thing I proposed to illustrate.

There can be no doubt that the *rest* here spoken of must be, at least, of equal extent with the *burden*, and include a deliverance from every cause of trouble to the soul. But this subject is an ocean without bottom or shore; we cannot measure the length or breadth of it, neither can its depth be fathomed; for "the riches of Christ are unsearchable;" and surely no tongue can express what the mind itself is unable to comprehend. Nevertheless, I shall attempt to say a few things which may be of use to help forward your comfort and joy, till eternity shall unfold the whole to your view.

Doth the guilt of sin, and the curse of the law, lie heavy upon thy soul? "Behold the Lamb of God which taketh away the sin of the world." In the sacrifice of Christ there is an infinite merit that can never be exhausted. He hath satisfied the most extensive demands of justice, and purchased a full and everlasting indemnity to every penitent and believing sinner: so that "now there is no condemnation to them which are in Christ Jesus." No sooner doth a soul *come* to him in the manner I described, than it "passeth from death to life." He spreads his righteousness over it, and, under that covering, presents it to his heavenly Father; from that happy moment it is no longer under the law, but under grace; "For Christ hath redeemed us from the curse of the law, by his being made a curse for us." And what a plentiful source of consolation is this! Well may the sinner "be of good cheer," to whom Christ hath said, "Thy sins are forgiven thee." Do you feel a law in your members warring against the law of your mind?

Are you harassed with temptations, and so environed with "a body of death," that you are made to cry out, as Paul once did, "O wretched man, who shall deliver me!" Look up to that Prince and Saviour, whom God hath exalted, not only to give remission of sins, but likewise to bestow repentance upon his people, and grace to help them in every time of need. Christ hath obtained the Holy Spirit, by whose almighty aid the Christian can do all things. He will plant that immortal seed in your hearts, which shall gradually kill the weeds of corruption: so that, according to his faithful word of promise, though sin may lodge and fight within you, yet it shall not be able to get "dominion over you."

Do you fear that some unforeseen cause may provoke him to forsake you, to withdraw his love, and the communications of his grace? Know that "the gifts and callings of God are without repentance." Christ is the "good shepherd, who carries the lambs in his bosom;" and therefore they cannot perish, because none is strong enough to pluck them out of his hand. The believer is not left to stand by himself; he who is the author, is likewise the finisher of his people's faith. Omnipotence is their guardian; and they are "kept," not by their own strength, but "by the power of God, through faith unto salvation."

These three are surely the *heaviest burdens* with which the soul of man can be oppressed; and you see that the Lord Jesus is able to remove them all. There are no doubt, many other causes of discouragement to which we are liable so long as we sojourn in this valley of tears; but as none of them are equal to those I have already named, we may certainly conclude, that he who performs the greater work, can, with infinite ease, perform the lesser also. And indeed, if I might stay upon this branch of the subject, it would be no difficult task to show, that in all other respects believers "are complete in Christ," and may by faith derive from him whatever is necessary either for their safety or comfort in this world: "For it hath pleased the Father, that in him should all fulness dwell," as it is written, Coloss. i. 19.

But if we would behold the *rest* here spoken of in its utmost extent, and highest perfection, we must look above us to that heavenly world, from which sin, and all the painful effects of it, are eternally excluded. "There remaineth a rest," said the apostle, "for the people of God." Great and manifold are their privileges even in this world; but beyond all these, are still more glorious and enriching blessings that await them in the next, which our "ears have not yet heard, neither can our hearts conceive." When we attempt to think of that exalted happiness, we can do little more than remove from it in our minds all those afflicting evils and grounds of discouragement which we presently feel; only we must conclude, that whatever the particular ingredients are, the happiness itself must be, in all respects, worthy of its glorious Author, and proportioned to the infinite price that was paid for it. Our Lord himself calls it a "kingdom," nay, a "kingdom prepared from the foundation of the world;" and the apostle Peter hath recorded three of its distinguishing properties, (1 Peter i. 4.) where he styles it an "inheritance incorruptible, undefiled, and that fadeth not away."

Such, my brethren, is that rest which Christ will finally bestow upon his people. They shall "enter into the joy of their Lord." All their burdens shall drop with their natural bodies; none of them can pass beyond the grave. Then faith and hope shall become sight and enjoyment; then love grown perfect shall cast out fear; and nothing shall remain of all their former trials, but the grateful remembrance of that friendly hand which supported them, and hath at length crowned their "light and momentary afflictions" with a "far more exceeding and eternal weight of glory."

And now, in the review of all that has been said, methinks every sinner who hears me should be ready to answer the call of my text in the language of Peter, "Lord, to whom shall we go but unto thee? for thou hast the words of eternal life." O that there were such hearts in us! But perhaps some humble soul may say, Gladly would I go to this Saviour, willingly would I throw myself at his feet and implore his protection; but such, alas! is my vileness and unworthiness, so long have I slighted his offers, and abused his grace, that I fear this call, kind as it is, doth not extend to me: my case is singularly bad, and my sins have been aggravated to such a degree, that my desponding heart hath already pronounced the sentence of condemnation; and the doom appears so just, so righteous, that I can see no ground to hope that ever it shall be reversed. For removing this obstacle, which seems to lie in the way of your return to Christ, let me beg your attention to the following particulars.

Consider the great condescension of this Redeemer. While he was upon earth, he never rejected any who sought relief from him; like a sanctuary whose gates stand continually open, he gave free, undebarred access to all, insomuch that his enemies, by way of reproach, styled him *the friend of publicans and sinners.* Neither did our Lord disown the character; on the contrary, he gloried in it, and proclaimed it openly to the world; declaring, upon all proper occasions, "that he was come to seek and to save that which was lost." For this end he assumed our nature; for this end he suffered and died; and upon the same benevolent design, he is now gone up to heaven, "where he appears in the presence of God for us;"— "that if any man sin, he may have an Advocate with the Father" to solicit his pardon, and to plead his cause. And may not these discoveries of his merciful nature expel your fears, and revive your hope? Has he in a manner laid aside the majesty of a sovereign, and put on the mild and amiable aspect of a tender-hearted, sympathizing friend? and may not this by itself encourage you to draw near to him, and to claim the blessings of that *rest* he hath obtained for his people?

But, lo! he hath prevented you even in this; for to all the proofs of his good-will to men, he superadds the most warm and pressing invitations, to come to him for relief from all their burdens. "In the last day, the great day of the feast, Jesus stood and cried, If *any man* thirst, let him come unto me and drink." "Behold," said he to the degenerated church of the Laodiceans, "Behold, I stand at the door and knock: If *any man* will hear my voice, and open the door, I will come in to him, and sup with him, and he with me." And in the concluding chapter of the Revelation, it is writtin, "The Spirit and the bride say, Come: and let him that is a-thirst, come: and *whosoever will*, let him come, and let him take the water of life freely." So that you see my text is not a singular instance of condescension; the Scriptures are replenished with invitations of the same kind; and they are all expressed in the most extensive and absolute terms, on purpose, as it were, to obviate every possible objection, and to remove all jealousy from the most desponding sinners, who might otherwise have suspected that the call did not reach so far as them.

But lest the offer of a Saviour, when viewed as a privilege, might still appear in the eyes of some a privilege too high for them to aspire to, therefore it hath pleased the Father to interpose his authority, and to make it our duty to embrace the offer: as we learn from that remarkable passage, (1 John iii. 23.) "This is the *command* of God, that we should believe on the name of his Son Jesus Christ." So that faith in Christ becomes an act of obedience; the law of the Supreme Governor is the sinner's warrant to come to the Saviour; and therefore it can be no presumption in any, however guilty they have been, to flee to this city of refuge, seeing he who hath appointed it, not only permits, but peremptorily *commands* them to repair to it.

And to crown all, our Lord himself hath declared in the most solemn manner, that none shall be rejected who come to him for salvation. These are his words, (John vi. 37.) "Him that cometh to me I will in nowise cast out." I will receive him with outstretched arms; I will tenderly embrace and cherish him, and so unite him to myself, that the combined force of earth and hell shall never be able to dissolve the union, or to separate my soul from his unchangeable love.

Lift up thy head, then, O *laboring and heavy laden* sinner! ponder, with due attention, those grounds of encouragement I have briefly suggested. Doth the Father *command* you to believe on his Son? doth the Lord Jesus invite, nay, entreat, you to come to him, and at the same time assure you that "he will in nowise cast you out?" and shall not this multiplied security remove all your doubts, and bring you to him with a humble, but steadfast, hope of obtaining that *rest* which he offers unto you? Say not henceforth, My burden is so heavy, and my guilt is so great, that I dare not go to him; but rather say, My burden is so heavy that I *must* go to him; for no other arm can remove it but his own. He offers you his help, because you are miserable; he invites you to come to him, not because you deserve, but because you need his aid. Arise, then, O sinners, and obey his call: cast your burden upon him who is mighty to save; yield yourselves, without reserve, to this faithful Redeemer, to be justified by his blood, and sanctified by his Spirit; "take his yoke upon you, and learn of him," and then you shall find *rest* to your souls.

But what shall I say to those who have never as yet felt the burden of sin? who, amidst the deepest poverty and wretchedness, imagine themselves to be "rich, and increased with goods, and to stand in need of nothing?" Alas! my friends, what can we do for such?—shall I denounce the curses of a broken covenant to alarm their fears?—shall I publish the terrors of the Lord, and by these persuade them to flee from the wrath to come? Indeed, considerations of this kind seem proper and necessary to rouse them from that deadly sleep into which they are cast. And believe it, O sinners! that no representations of this sort, however awful they might appear, could exceed, or even equal, the dreadful reality; "for who knoweth the power of God's anger?"

But as my text breathes nothing but clemency, I shall rather, upon this occasion, "beseech you by the meekness and gentleness of Christ," and fetch my arguments from the endearing condescensions of his mercy and grace.

Know then, O sinners! that after all the contempt you have thrown upon him, he is still willing to become your Saviour. Ungrateful as you have been, he once more opens his arms, and invites you to come unto him. He sends us forth this day to call after you in his name, and to entreat you in his stead to be reconciled to God. Behold, in the gospel-offer, he lays, as it were, his crucified body in your way, to stop you in your self-destroying course! And will you still press onward, "and trample under foot the Son of God!" Behold his blood, like a mighty river, flows between you and the place of torment! And will you force your passage to the everlasting burnings through this immense ocean of redeeming love! O sinners, think of this! all who perish under the gospel, must carry this dreadful aggravation along with them, that mercy was in their offer, and they would not accept it; nay, that they insulted and abused the mercy that would have saved them. And "can your hearts endure, or can your hands be strong, in the day that God shall deal with you" for this contempt? For the Lord's sake open your eyes in time; look upon him whom you have pierced by your sins, and mourn. I address you as the angels did Lot, when they brought him forth from Sodom; "Escape for thy life; look not behind thee, neither stay thou in all the plain:" "Flee to the Saviour, lest thou be consumed."

As for you who have already got within the walls of the city of refuge, I have one request to make to you, with which I shall conclude. Come now, and receive the new Testament in Christ's blood. For confirming your faith, and increasing your joy, he hath instituted this visible pledge of his love, this external seal of his gracious covenant; that, by the elements of bread and wine, the appointed symbols of his broken body and shed blood, he might invest his people with a full and unalterable right to all the blessed fruits of his sufferings and death. And, therefore, as you have come to Christ himself, you may lawfully consider the invitation in my text as your warrant and call to come to his holy table; and may hope to find, in this holy sacrament, something of that *rest*, or spiritual relief, which he is always ready to dispense to those who feel their need of it, and who know its worth. *Amen.*

SERMON VIII.

THE CAPTIVE'S HOPE.

ZECHARIAH IX. 12.—"Turn ye to the stronghold, ye prisoners of hope; even to-day do I declare that I will render double unto thee."

IN the 9th verse of this chapter proclamation is made that the Messiah is at hand; and the church is called upon to go forth to meet him with joy. "Rejoice greatly, O daughter of Zion; shout, O daughter of Jerusalem; behold, thy King cometh unto thee" And that the awe of his majesty might be no bar to their joy, they are told, for their encouragement, that he comes in such a form of condescension and grace, as serves rather to invite than forbid their approach to him: for "He is just, and having salvation; lowly, and riding upon an ass, and upon a colt, the foal of an ass." They are further assured, in the 10th verse, that as the ensigns of his royalty differ so widely from those which earthly monarchs use, so he shall govern his subjects, and subdue his enemies, not by external force, but by inward persuasion; not by "the chariot, the horse, and the battle-bow," for all these shall be "cut off;" but by the preaching of the gospel, accompanied with the powerful operation of the Spirit, which is emphatically called "speaking peace unto the heathen;" in consequence whereof, "his dominions shall extend from sea to sea, and from the river even to the ends of the earth." And to finish the description of this King of Zion, it is added, in the 11th verse, that the gracious aim of his government is to set men at liberty from the vilest slavery, and to release them from the most ignominious confinement, by opening their prison doors, and "sending them forth out of the pit wherein is no water." This too he is to perform in a way peculiarly endearing: he is to purchase their freedom with the price of his own blood; which, with great propriety, is styled "the blood of the covenant," as it ratifies and confirms that covenant of grace, whereby sinners are reinstated in the favor of God, and rescued from the power of all their spiritual enemies.

The like representation is given of the Messiah, .(Isaiah xlii. 6, 7.) "I the Lord have called thee in righteousness, and will hold thine hand, and will keep thee, and give thee for a covenant of the people, for a light of the Gentiles; to open the blind eyes, to bring out the prisoners from the prison, and them that sit in darkness out of the prison-house." And the Messiah himself is introduced, (Isaiah lxi. at the beginning) speaking to the same purpose, saying, "The Spirit of the Lord God is upon me, because the Lord hath anointed me to preach good tidings unto the meek, he hath sent me to bind up the broken-hearted, to proclaim liberty to the captives, and the opening of the prison to them that are bound."

In all these passages, he is plainly pointed out to us in the character of a Redeemer; and, as such, he issues forth the proclamation in my text: *Turn ye to the stronghold, ye prisoners of hope; even to-day do I declare that I will render double unto thee.*

In which words we have three things that deserve our notice.

First. A description of the persons whom he comes to redeem: They are *prisoners of hope.*

Second. The advice or command addressed to them: *Turn ye to the stronghold.* And,

Third. A gracious and encouraging promise; *Even to-day do I declare that I will render double unto thee.*

I propose, God willing, to make a few remarks upon each of these particulars, and to conclude with an improvement suited to the occasion of our present meeting.

First. The persons to whom the command is addressed are called *prisoners of hope.*

The description, you see, is of a mixed nature; it represents a state in the main bad, yet not so wholly bad as to be past recovery. We are all by nature in a state of bondage, condemned by the righteous sentence of the law, and slaves to Satan and our own corruptions. By our apostasy from God we sunk into a pit where indeed "there is no water:" There we sit "in darkness, and in the shadow of death," destitute of every thing that can afford real peace and joy to the soul. But though this pit doth not yield any water, yet water may be brought into it. The dew of divine grace may descend upon the prisoners, and "the day-spring from on high" may visit their dark abode, and guide them out of it into the way of peace and safety. Hence, unconverted sinners, though *prisoners*, may properly be called *prisoners of hope*, so long as their life is continued upon earth. It is true, that if death surprise them in that state, they shall then sink lower into another pit; of which it may be said, with an awful emphasis, that *there*—"there is no water;"—it yields none;—it admits of none;—not one drop can be brought into it to cool the tongue. But so long as they live, their case, though bad, is by no means hopeless; there is virtue enough in "the blood of the covenant" to save them; and though they are advanced to the last stage of impiety, yet, even there, Almighty grace can reach them, and snatch them like brands out of the burning. So that under this general denomination of *prisoners of hope*, every man or woman living upon earth is spoken to in my text. And indeed the gospel call is addressed to sinners indefinitely: "Unto you, O men, I call," says the Saviour, "and my voice is to the sons of men."—"Look unto me, and be saved, all ye ends of the earth." None are excluded from the offers of mercy; he invites all to come unto him; and him "who cometh he will in nowise cast out."

But, more particularly, the description seems to point at those who feel their misery, and earnestly look and long for deliverance. Many, alas! are lying in the pit of an unconverted state, without any sense or feeling of their woe; the darkness is so thick around them, that they see not the fetters by which they are bound.

Now, such must necessarily put away from themselves every offer of liberty, saying, in the scornful language of the Pharisees, "We be Abraham's seed, and were never in bondage to any man; how sayest thou then, Ye shall be made free?" I therefore reckon, that sensible sinners, humble, convinced souls, are spoken to for their encouragement under this designation of *prisoners of hope*, not only to distinguish them from those who are gone to the pit where there is no hope, but even from others, who, though they still dwell in the land of hope, yet, in some respects, may be reputed in a hopeless condition; because their pride and insensibility put them out of the way of help and deliverance. Whereas they who have got an affecting view of their guilt and misery, lie, as it were, in the very road of mercy; nay, the more painful their feelings are, the greater likelihood there is of a gracious and speedy relief: He whose office it is "to bind up the broken-hearted, and to proclaim liberty to the captives," will neither deny them his aid, nor defer their relief one moment beyond the time he knows to be best for them. And therefore sinners of this sort may, with peculiar propriety, be called *prisoners of hope;* because, whatever their own apprehensions are, Christ certainly looks upon them as his proper charge, and invites them to cast all their burdens upon himself, in these sweet, condescending words, "Come unto me, all ye that labor and are heavy laden, and I will give you rest."

By *prisoners of hope*, then, we may understand, more generally, all sinners, without exception, who are within the reach of divine mercy; and more especially those who are suing for mercy, under the felt burden of sin and misery.

But I add further, that even they who have obtained mercy, seem likewise to be included in the description of my text. The connection of this with the preceding verse leads me to this remark, and, I apprehend, lays a solid foundation for it; for the persons who are spoken *to* in this verse, are evidently the same who are spoken *of* in the preceding one; and yet here they are denominated *prisoners of hope*, though just before it was said of them, "that by the blood of the covenant they were sent forth out of the pit wherein is no water;" that is, cleansed from their guilt, and delivered from the darkness and misery of an unconverted state.

I need not observe to you, that the present condition of believers upon earth, is neither a state of perfect liberty, nor of uninterrupted peace. These are the blessed ingredients which constitute the happiness of the Zion above; but whilst they sojourn in this strange land, they are liable to various and painful distresses. Even after they have received "the Spirit of adoption," they may feel such returns of "the Spirit of bondage," as shall oblige them to cry out with David, "My spirit is overwhelmed within me;—Attend unto my cry, O God, for I am brought very low:—Bring my soul out of prison, that I may praise thy name."

The remembrance of past guilt, the present feeling of indwelling corruption, the hidings of God's face, and the assaults and buffetings of their spiritual enemies, are all so many different prisons, in which the dearest of God's children may be shut up for a season. And we find some of them recorded in holy writ, who, during the time of this spiritual confinement, have felt such exquisite agony, that with difficulty they have been kept from razing the foundation, and quitting all hope. Such was the case of Asaph when he thus expressed himself in the 77th Psalm, "I remembered God, and was troubled—I am so troubled that I cannot speak.—Will the Lord cast off for ever? will he be favorable no more? Is his mercy clean gone for ever? doth his promise fail for evermore? Hath God forgotten to be gracious? hath he in anger shut up his tender mercies?" And how distressing must we suppose the case of Heman to have been, when it drew from him such mournful complaints as these: "My soul is full of trouble, and my life draweth nigh unto the grave: Thou hast laid me in the lowest pit, in darkness, in the deeps: Lord, why castest thou off my soul? why hidest thou thy face from me? I am afflicted, and ready to die from my youth up: while I suffer thy terrors, I am distracted; thy fierce wrath goeth over me; thy terrors have cut me off."

These strong examples are sufficient to prove, that there are other prisons besides the pit of an unconverted state: Prisons where those who are near and dear to God, may, for wise and holy reasons, suffer a temporary confinement; on account of which they may be justly denominated *prisoners of hope.*

And if so, then my text speaks directly to every soul in this assembly; and the advice it gives to each of you is this:

Turn ye to the stronghold, ye prisoners of hope. And this is the

Second branch of the subject, which I am now to consider.

By the *stronghold* to which we are exhorted to turn, is undoubtedly meant "the blood of the covenant," spoken of in the preceding verse; or rather the new covenant itself, ratified and sealed by the blood of Christ.

This indeed is a *stronghold*, an impregnable defence to all who flee to it for refuge: It is "an everlasting covenant, ordered in all things and sure." Here an effectual supply is to be found for all the sinner's wants and necessities; an infinite sacrifice to expiate his guilt; all conquering grace to subdue his corruptions; unerring wisdom to guide him; irresistible power to protect him; unbounded goodness to relieve his present needs, and to crown him with glory and happiness hereafter. In short, "the whole fulness of the Godhead" is treasured up in the Mediator of this covenant; and "he is made of God," unto all who believe on him, "wisdom, and righteousness, and sanctification and redemption."

But instead of enlarging upon the description of this *stronghold*, I reckon it of greater importance to explain the advice here given to the *prisoners of hope*, which is the proper work and duty of the day. *Turn ye to the stronghold.* But how are we to do this?

1*st.* We must turn our back upon every thing else, and abandon all other means of deliverance as refuges of lies, which will miserably disappoint those who expect relief from them. Particularly we must renounce our own righteousness, and plead guilty in the presence of a holy God, acknowledging, that we must stand justly condemned by the tenor of the first covenant, and are neither able of ourselves to give any satisfaction for past offences, nor to yield an acceptable obedience for the future. "They that be whole," said our blessed Saviour, "need no physician, but they that are sick." The natural pride of our hearts opposeth our seeking aid from any thing without ourselves; nay, such is our disaffection to the great God, that even when aid appears necessary, we would rather be indebted for it to any other than to him. I believe I may venture to affirm, that the gospel sanctuary is always the sinner's last resort; and it is not till we are "shut up unto the faith," as the Apostle expresseth it, that is, hedged in on every side by an absolute despair of relief from any creature, that we come to think in good earnest of seeking it from Christ. This then is the first thing implied in *turning to the stronghold*, that we turn our back upon every thing else. It further imports in the

2*d* place, That we turn our eyes to this *stronghold*, and narrowly examine the security it affords.

The true flight of a soul to the Lord Jesus Christ, is not a rash and precipitate adventure, but the result of serious and mature deliberation: it is not curiosity, but pressing necessity, that sets the soul in motion. The awakened sinner sees the avenger of blood ready to seize upon him; and hearing of a *stronghold*, erected by infinite wisdom and grace, for the protection and safety of persons in his situation, he anxiously inquires into the truth of this report, and useth every means in his power to get certain information of it.

This, my brethren, is an essential part of the duty here enjoined. I cannot tell you of what importance it is to get clear and distinct apprehensions of the gospel-covenant, that *stronghold* pointed out to us in my text.

We should not only endeavor to know what we are allowed to expect from it, but likewise to see the firmness of that foundation upon which our faith and hope must stand. A wavering hope may balance a wavering apprehension of danger, but will not answer the necessities of an awakened sinner. But when we come to see that this *stronghold* is built upon the Rock of ages, and suported by pillars of invincible strength, even all the perfections of an unchangeable God; or, to drop the allusion, when we see that this covenant, which promises every blessing we need, is a sure, a permanent, and irrevocable deed, confirmed by the oath of the great *I AM*, and sealed with the blood of his own dear Son, "in whom all the promises are yea and amen;" here the soul finds something to lean upon; its anxious fears begin to vanish; it now knows with certainty where relief is to be found.

Having thus discovered the stability of the covenant, and that it is in all respects such a *stronghold* as we need, the

3*d*, and principal thing required is, That we actually flee to it, and improve it for all the purposes for which it was intended.

The two former advices I gave you, were only preparatory to this last and most important step, which is the sum and substance of the duty here enjoined, *Turn ye to the stronghold, ye prisoners of hope.*

You who are lying in the prison of an unconverted state, come hither to this sanctuary, whose gates stand open to receive you: "It is a faithful saying, and worthy of all acceptation, that Jesus Christ came into the world to save sinners:" He hath shed that blood which "cleanseth from all sin," and hath sealed that gracious and well-ordered covenant, which offers pardon and eternal life to every penitent, believing sinner. And now "all things are ready" for your reception and entertainment: The Father is ready to embrace you; Christ is ready to wash you in his blood; the Spirit is ready to heal your diseased natures; angels are ready to rejoice at your return; and we, as the servants of this King of Zion, are ready to welcome you into the family of God, and do now exhort and pray you, in Christ's stead, to flee for refuge, "to lay hold on the hope set before you." This is the call of my text to unconverted sinners.

As to the other *prisoners of hope* I spoke of, who, though they are rescued from the pit wherein is no water, yet find their souls cast down within them, and, by reason of various discouragements, cannot enjoy "the liberty wherewith Christ has set them free;"

The call to you is, *Turn* again *to the stronghold*, and once more look to "the Rock that is higher than you." The Redeemer, in whom you trust, is mighty to save; "all power is committed to him in heaven and in earth;" and he is constituted "head over all things for his church." "It hath pleased the Father, that in him all fulness should dwell;" and the whole fulness of the Godhead is treasured up in him, for this very end, that he may dispense to his people such gracious supplies as their various cases and circumstances may require. You are not straitened in him, be not "straitened in your own bowels."

Might I stay to examine your particular complaints, I believe I could show you that there is something in the covenant to answer them all. He who brought you out of the pit of an unconverted state, can easily deliver you from every other prison. What furnace can consume those who are sprinkled with that blood which hath already quenched the fire of incensed justice? He who "bore your sins in his own body upon the tree," will not suffer you to sink under the weight of them: He who "suffered, being tempted," will certainly succor you who are tempted! He who, under the hidings of his Father's face, cried out upon the cross, "My God! my God! why hast thou forsaken me?" cannot fail to sympathize with his people in the like circumstances; and he whose own "soul was exceeding sorrowful, even unto death," will, in due time, communicate that joy to you, the want of which was so painful to himself. If Christ is indeed precious in your esteem; if you can say without known guile, that your whole dependence is upon him, and him alone; then know, that he is equal to all the trust you can put in him, and he is faithful who hath said, *Even to day do I declare, that I will render double unto thee.* And this is the

Third and *last* branch of the text. Upon which I shall offer a very few remarks, and then conclude.

1*st*. I would observe, that the promise itself is most gracious, *I will render double unto thee.* We meet with the same expression, (Isaiah lxi. 7.) where I think the meaning of it is plainly ascertained: "For your shame ye shall have double; and for confusion they shall rejoice in their portion: therefore in their land they shall possess the double: everlasting joy shall be unto them." The chapter is introduced with that grand description of the Messiah's office, which I formerly quoted; "The Spirit of the Lord God is upon me," &c. The redemption of the Jews from the Babylonish captivity, and their return to their own land, appear from the sequel of the chapter to have been the events which the Prophet had more immediately in his eye. But we shall not be able to doubt that he looked a great deal farther, even to that spiritual redemption which Christ was to achieve for his church, if we turn over to the 4th chapter of Luke, 21st verse, where our blessed Lord, after reading this passage in the synagogue at Nazareth, made particular application of it to himself, in these remarkable words: "This day is the Scripture fulfilled in your ears." Hence it is obvious, that what the Prophet says in the 7th verse, viz. for "your shame ye shall have double," &c. falls to be understood in a spiritual sense too; and the meaning of it is, that the ransomed of the Lord shall not only be freed from bondage, and rescued from the hands of their spiritual enemies, but shall likewise be advanced to such honor and happiness, as shall wipe off all the shame of their servitude, and fill them with the most transporting joy.

In the 90th Psalm, at the 15th verse, Moses, the man of God, prays for the church in these terms: "Make us glad, *according* to the days wherein thou hast afflicted us, and the years wherein we have seen grief." He only asks joy *in proportion to* the grief they have felt; but the bounty of our gracious Lord doth far exceed the prayers and expectations of his servants; for here he says I will render unto thee, not barely *according* to, or in proportion to thy former sufferings, but I will render *double* unto thee. Even in this life, he may pour into your souls such measures of joy and consolation, as shall not only balance your past sorrows, but far outweigh them, and cause them to appear very light and inconsiderable. At any rate, he will render unto you *double* in another world; all tears shall there be wiped away from your eyes; your light afflictions, which are but for a moment, are, in the mean time, working for you a far more exceeding and eternal weight of glory; and, ere long, "you shall return and come to Zion, with songs and everlasting joy upon your heads; then shall you obtain joy and gladness, and sorrow and sighing shall flee away."

I would further observe to you, in the *2d* place, That the comfort of this promise is greatly heightened by the manner of publishing it; *Even to-day do I declare.* It is uttered with great solemnity, and expressed in the most resolved and peremptory manner.—I do not say it slightly: I *declare it;* I pledge the credit both of my power and faithfulness to make it good.

The circumstance of time, too, makes a remarkable addition. I declare it *even to-day;* in this dark and cloudy day, when your misgiving minds are meditating nothing but terror. Even on *this day*, when the event is most unlikely, I give you the promise of complete deliverance; *to-day*, when your hearts are emptied of self-confidence, when every other refuge fails, I give you my word, my oath, to lay hold upon; and I do it *to-day*, whilst your feelings are most painful, that the depth of your distress may help you to form some conception of the high joy that awaits you at that happy time when *I shall render double unto thee.*

But I apprehend there is still an emphasis on these words *to-day*, beyond any thing I have yet mentioned. Here God, as it were, prefixes a date to his promise, which, in human obligations, has always been judged an essential formality: as if he had said, let it be recorded, that *on this day* I have passed my word for your salvation; for though I need no tokens to remind me of my everlasting purposes of grace, yet, as you need them to strengthen your faith and hope, therefore, in pity of your weakness, I give you every kind of security you can ask from one another. Let it then be remembered, that *to-day, I declare I will render double unto thee.*

Upon the whole, then, let me once more repeat the call in my text, *Turn ye to the stronghold, ye prisoners of hope.* Bring all your cares, your doubts, your temptations, to that mighty Saviour on whom your help is laid. He hath declared to you in his word, *that he will render unto you double;* "for what things soever were written aforetime, were written for our learning, that we, through patience and comfort of the Scripture, might have hope." The promise, though addressed to believers many ages ago, extends even to us; because he who made the promise is always in one mind; "the same yesterday, to-day, and for ever." Nay, so great is his condescension, that he is just now willing to have it dated afresh under one of the authentic seals of his covenant.

Let us then, my brethren, humbly adore the goodness of God which hath provided so liberally for the relief and comfort of the *prisoners of hope;* and in the entrance to the solemn service of this day, let us look up to him who is "the God of hope;" praying, in the words which his own spirit hath indited, that he would "fill us with all joy and peace in believing, that we may abound in hope, through the power of the Holy Ghost." *Amen.*

SERMON IX.

THE WANDERER, AND HIS RETURN.

1 Peter ii. 25.—"For ye were as sheep going astray; but are now returned unto the Shepherd and Bishop of your souls."

Humility is both the strength and beauty of the soul; it is its best defence, as well as its fairest ornament. "Happy is the man that feareth always; but he that hardeneth his heart shall fall into mischief;" "for God resisteth the proud, but giveth grace to the humble." No sooner had David said, "I shall never be moved," than he suddenly experienced a sad reverse of fortune, and found cause to utter that mournful complaint, "Thou didst hide thy face, and I was troubled."

Various means have been employed in every age of the church, to banish pride from the hearts of men, and to beget and cherish that lowliness of mind which becomes dependent, guilty creatures. This was the obvious tendency of the most solemn rites under the old dispensation. The annual sacrifice of the paschal lamb, besides its typical use, or reference to the great atonement, had likewise an important moral signification; and the lessons it taught were *humility* and *gratitude.*

"It shall come to pass," said Moses, by the command of God, "that when your children shall say unto you, What mean you by this service? ye shall say, It is the sacrifice of the Lord's passover, who passed over the houses of the children of Israel in Egypt, when he smote the Egyptians, and delivered our houses." In like manner, when they brought the first fruits as an offering to the Lord, which was another solemnity that returned every year, the form of dedication was prescribed in these words: (Deut. xxvi. 5, 6, &c.) "A Syrian ready to perish was my father, and he went down into Egypt, and sojourned there with a few, and became there a nation, great, mighty, and populous. And the Egyptians evil entreated us, and afflicted us, and laid upon us hard bondage. And when we cried unto the Lord God of our fathers, the Lord heard our voice, and looked on our affliction, and our labor, and our oppression. And the Lord brought us forth out of Egypt, with a mighty hand, and with an outstretched arm, and with great terribleness, and with signs, and with wonders. And he hath brought us into this place, and hath given us this land that floweth with milk and honey. And now, behold, I have brought the first fruits of the land, which thou, O Lord, hast given me."

Thus did God train up his ancient people "to serve him with reverence, and to rejoice before him with trembling." Their thank-offerings, as well as their oblations for sin, obliged them to recognize the meanness of their original, and the ignominious servitude from which God had redeemed them; and every act of worship taught them to say, "Who am I, O Lord God, and what is my house, that thou hast brought me hitherto?"

The ordinances of grace in the New Testament church breathe the same spirit, and dictate the same language; nay, they do it with greater force and energy.

The gospel-passover, which we are this day to celebrate, commemorates a deliverance from spiritual thraldom; of which the release of the Jews from the Egyptian yoke affords but a faint and imperfect emblem.

In those complicated sufferings which were the price of our redemption, we not only discover the unsearchable riches of divine love, but we likewise behold the full demerit of sin, and all the horrors of that misery into which we had plunged ourselves by our fatal apostacy; so that our triumph in the great salvation, by recalling to our minds the low and helpless state in which mercy found us, gives check to every self-exalting thought, and constrains us to ascribe to the free and unmerited favor of God, the sole, the undivided praise of all that we have, or hope to enjoy.

To those views, and to this becoming exercise, we are naturally led by the words of my text; which have frequently occurred to me as a most proper form of address for introducing communicants to the table of their Lord. *Ye were as sheep going astray, but are now returned to the Shepherd and Bishop of your souls.*

These two widely different states,—what you *once were* by nature, and what you *now are* by grace, I propose to illustrate in the sequel of this discourse; from both which we may, with ease and certainty, discover what frame and temper of heart best suit our attendance upon this great Christian solemnity. Let me then call upon believers in Christ; for to them, and to them only, such language can be addressed; let me call upon them, in the

First place, Seriously to review their former condition, when *they*, as well as others, *were as sheep going astray.*

The fitness of this similitude, to exhibit the natural state of mankind, may justly be inferred from the frequent use that is made of it in the sacred writings. I shall not attempt to trace out the resemblance in all its extent; but some parts of it are so striking and expressive, that to overlook them altogether, or even slightly to regard them, would either betray very gross insensibility, or a perverse contempt of the divine condescension.

Thus, a sheep that hath forsaken the good pasture, and strayed into the parched and barren wilderness, presents to us, in the strongest and most affecting light, an emblem of indigence, perplexity, and disappointment. Now, such is the state of every natural man; "vanity and vexation of spirit" are his portion; he resembles one "who dreameth, and behold he eateth, but he awaketh, and his soul is empty." Disappointed in every pursuit, he goes from place to place, ever repeating the anxious question, *Who will show me any good?* There is a void within him that the world cannot fill; the flesh, after all the provision he can make for it, still cries with "the horse-leech, Give, give;" and like "the fire or the grave, never saith, It is enough." All the creatures are to him what the husks were to the prodigal; they yield a momentary relief, but no real nourishment; he endeavors to feed upon them, "but still he hath appetite, his soul is faint," and he perisheth with hunger.

Again, this figurative representation denotes a state of danger as well as of indigence and dissatisfaction. Few animals are beset with more enemies than sheep; and perhaps none are possessed of less cunning to elude, or of less courage to resist them. Their safety depends entirely upon the shepherd's care; for if they wander beyond the reach of his protecting arm, they become at once, to every ravenous beast, not only a tempting but an easy prey. With what awful precision doth this part of the similitude exhibit to us the state of unconverted sinners! Their spiritual enemies are both numerous and mighty; and the subtlety of the serpent and the strength of the lion are but faint representations of their craft and power; yet such is the presumption of carnal men, so fatal the security of those who are far from God, that instead of avoiding their blood-thirsty foes, they roam without fear through their most frequented haunts, and rush headlong into those snares that are laid for their destruction.

Once more;—Though sheep are not the only creatures that are prone to wander, yet it may justly be affirmed of them, that they, of all others, discover least sagacity in finding the way back to the place from whence they strayed; so that in them we likewise behold a proper and most descriptive emblem of man's helplessness and impotent state by nature, and of his utter inability, by any efforts of his own, to regain his primeval happiness and glory. That the apostle intended to convey this idea is more probable, from the form of his expression in the latter part of the verse; where, speaking of the recovery of wandering sinners, he doth not say, *ye have returned*, as if, by their own sagacity, they had discovered their error, and then rectified it by the activity of their own natural powers. But it deserves our notice, that he puts the word into the passive voice, *ye are* returned; that is, *converted*, or caused to return, as the same word is elsewhere rendered. For what our Lord said to his first disciples, may be addressed to believers in every age of the church: "Ye have not chosen me, but I have chosen you." "It is God that worketh in us both to will and to do of his good pleasure." "By grace we are saved, through faith; and that not of ourselves, it is the gift of God." Nor can any words be conceived more absolute and decisive than these, which are uttered by Christ himself: "No man cometh unto me, except the Father which hath sent me draw him."

In all these particulars, the resemblance can be traced with a critical exactness. But still there remains one other ingredient in man's apostacy from God, to which the similitude, comprehensive as it is, cannot be extended; the fatal ingredient I mean is *guilt*.

A sheep gone astray is an object of pity rather than of blame; the owner feels no emotion of anger against the simple wanderer; he doth not view it as faulty; but as unfortunate: he therefore seeks it with anxiety; and when he hath found it, so far is he from punishing it as a criminal, that he cherisheth it as a sufferer, takes it tenderly into his arms, and brings it home with joy. Whereas, in our departure from, God, evey crime is united that render us loathsome and odious in his sight. Man's apostacy was the effect not of weakness, but of wilfulness: the guilt that lieth upon us is nothing less than proud and obstinate rebellion: rebellion blackened with the vilest ingratitude; unprovoked rebellion against the Father of our spirits, and the former of our bodies, the God in whom we live, the generous author of those distinguished gifts, which, by the most impious abuse, we have turned into hostile weapons against him self.

Such monsters, my brethren, are all unconverted sinners. Happy! thrice happy they! of whom it can only be said, Such indeed ye *were;* "but ye are washed, ye are sanctified, ye are justified, in the name of the Lord Jesus, and by the Spirit of our God." To you, O believers, my text is addressed: look back to the waste and howling wilderness, "to the lions' dens," "and the mountains of leopards," where lately you wandered, "hungry and hard bestead," surrounded with enemies, and unable to resist them.—Now that you are established upon that Rock of ages, against which the gates of hell shall never prevail, it can surely do you no harm to cast your eye downward to the horrible pit and the miry clay, where you were ready to perish, when mercy interposed, and brought you seasonable relief; on the contrary, the remembrance of the dangers you have escaped, will heighten your gratitude, and only add solemnity to your present joy, while, from the humbling review of what you *were* by nature, I lead you to the contemplation of what you *are* by grace. Which was the

Second thing proposed in the method: *Ye are now returned unto the Shepherd and Bishop of your souls.*

The progress of a sinner in his return to God was formerly described, when I opened the import of these kind invitations. "Come unto me, all ye that labor and are heavy laden;"* and, "Turn ye to the stronghold, ye prisoners of hope."† My present aim is to comfort the souls of those who have already complied with the heavenly call, and to congratulate them upon the happy change that is wrought in their condition. Hail, ye blessed of the Lord!

Ye are returned to him who came from heaven to earth "to seek and to save that which was lost;" who, though infinitely offended by your criminal apostasy, hath himself made atonement for your past wanderings, and expiated your guilt with his own precious blood: "He was wounded for your transgressions, and bruised for your iniquities, that by his stripes ye might be healed." "This is that good shepherd who laid down his life for the sheep;" who "was made sin for us, though he knew no sin, that we might be made the righteousness of God in him:"—who "suffered, the just for the unjust, that he might bring us to God," with filial boldness, in the humble, yet assured hope, that we shall "obtain mercy, and find grace to help in every time of need."

Ye are *returned* to him,—who not only bore your griefs, and carried your sorrows, but hath likewise conquered all your enemies, and triumphed over them, as the chosen head and representative of his people. He hath in his own person, "spoiled principalities and powers;" and his success is a pledge of your final victory over them. Annoy you they may, but they cannot hurt you; by the blood of the Lamb you likewise shall overcome. Ere long "the God of peace shall bruise Satan under your feet," and put that new song into your mouth, "Now is come salvation, and strength, and the kingdom of our God, and the power of his Christ; for the accuser of the brethren is cast down, who accused them before our God day and night."

Ye are *returned* to him,—who will henceforth watch over you with peculiar care, and guard you as his property, which he purchased with his blood. "This *shepherd* of Israel, this *bishop*, this *overseer* of souls, never slumbers nor sleeps."—Many seasonable, though unknown deliverances, did he work for you, even while you ungratefully despised and rejected him. Often did he pluck you out of the jaws of the bear and the lion, before you were acquainted with him, or had any thought of craving his protection: but now his eye is continually upon you, his ear is at all times open to your cry, his everlasting arms are around and underneath you; and therefore you may boldly say, "the Lord is my light, and my salvation, whom shall I fear? The Lord is the strength of my life, of whom shall I be afraid? Behold, God is my salvation; I will trust and not be afraid: for the Lord JEHOVAH is my strength and my song: he also is become my salvation."

Ye are *returned* to him,—who hath not only almighty power to guard you against danger, but infinite compassion likewise to sympathize with you in all your distresses, and to comfort you in all your sorrows.

* Sermon vii. † Sermon viii.

He is meek and merciful, patient and condescending: "He gathers the lambs with his arms, and carries them in his bosom, and gently leads those that are with young." He pities their infirmities, and pardons their errors; he spares them when they are weary, and attends them when they are sick: nay, what no other shepherd can do, he imparts strength to the faint, and health to the diseased; and not only bestows food, but gives them an appetite to feed upon it: he also blesseth their provision, and causeth it to nourish them.

What shall I say more? This *shepherd and bishop of souls* continues to be their guardian even until death; neither doth he leave them at that awful period, but enters with them into the deep and darksome vale, supports them with "his staff," and so "comforts them with the rod of his strength," that they "walk through it with dignity, and fear no evil because he is with them." Many of the saints have been remarkably honored in this respect; even some, "who through fear of death were all their life long subject to bondage," have, in their latest moments, been enabled to triumph over this king of terrors, and to say with the apostle Paul, "O death, where is thy sting? O grave, where is thy victory? The sting of death is sin; and the strength of sin is the law. But thanks be unto God, who giveth us the victory, through Jesus Christ our Lord." Or if to any of them these evening-shadows are so thick, that they cannot see the hand that supports them; yet this momentary gloom shall only serve to heighten their surprise, their gratitude and their joy, when at the farther end of the valley, this good shepherd shall dispel the cloud, and stand before them revealed in all his glory; when he shall embrace them in his arms, and carry them upward to those greener pastures, and more fruitful fields of the heavenly Canaan; where, as it is beautifully expressed in the book of the Revelation, (chap. vii. at the close) "they shall hunger no more, neither thirst any more, neither shall the sun light on them, nor any heat. For the Lamb which is in the midst of the throne, shall feed them, and shall lead them unto living fountains of water; and God shall wipe away all tears from their eyes."

But I must not stay to enlarge upon these particulars; the imperfect account you have already heard, of the past and present state of believers in Christ, what they *were* by nature, and what they *are* by grace, may suffice to direct us to that frame and temper of heart, with which we ought to approach the table of the Lord. And it is obvious, in the

1*st* place, That we should do it with the deepest humility. This is the garb that sits most gracefully, and suits us best, whether we consider ourselves as lapsed, or restored; as sinners, or as saints. Are we pardoned? once we were condemned. Are we sanctified? once we were impure. Are we found? once we were lost. Are we made alive? lately we were dead; and still we live by an act of grace; it was God who quickened us, and not we ourselves: he only maketh us to differ; neither have we any thing but what we received from him. Surely, then, pride was not made for man.

2*dly.* We would perform this service with the warmest emotions of gratitude and love; giving thanks to the Father, who spared not his own Son, but delivered him to be a sacrifice and sin-offering for us: giving thanks to the Son, who spared not himself, but having taken upon him the form of a servant, submitted to hunger and thirst, to watching and weariness, to ignominy and torture: nay, to death and the grave: that through the merit of his death we might live for ever: giving thanks to the Spirit of all grace, who unites us to Christ, and applies to our souls that redemption he hath purchased, who renews our depraved natures, and renders us meet for the inheritance of the saints in light. How well doth that hymn of praise become the remembrance of Christ's death, with which the heavenly hosts celebrate the tidings of his birth? "Glory to God in the highest, on earth peace, good-will towards men."

3*dly.* Godly sorrows for past offences, and holy purposes to offend no more, should likewise attend us to the table of the Lord. Is Christ there set forth as crucified before our eyes? and can we "look upon him whom we have pierced," without mourning for those sins which were the cause of his sufferings? or can we mourn for them, without hating them, and resolving to forsake them? Should not this be the language of every sincere communicant? "What have I to do any more with idols?" "What I know not, Lord, teach thou me; if I have done iniquity, I will do so no more." But then, in the

4th place, These purposes must ever be accompanied with a sense of our own weakness, and of our absolute need of aid from above. Even after we are *returned* to the *bishop of our souls*, if left to ourselves we should quickly stumble and fall; the same hand that brought us back, when we were as *sheep going astray*, will always be necessary to uphold us in our journey, and to lead us forward till we arrive at the promised land. "Without me," said our Lord, even to those who were united to him, as the branches are to the vine, "without me," or separated from me, "ye can do nothing: as the branch cannot bear fruit of itself, except it abide in the vine; no more can ye, except ye abide in me." What is undertaken in self-confidence, shall certainly issue in shame and disappointment. The apostle Peter, who boasted, that "though all should forsake his Master, yet would not he," not only forsook him, but with oaths and imprecations denied that he knew him. "He that trusteth to his own heart is a fool:"—"Behold," said the prophet Habakkuk, "his soul which is lifted up is not upright in him." Needful, then, most needful, is that caution, "Let him who thinketh he standeth, take heed lest he fall." At the same time, in the

5th place, This diffidence of ourselves ought always to be qualified with a steadfast truth, an unsuspecting confidence, in the power and faithfulness of our great Redeemer. Paul, who disclaimed the ability of conceiving so much as one good thought, independent of God, did not however hesitate to say, "I can do all things through Christ that strengtheneth me." The same good shepherd who found us when we were lost, is able to "lead us in the paths of righteousness;" and he will do it "for his name's sake." He upon whom our help is laid, is styled "the faithful and true witness:" And these are his kind, encouraging words to all who are *returned* to him as the *bishop of their souls*, "My grace is sufficient for thee:"—"Fear not, for I am with thee; be not dismayed, for I am thy God; I will strengthen thee; yea, I will help thee; yea, I will uphold thee with the right hand of my righteousness."

Such, my brethren, is that temper of heart with which we ought to attend upon this great Christian solemnity: The deepest humility, and the warmest gratitude; godly sorrow on account of our wanderings in time past, and holy purposes to walk circumspectly for the time to come; a sense of our weakness, and of our absolute need of grace from on high, joined with a firm, unsuspecting reliance on the power and faithfulness of our glorious Redeemer, who hath promised the Spirit to them that ask it, and bid us "ask, and receive, that our joy might be full." Thus let us encompass the altar of God, praying that this gospel-feast may prove effectual, through his blessing, for confirming our faith, for inflaming our love, and enlivening our hope;—that, by the nourishment it affords, we may be strengthened to pursue our journey through this wilderness, till, having past the dark valley and shadow of death, we shall enter into the promised land of rest, where, face to face we shall behold the *shepherd and bishop of our souls*, and surrounding the throne of God and of the Lamb, bear our part in that grateful, triumphant song, "Unto him that loved us, and washed us from our sins in his own blood, and hath made us kings and priests unto God, and his Father; to him be glory and dominion for ever and ever." *Amen.*

SERMON X.

APPROACHING THE THRONE.

HEBREWS IV. 16.—"Let us therefore come boldly unto the throne of grace, that we may obtain mercy, and find grace to help in time of need."

THE great atonement we are this day to commemorate, is the sole foundation of that *throne of grace* to which the apostle invites us in my text; for it is only "in Christ Jesus, that God reconcileth the world unto himself." So that the subject I have chosen hath an obvious and peculiar reference to that sacred service in which we are shortly to be engaged. In order to render it profitable for our instruction and comfort, I propose, in dependence upon divine aid,

First. To explain what is meant by *coming boldly unto the throne of grace;* and,

Secondly. To consider the errand upon which we are invited to come; namely, *that we may obtain mercy, and find grace to help in time of need.* After which, I shall, in the

Third place, Illustrate the motives, or grounds of encouragement, suggested by the apostle in the foregoing context, upon which the exhortation appears to be founded:

And then direct you to the practical improvement of the whole.

I BEGIN with explaining what is meant by *coming boldly unto the throne of grace.*

You will easily perceive, that the *boldness* here recommended, must be something entirely different from fearless presumption, or headlong irreverence, in our approaches to God; for he hath expressly said, and confirmed the truth of it by many awful examples, "I will be sanctified in them that come nigh me, and before all the people I will be glorified."—"God is greatly to be feared in the assembly of the saints; he is to be had in reverence of all that are about him." We find this same apostle, towards the close of the epistle, concluding a most lofty and animated description of the dignity and privileges of the gospel-church, with this remarkable inference, "Wherefore, we receiving a kingdom which cannot be moved, let us have grace, whereby we may serve God acceptably, with *reverence and godly fear;* for our God is a consuming fire." Nay, the latter part of my text is sufficient to qualify the expression, and to guard us against any mistake about its true meaning and import.

In what character must we approach the throne of grace? Is it not as creatures that *need* both *mercy and grace?* If so, then surely the *boldness* with which we are exhorted to come, can be no other than the *boldness* of humble penitents; such as may consist with a conviction of guilt, and a sense of weakness; a *boldness* that takes its rise, not from any supposed goodness or worthiness in ourselves, but from the highest and most honorable conceptions of the greatness, as well as of the clemency, of that God whom we adore.

It is not then to filial awe and reverence, but to distrust and jealousy, that *boldness* is here opposed. The spirit becoming the gospel-state is not a spirit of bondage and fear, but a spirit of adoption, disposing and enabling us to "cry, Abba, Father." In this temper we should approach *the throne of grace;* not with terror and amazement, like criminals dragged before a tribunal of justice; but with a cheerful hope of obtaining pardon and acceptance, for the sake of him "who died for our sins, and rose again for our justification;" who suffered, the just for the unjust, that he might bring us to God."

Man's apostasy began with harsh and injurious thoughts of God; seduced by the tempter, he suspected his Creator both of falsehood and envy: And it is the office of faith to repair that injury, by recognizing his title to the entire and unreserved trust of the creature. It was for this end that "God, being willing more abundantly to show to the heirs of promise the immutability of his counsel, confirmed it by an oath, that by two immutable things, in which it was impossible for God to lie, they might have a strong consolation, who have fled for refuge to lay hold upon the hope set before them." It is his pleasure, that we rely upon him with an unsuspecting confidence; and we then honor him most, when, conscious of our own unworthiness, but depending at the same time upon his faithful word of promise; satisfied with the proofs he hath given us of his love, and encouraged by his kind and generous invitation; we come to his throne with a childlike freedom, to pour out our hearts before him, and to present our supplications for that mercy and grace, which he is always ready to bestow upon those who feel their need of such important blessings. But the full meaning and import of the exhortation will better appear, when I have opened the errand upon which we are invited to *come boldly unto the throne of grace.* Which was the

Second thing proposed in the method. The errand, you see, consists of two parts.

The *first* in order is, *that we may obtain mercy;* mercy to pardon our sins, and to reinstate us in the favor and friendship of God. This blessing is introductory to all others; for till we are reconciled to God through the great Mediator, we are incapable of holding communion with him; neither can we yield unto him any service that is acceptable: "Two cannot walk together except they be agreed;" and till *the blood of Jesus, who, through the eternal Spirit, offered himself without spot unto God, purge our conscience from dead works, we cannot serve the living God:* for "they that are in the flesh cannot please God." Nay, after we are justified and accepted in the Beloved, though we are thereby secured against final condemnation, yet we are not raised above the need of pardoning mercy; still we shall have this errand *to the throne of grace;* our repeated backslidings will always render it necessary to make repeated application to the blood of the covenant, for cleansing us afresh, and obtaining renewed intimations of pardon and acceptance.

But we have another errand besides this to *the throne of grace;* namely, *that we may find grace to help in time of need.* The form of expression implies, that there is no danger of a disappointment; assisting grace is already prepared; it waits our coming; and if we seek, we shall certainly *find it.* It farther seems to intimate, that we should be habitually in a posture of waiting upon God, according to that apostolic injunction, "Pray without ceasing;" for such is our weak, distempered state, that there is no portion of time in the whole duration of our life upon earth, which is not to us *a time of need:* should God withdraw his help for one moment, in that very moment we should stumble and fall.

One thing deserves our particular attention; namely, That the grace we are encouraged to ask, is grace for *present need*, and not present grace for *future supposed necessities.* This remark is of greater importance than is generally apprehended. It is no uncommon thing for serious people, who suspect their own sincerity, to forecast some trial of the severest kind, and to pass judgment upon themselves, according to the present state and temper of their minds with respect to that supposed trial. What shall I think of myself? saith one; it is required of a disciple of Jesus, that he take up his cross; but so feeble am I, that my nature shrinks at the remotest prospect of suffering; should persecution arise for righteousness sake, I should not be able to stand in that evil day; I should sink under the cross, and "make shipwreck of faith and a good conscience." Alas! saith another, instead of "desiring to depart, and be with Christ," Death is to me the "king of terrors;" when I think of dissolution, my heart dies within me; what shall I do when the fatal period is come? Were I in Christ Jesus, surely it could not be thus with me; have I not then cause to conclude that my religion is vain? By such unwarrantable experiments do many perplex and discourage their souls, and weaken their hands for present duty. I call them *unwarrantable experiments*, because they are not only beside the Scripture rule, but directly contrary to it. Our Lord hath commanded us, "to take no thought for the morrow, but leave the morrow to take thought for the things of itself; because sufficient unto the day is the evil thereof." When he forewarned his disciples that they were to be brought before governors and kings for his sake, did he require them to tell, at that very instant, what defence they could make? or did he even set upon them preparing answers to such questions as might be put unto them? No: on the contrary, he said unto them, "Be not anxious how, or what ye shall speak; for it shall be given you in that same hour what ye shall speak." When ye are brought to the trial and work of confessors, then you shall find the courage and wisdom of confessors. So it is, my brethren, with respect to us: grace to suffer, is for a suffering season: grace to die, is for dying moments: then, but not before, is the *time of need.* Are you solicitous about *grace* for future emergencies? let me ask you, I pray, have you got all the *grace* you need for present duty? If you think you have, I can, without further inquiry, assure you, that you are mistaken. At this very moment you need grace to cure your anxiety and distrust, to check your impatience and presumptuous curiosity. Cast your care upon God for every needful support, when you shall be called to suffer and die, and come to his throne for grace, that may enable you to live to some good and useful purpose in the mean time. Seek grace to mortify your remaining corruptions, to strengthen your faith, and to inflame your love; seek grace to perform all the duties of social life, to make you good neighbors, good friends, good parents, or good children, that you may serve and glorify God in those stations and conditions of life which his providence hath allotted you. These ought to be the immediate objects of your care; for till the present time cease to be a *time of need*, it is indecent, it is foolish, to look beyond it, and to distress yourselves with a premature anxiety about the morrow. Our errand, then, to *the throne of grace*, is no other than this, to obtain mercy for the pardon of past sins, and grace proportioned to our present necessity; either to subdue our corruptions, to resist temptations, to support us under the afflictions we feel, or to strengthen us for the duties we are called to perform. I now proceed in the

Third place, To illustrate the grounds of encouragement upon which the apostle's exhortation is founded. These are suggested in the two preceding verses: *We have a great High Priest, Jesus the Son of God.* This High Priest *is passed into the heavens:* and *he is not an High Priest who cannot be touched with the feeling of our infirmities, but was in all points tempted like as we are, yet without sin.*

The 1*st* thing to be considered is the personal worth and dignity of our High Priest. Of this we have a lofty description in the beginning of the epistle: there he is styled the *Son of God*, and the *Creator of the worlds*, the *brightness of the Father's glory, and the express image of his person, who upholdeth all things by the word of his power;* infinitely higher than the *angels*, inasmuch as he is their *Lord* and head, and they only *ministering spirits*, whom he employs as his servants, and *sends forth to minister unto the heirs of salvation.* Thus great is the Christian's High Priest: this is that exalted person who hath undertaken to mediate between God and sinners. Have we not here then one solid ground of encouragement, a firm foundation for our hope of the divine favor and acceptance? But this ground of encouragement receives a mighty addition, when, together with the personal dignity of our High Priest, we consider, in the

2*d* place, The value of what he did and suffered in that character. Having assumed our nature, "and taken upon him the form of a servant," he yielded a perfect obedience to that law which we had broken, and at last submitted to a painful, ignominious, and accursed death, that we might live through him. "He was made sin for us, who knew no sin, that we might be made the righteousness of God in him." Hereby the law was magnified, divine justice infinitely glorified, and a way opened for the free and honorable exercise of mercy and grace to a guilty world. The sufferings of the Son of God in our nature, and for our sins, afford a display of the divine holiness and justice, more bright and awful than if the whole human race had perished irrecoverably. While the law is not made void, but established, by what he *did*, at the same time by what he *suffered*, a public testimony is given to all intelligent creatures, that sin is an evil of such deep malignity, that nothing less than a sacrifice of infinite worth could expiate the guilt of it, or save the transgressors from endless misery: so that this dispensation, which provides so effectually for the glory of God, hath a powerful tendency to quiet our minds, and to cherish our hopes of pardon and acceptance; because now it appears, that God may be merciful without impairing the authority of his government; nay, perfectly just, as well as infinitely gracious, when he justifieth those who believe on Jesus. These hopes will appear to have a firmer foundation, if, to the dignity of our High Priest, and the inestimable worth of his obedience and suffering, we add, in the

3d place, That he was fully authorized to undertake this office; for, as we read in this same epistle, "Christ glorified not himself to be made an high priest; but he who said unto him, Thou art my Son, to-day have I begotten thee." Indeed, without such a divine constitution, the sacrifice he offered could have been of no benefit to us. The acceptance of one life in the place of another, dependeth solely upon him to whom the forfeiture is made. But, blessed be God, the designation of our Lord to the office of high priest, is so plainly and repeatedly asserted in Scripture, that there is no room left us to doubt of it. "He gave himself for our sins, according to the will of God." Hence he is styled the *Messenger of the covenant*, the *Servant*, and the *Elect of God.* In every part of his undertaking he acted by commission from his heavenly Father: "He came not to do his own will, but the will of him that sent him; which affords the strongest encouragement to draw near to God with filial boldness, and to hope for acceptance through this great High Priest of his own designation and choice, this "mighty One, upon whom he hath laid our help." Yea,

4thly. To remove every possible ground of jealousy, God hath testified in the most public and solemn manner, his perfect satisfaction with his whole conduct as Mediator; which is a circumstance of the utmost importance to give our hope a firm and lasting foundation. Though Christ had died on purpose to expiate our guilt, and to reconcile us to God; though his sacrifice had been of infinite worth in itself, and offered in consequence of his Father's appointment; yet, after all, something would have appeared wanting to assure our faith, if it had not been furnished with the strongest evidence that this sacrifice was really accepted. But, thanks be unto God, the certainty of this is put beyond all question in the sacred Scriptures. Twice was it proclaimed by an audible voice from heaven, "This is my beloved Son, in whom I am well pleased." The miracles wrought at his death, and that greatest of miracles, his own resurrection from the dead, are further confirmations of this comfortable truth; but, above all, his ascension into heaven, and his exaltation to the right hand of the majesty on high, remove every conceivable cause of fear, and do well support that triumphant challenge of the apostle, "Who shall lay any thing to the charge of God's elect? It is God that justifieth: Who is he that condemneth? It is Christ that died, yea rather, that is risen again; who is even at the right hand of God; who also maketh intercession for us." Which brings me to the

5th and *last* ground of encouragement, namely, That our great High Priest, who is passed into the heavens, is ever mindful of our interest, and lives and reigns for the benefit of his people. We are told in Scripture, that the legal high priest carried the names of the twelve tribes on his shoulder and breast-plate, when, on the great day of atonement, he made his solemn entrance into the holy of holies; that while God looked upon him, he might at the same time remember the tribes of Israel, accept his offering for the expiation of their guilt, and hearken to his prayers and intercession on their behalf. In like manner, our great High Priest, the Lord Jesus Christ, who is gone into the heavenly sanctuary, "appears in the immediate presence of God for us," sustaining the character of the second Adam, the head and representative of all his spiritual seed; and is raised to the highest dignity and power, that he may manage their affairs to the best advantage, and effectually secure their eternal salvation. He was a sufferer himself, and knoweth the heart of a sufferer, not by report, but by personal experience. He was tried with temptations even as we are; and though he conquered them all, yet he had proof of the skill, as well as of the malice of the tempter, and can make allowance for the disproportion betwixt himself and us. Nay, he stooped thus low, not only to make atonement for our guilt, and to open for us a passage to the mercy-seat; but that we, being assured of his perfect acquaintance with human infirmity, might have the most cheerful reliance upon his compassion and sympathy, and *boldly* approach *the throne of grace*, having such a friend to patronize us, and to plead our cause; "For we have not an High Priest who cannot be touched with the feeling of our infirmities, but was in all points tempted like as we are, yet without sin."

By such encouraging motives, my brethren, doth the apostle press the exhortation in my text.—"We have a great High Priest, Jesus the Son of God," who offered up a sacrifice of infinite worth; not officiously or at random, but by the express appointment of his heavenly Father, and in consequence of a solemn agreement or covenant.—This sacrifice was accepted for all the purposes for which it was intended; in testimony whereof our great High Priest hath "passed into the heavens;" where, amidst all the splendors of his exalted state, he kindly remembers his people upon earth, feels their infirmities, sympathizes with them in all their sufferings, and never ceaseth to make intercession for them. Have we not then reason *to come boldly unto the throne of grace, that we may obtain mercy, and find grace to help in time of need?*

But, after all, it must be confessed, that in this, as in most other things, the knowledge of our duty is far easier than the practice of it.

"Christ's flesh is meat indeed, and his blood is drink indeed;" but our Lord hath assured us, "that except we eat his flesh, and drink his blood, we have no life in us." A speculative knowledge will avail us nothing; a Saviour unapplied can be no Saviour to us. To think justly of Christ, and of the great things he hath already done, and continues to do, for sinners of mankind, is an attainment of no great difficulty; but to improve his mediation as the source of our joy, and the means of our comfortable access to God, requires greater skill than many who profess to believe on him are possessed of. This wisdom cometh only from above. Nevertheless, as God usually worketh by the ministry of the word, before I conclude this discourse, I shall endeavor to suggest a few hints that may be of use to you.

Are you overwhelmed with the glory and majesty of God? Are you ready to say, as Elihu did, "Behold! God is great, and we know him not?" Turn your eyes to the "Word made flesh," and see the divine glory veiled in the human nature of your Redeemer. We can have positive conceptions of Jesus Christ; and though we may not think that the Godhead is flesh, yet we may think of it as it appeared in flesh, and shone forth in its holiness and goodness to the world. In the person of our Mediator, God approacheth us familiarly, to invite us to come to him with humble confidence and reverend boldness. Christ did not assume a form of terror; women durst talk with him, sinners durst eat with him, the poor and the diseased durst ask his help; and though we must not debase the *dignity* of the Son of God, by imagining that it is as much obscured in heaven as it was upon earth; yet, even the glorified humanity of *the Word made flesh*, affords unspeakable comfort to the soul, that might otherwise shrink back, and tremble to draw near to God.

Doth the guilt of sin terrify you? Do you fear that a just and holy God can never accept such offenders as you have been? Here Christ is our relief; who was wounded for our transgressions, and bruised for our iniquities; who paid our debt, and hath purchased and sealed our pardon with his blood. The curse and condemning sentence of the law are indeed terrible; but if we have truly fled to Christ for refuge, he hath nailed them to his cross, and will give us a full and free discharge.

Are you discouraged with the infirmities you daily feel, the imperfection of your knowledge, the wandering of your thoughts, the coldness of your love, and the feebleness of your desires? Faith can still find a remedy in Christ Jesus, by reminding us, that our acceptance with the Father is through the merits of his Son;—and he, my friends, is worthy, though we are unworthy; his righteousness is perfect, and without spot; he is not weak when we are weak; he is not distempered when we are sick; our High Priest is unchangeable, "the same yesterday, to-day, and for ever."

Are you harassed with temptations, those fiery darts of the wicked one? Still faith can find a Saviour suited to your necessity. Our great Lord submitted, not only to be tempted by Satan, but to be tempted in a wilderness, where he had none to comfort him; nay, tempted to the most horrid blasphemy and wickedness, even to fall down and worship the devil himself. Look, therefore, to him "who is touched with the feeling of your infirmities, having been in all points tempted even as you are." He who made all temptations subservient to the triumphs of his own patience and conquering power, will support and succor his tempted servants, and make his grace victorious in the weakest hearts.

It sometimes happens that the soul is oppressed with griefs and fears which it cannot account for. Such was the Psalmist's case when he said, "I remembered God, and was troubled; I complained, and my spirit was overwhelmed. O my God, my soul is cast down in me; I am so troubled that I cannot speak." But even in this case faith can look to Christ, and remember that he too was in an agony; an agony more painful than any thing we can feel; and yet in that agony he prayed more earnestly. Faith will recollect the very words he uttered, *My soul is exceeding sorrowful, even unto death. Now is my soul troubled, and what shall I say!* It will remind us how he cried upon the cross, *My God! My God! why hast thou forsaken me?* though even then he was still the beloved of the Father, and suffered all this, that we might not be finally abandoned and forsaken.

After this manner we may improve the mediation of Christ, for bringing us, in all the variety of our circumstances, with humble *boldness to the throne of grace;* where, to our present comfort, and our everlasting joy, *we shall obtain mercy, and find grace to help* us *in* every season *of need.* Amen.

SERMON XI.

GOD'S GREATEST GIFT.

ROM. VIII. 32.—"He that spared not his own Son, but delivered him up for us all, how shall he not with him also freely give us all things?"

So bright and luminous are the principles of heavenly wisdom, that, like the sun, they are seen by their own light, and may rather be said to impart themselves to us than to be discovered by us. With regard to eternal things, the learned have no advantages above the unlearned. Neither the gifts of nature nor the improvements of art confer any precedency in the school of Christ. The comfort of a Christian doth not depend upon a process of abstract reasoning, but results immediately from the knowledge and belief of interesting facts attested by God, and faithfully recorded in the Scriptures of truth; for as it is the will of God, that all the "heirs of promise" should have a "strong consolation," therefore the grounds of their consolation are brought to the level of the weakest capacity, that all his children may have equal access to them, and feed like brethren at one common table. Accordingly, you may observe, that, in the passage I have now read to you, the apostle only reminds us of what God had already done for sinners of mankind; *He spared not his own Son, but delivered him up for us all.* And instead of reasoning in form, as if the import of this fact were dark or ambiguous, he takes it for granted that the most simple and illiterate will perceive it at once, and gives a defiance to ignorance, nay to distrust itself, either to pervert its meaning, or to draw from it any other conclusion than what he himself doth;—*how shall he not with him also freely give us all things!* My present design is, in dependence upon divine aid,

First, To illustrate this great foundation of the Christian's hope, *God spared not his own Son, but delivered him up for us all;* and then to show, in the

Second place, That the gift which God hath already bestowed upon sinners of mankind, affords every sincere believer the most absolute certainty, that nothing shall be withheld from him that is necessary to make him happy.

I begin with the great foundation of the Christian's hope, which is both the subject of my text, and the object presented to us in the holy sacrament of the supper: *God spared not his own Son, but delivered him up for us all.*

Amazing words! The *God* in whom we live and move,—the Father of our spirits, and the former of our bodies;—

who possessed an eternity of happiness and glory before we began to exist, and can neither be enriched by our services, nor impoverished by the want of them:—*He* whose goodness we had abused by the vilest ingratitude; whose omnipotence we have defied by the most insolent rebellion;—even *that God* who "spared not the angels that sinned, but hath reserved them in everlasting chains, under darkness, to the judgment of the great day," vouchsafed to pity and to *spare* the children of men: Nay, to make way for the exercise of this distinguishing mercy, *he spared not his own Son*, the Lord of angels, the creator of worlds; but, having substituted him in our place, clothed him in our nature, and "laid upon him the iniquities of us all," he *delivered him up* to contempt and persecution, to agony and torture, to death and the grave: and all this for our benefit, to redeem us from everlasting misery, and to reinstate us in that happiness and glory we had forfeited. These are the marvellous doings of the Lord, which the apostle here celebrates with gratitude and wonder, as the grounds of our faith, and hope, and joy.

But that our thoughts may not wander in too wide a field, let us at present confine them to the following particulars: 1*st.* The dignity of the sufferer; 2*dly.* The sufferings he endured; and 3*dly.* The persons for whom, and the ends for which, he was *delivered* to these sufferings. In each of these we shall discover a convincing proof of the love of God, a certain pledge of every necessary blessing.

1*st.* Let us consider the dignity of the sufferer. God, saith the apostle, *spared not his Son;*—his *own*,—his proper Son; "the brightness of his glory, and the express image of his person;" not a son by creation, adoption, or grace, but his "*begotten* Son," of the same essence with himself, and equal to him in power and in glory. Angels are called *the sons of God;* "but unto which of the angels said he at any time, Thou art my Son, this day have I *begotten thee?*" Nay, Christ is styled the "*only* begotten Son" of God; a title of peculiar significancy, importing, that he is not only infinitely great in himself, but likewise infinitely dear to the Father. Yet this is the person whom God sent to save us; and surely if the love of the giver is to be measured by the worth and value of the gift, we may justly say of God's love to us, that "it passeth knowledge." How loth was Jacob, a fond and indulgent parent to all his children, how loth was he to send Benjamin down to Egypt, even when his own life, and the preservation of his whole family seemed to depend upon it? yet Benjamin was not his *only* son; Jacob had many other children besides: but, behold! the great, the independent JEHOVAH, who would not suffer Abraham to offer up his Isaac, but provided and accepted a ram in his place, gives his *own*, his *only Son*, to be a sacrifice for us. Here the object is so high, that contemplation cannot reach it; so bright and dazzling, that it overpowers the sight: we can only say with David, "This is not the manner of men, O Lord God;" and must with reverence adore what we shall never be able fully to comprehend.

2*dly.* From the dignity of the sufferer, let us proceed to consider the sufferings he endured. Two words are employed by the apostle to convey to our minds a suitable apprehension both of their greatness and variety. God *spared him not*, but *delivered him up*. He *spared him not;* that is, he neither excused him from suffering, nor spared him while he suffered; he not only put the bitter cup into his hand, but kept it there till he had drunk up the dregs of it. With what awful severity did he stir up his justice! "Awake, O sword! against my shepherd, and against the man that is my fellow."—"It *pleased* the Lord to bruise him," saith the evangelical prophet, "and to put him to grief." He would not abate one tear, one groan, one drop of blood, any circumstance either of ignominy or pain, that was necessary to demonstrate the evil of sin, and to expiate that guilt which Christ, as our Surety, had appropriated to himself. Thus God *spared not his own Son;* nay, instead of sparing him, the apostle adds,

He *delivered him up.* But he doth not say to whom, or to what; because Christ was *delivered* into so many hands, abandoned or given up to such a variety of sufferings, that a minute detail of them would have obliged him to recite the whole history of his life; for in every period of it "he was *oppressed and afflicted;*" from his birth to his death "he was a man of sorrows, and acquainted with grief." He was *delivered* first into the virgin's womb; for even then, O Christians! did his passion begin; there was that temple framed, which afterwards, by wicked hands, was pulled down on mount Calvary; there that body was prepared, which was scourged, and bruised, and nailed to an ignominious and accursed tree. And being thus made flesh, and brought forth into the world, what was his after life but a repeated *delivery* of him to poverty, to reproach, to temptation, to persecution:—Such was the pomp, these were the harbingers which introduced him to the cross, and accompanied him to the grave. "Deliver me not," said David, "into the hands of mine enemies;" and his prayer was heard: But what David obtained was withheld from David's Son and Lord; for Christ was *delivered* into the hands of his enemies: He was *delivered* to Judas, who betrayed him; to the chief priests and rulers, who insulted and reviled him; to Herod and his men of war, who set him at naught; to Pilate, who condemned him; to the Roman soldiers, who crucified him:—Nay, more, he was *delivered* to such a sense of divine wrath, that wrath which was due to the sins of men, as, in the prophetic language of David, "withered his heart like grass, and burnt up his bones like a hearth." Sin is the sting of death, but the wrath of God is the sting of sin. When that seizes upon an awakened conscience, Oh! what a dark and disconsolate night doth it draw over the sinner's mind! or, rather, what a hell doth it kindle in his bosom! Yet it doth not, it cannot, appear in its full horror to us; as we see not all the malignity of sin, so neither can we see all the wrath that is due to it: but Christ had a full view of both in their utmost extent; and though he could not despair, for that indeed was impossible, yet the agony he felt was greater by far than any despairing sinner is capable of feeling, who bears only his own burden; whereas he lay pressed under the guilt of a whole world. It were impious to say, that the holy martyrs were more patient than their Lord; yet which of all that noble army ever uttered such disconsolate language as he did? Their torture was their triumph, their sufferings a recreation: Whereas the Son of God cries out in agony, "Now is my soul troubled, and what shall I say?" —"My God! my God! why hast thou forsaken me?" Whence these sad and mournful complaints? Did they proceed from any defect of magnanimity and fortitude? No, my brethren; it was the perfection of his mind that seemingly enfeebled him: the boundless extent of his understanding, which comprehended the full dimensions of sin and of wrath, was the sole cause of his deep and unparalleled distress. It was not the shame nor the torment of the cross that afflicted him; the thieves who suffered with him endured the same; but his soul, if I may be allowed the expression, was *crucified* more than his body: his heart had sharper nails to pierce it than his hands or his feet: in his body he felt the rage and cruelty of his murderers; but in his soul he felt sufferings of a more exquisite nature. Then he bore the griefs, and carried the sorrows of all his people; then he felt not the sins only, but the wounds also, of every broken heart; the torments of his martyrs, the reproaches of his saints, the poverty, distresses, and persecutions, which any, which all of them, have felt or shall feel, till the last trumpet shall sound, and he shall come again in his glory. Thus *God spared not his own Son;* to these inconceivable sufferings was the Lord of life *delivered.* But for whom, and for what ends, did the Son of God suffer? This was the

3*d* Thing I proposed to consider. And after what hath been already suggested, it is unnecessary that I should spend much time upon this head. It is evident that Christ did not suffer on his own account: "He was holy, harmless, undefiled, and separated from sinners." "He did not sin, neither was guile found in his lips." He suffered in the room of guilty man; he was delivered *for us*, saith the apostle, not only for our benefit, but in our place: "He was made sin for us, who knew no sin, that we might be made the righteousness of God in him." He suffered, the just for the unjust, that he might bring us to God." Do you ask, Why *God* *spared not his own Son?* The answer is, That he might spare us; he delivered him up to temporal sufferings, that we might be delivered from everlasting punishment: "For God so loved the world, that he gave his only begotten Son, that whosoever believeth in him, might not perish, but have everlasting life." Do you ask again, Who may lay claim to the benefit of this gift? I readily answer, Every child of Adam without exception, who feels his need of a Saviour, and is willing to accept him as he is offered in the gospel. The death, as well as the birth of Christ, "is good tidings of great joy *unto all people;*" to Gentiles as well as to Jews; to men of all kindreds, nations, and languages; to sinners of all sorts, the vilest not excepted; "He is the Lamb of God, which taketh away the sin of the *world.*" Every laboring and heavy-laden sinner is invited to come unto him; and "him that cometh he will in nowise cast out." In this sense, Christ is the "Saviour of all men;" though I apprehend, that as the apostle, in this passage, is writing purposely for the comfort of real Christians, this assertion, that *Christ was delivered up for us all*, is chiefly intended to signify, that all true believers have an equal interest in this gift of God; the weakest as well as the strongest; the dejected as well as the joyful; the convert of yesterday as well as the oldest servant in his family: for the inference he draws from it is expressly limited to those who have received Christ: *How shall he not* WITH HIM ALSO *freely give us all things?*—This leads me to the

Second branch of my subject; which is to show, That the gift which God hath already bestowed upon sinners of mankind, affords every sincere believer the most absolute certainty, that nothing shall be withheld from him that is necessary to make him happy.

The apostle, to give weight and emphasis to his conclusion, puts it into the form of a question, *How shall he not give?* It is impossible that he should not give; darkness and light may sooner become one, than that God should deny to believers in Christ aught that is conducive to their real felicity. He speaks, you see, in the language of assurance and triumph: and well he might; for if *God spared not his own Son, but delivered him up for us all*, what can be supposed to stop the current of his bounty? Is there any benefit too valuable for God to bestow?—That cannot be: the gift he hath already conferred is infinitely more precious than all that remains to be given. Other things may be estimated, but "the *riches* of Christ are *unsearchable:*" "In him dwelleth all the fulness of the Godhead bodily." Shall the unworthiness of the creature restrain his munificence? This objection is fully obviated by the free and gratuitous manner in which God hath bestowed his "unspeakable gift;" for it is evident, that we must have been far more unworthy of a Saviour than we possibly can be of any subsequent favor: and seeing *God spared not his own Son, but delivered him up for us all*, unmerited, nay, unsolicited, what bounds can be set to the Christian's hope? especially when we consider, that Christ was *delivered up* to sufferings and death, for this very end, that he might remove those obstructions that lay in the road of mercy, and render the exercise of it consistent with the honor of the divine government. The sacrifice of IMMANUEL afforded such a demonstration of the unchangeable holiness and justice of God, that without staining the glory of these perfections, he may now dispense to penitent believers all those blessings their circumstances can require; for what the apostle says of the pardon of sin, (Rom. iii. 25, 26.) may lawfully be extended to every other benefit: "God hath set forth his Son to be a propitiation, through faith in his blood, to declare his righteousness for the remission of sins; that he might be *just*, and the justifier of him who believeth in Jesus." Nay, my brethren, it is not only consistent with the justice of God, to do good to those who believe in Jesus; but, I speak it with reverence, it would be inconsistent with his justice to withhold good from them; for Christ hath actually purchased every blessing they need. He was *delivered up* "by the determinate counsel and foreknowledge of God;" not casually, or unadvisedly, but in consequence of a previous agreement or covenant; in which he freely consented, on his part, "to make his soul an offering for sin;" and the Father promised, that "he should see his seed;" that he should "prolong his days;" that "the pleasure of the Lord should prosper in his hand;" and that he should "see the travail of his soul, and be satisfied." Of which solemn transaction we have an authentic copy recorded by the prophet Isaiah, chap. liii. 10, 11.

What shall we then say to these things? —Hath God already bestowed the greatest of all gifts, the *unspeakable gift* of his own dear Son?—Did he bestow it freely, when there was nothing in the creature to merit or invite his love, but, on the contrary, every thing to provoke his holy indignation? Was this gift designed to pave the way for other blessings? Nay, further, were all other blessings actually purchased by the infinite sacrifice of this divine Saviour? How firm then is the foundation of the Christian's hope? With what humble, yet triumphant confidence, may the believer adopt the words of my text, and put the question, against all doubts, all fears, all temptations that may assail him, *He that spared not his own Son, but delivered him up for us all, how shall he not with him also freely give us all things?*

But we have not yet examined the grant itself. Shall I say the contents of it are large? The expression is too feeble; my brethren, they are boundless, they are infinite: these two words, *all things*, comprehend both heaven and earth in their bosom; and thus they are explained by this same apostle, (1 Cor. iii. 21.) "All things are yours, whether Paul, or Apollos, or Cephas, or the world, or life, or death, or things present, or things to come; all are yours; and ye are Christ's; and Christ is God's." And is the world too a part of the Christian's portion? Yes, my friends. But then it is the world conquered by faith, and "crucified to us by the cross" of our Redeemer. "The lust of the eye, the lust of the flesh, and the pride of life," are no parts of that world whereof the apostle there speaks, except it be in this sense, that they are subdued and mortified. Christ did not submit to hunger and thirst that we might riot in luxury; he did not become poor that we might possess great estates; he did not stoop to ignominy and to death, that we might be dignified with worldly honors. These are not included among the *all things* in my text. The truth is, they hardly deserve the name of *things;* they are mere ciphers, the creatures of opinion and fancy, which have no significancy, no price, but what mistake and delusion have wantonly set upon them. Our inheritance then is not diminished when all these are left out; nor hath the Christian any inducement to vitiate his charter, by interlining it with those carnal additions which a vain imagination is too apt to suggest. With Christ he hath *all things* which are subservient to the purposes for which Christ was *delivered:* pardon to remove his guilt; grace to aid him in the performance of duty; comfort to support him under the pressure of affliction; every needful supply during his journey through this world, and immortal life and happiness in the next. Hath not the Christian then "a goodly heritage," who hath God and the creature, grace and glory, time and eternity; who is safe among enemies as well as among friends; who lives in communion with God on earth, and shall dwell with him in heaven for evermore? Say, O Christians, hath such a man reason to complain of his portion?

But let it be observed, that all these things are given *with* Christ: his person and his benefits can never be divided. This is the order which God hath established;—He first gives us his own Son: and when that *unspeakable gift* is thankfully received, then, together *with his Son*, he *freely gives us all* other *things.* But without him, we have no right to any thing we possess; the food we eat, the raiment we put on, are not ours; we are usurpers, we are robbers; and as such, shall be severely reckoned with at last.—This shall be the condemnation of unbelievers at the great day, that they fraudulently seized upon their Master's goods, and rejected the Saviour, through whom alone they could have obtained a righteous title to them: and their condemnation shall be the heavier upon this account, that the Saviour was in their offer, and with him a full right to every benefit they enjoyed. Think of this, ye who forget God, and have hitherto turned a deaf ear to the calls of his grace.—And,

Let those who have complied with the gospel-invitation, and thankfully accepted the Lord Jesus Christ, take comfort from what has been spoken upon this subject, and approach the table of the Lord with enlarged expectations of obtaining all that is necessary to render them truly happy. God perfectly knoweth what we stand most in need of: he knoweth whether health or sickness, riches or poverty; whether cordials to cherish, or medicines of a different operation, are best for us. With respect to these, it is our duty and our interest to subject our choice entirely to his pleasure. This should be our chief, our only care, to renew from the heart our thankful acceptance of the Lord Jesus Christ; and then we may be assured that nothing can come amiss to us: For *he that spared not his own Son, but delivered him up for us all, shall* certainly *with him also freely give us all things.* Amen.

SERMON XII.

GOD'S FAVOR PERFECT SECURITY.

ROMANS VIII. 31.—"What shall we then say to these things? If God be for us, who can be against us?"

THIS chapter contains a large and animated detail of the privileges that belong to believers in Christ Jesus; and lays open those springs of true consolation with which the gospel-covenant is plentifully stored. Nothing is wanting that our present condition renders necessary or desirable; a suitable and an effectual remedy is provided both for our guilt and pollution. No sin can exceed the merit of a Redeemer's blood; no lust can withstand the power of his victorious grace; so that we may justly adopt the words of the returning prodigal, and say, as he did, that "in our Father's house there is bread enough and to spare."

In the two preceding verses, the Apostle leads us upward to the source and fountain of all those blessings we presently possess, or hope to enjoy; namely, the eternal love of an unchangeable God. It was his self-moving goodness that prompted him to devise the method of our recovery; and the scheme is so widely laid, so complete and finished in all its parts, that no power or policy can defeat the execution of it: "For whom God did foreknow, he also did predestinate to be conformed to the image of his Son, that he might be the first-born among many brethren. Moreover, whom he did predestinate, them he also *called;* and whom he *called,* them he also justified; and whom he justified, them he also glorified." So that the man whom God hath "*called* by his grace," is just as safe as Omnipotence can make him. Looking backward to God's purpose before time commenced, and forward to the glory that awaits him when time shall be no more, he may boldly bid defiance to every adverse power, saying, in the triumphant language of this Apostle, "Who shall lay any thing to the charge of God's elect?" and, "Who shall separate us from the love of God?"

The words I am to discourse upon, present the inspired author to our view in a very striking and agreeable light. Transported and overpowered with the greatness of the subject, he makes a sudden and solemn pause; and then asks the question, *What shall we say to these things?* Nothing can be said *against* them; and it is impossible to exceed in their just commendation. *What then shall we say* to *them?* What use shall we make of these comfortable truths? or what conclusion shall we draw from them? This I take to be the true meaning of the question. And an important question it is: Blessed be God, who put into the heart of his servant both to propose and answer it. Well, then, *what doth* a St. Paul *say to these things?* or rather what answer doth the Spirit of God indite? Let every believer in Christ listen with joy, and apply it to himself, *If God be for us, who can be against us?*

As the Apostle, through the whole of this chapter, speaks in the character of an assured Christian, the word *if* cannot be supposed to imply any doubtfulness or uncertainty about the truth of the proposition to which it relates; but rather taketh it for granted, and is of the same import as though the apostle had expressed himself thus: *Seeing that God is for us:* And therefore, instead of proving what none will deny, namely, that this privilege doth really belong to sanctified believers, I shall rather, in the *first* place, briefly unfold its meaning and worth; and then show, in the *second* place, what a solid foundation it lays for the joyful conclusion, or rather the triumphant challenge, in the close of the verse, *Who can be against us?*

I begin with unfolding the privilege itself. *God is for us.* And it necessarily implies, that

God is our friend. This is the very lowest sense the words will bear; and yet, my brethren, who can tell, nay, who can conceive the importance and worth of this single blessing? To be in a state of favor with the greatest and the best of Beings, the Father of our spirits too, upon whom we constantly depend for life and all things; how delightful the thought! How dismal to suppose ourselves in the opposite condition! As I speak at present to real Christians only, I need not enlarge upon this branch of your happiness. Many of you, doubtless, can remember the time when, lying under the sense of unpardoned guilt, and the fearful apprehensions of deserved wrath, you would have parted with ten thousand worlds like this, for one ray of God's countenance, for the remotest hint of pardon and acceptance. Such, I know, will require no commendation of the divine friendship: You have already learned from experience, the surest and most convincing teacher, that no enjoyment is comparable to the assurance of God's love; nay, that all other enjoyments are tasteless, or rather bitter, without it.

But the expression carries in it a higher meaning than this: It not only imports that God is reconciled to us, but that he likewise taketh our part, and is active for our good. *God is for us;* that is, he is *on our side*, and employs all his perfections for our safety and happiness. He not only graciously forgives what hath formerly been done by us against himself; but, as far as can consist with the perfection and happiness of his nature, he feels and resents what by others is at any time done against us: "He that toucheth you," saith he, "toucheth the apple of mine eye." And what shall we think of this? Balaam could say, "Surely there is no enchantment against Jacob, neither is there any divination against Israel;" for "the Lord his God is with him, and the shout of a king is among them." Yet this privilege is common to all believers in Christ: the Lord of hosts is their guardian as well as their friend; he chargeth himself with their protection; he adopts them into his family; and not only dignifies them with the title of children, but doth likewise enrich them with all the immunities and privileges which that high and endearing appellation imports. And what may they not expect from such a Father? whose wisdom is infinite, whose power is irresistible, whose "mercy is everlasting," and whose "truth endureth to all generations." And when I mention the truth of God, this leads me to observe another important sense, in which it may be justly said that *God is for us;* namely,

That he is our God in covenant, and hath pledged his veracity and faithfulness for every blessing our circumstances can require. It is comfortable to know that God is not only reconciled to us, but that he likewise taketh our part, and is active for our good. Nevertheless, as that jealousy which is inseparable from a consciousness of guilt might still suggest to us, that some unforeseen cause may throw us out of his protection; therefore, "God being willing more abundantly to show unto the heirs of promise the immutability of his counsel, hath confirmed it by an oath; that by two immutable things, in which it was impossible for God to lie, we might have a strong consolation, who have fled for refuge to lay hold upon the hope set before us." God hath not left us to spell out our privileges, or to reason ourselves into the hope of good things; he hath plainly told us what is in his heart; he hath put his merciful designs into the form of a covenant, and expressed them in a variety of gracious promises; by the help of which we may lay hold upon his truth, and plead the honor of the Godhead for every blessing we need. Nay, this covenant is sealed with the blood of his own Son; upon which account it sometimes gets the name of a *Testament;* that is, an irrevocable deed, made sure and unalterable by the death of the *testator.* Hereby the firmest foundation is laid for our faith and hope; and that our joy may be full, he hath instituted the holy sacrament of the supper, wherein visible pledges of his love are put into our hands, and by bread and wine, the appointed symbols of the broken body and shed blood of our Redeemer, Christ, and all the benefits of his purchase, are represented, sealed, and applied to believers.

These few hints may serve to give you some view both of the meaning and worth of this important privilege: *God is for us:* he is our friend; he is on our side; he is our God in covenant, and hath given us every kind of security our hearts could desire, for whatever is conducive to our real interest. In all, and in each of these respects, may the Christian say, that *God is for him.* Let us now consider, in the

Second place, The consequence of this privilege, or the joyful conclusion which the apostle draws from it, *Who can be against us?*

It is expressed, you see, in the form of a question or challenge. St. Paul, in the name of all true believers, gives a bold defiance to earth and hell, and triumphs in the assurance of their safety and happiness. The question doth not imply, that they who have God on their side, shall have no enemies at all; such an immunity would be inconsistent with a state of trial, and the Scripture gives us no warrant to expect any thing of this kind; on the contrary, they assure us, that "through much tribulation we must enter into the kingdom of heaven." "Our adversary, the devil, as a roaring lion, walketh about, seeking whom he may devour." "We wrestle not only against flesh and blood, but against principalities and powers, against the rulers of the darkness of this world, and against spiritual wickednesses in high places." And as, in the days of Abraham, "he that was born after the flesh, persecuted him that was born after the spirit; even so it is now." Nor shall this warfare cease till that great day of the Lord come, when "all his enemies shall be made his footstool." But the question, or defiance, may lawfully be considered as importing the following particulars.

1*st.* That none *shall be against us* whose favor is desirable.

That the children of God too frequently fall out among themselves, and squabble in the dark, is a melancholy truth; and that these contentions are unseemly and hurtful things, cannot be denied: But a little more daylight would soon put an end to the scuffle, make them ashamed of their mistakes, and unite them in the bonds of an everlasting friendship. The persons I speak of are they who are enemies to believers as such; and of them I say, that their favor is not worthy to be coveted, neither doth the want of it deserve to be regretted. What regard is due to the judgment of those who are so blind, that they see no beauty in the infinitely perfect God himself? especially when their enmity against us is only the natural effect of this woful stupidity; according to that assertion of the apostle John, "Therefore the world knoweth us not, because it knew him not." "If the world hate you," saith our Lord, "ye know that it hated me before it hated you. If ye were of the world, the world would love his own; but because ye are not of the world, but I have chosen you out of the world, *therefore* the world hateth you." And ought any wise man to be disquieted on that account? Nay, my brethren, did we view our enemies in this light, we should look upon them as objects of pity, rather than of fear or resentment; and any little hurt they could do to us, would scarcely be felt, whilst we thought of the infinitely greater mischief they were doing to themselves.

2*dly. If God be for us, who can* prevail *against us?* Who shall be able totally to subdue us, to deprive us of the glory and happiness we look for? Indeed, if the safety of believers depended on their own ability to keep hold of God; if they were left, as it were, to hang upon him by the mere strength of their own arms; a little force or cunning might soon loosen their grasp, and pull them away from him. But herein, my brethren, lies their security, an omnipotent God keepeth fast hold of them; they are committed to that good Shepherd "who gathers the lambs with his arms, and carries them in his bosom, and gently leads those that are with young:" They are joined to God by the bond of an "everlasting covenant, ordered in all things and sure;" and they who would attempt to tear them from him, must first of all make void that covenant, reverse the unchangeable purpose of God, and oblige the Almighty to resign his power. Such is the desperate enterprise in which the enemies of God's children are engaged; it is not the creature, but the Creator they have to cope with; Jehovah himself must be overcome, before the weakest believer can fall into their hands. Justly then might the Apostle say, as in the close of this chapter, "Who shall separate us from the love of Christ? shall tribulation, or distress, or persecution, or famine, or nakedness, or peril, or sword? Nay, in all these things we are more than conquerors through him that loved us. For I am persuaded, that neither death, nor life, nor angels, nor principalities, nor powers, nor things present, nor things to come, nor height, nor depth, nor any other creature, shall be able to separate us from the love of God which is in Christ Jesus our Lord." Nay, my text will allow us to advance a step farther, and to say, in the

3*d* place, *If God be for us*, who shall be able to do us any material hurt in the mean time? To be assured of final salvation, is indeed an unspeakable blessing; to know that our enemies shall not totally prevail against us, is a desirable privilege; yet a great addition would be made to our comfort, could we also be assured, that their malice and enmity, instead of hurting us, shall contribute as means to promote our true interest. Well, then, the Apostle, under the direction of God's unerring Spirit, hath asserted this in the strongest and most absolute terms: "We know," saith he at the 28th verse of this chapter; we do not barely hope, but "*we know*, that all things work together for good to them that love God, to them who are the called according to his purpose." Satan endeavors to blow out the spark of grace; but instead of that he kindles it into a flame, and only blows away the ashes that covered it. He plieth the saints with his fiery darts; but instead of killing them, he renders them more expert in the art of defence, teacheth them the use of "the shield of faith," and the other parts of their spiritual armor. In short, God effectually baffles every attempt of their enemies: He "beats their swords into plough-shares, and their spears into pruning-hooks;" that is, he converts their hostile weapons into instruments of husbandry, for the culture and improvement of his people, that in greater abundance they may bring forth "those fruits of righteousness, which are, through Jesus Christ, to his praise and glory."

Thus have I opened the joyful import of this question, or challenge, *If God be for us, who can be against us?* And in the review of all that hath been said, can we forbear to cry out with the holy Psalmist, "Happy is the people that is in such a case; yea, happy is that people whose God is the Lord!" What I further intend is, to give you a few plain and necessary directions about the use you ought to make of this comfortable subject.

But before I proceed to these, compassion to the souls of some who may be hearing me, obliges me to set before you a very different prospect, by inverting the question, and putting it in this form:

If God be against us, who can be for us?

"The Lord is in his holy temple, the Lord's throne is in heaven: his eyes behold, his eyelids try, the children of men. The Lord trieth the righteous: but the wicked, and him that loveth violence, his soul hateth. Upon the wicked he shall rain snares, fire and brimstone, and an horrible tempest: this shall be the portion of their cup." "Thine hand shall find out all thine enemies," saith the Psalmist; "thy right hand shall find out those that hate thee: thou shalt make them as a fiery oven in the time of thine anger; the Lord shall swallow them up in his wrath, and the fire shall devour them." How awful are these words, uttered by God himself! "I, even I, am he, and there is no God with me: I kill, and I make alive; I wound, and I heal; neither is there any that can deliver out of my hand. For I lift up my hand to heaven, and say, I live forever. If I whet my glittering sword, and mine hand take hold on judgment; I will render vengeance to mine enemies, and will reward them that hate me; I will make mine arrows drunk with blood." And "Can you stand before his indignation? Can you abide in the fierceness of his anger, when his fury is poured forth like fire, and the rocks are thrown down by him?" Consider this, ye that forget God, lest he tear you in pieces when there shall be none to deliver. Who can make you happy if God pronounce you miserable? Who can give quietness, if he cause trouble? Who can screen you from his justice? And, Oh! who can support you under the weight of his vengeance? For the Lord's sake, take a serious view of your condition; and then turn your eyes to that compassionate Redeemer, whose arms are yet extended to embrace you: Flee speedily to him as your only sanctuary: let the earth be acquainted with your bended knees; let the air be acquainted with your fervent supplications, till you have reason to conclude, that you are vitally united to the Lord Jesus Christ, who "of God is made," unto all who believe in him, "wisdom, and righteousness, and sanctification, and redemption."

As for you who are Christians indeed, to whom all the comfort of this text belongs, let me beg your attention to a few necessary advices, with which I shall conclude this discourse.

1*st*. Beware of despising your enemies; for that shall betray you into security and carelessness. Remember, that however weak they are in comparison with God, yet in themselves they are strong and formidable; insomuch, that were God to look on, and leave you to your own defence, you should quickly and easily be overmatched. In other armies, the strength of the general consisteth in the number and valor of his troops; but in the Christian army, the strength of the whole host, and every soldier in particular, lies in him who is the Lord of Hosts. We ought therefore to maintain an habitual jealousy of ourselves: we are never in greater danger than when we are most confident that we are out of danger; so that the caution which the Apostle gave to the Gentile converts is always in season: "Be not high minded, but fear;" and again, "Let him that thinketh he standeth, take heed lest he fall." At the same time, though you must not despise your enemies, yet neither, in the

2*d* place, Ought you to be afraid of them. The true Christian temper lies in the just medium, betwixt these opposite extremes: and therefore we are exhorted, not only "to watch," but also "to quit ourselves like men;" "to endure hardness as good soldiers of Jesus Christ;" and to be "strong in the Lord, and in the power of his might."—"Fear not," saith God, "for I am with thee; be not dismayed, for I am thy God: I will strengthen thee; yea, I will help thee; yea, I will uphold thee with the right hand of my righteousness." After this encouraging manner doth God speak to his children. Nay, he chides them when they betray the least timorousness in his service; as in Isaiah (chap. li. 12, 13.) "Who art thou, that thou shouldst be afraid of a man that shall die, and of the son of man which shall be made as grass? and forgettest the Lord thy Maker, that hath stretched forth the heavens, and laid the foundations of the earth? and hast feared continually every day, because of the fury of the oppressor, as if he were ready to destroy? And where is the fury of the oppressor?" Hear how David triumphs in the assurance of his safety, upon grounds which are common to all believers in Christ: "The Lord is my light and my salvation; whom shall I fear? The Lord is the strength of my life; of whom shall I be afraid? Though an host shall encamp against me, my heart shall not fear; though war should rise against me, in this will I be confident." Let the wicked tremble; they have reason to do so; but "let the heart of every one rejoice that seeks the Lord." Victory is insured to you; the great "Captain of salvation" hath already conquered all your enemies, and ere long he shall return, and bring you with singing into the heavenly Zion; then shall you obtain gladness and joy, and sorrow and mourning shall flee away. But as the strength by which you must overcome is not your own, this makes it necessary that I direct and exhort you, in the

3*d* place, To depend upon God, and to walk closely with him. For this end, "abide in Christ," for there it is alone that God and sinners can meet as friends. "God is *in Christ*," saith the Apostle Paul, "*reconciling* the world unto himself." Indeed he is nowhere else in the character of a *reconciler;* and consequently, if we wish to dwell under his shadow, it is necessary that *we* be *in Christ* also. This was one of the solemn advices which our Lord gave to his disciples a little before his death; "Abide in me;"—"as the branch cannot bear fruit of itself except it abide in the vine, no more can ye except ye abide in me;" for "without me," or separated from me, "ye can do nothing." In the

4*th* and *last* place, Seeing *God is for us*, let us be *for him;* let us appear openly on his side, and act with resolution and vigor in his service. God can do his work without us; he stands in no need of our assistance; yet such is his condescension, that he invites us to the honor of being "workers together with himself." And what can fire our ambition if this do not? He is just now calling aloud, both by his word and by his providence, "Who will rise up for me against the evil doers? Who will stand up for me against the workers of iniquity?" O! let each of us make haste to reply with the evangelical prophet, "Here am I, send me." At the same time, let us echo back the call, and humbly expostulate with him in the words which his own Spirit hath dictated; "Arise, O Lord, and plead thine own cause; remember how the foolish man reproacheth thee daily." "It is time for *thee* to work, for they have made void thy law." Thus doth God permit us to remind him of his own interest, while we ourselves are in a posture for active service; and such pleadings are highly pleasing and acceptable. Let us then, my brethren, in our respective stations, do what in us lies to advance the kingdom of Christ in the world, and to bear down every thing that stands in opposition to it. Let the "righteous be bold as lions;" and then may we hope that "Iniquity," as ashamed, shall hide her head, and "stop her mouth." At any rate, "our record shall be on high," and "our reward with our God." He will receive us unto himself "in that day when he maketh up his jewels;" and then shall an everlasting distinction be made "between the righteous and the wicked; between him that serveth God and him that serveth him not." *Amen.*

SERMON XIII.

THE GIRDED, WATCHING SERVANT.

LUKE XII. 35, 36, 37.—"Let your loins be girded about, and your lights burning; and ye yourselves like unto men that wait for their Lord, when he will return from the wedding; that when he cometh and knocketh, they may open to him immediately. Blessed are those servants whom the Lord, when he cometh, shall find watching: verily I say unto you, that he shall gird himself, and make them sit down to meat, and will come forth and serve them."

THE obvious design of this passage is, to excite us to a serious consideration about the awful solemnities of death and judgment. We are here directed to consider ourselves as servants who have a master in heaven; of whose return we have the strongest assurance, but are utterly ignorant of the precise time of his coming; and therefore it is both our duty and our interest to be always on our guard, and in a fit posture to receive him; the happy consequences of which shall be, that our Lord will not only approve of our prudent and zealous concern to please him, but he will even delight to honor us; he will not deal with us as servants, but as friends; and will bestow upon us a reward infinitely beyond what any services could entitle us to. So that here we have a short, but comprehensive account of the Christian's work and recompense; our duty and encouragement are both set before us.

Our duty is represented, by the diligent care of servants to have every thing in readiness for the reception of their absent master. As the Jews, and other eastern people, commonly wore long and loose garments, it was necessary, when they had any thing to do which required strength or agility, that they should tuck them up, and gird them close about them; now, says our Saviour, in allusion to this, *let your loins be girded about;* that is, lay aside every thing that may entangle you in your work: *let your lights* be continually *burning*, and ye yourselves, in every other respect, like servants who are anxious to please their Lord, and to be found diligent in their proper business, at whatever hour he shall come; that, *when he knocketh*, you may be ready to give him present admittance, and not to be surprised in any disorder.

The reward of the diligent and faithful servant is described in the same allegorical manner; *verily*, says he, when their master returns, and finds them thus employed, he will bestow on them some extraordinary marks of honor and regard. He will not consider them as mere servants "who have done no more than was their duty," but will advance them to the rank of friends; he will entertain them in the most liberal and gracious manner at his own table; yea, so condescending is he, that, in some respects, he will lay aside his superiority, as if he should *gird himself* like a servant, and *come forth* and wait upon them.

I shall at present confine myself to the first of these subjects; namely, the duty we owe to our absent Lord. It is this which more nearly concerns us in the mean time: the glorious reward mentioned in the latter part of my text belongs chiefly to our encouragement; and in that view I shall have occasion to speak of it before I conclude.

Now, by this figurative description of the duty we owe to our absent Lord, we are plainly taught, in the

1*st* place, That we should lay aside every thing that may incumber us in the service of our Master; *let your loins be girded about.* To the same purpose the Apostle Peter exhorts us (1 Peter i. 13.) "Wherefore gird up the loins of your mind, be sober, and hope to the end, for the grace that is to be brought unto you at the revelation of Jesus Christ." The New Testament abounds with many exhortations of the same kind; which will appear to have a peculiar propriety, if we consider those figurative representations of our work to which they are applied. It is called a *race*, a *strife*, a *warfare;* we must run, and wrestle, and fight; and therefore have need of all our strength and activity. Long garments are for ornament, but not for use; these must be gathered up or laid aside when a man addresses himself to any laborious business. Now such is the nature of our Christian work: "The kingdom of heaven suffereth violence, and the violence take it by force." We must do more than seek admittance; we must "*strive* to enter in at the strait gate; for many shall *seek* to enter in, and shall not be able." Think of this, my brethren; ponder the difficulties in your warfare; view the greatness of your work; consider the number and strength of your enemies; look through that large system of duties you have to perform; and then you must be convinced, that the most vigorous exertion of every active power is more than needful in such circumstances as ours. We must, therefore, I say, labor to get rid of every incumbrance, and to be always in a posture for active service. I need not tell you what these incumbrances are. In general, whatever unfits us for our duty, that must be laid aside. More particularly, an earthly mind, pride of heart, and the love of sensual pleasures, are three great enemies to holy diligence in the work of the Lord. Whilst our affections lie thus low, it is impossible we can do any thing to purpose; nay, if this be their prevailing bent, we shall act in direct opposition to the laws of our Master. In short, our first care shall be, to correct that disorder which is within us; to get our hearts purified by the Spirit of God, and raised above the profits and pleasures, and honors of this vain world; for "out of the heart are the issues of life;" and such as our affections are, such will the course of our actions be. But it is not enough to have our *loins* thus *girded about*, we must also, in the

2*d* place, Have *our lights burning.* This may import the care we should bestow to have our minds furnished with the knowledge of our duty; for as servants cannot work to any purpose in the dark, so neither can we be good and fruitful Christians, without a competent knowledge of that divine law which is the only infallible rule of our conduct. If we shall take this to be the meaning of the words, they no doubt teach us a most important and necessary lesson; namely, That we should carefully search the sacred Scriptures, and, with a sincere and humble temper of mind, labor to know what is the "good, and acceptable, and perfect will of our God."

But I rather incline to understand this expression as importing the lively and constant exercise of all our Christian graces. This is indeed the best preparation for our Lord's return. To have our repentance mourning over our past sins, and keeping the heart humble under a sense of guilt;—our faith applying the blood of Christ for pardon, and deriving, at the same time, strength from above for vanquishing our lusts, that "sin may no more have dominion over us;"—our love embracing an unseen Saviour, and extending to all his members; our hope casting anchor within the vail, and keeping the soul fixed and steady, amidst all the revolutions of this changing world;—our patience triumphing over sufferings;—our meekness passing by injuries, blessing and doing good to our most inveterate enemies;—and, by the happy influence of all these, the light of our external conduct adorning our profession, and engaging others to glorify our heavenly Father: This is to have our *lights burning* indeed; this will make us ready to meet our Lord. We shall not be backward *to open* at his call, when all is thus cleansed and in good order within. And this is the preparation we ought chiefly to study. Our readiness to work will not avail us by itself; we must be doing, our work must be advancing; for in vain do we trim the lamp, if it do not shine and give light; in vain are *our loins girded about*, if we have nothing to do, or neglect our business. Further, in the

3*d* place, We are here directed to be constantly on our guard, and to keep a strict and careful *watch* till our Master return.

Watchfulness is frequently in Scripture opposed to sleep: and that even the best Christians have need of this caution, we may learn from our Saviour's parable of the ten virgins; where it is said, (Matth. xxv. 5.) that "while the bridegroom tarried, *they all*," that is, the wise as well as the foolish, "slumbered and slept." Carnal and unregenerated sinners are represented in Scripture as being in a state of death; quite stupid and unfeeling; but even those who have got a principle of new life may suffer very sad decays; and though they do not totally expire, yet they may fall into that sleep which is the image of death. Though the precious oil which feeds the light will not suffer it to go out; yet, for want of trimming, it may grow so dim and obscure, that it shall scarcely be discernible. Now this, my brethren, is a very melancholy situation; and it highly concerneth us to guard against it with our utmost care. We read of some who lost their first love; nay, Paul complains of the Hebrews, that they had lost even their former knowledge, and had need "to be taught again which be the first principles of the oracles of God." "The hand of the diligent maketh rich; and he that is slothful is brother to him that is a great waster." Indeed, if holiness were natural to us, then it might abide with us, and grow up of its own accord without any care on our part; but as it is of a foreign extraction, and as our hearts are choked up with noxious weeds, this precious seed must be watched over, and carefully tended, otherwise it will starve and decay. The sleeping Christian cannot thrive; and if he be surprised in that condition when his Master calls, how great shall his disorder be! We should therefore beware of slothfulness; we have still work to do, and God hath not allowed us one moment more than is needful. Let us then awake to our business; let us never think we have finished our task so long as there is any part of the day to run; but let us imitate the great apostle of the Gentiles, who, notwithstanding his high attainments in religion, yet "did not think he had already obtained, either was already perfect; but, forgetting the things which were behind, and reaching forth unto those things which were before, he pressed towards the mark, for the prize of the high calling of God in Christ Jesus."

But we may consider *watchfulness* in another light, namely, as a duty arising from our present circumstances of danger. And in this view the necessity of it will appear unspeakably great; for though we could acquire such a stock of graces that we needed not make any further addition to them; nay, though we might even lie down and sleep, without any apprehension of their decay; yet, if we be in danger from without, if thieves may break through and steal our treasure, then of necessity we must be constantly on our guard; nor is it wise in us to drop our watch for one moment. And who can doubt that this is our situation? "Watch and pray," said our Saviour, "that ye enter not into temptation." So great is our danger, that our own vigilance is not sufficient to secure us; we must call in foreign assistance, we must implore the divine aid; for "unless an Almighty Guardian keep the city, the watchman waketh in vain." Yea, when Satan desired to have Peter, that he might "sift him as wheat," our Saviour himself, who had encountered this enemy, and knew his strength, prayed for his zealous disciple, that his faith might not fail. And if both *watchfulness* and *prayer* be necessary for our defence, alas! what shall become of those who neglect both? One compares the gracious soul to a ship richly laden; which is the greater temptation to pirates upon that very account. I say not this to discourage the sincere Christian; for greater is he that is with you than all that can be against you; but methinks it should excite you to double your watchfulness. If you have profited by the means of grace; if your treasure is increased; instead of growing secure, you should be the more humble and watchful upon that very account; for needful is that caution, "Let him that thinketh he standeth, take heed lest he fall." Once more, in the

4th place, Our Saviour here directs us to consider ourselves as fellow-servants and members of his family; and in this view another part of our preparation for his coming must lie in the performance of the duties we owe to each other, as well as of those duties which more immediately respect himself. This is more clearly pointed out to us in the 45th and 46th verses of this chapter, where we find a fearful threatening denounced against those who neglect this mutual relation; "But, and if that servant say in his heart, My lord delayeth his coming, and shall begin to beat the men-servants, and maidens, and to eat and drink, and to be drunken; the lord of that servant will come in a day when he looketh not for him, at an hour when he is not aware, and will cut him in sunder, and will appoint him his portion with the unbelievers." It appears from this passage, that the faithful discharge of social duties has a higher rank in religion than many seem to apprehend. It is not indeed the whole of religion; neither can it be called the most essential part of it; for no doubt the duties of the highest class are those which belong to the first table of the law, and arise from our first and most lasting relation. We were the subjects of God before we became members of human society; and if we prove unfaithful to God, it cannot surely give him any pleasure to behold confederated rebels living in the most perfect agreement among themselves: so that a man may, in several respects, prove an agreeable, perhaps an useful, member of society, and after all be condemned for his ingratitude to God, and rebellion against his Maker. Nevertheless, the discharge of those duties which we owe to one another, is of such importance in religion, that I can warrantably affirm, no man shall be saved who transgresses them, or even who wilfully and habitually neglects them. It is not to be expected, nor indeed is it necessary, that I should give you a detail of these; they are universally better understood than they are practised. Our duty here extends to all the different expressions of righteousness and love; and the rule is both short and plain; *All things whatsoever ye would that men should do unto you, do ye even so to them.* The best offices are those which promote our neighbor's spiritual and eternal interest; and therefore religious instruction, friendly advice, and seasonable reproof, cannot be dispensed with. Whatever tends to discourage vice, or to promote the interests of religion and virtue, is strictly incumbent upon us, according to the power and authority which our station gives us; and therefore he is but half a magistrate, and a poor half too, who resents only the injury that is done to men, and overlooks those horrid instances of impiety against God, which the good laws of our land authorize him to punish. In short, whatever be our condition in life, there are certain duties belonging to it which we must perform; and I shall only add, that as the obligation is mutual, both parties are equally bound, and neither can withhold from the other what is due without an injury; nor is the superior less strictly bound to those who are below him, than the inferior to those who are above him; and they who possess the highest stations are equally obliged, with the meanest of their brethren, to "live soberly, righteously, and godly, in the world," and to promote the glory of God, and the welfare of human society, by the faithful and conscientious use of all those talents which God hath put into their hands; and if they do otherwise, they shall be condemned and punished by their Master and Judge when he cometh again.

After this manner are we taught to make ready for the Lord's return.

We must lay aside every thing that may encumber us in his service; we must labor to know our Master's will, and to keep all our graces in lively and vigorous exercise;—particularly, we should guard against slothfulness and security, and, from a sense of our danger, keep a strict and habitual watch against the enemies of our souls; at the same time regarding each other as fellow-servants, and faithfully performing those social duties which belong to our several stations and relations. To all which I might further add, that we should earnestly look out for our Master's coming, and long for his second and glorious appearance, when we and all his faithful servants shall be admitted into his immediate presence, and be enabled to serve him without any mixture of sin, in another and a better world than this.

I COME now to exhort you to the practice of these duties; for which I offer the following motives and arguments:—

1*st* then, One great argument for the preparation here recommended may be drawn from the certainty of our Lord's return. This is asserted in so many passages of Scripture, that there is no room left us to doubt it. The present mixt state of things renders a future judgment not only probable to reason, but almost certain and necessary; and the apostle Paul, in the 8th chapter of his epistle to the Romans, derives a very ingenious, but substantial, argument in favor of this doctrine, from the present burdened state and weary face of the creation: nor can any who professeth Christianity pretend to question it. Should not this then oblige us to make ready for it? With these very eyes shall we see our Redeemer; and how shall we look him in the face, if we have been unfaithful during his absence, and lived at random, as if none had power over us? Nay, methinks this very consideration that he is now removed from us, should work upon our ingenuity, and excite us to the utmost care and diligence in his service. Every one will be doing while he sees the master present; the test of fidelity is, to mind the master's interest when he is at a distance; especially the interest of such a Master, who hath bought us from the most deplorable slavery with his own precious blood, and requires nothing at our hand, but what tends to make us happy here, and to fit us for eternal glory hereafter.

2*dly*. The uncertainty of the time of his coming should excite us to be always busy at our work, and in a fit posture to receive him. This argument is much insisted upon by our Saviour. He often compares his coming to that of a thief in the night, who studies secrecy, and will not give any previous notice: and this seems to be the meaning of that allusion in the 36th verse, where he likens himself to one who is attending a marriage-solemnity; because on such occasions people are not usually masters of their own time, which renders the season of their return to their own houses more uncertain. And if this be the case, can there be a more powerful motive to an habitual preparation? "Behold, I come as a thief," says our Saviour, in the book of the Revelation.—"Blessed is he that watcheth, and keepeth his garments, lest he walk naked, and they see his shame." Dost thou not know, O man! but that to-morrow thy Master may come to thee; or, which is the same thing, may call thee to him? and wilt thou not be busy? Show us thy security for one day, and then claim that day as thine own: but if thou canst not, how mad art thou to neglect thy business, or to leave any task unfinished, whilst it is in the power of thy hands to do it? Especially, if it be considered, in the

3*d* place, That when thy Master returns, thy working-time is over. What is then unfinished must remain so for ever. He comes to judge thee, according to what thou hast done, and not to call thee to perfect thy unfinished labors. This, my brethren, is a most awful consideration; we are now sowing the seed for eternity, and what we sow, that shall we reap. Our Master's order is, "*Occupy till I come:* that is the term; and we can neither get it protracted nor renewed; and if we be found unfaithful, dreadful shall our punishment be; and the more dreadful upon this account, that it shall be perpetual, without abatement and without end. But, as I would rather choose to allure than frighten you to your duty, I shall represent to you, as a

4*th* Motive to a diligent preparation for your Master's coming: The glorious advancement, and blessed reward, of the watchful servants, which is mentioned in the last part of my text; *Verily I say unto you.* It is introduced with a strong asseveration, to denote the absolute certainty of the thing; and, O how condescending is that which follows! *He shall gird himself, and make them to sit down to meat, and will come forth and serve them.* Surely this is a reward, not of debt, but of grace; for how can the most perfect obedience merit any thing like this? Those faithful servants shall be advanced to an honor, which, were it not promised, they could not lawfully hope for They shall be entertained by their Master at his own table; there shall they feast without any to disturb them. Here, indeed, whilst we are at our work, we obtain some foretastes of this heavenly banquet; but how soon is the table drawn! But it shall not be so in heaven.—Here we must eat, as the Jews did their passover, "in haste, with our loins girded, our shoes on our feet, and our staff in our hand."—But in heaven we shall sit down with Abraham, Isaac, and Jacob, and with all our dear fellow-servants, never more to rise again. O blessed rest! O glorious society! O delightful entertainment! But what can these words mean, *He shall gird himself, and come forth and serve them?*—Surely this cannot be literally fulfilled; yet it must have a resemblance to something that is real, otherwise it would not have been mentioned.

Thus much we know, that on that day Christ shall bestow some extraordinary marks of respect upon his servants, which "our ears have not yet heard, neither can our hearts conceive."

If "there is joy in heaven over one sinner that repenteth," though he is then only beginning his warfare, and has many a weary and painful step before him; if the prodigal is so kindly embraced upon his first return from feeding swine, and gets "the wedding-ring on his finger, and the best robe put on him;" what shall be the saint's honor in that day of the "manifestation of the sons of God!"

"If any man serve me," saith Christ, "let him follow me; and where I am, there shall my servant be. If any man serve me, him will my Father honor." But these matters are too high for us; the glories of the upper world are far beyond our sight. Yet surely those discoveries which have been imparted to us, are sufficient to invite our thoughts frequently thither; and especially to excite us to the most diligent preparation for our Lord's return, "who is gone before to prepare a place for us, and who shall certainly come again, and receive us unto himself, that where he is, there we may be also."

Well, then, my dear fellow-servants, *Let our loins be girded about, and our lights always burning;* ere long our work shall be at an end, and this glorious eternal reward shall begin. "Let us not be weary in well-doing: for in due season we shall reap if we faint not." Above all, let us guard against security and self-confidence; let us join prayer with our watching, depending upon him who hath said, "My grace is sufficient for thee." To whom, with the Father, and the ever-blessed Spirit, one God, be glory and honor, dominion and power, for evermore. *Amen.*

SERMON XIV.

SIMILITUDE OF THE RACE.

1 CORINTHIANS, IX. 24.—"So run that ye may obtain."

IN these words the Christian life is compared to a race, and the disciples of Jesus are warmly exhorted to press forward in their way to heaven, till they obtain the glorious prize for which they contend.

I shall therefore make it my business, in the following discourse,

First, To give you a general account of the race we have to run; and

Secondly, To illustrate the fitness and propriety of this similitude. After which, in the

Third place, I shall press the exhortation by some motives and arguments.

I NEED not spend much time upon the first of these particulars. In general, the race we have to run, comprehends the whole of that duty we owe to God; namely, obedience to his laws, and submission to his providence; doing what he commands, and patiently enduring whatever he is pleased to appoint. The charge which our great Master hath given us is expressed in these words: *Occupy till I come.* All the gifts of nature, of providence, and of grace, are talents put into our hands; which must not only be carefully kept, but diligently improved, for his glory and our own spiritual advantage; otherwise we shall be condemned, not only as slothful, but as wicked, servants, and punished accordingly. "To him that knoweth to do good, and doeth it not," saith the apostle James, "to him it is sin." It is not sufficient, barely "to deny ungodliness and worldly lusts:" the grace of God doth further teach us "to live soberly, righteously, and godly, in the world;" adding one Christian grace to another, abounding more and more in the work of the Lord, till we have perfected holiness in the fear of God. Thus extensive is the divine law, reaching to every part of our conduct, at all times, and in all places and circumstances. Wherever we are, it speaks to us; and if our ears are open, we may continually hear its voice behind us, saying, "Lo! this is the way, walk ye in it."

But the Christian life includes in it something more than the mere performance of duty; the cross lies in our way, and we shall never get to the end of the race, unless we take it up, and, with meekness and patience, carry it along with us. It must be owned, indeed, that this, at the first sight, hath rather the look of a clog or incumbrance; and the Christian, while under the cross, is very apt to think so: he feels his burden, and in his own apprehension, moves so heavily, that he is afraid he shall never get to the end of his journey; which frequently inclines him to wish that the load were removed, and some easier piece of service assigned him. But this in reality is a mistake: the cross is far from being a hindrance in our way to heaven; for though a heavy material load oppresses the body, yet in the spiritual race it often happens, that the burdened soul makes both the swiftest and the surest progress. "Tribulation worketh patience, and patience experience, and experience hope." The cross may be called a tree both of knowledge and of life: the fruit it bears hath no deadly quality; on the contrary, it gives both sight and health; it opens our eyes to see the good we ought to choose, and the evil we ought to shun; and is often made effectual, by the blessing of God, to purge away those fatal distempers which sin hath brought into our frame, to beget in us a loathing of every thing that is evil, and more ardent desires after higher measures of that holiness, which is at once the ornament and the happiness of our nature. The cross doth not enfeeble us, though we erroneously may think so; it only makes us sensible of our weakness, that we may depend upon him who is "the Lord our strength;" and instead of crushing us with its own weight, obligeth us to quit our hold of those real incumbrances which mar our progress, and hinder us to "run the race that is set before us."

Thus I have given you a general view of the race we have to run. It comprehends obedience to the laws of God, and submission to his discipline; doing what he commands, and patiently enduring whatever he is pleased to inflict. I am now, in the

Second place, To illustrate the fitness and propriety of this similitude; and to show, that the Christian life doth very much resemble a race in several important respects.

Thus, for example, one in running a race must strictly observe the course that is marked out to him: he is not at liberty to choose his own ground, but must confine himself to that which the judges have agreed upon; otherwise let him run ever so fast, he can acquire no right or title to the prize. Now here the resemblance is most exact. There is a certain limited way in which the Christian must run, emphatically called *the way of God's commandments.* This we must keep with the utmost precision, "neither turning aside to the right hand nor to the left." Mere activity will not avail us: we may be very keen and busy; but if we are not busy according to rule, we only lose our labor: God can never accept it as a service done to him. It is absolutely necessary that we be always in a readiness to answer that question, "Who hath required this at your hand?" Nothing is left to our own humor or fancy: "The law of the Lord is perfect;" and it is equally dishonored when we pretend to add to it as when we take from it. Arbitrary rules of strictness, for which we have no warrant in the word of God, are dangerous things, and seldom fail in the issue to supplant that religion which is solid and saving. By this officious overdoing, the church of Rome grew up by degrees into that monster which it is now become; for I am fully persuaded, that all those childish superstitions, which have long been advanced above the laws of God, were first introduced, many of them with a real design, and all of them under the specious pretext of giving aid to the divine law, and facilitating the observance of it. I am very sensible, that the humor of the present age doth not run this way: few need a caution against being "righteous overmuch." Nevertheless, as some serious, well-meaning people may be in danger of making snares for their own consciences, by laying down rules of conduct which are not warranted by the word of God, I am hopeful that this hint may not be altogether unuseful. Let the holy Scriptures be your constant study; and what these enjoin, observe with all the care and accuracy you are capable of. Let this be your business, to find out the duty of every season; and when you have found it, then do and spare not. Thus shall you run lawfully; and every step you make shall be an advance towards the prize.

Again; as running a race is a swift and constant progression, so ought the life of a Christian to be. "Whatever our hands find to do, we must do it with all our might." And we need never go far off to find work; there is enough on every side of us to keep us constantly employed. Let us not then be slothful in business, but "fervent in spirit, serving the Lord." "Let us never think we have already attained, either are already perfect; but forgetting the things which are behind, and reaching forth to those things which are before, let us press toward the mark, for the prize of the high calling of God in Christ Jesus." "The path of the just is as the shining light, that shineth more and more unto the perfect day." Our present attainments, instead of a resting-place, should only serve as a scaffolding to raise us up higher; and the nearer we advance to the prize, the more quick and accelerated should our motion be. Which leads me to mention another remarkable property in which the Christian life resembles a race; namely,

That there is no gaining the prize unless we hold out to the end. It signifies nothing to start briskly, and to run fast a great part of the way; the whole ground, you know, must be passed over, otherwise the person is reputed not to have run at all.—So it is in the Christian race. The temporary profession, or practice of religion, will not avail us; we must persevere to the last; for it is only he who endureth to the end that shall be saved: "To him that overcometh," said our blessed Lord, "will I grant to sit with me in my throne, even as I also overcame, and am set down with my father in his throne." The charge, as I formerly observed to you, runs in these words: "Occupy till I come;" and the promise exactly corresponds to it; "Be thou faithful unto the death, and I will give thee a crown of life."

Thus, in all these particulars, the Christian life may, with great propriety, be compared to a race. But then it is necessary to observe, that though the resemblance is sufficiently strong to justify the use of this figurative representation; yet there are several important respects in which the Christian race doth widely differ from all others: Such as,

1*st.* In other races, though many may start, and hold out to the end; yet none but the foremost receiveth the prize: *Know ye not*, saith the Apostle, in the first part of the verse, *that they which run in a race, run all, but one receiveth the prize;* whereas it is quite otherwise in the Christian race. There may be a great disparity among the candidates, but every one who endureth to the end shall be saved. He who is faithful over a little, shall be as certainly rewarded, as he who is faithful over much; each shall receive a crown as large as he can wear: Whosoever doth faithfully, is accounted by the Judge to have done well: for we find the same salutation that was addressed to the servant who had improved the many talents, addressed likewise to him who had improved the few: "Well done," (though not so much done) yet still it is said, "Well done, thou good and faithful servant; enter thou into the joy of thy Lord." Hence,

2*dly.* They who run in the Christian race have no envy, no jealousy among themselves; far less do they molest and hinder one another: on the contrary, the stronger help forward the weaker, and give them all the assistance and encouragement in their power. Now, in other races it is not so; the fall of one candidate gives joy to the rest; but they who run for the heavenly prize, would carry all the world along with them if they could. As the Psalmist "was glad when they said unto him, Let us go into the house of the Lord;" so every sincere candidate for immortal glory rejoiceth when he hears of many travellers by the way; and is ready to say to every one he meets, O come and let us go together to the Zion above, that city of the great King, where true riches and honors are only to be found.

3*dly.* They who run in other races have nothing but toil and labor till they obtain the prize; but in the Christian race, the exercise itself carries part of the reward in its bosom: "Wisdom's ways are ways of pleasantness, and all her paths are peace." Christ's yoke is easy, his burden is light, and his commandments are not grievous. Hear what holy David says, "Thy statutes have been my songs in the house of my pilgrimage."—Sometimes, indeed, they have dark nights and stormy weather; "without are fightings, and within are fears." But this is not the constant fear of them all, nor perhaps of any of them at all times: they have their seasons of joy as well as of grief: and they have this to comfort them amidst all their troubles, even the assurance that they shall work together for their everlasting benefit. Which leads me to mention a

4*th.* Distinguishing property of the Christian race; namely, the certainty of gaining the prize at last. Did the Christian run in his own strength, he might not only doubt but despair of success: but his whole dependence is on that almighty Saviour, upon whom the Father hath laid his help: He goes up through the wilderness, leaning upon the beloved; and therefore, under his felt weakness, and when every thing around him wears the most discouraging aspect, he is sometimes enabled to triumph in the language of Paul, and to say, as he did, "I can do all things through Christ that strengtheneth me." Perseverance is not only the duty, but the privilege of all who set themselves in good earnest to run for heaven: and though the law of God obligeth them, and the new nature habitually inclines them, "to keep under the body, and to bring it into subjection;" yet they have far better security than any efforts of their own. Omnipotence is their guardian: and they are kept by the power of God, through faith unto salvation." These, my brethren, are some of the endearing peculiarities of the Christian race: Let me now exhort you, in the

Third place, *So to run that you may at length obtain.* And, for this end, let us consider,

1*st.* That many eyes are upon us: We are surrounded with spectators, who narrowly observe every part of our behavior. The holy angels, those ministering spirits sent forth to minister to the heirs of salvation, look on us with a friendly concern; and as they rejoice at the first conversion of a sinner, so we may reasonably suppose, that all our strayings from the path of life are sorrowfully remarked and lamented by them. On the other hand, those malignant powers of darkness, which constantly go about "seeking whom they may devour," are no less attentive to our conduct. They too mark our steps, though from a different principle: not to help, but to ensnare us; not to applaud our fidelity and diligence, but to find matter of censure and accusation against us. Above all, the great and omniscient God hath his eye continually upon us; "he compasseth our path, and he is acquainted with all our ways." He besets us behind and before, and so holds us by his right hand, that we cannot fly from his presence, nor find any covering so thick as to hide us from his sight. Think of this, my brethren, and judge whether we have not cause to be continually on our guard. We perform every action, not only in the sight of innumerable witnesses, but in the presence of that glorious Being, by whom our final doom shall be pronounced: Ought we not then to quit ourselves like men? There is something in this motive so awful, and at the same time so animating, that I should think I affronted your reason, if I spent time in the illustration of it. We must feel its influence as soon as it is named: Did we see with our bodily eyes what we profess to believe, we should not wait for an exhortation to "run the race set before us."

Consider, in the 2*d* place, That many have already run this race, who are now in possession of the glorious prize. Paul exhorted the Christians in his day to be "followers of them, who through faith and patience inherit the promises." The way to heaven was not then an untrodden path; a great cloud of witnesses had passed that road before the Apostle began to write: and we may reasonably conclude, that vast multitudes have been following them during the seventeen hundred years which have elapsed since that time. And shall not their example encourage us to go and do likewise? We see plainly from their success, that there are no unsurmountable obstacles in the way. The saints now in heaven were once in the same condition with ourselves; they were men of like passions, and exposed to the same temptations. The grace that saved them is equally sufficient to save us; and (glory to God) it is as ready to be dispensed to us, if we ask and seek, and knock for it, as they did.

Where are all those illustrious persons recorded in Scripture? Where are the patriarchs, the prophets, and the apostles of our Lord? Where are those heroic spirits, of whom we read in the 11th chapter of the epistle to the Hebrews, "who through faith subdued kingdoms, wrought righteousness, obtained promises, stopped the mouths of lions, quenched the violence of fire, escaped the edge of the sword, out of weakness were made strong, waxed valiant in fight, and turned to flight the armies of the aliens?" Where are those faithful martyrs, "who had trial of cruel mockings, and scourgings, yea moreover of bonds and imprisonment; who were stoned, who were sawn asunder, who were tempted, who were slain with the sword; who wandered about in sheep-skins and goat-skins, being destitute, afflicted, tormented; of whom the world was not worthy?" Where are those holy souls, with whom we ourselves were personally acquainted, and whom we dearly loved, but who are now separated from our society, and have left us behind them in this vale of misery and tears? They are surrounding the throne of God most high, singing the song of Moses and of the Lamb; ascribing glory to him who washed them from their sins in his own blood, and made them kings and priests unto God, even his Father. Look above you, O Christians! to this glorious company; and the desire of being one day joined to them will reconcile you to all the hardships of the Christian course, and make you run with patience the race set before you.

Consider, in the 3*d* place, Who are your fellow-travellers. You are not only going to a glorious and triumphant society, but you go in company with persons of the greatest dignity and worth, "even the saints, those excellent ones in the earth," whom God hath chosen and set apart for himself. And this, my brethren, is an encouraging circumstance. We find, that even an Elias, when he supposed himself alone by the way, both wished and prayed for death, saying, "It is enough, now, O Lord God; take away my life; for I am not better than my fathers." And therefore God was pleased, in great condescension, to rectify the mistake of his servant, by assuring him, that there were many thousands unknown to him who had not bowed the knee to Baal; and that the road to the celestial country, even in that corrupt and degenerate age, was not so unfrequented and solitary as he imagined. The saints are not only hid from the world, but frequently mistaken by one another; which tempts many of them to think, that the kingdom of Christ is of a very narrow extent, and the number of his subjects exceeding small; but were our eyes opened, and the scales of pride and prejudice removed, we should see a far more goodly company than we expected. And ought not this to animate us in our Christian race? Have we all the saints on earth for our companions? are we going to saints and angels in heaven? and shall not this fire us with an heroic ardor *to run so as we may* at length *obtain?* Especially if we consider, in the

4th place, The nature of those duties which our Lord hath required of us; or if you please (to keep by the allusion) the goodness of that road in which we are to run for the heavenly prize. "The law is holy," saith the apostle Paul, "the commandment is holy, just, and *good;*" not only infinitely reasonable in itself, but infinitely kind and obliging to us, inasmuch as it enjoins nothing but what tends to purify and perfect our natures, and to qualify us for the enjoyment of a never-ending felicity. In the frame of the moral law, God appears rather like a father than a sovereign, exacting nothing as a test of our subjection to his authority, but what is so necessarily connected with our own true happiness, that a liberty to act otherwise would in reality be a license to destroy ourselves.

5thly. We have a kind, sympathizing and unerring Guide, who came from heaven to earth to teach us the way from earth to heaven; yea, he hath not only pointed out the road to us, but hath actually gone before us, and now calls upon us to follow his steps. "Behold," saith God by the Prophet Isaiah, "I have given him for a witness to the people, a leader and commander to the people." This is the peculiar office of our Lord Jesus Christ; and his mildness and condescension in the discharge of this office are beautifully described by the same prophet! "He shall feed his flock like a shepherd; he shall gather the lambs with his arm, and carry them in his bosom, and gently lead those that are with young." He doth not despise the weakness of his people; for he knoweth their frame, and "is touched with a feeling of their infirmities, having been in all points tempted like as they are." Like as a father pitieth his children, so the Lord pitieth those that fear him. "He doth not break the bruised reed, nor quench the smoking flax;" on the contrary, "he giveth power to the faint, and to them that have no might he increaseth strength." He will not suffer them to be tempted above what they are able; but in the emphatical language of holy writ, "he debates with them in measure, and stays his rough wind in the day of his east wind." When they pass through the fire, and through the water, he is with them; and though, for wise and holy reasons, their eyes may be holden that they cannot perceive him; yet with a powerful, though invisible hand, he supports and guides their weary steps; according to that gracious promise, "I will bring the blind by a way that they know not, and lead them in paths which they have not known; I will make darkness light before them, and crooked ways straight. These things will I do for them, and not forsake them." O what a joyful consideration is this! that the great Captain of salvation is our Guide, who can cover our head, and heal our wounds; raise us up when we fall, and perfect strength in our weakness. "Fear not," says he, "for I am with thee; be not dismayed, for I am thy God; I will strengthen thee; yea, I will help thee, yea, I will uphold thee with the right hand of my righteousness."

My *6th* and *last* motive shall be taken from the unspeakable worth of the prize to be obtained. This is no other than "heaven itself;" "eternal life;" "an exceeding and eternal weight of glory;" "an incorruptible crown;" "an undefiled inheritance;" "a glory which eye hath not seen, nor ear heard, neither can the heart of man conceive." "It doth not yet appear," saith the apostle John, "what we shall be; but we know, that when he shall appear, we shall be like him, for we shall see him as he is." Then shall we be thoroughly changed into the image of our Lord. We shall love him without measure, and praise him without end; we shall serve him without weariness, and those manifold imperfections which stain our most holy duties while on earth. Nay, our bodies being raised by the power and spirit of our Redeemer, who is the "plague of death, and the destruction of the grave," shall be fashioned like unto his own glorious body; whose presence we shall for ever enjoy, and whose matchless love, that passeth knowledge, we shall eternally celebrate with the church of the first-born.

This, my brethren, is the glorious prize for which we are called to contend. And can any thing fire our ambition if this do not? What bustle do men make for an earthly crown, when, lo! death is at hand to pluck it off their heads, and to throw it in the dust? and shall not we contend for a heavenly crown, a regal dignity and power, which, when once obtained, shall never be taken from us? "Wherefore gird up the loins of your mind, be sober, and hope to the end, for the grace that is to be brought unto you at the revelation of Jesus Christ." Let us henceforth "lay aside every weight, and the sin which doth so easily beset us, and let us run with patience the race that is set before us; looking unto Jesus, the author and finisher of our faith; who, for the joy that was set before him, endured the cross, despising the shame, and is set down at the right hand of the throne of God." To him let our waiting eyes be continually directed; and whilst we run in obedience to his command, let us humbly and fervently address him in the words of the devout Psalmist, with which I shall conclude: "Unto thee, O Lord, do I lift up my soul. O my God, I trust in thee, let me not be ashamed. Show me thy ways; Lord, teach me thy paths. Lead me in thy truth, and guide me; for thou art the God of my salvation, on thee do I wait all the day."—*Amen.*

SERMON XV.

FERVOR IN GOD'S SERVICE.

ROMANS XII. 11.—"Fervent in spirit, serving the Lord."

It usually happens, saith one, that in times of peace and outward prosperity, the church, like a river whose channel is enlarged, loseth as much in depth as it gains in breadth: I wish I could not add, that the present state of the church in our own land, serves not only to illustrate the propriety of this similitude, but likewise to confirm the truth of the observation. As we have long enjoyed, in a very distinguished manner, the protection and countenance of civil authority, the number of professors is indeed greatly increased; but though the *forms* of godliness are practised by many, there is too just cause to complain, that the genuine *power* of it is felt by few. Where are the persons who make religion their business, and apply themselves to it as the "one thing needful?" How few are to be found, who exemplify those scriptural representations of the Christian's work and duty; "fighting the good fight of faith;" "running with patience the race set before them;" "pressing toward the mark, for the prize of the high calling of God in Christ Jesus?" Alas! my brethren, the far greater number, if they be going forward at all, it is with such a slow and staggering pace, as can neither edify their brethren, nor yield any real comfort to themselves: "their light," instead of "shining before men," like the dim twinkling of a candle, sunk and expiring in the socket, is scarcely discernible.

For exciting such decayed and languishing Christians to "strengthen the things which remain, that are ready to die," I shall at present take occasion, from the words I have read to you, *first*, to explain; and, *secondly*, to recommend that *fervor of spirit*, with which the apostle exhorteth us to *serve the Lord.*

FERVOR, in general, is opposed to lukewarmness or indifference; and denotes that edge or keenness, that activity and diligence, which we commonly exert in the pursuit of any object we highly value and wish to possess. Now the *fervor* whereof my text speaks, hath religion, or the *service of God*, for its object: Love to God is the principle, the law of God is the rule, and his glory the end, of all its operations. The *fervent* Christian is habitually on the stretch to answer the great purposes for which he was made and redeemed; his understanding is employed in searching out the mind of God, so far as it regards the conduct of his creatures; his will is firmly and resolutely determined to perform whatever shall appear to be his duty; his affections are inspired with holy life and vigor: in consequence of which, his executive powers are all ready to perform their several parts; the tongue to speak, the hands to give, or to do what is required, and the feet to run in the way of God's commandments. In short, the whole man is engaged in the *service of God;* so that religion becomes his constant and most delightful occupation; he "strives" with all his might "to enter in at the strait gate;" and counts nothing too much to be done, or too hard to be endured, for the enjoyment of that God whom he most ardently loves, and to whom he is entirely devoted. This, my brethren, is to be *fervent in spirit.*

But as there are several counterfeits of this gracious temper, I shall endeavor to select those peculiar properties of true Christian *fervor* that chiefly distinguish it from those delusive appearances by which too many impose both upon themselves and others. Let it be observed then, in the

1*st* place, That as *the service of God* is the proper object of true Christian *fervor*, this renders it necessary that we be thoroughly acquainted with the laws of God, that we may know what particular services he requires of us, and will accept at our hands. A mistake here is of the most dangerous consequence; for if once we step aside from the path of duty, the faster we run, the farther we depart from the right way, and our return to it becomes more uncertain and difficult. Saul was very *fervent in spirit*, when he "breathed out threatenings and slaughter against the disciples of the Lord," and "verily thought that he ought to do many things contrary to the name of Jesus of Nazareth:" And yet this *fervor* of his, had not sovereign grace stopped him in his mad career, would only have hurried him downward to that hot and dark place from whence it most certainly sprung. We have heard of some who, according to our Saviour's prediction, "thought they did God service when they killed his people;" and the church of Rome continues at this day to afford an awful instance of this kind, whose *burning zeal*, as indeed it may literally be called, hath already consumed all that was mortal of some millions of saints; and yet, instead of being quenched by such a deluge of blood, doth still blaze out as fiercely as ever, where it is not controlled by superior force. I have quoted these strong examples for illustrating the difference betwixt true Christian *fervor* and that eagerness of spirit which frequently usurps its name; and to make you sensible how necessary it is that we study the "good and perfect will of God," for directing our zeal, and confining it to that sphere in which it may and ought to move.

2*dly*. As our *fervor* should be employed in the *service of God*, or in those duties that God hath plainly commanded, so it ought likewise to aim at his glory; otherwise it is an unhallowed passion, which corrupteth and debaseth every thing that proceeds from it. The want of a right aim appears to have been the principal error of the Scribes and Pharisees; for most of our Saviour's reproofs evidently turn upon this very thing. They prayed, they fasted, they gave alms, and "compassed sea and land" to gain proselytes to the Jewish religion; all which were very commendable in their own nature: But herein lay their fault, They did all "to be seen of men:" popular applause, and the advancement of their own interest, were the ends they aimed at; not the approbation of God, nor the advancement of his honor and interest in the world. Thus it often happens, when religion is in credit, that many use it as a political engine for helping them up into a higher place, and appear very warm in professing their regard to it; but no sooner is that carnal fuel withdrawn, than the flame expires, or perhaps is carried over to the opposite side, and burns as fiercely against religion as ever it seemed to do for it. Whereas true Christian *fervor* carries the person beyond himself to that God whom he adores; and instead of being cooled by the profane mockery, or hatred, or persecution, of wicked men, it rather becomes more vigorous and active, and exerts itself in proportion to the opposition it meets with. If God is glorified by his sufferings, the *fervent* Christian hath gained his end: like David, he is willing to be still "more vile," still more afflicted; and with the apostle Paul, he hath no higher ambition, than that "Christ may be magnified in his body, whether it be by life or by death." Which leads me to observe, in the

3*d* place, That this gracious temper extends its regards to all God's commandments. It declines no duty that bears the stamp of his authority; for as the glory of God is the great scope of all its actings, whatever tends to promote that, immediately becomes the object of its choice, and the matter of its most delightful and vigorous exercise. Now, here the hypocrite is always found halting; he picks out the easiest parts of duty, such as have least self-denial in them, and most of that outward splendor which attracts the observation of others. If he is rich, he may abound in alms-deeds, especially in those instances of charity which are most likely to make a noise in the world, that his fame may spread abroad, and bring him the tribute of praise from afar. He may attend upon the public ordiances of religion, and sit like one of the people of God, with a becoming air of warm devotion; but could your eye follow him into his own house, you should there behold a wonderful alteration, perhaps a total neglect both of family and secret prayer, or at best such a cold and lifeless worship, as scarcely deserved the name of "bodily exercise" itself. Whereas the upright Christian "is in the fear of the Lord all the day long." He considers his Judge as evermore present with him: this awakens his mind, and enlivens his devotion, and hath a more powerful influence upon his conduct than the applause or censure of ten thousand worlds: this makes him fervent in every part of duty; yea, as fervent in the severest acts of self-denial as in in those instances of obedience which are accompanied with the most immediate advantage or pleasure.

A 4*th* distinguishing property of true Christian *fervor* is this: It will make us peculiarly attentive to our own behavior, and begin with correcting what is faulty in ourselves.—Many exclaim against the vices of others, who are extremely partial and indulgent to their own. To such our apostle addresses a very sharp reproof, in the second chapter of this epistle, at the beginning: "Therefore, thou art inexcusable, O man, whosoever thou art that judgest: for wherein thou judgest another, thou condemnest thyself; for thou that judgest dost the same things. And thinkest thou this, O man, that judgest them which do such things, and dost the same, that thou shalt escape the judgment of God?" Nothing can be more disingenuous, than for people to profess a hatred of sin, and a mighty anxiety to have others reclaimed from it, when their own conduct proclaims that they do not hate it in themselves. That *fervor* which is of the right kind, will first "cast out the beam out of our own eye, before it will suffer us to behold the mote that is in our brother's eye." It will discover to us so many things amiss in our own vineyards, that we shall neither find leisure nor inclination to pry officiously into our neighbor's vineyard till these are amended. The *fervent* Christian will take no rest till the enemies of his God be subdued within his own breast: "He will never think that he hath already attained, either is already perfect; but, forgetting the things which are behind, and reaching forth unto those things which are before, he will press toward the mark, for the prize of the high calling of God in Christ Jesus;"—"giving all diligence to make his calling and election sure;"—and "working out his own salvation with fear and trembling."—Nevertheless, in the

5*th* place, Though true *fervor* begins at

home, yet it is not always confined there. It was the speech of a wicked Cain, "Am I my brother's keeper?" The warm-hearted Christian extends his good offices to all around him; and useth all that power and influence which his station gives him, to discourage vice, and to advance the kingdom of Christ in the world. —Is he a magistrate? he will not "bear the sword in vain," but faithfully employ it for the terror of evil doers, and the protection of those that do well.—Is he a minister? he will not "handle the word of God deceitfully;" but, without regarding the persons or passions of men, he will openly declare the whole counsel of God, and, by sound doctrine and good example, do what in him lieth to convince and reclaim the workers of iniquity, "that they may recover themselves out of the snare of the devil, who are taken captive by him at his pleasure."—Is he a parent or master? "he will walk within his house with a perfect heart," and adopt the resolution of holy David, (Psalm ci. 6, 7.) "He that walketh in a perfect way, he shall serve me; he that worketh deceit shall not dwell within my house; he that telleth lies shall not tarry in my sight." In short, whatever be his condition in life, he will embrace every opportunity that Providence affords him, of advancing the glory of God, and doing all the good he can, either to the souls or bodies of men. —Of this we have many eminent examples recorded in Scripture:—Righteous Lot was vexed from day to day with the unlawful deeds and filthy conversation of the Sodomites, among whom he lived; "Paul's spirit was stirred in him" when he beheld the city of Athens wholly given to idolatry; and Phinehas, the son of Eleazar, was both commended and rewarded, for executing righteous judgment in the camp of Israel, and obtained "the covenant of an everlasting priesthood;" for this express reason, *Because he was zealous for his God.*—But then I must add, in the

6*th* and *last* place, That this *fervor* must be always under the direction of Christian prudence, that it may not break out into indecent heats, and carry us beyond the limits of our office or station in the society to which we belong. If we step out of our proper sphere, we trespass against that subordination which the providence of God hath established; and no pretence to religious zeal can justify our conduct. Such fervor is not inspired by the Spirit of grace, but is the *strange* and unhallowed *fire* of disorderly passion, which can never find acceptance with that God, whose declared will it is, "that all things should be done decently and in order."

Such, my brethren, is that *fervor of spirit* with which the apostle exhorteth us to *serve the Lord.*

To recommend and enforce this gracious temper was the *second* thing proposed in the method.—And now that I am to enter upon this part of the subject, I would earnestly entreat your most serious attention. Consider that I speak not only *before* you, but *to* you; and that not in my own name, but in the name of that glorious Person "by whom God will judge the world in righteousness; whereof he hath given assurance unto all men, in that he raised him from the dead." That you may be ready for that awful trial, and appear with humble boldness in his presence, when careless and trifling sinners shall hang their heads, and stand speechless and self-condemned before his tremendous throne; this is the errand upon which I come to you; no other, no lower errand than this.—If the bare title of Christians would gain you admittance into the heavenly glory; if a cold and barren profession of religion, or the practice of some easy and common duties, would render you meet for the inheritance of the saints in light; if God deserved or required no more than what the world and the flesh can spare; I should be indiscreet for attempting to disturb your repose.—But if these things be otherwise; if it shall profit us nothing to "call Christ Lord, Lord," unless we "do the things which he saith;" if *sloth* be accounted *wickedness* by the righteous Judge of all the earth, and as such shall be punished by him in the great day of retribution;—then I should be unfaithful to God, and cruel to your souls, if I did not summon you to your duty, and vehemently urge you, in the words of my text, *to be fervent in spirit, serving the Lord.*—Consider, in the

1*st* place, That God deserves the most zealous and active service we can pay to him. Surely this assertion doth not require a formal proof; the evidence of its truth is so plain and obvious, that the most simple and illiterate must perceive it at once.—Dare any of you say that it is possible to render unto God more than you owe him? If you should, I need not go far for arguments to confute you; I can fetch them from yourselves, from every member of your bodies, from every faculty of your souls.—Who made thee, O man?—This is the first question that children are taught to answer; though, alas! it is to be feared that many grown people answer it like children, and need to be sent to school again to learn its meaning. Is God thy Creator? was it he who "clothed thee with skin and flesh, and fenced thee with bones and sinews?" Was it he who breathed into thy nostrils the breath of life, and made thee a living soul? Are all the endowments of thy mind, thy understanding, thy memory, thy will, and thy affections; are all these the fruits of his bounty? Doth his merciful visitation every moment preserve thy spirit, keep thy body from the dust, and thy soul from the place of anguish and despair?—And after all, is it possible, that thy soul or thy body can exceed in his service, or be employed with too much zeal for his honor? Stand forth, O man! and reply if thou canst. What! doth this plain, I had almost called it this childish, question put thee to a stand? How inexcusable then is thy sloth? How just, and, Oh! how dreadful, must thy condemnation be?

But, my brethren, these are not all the mercies you have received, and are daily receiving from God. He is not only your Creator, your Preserver, and Benefactor; but he hath bound you to his service by the still more endearing ties of redeeming grace and love: He sent his own Son into the world to save you, to save you by his death: Amazing goodness! to shed his blood for the expiation of your guilt: And can you exceed in your gratitude to such a friend? is it possible you can render unto him more than is due, or serve him with too great zeal and *fervor?*

But 2*dly*. God not only deserves such service as I am pleading for; he likewise demands it, peremptorily demands it, and will not be put off with any thing less.—"Be not deceived," saith this holy apostle, "God is not mocked; for whatsoever a man soweth, that shall he also reap: he that soweth to the flesh, shall of the flesh reap corruption; and he that soweth to the Spirit, shall of the Spirit reap life everlasting." If any imagine that Christ came into the world to relax their obligations to a holy life, they are grossly mistaken; and if they act upon that principle, they shall find themselves fatally disappointed at last. St. Paul knew of no such indulgence when he wrote to Titus, that "the grace of God, which bringeth salvation, teacheth us, that, denying ungodliness and worldly lusts, we should live soberly, righteously, and godly in this present world." Our Saviour gave countenance to no such opinion, when he exhorted his disciples to "strive to enter in at the strait gate;" and told them in plain and awful terms, that "except their righteousness should exceed the righteousness of the Scribes and Pharisees, they should in no case enter into the kingdom of heaven." This, my brethren, is the uniform language of holy writ; the words of my text are clear and strong; and it deserves our notice, that they are part of an epistle wherein the grace of the new covenant is most accurately described, and zealously defended; which, no doubt, must add a considerable weight to them. The slothful professor counteracts the whole design of the gospel; for the plan of man's redemption was so wisely laid, that not only the comfort of the Christian, but his improvement in holiness also, should be gradually advanced to full maturity. The design of Christ's death was not merely to reconcile God to us, but likewise to reconcile us to God; that his generous and unmerited love might overcome our enmity, make us ashamed of our ingratitude, and powerfully constrain us to live, "not unto ourselves, but unto him who died for us, and rose again."

A 4*th* motive to *fervor* and diligence in *the service of God*, ariseth from the difficulties that attend our duty. The

Christian's work is compared to a warfare; he must dispute every inch of ground, and fight his way through surrounding enemies. It is no easy matter "to pluck out a right eye, and to cut off a right hand;" that is, to renounce those sins to which we have been so long habituated, that they are in a manner become parts of ourselves, and no less dear to us than the most useful and necessary members of our body; yet to this we must consent before we can enter into the kingdom of heaven.—It appears a hard command that God gave to Abraham, "Take now thy son, thine only son Isaac, whom thou lovest, and get thee into the land of Moriah, and offer him there for a burnt-offering upon one of the mountains that I shall tell thee of." But is not that other command at least equally severe, Take now thy lust, thy beloved lust, from which thou hast promised thyself the greatest returns of profit or pleasure, bring it hither immediately, and slay it before me, without the ceremony of one parting embrace? This, my brethren, is difficult work indeed. Isaac lay meekly and patiently on the altar; but so will not our lusts; no, they will struggle, and cry, and plead for mercy, and use every insinuating method of address, to prevent, or at least to retard the stroke. But neither is this all: those inward corruptions, formidable as they are, yet are they not the only enemies we have to grapple with: The devil is an adversary both cunning and strong, very formidable by his power as "the roaring lion;" but still more formidable by his craft as that "old serpent," who can vary his shape, and put on the appearance of an angel of light, that, in a form so specious, he may get access to our hearts with greater ease, and fill them with his poison before we are aware.—This earth too upon which we tread is full of snares; and every state or condition of life hath some temptation or other peculiar to itself, as we learn from that well-conceived prayer of Agur, (Prov. xxx. 8, 9.) "Remove far from me vanity and lies; give me neither poverty nor riches, feed me with food convenient for me: *lest I be full and deny thee*, and say, who is the Lord? or, *lest I be poor and steal*, and take the name of my God in vain." Besides, in the ordinary course of events, "all that will live godly in Christ Jesus must suffer persecution" in one kind or other. The Christian is bound not only to avoid conformity to the world, but, on all proper occasions, to testify his dislike of its corrupt maxims and practices; which cannot fail to draw upon him a considerable share of hatred and resentment. Singularity is enough to beget ill will: but if a person shall not only use different manners, but likewise condemn the manners of those among whom he lives, which the most prudent and modest disciple of Jesus may sometimes find himself obliged to do; this will not easily be forgiven; such a one can expect no better treatment than Lot had from the Sodomites, who could not bear that a fellow, as they called him, "who came in to sojourn," should pretend to be their judge.—Such are the difficulties that attend religion; and do not these make zeal or *fervor* necessary?—I shall only add, in the

4th place, That we should be *fervent in spirit, serving the Lord;* because, as I have already observed, it is absolutely impossible that we can do too much. Were we in any danger of exceeding, there would no doubt be cause to moderate our zeal: but this is not the case; for after "we have done all those things which are commanded us," we shall still have reason to say, "We are unprofitable servants; we have done that which was our duty to do." True it is, that in particular exercises of religion there may be an overdoing; for one duty may justly be said to exceed, when it thrusts out another of greater, or even of equal importance, or which is more the duty of the season than itself; but so long as we regulate our services by the word of God, in which case alone they are proper acts of obedience, we need not be afraid of becoming "righteous overmuch." One thing is certain, that the most serious Christians, when they come to die, have always lamented their former negligence: and the time is at hand, when all the world shall confess, that holy diligence was the truest wisdom; and that they, and they only made a choice of the better part, who minded the "one thing needful," and were *fervent in spirit, serving the Lord.*

And now, my dear friends, my design, upon the whole, is to excite you to a proper concern about the salvation of your precious and immortal souls. It is not a system of opinions that will carry any man to heaven: our knowledge of the truth shall only serve to condemn us, if we do not receive the truth into our hearts, and suffer it to influence both our temper and practice. I am far from thinking that men may be saved in any religion, however false, provided only they be sincere in the belief, and obedient to the dictates, of that religion they profess; but of this I am fully persuaded, on the other hand, that no religion can save a man who is not serious in it, and who doth not yield himself entirely to its government. Can it avail us any thing, that we profess the *true* religion, if we ourselves are *false* to that religion? No, surely: The religion indeed is good, but it is not *our* religion; it is our book that contains the true religion, but not our heart; and therefore it can no more save us than the best food can nourish us, and preserve our life, which only standeth upon the table, or which never goeth farther than our mouth.

Let me therefore entreat you to comply with the apostle's exhortation in my text. I speak to you who are Christians *indeed;* because you alone are in a capacity of *serving the Lord;* for "they that are in the flesh," who were never cut off from the natural stock, and ingrafted into Christ the true vine, such persons, the apostle tells us (Rom viii. 8.), "cannot please God." They may perform the outward acts of duty, they may even do them with a considerable degree of *natural fervor;* but all the while their most specious services are only dead works, offered up with "strange fire," which cannot ascend to God with acceptance. I speak therefore to the living members of Christ, to those who are regenerated by the Spirit of God; and my request to you is, that, from this time forward, you should "stir up the gift of God that is in you," and be *fervent in spirit, serving the Lord.*

The declining interest of religion requires all the support you can give it. Men are wearing out of acquaintance with God; nor is it greatly to be wondered at, seeing his image is so faintly to be discerned, even upon those who are really his children. Look around you, and observe how active and violent wicked men are in the service of Satan; their pace, like "the driving of Jehu, the son of Nimshi, is swift and furious." With what zeal, with what carefulness, with what self-denial—I had almost said, with what fear and trembling—do many of them work out their own damnation! "drawing iniquity with cords of vanity, and sinning as with a cart rope!" And will you be cold and negligent, nay, timorous and shamefaced, in the service of the true and living God? Oh! how unseemly, how scandalous, how hurtful were this! hurtful to yourselves, hurtful to your fellow Christians, hurtful even to the wicked with whom you converse; they know that heaven and hell are in direct opposition, and consequently that the roads which lead to them must be widely distant from each other; and therefore they will never be persuaded that they shall be thrust down into utter darkness, if such as you, who in appearance are treading the same paths that they do, shall get to heaven at last. Ungrateful servants! how hath your Redeemer deserved this at your hands? Is this the way to gain men's hearts to the love of holiness? Would you wish the world to write after so imperfect and blotted a copy as you set before them? I beseech, I obtest you, by all the regard you have for the glory of God, your own comfort, and the good of others, that henceforth you would distinguish yourselves more visibly from "the men of the world who have their portion in this life." "Have no fellowship with the unfruitful works of darkness, but rather reprove them." Let Christianity be so deeply engraved on every part of your conduct, that he who runs may read whose servants you are, and thus God may be glorified in his saints. It is a mean, inglorious aim, merely to keep within the limits which divide the lawful from the forbidden ground. Show that you are men of "another spirit," by "following the Lord fully," and straining every nerve, as it were, to attain the highest perfection of which our nature is capable in its present imperfect state. Let faith realize to you the life of Jesus; and beg of God, for Christ's sake, that he, by his Spirit, may kindle that holy fire in your hearts, which shall gradually consume all your dross, and carry you swiftly forward to the Zion above, that imperial city of the great King, where, like those flaming ministers who surround his throne, you shall serve God day and night in his temple, without interruption, without imperfection, and without weariness. To which exalted felicity, may God, of his infinite mercy, bring us all in due time, through Jesus Christ our Lord. *Amen.*

SERMON XVI.

FOLLOWING GOD FULLY.

NUMB. XIV. 24.—"But my servant Caleb, because he had another spirit with him, and hath FOLLOWED ME FULLY; him will I bring into the land whereunto he went; and his seed shall possess it."

I PROPOSE to recommend to your imitation this illustrious servant of the most high God, whose name is recorded with such distinguished honor in the passage I have just now read in your hearing. *Caleb followed the Lord fully*, and obtained a glorious reward; and if we hope or wish to be rewarded as he was, reason teacheth us, that we should walk in his steps, and do as he did.

But what are we to understand by *following the Lord fully?* This question is first in order; and after I have endeavored to give a satisfying answer to it, I shall then proceed to press the duty by some motives and arguments.

LET us begin with inquiring what we are to understand by *following the Lord fully*.

And here I must observe in the entrance, that no man can *follow the Lord* at all till once he be acquainted with him; "For he that cometh to God must believe that he is, and that he is a rewarder of them that diligently seek him." A slavish, reluctant subjection there may be; but there cannot be a voluntary, far less an unreserved obedience, without affectionate trust and filial confidence. Before we can *follow God*, we must not only know that he is supreme, and hath a *right* to command; but we must likewise believe that he is *worthy* to command, and infinitely possessed of all those perfections which qualify him to govern the creatures he hath made. Two things we must be thoroughly persuaded of; *first*, That the laws of our Sovereign are righteous and good; and, *next*, That he is both able and willing to protect us in his service. And indeed, my brethren, had we never offended God, these views alone would have been sufficient inducements to *follow him fully;* but as we are guilty creatures, and liable to punishment, some farther discoveries are now become necessary. We need something to vanquish those fears of wrath, which would rather prompt us to fly from the presence of our Judge, than to make an uncertain attempt to pacify him by submission; some scheme of grace must be opened to our view, by which pardon may be dispensed to the guilty, and strength imparted to the weak, in a way that appears consistent with the honor of the divine government. Nay, we must not only know that such a scheme exists, but we on our part must cordially approve of it; and, by our personal consent, ascertain our claim to that mercy and grace which it offers to sinners; that, being at peace with God, we may no longer dread him as an enemy, but love him as a Father, and serve him with joy, being assured that "our labor shall not be in vain."

This being premised, as a necessary preparative for *following the Lord fully*, the duty itself may be considered as including the following particulars:

1*st*. That we acknowledge no other Lord beside him. One Lord we must have; for it is folly to imagine we can be independent and free. Man was made to serve; and nothing is left to him but the choice of his master. But more than one Lord we cannot have, unless by a derived or delegated authority. He who is supreme may appoint another to rule under him, and to enforce the observance of his laws; and when both concur in the same command, then both may be served by one act of obedience: but "no man can serve two *opposite* masters; for either he will hate the one and love the other, or else he will hold to the one and despise the other. We cannot serve God and Mammon." And therefore to *follow* *the Lord fully* is to follow him *only;* it is to make his will the sole and absolute rule of our conduct, in opposition to our own humor, the temptations of Satan, and the corrupt maxims of a world that lieth in wickedness.

2dly. To *follow the Lord fully* is to obey him without any reserve or limitation: it is to serve him with an affectionate and liberal heart; and to do this at all times. Each of these might be considered apart; but I have chosen to join them together under one head, as they serve to illustrate and support one another.

Our obedience, I say, must be without reserve or limitation; for unless we *follow the Lord* in *all* things, we cannot truly be said to follow him in *any* thing. We give cause to suspect, that when, in other instances, we perform the duties he enjoins, yet even in those we are governed by something else than a regard to his authority; and that, though we seem to *follow* him, yet, in reality, we are prosecuting some interested scheme of our own, and are seeking ourselves instead of serving our God. The universality of our obedience, then, is the only proof of our sincerity; for "whosoever shall keep the whole law, and yet offend in one point, is guilty of all." We do not *follow the Lord fully*, unless we follow him whithersoever he leadeth us, through the most rugged paths of self-denial and mortification, as well as in those smooth, delightful ways in which we find the most immediate advantage and pleasure. Again, we must serve him with an affectionate and liberal heart; continually asking such questions as these: "Lord, what wilt thou have me to do?" and, "What shall I render unto the Lord for all his benefits?" The term *following* plainly implies this. A person may be dragged or driven against his will, but to *follow* is an act of choice; it denotes a voluntary and cheerful obedience; a service of *love*, which is not sparing or niggardly, but always deviseth liberal things. Would we then *follow the Lord fully*, we must be "ready to every good work;" and not only embrace opportunities of service when they present themselves, but even seek out opportunities of improving those talents with which we are intrusted, that, as it is expressed in the parable, "when our Master returns, he may receive his own with usury." I further added, that we should behave after this manner at all times; that our conduct on every occasion may be consistent and uniform. The true servant of the Lord must always be *one man*, speaking the same language, and observing the same conduct in every place and in every company. Which leads me to a

3d Remark of considerable importance; namely, That to *follow the Lord fully*, is to follow him openly, and in the face of the world. We must not think of stealing to heaven by some clandestine, unfrequented path, as if we were ashamed of being seen, or afraid lest it should be known to what family we belonged: this is a sneaking, cowardly artifice; so base in itself, and so ungrateful to the kindest, as well as to the greatest and most honorable Master, that, were it not too commonly practised, one should scarcely think it needful to be mentioned.

There are two extremes into which people are apt to run, and both ought to be guarded against with equal care. Some proclaim their religion as on the house tops; they love to talk of their high attainments, and discover an anxiety to make themselves observable, and to gain the admiration and applause of their neighbors. This our Saviour expressly condemns. Matth. vi. from the 1st to the 19th verse, where he tells his disciples, that they who fast, or pray, or give alms, to be seen of men, only serve themselves; and what is the consequence? It is but just they should be left to reward themselves as they can; for duties done with such an aim can never be accepted by God as any part of that religious homage he requires. Others again, from a false modesty and bashfulness, or perhaps a pretended dislike of ostentation and hypocrisy, run into the opposite extreme; they hide their light (if any light they have), they hide it, I say, "under a bushel," as the Scriptures express it. They go as great lengths as they dare, in a servile compliance with the humors and customs of the world; and even keep at an affected distance from every thing that might betray any serious impression of God upon their minds.

Now, the duty I am recommending lies

at an equal distance from both these extremes. It is a profession that is neither ostentatious nor shame-faced; it neither courts observation nor avoids it. The true *follower of the Lord*, keeping the laws of his Master continually in his eye, performs every duty in its place and season. It appears a small matter to him to be "judged of man's judgment;" he endeavors "so to speak," and so to act, "not as pleasing men, but God, which trieth the heart." He doth not shun the view of his fellow-creatures, but is willing to give all who choose it an opportunity of learning, from his conduct, the nature and spirit of that religion he hath embraced. He feels, and practically acknowledgeth, the divine authority of such precepts as these: "Let your moderation be known to all men;" "Provide things honest in the sight of all men;" and, "Let your light so shine before men, that they may see your good works, and glorify your Father which is in Heaven." His soul is alarmed with that awful declaration of our Saviour (Luke ix. 26.) "Whosoever shall be ashamed of me, and of my words, of him also shall the Son of man be ashamed, when he shall come in his own glory, and in his Father's glory, and of the holy angels." Would we then *follow the Lord fully*, we must confess him openly, and dare to be holy in spite of devils and men. We must "be blameless and harmless, the sons of God, without rebuke, in the midst of a crooked and perverse generation,—holding forth the word of life." Once more, in the

4*th* place. To *follow the Lord fully*, is to cleave to him steadfastly when others forsake him; and to persevere in his service, even when it exposeth us to the world's hatred, and the persecution of wicked and unreasonable men. It was on account of this brave and honorable singularity that Caleb obtained the title of a man *of another spirit*. He was one of four, among some hundred thousands, who retained his loyalty to the King of heaven; for besides Moses and Aaron, and his own companion Joshua, it doth not appear that there was one dissenting voice in all the tribes of Israel; the revolt was universal, the whole congregation rebelled against their God. Nay, he was not only singular, but his singularity drew upon him the resentment of his brethren. Orders were given "to stone him to death;" and they were on the point of doing it, when "the glory of God appearing in the tabernacle," checked their fury, and protected the life of this illustrious saint. Thus it was that Caleb *followed the Lord fully;* and thus must we also do if we aspire to his reward. Instead of shrinking at persecution, if that should be our lot, we must rather "rejoice that we are counted worthy to suffer shame" in the cause of our Lord; and even esteem it a privilege, "that to us it is given, in the behalf of Christ, not only to believe in his name, but likewise to suffer for his sake."

The amount of all I have said is this: If we would *follow the Lord fully*, after the pattern in my text, we must acknowledge no other master besides him; we must obey him in all things; we must do this at all times; and serve "him with an affectionate and liberal heart; not grudgingly, or as of necessity;" for "the Lord loveth a cheerful giver." We must follow him openly, and in the face of the sun; and then we must persevere in our attendance upon him, though no man should join with us; nay, though earth and hell should unite their force, and both rise up in arms to oppose us.

You have now seen the aim of my discourse; and may I not hope to succeed in it? I am asking nothing that is unreasonable, nothing that you yourselves can find any pretence to refuse. All I ask is, in the

1*st* place, That you should be *honest men*.

You call yourselves Christians: and what is my request, but that you be Christians *indeed?* So that in reality it is the cause of your own honor I am pleading with you. A man of spirit and integrity is a character that universally commands esteem; but it is impossible to support that honorable character by any other means than by *following the Lord fully*. Enemies you may have; I ought rather to have said enemies you shall have, some, perhaps, perversely and maliciously, who may slander you as hypocrites: but a steadfast and uniform perseverance in holiness, if it disarm not their malice, will at length confute their reproach. Whereas your swerving from duty, either to gain the favor of men, or to avoid their displeasure, cannot fail to expose you to their contempt and scorn. Reward you they may; but Oh! how low must you sink in their esteem! And then what a triumph will it give to the wicked, who only wait for your halting? How will it whet their tongues, and give them an edge that shall pierce you to the quick? For this you may lay your account with, that their censures of you shall be far more severe and unmerciful than those they employ against others, who make no profession of religion; nay, their censures shall be more severely felt by yourselves, because you will find something within you that tells you they are just. The hardened sinner can assume an air of confidence and intrepidity; conscience being seared gives him no disturbance within; so that his external appearance is all he hath to attend unto; but the sense of having acted wrong will draw your attention inward, and leave your countenance to express every outward symptom of timidity and self-reproach. Whereas, by *following the Lord fully*, you shall by degrees acquire a firmness and independency of spirit, that will enable you at all times to behave with a genuine and well-supported dignity. This shall give you an irresistible superiority over the hearts of wicked men, which shall overawe them in secret, and constrain their homage, in the same proportion that it excites their hatred and envy. Thus we read, that "Herod feared John," even when he threw him into prison; and he feared him, as St. Mark informs us, purely upon this account, "because he knew that he was a just and holy man."

2dly. The duty I am recommending is equally necessary to secure the inward peace and tranquillity of your minds: it contributes to your interest no less than to your honor. How miserable is the man who hath war and discord within his own breast! This is worse than death, for that only tears the soul from the body, whereas this tears the health, the life, from the soul itself. Such a person resembles "the troubled sea when it cannot rest, whose waters cast up mire and dirt." Which way soever he turns his eyes, the prospect, on all hands, is dark and gloomy. Above, is the throne of an offended God: beneath, is the fire that shall never be quenched; and within, he feels the gnawings of the worm that dieth not: so that the creatures around him are his only resource; and these at best are "deceitful brooks;—broken cisterns that can hold no water;" "miserable comforters," which delude him for a moment, and forsake him at the time when he stands most in need of them. "There is no peace, saith my God, to the wicked;" but "light is sown for the righteous, and gladness for the upright in heart."—"Great peace," said one who knew it by experience, "great peace have they that love thy law, and nothing shall offend them;" even "the peace of God, which passeth all understanding, shall keep their hearts and minds, through Jesus Christ."

My brethren, we shall never taste the comforts of religion till we become thoroughly religious, and *follow the Lord* with all our heart. A half-religion must always be a joyless thing. Persons of this mixt character must in great measure be strangers to pleasure in any kind. They have just as much religion as maketh sin bitter, and as much sin as renders religion unpleasant: and what an insipid, disagreeable situation must this be! In respect of present enjoyment, the dissolute and unreserved slaves of the devil have manifestly the advantage of those half-converted people. They get a full taste, at least, of such dreggy pleasure as sin can afford; but the others cannot even get at that much, and at the same time their dry constrained formality supplies them with nothing to make up for the want of it. Whereas he who *followeth the Lord fully*, possesses a joy infinitely superior to what the creatures can yield; nay, a joy that is altogether independent on the creatures.

Moreover, religion, when it is genuine and cordial, heightens the relish of every lawful comfort. Besides that natural sweetness which God hath put into many of the outward benefits he bestows, the true Christian can look upon them as the gifts of a reconciled Father, and pledges of better things to come. He can say upon the receipt of every mercy,—This is mine, and heaven also: my God hath sent me this token of his love, to support and encourage me in my journey homeward; I shall soon be beyond the need of such inferior blessings, and possess the living fountain from whence those refreshing streams do flow. On the other hand, if his present allowance be scanty, he can say,—My Father knoweth what is good for me better than I do; blessed be his name, who in kindness withholds from me what his wisdom foresees would prove a snare to my soul. He seeks my *whole* heart, and he is worthy to possess it: it is my business to *follow* him; and the less I am encumbered, the faster I shall run. When I get home, I shall be comforted and satisfied to the full; famine may dwell in this wilderness, but is altogether unknown in that good land to which I am travelling: "In my Father's house there is bread enough, and to spare." To a person of this temper nothing can come amiss: he knows that his lot is ordered by that God "who is wise in heart, and mighty in strength;" and who hath expressly promised, that "all things shall work together for good to them that love him, to them who are the called according to his purpose." Distress falls with a crushing and deadly weight upon the man who steps aside from the road of duty; but he who keeps the straight and onward path, can take adversity by the cold hand, and welcome it as a friend, whose sober advice will guide him in his pilgrimage far better than the flattering lips of prosperity. He can say with the prophet Habakkuk, when every earthly comfort takes wing, and flieth away, "Although the fig-tree shall not blossom, neither shall fruit be in the vines, the labor of the olives shall fail, and the fields shall yield no meat, the flock shall be cut off from the fold, and there shall be no herd in the stalls; yet will I rejoice in the Lord, I will joy in the God of my salvation."—But there are other motives besides these which ought to have weight, and which will have weight with every ingenuous heart. Let me therefore remind you, in the

3*d* place, That our Lord hath in some measure intrusted us with his glory, and called the world to take notice of us, as the persons by whom he expects to be honored. O how should this fire us with a generous ambition to excel in holiness, that we may exhibit a just representation of the Master we serve, and show that he is in truth what the Scriptures report him to be, "altogether lovely," and is "fairer than the children of men!" Is it not, my brethren, matter of grief to you, that so many are to be found who "despise and reject the Saviour of mankind?" Would you not wish that all the world should know his excellence, that they might admire, and love, and choose him for their Master?—If you do, for the Lord's sake, for your own sake, and for the sake of the many thousands to whom he still appears "without form and comeliness," do not withhold the aid you can give. Him they cannot see, but you are always in their eye: permit them to behold his image in you. Would you not reckon it a high crime to blaspheme him with your mouths? I know you would: O then do not blaspheme and reproach him by your actions! Allow me to ask you, When you go with the multitude, and live as careless sinners do, trifling away your precious time in the giddy round of fashionable amusements; how would you have the world to judge? Would you have them to believe, that such behavior is agreeable to the laws of your Master? that he approves of, or even that he is but slightly displeased with it? What would you think of a minister who should preach in that manner, and labor to persuade his hearers that a careless, trifling, dissipated life, is perfectly consistent with true piety, and that any thing beyond it is unnecessary preciseness, and being "righteous overmuch?" Sure I am you would look upon such a minister with contempt, nay, with horror: and dare you practise what we dare not preach? We may, we ought to say every thing that is true. We dare not preach an uncommanded strictness; there is a curse denounced against those who "add unto the words of this book," as well as against those who "take from them." And if your behavior differ widely from what we are bound to recommend, I again ask the question, What judgment would you have the world to form?—They must necessarily condemn either us or you; us for requiring too much, or you for performing too little: they must either conclude that we misrepresent the religion of Jesus, or that you are not the disciples of Jesus. Will any of you be so candid as to take our part against yourselves, and honestly confess that you are wholly to blame?—will you go to your carnal neighbors, and tell them that what you do is utterly inconsistent with your holy profession; that the Lord, whose name you bear, acted in a different manner himself, and gave you laws of a quite different nature and tendency? I suspect you will hardly consent to this proposal; and yet justice demands it; nay, unless you either do something of this kind, or alter your course of life, and *follow the Lord fully*, you are criminal in the highest degree; you slander your Master, you bear false witness against him, and are chargeable with dishonesty, with perjury, nay, with blasphemy itself. And this suggests

A *4th* motive, which I beg you may attend to. I am now going to plead with you from love to your neighbors. This is a principle you profess to honor; nay, if I mistake not, the desire of obliging others, and of rendering yourselves agreeable to them, is your common apology for conforming to their manners, and avoiding the offensive singularity of *following the Lord fully*. This, my brethren, is a false expression of love; nevertheless, it discovers such a regard to others, as furnishes me with a handle to take hold of the true principle, and to plead it in support of the duty I am recommending. Surely it is no office of love to deceive another to his hurt, or to suffer him to continue in a pleasing mistake, which unavoidably must, and which may very speedily end in his ruin; such "tender mercies" would indeed be "cruelty." In the common affairs of life this maxim is universally acknowledged: and is it less cruel to deceive your neighbors in matters of infinitely higher importance? If, by the freedom you take, others are emboldened to sin against God, will the pretence of good-nature or courtesy be sustained as a defence against the charge of blood-guiltiness? No, my brethren. They who are thus misled by you "shall die in their iniquity;" but "their blood," at the same time, "shall be required at your hands." "Woe unto the world, because of offences; but, woe chiefly to him by whom the offence cometh." Hypocrites shall have the woe of everlasting punishment, even the children of God shall have the woe of sharp rebuke and chastisement. It is dreadful to think that the souls of any should perish eternally, and we be the cause of it: surely "it were better for that man, that a mill-stone were hanged about his neck, and that he were drowned in the depth of the sea." Do you then love your neighbor in sincerity? O teach him by your example to *follow the Lord fully*. Remember "that he who converteth a sinner from the error of his way shall save a soul fron death, and shall hide a multitude of sins;" and may hope to be crowned with distinguished honors in that day, "when they that be wise shall shine as the brightness of the firmament, and they that *turn many to righteousness* as the stars for ever and ever."

The *5th* and *last* motive with which I shall press this important duty, is the reward that awaits those who *follow the Lord fully*. They shall possess that good land of promise, whereof the earthly Canaan was only an emblem or type. "To them who by patient continuance in well-doing seek for glory, honor, and immortality, Christ shall render eternal life." "Blessed are they that do his commandments, that they may have right to the tree of life, and may enter in through the gates into the city." There shall they see Abraham, and Isaac, and Jacob, who shine with such lustre in the sacred records: there shall they see Moses, and Aaron, and Caleb, and Joshua, with all the holy prophets and apostles of our Lord. Nay, in heaven they shall behold, and delightfully converse with, "Jesus the Mediator of the new covenant," who, with the price of his own blood, obtained for them a right to that undefiled inheritance, and sent forth his Spirit to prepare them for the enjoyment of it. And shall not the prospect of such exalted felicity animate us in our Christian course, and powerfully incite us to "be the followers of them who through faith and patience inherit the promises?" Can we suppose that any of the saints who surround the throne of God, do now repent of their self-denial and mortification, or repine because they were despised and persecuted while on earth? No, my friends; they would not part with the feeblest ray of their present glory, for the everlasting possession of all the honors and pleasures that this earth can afford. What shall I say more? I have urged the most weighty motives that occurred to me; and could I think of any thing still more persuasive, I should add it with pleasure. But without the divine blessing, no arguments will prevail. All therefore that remains is, to turn my pleadings with you into prayers to God, that he may bestow upon you *another spirit*, and enable you by his grace *so to follow him* while here, that hereafter, in the heavenly world, you may *fully* enjoy him, through all the growing ages of a happy eternity. *Amen.*

SERMON XVII.

STRANGER AND SOJOURNER WITH GOD.

PSALM xxxix. 12.—"For I am a stranger with thee, and a sojourner, as all my fathers were."

HAD these words been spoken by one of the Rechabites, who were commanded by their father Jonadab, "That they should drink no wine, neither build houses, nor sow seed, nor plant vineyards, nor have any, but that they should dwell in tents all their days," we might perhaps have considered them as pointing merely at the *peculiarities* of that sequestered tribe, by which they were distinguished from the rest of mankind; but as they are the words of David, who himself was a king, one of the lords of this earth, who had every inducement to magnify his office, and to make his importance appear in its utmost extent, they can lie under no suspicion of partiality; and therefore challenge the greatest regard.

It must indeed be acknowledged, that David wrote this Psalm under the heavy pressure of affliction; which may induce some to think, that what he saith in my text is no other than the natural language of a dispirited man, whose mind was unhinged and broken by adversity; but if we attend to what is written, (Chron. xxix. 15.) we shall find him using the same language in the height of his prosperity: "We are strangers," said he, "before thee, and sojourners, as were all our fathers; our days on earth are as a shadow, and there is none abiding." Never did the Jewish nation appear to be more at home than at that time: As for David, his happiness was so complete, that, instead of asking any additional favors, he could hardly find words to express his gratitude for those he had already received. Yet, amidst all his affluence, when he possessed every outward comfort his heart could wish, still he called himself a *stranger* and a *sojourner* before God.

We must therefore consider the words of my text, as expressing the fixed and habitual sentiments of David's heart. In his most prosperous condition, he did not look upon this earth as his home; but extended his views to the heavenly world, that glorious and permanent inheritance of the saints, which is "incorruptible and undefiled, and which fadeth not away."

Among the various subjects of inquiry that might readily occur to us upon reading this passage, the two following appear to me the most interesting and profitable.

First. Whence is it that holy men consider themselves as *strangers and sojourners* upon earth? And,

Secondly. What manner of life is most expressive of this character, and best suited to the condition of *strangers and sojourners?* To these, therefore, I shall confine myself in the following discourse.

I BEGIN with inquiring, Whence it is that holy men, while they live upon earth, consider themselves as *strangers and sojourners with God?* And to account for this, one might declaim at great length upon the unsatisfying nature, and precarious duration, of every thing below the sun. I might remind you, that as we came but lately into this world, so we must shortly go out of it, and leave all our possessions to be enjoyed by others;

who, in their turn, likewise shall die, and part with them. I might descend to the various calamities that embitter human life, from which none of mankind are altogether exempted; and to these I might add the peculiar sufferings of the righteous, those sharp and painful trials to which the best of men are most frequently exposed in this state of discipline: But I am unwilling to enlarge upon topics of this nature; because I would not have it thought, that the godly consider themselves as *strangers and sojourners*, solely, or even principally, for such reasons as these. They renounce the world, not because it is unfriendly to them, but because it is unsuitable: they would despise its smiles no less than its frowns; they are not violently thrust out of it, but voluntarily resign it, and leave it to those who have nothing else for their portion. Accordingly you may observe that David styles himself not only a *stranger* but a *sojourner*. Every man is a stranger, who is not a native of the place where he resides: but a *sojourner* is one who maketh only a passing visit to a place, with a resolution to leave it again, and to proceed on his journey. Now, this last is the distinguishing character of the saints. Wicked men must leave this earth, they know they must, and wish it were otherwise with all their heart; and as they have no prospect of going to a better world, they do all they can to banish the thoughts of their removal from this, that they may relish their present enjoyments with as little alloy as possible. Whereas the godly, who are made citizens of the heavenly Jerusalem, can look forward without dismay to the time of their departure from this "strange land, knowing, that when the earthly house of this tabernacle shall be dissolved, they have a building of God, an house not made with hands, eternal in the heavens." They would not choose to live here always: they are *strangers* in affection, as well as in condition; their hearts are elsewhere; they desire, they even long, to be at home with God.

The saints justly account themselves *strangers* upon earth, because they are regenerated by the Spirit of God; they are "born from above," and therefore can find no place of rest while they live at a distance from their native country. Every thing tends naturally to the place of its original; and grace, which came down from heaven, leads the soul upward to heaven from whence it came. "Whatsoever is born of God," saith the apostle John, "overcometh the world." The dry and empty husks of earthly enjoyments cannot satisfy the desires of a heaven-born spirit: upon these the renewed man looks down with a holy disdain, and then lifts his longing eyes to that celestial country, where "is fulness of joy, and pleasures for evermore." There he knows his inheritance lies; there dwells his kindred, to whom he stands in the dearest and most intimate relation; "God the Judge of all, Jesus the Mediator of the new covenant, an innumerable company of angels, and the spirits of just men made perfect." And there also he is to make his everlasting abode. Here he sojourns for a while, till he is rendered meet for entering into "the purchased possession;" and when the appointed season comes, he gladly removes to his father's house, to dwell with his God for ever and ever.

Upon these accounts, my brethren, the children of God, while they live upon earth, consider themselves as *sojourners* in a strange land. Their sentiments in this matter are not the effects of disappointment and vexation, but the conclusions of an enlightened and renewed mind: they are willing to leave this world, because they have a home to go to, where their natures shall be perfected, and all their desires satisfied to the full.—Let us now inquire, in the

Second place, What manner of behavior is most expressive of this temper, and best suited to the condition of *strangers and sojourners?*—This branch of the subject opens a wide field of practical instruction, and will lead me to recommend to you some of the most important and difficult duties of the Christian life.

1*st*. If we look upon this earth as a strange country, through which we are only passing to our native home, it ought certainly to be our care, that we receive as little hurt in our passage as possible. This is a maxim of common prudence that nobody will dispute. Now the greatest hurt the world can do us, is to make us forget the place of our destination, or loiter too much by the way: and therefore its smiles are more to be dreaded than its frowns. "The prosperity of fools," saith Solomon, "destroyeth them." It is difficult to possess much, and not to overlove it: Hence that caution of the Psalmist, "If riches increase, set not your heart upon them." When our situation is so agreeable, that we find ourselves disposed to say, "Soul, take thine ease;" then indeed it is high time to look warily around us; the hook is not so curiously baited for no end. I do not mean to disparage the bounty of Providence; if it hath pleased God to distinguish any of you by riches or honors; or to crown your honest industry with uncommon affluence; it is certainly your duty to be thankful to that kind Benefactor, who "hath covered your table, and made your cup to run over." I only mean to execute that order which was given to Timothy, "Charge them that are rich in this world, that they be not high-minded, nor trust in uncertain riches, but in the living God, who giveth us richly all things to enjoy." I would only exhort you as Paul did the Corinthians, "To rejoice as though you rejoiced not; to buy as though you possessed not; and to use this world so as not to abuse it; because the time is short, and the fashion of this world passeth away." My sole aim is to remind you, that the more you have, the greater need there will be to keep a strict and jealous guard upon your hearts, lest they be debauched by those pleasing enjoyments, and alienated from God, who alone hath a right to them. But it is not enough that we receive no hurt in our journey through this strange land; it ought likewise to be our care, in the

2d place, To make all the provision we can for that better country to which we are travelling. The Holy Scriptures speak of "a meetness for the inheritance of the saints in light;"—of "making to ourselves friends of the mammon of unrighteousness;"—of "providing bags which wax not old, a treasure in the heavens that faileth not." In opposition to all this, we read of some, "who make provision for the flesh to fulfil the lusts thereof;" "whose God is their belly, and whose glory is in their shame, who mind earthly things." I need not inform you which of these two are the *strangers and sojourners.* Let it be our care, my brethren, who claim this character, "to grow in grace," and to bring forth "those fruits of righteousness, which are, by Jesus Christ, unto the glory and praise of God." Every advance in holiness is a step that leadeth upward to the heavenly felicity; for what is glory but grace in maturity? they differ only in degree; they are the same in kind, and the one grows up and ripens into the other. Our riches and honors, though they should accompany us to the last period of life, must leave us at death. "Naked we came into the world, and naked we must return;" but holiness shall pass with us beyond the grave, and attend us home to our Father's house, there to shine with increasing brightness through all the ages of eternity. Do we then aspire to the heavenly state? let us endeavor to enjoy as much of heaven as we can, even while we *sojourn* in this "house of our pilgrimage." Surely "every man that hath this hope in him,"—the hope of being thoroughly changed into the "likeness of his Lord, when he shall see him as he is" at his second appearance, must, by this hope, be excited to purify "himself even as he is pure." Let us then hearken to that affectionate exhortation of the apostle Peter, "Dearly beloved, I beseech you, as *strangers* and *pilgrims*, abstain from fleshly lusts, which war against the soul." Let us "add to our faith, virtue; and to our virtue, knowledge; and to knowledge, temperance; and to temperance, patience; and to patience, godliness; and to godliness, brotherly kindness; and to brotherly kindness, charity. For so an entrance shall be ministered unto us abundantly into the everlasting kingdom of our Lord and Saviour Jesus Christ."

3dly. It becomes *strangers and sojourners* to endure with patience and fortitude any hardships they may meet with on their journey homeward. We ought, indeed, my brethren, to lay our account with inconveniences by the way: our Master, who "was a man of sorrows," hath told us expressly, that "in the world we shall have tribulation." "Ye know," said he, "that the world hated me, before it hated you. If ye were of the world, the world would love his own; but because ye are not of the world, but I have chosen you out of the world, therefore the world hateth you." Yet however painful those sufferings may be, the prospect of the joy that awaiteth us, is more than sufficient to support us under them; especially when it is considered, that the afflictions of this present life, if wisely improved, shall exalt us to higher dignity in the kingdom of our Father. It is recorded of the primitive Christians, that "they took joyfully the spoiling of their goods," because "they knew in themselves, that they had in heaven a better and an enduring substance." "They were troubled on every side, yet not distressed; perplexed, but not in despair; persecuted, but not forsaken; cast down, but not destroyed;" as we read, 2 Cor. iv. 8, 9. And if any shall inquire, what it was that rendered them superior to these trials, they may be lawfully informed by St. Paul himself in the close of that chapter, where he saith, "For this cause we faint not, but though our outward man perish, yet the inward man is renewed day by day. For our light affliction, which is but for a moment, worketh for us a far more exceeding and eternal weight of glory; while we look not at the things which are seen, and are temporal, but at those things which are not seen, and are eternal."

4thly. If we view heaven as the place of our everlasting abode, we shall, above all things, be solicitous to be thoroughly acquainted with the way that leads to it. David prayed with the utmost propriety, when he thus expressed himself, (Psalm cxix. 19.) "I am a stranger in the earth, hide not thy commandments from me." He knew that "the word of God was a lamp to his feet and a light unto his path;" he therefore "hid it in his heart," as the most inestimable treasure he could possess, and made it the subject of his constant, delightful meditation: "Thy testimonies," said he, "are my delight, and my counsellors;" and "thy statutes have been my songs in the house of my pilgrimage." I do not deny that Reason, even in its present dark and corrupt state, may, in many important instances, lead a sober inquirer to the knowledge of his duty; but, alas! in a great variety of cases, he would find himself utterly at a loss, not knowing which road to take; for though Reason, unassisted, may still be able to trace out the capital lines of sin and duty, yet the confines of each, the precise boundaries which divide the lawful from the forbidden ground, require a more penetrating eye to discern them. But in the Holy Scriptures these are plainly marked out to us by the finger of God, who cannot err. The ten laws published from Sinai, which were afterwards explained and amplified by our Saviour in his sermon upon the mount, furnish us with a complete and unerring rule of life, and describe that "highway of holiness," in which we may walk without fear or diffidence. We need not perplex ourselves with the doubtful reasonings of our own minds; we may find an easy solution of all our difficulties in that written "law and testimony," according to which we shall be finally judged: for "the testimony of the Lord is sure, making wise the simple:" "the judgments of the Lord are true and righteous altogether." Such is the guide which God hath provided for directing his *pilgrims* in their way homeward; and if we are possessed of the temper of pilgrims, "we shall esteem the words of God's mouth more than our necessary food;" and say concerning them, "More to be desired are they than gold, yea, than much fine gold; sweeter also than honey, and the honeycomb. Moreover by them is thy servant warned; and in keeping of them there is great reward."

5thly. If we consider ourselves as *strangers and sojourners* here below, we ought certainly to behave like those who belong to a better country, and to show by our conduct, that we have a nobler birth and higher hopes than worldly men have. God frequently complained of his ancient people, that by the wickedness of their lives they had caused "his holy name to be profaned among the heathen." They who love their country, will be jealous of its credit in foreign parts, and carefully avoid every thing that hath a tendency to bring upon it the least stain or reproach. Accordingly, we are exhorted in Scripture, to "adorn the doctrine of God our Saviour in all things;" "to walk circumspectly, not as fools, but as wise;" and particularly, "to walk in wisdom towards them that are without." Indeed, as I formerly observed, our first care should be, that we ourselves receive no hurt; but I must now remind you, that something more is incumbent upon us than regard to our own safety: We ought not only to avoid or resist temptations to sin, but also to shine in all the virtues of a holy life, that by the light of our good works others may be excited to glorify our Father who is in heaven. We have two things that should engage our attention; *first*, our own welfare; and *next*, the credit and honor of that religion we profess: And he is too selfish to be a good Christian, who minds only the one, and overlooks the other. Wide, my brethren, is the compass of our duty; the spiritual *sojourner* hath many parts to perform; he must not satisfy himself with a retired and private virtue, but is bound by the strictest ties of gratitude, "to show forth the praises of that God who hath called him out of darkness into his marvellous light." Every step of our conduct is of the greatest importance, not to ourselves only, but to others also; and therefore we ought to move with caution and accuracy. It is not enough that we "cease to do evil;" we must likewise "learn to do well." Nor should we even think it enough to do what is simply good; we should aim at that good which is most seasonable and excellent. In fine, to live as becometh true pilgrims, is to walk with our rule continually in our eye, and never knowingly to deviate from it, either to the right hand or to the left: It is to ponder every step we take; to weigh every undertaking, with all its circumstances, in the balance of the sanctuary: It is to consider the consequences of our behavior with regard to others; to have our whole conversation, our words, and our actions, "seasoned with salt," as the Apostle hath expressed it; that is, not only innocent in themselves, but, as much as may be, edifying also, that they may minister grace to those who hear or behold us.

There is an affected singularity, which is conceited and disobliging, and does real dishonor to religion, representing it as childish, trifling, and capricious; on the other hand, there is a servile compliance with the maxims and fashions of the world, which is mean and pusillanimous, and represents religion as variable, timid, and irresolute: Betwixt these two extremes lies a middle plan of conduct, which expresseth the true genius of Christianity, representing it as generous, intrepid, and disinterested. When we dare avow the sentiments of our hearts, and obey the dictates of conscience, and the laws of our God, in the face of the sun; when our whole behavior is consistent and uniform, and shows that we have no other aim but to promote the honor of our heavenly Father, and to obtain his approbation; then we act up to the dignity of our Christian character; then we live as *strangers and sojourners* upon earth.

There is one thing in particular I would recommend to you as peculiarly suited to the condition of pilgrims; and that is a decent sobriety of manners, a grave and serious deportment, in opposition to what the Scriptures call a "vain conversation." I do not mean that you should be sad and dejected; blessed be God, the Christian hath a more extensive field of pleasure before him than Fancy itself can represent to the sensual mind. The seriousness to which I am pressing you is not opposed to joy, but to levity; I call you to delights that are pure, sincere, and inward, in opposition to "the laughter of the fool, and that delusive mirth that ends in heaviness." I would only have you to show, that you find a *present* reward in the service of God, and that the joys of religion are of too sublime a quality to mix and incorporate with the dead and polluted pleasures of sense; I would have you to behave with that spirit which becomes your high birth; like persons who know that God is their father, that Christ is their elder brother, and the Holy Spirit their comforter and guide. In short, I would have you to act like citizens of heaven, who are only passing through this earth, and have little more concern in it than to escape its pollutions, by keeping the strait and narrow road that leads to the promised land of rest. Why should you borrow, nay, why should you seem to borrow, water from the "broken" and dirty "cisterns" of the sensualist, who have access to "the fountain of living waters?" Is it not your duty, is it not your honor, to show the world, that no part of your happiness depends upon such low gratifications? that you find enough in God to quench your thirst, and to satisfy the most unbounded desires of your soul? This, my brethren, is the way, the only way, to awaken the attention of secure, besotted sinners. Let them see what true godliness can do by itself; and this may beget in them a conviction of its worth and excellence. But how shall they discover that religion hath any peculiar virtue to strengthen and comfort the soul, so long as they can observe those who profess it walking in the same road, and frequenting the same haunts of vanity with themselves? There is a majesty in strict and serious godliness, that commands esteem and reverence even from the worst of men: But when religion assumes the habit and complexion of the world, when it is blended with the fashionable follies of the age, it usually makes such a clumsy figure, such a motley appearance, that it becomes more ridiculous and contemptible than pure, unmixed folly itself. "Wherefore come out from among them, and be ye separate, saith the Lord, and touch not the unclean thing; and I will receive you, and be a father unto you, and ye shall be my sons and daughters, saith the Lord Almighty."

Once more, in the

6th place, If indeed we have turned our back upon this world, and are travelling to a better country, let us help one another by the way, and carry as many home with us as we can. Do we meet with any who are feeble and dejected? let us do every thing in our power to strengthen and encourage them. Are any doubtful and hesitating about the right path? let us give them our best advice, and, according to our ability, show them the way wherein they ought to go. Are any discouraged by the opposition they meet with, or the dangers they fear? let us take the road before them, and animate them to follow our example. Do we see any stopping short, or even looking aside to some alluring objects, that have a tendency to withdraw their hearts from God? let us, in the spirit of meekness, reprove and admonish them. Above all, let us beware of falling out with our fellow travellers; for that must necessarily mar the progress of both: if they and we are going to the same place, let that suffice to unite us in affection; and let it be agreed, that we may differ in lesser things.

But many, alas! take the opposite road, and walk in "the broad way that leadeth to destruction." How shall we behave with respect to these? Let us remember, my friends, that they are still our brethren; and that the time was when we ourselves were "foolish and disobedient," even as they are. Should we meet with one of our countrymen in a foreign land, living in a poor and abject condition, and at the same time knew that he was heir to a plentiful estate at home, would we not endeavor to make him sensible of his folly? would we not use every argument to persuade him to return with us?—Why, this is the very case. We see immortal creatures forgetting themselves, and the great things they may possess in the heavenly world, pleased and deluded with the veriest trifles, with lying vanities that perish in the using. They are really our brethren; and there is enough in our Father's house both for them and us. Indeed, if the provision were scanty, we might have some color of excuse for leaving them behind us; but the heavenly inheritance is sufficient for us all; nay, the number of coheirs, instead of diminishing, increaseth the happiness of each individual.

We had all wandered into "a far country," when our compassionate Father sent his *beloved Son* to invite us home. And if any of us have got our minds enlightened; if by grace we have been awakened from our fatal lethargy and determined to comply with the kind invitation; shall we not do what in us lies to awaken those who are still asleep? shall we not tell them the good news, and press them to go with us? Oh! it is terrible to think of an everlasting separation. Place yourselves before the judgment seat, and think how affecting that awful moment shall be, when the Judge shall pronounce the final doom, and send away from his presence some of those with whom we once were acquainted, perhaps intimately connected, nay, whom we dearly loved; send them, I say, from his presence, to the other side of that impassable gulf, from whence they shall never return! How that final parting shall then be felt by us, I know not; but surely the distant prospect of it is dreadful in the mean time. O then let us do what we can to prevent it! Let us imitate that *good Shepherd* "who came to seek and to save that which was lost:" *He* "gave his life for the sheep;" and shall any who have tasted the sweetness of his mercy, think it much to follow, with their warmest entreaties, those unhappy wanderers who, as they themselves once did, have left the good pasture, and continue to stray in the barren wilderness, where, without speedy relief, they must irevocably perish? God forbid. Let us have pity upon those who have not yet learnt to pity themselves; and to the most vigorous efforts we can use for their recovery, let us add our fervent prayers to God, that he may send forth his Spirit, to bring them into the way of peace and safety, and then to keep and guide them in that way, till he lead them at length into "the land of uprightness."

Thus have I endeavored to show, in a variety of instances, what manner of life is most expressive of the temper, and best suited to the condition of *strangers and sojourners.* May God accompany what hath been said with his effectual blessing, and enable us all so to behave in this "house of our pilgrimage," that when we shall have done with earthly things, we may be received into those "everlasting habitations, whither Christ hath gone to prepare a place for us." To whom, with the Father, and the Holy Spirit, the one living and true God, be ascribed, as is most due, all blessing, and honor, and glory, and power, both now and evermore. *Amen.*

SERMON XVIII.

JOSHUA'S ADVICE TO ISRAEL.

Preached on the day of National Thanksgiving, Nov. 29, 1759.

JOSHUA xxiii. 11.—"Take good heed therefore unto yourselves, that ye love the LORD your GOD."

These are the words of a soldier and a saint; a soldier, equally brave and successful; a saint, distinguished by the testimony of God himself. They are the words of Joshua, the victorious leader of God's ancient people, and make a part of that solemn valedictory speech which he pronounced in a national assembly of his countrymen a little before his death.

The same happy union of fortitude and piety which had rendered his active life so glorious, still shone forth with undiminished strength to adorn the concluding scene. Never did the magnanimity of the soldier, never did the piety of the saint, never did the generous zeal of the patriot, appear with more becoming grace and dignity, than when this great and good man rose up in the presence of all his brethren, and thus addressed the tribes of Israel:

"I am old and stricken in age; and ye have seen all that the Lord your God hath done unto all these nations because of you; for the Lord your God is he that hath fought for you. Behold, I have divided unto you by lot these nations that remain, to be an inheritance for your tribes, from Jordan, with all the nations that I have cut off, even unto the great sea westward. And the Lord your God, he shall expel them from before you, and drive them from out of your sight, and ye shall possess their land, as the Lord your God hath promised unto you. Be ye therefore very courageous, to keep and do all that is written in the book of the law of Moses, that ye turn not aside therefrom, to the right hand or to the left; that ye come not among these nations, these that remain amongst you, neither make mention of the name of their gods, nor cause to swear by them, neither serve them, nor bow yourselves unto them; but cleave unto the

Lord your God as ye have done unto this day. For the Lord hath driven out from before you great nations and strong; but as for you, no man hath been able to stand before you unto this day. One man of you shall chase a thousand; for the Lord your God, he it is that fighteth for you, as he hath promised you. *Take good heed therefore unto yourselves, that ye love the Lord your God.*"

"How forcible are right words!" Well did Solomon say, that "the tongue of the wise is health," and "a word fitly spoken like apples of gold in pictures of silver." An address more worthy of the speaker, or better adapted to those who heard it, cannot be devised, than that which these verses present to our view. The Jews were at this time in full possession of the promised land; every man dwelt safely under his vine, and under his fig-tree; neither was there any to make them afraid; for "the Lord had given them rest from all their enemies round about." By a train of the most astonishing victories, they had totally subdued the nations of Canaan, whose country they divided by lot among themselves. Such a valuable conquest, equally complete and glorious, afforded matter of joy and triumph to them all; but chiefly to Joshua, who conducted their arms, and to whose wisdom and valor, as the means under God, they were visibly indebted for all their success.

Here then was a theatre on which ambition and vain glory might have acted their parts to great advantage; nay, they might have done it almost without fear of detection or reproof. No claim of merit would have been thought excessive, no applause too high, no reward too great, for such an illustrious hero as Joshua; and had his speech been artfully framed to exalt *himself*, the effect of it would probably have been similar to that of Herod's oration, when "the people gave a shout, saying, It is the voice of a god, and not of a man."

But Joshua possessed "another spirit." Long had he been dead to pride and self-interest. He sought not his own praise, but the honor of his God, and the prosperity of his brethren. He reminds them indeed, that he had often led them to victory and triumph; but, with the same breath, he reminds them also, that "it was the Lord their God that fought for them." They got not the land by their own sword, neither did their own bow save them, but the right hand and arm of Almighty Jehovah." To him therefore the sole tribute of praise was due: this was the important truth which Joshua chiefly recommended to the attention of his hearers. And now knowing that the time of his departure was at hand, as the last and strongest proof of his affection and care, with the authority of a governor he commands, with the bowels of a father he entreats, and, with all the seriousness of a dying saint, he obtests them *to love the Lord their God.*

This, my brethren, is the charge which the best of kings, our truly magnanimous and most gracious sovereign, doth this day address to us. He hath called us together by his royal proclamation, to return public thanks to Almighty God, for the variety of great and public blessings which have enriched and distinguished this memorable year. The preceding year was indeed glorious; but of this it may be said with a peculiar emphasis, that it excels in glory. Even to the present day, the series of victory remains unbroken; no defeat hath stained our national honor, nor any public disaster interrupted our joy. Hitherto our sunshine hath been clear and unclouded. Amidst the tumults and horrors of surrounding war, blessed with uncommon plenty at home, we enjoy all the comforts of domestic peace; whilst every quarter of the world hath beheld our triumphs, and on every element, by sea and by land, success hath crowned the British arms. Success I say, of the best and most valuable kind; for the fruits of our victories are not the romantic and airy additions of military fame, but advantages of a substantial and more enduring nature;—the increase of our naval strength, which experience hath shown to be the surest means of our defence; the enlargement of our commerce, the great source of our wealth; the protection of our king's electoral dominions, unjustly invaded on our account; and the security of our colonies from the inroads and devastations of merciless *savages*, rendered still more savage by the instigation and example of perfidious Frenchmen. These are laurels which wither not; acquisitions of real and permanent worth, which, with humble boldness, we may publish to the world, and even avow to our own hearts, as becoming grounds of thanksgiving to that God, "who is righteous in all his ways, and holy in all his works; who executeth judgment for the oppressed, but the way of the wicked he turneth upside down."

This King of heaven, "who abaseth those who walk in pride; all whose works are truth, and his ways judgment;" we praise, extol, and honor this day, as the author of these signal and unmerited blessings. "Not unto us, O Lord, not unto us;" not unto the wisdom of our counsellors, not unto the valor of our troops, though both have equalled our wishes, and even exceeded our hopes; yet, not unto these, but "unto the name of God," is all "the glory" due. He it it was who taught our senators wisdom; He it was who girded our soldiers with strength; it was the Lord who fought for us in every successful enterprise; who, in *Germany* and *Canada*, revealed his mighty arm on our side; who hath thus far prospered our righteous cause, and made us to triumph over them that hate us.

Justly may we say with the church of old, "O sing unto the Lord a new song, for he hath done marvellous things; his right hand, and his holy arm, hath gotten him the victory. The Lord hath made known his salvation, his righteousness hath he openly shewed in the sight of the heathen: he hath remembered mercy towards" *Britain;* "all the ends of the earth have seen the salvation of our God."

But, my brethren, thanksgiving and praise are only a part of the tribute we owe. Joshua made a farther demand upon his countrymen. And as our situation, in some of its most important circumstances, is apparently similar to theirs; the same charge that was given to them, with the utmost propriety may be addressed to us:

Take good heed therefore unto yourselves, that ye love the Lord your God. For,

In the *first* place, It is for this very end that national mercies are bestowed. "Thou shalt love the Lord thy God with all thy heart, and with all thy soul," is the first and great commandment in the law; and Providence enforceth what the law demands. God speaks to us by his works as well as by his word; both are his messengers; and it happens, that the signs of the one are as expressive and intelligible as the language of the other. Hence a voice is ascribed to the rod by the prophet Micah, (Micah vi. 9.) "The Lord's voice crieth unto the city, and the man of wisdom shall see thy name; HEAR YE THE ROD, and who hath appointed it." Judgment is that stern messenger which speaks to us out of the whirlwind, saying, "Why should ye be striken any more? Will ye revolt still more and more?" But mercy hath a softer voice; in mildest accents it courts our return; and, with persuasive eloquence, disarms our enmity, bends the stubborn will, and captivates the heart. "When our wickedness corrects us, and our backslidings reprove us," then it is expected that we should "know and see what an evil and bitter thing it is to sin against God." After this manner do his judgments teach men righteousness. But his mercies have a higher office; to them it belongs to teach men love; they represent God as truly amiable, as the most worthy object of our supreme affection. Signal and unmerited favors, especially when conferred upon those who are not only unworthy of them, but who deserve the contrary, are justly compared to "coals of fire," which melt down every thing but dross. Even the malice of Saul was so far overcome by the generosity of David, that "he lifted up his voice and wept, and said unto David, Thou art more righteous than I; for thou hast rewarded me good, whereas I have rewarded thee evil." Now of this kind are all God's favors towards us. And shall favors of such a nature be heaped upon us in vain? Surely, when he whom we had offended, most basely offended, is not only merciful, but bounteous also; when he not only spares us, but even loads us with benefits; our hearts must be impenetrable, and void of all feeling, if they are not subdued to the love, as well as to the admiration, of such amazing generosity. We have been praising God for his goodness; but praise without love can never ascend to his throne with acceptance. Let us therefore *take good heed unto ourselves, that we love the Lord our God;* and the rather because,

In the *second* place, We are in danger of perverting his goodness to a very different purpose. The caution given in the text plainly implies this; and the subsequent history of the Jewish nation as plainly proves that the caution was necessary.

We read in the book of Judges, that, after the death of Joshua, "there arose another generation, which knew not the Lord, and they forsook the God of their fathers, which brought them out of the land of Egypt, and served other gods." This monstrous ingratitude Moses had suspected, and left many warnings on record to guard them against it. "It shall be," said he in one place, "when the Lord thy God shall have brought thee into the land which he sware unto thy fathers, to Abraham, Isaac, and Jacob, to give thee great and goodly cities which thou buildedst not, and houses full of all good things which thou filledst not, and wells which thou diggedst not, and vineyards and olive-trees which thou plantedst not; when thou shalt have eaten and are full, then beware that thou forget not the Lord thy God, which brought thee forth out of the land of Egypt and from the house of bondage." And in another place, after recounting many temporal blessings which God had promised to bestow upon them, he thus concludes: "Take heed to yourselves, that your heart be not deceived, and ye turn aside, and serve other gods, and worship them." "But Jeshurum waxed fat and kicked, and lightly esteemed the rock of his salvation." Israel, that was humble in the wilderness, tame and tractable in those lean pastures, grew proud and wanton in fruitful Canaan. When "they sucked honey out of the rock," as the prophet expresses it, "and did eat the fat of lambs, and kidneys of wheat, then said they, We are lords, we will come no more unto thee."

That prosperity should have another and very different effect upon us, I have already endeavored to show; and, blessed be God, examples of a wise and laudable improvement of prosperity are not altogether wanting. It is recorded to the honor of the good king Jehoshaphat, (2 Chron. xvii. 5, 6.) who had silver and gold in abundance, that "his heart was lifted up in the way of God's commandments." If we read the beginning of the 18th Psalm, in connection with the title prefixed to it, we shall discover another amiable instance of the most exact obedience to the command in my text. The title runs in these words: *A Psalm of David, the servant of the Lord, who spake unto the Lord the words of this song, in the day that the Lord delivered him from the hand of all his enemies, and from the hand of Saul; and he said,* (verse 1.) "I will love thee, O Lord, my strength." But few, alas! comparatively speaking, walk in the steps of these holy men. Even a pious Hezekiah "rendered not again according to the benefits done unto him, but his heart was lifted up;" for which cause "there came wrath upon himself, and upon Judah, and upon Jerusalem."

Great indeed is our national felicity; but equally great is our danger of abusing it. Scarcely had the Israelites escaped from the house of bondage, when those very spoils they had recovered from their task-masters were formed into an idol, which they basely worshipped in place of that God, whose outstretched arm had wrought their deliverance. And is it not possible, my brethren, that the fruits of that success with which God hath been pleased to favor us, may, by a like abuse, be perverted into weapons of rebellion against himself? Luxury is the common attendant upon affluence: This unfits the mind for serious thinking, and breeds a coldness and indifference towards spiritual things; in consequence of which, a secret disaffection to those laws which would restrain him, soon takes root in the heart of the sensualist, till, wearied with the struggle betwixt reason and appetite, he at length sets himself in opposition to God and his ways; reproaches, with the names of *ostentation* and *hypocrisy*, all serious religion and godliness in others; turns away his eyes from the light that reproves him, and even doth what he can to extinguish it altogether. Thus doth "the prosperity of fools destroy them:"

—"When men see no changes, they fear not God." What reason then have we to join trembling with our mirth, and to *take good heed unto ourselves*, lest our table become a snare to us, and the uncommon blessings we have received, instead of heightening our love, should cause us to forget the hand that bestowed them, and prove the means of alienating our hearts from God! To prevent this, let me beg your attention to what I have further to offer, in the

Third and *last* place, That to *love the Lord our God*, is not only the return he expects for his benefits, but the return he demands. It is not only just and reasonable in its own nature, but it is likewise absolutely necessary on our part; nay, it is the one thing needful; the withholding of which shall unavoidably be attended with the most fatal consequences.

This expresses the true spirit of the charge, and was certainly the important truth that Joshua meant to convey to his hearers. His great aim was to remind them, in the *first* place, that all the past successes were entirely owing to the favor of the Most High; and, *next*, to persuade them, that upon the continuance of his Almighty protection, their future prosperity would solely depend. He exhorts them indeed, (verse 6) to be "very courageous." But for what end? Was it only to fight against men? No; it was also that, in opposition to all dangers and difficulties of what kind soever, they might steadfastly obey the Lord their God. "Be ye therefore very courageous to keep and to do all that is written in the book of the law of Moses, that ye turn not aside therefrom, to the right hand or to the left." And then, says he, (verse 10.) "One man of you shall chase a thousand, for the Lord your God is he that fighteth for you" But he adds, in the verses following my text, "If ye go back, and transgress the covenant of the Lord your God, know for a certainty, that the anger of the Lord shall be kindled against you, and ye shall quickly perish from off the good land which he hath given you." Accordingly, we are told, in the second chapter of the book of Judges, that when the succeeding generation forsook the Lord, and served other gods, "then the anger of the Lord was hot against Israel, and he delivered them into the hands of spoilers that spoiled them, and he sold them into the hands of their enemies round about; so that they could not any longer stand before their enemies, and they were sore distressed." Now all these things happened to them for ensamples; and they are written for our admonition, upon whom the ends of the world are come. God is always the same; he is "in one mind, and none can turn him." His love to righteousness, his hatred of sin, are both unchangeable; and therefore the truth of that assertion must be equally unchangeable, that "righteousness exalteth a nation;" whereas "sin is the reproach," and, if obstinately persisted in, must prove the ruin "of any people."—"For wickedness burneth as the fire, it shall devour the briers and thorns, and kindle in the thickets of the forests, and they shall mount up as the lifting up of smoke; through the wrath of the Lord of hosts is the land darkened, and the people shall be as the fuel of the fire."—Isa. ix. 18.

Ought we not then *to take good heed unto ourselves, that we love the Lord our God?* Joshua gave this advice to the Jews a long time after the Lord had given them rest from all their enemies round about. We, my brethren, are still engaged in war, the issue of which is always doubtful. We have drawn the sword, and thus far have employed it with glory and success; but it was a prudent caution which Ahab gave to Benhadad, "Let not him that girdeth on the harness boast himself as he that taketh it off." Our enemies are weakened, but they are likewise greatly irritated; and still they are a strong and formidable people. We can look back upon a time when our own situation was very unpromising; when every alarm brought a panic along with it, till, roused by insult and a sense of danger, the national spirit at length awoke; vigorous measures were pursued; and, by the good hand of our God upon us, have wonderfully prospered. It is a thing impossible, it is even improbable, that similar causes may produce similar effects in the councils and measures of the nation with whom we contend?

Were they in reality weaker than we are

willing to suppose, it would ill become us to deny a truth, of which we ourselves have so lately had the happy experience, to wit, "That the battle is not always to the strong." Both at *Minden and Quebec*, every advantage for victory is now certainly known to have been on the side of our enemies. The fate of nations is not determined by the policy of men; the events of war are conducted and overruled by a higher hand than the arm of flesh. Hear what God said to the Jews by the prophet Jeremiah: "Though ye had smitten the whole army of the Chaldeans that fight against you, and there remained but wounded men among them, yet should they rise up every man in his tent, and burn this city with fire." "Without me," says he by another prophet, "they shall bow down under the prisoners, and they shall fall under the slain."

Blessed be God, we have large and manifold grounds of thanksgiving; but the very grounds of our thanksgiving are likewise monitors of humility, and press the necessity of securing the friendship of that Almighty Being, who "doth according to his will in the armies of heaven, and amongst the inhabitants of this earth." Pride and security are fatal presages of approaching ruin. "Before destruction the heart of man is haughty." How awful was the doom pronounced against Tyre! (Ezek. xxviii. 2. *et seq.*) "Thus saith the Lord God, Because thine heart is lifted up, and thou hast said, I am a god, I sit in the seat of God, in the midst of the seas; yet thou art a man, and not God, though thou hast set thine heart as the heart of God: behold, thou art wiser than Daniel; there is no secret that they can hide from thee: with thy wisdom, and with thine understanding, thou hast gotten thee riches, and hast gotten gold and silver into thy treasures: by thy great wisdom, and by thy traffic, hast thou increased thy riches, and thine heart is lifted up because of thy riches. Therefore thus saith the Lord God, Because thou hast set thine heart as the heart of God; behold, therefore, I will bring strangers upon thee, the terrible of the nations; and they shall draw their swords against the beauty of thy wisdom, and they shall defile thy brightness. They shall bring thee down to the pit, and thou shalt die the deaths of them that are slain in the midst of the seas."

Let *us* learn wisdom from *their* folly. Let their punishment admonish us to beware of that pride which God abhorreth: Let the manifold goodness we profess to celebrate this day, lead us to "that repentance which is never to be repented of;"—and let us fervently pray, "That the Holy Spirit may be given unto us, to shed abroad the love of God in our hearts," as an effectual principle of all holy obedience. Then we may hope, that the Lord of Hosts will go forth with our arms, and lead them on to new and still greater triumphs; till at length the desolations of war shall be happily terminated by a safe, an honorable, and lasting peace. Which may God of his infinite mercy grant, through Jesus Christ our Lord. *Amen.*

SERMON XIX.

SEPARATION OF THE PRECIOUS AND THE VILE

Preached in January 1773, when, in the city of Edinburgh, distress and dissipation were in the extreme.

EZEKIEL IX. 4.—"And the Lord said unto him, Go through the midst of the city, through the midst of Jerusalem, and set a mark upon the foreheads of the men that sigh, and that cry, for all the abominations that be done in the midst thereof."

THE apostle Paul having recited to the Christians at Corinth some of those awful judgments which God had inflicted upon his ancient church for their rebellion and obstinacy, subjoins these memorable words, (Cor. x. 11.) "Now all these things happened unto them for ensamples; (or *types*, as the world is rendered in the margin) and they are written for our admonition, upon whom the ends of the world are come." The Bible, though it records the actions of men, yet, properly speaking, is the history of God, and contains an account of his proceedings with his creatures in a great variety of instances; that from those acts of government, compared with what he positively declares concerning himself, we may be enabled to form the clearest and justest conceptions of his nature and will; and may learn, with undoubted certainty, what we have either to fear or to hope from him.

God is always the same; "with him there is no variableness, neither shadow of turning:" and therefore, in his past procedure, we see the plan of his present and future administration; which brings the passage I have been reading home to ourselves, and interests us deeply in the matter it contains.

In the preceding chapter, the prophet had got a full view of the abominations that were done in the midst of Jerusalem; and here he gets a visionary representation of their punishment. He beholds six men approaching the city, each of them armed with a destroying weapon, who are expressly commanded to *slay the inhabitants, both old and young, beginning at the sanctuary*. But before they proceed to execution, one, distinguished by his garb, *being clothed with linen, and having a writer's inkhorn by his side*, receives the gracious commission recorded in my text, to separate the precious from the vile, by *setting a mark upon their foreheads*, that they might not be involved in the ruin of their fellow-citizens.

Whether any sentence of wrath hath already gone forth against these sinful lands to which we belong, must be to us an impenetrable secret: "The heart of a king is unsearchable," said Solomon; much more is the heart of the King of kings. But surely it can never be unseasonable to lead your attention to a passage of scripture, where God's mercy to the penitent, and his peculiar concern for their safety, are set before us in so just and striking a light.

Godly sorrow for abounding iniquity is at all times a dutiful and becoming exercise; nevertheless there are certain seasons when the call to it may be considered as more loud and pressing. Some of these I shall mention in the *first* place.

Secondly. I shall inquire, with as much tenderness as regard to truth will permit, how the case stands with respect to the time and place in which our lot is cast: and if it shall appear that ill-boding symptoms of approaching danger are to be found among us in a very high degree, I shall endeavor, in the

Third place, To lay before you a few of the genuine symptoms and proper effects of the gracious temper I mean to recommend;—and then conclude the subject with some practical improvement.

First. If it shall be asked, When, or upon what occasions, the exercise of godly sorrow for sin is in a peculiar manner seasonable? I answer,

When transgressors are very numerous; when the body of a people is corrupted, so that, in the language of the prophet Isaiah, "the whole head is sick, and the whole heart is faint:" then all who fear God are loudly called upon *to sigh and to cry for the abominations that are done in the midst* of the land. If one Achan troubled the whole camp of Israel, what must a multitude of sinners do? If the disciples of our Lord were exceeding sorrowful when their Master told them that there was one traitor in their company, how afflicting must it be to the true lover of God, to behold the wicked so multiplied, that, in comparison of them, the godly are only a small remnant, a very "little flock," that can scarcely be discerned.

The call becomes still more pressing, when transgressors are not only numerous, but likewise bold and impudent; sinning, as Absalom did, "before all Israel, and in the sight of the sun." This is a fatal presage of approaching vengeance; for God will not always tolerate such insolent contempt of his authority. Judgment may be suspended, while vice skulks in darkness, as ashamed of the light; but when it appears in broad day, when sinners proclaim their sins as Sodom, and hide them not, then they may be said "to strengthen themselves against the Almighty, and to run upon the thick bosses of his bucklers." And it is not to be supposed that such insolent defiance can long escape without some open and awful rebuke. At such a time, then, mourning must be peculiarly seasonable.

Especially when sinners are not only numerous and impudent, but likewise guilty of those grosser abominations which in former ages have been followed with the most tremendous judgments. It is true, indeed, that "the wrath of God is revealed from heaven against *all* unrighteousness and ungodliness of men;" nevertheless there are *some* particular instances of ungodliness and unrighteousness, which God hath marked out, and distinguished from others, as the objects of his greatest abhorrence; and with respect to which he hath said more explicitly, both in his word and by his providence, that he will not suffer them to pass unpunished. I cannot pretend to give you a minute detail of these; only, if you read the Scriptures, you will find, that profane swearing, perjury, contempt of the Sabbath, theft, murder, and adultery, are all of this kind. The prophet Zechariah beheld a flying roll of curses, twenty cubits in length, and ten in breadth, which had a commission to enter into the house of the thief, and into the house of him that sweareth falsely by the name of God, there to remain till it had utterly consumed it, with the timber thereof, and the stones thereof. "By swearing, and lying, and killing," saith the prophet Hosea," by stealing and committing adultery, they break out, and blood toucheth blood. Therefore shall the land mourn, and every one that dwelleth therein shall languish, with the beasts of the field, and with the fowls of heaven; yea, the fishes of the sea also shall be taken away." And how highly God resents the profanation of his Sabbath, appears from the reproof and expostulation of good Nehemiah, which is recorded, (Nehem. xiii. 17, 18.) "Then I contended with the nobles of Judah, and said unto them, What evil thing is this that ye do, and profane the Sabbath-day? Did not your fathers thus, and did not God bring all this evil upon us, and upon this city? yet ye bring more wrath upon Israel by profaning the Sabbath." When therefore the same sins are frequent and open among any people, that must surely be a season for grief and lamentation. And still more,

When the persons that commit them are resolute and incorrigible. "He that being often reproved, hardeneth his neck, shall suddenly be destroyed, and that without remedy."—"Because I have purged thee," saith God by the prophet Ezekiel, "and thou wast not purged, thou shalt not be purged from thy filthiness any more, till I have caused my fury to rest upon thee. I the Lord have spoken it, it shall come to pass, and I will do it; I will not go back, neither will I spare, neither will I repent; according to thy ways, and according to thy doings, shall they judge thee, saith the Lord God." When the wicked are forewarned of their sin and danger; when, by the preaching of the word, their duty is plainly and faithfully set before them; when they are exhorted by others, and rebuked by their own consciences; when they are smitten with such rods as bear the most legible signature of their crimes; or when, in a milder way, they are admonished and warned by the punishments inflicted upon others for the same crimes; when, after *all* or *any* of these means employed to reclaim them, they still hold fast their iniquities, and will not let them go; then should the godly lament and mourn, and pray with redoubled earnestness for those miserable creatures, who have neither the ingenuity nor the wisdom to pray for themselves.

How far these causes of grief and lamentation are to be found among us, I might leave to the determination of those whose hearts are "wise to discern both time and judgment:" but I should reckon myself unfaithful to God, and injurious to the souls of men, if I did not hint a few obvious remarks relative to the time and place in which our lot is cast; which was the

Second thing proposed in the method.

I shall not compare our condition to that of Sodom, when ten righteous persons were not to be found in it; neither shall I compare it to the state of the Jews, when God said to the prophet Jeremiah, "Run ye to and fro in the streets of Jerusalem, and see now, and know, and seek in the broad places thereof, if ye can find a man, if there be any that executeth judgment, and seeketh the truth; and I will pardon it." Blessed be God this is not precisely the case with us. There is not only some, but, I trust, a goodly number throughout the land, who sincerely love God, and seek his glory: but this I dare venture to affirm, that they are few, very few, when compared with the wicked; and, which is still more afflicting their numbers are daily decreasing, while the opposite interest prevails, and visibly gains ground among all ranks and conditions of men.

It is too apparent to be denied, that the vices I mentioned under the former head, intemperance, lewdness, the most insolent abuse of the Christian Sabbath, lying, and even perjury itself, are more or less practised in every corner of the land.—These, and many other enormities, are so frequent and undisguised, that no man who comes abroad into the world can pretend to be ignorant that such *abominations are done in the midst of* us. I am far from supposing, that any of them were altogether unknown in former times; though I am verily persuaded, that all of them are now become more universal, and that some of them are carried to a much greater height than ever they were in the days of our fathers. However, as they cannot be strictly accounted the *peculiar* reproach of the present age, I shall remind you of some other instances of departure from God, which, with greater and more evident propriety, may be determined the *distinguishing characteristics* of the times in which we live.

I begin with *Infidelity*, which of late hath spread itself through all orders of men, the lowest not excepted. This article of charge needs no proof; for besides the multitude of professed infidels, who grasp at the character as a title of honor, and even struggle beyond the bounds of moderation to obtain it; besides these I say, the growing disregard of the ordinances of religion, the total neglect and disuse of them by some, and the hypocritical abuse, and formal, ineffectual attendance upon them by others, are fatal proofs of the prevalence of infidelity; and plainly show, that the generality, even of those who retain the Christian name, do either in their heart reject the gospel as false, or, which comes to the same purpose, reckon it a matter of small importance whether the gospel be true or not.

Again, is there not a visible *contempt of the authority of God?* If his laws contradict the humors of men, they refuse to be controlled by them; and say by their practice, "Who is the Lord, that we should obey him?" "As for the word which thou hast spoken to us in the name of the Lord, we will not hearken unto thee, but we will certainly do whatsoever goeth forth out of our own mouth." This is so notorious, that by many it is reputed a maxim of prudence, to give way to the prevailing humors of the times. Some sins, say they, have got such countenance, that it is dangerous to reprove them: they must be winked at; for were they to be roughly handled, they would either grow more headstrong and violent, or only be exchanged for other excesses, which might be fully as bad, or perhaps worse, than themselves. And though it betrays a disloyal, or at least a cowardly spirit, to be swayed by such crooked maxims; yet the currency they have got affords a pregnant proof, that *contempt of divine authority* is another unhappy characteristic which distinguisheth the present from former times.

Further, we seem, in a great measure, to have lost any proper sense of our *dependence upon God*. "When his hand is lifted up, we do not see." We forget him in prosperity; and in adversity we look no higher than the creature. We trust for deliverance to the arm of flesh, but never think of turning to the Lord who smiteth us. Nay, have there not been repeated attempts to prove, that a nation may prosper, not only independent of God, but even, as it were, in defiance of him? that the public interest is promoted by the vices of individuals? that *utility* is the measure of virtue, the only standard for determining what is right or wrong? I do not mention those schemes from any apprehension that the arguments by which they are supported are formidable in themselves; but whether men believe the principles or not, it is a certain truth, that the general practice doth unhappily correspond with them. One thing is obvious, that few consider a reformation of manners as any means of national prosperity; whereas, had we a just impression of our dependence upon God, *that* would readily occur to us, not only as one, but as the best, nay, the only effectual means, for securing the safety, and advancing the real honor and interest of our country.

To all these I must add the *Luxury*

and *Sensuality* which have been growing upon us for several years past, and have now spread their roots and branches so wide, that they may truly be said to fill the whole land. Pleasure is at length become a laborious study; and with many, I am afraid, it is their only study; for it leaves them no room to pursue any other. What new scenes of amusement are daily invented? How artfully are they ranged, so as to stand clear of each other, without leaving any vacant space between them? It is trifling to plead, that they are not criminal in their own nature, and may therefore be consistent with the service of God: I must call this a mean, disingenuous evasion, till they who plead it shall be pleased to inform us, what portions of time are left unoccupied, wherein they can find leisure to serve God if they would. The truth is, the present system of pleasure and fashionable politeness, appears absolutely incompatible with piety and devotion; an artful contrivance to banish reflection altogether, and to put it out of the power of sinful, dying creatures to think of God and an eternal world.

This unhappy distemper of the times in which we live, doth at present carry in its face some of the most alarming symptoms of danger. Instead of yielding to the most probable means of cure, it rather becomes more stubborn and infectious. Might it not have been expected, that the distress which hath prevailed in our nation for some months past, would at least have checked the growth of luxury? yet it seems to have produced the very opposite effect. While the poor are starving, while many who are willing to labor can find no employment, and not a few have abandoned their native country to seek that sustenance in foreign parts which they could not earn at home; still is pleasure pursued with increasing ardor, and no price is deemed extravagant that can purchase an addition to it. In short, men appear to be striving against God with their eyes open, and to have studied the design of his Providence on purpose to defeat it; for such an exact plan of contradiction discovers art and contrivance, and could hardly have been stumbled upon by mere accident.

Judge then, upon the whole, whether there be not cause more than sufficient *to sigh and to cry for the abominations that are done in the midst* of our land. It still remains, in the

Third place, That I lay before you a few of the genuine symptoms and proper effects of the gracious temper I mean to recommend. And,

1*st*. We can never be assured, that our grief for the sins of others is pure, and of the right kind, unless our hearts be duly affected with grief and sorrow for our own transgressions. It is this that distinguisheth the true mourners in Zion from censorious and ill-natured hypocrites, who are quick in discerning the smallest mote in their brother's eye, while they pay no attention at all to the great beam in their own. Godly sorrow is just and impartial; it always begins at home, and makes few visits abroad till domestic sins are first bewailed. Many, like the lapwing, are continually fluttering about, and, with artful screams, lament the vices of all around them, merely to draw off their attention from their own cage of unclean birds. Such pretended mourners are hateful to God; and every counterfeit tear becomes a drop of oil, which shall only serve to inflame the everlasting burnings: whereas the true mourner is more severe against himself than against any other person in the world, the vilest not excepted; yea, he never sees nor hears of the wickedness of others, but conscience immediately stirs within him, and he is ready to say with Pharaoh's butler, "I remember my own fault this day." He considers the worst of men as exhibiting a true picture of his own natural condition; and humbly acknowledgeth, that it was God only who made him to differ, and that he hath nothing but what he received from his bountiful hand.

2*dly*. Our grief is of the right kind, when it leads us to pray for transgressors; and when it hath not this effect, we have not only cause to suspect, but may conclude, without hesitation, that it is spurious and counterfeit. If, instead of the closet, it carry us abroad into company, to divulge our neighbor's faults, under the pretext of bewailing them; in that case we may assure ourselves, that our hearts are strangers to that godly sorrow whereof my text speaks. The true mourner desires, above all things, the reformation of his brother; and therefore he goes directly to God himself, who hath the hearts of all men in his hand, and can turn them as the rivers of water. He lays the sinner's case before the compassionate Saviour, not by way of complaint, but to move his pity, and to obtain his help. He uncovers the poor leper in the sight of the Physician who can heal him: and at the same time would be extremely well pleased, that his loathsomeness were hid from every other eye. True grief will restrain us from speaking evil of our neighbor, or detecting his secret faults, except in cases of absolute necessity, when the concealing them would either be hurtful to the innocent, or prejudicial to the public interest. Nay, it will be painful to us to hear of the miscarriages of our brethren; and we shall be very slow to believe any reports to their disadvantage, without the strongest and most convincing evidence; and after all, we shall neither despise nor hate them, far less expose them to the contempt and hatred of others; on the contrary, we shall pity them, and pray for them in secret, commending their case to the God of love, before whom all their sins are already naked and open, and earnestly implore his pardoning mercy and sanctifying grace in their behalf, with the same fervor and importunity that we ask these inestimable blessings for ourselves.

3dly. Our grief for the sins of others, if pure and genuine, will be accompanied with proper endeavors to reclaim them. Every true mourner will consider himself as "his brother's keeper," and will leave no means unattempted to prevent his ruin. He will not think it enough to plead with God for mercy to the sinner: he will likewise plead with the sinner to have mercy upon himself. He will set his guilt and danger before him in the most prudent and affecting manner he can; and though he meet with many repulses, nay, though his labor of love should be requited with scorn and hatred, yet he will repeat his application again and again, and take hold of every favorable opportunity that presents itself; remembering, that "he who converteth a sinner from the error of his way, shall save a soul from death, and hide a multitude of sins," and may look for more distinguished honor in that day, "when they that be wise shall shine as the brightness of the firmament; and they that turn many unto righteousness as the stars for ever and ever." Once more,

4thly. If we are in truth possessed of this gracious temper, if our grief for abounding iniquity flows from the pure fountain of love to God, and zeal for his glory, we shall own his cause in the most perilous times, and reckon nothing too dear to be hazarded in his service. That saying of our Lord will be continually sounding in our ears, "He that is ashamed of me and of my words, in this adulterous and perverse generation, of him also shall the Son of man be ashamed, when he cometh in the glory of his Father with all the holy angels." Many can weep in secret for the sins of others, who have not the fortitude to appear against them in public. But such persons would do well to consider, that neither their tears nor their prayers can avail them any thing, so long as they fold their hands like the sluggard, and neglect the proper means for obtaining what they ask. God permits, nay commandeth us, to cast our *care* upon him; but he giveth us no allowance to dispose of our *work* in that way. We must be doing in a humble dependence upon his grace; and then we may both ask and hope to obtain his blessing upon our endeavors. But if we pray, and sit still; if we lie howling upon our beds, when we should be abroad at our labor, we offend God instead of pleasing him; and can look for no other answer but this, "Who hath required these things at your hand?" This, my brethren, is very necessary to be attended to. There is hardly any man who maintains the profession of religion, who will not readily acknowledge, that we stand in great need of a reformation; yet where is the man to be found who seems heartily disposed to contribute his assistance? When God is calling, "Who will stand up for me against the evil doers? Who will rise up for me against the workers of iniquity?" instead of replying, with the prophet Isaiah, "Lord, here am I, send me," we are rather inclined to say, each one for himself, Lord, such another person is fitter for the work, send him; but I pray thee have me excused. I shall be accounted a zealot, saith one, if I engage in this service; I shall offend my friends, saith another: A third pleads the doubtfulness of the event: A fourth hath some worldly gain or preferment in view, and therefore it is too early to appear for God as yet; but he resolves, that after he hath got his aim in the service of the devil, then he will turn about, declare himself to be on the Lord's side, and confess him openly, when it can no longer hurt his secular interest. These maxims, however oddly they may sound, are in reality the hinges upon which the bulk of nominal Christians turn; by these despicable rules do they square their conduct, in a matter which, of all others, is the most weighty and interesting. Whereas the true mourner prefers the glory of God and the interest of his kingdom to every thing else. He is not governed by the low and flexible maxims of worldly policy; he doth not consult with flesh and blood, but makes the will of God, and the dictates of conscience, the rule and the only rule, of his conduct. He doth whatsoever appears right to him in the mean time, and leaves the issue with God. He is neither discouraged by the small number of the godly, nor intimidated by the multitude of transgressors; but in all cases, where he hath a call, and opportunity to act, publicly avows the master whom he serves; and under the banner of his Almighty Saviour, he valiantly contends with earth and hell, being assured of a triumphant victory at last. If this render him vile in the eyes of others, like David, he is willing to become yet more vile; and, with Moses, the man of God, he bravely prefers the reproach of Christ to all the fading riches, and honors, and pleasures, of a present world.

A GREAT variety of uses might be made of this subject; but I shall conclude with addressing a few words to three different classes of hearers, which may be supposed to comprehend the whole of this assembly.

I shall begin with those who think that there is no great cause to complain of the world at present; and consequently, that the duty I have been recommending is neither so necessary, nor so seasonable, as many others that might have been chosen. If you are very young, I partly excuse you; but if you are advanced in life, I am unable to devise any color of apology for you, but must necessarily charge you, either with amazing inattention, or more amazing perverseness; for it is notorious, that not the power only, but even the form of godliness, is under a lamentable decay, and hath been so for many years past: witness the general neglect of family-worship, the gross profanation of the Christian Sabbath, and sundry kinds of immorality, which were scarcely known in our country half a century ago. These ill-boding symptoms make it too evident, that we are a degenerate and backsliding people, who are fast filling up the measure of our iniquity; and it is an additional cause of grief that so few among us observe and are affected with it.

I shall next speak to those who make a mock of sin, who are obstinate and hard-hearted, and, instead of lamenting, glory in their wickedness. You perhaps suspect that I am going to address you with sharpness and severity; but you are really mistaken. God knows that I pity you, and have no other aim but to make you pity yourselves. You have long been deaf to warnings and reproofs: O let the sweet voice of mercy at length prevail! God hath sworn that he taketh no pleasure in your death; and this is his call to you after all your provocations, *Turn ye, turn ye, why will ye die?* Nay, he hath paved the way for your return to him with the blood of his own Son, "who suffered, the just for the unjust, that he might bring the chief of sinners to God." It is impossible you can prevail against him, or disappoint him of his glory; the weapons of your rebellion can only hurt yourselves; and, ere long, the proudest of his enemies shall bow down before him, and lick the very dust. Even you, my friends, must either bend to the sceptre of his grace, or be dashed in pieces with his rod of iron: those haughty looks shall shortly be humbled, either in mercy or in judgment; and if once his wrath begin to burn, there is no power that shall be able to deliver you out of his hand. Why then will you reject his gracious counsel? Why will you perish when mercy is in your offer? Why will you break the hearts of all that fear God, when, by your conversion, and flight into the true city of refuge, you might afford cause of great joy both in heaven and on earth? For the Lord's sake consider your ways, and be wise; "seek the Lord while he may be found, call upon him while he is near." The great enemy of your souls will probably suggest to you, that if you comply with this exhortation, your old companions will mock and ridicule you, in proportion to your former excess in sin; and this snare, I am afraid, is too fatally successful with many. But let not any suggestion of this kind deter you from doing what you plainly see to be your duty and your interest. The godly, with whom you join yourselves, will be far from upbraiding you with past offences; they will freely forgive all the injuries you have done to them, and teach you to magnify the riches of divine grace, which took hold of themselves when ready to perish, and advanced them to be heirs of everlasting salvation. "Wherefore come out from among the wicked, and be ye separate, saith the Lord, and touch not the unclean thing; and I will receive you, and I will be a father unto you, and ye shall be my sons and daughters, saith the Lord Almighty."

I now turn with pleasure to the mourners in Zion, who are deeply affected with their own sins and with the sins of those among whom they live. And I would say for your encouragement, that this becoming temper affords undoubted evidence of a work of grace upon your own hearts. Hereby it appears that you are the children of God, seeing the honor of your heavenly Father is so precious in your esteem. And know for your comfort, that none of these filial tears can be lost: God puts them into his bottle, as the Psalmist expresses it; and whatever be the fate of those on whose account they were shed, you shall at last receive joy for mourning, and garments of everlasting praise for your present spirit of heaviness. This holy grief, as you learn from the context, may be a means of securing you against temporal judgments; at any rate, it will sweeten them, and shall undoubtedly be succeeded with fulness of joy at God's right hand.

But you will remember, that grief for abounding iniquity, if pure and genuine, is always accompanied with vigorous endeavors to reclaim transgressors. This, then, my brethren, is what God demands and expects from you. Let every one in his station contribute his aid for the suppression of vice, and for promoting the interests of pure and undefiled religion. Let us join hand in hand in this necessary work and labor of love. Fired with zeal for the glory of God, and fervent charity to the souls of men, let us not only *sigh and cry for the abominations that are done in the midst* of our land, but do all that we can to prevent the ruin of a sinful nation.

Hereby we shall become public blessings while we live, and shall at last, through the mercy of God in Christ, have an entrance ministered unto us into that better world, where all tears shall be wiped away from our eyes, where the inhabitants are altogether unstained, and the joys absolutely perfect; where, with one heart, and one voice, we shall celebrate the praises of Zion's King; ascribing glory and honor, dominion and power, to him that sitteth upon the throne, and to the Lamb for ever and ever. *Amen.*

SERMON XX.

UNERRING MARK OF DEPRAVITY.

Eccl. viii. 11.—"Because sentence against an evil work is not executed speedily; therefore the heart of the sons of men is fully set in them to do evil."

Though God had not favored us with an explicit revelation of his will, yet that absolute perfection which Reason must attribute to the Supreme Being, would naturally lead us to conclude, that he cannot look upon sin without the greatest abhorrence; and, in consequence thereof, that his impartial justice, and almighty power, will not always suffer that abominable thing which he hates to pass unpunished. Accordingly we find, that the conscience of man, till a long habit of sinning hath rendered it callous and insensible, gives a reluctant assent to the equity of such punishment, by that anguish which it raiseth in the sinner's mind upon the commission of any gross and heinous transgression. This made Judas to cry out after his vile treachery, "I have betrayed innocent blood." Nay, so powerfully was his heart smitten with a sense of the demerit of his crime, that, despairing of pardon, he in a manner anticipated the sentence of condemnation, and became the executioner of divine justice, by laying violent hands upon himself. And the apostle Paul testifies concerning the Gentile world, that even they, by the light of Nature, and the dictates of unassisted Reason, "knew the judgment of God;" and universally acknowledged, with respect to many acts of atrocious wickedness, "that they who committed such things were worthy of death."

But the sacred records have put this matter beyond all uncertainty. *There* "the wrath of God is revealed from heaven against all unrighteousness and ungodliness of men:" and a curse is denounced against every one, without exception, "who continueth not in all things which are written in the book of the law to do them." So that a sentence is passed, and stands in force, against every evil work; and the words of Solomon, which I have chosen for the subject of the following discourse, represent to us, *on the one hand*, the marvellous patience of God in suspending the execution of this righteous sentence; and, *on the other hand*, men's vile abuse of his unmerited goodness. Instead of being led to repentance, they grow bolder in sin; and "*because* sentence against their evil works is not speedily executed, *therefore* their heart is *fully set in them to do evil.*

There is an awful emphasis in the last of these expressions: it denotes the extreme wickedness that sinners may arrive at; not only to commit sin when assaulted with violent temptations, but to make an habitual trade of it; nay, to employ themselves in it with delight. *Their heart is so fully set in them to do evil*, that all their faculties bend that way. Thus we read of some "who drink iniquity like water;" "who devise mischief upon their beds, and set themselves in a way that is not good; nay, who put themselves to incredible pains and hard labor, as it were, that they may exceed in wickedness: "they weary themselves to commit iniquity;" and "sin as with a cart-rope."

It must no doubt appear an incredible abuse of the divine goodness, to pervert that patience which should lead men to repentance, into an encouragement to sin more presumptuously; yet so it hath been in times past; and there is too just cause to complain, that it continues to be so still. Indeed, "when God's judgments are in the earth," the inhabitants thereof do *sometimes* "learn righteousness;" at least, so long as the rod lies heavy upon them, they may refrain from those sins which they imagine have subjected them to it; but no sooner is the rod laid aside, than they quickly relapse into their former course of living, agreeably to what the prophet Isaiah observes, "Let favor be shown to the wicked, yet he will not learn righteousness; in the land of uprightness will he deal unjustly, and will not behold the majesty of the Lord." What is written, (Luke xii. 45.) is too just a picture of the temper and practice of the bulk of mankind; "they say in their heart, The Lord delayeth his coming; and thereupon presume to beat their fellow-servants, and to eat, and drink, and to be drunken;" yea, not the *foolish* virgins only, but even the *wise*, are in danger of slumbering, while the bridegroom tarrieth, as we read, Matth. xxv. 5.

There is an unhappy tendency in our nature to forget God. The best find enough ado to overcome it; but the wicked give full scope to it; and nothing but chastisement, severe and present chastisement, will bring them the length even of a feigned submission to God. Hence the observation is drawn, that times of adversity have always been most friendly to religion; and they must know little of the history of the world in general, and of their own country in particular, who do not agree in this remark. National prosperity is certainly most desirable; we regard it as a blessing, we pray for the continuance of it; and it is our duty to do so: yet if we examine the annals of former times, and do not turn away our eyes from the real state of our own times, we shall be obliged to acknowledge, that a calm is often more hurtful than a storm, both to the church and people of God. True it is, that arts and sciences flourish, and a form of godliness may perhaps prevail; but, alas! the life and power of it decay apace; vices formerly unknown spring up like weeds in too rank a soil; even the best are apt to grow remiss and careless, wanton and secure.

What I apprehend to be most necessary upon this subject is, to inquire whence this unnatural abuse of the divine patience proceeds; and to detect some of those false reasonings by which sinners derive encouragement to do evil, from that very exercise of goodness which ought to produce the quite contrary effect.

Now the principal causes of this abuse, or the steps whereby sinners arrive at the amazing pitch of wickedness described in my text, seem to be these following.

The delay of punishment gradually weakens those impressions of *fear*, whereby the unpractised sinner is always alarmed at his entrance upon a wicked and flagitious course of life. No man becomes utterly profligate at once; conscience will remonstrate to the young transgressor; and the struggle is ofttimes sharp and long before this deputy of the Supreme Judge can be wholly put to silence. It were superfluous to prove what every man feels, or at least must have felt, in some period of his life. Depraved as we are, sins of a grosser kind are always committed with some reluctance at their first commencement, and followed with remorse and dread of punishment; but when, after repeated acts of sin, the transgressor still finds himself safe, these painful feelings abate by degrees; the man waxeth bolder day after day; and thus proceeds from evil to worse, till, like Job's war-horse, he at length "mocks at fear," and rusheth headlong in his wicked course without any restraint. This I take to be the leading abuse of divine patience; which paves the way to every subsequent step of departure from God, till the sinner arrives at the last stage of impiety, *an heart fully set in him to do evil.* For, as "the fear of God is the beginning of wisdom;" so the want of this fear may, with equal propriety, be styled the beginning of folly, or the introduction into a wicked and profligate life.

Having got thus far, he proceeds to call in question the *omniscience* of God, and to entertain some hope that his iniquities may pass unobserved. Of such we read, (Psalm lxiv. 5.) "They encourage themselves in an evil matter; they commune of laying snares privily; they say, Who shall see us?" And, (Psalm x. 11.) "He hath said in his heart, God hath forgotten; He hideth his face, He will never see it." He begins to think that God taketh no notice of human affairs when vice passeth long unpunished; and thence he derives fresh courage, and persists in his career with growing intrepidity.

At length he acquires the boldness to impugn the *holiness* of God, and to form an idea of him that suits the corrupt disposition of his own heart. He endeavors to persuade himself, that the remorse he used to feel after the commission of sin, was purely owing to the prejudice of education, and the influence of some narrow principles instilled into his mind by his parents or tutors, before he was capable of judging for himself.

This step to a total degeneracy is strongly marked, (Psalm l. 24.) where God saith, "These things thou hast done, and I kept silence; thou thoughtest that I was altogether such a one as thyself." Because God kept silence, and did not utter his anger in speedy vengeance, the sinner thought that he was altogether such a one as himself; that virtue and vice were fictitious names, framed by credulous or designing men; that God made no difference between them, but was every whit as well pleased with the one as with the other. Dreadful abuse of the divine patience! and yet I am afraid it is too prevalent in our day; else whence these secret whisperings among some who pretend to think above the common rate, that their constitution inclines them to such and such gratifications; which, therefore, cannot be criminal, seeing the author of their being hath implanted these appetites in their frame, and of consequence must be held as consenting to the indulgence of them? When punishment is long suspended, corruption too easily breeds such conceits as these; and nothing but the rod, a sharp and sanctified rod, will suffice to expel them. Thus many interpret a mere delay of punishment as a certain token that their conduct is approved of; and because God is not like man, weak and impotent to restrain his anger, hence, they impiously conclude, that he doth certainly resemble him in another respect; I almost tremble to mention it,—that he is a lover of impurity: nay, the very patron and author of sin.

From such premises as these, the determined sinner, without much hesitation, will eagerly draw the fatal inference, that the administration of the divine government shall always continue as it appears to his darkened mind at present; and that God doth neither mark iniquity now, nor will enter into judgment with sinners for it afterwards. We find the Psalmist proposing a question, (Psalm x. 13.) "Wherefore doth the wicked condemn God?" which he answers thus, "He hath said in his heart, Thou wilt not require it." One of the most eminent saints under the old dispensation, (as we learn from the 73d Psalm) was almost carried off his feet, upon observing the prosperity of the wicked, insomuch that he put the question, "How doth God know, and is there knowledge in the Most High?" Nay, he came the length to say, "Verily, I have cleansed my heart in vain, and washed my hands in innocence." And if holy men, whose minds have been enlightened by the Spirit of God, are thus apt, for a season, to suspect the wisdom and righteousness of his administration, surely it is not to be wondered at, that wicked men, "whose hearts are hardened through the deceitfulness of sin," should be so far deluded by temporal prosperity, as to dream that justice shall never awaken, and that sin shall always pass unpunished.

By a progress of this kind do sinners arrive at the dreadful pitch of wickedness spoken of in my text. When they observe that *sentence against an evil work is not speedily executed*, they draw such false conclusions from it as those I have mentioned, till at length every band that should restrain them is broken asunder, and their *hearts* become *fully set in them to do evil.*

From this account of the matter, you will be able to judge for yourselves, how far you are advanced in the road to a total, I had almost called it an irrecoverable, degeneracy. If you have made a shift to silence conscience, or even to render it more unfeeling than formerly it hath been, you have taken one very wide and dangerous step. But, as you love your own souls, oh! take not another. Beware of listening to any objections against the *omniscience*, the *holiness*, or the *justice* of God; for if you do, in your present state of spiritual deadness, your case is more hazardous than I am able to describe; you are not far from the desperate situation of those whose *heart is fully set in them to do evil.*

And now, my dear friends, as it is an undeniable truth, that this abuse of the Divine patience is too frequent in our day, let me beg your attention for a little, till I have set before you the *folly* and *baseness* of such conduct, and *fatal consequences* with which it must necessarily be attended. Consider then,

1*st.* That to grow bolder in sin because you are not *speedily* punished, is most *foolish;* for unless you have assurance of a full indemnity, and that sentence against your evil works shall never be executed, your conduct is obviously absurd and irrational. You have long escaped, through the patience and forbearance of God; but if you have the remotest suspicion that judgment may one day overtake you; nay, if you are not absolutely certain that it never shall; upon what principle of sound reason can you be easy for one moment? You do not know but that already you have committed the last act of wickedness that God is to tolerate, and that the next transgression will bring down the fatal stroke, and plunge you into remediless ruin. You live by a mere act of grace; your fate depends upon a reprieve which the Sovereign may protract or shorten at his pleasure; and how mad is it to presume upon so precarious a tenure? Or, if you have conceived any hope of escape, allow me to ask you, upon what ground is your hope built? It would need to be a strong foundation indeed that is to carry all the weight you are disposed to lay upon it. Have you any promise or declaration on the part of God, or any dictate of unprejudiced Reason, that saith you shall be safe? Produce your security, that we may know it. If you have nothing more to say than that you hope to escape, because you wish it, alas! this is nothing to the purpose; for we read of some fools, who say, or wish, in their heart there were no God; and yet a God there is, who will prove a *consuming fire* to them. You dare not say that sin never was punished; for all history, both sacred and profane, would contradict you; and it were easy to quote many examples of sinners who have escaped as long, perhaps longer than you, and yet have been punished at last; so that unless you have something altogether peculiar to yourselves, some special indulgence which the world hath never yet heard of, your conduct betrays the height of madness, a degree of frenzy which no term of reproach can fully express.

2dly, It is no less *base* than foolish. Ingratitude is universally condemned, and branded with infamy. We reckon it the mark of a base, disingenuous spirit, to forget favors received, or even to neglect making a proper return, when the obliged party hath it in his power to do it: but if one shall injure his benefactor, and render evil for good, such a person must become an object of universal contempt and detestation, and none will be found so hardy as to plead in his defence. And yet the abuse of divine patience, to which my text refers, is a species of baseness that exceeds ingratitude; and indeed, no word is to be found in any language I know, that is of sufficient force to express its malignity, or to convey an adequate idea of its abominable nature. No man ever injured his benefactor *because* he was his benefactor: interfering interests, or selfish views, may cause unequal returns for benefits conferred; but in the case before us, there is something entirely different from this. Sinners not only injure, or rather attempt to injure, their greatest benefactor, the God in whom they live and move, by whose power and goodness they are supported every moment; but his goodness to them in times past, and the hope of its continuance, are the very things that embolden them to offend him; and "*because* sentence against their evil work is not speedily executed, *therefore* their heart is *fully set in them to do evil.*" Devils may be *capable* of this, but *guilty* of it they are not; their forlorn condition hath put it beyond their reach; the immediate execution of the doom they had incurred afforded them no opportunity of trampling upon the mercy of God: so that, with regard to the *act* of sin, we plainly exceed them in this respect. O that men could be brought to view their conduct in its true light, I am sure they would loathe and abhor themselves on account of it. To burden God's patience *because* it is great; to load him with insults, *because*, out of pity to us, he is slow in resenting them; to harden our hearts by that very mercy which should dissolve and soften them; this is worse than *devilish;* there is something in this so perverse, so monstrous, so unnatural, that one would be tempted to suspect that some malicious slanderer of human nature had forged the accusation, were we not all conscious of the truth of it, and more or less convicted of this horrid baseness by the testimony of our own consciences. These considerations, methinks, should be sufficient to deter us from burdening the patience of God any more. But I have further to add, in the

3d place, That the *consequences* of this abuse shall, in the issue, be most fatal to the sinner himself. You cannot defeat the purposes of God, nor impair his glory in any degree; the weapons of your rebellion must recoil upon yourselves; for God will be magnified in them that perish, as well as admired in those who are saved. As the justice of his nature renders his mercy more wonderful, so mercy abused will make justice to shine forth with greater splendor. Sinners must stand speechless before the judgment-seat, and shall find nothing to plead in their own defence, when the Judge shall say to them, "Ye would not come unto me, that you might have life." Long did I stand at the door and knock, loudly did I call upon you to turn and live: but ye set at nought all my counsel, and would have none of my reproof; therefore now eat the fruit of your own doings, and fill yourselves with your own devices. Because when I called, ye refused; when I stretched out my hand, ye did not regard; therefore do I laugh at your calamity, and mock when your fear cometh, and leave you to inherit that wrath which you treasured up for yourselves, while mercy courted your acceptance, but did not prevail.

Thus far I have spoken, for the conviction and reproof of those who have hitherto been abusing the divine patience in the manner described in my text; and if such transgressors still remain unmoved, it is not because the considerations I have suggested want weight, but because they want feeling. May the exalted Prince and Saviour, who alone can give the spirit and grace of repentance, "open their eyes, and turn them from darkness to light, and from the power of Satan unto God, that they may receive forgiveness of sins, and inheritance among them which are sanctified through faith that is in him."

Upon the whole, let each of us give unto God the glory of his patience, and acknowledge, with humble gratitude, his sparing mercy towards himself in particular. O my friends! with what multiplied provocations are we all chargeable? Let us pitch upon the most innocent day of our life since we came to the full exercise of Reason, and say, if we dare, that we are willing to have our final state determined by the behavior of that one day, according to the measure of legal justice. Can conscience remind us of nothing that needs forgiveness or pardoning mercy? Surely none of us will be so hardy as to say this: our own hearts do, and must, condemn us; how guilty then must we appear in the sight of that God who is greater than our heart, and knoweth all things? Were we chargeable with nothing worse than omissions of duty, yet these alone might justly have stopped the current of his beneficence, nay, brought down his wrath upon such unfaithful and negligent servants; but when to these we add our many sins of commission, our sins against knowledge, conviction, and reproof, how great is their amount! how heinous their demerit! How astonishing then is the patience of God! The saints in heaven are amazed at it; the souls of them that were slain for the testimony which they held," who are better acquainted with the nature of God, and the order of his government, than we can be, are represented in the book of the Revelations, (chap. vi. 10.) as expressing the greatest surprise at the slowness of his wrath; nay, as being at a loss to reconcile his patience with his holiness and truth. "They cry with a loud voice, saying, How long, O Lord, holy and true, dost thou not judge, and avenge our blood on them that dwell on the earth?" And it can be owing to nothing but the grossest insensibility, if our hearts are not filled with amazement at those treasures of mercy which have already been expended upon us, and the overflowings of that goodness by which we are at this moment supported and preserved. How many of our companions have long ago been summoned away to receive their doom? yet we still live in the arms of mercy. How often has death been presented to our view, and the sentence (in our own apprehension) just ready to be executed, *Cut down this cumberer of the ground;* when, lo! mercy interposed, and prevailed for a farther respite and trial? What shall we say then? "He is God, and not man: and therefore it is that we are not consumed." O let our souls, and all that is within us, be stirred up to bless him, because he is good, and hath not executed sentence against our multiplied offences.

Let convinced sinners, in particular, take encouragement from the patience and long-sufferings of God. It is one of the deadly artifices of the adversary, who continually "goeth about seeking whom he may devour," to discourage the newly-awakened soul, by whispering, that the season of mercy is past, that the door is shut, and he is come too late. But be not dismayed, you are on the way to the fountain of love and grace; go on, and you shall find more than it is possible for you to conceive. You are going to him "who came to seek and to save that which was lost;"—that good Shepherd who laid down his life for the sheep, by whose merit and intercession you have been kept alive to this hour; who invites the chief of sinners to come to him; and hath expressly said, "Him that cometh to me, I will in no wise cast out." He is "the Lamb of God," meekness and gentleness itself.—"He will not break the bruised reed, nor quench the smoking flax." Did he spare you, while your heart was as hard as a stone? and will he destroy you, when, by the convincing influences of his own Spirit, it is softened, nay broken, with sorrow?—Impossible!—Go forward into his presence; cast yourself at his feet; implore his protection; and as God liveth thy soul shall be safe.

To conclude. The patience of God affords the strongest consolation to those who are already reconciled to him through the great Mediator. He who waited so long upon you, and at length gained your consent, will most assuredly keep you, and perfect his own work in your complete salvation. The mercy he is still exercising towards enemies, teacheth his friends what they may lawfully hope to receive. Great are your privileges; but, at the same time, great and manifold are your obligations. Hath much been forgiven you? then you ought to love the more, and to show the truth and fervor of your love, by an unreserved respect to all his commandments. "Be followers of God, as dear children." Remember that nothing is more unseemly, nothing more offensive, than the provocations of sons and of daughters. "See, then, that ye walk circumspectly, not as fools, but as wise;" and let the same goodness which led you to repentance, be continually present to your minds, that under its sweet, but powerful influence, you may bring forth in rich abundance all those fruits of righteousness, which are by Jesus Christ, to the praise and glory of God. *Amen.*

SERMON XXI.

JESUS CHRIST, THE MINISTER'S THEME.

Preached at the Introduction of the Reverend Mr. Charles Stuart to the Church of Cramond, the Sabbath after his Ordination, 1773.

2 Corin. iv. 5.—"We preach not ourselves, but Christ Jesus the Lord; and ourselves your servants for Jesus' sake."

When God descended upon Sinai to give laws to his ancient people Israel, the awful tokens of his presence, the thunderings and lightnings, the sound of the trumpet, and the smoking of the mountain, struck the whole camp with such consternation and dread, that they were constrained to remove and stand afar off. They could not bear the exceeding lustre of his glory, notwithstanding the thick darkness with which it was veiled; and therefore addressed Moses in these remarkable words: "Speak thou with us, and we will hear; but let not God speak with us, lest we die." From which authentic piece of sacred history we may justly conclude, that our nature is too weak, in its present state, to sustain an immediate intercourse with the Deity: for which cause, God, in great condescension, is pleased to speak to us by men like ourselves; that, on the one hand, we may not want the benefit of his instruction; and, on the other hand, that we may not be overpowered by the too dazzling splendor and majesty of the Teacher.

Under the old dispensation, besides the stated ministers of religion, God, "at sundry times," sent extraordinary messengers on special errands to the Jewish church; furnishing them with such credentials of their mission, as were sufficient to convince that highly-favored people that they came from God; and consequently, that in every thing relative to their particular message so attested, they were bound to hearken to them as unto God himself. This we have no warrant to look for under the Gospel: the whole counsel of God, so far as it regards the children of men, is clearly revealed, and committed to writing. Nothing is to be added to it, or taken from it; nay, could it be supposed that an angel were to come from heaven, and publish any thing that differed from, or even that was not already expressed in the Scripture record, instead of our being obliged to give him a hearing, we are told, that he himself would "be accursed" for so doing.

Nevertheless, that this complete and finished revelation might lack no advantage, and that all excuse might be taken away from those who should either contemn or counteract its dictates, our Lord Jesus Christ, "God manifested in the flesh," the great "Apostle and High-Priest of our profession," hath instituted the ordinance of a gospel-ministry, and committed to men the word of reconciliation, charging them to proclaim, in the ears of their brethren, "all the words of this life," which are already delivered in writing to the church; with a special promise, that in the faithful discharge of this important trust, "he will be with them always, even unto the end of the world." And to add greater weight to their holy ministrations, he hath expressly declared, that the doctrines and precepts of his word, which they publish in his name, are to be received with the same meekness and submission as if they were spoken immediately by his own blessed mouth: (Luke x. 16.) "He that heareth you, heareth me; and he that despiseth you, despiseth me; and he that despiseth me, despiseth him that sent me." I am sensible, that some proud, ambitious churchmen have, "with great swelling words of vanity," magnified their office beyond what is meet; laying claim to that kind of precedence which belongs to high rank, or other worldly distinctions, which men have devised for the benefit or embellishment of civil society. But this is only a false blazon, that doth by no means suit the ministerial character. "Be not ye called Rabbi," said the blessed Jesus; "for one is your master, even Christ, and all ye are brethren."—"Whosoever is great among you, let him be your minister; even as the Son of man came not to be ministered unto, but to minister, and to give his life a ransom for many." Your true dignity consists in your usefulness: and he that stoops lowest for the good of others, is highest in my esteem. Worldly pomp doth only tarnish the glory of my servants, as it cannot consist with those self-denying duties which belong to their employment. Do you reckon yourselves most honored, not when men give you title and place, but when they hearken to the instructions you receive from me, and embrace the saving message with which I have intrusted you. This, though in words somewhat different, is, in my apprehension, a genuine and summary account of what our Saviour taught the first ministers of his church, with regard to the nature and end of their office. And the language of Paul, in the passage before us, is obviously formed upon this original constitution: *We preach not ourselves, but Christ Jesus the Lord, and ourselves your servants for Jesus' sake.*

From an example of such unquestionable authority, we may justly, and without hesitation, conclude, that *to preach Christ Jesus the Lord*, is the distinguishing characteristic and proper employment of a gospel minister. And this is the observation which I propose to illustrate in the following discourse.

It may be affirmed with truth, that something concerning Christ hath been the principal subject of every revelation that came from God, downward from the original promise made to our first parents, that *the seed of the woman* should *bruise the head of the serpent.* The apostle Jude informs us, that "Enoch, the seventh from Adam, prophesied of these things, saying, Behold, the Lord cometh with ten thousands of his saints, to execute judgment upon all." Moses spake of him when he said unto the fathers, "A prophet shall the Lord your God raise up unto you, of your brethren, like unto me; him shall ye hear in all things whatsoever he shall say unto you." All the extraordinary messengers under the old dispensation were raised up by God for this very purpose, to foretell the coming of the promised Messiah, and, by the doctrine of repentance, gradually to prepare the world to receive him. The words of Peter to Cornelius are clear and strong upon this head, (Acts x. 43.) "To him gave all the prophets witness, that through his name, whosoever believeth in him, shall receive remission of sins." This, he tells us, was the subject of their own most delightful inquiry: (1 Pet. i. 10.) "Of this salvation the prophets have inquired, and searched diligently, who prophesied of the grace that should come unto you: searching what, or what manner of time, the spirit of Christ which was in them did signify, when it testified beforehand the sufferings of Christ, and the glory that should follow."

And if Christ was an object of such importance to those who lived before his manifestation in the flesh, it cannot surprise us to find, that they who could testify that he *was come*, and had finished the work that was given him to do, should in all their writings and discourses dwell upon him as their constant and most delightful theme. The author of this epistle informs the Corinthians, that "he determined not to know any thing among them but Jesus Christ, and him crucified." And elsewhere, he saith, that "he counteth all things but loss for the excellency of the knowledge of Jesus Christ his Lord." This was that "chosen vessel" whom the Lord converted in a miraculous way, and sent forth to bear his name before the Gentiles, and kings, and children of Israel; and his zeal and fidelity in executing his trust appear evidently from his writings. He made Christ the *foundation* of all his sermons, as we read (1 Cor. iii. 10, 11.) "I have laid the foundation, and another buildeth thereon. But let every one take heed how he buildeth. For other foundation can no man lay than that which is laid, which is *Jesus Christ;*" intimating, in the strongest manner, that all preaching which doth not refer to Christ, and lead to him, is like building a castle upon the loose sand, which may please the fancy for a little, but as it wants a foundation, will soon tumble down, to the equal disgrace and hurt of the builder. And as *Christ* was the foundation, so was he likewise the *end* of his preaching; and not of his only, but of all his brethren in the apostleship, and fellow-laborers in the ministry; as is fully expressed in the text: *We preach not ourselves, but Christ Jesus the Lord, and ourselves your servants, for Jesus' sake.* We seek not to advance our credit and interest; our sole aim is to render *Jesus* great and amiable in your esteem: and we desire to be considered in no other light than as *your* ministers or *servants for Jesus' sake.*

But what are we to understand by *preaching Christ?* This question I shall endeavor to answer in the first place; after which I shall show, that this is the proper employment and distinguishing characteristic of a gospel minister; and then conclude the subject with some practical improvement.

I begin with answering the question, What are we to understand by *preaching Christ Jesus the Lord?*

1*st.* It plainly imports that we make Christ the principal subject of our sermons.

It is by no means sufficient that we speak of him occasionally; we ought of set purpose to unfold the Scripture doctrines concerning him, that men may be acquainted both with his person and undertaking, and have clear and enlarged views of that glorious deliverer, to whom they are indebted for all they possess in a present world, and for all they hope to enjoy in the next. In particular, we ought frequently to remind our hearers, that he who came to seek and to save lost sinners of mankind, is "the beloved and only begotten Son of God," "the brightness of his Father's glory, and the express image of his person;"—"that *Word* which in the beginning was with God, and was God, by whom all things were made, and without whom was not any thing made that is made:" That in order to purchase redemption for us, he condescended to become the Son of man; or, in the emphatical language of the Holy Spirit, that "the Word was made flesh," and assumed our nature into a personal union with his own divinity: That this incarnate Word, or God manifested in the flesh, after he had published a most pure and perfect *law*, and exhibited an *example* of equal and as absolute perfection, at length laid down his life as a true and proper sacrifice to satisfy the justice of God, and to expiate the guilt of an elect world: That having thus made *his soul an offering for sin*, he soon after triumphed over death, and him that had the power of death, by rising from the grave, and ascending to his Father's right hand, where he now sitteth as a priest upon his throne, interceding for his people, and dispensing those gifts which he purchased with his blood; from whence he shall come again in the character of judge, taking vengeance upon them that obey not his gospel, "to be glorified and admired in those that believe," and to complete the consolation and joy of his saints. These important truths ought to be fully explained, and repeatedly insisted upon: "For this is life eternal, to know the only true God, and Jesus Christ, whom he hath sent." The natures and offices of our Redeemer, the glory of his Godhead, the merit of his blood, and the efficacy of his Spirit; the constitution of that government whereof he is Mediator, with all the promises thereof, which are exceeding great and precious; and especially the way or manner in which guilty, polluted creatures are vitally united to this all-sufficient Saviour, who, "of God, is made unto them wisdom, and righteousness, and sanctification, and redemption:" These, and doctrines connected with them, are as necessary to the souls of men, nay, infinitely more so, than food is to their bodies. Other things are perhaps desirable to be known; but these must be known, or people are undone for ever: and therefore none can be said to *preach Christ* who overlook these important, these essential truths, or treat them in a careless, superficial manner.

2dly. To *preach Christ Jesus the Lord,* is to handle every other subject of discourse in such a way as to keep Christ continually in the eye of our hearers. We must acknowledge him as the author of the truths we deliver, and improve them so as to lead men to him. It is not sufficient that we publish the laws of Christ, unless we publish them *as* his laws, and press obedience to them by those motives and arguments which are peculiar to his gospel. In recommending the great duties of morality, we should represent them as the genuine effects and proper evidences of faith in Christ, and love to God; directing our hearers at the same time to the Spirit of Christ for assistance, and to his merit for the acceptance of all their services: and, after all, we should remind them, that as they are at best "unprofitable servants," instead of depending upon any thing done by them, as the ground of their justification, in whole or in part, they must renounce all confidence in the flesh, and seek to be found in Christ alone; "not having their own righteousness, but that which is through the faith of Christ, even the righteousness which is of God by faith."

These are not trivial circumstances, as some represent them to be: on the contrary, they are essential to the right preaching of Christ; and, if they be omitted, I can easily conceive it possible for a minister to preach all his life long upon the moral precepts of Christianity, without any other effect, than to lead his people away from the Saviour, and to carry them hood-winked into everlasting perdition. The apostles of our Lord, and they surely are the best and most approved patterns of our imitation, introduced, upon all occasions, the peculiar doctrines of Christianity, both into their discourses and epistles; and never failed to press the duties they enjoined by those regards which are due to Christ himself. Thus, humility and self-denial are recommended by the lowliness and patience of Christ: Chastity is enforced by this consideration, "that our bodies are the members of Christ, and the temples of his Spirit." We are exhorted to abound in alms-deeds, "because Christ for our sakes became poor," and in testimony of our thankfulness to God "for his unspeakable gift." Husbands are charged to love their wives, "as Christ loved his church:" and servants are commanded to be faithful and diligent, "that they may adorn the doctrine of God their Saviour." In short, Christ is so deeply engraved upon every moral precept in the New Testament writings, that we must read his name upon every duty; nay, we cannot efface his name, without debasing, or rather vitiating, the duty itself, and casting away the most powerful inducement to the practice of it. I therefore said, that to *preach Christ,* is not only to publish what the Scriptures say concerning him, but likewise to handle every other subject of discourse in such a manner, as to keep Christ continually in the eye of our hearers; and they whose schemes of religion do not admit of this, may be assured, without any further examination, that their schemes differ widely from the gospel of Christ.

3dly. To *preach Christ Jesus the Lord,* is to make the advancement of his kingdom, and the salvation of men, the sole aim of our preaching. We must not seek our own glory, but the glory of him who sent us. If we serve ourselves, we must reward ourselves as we can. Such only can look for the approbation of Christ, who make the honor of his name, and the happiness of mankind, the ultimate aim of all their ministrations. They that usurp the sacred office from interested views, or merely to gain a subsistence in the present world, will find in the issue, that they have turned the best and most salutary employment into a very bad trade, and only entitled themselves to more and heavier stripes when the chief Shepherd shall appear. "We are ambassadors for Christ," saith our apostle, at the 20th verse of the following chapter, "as though God did beseech you by us, we pray you in God's stead, *be ye reconciled to God.*" This is our proper business, the errand upon which we are sent. The glory of God, and the salvation of men, are the great and good ends of the pastoral office; and he who loseth sight of these, or proposeth any end that is different from them, may acquire the reputation of a learned, an ingenious, or an eloquent orator, but cannot be styled *a preacher of Christ.* This will further appear from the

Second thing proposed: which was to show, That *preaching Christ* is the proper business, and the distinguishing characteristic, of a gospel-minister.

Can any thing be more reasonable, than that they who profess to derive their authority from Christ, should make him the principal subject of their sermons, and recommend him to the esteem and love of their hearers? And, on the other hand, can any thing be more unreasonable, can any thing be more unjust, than to assume the character of his messengers, while they seldom or never mention his name; or speak of him in such a way, as rather tends to breed contempt of him, than to render him precious to the souls of men? But what I would chiefly observe is, that *preaching Christ Jesus the Lord*, is the great means which God hath appointed for the conversion and final salvation of sinners: and therefore it is not only highly reasonable, but absolutely necessary; and they are cruel to men, as well as unfaithful to God, who do not make conscience of this important duty. Lectures upon morality may be of use to restrain men from scandalous sins, but it is the gospel alone that can save a sinner. A preacher, by discoursing well upon the duties that belong to *self-government*, and *righteousness*, may correct many outward disorders in the life, and produce such a change in the heart itself, as to convert those into *men*, who formerly were depraved to such a degree, that they differed very little from the *brutes* that perish. But after they become men, the greatest change doth still remain; those men must be converted into *saints;* they must be changed into the divine image; their very nature must be renewed, before they can be meet for the enjoyment of God: "Except a man be born again, he cannot enter into the kingdom of heaven;" and it is the gospel alone which the Spirit renders powerful for producing this effect. Morality grows out of faith in Christ, as the branches grow from the stock. This, and this only, is the principle of that holiness, without which no man shall see God. Whosoever, therefore, would preach morality with any hope of success, must begin here, and lay the foundation of it in that faith which purifieth the heart, and worketh by love; otherwise his sermons may supply fuel to pride and vain-glory, but shall never be the means of saving one soul. In vain do we attempt to improve the fruit till the tree be made good. Let sinners be first ingrafted into Christ, and then works of righteousness will follow in course; as our blessed Lord hath taught us (John xv. 4, 5.) "Abide in me, and I in you. As the branch cannot bear fruit of itself, except it abide in the vine; no more can ye, except ye abide in me. I am the vine, ye are the branches; he that abideth in me, and I in him, the same bringeth forth much fruit; for without me (or separated from me) ye can do nothing." Accordingly we find, that the *preaching Christ*, or the peculiar doctrines of the gospel, hath in every age been the means of convincing and converting sinners, and of building them up in holiness and comfort, through faith unto salvation; and in the same proportion that this hath been neglected, the power of godliness hath declined and languished, till a cold formality hath at length given way to the open profession of infidelity itself. It was the observation of a judicious and pious writer upon this subject, "That where a great and universal neglect of preaching Christ hath prevailed in a Christian nation, it hath given a fatal occasion to the growth of Deism and infidelity; for when people have heard the sermons of their ministers for many years together, and find little of Christ in them, they have taken it into their heads, that men may be very good, and go safe to heaven, without Christianity; and therefore, though they dwell in a land where the gospel is professed, they imagine there is no need they should be Christians." To which I may add, that it is no less observable, on the other hand, that wherever there has been any revival of religion, it hath uniformly been introduced and carried on through the blessing of God, by preaching the peculiar doctrines of Christianity. These, and these alone, have been, and ever will be, "the wisdom and power of God unto salvation."

THE application of what hath been said to the ministers of religion, is so direct and obvious, that I need not enlarge upon it; and therefore any further improvement I am to make of the subject, shall be addressed, not to them that *preach*, but to those that *hear*. And what hath been delivered may serve to inform them what sort of preaching they ought chiefly to value. I am afraid, that by many, the great and essential truths of the gospel are too little regarded: like the Athenians of old, they require something *new*, something that may gratify an itching ear, and furnish matter for a vain imagination to work upon. But this, my brethren, is equally perverse and foolish. Who should regard what a servant saith, if he doth not deliver the mind of his master? And yet I have often observed, that the greatest number of hearers never seem so well pleased, as when ministers speak of those things that are most foreign to their instructions. Did we come upon a disagreeable errand; were we charged with an embassy in which they to whom we speak have little or no concern, such conduct might be accounted for; but when the message we bring is not only most gracious, but likewise treats of matters in which they are immediately and most deeply interested, what words can express the folly and perverseness of those who shut their ears against it, while they greedily open them to every thing else? Hear what the angel said to the shepherds at Bethlehem, (Luke ii. 10.) "Behold I bring you good tidings of great joy, which shall be to all people." And what were these tidings which an angel was sent to publish, and introduced with such a high commendation of their importance and worth? They are recorded, (verse 11.) "Unto you is born this day, in the city of David, a Saviour, which is Christ the Lord." "And suddenly," as it follows, "there was with the angel a multitude of the heavenly host, praising God, and saying, Glory to God in the highest, on earth peace, good will towards men." And yet, be astonished, O heavens! blush, O earth! this gospel-sermon, which angels reckoned themselves honored to preach, and delivered with such rapturous exultation and joy, is, by multitudes in our day, thought trifling, and stale, and unworthy of their attention. To remedy this shameful, but growing evil, hath been the principal aim of my present discourse. I have told you what is our duty, that from thence you may learn your own; for the one must necessarily be suited to the other. The same authority which commandeth us to *preach*, doth virtually command and oblige you to *hear;* and if the pure doctrines of the gospel ought to be the subject of our sermons, it naturally follows, that you should neither expect nor desire any other. Ponder with due attention those awful words in the two verses preceding my text: "If our gospel be hid, it is hid to them that are lost: in whom the god of this world hath blinded the minds of them which believe not, lest the light of the glorious gospel of Christ, who is the image of God, should shine unto them." And let each of us pray in terms of the verse that immediately follows, that "God, who commanded the light to shine out of darkness, may shine in the hearts of both preachers and hearers, to give the light of the knowledge of his glory, in the face of Jesus;" that "we all, beholding, as in a glass, the glory of God, may be changed into the same image, from glory to glory, by the Spirit of the Lord." *Amen*.

SERMON XXII.

Preached on a Communion Sabbath.

CHRIST THE UNIVERSAL CREATOR.

COLOSSIANS I. 15–19.—"Who is the image of the invisible God, the first-born of every creature: for by him were all things created that are in heaven, and that are in earth, visible and invisible, whether they be thrones, or dominions, or principalities, or powers; all things were created by him, and for him. And he is before all things, and by him all things consist. And he is the head of the body, the church: who is the beginning, the first-born from the dead; that in all things he might have the pre-eminence. For it pleased the Father that in him should all fulness dwell."

OUR Lord Jesus Christ is uniformly represented to us in the sacred Scriptures as the Saviour of fallen man: a Saviour absolutely necessary; nay, as the ONLY Saviour. To this character he laid claim, in clear and express terms, when he said to Thomas, "I am the way, and the truth, and the life; no man cometh unto the Father but by me." And in this important light did Peter set him forth at the bar of the Jewish Sanhedrim: When speaking of him as the stone set at naught by the builders, which was now become the head of the corner, he added these memorable words: "Neither is there salvation in any other; for there is none other name under heaven given among men whereby we must be saved." Of the same import was the testimony of that illustrious prophet who was sent to prepare the way before him, and to introduce him to his public ministry by baptism: "He that believeth on the Son hath everlasting life; and he that believeth not the Son shall not see life; but the wrath of God abideth on him." Accordingly we are told by the Apostle John, that "this is the *command* of God," the first in order under the gospel-dispensation, and which claims the title of his peculiar commandment, "That we should believe on the name of his Son Jesus Christ."

It is, or at least it ought to be, unnecessary to observe, that this intimation of the divine will is sufficient, by itself, to constitute our duty. It surely belongs to the great Lord of all, to dispense his own grace by what hand, and in what manner, it pleaseth him; and in no case doth it become the creatures of his power to say unto him, What dost thou? or Why dost thou thus? Elihu spake the words of truth and soberness, when he said unto Job, "God is greater than man: why dost thou strive against him? for he giveth not account of any of his matters;" that is, he is not bound to explain the reason of his conduct; and none hath a right to demand that he should. But glory to his name, that with regard to the *greatest* of all his works, that dispensation of grace which angels desire to look into, and upon which the happiness of a whole order of his creatures doth depend, it cannot justly be said that he giveth no account of *this* matter. He hath not interposed his authority as Sovereign, and commanded sinners to believe on his Son, that they may be saved; but he hath likewise, in some measure, unfolded the secrets of his eternal counsel, and in particular, given us such encouraging views of that mighty One upon whom he hath laid our help, as render his command to believe on him at once the strongest and most endearing expression, both of his wisdom and of his love, so that they who refuse to comply with this command, counteract the soundest principles of reason, resist the clearest and most satisfying evidence, and shall be found, in the final issue of things, to have been equally chargeable with cruelty to themselves; with ingratitude, the vilest ingratitude, to their benefactor; and the most obstinate rebellion against their Sovereign Lord.

A few remarks upon the verses I have been reading, will serve to illustrate what I have just now said. And I have chosen this passage for the subject of my present discourse, in hope that God may bless it for the conviction of some who have hitherto rejected his gracious counsel; but chiefly with a view to confirm the faith, and to heighten the joy, of believers in Christ, by showing them, that he in whom they trust, is in all respects worthy to be depended upon, and will assuredly carry forward the work he hath begun, till it shall be perfected at length in their complete salvation.

The information that is here given us concerning our Redeemer, may be comprehended under the following heads.

First. What he is in himself; or, his original dignity.

Secondly. What he is to us; or, the station he holds in his church. And,

Thirdly. His qualifications for the discharge of what belongs to that station.

WHAT the Apostle saith upon the *first* of these particulars, amounts to something more than a simple assertion of our Lord's divinity. It is such an enlarged and accurate description of proper and essential Godhead, as cannot possibly be applied to any inferior being. The only expression that hath an appearance of difficulty is in the close of verse 15th, where Christ is styled *the first-born of every creature.* But the difficulty evanishes, when we attend to the explanation of that title which the apostle subjoins, or rather indeed to the reason he assigns for giving him that designation. No sooner has he called him *the first-born of every creature*, than he immediately adds, "For by him were all things created that are in heaven, and that are in earth, visible and invisible, whether they be thrones, or dominions, or principalities, or powers; all things were created by him, and for him." And that no room might be left for the remotest suspicion that he himself might have been created, *eternity*, in the most absolute sense of that word, is directly ascribed to him in the 17th verse; "And he is before all things, and by him all things consist." For surely he who existed *before all things*, must himself be without beginning, or from everlasting. Hence it appears, that this designation, *the first-born of every creature*, is of the same import with that other form of expression which the apostle useth, (Heb. i. 2.) where, having styled him the *Son of God*, he adds, "whom he hath appointed *heir* of all things." And both serve to denote that universal dominion which our Lord hath by inheritance, as the only begotten of the Father, of the same essence with himself, "the brightness of his glory, and the express image of his person;" an image so express, that when Philip said to our Lord, "Show us the Father, and it sufficeth us," he gave no answer but this, "Have I been so long with you, and yet hast thou not known me, Philip? he that hath seen me hath seen the Father: believest thou not that I am in the Father, and the Father in me?" Which is farther explained by what he said on another occasion, "I and the Father are one."

It would be highly improper, when we have such agreeable work before us, to enter into the thorny field of controversy; nevertheless, as so much of our comfort depends upon the persuasion we have, that he who came to save us is truly God, I cannot close this head without requesting you to compare what is written in the first verse of the bible, "In the beginning God created the heaven and the earth," with the introduction to John's gospel, "In the beginning was the Word, and the Word was with God, and the Word was God. All things were made by him; and without him was not any thing made that was made." And if to these you add that obvious conclusion of enlightened Reason, (Heb. iii. 4.) "Every house is builded by some man, but he that built all things is GOD,"—you will discover at once the true dignity of him in whom we are commanded to trust, and see with what strict propriety of language he is styled "the Son of the living God," "the great God and our Saviour," and "God over all, blessed for ever."

Having thus briefly illustrated his essential dignity, or what he is in himself, let us now consider,

Secondly, What he is to us. This we learn from the 18th verse, where the apostle calls him *the head of the body, the church;* which leads us to view him as "the seed of the woman;" "the Word made flesh;" the Son of God, by whom all things were created, uniting himself to human nature in the person of Jesus Christ; that as our kinsman and brother, he might redeem the forfeited inheritance; and by suffering in our room, the just for the unjust, might bring us to God. It is plain that the station here assigned to Christ belongs to him in the character of Emanuel, "which is, being interpreted, God with us," or, "God manifested in the flesh." Accordingly, he is styled, in immediate connection with his headship, *the first-born from the dead;* which necessarily supposes his previous incarnation and sufferings. And the church, which is here called *his body*, is expressly said by Paul, in the charge which he gave to the elders of Ephesus, to have been "purchased by him with his own blood." Here, my brethren, he is represented to us in such an endearing relation, as cannot fail, if we understand it aright, to fill our hearts at once with the highest admiration, the warmest gratitude, and most triumphant joy. Christ is said to be "the head of *all* principality and power," at the 10th verse of the following chapter; but it is not added, *these* are *his body*. In like manner, we are told, (Eph. i. at the close) that "God, who raised him from the dead hath set him at his own right hand in the heavenly places, far above all principality, and power, and might, and dominion, and every name that is named, not only in this world, but also in that which is to come; and hath put all things under his feet, and given him to be head *over* all things to the church." That is, he hath placed him at the head of all things, and given him supreme dominion over them; so that the highest angels are only ministers, or servants, in his kingdom, whom he sends forth to minister to the heirs of salvation. But his relation to his church, though it includes dominion, yet it carries in it a more close and intimate connection. He is not only head *over his* church, in respect of supreme authority, as a king is the political head over his subjects; but he is the head *of* his church in respect of vital influence; for so the apostle himself explains it in the following chapter, verse 19th; he is that head, "from which all the body by joints and bands having nourishment ministered, and knit together, increaseth with the increase of God."

But your time will not permit me to enlarge upon this subject; let it suffice at present to observe, that *what* Adam was in the first creation, *that* is Christ in the new creation. Hence he gets the name of the *second Adam;* and it is expressly said of the first Adam, (Rom. v. 14.) "that he was the *figure* of him that was to come." I shall not pretend to trace out the resemblance between these two different HEADS in all its extent; and yet it is obvious, that a great part of the Scripture language, which is employed to describe the nature of that station which Christ holds in the church, not only alludes to this resemblance, but is so much founded upon it, that without some just conception of the figure and type, our views of the antitype must be very dark and imperfect.

If we look at the state of things in the first creation, we shall find Adam placed in a station of the highest importance. Besides the dominion that was given him over the inferior creatures, he was constituted, in the most proper sense of the word, the *head* of mankind, inasmuch as "of that one blood were to be made all the nations of men that should dwell upon the face of the whole earth." The life of all his posterity was deposited in him. He was the root; and his descendants, in all their successive generations, are the branches which grow out of it. This is the plain account which the Scriptures give us; and the closeness of our connection with the first Adam is fatally illustrated by its effects, which cannot escape our observation. It is too apparent that life is conveyed to us under the same awful forfeiture which Adam incurred; for in consequence of the sentence pronounced against him on account of his transgression, "Dust thou art, and unto dust thou shalt return," we find, in fact, that "it is appointed unto all men once to die," and that "there is no discharge in that warfare."

This is the figure by which we are taught to form our conceptions of Jesus Christ, and of the place he holds in that new creation, which is here distinguished by the names of *his church* and *his body*. And to those who are acquainted with what the Scriptures say concerning Christ, many circumstances will occur from the hints I have already suggested, in which the resemblance between the first and second Adam may easily be traced with the most critical exactness. But, blessed be God, there is one circumstance of the greatest importance in which the resemblance doth not hold, as will appear from the information the apostle gives us concerning the *third* particular I took notice of, namely,

Thirdly. The qualifications of our Redeemer for performing what belongs to him as the *head* of his church.

It pleased the Father, saith he, verse 19, *that in him should* all *fulness dwell.*

The first Adam received the gift of life from God, which he held in trust for all his posterity, upon a condition the most gentle and easy that can possibly be imagined; but he failed in the performance of it; and thus "by one man sin entered into the world, and death by sin;" so that ever since that fatal trespass "death hath passed upon all men."

The SECOND ADAM received the grant of eternal life for his church, upon terms no less severe than his obedience unto death, even the death of the cross; that sin being condemned in the flesh, mercy and truth might meet together upon the apostate race, righteousness and peace might embrace each other. But difficult as the terms were, he not only punctually, but cheerfully, fulfilled them, insomuch that under all the pain and ignominy of the cross, he would not bow his head, and yield up the ghost, till, with a shout of triumph, he could say, "IT IS FINISHED."

"The first Adam was made a living soul; but the second Adam was made a quickening spirit." "The first man was of the earth, earthy; the second man was the Lord from heaven."

In the head of the first creation there dwelt indeed a *fulness*, but it was only the fulness of a creature; whereas *all fulness* resides in the Head of the new creation; or, as it is elsewhere expressed, in this same epistle, "in him dwelleth *all the fulness of the Godhead bodily.*"

Here, my brethren, expression fails; an ocean opens to our view that hath neither bottom nor shore, the Godhead! the fulness of the Godhead! all the fulness of the Godhead! How flat, how unmeaning, is the language of men, when applied to a subject which angels themselves are unable to comprehend? O glorious constitution of grace! worthy of him whose name, whose essence is love; and infinitely becoming the wisdom of that Sovereign, "whose work is perfect, and whose ways are judgment." With such an object in our eye, can we refrain from crying out, "Let Israel rejoice in him that made him; let the children of Zion be joyful in their king?" Well might Paul say, "I know in whom I have believed; and I am persuaded, that he is able to keep that which I have committed to him against that day." This is the endearing peculiarity of the gospel-covenant, that all the blessings of it are secured against forfeiture, in the hands of him who hath already fulfilled the terms of the grant, and finished the work which was given him to do: who, as he died to purchase those blessings, so he ever liveth to dispense them: ONE who by nature is God as well as man; and in whom, as the word incarnate and Mediator of the covenant, *it hath pleased the Father that all fulness should dwell*, for enriching, to the utmost capacity of created beings, all the members of that *body* whereof he is the *head.*

But what are the blessings of this well-ordered covenant? Let your own necessities dictate the answer. Say, my brethren, what do you need?

Is it the pardon of sin? Look back to the 14th verse of this chapter: "In Christ we have redemption through his blood, even the forgiveness of sins."—"He hath made peace by the blood of his cross," as we read verse 20th; and "the blood of Jesus cleanseth from all sin."—"He was made sin for us who knew no sin, that we might be made the righteousness of God in him." So that now "there is no condemnation to them that are in Christ Jesus." And O how blessed is the man whose iniquities are forgiven, whose transgressions are covered, and to whom the Lord imputeth not his sin!

This is a great, a necessary blessing; but great though it be, yet it is not commensurate to all the necessities of such creatures as we are. Man, by the apostasy, is not only liable to condemnation, nay, lying under sentence of death, but that sentence in part is already executed; his *soul* is dead, separated from God, the fountain of life. Thus it is written, "The natural man receiveth not the things of the Spirit of God; for they are foolishness to him: neither can he know them, because they are spiritually discerned." Nay, "the carnal mind is enmity against God; for it is not subject to the law of God, neither indeed can be." Can the death of a soul be expressed in stronger and more significant terms? Must not that spirit be dead, which is incapable of discerning the only objects that are suited to its nature, and of relishing the only enjoyments by which a spiritual being can subsist and be happy?

In this state every mere child of Adam cometh into the world; for "that which is born of the flesh is flesh," and can rise no higher by any means that nature affords. But as in the first Adam all die without exception, who, by the ordinary course of generation, are connected with him as their head; so in the second Adam, the quickening Spirit, and Lord from heaven, all who, by regeneration, are united to him, and become members of that body whereof he is the head, are in like manner made alive; for "that which is born of the spirit is," and must be, "spirit." Accordingly, Christ is styled *the Prince of Life;* not only the possessor of life, but the proprietor and dispenser of it. To him it belongs to raise the dead, and to quicken whom he will. Hear his own words, (John v. 25, 26.) "Verily, verily, I say unto you, The hour is coming, and now is, when the dead shall hear the voice of the Son of God; and they that hear shall live. For as the Father hath life in himself; so hath he given to the Son to have life in himself." And in this same epistle where my text lies, Christ is expressly styled *our life;* and the life of the believer is said to be *hid*, or treasured up *with Christ in God.*—Colossians iii. 3, 4. "Ye are dead," saith the apostle; dead to Adam, and the corrupted, perishing life you derived from him; dead to a present world, and the things on earth, which are no longer the objects of your affection. Thus are ye dead; but being raised with Christ to the things that are above, to a new life, and manner of living, "your life is hid with Christ in God; and when he who is our life shall appear, then shall ye also appear with him in glory."

Here we are again led into a subject to which no language is adequate, but such "unspeakable words" as Paul heard in paradise, "which it is not lawful for man to utter."

Should I attempt to enlarge upon it, I am afraid that I should only "darken counsel by words without knowledge." What hath already been said upon that *fulness* which dwelleth in Christ, may suffice to convince you that "his riches are unsearchable," and that nothing is wanting which sinners can either need or wish to possess. In him, as you have heard, they have both righteousness and strength: Righteousness for the guilty, complete and everlasting righteousness; for "by him all who believe are justified from all things:"—And strength for the weak, nay, life for the dead; with this peculiar advantage, that it is not left to their own keeping, but still resides in him who is the *head of the body*, and is imparted to them as his members, by that Spirit which is the indissoluble bond of their union; "for he that is joined to the Lord is one spirit." Accordingly he says, "Because I live, ye shall live also." And this was the foundation of that parting promise to his disciples, "I go to prepare a place for you; and if I go and prepare a place for you, I will come again and receive you unto myself, that where I am there ye may be also." This would lead me to speak of that high perfection at which the life they at present receive from him shall arrive in the heavenly world, when the body itself, which, by an irreversible decree, is condemned to return to the dust as it was, shall be raised again by the power and spirit of the Redeemer, and fashioned like unto his own glorious body, in that day when he, who once suffered to bear their sins, "shall appear the second time without sin unto salvation."

But I must not detain you any longer from the proper business of the day.

I have done what I could to render Christ precious to your souls: I have led you to view him in his essential dignity, as the Creator of all things; in his relation to believers, as the head of the body; and as possessing all fulness in that important character.

And here I would gladly expostulate with those to whom these things of the Spirit I have been talking of appear foolishness, and in whom the God of this world hath so far blinded their minds, that they see no beauty in this Saviour for which they should desire him. O that the hour might now come, in which every dead soul in this assembly should "hear the voice of the Son of God, and live." May he who at first commanded the light to shine out of darkness, while we speak in his name, shine into their hearts, to give them the light of the knowledge of his glory in the face of Jesus Christ, that in this glass, beholding the glory of the Lord, as the God of love, their darkness may be dispelled, their enmity subdued, and they be changed into the same image, from glory to glory, by his all-conquering Spirit.

But my chief concern at present is with the living members of Christ: For you a table is once more covered in the wilderness, for strengthening you to proceed in your journey to the Canaan that is above. This is one of the channels which your living head hath appointed for conveying his life to the members of his body. The ordinance itself affords you the strongest ground of hope: it is a representation of that sacrifice which Christ offered upon the cross: and he who loved you so well as to give his life *for* you, is certainly willing to impart life *to* you. "If while ye were enemies, ye were reconciled to God by the death of his Son; much more, being reconciled, you shall be saved by his life." Let not the sense of your unworthiness discourage you:—You come not here to give, but to take what is given. Nay, let me tell you, that the sense of your own emptiness is the very measure of your capacity for receiving his fulness: "He filleth the hungry with good things, but the rich," those who account themselves rich, "he sendeth empty away." Come therefore with longing desires, and enlarged hopes, to him who is full of grace and of truth, that out of his fulness you may this day receive grace for grace, to the glory of the giver, and to your own present and everlasting joy. *Amen.*

SERMON XXIII.

CHRIST'S POVERTY OUR RICHES.

2 CORIN. VIII. 9.—"Ye know the grace of our Lord Jesus Christ, that though he was rich, yet for your sakes he became poor, that ye through his poverty might be rich."

THESE words contain an accurate description of the *grace*, or free favor, of our Lord Jesus Christ, which all true believers are here said to *know; i. e.* they have not only heard the report of this grace, assented to the truth of the report, and are able to give some account of it to others; but they *know* it *experimentally*, having tasted its sweetness, and felt the power of it in their own hearts.

Several particulars are mentioned by the apostle in proof and commendation of the *grace* he celebrates, which I propose to illustrate in the following discourse.

I. THE *first* in order is the state of the Redeemer previous to his becoming poor. *He was rich*, but how rich no language can express, nor any mind but his own conceive. "In the beginning was the Word, and the Word was with God, and the Word was God. The same was in the beginning with God. All things were made by him: and without him was not anything made that was made;" John i. 1, 2, 3. It is expressly said of him, (Coloss. i. 16, 17.) "that by him all things were created that are in heaven and that are in earth, visible and invisible, whether they be thrones, or dominions, or principalities, or powers: all things were created by him, and for him. And he is before all things, and by him all things consist." The same representation is given of him by the apostle to the Hebrews, who styles him "the brightness of the Father's glory, and the express image of his person; whom he hath appointed heir of all things; by whom also he made the world; and who upholdeth all things by the word of his power."

We esteem a man rich, who, besides what is necessary for the supply of his own wants, hath wherewithal to relieve the necessities of others; but how rich must he be, who hath no wants to be supplied, and is at the same time possessed of such infinite treasures, that they can never be exhausted, nor in the least degree diminished, by being imparted to others! Nay, besides whom nothing exists, but what derived its being from him, and is necessarily dependent upon him, for all that it hath, or hopes to enjoy! Yet thus rich was he of whom the apostle speaks in my text.

II. The *second* thing to be considered, is the *poverty* to which he voluntarily submitted. The apostle John having introduced the history of our Saviour with that lofty description of his original and essential glory which I formerly quoted, makes a sudden transition, (verse 14.) and informs us, *how* he who was rich *became poor*, *viz.* by uniting himself to the human nature, and appearing in the likeness of sinful flesh. "The Word," says he, that same Word which in the beginning was with God, and was God, by whom all things were made; this "Word was made flesh, and dwelt among us."

Nothing can be more descriptive of the most abject poverty than the simple account we have of his birth, (Luke ii.) at the beginning; where, after being told, that, in consequence of a decree from the Roman emperor, Joseph went up from Nazareth unto Bethlehem, to be taxed with Mary, his espoused wife, who was great with child, the sacred historian thus proceeds, (ver. 6, 7.) "And so it was, that while they were there, the days were accomplished that she should be delivered. And she brought forth her first-born son, and wrapped him in swaddling clothes, and laid him in a manger, because there was no room for them in the inn." Nor did his after-life wear a different complexion from his birth: The same poverty, with respect to outward accommodation, which clouded his entrance into the world, accompanied him through every stage of his laborious journey, till at Calvary he finished his course upon the cross; insomuch that he could say, at the very time when his public ministry was most frequented and applauded, "The foxes have holes, and the birds of the air have nests, but the Son of man hath not where to lay his head." But this was not the only, nor even the worst kind of poverty, to which he voluntarily submitted. "He made himself," that is, he consented to be made, "of no reputation." For though multitudes occasionally admired and applauded him, yet these were generally persons in the lowest rank of life. The rich, the learned, and the powerful, among the Jews, were statedly combined to distress him on every side. They practised every art to defame his character, and to render both his person and his ministry the objects of popular contempt and hatred; till at length they were permitted to prevail so far, as to get him condemned by a sentence of the supreme court of their own nation, and then adjudged by the Roman governor to the death of a slave; which was executed with every circumstance of indignity and torture that the most inventive malice and cruelty could devise. Thus *poor* did our Lord *become;* not by constraint, or the hand of violence, for that was impossible; but of his own free choice; as it is written, (Phillip. ii. 6, 7, 8.) "He who was in the form of God and thought it not robbery to be equal with God, *made himself* of no reputation, and took upon him the form of a servant, and was made in the likeness of men; And being found in fashion as a man, *he humbled himself*, and became obedient unto death, even the death of the cross."

III. But for whose sake did he thus become poor? This is the *third* particular mentioned in the text; which manifests and commends the riches of his grace. It was for *us* the children of men, creatures but of yesterday, whose foundation is in the dust. We are indeed poor in every sense of the expression. Our life is the gift of another, and wholly dependent upon His sovereign pleasure. All the materials for supporting it lie without ourselves; we must go abroad in quest of them; and the same hand that provides them, can either withdraw them, or put them beyond our reach, or withhold that blessing which alone can render them effectual for the sustenance of that precarious life we possess: "If he hideth his face, we are troubled; if he taketh away our breath, we die."

Thus poor we all are, and necessarily must be, as creatures: but when I add that we are sinners, *poverty* is too feeble a word to convey the faintest idea of our forlorn condition. A person may be poor, and yet owe nothing to any man: but sin is not merely want; it is positively debt. Again, a man who is both poor and in debt, may be healthy and strong; so that by diligence and hard labor, he may not only procure the necessaries of life, but even be able in time to do justice to his creditors; but sin is disease as well as debt; it is the sickness of the soul, which wastes its strength, and renders it incapable of doing, nay, disinclined to attempt, any thing for the recovery of its health and vigor. Once more, the most insolvent debtor may, by flight, get beyond the reach of his creditor: but to what place can a sinner flee where God is not present? whose essential goodness is the irreconcilable enemy of sin, and only clothes itself with justice to condemn and punish it. In short, our Lord's description of the Laodiceans, "wretched, miserable, poor, blind, and naked," is the picture of every child of Adam in his natural state, with the same fatal inscription written over his head, "He knoweth it not." And did he who was rich; he whom we had offended; he who stood in no need of us; he who passed by creatures of a superior order, leaving them to inherit the misery they had chosen, and, in our punishment, as well as in theirs, might have displayed and glorified the perfection of his own nature;—did he, I say, *for our sakes become poor?* How astonishing this grace! —how impossible to be credited, if he himself had not declared it.

IV. Let us now inquire, in the *fourth* place, for what end was it that he did this?

It would justly have been deemed an act of uncommon generosity, had he simply discharged the debt we were unable to pay, that, being relieved of that burden, we might be at liberty to earn a scanty subsistence by our future labor and industry. It would have been a higher act of generosity, to raise us at once above poverty, and the fear of want, by supplying us from his own stores with the necessaries of life "feeding us," as Agur expressed his wish, "with food convenient for us." But *the grace of our Lord Jesus Christ* proposed an end still higher than this: *He became poor*, saith the apostle, "that we might be *rich*;" that is, possessed of every thing that could render us completely happy. Here it is that *grace* shines forth in its sweetest and most transcendent glory. But how shall we describe what "eye hath not seen, nor ear heard, neither hath it entered into the heart of man to conceive?" The best assistance I can give you, is to select from Scripture a few of those passages that speak of the riches which Christ doth at present confer upon his people; and then leave your own minds to imagine how immense their final portion must be, when Christ shall come again to complete their salvation.

"In him we have redemption through his blood, the forgiveness of sins, according to the riches of his grace; for by him all who believe are justified from all things." With pardon, which is the introductory blessing of the covenant, "peace with God" is inseparably connected; for "being justified by faith, we have peace with God through our Lord Jesus Christ." In consequence whereof, believers are received into the house and family of God; not as servants, but as children: for "to as many as receive Christ, to them gives he power to become the sons of God, even to them that believe in his name." "Behold," said the apostle John, "what manner of love the Father hath bestowed upon us, that we shall be *called* the sons of God." Nor is this a mere title of honor; believers have not only the name, but the nature of children. Accordingly they are said, by another apostle, to be "partakers of the divine nature." Christ dwells in them by his Spirit, in such a manner, that it is not so much *they* that live, as it is "*Christ* that liveth in them." Once more, as they have the name and nature of children, so likewise the portion that is connected with that relation; for, as Paul reasons, (Romans viii. 17.) "If children, then heirs, heirs of God, and joint heirs with Christ." And what is their portion? It is styled *eternal life;* "a treasure in the heavens that faileth not;"—"a kingdom that cannot be moved;"—an inheritance incorruptible, and undefiled, that fadeth not away."

These few quotations, which will be familiar to the ears of all who are conversant with the holy Scriptures, may serve to give us some notion of the *riches* which Christ doth impart to his people. I shall therefore conclude this head with two noted passages recorded in the preceding epistle to the Corinthians, which describe the provision that is made for believers in Christ, in terms more expressive than many volumes would suffice fully to unfold. The one is chap. i. 30. "Of him are ye in Christ Jesus, who of God is made unto us wisdom, and righteousness, and sanctification, and redemption." The other is chap. iii. 21. *et seq.* "*All things* are yours; whether Paul, or Apollos, or Cephas, or the world, or life, or death, or things present, or things to come; all are yours; and ye are Christ's; and Christ is God's."

V. The *fifth* and *last* thing in the text that remains to be illustrated, is the connection betwixt the *poverty* of Christ and the *riches* of his people, or the influence that the one hath upon the other: "He became poor, that we *through* his poverty might be rich."

This connection will appear, if we consider that his voluntary *humiliation*, in taking upon him our low nature, fulfilling all righteousness, and giving himself for us, an offering and sacrifice to God, hath so magnified the law, which we had broken, and given such full satisfaction to the justice of the lawgiver, that a way is now opened for the free and honorable exercise of mercy to the most guilty and polluted of the posterity of Adam. Hereby "sin was condemned in the *flesh*," that is, in the same nature that had offended: And God, by "setting forth his own Son, to be a propitiation through faith in his blood," doth now manifest his righteousness, no less than his mercy, in the forgiveness of sin; and appears to all his intelligent creatures to be infinitely *just*, as well as infinitely *gracious*, when he justifies those that believe in Jesus. The Son of God "was wounded for our transgressions, and bruised for our iniquities:" "He bore our sins in his own body upon the cross:" So that "now there is no condemnation to them that are in Christ Jesus;" for, as the Apostle reasons, (Rom. viii. 33, 34.) "Who shall lay any thing to the charge of God's elect? It is God that justifieth. Who is he that condemneth? It is Christ that died, yea, rather that is risen again, who is even at the right hand of God, who also maketh intercession for us."

And as the death or sacrifice of Christ absolves all that believe on him from the guilt of sin, which, as I formerly observed, is the fundamental and introductory blessing of the covenant; so his *exaltation*, which is the reward of his *poverty*, or voluntary humiliation, qualifies him to confer upon them all those consequent blessings which enrich them in time, and shall complete their happiness in the eternal world. Thus it is written, (Philip. ii. 8, &c.) that because "Christ humbled himself, and became obedient unto death, even the death of the cross;" therefore "God also hath highly exalted him, and given him a name which is above every name; that at the name of Jesus every knee should bow, of things in heaven, and things in earth, and things under the earth; and that every tongue should confess that Jesus Christ is Lord, to the glory of God the Father." And to the same purpose we read, (Eph. i. 21. *et seq.*) that "When God raised him from the dead, he set him at his own right hand in the heavenly places, far above all principality, and power, and might, and dominion, and every man that is named, not only in this world, but also in that which is to come; and put all things under his feet, and gave him to be the head over all things to the church, which is his body, the fulness of him that filleth all in all." When Christ ascended up on high, leading captivity captive, he then received gifts for men, even for the rebellious, that the Lord God might dwell among them. And now all power is committed to him, both in heaven and on earth: He not only appears in the presence of God as our great High-Priest, to plead the merit of his sacrifice, and to bless his people; but he sits at the Father's right hand, enthroned in glory, as "the King whom God hath set upon his holy hill of Zion;" from whence he sends forth his angels as "ministering spirits," to minister unto the heirs of promise during their continuance in this house of their pilgrimage, till they arrive at his Father's house in heaven, where they shall be advanced to sit with him upon his throne, and possess fulness of joy, and pleasures for evermore.

And now, my dear brethren, in the review of these five particulars, to which the Apostle directs our attention in proof and commendation of the *grace* which he celebrates, what improvement doth it become us to make of the subject?

Doth not *the grace of our Lord Jesus Christ* call for our humble and thankful *admiration?* The original and essential *riches* of the Redeemer, the *poverty* to which he voluntarily submitted, the character of those *for whose sake* he became poor, the *riches* he imparts unto them, and the *means* by which he doth it; are all so wonderful when separately considered, and kindle such a blaze of glory when combined and brought together, that angels themselves are dazzled with its splendor; and, through all eternity, will contemplate, with increasing wonder and delight, what neither they, nor we, shall ever be able fully to comprehend.

You must further be sensible, that this *grace of our Lord Jesus Christ* doth likewise invite, and should even constrain, our *imitation.* It was for this purpose that the Apostle introduced it into the subject with which my text is immediately connected. He is recommending love to the brethren, and in particular that instance of charity which consisteth in supplying the wants of the poor; and the argument or motive with which he presseth his exhortation, is the *grace of our Lord Jesus Christ, who, though he was rich, yet for their sake became poor, that they through his poverty might be rich.* And here, did your time permit, I might take occasion to show, that the gospel of Christ is so far from relaxing the obligations of those who receive it, to the practice of social duties, that, on the contrary, it strengthens these obligations, and carries the duties themselves to a sublimer height of self-denial, than the most refined moralist ever thought of, or perhaps would choose to adopt for the measure of his own conduct. I need only quote one passage of Scripture in proof of what I have said, where love to the brethren appears plainly to be raised by gospel-grace even above the standard of the original law itself. The *law* saith, "Thou shalt love thy neighbor *as* thyself." But what saith the *gospel?* You may read it, (1 John iii. 16.) "Hereby perceive we the love of God, because he laid down his life for us." To which it is immediately added, as a practical inference, "We *ought.*" The expression is emphatical, and imports, that it is not left to our choice, but is strictly due as a debt; "We *ought* to lay down our *lives* for the brethren." Such is the love that the gospel recommends. From whence it appears, that the purest and most sublime morality flows from faith in Christ as its native source, and will rise in exact proportion to the knowledge of his grace.

But do we *know* the grace of our Lord Jesus Christ? This question demands a serious and deliberate anwser.

It is too evident, that many who bear the title of Christians are grossly ignorant even of the doctrines of grace, and need to be taught "the first principles of the oracles of God." But besides these, we have just cause to fear, that not a few are to be found among us, who, though they have acquired a theory of Christian doctrine, and can talk of the great truths of the gospel with propriety and fluency; yet they cannot be said to know that grace whereof they are able to discourse to others.

The knowledge which the Apostle speaks of, is different from that which may be acquired by study, or mere human instruction. It is of a kind altogether peculiar to the real saint: It is produced by the Spirit accompanying the word, taking of the things of Christ, and not only showing them unto him, but writing them upon the "fleshy tables of his heart," and thereby transforming him into the divine image. Let me then ask you, or rather let me entreat you to ask your own hearts, as in the presence of God, Whether or not you ever were convinced of your need of this grace, your absolute need of it, to save you from the wrath to come? Did you ever see yourselves, by the light of God's word, to be wretched, and miserable, and poor, and blind, and naked; under a righteous sentence of condemnation, and unable, as of yourselves, to do any thing that could be effectual for your own recovery?—Under this conviction of your lost and helpless estate by nature, were your eyes opened to see the necessity and suitableness of the Lord Jesus Christ, the perfection of that sacrifice which he offered up to the Father; together with his ability and willingness "to save to the uttermost all that come unto God by him?" Animated by these spiritual discoveries of the Saviour, encouraged by his kind invitation to come to him, and constrained by the Father's command to believe on his name, did you humbly and thankfully receive him as the "unspeakble gift" of God to men? saying with the apostle Paul, "What things were gain to me, those I counted lost for Christ. Yea doubtless, and I count all things but loss for the excellency of the knowledge of Christ Jesus my Lord: And do count them but dung, that I may win Christ, and be found in him, not having mine own righteousness, which is of the law, but that which is by the faith of Christ, the righteousness, which is of God by faith." Was this acceptance entire and unreserved; did your heart consent that he should be made of God unto you, wisdom, and righteousness, and sanctification, and redemption; your prophet to instruct you, and your king to rule over you, as well as your priest to justify you by his blood? Have you relished, or do you now relish, the sweetness of his grace? Above all, let me ask you, have you felt its power and influence upon your temper and practice? The grace of the gospel is not only the parent of peace and joy, but an effectual principle of holiness in all who partake of it. This was the doctrine which Paul delivered to Titus, (Tit. ii. 11. *et seq.*) "The *grace* of God which bringeth salvation, teacheth us, that denying ungodliness, and worldly lusts, we should live soberly, and righteously and godly, in this present world." This is not only the most satisfying evidence, that we *know the grace of our Lord Jesus Christ;* but so essential an evidence, that where it is wanting, I can read nothing in the whole book of God to supply the defect, or that can be substituted in the place of it. I read of a *dead* faith,—a *presumptuous* hope,—a *false* peace,—and a *name* to live; but all these are refuges of lies, which ere long shall be "swept" away "with the besom of destruction." Whereas the true faith of the gospel is every where represented, as "working by love," and "overcoming the world." The hope of the gospel incites all who are possessed of it, "to purify themselves, even as he" whom they hope to enjoy "is pure."—"The peace of God which passeth all understanding, keeps," or guards "the heart and mind," and fortifies the believer against the fierce assaults of his spiritual enemies. And it is the distinguishing privilege of those who "are not under the law, but under grace," that "sin shall not have dominion over them:" "They have put off the old man with his deeds, and have put on the new man, which after God is created in righteousness and true holiness." They show, that they live in the Spirit, by walking in the Spirit; and give proof that they are "risen with Christ," and "know him in the power of his resurrection," by "seeking those things which are above, where Christ sitteth at the right hand of God." These are the words of truth; they are pure words, like silver tried in a furnace of earth, and purified seven times. And they are written in such capital letters, and expressed with such plainness and precision, that no sophistry can either darken their meaning or impair their force; unless it be to those unstable souls who are "ever learning, but never able to come to the knowledge of the truth;" "who like children are tossed to and fro, and carried about with every wind of doctrine, by the sleight of men and cunning craftiness, whereby they lie in wait to deceive." I therefore repeat upon this occasion, what I have often inculcated, and the Scriptures of truth uniformly teach, that the gospel-salvation is a *present* salvation; and that the Lord Jesus Christ is not only a deliverer from "wrath to come," but that, in the mean time, he saves all who trust in him, from that sin which renders them obnoxious to wrath; first, by expiating the guilt of it by his death, and next, by breaking the power of it in their hearts, through the operation of that Spirit which is the seal of their adoption, the earnest and first-fruits of their future inheritance.

These are the particulars upon which I would have you to examine yourselves impartially, as those who expect a judgment to come. Some of them are so essential to the character of a Christian, that every one who truly believeth in Christ, must have a consciousness of them in his own mind; for none was ever born into the family of God, without such a conviction of guilt, pollution, and weakness, as rendered the Redeemer both necessary and precious in his esteem. And though the enlightened mind will discover much imperfection, and many humbling blemishes, even in the fairest of those fruits which are the product of true and saving faith; yet (unless it be in those who are but newly entered into the school of Christ) the effects of his teaching must, in some degree, appear in such gracious fruits as I just now mentioned. And I should betray the trust committed to me, and reproach that *grace* I profess to magnify, if I encouraged any to conclude, that they are savingly acquainted with it, whose temper and practice have undergone no change, whatever pretensions they may make to faith in the Redeemer, and confident assurance of their final salvation; for all the saved of the Lord are expressly denominated "*God's workmanship*, created in Christ Jesus unto good works, which God hath before ordained that they should walk in them." And it will remain an invariable truth, to the confusion of all vain boasting hypocrites, that "whom God did foreknow, he also did predestinate to be conformed to the image of his Son, that he might be the first-born among many brethren."

But my chief business at present is with those who *know* by experience *the grace of our Lord Jesus Christ;* having both tasted its sweetness, and felt the power of it in their own hearts. To such I shall address a few short exhortations, and then proceed to the service for which we are assembled.

1*st.* Give glory to God, for what you *know* of his *grace;* and humbly acknowledge that it was he, and he only, who opened your eyes, and turned you from darkness to light. Who made you to differ from others? The proper answer to this question is to be found in the 4th chapter of this epistle, (verse 6.) "God, who at first commanded the light to shine out of darkness, hath shined into your hearts, to give you the light of the knowledge of his glory in the face of Jesus Christ." Not unto yourselves then, not unto yourselves, but to his free, distinguishing favor, is all the glory due.

2*dly.* Let this morning-dawn encourage you to hope for the perfect day. Christ would never have emptied himself, and *become poor*, without the most absolute assurance that some were to be *enriched* by him: and where he begins a good work, this may, and ought to be, considered as a certain pledge, that he will carry it forward to its full perfection; for he "who is the author" is also "the finisher of his people's faith." Rejoice, therefore, in hope of the glory of God. And till you are brought to the possession of it be careful, in the

3*d* place, To use all the means he hath appointed for obtaining larger measures of his *grace*, both in respect of knowledge and of influence. Among these means, the holy sacrament of our Lord's supper holds the most distinguished rank, as it was instituted for this very purpose, to exhibit a sensible representation of *the grace of our Lord Jesus Christ*, in becoming *poor for our sake, that we through his poverty might be rich.* Here we not only behold him in his lowest state of voluntary humiliation, evidently set forth as crucified before our eyes; but likewise presenting to us, and by visible symbols conferring upon us, all those unsearchable riches which he purchased with his blood, and secures by his intercession; which he actually possesseth as the "head of the church, which is his body;" and conveys, by his Spirit, to every member in due season, and measure, as their several necessities and circumstances require. Let us then approach the table of the Lord with faith, and love, and thankful praise; and while we bless him for the *grace* he hath already made known to us, let us pray for such further discoveries as may strengthen and comfort us in what remains of our journey through this wilderness, till we arrive at those blessed abodes of perfect light, and love, and purity, where we shall *see him as he is*, without the intervention of ordinances, and enjoy him fully, without interruption and without end. *Amen.*

SERMON XXIV.

FAITH AND HOPE ESTABLISHED.

1 PETER I. 20, 21.—"Who verily was foreordained before the foundation of the world, but was manifest in these last times for you; who by him do believe in GOD that raised him up from the dead, and gave him glory, that your faith and hope might be in GOD."

EVERY fabric must partake of the strength or weakness of its foundation. A house that is built upon the loose sand, will soon fall to the ground; nay, the higher it is raised, especially if the materials be weighty, the more sudden and ruinous will its fall be. It must therefore be of the last importance to the Christian, to be fully satisfied in his own mind, that the grounds of his *faith and hope in God* are sufficient to sustain all the weight he hath to lay upon them.

The *life* of the soul is no trivial matter; it is our ALL. Other things may be wanted, but this is the "one thing needful." The *death* of the soul, by which I mean its final separation from the only source of life and joy, is misery in the extreme; pure misery, without mixture or alloy.

To this death we all became liable by our apostasy from God. The loathsome disease, which if left to its own operation, will soon produce this fatal effect, is deep lodged in our nature; and we are directed to look up to the Lord Jesus Christ, not only for the cure of the disease, but likewise for all that exalted happiness besides, which, commencing in present reconciliation with God, and the renovation of the soul after his divine image, shall at length be perfected in the entire resemblance and full enjoyment of him in the heavenly state.

That the Lord Jesus is *able* to do these great things for us, is the professed belief of all who style themselves Christians.

The dignity of his person, as the "eternal Word made flesh;" the perfection of his obedience; the merit of his sacrifice; his resurrection from the dead; and his exaltation to the right hand of God, leave no room to doubt of his saving power; while his own account of the errand upon which he came into the world; his free choice of the office of Redeemer; his generous offers of mercy to the chief of sinners; together with the regret he always expressed when these offers were rejected—may justly lead us to conclude, that he is no less *willing* than "he is able to save to the uttermost all that come unto God by him."

These encouraging truths, which are written as with a sunbeam in the sacred Scriptures, present themselves to the view of every intelligent reader. Hence those general professions of gratitude to the Redeemer, and of dependence upon him, for the pardon of sin, and deliverance from wrath, which are so common among Christians of almost every denomination.

But I have had frequent occasion to observe, that these views of the Saviour, though just in themselves, are too often blended with indistinct, and even erroneous, conceptions of the great scheme of salvation, as revealed in the gospel. Many, while they look upon the *Son* as the generous friend of fallen man, are too apt to represent the *Father* to their own minds as severe and unrelenting; eager to punish his guilty creatures; yielding with reluctance to accept the offered ransom, and to receive from a Mediator, that satisfaction to his justice which was necessary to make way for such exercise of mercy as might consist with the authority of his laws, and the dignity of his government.

Sentiments of this kind are not only gloomy and uncomfortable to those who entertain them, but have likewise a most pernicious tendency in other respects. They thwart the very design of Christ's coming into the world; of whom it is expressly said, that "he suffered, the just for the unjust, that he might *bring us to God.*" It was not that our regard should terminate in his own person as Mediator; but that through him they should ascend to the eternal Father, who "so loved the world, that he gave his only begotten Son, that whosoever believeth in him might not perish, but have everlasting life." He came to demonstrate the love of God to sinners of mankind; that, by rendering the Father amiable to the convinced, enlightened soul, he might overpower its natural enmity, and, upon the ruins thereof, erect a throne for gratitude and love. Christ is indeed, said to be "the *end* of the law;" and the law, by showing us our guilt and depravity, and the necessity of a better righteousness than our own, to be pleaded as the ground of our acceptance with God, is very properly styled "our *Schoolmaster* to bring us to Christ." But when we are brought thus far by the discipline of the law, doth Christ then command us to stop short at himself, and to proceed no farther? No; he who is "the *end* of the law," is styled the *way* to the Father; for thus he describes his own character and office, (John xiv. 6.) "I am the *way*, and the truth, and the life; no man cometh unto the Father but by me." It is *God* in *Christ* reconciling the world unto himself by the ministry of the *Spirit*, that is the complete and adequate object of faith: and we do not understand "the word of reconciliation," till we see the undivided Godhead, *Father*, *Son*, and *Holy Ghost*, united in counsel, as they are in one essence; and each performing, in the character he sustains, a peculiar work of grace for the eternal salvation of an elect world.

It is the agency of the *Father* in this wonderful plan which "angels desire to look into," that the passage I have been reading leads us at present to contemplate. And it will readily occur to you, that four several acts of grace are here attributed to him.

First. He *ordained* his Son to the office of Redeemer.

Secondly. He *manifested* him to the world at the appointed season.

Thirdly. He *raised him up from the dead.* And,

Fourthly. He *gave him glory.*

Each of these particulars I shall endeavor to illustrate; and then show their joint tendency to establish our *faith and hope in God.*

First. It was the Father who *ordained* Christ to the office of Redeemer. You need only read from the 17th verse, to be satisfied that this was the doctrine the apostle meant to deliver; "If ye call on the *Father*, who, without respect of persons, judgeth according to every man's work, pass the time of your sojourning here in fear; forasmuch as ye know that ye were not redeemed with corruptible things, as silver and gold, but with the precious blood of Christ, as of a Lamb without blemish and without spot," *who verily was foreordained*, namely, by the *Father*, sustaining the character of the Supreme Lord and Judge, *before the foundation of the world.*

"Known unto God are all his works from the beginning." The scheme of redemption, and the several steps preparatory to its final execution, were fixed and adjusted before time commenced. This in part appears from the manner of its first publication in paradise, as Moses hath recorded it in the sacred history. The cool majestic solemnity with which the whole procedure was conducted on that important occasion, and especially the putting the gracious promise of a Deliverer to our guilty parents, into the form of a judicial sentence against the grand apostate who had seduced them, plainly showed, that the constitution which then commenced was not an after-thought, or newly-devised expedient, but that all was the result of previous counsel and design; that the rebellion had been seen before it was acted, and redemption decreed before the forfeiture was incurred.

Many passages might be quoted from the Old Testament writings, where the Father's choice and *ordination* of the Saviour are declared in the strongest and most explicit terms. In one place he is introduced, proclaiming his sovereign pleasure in these words: "Behold my Servant whom I uphold, mine elect in whom my soul delighteth: I have put my Spirit upon him, he shall bring forth judgment to the Gentiles." In another place, where Messiah himself is the speaker, the Father's commission is thus acknowledged by him: "The Spirit of the Lord God is upon me, because the Lord hath anointed me to preach good tidings unto the meek, he hath sent me to bind up the broken-hearted, to proclaim liberty to the captives, and the opening of the prison to them that are bound." And this last question is more remarkable, because the evangelist Luke informs us, that our Lord, after reading it publicly in the synagogue at Nazareth, directly applied it to himself, by adding these words: "This day is this Scripture fulfilled in your ears."—Luke iv. 21.

But there are other declarations of our blessed Redeemer, which, without any circuit, express the same truth, in terms so plain, that it is impossible for any body to mistake their meaning. "I proceeded forth," said he, "and came from God; neither came I of myself, but he sent me." "I do nothing of myself, but as the Father hath taught me I speak these things, and he that sent me is with me." "I came from heaven to do the will of him that sent me." "I have not spoken of myself, but the Father which sent me, he gave me a commandment what I should say and what I should speak." Such explicit acknowledgments from the mouth of "the faithful witness," which must be familiar to the ears of all who are conversant with the lively oracles of truth, are sufficient to illustrate the agency of the Father in framing the plan of man's redemption before time commenced, and in *ordaining* the Son to carry it into execution.

Secondly. His agency is no less conspicuous in *manifesting* the Saviour at the appointed season.

It was the original promise, that "the seed of the woman should bruise the serpent's head." Accordingly we read, (Gal. iv. 4.) that "when the fulness of the time was come, God sent forth his Son, *made of a woman.*" The propriety of which expression cannot fail to strike us with peculiar force, when we recollect what the angel said to Mary, after he had informed her of the high honor which God was about to confer upon her, (Luke i. 35.) "The Holy Ghost shall come upon thee, and the power of the Highest shall overshadow thee; therefore also that holy thing which shall be born of thee, shall be called the Son of God." All the predictions of the prophets concerning the time and place of the Messiah's birth, and the circumstances of the Jewish nation at that important period, were most exactly fulfilled, as might easily be shown.

A special messenger was sent to prepare the world for his reception; this was John the Baptist, (who had likewise been foretold in ancient prophecy) to whom the Father *manifested* the promised seed, by a visible descent of the Holy Ghost at his baptism, accompanied with a voice from heaven, which said, "This is my beloved Son, in whom I am well pleased." Which signal and most authentic attestation was immediately published by John to the men of that age; for this was the record he bare. (John i. 32, 33, 34.) "I saw the Spirit descending from heaven like a dove, and it abode upon him. And I knew him not; but he that sent me to baptize with water, the same said unto me, Upon whom thou shalt see the Spirit descending and remaining on him, the same is he which baptizeth with the Holy Ghost. And I saw, and bare record, that this is the Son of God."

But he had greater witness than that of John. "The works which his Father gave him to finish, the same works that he did, bare witness of him that the Father had sent him." It was to this divine attestation that our Lord himself most frequently appealed. When the Jews came to him in Solomon's porch at the feast of the dedication, and said unto him, "How long dost thou make us to doubt? if thou be the Christ tell us plainly;" his answer was, "I told you, and ye believed not: The works that I do in my Father's name, they bear witness of me." "If I do not the works of my Father, believe me not: but if I do, though ye believe not me, believe the works; that ye may know and believe that the Father is in me and I in him."

The miraculous appearances at his death had such an effect upon the centurion, and the soldiers who attended his crucifixion, that "when they saw the earthquake, and those things that were done," and in particular observed with what majesty he retired from life, voluntarily dismissing his Spirit, after he had cried with a shout of triumph, *It is finished*, "they feared greatly, saying, Truly this was the Son of God."

By these, and sundry other ways that might be mentioned, did the Father *manifest* and give testimony to the Saviour.

Thirdly. But it was chiefly by his *resurrection from the dead* that our Lord was declared to be the Son of God with power." And this is the *third* particular mentioned in the text; which, you see, is expressly attributed to the agency of the Father. It was *God*, saith the apostle, *that raised him up from the dead.* This doth not imply that our great Redeemer could not, or did not, by his own proper virtue, rise from the dead; for what he said to the Jews was strictly true in the most obvious sense of the words, "*I* have power to lay down my life, and *I have power to take it up again;*" and on another occasion, "Destroy this temple," pointing at his own body, "and in three days I will raise it up." Accordingly, the author of this epistle observes, (chap. iii. 18.) that he was "quickened by the *Spirit*," or that divine nature which was personally united to his humanity. And in his memorable sermon on the day of Pentecost, speaking of the resurrection of Christ, after he had said, (Acts ii. 24.) that the Father "loosed the pains of death," he immediately added, "because it was not possible he should be holden of it."

Nevertheless, as Christ sustained a public character, and died as the surety of fallen man, it was highly fit in himself and necessary for our comfort, that the agency of the Father should be clearly seen and acknowledged in his resurrection; and that his release from the grave should appear to be an act of righteous administration, rather than the mere exercise of Sovereign power. It was certainly most regular, that the same hand from which he received his commission should seal his discharge; for none else but the Father was qualified to judge whether or not the articles of agreement were fulfilled: He, and he alone, had authority to declare that the satisfaction was valid, and the debt paid to the uttermost farthing. This, I apprehend, was the reason why an angel was sent from heaven to roll away the stone from the door of the sepulchre. It was not surely to open a passage for our Lord, as though any stone, how great soever, could have confined his revived body to the grave; for we read, (John xx. 19.) that "on the same day at evening, when *the doors were shut*, where the disciples were assembled for fear of the Jews, Jesus came and stood in the midst of them." But what our Lord said to the people (John xii. 30.) concerning the voice which came from heaven, in answer to that prayer, "Father, glorify thy name;" *This voice came not because of me, but for your sakes*, may justly be applied to that appearance of the angel. It was not *because of Christ*, as though he needed his aid, but *for the sake* of the pious women who had come to visit the sepulchre; and I may add, for the sake of all whom their report shall reach, to make it evident, that his discharge was issued in due form, in testimony of the Father's infinite delight in him, and of his perfect satisfaction with his whole conduct as Mediator. This leads to the

Fourth and *last* particular; upon which it is as impossible to say enough, as it is unnecessary to say much; namely, *the glory he received* from the Father as the promised and merited reward of his obedience and sufferings.

Of this we have many lofty descriptions in Scripture. There we are told, that "God who raised him from the dead, hath set him at his own right hand in the heavenly places, far above all principality, and power, and might, and dominion, and every name that is named, not only in this world, but also in that which is to come: and hath put all things under his feet, and given him to be the head over all things to the church." "He is gone," saith our apostle, (in the 3d chapter of this epistle, at the 22d verse) "He is gone into heaven, and is on the right hand of God; angels, and authorities, and powers, being made subject unto him." He is constituted the final judge of men; for "God hath appointed the day in which he will judge the world in righteousness by that man whom he hath ordained; whereof he hath given assurance unto all men, in that he raised him from the dead." "Then shall the Lord Jesus be revealed from heaven, with his mighty angels, in flaming fire, taking vengeance on them that know not God, and that obey not the gospel of our Lord Jesus Christ: who shall be punished with everlasting destruction from the presence of the Lord, and from the glory of his power: when he shall come to be glorified in his saints, and to be admired in all them that believe." The donation of this glory by his heavenly Father, and its connection with his previous sufferings and death, are solemnly acknowledged by our Lord himself, in that prayer which he uttered in the hearing of his disciples, (John xvii. 4. 5.) "I have glorified thee on earth: I have finished the work which thou gavest me to do. And now, O Father, glorify thou me with thine own self, with the glory which I had with thee before the world was." And both are expressly asserted in the same connection, (Philip. ii. 6—11.) where the apostle first relates the several steps of our Lord's humiliation, and then adds, "Wherefore God also hath highly exalted him, and given him a name above every name: That at the name of Jesus every knee should bow, of things in heaven, and things in earth, and things under the earth; and that every tongue should confess, that Jesus Christ is Lord, to the glory of God the Father."

Thus I have endeavored to give you a short illustration of the agency of the *Father* in the work of man's redemption, as it is described in this passage. He *ordained* the Saviour:—he *manifested* him to the world;—he *raised him up from the dead;*—he *gave him glory.* And all those particulars are made known to us. For what end? *that our faith and hope may be in God.* Amazing goodness! What shall we say to this? "Lord, we believe; help thou our unbelief."

Can we entertain hard thoughts of that God, who hath not only done such great things for our recovery, but done them in a manner so demonstrative of his love, that it is impossible for the jealousy of guilt itself to find out any seeming defect in the encouragement they afford, or to devise any additional security, for dispelling the fears, and assuring the hopes, of the chief of sinners; who, conscious of deserved wrath, and confessing the justice of the sentence that condemns them, flee for refuge to that sanctuary erected by infinite wisdom and love, for the reception of those who look for protection nowhere else? Unbelief, when viewed in the glass of my text, changeth its aspect; and instead of *timid distrust*, plainly appears to be *daring presumption.* We give God the *lie*, when we put away from ourselves the calls of his mercy, and offers of his grace; Whereas, by humble and thankful acceptance of the Saviour, "we set to our seal that God is true;" and only render unto him the glory that is due to his name, as the God of love, the God who is love, even the God and Father of our Lord Jesus Christ, in whom he reconciles the world unto himself, not imputing their trespasses unto them.

A copious enlargement upon this branch of my subject would carry me far beyond the ordinary limits of a discourse: but as it is the will of God, that the heirs of promise should have "a strong consolation," I cannot conclude my remarks upon the agency of the Father in the work of man's redemption, without reminding you of "the grace of our Lord Jesus Christ, who, though he was rich, yet for our sakes became poor, that we through his poverty might be rich." He who was in the form of God, and thought it not robbery to be equal with God, made himself of no reputation, and took upon him the form of a servant, and was made in the likeness of men: and being found in fashion as a man, he humbled himself, and became obedient unto death, even the death of the cross." The Father indeed freely gave the Son *to us;* but with equal freedom the Son gave himself *for us.* With what alacrity did he accept the office of Mediator? "Lo, I come,—I delight to do thy will: thy law is within my heart." With what ardor did he execute the commission he had received! "I have a baptism to be baptized with, and how am I straitened till it be accomplished!" "I," said he, "am the good shepherd; the good shepherd *giveth* his life for the sheep." It is not violently taken from me; I voluntarily lay it down. Nay, he was not only a willing sacrifice, like Isaac, consenting to be bound, and laid upon the altar; but he himself was the priest that offered the sacrifice: for thus it is written in the epistle to the Hebrews, (chap. ix. 14.) "Through the eternal Spirit, he offered himself without spot unto God."

Here then is sunshine without a cloud. Around the throne of God, and of the

Lamb, all is bright meridian splendor. What pity is it that any gloom should sit upon our minds? "*In this was manifested the love of God towards us*, because that God sent his only begotten Son into the world, that they might live through him."—1 John ix. 9. *The love of Christ was no less clearly manifested in his* "GIVING himself for us an offering and a sacrifice to God, for a sweet-smelling savor."—Eph. v. 2.

These two memorable and interesting sentences, like the cherubims which covered the mercy-seat, have their faces looking one towards another; and both smile with complacence upon every returning prodigal. For to connect them together, and bring them home to ourselves, I need only direct your attention to a third passage of Scripture, where faith in the Son is expressly enjoined as an act of obedience to the will of the Father; (1 John iii. 23.) "this is the *command* of God, that we should believe on the name of his Son Jesus Christ." Let us this day unite them all in the serious meditations at the table of the Lord; and improve them, as we ought to do, for the establishment of our *faith*, and *hope*, and *joy*. We are not straitened in God: let us not be straitened in our bowels; for this is the call which he addresseth to each believer in particular, "Open thy mouth wide, and I will fill it." *Amen.*

SERMON XXV.

ETERNAL LIFE IN CHRIST.

I. JOHN, v. 11.—"This is the record, that GOD hath given to us eternal life: and this life is in his SON."

WHY do not all to whom these good tidings are published, receive them with humble gratitude and joy? Are they expressed in terms so dark and ambiguous, that their meaning and import cannot be fully ascertained? or is the offer of *life* loaded with such hard conditions, as exceed the powers of those to whom it is addressed? Were either of these the case, unbelief would be furnished with something more than a *plausible* excuse. But every body must be sensible, that neither of these objections can, with any color of justice, be charged upon the *record* as it lies before us in my text. To what then shall we attribute the cold reception it meets with from the bulk of mankind; the contemptuous rejection of it by many; and the violent opposition that is made to it by not a few.

I shall not pretend to enumerate all the different causes that might be assigned. There is *one* which, however it may appear a paradox to some, doth, in my opinion, unfold the most dangerous and fruitful source of infidelity. It is briefly this:—The gospel-record is *too plain* to be *understood* and *too gracious* to be *believed.*

Here is nothing above the level of the lowest capacity; nothing beyond the reach of the most degenerate among men. It requires no acuteness to discover what is meant by a *gift;* and if the gift be free and disencumbered, all to whom it is offered are equally qualified to receive it. This pulls up at once the deepest laid foundations of pride and vainglory, and thwarts that love of distinction and pre-eminence which, from the date of the apostasy, hath been the fatal inheritance of the human kind. We cannot bear the thought of being fed at a common table, how richly soever that table may be furnished. Each of us would wish to have a portion peculiar to himself; something that might denote a preference to others, and flatter that partial opinion which every one fondly cherisheth of his own personal importance.

Hence it is, that the *record* of God hath either been altogether rejected, or so interlined with the glosses of vain philosophy, as to alter its very frame, and render it not only ineffectual, but even adverse, to those salutary purposes for which it was intended.

The Almighty Independent Sovereign of the universe hath been tried at the bar of his own rebellious subjects. *There* it hath been decided what is fit and becoming the high station he holds. Plans of administration have been laid down for him, formed upon those systems of human government, which to each daring projector appeared the most complete: whereas the absurdity, as well as the arrogance, of all such attempts, are detected and reproved by two very plain questions, which the Apostle Paul proposes in the 11th chapter of his epistle to the Romans, at the close; "Who hath known the mind of the Lord? or who hath been his counsellor? Or who hath first given to him, and it shall be recompensed unto him again?" No man of common understanding will hesitate a moment in giving an answer to these questions, but will readily reply,—None hath been his counsellor, neither is there any who hath first given to God; "for," as it immediately follows, "of him, and through him, and to him, are all things." And yet how obvious, and how important, are the consequences of such acknowledgments?

For if none hath been his counsellor, it is plain that none can know his mind till he shall be pleased to reveal it; nor even then can it be known any further than it is revealed. To supply what is concealed, with conclusions drawn from the reasonings of our own minds, would be the height of presumption: We must take his counsel as it lies before us in the record he hath given us, without adding to it or subtracting from it. Again, if none hath first given to him, how erroneous must it be to measure the divine administration even by the most perfect models of government among men? Nay, if it would not seem another paradox, I could almost venture to affirm, that the more perfect any constitution of human government is, the less it is adapted to be a standard in this matter. We reckon that system the most excellent, because most agreeable to the soundest principles of reason, by which the original equality of all men by nature is most effectually preserved; where established law, to which the highest are subject, restrains the hand of violence, and supports the meanest individual in the possession of those privileges which, without such protection, he might be unable to defend. But here no parallel can be drawn with regard to the divine government; nor is there room to reason from the one to the other, even by the remotest analogy. The frame of human policy, the whole system of legislation, is built upon the basis of private right and property; whereas, in the kingdom of God, there is, there can be, no such thing as property on the side of the governed. All the subjects are the creatures of the Supreme Ruler; and whatever they possess, they derive from him. The more they receive, the greater debtors they are to his bounty; and when they improve their trust to the utmost extent of their capacity, they have no merit to plead; their fidelity can amount to nothing higher than innocence; while the least failure renders them criminal and liable to punishment.

So that, in the very nature of things, whatsoever God bestows upon the most perfect of his creatures, must be the effect of pure grace and favor. And if all be favor to the innocent, who have never left the station in which he placed them; surely what is bestowed upon the guilty must flow from the purest grace, the most condescending exercise of sovereign mercy.

And this is the light in which my text presents to our view the record of God with regard to fallen man; where the whole contents of the gospel constitution are comprehended in this short but emphatical sentence,

God hath given us eternal life: and this life is in his Son.

It consists, you see, of two parts.

1. *God hath given to us eternal life.*

2. *This life is in his Son.*

I. The first part of the record represents the great Lord of all, in the endearing character of a munificent benefactor and tender-hearted father, regarding his guilty creatures with an eye of pity, and graciously interposing for their relief, after they had wilfully destroyed themselves.

I need not detain you with a tragical description of the fatal effects of our apostacy from God. It may suffice to remind you of what is written, (Rom. v. 12.) "By one man sin entered into the world, and *death* by sin." This is the view which my text leads us to take of the present state of fallen man. He is not only become *mortal*, or liable to death, in the common acceptation of that term; but he is already dead, in the most important and awful sense of the word. He is separated, or cut off, from the only source of life; and though he is still alive in this material world, from which too he must soon remove, yet his connection is broken with the spiritual world; so that the dissolution of the body terminates at once his enjoyments and his hopes. Every thing beyond the grave must wear an aspect of horror: nothing remains for him after that fatal period, but "a fearful looking for of judgment and fiery indignation."

This may help us to a proper conception both of the nature and worth of the blessing here mentioned. The foundation of this *eternal life* is laid in reconciliation with God; for by that we pass from death to life; the essence of it consisteth in likeness to God; and it is perfected in the beatific vision, and full enjoyment of God in heaven.

The epithet *eternal*, sufficiently distinguisheth it from that precarious kind of life we at present find ourselves possessed of. It is a life that is not subject to death; neither is it interrupted for one moment by the dissolution of the earthly tabernacle: on the contrary, it acquires new vigor, by that stroke which separates the soul from the body; and then only arrives at full maturity, when the man ceaseth to be any more an inhabitant of this world.

But instead of enlarging upon the nature and excellence of this inestimable blessing, I would rather direct your attention to the manner in which it is bestowed. And here the record is abundantly plain, *God hath* GIVEN *to us eternal life.* The true import of the word *given*, is clearly decided by the apostle Paul, when he says, "The wages of sin is death; but the gift of God is eternal life;" where *wages* and *gift* are placed in direct opposition to one another; the first being an exercise of justice, the last an act of free and unmerited favor. And in this light the salvation of sinners is uniformly represented in the sacred writings. "It is your Father's good pleasure," said Christ to his disciples, "to *give* you the kingdom." "By grace are ye saved through faith," said St. Paul; "and that not of yourselves, it is the *gift* of God." And again, "Not by works of righteousness which we have done, but according to his *mercy* he saved us, by washing of regeneration, and the renewing of the Holy Ghost." Accordingly, eternal life is styled an *inheritance;* which is inseparably connected with the relation of children: and as by the apostacy we became enemies to God, it is not easy to conceive how enemies can be made children in any other way than by an act of the purest and most sovereign grace.

Were God in any respect weak or indigent, could he be impoverished by the revolt of his subjects, or hurt by the violent efforts of their enmity; it might be wisdom to court their return by the offer of a reward, and even to connect the reward with such gentle conditions as the proudest heart might easily digest: but this, you must be sensible, is not the case we are considering. God stands in no need of us, or of our services. It requires no exertion of strength to crush his rebellious subjects: if he withdraw for one moment the support of his power, they perish: for "in him they all live and move:" so that if punishment be deferred, and, still more, if benefits be conferred, no cause can be assigned for either but his own sovereign pleasure, the self-removing goodness of his nature.

Were these plain truths attended to, much vain jangling and strife of words might be prevented, and a ready solution found of many of those seemingly intricate questions, with which serious and awakened minds are ofttimes perplexed and discouraged.

It is one of the most obvious dictates of sound reason, that the creature owes its existence to the pure favor of the Creator. It is equally obvious that it can only live by those *means* which the Creator hath appointed. Every species of animals hath its *peculiar* aliment; so peculiar, that what is food to one species, is not only useless, but frequently noxious to another: a plain, convincing evidence of their immediate and absolute dependence upon the will of that Being whose workmanship they all are. Whence is it, that those materials upon which the elephant grows to a bulk so enormous, can afford no sustenance to the comparatively diminutive body of man? No answer can be given but this, The Creator hath not chosen and blessed them for that end. Every attempt to live by any other means than God hath appointed, is an attempt to live not only independent of God, but in defiance of his will. Adam tried the experiment, and thereupon became mortal: for it was not the quality of the forbidden tree, but the prohibition of the Creator, that armed his trespass with the fatal sting.

And can the nobler, and *Spiritual life*, be less intimately connected with its Author than the animal one? If that be lost by wilful transgression, doth it require less power or less grace to restore it? Or can the revolted creature plead any right to the institution of a benefit which was freely bestowed at first, and, even before it was forfeited, owed its continuance to the good pleasure of the giver? The absurdity is so glaring, that every one must perceive it as soon as it is mentioned. The blessing of eternal life is, and can be, no other than the *record* hath declared it to be, the free and sovereign *gift* of God.

An hard saying this to the vain sons of Adam, who would always find something in themselves to boast of! but absolutely necessary to bring them back to that cheerful dependence upon, and willing subjection to the Father of their spirits; which is the only healthful and orderly state of creatures; the happiness whereof they forfeited by aspiring to become gods. This appears to be the aim of all God's dispensations to the children of men; and is expressly declared to be the ultimate end of the gospel-constitution. (1 Cor. i. 30.) " Of him are ye in Christ Jesus, who of God is made unto us wisdom, righteousness, sanctification, and redemption: that, according as it is written, *He that glorieth, let him glory in the Lord.*"

These few remarks may serve to throw light upon the first part of the record, *God hath given to us eternal life.*

2dly. THE second branch of it doth further inform us, that *this life is in his Son.*

Though God acted as a Sovereign, in conferring so great a gift upon any of the dead posterity of Adam, and could not be influenced to this act of grace by any other motive than what he found in his own essential goodness; yet it became his wisdom to exercise mercy in such a manner, as should be expressive of his real character, and give a full and true representation of his other perfections to all his intelligent creatures.

Holiness belongs to God as well as *goodness;* and the sceptre of his kingdom if "a sceptre of *righteousness;*" and therefore Wisdom required, that while his mercy triumphed in the salvation of sinners, his holiness should at the same time shine forth in all its glory, by such a public and awful condemnation of sin, as should demonstrate his infinite abhorrence of that accursed thing, with no less convincing evidence, than if the sword of justice had descended with unabated force upon the guilty heads of the criminals themselves.

This was done in the most effectual manner by the sufferings of his only-begotten and well-beloved Son, in that very nature which had offended. When he "who was in the form of God, and thought it not robbery to be equal with God, made himself of no reputation, took upon him the form of a servant, and being found in fashion as a man, humbled himself, and became obedient unto death, even the death of the cross; "—*then* indeed was "sin condemned in the flesh," and the righteousness of God not only revealed, but magnified, as it is written, (Rom. iii. 25, 26.) " God hath set forth his Son to be a propitiation, through faith in his blood, to declare [or manifest] his righteousness for the remission of sins: that he might be just," and appear to be so, "when he justifies those that believe in Jesus."—Thus, the sacrifice of Christ is the meritorious cause of that justification of the sinner, which not only delivers him from present condemnation, and future wrath; but, in consequence of the grant annexed to the sacrifice, doth likewise invest him with a right to life that shall never end, and even introduce him to the possession of that inestimable blessing. Hence believers are said, in the preceding chapter, to live *through* Christ, as the *propitiation* for their sins. " In this was manifested the love of God towards us, because that God sent his only begotten Son into the world, that we might live *through* him."—" Herein is love, not that we loved God, but that he loved us. and sent his Son to be the *propitiation* for our sins."

But there is an obvious difference between living *through*, or by means of Christ, and having life *in* Christ; which last is the form of expression in my text. Nothing less can be meant by a phrase of such intense signification, than 1*st*. That the Son, as Mediator, is in full possession of all that life which is the gift of the Father; 2*dly*. That he is the sole fountain or source form whence life flows to sinners of mankind; and, 3*dly*. That in him life is so effectually secured for all who believe on his name, that no adverse power shall be able to deprive them of it. And if we consult the lively oracles of truth, we shall find each of these particulars not only implied, but asserted, in the clearest and strongest terms.

The *first* is written as with a sun-beam on almost every page of this sacred book. "The Word was made flesh," saith our Apostle, in the 1st chapter of his gospel, at the 14th verse, "and we beheld his glory, the glory as of the only begotten of the Father, full of grace, and truth :— and of his fulness have all we received, and grace for grace." It was our Lord's own declaration, (John v. 26.) that "as the Father hath life in himself, so hath he given to the Son to have life in himself." Accordingly, St. Paul, speaking of the Son in his official character as head of the church, thus writes to the Colossians, (Coloss. i. 19) "It pleased the Father, that in him should all fulness dwell." And that none might mistake the nature of that *fulness*, he explains it by another passage in that same epistle, (Coloss. ii. 9.) "In him dwelleth all the fulness of the *Godhead* bodily." To which he subjoins these emphatical words, "Ye are complete in him." It is written, (John iii. 35.) "The Father loveth the Son, and hath given all things into his hand." This was the testimony of John the Baptist concerning him: who informs us in particular, that the *Spirit*, by which the dead sinner is quickened, and born into a new world, "was not given *by measure* unto him." And we are further assured, that he is now in possession of that heavenly kingdom, where the spiritual life, begun at the new birth in the hearts of his people, shall arrive at full maturity, and be enjoyed in perfection through all eternity. Thus it appears, that the Son, as Mediator, is possessed of all that life which is the Father's gift to sinners of mankind.

2*dly*. We are taught with equal plainness, that the Son hath the entire disposal of life, and is the sole fountain or source from whence it flows. Thus our Lord said to the Jews, (John v, 21.) "As the father raiseth up the dead, and quickeneth them, even so the Son quickeneth whom he will." In his conference with Martha at the sepulchre of her brother Lazarus, he styled himself the *resurrection* and the *life;* and added, "He that believeth in me. though he were dead, yet shall he live; and whosoever liveth, and believeth on me, shall never die." The *manner* of imparting this life he illustrates by the similitude of a vine and its branches. "I," said he, "am the vine, and ye are the branches. As the branch cannot bear fruit of itself, except it abide in the vine; no more can ye, except ye abide in me: For without me (or separated from me) ye can do nothing." Accordingly he gets the name of the *head*, from which all the body, by joints and bands having nourishment ministered, and knit together, increaseth with the increase of God. The *closeness* of this *union* is thus expressed, (1 Cor. vi. 17.) "He that is joined to the Lord is ONE SPIRIT." And the apostle Paul, in describing his own life as "a man in Christ," (Gal. ii. 20.) after having said, "I am crucified with Christ," he immediately subjoins, "nevertheless I live; yet not I, but *Christ liveth in me;* and the life which I now live in the flesh, I live by the faith of the Son of God, who loved me, and gave himself for me." And this leads to the

3*d* Particular I mentioned, as included in that strong expression, *This life is in his Son*, namely, That in him it is effectually *secured* for all that believe on him, so that no adverse power shall be able to deprive them of it. Nothing can be more explicit upon this head than our Lord's own words, (John x. 27. *et seq.*) "My sheep hear my voice, and I know them, and they follow me. And I give unto them eternal life, and they shall never perish, neither shall any pluck them out of my hand. My Father which gave them me is greater than all; and none is able to pluck them out of my Father's hand. I and my Father are one." It is probable that Paul had this declaration in his eye, when he thus wrote to the Christians at Colosse, (Coloss. iii. 3.) "your life is *hid* (that is, safely lodged) *with Christ* in God." Indeed the treasure was too precious to be committed to any creature. Of this, the example of Adam, in his greatest perfection, affords a striking proof. How soon was his own life, and the life of all his posterity, forfeited in his hands? Not the highest seraph, none other but Immanuel, God in our nature, was equal to the trust. But with him it is in absolute safety. He is able to keep that which the Father hath committed to him; and therefore, "because he liveth, all who have fled to him for refuge shall live also;" and may be fully assured, that "when he *who is their life* shall appear, then shall they likewise appear with him in glory." Accordingly, the apostle subjoins to my text, *He that hath the Son hath life.* He doth not say, he *shall* have life at some distant period, but he *hath* it already in present possession. And well might he say so, when he recollected these words of our Lord, which his own pen had recorded in the 6th chapter of his gospel, "*I* am the bread of life. *I* am the living bread which came down from heaven: if any man eat of this bread, he shall live for ever. As the living Father hath sent me, and I live by the Father; so he that eateth me, even he shall live by me." For how can he die who feedeth upon that which giveth life? and he surely must have life in all its extent and perfection, whose sustenance or aliment is no other than essential life itself.

Hence it appears, how much they mistake the gospel-constitution, who represent eternal life as a distant reward, suspended upon the performance of certain conditions on the part of the creature: whereas salvation through Christ, though perfected in heaven, is a present salvation; of which the various particulars, which are commonly styled *terms* of acceptance with God, are in truth constituent parts, suited to the present state of Christians; and ought therefore to be considered as the genuine actings, and consequently the proper evidences of life received from Christ, but not as the conditions or means of obtaining it. That our apostle viewed the matter in this light is evident from the 13th verse of this chapter; where, in the review of the large account he had given of the special duties that belong to believers, and the characters by which they are distinguished, he thus concludes: "These things have I written unto you that believe on the name of the Son of God, (not that ye may obtain, but) that ye may *know* that ye *have* eternal life," by the free gift of the Father, in consequence of your union with his blessed Son, who hath the fulness of life in his hand, as the *proprietor*, the *dispenser*, and the *guardian* thereof. For eternal life doth really commence at that happy moment, when, by the new birth, we enter into the family of God, and become his children through faith in Christ Jesus.

THUS far have I endeavored to illustrate the *record* that God hath given concerning his Son. Permit me then to ask, after all you have been hearing, in what light doth the God and Father of our Lord Jesus Christ now appear to you? Is he that object of terror which the jealousy of an evil conscience is apt to paint him? Can you rationally conclude, or is there even room to suspect, that he is an enemy to your happiness? Oh! with what eyes do they read this sacred volume, who are capable for a moment of entertaining such a thought. Is it not the obvious tendency, as well as the declared purpose of every thing contained in the Scriptures of truth, to prove what the apostle twice repeats in the preceding chapter, GOD IS LOVE.

What kind of evidence would satisfy you? It is my earnest desire that the question should be fully tried. My interest in the decision is equal to yours: none hath more to gain or to lose than I have.

Devise the security that you esteem most valid: let nothing be omitted that you can suppose would be of avail for binding the most artful and fallacious of your fellow-men; and when you have done, I challenge you to mention one article among them all that is wanting in the security which God hath freely afforded you.

When a bare *declaration* of one's good intention doth not satisfy us, we may ask a *promise;* and if doubts still remain, we may proceed to require the interposition of an *oath*, but there we must rest as to verbal security: "An oath for confirmation is an end of all strife." Need I remind you, that without your solicitation, God hath been graciously pleased to give you all these? "For God being willing more abundantly to shew unto the heirs of promise the immutability of his counsel, confirmed it by an oath, that by two immutable things, in which it was impossible for God to lie, we might have a strong consolation who have fled for refuge to lay hold upon the hope set before us."

When personal obligation is not deemed sufficient, a *cautioner*, or surety, is another expedient which human wisdom hath devised. And is not such an one provided by the great God? Not a creature, though of the highest order, but his *own Son*, by whom all things were made, even Jesus, the Mediator of the new covenant, who is expressly styled the *surety* of a better testament.

If, after all, any jealousy remains, we must next, I suppose, have recourse to *legal* security, and may demand a written obligation, a deed executed with every essential formality. Now, what kind of deed hath greatest force and validity? None, I apprehend, is more universally held sacred and inviolable than a *testament.* This was Paul's opinion, when he said, (Gal. iii. 15.) "Though it be but a man's testament, yet if it be confirmed, no man disannulleth, or addeth thereto." And are not we furnished with this very species of obligation?—a testament confirmed and rendered unalterable by the death of the testator; with this additional security against its being abstracted, erased, or defeated, by the infidelity of those to whom the execution of it may be committed, (security which never did, nor ever can, exist in any other case) namely, that the testator, who died to give it force, revived, and liveth for evermore, to be the executor of his own deed in its utmost extent.

Can any thing further be required? If distrust be very great, one might perhaps wish to have a valuable *pledge*, something of equal worth put into his hand, till the obligation be fulfilled. What shall I say? Let unbelief blush and be ashamed to open its mouth any more, when it looks to the *unspeakable gift of God*, and hears how Paul reasons upon it, (Rom. viii. 32.) "He that spared not his own Son, but delivered him up for us all, how shall he not with him also freely give us all things?" It is really astonishing, that such profusion of evidence should not excite in men a greater curiosity to discover the true reason and design of it. Were a superior transacting with us in the way of bargain, though he should profess that he meant to do us a favor, would not the offer of such multiplied, superabundant security for the performance of his part of the agreement, discover such an anxiety to get the bargain concluded, as would naturally breed in us a secret suspicion, that however moderate and equitable the terms proposed might appear, yet, upon the whole, the chief advantage would accrue to himself? Now, it is agreed on all hands, that to impute any such interested views to the great sovereign of the universe, would be equally absurd and blasphemous: for how differently soever men have conceived of the gospel-constitution, it is universally admitted to be a covenant of *grace.* And yet, my brethren, if eternal life be not a gift absolutely free, but the wages of service to be done by us, I cannot help thinking, that, let the terms proposed be ever so moderate, yet such means employed for gaining our consent to them, could hardly fail to tincture our minds with some degree of these evil surmisings I have mentioned. Whereas, upon the plan of the *record*, as expressed in my text, every part of the divine procedure appears perfectly wise, consistent, and gracious. *God* and *man* are represented in their proper characters: *God*, infinitely good, and independently happy; showing mercy to the miserable who derived their existence from him, and have nothing to give but what his own bounty hath bestowed upon them: *Man*, on the other hand, in his fallen state, a guilty, and, of consequence, a fearful, suspicious creature; conscious that he deserves punishment, and hard to be persuaded that there is so much goodness with God as freely to pardon his offences, and receive him again into favor. These *fears* beget and cherish that *enmity* against God, which is the distinguishing characteristic of the *carnal mind.* We feel the effects of injuries upon our own hearts, and we are apt to judge of God by what we feel in ourselves.

It was to vanquish this distrust, that God condescended to deal with us in the manner I have represented; that by giving us every kind of assurance that jealousy itself can devise, we may be reduced to this necessity, either to give God the lie; or, being convinced that he *is love*, to rely upon his faithful word of promise; believing that he who bestowed life at first, by a free act of the purest bounty, hath goodness enough to restore life after it hath been forfeited, by another act of as free mercy and grace. This is the plain account which the Scriptures give us of faith in Christ. "If we receive the witness of man," saith our apostle in the 9th verse of this chapter, "the witness of God is greater:" and, (John iii. 33.) receiving the divine testimony, is said to be a *setting to our seal* that God is *true.* Accordingly, in the verse preceding my text, unbelief is represented as deriving its chief malignity from this very circumstance, that it denies the *truth* of God: For thus it is written, "He that believeth not God, maketh him a liar; because he believeth not the record that God gave of his Son." *And this is the record, that God hath given to us eternal life; and this life is in his Son.*

You see then, upon the whole, one great end of the holy sacrament of our Lord's Supper, and the use we ought to make of it. Here Christ is represented to us as the propitiation for our sins; "suffering, the just for the unjust, that he might bring us to God." And we are assured, that in consequence of his obedience unto death, whereby the unchangeable righteousness of God was fully displayed, and infinitely glorified, he is now exalted to the throne, and hath eternal life committed to his disposal, that he may impart it to all who are made willing to receive it as the gift of his Father, through the merit of his blood. Now, it is the express command of God, that we believe on the name of his Son Jesus Christ: and it is the no less express declaration of the Son, that he will in nowise cast out such as come unto him. Nay, in this condescending ordinance, he cometh to us; and under the visible symbols of bread and wine, gives himself, with all the fulness of life that dwelleth in him, to every believing soul. What then is the counterpart that belongs to us? Is it not to behold and admire the amazing love of God, that we may be no more faithless, but believing?—Is it not to do what the Israelite was directed to do, when he brought the appointed sacrifice to the high priest? He laid his hand upon the head of the victim; and, confessing his sin over it, acknowledged, that he was dead in law; and that what remained of life was to be held by him purely in virtue of that pardon which God had graciously annexed to the sacrifice. In like manner, let us go to the altar of God; and over the memorials of that infinite sacrifice, chosen and accepted by the Father, in which his own dear Son is both the priest and the victim, let us acknowledge our forfeiture of life, and justify the sentence whereby we are condemned to die; explicitly declaring, in the sight of God, angels, and men, that renouncing every other claim, we thankfully accept eternal life, as the gift of God through Jesus Christ; and consent to hold it solely by *his* right, who died that we might live through him. *Amen.*

SERMON XXVI.

THE NEW AND LIVING WAY.

HEBREWS x. 19,—22.—"Having therefore, brethren, boldness to enter into the holiest by the blood of JESUS, by a new and living way which he hath consecrated for us through the vail, that is to say, his flesh; and having an High Priest over the house of GOD; let us draw near with a true heart, in full assurance of faith, having our hearts sprinkled from an evil conscience, and our bodies washed with pure water."

EVERY thinking person, whose mind hath been enlightened to form just apprehensions of God and of himself, will be anxious to obtain a satisfying answer to the following questions:

1. What encouragement hath a sinner to draw near to God? and,

2. After what manner shall he draw near to him, so as to find acceptance?

Some, I know, look upon them both as very easy subjects of inquiry. They have such low conceptions of the divine purity, and so high an opinion of their own dignity and worth, that they see little, if any occasion at all, for a reconciling Mediator to introduce them into the presence of God. They admit, that repentance for what hath been amiss appears highly reasonable, and perhaps may be necessary; but when, like men of candor and probity, they have confessed their faults, and humbled themselves so far as to ask forgiveness, and to promise amendment, then, they presume, that God is too generous to require any further reparation; that he will readily pardon what is past, and receive them into favor, as if they had never offended him.

But however such persons may magnify their own foolish imaginations, and arrogantly style them the dictates of reason; yet it might easily be demonstrated, that this scheme is absolutely irrational, and incapable of giving satisfaction to any serious, unprejudiced mind. Nothing can be more obvious, than that the Source of all being deserves the supreme love, and the most perfect unceasing obedience, of the creatures he hath made. This is the true law of nature, that is, a law founded in the nature of God and of man. It is no arbitrary constitution, but infinitely fit and reasonable in itself; and therefore equally incapable either of repeal or abatement; so that, in the language of our shorter catechism, every deviation from it deserves God's wrath and curse, both in this life and that which is to come. Nor would it be consistent with the holiness and justice of God, to remit the punishment, and receive the transgressor into favor, without such a public satisfaction to justice, as may testify his abhorrence of all unrighteousness, and his resolution to support the authority of his law, as effectually as the due unabated punishment of the sinner himself could do. These are the dictates of sound reason; and therefore all whose minds have been awakened to serious consideration, will be solicitous to know what encouragement they have to draw near to a holy and righteous God; and how they should approach him so as to find acceptance.

Now, to each of these inquiries the passages I have been reading, afford a direct and satisfying answer.

1. If any shall ask, What warrant or encouragement hath a creature, conscious of guilt, to draw near to a God of unspotted holiness and inflexible justice?

The apostle will inform him, that the chief of sinners (for this was the title he assumed to himself, 1 Tim. i. 15.) hath *boldness*, or (according to the marginal reading) *liberty to enter into the holiest by the blood of Jesus, by a new and living way, which he*, in the character of *High-Priest over the house of God, hath consecrated for us through the vail, that is to say, his flesh*, or that human nature in which he suffered, as a propitiatory sacrifice, or sin-offering, in our place.

It will readily occur to you, that all these peculiar forms of expression allude to the instituted means of access to God under the Mosaic dispensation; and it were to be wished, that Christians were better acquainted with that ancient worship than they commonly are; for without some knowledge of this kind, much, I need not say of the beauty and energy of the New Testament language, but even of its true meaning and import, must escape their observation.

The principal service of this day will not permit me to spend so much time as would be necessary for tracing out the several parts of the allusion with perspicuity and accuracy: it must at present suffice to give you a general view of the apostle's reasoning in the foregoing part of this epistle, with which my text is evidently connected, as an obvious inference and practical conclusion.

There we are informed, that the correspondence with the God of Israel, in all the public exercises of religious worship, was maintained and conducted by the intervention of the high-priest. None of the other Jews, of whatever rank or office, were permitted in person to approach the symbols of the divine presence. To him alone it belonged to pass through the curtain or vail, which separated the first tabernacle, wherein the ordinary priest ministered, from the second tabernacle, or holiest of all, which had the golden censer, and the ark of the covenant, with the cherubims of glory over it, shadowing the mercy-seat. "Into this second tabernacle," saith the apostle, at the 7th verse of the preceding chapter, "went the high-priest alone, once every year, not without blood, which he offered for himself, and for the errors of the people." He then proceeds to observe, that the office of high-priest, the worldly sanctuary and the various ordinances of divine service which belonged to it, were only *figures for the time then present;* and plainly shows, that they were all typical of, derived their significancy from, and received their full accomplishment in, the priesthood and sacrifice of Jesus Christ; who "by a greater and more perfect tabernacle, not made with hands, that is to say, not of this building; neither by the blood of goats and calves, but by his own blood, entered in once into the holy place, having obtained eternal redemption for us." After which, he goes on to prove, with great force and perspicuity, that what he calls the *first covenant, or* the *Mosaic constitution*, carried in its very form or aspect the most legible marks of imperfection and decay. No *permanent* high-priest belonged to it, that office being exercised by men compassed about with infirmities; each of whom, by death, gave place to his successor. Besides, the gifts and sacrifices they offered were, in their own nature, so mean and inconsiderable, "that they could not make him that did the service perfect, as pertaining to the conscience; for it was impossible that the blood of goats and calves should," by any intrinsic virtue, "take away sin." Nay, the repetition of these sacrifices was a plain confession of their weakness and insufficiency; as the apostle reasons most conclusively in the beginning of this chapter. "For the law," saith he, "having a shadow of good things to come, and not the very image of the things, can never, with those sacrifices which they offered year by year continually, make the comers thereunto perfect. For then," adds he in the form of a question, "would they not have ceased to be offered? because that the worshippers, once purged, should have had no more conscience of sins. But in those sacrifices there is a remembrance again made of sins once every year." Whereas Christ is an ever-living and unchangeable high-priest. The blood which he offered is of infinite worth and efficacy, being the blood of Emmanuel, God in our nature. Accordingly there is no repetition of his sacrifice; for thus the apostle proceeds at the 11th verse, "Every high-priest standeth daily ministering, and offering oftentimes the same sacrifices, which can never take away sins; but this man," this God-man, "after he had offered one sacrifice for sins, for ever sat down on the right hand of God; from henceforth expecting till his enemies be made his footstool. For by one offering he hath perfected for ever them that are sanctified." He is now gone to the heavenly sanctuary, "having finished trangression, made an end of sin, made reconciliation for iniquity, and brought in everlasting righteousness." And nothing remains for him to do but to bless his people with the free and irrevocable remission of their sins, according to that promise of the covenant, quoted verse 17. *their sins and iniquities will I remember no more;* and to dispense to all who are willing to receive (and to hold it by his right) that fulness of life which is lodged in his hand, as the "Saviour of the body," and the "King and Head over all things to the church."

This short review of the apostle's reasoning serves to throw light upon the passage I am further to discourse upon. We see how the *blood of Jesus* gives boldness or freedom to enter into the heavenly sanctuary, even by removing that guilt which separates us from God, and renders us incapable of holding friendly communion or intercourse with him. We likewise see a reason, why the way of admittance into the holiest is called not only a *new* but a *living* way. The entrance into the worldly sanctuary was indeed by blood; for, as the apostle had observed at the 22d verse of the preceding chapter, "almost all things," under the old dispensation, "were purged with blood; and without shedding of blood there is no remission." But then it was the blood of animals, inferior to man; which, after they were slain, were utterly consumed, and could live no more: Whereas the blood by which we now enter into the heavenly sanctuary, is the blood of him who hath life in himself; who, though he voluntarily submitted to death for a season, yet soon rose again from the grave by his own power; "who is now alive, and behold, he liveth for evermore, and hath the keys of hell and of death." We further learn upon what account his *flesh*, or human nature, gets the name of a *vail*, through which the new and living way into the holiest is consecrated for us. It was by becoming man that he was qualified to suffer in our place for the expiation of our guilt. In him we behold God clothed with the character of a *reconciler*, as the God of love, the God who is love. His flesh then, is such a vail, as doth not exclude from, but opens to give us admittance to a throne of grace; nay, Christ himself is the true propitiatory or mercy-seat: the sacrifice, the altar, and the high-priest, are all united in his wonderful person. In short, "he is the way, the truth, and the life;" the true, the living, and the only way to the Father.

Here then we are furnished with a clear and satisfying answer to the first question proposed, viz: What warrant or encouragement hath a guilty creature to draw near to a holy and righteous God? *Jesus the high priest over the house of God*, who suffered for us in *his flesh*, or human nature, hath, by "that offering and sacrifice of a sweet-smelling savor," *consecrated a new and living way* of access, whereby we have *boldness to enter into the most holy place*, and *draw near to God* under the sprinkling of his blood.

II. The answer to the second question, which regards the *manner* of our approach, is no less clearly expressed in the following words: "Let us draw near with a true heart, in full assurance of faith, having our hearts sprinkled from an evil conscience, and our bodies washed with pure water."

The 1*st* qualification is *a true heart*.

Truth is directly opposed to dissimulation or falsehood. *A true heart*, then, in *drawing near to God by the blood of Jesus*, must be a heart that corresponds to the profession we make; and what that profession is, in the case before us, may, with ease and certainty, be collected from what was delivered under the former head.

When we profess to enter into the holiest *by the blood of Jesus*, we explicitly renounce all pretensions or hopes of obtaining admittance by any other means. We acknowledge the forfeiture we have incurred by our guilt, and subscribe to the justice of the sentence that condemns us; we confess, that we have done, and can do, nothing to recommend us to the favor of God, or that may found the remotest claim to pardon and acceptance. All our own righteousness we throw aside as filthy rags. In short, we plead guilty at a tribunal of justice, and adopt the language of the publican, as expressing our true character, and the only form of address that befits our state, *God be merciful to me a sinner!*

When the Jew brought the sacrifice which the law had appointed for his offence, to the door of the tabernacle; when he laid his hand upon the head of the victim, confessing his sin over it, and then delivered it to the high-priest, that its blood might be shed for the expiation of his guilt; what was the true meaning and intent of that service? Did not the offender present the victim that it might be substituted in his place? Did he not thereby acknowledge that he had incurred the penalty of death; and that the dying agonies of the devoted animal were only a faint representation of what was strictly due to himself? Was not this a virtual renunciation of any right to the continuance of life, but what arose from the acceptance of the sacrifice in his room, and the gracious promise of remission annexed to that acceptance? And can any thing less than this be meant by *drawing near to God by the blood of Jesus?* Was there more virtue in the typical than in the real atonement? Or is less to be expected from the substance than from the shadow? Did the offending Jew, when he made his confession over the head of the victim, look back to any instances of past obedience, or even forward to any purposes of future amendment, and conjoin these with the blood of the sacrifice, for rendering it more effectual to obtain pardon and acceptance? Surely none who attended to the nature and form of the institution, could be led by it to dream of any mixture of this kind. And can we suppose that the *blood of Jesus, by which we have boldness to enter into the holiest*, is only a joint cause with our own imperfect obedience, of our obtaining admission into the heavenly sanctuary? Is no more meant by his *consecrating for us the new and living way*, than that he hath repaired the old way which sin had broken; and by removing some obstructions, rendered it more smooth and accessible than originally it was? Hath he, instead of paying to the last mite what justice demanded, done no more by his sacrifice, than purchased an easy composition of the debt, that an hundred pence might be accepted for the ten thousand talents? Is it possible that human pride and vanity can give such a coloring to this motley scheme, as to make it pass with any reasonable creature, for that marvellous doing of the Lord, that highest exertion of wisdom and grace, which angels themselves desire to look into? To account for this, we must have recourse to what the apostle Paul writes, (1 Cor. ii. 14.) "The natural man receiveth not the things of the Spirit of God; for they are foolishness unto him: neither can he know them, because they are spiritually discerned." He is become vain in his imaginations, and his foolish heart is darkened. But they whose eyes are opened by the Spirit of truth, will cordially join with the same apostle, and say as he did, (Philip. iii. 7, 8, 9.) "What things were gain to me, those I counted loss for Christ. Yea, doubtless, and I count all things but loss, for the excellency of the knowledge of Christ Jesus my Lord: and do account them but dung that I may win Christ, and be found in him, not having mine own righteousness, which is of the law, but that which is through the faith of Christ, the righteousness which is of God by faith." This is the language of a *true heart, in drawing near to God by the blood of Jesus;* which may suffice to explain the first qualification here mentioned. I do not say that no more is included in it; but this I affirm, that such an absolute renunciation of every other ground of hope, is one principal thing implied in the true heart, as it stands connected with the apostle's reasoning, if not the very thing he had most directly in his eye.

2dly. To *a true heart*, the apostle adds *the full assurance of faith.*

This leads us back to the great objects of faith that have already been presented to our view, *viz., the high-priest over the house of God;* the *vail* of his human nature, which is the passage into the sanctuary; and the *blood* of his sacrifice, that emboldens us to enter in: And it is required, that our faith in this way of access be full and assured.

The *true heart*, giving a faithful verdict upon the demerit of sin, and subscribing to the justice of the sentence, whereby the sinner is excluded from the presence of God, acknowledgeth this to be the *only* way. But faith advanceth a step farther, and presents it to the enlightened mind, as a safe, a sure, and infallible way. Hear its genuine language from the mouth of our apostle, (1 Tim. i. 15.) "This is a faithful saying, and worthy of all acceptation, that Christ Jesus came into the world to save sinners; of whom I am chief." Faith, contemplating the dignity of the High-Priest, and the nature and design of the sacrifice he offered, can have no doubt of the *merit* of his blood; but may conclude firmly, and without hesitation, that it hath sufficient efficacy to cleanse from all sin. But when it proceeds farther, and reads the commission he received from the Father; when it weighs the evidence that ariseth from his resurrection and ascension, of the Father's infinite delight in him, and his perfect satisfaction with his whole conduct as Mediator; above all, when it follows him into the heavenly sanctuary, whither he hath carried his atoning blood, and sees the reward conferred upon him for his voluntary obedience unto death, a name given him above every name, and all things in heaven and on earth put under his feet: What shall I say? from this entire view of God in Christ reconciling the world unto himself, can any other conclusion be drawn, than what the apostle John hath done before us, viz.,

God is love? So complete is the evidence afforded us in the gospel of God's merciful nature, and of the good-will he bears to the children of men, that the most entire credit to his declarations upon this head is in effect no more than a *setting to our seal*, to what one should think the most obvious and self-evident of all propositions, *that God is true.* And is there a man to be found that denies this proposition? Dare any be so outrageously insolent and injurious as to call God a *liar?* Let me refer you to the same apostle, who testified that God is love, for an answer to this question, and he will inform you, (1 John, v. 10.) that every one who believeth not the record that God hath given of his Son, maketh him a liar. This is a repetition of the first transgression, with peculiar circumstances of aggravation. *Unbelief* was the root of Adam's sin; for had he truly believed that the threatening was to be executed, he would not have dared to incur the penalty. And can it be less criminal to charge God with falsehood in a profession of kindness than in a threatening of displeasure? Nay, is it not a worse species of deceit to flatter with delusive hopes than to frighten with unreal terrors? and yet an unbeliever of gospel grace doth in effect charge God with this very species of deceit; and that not only in the face of the strongest repeated declarations of good-will, but against every kind of confirmation that the most distrustful suspicion could require or devise. Adam had no other restraint but a naked threatening; he had seen no exertion of punitive justice; every thing around him was expressive of the perfect goodness of its Author; and there was no precedent or example of the penalty with which the prohibition was enforced. But what have we in support of the gospel record? or rather, let me ask, What addition could be made to the evidence already afforded us, that it is faithful and true? We have the promise of God confirmed by his oath; we have the gift of his own Son to be the propitiation for our sins! we are not only permitted, but invited, nay, commanded, to come to the Saviour, with this most endearing declaration, that such as come to him shall in no wise be rejected or cast out by him. And shall not this accumulated, this superabundant evidence, deter us from the presumption of calling God a liar, or rather shall it not produce in us that *full assurance of faith*, with which the apostle exhorteth us to draw near to God by the blood of Jesus?

The *third* qualification, expressed in these words, *having our hearts sprinkled from an evil conscience*, is an advance upon the other two, and implies a personal application of the blood of Christ to ourselves; for it is this alone that, (as we read verse 14. of the preceding chapter) *can purge the conscience from dead works*, and vanquish those fears of wrath, which by representing God as an implacable enemy, drive us from his presence, and render him an object of terror and aversion, rather than of desire and love.

This personal application of the blood of sprinkling is too commonly considered in the light of a *privilege*, rather than as *a duty*. And a privilege it surely is; but such a privilege as we are strictly bound in duty to make use of: *For this*, saith the apostle John, *is the command of God, that we should believe on the name of his Son Jesus Christ;* which certainly includes more than a general persuasion, however full and assured, that Jesus is a necessary and sufficient Saviour. It can mean no less, than that they to whom the command is given, should believe on the name of Christ for *themselves*, and put their trust in him, as one who is both willing and able to save them in particular.

But the question may be put, and it hath been put by many, How am I to know that this obliging command is addressed to *me?* It might suffice for an answer, to desire those who ask the question, to turn over to that part of Scripture where the words I have just now quoted are recorded, 1 John iii. 23. There it is written, "This is his commandment, that we should *believe* on the name of his Son Jesus Christ, and *love one another*, as he gave his commandment."

Now, nobody doubts, that the last of these precepts extends to him; and yet the same authority which enjoins mutual love, commands us to believe on the Lord Jesus Christ; and the apostle you see, unites them both in one sentence. How comes it, then, that any should make a difference between the two, in point either of extent or obligation, or limit the one commandment any more than the other.

But as this is a difficulty with which the truly serious only are apt to be distressed, I must not stop here, but beg them to consider, whether it would not be more reasonable to put the question in this form: How do I know, or rather, What ground can I find to suspect, that the commandment to believe on the Saviour doth *not* extend to me? It is undeniable, that none of the human race are excepted by name; the invitation or call is addressed to men indefinitely: " Look unto me, and be ye saved, all the ends of the earth."—" Unto you, O men, I call, and my voice is to the sons of men." Say, then, my friends, under what fatal denomination can you find yourselves excluded from the fountain opened for sin and for uncleanness? Surely not as *sinners;* for this denomination is common to all men, and " Christ came not to call the righteous, but sinners to repentance;" this was his very errand, "to seek and to save that which was lost." Neither can it be as *great sinners;* for Paul testifies, that Christ came to save the *chief* of sinners. " His blood cleanseth from all sin;" and many examples are recorded of the most infamous transgressors, who have been washed, and sanctified, and justified, in the name of the Lord Jesus, and by the Spirit of our God. Much less then can it be as *deeply-convinced* and *self-condemning* sinners; for under this denomination you are expressly invited to have recourse to him: " Come unto me all ye that labor, and are heavy laden, and I will give you rest." The commission he received was to bind up the broken-hearted, to bring forth the prisoners out of the prison-house, and to comfort those that mourn. Are you *wretched, miserable, poor, blind, and naked?* Such precisely was the state of the Laodiceans, with this only difference, from whence no discouraging inference can be drawn, that they *knew it not,* whereas you do: yet even to them were these gracious words addressed by our Lord himself, (Rev. iii. 18.) " I counsel thee to buy of me gold tried in the fire, that thou mayest be rich; and white raiment, that thou mayest be clothed; and to anoint thine eyes with eye-salve, that thou mayest see." Nay, (which methinks should put an end to all further questioning upon this head) the epistle directed to them concludes with that unlimited offer of gospel-grace, which might justly be introduced with a note of admiration, " BEHOLD, I stand at the door and knock; if *any* man will hear my voice, and open the door, I will come in to him, and sup with him, and he with me." Beware then of setting bounds where God hath set none. If you feel your need of Christ as the *only* Saviour; if your eyes have been so far opened, as to see that he is worthy to be depended upon, and " mighty to save," let no objections drawn from your own unworthiness, which, under the covert and semblance of humility, hides the daring presumption of giving God the lie, keep you back from this great *High-Priest,* or prevent your application of his atoning blood, for *sprinkling your hearts from an evil conscience,* and introducing you into *the holiest with* filial *boldness, by that new and living way which he hath consecrated for you, through the vail of his flesh.*

WHAT the apostle subjoins, *having our bodies washed with pure water,* may allude to those purifications enjoined by the law, which served to remind the Jews of the unspotted holiness of the God of Israel, and of that reverence which ought to possess their minds in all their approaches to his gracious presence; though I cannot help thinking, that these words were intended by the apostle to introduce a new exhortation; and ought therefore to be transferred to the following verse: in which case, without any straining, they obviously apply to the ordinance of baptism, and are urged, with great propriety, to enforce a steadfast, unwavering adherence to that faith which the converted Hebrews had professed with such solemnity, when, at their admission into the church of Christ, their *bodies were washed with pure water,* in the name of the Father, Son, and Holy Ghost.

But I shall not detain you any longer from the proper business of the day. Only let me call upon you, before I conclude, to look up to this great *High-Priest over the house of God*, for that Holy Spirit, without whom neither sermons nor sacraments have any virtue or efficacy. It is he alone that can bestow upon us the qualifications here required. Let each of us then plead the promise of the Father, begging, that the Spirit of all grace may be given, "to take of the things of Christ's, and to shew them unto us;" that from just views of our High-Priest, and of the new and living way he hath consecrated for us by his blood, we may be enabled to draw near to God *with true hearts, in the full assurance of faith;* and receive such tokens of his love while we sit at his table, as shall be an earnest and pledge to us, of that still more near and joyful approach to him in the heavenly sanctuary; where we shall no more see him in the glass of ordinances, but face to face; where we shall be thoroughly changed into his image, and enjoy him fully without interruption, and without end. *Amen.*

SERMON XXVII.

AS ENEMIES AND FRIENDS OF CHRIST.

ROMANS v. 10.—"For if, when we were enemies, we were reconciled to GOD by the death of his SON; much more being reconciled, we shall be saved by his life."

THE grounds of a Christian's faith and hope are not only sufficient to satisfy his own mind, but capable likewise of being described and vindicated, in such a manner as cannot fail to give full satisfaction to every sober unprejudiced inquirer.

Genuine Christianity is far from declining any means of trial, whereby truth is distinguished from delusion or imposture: on the contrary, it courts the light; and the more severely it is tried, the brighter it shines: "The words of the Lord are pure words, like silver tried in a furnace of earth, and purified seven times." The evidence by which our faith and hope are supported hath already stood the test of many generations; and the most violent attacks of its enemies, instead of shaking the foundation, have only served to show that it is laid by that same Almighty Hand which created and upholdeth these heavens and this earth. Nay, these heavens, and this earth, shall at length pass away; but one jot or one tittle, in these lively oracles of wisdom and truth, shall in no wise pass away till all be fulfilled.

The privileges of a Christian are not a picture drawn by fancy, neither doth his comfort take its rise from those inexplicable impressions to which the dreaming enthusiast is constrained to resort. The intelligent believer stands upon firm ground, and is always "ready to give an answer to every man that asketh him a reason of the hope that is in him."

Do you inquire into the *object* of his hope, he will tell you without hesitation, that he looks for a portion after death; in comparison whereof, this earth which we inhabit, and all that it contains, shrink into nothing, yea, less than nothing, and vanity.

Whatever we behold in this material world hath the seeds of dissolution sown in its very nature. Our bodies themselves are only tabernacles of clay, which ere long shall be crumbled into dust, and see corruption.

Here we breathe, as it were, in the midst of contagion and defilement; and the best things we enjoy are liable to be perverted, either into the instruments or occasions of sin. Honor tempteth to pride, power to oppression, and affluence to sensuality and criminal indulgence. Few, comparatively speaking, can carry with an even and steady hand the full cup of prosperity any length of way; like Jeshurun, they are apt to kick when they wax fat, and lightly to esteem the Rock of their salvation.

Nay, though they should escape the pollution of these earthly enjoyments, by using them with moderation, and employing them to the purposes for which they were designed; yet so precarious and fugitive are all sublunary things, that it is impossible for any man to promise upon their continuance. Who can say, "My mountain standeth strong, I shall never be moved?" Can any man guard himself at all times against secret fraud and open violence? Nay, every element, the wind, the fire, the water, may in a moment be armed with sufficient force to make the unwelcome separation betwixt us and the best of our worldly possessions.—Thus corruptible and defiled, thus uncertain and transitory, is all that is most admired and courted here below.

Not so the portion of the saints; the inheritance they look for is "incorruptible, undefiled, and fadeth not away." As it hath no principle of decay within itself, so neither can it be wasted by any thing from without. It is "reserved," or laid up, "for them in heaven:" a place of absolute safety, beyond the reach of every adverse power, and equally secured against deceit and rapine. *There* is no thief to steal, no spoiler to lay waste. In those regions of perfect light and love, no such piteous complaints are heard as these,—"My bowels! my bowels! I am pained at my very heart, because thou hast heard, O my soul! the sound of the trumpet, and the alarm of war." All above is order and harmony; there is nothing to hurt, nothing to destroy, through the whole extent of the heavenly Jerusalem, that imperial seat of Zion's King.—Such, can the believer say, is the *object* of my hope.

Do you inquire into the *grounds* of his hope, he hath an answer ready in the words of my text, and can say with the apostle Paul,—*If, when we were enemies, we were reconciled to God by the death of his Son; much more being reconciled, we shall be saved by his life.*

Here the reasoning is at once profound and obvious; it is simple and ingenious at the same time: so simple and obvious, that the mind, with one glance, perceives its force, and is satisfied; so profound and ingenious, that the more accurately it is examined, the more conclusive it will appear.

From the efficacy of Christ's death, which the apostle had proved at large in the foregoing part of this epistle, he infers, in this passage, the superior efficacy of his restored life: I say, his *restored life;* for the life here referred to, was not that life previous to his crucifixion, which he led upon earth in the form of a servant; but the life he now lives at the right hand of God, where he is exalted to the throne as a Prince and a Saviour, "having a name given him above every name, that at the name of Jesus every knee should bow, and every tongue confess, that he is the Lord, to the glory of God the Father."

Two comparisons are here stated; the *one* betwixt the past and present state of believers; formerly they were *enemies* to God, now they are become *friends.* The *other* comparison is betwixt the past and present condition of the Saviour; once he was *dead,* now he is *alive.* And the proposition that connects the two is this, That *reconciliation* to God was entirely owing to the death of Christ, as the meritorious procuring cause. These are the premises from whence the apostle draws his conclusion, and proves, with demonstrative evidence, the absolute certainty of the complete and everlasting salvation of believers.

The only principle he assumes, is what every one must admit as soon as it is mentioned, *viz.*, that reconciliation to an enemy is a more difficult exercise of goodness than beneficence to a friend. Upon which he thus reasons, That if the *death* of Christ had sufficient virtue to produce the greater effect, *viz.*, reconciliation to those who formerly were enemies, there can be no room to doubt that the *life* of Christ, which is a more powerful cause, must be sufficient to produce the lesser effect; lesser I mean in point of difficulty, namely, the continuance of the divine friendship and beneficence to those whom his death hath reconciled, till he bring them in due time to the full possession of the purchased inheritance.

Say then, my brethren, may not the hope of a Christian be justly denominated a rational hope, or, as the apostle terms it, (verse 5.) "a hope that maketh not ashamed?" And may not the believer reply, with holy exultation, to every one that asketh a reason of the hope that is in him, *If, when I was an enemy, I was reconciled to God by the death of his Son, much more being reconciled, I shall be saved by his life:* his death was the price of the inheritance I look for; and his restored life is my evidence that the price was accepted, and the purchase made. This renders my hope assured and vigorous. Did it depend upon any thing in myself, on the strength, or wisdom, or worthiness, of the creature, it would quickly languish and die; but as it leans upon him who rose from the grave to die no more, who ascended up on high, leading captivity captive, and is now exalted at the right hand of God, it is become "an anchor of the soul, both sure and steadfast:" for the Father raised him from the dead, and gave him glory, for this very end, that every ground of jealousy being removed, my faith and hope might be in God.—1 Pet. i. 21.

It must already have occurred to you, that none can apply this reasoning to themselves, but those who are previously *reconciled to God by the death of his Son.* Here begins the hope of a sinner; and here likewise must I begin to bring the subject home to our own hearts, by inquiring, who among us can say that we have experienced this blessed fruit of the Redeemer's death?

And for our assistance in this important trial, I shall endeavor, in few words, to mark out some of the principal steps, by which the soul is most usually led by the Spirit of God unto a vital union with the Lord Jesus Christ; who of God is made unto all that believe in him, wisdom, and righteousness, and sanctification, and redemption.

A deep conviction of guilt and misery doth certainly lie at the root of this important change. The sinner seeth himself to be all pollution, naked, and defenceless, having nothing to screen him from the wrath of that Almighty Being whom he hath offended. This constrains him to look about for deliverance. The wrath of God is intolerable: he cannot dwell with devouring flames, he cannot lie down in everlasting burnings; and though he is conscious that he hath justly merited this misery, yet self-preservation, that strong principle implanted in his nature by the great Author of his being, obligeth him to ask the question, Is there no hope?

Here, indeed, many steal away from under their burden, take shelter in some refuge of lies, and encompass themselves about with sparks of their own kindling; but the sinner that is under the conduct of the Spirit of God (and of such only I at present speak,) the more he considers his case, the more hopeless and desperate he findeth it to be. He indeed asketh the question, What shall I do? but feeling his impotence, answers, I can do nothing; or though I could do any thing, yet what would it avail me? Can the duty I owe at present make any reparation for the offences that are past? Will forbearing to contract new debt entitle me to a discharge of the old? Impossible! In short, when he casts his eyes abroad throughout the whole creation, he can find nothing at all to lean upon for deliverance. And thus, as the apostle expresseth it, (Gal. iii. 23.) he is "shut up unto the faith," hedged about, as it were, on every side; so that neither himself, nor any other creature, can make a way for his escape.

Being reduced to this condition, he listens with eagerness to the tidings of a Saviour. The name *Jesus* hath a different sound to him than ever it had before; and his very heart leaps within him, when he hears that "God was in Christ reconciling the world unto himself, not imputing their trespasses unto them." But he cannot rest satisfied with a general account of this matter. As his danger is real and pressing, he seeks a clear discovery of the method of deliverance. Felt distress breeds concern and anxiety; a self-condemned criminal cannot quiet his mind with the bare probability of a pardon: he therefore narrowly pries into the authority, the character, and the ability of the Saviour. He looks into his *commission*, and is wonderfully pleased to read such a plain declaration as this, (Isa. xlii. 6, 7.) "I the Lord have called thee in righteousness, and will hold thine hand, and will keep thee, and give thee for a covenant of the people, for a light of the Gentiles; to open the blind eyes, to bring out the prisoners from the prison, and them that sit in darkness out of the prison-house." He rejoiceth to hear the Father himself proclaiming with an audible voice from heaven, first at his baptism, and afterwards at his transfiguration, "This is my beloved Son, in whom I am well pleased." He then proceeds to consider his admirable fitness for the office and work of a Saviour, as being the eternal Word made flesh, Emmanuel, God in our nature. He reviews the whole history of his actions and sufferings; sees him offering up the sacrifice to divine justice; hears him cry on the cross, "It is finished;" beholds him rising from the grave in testimony of the divine acceptance, ascending up on high to receive the kingdom, where he ever liveth to make intercession for transgressors, and to dispense the gifts he purchased with his blood, having all power committed to him in heaven and on earth; from all which he discovers abundant reason to conclude that "he is able to save to the uttermost all that come unto God by him."

Having thus found a Saviour exactly suited to his necessities, he now begins to conceive some hope; he sees a possibility of obtaining salvation; and is satisfied, that if this Saviour will undertake his cause, he hath no reason to despair; he therefore anxiously inquires, how, or by what means, he may procure his aid, and be admitted to partake of the blessings he hath purchased. Here it is that the great adversary usually makes his most vigorous efforts, and puts forth all his force and artifice, to shipwreck the poor soul on the very shore of salvation. He endeavors to make that consciousness of guilt which first brought the sinner to see his need of a Saviour, now to appear an objection against coming to him for deliverance. He will tell him, that though others may be forgiven, yet surely he cannot; that the greatness of his sins, or his long continuance in them, place him beyond the reach of his saving power, or at least render him an improper object for his merciful interposition. Hereby the poor creature is either driven to despair, or else to a vain and fruitless search after something in himself to recommend him to the Saviour. And the last of these temptations is so adapted to the pride of our nature, which would always have something to boast of, that with many it proves too fatally successful; neither is it soon, nor easily overcome by any. But the soul that is guided by the Spirit of God, is here led to see the extent and freedom of the gospel-offer and call; that Jesus is a Saviour for the chief of sinners; that the wretched, the miserable, the poor, and blind, and naked, are the very persons to whom his gracious invitations and counsels are addressed; that he interposed for our relief, not because we were worthy of his aid, but because we needed his aid; and that a sense of extreme need, accompanied with a humble and thankful acceptance of the unspeakable gift of God to men, is all that is looked for on the part of the creature.

Upon this the sinner, renouncing his own righteousness as filthy rags, or, as it is elsewhere expressed, "having no confidence in the flesh," comes to him, judging and condemning himself, without any plea but his extreme necessity, and the infinite and undeserved mercy of God; having no answer to the law, but the merit of Christ's obedience unto death, nor any other shelter from avenging justice. This is what the apostle, in the verse following my text, calls *receiving the atonement;* because then the sinner is made a partaker of Christ's sacrifice, his peace-speaking blood is sprinkled upon him, and covers him so entirely, that from head to foot, if I may use that expression, no part of him is left exposed to that fiery indignation which shall finally consume all the adversaries of God.

And now let me ask, Who among you can say that you have experienced such a work of grace upon your hearts?—For the just encouragement of those who are thus *reconciled to God by the death of his Son,* I shall, in further illustration of the apostle's reasoning, endeavor to show the powerful influence of the *life* of Christ upon every thing that belongs to their complete salvation.

1*st.* The *justification* of believers, which was purchased by the death of Christ, is rendered sure and permanent by his restored life. Upon this the apostle lays a peculiar emphasis, (Rom. viii. 34.) where, in support of that triumphant challenge, "Who shall lay any thing to the charge of God's elect?" having said, "It is Christ that died," he immediately subjoins, "yea rather, that is risen again, who is even at the right hand of God, who also maketh intercession for us."

From whence can a sentence of condemnation proceed? Is it not from that very throne to which our once crucified Redeemer is raised, that he may confer that remission which he purchased with his blood? And now that he is entered into his glory, shall the indictment that he nailed to his cross be taken down from thence, and put in suit against those who, in obedience to his Father's command, have fled to him for refuge? Impossible! As he bowed his head upon the cross to expiate our guilt, so he lifted it up again when he rose from the grave, that he might effectually apply the merit of his sacrifice, and obviate every charge that could be brought against his people.

2dly. The life of Christ is no less available to insure the *sanctification* of all who believe on him. For what end did he enter into the heavenly sanctuary, but that from thence he might send forth his conquering Spirit to cleanse and purify the hearts of those whom he had washed with his blood; that as no guilt might be left to provoke the justice of God, so neither should there be any defilement to offend his holiness. It is impossible to doubt, that a Redeemer in glory will at length present to his Father "a glorious church, without spot, or wrinkle, or any such thing." Surely Christ is not gone to heaven, to leave that blood to run waste which he shed upon earth, or to be negligent in improving the virtue of his sacrifice. That prayer, "Father, sanctify them through thy truth," hath as loud a sound from his illustrious throne, as it had from the footstool, when he was just about to enter upon his agony and sufferings. He did not utter these words upon the confines of his kingdom, to forget or disuse them when he should enter upon the possession of it. What he prayed for in his humiliation, he hath power to dispense in his exalted state; and he will do it to all who put their trust in him; he will gradually adorn them with the beauties of holiness, and keep them by his power through faith unto salvation. Which leads me to observe,

In the *third* place, That the life of Christ doth effectually secure an honorable issue to all the *afflictions* and *temptations* of his people. It is the same person that was crucified on earth, who is now crowned with glory in the highest heavens; and though he dropped the infirmities of that body he had assumed, and left all the weakness of humanity behind him in the grave; yet he carried his pitying nature to the throne, and is still touched with the feeling of our infirmities, and disposed to help us in every time of need. "He will not break the bruised reed, nor quench the smoking flax." He knows our frame; he remembers that we are dust; and will therefore "debate with us in measure, and stay his rough wind in the day of his east wind."

And with regard to temptations, the life of Christ affords the most comfortable assurance, that over these we shall be finally victorious. He that suffered being tempted, will certainly be disposed to succor those that are tempted; and there can be no room to doubt, that he is as able as he is willing. If, while in the form of a servant, he defeated all the artifices of the cunning serpent, and repelled the most violent attacks of the roaring lion; if in his lowest state of abasement, even while he hung upon the cross, he spoiled principalities and powers, making a show of them openly; now that all power is committed to him both in heaven and on earth, can he want either wisdom or strength to bruise Satan under the feet of the weakest of his servants? Impossible! While the head of the body reigns in glory, we may be well assured, that no member can become the prey of any adverse power; so that every believer may adopt the language of Paul, and say as he did, "Who shall separate us from the love of Christ? shall tribulation, or distress, or persecution, or famine, or nakedness, or peril, or sword? Nay, in all these things we are more than conquerors, through him that loved us. For I am persuaded, that neither death nor life, nor angels, nor principalities, nor powers, nor things present, nor things to come, nor height, nor depth, nor any other creature, shall be able to separate us from the love of God, which is in Christ Jesus our Lord." Once more,

4thly. The life of Christ secures to his people the *resurrection* of their bodies, and the happiness of the whole man, in the full and everlasting enjoyment of God.

As Adam, by his apostasy, became the source of death to all his natural descendants; so Christ, by his expiatory sufferings, and the glory that followed, is become the fountain of life to all his spiritual offspring; who accordingly are said to be "begotten again to the lively hope of an inheritance that is incorruptible, and undefiled, and that fadeth not away; and that by means of his resurrection from the dead. Hence the second Adam is called *a quickening Spirit*, having the same virtue and efficacy to convey all the fulness of life to those who are new born into the family of God, that the first Adam had to transmit death to his posterity. It was not the soul of Christ only, but his body also, that was exalted and crowned with honor: in like manner shall the bodies of believers be rescued from the grave, and raised to glory, seeing these were redeemed by Christ as well as their souls. Nay, the bodies of the saints are said expressly to be "the temples of the Holy Ghost;" and it cannot be supposed, that these temples shall remain always under the ruins of death. He who honored them with his residence, will certainly rebuild them in due time: as the apostle reasons, (Rom. viii. 11.) "If the Spirit of him that raised up Jesus from the dead dwell in you; he that raised up Christ from the dead, shall also quicken your mortal bodies, by his Spirit that dwelleth in you." Then shall that song be sung by all the redeemed company newly raised from the dust, "Death is swallowed up in victory." "O death, where is now thy sting? O grave, where is now thy victory? The sting of death was sin, and the strength of sin was the law; but thanks be unto God, who hath now given us the victory through Jesus Christ our Lord."

Thus have I endeavored to lead you through a very extensive, but surely a pleasant and fruitful field, wherein a variety of objects have occurred, interesting to all, and peculiarly comfortable to the people of God; upon whom I therefore call, in the conclusion of my discourse, to praise and magnify that compassionate Saviour, and faithful High-Priest over the house of God, who ransomed them with his blood; and amidst all the splendors of his exalted state, is not unmindful of his charge upon earth, but continually appears in the presence of God for them; whose ear is always attentive to the voice of their supplications; whose mouth is ever open to plead in their behalf; and as if it had not been love enough to die for them, still lives and reigns for them, and even glories in being "the head over all things to the church, which is his body, the fulness of him that filleth all in all." To him, with the Father, and quickening Spirit, the one living and true God, be glory and honor, thanksgiving and praise, for ever and ever. *Amen.*

SERMON XXVIII.

THE CHRISTIAN'S RELATION TO IDOLS.

Hosea, xiv. 8.—"Ephraim shall say, What have I to do any more with Idols?"

If we compare the representation here given of Ephraim, with the account we have of him (ch. iv. 17.) we shall discover such a wonderful change, as must excite in us a desire to be acquainted with the cause of it. *There* it is said, "Ephraim is joined to idols;" *Here* we behold him throwing them away, with every symptom of contempt and abhorrence. Like a man awakened from a dream, or rather like one who had lost his reason, and was now restored to the right use of it, he saith, *What have I to do any more with idols?* —It is my disgrace, no less than my crime, that ever I had any thing to do with such lying vanities; but now I cast them from me with scorn and detestation, and with a determined purpose, that I shall never henceforth return to them any more.

How is this surprising change to be accounted for? When God said, "Ephraim is joined to idols," he immediatly pronounced that awful decree, "Let him alone." Hereby a restraint was laid upon every outward instrument. All the creatures were charged, by the highest authority, to give him no disturbance in the course of his idolatry, but to leave him entirely to his own conduct, and the unabated influence of the idols he had chosen. By what means then was his recovery brought about? Had Ephraim the honor to discover the delusion by his own sagacity, and to break the enchantment by his own strength? We find an answer to these questions, (chap. xiii. 9.) "O Israel, thou hast destroyed thyself, but IN ME is thy help." Had God said, *I am deter-*

mined to let Ephraim alone, there would have been an end of him at once, though the whole creation had been left at liberty to exert its utmost activity for his help; but it deserves our notice, that though God laid a restraint upon the agency of the creatures, yet he laid no restraint upon his own, but reserved to himself the full exercise of his essential and unalienable prerogative, to be the free and sovereign disposer of his grace.

In this character he is introduced at the first verse of this chapter, where he issues forth his royal command, and clothes it with power: "O Israel, return unto the Lord thy God, for thou hast fallen by thine iniquity." In order to encourage their hope of acceptance, he teacheth them in the following verses how to pray, and even dictates the very form of surrender they were to make; "Take with you words, and turn to the Lord; say unto him, Take away all iniquity, and receive us graciously; so will we render the calves of our lips. Ashur shall not save us, we will not ride upon horses, neither will we say any more to the works of our hands, Ye are our gods; for in thee the fatherless findeth mercy." After which, to remove that distrust and jealousy which necessarily spring from a consciousness of guilt, he goes on to declare his sovereign purpose, expressed in the most comprehensive and absolute terms, of dispensing to them, and conferring upon them, his pardoning mercy and sanctifying grace: "I will heal their backsliding, I will love them freely; for mine anger is turned away from him. I will be as the dew unto Israel," &c. In consequence whereof, he foretells, in the words of my text, that Ephraim, who, till then, had been joined to idols, should find himself disposed and enabled to say, not with his lips only, but from an effectual principle of new life in his heart, *What have I to do with idols any more?*

From this view of my text, as it stands connected with other passages in this book that relate to Ephraim, and more especially with the verses immediately preceding, four observations obviously arise, which I propose to illustrate in the following discourse.

1. That a sinner, in his natural state, is joined to idols.

2. That to separate a sinner from idols, is a work that is altogether peculiar to God.

3. That this separation is effected by the discovery and application of pardoning mercy and sanctifying grace. And,

4. That every one who is a partaker of these important benefits will, and must, adopt the words of Ephraim in their most extensive meaning, and say as he did, *What have I to do any more with idols?*

I. My first observation is, That a sinner in his natural state, is joined to idols.

Herein consisteth the essence of man's apostasy. Something that is not God is the object of his supreme love, and possesseth that place in his heart which is due only to the living and true God; and that thing, by what name soever it may be distinguished, is properly an *idol.* Now this world, and the things of the world, its riches and pleasures, and honors, which the apostle John, by a strong and significant figure, calls "the lust of the eye, the lust of the flesh, and the pride of life;" these are the great rivals of God, which, ever since the fatal apostasy, have usurped the throne in the human heart. I am unwilling to mention the profane rites by which some of these idols are worshipped by many: they are too shocking to be named, and, at the same time, so notorious as to render a detail of them superfluous. It is by no means necessary for proving the charge of idolatry, that I should lead your imagination through the various scenes of injustice, oppression, and cruelty, or into the foul haunts of lewdness and riotous excess. Many of these vices may be deemed *unnatural* to man even in his fallen state; and though the carnal mind may be enmity against God, yet I am verily persuaded, that the carnal mind itself doth often suffer a considerable degree of violence, before it can be fully reconciled to the practice of them. It is sufficient for my purpose to affirm, what daily observation puts beyond all doubt, viz., that this present world, in one shape or other, is loved and served in preference to God, by every man, without exception, who hath no other principle of life than what he derived from the first Adam. Here he finds the supply of his bodily wants, and all that kind of provision that suits his animal nature, and gratifies those appetites which he hath in common with the inferior creatures. And though he is often, or rather always, disappointed in his expectation; yet, being unacquainted with any better sustenance than this earth affords, he only makes new experiments, persists in seeking his portion here below, and will continue to do so, till, by some means or other, he get a mind to discern those spritual objects, and an appetite to relish those spiritual enjoyments, which are the proper food of the soul, the only aliment whereby its real life and well-being can be supported. Hence it already appears, in some measure,

II. That to separate a sinner from idols, must be the peculiar work of God himself; which was the second observation I proposed to illustrate.

The natural man, as I just now said, may change the *object* of his devotion; and having experienced the vanity of any particular idol, he may say concerning it, "What have I to do any more with thee?" Such a change as this is abundantly common, it is easy, nay it is necessary: it requires no exertion of strength: weakness itself is sufficient to produce it, being no other than the natural, the unavoidable, consequence of satiety and disgust. But amidst ten thousand changes of this kind, the man is only turning from one idol to another; and though he may pass from grosser ones to others more refined; from mere bodily indulgence to the amusements of science; or, perhaps, from the gratification of selfish and turbulent passions to the cultivation and practice of some public and social virtues; yet still he stops short of God: all the objects of his pursuit belong to the present state of things; and he aspires to no higher felicity than may be gathered from the materials of this earth which he inhabits.

Accordingly, the conversion of a sinner, or the turning him from idols to the true God, is every where throughout the Scriptures represented as the effect of omnipotent creating power. It is called a *new creation*, a being *born again*, a *resurrection*, a *passing from death to life*. Nor are these expressions metaphorical, but strictly just; they are the words not of truth only, but of soberness. The apostate creature is really *dead*, in the truest and most importent sense of that word. For what is natural death, as it is commonly styled? The soul, when separated from the body, doth not cease to exist; and though the body itself moulders into dust, yet no particle of that dust is annihilated or lost. The principal effect of that humiliating event, is to put an end to the creature's connection with a present world; the man ceases to be any more an inhabitant of this earth: and when we say he is dead, this is all we commonly mean to express.

Now sin hath broken our connection with the spiritual world, as really as the separation of the soul from the body will break our connection with this material world; and therefore, without any metaphor, sin is the death of the soul or spirit of the man, whereby it is cut off from the source of life, and utterly disabled to relish those employments or pleasures which alone can render a spiritual being happy. And in this state it must remain, till the same power that gave it existence at first shall create it anew, and restore those faculties which sin had destroyed, of acting and enjoying according to its true and proper nature.

The use of this observation is twofold; *first*, that those who are turned from idols may, with humble gratitude, give God the glory, and cheerfully trust in him for perfecting the change his grace hath begun; and, *secondly*, That they who are conscious that they are still joined to idols, may immediately, and without any circuit, go directly to the Fountain of life, even the Father of spirits, who is in Christ Jesus reconciling the world unto himself, and cry as they can, for new life, from him who quickeneth the dead, and calleth those things that be not as though they were.

But how doth God quicken the dead in trespasses and sins, and separate the sinner from his idols?

III. My third observation is the answer to this question. He doth it by the discovery and application of his pardoning mercy and sanctifying grace. I join these together, because they are so inseparably connected, that neither of them can exist apart; "for whom God justifies, them he also sanctifies." And both of them are expressly mentioned in the context, as the means by which Ephraim should be disposed and enabled to say, *What have I to do any more with idols?*

The discovery of pardoning mercy is the first means employed for working this change. Fear is the immediate consequence of guilt, which soon degenerates into hatred, or that emnity against God which is the distinguishing characteristic of the carnal mind. No sooner had Adam sinned than he became afraid of his Maker, and preposterously endeavored to flee from his presence. This fear is the natural inheritance of his children. God appears as an enemy to the guilty soul; and so long as he is viewed in that light, it is impossible that he can be the object of its love. But the report of pardoning mercy presents him in a light so suited to the necessities of the apostate creature, that in proportion as it is believed, the sinner is encouraged to look to him with hope. And when the evidence of this report is so fully seen, as to vanquish distrustful, tormenting fear; when the blessed record gains entire credit, "that God hath given to us eternal life, and that this life is in his Son," whom he hath set forth to be a propitiation through faith in his blood; that, without staining the honor of his justice, a way might be opened for the free exercise of mercy to the chief of sinners; then God becomes the object both of love and confidence, and appears so completely amiable, that, in comparison of him, those idols which the soul formerly desired, stripped of their delusive charms, are regarded with contempt, nay, renounced with abhorrence.

Now, if the believing views of God's pardoning mercy have this effect, how powerful must the experience of it be, when accompanied, as it always is, with his sanctifying grace? When the soul hath not only seen, but tasted, that the Lord is gracious, and that in him the fatherless findeth mercy; when God saith, (as in verse 4th) "I will heal their backslidings, I will love them freely, for mine anger is turned away;" especially when, as it follows, he becomes "as the dew unto Israel," causing the influences of his Spirit to descend upon the soul, whereby the barren wilderness is turned into a fruitful field; above all, when the great Lord of the vineyard comes into his garden, to eat his pleasant fruits; or, to drop the allusion, when the soul, washed, and sanctified, and justified, hath experienced the ineffable delights of fellowship with the Father, and with the Son, through the Spirit;—then the victory over the world is completed, and the person will be enabled to say without any reserve, *What have I to do any more with idols?*

IV. My fourth and last observation was, that these words of Ephraim, in their most extensive meaning, will, and must be adopted by all, without exception, upon whom God hath been pleased to confer his pardoning mercy, and his sanctifying grace. For these important blessings are not only the means by which the sinner is separated from idols, but they are means which can never fail to produce the effect. This happy change is not only their natural, but their necessary consequence; and therefore, if we be not turned from idols, however just and orthodox our speculative opinions concerning these points may be, it is certain, that we have not yet tasted that the Lord is gracious; for thus it is written, (Gal. i. 4) that Christ "gave himself for our sins," according to the will of God, "that he might deliver us from this present evil world;" and it is mentioned as the distinguishing character and real attainment of all his redeemed ones, (Gal. v. 24.) "They that are Christ's have crucified the flesh, with the affections and lusts."

By this time you will have discovered your concern in the subject, and the use you ought to make of it. I have showed that man, in his natural state, is joined to idols; that it is God alone who can separate him from them; and that he doth it by means of his pardoning mercy and sanctifying grace. Now it is by faith in the Redeemer that any of the children of Adam come to be interested in these great and inestimable benefits. Here then you are furnished with a plain decisive test, whereby you may judge of your Christian profession, and examine yourselves whether you be in the faith. If idols reign with full power in your hearts, the conclusion is unavoidable, that as yet you have neither part nor lot in the Saviour; you are utter strangers, both to pardoning mercy and sanctifying grace. On the other hand, though their dominion be taken from them, so that they cannot be said to reign within you; yet, in whatever degree their influence remains, you may certainly conclude, that so far your faith must be weak in proportion. Only this is your comfort, that he who hath begun the good work will carry it forward to perfection; for "he is the rock, his work is perfect, and all his ways are judgment." He who is the author, is likewise the finisher of his people's faith. To him therefore let your humble prayer be addressed. Say to him as the disciples did, "Lord, increase our faith." And you may do it in the assured hope of being heard; for he hath promised the Spirit to them that ask it. Let us then ask and receive, that our joy may be full.

From all that hath been said, we learn, 1*st*. How to account for that idolatry which is so prevalent in the world. While man remained innocent, he had free access to the Author of his existence; and, being assured of his friendship, he rejoiced in the displays of his glory; and all the creatures he beheld, instead of intercepting or dividing his love, served only to remind him how much he himself was indebted to the bounty of their Creator. But sin introduced a dismal revolution into the heart of man. Alienated from God, and conscious of deserved punishment, we either think not of him at all, or dread him in the tremendous character of a judge and avenger. At the same time we must have something to gratify our inbred desire of happiness; and finding among the creatures around us, not only the necessary materials for supplying our bodily wants, but likewise a variety of objects and enjoyments suited to the inferior part of our nature, our hearts cleave to them, we pursue them with eagerness, and hope to extract that pleasure from the possession of them which we despair of finding any where else. Hence likewise we learn,

2*dly*. That nothing can avail for this idolatry, which doth not relieve from the guilt of sin, and vanquish the tormenting fear of wrath, by representing God in a light wherein we can behold him with pleasure; nay, which doth not bring an object in view that outshines a present world, and will afford that kind of happiness which is adapted to the nature, and commensurate to the duration, of an immortal spirit. Reason is, in all respects, unequal to the task. It no doubt can discover, and may descant very plausibly, upon the vanity of the creature: but, alas! a hungry man will feed upon husks rather than starve; nay, Rsason itself will justify him in doing so. Something must be presented to him of real worth and excellence; something that can supply all his wants, and render him contented and happy, independent of the objects and enjoyments of sense. It must likewise be something attainable; and which, when once obtained, cannot be taken from him.

Upon the whole, then, we see, in the 3*d* place, the importance and use of faith in Christ. The sacrifice he offered lays a firm foundation for the hope of pardon to the chief of sinners. There we see sin condemned in the flesh, the law infinitely glorified, and the justice of the Lawgiver, not only receiving full satisfaction, but more illustriously displayed, and more highly exalted, by the sufferings of his own Son in our nature, than it could have been by the final condemnation and everlasting punishment of the whole apostate posterity of Adam. This hath an obvious and powerful tendency to remove those fears which necessarily spring from a sense of guilt; for when we discover a way in which God may righteously pardon the sinner, then we can look up to him with hope; we are no longer compelled to flee from his presence; the revelation of mercy and forgiveness invites our approach to him, and thereby weakens one of the strongest of those cords that bind us to a present world; especially when, to the intrinsic worth and value of Christ's sacrifice, we add, that it was offered up in consequence of a divine appointment: for "Christ glorified not himself to be made an High-Priest, but he who said unto him, Thou art my Son, this day have I begotten thee." This strikes at the very root of all distrust and jealousy. When we are well assured that "God so loved the world, that he gave his only begotten Son, that whosoever believeth on him might not perish, but have everlasting life;" what stronger evidence could the most suspicious mind require of his merciful nature, and kind regards to the children of men? Doth not this astonishing act of grace, this *unspeakable gift*, unmerited, and even unsolicited, amount to a full demonstration of what the apostle John repeatedly asserts, viz. GOD IS LOVE? Can any one that believes this, hesitate for a moment to draw the same conclusion from it that Paul did, (Rom. viii. 32.) "He that spared not his own Son, but delivered him up for us all, how shall he not with him also freely give us all things?" And this leads me to observe, that Christ's giving himself for our sins, according to the will of God, hath a mighty efficacy to separate us from idols; not only by laying a solid foundation for our hope of pardon, and representing the Father in such a light as cannot fail to vanquish that fear and jealousy which render the thoughts of him painful and alarming to the sinner; but further, by giving us the animating prospect, and the fullest assurance, of that incorruptible inheritance, which our great Redeemer hath purchased with his blood, and promised to bestow upon all without exception, who, acknowledging the original forfeiture, and the justice of the sentence which condemns them to die, are willing to receive new life from his hand, and to hold it by his right, as a free gift to them, through the merit of his obedience unto death in their place. This world, as I formerly observed, vain and unsatisfying as it is, will still appear of some importance to men, so long as they are unacquainted with any thing better. It is this that renders death the *king of terrors;* and they who cannot look with comfort beyond the grave, will not only cleave to a present world, but will even submit to the most grievous hardships and inconveniences, rather than consent to the dissolution of these earthly tabernacles: "Skin for skin, all that a man hath will he give for his life." Nothing can reconcile us to a removal from this world but the discovery of another, where we shall continue to live and to partake of enjoyments preferable to any of those we leave behind us. Now, for this discovery we are wholly indebted to the Lord Jesus Christ. Life and immortality are brought to light by his gospel. This great object darkens the delusive lustre of all seen things. What hath this earth to offer that can stand the least comparison with that fulness of joy which is at God's right hand? Animated by this prospect, the believing Hebrews "took joyfully the spoiling of their goods, knowing in themselves, that in heaven they had a better and more enduring substance." They did not regret the loss of those perishing trifles, for which carnal men contend with such eager and unremitting labor: they looked beyond them to permanent and substantial blessings, and rejoiced in the hope, "that when the earthly house of this tabernacle should be dissolved, they had a building of God, an house not made with hands, eternal in the heavens." But I must here add, that all these discoveries, which have so obvious a tendency to separate us from idols, derive their virtue and efficacy from that divine Spirit which Christ purchased by his sufferings and obedience unto death; whose office it is, not only to throw light upon the great truths revealed in the gospel, and to open or unvail our eyes, that we may see them in all their evidence, but likewise to carry them home into our hearts with such demonstration and power, that they shall become the type or mould wherein that new man is formed, which after God is created in righteousness, and true holiness. By this divine agent we are born into the kingdom and family of God, and are connected with the spiritual world as really as by our natural birth we are introduced into and connected with this material world. In consequence whereof, we become sons, not in name only, but in nature; and, as St. Paul reasons, upon a principle universally admitted, "If sons, then are we also heirs, heirs of God, and joint heirs with Christ Jesus." This powerful renovation pulls down at once every idol from the throne, and lays them all under the feet of the "man in Christ;" for every thing tends to the place of its original. "They that are after the flesh do mind the things of the flesh: and they that are after the spirit the things of the spirit:"—"They have not received the spirit of the world, but the spirit which is of God, whereby they know the things that are freely given them of God." And these they find to be a portion sufficient to fill the most enlarged capacity of their souls. Being risen with their Lord, they "seek the things which are above, where Christ sitteth at the right hand of God." They are dead to whatsoever is confined to their present state of existence; and the new life they have received, being "hid with Christ in God," they are enabled to conclude, with the most absolute certainty, "that when he who is their life shall appear, then shall they also appear with him in glory, and ever after be with the Lord."

"May he who at first commanded the light to shine out of darkness, shine into all your hearts, to give you the light of the knowledge of his glory, in the face of Jesus Christ," that each of you may be disposed and enabled to say, *What have I to do any more with idols?* And let those who have experienced the power of divine grace, show by their future conduct, that they find enough in their God and Saviour to render them completely happy; and that the draft they have got of the pure water of life, hath effectually quenched their thirst after the muddy pools of earthly enjoyments.

Beware, O Christians! of every thing that may sully your profession, or grieve the Spirit, and thereby breed in you a distrust of your personal interest in God's pardoning mercy and sanctifying grace: for it is "by faith you stand;" and in the same proportion that your faith fails, idols will gain their influence in your hearts. I shall therefore conclude with that affectionate exhortation of the apostle Jude, "Ye, beloved, building up yourselves on your most holy faith, praying in the Holy Ghost, keep yourselves in the love of God, looking for the mercy of our Lord Jesus Christ unto eternal life." *Amen.*

SERMON XXIX.

Preached at the opening of the General Assembly of the Church of Scotland, 1772.

MANIFESTATION OF THE SON.

1 John iii. 8.—"For this purpose the Son of God was manifested, that He might destroy the works of the Devil."

Among the various motives to the love and practice of universal holiness with which this sacred epistle abounds, the one I have now read to you doth certainly merit peculiar attention; and must to every ingenuous mind appear not only most persuasive, but likewise most animating. For who that hath any thirst for true glory, would not aspire to the high dignity of becoming a "worker together" with the *Son of God?* Or can any man have reason to entertain the least doubt of victory and triumph, who is engaged in a cause which the great Lord of heaven and earth hath undertaken to support?

1. I propose, therefore, in the *first* place, to offer a few remarks for establishing your faith of the important doctrine contained in my text.

2. *Secondly,* I shall give you some account of the principal means by which *the Son of God* hath hitherto conducted his salutary undertaking, and shall finally *destroy the works of the Devil.*—And then direct you to the practical improvement of the subject.

I *First,* then, that you may see the *evidence* by which the doctrine here asserted is confirmed and illustrated, in the clearest and most satisfying light, I shall lay before you the several parts of it, in the same method and order of time in which the Spirit of God hath placed them in the sacred Scriptures.

If we look back to the Old Testament writings, we shall find this doctrine published in paradise immediately after the apostacy of our first parents, when Satan's usurped domination commenced. Then it was that God said unto the serpent, "Because thou hast done this, I will put enmity between thee and the woman, and between thy seed and her seed: *It* shall bruise thy head, and *thou* shalt bruise his heel." This was an early intimation of a Saviour, who should defeat the malice of Satan, the grand adversary, and prevent the total ruin of mankind.

To prefigure the manner in which he was to achieve this great deliverance, it deserves our notice, that expiatory sacrifices were very early appointed. Thus we read, that "Abel offered unto the Lord the firstlings of his flock;" and when we consider that it was not till after the deluge that the use of animal food was permitted to man, we can hardly doubt, that the "coats of skins," which God is said to have made for Adam and Eve, must have been the skins of animals offered in sacrifice by his own direction and appointment. These were significant emblems, or types, of that great atonement which Christ was to make in due time by the sacrifice of himself; in allusion to which, he is styled, in the New Testament writings, *a Lamb*, "the Lamb of God,"—"the Lamb slain from the foundation of the world."

But lest these typical representations of the promised *seed* should prove too thick and obscure a vail, it pleased God gradually to unfold the purposes of his grace, by raising up prophets at different periods of time; who, though they separately bare witness to this illustrious person, yet they perfectly agreed in the report they gave of him; representing him as an irresistible conqueror, "who should divide the spoil with the strong," as "the King whom God had set upon his holy hill of Zion," as "the Lord strong in battle," and "mighty to save;" who should "proclaim liberty to the captives, and the opening of the prison to them that are bound;—who should finish transgression, and make an end of sins," or offerings for sin, "and make reconciliation for iniquity, and bring in everlasting righteousness."

Accordingly, when the fulness of time was come, *the Son of God* made his entrance into the world in the declared character of Saviour and Redeemer. A heavenly herald was employed to announce his appearance, and to appoint him a name expressive of his office: "Thou shalt call his name Jesus," said the angel to Joseph; "for he shall save his people from their sins." A special messenger was raised up to prepare the way before him, to bid Satan defiance, and to call upon men to "repent, because the kingdom of God was at hand." This was John, who soon after had the honor to introduce Christ by baptism into the field of battle, and to point him out to the men of that age as "the Lamb of God which taketh away the sin of the world."

And now let us review his personal conduct, and trace him through the course of his public ministry, where we shall behold the most striking proofs of the apostle's assertion, that *for this purpose the Son of God was manifested, that he might destroy the works of the Devil.* No sooner is he baptized, and consecrated to his office by the visible descent of the Holy Ghost, than he suffers himself to be "led by the Spirit into the wilderness," and continued there for the space of forty days "tempted of the devil." The circumstances of this combat, and the happy issue of it, are recorded by three evangelists, and are so generally known, that I need not stay to repeat them. This was the first signal defeat of the adversary; in the wilderness was the serpent's head broken as *tempter*, which on Calvary was afterwards bruised as *tormentor*.

Having thus vanquished the devil in single fight, our Lord forthwith invites men to fight under his banner. He chooseth twelve apostles, whom he appoints to be the stated attendants upon his person, and the principal leaders of the army under him. With these he joins seventy of a subordinate rank, to whom he gives orders to attack the enemy, and to exercise the power of his word and spirit against him. In obedience to his command, and relying upon his aid, they resolutely go forth two by two, into every city and place whither he himself was to come; and after a rapid and most successful progress, like young soldiers flushed with their first prosperous adventure, they return again with joy, saying, "Lord, even the devils are subject unto us through thy name."

Upon this the hotter part of the war begins. The old serpent puts forth all his strength and cunning, raiseth up enemies from every quarter, works upon the pride, envy, and prejudices of the Jewish rulers and teachers, and by their agency carries on a most furious persecution against him. Yet still this great Captain of Salvation maintains his ground, and, amidst all the opposition that is made to him, lays the foundation of a kingdom, against which the gates of hell shall never be able to prevail; till at length, by seeming to yield, he gives the enemy the mortal blow, pursues him into his own dominions; and, by a mysterious wisdom, "through death, he conquers him that had the power of death, that is the devil:" And having thus obtained a complete victory, he riseth from the grave in triumph, ascendeth up on high, leading captivity captive; where, seated on the right hand of the Father, he shall continue in the exercise of government as Mediator till all his enemies be made his footstool.

Thus, you see, that the doctrine of my text doth not lean upon a single testimony, but is supported by many clear and express declarations of holy writ, and beautifully illustrated by the whole of our Saviour's conduct during the time of his abode on this earth. Let us then proceed,

II. In the *second* place, To consider more particularly some of the principal means by which *the Son of God* hath hitherto conducted his salutary undertaking, and shall finally *destroy the works of the devil.*

1*st*. He hath given us the most certain and enlarged discoveries of every thing that is necessary to be known, believed, or done by us, in order to our present improvement and holiness, and the perfection of our happiness in a future state.

The devil is styled "the god of this world, who blindeth the minds of those that believe not," and by keeping the light from them, leads them captive at his pleasure. And Christ delivers them from this thraldom, "by opening their eyes, and turning them from darkness to light;" dispelling those clouds of ignorance, error, and prejudice, whereby Satan maintains his usurpations over the hearts of men.

"No man hath seen God at any time; the only begotten Son, who is in the bosom of the Father, he hath declared him." To him we are indebted for the fullest and most satisfying information concerning the nature and perfections of God Most High; the measures of his government, his relation to us, and the worship that is due to him; and that neither guilt nor distance might discourage our approach to the throne of his holiness, Christ hath opened to us, in his own blood, a precious fountain of sovereign virtue, in which the chief of sinners may wash and be made clean; and by revealing to us the mysterious union of the divine and human natures, in his own person as Mediator, he hath, as it were, thrown a bridge over that boundless infinite ocean, which separates the creature from the invisible Godhead: so that through the man Christ Jesus, who is also God's beloved Son, we may now address the Father of our spirits, without that dread of a repulse, and fear of offending him, which otherwise must have overwhelmed our minds. He hath given us a law which is holy, just, and good, utterly subversive of the kingdom of Satan, and contrary to all his works; "teaching us, that denying ungodliness and wordly lusts, we should live soberly, and righteously, and godly in this present world." This law he hath enforced with the most persuasive arguments. Every motive to obedience that can either encourage our hopes, or alarm our fears, is set before us in the strongest and most affecting light. Heaven is unfolded to our view, and destruction hath no covering: And that no incitement may be wanting to invigorate our opposition to the devil and his works, this great Captain of Salvation solemnly enlists us into his army by baptism; and hath appointed the other sacrament, not merely to represent his atoning sacrifice, and to remind us of the price with which we were redeemed, but likewise to afford us an opportunity of recognizing his title to our grateful homage and most loyal subjection; and to be a means of imparting to our souls those supplies of grace, which will enable us to quit ourselves like men, while we fight under his banner against the powers of darkness, till the God of peace shall in due time bruise Satan under our feet. Thus doth *the Son of God destroy the works of the devil*, by the doctrines, and laws, and ordinances he hath taught us. To which I add,

2dly. The bright and glorious *example* of his life.

It was the just reproach of the Jewish teachers, that "they bound heavy burdens, and laid them upon other men's shoulders, but they themselves would not touch them with one of their fingers." Whereas the example of our Lord was of equal perfection with his laws. He lived as he taught; and the whole of his conduct, from his birth to his death, was one continued lecture of the purest devotion, the sublimest morals, and the most extensive usefulness. But this opens a field too extensive to be entered upon. It must suffice at present to observe, that the principal virtues which the peculiar character and circumstances of our Lord gave him an opportunity to practise, were obviously adapted to counteract the devil's most favorite vices. How odious, how disgraceful, do human pride and vainglory appear, when set in opposition to the lowliness of Christ, who, "though he was in the form of God, and thought it not robbery to be equal with God, yet made himself of no reputation, and took upon him the form of a servant?" With what persuasive eloquence doth the contempt he poured upon the riches, and honors, and pleasures of this world, reprove and condemn the covetousness, the ambition, and sensuality of men? His condescension to the mean, and his sympathy with the miserable; his meekness in receiving and forgiving injuries; and his patience in enduring the most grievous sufferings, do all serve to expose the deformity of those opposite distempers which give Satan so much room in the hearts of most men. After this manner doth the perfect example of the Son of God in our nature contribute to the subversion of the kingdom of darkness. But,

3dly. It was by his obedience unto death that our Lord did most eminently *destroy the works of the devil;* as we learn from the passage to which I formerly alluded, (Heb. ii. 14.) "Through death he destroyed him that had the power of death, that is the devil." Accordingly, in the epistle to the Colossians, the cross of Christ is compared to a triumphal chariot, on which, having spoiled principalities and powers, he made a show of them openly. I shall therefore discourse at greater length upon this head, and endeavor to illustrate the efficacy of Christ's death, in counteracting and defeating the malice of Satan: 1*st.* As it advances the glory of God which he sought to impair; and, 2*d.* As it purchaseth and secures the salvation of men, in spite of all his attempts to ruin them. These subjects, which are no less delightful than interesting, will serve to unfold the meaning of that heavenly anthem with which angels celebrated the birth of our Lord: "Glory to God in the highest, and on earth peace, good will towards men."

1. First, then, let us view the death of Christ as a means of advancing the glory of God, or, to speak with greater propriety, of displaying it more fully to his intelligent creatures.

Satan, no doubt, triumphed in his victory over the heads of our race. He had seen with envy that fountain of beneficence flowing out towards them, which he knew was eternally shut against himself; and beheld, with vexation and rage, the complacency and delight of the Creator in his new made world. But now that the fatal trespass was committed, he would fondly conclude, that this blessed harmony between heaven and earth was for ever at an end. Man, would he think, is become no less guilty than I am. That tremendous justice, the severity of which I feel, stands as much in the way of this creature's happiness as of mine. God must rear up another world before he can make any further display of his goodness, for this world is effectually put beyond the reach of it. Thus we may suppose him glorying in his conquest, and his fancied disappointment of the divine purpose.

But, behold! by the death of Christ, the shameful disappointment recoiling upon himself. He had before seen goodness and justice displayed alternately, each acting in the most perfect manner upon their proper objects; but now he sees them ministering to each other's glory, and mutually conspiring to take advantage of his malice, that both might shine forth with more dazzling splendor. He sees mercy to the guilty (an exercise of goodness which till then he thought impossible) rejoicing against judgment, and judgment at the same time triumphing in a satisfaction of infinitely greater worth than the whole world of angels and men. He sees love bringing the sacrifice to satisfy justice; and justice, having nothing more to demand, giving place to love; nay, becoming bound to serve the purposes of love in the salvation of those whom it formerly sought to destroy. This is that mysterious object which angels contemplate with increasing wonder, and which devils must look at with shame and confusion. The Son of God suffers, that the sinner may escape; and thus mercy and truth, righteousness and peace, which are never to meet upon those apostate spirits, meet and embrace upon the cross of Christ; and God appears infinitely just, as well as infinitely gracious, when he justifies those who believe in Jesus.

In short, all the attempts of Satan to impair or darken the glory of God, serve only to furnish out a theatre for the more illustrious display of it. He pulls down his kingdom with his own hands, and builds up that which he meant to overturn.

It is impossible to know with certainty what views he had of the Messiah; but it is plain, that he thought his death would bring great advantage to himself. He very probably hoped, that by this horrid deed, God would be provoked finally to abandon the human kind. The Jews were the only society of true worshippers upon earth, the people whom God had chosen for his peculiar inheritance; and if their charter could be broken, by their ungrateful rejection, and barbarous murder, of their long-promised King, then of course they would fall to his share; and so the whole world would become his own, and God have no tribute of praise from men. But, O the depth of the riches, both of the wisdom and knowledge of God! Here again Satan is caught in his own snare; and by seeking to enlarge his kingdom, saps the foundation of it. Christ being lifted upon the cross draws all men unto him. The covenant of peculiarity doth indeed cease; but then it is succeeded by a better and more extensive one. The wall of partition that inclosed the Jews. and separated them from the rest of the world, is now broken down; and the divine goodness, which formerly ran in a narrow channel, now dilates itself, and embraceth a whole world, men of all kindreds, nations, and languages. Thus Satan, by overdoing, undoes his interest; by grasping at the Jews, he loseth his Heathen subjects: for as Paul writes to the Ephesians, (chap. ii. 13, 14.) "But now in Christ Jesus, ye who sometimes were far off," (being aliens from the commonwealth of Israel, and strangers from the covenants of promise) "are made nigh by the blood of Christ. For he is our peace, who hath made both one, and hath broken down the middle wall of partition between us." "Now therefore," as it follows, (verse 19.) "ye are no more strangers and foreigners, but fellow-citizens with the saints, and of the household of God." Christ, after his resurrection sent forth his apostles to preach the gospel to *every creature.* In obedience to his command, they flew abroad like lightning, invaded the kingdom of darkness on all quarters, and made an amazing progress in their own day. And we look by faith for still more glorious times, when the dominion of Satan shall be utterly subverted, and all the nations of the earth shall be brought to the knowledge of the only true God, and of Jesus Christ whom he hath sent, whom to know is life eternal. Thus doth the death of Christ *destroy the works of the devil,* inasmuch as it displays the glory of all the divine perfections, and enlarges the kingdom of God among men, by the very means which Satan employed to sully the one and to diminish the other.

2. The death of Christ is no less effectual to purchase and secure the salvation of men, in spite of all Satan's attempts to ruin them. This partly appears from what hath been already suggested. His blood is the price which redeems the soul; it expiates the guilt of sin, and gives full satisfaction to divine justice: so that now the grand obstacle is removed, which obstructed the sinner's access to God, and excluded him from any share in the fruits of his beneficence. But this is not all: The death of Christ doth likewise afford the most persuasive and effectual motives to that *holiness,* "without which no man

shall see God;" and thus directly *destroys the works of the devil.* Here we behold the frightful aspect of sin. Hell itself doth not furnish such an awful representation, either of its intrinsic malignity, or its heinous demerit. How deep, how black, must that stain have been, which nothing could wash away but the blood of Christ? How deadly the disease which no other medicine could cure? How tremendous that justice, which nothing less could satisfy than the death of him who created the worlds? In vain doth Satan tempt us to *presume*, if we duly attend to this. Here sin is made to appear exceeding sinful; and Christ from the cross proclaims God's infinite abhorrence of that accursed thing, and his resolution to punish it, with a louder and more alarming voice than even the howlings of the damned themselves can do. And then what an effectual remedy have we here against *despair?* This is another engine which the enemy of our souls seldom fails to employ. When he cannot hold us bound with the cords of presumption, he will next attempt to plunge us into the gulf of despair, and will be ready to say to us, (as Joshua said to the Jews with a very different aim,) "Ye cannot serve the Lord, for he is a holy God." Your sins are so multiplied, and your bad habits so strong, that it is a vain thing to think of amending now. But the cross of Christ suggests to the believer a sufficient answer to this objection. True it is, can he say, that my sins have been many and great; but here is blood that "cleanseth from all sin" My corrupt passions are indeed strong; but then my Redeemer "is mighty to save." He would not purchase an inheritance for me which I could not be rendered capable of possessing. He who died to prepare a heaven for his people, is certainly able to prepare his people for heaven. He knows my weakness, and yet calls upon me to follow him; and therefore I cannot, I dare not, despair of his help. I will go forward in his name, and he will make his grace sufficient for me. Thus doth the death of Christ destroy the works of the devil, inasmuch as it furnisheth his people with the strongest argument against sin, and the most persuasive motives to faith and holy obedience; and hath moreover merited for them that supernatural assistance, by which they are encouraged to *attempt*, nay, (as the apostle Paul assures us from his own experience) by which they are actually enabled to *do all things.* Which leads me to mention a

Fourth and principal means, by which *the Son of God destroys the works of the devil;* namely, the divine efficacy of the Holy Spirit, regenerating the souls of men, filling them with light, and love, and strength; casting down those proud imaginations which exalt themselves against God, and bringing every thought into captivity to the obedience of Christ. The Holy Spirit is Christ's vicegerent upon earth, sent forth by him to supply his place, and to erect his throne in the hearts of men upon the ruins of Satan's kingdom. This he doth, by opening their understandings to understand the Scriptures, and leading them to the knowledge of all necessary truths, by convincing them of their sin and misery, enlightening their minds in the knowledge of Christ, and renewing their wills; whereby he not only persuades, but effectually enables them to embrace Christ as he is offered; by shedding abroad the love of God in their hearts, furnishing them with strength to resist temptation, to overcome the world, to mortify the deeds of the body, and to crucify the flesh with the affections and lusts. These are some of the effects which the Scriptures attribute to the Spirit of Christ. By these the strong man armed is driven out of his palace; he is stripped of his armor, and his goods are spoiled. Thus the soul is rescued from the bondage of Satan, and the sinner is made willing by a day of power to yield himself unto God, and to walk in newness of life.

5thly. The Son of God will finally *destroy the works of the devil*, when he shall come the second time to judge the world in righteousness. Then shall the kingdom of darkness be plucked up by the roots; then shall the ransomed of the Lord be confirmed in a state of unchangeable purity and happiness. Satan shall no more vex and seduce them; but he, with all the workers of iniquity, shall be thrust down into those everlasting burnings, which the wrath of God, like a stream of brimstone, doth kindle and inflame, the smoke whereof ascendeth for ever and ever.

Thus have I illustrated the doctrine of my text, and taken notice of some of the principal means by which *the Son of God* hath hitherto conducted the war against Satan, and shall finally *destroy the works of the devil.* And now, in the review of all that hath been said, let us, in the

1*st* place, Praise and magnify our great deliverer, who came into the world upon so merciful an errand. "O the height and depth, the breadth and the length of the love of Christ!" It might justly have been feared, that if the Son of God was to visit this earth, it would have been for a very different end, even to display the glory of divine justice, by executing vengeance upon those ungrateful creatures who had risen up in rebellion against the God that made them. But behold, and wonder! He came to save, and not to destroy: "For God sent not his Son into the world to condemn the world, but that the world through him might be saved." Nay, he came to destroy those enemies who had vanquished us, and to rescue us out of their hands. "Lord, what is man, that thou art mindful of him?" My brethren, however coldly we may think or talk of these matters, angels, whom they less concern, contemplate them with ecstasy. They shouted for joy when the world was made, but they raise a higher note to celebrate the redemption of mankind. And shall men be silent while angels sing? O let us contend with those blessed spirits in the praises of our own Redeemer. He is their Lord, but he is our Saviour. Let our souls, and all that is within us, be stirred up to bless him, and let us, even at this distance, begin that grateful, triumphant song, "Unto him that loved us, and washed us from our sins in his own blood, and hath made us kings and priests unto God and his Father, to him be glory and dominion for ever and ever."

2*dly.* This doctrine yields the strongest consolation to every sincere Christian. He is engaged in a cause that must prevail; he follows a leader whom no might can withstand; he contends with a subdued and vanquished foe, who hath already received the mortal wound, and ere long shall be cast down and trampled under his feet. And will not this inspire you with courage and fortitude? You fight under a General whom Satan feareth; and though he uses every artifice to make others unbelievers, yet he himself believes and trembles. Remember the battles and victories of your Redeemer; consider the virtue of his blood, and the efficacy of his Spirit. Let faith behold him in his present exaltation at the Father's right hand, pleading your cause, and observing your conduct, covering your heads and healing your wounds, while he prepares for you those crowns of glory that shall never fade away; and then cry out with the apostle in holy triumph, "If God be for us, who shall be against us? Who shall separate us from the love of God? Shall tribulation, or distress, or persecution, or famine, or nakedness, or peril, or sword? Nay, in all those things we are more than conquerors, through him that loved us." Be bold, O Christians! in the cause of righteousness. Let the wicked blush; they have reason to do so, their work is base, and their wages deadly. But surely the disciples of Jesus have no cause to be ashamed, whether they consider the nature of their service, or the reward that attends it. And what a reproach is it, that the slaves of Satan should act more vigorously for their master than we do for ours! Their cause is not only bad in itself, but desperate too, as to any prospect of success; whereas the interest for which we contend is so just and honorable, that the very attempting to support it is glorious; and unless we were to suppose that Omnipotence may become weak, and the Creator be overmatched by the workmanship of his own hands, we are sure of victory. What then should we fear? Be strong, O believers! and of good courage. You fight the battles of the Lord of Hosts, and greater is he that is with you than all that can be against you. Say not that you are the sons of the Most High, and born from above, unless you can prove your descent, by daring to be holy in spite of devils and men. The battle may be hot, but it cannot last long. Death will soon come, and tell you that your warfare is accomplished; and angels, who now minister to you with joy, will carry you home in triumph to your Father's house; and the Redeemer, by whose blood and Spirit you overcome, will put the crown upon your heads, and "grant unto you to sit with him in his throne, even as he also overcame, and is set down with the Father in his throne."

3dly. The stability of the gospel-church is a necessary consequence of the doctrine in my text. Zion's King shall have a seed to serve him as long as sun and moon endure. The church he hath purchased with his blood is built upon a rock, against which the gates of hell shall never prevail. The heathen may rage, and the people imagine vain things; the kings of the earth may set themselves, and the rulers take counsel together, against the Lord, and against his anointed, saying, Let us break their bands asunder, and cast away their cords from us. But he that sitteth in the heavens shall laugh; the Lord shall have them in derision; and at length he shall speak unto them in his wrath, and vex them in his sore displeasure. The proudest of his enemies shall lick the dust, when he ariseth to plead the cause that is his own; and therefore his people may well rejoice under the heaviest pressure of affliction, and look by faith through the darkest cloud, to the complete redemption of Israel from all his troubles. "For Jerusalem shall be a burdensome stone for all people: all that burden themselves with it shall be cut in pieces, though all the people of the earth should be gathered together against it."

4thly. This important subject suggests a variety of useful instructions to all who bear office in the church of Christ, and more especially to those who labor in word and doctrine. To us is committed the ministry of reconciliation, that by the manifestation of the truth as it is in Jesus, the eyes of sinners may be opened, and they turned from darkness to light, and from the power of Satan unto God. We are commanded to "preach the word, to be instant in season and out of season, to reprove, rebuke, and exhort, with all long-suffering and doctrine." "In meekness instructing those that oppose themselves; if God peradventure will give them repentance to the acknowledging of the truth; and that they may recover themselves out of the snare of the devil, who are taken captive by him at his will."

This, my fathers and brethren, is the great aim of the sacred office we bear, to which not our public ministrations only, but every part of our conduct, ought to be subservient. Let us keep this aim continually in our eye, as a lamp to our feet, and a light unto our path; and, in particular, let us place it full in our view when we are assembled together in the name of our Lord, to deliberate and judge in matters which belong to his spiritual kingdom, remembering that, as all our authority is derived from him, so the exercise of that authority can be no further valid than as it is regulated by his will, and subordinated to *the purpose for which the Son of God was manifested;* and consequently, that every act and decision of an opposite tendency shall be finally disowned and reprobated by him who came *to destroy the works of the devil.* Amen.

SERMON XXX.

THE CHRISTIAN'S CONVERSATION.

PHILIPPIANS I. 27.—"Only let your conversation be as it becometh the gospel of CHRIST."

It will be to little purpose to inquire what kind of *conversation becometh the gospel of Christ,* till we be satisfied, in the first place, that this charge, which was originally addressed to the Philippians, may, with equal propriety, be addressed to us.

The qualifying particle ONLY, with which the apostle introduces the exhortation, plainly denotes, that, in his own judgment, the demand he made was no less moderate than it was just: *Only let your conversation be as it becometh the gospel of Christ.* This is all I require; and you cannot with decency ask, nor in reason hope, that less should be accepted. To this conclusion he was naturally led by the character and circumstances of those to whom he wrote. His epistle was inscribed, not to unbelieving Jews or Gentiles, but to *saints in Christ Jesus;* to men who had been converted to the Christian faith, as we learn from the foregoing part of the chapter. And it is material to observe, that as Christianity had been treated with peculiar indignity at Philippi, where Paul and his companion Silas were, by order of the magistrates, publicly scourged and cast into prison, therefore the profession of the gospel, in such a place, was justly entitled to the most favorable construction: for nothing less than a deep conviction of its truth and excellence could be supposed to have induced any inhabitant of that city to profess a religion that inevitably exposed him to those contemptuous, as well as painful sufferings, which a generous and feeling mind would of all others most anxiously wish to avoid.

Surely, then, the apostle could have no reason to suspect, that a demand so moderate would either offend or surprise them: *Let your conversation be as it becometh the gospel of Christ.* You have embraced the faith of the gospel, and continue to make an open confession of it, without any allurements of a temporal nature, nay, in the face of the most obvious and alarming discouragements; and therefore, as there can be no room to call in question either your belief of its doctrines, or your regard to its laws, I may, without presumption, hope to obtain your consent, when I *only* exhort you to act a consistent and uniform part, by suiting your conversation to the religion you have chosen, and have the fortitude to avow.

It is true, and it ought to be gratefully acknowledged, that our present situation in these lands is very different from that of the ancient Philippians. Christianity, as reformed from the corruptions of Popery, is the established religion of our country: so that if a man believe the gospel of Christ, he may, with the most perfect safety to his person and property, make as public a confession of his faith as he inclines. But it is equally true, that no man is compelled by the terrors of persecution to profess Christianity, if he do not believe it; nay, the profession of incredulity itself, if it break not forth into blasphemy, aggravated by sedition, doth not always prove an insurmountable bar in the way to any office, civil or military, which the person is otherwise qualified to fill, or hath interest to obtain; and therefore, though the mere profession of Christianity be not attended with any temporal inconveniences, yet as the want of such profession doth not exclude a man from any temporal advantages, and as neither the profession nor practice of Christianity can be said, in the ordinary course of things, to help any man forward in the line of worldly promotion; hence it follows, that every baptized person, who hath not openly renounced "the Lord that bought him," but still retains the name of *Christian*, and would complain of abuse and injury if his title to that appellation were either denied or called in question, must be considered as acting from the freest choice in the profession he makes; and can have no reason to be startled, far less to be offended, when we address him in the words of this holy apostle, *Let your conversation be as it becometh the gospel of Christ.* Should it be otherwise with any of us, the consequences are obvious; and upon every supposition we can make, must prove equally fatal to our peace and to our honor.

If we believe not the gospel, why do we profess it? To lie in any case is shameful, how great soever the temptation may be: but to lie deliberately, without any temptation at all, which, as I just now observed, is the present case; nay, to persist in that lie from day to day, when telling the truth could not hurt nor endanger any secular interest whatsoever, is a baseness the most superfluous, and consequently the most contemptible, that can possibly be imagined.

On the other hand, if we truly believe what we profess, what an odious as well as disgraceful appearance must we make, when our conversation is such as doth not *become the gospel of Christ?* By "holding the truth in unrighteousness," and counteracting the dictates of religion, and the conviction of our own minds, we expose ourselves to the lashes of that self-reproach which will not fail to occupy every lucid interval betwixt the tumultuous gratification of passion and appetite; while at the same time, by continuing to profess that gospel we counteract, we every day publish our shame and misery to the world around us, and virtually confess that we are guilty and self-condemned before all who have an opportunity of observing our conduct.

So that the subject of my text is one of the most important that can employ our attention, as our practical regard to this demand of the apostle is absolutely necessary to preserve the peace and purity of our own hearts, and to support that character which the most profligate reverence, and which all who can discern real beauty and excellence will covet to possess; I mean the venerable character of an *upright man.*

Having thus prepared the way, by showing, that the same charge which was primarily addressed to the Philippians, may, with strict justice and propriety, be extended to us; let us now proceed to examine, with attention and candor, the standard to which our conformity is enjoined; or, in other words, let us inquire into that *gospel of Christ* to which *our conversation*, that is, the whole of our external conduct, as expressing the inward temper of our hearts, ought to be suited.

Among the various particulars included in the gospel of Christ, the two following may be selected as the most distinguishing and comprehensive, namely,

I. The *Doctrines* we are taught to believe; and

II. The *Laws* we are commanded to obey.

Each of these particulars I shall examine apart; from whence we shall discover, with ease and certainty, what manner of *conversation* it is that may be said *to become the gospel of Christ.*

I. I BEGIN with the *doctrines* of the gospel, or the truths we are taught to believe. And without descending to the peculiar tenets, or modes of expression, by which Christians of any denomination have chosen to distinguish themselves, I shall confine myself entirely to those capital points, in which the sober and intelligent of almost every denomination will be found to agree.

Now the *gospel*, strictly so called, or that "word of reconciliation," the substance whereof the apostle hath elsewhere expressed in one short sentence, to wit, "That God was in Christ, reconciling the world unto himself, not imputing their trespasses unto them," necessarily supposes, that man is in a state of distance and alienation from God, liable to punishment in consequence of his apostasy; and so perverted and enfeebled, that he hath neither the disposition nor the ability to do any thing that can be effectual for his own recovery.

It informs us, that "God, who spared not the angels that sinned, but hath reserved them in everlasting chains under darkness to the judgment of the great day," so pitied the human race, "that he sent his only begotten Son into the world, not to condemn the world, but that the world through him might be saved." The nature and dignity of this great Deliverer are thus described by an inspired apostle: "In the beginning was the Word, and the Word was with God, and the Word was God. All things were made by him: and without him was not any thing made that was made." This "Word," adds he, "was made flesh, and dwelt," or tabernacled, "among men." "He who was in the form of God, and thought it not robbery to be equal with God, made himself of no reputation, took upon him the form of a servant, and was made in the likeness of men; and being found in fashion as a man, he humbled himself, and became obedient unto death, even the death of the cross." This death is uniformly represented by all the New Testament writings as an atoning sacrifice for the sins of men. Hence Christ is styled "the Lamb of God which taketh away the sin of the world." He is said to "have borne our sins in his own body on the tree," and "to have made peace by the blood of his cross;" to have "been made sin for us, who knew no sin, that we might be made the righteousness of God in him;" and "to have suffered, the just for the unjust, that he might bring us to God." The apostle John calls him "the propitiation for our sins;" and the author of this epistle, in another letter addressed to the Christians at Rome, (the principal aim whereof was to explain and vindicate this important doctrine) expressly says, that "we are justified freely by the grace of God, through the redemption that is in Christ Jesus, whom God hath set forth to be a *propitiation* through faith in his *blood*, to declare his righteousness for the remission of sin; that he may be just, and the justifier of him that believeth in Jesus."

The gospel doth every where present him to our view, as a *powerful*, a *suitable*, yea, a *necessary Saviour;* so *necessary*, that "there is not salvation in any other;" so *powerful*, that "he is able to save to the uttermost all that come unto God by him;" and so *suited* to the circumstances of fallen creatures, that they who are sunk into the most deplorable state of ignorance, guilt, pollution, and servitude, are rendered "complete in him," "who of God is made unto them wisdom, and righteousness, and sanctification, and redemption."

We are further taught, that *faith* in Christ, or a cordial acceptance of him, in the full extent of his character as Mediator, is the appointed means whereby we become interested in this all-sufficient Saviour. For "this is the command of God, that we believe on the name of his Son Jesus Christ." "He that believeth on the Son hath everlasting life; he that believeth not the Son, shall not see life, but the wrath of God *abideth* on him." Which last expression plainly implies, that the sinner is previously under a sentence of condemnation; and that by rejecting the offered ransom, the sentence remains in full force, and his former guilt becomes still more aggravated by his ingratitude and obstinacy: whereas upon our believing in Christ Jesus, we forthwith obtain the remission of sins; for "the blood of Jesus cleanseth from all sin." And "being thus justified by faith, we have peace with God through our Lord Jesus Christ:" nay, we are adopted into the family of God: for "to as many as receive Christ, to them gives he power to become the sons of God, even to them that believe on his name." Neither is this a mere honorary title; but they on whom it is conferred are actually enriched with all the privileges the title imports: together with the *dignity*, they receive the *nature* of children. They are regenerated by grace; the Spirit is given to them, both as a sanctifier and a comforter, to heal their diseases, and to make them "partakers of the divine nature;" "to shed abroad the love of God in their hearts;" and to bring them with filial boldness to the throne of grace, where they shall obtain mercy, and find grace to help them in every time of need, till the divine life, which is begun on earth, shall attain its full perfection in the kingdom of heaven, that undefiled and permanent "inheritance, which is reserved for all those who, being born of God, are kept by his power through faith unto salvation."

Once more, the gospel informs us, that this Jesus, "who died for our sins, *rose* again for our justification;" hereby giving the most authentic evidence, that he had finished his great undertaking, and was accepted by the Father in all that he taught, and acted, and suffered upon earth; "that he ascended up on high," as a triumphant conqueror, "leading captivity captive;" where, being constituted "head over all things for the church," he now sits enthroned at the right hand of God; from whence he shall once more descend to this earth, not in the form of a servant, but clothed with Majesty, and attended by all the holy angels, to gather together his elect, in whom he shall be glorified; while at the same time, as an awful and righteous Judge, he shall "take vengeance on them that know not God, and obey not his gospel; who shall be punished with everlasting destruction from the presence of the Lord, and from the glory of his power."

All who are acquainted with the Scriptures must be sensible, that in delivering this summary of Christian doctrine, I have done little more than repeated the words of the New Testament writers as they are translated into our own language; and therefore I may take it for granted, that those capital articles, to which many others might have been added, will readily be admitted to belong to *the gospel of Christ.*

It remains, then, to be inquired, What influence the faith of these interesting truths ought in reason to have upon our temper and practice? or, in other words, what manner of conversation is suited to such belief?

That we may be qualified to judge with

greater impartiality, let us at present endeavor to forget, if possible, our personal concern in the question; and having supposed that we had received information of other creatures in a state of apostasy from God, who were favored with a revelation of the same important truths which we have found to be contained in the gospel of Christ, let each of us inquire at his own heart, what effects the firm belief of these truths might be expected to produce in their temper and practice?

Would we not conclude, without hesitation, that a discovery of the awful forfeiture they had incurred would afflict their souls in the most sensible manner; and so possess them with grief, and shame, and the fearful apprehensions of deserved punishment, that all the enjoyments of a short precarious life would lose their relish, till they certainly knew that there was a possibility at least of obtaining the pardon of their sins, and of regaining the friendship of their offended Sovereign? Would it not occur to us as a probable, or rather a necessary consequence, of this inward distress, that, upon hearing the remotest intimation of a scheme for their recovery, they would anxiously inquire into the foundation of such report; and when they discovered the truth of it, that they would welcome the offered mercy with humble gratitude, and throw themselves at the feet of that generous friend who had interposed for their relief; resigning themselves, without reserve, to his disposal and government, in that very manner which is described and enjoined by the gospel of Christ?

Again, let me ask, What do you think would be the natural effects of pardon obtained, and peace restored to their troubled minds, upon that cordial acceptance of the remedy provided for them which I have just now supposed? Could any of us doubt that their hearts would be filled with the sincerest joy, and that out of the abundance of their hearts their lips would show forth the praises of their Deliverer, and utter the voice of gratitude and love in such language as this: "Bless the Lord, O my soul, and all that is within me bless his holy name. Bless the Lord, O my soul, and forget not all his benefits; who forgiveth all thine iniquities, who healeth all thy diseases, who hath redeemed thy life from destruction, and crowned thee with loving kindness, and with tender mercies." "Return unto thy rest, O my soul, for the Lord hath dealt bountifully with thee."

But here likewise I must ask, Do you not think that this joy of theirs would be of a nature so pure and delicate, as to disdain any alliance with carnal mirth and levity? Would it not be that kind of joy which a condemned criminal may be supposed to feel upon receiving the gracious pardon of his sovereign; who, while he tastes all the sweetness of his prince's clemency, and exults in the assurance of present safety, yet cannot help shuddering when he looks back to the dungeon where he lay imprisoned, and recollects the danger he hath happily escaped?

Surely all who have obtained mercy will perceive and acknowledge the propriety of that advice, "Serve the Lord with fear, and rejoice with trembling." None indeed have such rational grounds of joy; and they give an unfair representation of the privileges that belong to the sons of God, who walk in heaviness, and wear a dejected, melancholy aspect. But still the cheerfulness of those who have passed from death to life, will, and ought to have an air of composure and solemnity, that will easily distinguish it from the loose, intemperate mirth of the sensualist, which springs from no higher source than the gratification of those appetites he hath in common with the beasts that perish, or the increase of his corn, and wine, and oil. Besides, the prospect of a future judgment, which I mentioned as one of the great objects of belief, could not fail to overawe their minds, and to keep them in a sober and serious frame, rendering them no less attentive to their thoughts than to their words and actions; and constantly disposing them to "walk circumspectly, not as fools, but as wise;" to shun the doubtful as well as the forbidden ground, "abstaining even from the appearance of evil." While, at the same time, the animating hope of a glorious immortality would render them cool and indifferent to all the enjoyments of a present world; support them under every thing that is painful and afflicting; and powerfully incite them to run with patience the race set before them, till in due time they should obtain the end of their faith, even the complete and everlasting salvation of their souls.

Such, we might well conclude, would be the influence of Christian faith upon the habitual frame and temper of their hearts

But as my text speaks of a *conversation* becoming the gospel of Christ, let us inquire more particularly into those *visible effects* which the truths I formerly mentioned might naturally be supposed to produce in the conduct of those who sincerely believed them; *first*, with respect to God; and, *secondly*, with regard to their fellow-men.

First, with respect to God. We should hardly be able to doubt, that creatures redeemed from misery, dignified with such honors, and enriched with such privileges, would be fond of expressing their gratitude in the most public and significant manner, and embrace every opportunity of celebrating the praises of their great Deliverer. We should certainly take it for granted, that if any day was set apart for his more immediate worship and service, they would long for the return of that precious season, and "wait for it more than they that watch for the morning." We should not be able to suppose, that they would reckon it a burdensome institution, and say, "What a weariness is it?" or, "when will the Sabbath be over?" far less that they would waste it in idleness, profane it by gaming, intemperance, and lewdness; or even debase it by those employments which are lawful on other days. Such presumptuous ingratitude would appear so shocking, that we should not dare to suspect, and least of all should we believe, without ocular proof, that creatures endued with reason would be guilty of it.

Again, if any ordinance was appointed for the express purpose of commemorating redeeming love, and showing forth the death of that compassionate Saviour, who was "wounded for their transgressions, and bruised for their sins, that by his stripes they might be healed," could we doubt, that they would regard it as a distinguishing privilege, and attend upon it with reverence, love, and joy? especially if one great end of its institution was to confirm their faith of the divine friendship, by putting into their hands an authentic seal of that well-ordered covenant, which conveys to every sincere believer an irrevocable title to all the unsearchable riches of Christ? This appears so becoming, and withal so conducive to their personal comfort and interest, that one should think a bare permission to attend upon such an ordinance might suffice, and that there scarcely needed the authority of a dying command to enforce the observation of it.

Once more; might it not be hoped, that creatures who believed and confessed that they were redeemed from death by an act of pure grace, would judge it their indispensable duty to live unto him by whose mercy it was that they lived at all? that they would feel in their hearts, and practically acknowledge the constraining force of such exhortations as these: "Ye are not your own, ye are bought with a price; therefore glorify your Redeemer in your bodies and in your spirits which are his:" "Ye were some time darkness, but now are ye light in the Lord; walk as children of the light:" and, "If ye call on the Father, who, without respect of persons, judgeth according to every man's work, pass the time of your sojourning here in fear; forasmuch as ye know that ye were not redeemed with corruptible things, as silver and gold, but with the precious blood of Christ, as of a Lamb without blemish and without spot?" Would you think it creditable, or even possible, that with such great and interesting objects in their eye, they could deliberately and wilfully trample upon his authority, by breaking his laws; or arraign the wisdom and justice of his government by fretting and murmuring against any of his dispensations? Doth it not seem far more likely, that they would habitually be disposed to say, "Lord, what wilt thou have me to do?" "O that my ways were directed to keep thy statutes!" Or if at any time they should be exercised with trials and sufferings, that the language of their lips and hearts would be, "Here am I, let the Lord do unto me as seemeth good unto him:" "The Lord gave, and the Lord hath taken away, blessed be the name of the Lord?"

These conclusions appear so reasonable, and indeed so moderate, that, were it possible for us to forget that we ourselves are parties to the cause in question, I am verily persuaded this whole audience would readily acquiesce in them without one dissenting voice. Let us then proceed to inquire, in the

Second place, What influence the faith of the gospel might be expected to have upon the conduct of such creatures in their social intercourse one with another?

It might suffice to observe in general, that the supreme love to their God and Saviour, which the true faith of his rich and unmerited grace could not fail to inspire, would naturally, and even necessarily, lead them to listen with becoming attention and reverence to all the intimations of his will, and habitually dispose them to perform, with alacrity and zeal, what duties soever he should be pleased to enjoin. Upon this obvious principle, then, nothing more would be needful for the illustration of this head, than to collect from the sacred records the several laws concerning truth, justice, mercy, beneficence, and any other precepts that regarded them in their social state; as we should not be able to entertain a doubt, that, so far as the imperfection of their nature permitted, these would be the invariable rules of their conduct. But as the LAWS of the gospel are afterwards to be considered apart by themselves, I shall at present confine our inquiry to the influence which a serious relief of the great doctrines of Christianity might be supposed to have upon those kinds of intercourse which more immediately pertained to their common salvation. Say, then, doth it not appear highly probable, that they who relished the joyful tidings, while they made them the subject of their own delightful meditation, would likewise take pleasure in imparting them to others, especially to those with whom they were most intimately connected? that parents in particular would rehearse and commend them to their children; and that in every family, the God of all grace, and the Saviour of a lost world, would be presented with the morning and evening sacrifices of humble adoration, of fervent prayer, and of thankful praise?

How would they behave, do you think, to such of their brethren, if any such there were, who neglected the great salvation, and still remained in their natural state of distance and alienation from God? Would they regard them with supercilious contempt, or treat them with harsh severity? would they lay aside all concern for their recovery, and leave them to perish in their folly? or rather, would they not look upon them with an eye of the tenderest pity; and, regarding them as criminals, who, though at present under an awful sentence of condemnation, may nevertheless obtain mercy, even as they themselves have obtained mercy? would they not take hold of every favorable opportunity, nay, may we not conclude, that they would even seek out opportunities of awakening them to a sense of their guilt and danger, that they might feel themselves constrained to implore the protection of that good *Shepherd* who laid down his life for the sheep, and came from heaven to earth to seek and to save that which was lost?

View them once more in their intercourse with those who have obtained the same grace, and are become coheirs of the same incorruptible inheritance. Would you not take it for granted, that they could not be long together, without talking of those matters that most nearly concerned them? Surely none could suspect, that in a company of such persons, it would ever be reckoned a breach of good manners to introduce any thing that related to their Father in heaven; to his house with many mansions, where they all hoped to dwell; or to that precious Redeemer, who hath gone before to prepare a place for them. Might it not rather be expected, that besides occasional converse upon subjects of so interesting a nature, they would choose to set apart some portions of time for the sole purpose of "comforting themselves together, and edifying one another," according to the early practice of the Christians at Thessalonica, which our apostle so highly commends, 1 Thess. v. 11.?

THUS have I given you my cool, deliberate sentiments upon the practical influence of the great doctrines of the gospel, and that kind of conversation towards God and man which is best suited to the belief of them. Should any indeed be so perverse as to resist the influence of these doctrines, and counteract their native and most obvious tendency, while at the same time they acknowledged the evidence of their truth, it would not at all surprise me, to see them crowding, from day to day the public theatres, that the regularity and decorum of a fictitious representation might draw their attention away from that real and ill-conducted medley in which they themselves acted their disgraceful parts. I should not wonder to behold them flying with eagerness to cards and dice, and seeking aid from every engine of dissipation and noise, to conceal the lapse of time, and to bear down the clamors of an accusing conscience. It would not even surprise me to see them rushing headlong into the haunts of riot and debauch, that the intoxicating cup might either stupefy or madden their reason; which, if left to its sober exercise, would anticipate the evil day, and torment them before the time. Such things as these I should expect to see; but for none of them could I find any place at all in the natural and orderly state of reasonable creatures, whose temper and conduct, as I have all along supposed, were formed and regulated by the doctrines of the gospel.

How far my reasoning upon this branch of the subject hath been just will more fully appear afterwards. It no doubt exhibits to our view a state of things widely different from what we at present behold; which, I am aware, may furnish us all with matter of humbling and painful reflection. This, however, shall not discourage me from proceeding in my inquiry; as I well know, that if, "by the sadness of the countenance the heart be made better," we shall in the issue be infinite gainers, and obtain from him, who is "the comforter of those that are cast down," "the oil of joy for mourning, and the garments of praise for the spirit of heaviness."

May God dispose and enable us all to "judge righteous judgment." *Amen.*

SERMON XXXI.

THE CHRISTIAN'S CONVERSATION.

PHILIPPIANS I. 27.—"Only let your conversation be as it becometh the gospel of CHRIST."

We have already considered the most essential doctrines contained in *the gospel of Christ*, and the influence that the cordial belief of such interesting truths might be expected to have upon our temper and practice.

I am not sensible that any of the conclusions I drew were strained, or even obscure. To me they appeared, and, after the most serious and impartial examination, still do appear, so reasonable and obvious, and withal so moderate, that I cannot think they are liable to any just objection.

At the same time, as they present to our view a state of things so widely different from that which daily passeth before our eyes, I shall now proceed to consider the LAWS or precepts of our holy religion; that, from the review of these, we may discover, with still greater certainty, what the *conversation* is that may be said to *become the gospel of Christ.*

But before I descend to particulars upon this extensive subject, I must beg your attention to a few remarks I have to make upon the precepts or laws of the gospel in general.

With regard to their *authority*, there can be no doubt. He who enacted them hath an unquestionable right to our most perfect obedience: "In the beginning was the Word, and the Word was with God: and the Word was God: all things were made by him, and without him was not any thing made that was made." We are therefore his property in the most absolute and unlimited sense of that expression. He called us into being when as yet we were not, and every moment he sustains that existence which he gave us; for "in him we live and move." Nay, all that we possess is so necessarily dependent upon him, that with regard to soul, and body, and outward estate, we have nothing but what we daily receive from his liberal hand. Besides this original and unalienable right to govern us, there is another title, which, as Christians, we profess to acknowledge, and ought always to do it with the warmest and most humble gratitude; I mean, the right he hath obtained by redemption and purchase. As his natural subjects, we are bound to serve him to the utmost extent of the powers he hath given us; and this original obligation, instead of being relaxed or impaired, is rather confirmed and strengthened by the mercy he hath shown us as the objects of his grace: "We are not our own, we are bought with a price;" and are therefore bound, by the united ties of gratitude and justice, "to glorify our Redeemer, both with our bodies and spirits, which are his."

But what I would chiefly lead your attention to, is the *nature* and *properties* of those laws to which our subjection and obedience are required.

They are "all holy, just, and good," resulting from the very frame our Creator hath given us, and from the relation we bear to himself, and to other beings with whom his Providence hath connected us. Hence it follows, that they are equally incapable of repeal or abatement. The laws of men are local, temporary, changeable, and always partake of the imperfection of their authors. Some of them are so obscure, that they need another law to explain them; and it often happens that the commentary is darker than the text. The best of them take their aim from some temporal evil that is either presently felt, or foreseen in its cause; and the highest end they propose, is to restrain from injuries of the grosser kind: they do not even pretend to be a rule of moral conduct; they prohibit and denounce vengeance against theft, robbery, murder, and the like; but lay no restraint upon heart-hatred, covetousness, and envy. They tell us in what instances injustice or cruelty become excessive and intolerable; but where do we find it written in any body of human laws, "Thou shalt love thy neighbor as thyself;" and, "All things whatsoever ye would that men should do unto you, do ye even so unto them?" Whereas the laws of the gospel extend to the heart as well as to the life, and speak to all men without exception, at all times, and in every situation. They utter their voice with such precision and perspicuity, that none can be at a loss to discover their meaning. They do not bend to the humors of men, nor accommodate themselves to those flexible maxims and customs which by turns prevail in this or the other age and country; far less do they grow obsolete, as human statutes do, which by long disuse lose their force, and become void: like their great Master, what they were yesterday they are the same to-day: and in every succeeding period their efficacy will continue till time itself shall be no more. And, therefore, when I repeat the words of this sacred book, you are to consider them as spoken to yourselves in particular; and no less binding upon you in their most simple and obvious meaning, than they formerly were upon those to whom they were primarily addressed.

One thing further I would recommend to your notice, viz., that the laws I am speaking of are the laws of Him "who loved us, and gave himself for us, an offering and sacrifice to God of a sweet-smelling savor;" and therefore we may rest assured, that they are kind as well as righteous, and suited with perfct wisdom to be the means of promoting our truest interest. They are laws which he himself hath magnified and made honorable; not only by answering all their demands, so far as his high character would permit, or his peculiar circumstances afforded occasion; but likewise expiating the guilt incurred by the transgression of them, and bearing in his own person the punishment that was due to the offending creature.

This last consideration sets the obedience required of us in a most endearing point of light. It is not the servile task of a hireling who labors for his wages, but the ingenuous and grateful service of a loving child. Christ hath purchased the glorious inheritance; and to all who believe on him, eternal life is the free gift of God through the merit of his blood: so that nothing is required of them, but what tends to purify and perfect their natures, that, by a growing resemblance to the Father of their spirits in this state of discipline, they may be rendered meet for the full and everlasting enjoyment of him, when death, by dissolving the earthly tabernacle, shall pull down all that remains of the first Adam, and bring a final release from the body of sin.

HAVING premised these general remarks, I shall now proceed to remind you of those particular precepts to which our conformity is required by the gospel of Christ. And we are happily furnished with a short, but most comprehensive, summary of them, by the same apostle in his epistle to Titus, (chap. ii. 11, 12.) "The grace of God that bringeth salvation, hath appeared to all men; teaching us, that denying ungodliness, and worldly lusts, we should live soberly, righteously, and godly in this present world."

To these general heads, all the particulars may be reduced that belong to a conversation becoming the gospel of Christ. And here indeed I might stop short, and only call upon you to weigh, with candor and impartiality, the full meaning and import of the expressions here used.

What do you understand by *ungodliness and worldly lusts?* Do these terms reach no farther than to the grosser acts of impiety and sensual indulgence? And is nothing more intended by *denying* them, than a prudish reserve and shyness to comply with their demands; or such a feeble resistance as yields after a short and very imperfect struggle? Surely none of you can seriously entertain this opinion. You certainly must admit, that no exception is made of any species or degree whatsoever, either of *ungodliness* or *worldly affections;* and that by *denying* them, the apostle could mean nothing less, than such a refusal as proceeds from an inward abhorrence of them, even the most vigorous, determined, and persevering resistance of all their solicitation.

Again, What do you understand by *living soberly, righteously, and godly in this present world?* Doth *sobriety* mean no more than that species of moderation which is commonly opposed to surfeiting and drunkenness? Or admitting that it excludes every kind of excess in gratifying our bodily appetites, do you imagine that it leaves the mind at full liberty, so that we may lay the reins upon the neck of our passions, and suffer them to run wild without any control, in perfect consistency with that *sobriety* which the apostle recommends?

Will you call a man *righteous*, merely because he cannot be charged with any gross acts of fraud, injustice, and oppression, though perhaps, in the course of a lawful business, he may sometimes use a little artifice to impose upon the simplicity or ignorance of his neighbors? Or, supposing him to be strictly honest in his dealings, doth the *righteousness* which the gospel enjoins lay him under no obligation to feed the hungry, to clothe the naked, and to succor the distressed, according to his ability?

Is every man to be reputed *godly*, who doth not openly blaspheme, nor reproach the laws and ordinances of God; who gives regular attendance at church on the Lord's day, though his heart even then be running after his covetousness; and God receive no homage from him at all, either in his family or in the closet, through the rest of the week?

Were I to give such a loose interpretation of the apostle's words, I am confident, that the most partial offender who hears me, would not only condemn me in his heart, but even blush, or rather disdain, to plead my authority for defending or palliating his own misconduct.

But the true import of *sobriety*, *righteousness* and *godliness*, is ascertained beyond any possibility of a mistake, by what I may call the *statute-law* of the gospel: I mean, plain and explicit decrees, respecting particular instances of duty, under each of these general heads. Thus, in the

First place. With regard to *sobriety*, it is the express command of our Lord, "That we deny ourselves;" that we "possess our souls in patience;"—and be continually on our guard, "lest at any time our hearts be overcharged by surfeiting and drunkenness, and the *cares of this life*." It is required of us, "that we crucify the flesh with the affections and lusts;" that we lay aside anger, malice, envy, hatred, and revenge," and "put on, as the elect of God, bowels of mercy, kindness, humbleness of mind, meekness, and long-suffering." We are exhorted, "not to think of ourselves more highly than we ought to think, but to think *soberly*, (mark the expression) according as

God hath dealt to every man the measure of faith." "Let nothing be done through strife and vain glory," saith this same apostle, at the 3d verse of the following chapter; "but in lowliness of mind, let each esteem other better than himself. Look not every man on his own things, but every man also on the things of others;" and then adds, "Let this mind be in you which was also in Christ Jesus." These few quotations, which must be familiar to all who are acquainted with the New Testament writings, may suffice to give you some view of the extent of *sobriety*, as including every thing that belongs to the right government and discipline both of the outward and inward man.

Secondly, With respect to *righteousness*, we are plainly taught, that it not only restrains from the outward acts of injustice, oppression, and cruelty, but that we are thereby obliged to render unto all their dues, and to do unto others, as with good reason we would expect or desire that they, in like circumstances, should do unto us. It belongs to righteousness, "to comfort the feeble-minded, and to support the weak," as being members one of another; for thus it is written, (Gal. vi. 2.) "Bear ye one another's burdens, and so fulfil the law of Christ." We are commanded to "be of the same mind one towards another:" "to rejoice with them that rejoice, and to weep with those that weep;" "to do good to all as we have opportunity, especially them who are of the household of faith." "As every man hath received the gift," saith the apostle Peter, "even so minister the same one to another, as good stewards of the manifold grace of God." Nay, the apostle John carries the matter still higher, and speaks of it as a *debt*, an act of justice, in certain cases, to lay down our *lives* for the brethren: (1 John iii. 16.) "Hereby perceive we the love of God, because he laid down his life for us; and we *ought* to lay down our lives for the brethren." It is an error to imagine, that God bestows on us the good things of this life, merely for our personal accommodation and use; or that he opens his hand, and fills our basket, that the blessings of his Providence may there stagnate and putrify. We are not *proprietors*, but *stewards*, as I just now observed, who shall one day be called upon to give an account of our stewardship. And though the griping miser cannot be arraigned at any human bar, yet at the tribunal of Jesus Christ, he who doth not feed the hungry, and clothe the naked, shall be tried, and condemned to everlasting banishment from the presence of the Lord, and from the glory of his power.

You say, you wrong no man by keeping your own. I answer, You wrong the King of kings, if you suffer a subject of his to perish, when it is in the power of your hand to prevent it: and though the laws of men permit you to give or to withhold, according to your pleasure, whatsoever you possess independent of others; yet if you consult the lively oracles of God, you shall there find, that you are as much bound to do good to your neighbors, as not to injure them; to supply their wants, as not to rob them; to stretch forth your hand to help them, as not to smite them with the fist of wickedness. "To him that knoweth to do good, and doth it not, to him it is sin." "If thou forbear to deliver them that are drawn unto death, and those that are ready to be slain; if thou sayest, Behold we knew it not:—doth not he that pondereth the heart consider it? and he that keepeth thy soul, doth not he know it? and shall not he render to every man according to his works?" Prov. xxxiv. 11, 12. How awful are these words of the apostle John: "Whoso hath this world's good, and seeth his brother have need, and shutteth up his bowels of compassion from him, how dwelleth the love of God in him?" To which he subjoins the following exhortation, whereunto we do well that we take heed: "My little children, let us not love in word, neither in tongue, but in deed and in truth; and hereby we know that we are of the truth, and shall assure our hearts before him." Thus far is the law of *righteousness* extended by the *gospel of Christ*.

Thirdly. With regard to *godliness*, none who are acquainted with the New Testament writings can be at a loss to discover, either wherein it consists, or how it ought to be expressed. Love to God in the renewed soul, springing from faith in the Lord Jesus Christ, is the root, or vital principle, of godliness: not a common subdued love, but a fervent, supreme, and ruling love, that exalts God to the throne in the heart, and desireth nothing so much as that he should keep it in full and everlasting possession. As creatures, we are bound to love the Lord our God with all our heart, and soul, and strength; And we are further obliged, as *guilty* creatures, humbly to acknowledge the forfeiture we have incurred, to justify the law by which we are condemned, thankfully to accept the Lord Jesus Christ as the only Mediator between God and Man, and carefully to observe and improve all those ordinances which God hath appointed, as the methods of testifying our subjection and gratitude, or as means of receiving the communications of his grace, for healing our diseased natures, and rendering us meet for the enjoyment of himself in heaven. These are essential parts of the religion of a sinner; and must therefore be considered as the genuine and necessary expressions of godliness, or of a right temper of heart towards the Father of our spirits, the God in whom we live, the God and Father of our Lord Jesus Christ.

All the duties we owe to our fellow-creatures lean upon this as their proper foundation; and are so dependent upon it, that neither our righteousness, nor beneficence, can avail us any thing, unless they flow from a living principle of devotion in the heart. They may profit others, and render ourselves amiable in the eyes of men; but if they be not animated with love to God, and accompanied with suitable expressions of regard to him, it is impossible they can meet with the divine acceptance. For let it be observed, that the *practice* of these duties became necessary *only* through man's apostasy. Had we kept our first estate, there would have been no room for the exercise of either justice or mercy in any of those instances which our present distempered condition requires. Men would have lived together as one great family without strife or emulation, each rejoicing in the happiness of his brother. There would have been no temptation to fraud or injustice; every inhabitant of the earth possessing all that his heart could wish. There would have been no occasion for redressing wrongs; for punishing the injurious, or protecting the injured; for relieving the poor, or sympathizing with the afflicted: love would have had no other employment but complacency and delight in seeing each one blessed to the full extent of his capacity: and therefore it can never be supposed, that the practice of those duties, which the bitter consequences of our guilt *alone* have rendered necessary, should be the whole, or even the most essential part, of that obedience which is pleasing to God.

Indeed, were we to look upon the present state of the world as the original constitution, we might be apt to conclude, that our chief business upon earth consisted in the exercise of those social virtues which knit men together, and enable them to provide most effectually for their common defence against those numberless evils to which they are continually exposed. But if we view the present state as the ruins of one far more perfect and excellent, which we forfeited by our unprovoked and criminal revolt from the great Author of our existence, we must be sensible, that the bare performance of those social duties we owe to one another, can be of little account in the sight of God, so long as we persist in our rebellion against himself, and neglect those higher duties which arise from our first and most lasting relation.

Godliness, my brethren, is the one thing needful: did *that* prevail in its power, *sobriety* and *righteousness* would follow of course, and maintain their ground against every assault, having so firm and permanent a basis to lean upon: but till godliness be laid as a foundation, any attempt to introduce or establish either of the other two must be vain and fruitless.

Loud and general hath been the cry for some time past, after public spirit, disinterested patriotism, and integrity, which can neither be bribed nor overawed, among those who move in the upper ranks of life. These qualities, it must be confessed, accompanied with a large proportion of wisdom, are truly desirable, and might be eminently useful; and when it shall please God to bestow them, they will no doubt appear very beautiful in their season; but if all who join in the cry, would endeavor in the first place, to get their own hearts possessed with real godliness, and then pray for the same blessing to others, with as much fervency as they utter their complaints, I can assure them they would be taking by far the nearest road to success. "The fear of the Lord is the beginning of wisdom," and love carries it to perfection; but when these find no place in the hearts of men, what can be looked for in such a world as ours, but the rankest growth of folly and wickedness, both in public and private life?

From this general review of the LAWS of Christ, you must be sensible, that the same temper and conduct which we formerly supposed to result from a cordial belief of the DOCTRINES of the gospel, now appear to be expressly enjoined by plain and positive statutes: so that, upon the whole, we are furnished with a decisive test of genuine Christianity, and may clearly see, by the light of God's word, what the *conversation* is that *becometh the gospel of Christ.*

It gives me pain to repeat the observation I have more than once hinted at, (and yet the evidence of its truth is too glaring to be concealed) namely, that among the multitudes who bear the title of Christians, the conversation of by much the greater part is so far from expressing the true spirit and genius of our holy religion, with regard either to the doctrines it reveals, or the duties it requires, that the character of the Cretians may too justly be applied to many of them, (Tit. i. 16.) "They profess that they know God; but in works they deny him, being abominable, and disobedient, and unto every good work reprobate." To such inconsistent usurpers of the Christian name, the obvious remarks with which I introduced my first discourse upon this subject administer a severe, but just reproof: and therefore I might here dismiss them without further admonition, were it not that numbers are to be found in that unhappy class of men, who, not contented with publishing their own shame, by counteracting the principles of that religion they profess, are bold enough to scoff at true godliness in others, and do every thing in their power to enfeeble the hands of real Christians, while they are humbly endeavoring, by the grace of God, to have their *conversation as it becometh the gospel of Christ.* I know how difficult it is to get access to those who are proudly seated in the scorner's chair; nevertheless I shall take the liberty to beg their attention to a few plain questions, praying that God may carry them home to their hearts with power, and so bless them for their conviction, "that they may yet recover themselves out of the snare of the devil, who are taken captive by him at his will."

Do you really think it possible that any man can love God too well, or serve him with too much zeal and diligence? Do you think, that there is a saint in heaven who repents of his zeal and diligence while on earth? or a sinner in hell, that justifies his scoffing at serious religion? or do you suppose, that you yourselves shall approve of such conduct when you come to die, and boldly defend it at the tribunal of Christ? What can be more unfair, than to scoff at men, for being, in truth the very thing that you pretend to be? You call yourselves Christians, and at the same time deride those who are Christians indeed: It is your professed belief, that Christ shall judge the world; and when others are giving all diligence that they may be found of him in peace, they are mocked and reviled, and hated by you upon that account; nay, which is still more injurious, they are branded with the odious name of *hypocrites*, by those very persons who themselves are the most impudent hypocrites upon earth. For tell me, thou who retainest the name of Christian, what grosser hypocrisy can be imagined, than to hate the serious practice of thy own profession, and to reproach others for living by the influence of those very principles which thine own false tongue professeth to believe?

These are all the questions I shall put to you at present; and the main thing intended by them, is to give you such a view of the folly and inconsistency of your character, that if modesty be not altogether banished, I may at least bring you the length of being ashamed of your conduct. But though modesty should be gone, yet as fear and self-love are still left behind, I shall endeavor, in a few words, to give you a just representation of the peculiar malignity of such a course, and of the fatal consequences with which an obstinate continuance in it must necessarily be attended.

Know, then, that to scoff at the sanctifying work of the Spirit of God, is a sin of so deep a tincture, that it approacheth near to the confines of "the great transgression." This much I may with confidence affirm, that so long as you persist in it, there is no room for any rational hope that you shall be saved. With God indeed all things are possible; he is able of such stones to raise up children unto Abraham; and therefore some hope is left that you may be converted; but that you should be saved in your present course, is just as impossible as it is for God to lie, as impossible as for the devils to be saved. It is an astonishing proof of the power and cunning of the grand deceiver, that he should be able to hide this alarming truth from your own eyes. The scorner bears upon his forehead one of the most distinguishing marks of a son of perdition. Of such transgressors it may be said with an awful emphasis, "their spot is not the spot of children." Other sinners may find some cloak to throw over their guilt; the recorded failings of some eminent saints may be so far perverted as to cherish the presumption and soothe the consciences of various kinds of sinners; but where do we read of any among the saints who scoffed at holiness, or spake reproachfully of the ways of God? Surely no man of common understanding can suppose, that a scorner of a holy life is himself possessed of that holiness which he derides. I would not for a world, said one, be in the case of that wretch who speaketh well of holiness in others, while he himself lives in sensuality and wickedness; but I would much less, for a thousand worlds, be in the case of him that is neither godly, nor can speak well of godliness; who is not only void of the image of God, but hates, and reviles, and persecutes it in others. Consider, O sinners! while yet there is hope, how terrible your eternal state must be, if death overtake you in this malignant course. The Lord Jesus is now calling upon you in mercy, and saying unto you, as once he said to Saul, "Why persecutest thou me?" But if you do not hearken to his voice, and tnrn from your evil way, ere long "he will speak to you in wrath, and vex you in his sore displeasure:" for "behold, the Lord cometh with ten thousands of his saints to execute judgment upon all, and to convince all that are ungodly among them, of all their ungodly deeds which they have ungodly committed, and of all their *hard speeches* which ungodly sinners have spoken against him." There is an alarming passage, (Psal. vii. 11, 12, 13.) which I would recommend to your serious perusal: "God judgeth the righteous, and God is angry with the wicked every day. If he turn not, he will whet his sword: he hath bent his bow, and made it ready. He hath also prepared for him the instruments of death; he ordaineth his arrows against the *persecutors.*" God himself hath undertaken the defence of the just: Christ will finally be glorified in his saints, when all their enemies shall be cast out of sight, overwhelmed with shame, and doomed to everlasting contempt and misery.

THUS far have I spoken for the conviction and reproof of those who have the boldness to scoff at vital religion and practical godliness; and shall now conclude the subject with a few words of advice and encouragement to the true servants of Christ, who feel the influences of his gospel, and are determined, through grace, to live unto Him who died for them.

Let me then call upon you to lay your account with opposition in your way heavenward. Marvel not, my brethren, if the world hate you; but rather rejoice, in as much as ye are partakers of the sufferings of your Lord,. that when his glory shall be revealed, ye may be glad also with exceeding joy. You have good company, you have powerful assistance, and glorious hopes: "If ye be reproached for the name of Christ, happy are ye; for the Spirit of God and of glory resteth upon you." "Stand fast," therefore, as the apostle exhorts you in the words following my text, "in one spirit, with one mind, striving together for the faith of the gospel, and in nothing terrified by your adversaries; which is to them an evident token of perdition, but to you of salvation, and that of God.

For unto you it is given, in the behalf of Christ, not only to believe on him, but also to suffer for his sake." Beware of courting the favor of the wicked, by conforming in any degree to their corrupt maxims and practices; but keep up the majesty of true godliness, and study so to live, that they may find no occasion against you, except it be concerning the law of your God. "Be blameless and harmless, the sons of God, without rebuke, in the midst of a crooked and perverse nation, among whom ye shine as lights in the world, holding forth the word of life." "Finally, brethren, whatsoever things are true, whatsoever things are honest, whatsoever things are just, whatsoever things are pure, whatsoever things are lovely, whatsoever things are of good report: If there be any virtue, and if there be any praise, think on these things;" "and the God of peace shall be with you." *Amen.*

SERMON XXXII.

IN LIFE OR DEATH THE LORD'S.

ROM. XIV. 8.—"Whether we live, we live unto the LORD; and whether we die, we die unto the LORD: Whether we live therefore or die, we are the LORD'S."

THE following verse will inform you *who* that Lord is of whom the apostle speaks in this passage. "To this end," saith he, "Christ both died and rose, and revived, that he might be *Lord* both of the dead and living." He is the king whom God hath set upon his holy hill of Zion, and appointed to be the head over all things to the church; for as Paul wrote to the Philippians, in regard of his humbling himself, and becoming obedient unto death, even the death of the cross; "therefore God also hath highly exalted him, and given him a name, which is above every name, that at the name of Jesus every knee should bow, of things in heaven, and things in earth, and things under the earth; and that every tongue should confess that Jesus Christ is *Lord*, to the glory of God the Father." This doctrine we all profess to believe; nay, the designation we bear imports an acknowledgment that Christ is our Master. But something more than the appellation of Christians is necessary to prove that we are in truth his servants. The proper, the only decisive test, is that which lies before us in the words of my text; where one who knew well what Christianity was, thus speaks in the name of all sincere believers: *Whether we live, we live unto the Lord, and whether we die, we die unto the Lord: Whether we live therefore or die, we are the Lord's.*

It is the comprehensive description of the Christian's life expressed in these few but emphatical words, *We live unto the Lord*, which I have chosen for the subject of the following discourse. And my design is,

I. To inquire into the import of *living unto the Lord;* and,

II. To apply the character as a measure, or standard, for helping us to judge of our spiritual condition.

I. *Living unto the Lord* may be considered as including the following particulars:

1*st.* That we make his will the rule, the only rule of our conduct.

Our Lord hath intrusted us with various talents, and requires that we should improve them to the best advantage, for the important purposes for which they were bestowed. We are *his* servants, and have a task assigned us, for which we must be accountable to him at last. It is not left to our own choice what pieces of service we shall perform; but we must at all times wait upon him for direction; saying, as Paul did when struck to the ground, "Lord, what wilt thou have me to do?" Neither is it enough that we do the things he requires, unless we do them *because* he requires them. The laws of our Lord are so wisely calculated to promote the private interests of individuals, and the public welfare of human society, that they who are most disaffected to his government, will choose, for their own sake, to comply with many of his sacred injunctions; but they, and they only, *live unto the Lord*, who realize his authority, and do every thing he enjoins, as an act of willing and cheerful obedience, as a part of that homage they owe to their Master.

2dly. To *live unto the Lord*, is to make his approbation our governing aim, and to study to please him in all that we do.

I need not tell you that we early contract a love for many things which are hurtful to our souls, and stand condemned by the laws of our sovereign. This renders some parts of duty so painful to the flesh, that they are compared in Scripture to the "cutting off a right hand, and the plucking out a right eye;" operations which no man would submit to, far less perform them himself, unless the preservation of the rest of his body rendered them absolutely necessary. Other parts of duty are attended with inconveniences of a different kind: they may draw upon us the scorn, the hatred, and persecution of a partial, blind, malignant world; so that if we listen either to the corrupt part of our own nature, or to the voice of the multitude, we shall unavoidably be persuaded to leave them undone, or rather to do the contrary. Nothing else than a prevailing habitual desire to please *the Lord* can reconcile us to the practice of these self-denying duties. But if this principle be deeply rooted in our hearts, the roughest paths of obedience will soon become smooth; with resolution, nay, with cheerfulness, we shall address ourselves to our work; declining no service, how painful or difficult soever, that we know will be crowned with the approbation of our Judge. Thus did the primitive Christians *live unto the Lord*. It appeared a small matter to them to be judged of man's judgment; this was their labor; that, whether present or absent, they might be accepted of their Master. They so spake, and so acted, not as pleasing men, but God, who trieth the hearts of his creatures, and will render unto every one according to his works.

3dly. To *live unto the Lord*, is to make his glory our end in every thing we do.

Paul expressed the genuine spirit of Christianity, when, with a dignity becoming the character of an apostle, he thus wrote to the Philippians: "I would ye should understand, brethren, that the things which happened unto me, have fallen out rather unto the furtherance of the gospel; so that my bonds in Christ are manifest in all the palace, and in all other places; and many of the brethern in the Lord, waxing confident by my bonds, are much more bold to speak the word without fear. Some indeed preach Christ even of envy and strife; and some also of good will. The one preach Christ of contention, not sincerely, supposing to add affliction to my bonds; but the other of love, knowing that I am set for the defence of the gospel. What then? notwithstanding every way, whether in pretence, or in truth, Christ is preached; and I therein do rejoice, yea, and will rejoice. For I know that this shall turn to my salvation, through your prayer, and the supply of the Spirit of Jesus Christ, according to my earnest expectation, and my hope, that in nothing I shall be ashamed, but that with all boldness, as always, so now also, *Christ shall be magnified* in my body, whether it be by life or by death. For to me to live is Christ, and to die is gain." (Phil. i. 12–21.) If *we live unto the Lord*, we shall not seek great things for ourselves. This will be our only concern, that the Lord may be *magnified* in us, and by us, either by our doing or suffering; by our life or by our death. We shall be contented to be employed in any station his wisdom shall choose for us, and study to honor him in that station by the diligent performance of the duties that belong to it. Though we occupy the meanest office in his family, we shall with pleasure apply ourselves to the work of that office, without repining at those who are dignified with a higher place; nay, instead of looking at them with envy, we shall rejoice to behold their diligence and success. If our Lord be well served, if much work be done, that will satisfy us, by whatsoever hands the work is carried on. We shall execute what falls to our own share in the best manner we can; and pray for larger measures of grace to those who have the honor to be employed in higher pieces of service.

4thly. To *live unto the Lord*, is to be wholly resigned to his disposal, blessing him at *all* times, in adversity as well as in prosperity, making him as welcome to take from us as to give unto us.

How well our apostle had learned this important lesson, appears from his own words, (Phil. iv. 12.) "I know both how to be abased, and I know how to abound; every where and in all things I am instructed, both to be full and to be hungry, both to abound and to suffer need." It is rebellion against our Lord to repine at any of his dispensations, how afflicting soever. What have we that we did not receive from him? and is it not lawful for him to do what he will with his own? David, after contemplating the heavens, the work of God's fingers, the moon and the stars which he had ordained, breaks forth into this exclamation, (Psal. viii. 4.) "What is man, that thou art mindful of him; and the son of man, that thou visitest him? For thou hast made him a little lower than the angels, and hast crowned him with glory and honor." He there celebrates the goodness of God, in assigning to man, at his first creation, so high a rank among the variety and immensity of his works. The form of expression is a little varied, (Psal. cxliv. 3.) where, speaking of God's condescension to man in his fallen and degraded state, he saith, "Lord, what is man, that thou takest knowledge of him? or the son of man, that thou makest account of him? Man is like to vanity; his days are as a shadow that passeth away." This reflection arose from the experience he had of God's unmerited kindness to himself, "who had taught his hands to war and his fingers to fight;" who had raised him from the sheepfold to the throne of Israel, and had "subdued his people under him." But I am persuaded you will agree with me, that what Job saith (Job vii. 17, 18.) is more striking and emphatical than either of the former two; when, in the deepest adversity, he expressed himself thus: "What is man that thou shouldst magnify him? and that thou shouldst set thine heart upon him? and that thou shouldst visit him every morning, and try him every moment?" David, speaking of the Divine *beneficence*, calls it a being "mindful" of man, "taking knowledge" of man, and "making account" of him; but when Job speaks of *correction*, and chastisement, he raiseth his style, and calls it God's "magnifying man," and "setting his heart" upon him. He wonders that God should bestow such attention upon a sinful creature; that he should stoop so low as to become his physician; nay, that he should visit him every morning, to administer medicine for the recovery of his spiritual health, afflicting his body for the good of his soul. In this light will the true disciple of Jesus Christ view the most distressful events of Divine Providence. Convinced that his Lord knows what is good for him better than he doth, he will kiss the rod, and make every dispensation welcome; and though nature may shrink a little, and even wish that the bitter cup might pass from him, yet grace will teach him to consent, and dispose him to say, "Nevertheless, not my will, but thine be done." Once more,

5thly. To *live unto the Lord*, is to be so thoroughly devoted to him, as to account that we *live not* at all, but in so far as we serve him, and show forth his praise.

This, I apprehend, expresseth the true spirit of the apostle's words. He reckoned nothing worthy to be called *living* that was not subservient to the great purpose for which life was bestowed. He measured his time, not by days, or months, or years; but by a succession of services to his dear Master, by those acts of obedience he was enabled to perform. What portions of time were otherwise employed, he did not esteem to be living at all; these he reckoned among the vacancies of life, like the hours that pass away in sleep, which is the image of death. The true Christian prefers one day in the courts of the Lord to a thousand any where else, and would rather be a door-keeper in the house of his God, than dwell in the tents of wickedness.

Thus have I told you what is included in *living unto the Lord.* I shall now proceed,

II. In the *second* place, To apply this description of genuine Christianity as a measure or standard for helping us to judge of our spiritual condition. For this end, I must beg your attention, and the answer of a true conscience, to the following questions.

1*st.* Of what weight is the authority of God in your hearts?

I am not inquiring, whether the things you do are commanded by God? I formerly observed, that there may be a deception here. God enjoins many things as duty, to which human nature, even in its present state, feeleth no aversion; for our apostasy was chiefly from God himself; and though some fierce and unsocial passions have sprung from this bitter root, yet, in the main, we are not naturally disaffected to our fellow-men, but rather disposed to wish them well, and even to do them good, provided our personal interest be not hurt by it. And therefore no man can be said with certainty *to live unto the Lord*, merely because he performs the common offices of justice, humanity and beneficence, towards others with whom he is connected; for these things have a comeliness in them that is obvious to the dimmest eye; they are of good report among all men; and, in most cases, a man cannot serve himself more effectually than by practising them. But if he practise them merely, or even principally, to promote his own interest, he must not pretend that he liveth unto the Lord; he only serves himself, and must therefore be left to reward himself as he can. If he do not mean to serve the Lord, if he do not act from love and loyalty to his Sovereign, he can have no ground to expect any reward at his hand.

2dly. Whom do you seek to please, and whose approbation do you principally covet?

If you only, or even chiefly, court the applause of men, it is plain that you do not *live unto the Lord.* "We labor," saith the apostle Paul, in the name of all true believers, "that whether present or absent, we may be accepted of Christ;" 2 Cor. v. 9. The Pharisees gave much alms; they were frequent, and loud, and long in their prayers; but they did all "to be seen of men;" and therefore our Lord styled them *hypocrites*, and denounced many awful woes against them. I am sensible that this species of hypocrisy is not the disease of the present age: there are few that make much noise about their prayers or their alms; and there are still fewer, I suppose, that can justly be charged with excess in either; so that a caution against being righteous overmuch seems quite superfluous. But can you discover nothing in yourselves that is akin to this hypocrisy? Are you as ready to perform the most self-denying duties as those that are accompanied with immediate pleasure or advantage? Are you the same in secret that you appear, or wish to appear, in public? Or rather, do you not suit your behavior to the humor of the times? Can you charge yourselves with no instances of a timid compliance with the prevailing maxims and manners of the world? Hath not *fashion* some weight with you, to draw you into many things which you do not inwardly approve? and are you not often restrained from doing what conscience tells you ought to be done, by the fear of incurring the ridicule and censure of others, even of those whom, in your hearts, you do not, and cannot esteem? If so, then these very hearts must testify against you, that hitherto you have not been *living unto the Lord.*

3dly. What regard do you feel for the honor of your Lord?

Are you willing to become any thing, to do any thing, and to suffer any thing for his sake? Are you contented to serve him in the meanest station of his family? or if you aspire to an higher place, is it solely to enlarge your sphere of usefulness, that you may labor more abundantly, and serve him to greater advantage, than your present inferior situation will permit? When we see you climbing upwards as fast as you can, may we really suppose that this is your aim? That it ought to be your aim, is obvious; for he who came not to be administered unto, but to minister, keeps no idle attendants about his person for mere parade and show. Earthly princes, who are made of the same materials with other men, need many external appendages to eke them out, as it were, and to give them bulk and importance in the eye of the world; but he who made the heavens and earth, infinitely disdains to borrow any significancy from the workmanship of his own hands. The angels that excel in strength do his commandments, hearkening unto the voice of his word: the highest seraph hath his task: "They are all ministering spirits, sent forth to minister for them who shall be heirs of salvation." And can any of the sons of men be so befooled by temporal prosperity, as to imagine that any little elevation they can attain on this footstool, relaxes their obligation to serve God so strictly as meaner men do? They may imagine it; and when we survey the upper ranks of life, we find too just cause to suspect, that this absurd and impious conceit is entertained by many; but the faithful and true Witness hath assured us, "that unto whomsoever much is given, of them much will be required;" and that the greater talent, if not faithfully improved, shall only heighten the condemnation of its possessor, and entitle him to more and heavier stripes. Once more let me ask,

4thly. What is it that gives the highest value to every thing in your esteem?

"One thing have I desired of the Lord," said David, "and that will I seek after, that I may dwell in the house of the Lord all the days of my life, to behold the beauty of the Lord, and to inquire in his temple."—"I count all things but loss," said the holy apostle Paul, "for the excellency of the knowledge of Christ Jesus my Lord; for whom I have suffered the loss of all things, and do count them but dung that I may win Christ." If you are sincerely devoted to the Lord Redeemer, you will value other things in exact proportion to their connection with him, and the relation they bear to him. You will prefer the Bible to all other books, because it is the word, the testament of your *Lord.* You will rejoice at every return of the Sabbath, because it is the *Lord's* day. You will delight in his saints, and account them the "excellent ones in the earth," because they are dear to your *Lord,* and bear his image. Prayer will be your sweetest entertainment, because it is the means of correspondence and intercourse with your *Lord:* And doing good to the bodies, and more especially to the souls of men, will be relished by you as the most pleasant and honorable employment, because it renders you most like unto your *Lord,* "who went about doing good," leaving us an example that we should follow his steps. And thus will you estimate all other things.

These, and such like questions, I would have you to put to your own hearts, as in the presence of that God who is already perfectly acquainted with you; who will shortly cause you to know yourselves, and will make all others to know you too, in that day when every disguise shall be torn off, and your real character shall be published in the presence of an assembled world.

I SHALL conclude this discourse with reminding you of those peculiar obligations that lie upon all who name the name of Christ, *to live unto the Lord* in the manner I have endeavored to describe.

1st. Unless we *live unto the Lord,* we shall counteract the very design of that marvellous love he hath manifested towards us, in giving himself for us an offering and sacrifice to God for a sweet-smelling savor. "He bore our sins in his own body on the tree, that we being dead to sin, should live unto righteousness." "He gave himself for us, that he might redeem us from all iniquity, and purify unto himself a peculiar people, zealous of good works."—"He died for all, that they who live," by the merit of his death, "should not henceforth live unto themselves, but unto him who died for them, and rose again." This is so much insisted upon in the New Testament writings, that the Socinians have represented it as the *sole* end for which our Lord both lived and died. But though we justly maintain, in opposition to them, that the death of Christ was, in the strictest propriety of language, a true propitiatory sacrifice for expiating the guilt of sin, and rendering the exercise of mercy to the sinner consistent with the holiness and justice of God; yet in expressing our abhorrence of their error, we must beware of running into the opposite extreme; for nothing can be more clearly asserted in the oracles of truth, than that "the Son of God was manifested for this purpose, that he might destroy the works of the devil;" or, in other words, that he might prepare men for heaven, by the sanctifying influences of his Spirit, as well as that he might purchase a heaven for them by the merit of his blood. And it deserves particular notice, that though the main difficulty the first preachers of Christianity had to struggle with among their own countrymen, was to bring them off from a proud dependence upon their own righteousness, that they may rely upon Christ alone for pardon and acceptance; yet in declaring this doctrine, they never failed to establish the inseparable connection between faith and holiness, lest any should turn the grace of God unto wantonness, and, by claiming the privileges of the gospel while they refused subjection to its laws, should represent Christ as the minister of sin.

2*dly*. We are further obliged *to live unto the Lord*, as we regard the honor of our Master, and the credit of that saving religion which he taught. For hereby we most effectually stop the mouths of gainsayers, and cut off occasion from those that desire occasion to blaspheme that worthy name by which we are called ; presenting to their view a convincing proof, that Christianity is an effectual means of salvation, and that Christ is truly and properly a Saviour. The death of Christ appears to have a mighty efficacy indeed, when it maketh those that believe on him to die unto sin. And it is impossible to doubt that he is alive, and hath all power committed to him in heaven and in earth, when he visibly lives in his members by his all-conquering grace, and causeth them to live unto him : Whereas a contrary behavior doth the greatest possible injury to the cause of truth, furnishing the world with a handle to say, that Christianity is nothing more than an airy speculation, and that the religion of Jesus is of no effect towards reforming the hearts and lives of its professors.

2*dly*. I shall only add, that we are bound to live in the manner I described by the strictest ties of justice and equity. "Ye are not your own," saith our apostle, (1 Cor. vi. 19, 20.) "for ye are bought with a price." From whence he draws this practical inference, "Therefore glorify God in your body, and in your spirit, which are God's." As creatures who derived their being from God, we are bound to love him with all our heart, and to serve him to the utmost extent of the powers he hath given us. But his redeeming grace brings us under a new and still more endearing obligation to his service. When we had destroyed ourselves, and lay exposed to all the dreadful effects of his righteous displeasure, having no eye to pity, and no hand that could help us, then did he pity us, and his own arm brought salvation. He issued forth the gracious command, "Deliver them from going down to the pit, for I have found a ransom." And in the fulness of time our Lord Jesus Christ, "the Lamb slain" in decree "from the foundation of the world," appeared in our nature ; and with the infinite price of his own precious blood, redeemed us from the hand of justice, and purchased for us complete and everlasting salvation. And now, with what face can we decline his service or refuse subjection to any of his laws? It is purely by his merit that we live at all : and shall we reckon it grievous to walk by his direction? Surely nothing can appear more just and equitable, than that he who bought us should possess us, and that the ransomed should be entirely devoted to their Redeemer.

Let these considerations prevail with us to *live unto him* who "died, and rose, and revived, that he might be Lord both of the dead and living." And while we look up to him for that divine aid, which he hath not only encouraged us to ask, but commanded us to expect, let us go forward in his strength, making mention of his righteousness, even of his only ; that when we die, we may fall asleep in that Jesus, unto whom we now live, and commit our bodies to the dust, in the assured hope of a glorious resurrection : when that promise shall be fulfilled in its largest extent, "If any man serve me, let him follow me ; *and where I am, there shall also my servant be.* If any man serve me, him will my Father honor." *Amen.*

SERMON XXXIII.

THE CHRISTIAN CHRIST'S CARE.

1 Peter v. 7.—"Casting all your care upon him, for he careth for you."

Exhortations of this kind, which frequently occur in the sacred Scriptures, represent our holy religion in the most amiable light. It appears, in all respects, suited to our present necessities, and friendly to our highest, our most important interests. How deplorable would be the state of men upon earth, were they left to struggle in their own strength with the trials and sufferings to which they are continually exposed? In prosperity, when the mind is vigorous and undisturbed, *Reason* may discover a variety of arguments for bearing affliction with patience and fortitude, and may even suggest some topics of consolation, which, in the distant view of adversity, seem to promise a seasonable and effectual relief; but these are rather specious than solid, and when brought to the test, have always been complained of as feeble and unavailing. The best of them are those which lead our thoughts upwards to the Supreme Disposer of all events, the wise and righteous Governor of the world. But as it is impossible for a creature, conscious of guilt, to separate the idea of punishment from suffering, it is not easy to conceive how the mere persuasion, that our sufferings proceed from one who is incapable of doing wrong, should yield us any comfort, unless we are assured, that while he punisheth our sins, he is at the same time willing to be reconciled to us; nay, that the correction itself is the fruit of his love, and graciously intended for the cure of our souls. But here Reason, unassisted, is unable to move one step upon firm ground; and though it could, yet, as the mind itself is too commonly unhinged and broken by adversity, any aid that depended upon a process of reasoning would come by far too slow to our relief. "The spirit of a man will sustain his infirmity; but a wounded spirit who can bear?"

In this distressed situation, when every other refuge fails, divine revelation comes seasonably to our assistance. So bright are the objects it presents to our view, that they prevent the labor of a tedious inquiry: The mind sees them at once; and though greatly disturbed, can with ease discover both their nature and their use. The import of a striking fact is much sooner comprehended than the force of an argument. Thus when we are told "that God spared not his own Son, but delivered him up to the death for us," we no sooner hear and believe the fact, than we are sufficiently prepared to draw the same conclusion from it that Paul did, "How shall he not with him also freely give us all things?" But the Scriptures do not stop here: they not only relate what God hath already done, and thereby furnish us with proofs of his mercy and grace; they likewise contain explicit declarations of what he hath purposed and determined to do. They abound with great and precious promises, confirmed by the oath of an unchangeable God, "that by two immutable things, in which it is impossible for God to lie, they may have a strong consolation, who have fled for refuge to lay hold on the hope set before them."

Of this kind is the argument with which the apostle presseth the exhortation in my text, *Casting all your care upon God*, saith he, FOR *he careth for you.* Nothing can be more simple; and, at the same time, nothing can be more persuasive. No acuteness is requisite for discovering the meaning of the argument. And then its strength is irresistible; "for if God be with us, who can be against us?" If the great Lord of heaven and earth vouchsafe to become our friend, nay, our guardian, then surely, with a cheerful and unreserved confidence, we may resign ourselves wholly to his disposal and government. The objects of his paternal care must always be safe; no real evil can befall them, neither shall any thing that is truly good be withheld from them. But to whom doth the apostle address his exhortation?

This question is of importance, and must be answered in the *first* place.

Secondly. I shall lay open the nature and extent of the duty here enjoined, and show what is included in *casting all our care upon God.*

Thirdly. I shall illustrate the propriety and strength of the motive with which the exhortation is enforced, *God careth for you.*

And then direct you to the practical improvement of the subject.

NOTHING would give me greater pleasure than to say to every one that hears me, Thou art the person who art invited to *cast thy care upon God:* but it is truth, and not inclination, that must dictate what I say. The great Prophet of the church compares the office of a minister to that of a steward, whose business it is to feed those committed to his care, by giving unto each "his portion of meat in due season." A promiscuous distribution of the bread of life, is not merely unprofitable, but in many cases hurtful, to the souls of men: And give me leave to add, that in no case is it more likely to be hurtful, than when the subject, like the present one, is soothing and agreeable. And therefore, that this word of truth may be rightly divided, it will be necessary

I. In the *first* place, To inquire who the persons are to whom the exhortation may properly be addressed.

It is certain, that as there are *privileges* peculiar to sanctified believers, so there are many *duties* enjoined in Scripture, which the impenitent and unbelieving are incapable of performing; and, I apprehend, there is no duty whatsoever that lies farther beyond their reach, than the exercise of trust and hope in God; for every part of his word denounces wrath against them so long as they persist in their rebellion and enmity. "God is angry with the wicked every day. He hath bent his bow, and made it ready; he hath also prepared for him the instruments of death." And therefore, to persons of this character, a previous exhortation is necessary. I must address you in the words of Eliphaz to Job, "Acquaint now thyself with God, and be at peace, and hereby good shall come unto you." At present my text doth not speak to you at all. If you look back to the foregoing part of this epistle, you will see the persons described whom the apostle had in his eye. He doth not write to all promiscuously, but "to the elect, according to the foreknowledge of God the Father, through sanctification of the Spirit unto obedience, and sprinkling of the blood of Christ." He writes to those "who are born again, not of corruptible seed, but of incorruptible, by the word of God, which liveth and abideth for ever." He addresseth his exhortation to believers in Christ Jesus, "who loved him though unseen," having tasted of his grace; whom he distinguished by the honorable appellations of "a chosen generation, a royal priesthood, a holy nation, a peculiar people." These are the objects of God's paternal care; and they only are qualified to *cast their care upon him.*

I speak not thus to drive any, even the worst of you, away from God, or to discourage your application to him when trouble overtakes you. A time of distress is a very proper season for seeking acquaintance with God. His rod hath a voice as well as his word, and both speak the same language, "Turn ye, turn ye, why will ye die?" All I affirm is, that you cannot *cast your care upon God* till your acquaintance with him be begun; and by telling you, that the saints are possessed of privileges which at present do not belong to you, my sole aim is, "to provoke you to jealousy," as Paul expresseth it, and to make you ambitious to cast in your lot with "these excellent ones in the earth," that ye also may partake of their joy. "This is the command of God," and the first in order under the gospel-dispensation, "that we believe on the name of his Son Jesus Christ:" and it is only in consequence of our obedience to this command, that we obtain an interest in the blessings he hath purchased. Christ is that unspeakable, comprehensive gift, in which all other gifts are virtually included. It is our thankful acceptance of the Mediator of the covenant, that both manifests our claim to the promises of the covenant, and qualifies us to perform the duties it requires. From this account of the persons who are invited *to cast their care upon God*, we shall with greater ease and certainty discover,

II. The nature and extent of the duty itself; which is the *second* thing I proposed to illustrate.

It differs entirely in its *nature* from that carelessness and insensibility which the bulk of mankind too generally indulge. Many indeed enjoy a fatal tranquillity, having no concern at all about their eternal interests. Their inquiries are abundantly anxious with regard to the things of a present life; saying, "What shall we eat, and what shall we drink, and wherewithal shall we be clothed?" But they were never brought in good earnest to ask the infinitely more interesting question, "What shall we do to be saved?" Or if at any time a serious thought, tending to this inquiry, force itself upon their minds, they immediately encounter it with the presumptuous hope of the divine mercy, and endeavor to persuade themselves, by some fallacious reasonings, that it may be well with them at last, though they go on in their trespasses. Now the faith of such persons is not only dead in itself, but likewise poisonous and killing to their souls. They are perishing, and will not believe it, till the unquenchable fire awaken them from their security, and put it out of their power to deceive themselves any longer. We must not cast our *work* upon God, and presume that he will save us in the way of sloth and carnal indulgence; on the contrary, we are commanded "to work out our own salvation with fear and trembling." It is only "in well-doing" that we can regularly "commit the keeping of our souls to God," as the apostle hath taught us in the close of the preceding chapter. We are exhorted to cast our *care* upon him, not that we may enjoy the base rest of the sluggard, "who desireth and hath nothing, because his hands refuse to labor;" but that, having got our hearts enlarged, and freed from a load that pressed them down, we may quicken our pace, and run with greater alacrity in the way of God's commandments.

The character of the persons to whom this exhortation is addressed, doth likewise serve to limit the *extent* of the duty. It is not every sort of care that we are invited or permitted to cast upon God, but only the care of those things which the Christian dare avow in the presence of his Father, and humbly ask of him by prayer and supplication. We read, (Matth. xviii. at the beginning) that the disciples of our Lord came to him in a body, inquiring which of them should be "*greatest* in the kingdom of heaven." This was a vain, self-interested anxiety, to which our Lord gave a sharp and sudden check, by telling them in plain terms, that till they should lay aside that ambitious *care*, they were not fit to possess the *lowest* place in his kingdom. "He called a little child unto him, and set him in the midst of them, and said, Verily I say unto you, that except ye be converted, and become as little children, ye shall not *enter* into the kingdom of heaven." We have an account of another very *careful* man, (Luke xii. 16–20.) where his picture is drawn with inimitable strength. He is represented in a musing posture, thinking within himself, and saying, "What shall I do?" The question betrays the greatest uneasiness and perplexity. A poor starving beggar, who had not a morsel of bread, nor knew where to find it, could have said nothing more expressive of distrust and anxiety. And what do you really think ailed this man? Did he want bread? Quite the contrary; he had got too much: his barns were not large enough to contain the product of his ground: "I have no room," said he, "where to bestow my fruits." And it was this that made him cry out, "What shall I do?" If you desire any further information concerning him, you will find it at verse 20. "But God said unto him, *Thou fool*, this night thy soul shall be required of thee; then whose shall those things be which thou hast provided?" It would appear, that his situation with respect to an heir was similar to what Solomon describes, (Ecclesiastes iv. 8.) "There is one alone, and there is not a second; yea, he hath neither child nor brother; yet there is no end of all his labor," &c. But whatever became of his *fruits*, we know that his *folly* proved a lasting estate, for it continues to be the inheritance of many at this day. I believe there are numbers among ourselves, whose minds are continually on the rack, so that they cannot sleep with laying schemes about the merest trifles in the world. In this age of gayety and frivolous ostentation, I make no doubt, that the superfluities of dress, furniture, equipage, and the like, employ the thoughts of the rich (or of people of fashion, whether they be rich or not) as anxiously, as the clothing that is necessary to cover their nakedness employs the thoughts of the poor and destitute. It is the care of some to overtop their neighbors; it is the care of others to overreach at gaming; and indeed the mind of a gamester must be in perpetual suspense and agitation. Surely I need not tell you, that it would be impious to *cast* such *cares upon God*. We are not at liberty to choose at random whatsoever is agreeable to fancy or appetite; and, when our passions are inflamed, and our hearts overcharged with disquieting cares, attempt to roll these over upon God. We must first examine the object of our desire, whether it be good in itself, and fit for us; whether it be consistent with and subservient to our spiritual interest: and if, upon inquiry, it shall appear that these qualifications are wanting, we must neither cast the care of it upon God, nor keep it to ourselves, but throw it away altogether; praying that our folly may be forgiven, our diseased affections healed, and led forth to other objects more worthy of our pursuit. This being laid down, then, as a fundamental principle, that the object of our desire must be lawful and good, the *practice* of the duty which my text recommends may be considered as including the following particulars.

1*st*. A steadfast persuasion, that all events are ordered and directed by God; that we and all our interests are continually in his hand; and that nothing can befall us without his appointment or permission. This was the foundation of David's confidence, when he said, "Into thine hands I commit my spirit: thou hast redeemed me, O Lord God of truth. I have heard the slander of many; fear was on every side; while they took counsel totogether against me, they devised to take away my life. But I trusted in thee, O Lord: I said, Thou art my God, my times are in thy hand." Herein lies the difference betwixt the judgment of sanctified believers and that of worldly men: the last, confining their views to the objects of sense, place their whole dependence upon weak and mutable creatures like themselves. They court the smiles, and tremble at the frowns, of those who are raised a little above them; and have no higher aim than to recommend themselves to the favor and protection of such persons as are most likely to gratify their ambition or covetousness; whereas the believer, knowing that God is supreme, and that the highest creatures are only instruments which he employs at his pleasure, keeps his eye continually fixed upon him, and hath no other concern than to be found walking in those ways which he hath appointed; being fully assured, that all events, of whatever kind, are ordered by his reconciled Father in Christ Jesus, and shall infallibly work together for his spiritual improvement in this state of discipline, and issue in his complete and everlasting felicity.

2*dly*. To *cast our care upon God*, is to make his will the guide and measure of ours. We may desire, we may ask, what appears to us good in its own nature, and conducive either to our comfort or usefulness in a present world; we may lawfully wish to be delivered from trouble, to enjoy health of body, composure and cheerfulness of mind, the pleasures of virtuous friendship, and a competent portion of the good things of this life: but still we must desire and ask these blessings with due submission to the will of God, leaving it entirely to his unerring wisdom to give or to withhold them, as seemeth good unto himself. We have a lovely example of this temper in the behavior of David upon a very trying occasion. When the unsuspected rebellion of his unnatural son Absalom, which threatened him with the immediate loss, not of his crown only, but also of his life, obliged him to leave Jerusalem in haste; we are told, that among the few that accompanied him in his flight toward the wilderness, was Zadock the priest, and with him all the Levites, bearing the ark of the covenant of God. In this time of great distress, when his situation was so affecting, that, as we read (2 Sam. xv. 23.) "all the country wept with a loud voice" while they beheld him passing over the brook Kidron, the sacred historian informs us, (ver. 25, 26.) that the king addressed Zadock in the following words: "Carry back the ark of God into the city; if I shall find favor in the eyes of the Lord, he will bring me again, and show me both it and his habitation. But if he thus say, I have no delight in thee, behold, here am I, let him do to me as seemeth good unto him."—What shall be the issue of this formidable conspiracy I know not; but I *cast my care*, my all, upon my God: in the mean time, let the ark of the covenant be carried back to its place. The *presence* of the God of Israel is not confined to this symbol of his grace; and that I trust shall encompass me whithersoever I go, to support and cheer me in this melancholy flight. Whether or not I shall be restored to my house and throne, I cannot at present foresee: but this I know, that in either case it shall be well with me. If I return to Jerusalem, I shall again behold this ark, and enjoy the Lord my God in his ordinances; but if my God hath no farther service for me on this earth, I shall go to that place where there is no occasion for external means of correspondence and intercourse. Behold, here I lie at the disposal of my Father and my King, equally prepared to live or to die; to reign once more in the earthly Jerusalem, or to take up my eternal residence in the Jerusalem that is above.—This unlimited resignation to the will of God makes an essential part of the duty which my text recommends. It further implies,

3*dly*. That we renounce all confidence in the creature, and place our trust in God alone. We are required, you see, *to cast* ALL *our care upon him;* not a part, but the whole. For thus it is written, (Jer. xvii. 5, 8.) "Cursed be the man that trusteth in man, and maketh flesh his arm, and whose heart departeth from the Lord. For he shall be like the heath in the desert, and shall not see when good cometh, and shall inhabit the parched places in the wilderness, in a salt land and not inhabited." Whereas, "Blessed is the man that trusteth in the Lord, and whose hope the Lord is. For he shall be as a tree planted by the waters, and that spreadeth out her roots by the river, and shall not see when heat cometh, but her leaf shall be green, and shall not be careful in the year of drought, neither shall cease from yielding fruit." A divided trust between God and the creature, is as foolish and unsafe, as to set one foot upon a rock and the other upon the quicksand. We must, as I formerly observed, be diligent in the use of means; for thus the commandment runs, "Trust in the Lord, and do good;" but at the same time we must look beyond and above all means to God himself for success; saying, as David did, "My soul, wait thou *only* upon God; for my expectation is from him. He *only* is my rock and my salvation; he is my defence; I shall not be moved. In God is my salvation and my glory; the rock of my strength, and my refuge is on God." Once more, in the

4*th* place, To *cast all our care upon God*, implies a full and unsuspecting dependence upon his wisdom and goodness; such a dependence as quiets the mind, disposing it to wait patiently upon God, and to accept with thankfulness whatsoever he is pleased to appoint. The Christian who hath learned this important lesson, not only brings his cares to the throne of grace, but there also he leaves them, and, like Hannah, returns with his countenance no more sad. Having, "by prayer and supplication, with thanksgiving, made his requests known to God," his mind is at rest, "he is careful for nothing;" he hath put all his interests into the best hands; he hath committed them to One, who is too wise to bestow what is hurtful, and too kind to withhold what is good. In consequence whereof, "the peace of God, that passeth all understanding, keeps his heart and mind through Jesus Christ." This gracious temper brings not only rest, but liberty to the soul. It breaks all those fetters in pieces, by which the covetous, the ambitious, the voluptuous, are chained to a present world, and dragged at the heels of those worse than Egyptian taskmasters, "the lust of the eye, the lust of the flesh, and the pride of life." Whatever God willeth is pleasing to the sanctified believer; and the light of his Father's countenance, amidst the deepest and most complicated distress, puts greater gladness into his heart than the sensualist can feel, or is capable of conceiving, when his corn and wine do most abound. It is this that gives the Christian the true enjoyment of life. No man can have the proper relish of any earthly comfort, who is not prepared to part with it. This looks like a paradox, but will be found upon examination to be a weighty truth. Where fear is, there is torment; and nothing mars our joy so effectually as the prospect of being separated from what we greatly love. Talk to a carnal man of death, and the poor creature's spirit dies within him; the awful prospect of dissolution, like the handwriting upon the wall which Belshazzar perceived while he was drinking wine with his princes, his wives, and his concubines, will, in the height of his gayety, change his countenance, loosen the joints of his loins, and make his knees to smite against one another. Whereas the man who hath been taught to *cast his care upon God*, can sit cheerfully at the feast which Providence affords him, and think of his dying hour without diminishing the relish of his present enjoyment. Like David, (Psal. xxiii.) he can look forward without dismay, to his walk through the valley and shadow of death; and, while the gloomy object is in his eye, he can say to his God with thankful praise, "Thou preparest a table before me in the presence of mine enemies; thou anointest my head with oil, my cup runneth over: surely goodness and mercy shall follow me all the days of my life; and I will dwell in the house of the Lord for ever."

Thus have I opened the meaning of the exhortation, and at the same time attempted to give you a general view of the dignity and excellence of the temper it recommends. But the most persuasive motive to the practice of this duty, is that which the apostle himself maketh use of in the close of the verse, where he giveth full assurance to believers in Christ, that God, in a peculiar manner, *careth for them.* To this I shall proceed in my next discourse. May God lead us by his Spirit to the knowledge of our duty, and dispose us by his grace to the love and practice of it, for Christ's sake. *Amen.*

SERMON XXXIV.

THE CHRISTIAN CHRIST'S CARE.

1 Peter v. 7.—"Casting all your care upon him, for he careth for you."

These words contain a pressing exhortation to an important duty, and a most persuasive argument to enforce the practice of it. It was an apostle of Christ who gave the exhortation, and he addressed it to believers in Christ; not to those who barely professed Christianity in opposition to Heathenism, but to real saints, as distinguished from mere nominal Christians, "who have a form of godliness, but deny the power thereof." What their condition was with respect to external things, partly appears from the inscription of the epistle, where they are called "strangers, scattered abroad throughout Pontus, Galatia, Cappadocia, Asia, and Bithynia." Such persons were not likely to enjoy much worldly ease or affluence; and indeed we have positive evidence that they did not; for we are told expressly, that "they were in heaviness through manifold temptations," reproached as evil-doers, and cruelly persecuted for the name of Christ. Nay, as if these trials had been only the beginning of sorrows, the apostle forewarns them, at the 12th verse of the preceding chapter, that they were soon to enter upon a new scene of sufferings; the severity of which should far exceed any thing they had yet felt. "Beloved," saith he, "think it not strange concerning the *fiery trial* which is to try you, as though some strange thing happened unto you; but rejoice, inasmuch as ye are partakers of Christ's sufferings; that when his glory shall be revealed, ye may be glad also with exceeding joy."

We can hardly doubt, that such an awful prospect would beget many anxious, disquieting thoughts. *Cares* it behooved them to have; not about the trivial accommodations of a present life, *theirs* would be of a more serious and important nature: How they should quit themselves like men, and maintain their ground against the craft of seducers, and the furious attacks of persecuting zeal; how they should adorn the doctrine of God their Saviour, and "cut off occasion from those who desired occasion to blaspheme that worthy name by which they were called;" above all, how they should recommend religion to the esteem and choice of their enemies, and become the instruments of saving from eternal death those who thirsted for their own blood, and treated them like the filth and offscouring of all things. Such, we may suppose, would be the principal cares of persecuted saints; and all these they are exhorted to cast upon God: *For*, adds the apostle, *God careth for you.*

This is the argument which I shall now endeavor to illustrate,

1. By laying before you the evidence of its truth; and,

2. By showing its propriety and strength for engaging us to *cast our care upon God.*

I. When we consider the character of the persons to whom this exhortation was originally addressed, it will readily occur to us, that the apostle means something more by the *care* of God, than that general providence which extends to all the creatures he hath made. The *care* he speaks of, is that peculiar and affectionate regard to the saints which he had before described, (chap. iii. 12.) "The eyes of the Lord are over the righteous, and his ears are open unto their prayers; but the face of the Lord is against them that do evil." Thus it is written, that "he withdraweth not his eye from the righteous." "The Lord is God," saith the prophet Nahum, "a strong hold in the day of trouble, and he knoweth them that trust in him." Many other passages might be quoted which assert, in the most explicit terms, that God *careth* for his saints in another manner than he doth for the rest of the world. But that you may have a more extensive and encouraging view of the evidence of this truth, consider

How intimately the saints are related to God. "Behold," saith the apostle John in name of all the faithful, "behold, what manner of love the Father hath bestowed upon us, that we should be called the *sons* of God." Nor is this a mere title of honor; the persons on whom it is conferred are invested with a full and unalterable right to all those privileges which the title imports; for, as St. Paul reasons, "If children, then heirs, heirs of God, and joint heirs with Christ." And can it be supposed, that the Father of mercies will abandon his own offspring? Do earthly parents care for their children? and can he who hath implanted that disposition in their nature, be unconcerned about those whom he hath adopted into his family, and regenerated by his Spirit? Is it possible that the streams should have more sweetness than the fountain whence they flow? No, surely. "If men, being evil, know how to give good gifts to their children, much more will the Father of mercies give good things unto them that ask him." And is not this a solid ground of confidence and hope? Every believer in Christ may expect all from God, and infinitely more, than any child can expect from the most affectionate and tender-hearted parent upon earth. But this is not all: for

Our Father in heaven hath in a manner laid open his heart to us, and told us plainly what we may lawfully ask and hope to obtain. He hath published his good-will in a variety of great and precious promises; promises that extend to all the necessities of his children; insomuch, that be their condition what it will, they may find some gracious declaration of what God hath purposed to do, which suits their case with as much precision and exactness, as if their particular distress had been the immediate occasion of it. Or if any calamity should present itself to their imagination, against which no effectual provision appears to have been made, there is one promise upon record, to which the believing soul may at all times retreat, (Rom. viii. 28.) "We know that all things work together for good to them that love God, to them who are the called according to his purpose." These are the words of him who is unchangeable, "the same yesterday, to-day, and for ever, without any variableness or shadow of turning." Hear what he saith, (Isa. xlix. 15.) "Can a woman forget her sucking child, that she should not have compassion on the son of her womb? yea, they may forget, yet will I not forget thee." And that we may have fuller assurance of this, we are told by the prophet Malachi, that a book of remembrance is written before God, for them that fear the Lord, and that think upon his name." Nay, the Scriptures inform us, that there is One in heaven, infinitely dear to the Father, who is not only a faithful Remembrancer, but a powerful Advocate, and unwearied Intercessor, in behalf of all who come to God by "him."

And this may be considered as an additional ground of assurance that believers are the objects of God's peculiar care. "We have a great High-Priest, who is passed into the heavens, Jesus the Son of God, who constantly appears in the presence of God for us." Thus John beheld him in vision, "standing in the midst of the throne, as a Lamb that had been slain," displaying those wounds which he received, when "he bore our sins in his own body on the tree," as so many mouths filled with the most prevailing arguments for mercy and grace to his redeemed ones, whom he then did, and still doth, represent. We have a specimen of his intercession recorded by that apostle in the 17th chapter of his gospel; where, among other tender and affectionate requests, we find the following remarkable words: "Now I am no more in the world, but these are in the world, and I come to thee. Holy Father, keep through thine own name those whom thou hast given me. I pray not that thou shouldst take them out of the world, but that thou shouldst keep them from the evil. Neither pray I for these alone, but for them also which shall believe on me through their word." In such terms did our Lord recommend his immediate followers, and all his disciples in succeeding generations, to the protection and care of his heavenly Father. And may not this beget in us the fullest and most joyful assurance, that God doth, and always will, care for them? And still more, when we consider, that he who thus intercedes in their behalf, is himself possessed of all power in heaven and in earth, and is constituted Head over all things for the church. "I am he," said he, "that was dead and am now alive, and behold I live for evermore, and have the keys of hell and of death."

These are some of the evidences which the Scriptures afford us, that God careth for sanctified believers. The relation he bears to them, the promises he hath given to them, the constant prevailing intercession of his Son, together with the power committed to him as King of Zion, all concur to secure this important benefit.

But I have further to add, that we have the evidence of *facts*, as well as of arguments, to establish our faith of the divine care and protection. The sacred records bear witness, that God hath been the dwelling-place of his people in all generations, and give us abundant reason to say, with David, "Our fathers trusted in thee; they trusted, and thou didst deliver them. They cried unto thee, and were delivered; they trusted in thee, and were not confounded." And God is always in one mind: "He is the rock, his work is perfect, and all his ways are judgment; a God of truth and without iniquity, just and right is he."

What signal appearances hath he made in every age for the protection and safety of his peculiar people? Nothing can be conceived more formidable than Pharaoh's preparation against the Israelites; the whole strength of an extensive and potent empire employed against an undisciplined company of fugitives, who had long been dispirited by oppression and slavery: but though the bush was all in flame, yet it was not consumed. when the enemy said, "I will pursue, I will overtake, I will divide the spoil, my lust shall be satisfied on them, I will draw the sword, my hand shall destroy them:"—*then* the sea opened a passage for their escape, and overwhelmed their enemies; "God did blow with his wind, the sea covered them, they sank as lead in the mighty waters." How wonderful were the steps of Joseph's advancement to which his father and brethren owed their preservation in a time of famine? And no less wonderful was the defeat of Haman's wicked attempt to cut off the whole nation of the Jews as one man. In either case the failing of one circumstance would have varied the event; and yet each circumstance in both, when viewed apart, seems purely accidental; nay, some of them appear at first sight rather adverse than favorable. And lest any should imagine that these, and other deliverances of the like nature, were really casual, and therefore no proofs of God's gracious protection, let it be observed, that in two of the instances I have mentioned, the events were the direct and immediate answers of prayer. Thus the Red Sea was divided when Moses and the children of Israel "cried unto the Lord." And Haman's plot was detected and broken on that very day which Esther and Mordecai had set apart for fasting and prayer. To which I may add, that Asa obtained a complete victory over his enemies, after he had uttered that fervent supplication, "Help us, O Lord our God." And the apostle Peter was brought out of prison by the ministry of an angel, on that very night when prayer was offered up by the church in his behalf.

You see, then, upon the whole, that the truth of the apostle's assertion in the text is supported and confirmed by every kind of evidence we could wish to obtain. Let us now consider,

II. The propriety and force of the argument for engaging us to *cast our care upon God.* This branch of the subject will need little illustration. For,

1*st.* If *God careth for us*, then we have one to *care* for us who is infinitely wise, who is perfectly acquainted with all our wants, and can never mistake in judging what is best for us. We may choose many things apparently good, the possession of which would prove hurtful to our souls; for, as Solomon observed long ago, (and daily experience confirms the observation) "No man knoweth what is good for man in this life." There are many latent seeds of corruption in our hearts that we do not at present suspect, and perhaps shall never discover, unless a proper temptation bring them forth to our view. David, whose conscience was so tender in the wilderness, that it smote him for cutting off the skirt of Saul's garment, continued insensible for a long time under the most aggravated guilt, after he was fixed in the peaceable possession of a throne. Hezekiah, whose devotion was so humble and ardent in the time of his sickness, waxed proud and vain-glorious when restored to health; insomuch that "he brought wrath upon himself, and upon Judah, and upon Jerusalem." Many who, in a low estate, were humane and kind, and did good with the little they possessed, have been so intoxicated with the full cup of prosperity, that, for a season at least, they have forgotten themselves, their neighbor, nay, their God, and become quite the reverse of what they formerly appeared to be. One thing is certain, that if left to our own choice we should never feel distress or affliction of any kind; and yet the Scriptures assure us, and our own observation may convince us of the truth of it, that adversity is more friendly to religion than prosperity. Our diseased nature requires bitter medicines much oftener than cordials; even the best need frequently to be dieted, and brought low, to keep their feverish passions and appetites within bounds. Now God is perfectly acquainted with all the tendencies of our nature, and can therefore judge with unerring skill what things are best for us, and most conducive to our interest. He knows what measure of health, or riches, or honors, we shall be able to bear, or be disposed to improve; when, and in what proportion, pain, or sickness, or poverty, or reproach, are necessary to expel some spiritual distemper, to exercise and strengthen some languishing grace, or to make room in the heart for his own divine presence. Again, let our enemies plot against us in the most secret manner; let them shut themselves up in the closest retirement; yet it is impossible for them to hide their consultations from God, "who discovereth deep things out of darkness, and bringeth to light the shadow of death." When Benhadad had failed in his repeated attempts to cut off the armies of Israel by surprise, his heart was sore troubled; and suspecting treachery in his own court, he called his servants together, and said unto them, "Will ye not shew me which of us is for the King of Israel?" To which one of his servants replied, "None, my Lord, O King; but Elisha the prophet that is in Israel, telleth the king of Israel the words that thou speakest in thy bed-chamber." Nay, he can preserve his people from the effects of their own folly, as well as from the craft and malice of their enemies. "The Lord knoweth how to deliver the godly out of temptation:"—"He leadeth the blind in a way that they knew not:"—"He giveth understanding to the simple:"—"The meek will he guide in judgment, the meek will he teach his way." And if infinite Wisdom take the disposal of our lot, if he who cannot err vouchsafe to become both our guardian and our guide, with what unsuspecting trust may we commit ourselves into his hands, and cheerfully acquiesce in all the determinations of his Providence? Especially when we consider,

2*dly.* That his *power* is equal to his *wisdom.* "Whatsoever the Lord pleaseth, that doth he in heaven, in the earth, and in the sea, and in all deep places." He causeth the wrath of man to praise him; and the remainder thereof he is able to restrain. All the power of the creatures is derived from him, and dependent upon him. The haughtiest tyrant upon earth is only the rod of his anger, which he employs for a season, and then breaketh in pieces, and throws it away. When Pilate said to our Lord, "Knowest thou not that I have power to crucify thee, and power to release thee?" he at once detected and reproved his ignorance and pride, by answering him, "Thou couldst have no power at all against me, except it were given thee from above." And as the power of God is supreme, so is it likewise everlasting. "The Lord, the Creator of the ends of the earth, fainteth not, neither is weary." His arm is never shortened that it cannot save; neither age nor exercise can impair its vigor; what he did yesterday he can do to-day, and repeat it as often as his people have occasion for it. This was the foundation of that expostulatory address, (Isaiah li. 9.) "Awake, awake, put on strength, O arm of the Lord; awake as in the ancient days, in the generations of old. Art not thou it that hath cut Rahab, and wounded the dragon?" To which God replied, "I, even I, am he that comforteth you: who art thou then that thou shouldst be afraid of a man that shall die, and of the son of man which shall be made as grass? and forgettest the Lord thy Maker, that hath stretched forth the heavens, and laid the foundations of the earth? and hast feared continually every day, because of the fury of the oppressor, as if he were ready to destroy? And where is the fury of the oppressor? I am the Lord thy God, that divided the sea, whose waters roared: the Lord of Hosts is my name." His power reacheth to the heart of man, to which no creature can have immediate access: even the hearts of kings are in his hand, and he turneth them as the rivers of water. Thus he promised to Jeremiah, "that he would cause the enemy to entreat him well in the day of evil." Who but the Lord of man's heart could have said unto Moab, and said it with efficacy, "Let mine outcasts dwell with thee, Moab; be thou a covert to them from the face of the spoiler?" Thus, when it pleaseth him, he can open a sanctuary for his people in the midst of their foes, and make these very foes the protectors of his people. In short, "with God all things are possible." He is able to do exceeding abundantly above all that we can ask or think. This good old Jacob gratefully acknowledged, when he met with his darling son Joseph, whose supposed death he had long and bitterly lamented: "I had not thought to see thy face, and lo! God hath showed me thy children also." "When the apostles had the sentence of death in themselves," God dispelled their fears, and preserved their lives, in spite of all the rage and cunning of their persecutors. And thus, "in the mount of the Lord" it hath often "been seen:" deliverance came when death was expected; or, according to the prophetic style of Zechariah, (chap. xiv. 7.) "at evening time:" when, according to the course of nature, nothing was looked for but deepening shades and increasing darkness, "light" hath suddenly sprung up, and the thick clouds have fled and vanished away. Here then is a solid ground of confidence and hope: He *that careth for us*, not only *knoweth* all things, but *can do* all things. He giveth power to the faint, and to them that have no might he increaseth strength. "Fear not," saith he, "for I am with thee: be not dismayed, for I am thy God: I will strengthen thee, yea I will help thee, yea I will uphold thee, with the right hand of my righteousness." Have we not then the most powerful encouragement to *cast our care*, our whole *care, upon God?* And still more, when I add,

3*dly*. That he who is so wise in heart, and mighty in strength; so wonderful in counsel, and excellent in working; is likewise possessed of infinite goodness. Like as a father pitieth his children, so the Lord pitieth them that fear him. "God is love," said the apostle John; and well might he say so, who was one of the heralds of that joyful proclamation, "God was in Christ reconciling the world unto himself, not imputing their trespasses unto them." Here then is a foundation that is able to carry all the weight a believer can lay upon it; for "if God spared not his own Son, but delivered him up for us all, how shall he not with him also freely give us all things?" What can he withhold from those upon whom he hath already bestowed his own dear Son, and enabled, by his Spirit, thankfully to receive him as the "unspeakable gift" of God to men. How firm then are the grounds of the believer's hope? With what humble, but triumphant confidence, may he *cast his care upon God*, whose *wisdom* knoweth all things, whose *power* can do all things, and whose unbounded *goodness* doth constantly incline him to bestow every needful blessing upon his people?

As I have made it my business, in every branch of the subject, to keep the persons in your eye to whom the exhortation is addressed, it is almost unnecessary to remind you, in the conclusion, that the comfort of all I have said must be confined to those who are Christians indeed. None else are the objects of that peculiar care which the apostle speaks of; and therefore to them only the privilege belongs of *casting all their care upon God.* Permit me now to add, that as it is their privilege, so it is likewise their duty; and they dishonor themselves, and reproach their Father, when they give way to anxious, disquieting cares upon any account whatsoever. We may justly say to such, as Jonadab said to Amnon, "Why art thou, being the king's son, lean from day to day?" Carry all your grievances to him who is both able and willing to redress them. Make use of thy birth-right, O Christian! and *cast thy cares upon him that careth for thee.* Your very reliance upon him, in the way of duty, your leaning upon his arm, if I may so express it, while you are using the appointed means, insures his protection according to that gracious promise, (Isaiah xxvi. 3.) "Thou wilt keep him in perfect peace, whose mind is stayed upon thee, because he trusteth in thee."

But what shall those do who are of an opposite character? May not they too *cast their care upon God*, as the God of nature, the Father of their spirits, and the former of their bodies, in whom they live and move? Doth not his providence extend to all the creatures he hath made? Doth he not clothe the lilies, and feed the ravens, and hear the lions when they cry to him for food? All this is true; and, in one sense, all men without exception are the objects of his care. But this can yield no comfort to impenitent, unbelieving sinners; for the same God who sustains them in life, and gives them what they possess, and most ungratefully abuse, hath expressly declared, "that though hand join in hand, the wicked shall not pass unpunished." I appeal to yourselves, is it reasonable to expect, that God shall take the burden of your cares, while you deny him your hearts, and even fight against him with the fruits of his bounty? If you think coolly upon the matter, I am almost persuaded you will blush to ask it.

How then are you to dispose of your cares?—What shall I say? I might tell you, that your anxiety will do you no good; and therefore it were best to lay it aside, and take things as they happen, without murmuring. But this were only to amuse you; for the burden would still press you with its weight, and all my reasoning would amount to nothing more than a cold, unavailing advice to struggle with it as you can. But if your cares be very painful, though I cannot encourage you to go directly to God with them in your present state, yet I shall suggest a hint which by the blessing of God may be of use to you. It hath often been observed, that one great care will swallow up many others of smaller importance, and even banish them from the mind altogether. Thus, in a storm at sea, the most covetous worldlings have been known to throw their most precious goods overboard with their own hands, when no other means could be found to keep the ship above water. This points out a remedy; and it is the only remedy that occurs to me. Were you awakened to a proper concern about the life of your souls, this would have a powerful influence to cure your anxiety about lesser things. Were you brought to cry out with the jailor, "What shall I do to be saved?" you would find neither leisure nor inclination to ask these disquieting, anxious questions, "What shall I eat? and what shall I drink? and wherewithal shall I be clothed?" All these would be swallowed up in your concern for "the one thing needful." And give me leave to add, that when this becomes your care, I shall then be at full liberty to invite you to *cast it upon God;* nay, I shall be able to assure you, that he will not only accept the charge, but likewise give you what you care for, even a complete and everlasting salvation. O then "seek the Lord while he is to be found; call upon him while he is near."

May God determine and enable you to take this course, and make your worldly cares the means of leading your hearts beyond and above this world, to seek rest and happiness in himself. *Amen.*

SERMON XXXV.

SUFFICIENCY OF GOD'S GRACE.

2 Corin. xii. 9.—"He said unto me, my grace is sufficient for thee."

In the foregoing verses of this chapter, the apostle relates an extraordinary revelation he had been favored with, above fourteen years before the date of this epistle. He informs us, that "he was caught up into paradise," or "the third heaven (whether in the body, or out of the body, he could not tell), where he heard unspeakable words, which it is not lawful," or possible, "for a man to utter." This probably happened soon after his conversion; and was graciously intended, either to remove those doubts and fears which the resemblance of his former conduct might naturally occasion, or rather to fortify his mind against the trials and sufferings he was afterwards to meet with in the course of his ministry. One should imagine, that such a glorious manifestation could not be liable to any abuse. When Satan would have tempted our Lord to worship him, it was by giving him a sight and offer of all the kingdoms of *this* world; and we readily admit, that such a temptation might prove very fatal to us. Earthly objects have indeed too powerful a tendency to inflame our sensual appetites, and to alienate our hearts from God; but surely no danger can be apprehended from a view of heaven. The glories of the upper world, a display of those things above upon which God himself hath commanded us to set our affection, cannot be supposed to have any bad effect.

And no doubt this will be the case, when we shall be perfectly freed from all remainders of corruption. But we learn, from what follows, that in our present state of weakness and depravity, even a view of heaven might prove a snare to our souls. Holy Paul, as we read (verse 7.) was in danger of being "exalted above measure through the abundance of the revelations; for which cause "there was given to him a thorn in the flesh, the messenger of Satan to buffet him." What this particular exercise was is not material for us to know. The words plainly import, that it was both violent and painful; and the effects it produced as evidently show, that it was appointed in mercy, and wisely calculated for his spiritual advantage. This eminent saint, who but a little before was caught up into paradise, now humbles himself as low as the dust. He falls down upon his knees, and earnestly implores deliverance from this trial. Once and again he repeats his supplication, but gets no answer. This could not fail to heighten his distress. A messenger of Satan is sent to buffet him; and God, by his silence, seems deaf to his entreaties. But still this is made to work for his good: He becomes more and more sensible of his own weakness; he draws nearer to a throne of grace, and renews his suit with increasing fervor and importunity. "For this thing," says he, (verse 8.) "I besought the Lord thrice, that it might depart from me." At length the answer comes in the words of my text: *And he said unto me, My grace is sufficient for thee.*

You will observe, that, after all his entreaties, the Lord did not grant him the precise thing he had asked; but he gave him what was better, and more suited to his condition. Paul needed an antidote against spiritual pride; and as the thorn in the flesh was necessary for that end, it would have been no act of kindness to have taken it away: and therefore our Lord, who knew his servant better than he knew himself, prolongs the trial, but at the same time assures him of grace to support him under it. This messenger of Satan must not be sent away, lest thou shouldst forget thy dependence upon me; but I will stand by thee, and strengthen thee to bear his assaults and buffetings; that, feeling thine own weakness, and the power of *my grace*, thy soul may be kept at an equal distance from *presumption* on the one hand, and from *distrust* on the other; both which extremes are utterly inconsistent with the duties of my service, and the happiness of my people.

According to this view of the words, I propose, in dependence upon divine aid,

I. To guard you against pride and self-confidence, by giving you a true representation of that weak and impotent state into which we are fallen by our apostasy from God; and,

II. For your encouragement, I shall lead your thoughts to that *all-sufficient grace* which is treasured up in Christ, whereby the weakest of his people are enabled to endure the buffetings of Satan, and shall finally prevail against all their spiritual enemies.

I. That I may guard you against pride and self-confidence, I shall lay before you a plain and scriptural account of that weak and impotent state into which we are fallen by our apostasy from God.

It were easy to quote a variety of passages which expressly assert the corruption of human nature, and man's utter inability to do any thing that can be effectual for his own recovery: but I need only appeal to every man who reads the sacred oracles with seriousness and impartiality, whether this doth not appear to be a Scriptural doctrine from the very face of the revelation, and the uniform strain of the word of God.

Doth not the method of salvation by Jesus Christ necessarily suppose the whole human race to be in a state of guilt, pollution, and weakness? Do not the promises of taking away the heart of stone, and giving a heart of flesh, plainly imply, that these works are peculiar to God, and that man is unable to do such great things for himself? Would God command us to pray to him for these inestimable blessings, if we were able to procure them by our own wisdom and strength? nay, would it not be a mocking of God to apply to him for that which we are already possessed of, or may acquire when we choose, without his interposition or aid? Besides, are we not told, that "every good and perfect gift is from above, and cometh down from the Father of lights?" Is not our sanctification every where attributed to the Spirit of God? and are not the saints denominated "God's workmanship, *created* in Christ Jesus unto good works, which God hath before ordained, that they should walk in them?" Are not "love, joy, peace, long-suffering, gentleness, goodness, faith, meekness, temperance," expressly said to be "the fruits of the Spirit?" nay, are we not told, that it is God who worketh in us "to *will* and to *do* of his good pleasure?" Surely, my brethren, if we judge of the Scriptures by the same rules that we judge of any other books; nay, unless we suppose that they were artfully contrived to mislead us; we must be sensible, that the absolute necessity of supernatural grace, is not only clearly asserted in Scripture, but that this doctrine is so intimately connected with all the other parts of divine revelation, that the whole must stand or fall with it.

This is further confirmed by the concurring testimony of all the saints of whose experiences, in the spiritual life, we have any accounts recorded in Scripture. They all join in the most humiliating acknowledgments of their guilt, pollution, and weakness; disclaiming the praise of any good thing that was in them, and ascribing the undivided glory of all that they possessed, or hoped to enjoy, to the free unmerited grace of God. How pathetically did David bewail the corruption of his nature, (Psal. li. 5.) "Behold, I was shapen in iniquity, and in sin did my mother conceive me." And what a deep sense did he express of his inability to cleanse or purify himself, when he addressed God in such terms as these, (verse 10.) "Create in me a clean heart, O God, and renew a right spirit within me." But lest any should be so injurious as to suspect that David might have spoken after this manner, to apologize for his criminal conduct in the matter of Uriah, which gave occasion to that psalm; let us hear what the apostle Paul saith of himself, whose character is not liable to any such objection, (Rom. vii. 18. *et seq.*) "I know, that in me (that is, in my flesh) dwelleth no good thing; for to will is present with me; but how to perform that which is good, I find not.—I find then a law, that when I would do good, evil is present with me. For I delight in the law of God, after the inward man. But I see another law in my members, warring against the law of my mind, and bringing me into captivity to the law of sin, which is in my members." Upon which he cries out, "O wretched man that I am, who shall deliver me from the body of this death!" Here then is one who was not behind the very chief apostles; who, before his conversion, lived a Pharisee, and afterwards could say at the bar of the Jewish Sanhedrim, "I have lived in all good conscience before God unto this day;" who, conscious of the grace he had received, expressed himself thus in the presence of Agrippa, "I would to God, that not only thou, but all that hear me this day, were both almost and altogether such as I am, except these bonds." Yet this chosen vessel ingenuously confesseth his natural depravity, mourns over the remainders of a body of sin, and ascribes those eminent gifts and graces with which his soul was so remarkably enriched, to God, and to him alone, saying, (1 Cor. xv. 10.) "By the grace of God I am what I am: and his grace which was bestowed upon me, was not in vain; but I labored more abundantly than they all: yet not I, but the grace of God which was with me." Now what should have induced Paul to speak after this manner if it had not been true? Surely this was not the way to make a figure in the world. Had that been his aim, it would have answered his purpose far better to have represented his high attainments as the fruit of his own labor and diligence, rather than a mere alms to which he had no previous title. Surely nothing but a regard to truth could have drawn from him such humble, repeated acknowledgments; and therefore his testimony is altogether beyond exception. And when I add, that he wrote under the immediate direction and influence of the Spirit of God, we are furnished with the most convincing evidence of the absolute necessity of divine grace, for beginning and carrying forward a work of sanctification in the soul of an apostate creature.

They whose religion lies wholly in speculation, who have acquired a refined system of opinions, but never tried in good earnest to reduce them to practice, may dispute against this doctrine, and flatter themselves into a vain conceit of the vigor and sufficiency of the natural powers they possess. But all who are exercised to godliness, who have put their strength to the trial, (and they only are competent judges in a question of this nature) know the truth of what I have been proving, and will be ready to attest it from their own experience. Nevertheless, as pride is the last part of the old man that dies, it will be profitable even for such persons to "be put in remembrance of these things, though they know them, and be established in the present truth." Have you experienced the power of divine grace? have you tasted and seen that the Lord is good? then surely it is meet that your souls should bless him. But, O be humble! and give check to any self-exalting thoughts. Consider both where and what you are. You are still upon earth, part of the wilderness lieth before you, and you must pass through the valley and shadow of death before you can enter into the promised land. Many seeds of corruption still lodge in your nature; many enemies beset you, both within and without; the fiery darts of the wicked one fly thick on every side: and nothing less than Omnipotence can protect and sustain you, and carry you forward in safety to the end of your journey. If you trust in any measure to yourselves, if you depend upon the grace you have already received, as if that would be sufficient for the time to come, you shall soon get a proof of your ignorance and folly. You need daily grace as much as daily bread; for, separated from Christ, you can do nothing. Beware, O Christians! of undertaking any thing in your own strength; for that which is begun in self-confidence will most assuredly end in shame and disappointment. Go forth in the name of the Lord of hosts, saying, with good king Jehoshaphat, (2 Chron. xx. 21.) "O Lord, we know not what to do, but our eyes are towards thee." And for your encouragement, I shall now,

II. In the *second* place, Lead your thoughts to that all-sufficient grace which is treasured up in Christ; whereby the weakest of his people are enabled to endure the buffetings of Satan, and shall finally be made to triumph over all their spiritual enemies.

This is a most comfortable doctrine, and cannot fail to beget joy and confidence in every believing soul. How completely wretched would the discovery of our weakness make us, had we no knowledge where help is to be found, or no hope that help would be granted to us! But, blessed be God, neither of these is the case. For,

1*st.* An overflowing fountain of *grace* is set open to our view. "The Word was made flesh," saith the apostle John, "and dwelt among us, (and we beheld his glory, the glory as of the only begotten of the Father) full of *grace* and truth." "It hath pleased the Father," saith the apostle Paul, "that in him should all fulness dwell." Nay, "In him dwelleth all the fulness of the Godhead bodily." Coloss. ii. 9. Here then is not only fulness, but all fulness; nay, the whole fulness of the Godhead dwelling in Christ Jesus: and what words can import a *sufficiency* of grace, if these do not? But may we hope that this grace shall be imparted to us? Yes, we may. For, in the

2*d* place, The Scriptures assure us, that all this grace is treasured up in Christ for the behoof of his people. I need not mention particular passages of Scripture for the proof of this, seeing it evidently appears from the whole strain of divine revelation, where Christ is uniformly represented as a public person, sustaining the character of Mediator or Surety, living and dying, not for himself, but for the sake of those whom the Father had given him. Hence he is called the *head*, and believers are styled the *members* of his body. He is compared to the *vine;* and, in a suitableness to this figurative representation, believers are denominated *branches* which grow out of this vine, and derive all their sap and nourishment from it. That remarkable prophecy of Isaiah, (chap. lxi. 1,—3.) which our Lord applied to hinself in the synagogue at Nazareth, is a clear and strong confirmation of this truth: "The Spirit of the Lord God is upon me, because the Lord hath anointed me to preach good tidings unto the meek; he hath sent me to bind up the broken-hearted, to proclaim liberty to the captives, and the opening of the prison to them that are bound; to appoint unto them that mourn in Zion, to give unto them beauty for ashes, the oil of joy for mourning, the garment of praise for the spirit of heaviness; that they might be called trees of righteousness, the planting of the Lord, that he might be glorified." Here is a plain declaration, that Christ was anointed, and filled with the Spirit, for this very end, that he might dispense to his people those supplies of grace which their various cases and necessities might require. We are further assured,

dly. That Christ, upon all occasions, is willing and ready to impart his grace unto them according to their need. Ignorance of this keeps many Christians in a languishing, dejected state. Though they know that the fulness of the Godhead dwelleth in Christ, and that all grace is treasured up in him for the benefit of his people, they are nevertheless haunted with fears and jealousies about his willingness to communicate this treasure to them. These partly arise from the sense of their own unworthiness, and partly from the misrepresentations of Satan, the great adversary, who doth every thing in his power to cherish and strengthen those evil surmisings which keep sinners at a distance from the fountain of mercy, and drive them away from that Almighty Saviour upon whom their help is laid. But, blessed be God! the Scriptures furnish us with arguments more than sufficient to refute all the suggestions of Satan upon this head. The good will of our Lord shines with such glory in every page of this sacred book, that there can remain no rational ground to doubt of it: "In the last day, that great day of the feast, Jesus stood and cried, saying, If *any* man thirst, let him come unto me and drink. He that believeth on me, out of his belly shall flow rivers of living water. This," adds the evangelist, "spake he of the Spirit, which they that believe on him should receive." John vii. 37, 38, 39. He is represented, in the book of the Revelation, as standing at the door, and knocking, with these gracious words in his mouth, "If *any* man will hear my voice, and open the door, I will come in to him and sup with him, and he with me." How sweet is his name, *Jesus*, a Saviour! how endearing the relations he stands in to his people, as their Shepherd and Friend, their Husband, their Brother? Was he not tempted, that he might succor those who are tempted? And can we have any reason to question his love to us, who became flesh of our flesh, and bore our griefs, for this very end, that he might be gracious? Nay, we may appeal to facts for the proof of this doctrine. All the ransomed around the throne, who overcame by the blood and Spirit of the Lamb, give testimony to this great and important truth; and I trust there are many thousands upon earth, who, with humble gratitude and joy, can attest the same, and say with the apostle John, "Of his fulness have all we received, and grace for grace." More might be said upon this head; but you have heard enough to show, that believers in Christ have all possible encouragement to come boldly to a throne of grace, in the assured hope that they shall obtain mercy, and find grace to help them in every time of need. And therefore I shall only add,

4thly. That this grace of Christ, when once obtained, shall infallibly prove victorious, and finally prevail against all opposition. He who is the author, is likewise the finisher of his people's faith; for "his gifts and calling are without repentance." "He will not break the bruised reed, nor quench the smoking flax, till he bring forth judgment unto victory." *Grace*, though a small rivulet in appearance, is fed with an everlasting spring. Where the Lord Jesus begins a good work, he will carry it on to perfection, and never leave the objects of his love till he hath made them like himself, all glorious both within and without, and presented them to his Father without spot and blemish.

Thus have I laid before you two impotant points of Christian doctrine; *first*, Our weakness in ourselves; and, *secondly*, That sufficiency of grace which is to be found in Christ Jesus. The Spirit was not given by measure unto him; and the precious oil was poured upon his head, that from thence it might flow down to the remotest skirts of his garments, and be communicated to all the members of his body. Nay, he is, upon all occasions, most willing and ready to dispense to his people this inestimable blessing: none who come to him under a sense of need shall be sent empty away. And the first fruits of his *grace* are a certain pledge and earnest of future glory; for "whatsoever is born of God overcometh the world." It is not so much the Christian that lives, as Christ that liveth in him; and because he lives, all who believe in him shall live also. "They are kept," not by their own strength, but "by the power of God, through faith unto salvation."

How completely amiable doth the Lord Jesus appear when viewed in this light! How safe and happy are they who are vitally united to him! "The young lions do lack and suffer hunger; but they that fear the Lord shall not want any good thing." "O sing unto the Lord a new song, and his praise in the congregation of his saints: Let Israel rejoice in him that made and redeemed him; let the children of Zion be joyful in their King." These reflections are just and natural; but as I must not stay to enlarge upon all the uses that might be made of this subject, I shall at present confine myself to what appears most important and seasonable; namely, a few advices to Christians in general, and more especially to those who have newly entered upon a religious course. And,

1*st*. I would forewarn you of the opposition you are likely to meet with in your way heavenward. You have begun a warfare; and "every battle of the warrior is with confused noise, and garments rolled in blood." Corruption will no doubt assail you from within; but I am to warn you of danger from another quarter. We read, that when Jesus was born, "Herod the king was troubled, and all Jerusalem with him." In like manner, when Christ is formed in any heart, all hell is in an uproar, and the malignant brood of the old serpent upon earth will not fail to spit out their venom against that person as lavishly as they can. The wicked among whom you live will mock and ridicule you; and it is probable that your former companions in sin will taunt you with past and pardoned faults (for pardoned they are if you have come to Christ), and will exert their utmost strength and cunning to mar your confidence, if they cannot carry you back into the same excess of riot with themselves; nay, with hellish spite they may even forge lies to blacken your character, that they may not seem to have suffered any loss by your revolt from their party. All this you have reason to expect; and I speak of it beforehand, that when it happens, you may not be surprised or discouraged, as though some strange and unusual thing had befallen you. It is, and always hath been, the lot of God's children; and when you suffer in this manner, you have the honor to suffer in the best of causes, and with the best of company. "Marvel not, my brethren, if the world hate you;" it hated your Lord before it hated you, and the servant is not greater than his Master. If ye were of the world, the world would love its own; but because ye are not of the world, and because Christ hath called you out of the world, upon these accounts the world hateth you. "Rejoice, therefors, and be exceeding glad; for great is your reward in heaven."

2dly. Maintain a constant sense of your own weakness. Remember that caution of the apostle, "Be not high-minded, but fear." You can only work to purpose when you work upon a present strength; the grace you receive to-day will need a fresh supply of grace to revive and actuate it to-morrow; for Christ always dispenseth his peculiar gifts in such a way as to remind his people of their constant dependence upon him, and to render them diligent in the use of all the means he hath appointed for promoting the divine life in their souls. At the same time,

3dly. Think honorably of your Lord, in whose service you are engaged. Believe it, whatever Satan may suggest to the contrary, that his heart is kind, and his hand liberal. It is of the highest importance to have just conceptions of Christ, and to know what mercy and strength are laid up for us in him. Look not so much to your enemies as to the Captain of your salvation; set his promises against their threatening, his omnipotent grace against their impotent malice. Be ye therefore bold and very courageous; victory is insured to you; it is already sown in that new nature you have got; and ere long the Prince of Peace, the Lion of the tribe of Judah, shall bruise Satan underneath your feet, and put that triumphant song into your mouths, "Now is come salvation and strength, and the kingdom of our God, and the power of his Christ; for the accuser of our brethren is cast down, which accused them before our God day and night."

4thly. Remember, that all this sufficient grace is only to be obtained by prayer and supplication: "For this," saith God, "will I be inquired of by the house of Israel to do it for them." Paul, you see, besought the Lord thrice before he received the answer in my text. Prayer keeps the communication open between the head and the members; it is the messenger that goes from earth to heaven, and returns with all necessary blessings from thence. Beware, then, of neglecting this necessary duty. Pray in faith, pray in the name of Christ, pray without ceasing: and beg of Christ to teach you to pray aright, that you may ask and receive, and then your joy shall be full.

Now, brethren, I commend you to God, "and to the word of his grace, which is able to build you up, and to give you an inheritance among all them which are sanctified." And to him who is able to keep us from falling, whose *grace is sufficient* for all his people, at all times, and in all circumstances, to the only wise God and our Saviour, be glory and honor, dominion and power, for ever and ever. *Amen.*

SERMON XXXVI.

THE GREAT TRUST.

1 Thessalonians, ii. 4.—"But as we were allowed of God to be put in trust with the gospel, even so we speak, not as pleasing men, but God, which trieth our hearts."

When we compare ourselves with the primitive Christians, we are obliged to confess, that, in every respect, we fall greatly short of their attainments. We seem to be creatures of a lower rank, incapable of reaching the same degree of perfection with them: And indeed it is to be suspected, that through a false and vicious modesty, we look upon these ancient worthies as examples which, though we ought to imitate, we can never hope to equal. Hence we rest satisfied with any distant resemblance we can attain, thinking, that if we are not altogether unlike to them, it is all that a modern Christian can expect.

This is a gross and most pernicious mistake. The gate of heaven is no wider now than it was seventeen hundred years ago. The law of God extends as far as it did when the apostles lived; and I know of no indulgence granted to us which did not exist in the earliest times of Christianity. The church of Rome indeed hath taught, that some eminent Christians have done more than was strictly necessary for their own salvation. But no such doctrine is to be found in Scripture: Nay, on the contrary, we are told, that when we have done all, we are still unprofitable servants, and have done no more than what was our duty to do. To this day, therefore, we are bound to the same strictness and purity, to the same mortification and self-denial, to the same zeal and steadfastness, which distinguished the primitive Christians; and it is impossible to devise any excuse for our degeneracy from their bright example. They were all men of like passions with ourselves: they had the same corrupt nature to strive against, the same temptations to resist, the same enemies to overcome. Their advantages for performing their duty were not greater than ours: on the contrary, besides all that they possessed, we have the benefit of their example and experience. God's hand is not shortened, the blood of Christ hath lost none of its virtue, his intercession is no less prevalent, nor is the power of his Spirit in the least impaired by length of time and constant exercise. "He is the same yesterday, to-day, and for ever:" So that we are entirely without excuse, if we do not both aim at it, and actually attain the same degrees of holiness and purity with any of those that have gone before us.

Let us then consider all those persons celebrated in Scripture history, as examples which we not only ought to copy after, but may, through God's grace, hope to equal: and, instead of being dazzled with the lustre of their virtues, let us search into the principles which influenced their conduct, that, by cherishing these, we may be animated to go on, and do as they did.

The apostle mentions, in the text, one of distinguished efficacy, which I propose to make the subject of this discourse: A supreme desire to please God, who trieth the heart, without regard either to the praise or censure of men. It was this which supported him under the ignominious treatment he met with at Philippi, which he mentions in the second verse of this chapter, and encouraged him to persist in preaching that gospel which he had received in trust from God. It was this which rendered the first Christians superior to adversity in all its frightful forms; and it is the same divine principle, which, if once it got the entire possession of our hearts, would be a constant spring of holy obedience, and enable us, by the blessing of God, to follow the cloud of witnesses who have gone before us, through the most rugged paths of virtue, untainted with that meanness and inconstancy of behavior which are the reproach of so many professing Christians in our days.

I propose, therefore, through divine assistance, 1*st*, To open the nature and extent of the divine principle mentioned in my text; 2*dly*, To represent the happy effects which would flow from our being animated with this steady and prevailing desire. After which I shall conclude with a practical improvement on the subject.

I BEGIN with opening the nature and extent of the divine principle mentioned in the text. And to prevent any mistakes on this head, it may be needful to observe, that our making the approbation of God our principal aim, does not exclude all regard to the opinion or judgment of our fellow-creatures. We are certainly bound by that great law of our religion, "Thou shalt love thy neighbor as thyself," to make the pleasing of our brethren, by every lawful means, an object of attention, and a subordinate end of our conduct. And as our neighbor is commanded to love us as himself, both reason and religion teach us to render ourselves as amiable to him as we can, that so we may facilitate his performance of that important duty.

Neither, on the other hand, are we wholly to disregard the censures of men, or be altogether unconcerned, when our reputation is blackened by injurious calumnies. "A good name is better than precious ointment." It is a special blessing which we are to receive with thankfulness from the hand of God; and it is our duty to preserve it as carefully as we can. Without a good name, no man can be useful in the world. To neglect it therefore, where it does not proceed from a consciousness of guilt, is certainly in most cases a very culpable indifference. Thus far, then, the judgment of men is to be regarded; but then we must please our brethren only so far as it is pleasing to God. In every case we must state the matter thus: Whether it is wiser to obey God or man? to fear those who, after they have killed the body, have no more that they can do? or to fear him who, after he hath killed, can destroy both soul and body in hell? We must not only contemn the favor of men when compared with the approbation of God, but learn to value it among those transitory things which are only desirable as means for attaining a higher end.

In like manner, the displeasure of men, if unjust, must be reckoned among our light afflictions, which are but for a moment. In such circumstances, it must appear a small matter to us to be judged of man's judgment: "We have one that judgeth us, even God." That prophecy of our Saviour must be constantly remembered, that the world will hate us; and his example must be ever before our eyes, who condescended to be scorned, and buffeted, and slandered as an impostor and blasphemer; who made himself of no reputation, but endured the cross, and despised the shame, leaving us an example that we should follow his steps. In a word, God must be pleased by all means; his approbation is the one thing needful; he is now our Witness, and will ere long be our Judge; and in these two characters we ought constantly to set him before us.

This is the temper which the apostle expresseth in the text. I proceed now, in the

Second place, to represent the happy effects which would flow from our being animated with this steady and prevailing desire of pleasing God.

And, in the 1*st* place, This would make us ready to every good work, by removing all those grounds of hesitation and suspense, whereby double-minded people are perplexed and retarded in their way. A man must be very slow in his motions, when every step is burdened with such questions as these: What will men think or say of me, if I act in this manner? Will it endanger my reputation, or hurt my interst, or prevent my rising in the world? You will easily see that a considerable time must elapse before all these difficult points can be settled. Weheras the man whose single aim is to please God, is at once freed from all these incumbrances. He no sooner discovers the will of God, than he proceeds immediately to action; and whilst the other is bewildered with numberless conjectures, he goes cheerfully forward, leaving all his temporal concerns in the hands of that God by whose law he is governed, and to whose disposal he is entirely resigned. And is not this an unspeakable advantage, towards abounding in the fruits of righteousness? How free is the mind of such a man? how firm are his steps? He walks straight forward, without deviating into by-paths; and whilst his conscience tells him that he is accepted of God, he enjoys a pure and unmixed tranquillity, which the world can neither give nor take away.

A 2*d* happy effect that would flow from our being animated with a steady and prevailing desire of pleasing God, would be, that our conduct would thereby become consistent and uniform. God alone is invariable. What pleased him yesterday, pleaseth him to-day as well; and though his commandments are exceeding broad, yet they perfectly agree among themselves, and make one beautiful and harmonious system. Whereas men not only differ from one another, but at times from themselves also, and require opposite and contradictory things, which makes it absolutely impossible to please any number of them at one time, or even to continue long in the favor of any one of them, without the most disgraceful inconsistencies in our conduct; but he, whose single aim is to please God, in some measure resembles the Father of lights, "with whom is no variableness, neither shadow of turning." "His path is as the morning light, that shineth more and more unto the perfect day." His character is still brightening; he advanceth from one degree of grace to another; and is every moment drawing nearer to the enjoyment of that God whose approbation he constantly sought.

In the 3*d* place, The divine principle

mentioned in my text would produce an universal obedience to the laws of God, because they are but various ways of compassing the important end at which it aims.

The man who is truly animated with it, will, like David, have a "respect to all God's commandments;" and instead of complaining that they are grievous, will rather rejoice at being furnished with such a variety of opportunities for promoting the glory of his heavenly Father. This divine principle will have influence upon him in the most secret retirement, as well as when he acts in the open view of the world. The hypocrite, who courts the approbation of men, may be very exact and punctual in the outward exercises of religion; but he who seeks to please God will not rest in these. He knows that his Father seeth him in secret; he rejoiceth in the thought of it, and therefore omits no duty that bears the stamp of his authority: Yea, his heart is as much engaged in the severest acts of self-denial, as in those instances of obedience which are accompanied with the most immediate pleasure and advantage. And this leads me to observe, in the

4th place, That a sincere desire of pleasing God would likewise lessen the difficulties of obedience, and support us under all the sufferings to which our duty may at any time expose us. Perhaps our duty may be accompanied with much pain and trouble in the world; perhaps, like Paul, we may be shamefully entreated, and, like the rest of the apostles, looked upon as the filth and offscouring of all things. But still the Christian reasons thus: "What are these things to me? Is it not better to please God, than to indulge this corrupt flesh, or to seek the approbation of man, "whose breath is in his nostrils?" Should I please men, I could not be the servant of Christ. Those hardships and difficulties which I now suffer will soon be at an end; and though my good things are not in this life, yet hereafter I shall be comforted in that state, "where the wicked cease from troubling, and the weary are at rest." Was I not forewarned by my blessed Saviour, that the way to his kingdom lay through many tribulations; and shall I now faint because I find it to be so? Where can I enjoy so good an opportunity of showing my regard to my Lord, as by serving him now that I am brought to the test? He is now saying to me, as once he said to Peter, "Lovest thou me more than these?" Awake then, O my soul, and answer with that apostle, "Thou, Lord, who knowest all things, knowest that I love thee;" and I adore thy goodness in granting me this opportunity of testifying the strength and sincerity of my love, to thy glory and my unspeakable comfort. Such will be the sentiments of the man whose single aim is to obtain the approbation of God. He will continue firm and unshaken amidst the greatest sufferings; whilst the hypocrite, like the base multitude who followed Christ only for the loaves, will be offended, and fall off, when a day of trouble comes. I shall only add, in the

5th and *last* place, That this divine principle will make a man easy and satisfied, whatever be his outward condition in the world. He knows that his lot is appointed by God, and his only anxiety is to perform that part which hath been assigned to him; being fully assured that God, who is no respecter of persons, will graciously accept his sincere endeavors to please him, whether his station be high or low, whether his circumstances be rich or poor. His only concern is, that Christ may be magnified in his body. Like a determined traveller, he takes the road as he finds it, and makes no complaints, provided it lead him to the end of his journey.

These are some of the advantages which would flow from a sincere and steady desire of pleasing God, and him only. But to set these advantages in a more striking light, let us a little examine the opposite principle, and take a view of the man whose great aim is to obtain the approbation of his fellow-creatures. Consider, then,

1st. To what a drudgery he subjects himself, and what a strange and inconsistent part he must act. He makes himself the servant of every man, whose censure he fears, or whose praise he covets. He renounceth his own will and reason: and to whom? Not to God, who requires nothing but what is holy, just, and good; but to creatures like himself, ignorant, perverse, and capricious. He who is resolved to please men, must follow them through all their jarring inconsistent humors. He must undo to-morrow what he does to-day; he must assume a different appearance in every company; he must be the servant of servants, contemptible in the sight of God, and often despised by those very men whose approbation he courts. For it is to be observed, that respect and esteem are sooner found by an honest indifference about them, than by an anxious pursuit of them. They who are satisfied with the approbation of their heavenly Father, who seeth them in secret, are for the most part rewarded by him openly, according to what the wise man saith, "When a man's ways please the Lord, he maketh even his enemies to be at peace with him." Whereas it holds almost universally true, that men lose respect in proportion as they are observed to court it with anxiety, and sink thereby into greater contempt than otherwise they would have done. But,

2dly. Let us suppose that they obtain what they covet so earnestly. How trivial is the acquisition! "Verily," saith our Lord concerning men-pleasers, "they have their reward." Ah! poor reward! to obtain the favor and friendship of dying men, instead of the approbation of God, and the testimony of a good conscience; to remember, in hell, that they were well spoken of on earth, and that the sentence of their Judge was the first thing that undeceived their fellow-creatures as to their true character. This is the whole amount of their gain, even supposing that they succeed in their pursuit. But I must now add, in the

3d place, That this is only a supposition; for so great is the difficulty of pleasing men, that, after all your pains, it is ten thousand to one but you shall fail in the attempt. The very number of those whom you would please, renders it almost impossible to succeed in it.

We cannot at one time observe all who observe us, and expect to be pleased by us. We are like a person who has but a few pieces of money in his pocket, and a crowd of beggars about him. If, according to his best judgment, he divides the whole among the most needy, that he may please God, he is sure of attaining his end; but if he attempts to manage so as to please them, he will be miserably disappointed. For though the few that shared of his bounty may possibly be satisfied with their proportion; yet the rest, who got nothing, will revile, and perhaps curse him as penurious and unmerciful. Besides, the different parties and interfering interests of men, make it impossible to please all. If, in any case, you join with one party, the other, of course, will be offended; if you keep yourself disengaged from either side, you will probably incur the resentment of both; or, if you think to keep the good-will of both by trimming, making each believe that you are on their side, besides the baseness of the practice, which must set a man at irreconcilable variance with himself, you must live in a perpetual fear of discovery; and when you are detected, both will hate you worse than they do each other. Nay, in the

4th place, Should you give up the idea of obtaining universal favor, and content yourselves with pleasing a few; yet such is the mutability of men's tempers, that your success, even in this limited attempt, is very precarious. For how variable is the mind of man? ever shifting about, and alternately pleased and displeased with the same thing. When you have spent the best of your days in building upon this sand, one blast shall throw down the laborious fabric in a moment. For difficult as it is to gain the favor of men, it is still more difficult to preserve it, or to regain it when it is lost. Serve them as submissively as you can, yet some cross accident, some failure in gratifying their unreasonable expectations, may suddenly turn all your honors into disgrace, and leave you to complain, as cardinal Wolsey did, "Had I served God as faithfully as man, he would not thus have forsaken me in my old age." Nay, the perverseness of many is so great, that they require contradictions ere they will be pleased. If John come fasting, they say, "he hath a devil:" If Christ come eating and drinking, they say, "Behold a man gluttonous and a wine-bibber, a friend of publicans and sinners." If your judgment and practice be accommodated to your superiors, some will call you supple and temporizing: if it be otherwise, you will perhaps be reproached as discontented and seditious.

Thus, you see, that it is impossible to please all men, or even any considerable number of them at one time. Nor have we cause to wonder at this, when we consider, that our blessed Saviour himself, notwithstanding his perfect innocence and wisdom, was more reviled than any man. Can you do more to deserve the favor of men than Christ did? or can you expect to please those who are displeased with God himself? For is not God daily displeasing men in the course of his Providence? and what is there that they quarrel with more bitterly than with his word? In fine, how can we expect to please any number of our fellow-creatures when we cannot even please ourselves constantly? And for the truth of this, I appeal to your own experience. You must be singular indeed, if you never fall out with yourselves; I mean singularly inattentive (to give it no harsher name), for with the best I am sure there is too often just cause for it. If then we are not able to preserve our own esteem at all times, how can we expect to preserve the approbation of other men?

And now what is your judgment upon the whole? Is not man-pleasing both a mean and fruitless attempt? Is it wise to have for your aim a thing so disquieting, and so very precarious? Is it not by far the wiser course to seek the approbation of God, who trieth your hearts, whom you please most effectually when you pursue your own best interest? He is not variable in his affections, like men. Whom he loves, he loves unto the end. "Neither death, nor life, nor angels, nor principalities, nor powers, nor things present, nor things to come, nor height, nor depth, nor any other creature, shall be able to separate us from his love, which is in Christ Jesus our Lord."

Let me then address you in the words of this same apostle on another occasion, "Ye are bought with a price, be not ye the servants of men." Remember what our Lord said to his disciples while he was on earth; "One is your Master, even Christ." To him you owe all your homage; him only you are bound to please. And is not his favor a sufficient portion? Did he suffer, and bleed, and die, that your hearts might be his, and will you refuse him that which he hath so dearly bought? Where can you find a better Master, or one that you can be so certain of pleasing, if you apply yourselves to it? He requires no contradictory or impracticable services. He hath left you in no uncertainty about your duty. You need not say, "Wherewith shall we come before the Lord? He hath shewed thee, O man, what is good, and what he requires of you," even in his written word, which he hath given to be "a lamp to your feet and a light unto your paths." He makes also the most gracious allowances for your infirmities. The willing mind is accepted by him; and although through weakness you fall short of your own good purposes, yet he will say to you as he did to David, when he purposed to build him an house, "It was well that it was in thine heart."

Who then would not apply himself to gain the approbation of such a master? This aim, well established, would be a constant principle of holy obedience, and make us to abound in all those fruits of righteousness, which are through Christ to the praise and glory of God. Let this henceforth then be our sole ambition, to approve ourselves to him, by whose sentence our final condition must be determined. And let it be our constant request at the throne of grace, that God by his almighty Spirit may exalt our souls above every mean and sordid view, and enable us always so to speak and act, "not as pleasing men, but God who trieth our hearts."—Then the peace of God, which passeth all understanding, shall keep our hearts and minds through Christ Jesus; and amidst all the changing scenes of life, we shall have this for our rejoicing, even the testimony of a good conscience, that in simplicity and godly sincerity, not with fleshly wisdom, but by the grace of God, we have had our conversation in the world. *Amen.*

SERMON XXXVII.

THE APOSTLE'S EXHORTATION.

ACTS XI. 23.—"And exhorted them all, that with purpose of heart they would cleave unto the LORD."

IT is not easy to conceive a more complete or amiable character than that which is given of Barnabas in the following verse: "He was a good man, and full of the Holy Ghost, and of faith." And as a good man, out of the good treasure of his heart, bringeth forth good things; so this faithful minister of Christ, who had been sent by the church in Jerusalem to visit the new converts at Antioch, having seen those real effects of the grace of God among them, of which he had formerly heard the agreeable report, was filled with joy; and, like a true "son of consolation," which his name signifies, he "exhorted them all, that with purpose of heart they would cleave unto the Lord."—My design in discoursing from these words is,

1*st.* To explain the exhortation contained in them; 2*dly.* To enforce it by some motives and arguments; and, 3*dly.* To offer some directions which, through the blessing of God, may be useful to those who are desirous of complying with it.

I BEGIN with explaining the exhortation contained in the text. And,

1*st.* It is obvious, that it supposeth those to whom it is directed to be already entered upon a religious course of life. Barnabas addressed his discourse to persons who were real converts to Christianity. It appears from the 21st and 22d verses, that the tidings which had come to Jerusalem concerning them, expressly affirmed, that "a great number had believed and turned unto the Lord:" and Barnabas, soon after his arrival at Antioch, received full conviction that this report was true; for "he saw the grace of God, and was glad." The form of his exhortation indeed sufficiently distinguisheth the character of those to whom it was addressed; for such as had never been joined to the Lord could not, with any propriety, be exhorted to cleave or to adhere to him. And as this exhortation, when addressed to us, supposeth that we have already chosen the ways of God; so it implies also, that our choice is the fruit of mature and solid consideration. "This purpose of heart," with which we are to "cleave unto the Lord," is not a blind and obstinate bigotry, which pusheth men headlong in a way which they know not. Persons of this character may have a fair show in the time of prosperity; but when they are brought to the trial of adversity, they will relinquish against reason what they began without it; and will turn as violent in opposing religion, as ever they seemed zealous in promoting it. In the

2*d* place, The exhortation in my text requires the habitual exercise of all the graces of the Christian life; the constant performance of every commanded duty. It is not enough that we draw near to the Lord on some stated occasions, or have some transient flashes of devotion, like the Israelites of old, concerning whom it is said (Hosea vi. 4.) that their goodness, like "the morning cloud and early dew," appeared for a little, and then "vanished" away. We must cleave to the Lord at all times; devotion must be the prevailing temper of our minds; and our habitual practice must correspond to it. It must be our fixed design, and sincere resolution, to keep all God's commandments, at all times, and in all places and circumstances.

Some there are who lay down resolutions for the performance of *certain* duties, with a designed exception of others: Or perhaps they purpose to perform all the branches of duty for a particular season, with a secret reserve, that when that time shall be elapsed, they will then return to their former course of life. But all such resolutions are an abomination to God, as being hypocritical and insincere; and plainly show that the first step in religion is not yet taken. For at the least, it is essential to the character of a true Christian, that there be a fixed and peremptory design to adhere to all duty at all times. Grievous failures and sins there may be, even where there are such honest and upright purposes; but if these are wanting, our profession of religion must be altogether vain. In the

2*d* place, The exhortation in my text requires that we make an open and honest profession of our adherence to the Lord. And I mention this, not only because of the importance of the thing itself, but also on account of the shameful and pernicious failure even of some good people in this matter. Instead of confessing Christ boldly before men, they take as wide steps as their consciences will allow them, to speak the language, and to act the manners, of a corrupt generation, from the dread of appearing singular, or of incurring the charge of ostentation or hypocrisy. But this method of concealing, or rather indeed of giving away, a part of our religion, to secure the reputation of the rest, is neither honest nor wise. Honest it cannot be; for it is just as fraudulent to impose upon men, by seeming worse than we are, as by seeming better: and surely it is not wise; for if we resolve to have the appearance of no more religion than corrupt minds will allow to be sincere, I am afraid we must give it up altogether, and preserve the opinion of our honesty, by appearing to have no religion at all. Hypocrisy is a bad thing, not because it wears the form of religion, but because it wants the power of it; and the way to avoid hypocrisy, is not by doing less than the hypocrite, but by doing more and better. Our Saviour, who spent whole nights in prayer, cannot be supposed to condemn the Pharisees for praying long; but for making their prayers a cloak to cover their covetousness and oppression. He does not find fault with them for their outward beauty, but for their inward pollution and deformity. If holiness be really within us, we have no occasion to dread any harm from its appearing outwardly. It will at length overcome the malice of the world, and prove its divine original, both by its native lustre, and its powerful influence, upon those who behold it. Once more, in the

4th place, The exhortation in my text requires, that we persevere in our adherence to the Lord to the end of our lives. It is not sufficient that we begin well, and continue faithful for a while; we must hold on our way, and wax stronger and stronger as we proceed. We must not be wearied with the length of the way, but, "lifting up the hands that hang down, and strengthening the feeble knees," we must run without wearying, and walk without fainting, "pressing toward the mark, for the prize of the high calling of God in Christ Jesus." We must not give up religious exercises, either because of the frequent repetition of self-denying duties, or of the bodily decay which old age brings on, or of the increasing infirmities of the mind. We must not give over our work in despondency, because of the slowness of our progress, the smallness of our success, or the number and strength of our enemies. For all these discouragements will soon be over, "and in due time we shall reap, if we faint not, a glorious and everlasting reward." Having thus explained the exhortation in my text, I proceed now, in the

Second place, To enforce it by some motives and arguments. Consider then,

1*st.* That the same reasons which at first determined you to choose the ways of God, are equally forcible for inciting you to persevere in them to the end. Upon what grounds did ye embrace your religion at first? Why was it that ye ratified, when ye came to years, that profession into which ye were baptized? Was it because of the divine authority upon which your religion rests? This reason surely still holds to make you adhere to it amidst the strongest temptations; for divine authority is always to be obeyed, whatever difficulties lie in the way; nay, though the commands of the highest powers on earth should interfere with it. Was it concern for your eternal salvation, and a conviction that "there is no other name under heaven, given among men, whereby you can be saved, but the name of Christ?" and does not this reason bind you as much to cleave to the Lord as to come to him at first? "The Lord is with you while ye be with him; and if you seek him he will be found of you; but if ye forsake him, he will forsake you." He that endureth to the end," saith Christ, "shall be saved." "But if any man draw back, my soul shall have no pleasure in him." Nay, the case of apostates is represented every where in Scripture as inconceivably more dreadful than that of any other sinners. Once more, did you enter upon a religious course of life, because your consciences would not suffer you to be at peace till you had done so? This reason also binds you to persevere as you have begun; for the more faithfully you cleave to the Lord, the more steadfastly you resist temptation, the greater peace and tranquillity you will have in your own minds. Nay, the obstacles which now make your progress difficult and painful, will gradually disappear, and at length you shall find, that "Wisdom's ways are ways of pleasantness, and that all her paths are peace." In a word, whatever good reason we had to set out in the Christian course, the same reason will hold for our perseverance in it. If we began it from bad or from worldly motives, our religion is but an empty profession, without any reality. In this case we are not yet Christians; and therefore the exhortation in the text doth not belong to us. Consider, in the

2*d* place, That all the bribes which can be offered, in order to seduce you from your adherence to the Lord, are vain, precarious, and unsatisfying. How often have men "made shipwreck of faith and of a good conscience," for a mere shadow of expectation, which was never realized to them? But though you should obtain all that this world can present to you, yet how bitter is that advantage which is purchased at the expense of inward peace and tranquillity? Nay, how vain and precarious are the enjoyments of this world at the best? "Riches often make to themselves wings and flee away;" and then they leave the person much more unhappy than they found him, under the dominion of inflamed appetites, without the proper objects to satisfy them. The joy of the wicked is like the "crackling of thorns under a pot;" vain whilst it lasts, and soon at an end. Balaam loved the reward of unrighteousness, and he obtained it: but what did he reap from it at last? he returned to his own country loaded with riches, but all his enjoyments were embittered by "an evil conscience," and he himself was soon after brought to an untimely end by the victorious arms of the Israelites. So deceitful are the offers with which this world would seduce you from your adherence to the Lord. But in cleaving to the Lord, you can never be disappointed in your expectations; for he hath said, "I will never leave thee nor forsake thee." Consider, in the

3*d* place, What obligations you lie under to this Lord to whom you are exhorted in the text to "cleave with purpose of heart." He it was that befriended you in your greatest necessity, and that brought salvation with his own arm, when there was no other eye to pity you, nor any other hand that could help you. Think on the greatness of the love of Christ, and on the costly proofs he gave of it, in condescending to become a man, and "a man of sorrows," and at last to die under the bitterest agonies, for the redemption of your souls; and then let gratitude suggest to you what returns may reasonably be expected from creatures so infinitely indebted to him as you have been. Did the Lord Jesus, without any importunity from us, and even contrary to our desires, persist in his gracious design of saving us, till he could say upon the cross, "It is finished?" and shall not we persevere with steadfastness in our duty and allegiance to him? Surely, if his heart clave to us, when he had nothing to merit or invite his love, much more should our hearts cleave to Him, who is not only infinitely amiable in himself, but, which is still more interesting, infinitely kind and gracious to us. Once more, in the

4*th* place, Consider that this duty, although difficult, is by no means impracticable. Thousands of our brethren, all men of like passions with ourselves, have perservered to the end in cleaving to the Lord, and are now enjoying the glorious reward of their steadfast adherence to him. All necessary aid is provided for you, and ready to be conveyed to you as often as you shall ask it. For "God is faithful, who will not suffer you to be tempted above what ye are able to bear, but will with the temptation also make a way to escape, that ye may be able to bear it." Indeed, had you no other strength but your own, to exhort you to "cleave unto the Lord," would only be to mock your misery. But help is laid for you on One who is mighty, and is no less willing than powerful, to support you under all your trials. He can perfect strength in your weakness; and whilst you are stretching forth your feeble arms to embrace him, he will inclose you in the arms of his Omnipotence, and work in you effectually "both to will and to do of his good pleasure."

Having thus explained the exhortation in the text, and endeavored to enforce it by some motives and arguments, I proceed now, as was proposed, in the

Third place, To offer some directions, which, through the blessing of God, may be useful to those who are desirous of complying with this exhortation. And, in the

1*st* place, Labor to have your minds as richly furnished as possible with true Christian knowledge. Study the nature and the reasons of the religion which you profess, that you may be able to confute gainsayers, or at least to withstand their attempts to seduce and pervert you. Knowledge must lie at the root of our steadfastness; otherwise, let the cause in which we are engaged be ever so good, our adherence to it is nothing else than obstinacy of temper; which can neither please God, nor bring any real advantage to ourselves. In such a case, if a man is in the right, it is merely by accident: he might as readily have been in the wrong; and it is very possible, nay extremely likely, that some new "wind of doctrine" may seduce him, and that he may become as violent in his enmity to the gospel as he was once warm in supporting it. It is true, indeed, there may be a great deal of sound knowledge in the head, where there is no real grace in the heart. A foreigner may learn to speak the language of Zion so well, that it will be difficult to distinguish him from one who is "an Israelite indeed." But, on the other hand, it is absolutely certain, that grace cannot consist with gross ignorance: For the first operation of the Spirit of God is to open men's eyes, and to turn them from darkness unto light: Consequently, where there is no light, it must be concluded that there is no grace. Some exceptions there may be; and there have been examples of persons, in whose temper and practice the lineaments of the New Creature could plainly be discerned, who, by reason of their natural dulness, were incapable of acquiring any distinct knowledge of the principles of religion, or at least of expressing what they knew to the satisfaction of others. This rule of judging must not therefore be extended to those whose understandings are visibly weak, and unapt to receive or to retain instruction; for out of the mouths of such babes and sucklings, God may, and often doth, perfect his praise. But when men are quick enough to learn other things, and yet remain ignorant of the great truths of Christianity; when they discover no anxiety, nor use any proper endeavors, to acquire the knowledge of them; this voluntary ignorance, whatever they may pretend, is a plain proof of an unconverted state. Let none who acknowledge and lament their ignorance, and who use the means to have it removed, be discouraged at what I have now said; for they are not the persons concerning whom I speak. But if I could meditate a reproof of more than ordinary sharpness, I would address it to those who, amidst Bibles and Sermons, and other excellent helps for their spiritual improvement, remain stupidly ignorant of the most essential points of Christianity, without any shame and concern. And, alas! what numbers of this description are to be found among us? How many claim the peculiar privileges of Christians, who know little more of Christianity than the name? Nay, is it not to be feared, that many who partake of the holy sacrament of the Lord's Supper are so grossly ignorant of the nature of that ordinance, that, with respect to them, the communion-table itself may bear the same inscription which Paul found upon the altar at Athens, "To the unknown God." This, my brethren, yields us a very melancholy prospect: for surely they are not likely to prove steadfast Christians, who know so little of Christianity, that it is hard to find out upon what grounds they are Christians at all. I would therefore recommend it to you, with the greatest earnestness, to study the principles of that religion which you profess. Spare no pains that may be necessary to get a thorough acquaintance with them, and then you will be in less danger of forsaking them when an hour of trial comes. "They that know their God," said the angel to Daniel, "shall be strong and do exploits." "For understanding shall keep thee," saith Solomon, "to deliver thee from the way of the evil man, from the man that speaketh froward things, who leave the paths of uprightness, to walk in the ways of darkness." But,

2dly. Besides the speculative knowledge of divine truths, you must also labor to acquire an inward experience and relish of them. Did we truly feel their influence upon our own hearts, it would serve in place of a thousand arguments to prove their divine original. He would be a cunning sophister, indeed, who could persuade a man that honey was bitter, whilst he tasted the sweetness of it in his mouth. It is an experimental conviction of the truth of the gospel, which fortifies the true Christian against all the arts of seducers. He hath a witness within himself, and can bring a proof from his own heart, both of the truth and excellence of the religion which he professeth. It was a stubborn question which Athanasius put to the heathens of his time, who denied the resurrection of Christ. "If Christ be not alive," said he, "how doth he yet destroy your idols, and cast out devils, and convert and subdue the world to himself? Are these the works of a dead man?" In like manner can the sanctified soul say, "Have I felt Christ opening my blind eyes, binding the strong man, and casting him out? Have I felt him stamping his image upon my soul, and bringing me with boldness into the presence of that God whom I had offended? And after this, shall I doubt whether there be a Christ, or whether this Christ be able to save me?" Thus can the true believer, who hath felt the power of Christianity, bring unanswerable arguments for its truth from his own experience: arguments which neither the temptations of Satan, nor the cavils of wicked men, will be able to overthrow.

3dly. If you would cleave with steadfastness unto the Lord, attend constantly to the inward frame and temper of your hearts. Make conscience of watching over your most secret thoughts. Suffer them not to wander without control, or to spend their strength upon things which cannot profit you; otherwise you will open a wide door to the enemy, and even furnish him with weapons which he will not fail to improve against you. I am afraid the importance of this direction is too little considered by the generality of Christians. We commonly think ourselves secure when out of the way of external temptations, and suffer our minds to roam at large wherever fancy presents an amusing object. Whereas we ought to consider, that whatever inflames our passions, or gives them an improper direction, is equally hurtful to the soul, whether the cause be real or imaginary. Nay, I am persuaded, that the tempter doth often make greater havoc in our hearts, by mingling his poison with the suggestions of our own minds, than by all the other methods of temptation. If we would keep our hearts indeed, we must watch their motions as carefully when we are alone, as when we are abroad, and in the midst of danger. The presence of God should constantly overawe our most secret thoughts, and have equal influence on us in our retirement, as when we act in the open view of the world.—A

4th direction I shall give you in the words of the apostle Paul, (Romans xi. 20.) "Be not high minded, but fear." Remember what our blessed Lord said to his disciples, "Without me ye can do nothing." Nothing is more offensive to God than pride. When our hearts begin to swell with an high opinion of our own strength, he is provoked to withhold his grace from us; because all that is poured into the proud soul runs over in self-applause, and so is like water spilt on a rock, with respect to any good that it doth to a man himself, or any glory which it brings to God. The proud heart, like the towering cliff, is never fruitful. If we would in due time be exalted, we must first humble ourselves under the mighty hand of God. This is the way to obtain fresh supplies of his supporting grace. "Happy is the man," saith Solomon, "who feareth always." A holy diffidence of ourselves is the true temper of a Christian, and will both serve to keep us out of the way of temptation, and teach us to act with the caution of men who perceive their danger, and are careful to shun it.

5thly. Avoid, as much as possible, the fellowship of wicked men. This is an advice which I am inclined to repeat as often as I can find occasion for it; and indeed it is scarcely possible to insist upon it as much as its importance deserves. A man who is careless of his company, disregards his own soul. If therefore you would cleave unto the Lord, imitate the holy Psalmist, and give charge to evil-doers to depart from you. Let the saints, the excellent ones of the earth, be the men of your counsel. We stand much in need of all the assistance which we can derive from our fellow Christians: "Woe to him that is alone when he falleth," saith the wise man, "for he hath not another to help him up." Whereas, when Christians join together in holy communion, like trees planted in a thicket, they shelter and defend one another. They have boldness to face their adversaries, as well as strength to baffle their attempts to seduce them. "Let us then exhort one another daily, lest any of us be hardened through the deceitfulness of sin." Like brethren, let us dwell together in love and unity, having all our spiritual goods in common, being "ready to distribute, willing to communicate," according to the measure of gifts and graces which it hath pleased our heavenly Father to bestow on us.—In the

6th and *last* place, If we would obey the exhortation in the text, we must beware of neglecting the instrumental duties of religion. Let us carefully read the Holy Scriptures, which God, in mercy, hath given us to be a "lamp to our feet, and a light unto our path." "The law of the Lord is perfect, converting the soul: the testimony of the Lord is sure, making wise the simple." To reading you must join the hearing of the word preached; that powerful ordinance which God hath so remarkably countenanced in all ages of the church, and made effectual, by his blessing, both for the conversion of sinners, and for the establishment of his own people. Under this head I would particularly recommend to you a devout attendance upon the holy sacrament of the Lord's Supper, which is so peculiarly calculated to strengthen our faith, and to build us up in holiness and comfort, unto eternal life. This hath been found, in the experience of all the saints, to be a most blessed institution, which hath in every age enabled men to hold on their way with alacrity and joy, and in every situation hath assisted them to renew their strength. To all this we must add constant and fervent prayer to God. By this we maintain correspondence with the "Father of lights, from whom cometh down every good and perfect gift." Prayer is the messenger which he hath appointed for conveying to us help in every time of need. He hath promised his Spirit to them who ask it. Let us "ask and receive, that our joy may be full."

Thus, my brethren, I have suggested to you a few plain directions, which, through the blessing of God, may be of use to assist you in maintaining that firm adherence to the Lord which my text recommends. All that now remains is, that I entreat you to reduce them to practice. And what motive can I present to you so powerful as the consideration, that "to them who, by a patient continuance in well-doing, seek for glory, honor, and immortality, God will render eternal life."—"To him that overcometh," saith Christ, "will I grant to sit down with me on my throne, even as I also overcame, and am set down with my Father on his throne." The time draweth near, when you shall be placed beyond the reach of temptation, when your warfare shall be accomplished, and your struggles at an end; and who would not sustain a short, though it were a sharp conflict, that he might obtain a triumphant victory? Some of us perhaps have but a few more efforts to make, and a few more assaults to sustain, before Christ shall call us home to receive the enriching reward—a reward not of debt but of grace; even that exceeding and eternal weight of glory, with which our light and momentary afflictions are not worthy to be compared. Let us all then be persuaded, "with purpose of heart to cleave unto the Lord." Let us count all things but loss, that we may win Christ, and be found in him, not having our own righteousness, but that everlasting righteousness which he hath prepared for them who "cleave to him." Let us go from this place, saying as Peter did, only with more humility, "Though all men should forsake thee, yet will not we." And "now unto him that is able to keep you from falling, and to present you faultless before the presence of his glory with exceeding joy: To the only wise God our Saviour, be glory and majesty, dominion and power, both now and ever." *Amen.*

SERMON XXXVIII.

THE IMPORTANT INQUIRY.

Micah vi. 3.—" O my People, what have I done unto thee? and wherein have I wearied thee? Testify against me."

It is impossible to predict what impression the same truth will make upon the different minds of men. That word, which will pierce one man to the " dividing asunder of the soul and spirit," may have no edge at all when addressed to another. But were I to judge from my own feelings, I should think, that all the terrors of God could not more effectually awe the heart of a sinner, than the passage of Scripture which I have now read. It strikes my ear like the last sound of God's mercy. Doth the Almighty command and threaten? I fear and tremble: yet I have still some expectation that his compassion may interpose in my behalf.—But doth he put off his terrible Majesty, and, instead of vindicating the authority, condescend to plead the reasonableness of his law? then I am sure that his forbearance is almost exhausted, and that my day of grace is drawing near to an end. For as he neither wants power to punish, nor provocation to justify the punishment he might inflict, his design in stooping so low, can only be to render my condemnation consistent with the utmost extent of his mercy. In the words of the text, the Supreme Lord of heaven and earth appeals to sinners themselves for the mildness and equity of his government: and challengeth them to produce one instance of undue severity towards them, or the least shadow of excuse for their undutiful behavior towards him. " O my people, what have I done unto thee? and wherein have I wearied thee? Testify against me." And doth the infinitely wise God condescend to be tried at the bar of human reason? Can it then be supposed that his cause is doubtful, or that he runs the least hazard of being cast in judgment? Have we not reason to conclude, that the evidence of his goodness must be clear and irresistible, when he offers it to trial before the most partial tribunal, and submits his vindication to those very persons who cannot justify him without condemning themselves?

But as sinners are naturally supposed to shun the light, and to turn away their eyes from every thing that hath a tendency to humble and abase them; it may be of use to bring this cause to a fair and open trial: Which, through divine assistance, I propose to do.

First. By giving you a direct proof of the goodness of God, and of his tender concern for the welfare of his creatures.

Secondly. By examining some of the most plausible objections which are urged against the mildness and equity of the divine administration.

I will then conclude with a divine and practical improvement of the subject.

I begin with giving you a direct proof of the goodness of God, and of his tender concern for the welfare of his creatures. This appears, in the

1*st* place, From the unwearied patience which he exerciseth towards transgressors. How easily could he arrest them in the midst of their mad career, and hurry them to judgment with all their provocations on their heads? Might not God have seized thee, O sinner, in the very act of sin, with a curse or a lie in thy mouth, and have stopped that breath with which thou wast insulting his name and his laws? How often might he have summoned thee to his dread tribunal in a fit of drunkenness; and made thee sober in that place of torment where there is not a drop of water to cool the thirsty tongue? Ah, how easy a matter it is for the Almighty to bring down the proudest of his foes? to silence the profane, injurious railer? to bind the hands of the oppressors, and to make them know that they are but worms? We read of one angel destroying in one night an hundred and fourscore and five thousand Assyrians; and myriads of angels stand continually before his throne ready to execute whatever he commands. He is the Lord of Hosts, " who doth according to his will in the army of heaven, and among the inhabitants of the earth." How easily can he throw thee into a bed of languishing? and waste thy strength under such a pining sickness, or racking pain, as to make thee cry for mercy to him whom thou blasphemest, and even beg the prayers of those whom thou wast wont to scorn? But God hath as yet done none of these things. By his merciful visitation he preserves thee in the land of the living and in the land of hope. He supplies all thy wants, and loads thee with increasing benefits. He gave thee that breath which thou hast breathed out against him, and every moment of that time which thou hast squandered away in idleness, sensuality, and the works of the flesh. Why doth he yet wait to be gracious, if he were not tenderly solicitous for thy welfare? Surely his sparing mercy must be intended to bring thee back to himself: He restrains his wrath, that his goodness, like coals of fire, may melt down thine impenitence, and thy hardness of heart: "The Lord is not slack concerning his promise, (as some men count slackness) but is long-suffering to us-ward, not willing that any should perish, but that all should come to repentance."

2dly. The goodness of God, and his tender concern for the welfare of his creatures, is still more illustriously displayed in the sufferings and death of our Lord Jesus Christ, whom God sent into the world for this very end, "that whosoever believeth on him might not perish, but have everlasting life." There we see a proof, the most strong and convincing that God himself could give, of his having "no pleasure in the death of the wicked, but rather that he should turn from his way and live." Would he have ransomed sinners at so costly a price as the blood of his only begotten Son? would he have astonished angels with so wonderful an act of condescension, as to send Him who was the "brightness of his glory, and the express image of his person," to assume the likeness of sinful flesh, to submit to the infirmities of our low nature, nay, to the ignominy and pain of the cross? had not our everlasting welfare been an object of his tenderest concern. This surely, if duly considered, must remove all suspicions of his goodness, and destroy the jealousies even of the most mistrustful mind. Behold Christ weeping over the impending fate of Jerusalem, and bemoaning the hardness of heart of those who attended his ministry; view him in his agony, and in his conflict with the powers of darkness; hear him on the cross praying for his enemies; and then suppose, if you are able, that your ruin can be pleasing to him who hath done so much to prevent it. But, in the

3d place, The various means which God employs for reclaiming men from their ways of folly and vice, afford another proof of his goodness, and of his tender concern for their welfare. He is not only the Author of the gracious plan of our redemption, but he hath likewise set before us the most powerful motives to persuade us to embrace his offered favor, and to comply with his designs of mercy. Every consideration which can be supposed to work, either on our hopes or our fears, is set before us in the most striking light. The veil is removed from the invisible world; the joys of glorified saints, and the torments of despairing sinners, are made the subject of a clear revelation. How affectionately doth he invite men to turn unto him and live? "Come now, and let us reason together, saith the Lord: though your sins be as scarlet, they shall be as white as snow; though they be red like crimson, they shall be as wool." "Wherefore do ye spend money for that which is not bread? and your labor for that which satisfieth not? Hearken diligently unto me, and eat ye that which is good, and let your soul delight itself in fatness. Incline your ear, and come unto me; hear, and your soul shall live." Even the threatenings of God are not so much the thunderings of his justice, as the loud rhetoric of his mercy. He shakes the rod over us, that, by a timely submission, we may avert the stroke. And when all the methods used to reclaim a sinner have proved ineffectual, with what reluctance doth he at last execute his threatened vengeance? "How shall I give thee up, Ephraim? how shall I deliver thee, Israel? how shall I make thee as Admah? how shall I set thee as Zeboim? Mine heart is turned within me, my repentings are kindled together." Nay, after the fierceness of his anger hath consumed the transgressors, what regret doth he express that they should have extorted from him their own punishment? "O that my people had hearkened unto me, and Israel had walked in my ways!" He utters these words as it were with a sigh, lamenting the folly and perverseness which had compelled him to such measures of severity against them: Not that God is influenced by any human passions; but because he could not otherwise communicate, in a manner intelligible to us, the deep concern which he takes in our welfare.

Nor are these mere expressions of kindness, which are unaccompanied with deeds to prove their sincerity, and to render them effectual: he hath instituted an order of men to carry the glad tidings of salvation to every corner of the earth; to beseech sinners, in his name, to lay aside their enmity to him, which can only hurt themselves, and to return to that Almighty Being, who, though he stands in no need of them, is most sincerely willing to receive them into his favor, and to bestow on them everlasting happiness. "We are ambassadors for Christ, as though God did beseech you by us; we pray you in Christ's stead, be ye reconciled to God." We are commanded to "preach the word, to be instant in season and out of season, in meekness instructing those that oppose themselves, if God peradventure will give them repentance to the acknowledging of the truth." And to excite us to be diligent and faithful in the exercise of this office, he hath assured us, "that when the chief Shepherd shall appear, we shall receive a crown of glory that fadeth not away."

Is not this then an unanswerable proof that God hath no pleasure in the death of sinners? What stronger evidence of it could he give, than to send to them so many messengers, to beseech them in his name to turn and live? to employ on this kind errand creatures of the same nature with themselves, subject to the same passions, exposed to the same temptations, who have the advantage of familiar intercourse with them, and who are always at hand, to help, to comfort, and to quicken them? Nay, he hath made it the duty of every man, in his place, to do all that he can for the conversion of others. "Exhort one another daily," saith an apostle, "while it is called to-day, lest any of you be hardened, through the deceitfulness of sin." "Brethren," saith the apostle James, "if any of you do err from the truth, and one convert him, let him know, that he which converteth a sinner from the error of his way shall save a soul from death, and shall hide a multitude of sins." Nor shall this labor of love pass without a reward; for, "they that be wise shall shine as the brightness of the firmament, and they that turn many to righteousness as the stars for ever and ever." But that nothing may be wanting to beget in us the firmest persuasion of the goodness of God, and of his tender concern for the welfare of his creatures, let it be observed, in the

4th and *last* place on this head, That he hath selected some of the most notorious offenders in the different ages of the world to be monuments of the riches of his grace, that the chief of sinners might be encouraged to apply to him for pardon and eternal life; who, without such examples, might have been ready to look on their case as desperate. How many, who were once sunk into the lowest degeneracy, are now in heaven, singing that grateful triumphant song, "Unto him that loved us, and washed us from our sins in his own blood, and hath made us kings and priests unto God and his Father; to him be glory and dominion for ever and ever. Amen." There is Manasseh, one who used enchantment and divination, and who deluged the streets of Jerusalem with innocent blood. There is Saul, once a blasphemer and a persecutor, who thus testifies of himself, "For this cause I obtained mercy, that in me first Jesus Christ might shew forth all long-suffering, for a pattern to them which should hereafter believe on him to life everlasting." There are some of those Corinthians who were once the scandal of their country, and the reproach of human nature, (1 Cor. vi. 11.) but being "washed and sanctified, and justified in the name of the Lord Jesus, and by the Spirit of our God," are now walking in white, following the Lamb whithersoever he goeth, and contemplating with wonder and joy the extent of that love "which passeth knowledge." Nay, there are some of the murderers of the Lord of glory, three thousand of whom were converted by the ministry of Peter in one day: and now they are rejoicing in the presence of that Jesus whom they crucified, and ascribing their eternal salvation to that blood which was shed by their own wicked hands. In one word, with such examples as these the Scripture is replenished; and God every where appears, like the father in the parable, stretching forth his arms to the prodigal son, and delighting to display the riches of his grace.

Such then are the positive and direct evidences of the goodness of God, and of his tender concern for the welfare of his creatures. I proceed now, as was proposed, in the

Second place, To examine some of the most plausible objections which are urged against the mildness and equity of the divine administration.

Say, then, O sinner, wherein hath God dealt rigorously with you? and what cause he hath ever given you to charge him with severity? "Testify against him," in what respect he hath shown himself an enemy to your happiness?

1*st*. Is it the holiness and perfection of his law that you complain of? Hath he given you too accurate a rule of life? and laid too many restraints upon your natural inclinations? This complaint is both foolish and ungrateful. The law of God requires nothing but what tends to make us happy; nor doth it forbid any thing which would not be productive of our misery. The very design of it is to describe and recommend that holiness, "without which no man shall see the Lord:" so that the perfection of it is no less a proof of the goodness than of the wisdom of its Author. Were holiness indeed unnecessary, or were vice the road to happiness, the objection would in that case be just. But as there is an inseparable connection between sin and misery; and as holiness is indispensably necessary to qualify us for the enjoyment of God; it must follow, that to find fault with the purity of his law, is to find fault with it for being too much adapted to our interest. It is not therefore less absurd, than if a scholar were to blame his master for the excellence of the example which he had given him to copy; or, than if a traveller should quarrel with his guide, for directing him with too much exactness in the way.

2*dly*. Do you complain of the threatenings with which this law is enforced? Doth God appear severe, because he hath said, that the wicked must either turn from his evil ways or die? This complaint is surely as unreasonable as the former. Shall God be reckoned an enemy to your happiness, because he useth the most effectual means to promote it? Can he be supposed to desire your misery, who so earnestly warns you of your danger, and who so warmly pleads with you to avoid it? Should one find you running towards a precipice in your sleep, would you blame him for stopping you, though perhaps he might interrupt you in the enjoyment of some pleasant dream? Were you ready to sink in deep water, would you not reckon that man your friend who should save you from drowning, even though he dragged you out by the hair of the head? This is the very purpose, or the friendly design of all God's threatenings. He publisheth them, that they may never be executed; he makes them terrible, that the terror of them may persuade men to avoid them. Had God published a law, and concealed the importance of it, with respect to our happiness or misery; would not the objection, in that case, against his goodness, have been far more just and rational? If his threatenings prevail with you, never shall you have cause to complain of their severity; and if they do not prevail, with what face can you allege, that the penalties are too high, when, at the same time, your own practice confutes you, and proves, that they are not high enough to restrain you from incurring them. But,

3*dly*. Perhaps your objection doth not lie so much against the publication of the threatenings, as against the final execution of them. You see their use to overawe mankind in this world; but you think that it would be cruel in God to inflict them in good earnest, and to punish men eternally, for sins committed during the short period of their abode on earth. Now, in answer to this, let me only ask you, whether those threatenings would be of any use at all, if the sinner knew that they would never be executed, or even if the execution of them were in the least degree doubtful? He who can make subjects believe that their governor means only to frighten them with his penalties, will easily make his laws of no effect, and set offenders loose from every restraint. The belief of the execution is therefore absolutely necessary to the efficacy of the law, which otherwise could only be an engine to work upon fools. And if it be necessary in all cases that subjects should believe that the law will be executed, then it follows in the present case, that the threatenings of God shall certainly be executed at last. For God cannot lie, nor make it the duty of mankind to believe a lie. He has no need of such base means to keep the world in order. If the penalties, as they are described in the law, be consistent with the goodness of God, the inflicting of them at last cannot in reason be sustained as an objection against it. Say then, O sinner, what farther hast thou to allege against God? The appeal is made to you in the text, and a challenge given to you to bring forth all your objections against his laws and government. Do you blame him, in the

4th place, For the temptations you meet with in the world, and those circumstances of danger with which you are surrounded? Let us consider a little the justice of this complaint. The strongest temptations, you must allow, have no compulsive efficacy; all that they can do, is to solicit and entice us: And are there not addressed to us far more weighty arguments and solicitations to forsake sin, and to walk in the paths of wisdom? If we cannot resist the devil and the flesh, how can we refuse what God demands, who pleadeth with us by infinitely stronger motives than they can present to us? for he sets before us the endless joys, or the endless torments, of a future state of existence. Doth not the undefiled inheritance of the saints in light infinitely transcend all that earth or sense can promise us? and yet shall we pretend to justify ourselves, when, contrary to all reason, we prefer the pleasures of sin, which are but for a moment, to the eternal happiness and glory of the world to come? Once more, in the

5th place, Do you object, that you cannot reclaim or convert yourselves? that man can do nothing towards his conversion, unless he shall receive power from on high? that therefore you are excusable until God shall impart his assistance? and that if you perish, it is not your fault?

My brethren, we must not speak falsely even for God; nor suppress or disguise the doctrines of his word, however they may be abused by carnal and obstinate sinners.

It is true that man in his natural state cannot do any thing that is spiritually good; for "they that are in the flesh cannot please God." It is equally true, that God is a debtor to no man, but is the free disposer of his own grace, giving it when and to whomsoever he pleaseth. But it is no less true, that there are certain means of his appointment, in the use of which alone we have reason to expect his aid; and he who doth not improve these faithfully, complains with a very bad grace, at least, and is justly chargeable with his own damnation.

You cannot convert yourselves;—but cannot you forbear to curse and blaspheme the name of God? Cannot you restrain yourselves when your nature is duly refreshed with meat and drink? Cannot you keep at a distance from evil company, and avoid many occasions of sinning, and temptation to sin? It is certainly in your power to perform many of the external acts of religious worship. You can go to church, if you are so disposed, as easily as you can stay at home, or ride about for amusement. You can go to your closet as easily as to the tavern. What hinders you to read your Bible as well as any other book? to meditate on what it contains, and on its vast importance to your everlasting interest?

Have you then done these things, or have you not done them? Have you avoided the tempting occasions of evil; Have you used the means of grace, and attended seriously upon the ordinances of God's worship? If you have neglected to employ the powers you possess, whom can you blame for it, that you have not obtained more extensive powers? God will make you one day to know, that it was not he who carried you to the haunts of riot, intemperance, and lewdness; that it was not he who tempted you to swear profanely, or to rail at goodness, or to quarrel with the Word that should have saved you; but that all this was owing to the voluntary and obstinate wickedness of your own corrupt hearts. And, whatever excuses sinners may now feign to themselves, they must all stand speechless at last. None shall be able to plead, " Lord, I applied to thee for converting grace, but it was refused me." No, God will be clear when he judgeth; and every mouth shall be stopped in that day when he passeth sentence on an assembled world.

Thus have I examined and endeavored to refute some of the most plausible objections which are commonly alleged against the mildness and equity of the divine administration; and from all that has been said, I hope it now appears, that nothing can be more unreasonable and blasphemous than to lay the blame of the sinner's destruction upon God. " The foolishness of man," saith Solomon, " perverteth his way; and his heart fretteth against the Lord." Prov. xix. 3. This is the true account of the matter. The sinner destroys himself by his own wilful and obstinate folly, and then he accuses God, as if he were the cause of his misery; although God hath done every thing to save him, which could have been done by the righteous Lawgiver and Governor of the world.

The lying lips shall ere long be put to silence. The workers of iniquity shall stand self-condemned before the awful tribunal; and all their vain and impious pretexts and excuses, instead of availing them in that day, will only serve to increase their shame and confusion. With what inconceivable remorse and anguish will the sinner then review his past conduct? How contemptible will those temptations then appear to him, which he once magnified so much, when he shall compare them with the powerful motives and encouragements to a holy life, which were in vain so often and so plainly set before him? when he shall recollect the various means and instruments which were employed to save him from ruin; the full and free offers which were made to him of pardoning mercy and of sanctifying grace; the earnest calls and invitations which he received to turn from his evil way and live? when he shall view that precious fountain, in which thousands, as guilty as himself, have been washed and made clean; and shall reflect that all these advantages are for ever lost; how shall he then hang down his head, and smite his guilty and despairing breast? saying, in the bitterness of his soul, " How have I hated instruction, and my heart despised reproof? and have not obeyed the voice of my teachers, nor inclined mine ear to them that instructed me?" Prov. v. 12, 13. Then shall all his complaints be turned against himself; and, instead of resting on his wonted excuses, he shall then call, but call in vain, " on the mountains and on the rocks to fall on him, and to hide him from the face of him who sitteth on the throne, and from the wrath of the Lamb." O that men were wise, and would consider these things, so as to prevent, by a timely repentance, the horrors of that awful day which is hastening fast to surprise a sleeping world.

My brethren, I have represented your danger to you as plainly as I could. I have endeavored to expose the weakness of those pitiful evasions by which many of you endeavor to support a vain hope, or at least to lessen the awful apprehensions of a judgment to come. I have spoken to your ears: God alone can speak to your hearts; and to his mercy and grace I commend you.—Allow me, before I conclude, to beg your attention to the following considerations.

Consider, that to be your own destroyers is to counteract the very strongest principle of your natures, the principle of self-preservation. Every creature naturally desireth its own felicity; and will you obstinately rush upon manifest ruin through all the obstacles that are placed in your way? Assistants you may find in accomplishing this desperate purpose; but without your own consent and active concurrence, it never can be accomplished, even though the whole world, and all the host of apostate spirits, were combined against you. Will you be worse than devils to yourselves? What pity can you expect to meet with, who have no pity for your own souls? The unfortunates are objects of compassion; but wilful self-destroyers neither deserve compassion, nor can expect it. Consider what an aggravation this will be of your misery in a future state? How terrible will it be to recollect, in the regions of everlasting woe, that ye have brought all your misery on yourselves? that you were forewarned repeatedly, and awfully forewarned, of the fatal issue of your conduct, but without effect? that Christ and eternal salvation were freely offered to you, but were contemptuously despised and set at naught? These considerations will add a continual fuel to the tormenting flames, and will make them burn with insufferable violence. O then be wise in time! "Seek the Lord while he may be found, and call upon him while he is near. Let the wicked forsake his way, and the unrighteous man his thoughts, and let him return unto the Lord, and he will have mercy upon him, and to our God, for he will abundantly pardon."—To conclude: Ponder the wholesome advice recorded in Prov. viii. 33, 36. "Hear Instruction, and be wise, and refuse it not. Blessed is the man that heareth me, watching daily at my gates, waiting at the posts of my doors. For whoso findeth me, findeth life, and shall obtain favor of the Lord. But he that sinneth against me, wrongeth his own soul. All they that hate me, love death." *Amen.*

SERMON XXXIX.

Preached on the Evening of a Communion Sabbath.

OUR WORKS TO BE VERIFIED.

Galatians vi. 4.—"Let every Man prove his own Work."

Before I enter upon the subject of this text, it may not be improper to mention some of the reasons which have led me to it at this time.

1*st.* As many, who call themselves Christians, discover so little of Christianity in their lives, that we are often at a loss to reconcile their conduct with their professions; I thought it might be of use to those who are in any degree distinguished by their religious conduct, if I could lead them into such a scrutiny of themselves as this text suggests to us; or persuade them to inquire, whether their works, which are apparently good, are such as will abide the test: whether they proceed from the Spirit of God, or from the spirit of the world: whether they are animated by a "simplicity and godly sincerity," or by the unhallowed principles of self-love, and the desire of recommending themselves to the esteem of men.

2*dly.* It is evident from Scripture, that a man may go far in the outward performance of his duty, and yet be actuated by such motives as afford him greater cause of grief and of shame than of that rejoicing which is mentioned in the clause following my text. I read in the preceding verse, that it is possible for a "man to think himself to be something when he is nothing." I find in fact, that the Laodiceans imagined themselves to be "rich and increased with goods, and having need of nothing," when, in truth, they were "wretched, and miserable, and poor, and blind, and naked." And there are too many reasons to suspect, that, like those, multitudes of this present generation are "pure in their own eyes, and yet are not washed from their filthiness;" have a "name that they live" while "they are dead;" and have "the praise of men" while "their hearts are not right with God."

3*dly.* I foresee the time when thousands shall wish that they had followed the apostle's advice in my text. "Yet a little while, and he that shall come will come, and will not tarry."—"The Lord himself shall descend from heaven with a shout, with the voice of the archangel, and the trump of God; to judge the world in righteousness. In that day many shall say to him, Lord, Lord, did we not eat and drink in thy presence, have we not prophesied in thy name, and in thy name done many wonderful works?" But when they receive that awful reply, "Depart from me, I know you not whence ye are," with what inconceivable anguish will they then cry out, Oh! that we had tried and proved those specious works in which we trusted. We thought them good and acceptable to God; alas! too late, we find our unhappy mistake. The time was, when this discovery might have profited us; but now the doom is passed; our state is fixed; and nothing remains for us but a fruitless remorse, and the galling remembrance of our former sloth and security.—And,

Lastly. When I consider that I was to speak to communicants, who have this day sealed either their friendship or their enmity with Christ at his own table, it determined me to address to you a pressing and earnest call to prove this part of your work in particular; that such as have been properly employed in this holy service may, after trial of themselves, lay hold of the comforts which belong to them; and that others may receive such a view of their guilt and of their danger, as, by the grace of God, shall constrain them to have immediate recourse to that injured, but compassionate Saviour, whose blood, instead of crying for vengeance, pleads for mercy to the chief of sinners. On all these accounts let me entreat, not only the hearing of your ears, but the attention of your minds, whilst I endeavor, through divine aid,

1*st.* To explain the full meaning or import of the apostle's exhortation—" Let every man prove his own work."

2*dly.* To give you some directions with regard to the manner of conducting the inquiry to which the exhortation relates; and then to point out to you the practical improvement of the subject. I begin with the exhortation itself, " Let every man prove his own work."

There is a particular emphasis in these words, which must not be overlooked. It is his *own* work that a man must prove. We are sufficiently-ready to examine, and to pass sentence upon the works of others. We are often abroad, but are seldom at home, where our chief business lies. Like some travellers, who are well acquainted with foreign countries, but shamefully ignorant of their own, we know more of others than we are willing to know of ourselves, and persuade ourselves, that the study of our own hearts is a dull and melancholy business, which may incite within us many uneasy thoughts, and can give us no pleasure at all.

Alas! how low are we sunk by our apostasy from God! and with what little and false consolations may a degenerate mind be soothed! Instead of looking inwards for positive evidence of our favor with God, we learn to regulate our judgment of ourselves by what we perceive in the characters of other men. If the image of the devil is more visibly formed on others than on ourselves, we have little anxiety to discover the image of God upon our own hearts. The bulk of men think it enough to know that some of their brethren are worse than they are, as if their characters would rise in proportion as the characters of others are debased. We must relinquish this false rule of judging, if we would either enter into the spirit of the exhortation in the text, or would not be fatally disappointed at last. We must learn to rejoice in ourselves and not in others; and we must call in our thoughts from the state of other men, and "prove every man his own work."—" Every man," saith the apostle, " shall bear his own burden." Each of us shall give an account of his own conduct to God, and shall be judged according to his own personal behavior, without regard to any comparative goodness or attainments which may belong to him.

But here, perhaps, some may ask the question, To what works do you refer? If they are works of a doubtful nature, we acknowledge that they ought to be tried, and that those are highly to blame who neglect to try them. But are there not other works, so eminently good and excellent in themselves, that the person who doth them may conclude, without hesitation, that they are certainly pleasing and acceptable to God? This, my brethren, is a rock upon which thousands have made shipwreck. It would make one sad to think what multitudes will be surprised with the everlasting burnings, who, in consequence of this very opinion, flatter themselves, while they live, with the hopes of heaven. You must therefore allow me to retort the question, and to ask, What are those works which are so eminently good and excellent, that there is no need to prove them? or rather, Are there any duties of an external nature, which an hypocrite cannot perform as well as you? Do you frequent the church, and attend upon the preaching of the word? So did the impenitent Jews in the days of the prophet Ezekiel, with as much decency, perhaps, and apparent devotion, as are seen in you. For thus said the Lord unto that prophet, " They come unto thee as the people cometh, and they sit before thee as my people, and they hear thy words, but they will not do them: for with their mouth they show much love, but their heart goeth after their covetousness." Are you strict observers of the Sabbath? We read of some who persecuted our Saviour for working a miracle of mercy on the sabbath-day: and surely you pretend not to a greater degree of strictness than this. Do you pray? So did the Pharisees; they made long prayers, and they prayed with a loud voice. Do you fast before the observation of the Lord's Supper? The Pharisees did more: They fasted twice in the week. Do you partake of that holy sacrament? Many think that Judas did so too: we know at least that he was present at the passover, which was also a solemn rite of religion: And therefore no certain conclusion can be drawn from the outward exercises of religious worship.

Where then shall we go next? Will we judge with more certainty from the duties of the second table of the law of God?

Here, my brethren, the matter may be brought to a very short issue. We read of a young man who professed, in the presence of our Lord, that he had kept all these commandments from his youth: and yet we learn from the sequel of his story, that he preferred the possessions of this earth to the enjoyment of God; for he refused to sell his lands for the relief of the poor, although our Saviour had assured him of treasure in heaven. But you have perhaps to say for yourselves, that you are charitable and kind to the poor; and ask if this is not a duty applauded in Scripture? I confess it is much applauded. But were not the proud and hypocritical Pharisees also charitable? They gave alms; and more liberal alms than most of us; otherwise, I suppose, they would have sounded the trumpet as little as we do. We may therefore conclude, that none of all these outward deeds are sufficient, by themselves, to distinguish us from the hypocrite: But the question will return, May we not join all these works together? and in that case, may we not draw from them a certain conclusion?

My brethren, if I were now speaking of the judgment which others ought to form of your characters, from what they see in your actions, I would certainly say, that those favorable appearances ought to persuade them that you are real Christians. But as I speak of the estimate which you are to make of yourselves, I must tell you, that all this fair show may certainly consist with a heart that is not " sound in God's statutes." For Amaziah the king of Judah was not far short of this, of whom we read (2 Chron. xxv. 2.) that he " did that which was right in the sight of the Lord;" but (observe what follows, he did it) " not with a perfect heart." What a promising appearance was here blasted! Amaziah gave God every thing but his heart; the very thing which God valued, and without which all that he could give besides was insignificant. Does not this shake the foundation of your confidence, and make you, like one newly awakened out of a flattering dream, summon up all your attention to see whether you are in the unhappy situation of Amaziah, or are really in the circumstances in in which your own fancy hath represented you? This, my brethren, is the very thing which I have been aiming at. I foresee the day, when many who were something in their own eyes, and trusted in themselves that they were righteous, will present their specious roll of outward duties to the heart-searching Judge, saying, Lo! this is the life which we spent in the flesh; who will not be able to add, This life was " by the faith of the Son of God." Methinks I hear the Judge say to them, These are indeed the duties which I enjoined; but where is the spirit which should have animated them? These are the sacrifices which I appointed; but the strange fire with which you offered them can find no acceptance here. Ye have not served me, but yourselves. " I never knew you." And therefore ye can receive no reward.

What hath been said may be sufficient to explain the apostle's exhortation; and to show both the reasonableness and the necessity of proving even our best works. I proceed now,

Secondly, To give you some directions with regard to the manner of conducting this important inquiry.

Now, before a man can be qualified for proving his own works, two things are indispensably necessary. The

1*st* is, That he should be well acquainted with the holy Scriptures; for it is by the Scriptures alone that we know with certainty what is good and acceptable to God. "Wherewith shall a young man cleanse his way?" said David. The answer is, "By taking heed thereto according to thy word." Scripture is that unerring rule which points out to us the road of duty, and which discovers to us the straightness or the crookedness of our own paths. A considerable degree of acquaintance with it, is therefore absolutely necessary to enable us "to prove" and to judge of our own works. But,

2*dly*. It is also requisite that we should be constant and diligent observers of what passeth in our own hearts; for "out of the heart are the issues of life." The heart is the fountain from which all our actions flow, and from which alone they can be truly denominated either good or bad. I observed formerly, that there is no outward duty which a hypocrite may not counterfeit: And we have a remarkable example (2 Kings x.) of the same action being good in one man and bad in another, from the different dispositions with which it was performed. We find two men riding in the same chariot, and both of them engaged in the same expedition, Jehu and Jonadab. But though the work they were executing was the same, the different ends which they aimed at, made that which was an excellent duty in Jonadab an act of mere cruelty, and of vile hypocrisy, in Jehu. Jehu was impelled, not by zeal for the Lord, but by ambition to wear a crown. We must therefore retire into our own breasts, and carefully observe the various operations of our minds. We must consider the motives that influence our conduct; the ends we propose in our actions; and the temper and frame of spirit with which every duty is performed. For in vain do we know the rule, unless we also know the thing to which it must be applied; in vain do we read and study the Scriptures, unless we likewise read and study our own hearts. The duty I am recommending, consists in comparing them together, that we may discover how far they agree, and wherein they differ. This is indeed a work of great difficulty; but, though difficult, it is not impracticable. He who gave the command, will likewise grant his assistance to those who, in a humble dependence on his grace, apply themselves heartily to this necessary duty. Let it then be your

First care, to get your minds thoroughly awakened when you enter upon this work. Never was time put to a higher improvement; never were thoughts spent upon a more important business. Compared with this, the trial of men for their lives at a human bar is a mere trifle; for here nothing less than an eternal interest depends on the issue. Summon up all the powers of your souls, bring your thoughts to the subject as intensely as you can, let your minds be divested of every other care; and above all—O be honest with yourselves, and resolve to pass an impartial sentence, as the evidence shall appear, whether it should be in your favor or against you. Remember that your great Judge knows the truth of your condition, and that therefore you can gain nothing by hiding it from yourselves.

When your hearts are once seriously engaged, then fall down before God, and plead the assistance of his good Spirit, to enlighten and direct you in the knowledge of yourselves; to keep you from mistakes, both on the one hand and on the other; and to guide you to a just and an affecting view of your true condition.

Having thus prepared yourselves by meditation and prayer, proceed immediately to the inquiry itself, before your hearts begin to cool, or the impressions of the divine presence are effaced. Set the word of God before you as the rule, and then put the question, Do my actions and dispositions correspond to this rule, or are they inconsistent with it? Take your actions, and the sources of them, one by one, and bring them to this standard; suffer not your hearts, in any case, to start aside, till they have given an explicit answer; lay the command of God upon them, and charge them to obey upon pain of his wrath.

When, by these means, you have discovered the truth, then pass the sentence on yourselves, and labor to have your hearts properly affected with it. Do not think it enough to have discerned your true condition, but endeavor to feel what God hath made you to know. If you find that you have been all along formal and hypocritical in your obedience; that instead of serving God, you have been serving yourselves that instead of seeking his approbation, you have been courting the applause of men; that instead of sowing to the Spirit, you have been sowing to the flesh;—O lay this conviction home to your hearts. Think what a dreadful state you are in; unpardoned, unsanctified, and, if death should now surprise you, ruined for ever.

But, whilst you thus endeavor to know the very worst of your condition, beware, at the same time, of giving way to gloomy and desponding thoughts. Let none of you say, "Because I am ungodly, I shall die so; because I am an hypocrite, I shall continue so;" for such despondence is no less unwarranted than your former presumption. You have another work to do, which is to flee speedily to Christ, and to break off your hypocrisy and wickedness by repentance. If you find that you haye been hitherto out of the way, do not sit down and despair, but make the more haste to turn into it. Christ is still in your offer, and you cannot be more willing to receive him than he is to accept of you.

But, on the other hand, if you find reason to conclude, after a strict and impartial examination, that you have been sincere in the practice of your duty, that your inward dispositions have corresponded to your outward actions, and that both have been according to the rule of Scripture, take the comfort of so happy a discovery. This is a good evidence that you are sanctified and renewed by the Spirit of God: This is a proof that you are united to Christ, who is "the true vine;" for none but those who are united to him can bring forth such good fruit. Consider into what a blessed state the Lord hath brought you; to be his children and his friends; to be pardoned, and sanctified, and sure of being saved. What more can you desire? Doth not the assurance of such a blessed condition deserve all the labor and pains which the inquiry can cost you? One caution, however, I must give you. Do not trust so much to one discovery of this kind as to give up all further trial. No. "To prove your own works" must be your daily employment. Renew the inquiry often; make frequent proof of yourselves; compare the result of your observations at different times, and let them serve to rectify one another.

Thus, my brethren, I have given you the best directions which I could think of, with regard to the method of conducting this important inquiry. And here it might be proper to subjoin some of those Scriptural marks or characters by which "every man ought to prove his own works." But this would lead me beyond the limits of one discourse. I mean therefore at present to confine myself to the circumstances or marks by which you ought to try the important duty in which you have been this day employed.

Allow me then, in the conclusion of this solemn service, to put a few plain, but necessary questions to you, and to call on you to answer them, as you hope to speed at the bar of God's judgment.

1*st.* By what motives were you determined to come here this day? Was it by a sense of duty, and in obedience to the command of a crucified Saviour? Was it from a mind "hungering and thirsting" after Christ and his righteousness? Or was it only in compliance with the custom of the country, and from a desire of appearing religious in the eyes of men? Would to God there were less cause than there is for this question, gross and reproachful as it may appear!

2*dly.* What pains were you at in preparing yourselves for this near approach to God? Were you careful to stir up in yourselves those holy and humble dispositions which constitute the "wedding garment" of those who are bidden to the feast? Or, have you, without any previous examination, or any regard to the awful fence which surrounds this table, fearlessly taken your seat among faithful disciples, without asking the Master's welcome, or dreading his displeasure?

3*dly*. What benefit did you propose to reap from your attendance upon this solemn ordinance? Did you only wish to pacify your natural conscience, by doing what you apprehended to be an acceptable duty? Or did you mean to offer an outward compliment to the Almighty, in order to induce him to pardon what is past, that you might sin, as it were, on a new score? Or, on the other hand, did you come here in the hope of meeting him whom your soul loves, to take upon you "his yoke which is easy, and his burden which is light?"—to implore, over the pledges of your Saviour's love, his mercy to pardon, his Spirit to sanctify, and his grace to strengthen you? Did you come that this holy service might have some influence to assist you in crucifying "the old man with his deeds," and to confirm the image of God on your souls? Once more,

4*thly*. How were you employed while you sat at this holy table? Did you seek the Lord with your whole hearts? Did your "souls follow hard after him?" And if any vain intruding thought arose within you, did you instantly check it with abhorrence, and renew your repentance for that mixture of infirmity in your holy service? When you heard these affecting words, "This is my body broken for you, this is my blood shed for the remission of your sins," were your hearts wrung with grief for the sins which were the cause of your Redeemer's sufferings? Did you give yourselves entirely up to him who gave himself for you an offering and a sacrifice to God? Did you accept of him as your only peace-maker with the Father, and resolve to build all your hopes of happiness upon the merits of his sufferings and obedience? Did you renounce all his enemies, and devote yourselves entirely to his service, to be governed by his laws, as your only Lord and King?

Finally. Was all this done from a deliberate and a confirmed choice, and not from a mere transient flash of devotion? Then, indeed, you have been well employed; and we desire to give glory to God on your account.

But if, on the contrary, your hearts have been cold and insensible, and your thoughts have been wandering without control upon the mountains of vanity; if you have felt no grief for sin, no love to the Redeemer, or only such a grief and love as a moving tale might have occasioned; if what you have felt hath not led you to bind yourselves irrevocably to the service of that Redeemer who encountered the wrath of God for you—this was not to eat the Lord's Supper. Alas! my heart bleeds for you. Ye have been mocking him who hath declared that he will not be mocked with impunity; and who, unless you repent, will certainly convince you of this in another world.

These are all the questions which I shall put to you at this time; and in whatever way you may find reason to answer them, the inquiry must turn out to your advantage. If, upon search, you discover the unsoundness of your hearts, even in that very sad discovery you have the greatest advantage for salvation that you have ever had in the course of your lives. For now, your vain confidence being overthrown, you lie open to a deep and effectual conviction, which is the mercy introductive of all other mercies to your souls. Your chief danger lies in judging too favorably, or in judging falsely, of yourselves. But if you do so, how severely will you suffer for the short-lived deceit, when God shall himself prove your works, or when he shall say to you as he said to the carousing king, "Thou art weighed in the balances, and art found wanting!" How confounded will you be if this sentence shall be pronounced? and how passionately will you then wish for such an opportunity of "proving your own works" as you now enjoy?

But if, on the other hand, you can, upon good grounds, conclude, that notwithstanding many imperfections in your holy service, you have been sincere and upright on the whole, how great may your comfort be? For God will not cast off the upright man. That which is the terror of the wicked will be your joy. As the son of a king rejoiceth in his father's power and magnificence, so may you rejoice in those displays of the divine Majesty, which scare a guilty world. How comfortable will the thoughts of a Saviour be, when you can say, "My beloved is mine;" when by faith you can, like Thomas, "put your hand into his side, and your finger into the print of the nails, and say unto him, My Lord, and my God?" With what joy will you read the Holy Scriptures, as the charter of your future inheritance, and ponder that "exceeding and eternal weight of glory," which you shall one day possess? With what holy boldness may you approach the throne of Grace, when you can address God as your reconciled Father in Jesus Christ? How cheerfully may you endure affliction? How calmly may you leave this world?

If then any of these comforts are dear to you; if you would enjoy them in a sound state, or would have a clear and lively impression of them, let me beseech you to comply with the apostle's exhortation, and to "prove your own works." So shall ye have your rejoicing in yourselves, and never be ashamed. *Amen.*

SERMON XL.

THE RESPONSIBILITY OF KNOWLEDGE.

JAMES IV. 17.—"Therefore to him that knoweth to do good, and doeth it not, to him it is sin."

THE unfruitful lives of professing Christians is a very general and a just complaint. But few of those who retail this complaint are heartily inclined to remove the cause of it. We are melancholy examples of that which we pretend to lament; and we cease not to strengthen the interests of a party which we condemn. David, when he was treating with Araunah the Jebusite, for the purchase of his threshing floor, in order to rear an altar to God, refused to accept of it without a price, because he would not "offer burnt-offerings unto the Lord his God, of that which cost him nothing." But, alas! our general contest seems rather to be, who shall be most penurious in his offerings to God, and who shall purchase heaven with the easiest service. Many have unhappily deceived themselves into an opinion, that nothing but positive acts of rebellion will subject them to punishment. They place much confidence in what is called a harmless inoffensive life, as if it were virtue enough not to be abandoned to vice. They seem to aim at nothing higher than that of which the Pharisee made his boast, when he gave thanks to God that he was not as other men, nor even as the humble publican. But, in the passage which I have now read to you, the apostle directs us to a much safer test of our conduct; a test which leaves us no room for mistake. The question is not, What vices have you forborne? but, What virtues have you practised? You say that you are not idolaters.—Well—but do you reverence and love the true God? You are not adulterers;—but do you study temperance and sobriety in all things? You are not slanderers;—but are you as tender of your neighbor's good name as of your own? If ye are strangers to these positive virtues, then all the advantage ye can pretend to is this; ye are sinners of a lower order, than if ye had added positive transgressions to your neglect of doing good: but still you are sinners; for, according to the apostle, not to do good is sin.

This text evidently contains the two following propositions:

1*st.* That men sin not only when they positively transgress the law of God; but also, when they do not fulfil the duties which the law requires to the utmost of their power. And,

2*dly.* That our guilt is more highly aggravated, when we neglect the duties which are known to us; or when we decline opportunities of doing good, though we know that it is our duty to embrace them.

These propositions I will endeavor to illustrate and confirm; and will then conclude with a practical improvement of the subject.

First. I begin with showing you that men sin, not only when they positively trangress the law of God, but also, when they do not fulfil the duties which the law requires to the utmost of their power.

Were we to look upon God as an austere and selfish Being, who employed his laws only as a fence about his own private interests; then indeed, not to violate them might be considered as sufficient to comply with their design. The kings of this earth are forced to inclose their little allotment of honor, and to use their authority as a flaming sword, to ward off insults from their prerogatives. But it is not so with God. The Creator of heaven and of earth can have no dependence on the workmanship of his own hands. His prerogative cannot suffer, nor can his glory be impaired, by the feeble and impotent attempts of his creatures. His laws therefore could never be intended for his own security, but for our benefit. They are expressions of his goodnessr ather than of his sovereignty; and his great view in enacting them, seems to have been, to bind us by his authority to consult our present interest, and to render ourselves capable of everlasting felicity. Judge then whether a law which hath in view this kind and generous object, doth not challenge our most cordial acceptance and entire subjection; and whether gratitude, as well as duty, should not prompt us to fulfil every part of it to the utmost of our power.

Indeed, if we consider God as a severe task-master, as I am afraid too many of us do; in that case, whatever he enjoins, will appear to be an hardship or a burden. But if we view him in his true character, as a wise and good parent, who in every thing consults the real advantage of his children, then his yoke will appear to be easy indeed, and his burden to be light. The cords of love will draw us on to obedience; and gratitude, which is ever ingenious in finding out ways to express itself, will constantly prompt us to the most dutiful observance of his will.

Show me the man whose ingenuous mind, not only expects a future reward, but feels a present joy in the service of his God; and to that man I will address the words of unfeigned salutation. I will say to him, "Hail thou favored of the Lord," thine is the true "spirit of adoption," which deviseth liberal things; thine is that soul which is born from on high, and which doth not commit sin; thine is that love which fulfilleth the law, and which perfecteth the saints.

But show me the man whose servile soul is moved only by the fear of punishment, to yield a grudging and penurious service to his Maker; and to that man I must be sparing of consolation. I must remind him, that it is the heart which God requires; that God hath respect to the offering of a liberal giver; but that he hath no regard to the churl, or to his offering.

Thus far I might argue upon general principles, that we ought not only to abstain from what the law of God prohibits, but also to fulfil, to the utmost of our power, what the spirit or intention of the law requires. But as I speak to Christians I will now resort to an authority which they must acknowledge to be valid, and sufficient to decide the question.

The proposition which I have laid down then, is not deduced by remote inference, neither does it depend upon a single testimony; but is both supported and illustrated by a multitude of clear and express declarations of Scripture.

We are commanded not only to "depart from evil," but "to do good;" not only to cleanse ourselves from all filthiness of the flesh and spirit, but also "to perfect holiness in the fear of God." Christ is proposed to us as our example; and what was his character? "He went about doing good, and persisted, till he had finished the work which was given him to do." Nay, he saith himself (John ix. 4.) "I *must* work the works of him that sent me." And if he, who voluntarily came under the law, was bound to this active and extensive service, shall we who are its necessary subjects, plead an exemption from it? Paul, in his epistle to Titus (chap. ii. 11.) informs us, that "the grace of God, which hath appeared to all men, bringing salvation, teacheth us not only to deny ungodliness and worldly lusts, but to live soberly, and righteously, and godly in the world;" and that Christ gave himself for us, for this end, "that he might redeem us from all iniquity, and purify to himself a peculiar people, zealous of good works."

These passages of Scripture need no commentary, all of them point out the necessity of a positive and active obedience.

But this is not all: Our blessed Lord, who well knew what was in man, seems to have directly calculated some of his discourses to prevent the possibility of a mistake on the subject. The parables of the rich man and Lazarus, of the talents, and of the barren fig-tree, plainly appear to have been delivered with this view.

We are not told that the rich man was in any respect injurious or oppressive to Lazarus: his guilt lay in his not extending his kindness to supply his wants. The unprofitable servant was cast into outer darkness, not for losing or squandering away his talent, but for hiding it in a napkin, and neglecting to improve it. And the fig-tree was cut down, and cast into the fire, not for producing bad fruit, but because it produced no fruit at all. But lest the allegorical dress of these instructions should leave men at too great liberty to explain away the force of them, this wise and provident Teacher, in a serious and awful discourse on the process of the last judgment, resumes the same argument, (Matth. xxv. 31.—) There he tells us expressly, that men shall not only be punished for doing evil, but also for neglecting to perform active service; and in particular, for neglecting to perform the offices of humanity to their brethren. For the charge runs in these words: "I was an hungered, and ye gave me no meat; I was thirsty, and ye gave me no drink; I was a stranger, and ye took me not in; naked and ye clothed me not; sick, and in prison, and ye visited me not."—"For inasmuch as ye did it not to the least of these my brethren, ye did it not to me." And then follows the doom to be pronounced on those against whom this charge is brought; "These shall go away into everlasting punishment."

From these passages of Scripture, we learn with assurance, that unless life is filled up with good works, death, which introduceth us to judgment, must approach to us with a dark and gloomy aspect. When conscience, awakened with the dawning of an everlasting day, shall prompt us to inquire, What we have done? How we have improved our time, our talents, and the means of grace with which we have been favored? If in this review of ourselves, we shall be able to discover nothing but the traces of vanity and impertinence, how must we shrink back, and tremble on the awful state before us? If God will judge every man according to his works, alas! what must become of the unhappy sluggard, who hath no works to show: who hath slept, and trifled, and squandered away all his time? "O that men were wise, that they understood this, that they would consider their latter end!"—"How long, O ye simple ones, will ye love simplicity?" How long, O sinner, shall that precious time on which eternity depends, be wasted in the pursuit of lying vanities? O think, how swiftly it passeth away, and how passionately thou wilt one day wish to recall it. Who can assure thee that the decree is not already gone forth against thee, "Cut him off, why cumbereth he the ground."—"Thou fool, this night thy soul shall be required of thee."

Pardon me, then, if I speak to you as short-lived, or as dying creatures; some of whom I may never see again till we meet before the judgment-seat of God. Under this impression, let me deal freely with you, and call on you to review your past conduct, as if the Lord himself were demanding an account of it.

Say, then, hath it been suitable to the rank you hold in life? Hath it even been rational? such as became those high intellectual powers by which you are raised above the beasts that perish? Would you consent to have it published before this congregation? Or rather, are there not some parts of it which you would wish to hide from your most intimate friends? lest, partial as they are to you, the knowledge of them should quench their affection, and render you contemptible in their eyes? Are you then ready to appear in judgment, and to have all your thoughts, and words, and actions laid open and canvassed before an assembled world?

I shall not suppose you guilty of gross acts of wickedness. Perhaps the influence of education, the power of natural conscience, and the restraints of Providence, have hitherto kept you back from these. I at present charge you with nothing worse than the omission of duty, and the neglect of opportunities for cultivating and improving the talents which God hath given you. You have been thoughtless and inconsiderate, unmindful of the God who made you, and of the Redeemer who bought you with his blood. You have forgotten the end for which you were sent into the world. You have suffered the cares and pleasures of the present life, the business or amusements of this fleeting scene of vanity, to divide your hearts, and engross your time, as if the soul had been destined to serve the body; or as if this earth had been designed for your only residence and portion.

Can you then review such a life without blushing and shame? When you think of it, doth it not appear mean and despicable even in your own eyes? And can it then be pleasing; or rather, must it not be highly offensive, to that Almighty Being, who gave you a nature fitted for the performance of nobler services, and for the relish of higher enjoyments, than any with which your have been hitherto acquainted?

For the Lord's sake open your eyes, and take a serious and impartial view of your condition. Blessed be God it is not yet too late. The door of mercy is still open; and though, like the prodigal son, you have hitherto been feeding upon husks; yet when, like him, ye shall return to your Father's house, and to the faithful and affectionate duty of children, your past wandering and unprofitable life shall be forgiven; and ye may yet enjoy the honors and privileges of your Father's sons.

Having thus confirmed and illustrated the first propositions contained in the text, namely, that men sin, not only when they positively transgress the law of God; but also when they do not fulfil the duties which the law requires to the utmost of their power; I now proceed to show you, as was proposed,

Secondly. That our guilt is more highly aggravated, when we neglect the duties which are known to us; or when we decline opportunities of doing good, though we are convinced that it is our duty to embrace them.

He who doth not seek for opportunities of doing good, is a sinner; that is, he counteracts the obvious intention of his Maker in sending him into the world: and therefore shall be dealt with as an unfaithful servant, who hath not applied his talents to the purposes for which they were given him. And if this be the case, then surely the person who hath a known opportunity of doing good, and yet wilfully neglects it, must contract greater guilt, and be liable to a severer punishment. If that man be culpable, who is careless of doing all the good which by an exertion of his talents he is able to do; is not that man much more culpable, who presumptuously omits to do the good to which he has opportunities to solicit him? But why should I spend time in establishing so plain a truth, especially when it is confirmed by the highest authority? Our blessed Lord himself expressly tells us, (Luke xii. 47.) that "the servant who knew his Lord's will, and prepared not himself, neither did according to his will, shall be beaten with many stripes."

The only question that remains then is, Whether this be a supposition that can be made? Is it to be thought, that any man is capable of deliberately resisting his own conviction, and of declining obedience to a law which he both knows and believes to be binding on him?

I confess, indeed, that a superior Being, if we could imagine him to be altogether unacquainted with human affairs, might reject this supposition as improbable. But surely *we* have no cause to object against the representation as forced, or beyond the life. Our own observation, unless we have been extremely inattentive, cannot fail to furnish us with numberless proofs of this determined neglect of duty. We need not go from home to bring our examples from persons in high and public trust, who have been known to sacrifice the acknowledged interest and honor of a whole nation to their own private resentment or personal advantage. They are farther seen, for no other reason but because they are placed higher. The importance of their station renders their faults the more conspicuous, while a groaning community points out, as with the finger, the authors of its distress. But let each of us look into his own breast; and if conscience is not asleep, it will say to us as Nathan said to David, "Thou art the man." Thou thyself hast neglected the fairest opportunities of doing good, when thou hadst the strongest conviction that it was thy reasonable duty.

I mean not to pry into the secrets of your hearts, any more than to divulge the secrets of my own. But I speak from a thorough conviction, that all of us pass too slightly over our omissions, even in the most serious review which we take of our conduct. We are, alas! too fruitful in excuses, and too ready to gloss over our most culpable neglects, with the specious color of ignorance or incapacity. But God, to whom the night shineth as the day, knows the conviction of mind against which we sin; and our most dexterous arts of concealment cannot screen us from his penetrating eye. A just impression of this would prevent many fatal mistakes in our conduct.

I have now, for example, an opportunity of doing good; and my conscience tells me, that I ought to improve it. On the other hand, I have many strong temptations to neglect it. It would put me to too much cost or trouble; it would involve me in a train of action against which my indolence revolts; or it would divert me from other employments more agreeable to my inclination. On which side shall I resolve? May I not so manage it that the neglect shall escape the observation of my neighbor? Or if he should perceive it, may I not put a good face upon it, and find out some excuse to save me from his censure? Ah! but here is the check. The Searcher of hearts knows my present conviction. In vain shall I attempt to prevaricate with him. I may elude the censure of man; but I never can escape the just judgment of that God who is greater than my heart, and knoweth all things. Such reasoning as this, if it were once become habitual to us, would be a constant and powerful incitement to all holy obedience; and would prevent the deep guilt of neglecting to do good, even when we know the extent and obligation of the law of God, and are convinced that it is our duty to comply with it.

Having thus endeavored to illustrate and confirm the two propositions contained in my text, I proceed now to the practical improvement of the subject. And,

1*st*. This subject administers a sharp reproof to those who, in any case, attempt to evade their convictions of duty. "To him that knoweth to do good," saith the apostle, "and doth it not, to him it is sin." For, consider what kind of disposition this conduct betrays. Is it not evidently the disposition of a slavish and mercenary mind? You do no more in the service of God than you suppose to be necessary, in order to escape eternal misery; and this is the only consideration which deters you from open transgressions of his law. You have therefore no regard for him, but only a concern for your own safety. Your plan of conduct is to offend God as far as you can, without incurring his vengeance: So that any appearance of goodness about you is nothing more than the effect of a natural timidity. Do ye thus requite the Lord, O foolish people and unwise? Doth his goodness challenge no better return from you, than merely to refrain from acts of open rebellion against him? Consider, I beseech you, the baseness and ingratitude of this conduct; and if your hearts retain any spark of ingenuity, you will surely be persuaded to yield him a more faithful and generous service in time to come. But,

2*dly*. This subject administers reproof also to the slothful and inactive servant, who rests contented with low attainments in religion. You perhaps flatter yourself, that although you are remiss in seeking out opportunities of doing good, yet you are not unfaithful to any known obligation. But in this case you greatly deceive yourself. For is it not a known obligation, that we should aim at as much perfection as we are capable of attaining? But you have renounced this desire altogether. In other words, you have deliberately left off that work to which our Saviour hath expressly commanded us to devote ourselves. For, are not these his words? "Be ye perfect, even as your Father who is in heaven is perfect." Once more,

What hath been said on this subject ought to quicken the zeal and activity even of those who have made the greatest progress in the good ways of God.

The declining state of religion calls loudly on all who are its real friends, to exert themselves to the utmost, in order to revive its influence in the world. Nothing, be assured, will be so effectual for accomplishing this desirable object, as the bright and exemplary lives of professing Christians. Are you then zealous for the glory of God? be "zealous of good works." Let it appear that your religion gives authority to your conscience, by your being more just, and humane, and generous than other men. "Ye are the salt of the earth, ye are the light of the world." Your divine Master hath intrusted you with the honor of that religion which he taught on earth, and expects that you should display it in an amiable light. But surely a mere negative degree of virtue will never convince men that your principles have any excellence superior to their own; and that professing Christians satisfy themselves with a virtue of this sort, is, I am afraid, in no small degree, the cause to which the rapid growth of infidelity in these times must be ascribed.

If this is at all the fact, doth it not afford us a subject of the most serious lamentation? "It is impossible but that offences will come, but woe unto him through whom they come. It were better for him that a millstone were hanged about his neck, and he cast into the sea." O then, study to adorn the doctrine of God your Saviour in all things. "Let your light so shine before men, that they may see your good works, and glorify your Father which is in heaven." "Whatsoever things are true, whatsoever things are honest, whatsoever things are just, whatsoever things are pure, whatsoever things are lovely, whatsoever things are of good report, if there be any virtue, and if there be any praise, think on these things," and do them. This will administer to you true pleasure in life, and solid hope in death; and hereafter the sound of the last trumpet, the terror of the negligent and unfaithful servant, will be the triumphant signal of your release from the grave, and the summons of your Lord to enter into his joy. *Amen.*

SERMON XLI.

THE ANT AN INSTRUCTOR.

PROVERBS VI. 6, 7, 8.—"Go to the Ant, thou Sluggard; consider her ways, and be wise: which, having no guide, overseer, or ruler, provideth her meat in the summer, and gathereth her food in the harvest."

MAN was created with more understanding than the beasts of the earth: But our minds are so debased by our apostasy from God, that the meanest creatures may become our teachers. And accordingly, the Spirit of God, in the Scriptures, doth frequently send us to learn our duty from the example of the beasts of the field, and of the fowls of heaven. Thus, ingratitude is reproved by the example of those animals which are accounted the most stupid and intractable, (Isaiah i. 3.) "The ox knoweth his owner, and the ass his master's crib; but Israel doth not know, my people doth not consider." An inattention to the conduct of divine Providence, and a neglect of the proper seasons of activity, are in like manner condemned by the example of the fowls of heaven. "The stork knoweth her appointed times, and the turtle, and the crane, and the swallow, observe the times of their coming; but my people (saith God) know not the judgment of the Lord." Jerem. viii. 7. To cure us of excessive carefulness and anxiety, our Saviour sends us to "consider the ravens; they neither sow nor reap; they have neither storehouse nor barn; yet God feedeth them: How much more," saith he," "are ye better than the fowls?" Luke xii. 24. And in my text, to cure us of negligence and sloth, Solomon sends us to a creature of the smallest size, but of most wonderful activity. "Go to the ant, thou sluggard; consider her ways, and be wise: which, having no guide, overseer, or ruler, provideth her meat in the summer, and gathereth her food in the harvest."

In discoursing of these words, I will,

1*st.* Consider the character of the person whom the wise man here addresses. And,

2*dly.* The counsel or advice which he gives him; and will then conclude with a practical improvement of the subject.

I Begin with the character of the person to whom this advice is addressed. "Go to the ant," saith Solomon, "thou sluggard:" and the character of the sluggard is so minutely described in this book, and in the book of Ecclesiastes, that any of us may soon be acquainted with it.

Solomon observes in general, that sloth casteth into a deep sleep; and he represents the sluggard in this state in the verses immediately following my text. When it is said to him, "How long wilt thou sleep, O sluggard? when wilt thou arise out of thy sleep?" Instead of being affected with the just reproach, he begs earnestly for farther indulgence, "Yet a little sleep, a little slumber, a little folding of the hands to sleep." "As the door turneth upon its hinges, so doth the slothful man upon his bed." At length, when sleep itself hath become wearisome, and he hath risen from his bed, he hath changed his situation only to give a new indulgence to his sloth. "He hideth his hand in his bosom," and will not so much as "bring it to his mouth again." He spends his time in fruitless wishes: The soul of the sluggard "desireth and hath not." To-morrow is always a day of labor, to-day is always spent in idleness: And thus "the desire of the slothful killeth him, because his hands refuse to labor." He is discouraged by the least opposition; "The way of the slothfull man is as a hedge of thorns." Every difficulty furnisheth him with an excuse for his idleness: "The sluggard will not plough by reason of the cold." Nay, rather than want an excuse, he creates imaginary dangers to himself: he saith "There is a lion without, I shall be slain in the streets." At length, "By much slothfulness the building decays, and through the idleness of the hands the house droppeth through."—"His field and his vineyard are grown over with thorns: nettles cover the face thereof; and the stonewall is broken down." Thus, "Poverty cometh upon him like one that travaileth, and his want as an armed man, till drowsiness at last clothes him with rags."

Such is the picture which Solomon draws of the sluggard; and the features are so strongly marked. that there is no room to doubt that it was drawn from the life.

Whether there are persons in the present state of society to whom all the parts of this character agree, is a question which every man will answer to himself, either from his knowledge or experience. The charge is indeed so complex, that it might be difficult perhaps to prove it in its full extent against any one individual.

We know well who they are whose hands refuse to labor, who are clothed with rags, and make poverty not only their complaint, but their argument. But though the idle vagrant is plainly described and condemned by these articles, there are other parts of the charge against which he might offer a plausible defence.

He might answer to the charge of excessive sleep, that he riseth as early, or at least is as soon abroad, as any from whom he can expect an alms: and that he is so far from hiding his hand in his bosom, that he stretcheth it forth from morning to night, to levy contributions from every passenger he sees. Nay, to strengthen his defence, might he not argue, that as the Preacher was a king, persons of a higher rank were far more likely to be the objects of his attention, many of whom eat the bread of idleness, and labor as little as the beggar? And as he speaks of fields and vineyards, that this shows him to have had sluggards of a superior order in his eye, who originally possessed some property, and a station above the lower tribes of the people. By this defence, he will certainly elude some articles of the charge. Enough, however, will still remain to evince his right to the character in the text. And what he throws off from himself doth not fall to the ground, but will bear hard on the idle and voluptuous in the higher ranks of life. At the same time, there are some articles in the charge, to which those of a better station would no doubt object in their turn. They might attempt to evade the charge of sluggishness, by alleging, that though indeed they apply themselves to no active business or employment, yet the fatigues of dress, of ceremony, and equipage; the anxieties of gaming, and the attendance on fashionable amusements, render the pursuit of pleasure in the present age as toilsome and laborious as any mechanical employment whatsoever. And that so far from being clothed in rags, which Solomon makes the badge of a sluggard, the fact is, that Solomon himself, in all his glory, was not arrayed like one of them.

Were this a controversy of any importance, it would be an easy matter to detect the fallacy of these reasonings, and to show, that the defences on both sides are weak and frivolous. But this would be an idle waste of time; for as neither of the parties can deny that some parts of the description apply to them, it is of little consequence to which of them the larger share of it belongs.

But sloth is not confined to the common affairs of life, nor the character of a sluggard to men in any particular station. There is sloth in religion as well as in common life; and the description in my text applies to all, without exception, who, however active and industrious in their secular employments, neglect the one thing needful, the care of their precious and immortal souls.

The laborious mechanic, the busy merchant, the painful student, and the bustling statesman, are all sluggards in a spiritual sense, unless they are active in the love and service of the God that made them; and unless the advancement of his glory, and the final enjoyment of his favor, are the ends to which all their pursuits are directed.

Here we are only to sojourn for a short time. Our great Creator hath made us for higher occupations and better joys than the present world affords us. He hath formed us for the knowledge and enjoyment of himself in an eternal and unchangeable state, and hath instructed us how we may attain this glorious object of our being. And therefore, however busy a man may be for himself, however industrious for his family, however active for the public; yet if all his views terminate in this present life, he is still a sluggard in the eye of God. For he who labors only for the meat that perisheth, doth as fatally counteract the end of his creation, as he that sleeps on the bed of sloth, or as he that fatigues himself in pursuing the vain and fugitive pleasures of this world. I will add, that even those who have chosen the better part, and who seek the kingdom of God and his righteousness in the first place, do often incur the imputation of sluggishness, by the omission or careless performance of what God hath required of them. For, alas! where is the man who doth "whatsoever his hand findeth to do" in the business of religion, "with all his might?" Where is the man who "strives," as in an agony (for so the original word imports) "to enter in at the strait gate?" or who "gives all diligence to make his calling and election sure?" We see much activity in the pursuits of the world; but a very small portion of it, indeed, in that pursuit which most requires and deserves it.

I may therefore venture to affirm, that there is not one in this assembly to whom my text is not addressed in one view or another. And, therefore, without questioning the propriety of the description, let us go on, as was proposed,

Secondly. To consider the counsel or advice which the wise man hath given us: "Go to the ant, thou sluggard; consider her ways, and be wise; which, having no guide, overseer, or ruler, provideth her meat in the summer, and gathereth her food in the harvest."

He directs us to a creature, indeed, of the most diminutive size and appearance, but whose sagacity and unremitting activity strike the eye of every beholder. The ant instructeth us, not by speech, but by actions; and therefore we are called upon "to consider her *ways;*" how she is employed, and for what end she is active: not merely that we may gratify our curiosity, or even extend our knowledge of the natural world; but that we may become wiser and better. The wisdom we learn from the ant is the wisdom of living well: the wisdom of acting suitably to our superior nature, and our glorious hopes.

There are three very important lessons which we learn from the conduct of the ant. The

1*st* is, A foresight and sagacity in making provision for the time to come. The ant gathereth more than she hath present occasion for; and in the summer and harvest lays up a store for the approaching winter. Thus she arms herself against the rigors of the inclement season; and whilst the grasshoppers, that sung and sported in the summer and harvest: nay, whilst many creatures of larger size and greater strength, perish for want of food, she lives on the fruits of her industry, and reaps the reward of her care and providence. O that this wisdom were more common among men! and that we could be persuaded, while the season of action lasts, to "lay up in store for ourselves a good foundation against the time to come, while the evil days come not, nor the years draw nigh, when we shall say we have no pleasure in them." How dreary must the winter of life be, when the previous seasons have been passed in sloth, in idleness, or in folly; when the body languishes under poverty and wretchedness; or when the mind, unfurnished with knowledge, and virtue, and faith, and devotion, sojourns in a crazy tabernacle, tottering to the dust? A

2d lesson to be learned from the conduct of the ant is activity and diligence. The ant never intermits her labors as long as the season lasts. In summer, when the weather is hottest, at sultry noon, as well as in the cool of the morning and of the evening, this busy creature is continually in motion, either seeking her food abroad, or disposing it in her cells at home. Nay, her labors end not with the day, but, as naturalists have observed, she often takes the benefit of the moon, and plies her work with a surprising alacrity. Happy were it for man, that he as faithfully employed that precious time which is given him, either to render himself useful in this world, or to prepare for eternity. Then would he not be seen encroaching on the day by sloth, nor turning it into night by intemperance and riot. The

3d lesson which we learn from the conduct of the ant is sagacity in making use of the proper season for activity. Opportunity is the flower of time; or it is the most precious part of it, which if once lost may never return. This the ant knoweth how to seize with admirable skill. She goeth forth in quest of food when it can be had with ease and certainty: She employs her labor at the time when she knows that it will be effectual. Unlike to man, whose folly prompts him to neglect the season in which his talents might be usefully employed, till he hath lost it for ever; and who spends on trifles the day of his merciful visitation, till the things which belong to his peace are for ever hid from his eyes.

All this foresight, diligence, and sagacity, the ant employs by an instinct of nature, untutored and unawed. She hath neither guide, overseer, nor judge: There is none to go before and mark out her task; none to superintend and prompt her to her labor; none to require an account of her industry, or to punish her either for her neglect or miscarriages. This circumstance the wise man mentions with a peculiar emphasis, on purpose to draw the sluggard's attention to it. For surely nothing can be suggested of greater force and efficacy to rouse him from his lethargy, and to convince him that his sloth is not only criminal, but without excuse.

The ant hath no guide; but we, my brethren, have many guides. "There is a spirit in man, and the inspiration of the Almighty giveth them understanding." Our Maker hath endued us with reasonable souls, capable of discerning betwixt good and evil. He hath favored us with a complete revelation of his will, and hath showed us "what is good, and what the Lord our God requireth of us."—"The law of the Lord is perfect, converting the soul; the testimony of the Lord is sure, making wise the simple." He hath sent his Son into the world to show us the path of life, not only by his doctrine, but by his example *too*. And he offers us his Spirit, to lead us into all truth, to open our eyes, and to turn us from darkness to light, by taking of the things of Christ, and showing them unto us. He hath assured us of his willingness to assist and to guide us. "If any man lack wisdom, let him ask it of God, who giveth to all men liberally, and upbraideth not, and it shall be given him." If men therefore are sluggards, and loiter in their work, they can neither pretend ignorance of their duty, nor the want of a guide to direct them in it.

Again, the ant "hath no overseer;" but man acts under the immediate inspection of him, "whose eyes are as a flame of fire."—"The eyes of the Lord are in every place, beholding the evil and the good."—Can any man hide himself in secret "places that I shall not see him? do not I fill heaven and earth, saith the Lord?"—"Yea, the darkness hideth not from thee, O Lord, but the night shineth as the day." Besides, God hath placed an overseer in our own breasts, which acts within us as his deputy; for the voice of conscience is the voice of God. This bosom-witness marks our steps, reminds us of our duty, condemns us when we do wrong, and never fails to render those unhappy whom it fails to keep faithful to their duty. For conscience at first speaks forcibly to every human being; and many a hard struggle doth it cost even the worst of men, before this awful monitor can be silenced. Thus we have not only a guide to point out the way to us, but an overseer to attend us in every step; and therefore, if we either loiter or turn aside, we must be without excuse: "our own hearts condemn us, and God is greater than our hearts, and knoweth all things."

Once more, the ant "hath no ruler" or judge to call her to account for her conduct; but every one of us must give an account to God. "God hath appointed a day in which he will judge the world in righteousness, by that Man whom he hath ordained, whereof he hath given assurance unto all men, in that he raised him from the dead." "We must all appear before the judgment-seat of Christ, that every one may receive the things done in the body, according to that he hath done, whether it be good or bad." And it deserves our notice, that the sluggard is particularly pointed out in Scripture as one of those who shall certainly be condemned in that decisive day. This is clearly intimated to us in the parable of the talents. The unprofitable servant, who is condemned to utter darkness, is not accused of having squandered his talent, or of having applied it to wicked purposes: on the contrary, he had preserved it entire, and returned it unimpaired to his master: his crime was, that he had not improved it. He was a wicked servant, because he had not been active for the interest of his Lord: he was, in short, the sluggard here addressed by the wise man; and his doom was just. For it is only "to those who, by a patient continuance in well-doing, seek for glory, honor, and immortality, that God will render eternal life, in the day when he shall judge the secrets of men by Jesus Christ."

Thus, then, the ant, which, without a guide, overseer, or judge, labors with such diligence, sagacity, and foresight, for the preservation of a life which must soon come to a final period; instructs, reproves, and condemns those who, having all the advantages which are denied to her, are yet remiss and negligent in the great business assigned them: on which depend not their present interests only, but the interests and the life of their immortal spirits—of their spirits, which shall survive the dissolution of their bodies, and shall last through eternal ages.

These observations may be sufficient both to illustrate the meaning, and to show the propriety of Solomon's advice. Let me now, as the improvement of the subject, press you to reduce to practice the lessons which I have been considering. And for this end, I would represent to you,

1*st*. THAT the sluggard sins against the very nature which God hath given him. For what are all the high powers and faculties with which we are endowed, but so many tokens that we were formed for active service? The nature of things has evidently in this respect the force of a law; since it is impossible to conceive, that powers and capacities were given us, which were not meant to be exerted and improved. Even in the state of innocence, man had his task assigned him, whilst the inferior animals were left to roam at large, without being accountable for their conduct. And as our natures are formed for action, so our inclination evidently prompts us to it. This is plain from the various methods by which those who will not labor endeavor to relieve themselves from the oppressive load of idleness. Their time itself is a misery: and there is nothing so impertinent to which they will not fly, that they may be free from it. The burdens of the most laborious slaves are light, when compared with the burden which the sluggard carries about with him in an enfeebled body, and a vacant, discontented mind.

2dly. The sluggard sins against the manifest design of Providence. God hath indeed made a liberal provision for the supply of all our returning wants. But he hath done this in a way that requires industry on our part, in order to render that provision effectual. The earth, by the blessing of God, is fruitful of herbs and grain for the use of man. But man must be careful to do his part in the labor of the field, that it may yield him a regular or a certain produce. The rough materials of all things necessary and convenient for the purposes of life are laid plentifully at our hands; but the skill and industry of the workmen must bring them into form, and render them fit for use. "All things are full of labor." Who then art thou, O sluggard, to counteract the designs both of Nature and of Providence?

But some may say, perhaps, We have nothing to do. Our wants are abundantly supplied from the patrimony which we have inherited; and nothing remains for us but to enjoy what we have. Do you then indeed believe, that any human being can have a right to live idle on the earth? If ye believe this, ye have yet to learn this fundamental principle of common sense, That all obligations are reciprocal. Ye sluggards, why cumber ye the ground? Shall God give you all things richly to enjoy, and is there no active service which he requires of you? Must the labor of the husbandman nourish, and the art of the manufacturer clothe you? Must all ranks of men labor for your convenience; and are there no obligations which ye are bound to discharge to them in return for so many, and so important services? For what end then do you live? Your being is an embarrassment and burden to the creation. "For if any man will not work, neither should he eat."—Once more, in the

3*d* place, The sluggard sins against the great design of the Gospel. For we have not only a Guide to instruct us, an Overseer to observe us, and a Judge to whom we are accountable; but we have also a great Redeemer, who shed his blood for the ransom of our souls, and who gave himself for us, not to purchase our release from duty, but to "purify unto himself a peculiar people, zealous of good works." Christ spoiled principalities and powers, "that we, being delivered out of the hands of our enemies, might serve him without fear, in holiness and righteousness before him all the days of our lives." Let us hear and reverence the language of the Gospel. "Ye are not your own: ye are bought with a price: therefore glorify God in your body and in your spirit, which are God's. Work out your own salvation with fear and trembling: for it is God that worketh in you, both to will and to do of his good pleasure. And beside this, giving all diligence, add to your faith virtue, and to virtue knowledge, and to knowledge temperance, and to temperance patience, and to patience godliness, and to godliness brotherly kindness, and to brotherly kindness charity. For so an entrance shall be ministered unto you abundantly, into the everlasting kingdom of our Lord and Saviour Jesus Christ."

Let us then be no longer "slothful in business, but fervent in spirit, serving the Lord." *Amen.*

SERMON XLII.

FATALITY OF PROCRASTINATION.

James iv. 13, 14, 15.—"Go to now, ye that say, to-day or to-morrow we will go into such a city, and continue there a year, and buy and sell, and get gain. Whereas ye know not what shall be on the morrow. For what is your life? it is even a vapor that appeareth for a little time, and then vanisheth away. For that ye ought to say, If the Lord will, we shall live, and do this or that."

The obvious design of this passage is to detect the folly and presumption of those who lay schemes for futurity, without a proper acknowledgment of their dependence on the providence of God. The particular scheme, which the apostle represents and condemns, is one of the most plausible that can well be imagined. A merchant resolves on a journey to some city, in which he can carry on his trade to advantage. That he may lose no time, he saith, "To-day," or, at farthest, "to-morrow, I will go into such a city, and continue there a year, and buy and sell, and get gain." There is no intimation that he meant to enrich himself by fraud or extortion. The gain he had in view may be supposed to have been the profits of a fair and honorable commerce; the honest reward of his attention and diligence.

I apprehend that none of us would be greatly startled, though we should hear some of our friends talking in the manner which is here represented. There are few of us, perhaps, who have not on some occasions held such a language, without suspecting that it was either presumptuous or wrong. In order, therefore, to discover what is faulty in it, and to enter into the spirit of this text, let us examine with attention,

1*st.* The form of expression which the apostle condemns. And,

2*dly.* The amendment which he suggests. And if it shall please God to afford us the assistance of his Spirit, I am persuaded that several remarks will occur to us in the course of this inquiry, which may be "profitable for doctrine, for reproof, for correction, and for instruction in righteousness." Let us then attend,

First. To the form of expression which the apostle condemns. "Go to now, ye that say, to-day or to-morrow we will go into such a city, and continue there a year, and buy and sell, and get gain."

In general, we may observe, that this language relates altogether to a worldly project. The principal object is gain: "not the true riches;" or "that good part" which shall never be taken from those who choose it; but the gain of this world, the gain which is acquired by buying and selling. They say nothing of the measure of gain that would satisfy them, and nothing of the use to which they meant to apply their wealth. For any thing that their expressions imply, their desires might be without bounds, and their sole aim might be to "heap up silver as the dust, and fine gold as the mire of the streets;" or, in the language of Isaiah, "to join house to house, and field to field, till they were placed alone in the midst of the earth.'

If this remark is just, we have already discovered one capital error in the expressions before us.—To seek gain by honest industry, either for the supply of our own wants, or to enable us to relieve the necessities of others, is not only lawful but honorable: But to seek wealth for its own sake, and merely for the sordid pleasure of possessing it, betrays a mean and selfish spirit, unworthy of a man, and much more unworthy of a Christian.

Supposing this then to be the end in view, there can be no doubt that it is in a high degree culpable. But as the apostle is silent on this head, we shall admit, that the persons who hold the language before us, might intend to make a proper use of their riches, and proceed to examine the means by which they propose to obtain them. "To-day," say they, "or to-morrow, we will go into such a city." These words may pass in common conversation; but when we seriously weigh the import of them, as at present we are called to do, we shall find that they are chargeable both with folly and presumption.

The great Lord of all has no part in this scheme. These little arrogant words, WE WILL, thrust him out at once, and occupy his place. And for what do the persons here described undertake? They undertake, without hesitation, to insure their lives against death, their bodies against sickness, and their effects against every casualty or hazard. They speak of the morrow as if they had the absolute property of it. They promise themselves, that to-morrow they shall not only be alive, but in health, to set out on their journey; that they shall meet with no cross accidents by the way; that the goods which they carry along with them shall be protected against thieves and robbers; and that in due time they shall arrive at the city where their plan of business is to be carried into execution. But what follows is still more extravagant. They promise upon life for a full year: "We will continue there a year:" and not upon life only, but on health of body, and soundness of mind, during all that time. No allowance is made for the change of climate, or the fatigues of business: they are always to be in a condition to buy and sell, and to manage their affairs with activity and prudence. Nay, more, they assure themselves of success. "We will buy and sell, and get gain." They undertake, not for themselves alone, but for all whom they shall employ, or with whom they shall have commerce—that they shall have diligent and faithful servants; that they shall have large profits from those to whom they sell, and cheap bargains from those of whom they buy. In a word, they speak as if every thing relating to themselves and others were so dependent on their will, that they might command the events which they desired, and dispose of all things according to their own pleasure.

Well might the apostle give this the name of boasting, as he doth at the 16th verse of this chapter; and had it suited the gravity of an inspired writer, he might have examined the different parts of the scheme, computed the risks which were plainly against them in every step, and thus turned the whole design into matter of contempt and ridicule. But instead of this, he arrests them at the very first outset. You talk of "going to such a city, of continuing there a year, of buying, of selling, and getting gain:"—"whereas ye know not what shall be on the morrow." The present moment is all that ye can call your own. This night your souls may be required of you: to-day you *are;* but to-morrow ye may be numbered with those who *have* been. He would not trifle with miserable men, who might die whilst he was speaking to them. He therefore seizeth one important truth, the force of which could not be denied, and instantly placeth it full in their view. "What is your life?" saith he, "it is even a vapor." At present it appears; but while I yet speak to you it may vanish away. Cease then, vain boasters, to talk of a year hence, until ye can say something with certainty of the succeeding day. Thus the visionary Babel falls to the ground. This plain proposition, "Life is a vapor," undermines it at once, and overwhelms the proud builders with shame.

It hath often given me pleasure to observe, that the truths which are best fitted to touch the heart, and to influence the life, are universally the most simple and obvious, and lie so near us, that we need only to stretch forth our hand to take hold of them. God knows, that we have much work to do, and little time to do it in: and therefore, that we may lose no part of it, the most useful and necessary things are scattered around us with the greatest profusion. Were it otherwise, the opportunity of acting might frequently pass away before the means of action were ready. Yet such, alas! is our folly and perverseness, that overlooking what is near, we roam abroad, and always grasp most eagerly at those things which are farthest from us. Thwarting the merciful designs of God, we despise common truths, merely because they are common; and wander in pursuit of abstruse and intricate speculations, which puzzle the understanding, and amuse the fancy, but leave the heart cold and insensible. How much better was the course which the apostle took with those who held the language of the text, in order to bring them to a sense of their folly? He doth not go about in quest of remote objects, nor seek to surprise them with new and uncommon discoveries; but he surprised them most effectually, by pointing to an object just at hand, one view of which was sufficient to check their presumption,—an object which stood always before their eyes, though overlooked through the pride, or inattention, or perverseness of their minds.

It hath already been observed, that the matter of the project, here represented by the apostle, is in itself plausible; and that his reproof is chiefly aimed at the form or manner of expressing it. And if he treated this with so much severity, what would he have said, had the end proposed been criminal in its own nature, or the means of obtaining it base and dishonorable? What would he have said to those who puzzle themselves with schemes to get rid of their money, or to throw it away upon the most ridiculous trifles? who have no higher objects than the superfluities of dress, the luxury of entertainments, the multiplicity of diversions, and all the expensive arts of dissipation and sensuality? What would he have said to those who, in the same presumptuous style, lay deliberate schemes for low vice and debauchery, for drunkenness and whoredom, and other works of the flesh? What would he have said to those who devise methods of making gain by secret fraud or open violence? to those who practise deceit in buying and selling, or who, without either buying or selling, support a useless and pernicious life by the base and infamous occupation of gaming? Compared with these, the scheme which the apostle condemns is wisdom, and honor, and virtue.

But the apostle doth not rest in censuring what was wrong. He goes on at the 15th verse to correct what was faulty, and to supply what was defective. "For that ye ought to say," adds he, "If the Lord will, we shall live, and do this or that."—This amendment, suggested by the apostle, was the

Second thing which I proposed to consider.—And,

1*st*. It furnisheth us with a rule by which all our undertakings ought to be examined. Whatever scheme we have in view, to which we cannot prefix this preface, "If the Lord will," we may be assured is essentially wrong, and ought to be abandoned without delay. There is nothing truly good or profitable to us, for which we may not address God by prayer. Let us then convert the views which we have in any undertaking into the form of a petition, and try whether we can, with decency or propriety, offer up such a petition to God. Let us consider, whether the means by which we propose to compass these views are of such a nature, that we may ask or expect the divine blessing to accompany them. Happy were it for us, that all our schemes and projects were brought to this test. We should then be seasonably delivered from that fatal enchantment which first engageth us in unlawful pursuits, and then stimulates us to persist in them against the remonstrances of our own consciences.

We should then escape from those fatal snares into which our rash unadvised plans betray us. For who would dare to say, "If the Lord will, I shall live," and rob and steal, game and defraud, oppress and overreach my neighbor? Such a connection of thought would startle the mind at the first conception of lust, before it had brought forth sin. And I am persuaded, that if men were faithfully to practise this one easy and reasonable precaution, they would at least avoid many of those presumptuous offences which lay waste the conscience, and destroy the peace of the soul.

2*dly*. This amendment, which the apostle suggests, teacheth us to consider the shortness, and particularly the uncertainty, of life. "Ye know not," saith he, "what shall be on the morrow. For what is your life? it is even a vapor which appeareth for a little time, and then vanisheth away." Thus David describes the life of man by those things which are most frail and fugitive in nature. "As for man, his days are as grass." Nay, as if the grass, which endures for a season, were too permanent an object of comparison, he immediately corrects the similitude, "As the flower of the field, so he flourisheth:" As the flower of the field, which is exposed to the foot of every passenger, to the tooth of every wild beast, to the wanton hand of every destroyer. It is not by rare and striking events only that the thread of life may be broken. There is no need that the thunder should break on you, or that the fire should devour you, or that the earth should open and swallow you up. Things far more common and familiar are sufficient for so easy a purpose, as that of cutting off your days. There is not an element so friendly, nor a circumstance so trifling, that it may not become the minister of death. Ought not this manifest uncertainty of life, then, to cool our pursuit of earthly projects? We are apt to meditate great and complicated schemes to attain wealth, or power, or honor in the world. But could we penetrate a little into futurity, we might perhaps see our grave opened far on this side of half way to the objects of our keenest pursuit. "For what is our life? it is even a vapor that appeareth for a little time, and then vanisheth away. For that we ought to say, If the Lord will, we shall live, and do this or that."

3*dly*. This amendment, suggested by the apostle, teacheth us to live in an habitual dependence on God, not only for life, but also for activity and prudence to carry our lawful designs into execution. There are two assertions in the 10th chapter of the book of Proverbs, which have a seeming opposition to each other. At the 4th verse, it is said, that "the hand of the diligent maketh rich;" where it would appear, that prosperity, in our worldly callings, is to be ascribed to our own activity and skill. On the other hand, it is asserted at the 22d verse, that "the blessing of the Lord, it maketh rich; and he addeth no sorrow with it." These two assertions are not opposed; but the one is subordinate to the other; and the meaning is, that the hand of the diligent, by the blessing of God, is the means of gaining wealth and honor. Accordingly, we find that God gave this caution to his ancient people. "Beware that thou say not in thine heart, when thy herds and thy flocks multiply, and thy silver and thy gold is multiplied, and all that thou hast is multiplied, My power, and the might of my hand, hath gotten me this wealth. But thou shalt remember the Lord thy God, for it is he that giveth thee power to get wealth." How often do we see the best laid schemes miscarry; while others, far less flattering, succeed in a wonderful manner? One man shall toil with incessant industry, rise early, and sit up late, and eat the bread of carefulness, and yet all in vain. Another, who, compared with this man, hath neither a head to contrive, nor hands to execute, shall prosper in all his plans. "I returned, and saw under the sun, that the race is not to the swift, nor the battle to the strong; neither yet bread to the wise, nor yet riches to men of understanding, nor yet favor to men of skill; but time and chance happeneth to them all." Men are too apt "to sacrifice to their own net, and to burn incense to their own drag." In great mercy, therefore, God denies riches to those who may be said to live for no other end but to obtain them; while, on the other hand, they sometimes drop, as it were, into the lap of others, who have no talents and little anxiety to acquire them. These observations are not meant to discourage industry or skill in the management of our lawful business. For it is still true, notwithstanding what hath been said, that wisdom excelleth folly, as much as light excelleth darkness; and that without proper means being used, we have no title to expect the blessing of God upon our affairs. But they ought to teach us to "commit our ways unto God" in well doing; to trust also in him that he may bring it to pass; to acknowledge him in all our ways, that he may direct our steps."—In the

4th and *last* place, This amendment, suggested by the apostle, teacheth us to resign ourselves entirely to the will of God, and to submit all our schemes to him, to prosper or to disappoint them as seemeth good to him. This is the true spirit of the text. "If the Lord will, we shall live, and do this or that." Resignation to the will of God frees the mind from a grievous bondage, the bondage of earthly pursuits and expectations. Whatever God wills, is pleasing to the resigned soul; and when a Christian hath, by prayer and supplication, made known his requests to God, then the peace of God which passeth all understanding keeps his heart and mind through Jesus Christ. Then only is life truly enjoyed, when we relish its comforts, at the same time that we are prepared to part with them. The anxieties of the worldly man torment him with the pangs of a thousand deaths. His soul dies within him as often as he conceives the apprehension of losing those good things which he would wish always to enjoy. Whereas he who hath resigned his will to the will of God, "eats his bread with joy, and drinks his wine with a merry heart." Even the thought of his dying hour throws no damp on the joys of his mind From the contemplation of God's goodness to him in life, he can pass without terror or amazement to the thought of his protection in the dark valley and shadow of death. Even in that gloomy passage he fears no evil; but commits himself to the Lord his shepherd, who will make goodness and mercy to follow him all the days of his life, and at last will bring him to dwell in his house above for ever.

These are some of the instructions which we may derive from the amendment here suggested by the apostle: "For that ye ought to say, If the Lord will, we shall live, and do this or that."

From what hath been said, let us learn, in the

1*st* place, To guard against that extravagance in laying down schemes for the time to come, which, upon cool reflection, appears so unjustifiable in the example before us. Had the persons here described, upon finding it inconvenient to set out immediately, asked themselves this question, What assurance have we of another day? this might have given them a timely check. But their imagination having taken possession of the morrow, it carried them forward without the least interruption, brought them safe to the end of their journey, fixed their residence, transacted business, and reaped the profits of the whole ensuing year. One presumptuous step leads on to another. The first object is near, and appears to be within our reach: but if we assure ourselves of possessing that before it actually become ours, then we see another object a little farther on, which appears as near to it again; afterwards a third but a little beyond that; and thus we proceed step by step, till we have passed the utmost bounds of probability, before we begin to suspect that we have gone any length at all. Let us then, in the

2*d* place, Realize this awful and important truth, That our life is but "a vapor, which appeareth for a little time, and then vanisheth away." Die we must, and we know not how soon. Our worldly enjoyments must be relinquished, our worldly plans and projects must perish. "The wind shall pass over us, and we shall be gone, and our place shall know us no more." Nature will look on the day of our decease as it ever did; the business of the world will go on as briskly as before; our habitations will make our successors as welcome as they made us; and even our names, in a few years, shall perish as if we had never been. What wise man, then, would build his house on such unstable sand? How wretched must that man be, whose inheritance lies wholly upon earth? What pangs must he feel at the parting hour? with what horror must he hear the summons of dissolution?

Let us then be persuaded to raise our affections above the things of the earth to those things which are above. Let us plan for eternity, and let us choose the unchangeable God for our portion. Knowing that we have here no continuing city, let us seek one to come; a city which hath foundations, whose builder and maker is God. Let the Lord Jesus be our leader and guardian; under his conduct let us presently set out for the heavenly Jerusalem; and in due time he will bring us safe to the city of the great and universal King, where we shall continue, not for a year only, but for ever; and where we shall get possession of substantial gain, even that glorious inheritance of the saints in light, which is incorruptible, and undefiled, and which fadeth not away. *Amen.*

SERMON XLIII.

THE SABBATH REMEMBERED AND KEPT.

Exodus xx. 8.—"Remember the Sabbath-day, to keep it holy."

The too general and growing abuse of the Christian Sabbath, must render a discourse on this subject both seasonable and necessary; and I propose therefore, in dependence on divine aid,

1*st.* To inquire how far the precept in this text is binding on us.

2*dly.* To show how this commandment ought to be kept or observed. And,

3*dly.* To enforce the observance of it by some motives and arguments.

First. I begin with inquiring how far this precept of keeping holy the Sabbath-day is binding on us.

Although your stated attendance on this day, for the worship of God, may be interpreted as a public declaration on your part, that you reckon this commandment binding on you, yet the inquiry I have proposed is by no means superfluous. We are exhorted in Scripture, not only "to sanctify the Lord God in our hearts," but likewise "to be always ready to give an answer to every man who asketh us a reason of the hope that is in us." And if we should at all times be ready to declare the grounds of our hope, we should certainly be at least equally ready to explain and to justify the reasons of our practice. Besides, although in the judgment of charity, "which thinketh no evil," your weekly attendance on this day for public worship may be supposed to flow from a religious principle ; yet in our present situation, it is easy to conceive, that something else than a sense of duty may occasion our meeting together in this manner. The laws of our country not only permit, but require, the observance of the Christian Sabbath : so that human authority, the manner of our education, a regard to decency, or even motives inferior to any of these, may bring people to church who have never seen themselves to be bound by any divine law to keep holy the Sabbath-day. And I am sorry to add, that there is too great cause to suspect this to be the case with many who frequent our religious assemblies, from their defective and partial observance of this holy day. I therefore judge it to be of the highest importance, to set the authority of this precept in a clear and striking light. For until we view the Sabbath as a divine institution, we shall never either pay to it that regard which it deserves, nor reap any spiritual advantage from the most exact outward observance of it. I suppose it will not be denied, in the

1*st* place, That some part of our time should be employed in the immediate worship of God. Reason must necessarily teach us, that such homage is due to that Almighty Being on whom we depend for life, and breath, and all things. In order to secure the regular performance of this worship, the same principle of reason will naturally suggest the propriety of allotting certain stated seasons for that purpose. If any shall dispute the necessity of this, they will at least allow us to affirm the expediency of it : for it is a common and true observation, that what is left to be done at any time is in great danger of being done at no time. I may likewise take it for granted, in the

2*d* place, That the right of determining what proportion of time, or what stated seasons should be employed in divine worship, will be readily admitted to belong to God. This is so evident, that it scarcely needs an illustration. If we can live one moment independent of God, we may call that moment our own, and claim the disposal of it : But if we cannot draw one breath without his aid ; if his constant visitation is necessary to preserve us ; the consequence is unavoidable, that the whole of our time is due to God, and that his right is absolute to reserve any part of it which he pleaseth for his own worship. And this leads me to observe, in the

3*d* place, That God hath actually interposed his authority in this matter : and by a clear and positive law, part of which I have now read to you, hath reserved for himself one day in seven ; that he hath consecrated or set apart this portion of our time, by his precept, example and blessing, for a holy rest or cessation from secular employments, and for such acts of religious worship and adoration as creatures owe to their great Creator.

It is confessed by all who admit the inspiration of the Old Testament, that this law was strictly binding upon the Jews, to whom it was delivered by the ministry of Moses. But some have made it a question, whether it continues to be binding under the Christian dispensation. We maintain that it is still in force, inasmuch as it contains a declaration of the will of God, that one day in seven, or the seventh part of our time, should be separated from common use, and dedicated to religious purposes. With regard to the particular day to be observed, all days being alike in themselves, the appointment of it must be of a positive nature, and may therefore be varied at the pleasure of the Lawgiver. Accordingly we find, that in this circumstance the law hath received an alteration. The seventh, or last day of the week, is now become common ; and in commemoration of our Saviour's resurrection from the dead, the holy rest is transferred to the first day of the week ; which hath ever since been called, by way of eminence, *The* LORD's *day*. Whether this remarkable change is sufficiently supported by divine authority, admits of farther inquiry. What I have hitherto said, is only intended to prove our obligation to keep one day in seven holy to the Lord ; and for this, I think I have given you very satisfying evidence. It is a natural principle, that God ought to be worshipped ; and as it is highly necessary to secure the performance of such an important duty, reason farther teacheth us, that some stated times ought to be set apart for that end. The right of determining these doth certainly belong to God himself; and he hath actually been pleased to give a plain intimation of his will in this matter, claiming, by a distinct and peremptory statute, one whole day in seven, for the peculiar exercises of religious worship. Thus far, then, the commandment is strictly moral; and therefore still binding upon us, inasmuch as it only enjoins a natural duty, and prescribes the most effectual means for securing the performance of it.

Having established this point, the way lies more open to the other subject of inquiry; and I expect to find less difficulty in satisfying you about the alteration of the day. Some Christians, indeed have maintained, that both days ought to be kept; but I reckon there will be no need to guard you against a mistake of this kind. You will easily convince yourselves that there is but one Sabbath in the week.

As to our practice in observing the first, instead of the last day in the week, which was the Jewish Sabbath, the reasons of it may be reduced under these following heads.

1*st.* We learn from Scripture, that this was the day on which the apostles and primitive Christians held their solemn assemblies for the public exercises of religious worship. Thus we read, (Acts xx. 7.) that "upon the first day of the week, when the disciples came together to break bread," *i. e.* to celebrate the sacrament of our Lord's Supper, "Paul preached unto them, and continued his speech until midnight;" where it is observable, that their meeting together on that precise day is not spoken of as a thing extraordinary, or merely occasional, but as a stated and ordinary practice. It was their custom so to do; and Paul being on the spot, met with them, and presided in their assembly. It farther appears that this was the day on which they laid up their public charity, and contributed for the relief of their needy brethren; and this by an express apostolical injunction. For thus Paul writes to the Corinthians, (1 Cor. xvi. 1, 2.) "Now concerning the collection for the saints, as I have given order to the churches of Galatia, even so do ye. Upon the first day of the week, let every one of you lay by him in store, as God hath prospered him, that there be no gathering when I come." In this passage, there is not only a practice of the church described, but likewise the appointment of an inspired apostle ratifying and confirming it. For if the words extend to the religious observance of that particular day, then we have a plain scriptural command for our warrant: or if they refer only to the collecting alms on that day, which is the lowest sense that they will bear, they necessarily imply, that this was a weekly holy day then in use, on which Christians ceased from their worldly business, and met together for the social worship of God; that the apostle justified and approved of this practice, and thereby testified his opinion that it was perfectly agreeable to the will of Christ.

Besides, we find that this day was, in the earliest times, distinguished by the title of *The* LORD'S *day;* for this appears from Rev. i. 10, where John informs the churches, that he "was in the Spirit on the Lord's day;" that well known day, sacred to the memory of the Lord Redeemer; the day on which he triumphed over death, and which he dignified, by his resurrection, above all other days. From these circumstances taken together, it appears, that this change took place in the apostolic age; and that the first day of the week was then esteemed holy to the Lord, and separated from the rest for religious purposes; so that though we cannot find any express command, appointing the alteration in so many words; yet we have the most convincing evidence, that it was either part of the instruction which Christ gave to his disciples before his ascension, when he was seen of them forty days, as the sacred history informs us, and spake of the things pertaining to the kingdom of God; or else that it was afterwards enacted by the apostles, in virtue of their authority derived from Christ, and under the infallible direction of his blessed Spirit.

2*dly.* There appear to be many great and weighty reasons for such a change. Under the Old Testament, the seventh day was kept holy in memory of the creation, because on that day God rested from all his works; and is it not equally reasonable and fit, that the first day should be sanctified under the gospel dispensation, seeing on that day the great God and our Saviour rested from all the labors of his suffering state, and rose from the dead, in testimony that man's redemption was fully accomplished? Surely the renovation of the world, after sin had in a manner broken it in pieces, is a work as glorious and divine as the first creation of it, and as worthy to be gratefully remembered by us.

3dly. It is of some moment to observe, that this day has been uniformly kept as the Christian Sabbath from the apostolic age down to the present time. This fact is proved by the concurring testimony of historians in all the different periods of the church. At the same time, they tell us what hot disputes arose about other matters, particularly about the institution and observance of holy days. We find the Eastern and Western churches so divided with regard to the time of keeping Easter, as to proceed to excommunicate each other: but we hear of no controversy about observing the first day of the week; for in this they were all agreed. Now, what could have produced such perfect uniformity, especially in those ages, when there was no Christian magistrate to interpose his authority, but a clear conviction, and a well-grounded belief, that this was really a divine institution delivered by Christ, or his apostles, to the church? Once more, in the

4th place, God hath remarkably hallowed this day, by many acts of grace done to his people, when employed in the religious observance of it. On this day, when "the disciples were all with one accord in one place," the Spirit of God descended upon them, insomuch that they were filled with the Holy Ghost, to their own unspeakable comfort, and the admiration of all who saw and heard them. On the same day, "the arm of the Lord was" gloriously "revealed," in the conversion of three thousand souls, who were brought from a state of enmity to Christ into the bosom of the church, by the plain and powerful preaching of the apostle Peter. On this day John was inspired with the spirit of prophecy, and had visible representations of the various revolutions in the church of Christ, down to the final consummation of all things. And in latter times God hath signally blessed his people when met together on this holy day; making all his goodness to pass before them, and giving them such views of his power and glory in the sanctuary, that they have been obliged to say with Jacob at Bethel, "This is no other than the house of God, and this is the gate of heaven;" a foretaste of the everlasting Sabbath, an earnest of that rest which remains for the people of God. And is it to be supposed, that the holy and righteous Governor of the world would countenance his creatures in a superstition of their own contrivance, to the open and weekly neglect of a plain and positive law? No, surely: These tokens of the Divine presence and favor dispensed on this day, are sure indications that this is the day which God himself hath made, and which he hath separated, by his authority, for the Christian Sabbath.

Thus have I finished the first thing proposed in this discourse; which was to inquire how far the precept in the text is binding on us; and I hope I have said enough to satisfy every unprejudiced mind, that it is still in force, as to the great scope and design of it; and that the change of the day, which is only circumstantial, bears such evident marks of divine authority, as sufficiently justify the uniform opinion, and uninterrupted practice, of all the Christian churches. I proceed now to the

Second thing proposed, Which was to show how this commandment ought to be kept or observed, "Remember the Sabbath-day, to keep it holy."

This, as it is the first, so it is likewise the principal and most important branch of the precept. Nay, the full scope and design of the law is probably expressed in these few significant words. For I cannot help thinking that the bodily rest or cessation from labor, which is afterwards enjoined, derives its chief value from its subserviency to those spiritual exercises by which the Sabbath is most eminently sanctified; and that it ought principally to be considered as a description of the means to aid us in the duties of religious worship. I think it proper to mention this distinction, because some have contended, that resting from labor is all that is meant by keeping holy the Sabbath: but surely it cannot be thought that God, who is a pure and holy Spirit, would deliver a law with such solemnity, for so mean and low a purpose as this. He who so frequently declares, that the rites and ceremonies of his own appointment were no farther acceptable to him than as they represented spiritual blessings, and were improved for promoting internal purity, cannot be supposed to take pleasure in mere inactivity, or to have appointed a weekly day of rest, solely for the indulgence of the body. Besides, this expression of *sanctifying* or *keeping holy*, not only imports a separation from common use, but likewise a consecration to a sacred or religious use. In this sense it is always employed in the Old Testament, either when it is applied to the persons of the priests, or to the vessels of the sanctuary; and no reason can be given why it should be taken in a lower sense here, or why it should import any thing less than that the day is set apart for the service of God, and ought to be employed in the duties of religious worship—I shall, in the

1*st* place, Give you a general account of these duties. And then we shall see more clearly, in the

2*d* place, What things ought to be avoided by us, as inconsistent with the scope and design of this commandment.

In general, then, we are bound to sanctify this day, by assembling together for the public worship of God, that as many as can conveniently meet in one place may join in paying homage to their common Lord; and thus contribute their endeavors to make him glorious in the eyes of the world around him. For this we ought to prepare ourselves, by the more private exercises of family worship. And because our hearts are naturally indisposed for such divine and heavenly employments, it is both reasonable and necessary, that each person apart should spend a competent time in reading and meditating on the word of God, and implore his presence and his blessing, by humble prayer, in the secret retirements of the closet. It will also be of considerable use, to render these several kinds of religious worship more beneficial to us, that, when occasion offers, we should discourse together on divine subjects, in order to increase our knowledge of spiritual things, and to fix upon our minds a more lively sense of God and of our duty.

1*st*. I say, we are bound to sanctify this day by a punctual and devout attendance upon the public ordinances of religion, assembling together in the name of the Lord, to offer up the sacrifices of prayer and praise; to hear his word explained and applied; and especially to partake, as often as we have opportunity, of the holy sacrament of the Lord's Supper, the memorial of our Saviour's death, and the pledge of his second coming. In such duties as these, did the people of God in former times chiefly employ themselves on the Holy Sabbath. Under the old dispensation, sacrifices were offered, and incense burnt in the temple, and the law was publicly read and explained, both at Jerusalem and other cities of Judea, where synagogues were built for that very end. After the resurrection of Christ, the apostles and primitive Christians met together statedly on the first day of the week, that they might join in celebrating that great and propitious event, and in performing other acts of social religion. And ought not we to sanctify the Lord's day in the same manner? We are blessed with the ordinances of the gospel regularly, and I hope, purely dispensed. We have places set apart for public worship, and are countenanced in the exercise of it by lawful authority, and therefore it must discover a strange perverseness of temper, and an unpardonable contempt both of God and man, to withdraw from the place of public worship, and, on any pretence whatsoever, to refuse to bear a part in such a becoming and rational service. But,

2*dly*. That the public worship may have a greater efficacy, and that our minds may be better disposed to enter into it, it is the duty of each family apart to spend some time, both before and after the public service, in reading the Holy Scriptures, and in joining together in prayer and thanksgiving to God. Were this practised in a serious and devout manner, we might expect to see better days, and more fruitful and joyful Sabbaths than any we have yet seen. A congregation composed of a number of holy families, just come from conversing with God at home, to worship him together in the house of prayer, would be indeed a lovely sight, and could not fail to be honored with the special marks of divine favor. We have some illustrious examples of family religion recorded in the Old Testament; but what chiefly ought to engage the attention of Christians is, that our blessed Lord himself was pleased to become a pattern to us in this matter. In the intervals of his public work, we find him frequently retiring with his little family, praying with them, and teaching them to pray, and instructing them in things pertaining to the kingdom of God; in this, as in all other things, leaving us an example that we should follow his steps. Family-religion, therefore, a duty incumbent on us at all times, must be in a very peculiar manner seasonable and necessary on the holy Sabbath. It deserves our notice, too, that this command is particularly addressed to heads of families; and as they are expressly enjoined to suffer nothing to be done by any under their inspection, which is inconsistent with the due observance of the Sabbath, this injunction plainly implies, that, in their station and character, they ought to employ their natural authority, as well as every other means, to promote the great ends of this holy commandment. I add, in the

3d place, That as our hearts are naturally indisposed for spiritual exercises, we ought each of us, by ourselves, to make conscience of the secret duties of the closet. There we ought to meditate on the marvellous works of God; on his glorious perfections, as they are displayed to us, in creation, providence and redemption; above all, on that great "mystery of godliness, God manifest in the flesh, justified in the Spirit, seen of angels, preached unto the Gentiles, believed on in the world, received up into glory." In this sacred retirement, we ought to revolve in our minds the various steps of our Lord's humiliation, from his birth at Bethlehem to his burial on Mount Calvary. Thence we should proceed to view the triumphs of his cross, where he bruised the old serpent's head, finished transgression, made reconciliation for iniquity, and brought in everlasting righteousness." To confirm our faith, and increase our joy, our meditations ought to follow this Mighty Conqueror, and to contemplate him breaking the bands of death, and rising from the grave on this first day of the week, ascending up to heaven in the sight of his disciples, and sitting on the right hand of God the Father; from whence he shall come, in power and great glory, to judge the world in righteousness, according to this gospel which is now preached in his name. When, by such meditations as these, our hearts are warmed and enlivened, we should then, with all humility and reverence, approach the throne of grace; imploring those mercies which we need for ourselves, and begging a divine blessing to accompany the outward means of grace, that with our fellow-worshippers, we may be made to taste of the fatness of his house, and may find his ordinances to be indeed the wisdom and the power of God, "the savor of life unto life" to our souls.—The

4th and *last* particular which I mention, is mutual conference upon divine things. This is of great use to make the truths of religion plain and familiar to us. It stirs up our affections, and makes our knowledge more lively and more operative, both on our hearts and lives. It confirms and strengthens our faith, and brings much joy and comfort to our souls, by showing us, that as face answereth to face in water, so doth the heart of one true Christian to that of another. In this exercise holy men of old have employed themselves, and met with singular tokens of divine favor and acceptance. At no time surely can such conference be more seasonable than on the Christian Sabbath: and it is owing probably to the neglect of this, that the preaching of the word, and other parts of public religious service, are so generally fruitless and unsuccessful. I have thus given you a general account of the manner in which the Sabbath ought to be sanctified. In the *next* discourse, I shall consider the prohibitory part of the commandment, and endeavor to enforce the observance of it by some motives and arguments. *Amen.*

SERMON XLIV.

THE SABBATH REMEMBERED AND KEPT.

Exodus xx. 8.—"Remember the Sabbath-day, to keep it holy."

I have already endeavored to prove that we are strictly bound by this divine precept to keep one day in seven holy to the Lord; and that the change of the Sabbath, from the seventh to the first day of the week on which our Lord rose from the dead, bears such evident signatures of divine authority, as are sufficient to justify the uniform opinion, and uninterrupted practice of all the Christian churches in this matter. I have also endeavored to explain the commandment itself, and to give you an account of the manner in which the Sabbath ought to be sanctified. I now proceed to consider the prohibitory part of the commandment, and to enforce the observance of it by some motives and arguments.

The prohibition chiefly respects bodily labor. "The Sabbath-day is the Sabbath of the Lord thy God," saith the Supreme Lawgiver; "in it thou shalt not do any work." It is expressed, you see, in very strong and absolute terms, and was for a long time understood by the Jews in a very rigid sense, insomuch that they thought it even unlawful to defend their lives when they were attacked by their enemies on that day. So universally did this opinion prevail among them in the beginning of the wars of the Maccabees, that, in some instances, it proved fatal to many of them. But this was afterward, by the universal consent of the learned in their law, declared to be a mistake: and indeed, from the design of the precept, from other passages of Scripture, and especially from our Saviour's instruction and example, it appears, that some kinds of work are perfectly consistent with the rest which is here enjoined. Of this nature are works of necessity, *i. e.* works which cannot be done the day before, nor delayed till the day following. Thus, for instance, should a fire break out on the Sabbath, we may and ought to use every mean to extinguish it. Should our enemies attack us, it is lawful to resist them: if we are at a distance from church, we may travel as far as is necessary, in order to hear the word of God, and to join with others in public worship. For, as our Saviour tells us, "the Sabbath was made for man, and not man for the Sabbath;" and the means are never to be set above the end; nor is resting on the Sabbath to be interpreted so as to exclude the religious employment of it.

In like manner, works of charity and compassion are lawful on this day. Our Lord wrought many miracles of mercy on the Sabbath, and vindicated his conduct against those who found fault with him, by such maxims as plainly show, that offices of charity are not only allowable but praiseworthy, and are perfectly consistent with the rest which is here enjoined.

But then it is absolutely unlawful to pursue our worldly business on this day; because this thwarts the great end and design of the commandment, which ordains the seventh part of our time to be statedly employed in the immediate service of God, that we may thereby become better acquainted with him, and may become more fit for an eternal communion with him in heaven. The very intention of the law is to set apart a certain proportion of our time for the care of our souls; which, amidst the hurry of our secular affairs, we are too apt to neglect.

To apply ourselves therefore to our ordinary business on the Sabbath, to talk of it, or even to spend our thoughts on it, is doing what we can to frustrate the gracious designs of the Lawgiver, and must necessarily be of infinite hurt and prejudice to our souls. And if our worldly employments, which are not only lawful, but even necessary on other days of the week, are criminal on this day, you will easily perceive, that sports and recreations must certainly be considered as included in the prohibition: for these are still more opposite to the proper business of the Sabbath, and have not the remotest pretence either to necessity or usefulness. To have recourse to amusements on this day, is wantonly to throw away our time without any advantage; and carries in it a plain declaration, that we have no relish for spiritual things; and that, rather than think of God, and the concerns of our souls, we will banish reflection altogether, and study to forget both God and ourselves. It was the judgment of one of the fathers, that it was more lawful to plough than to dance on the Lord's day; and the same thing may be said of all other diversions, which entirely withdraw us from the business of religion, and will not suffer our minds to be serious and composed. If it is criminal to work or to labor on this day, it must evidently be still more so to waste the time in carnal mirth, or in indolence and sloth, or in vain and trifling amusements. In a word, whatever is foreign to religion, or has not a direct tendency to glorify God, and advance our own spiritual interest, ought carefully to be avoided on this holy day, as we regard the approbation of God, and our own present and eternal happiness.

Having thus laid your duty in this matter before you, it only remains, in the

Third and *last* place, That I enforce the practice of it by some motives and arguments. And,

1*st*. Allow me to observe, that though this commandment were to be considered as a mere positive institution, or only as a test of our obedience and subjection to God; yet the portion of time which is thereby separated from common use, is so very moderate, that we have not the remotest cause to complain of it. I am even persuaded, that were God to refer the matter to ourselves, and, after having represented that he had brought us into being, and would allow us a certain term of life in his world, were to ask us what portion of our time we would freely resign to his disposal, as an acknowledgment of his righteous title to the whole, we should be ashamed to offer so little as he hath been pleased to demand. I am apt to think, that, instead of every seventh day, we should have thought every other day, or the full half of our time, the least that could be offered in return for such undeserved goodness. Put the case, that any of you were lying on a death-bed, and God should say to you, How much of your time will you consecrate to my service in future, if I shall now be pleased to restore you to health again? I suppose most of you would reply, without any hesitation, Lord, I make no conditions: I put myself wholly into thy hands: demand of me whatsoever thou wilt. Hear how Hezekiah expresseth himself, after his miraculous recovery from a deadly disease, (Is. xxxviii. 19, 20.) "The living, the living, he shall praise thee as I do this day. The father to the children shall make known thy truth. The Lord was ready to save me; therefore we will sing my songs to the stringed instruments all the days of our life in the house of the Lord." He doth not limit his resolutions of thanksgiving and praise to the Sabbath-day: he thought all the days of his life a tribute of consecrated time small enough in return for the goodness which had rescued him from the grave. And is it possible, that any of us should judge one day in seven too much, even though the duties required on it were in their own nature disagreeable, and had nothing to recommend them but the mere authority of the Lawgiver? Nay, my brethren, I shall put the case a little stronger. Suppose yourselves in the immediate prospect of death, either by sickness or some external cause, and that God should say to you in these circumstances, I will save you from this danger, on condition that every seventh day you will quietly submit to the torments of some acute distemper, as long as I shall continue you in the world. Do you imagine that you would reject these terms? God knows, and yourselves know, that you would not reject them; the offer would appear too good to be refused. If God then requires nothing more severe than this, your own reason must tell you that there is no cause to complain. But what are the duties which God requires of us? Are they disagreeable in their own nature? Have they no value or excellence in themselves? On the contrary, they are infinitely fit and reasonable, and every way calculated to give the truest satisfaction, the most sublime pleasure, to the soul of man. This I shall state as a

2*d* Argument for enforcing obedience to the commandment in the text. What can be more rational or delightful to a well-informed mind, than to contemplate the wonderful works of God in creation, providence and grace? What can be more becoming, than to join with others in adoring the perfections of the Father of our spirits, and in ascribing that glory which is due to his name? Can any thing be more pleasant, than to retire from the hurry of a vain world, that without reserve we may pour out our hearts, and lay open the secret desires of our souls, in the presence of that great Being, whose nature disposeth him to pity us, and whose power enables him to bestow upon us, in the fullest and most effectual manner, every blessing that can promote our most important interests? Can any entertainment be more rational, more truly divine, than to read the lively oracles of God, and to converse with our fellow-Christians, upon the most interesting of all subjects, the salvation of our souls, and the means of securing an "inheritance incorruptible and undefiled, and that fadeth not away?" One should think that a bare counsel, nay, even a permission to spend one day in seven in such pleasant and profitable exercises, would be regarded as a singular privilege that deserved our warmest returns of gratitude and praise. The force of this argument is not weakened, because those who are alienated from the life of God have no relish for the pleasures which arise from the exercises of devotion. It is not the reason of the thing which leads the depraved mind to account "the Sabbath a weariness," or to say, "When will the Sabbath be over?" After six days spent in provision for the body, is one day too long to care for the soul? Nay, after deducting the time which is necessarily employed in sleeping, and eating, and drinking, can we not find as much in God, in Christ, and in heaven, as may afford us entertainment for the scanty remainder of twenty-four hours? Alas, my brethren, how shall we employ an everlasting Sabbath, if one Sabbath in the week is so tedious and burdensome? Can those be candidates for immortal glory, who think one day too long for the work of heaven, unless they relieve themselves, by consuming the greater part of it in idle conversation or trifling amusements?—My

3*d* Argument to enforce this commandment shall be taken from the many advantages which flow from the religious observance of the Sabbath. Hereby we shall obtain the blessing of God, according to that large and comprehensive promise, (Isaiah lviii. 13, 14.) "If thou turn away thy foot from the Sabbath from doing thy pleasure on my holy day, and call the Sabbath a delight, the holy of the Lord honorable, and shalt honor him, not doing thine own ways, nor finding thine own pleasure, nor speaking thine own words; then shalt thou delight thyself in the Lord, and I will cause thee to ride upon the high places of the earth, and feed thee with the heritage of Jacob thy father; for the mouth of the Lord hath spoken it." If we honor God on this separate day, which he claims as his special property, then may we expect to be honored by him on the other days of the week, which he hath given us for our own use. The truth of this hath been frequently experienced by the people of God; and among these, too, by some of the most eminent characters, not only for piety, but also for learning and taste, and knowledge of the world. I shall mention one who was highly respected in his own time, and whose character and writings are to this day universally esteemed. The learned Judge Hales, speaking of his experience on this subject, hath these words: "I have found," saith he, "by a strict and diligent observation, that a due observing the duty of this day, hath ever had joined to it a blessing upon the rest of my time; and the week that hath been so begun, hath been blessed and prosperous to me. And, on the other side, when I have been negligent of the duties of this day, the rest of the week hath been unsuccessful and unhappy to my secular employments; so that I could easily make an estimate of my successes in my own secular employments the week following by the manner of my passing this day. And this," adds he, "I do not write lightly or inconsiderately, but upon a long and sound observation and experience." Nay, the right observance of this duty will procure national as well as personal blessings: for so God promised to his ancient church, (Jer. xvii. 24, 25.) "If ye diligently hearken unto me, to bring in no burden through the gates of this city on the Sabbath day, but hallow the Sabbath day, to do no work therein; then shall there enter into the gates of this city kings and princes sitting upon the throne of David, riding in chariots, and on horses, they and their princes, the men of Judah, and the inhabitants of Jerusalem, and this city shall remain for ever." I do not mean by these arguments to bribe you into a mercenary or political observance of the Christian Sabbath. Should you spend the whole day in reading, praying, praising, or any other forms of religious worship, merely, or even principally from a regard to your own private interest, or to the public prosperity of the nation to which you belong, I must be so faithful as to tell you, that it would not be accepted. Nay, God would number these hypocritical services amongst your most provoking sins. For it is the heart which God requires; and if that be withheld, he will accept of no outward homage. But I mention these things to show you, that Sabbath-breakers must be utterly inexcusable, when they transgress a law, which is not only most reasonable in itself, but which hath also peculiar promises annexed to it, of temporal prosperity and happiness. And with the same view I am now going to add a

4th Consideration for enforcing obedience to this commandment, namely, That the transgression of it is attended with many sad and fatal consequences. God hath frequently punished this sin, by inflicting very awful judgments both upon societies and particular persons. There was an express statute in the Jewish law, appointing the Sabbath-breaker to be put to death, (Exodus xxxi. 12, 16.); and this punishment was actually inflicted upon one who was found gathering sticks on that holy day: "all the congregation brought him without the camp, and stoned him with stones, and he died, as the Lord commanded Moses." Num. xv. 32, 37. How alarming is that threatening, (Jerem. xvii. 27.) "If ye will not hearken unto me to hallow the Sabbath-day, and not to bear a burden, even entering in at the gates of Jerusalem on the Sabbath-day; then will I kindle a fire in the gates thereof, and it shall devour the palaces of Jerusalem, and it shall not be quenched." Accordingly, Nehemiah imputes all the calamities which befell the Jewish nation to this, as one of the principal causes of God's anger against that people. "Then, (saith he) I contended with the nobles of Judah, and said unto them, What evil thing is this that ye do, and profane the Sabbath-day? Did not your fathers thus, and did not our God bring all this evil upon us, and upon this city; yet ye bring more wrath upon Israel by profaning the Sabbath." And I am verily persuaded, that many of the national calamities with which we have been visited, may justly be attributed to the same cause. Nor is it greatly to be wondered at, when we consider, that this sin is not only an act of rebellion against the authority of God, but also a bold and sacrilegious invasion of his property, in applying to common use that proportion of time which he hath reserved for himself, and set apart for the immediate exercises of his worship.

But besides this, the abuse or neglect of the Sabbath must be attended with pernicious consequences on several other accounts. To this gracious institution it is in a great measure owing that any sense of God, and of divine things, is preserved in the world. Were this day rendered common, the bulk of mankind would soon sink into Atheism or utter profaneness. What would become of the lower ranks in society, whose servitude and bodily necessities oblige them to work hard for daily bread, were it not for this separated day, on which they are invited and commanded to care for their souls? I am even afraid, that the tyranny and covetousness of many masters would incline them to deny their servants any leisure whatsoever, either for the rest of their bodies, or the improvement of their minds, had not God, in mercy, made a law for one day of rest and liberty in the week. In proportion as this law is despised and neglected, in the same proportion will religion fall into decay, the impressions of God become feeble and languid; while ignorance, brutality, oppression, and all the evils which unrestrained corruption can produce, will prevail, and render this earth the very suburbs of hell.

These are all the arguments which I

shall at present use with you, for enforcing the observance of the Christian Sabbath. The proportion of time is so moderate, that even upon the supposition that the duties required were painful, there could be no just cause of complaint. Yet so far is this supposition from being true, that, on the contrary, the work assigned us on this holy day is most pleasant and delightful; insomuch that were our minds in a right temper, we would count it our happiness to spend our whole time, nay, a whole eternity, in such heavenly employment. Besides, the religious observance of this holy day is accompanied with many signal advantages, and is a mean of deriving the blessing of God, both upon individuals and communities; whereas the profanation or neglect of it is in every respect pernicious, both to particular persons and to societies.

And if these things are so, how many who now hear me ought to blush, and be ashamed to lift up their faces either before God or man? But as reformation is the great object which I have in view, I shall spare the reproof which I once intended to give; and instead of upbraiding you for the time past, I shall rather entreat you by the meekness and gentleness of Christ, to behave more dutifully for the time to come. And my exhortation shall be chiefly directed to parents and masters of families, to whom the commandment seems to be principally addressed. It is true, the expression "within thy gates," may relate to the gates of a city as well as of a particular house; and then it would intimate to us this truth, that it is the duty of magistrates to secure the observance of this day, by the exercise of that power and authority with which their public station invests them. But as there would be less occasion for the interposition of civil authority, if parents and heads of families would mind their proper work, to these I shall more directly address what I have to say. And I must tell you in the name of God, that you are strictly accountable, not only for your own conduct, but likewise for the conduct of all within your houses on this holy day. Hear how the commandment runs: "Remember the Sabbath-day to keep it holy; six days shalt thou labor and do all thy work; but the seventh day is the Sabbath of the Lord thy God; in it thou shalt not do any work, thou, nor thy son, nor thy daughter, thy man-servant, nor thy maid-servant, nor thy cattle, nor the stranger that is within thy gates." You see that you are charged with the immediate inspection, not only of your children and servants, but likewise of the stranger who sojourns with you, over whom you have no jurisdiction or authority through the rest of the week.

I should be glad to know what those who keep houses of public entertainment think of this doctrine. A respectful complaisance and readiness to serve are the general duties of your station. But there is one day of the week on which God permits, nay, commands you, to take rest to yourselves, and to keep your doors shut against the idle and profane, of what rank soever, and to restrain such as necessity brings to your houses from every thing that is profane, either in speech or behavior. If any shall question your authority, this precept is your charter, vesting you with the same power over the stranger that is within your gates, as over your own children and servants; and even charging you to exercise that power, as you would not incur the wrath of Almighty God. Did you know that you possessed so high a privilege? I hope, for your own sakes, that you did not; and now that I have told you the secret, I pray that God may give you wisdom and courage to improve it.

To conclude: Let all of us be persuaded to pay a proper regard to this divine precept. If we have any concern for the glory of God, for the honor of our Redeemer, for the welfare of our country, or for our own comfort and happiness, either in this world or the world to come, let us make conscience of the important duties of the Lord's day; that after having finished our course on earth, we may be fixed as pillars in the temple above, and may spend an eternal Sabbath in the presence of God and of the Lamb. *Amen.*

SERMON XLV.

DAVID'S DOMESTIC PIETY.

2 Samuel vi. 20.—"Then David returned to bless his household."

From the example of this great and good man, I propose to recommend to you the important, but much-neglected duty of family-worship. And I have chosen the example of a king for two reasons.

1*st*. Because the actions of one in that elevated station are commonly more regarded than those of a meaner person. "The poor man's wisdom is despised, and his words are not heard;" but if one arrayed in royal apparel make an oration from a throne, the people shall give a shout, saying, "It is the voice of a god, and not of a man." This partial regard is indeed a sore evil under the sun; but in the present case, it is possible to bring good out of it, by making that pomp or splendor, which so often covers the deformity of vice, a means of throwing a lustre upon religion, and of rendering a thing, so truly excellent in itself, more respectable in our eyes.

2*dly*. It is but too obvious, that the neglect of family-worship prevails chiefly among those who either are, or imagine themselves to be, of a better rank than others; nay, some who were punctual in the performance of this duty while their station and circumstances were low, have been observed to lay it aside, when, by the bounty of Providence, their state became more prosperous. This presents us with a very melancholy prospect, and threatens nothing less than the utter extinction of family-religion. For if once it becomes a maxim, that this duty is below the rank of a gentleman, then every one who affects to be thought of that rank will forbear it. In this case, it is impossible to see where the evil may stop; as there are few people in the world who do not imagine that they either are, or deserve to be, of equal consideration with their neighbors. I have therefore thought it necessary to pitch upon nothing lower than a royal example, that the vanity of no man may take it amiss when I call upon him to follow it.

We have an account, in the preceding verses, of David's bringing up the ark of God from the house of Obededom into his own city. This was done with shouting, and with the sound of the trumpet; the king himself, girded with a linen ephod, attending the solemnity, with the highest expressions of thankfulness and joy. When the ark was set in its place, in the midst of the tabernacle that was prepared for it, then David, as we read in the 17th verse, offered burnt-offerings and peace-offerings before the Lord, and afterwards dismissed the assembly with presents, which he dealt among all the people, having first blessed them in the name of the Lord of Hosts. This he did as the Father of his people. But he did not stop here. The duties of his public office and character did not make him forget what was incumbent upon him in his private capacity; for, as my text informs us, "Then David returned to bless his household;" *i. e.*, to pray with them and for them, and probably to offer up his family-thanksgivings for the great national mercy which he had been celebrating in the public assembly. From this plain and instructive passage of Scripture history I shall take occasion, in the

First place, To prove, that it is the indispensable duty of all to whom God hath given families, to worship God publicly in their own houses; or, that every man is bound, according to the example of David, "to bless his household." In the

Second place, I shall show you the reasonableness of this duty. And then, in the

Third place, I shall represent to you the advantages which accompany the practice of it, and the pernicious consequences which must follow from the neglect of it.

I begin with proving, that it is the indispensable duty of all to whom God hath given families, to worship God publicly in their own houses. This is a truth which even the light of Nature doth very plainly teach us. A family is a society connected together by such strict ties, that every argument for the propriety of private prayer is equally conclusive for that of family devotion. Of this even the heathens were sensible; for besides their tutelar deities, who were supposed to reside over cities and nations, and who had public honors paid to them in that character, we read of household-gods, whom every private family worshipped at home as their immediate guardians and benefactors.

But the light of Scripture affords us a more clear and satisfying discovery of our obligations to this duty, as well as of the proper manner of performing it. It reveals to us that great Mediator, by whom we have access to the throne of grace, and through whom all our religious services are accepted by God. It not only represents prayer as a privilege which we are permitted to use, but expressly requires it as a duty which we are bound to perform. Thus we are commanded, "In every thing, by prayer and supplication, with thanksgiving, to make our requests known unto God; to pray always, with all prayer and supplication in the Spirit, and to continue in prayer." And it is observable, that this last exhortation is particularly addressed to masters of families, as you may read, (Coloss. iv. 1, 2.) "Masters, give unto your servants that which is just and equal, knowing that ye also have a Master in heaven." The apostle goes on, still addressing them in the same character; "Continue in prayer, and watch in the same, with thanksgiving." In the same strain Paul writes to Timothy, (1 Tim. ii. 8.) "I will therefore, that men pray every where, lifting up holy hands, without wrath or doubting." And surely, if in all places men ought to lift up holy hands unto God, much more ought they to do so in their own families, which are immediately under their care, and for whose spiritual as well as temporal interest they ought to be chiefly concerned. Accordingly, we learn from the sacred history, that this has been the uniform practice of good men in all ages of the world. The care of the ancient Patriarchs, to keep up family religion, is very remarkable. We find Abraham rearing up altars wherever he came: And for what end did he this, but that on these altars he might offer sacrifices, and call upon God with his household? We have another bright example of this in Job, of whom we read, (Job i. 5.) that "he sent for his sons, and sanctified them, and rose up early in the morning, and offered burnt-offerings for each of them." And lest it might be thought that his family-worship was only occasional and accidental, it is added at the close of the verse, "Thus did Job continually." Nor was this peculiar to the patriarchal state, when each family was a church by itself; but the same good practice was continued after the Jews were formed into a national church, and had priests appointed to preside in the public worship. Thus Joshua vowed, not only for himself, but likewise for his house, that they would serve the Lord: which plainly imports a resolution on his part to use all the means in his power to make his family do so: particularly to worship God before them, and to take care that none should dwell in his house who would not join in this holy service. The example of David in the text is abundantly plain; for though he had priests and Levites about him, yet did he not devolve the work upon them, but he himself, as head and master of the house, "blessed his household."

In the New-Testament writings it is very usual to give private families of devout Christians the name of *Churches*. But surely this would have been a most improper appellation, if God had not been publicly acknowledged, and the daily sacrifices of prayers and praises had not been offered in them.

These, I think, are sufficient intimations of the will of God in this matter; and may serve to convince any man, who acknowledgeth the divine authority of the Scriptures, that it is the unquestionable duty of all who have families, to maintain the worship of God in their houses. The reasonableness of this duty was the

Second thing which I proposed to show: and this, I hope, will appear from the following considerations.

1*st.* Families are natural societies, formed originally by God, and held together by his Providence. Previous to all civil or religious establishments families subsisted. All the obligations incumbent on communities of any kind were originally, and still continue to be, incumbent on particular families. Were the present state of society to be dissolved, and the patriarchal state restored, it is evident that family-worship would be the only worship of God: Is it possible, then, that this original obligation can ever be cancelled? What is there to be plead as a reason for cancelling it? Will you say, that the private duty is superseded by the public ordinances which we have the opportunity of attending? This argument might as well be used to disapprove the obligation to secret and personal devotion: and therefore, by proving too much, it proves nothing at all. For can any person seriously be of opinion, that the providence of God hath bestowed these public advantages on us, in order to relax the obligations which we owe to him in our houses and in our closets? But,

2dly. As God is the founder, so he is likewise the gracious benefactor of our families. All the blessings which we enjoy flow from his bounty, and depend entirely on his favor. Surely, then, if personal blessings claim the private acknowledgments of the person who receives them, family blessings ought in like manner, to be acknowledged by united thanksgivings in our household. Were a man, having a numerous offspring, to receive some signal favor from an earthly benefactor, by which his circumstances were changed from meanness and want to an easy or a decent competence; would it not be a natural acknowledgment for him to bring his family and children in their best apparel, and present them to his benefactor, fed and clothed with his bounty, to offer him their united thanks? Would not such a scene be delightful on both sides? Would it not be enjoyed as a very lovely appearance, even by a mere spectator? And is there less beauty or propriety in the same acknowledgments offered to the God in whom we live and breathe, and who giveth us all things richly to enjoy? Doth he set the hedge of his protection around us, and defend us from the many evils to which we are continually exposed; and shall he yet have no tribute of praise offered up from those houses in which he maketh us to dwell in safety? How disingenuous and unreasonable must this appear to every candid and grateful mind!

3dly. As we receive all our family blessings from God, so we are guilty also of many family sins against him; and ought therefore to join together in the penitent confession of our sins, and in deprecating the judgments which we have deserved. In a word, whatever reason there is for single persons to worship God, there is the same reason for families to do it. As there are personal sins, and wants and mercies, so there are family sins, family wants and troubles, family mercies and deliverances; and therefore it must appear highly reasonable, that the members of each family should unite together in humiliation and prayer and thanksgiving. Those who sin together, should ask forgiveness together; and those who receive mercies together, should join in praising their common benefactor.

Thus have I endeavored to show, that family-worship is not only a duty by virtue of the divine command, but is so fit and becoming in itself, that although the authority binding us to it were less apparent, yet every man who allows himself to think, must immediately be convinced, by his own reason and conscience, that such homage is certainly due to God, and that they are highly criminal who refuse or neglect to offer it. I proceed now, in the

Third place, To represent to you the manifold advantages which accompany the practice of this duty, and the pernicious consequences which flow from the neglect of it.

1*st*, Then, the practice of this duty would be of great us to promote even your temporal and worldly interest. I address myself to you who are parents or masters; and surely this consideration must appear in your own eyes to merit some regard. I need not stay to prove to you, that your prosperity, as well as your comfort, depends very much upon the dutiful behavior of your children, and the fidelity of your servants. This, I suppose, you will readily acknowledge. Now it is evident to a demonstration, that nothing can contribute more effectually to this than the good practice which I am recommending to you. Bring the fear of God into your families, and that will secure your authority better than any thing else can do. The influence of a religious principle will be as powerful and operative when you are absent from them as when you are present, because God is always present; and consequently the obedience which flows from a regard to him, must in every place, and at all times, be the same. Hereby, too, you will gain their esteem and love; which are the most powerful and permanent of all bonds of duty. There is a certain majesty in the image of God, which commands reverence to itself, even from the worst of men. Thus, we are told of Herod (Mark vi. 20.) that he feared John, because he knew him to be a holy and just man. And if this wicked prince was so much overawed by the exemplary holiness of a mean subject, how venerable must a devout parent or master appear in the eyes of his own family, when, besides that authority which his station gives him, they see him adorned with that piety and regard to God, which of themselves would dignify him, and render him worthy of their esteem and honor? How must it endear him in their hearts, to behold his anxious concern for their welfare; to hear him morning and evening commending them to the protection of Almighty God, imploring the pardon of their sins, and earnestly soliciting the same blessings for them which he begs for himself? And how must this esteem and love influence their whole behavior, and make them not only faithful, but cheerful, active, and zealous in every part of the duty and service which they owe him? I am aware, that many think to maintain their authority in their families by other sort of prayers than those I am recommending: I mean, by horrid curses and imprecations; yea, some are so abandoned as to plead the necessity of these to render their orders effectual. But this practice must appear so absurd and odious to every thinking person, that, I am persuaded, I need not spend your time in exposing it. Such a vile and impious habit must evidently destroy at once all that esteem and love, which are the only sure and permanent principles of obedience. Their whole authority, therefore, must lean on the precarious foundation of a servile fear, which God, who hath the hearts of all men in his hands, can remove when he pleases; and then they shall become utterly contemptible, and may curse on without having any person to regard them, till their own curses overtake them. But,

2dly. As the practice of worshipping God in your houses would contribute much to your worldly prosperity, in the manner I have just now explained; so it has likewise a manifest tendency to promote your spiritual and eternal interest. It is not only a considerable branch of that homage which you owe to God, but it may be also of great use to restrain you from sin, and to render you cautious and circumspect in every part of your behavior. A man will be ashamed to do any thing against the honor of that God whom he so publicly acknowledges before his family; and the very desire of appearing consistent with himself in the eyes of his children or servants, will hardly fail to produce at least an outward decency, and to restrain him from many of those scandalous sins, which he might otherwise be in danger of committing. So that though family-worship served no higher purpose than to hedge in our practice before our household, I should even think that a considerable recommendation of it; and every wise and good man must esteem and value it upon that account. But this is one of the least of its happy effects. The practice of this duty would not only render our outward conduct cautious and decent, but would also tincture our minds deeply with a sense of God, and of divine things. It would give us greater boldness, too, in our secret approaches to the throne of grace. How can that man have any confidence or enlargement of heart in secret prayer, whose conscience reproacheth him with never having honored that God in public, from whom he is now going to ask the most unmerited favors? It is true indeed, that our Lord, in great condescension, granted a private audience in the night season to Nicodemus, who had not the courage to own him in the face of the day; but no man hath reason to expect the same indulgence now. Nay, however uncharitable it may be thought, I must declare it as my opinion, that the neglect of public duties gives too just ground to suspect, that those of a more private nature are either little minded, or superficially performed. For, did you obtain access to God in secret prayer, and taste the sweetness of holy communion with him in your closets, there can be no doubt that you would thereby be disposed to the duties of social worship.—A

3*d* Advantage of family-worship is, That under the influences of the divine Spirit, it is one of the most effectual means of promoting the salvation of all your household. Many godly persons have ascribed their own vital impressions of religion to their living in a devout family; and many a sinner, ruined by vice and evil habits, has too justly laid the blame of it on the wickedness of those with whom he dwelt. What numbers of children and servants have been lost for want of that good example which it was the duty of their parents or masters to have given them? As in a profane and sensual family there are continual temptations to sin, to swearing, lying, intemperance, and contempt of God; so in a devout, well governed house, there are continual incitements to a holy life, to faith, love, sobriety, and heavenly-mindedness. The authority of the heads of the family, and the conversation and example of all the members of it, are powerful inducements to a religious temper and behavior. As in a well discipled army, even the cowards are constrained to stand to their arms, and to act valiantly, by the general order of the whole; so in a religious household, a wicked man can scarcely contrive how to live wickedly, but seems to be almost a saint, by being continually among those who appear to be saints. O how easy and well-paved (if I may use the expression) is the way to heaven in such a gracious society, in comparison of what it is to those who dwell in the houses of the profane and sensual! In the former, the advantages of instruction, authority, example, and conversation, are all on the side of God and religion: in the latter, the same powerful circumstances are all on the side of corrupt nature, and push men forward in the broad way that leads to destruction.

If then you would not be guilty of bringing ruin on immortal souls; if you wish to have the blessing of them who are ready to perish for ever, to come upon you; if you desire that your children and servants should be pious and happy; if you would have your whole domestic society blessed;—let your household be daily consecrated by fervent prayer to Almighty God.—The

4*th* and *last* advantage of family religion which I shall mention, is its tendency to form an holy church and people, and to propagate religion from generation to generation. The public state of religion in the world must entirely depend on the care bestowed on the cultivation of it in private families. If the nursery be neglected, how is it possible that the plantation should prosper? Such as the families are, of which congregations, churches, and kingdoms are composed, such will be the flourishing or the decayed state of religion in these larger communities: And consequently it is as clear as noon-day, that the disregard shown to God in our households, is the fatal source of that amazing corruption of manners in the present age, which almost every one pretends to lament, but almost none sets himself in earnest to reform. Would you then put a stop to abounding iniquity, and promote the cause of God and religion, begin at home, and let your Maker have that honor in your families to which he is entitled.

Had we, who minister in the public worship of God, only to lay those stones in order in the building, which parents and masters of families had previously polished, how easy and delightful would be our task? how comely and beautiful would our worshipping assemblies appear? how pure and comfortable would their communion be? But if these shall neglect to exert their proper influence; if the work of hundreds or thousands shall be left to be performed by one or two, what a tedious labor must it prove? What effect can divine truths, delivered once a-week, have, unless the impression of them be afterwards kept alive by family-devotion and domestic religion? It is no wonder that a tender plant should wither and die which is seldom visited or watered: and it is as little wonderful, that those should continue wicked and impenitent, who but once a-week come under the influence of a religious ordinance; and who neither see nor hear any thing of God, but when the stated season of public instruction returns. If religion die in families, how can it live in nations? Is it not an inevitable consequence, that all our pubic devotions must in this case dwindle away into mere hypocrisy and lifeless, unavailing forms of worship?

I have thus endeavored to represent to you the manifold advantages which would arise from maintaining the worship of God in your families. And I have now only to add, that though you were willing to be without these advantages, yet this loss is not the whole penalty which must attend the neglect of that duty. This avowed disregard of God will not always pass unpunished. The day is coming, when "God will pour out his fury upon the Heathen that know him not, and upon the families that call not upon his name." — "Consider this, ye that now forget God, lest he tear you in pieces, when there is none to deliver."

I would now conclude the subject by pressing you, with all the earnestness of which I am capable, to the performance of this necessary and important duty, were it not that I think it may be of use to consider some of those excuses by which the neglect of it is commonly defended.

Some plead their rank and station in the world, but on what principles I could never yet discover. I cannot conceive any principle of reason more strong and obvious, than that uttered by our Saviour, (Luke xii. 48.) "Unto whomsoever much is given, of him shall much be required; and to whom men have committed much, of him will they ask the more." And certainly if benefits conferred deserve any return, they at least deserve thanks: if God hath placed us in a more distinguished station, we owe to him a more solemn and devout acknowledgment. Riches and honors, instead of setting a man above the obligation of family-worship, rather bind it more strictly on him: and that it is below no man of any station whatsoever to perform this office, appears by the example in my text; the example of one in the most elevated station known among men, returning from the public worship of God to bless his household.

Others plead, that it has not been the practice of their families, and that they are not inclined to bring a new custom into it. To these I answer, that the reason of this duty is as old as eternity itself, and the practice of it is as ancient as the first family of mankind. In every succeeding age, down to the present day, there have been families in which God was worshipped, and there will be such until the end of the world. Nay, I dare venture to affirm, that there are few now hearing me, whose fathers or grandfathers did not at least maintain the form of this duty. For, however much it is despised now, it is certain, that it was in reputation about an hundred years ago, and generally practised by men of all ranks. It deserves, therefore, to be inquired into, when, or by whom, and for what cause, this good old custom was laid aside? what was the shameful period in which the worship of God was turned out of doors to make way for irreligion, and a contempt of divine things? Then, indeed, a most base and dishonorable innovation was made in your families: and therefore it must be your glory to restore things to their ancient state, and to give the worship of God that room in your houses which it formerly possessed.

But if it be really true, that this important duty has been always neglected in your families, believe me it is now high time to introduce it. Your danger is greater than you are aware of. Punishment loseth nothing by delay; the slower it advances, the heavier it will prove. And therefore you have reason to fear, that the wrath of God, which has been so long restrained, shall at length break forth with double violence, if it is not prevented by a speedy reformation.

Another excuse, by which some defend their neglect of this duty, is their inability to perform it well. They cannot pray to God in public in so decent a manner as they would incline. In answer to this, I need only observe, that, next to the divine blessing, nothing contributes more to teach men to pray than frequent practice and use. So that, if upon this account you neglect the duty, your inability can pass for nothing else than a feigned pretence to cover your unwillingness; for, were you as willing to learn to pray, as to acquire the knowledge of any art, you would soon by diligent endeavors obtain a competent measure of this excellent gift. Besides, if there is first a willing mind, it is accepted according to what a man hath; it is the sincerity of your desires which God regards, and not the expressions with which you clothe them; and if you set about this duty in good earnest, and in the best manner you can, though perhaps you may come short of what you wish, God will both accept and assist you in your humble and well-meant attempts to honor him.

Upon the whole, then, may I not hope that you will hearken to what I have said? God is now offering himself to be your guest; and is, by us, demanding an entrance into your hearts and into your houses. And can you resolve on refusing him? Shall the great King of heaven thus stand at your doors and knock, and yet meet with a repulse? If the authority of God has any weight with you; if your reason can prevail with you; if your own immortal souls, or the souls of those who dwell with you, appear worthy of your regard; in a word, if duty, gratitude, or interest, can move you, all these conspire to enforce my exhortation, and to plead the cause of family-worship. And must these powerful advocates plead in vain? must they turn evidences against you, and appear at last in judgment to condemn you? God forbid. I desire to hope better things of you, and things that accompany salvation, though I thus speak.

May the spirit of all grace seal these instructions, and powerfully determine you to the practice of this duty, that, by the exercise of social worship here below, you may be gradually prepared for the more exalted worship of the triumphant society above, who all with one heart, and one voice, ascribe salvation to him that sitteth on the throne, and to the Lamb for ever and ever. *Amen.*

SERMON XLVI.

Preached before the Society in Scotland for propagating Christian Knowledge, January 4, 1784.

PRAYER FOR CHRIST'S KINGDOM.

MATTHEW VI. 10.—"Thy Kingdom come."

THE correspondence between heaven and earth is preserved and conducted by Christ alone; "For no man cometh," or can come, "to the Father but by him." John xiv. 6. It is he who presents all our homage to God; it is he who transmits to him all our petitions; and by his hands all mercy and grace are conveyed to us. Our most fervent prayers, the devoutest breathings of our souls, must not only be purged from that defilement which cleaves to them, but even in their greatest purity, they must be offered up in his censer, in order to their acceptance, and can only ascend by the incense of his sacrifice.

It should therefore be our first care, in all our approaches to the throne of grace, to solicit the favor of this powerful Mediator, and to procure his friendly interposition in our behalf; and then we shall have no cause to dread a repulse; for his intercession is, and must be, always prevalent. The dignity of his person, his relation to the Father, and especially the perfection of that sacrifice upon which his intercession is founded, effectually secure acceptance to us; so that if once we are fully persuaded that our requests are framed according to his will, we need have no distrustful anxiety about their success, for he will enforce them with all the merit of his own blood; and therefore we may confidently hope to obtain what we ask, in that time and way which unerring Wisdom sees best for us: "For this," says the apostle John, "is the confidence which we have in the Son of God, that if we ask any thing according to his will, he heareth us; and if we know that he heareth us, we know that we have the petitions we desired of him."—1 John v. 14, 15.

This, my brethren, is an abundant source of consolation and joy; and though our desires are limited to such things as are agreeable to the will of our Redeemer;

yet by this very limitation our comfort is extended, and prayer becomes a privilege of infinitely greater value than otherwise it would be An unconfined liberty in our addresses to God would, in most cases (to such ignorant and unthinking creatures as we are) amount to nothing better than the choice of the means and manner of our own destruction. (Eccl. vi. 12.) "For who knoweth what is good for a man in this life?" Whereas our glorious High Priest, who is perfectly acquainted with our state, can never be at a loss to know what is good for us; and the costly proofs he hath already given of his mercy and love, leave us no room to suspect his concern for our welfare. The least reflection on his sufferings may easily convince us, that he sincerely intends our happiness, and can disapprove of nothing but what is hurtful to our interest. Neither hath he left it to the uncertain conjectures and doubtful reasonings of our own minds, to find out what is agreeable to him; this is clearly revealed to us in the holy Scriptures: and to render the discovery of it still more easy to us, he hath furnished us with a short but perfect model of devotion in this comprehensive prayer which he taught his disciples; by attending to which, we may learn from his own mouth after what manner we should address the throne of grace, and what ought to be the matter and order of our desires. Hereby the surest foundation is laid for our confidence and hope; and whatever is according to this divine pattern, we may ask with full assurance of faith, being confident that he who hath secured for us all the blessings which we need, will certainly listen to those desires which he himself hath excited and authorized. "And if we know that he heareth us," we may from thence certainly conclude, "that we shall have the petitions we desired of him."

I shall not detain you with any account of the several parts of this excellent prayer, nor the particular design for which our Lord introduced it in this sermon: Only, to make way for the instructions I propose to lay before you on this occasion, I shall observe in general,

That prayer is not only an acknowledgment of our dependence upon God for the blessings we ask, but it likewise imports a sincere resolution on our part to put ourselves in the way of those blessings, and to use all proper means for obtaining them. Thus, when we pray for daily bread, we do not mean, that God should indulge our idleness, and feed us in a miraculous way; but only, that he would countenance our honest endeavors, and prosper them by his blessing, which alone maketh rich. In like manner, when we pray, as in my text, that the kingdom of God may come, we certainly intimate our own consent to be employed as instruments in carrying on this design, and must be understood as binding and obliging ourselves, by this petition, to do every thing in our sphere that may contribute to promote it.

Accordingly, I shall endeavor, in dependence upon the divine aid,

First. To explain and illustrate the petition itself. And,

Secondly. To show what may reasonably be expected from us in consequence of our using it. Or rather indeed, what is absolutely necessary to prove that we are sincere, when we thus pray "thy kingdom come."

It is scarcely to be supposed, that any who read their Bibles, can be ignorant of what is here meant by the kingdom of God. This form of speech was very common among the Jews, especially about the time of our Saviour's appearance; and was used by them, to signify that grand revolution foretold in ancient prophecy which was to be brought about by the Messiah, their long expected king. Thus we find the Pharisees (Luke xvii. 20.) inquiring "when the kingdom of God should come;" that is, as the context explains it, when the reign of the Messiah should commence. And John the Baptist proclaimed the approach of this glorious Person in the same style; saying, "Repent ye, for the kingdom of heaven is at hand." Matth. iii. 2. There are several other passages in the New Testament, where the same phrase occurs; from which it doth still more plainly appear, that by the "kingdom of God" is meant the gospel-dispensation, in which subjects were to be gathered to God by his Son as the reconciling Mediator, and by him formed into a church or spiritual kingdom, against which the gates of hell shall never prevail; which is to subsist on earth, and enlarge itself in spite of all opposition, till at length it shall become perfect in heaven, and triumph in eternal glory.

Now, this kingdom is either External, comprehending all who make an open profession of faith in Christ, and submit to the ordinances which he hath instituted; or Internal, consisting in that dominion which he exercises over the hearts of his subjects, converting them by his grace to the faith and obedience of the gospel, enlightening their minds, renewing their wills, and purifying their affections; filling them with "righteousness, and peace, and joy in the Holy Ghost;" that is, with true Christian virtue, and all the blessed fruits and effects of it. And no doubt the petition respects both these views of the kingdom of God: for though the last, *viz.*, the dominion of grace in the heart, or the dominion of God within us, is beyond comparison the most valuable of the two, and therefore chiefly to be desired by us; yet, as the kingdom is introduced and established by means of the ordinances which Christ hath appointed, we ought likewise to be much concerned for the preservation and enlargement of the visible church, or that external kingdom within which these ordinances are dispensed, and to pray for the one in order to the other.

So that this petition may be considered as directing us to pray for these following things:

1*st.* That the gospel may be propagated throughout the world, and all nations brought to the knowledge of the only true God, and of Jesus Christ whom he hath sent.

It appears from the prophetic writings of the Old Testament, that no less than universal dominion was promised to the Lord Redeemer. "Ask of me," says God, (Psal. ii. 8.) "and I shall give thee the Heathen for thine inheritance, and the utmost parts of the earth for thy possession." It was foretold, (Psal. lxxii. 8, 11, 17.) "That his dominion should reach from sea to sea, and from the rivers to the ends of the earth; yea, that all kings should bow down before him, and all nations should serve him; that men should be blessed in him, and all nations call him blessed." And that remarkable passage (Dan. vii. 13, 14.) is a clear and express declaration on this head. "I saw," says the Prophet, "in the night visions, and behold, one like the Son of man came with the clouds of heaven, and came to the Ancient of Days, and they brought him near before him; and there was given him dominion, and glory, and a kingdom, that all people, nations, and languages, should serve him." Now, it is evident, that the extent of his kingdom doth not yet equal these magnificent descriptions of it. There are still many dark corners of the earth upon which the Sun of Righteousness hath never arisen; others, which were once visited with his healing and comforting light, have had their candlestick long removed; and the Jews, whose return to their own Messiah shall so remarkably enrich the church, and give such life and beauty to it, that Paul compares it to a "resurrection from the dead," (Rom. xi. 15.) do still retain their prejudice against him, and obstinately refuse subjection to him.

We ought therefore to pray that the gospel, which hitherto has been confined within very narrow bounds, may gradually spread and extend itself on every side, till at length it obtain possession of the whole earth, and "all the the kingdoms of this world become the kingdoms of our God, and of his Christ." Rev. xi. 15. But,

2*dly.* We are more especially to pray for a divine blessing to accompany the means of grace,

That the gospel may come to men, not in word only, but also in power, and prove effectual for turning "them from darkness unto light, and from the power of Satan unto God." That where Christ doth already reign in his external ordinances, there he would also erect his throne in the hearts of men, subduing sinners to himself, and training up his saints, by the influences of his holy Spirit, to a meetness for that undefiled inheritance which he hath purchased for them. And,

3*dly.* We are likewise authorized by this petition to pray, that whatever stands in opposition to the kingdom of our Redeemer, either with respect to the extent or influence of it, may be removed out of the way:

Particularly, that Antichrist, that "man of sin and son of perdition, who opposeth and exalteth himself above all that is called God," (2 Thess. ii. 3, 4.) and hath long been "drunk with the blood of the saints,' (Rev. xvii. 6.) may be brought to the ground, and never arise any more: that the delusions of the false prophet, and blasphemous impostor Mahomet, which have overspread so great a part of the world, may at length be detected, and his kingdom of darkness and violence plucked up by the roots.

And though it doth not belong to us to choose the time, or means, or manner of doing it, for these must be wholly submitted to Him "who is wonderful in counsel and excellent in working;" yet surely it is lawful for us, to desire in general, "that God would arise and scatter all his enemies" (Psal. lxviii. 1.): and even to make mention of those enemies in particular whom he hath described in Scripture by such plain and legible characters, that we can be in no danger of mistaking them; and to plead, that what he hath purposed and spoken concerning them may be fulfilled in the most speedy and effectual manner. In a word, whatever is conducive to the present glory of the Redeemer, and the prosperity of his kingdom upon earth, may justly be comprehended in this petition; and it will never cease to be of use in the church, till all the Redeemer's enemies are made his footstool; and then it shall be exchanged for that triumphant song, (Rev. xii. 10.) "Now is come salvation and strength, and the kingdom of our God, and the power of his Christ. Alleluia! for the Lord God Omnipotent reigneth. Let us be glad, and rejoice, and give honor to him; for the marriage of the Lamb is come, and his wife hath made herself ready." Rev. xix. 6, 7.

Thus I have endeavored to give you a short account of the sense and import of this petition. Let us now proceed, in the

Second place, To consider more largely what may reasonably be expected from us in consequence of our using it; or rather, indeed, what is absolutely necessary to prove that we are sincere when we thus pray, "Thy kingdom come." And,

1*st*. It is necessary that we should become the subjects of this kingdom, not in name only, but in deed and in truth, otherwise we cannot wish the prosperity and advancement of it.

This King of Zion, who sways a sceptre of grace over those who cordially submit to him, is likewise armed with a rod of iron, to dash in pieces his obstinate enemies; and therefore, to all such, his coming must be most terrible; and neither their inclination nor interest will suffer them to desire it. No man can wish the increase of a power which he knows to be opposite to him, especially when the opposition is so great, and the difference so irreconcilable, as that which subsists between the kingdom of Christ and the kingdom of Satan; for the one must necessarily be built upon the ruins of the other.

Let us then, my brethren, throw down the weapons of our rebellion, and yield ourselves to this gracious Sovereign; and then the increase of his power shall become the matter of our joy. Let us invite him into our hearts, and erect a throne for him there; or rather, let us beseech him to erect one for himself, to cast down every thing within us that would exalt itself against his authority, and to take the full and perpetual possession of our souls. Let us unfeignedly accept of him, in the whole extent of his office as Mediator; that, standing related to him as the members of his body, we may derive from him wisdom, and righteousness, and sanctification, and every thing necessary to our complete redemption. Let us secure to ourselves a title to the protection and privileges of his government, by submitting to the laws and constitutions of it; and then it will become easy and natural to us, to pray for the prosperity of a kingdom to which we belong, and the glory of a Sovereign who employs all his power and authority for our good.

2*d* Duty incumbent upon us, in consequence of our using this petition, is to endeavor, by all the methods we can, to persuade others likewise to become the subjects of this kingdom.

Many indeed call Christ, "Lord, Lord; but few," alas! "do the things which he says: they profess that they know God, while in works they deny him,—being abominable, and disobedient, and to every good work reprobate." And shall not this move our pity and compassion? Can we look around us, even within the limits of the visible church, and see human nature exposed in every deformed and sickly shape? Can we behold multitudes of men, who are called by the name of Jesus, counteracting the most sacred obligations of conscience, and even pouring contempt upon the only Saviour of lost sinners? Can we see all this, I say, and not afford our helping hand? Do we pray that the kingdom of God may come, and will we do nothing to introduce it into the hearts of others, who by nature are less disposed to entertain it than we ourselves once were? If we are sincere in using this petition, let us show our sincerity by our endeavors to obtain what we ask. Let us labor, with all our might, to awaken poor sinners to a sense of their danger, that they may fly to the protection of that merciful Saviour, who hath expressly said, "Him that cometh unto me I will in no wise cast out." (John vi. 37.)

Various are the means which may be used for this purpose: I shall mention one, which all of us may employ, and that is a holy and exemplary life. There is grandeur and majesty in the image of God, which exacts homage to itself from every heart. There is something within us, which, in spite of our degeneracy, confesses and approves of what is right; truth in our speech; justice and honesty in our commerce with others; patience under affliction, and pity to the afflicted; a generous contempt of the world, and a readiness to do good to all. These are virtues which the worst of men secretly honor, and the practice of them explains them better, and enforces them more, than words can do. Would we then prevail with men to become Christians indeed, let us draw out Christianity in our lives, and make it visible to their eyes, and it will speak for itself more intelligibly and convincingly than we can do: for men, by beholding it, will see at once, that it is not only excellent, but, by the grace of God, practicable too. This is an argument that hath more persuasion in it than any other can have; and then it is recommended to us by our Lord himself, (Matt. v. 16.) "Let your light so shine before men, that they may see your good works, and glorify your Father which is in heaven."

3dly. If we sincerely desire the prosperity and advancement of Christ's external kingdom, we will manifest this by our endeavors to support and maintain it where it is already established, especially among ourselves.

This is an evidence which may reasonably be expected from us; and indeed without it, all our professions of love to the Redeemer, and of zeal for his glory, must pass for vain and flattering pretences, which deserve no credit. We only mock God, when we pray that the religion of his Son may become universal, and fill the whole earth, if at the same time we do not discover, by our conduct, a hearty concern for its continuance in our own land; yea, if we do not actually resist and oppose all attempts whatever to carry it away from us.

It hath pleased God to distinguish us by our religious privileges above most other nations in the world. They were purchased by our fathers, with the expense of much blood and treasure; and it would be highly criminal in us to resign them tamely, but far more to throw them away with our own hands: yet forgive me to say, that they are chargeable with a crime not less than this, who either openly attempt, or secretly wish, to bring one to the throne of these kingdoms, whose principles oblige him to pull down what we apprehend to be the kingdom of Christ, and to carry us back to that anti-christian slavery, from which we have so happily escaped.

There is such a manifest inconsistency between this petition and the practice of such people, that it is surprising they do not observe it; and it must appear still more wonderful, when we consider that the persons who are chiefly chargeable with this inconsistency among us, cannot be supposed ignorant of the meaning of this excellent prayer, which, by their ordinances, they oblige themselves to use so frequently, and even press as a necessary form upon others. But surely to pronounce the words of it cannot be of such efficacy as to atone for actions which contradict the sense of it; nor indeed do I suppose that they expect this from it. I rather believe, that inveterate prejudice and strong delusion hinder many of them to perceive this obvious inconsistency.

But let us, my brethren, " stand fast in that liberty wherewith Christ hath made us free, and not suffer ourselves to be entangled again with the yoke of bondage." Let us show our sincerity in using this petition, by resisting all attempts to remove the candlestick from among ourselves; let us bless God for the religious privileges we enjoy, and not suffer them to be violently wrested out of our hands, under any pretence whatever: let us not even expose them to the smallest danger, but guard them as the most valuable part of our property; and especially, let us be careful so to improve them, that we may never provoke God himself to deprive us of them. In the

4th and *last* place, Let us extend our regards to those dark and miserable corners of the earth, which are full of the habitations of cruelty and wickedness.

Let us not only pray, that the gospel may be sent to them; but let us do what we can to make our prayers effectual, by embracing every opportunity which the providence of God affords us, of conveying to them this inestimable blessing. It is our honor and happiness to have a Society for Propagating Christian Knowledge erected among us by royal letters patent, (and countenanced by an annual donation from his majesty of one thousand pounds sterling) whose business it is to attend to this very thing. The progress they have already made, is at once a convincing proof of their fidelity, and a manifest token of the divine favor and acceptance; hitherto, indeed, their pious endeavors have been mostly laid out in the remote and barbarous parts of our own native land, though they have not been wholly confined to these. They have been enabled to employ some missionaries abroad; of whose success among the Indians, especially of late, they have received such agreeable accounts, as gives the delightful prospect of a large accession to the kingdom of our Redeemer. The fields are already growing white in those parts, and promise a rich and plentiful harvest, were more laborers employed to gather it.

Here then is an opportunity, which God, in his providence, affords us of obtaining the answer of our own prayer. By this Society, he demands a proof of our sincerity, and, as it were, offers us the honor to become fellow-workers with himself in gaining new subjects to his Son. Let us with thankfulness embrace the offer, and contribute as liberal an assistance as we can for carrying on this glorious design.

You must all be sensible, that your substance cannot be employed to a better purpose, nor indeed laid out in a way more truly advantageous to yourselves. This is charity to the souls of men, and, in the noblest sense, "lending to the Lord," (Prov. xix. 17.) who will not fail to repay with usury.

There is a certain way of laying " up for yourselves treasures in heaven, where there is no corrupting moth nor rust, and where thieves cannot break through to steal." What is thus devoted to the immediate service of the Redeemer, can never be lost to the giver, but shall descend in showers of blessings upon his own head. " The liberal soul shall be made fat, and he who watereth shall be watered also himself." (Prov. xi. 25.)

Such liberality will afford us, in the mean time, a most refined and delicate pleasure; an enjoyment not confined to a day, but which lives and improves by reflection: and then it shall be amply recompensed at the resurrection of the just, (Dan. xii. 3.) " When they that are wise shall shine as the brightness of the firmament, and they that turn many unto righteousness as the stars for ever and ever."

Yea, this will bring down the blessing of God upon our land; the vigorous prosecution of this noble design will be a better defence to us than the most potent fleets or numerous armies, as it will engage the Lord of Hosts on our side, "who will be a wall of fire about us, and the glory in the midst of us."

But I hope I need not multiply arguments to persuade you to so reasonable a duty: the glory of the Redeemer, the salvation of precious and immortal souls, our own present and eternal interest, all unite their force in exciting us to it. Let us then, whilst we pray " Thy kingdom come," do every thing in our sphere that may contribute to promote it; and then shall we triumph in eternal glory, when the body of Christ shall be completed. *Amen.*

SERMON XLVII.

Preached Dec. 12, 1776, being the first public Fast after the commencement of the American War.

SUPPLICATION FOR ZION.

PSALM li. 18.—"Do good in thy good pleasure unto Zion: build thou the walls of Jerusalem."

THERE is an advice becoming the wisdom of Solomon, (in Eccl. v. 2.) "Be not rash with thy mouth, and let not thine heart be hasty to utter any thing before God; for God is in heaven, and thou upon earth: therefore let thy words be few." To pray to the Most High God is a very solemn thing, even when we view him as seated on a throne of mercy. He is always present with us, whether we think of him or not: but when we pray, we, by our own deed, place ourselves in his sight, and solicit his attention. And is not this a very solemn and awful thought? We speak to one who looks immediately into the heart, and who requireth "truth in the inward parts." Nay, we appeal to him as the Searcher of hearts, for the truth of every word which we utter before him, and challenge his omniscience to take cognizance, whether what we say doth not express the real sentiments and desires of our hearts. I say *the desires of our hearts;* for these, and not the language in which we clothe them, are our prayers to God. Nay, the better the words are which we use in prayer, the more insolent is the profanation, if they are not animated by the desires which they ought to express. Too many are apt to imagine, that they have succeeded well in the exercise of devotion, if they have been able to address God by his proper titles, and to recollect those words indited by the Spirit of God, in which holy men of old expressed their desires, and which they committed to writing for the use of the church. But they do not consider, that the very end for which those accepted prayers were recorded, was to regulate our hearts instead of directing our lips; and that it is our most immediate business, when such petitions occur to our minds, to try our hearts by them, that we may truly feel what they express, before we adventure to present them to God.

It is the character of hypocrites, whom God abhorreth, that they "draw near to him with their mouths, and honor him with their lips, while their hearts are far from him." This is to add abuse and insult to all their other sins; and those prayers which have proceeded from feigned lips, will, in the great day of judgment, stop the mouths of transgressors more effectually, than all the other offences with which they shall be found chargeable.

The articles of a man's belief may not always be present to his mind; or at least the practical inferences which may justly be drawn from them, may not be all so obvious as to command his uniform attention. To counteract indeed a plain and positive law, is such a flagrant rebellion as admits of no excuse: and yet even in this case, the sinner may pretend to plead, in alleviation of his crime, that the law appeared to him so strict and rigorous, that he could not bring his mind to consent to its demands.

But what evasion can a man find for contradicting his own prayers? Or what shall he be able to answer, when God shall say to him, "Out of thine own mouth do I condemn thee, thou wicked servant?" Every request which we make to God, is not only an explicit declaration that we highly esteem, and ardently desire the benefits we ask, but likewise implies an obligation on our part, to put ourselves in the way of receiving what we ask, and to use all the means in our own power to obtain it. When therefore we do not endeavor to obtain the blessings which we ask, we plainly declare that we do not heartily desire them. And by asking what we do not desire to obtain, we make it evident that we are presumptuous dissemblers, who use greater freedom with the all-perfect Being, than we dare to use with any of our fellow mortals, who is possessed of sufficient power to resist such unworthy and abusive treatment.

I have just now read to you a prayer of the royal Psalmist, which none of us, I suppose, will hesitate to adopt. It consists of two distinct petitions; the one respecting the spiritual, the other the temporal prosperity of the people over which the providence of God had placed him. And it will readily occur to you, that both these important interests of the nation to which we belong, are recommended to our attention in the royal proclamation which hath brought us together this day. What I propose in the following discourse is to make a few remarks,

First. On the matter of David's prayer.

Secondly. On the order observed in the petitions contained in it.

Thirdly. On the temper of mind with which this prayer appears to have been accompanied. I will then show what is incumbent on those who address the same request to God, in order to prove the uprightness of their hearts, and that they sincerely wish to obtain what they ask.

I begin with the matter of David's prayer; "Do good in thy good pleasure unto Zion: build thou the walls of Jerusalem."

The first of these petitions hath an obvious reference to the tribes of Israel, considered in their spiritual state, as a religious community, or the true church of God. To those who are acquainted with the language of Scripture, it will not be needful to prove, that this is the common acceptation of the term Zion, when it is used in distinction from Jerusalem. Zion was the unalterable station of the tabernacle, the city of David, and the emblem of that spiritual kingdom which David's Son and Lord was to erect in future times. The blessing prayed for by the Psalmist is, that it would please God to do good unto Zion.

This short, but comprehensive request, in the mouth of a British and protestant Christian, includes more particulars than the limits of one discourse will permit me to enumerate. I shall select a few leading petitions, in which all who come under this description will cordially unite; namely, That God, of his infinite mercy, may establish and perpetuate what his own right hand wrought for us in the days of our fathers, at the two illustrious eras of the reformation from popery, and what is justly styled the Glorious Revolution; That the word of the Lord may have free course, and be glorified in these lands, as long as the sun and moon endure: That the great truths of the gospel of Christ may be faithfully published, and successfully defended, both against the attacks of open enemies, and the secret artifices of those who lie in wait to deceive: That the ordinances of religion may not only be dispensed in purity, but may be accompanied with power, and rendered effectual for the conviction of sinners, and for building up saints in holiness and comfort through faith unto salvation: That the wickedness of the wicked may come to an end, and the just be established: That the spirit of division may cease, and that the whole multitude of believers may be of one heart and one soul, "following after the things which make for peace, and things whereby one may edify another." In fine, that our Zion may be a "quiet habitation, and a tabernacle that shall not be taken down, none of the stakes whereof shall be removed, neither any of the cords broken: that God may appoint salvation for walls and bulwarks to her, and be himself the glory in the midst of her;" "Clothing her priests with righteousness, that all her saints may shout aloud for joy." In these, and such particulars, consisteth the good of Zion. "Christ loved his church, and gave himself for it, that he might sanctify and cleanse it with the washing of water by the word; that he might present it to himself a glorious church, not having spot or wrinkle, or any such thing; that it might be holy and without blemish." For this end he lived, and for this end he died, "That he might redeem us from all iniquity, and purify unto himself a peculiar people, zealous of good works."

The other petition contained in the text, "build thou the walls of Jerusalem," hath a reference to the civil state of the Jews as a commonwealth or kingdom, and is a prayer for their national safety and prosperity.

This request, like the former, comprehends a great variety of particulars.

It will be readily admitted, that a form of government, by which the natural rights of men are most effectually secured, and in which the impartial administration of established laws guard the life, the liberty, and the property of the meanest individual, may, without straining the metaphor, be included in the idea of walls and bulwarks, which contribute at once to the defence and ornament of a city. With regard to the "walls or bulwarks" of our civil constitution, it gives me pleasure to acknowledge that they are not only entire, but in several respects more fair and durable than those of any other nation upon earth. In other lands, the walls of government are built on the surrender of some of the most precious rights of human nature: but in this happy country, we have not bought the protection of government at so dear a rate; nor is the hard hand of the oppressor either felt or feared by the meanest member of the community. And must not the heart of that man then be hard and unfeeling, who doth not wish and pray that such an invaluable constitution may be built up and preserved entire to the latest generations?

But the expression used in the text, calls upon us to look with weeping eyes and sorrowful hearts, upon that awful rent in the British empire, which is the immediate occasion of our meeting together at this time. We have seen a cloud rise out of the west, at first no bigger than a man's hand; but, like that which the Prophet's servant saw, it hath overspread the face of heaven, and carried tempest and desolation in its progress. When I mention this great calamity, I do not mean to fix your attention on it as an object which presents nothing to our view but complicated distress and danger. Much as I disapprove of that levity which "despiseth the chastening of the Lord," I am yet no friend to that despondency which would make us "faint when we are rebuked of him." The same expression in my text, which reminds us of the alarming breach which we deplore, doth at the same time lead us to look beyond and above it, to him who is able to repair it; to that God who "hath the hearts of all men in his hands, and turneth them as the rivers of water." With him it is a small matter, not only to fill up the gap which hath separated Great Britain from her American colonies; but if it seem good in his sight, he can, with infinite ease, make this temporary separation the occasion and the means of establishing a firm and permanent union; an union which neither political artifice, nor selfish ambition, nor the pride of independence, will be able to dissolve. This is the desirable issue to which our wishes may lawfully direct us, when we pray, in the language of the royal Psalmist, "Build thou the walls of Jerusalem."

Having made these remarks on the import of David's requests, let us attend, in the

Second place, To the order in which they are placed. He begins with praying for the good of Zion, and then offers his supplication in behalf of Jerusalem. Nor is this an accidental or arbitary arrangement. The same subordination of temporal to spiritual blessings, is uniformly observed through the whole of the sacred record, both in the promises of God, and in the accepted prayers of his people: and it deserves our notice, that, in this order, we are called upon by his majesty's proclamation to conduct the devotional exercises of this day. For, previous to any particular request respecting the political state of the British empire, we are admonished by our gracious sovereign, "To humble ourselves before Almighty God on account of our sins: to implore his pardon, and to send up, in the most devout and solemn manner, our prayers and supplications to the divine Majesty, for averting those heavy judgments which our manifold sins and provocations have most justly deserved."

It may be remembered by some now present, that in the year 1759, when Great Britain sat as queen among the nations, we were called together by a proclamation from the throne, to return public thanks to Almighty God, for the great and public blessings which enriched and distinguished that memorable year.

It was then my object, to warn my fellow citizens against the criminal abuse of our national felicity, by perverting, into weapons of rebellion against God, the fruits of that success with which he had been pleased to favor us.

Since that time we have enjoyed a period of very uncommon prosperity as a kingdom. While riches have been flowing to us from all quarters, luxury and dissipation, advancing with an equal pace, have proved at once the propriety and the neglect of that warning. Enormous fortunes, suddenly acquired in our foreign settlements, have accelerated that corruption of manners, which is the usual concomitant of prosperity. Successful adventurers, coming home with sums almost beyond the calculation of a moderate mind, produce a disdain of the slow and sober paths of industry: and "men hastening to be rich fall into temptation, and a snare, and into many foolish and hurtful lusts, which drown them in destruction and perdition." Our table hath indeed become our snare; and the uncommon blessings conferred on us, instead of heightening our gratitude, have only caused us to forget the hand that bestowed them, and proved the means of alienating our hearts from God.

For this abuse of prosperity, the land doth mourn this day. They must be blind indeed, who do not see the uplifted hand of God, and even read, on the rod with which he hath smitten us, our national guilt engraved in such deep and legible characters, that it may be truly said, "Our own wickedness hath corrected us, and our backslidings have reproved us."

Do we complain of the ingratitude of our American colonies, which have flourished so long, and prospered so much in a state of union with the mother-country, and as the free subjects of a free state? In what words can we utter our complaints more expressive than those which are preoccupied, if I may so speak, by the great Lord of heaven and earth, in that solemn appeal which is recorded (Isaiah i. 2.), "Hear, O heavens, and give ear, O earth, for I have nourished and brought up children, and they have rebelled against me." So that the very expressions with which we would naturally reproach our rebellious colonists, may justly remind us of that more aggravated rebellion, wherewith we ourselves are chargeable against that God, who hath not only planted, but cherished, and protected us in a good land unto this day.

Now, whatsoever things were written aforetime, were written for our admonition, upon whom the ends of the world are come. God is always the same. He is in one mind, and none can turn him. His love to righteousness, and his hatred of sin, are both unchangeable, and therefore, the truth of that assertion must be equally unchangeable, that righteousness exalteth a nation; whereas sin is the reproach, and without repentance must, in the issue, be the ruin of any people. Would we then pray with acceptance for the peace and prosperity of our Jerusalem, let us begin with praying for the good of Zion; that it may please God to pour down the spirit of repentance and reformation on men of every rank. Until we thus turn to God, solid prosperity will not return to our land. There may be gleams of transient success: but these interruptions of calamity will only aggravate our final doom. Whereas, if we sincerely repent of our evil ways, and return to that God from whom we have revolted, he will stay his hand, now lifted up in wrath, "and God, even our own God, shall bless us."—"Behold the hand of the Lord is not shortened, that it cannot save; neither is his ear heavy, that it cannot hear; but our iniquities have separated between us and our God." We have a most gracious and explicit promise to encourage us, (Jerem. xviii. 7, 8.) "At what instant (saith God) I shall speak concerning a nation and concerning a kingdom, to pluck up and pull down, and to destroy it: if that nation against whom I have pronounced, turn from their evil, I will repent of the evil that I thought to do unto them."

Here then is a large field, in which every man may labor for the good of his country. In this view, the meanest subject has the consolation to think, that he may become useful to the community with which he is connected. The meanest subject may so order his life and conversation, as to render himself, in the eyes of his Maker, one of the "excellent ones of the earth," one of that "holy seed which is the substance of the land." The meanest subject may put up the fervent supplications of a pious, pure, and humble soul, to the throne of grace; and with that holy ardor, which alone will find acceptance, solicit the Supreme Disposer of all events, for blessings and benefits of every kind to his country. The meanest subject can "walk with God" in the duties of devotion, can display the beauty of holiness, and stir up others to imitate the example of his virtue and piety.

Thus far I have considered both the matter and order of the two petitions in my text. The

Third thing proposed was, To make some practical observations on the temper of mind with which they appear to have been accompanied. And it is obvious, in general, that David had a just impression of his absolute dependence on God, and that he did not trust in the arm of flesh, but looked for help from God alone. No man possessed larger measures than David, either of political wisdom or warlike skill; but he did not confide in his own talents for building or defending the walls of Jerusalem: He knew, as he expresseth it in another of his Psalms, that "except the Lord build the house, they labor in vain that build it; and except the Lord keep the city, the watchman waketh in vain." He therefore looks directly to the God of Zion, and commits Jerusalem, and her walls, to his keeping, who neither slumbers nor sleeps, even the Creator of the ends of the earth, who fainteth not, neither is weary.

The form of his address doth likewise discover the deep conviction he had of his own unworthiness. He pleads with God, as a humble supplicant, with that penitent and contrite heart, of which he speaks in the verse preceding my text. He claims nothing upon the terms of justice, but applies solely to the mercy and free favor of God. "Do good," saith he, "*in thy good pleasure*, unto Zion."

This expression may be further considered, as denoting that submissive and resigned frame of spirit with which he puts up his requests both for Zion and Jerusalem. He did not presume to limit the Holy One of Israel; but left it entirely to his own wisdom and goodness, to grant the matter of his prayer at what time, and in what manner, or by what means, he should choose.

In all these respects, he presents to our view an approved example for our imitation in similar circumstances.

It now only remains that I should inquire, what is incumbent on those who adopt the Psalmist's prayer, in order to prove the uprightness of their hearts, and that they sincerely wish to obtain what they ask.

I observed, in the introduction to this discourse, that every request which we make to God, is not only an explicit declaration that we highly esteem, and ardently desire, the benefits which we pray for, but doth likewise imply an obligation and promise on our part to use all the means in our power to obtain them.

As to what concerns the public state of the nation, and the means of building up and cementing the walls of our Jerusalem, these matters I leave to those who have the constitutional charge of them. The best aid I can contribute in my sphere, is to pray for wisdom to direct the public counsels, and to do what I can for the good of Zion; and in this you all may and ought to be workers together with me. If, then, we have any love for our country, or any sincere desire of saving her from impending calamity, let us now form hearty and vigorous resolutions of correcting and amending our ways. Let our reformation begin in those points from which our corruption may be traced. Remember, that piety towards God is the best support of all those virtues which form the good man, or the useful citizen. Legislators may devise what regulations they please; but if there is no sense of a God or of a providence among the subjects, they will never be able to execute their plans, or to attain their ends. Let personal reformation, therefore, be our first care; and having given all diligence to make our own calling and election sure, let us, in our respective stations, join heart and hand to discourage vice in every form, and to promote the interests of pure and undefiled religion in our land. Unless we do this, our national fast, instead of ascending to God with acceptance, will sink down into the measure of national guilt, and will only hasten the execution of that fatal sentence, "Put ye in the sickle, for the harvest is ripe, the press is full, and the fat overflows, for their wickedness is great," On the other hand, by turning to God through Jesus Christ, and bringing forth fruits meet for repentance, we may not only avert those heavy judgments with which we are threatened, but on scriptural grounds may take encouragement to hope, that God will return in mercy to Zion, and will yet make our Jerusalem a praise on earth. *Amen.*

SERMON XLVIII.

Preached before the Managers of the Orphan Hospital of Edinburgh, August 7, 1775.

WHO MAKETH THEE TO DIFFER?

1 Cor. iv. 7.—"Who maketh thee to differ from another? and what hast thou that thou didst not receive?"

It is not to be supposed, that any person endowed with reason can be in suspense for a moment about an answer to these questions. I am confident that there is not one in this assembly who is not ready to reply, It is God alone who maketh me to differ from any other; and I have nothing which I did not receive from his bountiful hand. No man who believes that God is, will hesitate to confess, with the apostle James, "that every good gift, and every perfect gift, is from above, and cometh down from the Father of lights." Yet so little attention is paid by the bulk of mankind to the consequences of this commonly acknowledged truth, that I shall make no apology for employing the *first* part of my discourse, in reminding you of the evidence by which it is supported:—I shall *then* lay before you some of those practical lessons, equally obvious and important, which with ease and certainty may be deduced from it:—And *conclude* with that improvement of the subject which hath a more immediate reference to the occasion of our meeting together at this time.

First. I begin with reminding you, that every blessing we possess is the gift of God, and that we have nothing which we did not receive from him.

That this is the case with respect to natural endowments, will readily be admitted. Men are apt enough to boast of the improvement of their faculties; but the faculties themselves are universally acknowledged to be the gifts of God. "There is a spirit in man," said Elihu in the book of Job, "and the inspiration of the Almighty giveth him understanding." A quick apprehension, a retentive memory, a lively imagination, and other mental powers, these are favors which the great Author of our being dispenseth to whom, and in what measure it pleaseth him; and never was any man so arrogant as to pretend, that he bestowed these qualities upon himself.

It is no less evident, that the light of divine revelation is an additional blessing, which flows immediately from the same fountain of beneficence; according to that grateful acknowledgment of the Psalmist, "He showeth his word unto Jacob, his statutes and his judgments unto Israel: He hath not dealt so with any nation." And we must be sensible, that it is purely owing to "the tender mercy of our God, that the day-spring from on high hath visited us, to give light to us, whose fathers sat in darkness and in the shadow of death, to guide our feet into the way of peace."

Nay, we are taught, that the virtue and efficacy of this external light must be wholly attributed to the blessing of God. This is plainly and strongly asserted at the 6th and 7th verses of the preceding chapter: "I have planted, Apollos watered; but God gave the increase. So then, neither is he that planteth any thing, neither he that watereth; but God that giveth the increase."—"It pleased God," saith our apostle, speaking of himself, (Gal. i. 15.) "who separated me from my mother's womb, and called me by his grace, to reveal his Son in me." And in another part of his writings, "By the grace of God I am what I am." Nor did these expressions of humility take their rise from the peculiar circumstances of his own conversion; for he applies the same principle to the Christians at Corinth, and urgeth it as an argument against every degree of boasting or self-attribution, (1 Cor. i. 26, &c.) "For ye see your calling, brethren, how that not many wise men after the flesh, not many mighty, not many noble, are called. But God hath chosen the foolish things of the world, to confound the wise; and God hath chosen the weak things of the world, to confound the things which are mighty; and base things of the world, and things which are despised, hath God chosen, yea, and things which are not, to bring to naught things that are: that no flesh should glory in his presence." And then adds, "But of him are ye in Christ Jesus, who of God is made unto us wisdom, and righteousness, and sanctification, and redemption: that, according as it is written, He that glorieth, let him glory in the Lord."

Were it necessary to descend to other particulars that might be named, it would be easy to show, that all our advantages, of what kind soever, whether they belong to the body or outward estate, are equally derived from God, and dependent upon him. Hear what God said to Moses, (Exod. iv. 11.) "Who hath made man's mouth? or who maketh the dumb, or deaf, or the seeing, or blind? have not I the Lord?" How sublime, and how just were the sentiments which Hannah expressed! (1 Sam. ii. 3. &c.) "Talk no more so exceedingly proudly, and let not arrogancy proceed out of your mouth: for the Lord is a God of knowledge, and by him actions are weighed. The Lord killeth, and maketh alive: He bringeth down to the grave, and bringeth up. The Lord maketh poor, and maketh rich; he bringeth low, and lifteth up. He raiseth up the poor out of the dust, and lifteth up the beggar from the dunghill, to set them among princes, and to make them inherit the throne of glory; for the pillars of the earth are the Lord's, and he hath set the world upon them." And with what humble, but elevated devotion did David, in the height of his prosperity, ascribe all that he possessed to the free bounty of God, when he blessed the Lord, and said before all the congregation of the children of Israel, "Thine, O Lord, is the greatness, and the power, and the glory, and the victory, and the majesty; for all that is in the heaven, and in the earth, is thine; thine is the kingdom, O Lord, and thou art exalted as head above all. Both riches and honor come of thee, and thou reignest over all; and in thine hand is power and might, and in thine hand it is to make great, and to give strength unto all. Now therefore, our God, we thank thee, and praise thy glorious name. But who am I, and what is my people, that we should be able to offer so willingly after this sort? for all things come of thee, and of thine own have we given thee. O Lord our God, all this store that we have prepared to build thee an house for thy name, cometh of thine own hand, and is all thine own."

I might quote many other passages to the same purpose; but you have heard enough to satisfy you that I am supported by the highest authority when I say, that all the blessings we possess are the gifts of God, the effects of his free and unmerited liberality.

This doctrine, as I observed in the entrance, hath none of the charms of *novelty* to recommend it. But is it on that account less needful to be insisted upon? Most assuredly it is not. I believe we shall find, upon inquiry, that the most obvious truths are universally the least regarded, and therefore have most need to be frequently brought in view, that men may be constrained to bestow some attention upon them, and to consider the influence they ought to have upon their temper and conduct. I am afraid that we judge of spiritual things in the same absurd manner that we judge of temporal things; I mean, that we put a fanciful value upon them, and do not rate them according to their intrinsic worth and real usefulness.

We see every day, that earthly things are estimated, not by their use, but by their scarcity; insomuch that, in common language, the words *rare* and *precious* are convertible terms; though, in fact, the things that are truly precious, because most necessary, instead of being rare, are scattered abroad with the greatest profusion. Thus doth God dispense temporal benefits; the best, that is, the most useful, are universally given out in greatest abundance. And it may justly be affirmed, that spiritual blessings are dispensed in the same way. The most comprehensive blessing, the *unspeakable* gift of Jesus Christ, is of all others the most free and liberal, being offered "without money and without price," to every sinner of mankind, without exception; and actually conferred upon all who, feeling their need of a Saviour, are made willing to receive and rest upon him alone for pardon, and peace, and complete salvation. In like manner, the great rules of duty, and the truths that are best adapted to purify our hearts and reform our practice, are dispersed as it were around us in the greatest plenty and variety. God, who hath appointed our work, hath likewise limited the season for doing it; and therefore, that we may not lose a moment, the most useful and necessary instruments of action are laid so near us, that we need only stretch forth our hand to take hold of them. Were they placed at a distance, the opportunity of acting might frequently pass away before the proper means and instruments were got ready. But such wise and effectual provision is made, that no man shall have it in his power to plead this excuse. If any piece of duty be left undone, it cannot be owing either to the want of a plain rule to direct our conduct, or of sufficient arguments and encouragements to move us to action, but to the inattention, or pride, or stubbornness, of our own hearts.

This affords a glorious display of the wisdom and goodness of our great Lawgiver and Judge. But, alas! we thwart his merciful intentions. Overlooking what is near, we roam abroad in quest of other things, that lie at the remotest distance from us, and have the feeblest influence upon our temper and practice. Such is our folly and perverseness, that, despising the most important truths, because they are common and obvious, we run away in the vain pursuit of abstruse and intricate speculations, which have no other effect than to puzzle the head, or to warm the imagination, while they leave the heart dark, and cold, and insensible.

To correct this false taste, by recalling men's attention to the most simple and practical truths, ought, in my apprehension, to be the principal aim of a gospel-minister. When these have got full possession of men's hearts, and appear in the fruits of a holy life, then, if we find leisure, we may seek after new discoveries; but surely necessity should have the first disposal of our study and labor. Life is short, and souls are precious; and therefore things of eternal consequence ought in all reason to be preferred. They who choose to gratify the curious, by telling them new and strange things, may indeed raise the reputation of their own *invention;* but they do it upon the ruins of a far more excellent thing, I mean, that *charity* "which vaunteth not itself, is not puffed up, and seeketh not her own;" and as they have no higher aim than to serve themselves, it is but just they should be left to reward themselves as they can.

We are commanded in Scripture, to be "*ready* to every good work:" that is, to be in such an habitual posture for service, that with facility we may enter upon action so soon as an opportunity presents itself. But we shall never acquire this promptness and facility, till the mind be furnished with some fruitful principles of action; and the more simple and obvious these principles are, the more readily will they occur to us, and the greater authority and influence will attend them. Of this kind is the proposition I have been endeavoring to illustrate. The truth of it is obvious to the meanest capacity; and yet such is its fruitfulness and energy, that some of the sublimest duties of the Christian life are virtually included in it, and may with ease and certainty be deduced from it.

To select some of these practical lessons was the second thing proposed; to which I now proceed.

1*st.* If all the blessings we possess be the gifts of God, the effects of his free and unmerited bounty, then surely we ought to be *humble.* This is the particular improvement which the apostle directs us to make of this doctrine in the close of my text: "Who maketh thee to differ from another? and what hast thou that thou didst not receive? *Now if thou didst receive it, why dost thou glory, as if thou hadst not received it?*"

This reasoning is so plain and simple, that a child may understand it; and yet so perfectly just, that it will abide the severest trial; nay, the more accurately it is examined, the stronger will it appear. Did we keep this single principle in our eye, that it is God *who maketh us to dif-*

fer, that alone might be sufficient to give a check to our pride, and to inspire us with humility. Did we view all our present advantages as gifts freely bestowed, to which we had no previous title or claim; then every additional blessing would only remind us of our indigence before we received it; and the greater and more numerous the benefits conferred upon us were, the greater debtors should we judge ourselves, the more deeply should we feel our dependence upon God, and the less disposed should we be to glory in ourselves.

2dly. From the same principle, and with equal ease and certainty, we may deduce our obligation to *thankfulness* and praise. Humility and gratitude, those kindred graces which constitute the proper temper of a Christian, are inseparable companions. They give mutual aid and support to each other, and both take their rise from the persuasion of this truth. For how can we think of our kind and unwearied benefactor, who condescends to make us the objects of his care, who daily loads us with his benefits, though he is altogether independent of us, and can neither be enriched by our services, nor impoverished by the want of them; how can we think of him, I say, without the most fervent love and humble gratitude?

3dly. To humility and gratitude, I add *resignation* to the will of God. This was the inference which holy Job drew from the doctrine I have been illustrating: "Shall we receive good at the hand of the Lord, and shall we not receive evil also? The Lord gave, and the Lord hath taken away, blessed be the name of the Lord." Surely if no wrong be done us, we have no right to complain. We ought rather to adore that goodness which at first bestowed the gift, gave us the comfortable enjoyment of it, and continued it with us so long; and to say with the saints of old, when our distress is greatest, "I will bless the Lord at all times; his praise shall continually be in my mouth." Wherefore doth a living man complain, a man for the punishment of his sins?" "It is the Lord, let him do what seemeth him good;" and, "Good is the will of the Lord."

4thly. Did we attend to this truth, we should not dare to employ any means that are unlawful for improving our circumstances, or acquiring the good things that belong to a present world; and even in using the means that are lawful, we should constantly look up to God for success, and implore his blessing upon our honest endeavors; remembering, on the one hand, "that the getting of treasures by lying lips, is a vanity tossed to and fro of them that seek death; and, on the other hand, that the blessing of the Lord maketh rich, and he addeth no sorrow with it." Which leads me to observe,

5thly, The importance of enjoying the blessing of God, with all the gifts which his bounty bestows upon us. From this alone ariseth their value, and nothing else can impart to them that sweetness which renders the possession of them so truly desirable. Happiness cannot be extracted from the creatures themselves; they are all broken cisterns that can hold no water: "The eye is not satisfied with seeing, neither is the ear filled with hearing."—"He that loveth silver, shall not be satisfied with silver; nor he that loveth abundance with increase." Solomon records it as one of the evils he had seen under the sun, namely, "riches kept for the owners thereof to their hurt." And he supposeth it a very possible case, that amidst the greatest abundance of earthly things, "a man may all his days eat in darkness, and have much sorrow and wrath with his sickness." How awful is that threatening, (Mal. ii. 2.) "If ye will not hear, and if ye will not lay it to heart to give glory unto my name, saith the Lord of hosts, I will even send a curse upon you, and I will curse your blessings!" And when this threatening is executed upon any, then "their table becomes a snare to them; and that which should have been for their welfare becomes a trap," insomuch that their prosperity proves both the occasion and instrument of their destruction: "Whereas the Lord blesseth the habitation of the just;" in consequence whereof, "the little that a righteous man hath, is better than the riches of many wicked." It is a significant saying of David, (Psalm xxxvii. 22.) "Such as be blessed of the Lord shall inherit the earth." They hold their portion of it by a different tenure than other men; they possess it as the children of him who is Lord of all; and their Father, while he feeds them with food convenient for them, gives them at once the proper enjoyment, and the sanctified use of it. This is the peculiar privilege of believers in Christ Jesus; for "as many as receive him, to them gives he power to become the sons of God, even to them that believe in his name." And as the apostle Paul reasons, "If children, then are they also heirs, heirs of God, and joint-heirs with Christ Jesus;" so that, in the most common bounties of Providence, they can taste the sweetness of special love, and may lawfully consider every benefit conferred upon them as a token of their Father's affection, and a pledge of that fulness of joy that awaits them in a future state. How much then doth it concern us, even as we regard our present comfort, "to give all diligence to make our calling and election sure," that on every gift, whether small or great, reading the precious name of him who bestows it, we may have the true relish of the provision afforded us in the course of our journey through this strange country, till we arrive at our Father's house above, where we shall obtain possession of that glorious inheritance of the saints, which is incorruptible, and undefiled, and fadeth not away.

These are a few of the practical lessons, which, with ease and certainty, may be deduced from the doctrine of my text.

PERMIT me now to apply the subject to the particular occasion of our meeting together at this time.

Hitherto I have been speaking of the blessings we possess as gifts freely bestowed. But there is another important light in which we ought likewise to view them. They are talents committed to us for special ends and purposes; and it is both expected and required that we be diligent and faithful in improving them, as it becomes those who must one day give an account of their stewardship. There is an essential difference between God's giving to us, and our giving to our fellow-men. We renounce our interest in what we give to another: it ceaseth to be ours, and becomes the property of the person upon whom we bestow it. But God giveth nothing away after this manner. His giving to his creatures doth not make the benefit conferred a whit the less his own than it originally was. God is the entire and absolute proprietor of all things: they are his, because he made them; and what is styled *property* among men, must necessarily be derived, limited, and dependent. This dominion is so essential to God, that he cannot divest himself of it. Earthly rulers may resign part of the jurisdiction that belongs to them. Thus Saul proclaimed, that whosoever should fight Goliath the Philistine, and kill him, "he and his house should be made free in Israel." But no creature can be released from its obligation to serve God; for absolute dependence and unlimited subjection are so intimately connected, that they cannot exist separately. As we necessarily depend upon God, so we are necessarily bound to submit to his authority, and to serve him to the utmost extent of the powers he hath given us. No creature can say of any thing he possesseth, This is fully mine, to dispose of it as I please. The benefits conferred upon us are so far our property, with respect to our fellow-servants, that, unless they can produce an order from the great Master of the family, none of them may take them from us, neither can they righteously possess them without our own consent; but, with regard to God, they still belong to him, and are ours only for the ends and purposes he hath appointed. They were not given merely as an alms to the needy, but as instruments are given to a servant for doing his Master's work. This is clearly expressed, (1 Peter iv. 10.) "As every man hath received the gift, even so minister the same one to another, as good stewards of the manifold grace of God."

The nature of the gifts bestowed upon men, plainly shows, that they were not intended for pomp, but for use; and it appears from the manner in which they are distributed, that none of them are bestowed to gratify the pride of individuals, but to establish such a mutual connection and dependence, as may render every one in his place useful to the community. We have a lively illustration of this, (1 Cor. xii. 8. *et seq.*) "To one is given by the Spirit the word of wisdom; to another the word of knowledge by the same Spirit; to another faith by the same Spirit; to another the gifts of healing by the same

Spirit; to another the working of miracles; to another prophecy; to another discerning of spirits; to another divers kinds of tongues; to another the interpretation of tongues. But all these worketh that one and the self-same Spirit, dividing to every man severally as he will." Thus each hath his distinct office and use, that, as it is expressed, (ver. 25.) "there should be no schism in the body; but that the several members should have the same care one for another," and maintain mutual love, whilst all in their way contribute to the good of the whole. "The eye cannot say unto the hand, I have no need of thee; nor again the head to the feet, I have no need of you." To every one something is given, to recommend him to the respect of others; and from every one something is withheld, to keep him modest and humble; for God hath so ordered the distribution of his benefits, that each may feel his need of that excellence which he hath not in possession, and at the same time have the aid of those gifts, by the ministry of others, which he himself wants.

"The rich and the poor meet together," saith Solomon, "the Lord is the maker of them both." Hence, "he that mocketh the poor" is said "to reproach his Maker;" that is, he throws an injurious reflection upon the wisdom and goodness of divine providence, which hath appointed this inequality of conditions among men, for exercising, on the one hand, the patience and resignation of the poor; and that the rich, on the other hand, may be furnished with constant opportunities of acknowledging their obligations to God, and their dependence upon him for all they possess, by distributing what they can spare from their own necessary uses, for the relief and comfort of their needy brethren. That this is the proper improvement of wealth, and the purpose for which it is bestowed, appears from Paul's directions to Timothy, (1 Tim. vi. 17.) "Charge them that are rich in this world, that they be not high-minded, nor trust in uncertain riches, but in the living God, who giveth us all things richly to enjoy: that they do good, that they be rich in good works, ready to distribute, willing to communicate; laying up in store for themselves a good foundation against the time to come, that they may lay hold on eternal life." And how provoking it is to God, when men abuse the gifts of his providence, we learn from that complaint and threatening, (Hosea ii. 8, 9.) "She did not know that I gave her corn, and wine, and oil, and multiplied her silver and gold, which they prepared for Baal. Therefore will I return, and take away my corn in the time thereof, and my wine in the season thereof, and will recover my wool and my flax given to cover her nakedness."

The application of these truths to the purpose for which we are at present assembled, is so obvious, that I am confident it must already have occurred to the most inattentive of my hearers. Were we to consider the good things we possess, merely as gifts freely bestowed, and left entirely to our own disposal; yet gratitude should prompt us to employ them in such a way as might be most acceptable to our kind and generous Benefactor. But I am furnished, you now see, with a more persuasive argument; the plea of gratitude comes enforced with the claim of justice, while regard to our own interest solicits our compliance with their united demands: "For we must all appear before the judgment seat of Christ, that every one may receive the deeds done in his body, according to that he hath done, whether it be good or bad." In that day, "unto whomsoever much hath been given, of him also much will be required:" and the unprofitable servant, who did not improve the talent committed to him, but buried it under ground, or wrapt it in a napkin, shall be cast "into outer darkness; there shall be weeping and gnashing of teeth."

Seeing then these things are so, ought we not to reckon it an additional ground of thankfulness to God, when, besides the favors conferred upon us, he is at any time pleased to afford us an opportunity of employing the fruits of his liberality in such a manner as contributes most effectually to answer the highest and most important purposes for which they were bestowed? An opportunity of this kind is just now presented to you by the much-to-be respected Managers of the Orphan

Hospital, at whose desire I address you this day. The objects of their care are there placed in your view; and surely to provide for the Christian education of so many helpless children, and for their decent clothing and maintenance, till they be trained up to earn a subsistence for themselves, as it is an exercise of the truest mercy to them, so it cannot fail to be highly acceptable to that God who disdains not to style himself the Father of the fatherless.

The peculiar excellencies of this species of charity were fully illustrated, on a former occasion of this kind, from that prayer of the Psalmist in behalf of the Jewish nation, (Psal. cxliv. 12.) "That our sons may be as plants grown up in their youth; that our daughters may be as corner-stones, polished after the similitude of a palace."* Then it was shown, That a permanent provision for the Christian education of destitute children, is a charity which tends to prevent misery; and must therefore be preferable to that which only alleviates present distress, or procures it a short and uncertain relief. This is charity to the souls of our fellow-creatures, and the noblest imitation of Him who came from heaven to earth, to seek and to save that which was lost. Besides, it is a charity which, of all others, is in least danger of being misapplied or defeated. This renders the prospect of doing good by it in the highest degree probable. And then its influence is of the largest extent; for while it serves to advance the glory of God, and the interests of pure and undefiled religion in the world, it promotes at the same time, in the most effectual manner, the spiritual improvement and happiness of individuals, and even the temporal prosperity of the nation to which we belong.

To such powerful recommendations any addition would be superfluous. And they who, influenced by these motives, contribute according to their ability for the support of an institution so pious and salutary, may be assured, that what they give is, in the most proper sense of Solomon's words, "lent to the Lord, and that which they give will he pay them again."

* Dr. Erskine's Sermon, preached before the Managers of the Orphan Hospital, at Edinburgh, *May*, 18, 1774.

Upon the whole, then, let it be our first care to have our own hearts filled with love to God, as the Father of our Lord Jesus Christ, and our Father in Christ; for unless this be the source of our charity to others, our beneficence may be profitable to them, but cannot avail ourselves. And if once this principle be deeply rooted in our hearts, then it will become easy and delightful to us, to communicate good to our fellow-men, in obedience to the command of God, and in imitation of his example. Let us always bear in mind "the grace of our Lord Jesus Christ, who, though he was rich, yet for our sakes became poor, that we through his poverty might be rich." Let us consider the uncertainty of all earthly things, and this will dispose us to employ them with greater cheerfulness for the relief and comfort of our needy brethren, before they be taken from us, or we by death be divorced from them. Above all, let us beg of God the influences of his Spirit, which alone can vanquish that selfishness which is the great opposer of charity, and incline our hearts to all those acts of compassion and kindness which adorn our Christian profession, and by their beauty and usefulness engage others to glorify our heavenly Father. *Amen.*

SERMON XLIX.

Preached on a Communion Sabbath.

THE GOOD SHEPHERD'S GREAT SACRIFICE.

JOHN x. 11.—"I am the Good SHEPHERD: the Good SHEPHERD giveth his life for the Sheep."

THOUGH Christ is in every view precious to them that believe, yet some of the characters which he sustains, present him to us in a milder light than others, and render him comparatively more lovely and estimable. And amidst the variety of titles given him in Scripture, there is perhaps none more expressive of condescension and grace, than that which he is pleased to assume in my text.

As many of the Jews were shepherds by occupation, language of this description would be obvious to them all. And they who were enlightened by the Spirit of God, would not only perceive the propriety, but likewise relish all the sweetness of this endearing designation.

To us, indeed, an allusion to the pastoral life can hardly appear with equal beauty and strength. Many circumstances of resemblance would strike those who were acquainted with rural affairs, which must necessarily be supposed to escape our observation. But though we cannot trace them all with a critical exactness, yet by the light which the Scriptures afford us, I hope I shall be able to bring as many proofs of our Lord's care and tenderness, as may suffice to illustrate the propriety of the allusion, and show with what justice this title of the Good Shepherd is claimed by our Redeemer.

I BEGIN with that to which our Lord himself appeals in the text. "I," says he, "am the good Shepherd: the good Shepherd giveth his life for the sheep."

It was a signal proof that David gave of his care and tenderness, when he ventured his life for the sake of his sheep, and encountered a bear and a lion in their defence. But though the attempt was hazardous, it was not altogether desperate; he had hope of success, and actually prevailed. Besides, the charge committed to him was his father's property, part of which would one day fall to his own share: so that his personal interest was connected with the preservation of it; for if the flock decreased, his part of the inheritance would have been diminished in proportion.

But our blessed Lord had no inducement of this nature. His interest was in no shape connected with our welfare; his glory and happiness were independent of us. He could neither be enriched by our homage, nor impoverished by the want of it. Besides, we had forfeited all title to his protection, and, by the most wicked and unprovoked rebellion, had rendered ourselves the objects of his just displeasure. Yet such was his free and unmerited goodness, that he not only hazarded his life in our behalf, but voluntarily resigned it, that we might live through him. "All we like sheep had gone astray," says the evangelical prophet, "we had turned every one to his own way." But "he was wounded for our transgressions, he was bruised for our iniquities;" or, in the language of the New Testament, "He who knew no sin" became a sin-offering for us; the just One suffered for the unjust, "that he might bring us to God."

Had our case been merely unfortunate, like that of a weak and harmless lamb seized by a lion, whom it could neither resist nor avoid, pity might have inclined a generous heart to attempt something for our deliverance. But our misery was the effect, not of weakness, but of voluntary wickedness. We chose it in its cause. We sinned, though we were forewarned that death would be the issue. We were not caught by surprise, but deliberately surrendered, or rather sold, ourselves to the adversary. Yet in this situation, when we had nothing to invite, far less to deserve, his regard and affection, did the blessed Jesus fly to our relief; and descending from the throne, put on the form of a servant, that in our place he might suffer and die on this earth which he had made.

Besides, the fatal deeds which forfeited our happiness were sins committed directly against himself. It was his own law we transgressed, his own royalty we invaded; we fought against him with his own arms, and joined in confederacy with his most inveterate enemies. So that every obstacle that can be imagined lay in the road of mercy; the blackest ingratitude, the most outrageous insolence; in a word, all the circumstances were united which could aggravate our guilt, and inflame the wrath of him against whom we sinned; and conspired to render our punishment not only a righteous, but even a wise and necessary exercise of severity, for vindicating the honor of the Sovereign, and for maintaining the credit and influence of his government. Nay, as the threatening was published before the penalty was incurred, truth as well as justice demanded the execution of it.

Such were our circumstances, when this Friend of sinners, but the enemy of sin.

came upon the wings of love to save us. "Deliver them," said he, "from going down to the pit," and against me let the sword of justice be unsheathed. Here was goodness, generous, disinterested goodness, that never had, and that never can have, a parallel. "Scarcely for a righteous man will one die, peradventure for a good man some would even dare to die;" but who hath ever heard of one dying for an enemy? Or if such a prodigy could be found among men, yet the generosity even of this person would fall infinitely short of the example in my text. Such a one might be said to resign a life; but then it is a precarious, dependent life; a debt payable on demand; a lease revocable at pleasure. A mere creature can give away nothing that is properly his own, because he has nothing but what he received. Whereas our dearest Lord not only died in the room of enemies, but by dying resigned a life that, in the strictest sense, was his property: for so he says in the 18th verse of this chapter, "I have power to lay down my life, and I have power to take it up again." He had an estate of his own, (so to speak) an original, and therefore an absolute right to his life. This, as it gave merit and efficacy to his death, so it qualified him to exhibit that mystery of love, which angels contemplated with increasing wonder, when he assumed our nature, and became our Shepherd, and in that character gave his life for the sheep.

But did the blessed Jesus stop here? Did he merely restore sinners to a capacity of happiness, by expiating their guilt, and paving the way for their return to God? Or, to carry forward the allusion, does the good Shepherd satisfy himself with rescuing his sheep from the jaws of the lion, and then leave them to their own conduct, to find the road back to the fold from whence they had strayed? No —For in the

2*d* place, He also becomes their Guide; and, as it is beautifully expressed in the 23d Psalm, "He leads them in the paths of righteousness for his name's sake."

How amiable does he appear when introduced by Ezekiel, speaking after this manner: "Behold I, even I, will both search my sheep, and seek them out: as a shepherd seeketh out his flock, so will I seek out my sheep, and will deliver them out of all places where they have been scattered in the dark and cloudy day. I will seek that which was lost, and bring again that which was broken, and strengthen that which was sick." Of the same mild and gracious import is that tender representation in the prophecy of Isaiah: "He shall feed his flock like a shepherd; he shall gather the lambs with his arms, and carry them in his bosom, and gently lead them that are with young." In allusion to these prophetical descriptions of the Messiah, our Lord himself hath declared in the New Testament, that, "the Son of man is come to seek and to save that which was lost." And having in this chapter assumed the title of a Shepherd, he says in the 16th verse, "Other sheep I have, which are not of this fold, them also I must bring, and they shall hear my voice."

And indeed this exercise of his pastoral office is no less necessary than it is kind; for such is the enmity of our hearts, such the perverseness of our natures, that after all he has done without us, to bring us to God, yet if his Spirit did not work within us, none of us would ever think of returning to him. "The carnal mind is enmity against God; for it is not subject to the law of God, neither indeed can be." Accordingly Paul reminds the converts at Ephesus, that till Christ quickened them, they too were "dead in trespasses and sins, and children of wrath even as others." Hear the language of our Lord to his disciples of every tribe of men, "Ye have not chosen me, but I have chosen you;" and that assertion of the apostle which is universally true, "By grace are ye saved through faith, and that not of yourselves, it is the gift of God." And does he not merit the designation of a good Shepherd, who not only saves his flock from destruction, and opens to them the door of his sheepfold, but goes after them into the wilderness, pursues them whilst they are flying from their own happiness, and never gives over his search till he finds them, and then leads them in safety to a place of rest, where every thing is provided that their necessities require? For this is a

3*d* proof of his love to his sheep: Having brought them into his fold, he supplies all their wants, and feeds them with food convenient for them. How sweetly did David sing under the sense of this privilege, "The Lord is my shepherd, I shall not want: he maketh me to lie down in green pastures; he leadeth me beside the still waters." "The young lions may lack and suffer hunger, but they that fear the Lord shall not lack any good thing." "I will feed them," (said God by the prophet Ezekiel, chap. xxxiv. 14.) "I will feed them in a good pasture, and upon the high mountains of Israel shall their fold be: there shall they lie in a good fold, and in a fat pasture shall they feed upon the mountains of Israel." Here peace and affluence are represented in the most striking and agreeable colors. And that this promise has a spiritual meaning, and extends to the gospel church, appears from verse 23d, where the Messiah, under the well-known title of David, is brought fully into view, as the person by whose hand these blessings are dispensed. "I will set up one shepherd over them, and he shall feed them, even my servant David, he shall feed them, and he shall be their shepherd. And I the Lord will be their God, and my servant David a prince among them: I the Lord have spoken it. And I will make with them a covenant of peace, and cause the evil beasts to cease out of the land: and they shall dwell safely in the wilderness, and sleep in the woods. And I will make them, and the places round about my hill, a blessing; and I will cause the shower to come down in his season: there shall be showers of blessing. And I will raise up for them a Plant of Renown, and they shall be no more consumed with hunger in the land." It is not improbable that our Lord had this prophetical description in his eye, when he said in the 9th verse of this chapter, "I am the door (of the sheep:) by me if any man enter in, he shall be saved, and shall go in and out, and find pasture." But how must it amaze us, to hear from his own lips, that he is not only the door by which the sheep enter into the pasture, but is himself the pasture upon which they feed; yet these are his words, in the 6th chapter of this gospel, at the 51st and following verses: "I am the bread of life, the living bread which came down from heaven; if any man eat of this bread, he shall live for ever: and the bread that I give is my flesh, which I will give for the life of the world: Verily, verily, I say unto you, except ye eat the flesh of the Son of man, and drink his blood, ye have no life in you. Whoso eateth my flesh and drinketh my blood, hath eternal life: for my flesh is meat indeed, and my blood is drink indeed." Nay, is not this precious food to be dispensed to us this day, in the holy sacrament, under the significant emblems of bread and wine, when the good Shepherd shall say, and say it with power, to those who believe in him, and know his voice, "Take and eat; this is my body broken for you: and this cup is the New Testament in my blood; drink ye all of it." I suppose I need not inform you, that these expressions are figurative. You have long been taught, that the Lord's supper is a sacrament, wherein by giving and receiving bread and wine, according to Christ's appointment, his death is showed forth, and the worthy receivers are not after a corporeal and carnal manner, but by faith, made partakers of his body and blood, with all his benefits, to their spiritual nourishment, and growth in grace. This is not the worldling's portion, the whole amount of which is vanity and vexation; no, this is substantial food, even all the blessings of the new and well ordered covenant, the justification of our persons, the renovation of our natures, adoption into the family of God, assurance of his love, peace of conscience, joy in the Holy Ghost; in a word, all the unsearchable riches of his grace. Thus doth Christ feed his sheep; he invests them with a right to all the blessings of his purchase, and distributes these blessings as their necessities require, till, as Paul hath expressed it, (Eph. iii. 19.) "They are filled with all the fulness of God."—But farther in the

4*th* place, It belongs to a good Shepherd to defend his flock, as well as to feed them. And this office he likewise performs in the most effectual manner. He watches over them by night and by day; for "he that keeps Israel, neither slumbers nor sleeps."—"Fear not," says he, "for I am with thee, be not dismayed, for I am thy God: I will strengthen thee, yea I will help thee, yea I will uphold thee with the right hand of my righteousness." Their enemies indeed are many and strong, but he is mighty on whom their help is laid. He makes his grace sufficient for them, and will keep them by his power through faith unto salvation. Hear his own words in the 27th and following verses of this chapter, "My sheep hear my voice, and I know them, and they follow me. And I give unto them eternal life, and they shall never perish, neither shall any pluck them out of my hand. My Father who gave them me, is greater than all; and none is able to pluck them out of my Father's hand. I and my Father are one." He foresees the trials which are coming upon them; and prays for them effectually, that their faith may not fail. He gives power to the faint, and to them that have no might he increases strength. And when at any time they stumble and fall, he comes seasonably to their relief, lifts up their hands which hang down, and strengthens their feeble knees; and having enlarged their hearts, enables them to run in the way of his commandments. Thus does he conduct them through the slippery paths of life, and continues to be their guardian even until death. Neither does he leave them at the hour of death. For,

5*thly*. When they walk through the valley of the shadow of death, his rod and his staff comfort and sustain them. He fortifies and cheers their departing spirits; and when the evening shadows gather thick around them, the Holy Ghost, the Comforter, is sent to say to them, that death as well as life is theirs. Nay, "the good Shepherd himself, who gave his life for the sheep," will say to them in this awful hour, "Fear not, I am he that liveth and was dead; and behold, I am alive for evermore, and have the keys of hell and death:—I am the resurrection and the life: he that believeth on me, though he were dead, yet shall he live." What a multitude of saints who now inherit the promises, have in their last moments experienced the effect of these gracious and joyful assurances! In how many instances hath a lively and unexpected view of the promises of God, and of the great redemption, sustained and even elevated a dying saint, who from the infirmities of the body, or other causes, was, through fear of death, subject to bondage all his life! The sensible presence of the good Shepherd, in these awful moments, will support the most fearful, and the feeblest of the flock. It will enable him that hath no might, to triumph over death, and him that hath the power of death; and, even in the presence of the king of terrors, it will teach him this song of victory, "My flesh and my heart faileth; but God is the strength of my heart and my portion for ever."—"Thanks be unto God, which hath given me the victory, through Jesus Christ my Lord."—"For I am persuaded, that neither death, nor life, nor angels, nor principalities, nor powers, nor things present, nor things to come, nor height, nor depth, nor any other creature, shall be able to separate me from the love of God, which is in Christ Jesus my Lord." It is true, the saints of God have not all the same degree of sensible comfort at the hour of death. The wisdom of heaven may sometimes permit them to shut their eyes, without perceiving the full extent of the blessedness of them who die in the Lord, or without having received those sensible tokens of their victory over death. But "though weeping may endure for a night," while they are yet struggling to be released from the mortal tabernacle, their spirits shall awake to everlasting joy For, in the

6*th* and *last* place, When the morning of the day that never ends shall dawn, they shall again see the good Shepherd stretching out his arms to receive them into everlasting habitations. "They shall see him as he is:" they shall "be satisfied with his likeness." The mansions which he is now preparing for them will then be ready. Each of them shall enter into the blessed abode provided for him. "They shall go no more out for ever;" and "the Lamb which is in the midst of the throne shall feed them, and shall lead them to living fountains of water: and God shall wipe away all tears from their eyes." Then shall they sing together, with united gratitude and joy, the triumphant and eternal song of praise, saying, "Worthy is the Lamb that was slain, to receive power, and riches, and wisdom, and strength, and honor, and glory, and blessing: for thou hast redeemed us to God by thy blood, out of every kindred, and tongue, and people, and nation. Salvation to our God, which sitteth upon the throne, and unto the Lamb."

And now say, my dear brethren, in the review of what you have heard, is not the Lord Jesus a good Shepherd indeed? He redeemed his flock with his blood, and guides them by his Spirit, and feeds them with all the rich fruits of his purchase. He defends them in life, accompanies them through death, and conducts them to those regions of light and love, where they shall dwell in his presence for evermore, eating the fruit of the tree of life, and drinking the water of the river of life, following the Lamb whithersoever he goeth.

Thrice happy they who are the sheep of his pasture; who, allured by his love, and aided by his grace, have returned to him as the "Shepherd and Bishop of their souls."

Let me then call upon such; for of such, I trust, a goodly number are assembled in this place; let me, I say, call upon them to reflect, with gratitude and joy, upon the proofs they have already received of his care and tenderness. Remember how he found you wandering in the wilderness, exposed to every beast of prey, insensible of your danger, and unable to avoid it. Remember how he opened your eyes to see your misery, and not only discovered the all-sufficient remedy, but powerfully determined and enabled you to apply it. And let these past experiences endear him to your souls, and strengthen your dependence on him, for whatever else may be necessary to complete your salvation.

This is the natural tendency of the representation I have given you, and this is the improvement of it that best suits the occasion of our present meeting. The good Shepherd is this day to feed his own sheep, in the fattest part of that pasture which his love hath prepared for them. The ordinance now before us, doth not merely exhibit the riches of his grace, but seals and applies them to each believer in particular, that, having this security superadded to the unchangeable promise and oath of God, they may "have a strong consolation, who have fled for refuge, to lay hold on the hope set before them."

With this view, then, let us approach the table of the Lord, and pray, that this gospel-feast may prove effectual, by his blessing, to confirm our faith, to inflame our love, and to enliven our hope; that, by the nourishment it affords, we may be strengthened to pursue our journey through this wilderness, till, having passed the Jordan of death, and arrived at the heavenly Canaan, faith and hope shall become sight and enjoyment, and love, ever growing with the ages of eternity, shall embrace, with increasing vigor and delight, the good Shepherd, who gave his life for the sheep. *Amen.*

SERMON L.

THE IMMUTABLE PROMISE.

HEBREWS XIII. 5.—"He hath said, I will never leave thee nor forsake thee."

THIS comfortable declaration or promise is introduced by the apostle, to enforce the duty of contentment, to which he had exhorted the Hebrews in the preceding part of the verse. Nothing can be more unbecoming in a child of God, than dissatisfaction with his present condition, or anxiety about his future provision in the world. It is no wonder to see worldly men, whose portion of good things lies wholly upon earth, loading themselves with thick clay, and eagerly grasping every thing which their craving appetites demand. Such persons cannot but be uneasy when they meet with disappointments; because, having nothing desirable in prospect beyond the grave, in losing their present enjoyments they lose their *all.* But the Christian, who knows of a treasure in heaven, a treasure incorruptible in its own nature, and which no fraud nor force can take from him, may and ought to look down, with a holy indifference, upon every thing here below, resigning himself entirely to the disposal of his Heavenly Father, who not only knows what is best for him, but hath likewise obliged himself, by covenant and promise, to make all things work together for the eternal advantage of those who love him and confide in his mercy.

It was this argument which Christ used with his disciples, to dissuade them from an anxious solicitude about their temporal concerns, (Matthew vi. 31.) "Take no thought, saying, What shall we eat? or what shall we drink? or wherewithal shall we be clothed? For after all these things do the Gentiles seek, and your Heavenly Father knoweth that ye have need of all these things. But seek ye first the kingdom of God, and his righteousness; and all these things shall be added unto you." God will support and maintain his own people as long as he has any service for them in this world. He knows all their wants; and as his goodness constantly inclines him, so his power doth at all times enable him, to bestow every needful supply in its season. And can our interest be lodged in better hands? Who that believes this, would choose to be the disposer of his own lot? "The Lord reigneth," says the Psalmist, "let the earth rejoice." And surely they who can say, This God is our God, our Father and our Friend, have cause to rejoice in every condition, and must act very inconsistently with their profession and hopes, if any thing from without can disturb their inward peace and tranquillity. I propose, therefore, in dependence upon divine aid,

First. To show the import of this gracious promise, "I will never leave thee nor forsake thee."

Secondly. I shall inquire who the persons are that may apply the comfort of this promise to themselves.

Thirdly. I shall lay before you some ot those grounds of assurance on which the people of God may depend for the accomplishment of this promise; and then direct you to the practical improvement of the subject.

I BEGIN with the import of the promise itself, "I will never leave thee nor forsake thee." And,

1*st.* It is here supposed, that all other things may forsake us; for in this promise God plainly intends to distinguish himself from the creatures, by claiming this perfection of constancy or unchangeableness, as an attribute peculiar to himself. Vanity is engraved in deep and legible characters upon every thing below the sun. All things on earth are perishing in their own nature; and so fleeting and deceitful, that they who lean upon them, only secure to themselves a more intense degree of pain and vexation; for sooner or later they will slide from under them, and leave nothing in their room, but the disgrace of a foolish choice, and the bitterness of disappointed hope. History affords us innumerable proofs of this. The wisest men in every age have observed and lamented the mutability of all earthly things; and we need only keep our eyes and our ears open, to learn this truth, by some fresh example every day we live.

How often do we see riches take unto themselves wings, and fly away as an eagle towards heaven? What a variety of accidents may suddenly deprive a man of all his substance, and reduce him to the lowest state of poverty and want? A storm at sea or a fire at land will in a few hours consume the labors of many years; and he who, whilst I speak, possesseth plenty of all things, and promiseth himself a long succession of prosperous days, may, before to-morrow's sun, find himself stripped of all his substance, and obliged to depend upon the bounty of others for the common necessaries of life. How many who boasted that their mountian stood strong, have suddenly been thrown down from the highest pinnacle of power and greatness? Even princes, when they least dreamt of it, have been forced to exchange their palace for a prison; and have learnt, by sad experience, that crowns are but tottering emblems of power, and that royalty itself hath no exemption from the vicissitudes of sublunary things. Reputation and friends, health and all bodily advantages, yea reason, with all the endowments of the mind, are so uncertain and mutable, that no man can promise on the possession of them. The fairest character may be sullied with the breath of calumny; our friends may prove false or abandon us through mistake; or, when they are faithful, and in all respects comfortable to us, yet death may snatch them from us one after another, till we are in a manner left solitary in the midst of the earth. Health and strength, and whatever else belongs to the body, are of all things the least durable, and the most subject to change. Life itself is but a vapor, which, for any thing we know, may vanish into air the very next breath we draw. We see frequently also, that the mind, as well as the body, is liable to many sad disasters. In some men, the intellectual powers are so blunted and impaired, that they seem to be almost totally extinguished; and, in others, so strangely disordered, that, instead of being of use to them, they serve only to render them more completely wretched. In a word, our condition upon earth is liable to continual alteration, and there is nothing we can be secure of so much as for one moment. How foolish, then, are they who promise themselves any durable happiness in this world? Such persons may truly be said to build their house upon the sand; and though, perhaps, they may be allowed to raise it to some height, yet, ere long, some sudden unforeseen storm shall lay it in ruins, and bury all their vain expectations under it.

But what I would chiefly observe on this head is, that frequently the people of God are exercised with the severest trials, and meet with the sharpest afflictions while they remain upon earth. For this mutability of the creatures is not the effect of *chance* but of *design*. God thereby designs to render all those inexcusable who choose them for their portion: and when his own children are in danger of being ensnared by them, he pulls them, as it were, with violence out of their hands, that they may be aware of contracting too close an alliance with them in future. He will not suffer them to continue long in so dangerous an error; and he sends the rod to undeceive them: he frequently repeats the stroke, to remind them that they are only sojourners in a strange land, and to quicken their desires for their Father's house above;—for their Father's house, where alone they shall have fulness of joy and pleasures for evermore.

2dly. As the inconstancy of the creatures is here supposed, so this promise necessarily implies, that the presence of God with his people is a sufficient ground of consolation in every state and condition of life. David was sensible of this when he said in the 23d Psalm, "Though I walk through the valley of the shadow of death, I will fear no evil, for thou art with me:" and upon the same principle, the prophet Habakkuk triumphs in the name of the church. "Although the fig-tree shall not blossom, neither shall there be fruit in the vines, the labor of the olive shall fail, and the fields shall yield no meat, the flock shall be cut off from the fold, and there shall be no herd in the stalls; yet will I rejoice in the Lord, I will joy in the God of my salvation."

We read in the book of Daniel, that after Nebuchadnezzar the king had caused Shadrach, Meshech, and Abednego, to be cast into the burning fiery furnace, he was astonished, and rose up in haste, and said unto his counsellors, "Did we not cast three men bound into the midst of the fire? And lo! I see four men loose, walking in the midst of the fire, and they have no hurt; and the form of the fourth is like the Son of God." Is there a man who reads this passage, that does not prefer the condition of these captives to all the splendors of the Babylonish throne? How little does the trembling monarch seem, though surrounded with his counsellors? How glorious do the three young Jews appear, whilst walking amidst flames with their God and Saviour? How would they rejoice in this exalted privilege? And yet, my brethren, all the saints who have God really present with them, although they cannot see him with their bodily eyes, have equal cause to rejoice in the midst of tribulation. For if God be with them, then he is with them who is infinitely wise, who is perfectly acquainted with all their wants, and can never be at a loss to know what is good for them. He is with them who is infinitely powerful, and can easily perform whatever his unerring wisdom shall suggest. He is with them who is perfectly good, yea goodness itself; who is always disposed to employ his wisdom in contriving, and his power in executing, whatever is necessary for their interest and happiness. Yea, he is with them who hath already bestowed on them the greatest of all blessings, even Jesus Christ his unspeakable gift; and as the apostle reasons, "If God spared not his own Son, but delivered him up for us all, how shall he not with him also freely give us all things?" And is not the presence of such a God sufficient for the comfort of his people at all times? Who would mourn the loss of a taper, who enjoys the light of the sun? All the creatures are nothing without God; whereas he is all in all: "In his favor is life, and his loving kindness is better than life." Even Balaam was constrained to confess this truth in the presence of Balak (Numbers xxiii. 23.) "Surely," says he, "there is no enchantment against Jacob, nor any divination againt Israel; for the Lord his God is with him, and the shout of a king is among them." If the happiness of Solomon's courtiers excited the admiration of the queen of Sheba, because they had access to the presence of so wise and magnificent a king, how inconceivably more happy are the friends, nay, the children of the King of kings, who have the infinitely perfect and all sufficient Jehovah continually near to them? Which leads me to observe, in the

3*d* place, That the constant presence of God with his people is the blessing expressly contained in his promise, "I will never leave thee nor forsake thee." All other things may forsake you. Riches may take wings and fly away; friends may desert you, or they may die; your reputation may be blasted; your health and strength may fail and decay; yea, memory, judgment, and all the faculties of your mind, may be weakened or destroyed: "But I will never leave you, I will never forsake you;" my friendship is unchangeable; "And whom I love, I love to the end." All this, saith the apostle, God hath said; but he doth not tell us when or where he hath said it, because he hath said it so often, and upon such various occasions, that it is to be met with almost every where in Scripture, and in a manner sounds through the whole revelation of his will. And indeed I cannot illustrate this head better, than by reciting some of those passages where this general and comprehensive promise is particularly applied for the comfort of God's people, under the various trials and afflictions to which they are exposed in this world. All who are acquainted with their Bibles, will remember to have read such passages as these: "When thou passest through the waters, I will be with thee; and through the rivers, they shall not overflow thee; when thou walkest through the fire, thou shalt not be burnt, neither shall the flame kindle upon thee; for I am the Lord thy God." "When the poor and needy seek water, and there is none, and their tongue faileth for thirst, I the Lord will hear them, I the God of Israel will not forsake them. I will open rivers in high places, and fountains in the midst of the valleys: I will make the wilderness a pool of water, and the dry land springs of water." "The Lord will be a refuge for the oppressed, a refuge in time of trouble." "The Lord will not suffer the soul of the righteous to famish." "He shall dwell on high, his defence shall be the munition of rocks. Bread shall be given him, his waters shall be sure." "The Lord will strengthen him upon the bed of languishing. Thou wilt make all his bed in his sickness." "A father of the fatherless, a judge of the widows, is God in his holy habitation."—"Fear not," saith he, "for I am with thee; be not dismayed, for I am thy God. I will strengthen thee; yea, I will help thee; yea, I will uphold thee with the right hand of my righteousness."

I might quote many other texts, where God promiseth to be with his people in every case of distress that can be supposed; but I shall have said enough to give you some notion of the vast extent of this comfortable promise, when I have added, that it reacheth beyond the grave, and comprehends no less than eternity itself. As God will not leave his people in life, as he will not forsake them at death; so he will at last receive them into glory, and make them to dwell for ever in his immediate presence. But who are his people? Who are the happy persons that may apply the comfort of this promise to themselves? This is the

Second thing I proposed to inquire into.

And, in general, this promise is addressed to believers in Christ Jesus, and to them only, exclusive of all others; for this is the order which God hath established. He first gives us his Son; and when this "unspeakable gift" is thankfully received, then, together with him, he freely gives us all other things." Men may fancy themselves in good terms with God upon account of some moral qualifications of which they are possessed; and I greatly suspect, that many among us are ruined by this mistake: but I am not afraid to affirm, that no moral qualifications whatever can reconcile a sinner to God, or entitle him to plead any one promise from the beginning of the Bible to the end of it. The reason is plain: All the blessings promised in the gospel were purchased by Christ with the price of his own blood. To him they belong of right; for in regard of "his humbling himself, and becoming obedient unto death, even the death of the cross, God hath highly exalted him," and "hath put all things under his feet, and hath given him to be head over all things to the church." Accordingly Christ himself says (Matth. xi. 27.) "All things are delivered unto me of my Father;" and (Matth. xxviii. 18.) "All power is given unto me in heaven and in earth." Every good and perfect gift, therefore, must be conveyed to us through his hands; and it is not only a vain, but I may even call it an impious attempt, to address God immediately for those blessings which he hath already given to his Son, and committed to his disposal as King of Zion, for the behoof of his true and spiritual subjects. All the promises in Scripture must necessarily be explained in a consistency with this great fundamental truth: and when the persons to whom they are addressed are described by any moral qualification, such as righteousness, mercifulness, and the like, it must always be understood, that they are previously in a state of friendship with God; and that these qualifications are mentioned, not as the terms of their acceptance with him, but only as the fruits and evidences of that faith which unites them to Christ, in whom all the promises are "Yea and Amen."

Would any then know, whether they may apply to themselves the gracious and comfortable promise in my text, they must first of all try their relation to Christ. If they are still unacquainted with this great and only Mediator between God and man; if they have never fled to him as their city of refuge, nor accepted of him as the "Lord their righteousness and their strength;" it is certain that they have no part nor lot in this matter. For nothing can be more express than those words of John the Baptist, (John iii. 36.) "He that believeth on the Son hath everlasting life; but he that believeth not the Son, shall not see life, but the wrath of God abideth on him." Whereas, on the other hand, if, from a deep conviction of your guilt and misery, you have cordially accepted the Lord Jesus Christ for all the purposes of a Saviour; if you can say without any known guile, that, renouncing all other grounds of confidence, you depend on him alone for pardon and peace, for grace and glory, and every good thing; if you have the evidence of your faith in Christ, and of your union to him, which arises from the sanctifying power of the Holy Ghost on your tempers and your lives, determining you to deny ungodliness and worldly lusts, and to live soberly, and righteously, and godly in the world; then are you the friends of God, and may lawfully consider yourselves as the persons to whom he hath said, "I will never leave thee nor forsake thee." And, for your farther encouragement, I shall now go on to the

Third general head, and briefly suggest to you some of those grounds of assurance upon which you may confidently rely for the accomplishment of this promise. Consider, then,

1*st*. Who he is that hath said this. "He is not man, that he should lie, nor the son of man, that he should repent." These are the words of God himself, who is incapable of deceit, and with whom "there is no variableness, neither shadow of turning."—"He is the rock, his work is perfect, for all his ways are judgment, a God of truth, and without iniquity, just and right is he."—"The mountains shall depart, and the hills be removed; but my kindness shall not depart from thee, neither shall the covenant of my peace be removed, saith the Lord, that hath mercy upon thee." And is not the word, the promise of such a God, a sufficient ground of trust? Yea, he hath not only said it, but he hath also sworn it. "For God being willing more abundantly to show to the heirs of promise the immutability of his counsel, hath confirmed it by an oath, that by two immutable things, in which it was impossible for God to lie, they might have a strong consolation, who have fled for refuge to lay hold on the hope set before them." And can our souls desire a better security? What can establish our faith, if this doth not establish it?

2dly. Believers in Christ Jesus are the children of God, adopted into his family, and beautified with his image: and this is another pledge of his gracious promise; for surely he will never abandon his own offspring. "Can a mother forget her sucking child," saith God, "that she should not have compassion on the son of her womb? Yea, she may forget, yet will not I forget thee." The affection and tenderness of an earthly parent are but faint resemblances of God's paternal love. In him love is an infinite overflowing fountain of beneficence. And then his love is as permanent as it is extensive. He is always in one mind, and therefore can never leave nor forsake his people.

3dly. The constant intercession of our glorious High-Priest effectually secures the accomplishment of this promise. By his death he obtained the Holy Spirit to dwell in his people, and to abide with them. This he intimated to his disciples, for their comfort and encouragement, when they were about to lose his bodily presence, (John xvi. 7.) "It is expedient for you that I go away; for if I go not away, the Comforter will not come unto you; but if I depart, I will send him unto you." And, in another place, "I will pray the Father, and he shall give you another Comforter, even the Spirit of truth, who shall abide with you;"—who shall abide with you, and that not for a season only, but "for ever."

With what tenderness did he recommend them to his heavenly Father, in his last intercessory prayer upon earth, (John xvii. 11.) "And now I am no more in the world, but these are in the world. Holy Father, keep through thine own name those whom thou hast given me." Is it possible, then, that God should forsake those for whom his well-beloved Son pleads with such earnestness and affection? Especially if it be considered, in the

4th and *last* place, That his own glory is interested in the accomplishment of this gracious promise. I mean that glory which consists in making effectual the purposes of his grace towards those whom he hath chosen out of the world. For were he to leave or forsake his people, they must fall a prey to their spiritual enemies, and yield to the adversary of God and man, that triumph which he hath sought from the beginning. That apostate spirit never deserts his purpose of ensnaring and destroying the souls of men. He is ever on the watch to seize them in a defenceless moment; so that were God to leave them without his protection, they would fall easy victims to his artifices. And will he suffer his purposes thus to be baffled by his declared foe? It cannot be; and therefore he never will leave nor forsake his people.

I shall now conclude this discourse with a short practical improvement, addressed to two different classes of people. And the

1st Sort of persons to whom I will address myself, are those who are yet in a state of alienation from God. It is possible, that at present you may not see the value of this promise which I have been unfolding. You have never, perhaps, been sensible of the vanity of earthly enjoyments; or if you have been weary of some of them, you promise yourselves a permanent satisfaction in others. Alas! this is a delusive expectation; for happiness never can be extracted from the creatures. God hath pronounced an irreversible decree of vanity upon them all. Ye are therefore pursuing what will for ever flee from you;—ye are feeding upon mere husks, which can neither nourish nor satisfy you. But though you should even be contented with this poor and empty portion, yet you cannot always enjoy it; for what will you do when every earthly prop is tottering and ready to sink under you? What will ye do at that period, when neither riches, nor power, nor friends, nor any thing that this world affords, will be able to give you the least relief? Let me therefore entreat you speedily to seek the favor of that God who is the only adequate portion of an immortal soul. Listen to that kind expostulation and advice, (Isa. lv. 2, 3.) "Wherefore do you spend money for that which is not bread? and your labor for that which satisfieth not? Hearken diligently unto me, and eat ye that which is good, and let your soul delight itself in fatness. Incline your ear, and come unto me; hear, and your souls shall live: and I will make an everlasting covenant with you, even the sure mercies of David." But I now address myself, in the

2*d* Place, to those happy persons who are in a state of friendship with God. To you then I say, that this gracious promise should both excite and encourage you to steadfastness in the way of religion. "For if God be with you, who can be against you?" "Be strong then in the Lord, and in the power of his might." All necessary aid is provided for you in the tenor of the well-ordered covenant, and will not fail to be imparted to you in the time of your need. Your help is laid on one who is mighty to save, and who is no less willing than able to support you under all your trials, "Wherefore, gird up the loins of your mind, be sober, and hope to the end." But the principal improvement which you ought to make of this promise, is to put away from your minds all dissatisfaction with your present condition, or anxiety about your future provision in the world. God hath charged himself with the care of providing for you while you are here. He hath not, indeed, promised you an exemption from poverty, hardships, or afflictions; but he hath assured you, that these things are no tokens of his displeasure; nay, on the contrary, that they are intended for your greatest good, and that he is never nearer to his people than when they are in the furnace of affliction. What abundant reason then have you to be contented with whatever lot he is pleased to appoint you in the world, and to look beyond all the momentary distresses you now suffer, to that incorruptible inheritance which is reserved for you in heaven. "Let your conversation then be without covetousness; and be content with such things as ye have: for he hath said, I will never leave thee nor forsake thee."

SERMON LI.

Preached on a Day of Thanksgiving, after the dispensation of the Lord's Supper.

CRUCIFIXION OF THE FLESH.

GALATIANS v. 24.—"And they that are CHRIST'S have crucified the flesh, with the affections and lusts."

No man, who hath experienced the deceitfulness of his own heart, will think the subject of this text improper for the present occasion. It is true this day is set apart for thanksgiving; and with the highest pleasure would I enter on the delightful theme of divine love and condescension, which shall employ the praises of the redeemed through endless ages. But a solicitous concern, that your joy may be well founded, hath induced me to propose to you a strict examination of yourselves, whether you have indeed an interest in him, through whom all favor and goodwill to sinners is conveyed. The text furnisheth us with an infallible rule to direct our judgment in this inquiry. "They that are Christ's," not all who are called by his name, but they who are united to him, as the branches are united to the vine, who are governed by his Spirit, and have a right to the benefits of his purchase, are distinguished by *this* attainment, "They have crucified the flesh with the affections and lusts."

In discoursing on these words, I propose,

First, To show what is meant by crucifying the flesh, with the affections and lusts.

Secondly, To show, that it is the distinguishing character and the real attainment of all who are Christ's, to crucify the flesh, with the affections and lusts. And then to conclude with an improvement suited to the occasion of our present meeting.

I BEGIN with inquiring what is meant by "crucifying the flesh, with the affections and lusts." By "the flesh," we are to understand the corrupt nature of man; and by "the affections and lusts," those depraved appetites which maintain their power within us, until the renewing grace of God implant in us those seeds of holiness, by which the image of God is formed in our soul. When man came first from the hands of his Maker, his reason, pure and uncorrupted, was the governing principle of his mind. But by transgressing the original commandment, and eating the forbidden fruit, in compliance with a mean corporeal appetite, the sensitive part of his nature obtained that dominion or predominancy which it still maintains in every unrenewed man. Accordingly, we find our natural condition opposed in Scripture, to our regenerated state, under the metaphorical expressions of *flesh* and *spirit.* "That which is born of the flesh is flesh; and that which is born of the Spirit is spirit." The meaning is plainly this: the temper and dispositions which we bring with us into the world by ordinary generation, are, since the fall, carnal and depraved; whereas the temper and dispositions which we receive by the regeneration of the Holy Ghost, are, like their original, spiritual and holy. The same idea is expressed in the 17th verse of this chapter; where it is said, "the flesh lusteth against the spirit, and the spirit against the flesh; and these two are contrary the one to the other." It appears, then, that by the "flesh, with the affections and lusts," we are to understand the corrupt state of man's mind since the first transgression, and all those depraved dispositions and affections which naturally flow from the corrupt principle, and which incline us to seek happiness from earthly things, independent of God. We learn too what is meant by "crucifying the lusts and affections of the flesh;" namely, that this natural depravity of mind is subdued; that the carnal principle, like a crucified malefactor, languishes and decays; until, by degrees, gracious or renewed habits are formed in us, which at last obtain the full possession of our minds.

What hath been said may suffice to give a plain and intelligible explanation of the terms in the text; and to pursue the metaphor farther, would neither be profitable to you nor agreeable to myself. The words thus explained give us a very distinguishing character of a true Christian. He is one who, by the grace of God, hath obtained the victory over his corrupt appetites and inclinations. He is in a great measure rescued from the ruins of the fall, and is no longer a servant of sin, that he should obey it in the lusts thereof. "He hath put off, concerning the former conversation, the old man, which is corrupt according to the deceitful lusts; and being renewed in the spirit of his mind, hath put on the new man, which after God is created in righteousness and true holiness."—"The law of the spirit of life, which is in Christ Jesus, hath made him free from the law of sin and death." Conscience, long dethroned by imperious passions, hath reassumed its authority; and all the faculties of his mind, purified and exalted, unite in the pursuit of spiritual enjoyments.

And now, my brethren, let me entreat you to stop your ears for a little against the suggestions of self-love, and let conscience bear testimony, whether you have indeed a claim to this character. Alas! if you have no claim to it, this can be no day of thanksgiving to you. If you have adventured to approach the table of the Lord with all your unmortified lusts about you, ye have been guilty of the body and blood of Christ; ye have sealed the sentence of your own condemnation; and lamentation becomes you better than the voice of praise. You may, perhaps, complain of this as a severe and heavy message; but dare any of you say that it is a message without a warrant? Shall I speak peace to those to whom God hath not spoken peace? Shall I soothe you with false comforts, which might lead you down to the grave with a lie in your right hand? No; I remember too well the woe pronounced against the prophet "who dealeth falsely, and healeth the wound of the daughter of God's people slightly." I should not wish to be an eternal subject of imprecation to hopeless souls, which I should well deserve to be, if I spoke any other language to you than what I now speak.

But you have as yet no cause to complain: I have indeed set before you the danger, but I have not said you must despair. On the contrary, my only object is to prevent your everlasting despair, by awakening your fears ere it be too late, and the door of mercy be shut against you. That door is still open, and the call is yet, "To-day hear his voice." O then harden not your hearts against conviction. Decline not an impartial scrutiny into your real state. Let this passage of Scripture inform you, whether you indeed belong to Christ. If you do possess the marks of those who are his, take the comfort of your sincerity, and give God the glory. But if the issue of the inquiry should turn out otherwise, O beware of resting in this dreadful condition. Give no sleep to your eyes, nor slumber to your eye-lids, till you have secured an interest in that blood of sprinkling which cleanseth from all sin.

Need I enter on a detail of those lusts and affections which flow from a corrupt and depraved principle within? "The works of the flesh," saith the apostle, (at the 19th verse of this chapter) are "manifest; which are these, adultery, fornication, uncleanness, lasciviousness, idolatry, witchcraft, hatred, variance, emulations, wrath, strife, seditions, heresies, envyings, murders, drunkenness, revellings, and such like; of the which I tell you before, as I have also told you in time past, that they which do such things shall not inherit the kingdom of God."

I am sensible, that, after the recital of so black a catalogue of crimes, the most of you will already have acquitted yourselves of such enormous degrees of guilt. And I am afraid, that this general acquittal from the charge of heinous transgressions, lulls the consciences of many into a fatal security. I will not go so far as to say, that it were better for the unconverted sinner, that his conscience could charge him with some of these glaring iniquities, although our Saviour's saying seems to imply as much, viz., That the publicans and harlots go into the kingdom of heaven before the scribes and pharisees. All that I assert is, that you ought not too hastily to conclude that the flesh is crucified with its affections and lusts, merely because your lives have not been spotted with any of those gross and scandalous sins. In these days of light and knowledge, Satan doth not find it for his interest to push men to the extremities of vice. He rather endeavors to keep the garrison in peace, by blunting the edge of conviction with the fair shows of outward decency and formality.

Be persuaded then to go deeper into your inquiry. Search the very inmost corners of your hearts. Put the authority of God in one scale, and the interests of the flesh in another, and see which of the two weighs heavier in your affections. You frequent the church, you attend on ordinances, and perform the external parts of religion with an apparent relish and alacrity. All this is good; but beware of building too much on it. Consider that these observances do not in any great degree thwart the interests of the flesh. The laws and customs of the land favor you; your estates are not thereby impaired, nor your lives endangered; nor is your reputation hurt, but rather advanced. But suppose the case to be otherwise, and let your hearts give the answer. Would you persist in the same course at all risks, though your estates were exposed to confiscation, though your names were to be branded with every term of reproach that malice could devise; yea, though all the engines of torture lay in the road of duty? Would no prospect of gain, however secure from human discovery, tempt you to encroach on the divine rules of justice and equity? Can you bless them that curse you, and render good for evil, and forgive the most galling injuries, even when Providence puts your enemies in your power? Did the objects of criminal desire not only tempt but solicit you; were you favored with every circumstance of time and place, could you check the career of passion, with Joseph's reflection, "How can I do this great wickedness, and sin against God?" These, indeed, are sure signs that the flesh is crucified with the affections and lusts. But if, on the contrary, the fear of man's censure or punishment would turn you aside from the practice of your duty, if the prospect of secret gain could tempt you to lie or cheat or dissemble; if any injury appears too great to be forgiven, or any sensual appetite too importunate to be denied; in a word, if any temptation, be its circumstances what they will, would prevail on you to indulge yourselves in the deliberate omission of any known duty, or in the practice of any known sin; then, whatever your pretences are, the flesh, with its affections and lusts, is not yet crucified in you. But do not mistake me, as if I meant to assert, that none have crucified the flesh but those who are perfect in holiness. No; the righteous man falleth seven times a day, and riseth again. Nay, there is not a just man upon earth that doth good, and sinneth not. And therefore I speak not of those false steps to which the best are liable through the remainders of corruption; but of known and habitual sins, committed with the full bent and inclination of the will. These plainly betray the predominancy of the flesh, with its affections and lusts; and show, that the person who is under the dominion of them, has no just or scriptural claim to an interest in Christ. For a worldly Christian, or a carnal Christian, or a dishonest Christian, are as gross contradictions in terms as an infidel Christian. And this naturally leads me to the

Second thing proposed; which was to show that it is the distinguishing character and the real attainment of all who are Christ's, to crucify the flesh, with the affections and lusts. This is so much the uniform language of the New Testament, that one should hardly think it required a proof. The great lesson which our Lord taught his disciples was expressed in these words: "If any man will come after me, let him deny himself, and take up his cross and follow me." This he repeated on various occasions, as a subject that ought to employ their constant attention. "He that taketh not up his cross and followeth after me, is not worthy of me."—"If any man come after me, and hate not his father and mother, and wife and children, and brethren and sisters," those nearest and dearest relations according to the flesh, "yea, and his own life also," when the preservation of it becomes inconsistent with the duty he owes to God, "he cannot be my disciple." And again, "Whosoever he be of you that forsaketh not all that he hath," namely, habitually in affection, and actually too, when God calls him to it, "he cannot be my disciple." These are the permanent, the invariable laws of Christ's spiritual kingdom, and are equally binding on us, as on those to whom they were originally addressed. For had our Lord ever intended to relax or mitigate them in any degree, he would certainly have done it in favor of his first disciples, when his church was yet in its infant state, and therefore stood in need of greater indulgence. But these seemingly hard sayings express the true spirit of Christianity, and afford the most convincing proof of its divine original. Man fell by seeking himself, and must therefore be raised in the way of self-denial. He forfeited his innocence and happiness by hearkening to the solicitation of a fleshly appetite; and, before he can regain happiness, the flesh must be crucified with the affections and lusts.

Accordingly, we find that our Saviour's meaning was well understood by his immediate followers; and their practice is the best commentary on his injunctions. What he recommended, they labored to attain. Thus Paul writes to the Corinthians, "I keep under my body, and bring it into subjection, lest when I have preached to others, I myself should be a cast-away." The remainders of corruption within him, made him cry out with all the emphasis of distress, "O wretched man that I am, who shall deliver me from the body of this death?" Nay, so sensible was he of the importance and necessity of this deliverance, that, as he expresseth it himself, "He counted all things but loss and dung;" first, "That he might win Christ, and be found in him not having his own righteousness, but that which is through the faith of Christ, the righteousness which is of God by faith." And next, "That he might know Christ" experimentally, "and the power of his resurrection, and the fellowship of his sufferings, being made conformable unto his death." Nor was this only his *wish;* we find also that it was his real attainment. "I am crucified," says he, "with Christ: nevertheless, I live; yet not I, but Christ liveth in me: and the life which I now live in the flesh, I live by the faith of the Son of God, who loved me, and gave himself for me." "And God forbid that I should glory, save in the cross of our Lord Jesus Christ, by whom the world is crucified unto me, and I unto the world." Neither was Paul singular in this. It appears to have been the common attainment of all true Christians in his time. For it is spoken of in my text as the badge of Christianity, the very thing which distinguished Christians from all other men. "They that are Christ's have crucified the flesh, with the affections and lusts." I have given a recital of these passages of Scripture, as they serve to explain one another: and I hope that when they are compared together, and duly considered, they will appear to be a sufficient demonstration, that none whose flesh is not crucified, with its affections and lusts, can, with a Scriptural warrant, lay claim to an interest in Christ.

Thus have I endeavored to explain what is meant by "crucifying the flesh, with the affections and lusts:" and have shown you, that this is the actual attainment of every true Christian. Allow me now to conclude this discourse with a practical improvement of the subject. From what has been said, then, we learn in the

1*st* place, What is the true nature of our holy religion. It is not a mere bodily exercise, consisting only in external ceremonies or observances. Earthly rulers can ask no more but an outward homage: but the Searcher of hearts challengeth the sincere adoration of the inner man. He who is a Spirit must be worshipped in spirit and in truth. So that to attend the church, to partake of religious ordinances, and to perform the external duties of religion, will be of no avail in the sight of God, unless those outward services proceed from a heart warmed with his love, in which every usurping lust, that would share his place, is vanquished and dethroned. To be a real Christian, therefore, is not so easy an attainment as many seem to imagine. Flesh and blood must be wrestled with and overcome; "for flesh and blood cannot inherit the kingdom of heaven." Every gratification that is contrary to the holiness of the divine nature, although dear to us as a right hand or a right eye, must be denied. Nay, the very inclination to vicious indulgences must be subdued, otherwise our abstaining from the outward acts of them will be of no avail. It is the heart that God requires; and if we deny him this, we can give him nothing that is worthy of his acceptance.

An inoffensive outward deportment may soothe your consciences, and prevent the uneasy feelings of remorse, but will not save you from final ruin. The very interest of the flesh may make a man forbear disgraceful sins, and may, for a time, chain up, without weakening, the vigor of corruption. You may be possessed of many amiable qualities, by which you deserve well of society, and yet be total strangers to that character of real Christians which is given in this text. If temporary good impressions, or restraints of the flesh for a season, would amount to that character, then Felix, who trembled under conviction, and Herod, who did many things in consequence of the Baptist's preaching, had been real Christians. If the estimable qualities of social life were a proof that Christianity had its full effect on the mind, then the young ruler, who had kept the second table of the law from his youth upwards, would have had an unreserved approbation from our Lord. But Felix and Herod relapsed under the dominion of their lusts; and through the love of this world, the young ruler fell short of the kingdom of heaven. In the

2*nd* place, From what hath been said, let each of us be prevailed on to try how matters stand with himself. You see that it is not a point to be lightly taken for granted, that a man hath a real interest in Christ. I have already mentioned several things under my first head of discourse, which may serve as hints to direct you in this trial. All that I have further to beg of you is, that you would judge yourselves impartially, as those who expect a judgment to come. Try every ground of hope upon which you have hitherto rested; let every rotten pillar be removed, or else the whole building, however glorious in appearance, will shortly fall to the ground. Self-love may, for a season, blind your eyes; but remember, that it will throw no veil over that impartial judgment which will overtake you at the bar of God. Compare, then, your actions and dispositions with that holy and spiritual law which flatters no man; and then, if conscience gives an unbiassed judgment, I have little doubt that numbers in this assembly will discover, that "the flesh, with its affections and lusts," is not only alive, but in full vigor. Nay, the very best will find cause to conclude, that the corrupt principle is not yet crucified as it ought to be.

As for those of the first class now mentioned, if the text itself does not furnish them with a sufficient motive for crucifying the flesh, I despair of being able to offer any other which will be more powerful. I might tell you, how mean it is to let sense give law to reason, and to prefer the earthly tabernacle to its immortal inhabitant. I might assure you that you are serving an ungrateful master, whom you can never satisfy; that, while you feed one lust, you must starve another, whose importunate cravings will destroy the relish of your imagined happiness. I might tell you, that the flesh must ere long be reduced to rottenness and dust, and be buried under ground, that it may be no offence to the living. But what are all these arguments compared with that motive which is implied in the text, that, unless you crucify the flesh, you do not belong to Christ; and if you have no interest in Christ, God is a consuming fire? So that this furnisheth me with an address, to the same purpose with what a brave officer made to his soldiers in the day of battle, "Unless ye kill your enemies," said he, "they will kill you." In like manner, I say unto you, Unless ye crucify the flesh, it will be your everlasting ruin. "For if ye live after the flesh, ye shall die."

As for you who are mourning over the remainders of corruption, and struggling to get free from them, I know that you will require no motives to engage you to go on in this opposition to the carnal principle. I shall therefore only offer you a few directions, with which I will now conclude.

Keep a strict watch over your senses. Let nothing enter into the soul by these avenues without a strict examination. Avoid with the utmost caution all those things which may inflame your passions, and accustom yourselves to contradict them in their first tendencies to evil. A spark may easily be quenched, which, after it hath kindled a flame, will baffle all your industry. Improve that holy ordinance, which you have been celebrating, to this salutary purpose. The contemplation of a crucified Saviour, is an excellent mean to assist you in crucifying the flesh. When your appetites solicit any unlawful indulgence, remember him who had not even the common accommodations of nature. When your flesh requires ease and pleasure, think of him who pleased not, or minded not himself, but for your sakes submitted to hunger and thirst, weariness and watching, pain and reproach, and at last to an ignominious death. When riches inflame your desires, reflect on the history of Jesus, "who, though he was rich, for your sakes became poor, that ye through his poverty might be made rich." When the desire of applause, or the fear of censure from man, tempt you to desert the path of duty, then remember him, who for you made himself of no reputation, gave his head to be crowned with thorns, and his body to be arrayed with the garb of derision, and was suspended on the cross in the company of malefactors. In all these views, let your eyes be directed to Jesus, the author and finisher of your faith. Above all, depend much on the grace of God, and pour out your souls in fervent supplication for the Spirit of Promise, by whose assistance alone you can mortify the deeds of the body, and crucify the flesh, with its affections and lusts. Principles of philosophy may restrain our evil passions; but nothing less than the Omnipotent power of divine grace can overcome them. Plead, therefore, earnestly, that he who is now ascended up on high, and hath received gifts for men, may grant you every needful supply in this difficult warfare; that so when you have fought the good fight, and overcome your enemies, both within and without you, you may be publicly acknowledged and acquitted in the day of judgment, and made perfectly happy in the full enjoyment of God for ever. *Amen.*

SERMON LII.

THE CONTRADICTING WITNESSES.

PSALM IV. 6, 7.—"There be many that say, Who will show us any good? LORD, lift thou up the light of thy countenance upon us. Thou hast put gladness in my heart, more than in the time that their corn and their wine increased."

THE chief distinction between a child of God and a man of the world, lies in the prevailing tendency of their desires. Both of them are engaged in the pursuit of happiness. But the one aims at nothing higher than the present gratification of his appetites, while the other rises above this world, and aspires at the supreme felicity of his immortal nature. The one seeks information from every quarter concerning the object of his pursuit; the other asks the blessing directly from the Giver of all good. The one seeks a happiness separated from God: the whole earth, without the light of God's countenance, would appear to the other a barren wilderness, and a place of exile. I propose, in discoursing on this subject,

First, To make a few remarks on the Psalmist's description of these opposite characters.

Secondly, To illustrate the two following propositions which naturally arise from the text, namely, That worldly men have little cause to rejoice in the temporal advantages which they possess; and that the light of God's countenance is sufficient to gladden the heart of a saint in all circumstances whatsoever.

The illustration of these particulars will give rise to a practical improvement of the subject. Let us,

First, Attend to the description of worldly men in the first part of the 6th verse, "There be many that say, Who will show us any good?" It is obvious, in the

1*st* place, That this question betrays a great degree of inward dissatisfaction and perplexity. They speak like men who have no relish for what they possess, and who are utterly at a loss to what hand to turn to for enjoyment. They do not ask, Who will show us the *chief good?* But, "Who will show us *any good?*" any thing to fill up the craving vacuity of our minds: a plain intimation that hitherto they have been miserably disappointed in their pursuits, and that at the time of the question, they cannot find any thing in their lot that deserves the name of good. They are unacquainted with happiness, though they have been always in search of it, and neither know wherein it consists, nor how it is to be obtained. It deserves our notice,

2*dly*. That the only good which they inquire for is some present sensible enjoyment, which may be pointed out to the eye of sense, and may be immediately laid hold of. "Who will *show* us any good?" They are strangers to the operation of that faith, which is "the substance of things hoped for, and the evidence of things not seen." They look not "at the things which are unseen and eternal;" their views are confined within the narrow limits of this present life; and they covet no other portion than they suppose may be found in the world of sense. It may be observed,

3*dly*, That they make no discrimination of the objects which they seek after. *Any good* will be welcome to them; let it be good food, or good clothing; a good estate by lawful means, or a good estate by any means whatever; a good bargain in business, or a good booty by theft or plunder: no matter what it is, provided it gives them pleasure in the mean time, or relieves them from the irksome labor of thinking on themselves, and on the great end for which they were made. Once more, in the

4*th* place, You observe, that amidst all their dissatisfaction with their present state, and their eager desires after something better, they do not turn their thoughts at all to God, but seem rather determined to banish the remembrance of him from their minds. They seek counsel from others, but none from him: they inquire at weak and erring mortals like themselves, but they neither ask wisdom nor grace from God.

Such is the representation which the Psalmist gives us of the temper and of the language of worldly men. He further tells us, that the character of which he gives this description was a common one in his time: "There be many that say, Who will show us any good?" And it is but too apparent, that multitudes of men do still exhibit the same temper. They have no relish for spiritual and divine enjoyments; their only care is, "What they shall eat, and what they shall drink, and wherewithal they shall be clothed."—"They labor abundantly for the meat which perisheth, but not at all for that meat which endureth unto everlasting life." And though they meet with repeated disappointments in every new experiment; yet instead of seeking after happiness where it is alone to be found, they still renew the fruitless search among the creatures around them, and cry out with as much keenness as ever, "Who will show us any worldly good?"

Let us now turn our eyes to a different object, and consider the temper of a child of God, as it is beautifully described by the Psalmist. Whilst others say, "Who will show us any good?" the language of his heart is, "Lord, lift thou upon me the light of thy countenance." He, too, seeks what is good; for the desire of happiness is common to all. But you will observe,

1*st*, That it is not *any* good that will satisfy him: he cannot feed upon husks; it is a real and substantial good that he seeks after. Nay, it is the chief good. He disdains the thought of having any thing less than this for the portion of his soul. He knows that all other sources of enjoyment are no better than "broken cisterns, which can hold no water;" adapted indeed to supply the wants of the body, but in no respect suited to the immortal spirit, either as the objects of its choice, or the sources of its happiness. And as nothing can satisfy him but a real and permanent good, so we find,

2*dly*, That he knows where that good is to be found. He has no need to solicit information from every one he meets. He knows that the favor of God, and the sense of his loving kindness, are the only sources of true happiness. Here therefore he fixeth his choice, and is perfectly satisfied that he is right in doing so.

The worldly mind is in a state of perpetual fluctuation. Having no determinate object in view it runs wild in pursuit of every delusive image of good; and when disappointed in one object, only feels a more intense desire to seek its gratification in another.

But the enlightened mind seeth vanity engraved in deep and legible characters, on all things below the sun; and therefore looks beyond and above them for its portion, saying with the devout Psalmist, "Whom have I in heaven but thee? and there is none upon earth whom I desire beside thee. My flesh and my heart faileth; but God is the strength of my heart, and my portion for ever." I observe, in the

3*d* place, That a child of God goes directly to God himself, and begs the blessing from him. He loses no time in wandering among the creatures, or in making experiments of sensual pleasure; but takes the shortest road to the object he pursues. He flies to the arms of his father, and implores that he would smile on him, and grant him his salvation. Sensible at the same time of his unworthiness, he claims nothing as a debt; but what he asks, he prays for as a free unmerited gift, fetching all his arguments from his mercy, and pleading with him for his own name's sake, "O Lord, lift thou upon me the light of thy countenance." Once more, in the

4*th* place, It deserves our notice, that the Psalmist, in the name of all the godly, useth this prayer in direct opposition to the carnal language of worldly men, who are continually crying, "Who will show us any good?" Hereby intimating to us, that a child of God can relish no sweetness in any inferior good, till he be assured of the divine favor; and that when this great blessing is obtained, nothing amiss can come to him. Even amidst the abundance of outward things, he mourns and languisheth, as long as he apprehends God to be at a distance from him. And no sooner doth he behold his reconciled countenance, than he forgets every outward calamity, and can rejoice in the lowest state of poverty and distress.

In a word, to the spiritual man the favor of God is the one thing needful. As to other things, which may be either good or bad, as they are used, he dares not be peremptory in his choice; "For who knoweth what is good for man in this life?" But the favor of his God he cannot want. Here all his desires centre, and here he hath treasured up all the wishes of his heart.

Having thus considered the Psalmist's description of these two opposite characters in the text, let us now proceed,

Secondly, To illustrate the propositions which arise from this comparison. The

First which I mentioned was, That worldly men have little cause to rejoice in the temporal advantages which they possess.

Stretch your imaginations to the utmost; fancy to yourselves a man raised above all his fellows, enjoying every thing that his heart can wish, obeyed and honored by all around him; let luxury furnish out his house and table; let prosperity attend his steps and crown his undertakings with glory. Add to these advantages, if you will, the splendid titles of king and hero; and when you have finished the gaudy picture, say, what doth the value of it amount to?

1*st*. May not all these outward things consist with present misery of the person who possesseth them? May not the man who hath reached the summit of earthly grandeur be the wretched slave of his own passions, and suffer all the torments of a diseased mind? Who have, in fact, held the most complaining language on the subject of human life? Have not those who have drunk deepest of the cup of prosperity, and whose minds, satiated with pleasure, have become the prey of spleen and disappointment? Unless, therefore, we can finish the description of the prosperous man, by saying, that his soul is as flourishing as his body, and that his eternal interest is as well secured as his temporal advantages seem to be, all that we have supposed him to possess must go for nothing. He is indeed more sumptuously miserable than any of his fellow-creatures, but cannot be allowed to have the least reasonable cause of joy.

God seeth not as man seeth. Man looketh on the outward appearance, but God searcheth the heart. Accordingly, he speaks a language very different from the men of the world, and calls those "wretched, and miserable, and poor, and naked," who think themselves, and perhaps are thought by others, to be "rich, and increased in goods, and to stand in need of nothing." And will any wise man, then, rejoice in these outward circumstances, which may so easily consist with the real misery of the person who possesseth them? Especially if we consider,

2*dly*, That these very things are frequently the means of making men miserable, and of fixing them in that deplorable state. How many have been fruitful in the low valley of adversity, who have proved barren, after they removed their habitations to the high mountains of prosperity? And should any man rejoice, because he must pass to heaven as a camel must pass through the eye of a needle? Is it not difficult enough to keep our hearts and affections above, even when we have little or nothing to confine them below? And should we, who already stumble at a straw, rejoice that we have rocks of offence, and mountains of provocation cast in our way? How few are advanced to higher measures of faith and holiness, by their advancement in the world? How strangely doth prosperity transform men, and make them forget their former apprehensions of things, their convictions, their purposes, and their vows; nay, their God, their happiness, and themselves? While men are low in the world and live by faith, they do good with the little which they possess, and have the blessing of a willing mind: Whereas, when they are lifted up, they often lose the inclination, in proportion as they increase in the inability of doing good, and use their superior talents only to bring upon themselves a heavier condemnation. The carnal mind commonly grows with the carnal interest, and the greatest opposers of God have in all ages been the very persons who were most indebted to his goodness. Rejoice not then in the possession of these common mercies for their own sake; and learn to value them only as they are made subservient to your real usefulness and to your spiritual joy. For, in the

3*d* place, All these things may end in misery, and leave the owner in everlasting woe. He who to-day "is clothed in purple and fine linen, and fares sumptuously," may to-morrow "lift up his eyes in torments." "Weeping, and wailing, and gnashing of teeth" may succeed to his carnal mirth. If this shall happen, he shall then cry out, O that I had lain in mendicinal rags, instead of having got this mortal surfeit of prosperity! Alas! are all my pleasant morsels to be for ever exchanged for this gall and wormwood? O deplorable state! O wretched issue of a carnal life!

Think not that I am an enemy to your joy in urging these remonstrances. My sole aim is to lead you to that fountain, which will at all times supply you with the most exalted delight; the sense of the love of God, and the sure prospect of immortal felicity. Were you in this happy condition, then should I bid you rejoice even in those temporal mercies, as the gifts of your Heavenly Father, the tokens of his love, and the pledges of your future inheritance. I would then address you in the words of the preacher, "Go thy way, eat thy bread with joy, and drink thy wine with a merry heart; for God now accepteth thy works." But until you have made sure of this one thing needful, I must be an enemy to your secure and carnal joy. The frantic mirth of a madman is an object that will cast a damp on a mind most addicted to gayety; and I appeal to yourselves, whether it be reasonable for a man to rejoice, who, in the midst of all his pleasures, cannot have the smallest assurance that he shall be the next moment out of hell. A wicked man, suffering the horrors of an awakened conscience, is indeed an object of commiseration: but a far greater object of commiseration is that man, who, in the depths of misery, and on the very brink of perdition, still retains his thoughtless and insensible gayety of heart. This is that laughter of which Solomon might well say, "It is mad;" and that mirth of which he saith, "what doth it?" How many are now in sorrow, by reason of this unseasonable and sinful joy? They were too gay to listen to the grave admonitions of God's word; too eagerly bent upon their delusive pleasures to attend to the motions of his Holy Spirit; and, therefore, because when God called they would not hear; so now he laughs at their calamity, and mocks when their fears are come upon them. It is the awful apprehension of this which constrains me to be earnest with you in my present argument. The pleasure which you take in the enjoyment of sense, is that which makes you careless of the pleasures of religion. Could I for once prevail with you to enter into your own breasts, to abstract yourselves from the business and pleasures of this vain world, and to think seriously for one day upon your everlasting state, I should not despair of convincing you, that this earth can afford nothing which can be an equivalent for your immortal souls. But, alas! your sensual dissipated mirth banishes all reflection, and makes you deaf to the sober voice of reason. When you are confined to a bed of sickness, indeed, or languishing under some painful disease, it is possible for a religious monitor to obtain something like a patient hearing from you: but when your flesh is in vigor, and capable of relishing outward pleasures, this docile season is no more, and all the truths which relate to another world become grating and offensive to your ears, like the sound of an instrument out of tune. I have only to add, on this head, that were your mirth, such as it is, to endure for any time, I should wonder the less at your rejecting this admonition. But, alas! to be jocund, or even happy, for a day, and then to lie down in endless torment, is a dismal prospect indeed. To see a man laugh and play, and brave it out, in a vessel which is so swiftly running down a stream which terminates in a gulf of endless horror, is a shocking spectacle, and calls loudly on every one who sees it to warn the unhappy person of his danger. This hath been my office to you; and could I be your friend if I did less? If I did not obtest to you, with all the earnestness of which I am capable, to secure your interest in another world than this, and to derive your joys from something better than the portion of the sensualist?

Let us now turn our eyes to a more agreeable object, and survey those solid grounds of joy which belong to the people of God.—For the

Second proposition which I proposed

to illustrate was, that the light of God's countenance is sufficient to gladden the heart of a saint in all circumstances whatsoever. For this purpose let us consider from what sources the joys of a saint proceed.

1*st*, Then, he is possessed of the joy which results from comparing his present happy condition with the misery in which he was once involved. He remembers a time when, like others, he wandered in the vanity and darkness of his mind, still putting the anxious question, "Who will show me any good?" When, like a sheep, he went astray, in the dark and howling wilderness; when he fed upon mere husks, and spent his money for that which is not bread. "But now he is returned to the Shepherd and Bishop of his soul." He is passed from death to life: the Judge of the universe is at peace with him, and hath cast all his sins into the depths of the sea. He hath got within the walls of the city of refuge, where the avenger of blood cannot enter; the sword of justice is put up in its scabbard; and that Almighty being, upon whom he constantly depends, hath laid aside his wrath, and beholds him with a pleasant countenance. And, therefore, "Although the fig-tree shall not blossom, neither shall fruit be in the vines; the labor of the olive shall fail, and the fields shall yield no meat; the flock shall be cut off from the fold, and there shall be no herd in the stalls; yet will he rejoice in the Lord, he will joy in the God of his salvation."—But a

2*d* Source of joy to a child of God consists in the actual honors and privileges conferred upon him. He is advanced to the dearest and most intimate relation to God, adopted into his family, and invested with all the rights of a son. In him that life is begun, which, being hid with Christ in God, shall be preserved and improved, till at length it be perfected, in the heavenly world. Rejoice in the Lord, O ye righteous; and shout for joy, all ye that are upright in heart." To you it belongs to come boldly to a throne of grace, in the assured hope that you shall obtain mercy, and find grace to help you in every time of need: by the blood of Jesus you can enter into the holiest, and in every thing by prayer and supplication, with thanksgiving, make your requests known to God; casting all your care upon him, because he careth for you. He is yours who possesseth all things, and what can you want? He is yours who can do all things, and what should you fear? He is yours who is goodness and love itself, how then can you be miserable, or what imperfection can there be in your felicity? His faithfulness is pledged to make all things work together for your good. The most afflictive events, like the furnace or pruning hook, shall only purge away your dross, or render you more fruitful. So that you may glory in tribulation, "knowing that tribulation worketh patience, and patience experience, and experience hope that maketh not ashamed." To conclude this detail of the privileges of a saint, hear how the apostle to the Corinthians describes them, (1 Corinth. iii. 24.) "All things are yours, whether Paul, or Apollos, or Cephas, or the world, or life, or death, or things present, or things to come; all are yours; and ye are Christ's; and Christ is God's." Once more,

3*dly*. The joy of a saint proceeds from the contemplation of those future blessings which as yet are only the objects of hope. But in speaking of these, where shall we begin? Shall I pass beyond the dark and lonely grave, which Job hath styled "the house appointed for all living," and lead you upwards at once to the realms of light and joy, to survey that house, with many mansions, whither Christ is gone to prepare a place for his people? No; in the passage I last quoted, we find death reckoned among the possessions of believers. To those who belong to Christ, death ceaseth to be the king of terrors. The stroke he gives doth indeed put an end to the existence of the old man; but by that very stroke, the fetters which galled the new man in Christ are broken asunder, and the life imparted by the second Adam comes to full maturity, when that which was derived from the first Adam concludes. When, therefore, we view death and the grave as consecrated by Christ, who died and was buried, they are no more to be ranked among the articles of the curse denounced against the original apostasy, but fall to be enrolled among the "things to come;" of which every believer may say, They are mine. In this light did Paul behold them, when he said, "To me to live is Christ, and to die is gain.—I desire to depart, and to be with Christ, which is far better."—"While I am at home in the body, I am absent from the Lord. I am, therefore, confident and willing, rather to be absent from the body, and present with the Lord."—"O death, where is thy sting? O grave, where is thy victory? The sting of death is sin, and the strength of sin is the law. But thanks be unto God, who giveth us the victory, through Jesus Christ our Lord."

But it is the resurrection which shall complete the triumph of the saints, when that which is sown in weakness, in dishonor, and corruption, shall be raised in power, in glory, and incorruption. In that day of the manifestation of the sons of God, when our vile bodies shall be changed and fashioned like unto Christ's glorious body, "when this corruptible shall have put on incorruption, and this mortal shall have put on immortality, then shall be brought to pass the saying that is written, Death is swallowed up in victory." But how shall we speak of the glory yet to be revealed, "which eye hath not seen, nor ear heard, neither hath it entered into the heart of man to conceive." Should I attempt any description of it, I should only "darken counsel by words without knowledge."—"It doth not yet appear," saith the apostle John, "what we shall be: but this we know, that when he shall appear, we shall be like him; for we shall see him as he is." Here, then, let us stop. To be made like the Son of God, to behold his unveiled glory, and to be for ever with him: these particulars must surely include every ingredient which can belong to the highest perfection and happiness of a creature. With this great object in our eye, how well doth it become us to adopt the language of the apostle Peter, and to say with fervent gratitude, as he did, "Blessed be the God and Father of our Lord Jesus Christ, which according to his abundant mercy hath begotten us again unto a lively hope, by the resurrection of Jesus Christ from the dead, to an inheritance incorruptible, undefiled, and that fadeth not away."

These are the peculiar sources from which the godly man derives his joy. And may I not now appeal to you, whether they are not of such a nature, as that no outward distress or calamity can take them away? Even when the heavens shall be rolled together like a scroll, and the elements shall melt with fervent heat, he will be able to look at the mighty desolation, and say, when all these materials are consumed, I shall have lost nothing; "God liveth, blessed be my rock." "The Lord is the portion of mine inheritance," and in him I possess and enjoy all things.

And now what improvement are we to make of this subject?—In the

1*st* place, Let us inquire which of the characters described by the Psalmist belongs to us. Are we among the many that say, "Who will show us any good?" or are we among the happy few who seek the light of God's countenance above all things? There is no neutral person in this case. Every man that liveth upon the earth is either "carnally minded, which is death; or spiritually minded, which is life and peace;" either a child of God, or a drudge and slave to the world. To which party, then, do you belong? What are your hearts principally set upon, and whither do you bend your chief and most vigorous endeavors? If you can find but little leisure for the service of God, and the care of your souls; if you can spend whole days without calling upon God, or reading his word; if the Sabbath appears burdensome to you, and you join in your hearts with those profane persons whom the prophet Amos describes, as saying, (viii. 5.) "When will the new moon be gone, that we may sell corn? and the Sabbath, that we may set forth wheat?" If you are conscious that it is thus with you, I need scarcely inform you, that you must be classed with those whose language it is, "Who will show us any good?" A

2*d* Use, therefore, which I would make of this subject, is to exhort you, who are yet carnally minded, to think seriously of your condition. Ye are pursuing what will for ever flee from you. Ye are combating with a decree of him who is Almighty, even that irreversible decree which hath pronounced vanity on all things below the sun. Ye are opposing the experience of all who ever made the same trial before you; ye are struggling with the very feelings of your own hearts, which as yet have never found that permanent satisfaction which they require. O then be persuaded to relinquish those false plans of happiness by which you have been hitherto deluded, and to seek the favor of that God who is the only adequate portion of an immortal soul. Listen to that expostulation and advice, (Isa. lv. 2, 3.) "Wherefore do ye spend money for that which is not bread, and your labor for that which satisfieth not? Hearken diligently unto me, and eat ye that which is good, and let your soul delight itself in fatness. Incline your ear, and come unto me; hear, and your soul shall live; and I will make an everlasting covenant with you, even the sure mercies of David."

Lastly, Let me call on those who have been taught to value the light of God's countenance above all things, to be humble and thankful. Often recollect that mercy which plucked you as brands out of the burning, and set you apart to see the glory of the Lord, and to show forth his praise. Often acknowledge that Sovereign grace by which you were arrested in the broad way that leads to destruction, and led to him who alone hath the words of eternal life. "Who made thee to differ, and what hast thou that thou didst not receive?" If he who commanded the light to shine out of darkness hath shined into your hearts, to give you the light of the knowledge of his glory, as it shines in the face of Jesus; adore and praise this distinguishing goodness; acknowledge, with humble gratitude, that it was the doing of the Lord. And if you would continue to enjoy the comfort which ariseth from the light of God's countenance, be careful to abound in all those "fruits of righteousness, which are through Christ to the praise and glory of God." Our duty and our comfort are wisely and graciously connected together. "Great peace have they that love thy law," saith the Psalmist, "and nothing shall offend them." "The work of righteousness shall be peace, and the effect of righteousness, quietness, and assurance for ever." As many as walk according to this rule, peace shall be on them, and mercy, and on the Israel of God. *Amen.*

SERMON LIII.

Preached on the Evening of a Communion Sabbath, March 16, 1783, a few days before the Author's death.

SECOND COMING OF CHRIST.

HEBREWS IX. 28.—"CHRIST was once offered to bear the sins of many; and unto them that look for him shall he appear the second time, without sin, unto salvation."

THERE are two things which we are taught to believe concerning Christ. The *first* is, That he once appeared in this world, clothed with our nature; that he published to sinners of mankind a pure and heavenly doctrine; and after exhibiting, in his own conduct, a fair and unblemished example of holy obedience, at last offered up himself a sacrifice to God, to expiate our offences, and purchase our eternal redemption. The *second* is, That this same Jesus, who was dead, is now alive, and sitteth on the right hand of the Majesty on high, from whence he shall come at the end of the world, crowned with glory and honor, and attended with all the host of heaven, to judge the quick and the dead.

We were this day commemorating, in the Holy Sacrament of the Supper, what Christ hath already done for the redemption of his people. There we beheld him "evidently set forth as crucified before our eyes," bearing our griefs, and "wounded for our transgressions." And now to display the riches of his grace, and our infinite obligations to love and serve him, let us with joy contemplate what he is farther to do, as it is shortly expressed in the latter part of my text: "Unto them that look for him, shall he appear the second time, without sin, unto salvation.' The

First thing that claims our attention is

the certainty of our Lord's return. "He shall appear the second time." And, blessed be God, this comfortable truth doth not depend upon any doubtful process of reasoning, but is both supported and illustrated by a variety of the most clear and express declarations of holy writ. The apostle Jude informs us, that Enoch, the seventh from Adam, by faith foresaw this great event, and said by divine inspiration, "Behold, the Lord cometh with ten thousand of his saints, to execute judgment on all." It was Christ's promise to his disciples, "In my Father's house are many mansions; if it were not so, I would have told you. I go to prepare a place for you. And if I go and prepare a place for you, I will come again, and receive you unto myself, that where I am there ye may be also." The angels who attended him at his ascension into heaven bare witness to the same truth. "Ye men of Galilee," said they, "why stand ye gazing up into heaven? This same Jesus, which is taken up from you into heaven, shall so come in like manner as ye have seen him go into heaven." Nay, we are told, that the Father hath appointed the very day in which "he shall judge the world in righteousness, by that man whom he hath ordained." In a word, this doctrine is not only frequently asserted in Scripture, but is so intimately connected with all the other parts of revelation, that the whole must stand or fall with it. Is not the Sacrament of the Supper a visible pledge of our Lord's return, as well as a memorial of his sufferings and death? And do we not profess an equal belief of both, every time we partake of that holy ordinance? "For as often as we eat this bread, and drink this cup, we do show the Lord's death till he come;" that is, we commemorate his death in the faith of his second and glorious appearance.

This, my brethren, is an interesting truth, and doth justly challenge our most serious attention. It is not more certain that we are met together in this place, than that we shall all meet again at the tribunal of Christ, where every one of us shall appear in his true colors, without any mask or disguise. At present we are but little acquainted with ourselves, and frequently mistaken by others; but the sentence of the supreme Judge will rectify all mistakes, and at once put an end to the presumptuous hope of the hypocrite, and to the fears and anxieties of the humble self-suspecting soul. Whom he then justifies, none can condemn; and whom he then condemns, none dare justify, neither is there any that can deliver out of his hand. What a mighty influence ought this to have on our temper and practice? Were any of us to be tried for our lives at a human bar, I am persuaded that the thoughts of it would so fully possess our minds, as to leave room for almost nothing else. Yet the most that a judge can do in such a case, is to determine the day beyond which we shall not live; while neither he, nor any man in the world, can say with certainty, that we shall live till that day come. One of a thousand accidents may cut us off, and prevent the execution of his sentence; so that the legal date of our lives may be considerably longer than the term which the Author of our lives hath appointed. But the issue of that trial, which we must undergo at the second appearance of Christ, is of eternal consequence to us. Our final state is determined by it; aad no power in heaven or on earth is able to defeat or alter the sentence. And is it possible that we can banish the thoughts of this for one moment, or that we can think of it with cold and unaffected hearts? The

Second thing that deserves the peculiar notice of believers, is the gracious design of our Lord's appearance.—"He shall appear the second time unto salvation." Some may, perhaps, be at a loss to conceive what should remain to be done for the salvation of the saints, after their souls are admitted into heaven. But if we reflect a little, we shall be sensible, that even after the soul's admission into heaven, there are several things to be done by Christ for his people, which will increase their happiness, and render their salvation more perfect.—For,

1*st*, At his second coming, Christ will raise the dead bodies of his servants, which will, without doubt, be a considerable addition to their felicity. The souls of the saints are represented in Scripture as waiting and longing for the resurrection of their bodies. Hence their flesh is said to rest in hope; and, therefore, when this hope is fulfilled at Christ's second appearance, we may justly conclude, that the joy of the soul shall be heightened and improved; especially when we consider the wonderful change which shall be wrought upon the body itself. When, in the morning of the resurrection, the trumpet shall sound, and the graves shall be opened; when that which was sown in weakness and dishonor, shall be raised in power and glory; when the formerly vile body shall not only be refined, but fashioned like unto the glorious body of the Redeemer, with what triumph and exultation shall that song be sung! "Death is swallowed up in victory."—"O death, where is thy sting? O grave, where is thy victory? The sting of death is sin, and the strength of sin is the law. But thanks be to God, which giveth us the victory, through our Lord Jesus Christ."

2dly. In that day the Church, which is called the body of Christ, shall be complete; which must add to the happiness of every saint in particular. For the several members of that spiritual body being closely united, not only to the head, but also to one another, each of them must necessarily partake of the happiness and glory of the whole. Must not every child of God be more joyful when the whole family is assembled in the immediate presence of their Father, and not one member is wanting? If there is joy in heaven at the conversion of one sinner, though afterwards he hath a waste and howling wilderness to pass through, and many a toilsome and dangerous step to take, ere he arrive at the end of his journey; how much greater joy shall there be in the heavenly Jerusalem, when the many sons of God are all brought home to glory?

3dly. Then also shall believers be solemnly acquitted by the Judge himself, and publicly acknowledged in the presence of an assembled world. "They shall be mine," saith the Lord, "in that day when I make up my jewels." Having washed them with his blood, and sanctified them by his Spirit, he will not be ashamed to call them brethren, but will confess them before his Father, and present them at his throne without spot and blemish.—And

4thly, To complete the happiness of the saints, then shall there be the clearest discovery of all God's works, and the most full and open manifestation of his glorious perfections. When all his great designs are accomplished and brought to their intended issue, then shall the wise order, and harmonious contexture, of divine Providence be clearly discerned, the most intricate and perplexed dispensations shall be explained and vindicated; and it shall then appear, to the full conviction of the whole admiring family of God, that all things have wrought together for their spiritual improvement and eternal felicity. This shall be the day of solemn triumph, the grand jubilee, upon the finishing of all God's works from the creation of the world, upon which ensues the resignation of the Mediator's kingdom. For although Christ shall continue through eternity to be the head of his church, yet the present manner of his administration shall then cease. He shall then deliver up the kingdom to the Father, that God, or the undivided Godhead, Father, Son, and Holy Ghost, may be all in all. This fact is distinctly asserted (1 Cor. xv. 24—28.) "Then cometh the end," saith the apostle, "when Christ shall have delivered up the kingdom to God, even the Father; when he shall have put down all rule, and all authority and power. For he must reign, till he hath put all enemies under his feet. The last enemy that shall be destroyed is death. For he hath put all things under his feet. But when he saith that all things are put under him, it is manifest that he is excepted which did put all things under him. And when all things shall be subdued unto him, then shall the Son also himself be subject unto him that put all things under him that God may be all in all."

Thus you have heard how Christ's second coming shall complete the salvation of his people, and increase that happiness at the resurrection which commenced at their new birth; and which, though greatly improved by the release of the soul from the earthly tabernacle, was not carried to its full perfection at death.—The manner of our Lord's appearance, when he comes upon this gracious design, is the

Third particular in the text, which comes now to be considered. "He shall appear the second time, *without sin*, unto salvation." When in the fulness of time God sent forth his Son into this world, although he was absolutely pure and spotless in himself, yet then he "bare the sins of many;" and "he who knew no sin, was made sin for us." Appearing in the likeness of sinful flesh, he was numbered with transgressors, and treated as if he had been the worst of criminals: But by his sufferings and death, having fully expiated the guilt of sin, he obtained a public and legal discharge, by being released from the prison of the grave, and "set at the right hand of God in the heavenly places, far above all principality and power, and might and dominion, and every name that is named, not only in this world, but also in that which is to come." When, therefore, he cometh again, he shall appear "*without sin*," without that guilt which was charged upon him, while he sustained the character of Surety, and stood in the place of sinful man.

He shall likewise appear without any of the effects of sin, such as pain, poverty, reproach, or infirmity of any kind. It shall not be such an appearance as his first was, when he "made himself of no reputation, took upon him the form of a servant," and submitted to all the indignities attending that mean condition. He will not come to be buffeted and scourged, and spit upon, and crowned with thorns. He will not come, O careless and ungrateful sinners! to be despised and rejected in all his gracious offers. No; he shall come in the clouds, with great power and glory; he shall be revealed from heaven with his mighty angels; he shall appear in all the splendor of Zion's King, arrayed with that glory which he had with the Father before the world was. Then shall the reproach of the cross be wiped off, and all his sufferings fully recompensed. In this humble state, he was attended by twelve poor and illiterate men; but then shall he come with "ten thousands of his saints, and all the holy angels with him." He was introduced to his public ministry by the "voice of one crying in the wilderness;" but then shall his approach be announced by the "voice of the archangel and the trump of God." And he who on Mount Calvary was lifted up on the cross between two thieves, shall then ascend his "great white throne, high and lifted up;" from whence, with unerring wisdom, and almighty power, he shall separate the righteous from the wicked, adjudging the one to everlasting life, and the other to endless misery.

Thus shall he appear, when he "comes the second time, without sin, unto salvation." And ought not the prospect of this to have a mighty influence upon us in the mean time? "Behold he cometh with clouds, and every eye shall see him, and they also who pierced him, and all kindreds of the earth shall wail because of him." How great will be the confusion of ungodly men, when they see that Jesus, whose grace they despised, coming to fix their everlasting state. The multitude that came determined to apprehend him in the days of his flesh, went backward, and fell to the ground, when, with an air of majesty, he only pronounced these few words, "I am he." And if the Lamb's voice was so terrible, how dreadful will he appear when he roareth as a lion? If his voice shook the earth when he published the law from Mount Sinai, how must it shake the hearts of his enemies, when he pronounceth the sentence of the law, and dooms to those punishments which the law hath awarded?

But the prospect of this appearance is no less comfortable to believers, than it is terrible to the ungodly. Then shall his own people lift up their heads, and behold his glory with exceeding joy. His coming shall be to them the dawning of an everlasting day. They know that he brings salvation with him, the full harvest of that light and gladness which were sown for them in time. He comes to wipe away all tears from their eyes, to complete their victory over death and hell, and to put their whole persons, souls and bodies, in full possession of that heavenly inheritance, "which is incorruptible, undefiled, and that fadeth not away."

If it is comfortable at present to hear of him, to think of his love, to commemorate his death, and to behold his beauty in the ordinances of his grace; what must it be to see him in all the glory of his exalted state? When a dear relation, who hath been long absent in a far country, returns to his kindred and friends, how do all concerned hasten to meet him, and to express their joy at his arrival? And will not the saints then rejoice at the coming of their Saviour? With what transports of gladness will they cry out, Behold, yonder he comes! He whose blood hath redeemed, and whose Spirit hath sanctified us. Yonder he comes in whom we trusted, and for whom we have long waited; and now we see that he hath not deceived us, and that he hath not made us wait in vain. "Even so come, Lord Jesus." And this leads me to the

Fourth and *last* particular in the text, which is the character of those to whom this second appearance of our Lord shall be comfortable. They are such as "look for him." This short but significant description may be considered as including,

1*st*, A firm belief of this event. One who looks for it in the sense of the apostle's words, is as thoroughly persuaded of its certainty, as he is that the sun, which sets to-night, shall rise again to-morrow. His faith is built on the surest foundation, the word and promise of his Saviour himself; and, therefore, his heart is impressed with Christ's second appearance as much, at least as really, as if he already saw him coming in the clouds of heaven. But,

2*dly*, The expression denotes the love and desire of this event. The saints take pleasure in the prospect of it, and accordingly are described by the apostle Paul, (2 Tim. iv. 8.) by this very circumstance. They are such as "love his appearing." If the saints under the old dispensation longed for the manifestation of our Lord in the flesh, how much more ought we to long for that more glorious appearance which he shall make in the end of the world. The Atheist rejects this doctrine altogether; the profane scoffer says, "Where is the promise of his coming?" Carnal sinners are afraid of it, when alarmed with the rebukes of conscience; as when Paul preached of righteousness, temperance, and judgment to come, Felix trembled. But to the godly it is not matter of terror, but of delight. Nay, they would even hasten its approach, if it were in their power. A believer, when his heart is right, will say, like the mother of Sisera, when she cried through the lattice, "Why is his chariot so long in coming? Why tarry the wheels of his chariot?" At the same time,

3*dly*, This expression imports a patient waiting for his appearance, in spite of all discouragements. Love makes the believer to long; but faith enables patiently to wait for his Lord's coming. What though he dwells in an unkind world, wounded with sharp afflictions, harassed with temptations, and oppressed with a body of sin and death? Yet all this notwithstanding, he still looks and waits with patience and resignation. He knows that the second coming of his Lord will abundantly compensate all his present delays and discouragements; and "that this trial of their faith, being much more precious than of gold that perisheth, though it be tried with fire, shall then be found unto praise, and honor, and glory." But the most essential part of the character of those to whom the second appearance of our Lord shall be comfortable, is, in the

4*th* and *last* place, An habitual preparation for this event. They will endeavor "to have their loins girded about, and their lights burning, and themselves like unto men that wait for their Lord, that when he cometh and knocketh, they may open unto him immediately." The best evidence which we can give that we truly look for him with faith and love, is our being diligent, that we may be found of him in peace, without spot, and blameless. As the proper improvement, therefore, of all that hath been said, let me address to you this concluding exhortation. "Give all diligence to make your calling and election sure."—"Take heed to yourselves, lest at any time your hearts be overcharged with surfeiting and drunkenness, and the cares of this life, and so that day come upon you unawares."—"Let your whole conversation be such as becometh the gospel of Christ." Never think "that you have already attained, either are already perfect; but forgetting the things which are behind, and reaching forth to those things which are before, press towards the mark, for the prize of the high calling of God in Christ Jesus."—"Set your affections on things above, not on things on the earth, that when he who is your life shall appear, ye may also appear with him in glory." *Amen.*

SERMON LIV.

Preached at the Author's admission at South Leith.

THE FAITHFUL STEWARD.

1 CORIN. IV. 1, 2.—"Let a man so account of us as of the ministers of CHRIST, and stewards of the mysteries of GOD. Moreover, it is required in stewards that a man be found faithful."

THE just conception and faithful discharge of the reciprocal duties in society, are the foundation both of private and public happiness. In this respect, the church of Christ is not different from other communities among men. Although Christians acknowledge but one supreme Master, yet they are taught to acknowledge among themselves subordinate degrees of authority on the one hand, and of submission and respect on the other. The God whom we serve is a God of order, not a God of confusion; and he hath pointed out, both in his word and in his providence, the necessity of doing all things decently and in good order. The text, and the occasion likewise, lead me to speak of the mutual regards and duties which ought to subsist between a minister of Christ, and the people committed to his charge; in doing which I shall, through divine assistance,

First, Explain the account given us in the text, of the nature of our office as ministers of Christ, and stewards of the mysteries of God. And,

Secondly, Point out the corresponding obligations incumbent on Christians, with regard to those intrusted with this ministry.

The illustration of these particulars will tend to produce a just conception, and I trust, through the blessing of God, the faithful discharge of those important duties which you and I will henceforth owe to each other.

I am *first,* to explain the account given in my text, of the nature of our office as ministers of Christ, and stewards of the mysteries of God.

And in order to have clear apprehensions of this subject, it will be necessary to look back to the origin of the office, and see wherein it differed, at its first appointment, from the circumstances in which it exists at present. I set out with observing, that the ministry of the word is in all essential points the same, ever since it was ordained as an employment. At the same time it is plain, that several circumstances attending it are considerably varied. The ordinary call to the office, which now takes place, is very different from the miraculous mission by which men were consecrated to it in former times. Their vocation was more immediate, more striking, attended with more ample powers, as well as more splendid effects. From their immediate inspiration, an authority was derived to their words, to which none of us can justly pretend. They promised, and the blessings of time and eternity were conveyed with their words; they threatened, and vengeance from heaven followed without delay. Besides, the first teachers of the gospel enjoyed from their divine Master the communication of his own powers over nature. "Having called the twelve disciples, he gave them power against unclean spirits, and to heal all manner of sickness and disease." Accordingly, the whole history of their lives is one train of miracles, verifying the reality of these powers, and displaying the fulfilment of that splendid promise, "Verily, verily, I say unto you, he that believeth on me, the works that I do shall he do also, and greater works than these shall he do, because I go to my Father." All these extraordinary powers have now ceased. The pastors of the Christian church, in these later ages, are neither possessed of the immediate inspiration, nor of the power of working miracles, enjoyed by the apostles. They are now men in all respects like yourselves, to whom God hath conveyed, by the hands of other men, authority to preach the word, to dispense the sacraments, and to preside over the congregations in which his providence may place them. Here then is a very manifest difference, and an evident inferiority on our side. Still, however, the original proposition stands true, that the office is in all essential points the same as exercised both by them and us. For it is easy to conceive, that the superior prerogatives which have been mentioned, vary some circumstances in the ministry only, but do not in any degree alter its nature. The essence of this sacred office, the foundations of the pastoral authority, remain unimpaired. The mission is one and the same by Jesus Christ, to all his faithful servants in this employment. His promise is unalterable, "Behold I am with you always, even to the end of the world." From his holy hill, where he sits as King of Zion, he provides for the perpetuity of his church, "giving some apostles, and some prophets, and some evangelists, some pastors and teachers, for the perfecting of the saints, for the work of the ministry, for the edifying of the body of Christ."

This then is the origin of that sacred office, which is still exercised among you. This is the source from which the authority is derived that is necessary for sustaining the character. It is this which constitutes our mission the same with that of the apostles, and confers on the truths which we deliver the authority of the word of God. So that if the doctrines which we set forth are agreeable to the Scriptures, if the morality which we enforce is a conversation becoming the gospel, we are in all respects to be accounted of as "ministers of Christ, and stewards of the mysteries of God."

But these titles, so ennobling to him who supports them, are not without very solemn considerations to correct the levity of confidence and self-applause. "It is required in stewards," saith the apostle, "that a man be found faithful." What a variety of important duties are included in this requisition? When we speak of a faithful minister, we speak of the rare and happy union of ability and attention, of zeal and knowledge, of meekness and firmness, in the same character; for all these are necessary to sustain the office with propriety. And are these qualities to be attained with a slight degree of application? Is it a small demand on the conscience of a man, to give its testimony to his faithfulness, in such arduous and important respects? These considerations may well give rise to that emphatical question, "Who is sufficient for these things?" especially when to all this we take likewise into view the awful threatenings denounced against the unfaithful discharge of this office. "Son of man," saith the Almighty to each of us, as he said to his prophets of old, "I have made thee a watchman unto the house of Israel, therefore hear the word at my mouth, and give them warning from me. When I say unto the wicked, thou shalt surely die, and thou givest him not warning, nor speakest to warn the wicked from his wicked way, to save his life, the same wicked man shall die in his iniquity, but his blood will I require at thine hand. Woe be to the shepherds of Israel that do feed themselves; should not the shepherds feed the flocks? Thus saith the Lord God, Behold I am against the shepherds, and I will require my flock at their hand, and cause them to cease from feeding the flock, neither shall the shepherds feed themselves any more."

Thus have I endeavored to set before you the nature of our office, as ministers of Christ, and stewards of the mysteries of God. No man can boast of a more honorable employment. At the same time, none can aspire to one that requires higher attention, involves more difficulty, or subjects to a more awful account.

But you are not to imagine, my brethren, that while such high obligations are laid on the ministers of the gospel, no duties are, on the other hand, required of you towards those who hold that station. "Let a man," saith the apostle, "so account of us as ministers of Christ, and stewards of the mysteries of God." The plain meaning of which exhortation is, that Christians are required to entertain sentiments corresponding to that relation in which they stand to those who labor among them in word and doctrine.

I. The same authority which lays such arduous obligations on your pastors, requires of you to entertain a spirit of equity and candor towards them. It is certainly but fair to judge of every person according to the character he assumes, and the pretensions with which he sets out. What these are on our part, you have already heard. I have shown those circumstances in which we acknowledge our inferiority to the first teachers of the gospel. I have pointed out those also, in which we maintain our commission to be equal to theirs. The sum is this, that, on the one hand, we profess ourselves to be no more than ordinary, uninspired, fallible men, like yourselves; but at the same time contend, on the other hand, that we possess the same authority to preach the doctrines of revelation, and to dispense the ordinances of religion, which the most distinguished apostle ever enjoyed. What we expect then of your equity and candor, is, that you would judge of us on these grounds, and expect nothing from us but what is consistent with them. You may perhaps ask, In what respects is there any danger of your transgressing this rule? To which I answer, 1*st*, That this rule is transgressed, when you confine the respect to which the office itself is entitled, entirely to the personal qualities and accomplishments of mind bestowed on those who are invested with it. When I speak of personal qualities, I do not mean that you should understand me as referring to sanctity of conduct. You cannot make any demand on us on this head, beyond what is just and incumbent. God forbid that any of us should incur the application of our Lord's saying, as to the scribes and pharisees: "The scribes and pharisees sit in Moses' seat; all therefore whatsoever they bid you observe, that observe and do; but do not ye after their works, for they say and do not." We acknowledge that we ought to be ensamples to believers, not only in word, but in conversation, in charity, in spirit, in faith, in purity. In this respect, therefore, your severest demands do us no injustice. But is there not a want of equity in withholding your respect from those who do not embellish this office with shining and superior endowments of mind? Is not this the very thing against which you are warned, when you are told that you have the treasure of the "gospel in earthen vessels, that the power and excellency may appear to be of God?" Why should it be expected, then, that ministers should understand all mysteries, and all knowledge, even as the superior intelligences of heaven, who stand before the throne of God? Why should you be dissatisfied, except we can employ all the most exquisite arts of oratory to soothe your ears, and amuse your imaginations? Where are you taught to expect this from us? These are not our pretensions; this is not the character we assume. For let not any man account of us as orators or declaimers, plausible and artificial discoursers, who have nothing in view beyond their own credit, and are eloquent and ingenious by profession. We profess a character more humble indeed, as to any personal importance we can assume from it; but, at the same time, infinitely more serious and weighty, even that of ministers of Christ, and stewards of the mysteries of God. But,

2*dly*, This rule of equity and candor is transgressed in a still higher degree, when you expect of us to preach doctrines accommodated to your passions, or to refrain from delivering those truths which are unacceptable or alarming. You complain, perhaps, that we disturb your repose, and interrupt your pleasing dreams of happiness; but this complaint is both unjust to us, and injurious to yourselves; and though at first sight it may seem levelled against us, is in truth levelled against God himself. For whose words, I beseech you, are these words? "He that believeth not, shall be damned."—"If ye live after the flesh, ye shall die."—"Without holiness no man shall see the Lord." These, indeed, are alarming sentences; but you will keep it in mind, that they were not devised by us. They are among those mysteries of God, which are intrusted to us as stewards, and surely no less can be expected than that we should dispense them faithfully. God hath assured us, that if we do not speak to warn the wicked from the evil of his way, that wicked man shall die in his iniquity, but his blood he will require at our hands. Would you then in good earnest desire that we should forfeit our own souls, and incur the wrath of Almighty God, from a false tenderness to your delusive peace? No, my brethren, this cannot be done; or if it be done, eternal woe will be our portion, eternal reproaches will pass between us. I had rather hear from one in the spirit of Ahab, "Feed him with the bread and water of affliction;" or from one in the spirit of Amaziah, "Forbear, why shouldst thou be smitten;" than to hear from my own conscience, Thou hast betrayed souls to damnation; than to hear from an incensed God, "Their blood will I require at thine hands;" than to hear from the chief Shepherd, when he shall appear, "Cast the unprofitable servant into outer darkness, there shall be weeping, and wailing, and gnashing of teeth." Let a man, therefore, so account of us in the spirit of candor and equity, "as ministers of Christ, and stewards of the mysteries of God."

II. Christians, you are required to entertain a just esteem for the office and character which we bear. I am aware how delicate a subject it is to talk of that estimation which we claim from you on this account. I am sensible that our highest glory consists in our humility, and our best dignity in stooping to be useful: "For we preach not ourselves, but Christ Jesus the Lord, and ourselves your servants for Jesus' sake." We claim no obsequious homage, we arrogate not dominion over your faith, but we expect that no man should despise us; we account our office venerable enough to entitle those to respect, who do the duties of it with propriety. Indeed we have not diffidence enough to apprehend, in the least degree, that such respect will be denied, where the proper virtues of our station appear in our conduct; and we know it to be both vain and absurd to expect it on any other terms.

Leaving therefore a theme, which cannot be pursued long to advantage, we are still more desirous,

III. That you would make a proper improvement of the truths which we deliver. Take heed then, brethren, how ye hear. The time is coming, when we must all meet before the judgment-seat of God, to give an account of the advantages which we have enjoyed, and of the manner in which we have improved them. In what way this decisive trial shall be conducted, cannot be certainly known in the present time. We are told in general, that the great Shepherd, who shall then sit in judgment, will separate the sheep from the goats, placing the one on his right hand, and the other on his left. But besides this grand division, it seems probable from the analogy both of reason and Scripture, that those who were members of the same Christian society, and enjoyed the same ordinances and means of grace, shall then be brought together and confronted, that the evidence upon which the different sentences shall proceed, may be the more unexceptionable and convincing to all. The impenitent sinner shall then have nothing to plead in his own defence, when it shall appear that many of those with whom he lived have been converted and saved by those very means which he neglected and abused. It will be impossible for him to plead any singularity in his own case, when he shall behold some of those persons crowned with glory, whom he remembers to have seen in the same church he frequented, receiving the same ordinances of religion which he did, and who perhaps, in many outward respects, had fewer advantages for salvation than himself. This, my brethren, is a very solemn consideration, and, if duly attended to, can hardly fail to have a powerful influence on our minds. We who are intrusted with the care of your souls, shall then be called to give an account of our stewardship. But you, too, my dear friends, must then appear with us; and as we must declare the message we have delivered, so you must answer for the reception you gave it. Woe will be unto us if we did not preach the gospel, and if we did, woe will be to you if you did not receive it. In these views, it is no slight or transient relation which was solemnized so lately in this place; and happy indeed will it be, if the same sentence of the Judge shall acquit us both at the great day.

In the mean time, remember, and lay it to heart, that my task is not to please or to amuse you, but to dispense to you the word of life, which is able to save your souls.

Many, I doubt not, will come to this, as to other churches, merely to sit in judgment as critics of the speaker's abilities. But I hope God will save us from an undue respect to any of you in this capacity.

I hope he will save you from that disdainful nicety which scorns to be instructed with plain exhortations. A professed declaimer may justly be censured if he fails to entertain his audience. For this purpose, it is his part to make what excursions he pleaseth into the regions of imagination. But we have a dispensation committed to us, a form of sound words, from which we must not depart; a doctrine which we must deliver with uncorruptness, with gravity, with sincerity. Permit us, therefore, to aim only at the praise of faithfulness, wishing indeed to please you, but at the same time to please you only to edification.

Brethren, pray for us that we may be found faithful. Pray for yourselves, that ye may be able to suffer the word of exhortation, and profit thereby. And may the great Master of the vineyard watch over us with a propitious care, to direct our labors, and in you to give the increase of fruit unto holiness, and in the end everlasting life. *Amen.*

SERMON LV.

THE TRUE SOVEREIGN OF THE BODY.

ROMANS VI. 12, 13.—"Let not sin therefore reign in your mortal body, that ye should obey it in the lusts thereof: neither yield ye your members as instruments of unrighteousness unto sin; but yield yourselves unto GOD, as those that are alive from the dead, and your members as instruments of righteousness unto GOD."

THE apostle had, in the preceding part of the Epistle, opened at great length that fundamental doctrine of our holy religion, the justification of a sinner through faith in Jesus Christ. In the chapter from which the text is taken, he proceeds to guard the Christians to whom he wrote against those false conclusions which they might be in danger of inferring from this doctrine. And, that none might pretend to turn the grace of God into lasciviousness, he shows, with great strength of evidence, that the truths which he had been stating, so far from giving encouragement to a licentious life, on the contrary, laid peculiar obligations on all who embraced them to a strict and universal holiness. This he argues from the nature of Christian baptism, the initiating seal of the covenant of grace, showing, that by this rite we are solemnly engaged to die unto sin and live unto righteousness, in conformity to Christ's death and resurrection, signified in that ordinance. Afterwards he goes on to dissuade them from giving indulgence to sin in any kind or degree, and to enforce the obligations to universal purity by a variety of weighty arguments. "Let not sin therefore reign in your mortal body." Sin is said to *reign*, when it bears chief sway in the soul, and the person is wholly subject to its influence. The best and most sanctified Christian on earth hath still some remainder of corruption abiding in him: For perfection doth not belong to the present state; and he that saith he hath no sin, deceiveth himself, and the truth is not in him. The apostle therefore expresseth himself in this qualified manner, Let not sin *reign* in your mortal body, that ye should obey it in the lusts thereof. Beware of giving way to your sensual appetites, otherwise you forfeit all the comfort of the doctrine which I have been teaching, and must be concluded strangers to that grace of God which effectually teacheth those who are partakers of it, to "deny ungodliness and worldly lusts, and to live soberly, righteously, and godly, in the world."

Let not sin therefore reign in your mortal body, that ye should obey it in the lusts thereof: neither yield ye your members as instruments of unrighteousness unto sin; "but yield yourselves unto God." It is this last exhortation which I propose to make the subject of the present discourse: and I intend, in the

First place, To explain what is implied in yielding ourselves to God;

Secondly, To offer some directions as to the right manner of performing this duty; and

Thirdly, To enforce the exhortation by some arguments.

I begin with explaining the duty itself. And, in general, it implies, that whatever we possess, all that we are, or have, or can do, should be consecrated to God, and devoted to his service and honor. The being which we have is derived from him; every blessing which we enjoy is the fruit of his bounty; every talent with which we are distinguished was freely bestowed by him. To him, therefore, they ought to be entirely surrendered, and in the advancement of his glory at all times employed. When we serve God with the best of our faculties, and with the most valuable of our possessions, what is the whole amount of our offering? Surely if ever self-complacent thoughts on this point might have been indulged, David might have indulged them, when he, and a willing people with him, offered unto the Lord of their most precious substance with a perfect heart. Yet hear how humbly he speaks of all the costly oblations which he had brought. "Who am I, and what is my people, that we should be able to offer so willingly after this sort; for all things come of thee, and of thine own have we given thee. Thine, O Lord, is the greatness, and the power, and the glory, and the victory, and the majesty; for all that is in the heaven and the earth are thine: thine is the kingdom, and thou art exalted as head above all."

More particularly, we must yield to God our immortal souls, with all the intellectual powers which they possess. We must dedicate our understanding to the Father of Lights, to be illuminated by him with saving knowledge, to be employed in contemplating his nature and perfection; above all, to know Jesus, and him crucified, in whom are hid all the treasures of wisdom and knowledge. We must dedicate our will to that holy rule of resignation which David expressed when he said, "Here am I, let the Lord do unto me what seemeth good in his sight;" and which David's Lord expressed in circumstances infinitely more trying: "Father, not my will, but thine be done." We must consecrate our memories to be treasuries of divine truth, our affections to the pursuit of those things which are above, our senses to the salutary discipline of self-denial, and our members as instruments of holiness to God.

All our possessions and enjoyments must be devoted to God. Our wealth and power, our time and our faculties, nay life itself, which is the foundation of all our comforts, must be entirely resigned to him. Neither must we count death itself grievous, so that we finish our course with joy and true honor. We must yield ourselves to God in all capacities and relations wherein his providence may have placed us, and improve the advantages of our different conditions in life for the advancement of his glory. Are we masters or servants, parents or children, pastors or people, rulers or subjects, let us, in all these relations, be devoted to God, and discharge the various duties which result from them with fidelity and zeal, that we may glorify our Father in heaven, who hath appointed to every man his proper work, and will at length demand an account of the manner in which we have performed it.

If it be inquired for what purposes we are thus to yield ourselves unto God, the following particulars will furnish the answer.

1*st*. We are to yield ourselves to God, to do whatsoever he commands; in all instances of duty, to give a prompt and cheerful obedience to his authority. It ought to be sufficient for us, in every case, to know what God hath pronounced to be an obligation, whatever the world or the flesh may have to say against it. This is the true way to keep our minds in a steady decisive frame. "A double minded man is unstable in all his ways." He who seeks to ascertain other points besides his duty, will find himself perplexed with perpetual difficulties. Embarrassed with attending to distracting and opposite counsels, his conduct will neither be firm nor graceful; and, even when he does what is right, he will be unable to enjoy the satisfaction of it, conscious that he did it not in that simplicity and godly sincerity which alone can render our obedience acceptable, We are therefore to yield ourselves to God as our supreme Lawgiver, who hath an unquestionable title to the service of all our active powers, saying with Samuel, "Speak, Lord, for thy servant heareth;" and with the apostle Paul, "Lord, what wilt thou have me to do?"

2*dly*. We must yield ourselves to God not only to do but to suffer his will. The rewards of active obedience are not found in the present life: on the contrary, the most faithful servants of God are often visited with the severest dispensations of

Providence. We must therefore not only have our loins girt about for cheerful obedience, but our minds prepared also for patient suffering. We must be ready to resign our most valuable possessions, and our dearest comforts, the moment that they are reclaimed by him who first bestowed them, saying with Job, "The Lord gave, and the Lord hath taken away, blessed be the name of the Lord;" and, with David, "I know, O Lord, that thy judgments are right, and that in very faithfulness thou hast afflicted me."

We are already in the hand of God, by our essential dependence, as the clay is in the hands of the potter; let us likewise be so by our own consent and choice. This is the true balm of life. It is this that softens adversity, and alleviates the load of sorrow. In this we unite the noblest duty which we can perform, and the most precious benefits which we can reap. What wisdom can compare with the wisdom of resignation, which not only softens inevitable evils, but turns them into real and permanent good; which not only soothes the sense of suffering, but secures a happy and a glorious reward.

3*dly*. We must yield ourselves to God, to be disposed of by his providence, as to our lot and condition in the world. "He hath made of one blood all that dwell upon the face of the earth." He hath fixed the precise issues of life and death, and hath appointed where we shall dwell, and what station we shall occupy in the world. To one he saith, Be thou a king; and to another, Be thou a beggar. All these things come forth of the Lord of Hosts; and in his will we must cheerfully acquiesce, with a firm and meek resolution to be disposed of as he sees meet, and to glorify him in the place and station which he hath assigned us; to serve him cheerfully, while he hath service for us to perform in this world; and at last to resign our souls into his hands, when he shall require them.

4*thly*. As we must be resigned to the will of God with respect to our outward lot, so we must be satisfied with his disposal, as to the measure of spiritual gifts which he is pleased to bestow on us. Should he make us but as the foot, we must be as well contented as if he had made us the hand or the head, and rejoice that we are found qualified for being even the least honorable member in Christ's mystical body. We must not envy our brother for being wiser or better than we, more than for being richer or nobler. And though we may covet earnestly the best gifts, yet if, in the use of appointed means, we cannot attain to them, we ought, with resignation to the Father of lights, to make a diligent and faithful use of what God hath given us, trusting that they who have been good stewards over a little, shall not fail to receive their proportional reward in the day of retribution. Every vessel of honor hath not the same capacity, but every vessel of honor shall be completely filled. None shall have a mean station in the heavenly temple, although some shall be more gloriously distinguished than others. They shall all be kings and priests unto God, and mansions shall not be wanting to accommodate every class of guests in the New Jerusalem.

I proceed now to give you some directions as to the manner in which we ought to perform this duty, of yielding ourselves unto God.

I. Before we can perform this duty in an acceptable manner, it is necessary that we have just views both of God and of ourselves. In a particular manner, we must have a deep sense both of our original apostasy, and of the actual transgressions with which we are chargeable. We must yield ourselves to God, like condemned rebels, who cast themsleves on the mercy of their sovereign. Yet while we are sensible of our miserable and condemned state, we must also have a view of those riches of mercy which are open to the chief of sinners. We are to remember, with faith and gratitude, that God so loved the world, as to send his only begotten Son, not to condemn the world, but that the world through him might have life; that he only is the way, the truth, and the life; that he is able to save to the uttermost all who come unto God by him; that in him dwelleth all the fulness of the Godhead bodily; and that he is made of God to all that believe on him, wisdom, and righteousness, and sanctification, and redemption. The knowledge of these fundamental truths must influence the surrender which we make of ourselves to God, that it may be an act of our understanding, accompanied both with humility and with hope. But,

II. We must yield ourselves unto God with serious, attentive, and awakened minds. It is seldom that any permanent good is obtained, in consequence of a hasty choice. Even when the object of our choice is just and valuable, our esteem of it is apt to decline, if it has been embraced at first with too rash and violent an affection. In proportion as the charms of novelty fade, our attachment to it subsides, and indifference or aversion succeed to the eagerness of a prompt and hasty passion. If therefore we would prove steadfast and faithful, we must not be precipitate, but weigh every circumstance with care, and ponder well ere we fix our choice. We must remember, that yielding ourselves to God, will involve in it the renouncing of many favorite engagements, the performing of many difficult duties, and the mortifying of many desires, which hitherto, perhaps, it has been the whole plan of our lives to gratify. Let us, therefore, represent to ourselves the probable consequences, before we embark in so important and solemn a transaction. Consider the self-reproach, the censures of others, and, above all, the displeasure of God, which you must incur, if you retract from such a deep engagement. God doth not wish to ensnare you into his service. He does not allure you by flattering prospects of ease. He does not conceal from you the hardships which you must endure. It is plainly therefore his will, that ye should consider these things, and that before ye devote yourselves to him, ye should count the cost, and see whether ye are able to fulfil the engagement.

3dly. In yielding ourselves unto God, our hearts must be humbled, with serious and deep repentance, for having so long gone astray from him and his service. We ought to imitate the example of those penitents mentioned in the 50th chapter of Jeremiah, (verse 4.) "In those days, and in that time, saith the Lord, the children of Israel shall come, they and the children of Judah together, going and weeping, they shall go and seek the Lord their God. They shall ask the way to Zion with their faces thitherward, saying, Come and let us join ourselves to the Lord in a perpetual covenant that shall never be forgotten." God will not accept of us, unless we be truly weary of our burden, and sensible of our absolute need of a Saviour. To such, the calls of the gospel are peculiarly addressed: "Come unto me, all ye that labor and are heavy laden, and I will give you rest."—"For thus saith the high and lofty One that inhabiteth eternity, whose name is Holy, I dwell in the high and holy place; with him also that is of a contrite and humble spirit, to revive the spirit of the humble, and to revive the heart of the contrite ones."

4thly. We must yield ourselves unto God without any secret reserve or limitation, imploring that he may take the full possession of our hearts, and cast out of them whatever opposeth or exalteth itself against him. We ought to say to him, O Lord, our Lord, other lords have had dominion over us; but henceforth we will make mention of thy righteousness, even of thine only." He who hath only consistent pursuits, may follow them with a prospect of success; but a mind divided between contrary principles of action, can expect nothing but to be for ever drawn backward and forward, as they happen alternately to prevail. In this view it is impossible to yield ourselves to God, if at the same time we yield ourselves to sin in any degree. Perhaps indeed we propose to dedicate ourselves to God in general, and only to spare ourselves the mortification of renouncing a few trifling indulgences. But these indulgences have unforeseen connections with others that are not trifling, and these again with more. Or supposing that they had not, yet the truth certainly is, that when we deliberately become unfaithful to our consciences in any one instance, we lose every firm ground on which we can withstand temptation in any other instance. We lose gradually both the power and inclination to resist evil. God withdraws the good aids of his Spirit, we decline from evil to worse, and our last state becomes worse than our first. Such only, therefore, as yield themselves wholly to God, and acknowledge, after all, that they are but unprofitable servants, entitled to acceptance only through the merits of a gracious

Redeemer, have cause to hope well. All others build on the sand, but they on a rock. Their superstructure may be raised to the greatest height, and stands both firm and graceful. God will pardon their unavoidable infirmities, and assist their endeavors. They will of course make continual progress, and for every step of that progress enjoy an increase of peace and joy here, and of unfading glory hereafter.

5thly. All this must be done with an explicit regard to the Lord Jesus Christ, through whom alone we have access to the Father: "For there is none other name given under heaven whereby we can be saved, but the name of Jesus." Without this Mediator, God could have no friendly intercourse with man. The weapons of our rebellion must be surrendered into his hands; for it is in him alone that God reconciles the world unto himself. It is by the blood of Jesus that we have boldness to enter into the holiest. We are accepted only in the beloved. The Father receives no offering but at the hand of this great High Priest.

Having thus explained the duty of yielding ourselves unto God, and shown in what way it ought to be performed, what remains but that I enforce the exhortation by some motives and arguments.

Need I to represent to you the necessity of this duty? Can you withdraw yourselves from being the property of God as his creatures? Can you evade the dispensations of his providence, or snatch from him those issues of life and death, which are uncontrollably in his hands? If so, then you may consult whether you should yield yourselves to him or not? But if your present and your eternal happiness depends on his favor; if you cannot secure an interest in his favor otherwise than by complying with this exhortation; if you must otherwise be left to struggle as you best can, with all the evils of life, and at last be banished his presence for ever, to spend a miserable eternity with reprobate spirits, what choice is left? Can you hesitate a moment to comply with what you cannot alter, and to surrender yourselves to Him, who will either glorify himself in you as vessels of mercy, or as vessels prepared for destruction?

Consider, in the *2d* place, the reasonableness of this duty. This is the argument of the apostle to the Romans: "I beseech you, therefore, brethren, by the mercies of God, that ye present your bodies a living sacrifice, holy, acceptable unto God, which is your reasonable service." And what can be so reasonable as to consecrate to God that being, those faculties, those possessions and enjoyments, which we derive from his bounty. If there is reasonableness in acknowledging our debts, and in being thankful for our benefits; if there is reasonableness in submitting to be guided by unerring wisdom, and to be disposed of by infinite goodness; in a word, if there be any thing superior in reasonableness to any other that reason requires, it is this, that we should yield ourselves to that God who made us, who preserves and hath redeemed us, and hath pledged his faithfulness to conduct all those to happiness who put their confidence in him. And this leads me to the last argument which I shall use for enforcing this exhortation, which is the advantage with which it will be attended. At the same time that we yield ourselves to God, he gives himself to us in all the fulness of his grace; for this is the tenor of his well ordered covenant, "I will be your God, and ye shall be my people." And what an infinite portion is this? If all the treasures of grace were open to our choice, would it be possible for to pitch on any blessing so rich and compendious as this, that God would accept of us as his property, and provide for us as he provides for his own? Surely then we cannot want any good thing. His wisdom can guide us through all the perplexing paths of life; his power can support us in every danger and difficulty; and his goodness is more than sufficient to bestow on us all things richly to enjoy.

I have only to add, that the exhortation in the text belongs in an especial manner to you who are as yet in early and vigorous years. Now your understandings are capable of the firmest impressions. Now your wills are most pliable. Now your affections are most patient of discipline. Now your bodies are most useful to your minds. Now your minds are most unfettered, and your whole man most susceptible of good impressions, and most capable of exerting them in action. Lose not, therefore, your irrecoverable advantage. Answer now when God calls you with most affection. Offer yourselves while you are most worth the offering. Govern your appetites before the evil day come. Now you may gird them, and carry them whither you will; but if you neglect this precious season, they will hereafter gird you, and carry you whither you would not. An early virtue is the most worthy and valuable offering, honored and blessed with the kindest acceptance of God. But when a man shall look into himself, and find his faculties depraved and weakened, stained with the pollution, wearied with the service, sick with the disappointments, and darkened with the impostures of sin, how comfortless a task must he have in preparing an offering to God from among such a lame and diseased herd. "Remember therefore now thy Creator in the days of thy youth, ere the evil days come, and the years draw nigh in which thou shalt say, I have no pleasure in them." *Amen.*

SERMON LVI.

Preached on a Day of Humiliation before Celebrating the Lord's Supper.

THE REWARD OF HUMILITY.

LUKE XVIII. 19.—"He that humbleth himself shall be exalted."

As man fell by *pride*, it is reasonable to conclude that he can only rise again by *humility:* and here we are taught that this is the express ordination and appointment of God; for thus saith the faithful and true Witness, "Every one that exalteth himself shall be abased; and he that humbleth himself shall be exalted." I cannot therefore employ your time to better purpose, especially upon such an occasion as this, than in opening the nature of true humiliation, and endeavoring to illustrate the necessity and use of it, to prepare our hearts for those enriching communications both of mercy and grace, which our Saviour, in this passage, encourageth us to expect.

I BEGIN with opening the nature of true humiliation. This takes its rise from spiritual discoveries of the evil of sin, as the transgression of a law which is holy, just, and good; as an act of outrageous and unprovoked rebellion against the mildest, as well as the most righteous administration; as the basest ingratitude to our kindest Benefactor, the Author of our being, and of all that we possess; and especially as it renders us unlike to him who is not only the standard but the source of perfection, and consequently incapable of any friendly correspondence with the Father of our spirits, the Fountain of light, of life, and of joy.

These spiritual discoveries of the evil of sin, produce a fixed and solid apprehension of our own ill deserving because of it. We see the justice of the sentence which condemns us, and cannot help acknowledging that we are unworthy of the least of all God's mercies, and liable to that tremendous wrath which is revealed from heaven against all unrighteousness and ungodliness of men. Hence arise grief and shame, and all that inward distress which necessarily attend the consciousness of guilt, the present sense of forfeited happiness, and the fearful prospect of that unknown misery which awaits transgressors in the world to come.

To all which must be added, such a deep conviction of our utter inability to do any thing that can be effectual for our own recovery, as issues in a despair of relief from every other quarter but the free mercy of God, extended to sinners through Jesus Christ, and the effectual operation of his renewing grace. We are not truly humbled, till we feel ourselves wretched, miserable, poor, blind, and naked, equally destitute of righteousness and strength, incapable of making any satisfaction for past offences, and having no power of our own to rectify that fatal disorder in our frame, which is the bitter fruit of our apostasy from God.

Such was the state of the publican's mind, who is presented to our view in the foregoing parable, as an approved example for our imitation; whilst the Pharisee, who trusted in himself that he was rightcous, standing apart from his fellow-worshippers, as one who disdained to hold communion with them, boldly addressed the Divine Majesty, and, under the specious form of thanksgiving, poured forth the pride and uncharitableness of his heart. The publican, we are told, stood afar off; and, though his face was turned towards the mercy-seat, yet, conscious of his unworthiness, he would not so much as lift up his eyes unto heaven, but smiting upon his breast, as the seat of his disease and pain, from whence he despaired of fetching any relief, he as it were flies from himself to the God of all grace, and gives vent to his penitent and humble hope, in these few but emphatical words, "God be merciful to me a sinner." But the nature of true humiliation will more fully appear from the salutary purposes for which it is intended, which was the

Second thing I proposed to illustrate; and hence likewise we shall discover how necessary it is, in order to our regaining that happiness we have forfeited. And,

I. It is of use to disgrace and mortify carnal self, that usurping idol which sits on the throne of God, and reigns in the heart of every natural man. Herein lies the essence of man's apostasy. He is fallen from God to self. Dissatisfied with the rank which God had assigned him, he attempted to break loose from the Author of his being, and to seize upon knowledge, immortality, and happiness, without any dependence upon the hand that formed him. This, my brethren, is the original disease of our nature; in this consisteth the sinfulness and the misery of man. He loveth himself supremely, he liveth to himself ultimately: the genuine language of his heart is, "Who is the Lord, that I should obey him?"

He begins indeed to alter his tone, when conviction, like an armed man, forceth its way into his soul; then he feels his dependence, and wisheth to be at peace with that Being whom he finds he is unable to resist. For this end he will part, at least for a season, with many of the members of the body of sin. Nay, so far as the external act extends, there are few duties perhaps which he will not consent to perform. But, when he is driven from the outworks, he only retires to the chief fortress of sin. Still self is worshipped in a different form; and, though he sees that it cannot possess the throne by violence, yet he hopes that it may be able to purchase it with a price. Thus the homage that was paid to sinful self, is only transferred to righteous self; and now the idol which was formerly black as hell, being whitewashed, and decked with some forms of godliness, is permitted to wield the sceptre in peace, till either grace or vengeance wipe off the false coloring, and stripping the deceiver of his gorgeous apparel, cast him down to the ground, and put a final period to his usurped domination.

Of all the parts of mortification, self-denial is by far the most painful and difficult; indeed all the rest are virtually contained in it. Were it only riches or honors, or even the fruit of the body for the sin of the soul, a carnal mind, stung with remorse, and terrified with the prospect of impending wrath, might be brought to part with them; but to part with his all, with his life, with his self, this indeed is a hard saying, and more than enough to make him go away sorrowful.

Now herein appeareth the end and the necessity of such humiliation as I endeavored to describe. This layeth the whole load upon self, and breaketh the very heart of the old man; it setteth the house on fire, in which we both trusted and delighted, and maketh us not only to see, but to feel that it is time for us to abandon it, lest we be consumed. This then is the first office of humiliation, to hide pride from our eyes, by showing us that we are our own destroyers, and giving us such discoveries of our guilt and pollution, that we are made to abhor ourselves in dust and in ashes, and to cry out with the publican, God be merciful to us sinners. This leads me to mention a

Second, and more salutary end of humiliation, which indeed may be called its ultimate end, because the self annihilation I have been speaking of, derives its chief importance from its tendency to promote it, and that is, true humiliation prepares the soul for the honorable reception of Christ and his grace.

I say, for the *honorable* reception of Christ; it is not meet that he should come into an unhumbled heart; for, though his errand be to heal us, yet he must have the welcome that is due to a physician. He comes indeed to save us, but he comes at the same time to be honored in our salvation. Though his grace be free, yet he will not expose it to contempt, but have the fulness and the freedom of it acknowledged and glorified. Faith indeed accepts the gift, but then it must be a humble faith that is sensible of its worth; a thankful faith, that magnifieth the Giver; and an obedient faith, that will practically improve the mercy bestowed. Christ hath no grace so free as to save those who neither feel their need of it, nor know its worth. Christ's benefits are not applied in the same way they were purchased. When he came to ransom us, he consented to be a sufferer; for then he bore our griefs, and carried our sorrows; the chastisement of our peace was laid upon him, as the substitute and surety of guilty man; but when he comes, by his saving grace, into the soul, he will not then be entertained with contempt. He came in the flesh on purpose to be humbled; but when he comes in the spirit, it is that he may be exalted. On the cross he was reputed a sinner, and bore the punishment that was due to sin; but, in the soul, he is the conqueror of sin, and comes to take possession of his own, and therefore must be treated according to his dignity. It was the hour and power of darkness while he suffered; but, when he enters into the heart by his quickening Spirit, that is the hour of triumph, and the prevailing power of heavenly light; and, therefore, though in the flesh he submitted to contempt and reproach, yet he will not endure to be slighted in the soul. No; there he must be enthroned in our most reverend esteem, and crowned with our highest gratitude and love. The cross must there be the portion of his enemies. The crown and sceptre which he purchased must be yielded to him; and every thought must be captivated to the obedience of his will.

This is the end of humiliation, to employ the soul for the fuller entertainment of the Lord that bought it; to prepare the way before him; to whip the buyers and sellers out of the living temples of our hearts, that they may become holiness to the Lord, a fit habitation for the King of Glory.

From this account of the nature and use of humiliation, you may be able to judge what measure of it is absolutely necessary. It must at least go so deep as to undermine our pride, and bring us so low, that the blood of Christ, and the favor of God, shall become more precious in our esteem, than all the riches, and honors, and pleasures of a present world. At the same time, we must beware of ascribing to our own humiliation any part of the office of Christ, or of the honor that is due to him. We must not think that we can recommend ourselves to the favor of God by the worth of our sorrows, though we should weep even tears of blood. It is not true humiliation, if it lead us not wholly beyond ourselves, to seek pardon and life from Christ alone; and, therefore, it would be a plain contradiction, if humiliation should assume the place of satisfaction and merit, or be in any degree relied upon instead of the Saviour, or so much as associated with him in procuring our salvation.

Hence likewise we learn, that humiliation becomes excessive, and counteracts its chief end, when it confines our attention so entirely to our own unworthiness, as to darken our views of gospel grace, and prevent or obstruct our application to Christ. But as few, comparatively speaking, err upon this side, I shall rather take occasion, from what has been said, to point out some of the symptoms of the opposite extreme, and then call upon those whose humiliation, upon trial, shall appear to be defective, to beg of God the blessing of a broken and contrite heart, which is the professed design of our assembling together this day.

1*st*, then, They may certainly conclude that they are not sufficiently humbled, who suffer their hearts to be lifted up with their duties or attainments, and are not suitably affected with those imperfections and blemishes which necessarily cleave to their best performances. The true Christian grows downward in humility, in the same proportion that he abounds in the fruits of righteousness. The nearer he approaches to a holy God, the more clearly he discovers his own guilt and pollution. Thus holy Nehemiah, after he had been recounting, to the praise of divine grace, the many eminent services he had been enabled to do for the church, addresses to God this humble prayer, "O spare me, according to the greatness of thy mercy!"

2d. When you are apt to murmur and repine, because your duties are not accompanied with a present reward; when you are ready to say, in the language of the Jews of old, "Wherefore have we fasted and prayed, and thou regardest not;" this is another symptom that secretly you entertain an opinion of some worthiness in yourselves; for, where nothing is due, there can be no right to complain when the favor is either delayed or refused.

3d. When you begin to think that any of Christ's sayings are hard, and to wish that his laws were less strict and extensive, and are hesitating whether you should yield to them or not; when you are unwilling to take up his cross, and to forsake all for the hopes of glory, but are set upon a thriving course in the world, and suffer your hearts to be overcharged with the cares of this life, and are cumbered about many things through your own choice, this shows that you are not yet sufficiently humbled, otherwise you would not stand thus trifling with Christ; and, if God have mercy upon you, he will bring you down, abase your earthly appetite, teach you to know that one thing is needful, and constrain you to choose the better part.

4th. When you grow heartless and dull in the service of God, and relish no sweetness in the exercises of religion; when you begin to be indifferent about communion with God, and have little anxiety to know whether your services be accepted; when you can pray without looking after your prayers, and attend upon ordinances almost merely from custom, or to keep conscience quiet, without a real concern to find God in them, or to receive benefit from them; especially if you are so far indifferent about the spiritual consolation of the saints, that vain company, or amusing diversions, can make up for the want of them, and keep your minds easy and satisfied without them; it must be obvious to yourselves, that you need a sharper rod than you have ever yet felt, that you may be effectually taught to know your true home, and to take greater pleasure in the fellowship of your Father and brethren, than in strangers and enemies to God and your own souls. Once more, in the

5th place, When, instead of feeding upon ordinances, and receiving them thankfully, you rather pick quarrels with them, and those that dispense them; when you cannot bear to have your faults laid open, but hate and revile the faithful reprover; when you grow censorious and uncharitable, like the Pharisee in the context, treating others with contempt, aggravating their failings, and extenuating their graces; especially when men begin to grow wanton in matters of religion, itching after novelties, and affecting singularity; when they think themselves fitter to teach than to learn, and that the church is not pure or good enough for their company: all this cries aloud for farther humiliation. And, when it shall please God to lead them into the chambers of imagery, and expose the hidden contents of them to their view, he will make them to stoop to the very persons whom once they slighted, and to judge themselves unworthy of the communion of those whom they formerly despised as unworthy of theirs.

These are a few marks by which I would have you to try yourselves; and, if you find that any of them are partly applicable to you, or, if by any other means you can discover that pride and self-exaltation still retain too much power in your hearts, let me now beseech you to cry earnestly to God for that humble and contrite spirit which he expressly requires, and hath graciously promised to accept.

Grief, I know, is an unwelcome guest to nature; but grace can see reason to bid it welcome, as a necessary consequence of our past sins, and an essential preparative for our future recovery.

You will submit to the severest regimen, and take the most loathsome potions, for the health of your bodies; and should you not submit to the bitterest sorrows, and the keenest rebukes, for the saving of your souls? It is true, as I formerly observed, that your deepest humiliation merits nothing, and can make no amends to God for your sins; neither is it for any want of sufficiency in the blood of Christ that it is required: but it is part of the fruit of his blood upon your souls; for if his blood do not melt and break your hearts, you have no part in him.

Consider whence you are coming. Is it not from a state of enmity against God? and is it decent, is it ingenuous, to leave such a state, without lamenting that you staid in it so long?

Consider what sorrows they be which these sorrows are intended to prevent, and what those are now suffering in hell, who felt not this godly sorrow upon earth. Yours have hope, but theirs are sharpened with despair; yours are medicinal, but theirs are tormenting; yours are of short duration, but theirs are eternal. Grudge not then at the opening of a vein, when so many shall bleed at the heart for ever. Besides, who was it that brought you to the necessity of this sorrow? Who was it that sinned, and laid in the fuel of after remorse? God did not do this. All the pain you can feel, is of your own preparation. God only undoes what you have been doing.

Consider farther, that you have a wise and tender-hearted physician, who perfectly knows what sorrow and grief are; for he himself was a man of sorrows, and acquainted with griefs, and is therefore disposed to pity them that are in sorrow. He delighteth not in your trouble, but in your cure and after consolation, and therefore you may be assured that he will deal gently with you, and put no more bitterness into the cup than is necessary for your recovery. He was sent to heal the broken-hearted, and he invites the laboring and heavy laden to come to him for rest. When he hath wounded you, he will bind up your wounds as tenderly as you can desire. He hath not, indeed, that blind fondness for you which you have for yourselves. He will not be so cruelly merciful as to save you from that sorrow which is necessary to save your souls from perdition; but at the same time, he will not suffer you to taste one drop of vinegar and gall, nor to shed one tear, but what tends to your future comfort and joy.

Remember that the more you are humbled after a godly sort, the sweeter will Christ and all his benefits be to you while you live. One taste of his healing love will make you bless those medicinal sorrows that prepared for it. Christ is not equally esteemed by all whom he will save; and would you not rather be yet more emptied of yourselves now, that hereafter you may be fuller of Christ and his grace? for our Saviour here assures us in the text, that a thorough humiliation is a certain forerunner of future exaltation. "Every one that humbleth himself shall be exalted." When men propose to build high, they dig deeper for the foundation. Paul was laid exceeding low at his conversion, that he might be better fitted for the important services to which he had afterwards the honor to be called.

Let these considerations reconcile you to the humbling work of the Spirit of God. And if any thing you have heard hath touched your hearts, seek not relief among foolish companions, but retire to your closets, and on your bended knees beseech the Lord to perfect the good work he hath begun; and He who comforteth those that are cast down, will not leave you in the Red Sea, but carry you safely through to the farther side, and put the Song of Moses and of the Lamb into your mouths, "giving you beauty for ashes, the oil of joy for mourning, and the garments of praise for the spirit of heaviness." *Amen.*

SERMON LVII.

Preached after the Celebration of the Lord's Supper.

DAVID'S CHOICE AND DELIGHT.

PSALM cxix. 173, 174, 175.—"Let thine hand help me; for I have chosen thy precepts. I have longed for thy salvation, O LORD; and thy law is my delight. Let my soul live, and it shall praise thee; and let thy judgments help me."

THESE words were immediately addressed to God, most High, whose workmanship we all are, even to him that quickeneth the dead, and calleth those things that be not as though they were. Here David appeals to the Searcher of hearts, and lays before him not the product of his own labor and skill, as though he possessed something whereof he might glory before God, but what he gratefully acknowledges to be the doing of the Lord; a heart in some measure renewed after his image, and panting after a nearer and still more perfect resemblance.

I shall therefore consider this account, which, in the form of a solemn address to God, the Psalmist here gives of his own temper and conduct, as an approved model or pattern for our imitation. What this holy man was, that ought we to be; and such we shall certainly endeavor to be, if we aspire to the character whereby David was distinguished by the Supreme Judge himself, when he dignified him with the most honorable of all appellations, even that of the man after his own heart.

The passage contains,

I. The distinguishing character. And,

II. The leading requests of a truly godly man.

Each of these I shall briefly illustrate and improve; the one for the present trial, and the other for the future direction, of those who have this day made a public profession of their faith in Christ, over the sacred symbols of his broken body and shed blood, in the holy sacrament of his supper.

I BEGIN with the distinguishing character of a truly godly man: and you will observe the following particulars distinctly marked, viz. The matter of his choice—The object of his desires—and, The source of his joy.

The godly man's choice—is the precepts of God. David had said, (verse 3.) That he had chosen the testimonies of God for his heritage; by which he probably meant the promises of that everlasting covenant, ordered in all things and sure, to which he afterwards resorted in the immediate prospect of death, as all his salvation, and all his desire. These promises are indeed exceeding great and precious, suited to all the necessities of the saints, and extending to every blessing that can be denoted by these two significant and most comprehensive words, GRACE and GLORY. But one may choose, or rather covet, the heritage of a child, who hath an aversion to the duties that result from that relation; and therefore the choosing the *law* or *precepts* of God, for regulating the heart and life, is, of all others, the most discriminating character of a true child of God; for there can be no doubt, that one who sincerely devotes himself to the service of God, will most sincerely and ardently wish to be happy in the possession of the promised inheritance.

Let us next attend to the object of the godly man's desire. "I have longed," said David, "for thy salvation;" a present salvation from the guilt and power of sin; and future salvation, in the full and everlasting enjoyment of God in heaven. David was already possessed of the first of these; for he spake from his own experience, when he said, "blessed is the man whose transgression is forgiven, whose sin is covered, unto whom the Lord imputeth not iniquity, and in whose spirit there is no guile." He had the happiness to be a partaker, both of pardoning mercy and of sanctifying grace; yet still he longed for more of this salvation, that is, for a more assured faith of pardoning mercy, and larger measures of sanctifying grace. It is a just observation, with respect to earthly things, that NATURE is contented with a little, and GRACE with less. But it is quite the reverse as to spiritual things. Here grace is not contented with a little; on the contrary, it is insatiable; the more it hath received, the more it desires to receive. Enjoyment, instead of surfeiting, sharpens the appetite. Nay, so sweet is their relish, that every renewed taste of it abates and quenches the thirst for other things. "There be many that say, who will show us any good?" This is the voice of the mere child of Adam. But what saith the new man in Christ? "One thing have I desired of the Lord, and that will I seek after.—As the hart panteth for the brooks of water, so panteth my soul after thee, O God.—Whom have I in heaven but thee? and there is none upon earth that I desire besides thee."

This leads us forward to the source of the godly man's joy. "Thy law," saith David, "is my delight." Here he chooses the term *law* for denoting the whole revelation of God's will, to remind us of the inseparable connection between privilege and duty, faith and obedience, holiness and comfort; and to teach us, that we ought to be thankful to God for the direction he hath given us in the road to heaven, no less than for the promises by which we are assured of the possession of it. But what I would chiefly observe is, that the joy of a saint is not extracted from such base and perishing materials as corn, and wine, and oil; it flows spontaneously from the fountain of living water, from the pure source of that word of God, which liveth and abideth for ever. Nay, so little is it dependent upon, or even connected with, any thing that belongs to the present world, that "although the fig-tree should not blossom, neither should fruit be in the vine; the labor of the olive should fail, and the fields should yield no meat; the flock should be cut off from the fold, and there should be no herd in the stall;" yet still the saint can rejoice in the Lord, and joy in the God of his salvation. Nay, when the heaven shall be shrivelled up like a scrawl when it is rolled together, and every mountain and island shall be moved out of their places; he can look at the universal desolation, and say, when these materials are consumed, I shall have lost nothing. "All things are mine, for I am Christ's, and Christ is God's.—God lives, blessed be my rock—The Lord is the portion of my inheritance," and in him I possess and enjoy all things.

These three particulars, respecting the matter of the godly man's choice, the object of his desire, and the source of his joy, may help us to form a just estimate of ourselves; and this is the improvement I would have you to make of this branch of the subject.

How are your hearts affected towards the precepts of God's word? an outward reluctant obedience there may be, compelled by the slavish fear of wrath: but do you serve God from choice, with a free and liberal mind? Doth the Lord Jesus appear as amiable with the crown upon his head, and the sceptre in his hand, as when clad with his garments rolled in blood?

Is salvation, in all its extent, the chief object of your desire? even the present salvation of an inward growing light, and love, and purity; as well as the future salvation of deliverance from the fire that is not quenched, and the enjoyment of those positive pleasures which are at God's right hand for evermore.

Do you know what it is to hunger and thirst after righteousness? "They that are after the flesh do mind the things of the flesh, but they that are after the spirit do mind the things of the spirit.—If you be risen with Christ, you will seek the things that are above." You will never think you have already attained, either are already perfect; but forgetting the things that are behind, and reaching forth to those things which are before, you will press towards the mark for the prize of the high calling of God in Christ Jesus.

Once more, from whence do you derive your comfort and joy; from the wells of salvation, that issue forth from beneath the throne of God and the Lamb, or from the polluted streams that spring out of this footstool upon which we tread?

By this unerring touchstone of God's word let us examine and prove ourselves; and if the Spirit bears witness with our spirits, that these lineaments of the new creature, though too much blended and marred with the features of the old man, are nevertheless legible on the fleshy tables of our hearts, let us give glory to God, who hath thus far formed us for himself, and trust, that he who hath begun a good work in us will carry it on till it be perfected in the heavenly glory. And let the many blemishes we must unavoidably discover, while they humble us in the presence of a holy God, urge us forward, at the same time, to a throne of grace, that we may obtain mercy for the pardon of past offences, and find grace to help us in every future time of need.

Having thus endeavored to illustrate, and to improve, for self-examination, the distinguishing character of the godly man, as it lies before us in this passage, let us now attend, for our direction, to his leading requests.

1*st.* He prays for strengthening and upholding grace, "Let thine hand help me."

Dependence upon the Creator belongs to the essence of every creature. None of them subsist by themselves, neither do they possess any thing that they can claim as their property. The highest seraph that ministers before the throne, must adopt the language of the apostle Paul, and say as he did, " By the grace of God, I am what I am." We read of " angels who kept not their first estate, but left their own habitation, being reserved in everlasting chains under darkness, unto the judgment of the great day." Adam, created after the image of God, and furnished with every advantage suited to his rank, seduced by an apostate spirit, forfeited at once both his innocence and happiness, in consequence whereof all his posterity come into the world involved in the forfeiture he incurred, equally destitute of righteousness and strength, according to that saying of the apostle Paul, (Romans v. 6.) "When we were without strength, in due time Christ died for the ungodly." And though this weakness is in part removed by the renewing influences of the Spirit of God, yet there will always be need for that caution, " Be not high minded, but fear." Who can say, " My mountain standeth strong, I shall never be moved?" The most eminent saints have not only failed, but failed in those very graces for which they were most eminent, and that too by means of temptations far inferior to others which they were enabled to resist. The faith of Abraham, the patience of Job, the meekness of Moses, and the courage of Peter, were all found unequal to the conflict, when left alone in the hour of trial. These examples are recorded for our admonition; and on each of them we may read the solemn warning, " Let him that thinketh he standeth take heed lest he fall." Remember who it was that said, " Without me ye can do nothing. As the branch cannot bear fruit of itself, except it abide in the vine, no more can ye, except ye abide in me." Blessed be God for the assurance we have that help is laid for us upon one that is mighty; upon him let us lean in our journey through the wilderness; to his hand let us look for the help we need, and he will make his grace sufficient for us. Animated by this hope, the same apostle who said in one place, " I know that in me, that is, in my flesh, dwelleth no good thing:" in another place, setting his foot upon the neck of his enemies, utters the shout of victory in those triumphant words, " I can do all things through Christ which strengtheneth me." Let us go and do likewise. To the prayer for upholding grace, David adds,

2dly, A desire for quickening grace; for this I take to be the true import of the request, " Let my soul live." Sometimes, indeed, we find him praying for the life of the body, as when he says, " O spare me that I may recover strength, before I go hence and be no more:" But here the expression is too strong to be limited to a sense comparatively so low.

Life, or conscious exercise, though a valuable gift in itself, is a gift we possess in common with the worst of our own kind, and with the meanest and most noxious of the inferior creatures. Nay, devils partake of it in a higher degree than man. Besides, the life of man, since the apostasy, is become short and precarious; and though it holds true in general, that " skin for skin, all that a man hath will he give for his life:" yet the bitterness of affliction hath caused many to grow weary of it, insomuch that their souls have chosen strangling and death rather than life. But in all these respects, the life of the soul is entirely the reverse. It is not a privilege common to all, but the gift of special distinguishing love. It was purchased for condemned sinners by the blood of Christ; and is produced in dead sinners by his renewing Spirit. So far is it from being short and precarious, that its duration is eternal. It is a " life hid with Christ in God; and because he lives, all who believe in him shall live also." The longer it is enjoyed also, the more it is esteemed. Who was ever heard to say of spiritual life, " I loathe it—I would not live always?" Nay, it is the life of the soul alone that gives a relish to the life of the body, and enables the believer, under the heaviest pressure of affliction, either to possess it with thankfulness, or to resign it with joy.

This was the life for which David prayed; a confirmed sense of pardoning mercy, larger measures of sanctifying grace, communion with his God in a present world, and the full and everlasting enjoyment of him in heaven. The life for which he prays, is no other than the salvation for which he longed. He had tasted of its sweetness, and he thirsted for more. "Let my soul live," saith he; to which he subjoins, "and it shall praise thee." From which words we learn, for our farther direction,

3dly, The ultimate end for which David was so earnest in his requests for help and life, and the improvement he proposed to make of both. There were no doubt blessings that would greatly contribute to his own honor and comfort; but every private and personal interest was in him subordinated to the glory of God. He prayed for upholding and quickening grace, that he might be better qualified for the service of his God, to whom he had devoted himself and his all. Thus he prays, (Psal. li.) "Restore unto me the joy of thy salvation, and uphold me by thy free Spirit; then will I teach transgressors thy way, and sinners shall be converted unto thee. Lord, open thou my lips, and my mouth shall show forth thy praise." And the principal reason for which he was desirous to obtain divine consolation, appears from the use he intended to make of it, (verse 32 of this Psalm) "I will run the way of thy commandments, when thou shalt enlarge my heart."

I shall therefore make this my concluding exhortation to you.—By your solemn profession at the table of the Lord, you have publicly acknowledged that you are not your own, but bought with a price; in consequence whereof, you are strictly obliged to live not unto yourselves, but to him that bought you; to glorify your Redeemer, both with your bodies and spirits, which are his. He says concerning you, "This people have I formed for myself, to show forth my praise." He calls the world to take knowledge of you, as the persons by whom he expects to be honored. "Ye are a chosen generation, a royal priesthood, an holy nation, a peculiar people; that ye should show forth the praises of him who hath called you out of darkness into his marvellous light. I beseech you therefore by the mercies of God, that ye walk worthy of the vocation wherewith ye are called, with all lowliness and meekness, with long-suffering, forbearing one another in love. Adding to your faith, virtue; and to virtue, knowledge; and to knowledge, temperance; and to temperance, patience; and to patience, godliness; and to godliness, brotherly kindness; and to brotherly kindness, charity:"—abounding in all those fruits of righteousness, which are through Jesus Christ, to the praise and glory of God; shining as lights in the midst of a perverse and a crooked generation; holding forth the word of life. After this manner improve the help and life you have received, in your attendance upon this precious means of grace. "Whatsoever things are true, whatsoever things are honest, whatsoever things are just, whatsoever things are pure, whatsoever things are lovely, whatsoever things are of good report; if there be any virtue, and if there be any praise, think on these things." And "let your light so shine before men, that they may see your good works, and glorify your Father which is in heaven." *Amen.*

SERMON LVIII.

Preached at the Celebration of the Lord's Supper.

CHRIST'S PRAYER FOR HIS PEOPLE.

JOHN XVI. 26, 27.—"At that day ye shall ask in my name: And I say not unto you, that I will pray the Father for you; for the Father himself loveth you, because ye have loved me, and have believed that I came out from GOD."

THESE words spake Jesus, to support the drooping spirits of his disciples. We are told in the 6th verse, "that sorrow had filled their hearts." Although they did not fully understand the intimations he had given them of his approaching sufferings and death, although their warm affection for him made them slow to believe an event so contrary to their expectations and desires; yet the manner in which he had been speaking to them for some time past, and the unusual tenderness which had of late appeared in his discourses to them, left them no room to doubt, that some sore and heavy trial was at hand. Jesus perceiving their grief, begins to tell them more plainly of his departure from them; but at the same time gives them such good reasons for it, as could not fail to quiet their minds, and to convince them that his leaving them, instead of being a disaster, was every way necessary for their best interests and happiness. "It is expedient for you," says he, in the 7th verse, "that I go away; for if I go not away, the Comforter will not come unto you; but if I depart, I will send him unto you." As if he had said, "The work given me to do is not yet finished: I must yet suffer more before I can reign; but after my exaltation, to which my death is a previous and necessary step, I will send forth the Comforter, who shall fully supply my place, and make up to you for my bodily absence. What though you shall no more hear instruction from these lips, you shall have a teacher within you, even the Spirit of truth, who shall guide you into all truth. Whilst I am yet with you, you have indeed ready access to me, for counsel and direction, in every case of hazard and perplexity; and perhaps you fear that when I am taken from you, you shall want a friend to apply to; but know and rejoice, that I go to my Father who is greater than I, to him you shall have free access for my sake; and whatever ye shall ask in my name, he shall give it unto you. If I have befriended you so much in my present humble condition, what may you not expect from me, when I am exalted at my Father's right hand."

It is this last ground of comfort which our Saviour enlarges upon in the verses now under consideration; and the design of them is, to confirm his disciples in the belief of this, that whatever suitable prayer they shall offer up to the Father in his name, they may assuredly expect a gracious answer. The argument he uses for this purpose is very conclusive, and is no where else in Scripture, that I know of, expressed with the same degree of energy and force. "I say not unto you, that I will pray the Father for you, for the Father himself loveth you." That is, My Father is so fully satisfied with my undertaking for the redemption of the world, and my sufferings and obedience are so meritorious and acceptable in his sight, that even though I were to conceal from you that I am to be your constant intercessor and advocate in heaven, all of you who love me and believe in me, have abundant reason to expect a favorable hearing from the Father himself: "for the Father himself loveth you, because ye have loved me, and have believed that I came out from God." And if the Father is already so much disposed to hear our prayers, how great must *their* encouragement be, and how strong *their* consolation, who know besides that their Redeemer liveth to enforce their requests; that he maketh intercession for them, according to the will of God; that his mediation must be always effectual; and that him the Father heareth always. These are joyful tidings indeed, and must make a strong impression on every one whose conscience testifies that he loves the Redeemer, and believes that he came out from God. The Father is fully reconciled to him, the Son constantly prays for him at the throne of heaven; and what may he not then expect from the fulness of him who filleth all in all? But that we may have a more complete view of the comfort which this text presents to us, I shall separately consider

I. The love of the Father.

II. The intercession of the Son.

III. The security which believers derive from them both, as inseparably united together.

I. then, Let us take a view of the love of God separately from the intercession of our blessed Redeemer. And, for our better conceiving of this, let us consider that remarkable declaration which we have, (John iii. 16, 17.) "God so loved the world, that he gave his only begotten Son, that whosoever believeth in him should not perish, but have everlasting life; for God sent not his Son into the world to condemn the world, but that the world through him might be saved." It was the Father who laid the plan of our redemption. It was he who sent his Son into the world, not in anger, but in love, that his poor lost creatures might be recovered and saved from that dreadful gulf of misery into which they had plunged themselves. Many look upon the Father as an austere and rigid Being, who has no compassion, who delights in punishing, and even suffers a sort of violence in admitting Christ to be surety for sinners. But it appears from the fore-cited passage, that this is by no means the light in which the Scriptures represent him to us. No; goodness and mercy are the attributes in which he glories. "God is love," saith the apostle. He is not only represented as accepting the offer when made by the Redeemer, but as being the first mover and spring. How does he rejoice that he has found out a ransom! what special delight does he express towards the Son, when employed in this favored undertaking! "This," says he, by an audible voice, "is my beloved Son, in whom I am well pleased." He sent forth his angels from heaven to proclaim the news of good will to men, to minister to the tempted Saviour, to strengthen him under his agony in the garden, and at last to conduct him in triumph to his own right hand. All these are unquestionable proofs of the Father's love. And if God so lòved mankind whilst they were enemies, how much more must he love them when they become friends, when they comply with the terms which he has graciously established for their recovery, by loving and believing in him whom he hath sent? With what delight and complacency must he look upon them? He views us now as ransomed by the blood of his own equal. He looks upon us in the face of his Anointed; and whilst he does so, how warm and affectionate must his regard be! And O what comfort arises to us from this! If our hearts do not condemn us, what confidence must we have towards such a God! When the sight of our distress, worthless and wicked as we were, moved him to find a Redeemer, will he now reject us when we cry to him, and plead the merit of his own gift? No: "He that spared not his own Son, but gave him up to the death for us all, will certainly with him likewise freely give us all things." Thus the love of God, considered singly by itself, gives us the greatest ground of expectation from him, even though the intercession of Christ were less certainly revealed to us than it is. Let us now, in the

II. place, Take under our consideration the intercession of Christ, than which there is nothing more clearly held forth to us in sacred Scripture. He himself says to his disciples, in the 16th verse of the 14th chapter of this gospel, "I will pray the Father, and he shall give you another Comforter." This is a special part of his office, as our great High Priest, to intercede for his people; and his saving ability is particularly concluded from this, "that he ever liveth to make intercession for us." Heb. vii. 25. Indeed, we have both an example and proof of his intercession in the chapter following, which is wholly employed in prayers for his people. Let us now make the supposition that the Father's love was more doubtful; yea, that there were even some ground to suspect that his affection was quite alienated from the children of men, yet, unless we were to suppose that he had likewise thrown aside all regard to his only begotten Son, we have still ground enough to conclude, that for HIS sake he will bestow whatever he asks upon those who love him and believe on him. When he presents that body in which he suffered so much—when he pleads the merit and sufficiency of that sacrifice which he offered up—when he urges the memory of the shame, the pain, and the cursed death he underwent to satisfy the justice of God, and to magnify his law, how prevalent must his suit be! Can the Father turn a deaf ear to his beloved Son, whilst he enforces his plea with such powerful reasonings? Can he behold the prints of that bloody punishment which himself inflicted upon him, and be insensible of their merit? Now that the most rigorous demands of stern justice are answered, will not mercy be awakened at the entreaty of such a suitor? It were absurd to think so. No; the Father's love to our Redeemer, nay, impartial justice itself, secures the success of the Saviour's intercession, though God were more averse to a reconciliation than the most gloomy self-tormenting mind can conceive.

We have a famous story recorded of two brothers at Athens, which as it serves to illustrate what I have been saying, I shall briefly relate it to you.—One of them, for some high misdemeanor, was condemned to lose his life, and was going to be led to execution, when his brother, who had lost his hand in the defence of his country, and had been a great mean of gaining a victory which was of the last importance to the state, came suddenly into the court; and without saying a word, but barely holding up his mutilated arm, so prevailed with the judges by this remembrance of what he had formerly done, that they instantly discharged the delinquent brother, though he had forfeited his life. Thus far does the intercession of man prevail with men; and shall not the constant presentation of the Lamb that was slain, for so our Saviour's appearance in heaven is described in the book of Revelation, shall not this be as operative and powerful with the loving Father? The Redeemer thus pleads, "Behold me, O my Father, behold me in a form thus different from that in which I originally was! Behold me now dwelling in human flesh, which I have assumed; and how it was treated for the atonement of thy justice, and the salvation of these my people; and now, let not all my sufferings be in vain, but for my sake receive them into thy favor, and bestow upon them those blessings which have cost me so much." Can any consider the force of this intercession, and yet doubt of its success? Let us, in the

III. place, join both these together, viz. The assured love of the Father; and —The constant prevailing intercession of the Son. And O, how great is the amount! Either of them singly give us good ground to hope; but when the two are united, how certain, how infallible is our assurance? When the advocate's plea is just and fairly urged, when the Judge is sufficiently qualified, and perfectly well disposed, how safe is the client, how secure of success! If God himself loves you, and the Redeemer never leaves importuning him for you, how is it possible that your prayers should be rejected, or any of your interests miscarry? It is needless to insist any longer in the proof of this; the conclusion is so strong and evident, that you must all of you have made it before I could speak it. I shall therefore suggest to you, in a few particulars, the natural use and improvement of this comfortable subject.

And now, my dear brethren, upon the review of all that has been said, is not this the secret language of your hearts:—These indeed are blessed news, but what interest have I in them? Does the comfort of them belong to me in particular or not? This is as it should be. In so far you are on the road to the best and most necessary improvement that I can suggest to you. The Scriptures will inform you, that this is the children's bread, in which the dogs can pretend no share. You see it is not a common privilege. It is peculiar to those who love the Redeemer, "and believe that he is come out from God." This is the test.

Here then is the great and important question, which in the name of the living God, the Searcher of hearts, I put to every soul who now hears me. Is it your character, or is it not? I do not ask you if you believe the existence of a God, or even the truth of the Christian religion. This is a faith which may go down with you to hell, where the devils themselves believe and tremble.

Neither do I ask you, if you have felt some passing motions of love to Christ, some faint desires after an interest in him. There is a desire of the slothful, says Solomon, that kills him, while it only serves to increase his present uneasiness, and his after punishment. But do you really know Christ, and love him in sincerity? Do you cordially approve of the methods of his saving grace? Do you know what it is to lay down your guilty souls, as under the effusion of his blood, and the covert of his righteousness? Do you know what it is to strip yourselves of pride and self-confidence in his sight, that your nakedness may be clothed with his most perfect righteousness? Do you know what it is to bow to his sceptre, as his obedient subjects; to take the law of your direction from his mouth, and to rejoice that you have such a governor or instructor? And do you feel the necessity of a constant application to him as your great Head, on whose influences you live, and by whose Spirit you must be perpetually aided to all the purposes of a divine life?

Can you say to him, as Peter did, "Thou, Lord, who knowest all things, knowest that I love thee?" Does this faith and love govern your practice, and appear in the fruits of holy and virtuous conversation? Have you, by these, been kept only from the grosser habits of falsehood, drunkenness, swearing, uncleanness, and other rank sins? but is the very inclination to them mortified, and can you say that it is your principal aim and study to maintain consciences void of offence both towards God and man? Do you know what it is to pray in the name of Christ; not barely to pronounce the words, as many do a spell, as if God were to be charmed by a sound; but with a humble sense of your own unworthiness, a firm persuasion of his infinite merit, and a hopeful expectation of being graciously heard for his sake?

These are the marks by which each of you may be known to himself.

And now that I have held up the mirror, I suppose I may warrantably class this whole audience into three different sorts of people.

1*st.* Those who are yet doubtful of their state, and know not what judgment to pass.

2*d.* Those who are sensible that the marks that I have given do not at all agree to them. And,

3*d.* Those with whose spirits the Holy Spirit doth witness, that in truth they love the Redeemer, and believe that he came out from God. And this directs me to a threefold address.

1*st.* As for you who are yet uncertain about your state, who have not accustomed yourselves to this strict reckoning, and therefore know not what judgment to form of yourselves, What have you been doing? How can you answer this neglect? Ah! shame upon you, to delay an inquiry upon which all the comfort and safety of your souls does depend. How inexcusable is this? If the Scriptures had told us that it was only some few that should miss salvation; yea, if it had been said, that it was only one of ten thousand that was in danger of hell-fire, yet methinks the hazard is so dreadful, that each of us should be crying out, "Lord, is it I?" But when the Spirit of God tells us, that the common course of the world must convince us, that comparatively there are few, very few, that shall be saved! O how solicitous should every one of us be to know whether we be of that happy number! and how utterly inexcusable are they who neglect it. Well then, let the time past suffice. Speedily set about the most serious examination. Never be at rest till you have come to a just sentence on your case. The discovery will repay all the time and pains you can bestow upon it.

2*dly.* As for you who are past doubting in this matter, whose full-blown sins testify to your foreheads, that you cannot lay the most distant claim to the character in the text; who neither love the Redeemer, nor believe to any saving purpose that he came out from God, how deplorable is your present case! What! cannot self-love conceal your condition from you? Has it no covering to throw over you, no lurking-place to hide you in? O then bethink you, how open you must be to that God, whose eyes are as a flame of fire, penetrating into the innermost foldings of the most deceitful heart, and marking him for a hypocrite who calls, yea thinks himself just? How does this discovery affect your souls? Canst thou dwell with devouring flames? Canst thou lie down in everlasting burnings? Canst thou bear the heavy hand of Omnipotence upon thee without shrinking? or, if thou canst not, say, hast thou the most distant hope that possibly thou mayest be saved, notwithstanding thy unbelief and wickedness? The issue of this matter is very short, and requires no great degree of penetration to perceive. If the gospel be not true, thou canst have no ground for any hope at all. And if it be true, thou art utterly cut off from all the hope of it, so long as thou continuest in thy present state. The Saviour, the almighty Saviour himself cannot save thee. He cannot overturn the whole tenor of the gospel, and make himself the minister of sin.

And are thy unavailing hopes cut off? What course wilt thou then betake thyself to next? Even while I speak, thou art on the brink of destruction, the wrath of God abideth on thee. Behold a black storm of vengeance is gathering around thee, and thou art excluded from the only ark in which thou canst escape. And what excludes thee? Hear, and blush, O sinner, even thine own obstinate folly. Nothing else can; all the devils in hell cannot shut thee out unless thou wilt; and from heaven thou canst meet with no hindrance, where all is love and goodness; so that, if thou dost perish, it must be by thine own merciless hands. And wilt thou be thine own murderer? Wilt thou destroy an immortal soul? Desperate madness! O stop in time, and yet repent and believe, and all that is past shall be forgiven thee. This is the voice of the gospel. These are the tidings which I am warranted to deliver. The much injured Saviour himself shall pray for thee—and he has been praying for thee. For had he not, from year to year, procured saving mercy by his intercession, thou hadst been long ere now cut down as a cumberer of the ground. O then, let this melt down thy heart to an ingenuous sorrow for what is past, and sincere resolutions of amendment for the future. Throw thyself at the feet of this compassionate Saviour; commit thy cause to this prevailing High-Priest. None ever perished that did so. Neither shalt thou, unless almighty power be weakened, or infinite compassions exhausted. Let this be the day of thy return. Speedily break covenant with hell and death, that thou mayest be enrolled among those whom the Father himself loves, and for whom the Son does in a peculiar manner constantly pray.

3*dly*. As for you who sincerely love the Redeemer, and believe that he is come out from God, to you belongs all the comfort of these gracious words: Whatever you ask in the name of Jesus shall be freely given you; for the Father himself loveth you, and his blessed Son constantly prays for you. Whatever carnal men may think of this, yet surely it is a privilege of which I hope you know both the value and use. To be allowed access to God at any rate, is a prodigious favor; but to come before him hopefully, with good assurance of being accepted, this is a signal blessing, which is peculiar to yourselves. Lift up thy head, then, O sincere believer. Does thy conscience bear testimony that thou lovest Jesus, and believest that he is the sent of God? Apply then these gracious words to thyself. The Father himself loveth thee, and makes thee welcome to use the prevailing name of his once suffering but now exalted Son. In all thy difficulties come freely to him. "Be careful for nothing, but in every thing, by prayer and supplication, with thanksgiving, make thy requests known to God." The Redeemer, too, enforces thy requests, and is more mindful of thee than thou canst be of thyself. He sympathizes with thee in all thy infirmities and distresses; and when thou canst not uttter thy desires, yet he understands the groanings of his own Spirit within thee. He forms thy petitions, and urges them with all their force; yea, thy very need has a language which he can interpret. He foresees the trials that are coming upon thee, when thou dost not. Thus, whilst Peter was glorying in his strength, his Saviour, knowing his weakness, and the malice of Satan, was praying for him that his faith might not fail. The like provident tenderness will he show to thee.

Even now, O believers, he is pleading on your behalf, whilst the Father listens with delight and approbation. He kindly accepts of this testimony of your love, in keeping up the memory of his bitter passion; and no doubt all your well qualified prayers have been this day powerfully enforced by your faithful High-Priest.

What shall I say more to you? Praise and thanksgiving is your duty at this time. Let your souls, and all that is within you, be stirred up to bless your heavenly Father, whose love was the fountain and spring of your happiness, and is still the foundation of your truest comfort.

Let your souls, and all that is within you, be stirred up to bless your gracious Redeemer, who hath ransomed you by his blood, and who, amid the exaltation of heaven, the splendor of his Father's right hand, still kindly remembers his humble followers, whose ears are ever open to their prayers, whose mouth is ever ready to plead their cause, and, as if it were not love enough to die for them, who also lives and reigns for them, yea, and even glories in being made head over all things to the church. Alas! our praises are so feeble and low, that we may blush and be ashamed to offer them.

But do you not long for heaven, that with a more elevated song than this dull state can admit, you may join in praising this object of your love? Continue yet a little longer—have patience for awhile, give some farther testimonies of your faith here, and he who intercedes for you will receive you to himself; and that you may not doubt of this, read and ponder these gracious verses with which I conclude, (John xvii. 24.) "Father, I will, that they also whom thou hast given me, be with me where I am, that they may behold the glory which thou hast given me; for thou lovedst me before the foundation of the world."

To Father, Son, and Holy Ghost, one God, be glory and honor, dominion and power, for ever. *Amen.*

SERMON LIX.

THE KINGDOM, GRACE, AND SERVICE.

HEBREWS xii. 28, 29.—"Wherefore we, receiving a kingdom which cannot be moved, let us have grace, whereby we may serve God acceptably with reverence and godly fear: for our God is a consuming fire."

THE gospel of our salvation, which contains the wholesome words of our Lord Jesus Christ, is expressly styled the doctrine which is according to godliness. It manifests the grace of God to sinners of mankind; but all who receive that grace are thereby taught effectually to deny ungodliness and worldly lusts, and to live soberly, and righteously, and godly in this present world. It abounds with great and precious promises; but all these promises have a practical tendency, that by the belief and improvement of them, we may be made partakers of the divine nature; having escaped the pollution that is in the world through lust. Hence that exhortation, (2 Cor. vii. 1.) "Having therefore these promises, dearly beloved, let us cleanse ourselves from all filthiness of the flesh and spirit, perfecting holiness in the fear of God." If we look through the whole of divine revelation, we shall find in every part, privilege and duty inseparably connected, and the latter uniformly inferred from the former. This connection is clearly established in the passage I have read to you, which contains,

I. The distinguishing privilege of believers in Christ. "We," saith the apostle, in the name of all true Christians, "receiving a kingdom which cannot be moved."

II. An exhortation to duty, founded upon this privilege, and the motives with which it is enforced: "Let us have grace whereby we may serve God acceptably with reverence and godly fear: for our God is a consuming fire."

BOTH these subjects are so extensive, that each of them might furnish materials for many discourses. All I can at present propose is, to give some assistance to your minds when you meditate upon them in private, by weighing the import of the words in which they are expressed; every one of which appears to be strongly emphatical, and full of the most instructive and comfortable meaning.

I begin with the privilege of believers in Christ Jesus, expressed in these words, "We receiving a kingdom that cannot be moved." Where you will observe,

1*st*, The designation that is given to their portion. It is styled a kingdom, which, among earthly possessions is universally admitted to hold the first rank; but what is the highest dignity, and the greatest affluence that this earth can afford, when compared with the kingdom whereof my text speaks? Would you know the extent of it? you may learn it from (1 Cor. iii. 21, &c.) "All things are yours." And it must be so, for God himself is the portion of his sainst; for as many as receive Christ, "to them gives he power to become the sons of God, even to them that believe on his name;—and if sons, then are they also heirs, heirs of God, and joint heirs with Christ Jesus." Accordingly they are said, by the apostle Peter, "to be begotten again to the lively hope of an inheritance, incorruptible, undefiled, and that fadeth not away." Which last expression agrees with the description here given by the apostle, where he calls it a kingdom that cannot be moved; and the stability of it is explained by Peter, in the passage I just now alluded to, where he not only informs us, that this inheritance is reserved in heaven, beyond the reach of every adverse power; but likewise, that all who are begotten again to the hope of it, "are kept by the power of God through faith unto salvation."

You will further observe, that believers are said to receive this kingdom. They have no natural right to it; on the contrary, by the fatal apostasy they are children of wrath and heirs of destruction. They have no price to give for it; for they are not only wretched and miserable, but poor, and blind, and naked. It is a gift altogether free and unmerited on their part. "It is your Father's good pleasure," said Christ to his disciples, "to give you the kingdom;" and eternal life is expressly said to be "the gift of God through Jesus Christ our Lord."

Once more, you will observe, that this inheritance is not altogether future. The apostle speaks of it as a present possession. He doth not say, We looking for a kingdom that cannot be moved; but, we receiving it in the mean time. This is perfectly agreeable to what he had said, (ver. 22.) "Ye are come unto mount Zion, and unto the city of the living God, the heavenly Jerusalem, and to an innumerable company of angels, to the general assembly and church of the first born, which are written in heaven, and to God the Judge of all, and to the spirits of just men made perfect, and to Jesus the mediator of the new covenant, and to the blood of sprinkling, that speaketh better things than that of Abel." Believers have not only a title to the glory that shall afterwards be revealed, but they possess the earnest and first fruits of it in the mean time. Heaven is already begun in their hearts; the kingdom of God is within them, that kingdom which "consisteth not in meats and drinks, but in righteousness, and peace, and joy in the Holy Ghost.—He who loved them, and washed them from their sins in his own blood, hath also made them kings and priests unto God.—By beholding his glory with the eye of faith, they are "changed into the same image, from glory to glory," while they sojourn here below, as we read 2 Cor. iii. 18. This resemblance, at present indeed imperfect, shall continually advance, through the influences of the divine Spirit, till, being released from the prison of the body, they shall no more see darkly as through a glass, but face to face; and by seeing him as he is, shall be fully transformed into his image, which will render them completely happy, as it is written, (1 John iii. 2.) "Beloved, now are we the sons of God; and it doth not yet appear what we shall be, but we know, that when he shall appear we shall be like him, for we shall see him as he is."

Thus have I opened the import of the terms by which the apostle describes the dignity and happiness of believers in Christ Jesus. By their new birth, and in consequence of their union with the Lord Jesus Christ, they are constituted heirs of a kingdom, which it is their Father's good pleasure to bestow upon them by free gift; this kingdom cannot be moved; it was prepared for them before the foundation of the world; it is reserved for them in heaven, and they are kept for it through faith by the power of God: and though the full possession of it, in all its glory, awaits them in a future state, yet they have their maintenance and provision out of it in the mean time; the new nature they have got is not only the pledge, but the interest of the inheritance, being of the same kind with that glory which is afterwards to be revealed; they at present receive eternal life, a life that cannot die, but, like the morning light, shall continue to shine with increasing brightness, till in heaven it shall arrive at the perfect day.

Such is the present dignity and happiness of all true believers in Christ Jesus; in this sense the weakest, as well as the strong, receive a kingdom which cannot be moved.

II. Let us consider the exhortation to duty, founded upon this privilege, "Let us have grace."

1*st.* We are called upon to serve God. Believers, though kings, are still the subjects of the King of kings; and the honor conferred upon them, instead of relaxing their obligation to duty, rather binds them to serve him with greater zeal and activity. Their very royalty consists in their release from the enemies of God, which formerly enslaved and led them captive at their pleasure. Hence that exhortation of the apostle, "Let not sin reign in your mortal bodies." They are styled, in the book of the Revelation, "kings and priests to God, even the Father:" and dominion is given them, not in respect of God, to render them independent on him, but in respect of sin, Satan, the world, and death, over all which they are made conquerors through him that loved them, and washed them from their sins in his own blood. They are indeed a chosen generation, and a royal priesthood; but for what end? It is, that by bringing forth the fruits of righteousness, "they may show forth the praises of him who hath called them out of darkness into his marvellous light."

2dly. We are reminded of the qualification that is requisite for serving God acceptably. We cannot do this by any strength that is inherent in us. "We are not sufficient of ourselves to think any thing as of ourselves." We are indeed exhorted to work out our own salvation; but at the same time we are told, "that it is God who worketh in us both to will and to do of his good pleasure." The apostle's words are chosen with the most significant propriety. He doth not say, Let us take strength to ourselves; or, let us purchase it from another; but, let us have it; *i. e.*, Let us ask it of him who giveth liberally—Let us possess it, by receiving the gift that is offered; or, having received it, let us hold it fast, as the word is rendered in the margin, and improve it to the purposes for which it was bestowed.

3dly. We are directed to the manner of serving God, so as to be accepted of him, viz., "with reverence and godly fear:" *i. e.*, with a deep sense of his infinite greatness, and of our own meanness and unworthiness. We are indeed exhorted and encouraged to come boldly to a throne of grace; but it must be such a boldness only as becometh those who stand in need both of mercy and grace; of mercy to pardon what hath been amiss, and of grace to help them in every time of need. "There is forgiveness with thee," said the Psalmist, "that thou mayest be feared." And indeed mercy is dispensed in such a way, as renders God no less awful than he is amiable to the pardoned sinner. The sacrifice of Christ, while it manifests the love of God in giving his Son to be the propitiation for our sins, affords, at the same time, the strongest proof and demonstration of his holiness and justice. The new and living way of access to God is consecrated for us through the veil of Christ's flesh. The blood that cleanseth from all sin, by which we have boldness to enter into the holiest, is the blood of Emmanuel, the Word made flesh, by whom all things were made, and without whom was not any thing made that is made. A proper attention to this, will show both the meaning and propriety of the apostle's direction to serve God with reverence and godly fear; not the tormenting fear which cherisheth that enmity against God, whereby the carnal mind is characterized; but that filial reverence which flows from a supreme love to God, as a reconciled father, and desire to please him, which consists in a holy jealousy of ourselves, an abhorrence of every thing that is offensive to God, and produceth a carefulness to avoid every temptation to sin, and to shun not only the forbidden, but even the doubtful ground, according to that just description which is given of it, (Prov. viii. 12.) "The fear of the Lord is to hate evil." And the genuine effects of this fear are fully expressed in those advices of the Wise Man, which are recorded, (chap. iv. at the close) "Keep thy heart with all diligence—Let thine eyes look right on, and let thine eyelids look straight before thee. Ponder the path of thy feet, and let all thy ways be established. Turn not to the right hand nor to the left; remove thy feet from evil." Such is the reverence and godly fear with which we are directed to serve the Lord.

Let us now briefly consider the arguments with which the exhortation is enforced; and these are two—The one respecting the matter of duty in general—And the other, the manner in which the service that is due to God ought to be performed.

1*st.* We are exhorted to serve God, in testimony of our gratitude for the inestimable benefits his grace hath conferred upon us. This argument is plainly addressed to believers in Christ, who have received that kingdom which cannot be moved. The apostle doth not say, Let us serve God that we may obtain a kingdom; but, having received it as the free gift of God, through faith in his Son, who purchased it with his blood, let us express our thankfulness, by devoting ourselves, and all that we have, or can do, to his service. This is the plain and obvious meaning of the apostle's argument; and in order to make this passage of Scripture speak the language of that scheme of religion which is too current in the world, the words of it would need to be transposed and varied in some such manner as this:

Prompted by self-love, and the tormenting fear of future punishment, let us resolve in our minds, for we neither need nor expect supernatural grace, that henceforth we will serve God, as well as the world and the flesh will permit, that so we may escape damnation, and procure a title to, or at least the probable chance of a kingdom, which, after all, may not only be moved, but so agitated and shaken that without a vigorous exertion of the powers we possess, we ourselves may be tossed out of it, and fall into perdition.—Thus ridiculous are the best efforts of human wisdom, to corrupt the plain meaning of Scripture language, and to accommodate the constitution of gospel grace to that pride and self-idolatry, which, ever since the apostasy, reign in the heart of every natural man.

Whereas the gospel of Christ binds us to duty by the cords of love; and while it presseth holy diligence and activity in the service of God, by the most persuasive arguments, it animates us, at the same time, with the most comfortable assurance that our labor shall not be in vain in the Lord. Help is laid for us upon one who is mighty, even that good Shepherd who laid down his life for the sheep, who gathers the lambs in his bosom, and gently leads those that are with young. Therefore they shall never perish, because none are able to pluck them out of his hand. He gives unto them eternal life, and they enter upon the possession of it at their new birth, when, by believing on his name, the power, or rather the privilege is given them, to become the sons of God. His grace is sufficient for them at all times, and in every situation. He is gone to his Father's house to prepare a place for them; and he will come again and receive them to himself, that where he is, there they may be also, to behold that glory which his Father hath given him. "Wherefore we, receiving a kingdom which cannot be moved, let us have grace whereby we may serve God acceptably with reverence and godly fear."

2*d*. The argument, which respects the manner of our service, is continued in these words, "For our God is a consuming fire." This, at first sight, does not seem to accord with the other argument, which is addressed to the ingenuity and gratitude of a renewed heart; but appears rather adapted to the spirit of bondage, than to that spirit of adoption which believers in Christ receive, whereby they are disposed and enabled to call God, Father. But I shall direct you to two passages of Scripture, which, I apprehend, will remove this difficulty, and lead us to the true meaning and intent of the apostle's argument.

One is Isaiah xxxi. 9, where it is said as a ground of fear to the enemies of Zion, and consequently as a ground of encouragement to her children, that "the Lord hath his fire in Zion, and his furnace in Jerusalem."

The other is Mal. iii. 2, where the messenger of the covenant and King of Zion is compared to a refiner's fire, and fuller's soap. "He shall sit as a refiner and purifier of silver, and he shall purify the sons of Levi, and purge them as gold and silver, that they may offer unto the Lord an offering in righteousness." In this sense, he is a consuming fire to the godly; he refines them by consuming their dross. This view of God indeed is terrible to the wicked, who are all dross; but it hath another aspect to the godly, who are made partakers of the divine nature. The fire that burns up the enemies of God altogether, shall only consume the dross that still cleaves to them, and from which they will never be wholly separated, till death dissolve their earthly tabernacles. Nevertheless, this is urged, with great propriety, as an argument for serving God with reverence and godly fear: for the means of purifying may be very painful in the mean time, and it is written, (Psalm xcix. 8.) "Though he forgives their sins, yet he will take vengeance of their inventions." The children of God may be assured of it, that the rod shall not be withheld—their own backslidings shall be made to reprove them; "for whom the Lord loveth he chasteneth." And therefore they should serve God with reverence, that a moderate furnace may suffice to purge away their dross, and that it may not become necessary that God, for their correction, should wound their hearts in the tenderest part, by taking from them their dearest earthly comforts, or withdrawing the light of his countenance utterly from them. "Wherefore we, receiving a kingdom that cannot be moved, let us have grace whereby we may serve God acceptably with reverence and godly fear; for our God is a consuming fire."

SERMON LX.

Preached on a Public Fast-Day, in the time of the American War.

THE ALARMING DENUNCIATION.

Isaiah xxii. 12—14.—"And in that day did the Lord God of Hosts call to weeping, and to mourning, and to baldness, and to girding with sackcloth; and behold joy and gladness, slaying oxen, and killing sheep, eating flesh and drinking wine; let us eat and drink, for tomorrow we shall die. And it was revealed in mine ears by the Lord of Hosts, Surely this iniquity shall not be purged from you till ye die, saith the Lord God of Hosts."

This passage is introduced with a loud and pressing call to repentance. It describes the contemptuous behavior of the people to whom the call was addressed; and concludes with an alarming denunciation of wrath against those perverse and obstinate transgressors.

Each of these particulars I shall briefly illustrate, and then point out our immediate concern in the subject, and the practical improvement we all ought to make of it.

The *first* thing that occurs is the call to repentance, (verse 12.) "In that day did the Lord of Hosts call to weeping, and to mourning, and to baldness, and to girding with sackcloth."

The day here referred to was a season of abounding iniquity, as we learn from the first chapter of this book of prophecy, which begins with a heavy charge against the nation of the Jews, published with awful solemnity by God himself, in the following words: "Hear, O heavens, and give ear, O earth, for the Lord hath spoken! I have nourished and brought up children, and they have rebelled against me. The ox knoweth his owner, and the ass his master's crib; but Israel doth not know, my people do not consider. Ah, sinful nation! a people laden with iniquity, a seed of evil doers, children that are corrupters. They have forsaken the Lord, they have provoked the Holy One of Israel to anger, they have gone away backward." Accordingly the prophet, in bespeaking their attention to the message he was about to deliver, addressed them, in terms of severe reproach, (verse 10.) "Hear the words of the Lord, ye rulers of Sodom; give ear unto the law of our God, ye people of Gomorrah." And the lamentation he utters, (verse 21.) shows with what justice and propriety those titles of ignominy were applied to them. "How is the faithful city become an harlot! It was full of judgment, righteousness lodged in it, but now murderers. Thy silver is become dross, thy wine mixed with water. Thy princes are rebellious, and companions of thieves; every one loveth gifts, and followeth after rewards."

Their boldness and impudence in sinning are particularly taken notice of, as high aggravations of their guilt, (chap. iii. verses 8, 9.) "The show of their countenance doth witness against them, and they declare their sin as Sodom; they hide it not. Their tongue and their doings are against the Lord, to provoke the eye of his glory." Neither was this accusation limited to the men in that age; for, (ver. 16.) even the daughters of Zion are represented as "haughty, walking with stretched forth necks and wanton eyes, walking and mincing as they went," under the cumbersome load of tinkling ornaments, chains and bracelets, and the many other superfluous articles of dress, of which a catalogue is left on record from the 18th verse downward, till, at the 24th verse, the fantastic inventory is closed with that humiliating doom: "It shall come to pass, that instead of sweet smell, there shall be stink; and instead of a girdle, a rent; and instead of well set hair, baldness; and burning instead of beauty."

This leads me to mention another circumstance, by which the day referred to in my text is distinguished. It was a day of sore rebuke, as well as of abounding iniquity. "Look away from me," said the prophet, ver. 4 of this chapter, "I will weep bitterly, labor not to comfort me, because of the spoiling of the daughter of my people; for it is a day of trouble, and of treading down, and of perplexity, by the Lord God of Hosts in the valley of vision."

Such was the day in which the Lord God of Hosts did call to weeping and mourning, and to baldness, and to girding with sackcloth, *i. e.* to the deepest humiliation on account of their sins, to the most unfeigned repentance, and amendment of life. That this is the true import of the call, appears from a similar exhortation, (Joel ii. 12.) where, after the Lord had given commandment to blow the trumpet in Zion, and to sound an alarm in his holy mountain, that all the inhabitants of the land might tremble in the prospect of that day of darkness and gloominess, which was soon to be spread over them; he addresses them in these words: "Turn ye even to me with all your heart, with weeping and with mourning, and rend your hearts and not your garments, and turn unto the Lord your God."

In every age, and in every climate, weeping and mourning are the natural expressions of inward sorrow. In the eastern countries, and especially among the Jews, when grief rose to a great height, tears of lamentations were usually accompanied with rending their clothes, plucking out their hair, and covering their bodies with sackcloth. And though these outward signs are only the trappings of woe, which are no further acceptable than as they truly express the sorrow and contrition of the heart, yet, in the case before us, they are expressly required of that impudent and hard-hearted people, that as their tongue and their doings had been against the Lord, to provoke the eyes of his glory, so their shame and sorrow might be proclaimed as openly as their sin, and their penitent return to God might be no less apparent than their proud and insolent revolt had been.

Having made these remarks upon the import of the call, and the state of the Jews in the day it was published to them, let me now,

II. Lead forward your attention to the account that is given us of the reception it met with, (ver. 13.) "And behold!" It is introduced, you see, with a note—what shall I call it?—Whether doth it bespeak our admiration or astonishment? The object must surely be wonderful, either for beauty or deformity, to which the great God himself demands our attention with such solemnity.

Say then, my brethren, were you not already acquainted with what follows, would you not expect to see a multitude of humble penitents, prostrate on the ground, and covered with sackcloth, while, with weeping and mourning, they say one to another, in the language of genuine repentance, "Come, and let us return unto the Lord, for he hath torn, and he will heal us; he hath smitten, and he will bind us up." But what do we really see? Be astonished, O ye heavens, at this, and be horribly afraid. Instead of mourning and weeping, behold joy and gladness; instead of baldness and girding with sackcloth, behold every kind of riotous excess, slaying oxen and killing sheep, eating flesh, and drinking wine.

There is no room to suppose that they had given no attention to the message delivered by the prophet. It would rather appear that they had attended to it with accuracy, nay, studied its meaning, on purpose to counteract it; for a contrast so minutely exact, a scheme of contradiction so completely adjusted, could hardly have been stumbled upon by mere accident. And indeed the latter part of the verse puts this beyond all doubt. "*Let us eat and drink*," said they, *for to-morrow we shall die*."

We are not to imagine that these words were spoken seriously by one of those presumptuous and boasting rebels. The most daring amongst them must have been conscious, that the aspect of the king of terrors, at their most sumptuous entertainments, would leave them no appetite for flesh or wine. They meant it as a scoff, a witty saying, for turning into ridicule the warning they had received, but which they did not believe. The prophet hath been telling us of desolating judgments just at hand, and with the same breath he calls us to weeping, and mourning, and girding with sackcloth. How absurd, how unreasonably cruel is the demand! Will not the evil day come soon enough, though we should not anticipate the sorrows of it, by afflicting ourselves unnecessarily before its arrival? Nay, rather, if life is to be cut short, let us make the most of it while it lasts. If we must die to-morrow, let us eat and drink, and be merry to-day, and crowd into the few scanty hours that remain as much festivity and pleasure as we can.

Surely it is not needful that I should lengthen out this picture of deformity in all its dimensions. Its most distinguishing features are abundantly obvious; and I am confident, that the few sketches I have given you, will suffice to render the generation it represents, the objects of contempt and abhorrence to all; those very persons not excepted, who, in the portrait drawn for them, may perhaps discover their own true likeness. For it is common enough to condemn with just, though partial severity, the same faults in others, which we easily forgive, nay cherish in ourselves. At any rate, I suppose none of us will be surprised to hear the alarming denunciation of wrath against those perverse and obstinate transgressors; which is the

III. Particular contained in my text, (ver. 14.) "It was revealed in mine ears by the Lord of Hosts, surely this iniquity shall not be purged from you till ye die, saith the Lord God of Hosts."

We meet with another threatening of the same import, (Ezek. xxiv. 13.) "Because I have purged thee, and thou wast not purged, thou shalt not be purged from thy filthiness any more, till I have caused my fury to rest upon thee. I the Lord have spoken it, and it shall come to pass, and I will do it. I will not go back, neither will I spare, neither will I repent, saith the Lord God."

These wicked men had not only resisted the means of conviction, but they had perverted those means and extracted poison from the medicine intended for their cure. They drew iniquity with cords of vanity, and sinned as it were with a cart rope. By their scoffing reply to the call that was given them, in the name of the Lord God of Hosts, they said in effect, with insolent contempt and proud defiance, "Let him make speed and hasten his work, that we may see it; and let the counsel of the Holy One of Israel draw nigh and come, that we may know it." The prophet therefore proclaims, as on the house top, what God had revealed in his ears, that from that time forward, vengeance should pursue those impious men, till, like their rebellious forefathers, whose carcasses fell in the wilderness, they should be utterly consumed from off the face of the earth.

Thus have I endeavored briefly to illustrate the several parts of the passage before us.

But what concern have we in these things? and what improvement shall we make of them?

For an answer to these questions, I need only refer you to 1 Corinthians, chap. x. where, after reciting some of those awful judgments which God had inflicted upon his ancient church, the apostle subjoins those memorable words, (verse 11.) "Now all these things happened unto them for ensamples, and they are written for our admonition, upon whom the ends of the world are come."

"The Lord is known by the judgments which he executes." God is always the same: with him there is no variableness, neither shadow of turning. And therefore, in his past acts of government, as they are explained by his word, we behold a plan of righteous administration; from whence we may learn, with some degree of certainty, what kind of treatment, in similar circumstances, we ourselves have reason to expect.

They must know little of what passes in the world, who do not observe a very striking resemblance between the present state of our own nation and that of the Jews, in the day to which my text refers.

Ingratitude to God, for the great things he hath done in our behalf, and for the distinguishing privileges we have long enjoyed, is too apparent to require any proof. Our deliverance from popery at the Reformation, and the full establishment of our civil and religious liberties at the Revolution; these marvellous doings of the Lord are either forgotten by many, as a dead man out of mind, or at least remembered with cold indifference; nay, treated with marks of disaffection by some, while the character of those illustrious men, whom God honored to be the instruments in bringing about those glorious events, have been canvassed with the utmost severity of criticism, and under the specious pretext of candor and impartiality, set forth to public view in the most unfavorable light.

Have not vice and immorality grown up among us to an amazing height? Do not multitudes proclaim their sins as Sodom; and, instead of hiding them, do they not rather glory in their shame, as if they accounted it an honor to excel in one species of wickednesss or another? I do not aggravate the charge: every one's observation may convince him of the truth of it. Is there not a visible and growing contempt of the blessed gospel? Are not its ordinances despised by some, and profaned by others; nay, is it not by many deemed a mark of superior genius to reject the whole of divine revelation as a cunningly devised fable, and to employ all their influence in proselyting others to their opinion?

What small success attends the preaching of the gospel even among those who profess to believe? Into how many sects and parties are they divided? With what zeal do they build up their walls of partition? With what animosity do they contend for their own peculiarities, as points of new and important discovery, though in fact most of them might lay claim to a very ancient date, have been often republished, and as often refuted? Now, union is the strength of the religious, as well as of the civil community; and there is reason to fear that God will suffer that candlestick to be removed from among us, about which we quarrel and fight with one another, instead of walking by the light it affords, and performing the work which was given us to do.

I shall not waste any part of your time upon the mere triflers of either sex, who literally walk in a vain show, and ought rather to be regarded as the scenery or decorations of the theatre, than as actors sustaining any character upon the stage. Yet even they, light as they may seem, make some addition to the load of national guilt, as we learn from the passage respecting the daughters of Zion, in the third chapter of this prophecy, which I formerly quoted. Enough has been said to prove, that we are a sinful nation, a people laden with iniquity, and that the call to repentance is proper and seasonable, and belongs to the very day in which our lot is cast.

Indeed our very meeting together in this place is a public acknowledgment of it. For what purpose are we convened by royal authority? Is it not that we may humble ourselves before Almighty God, and send up our prayers and supplications to the divine Majesty, for obtaining pardon of our sins, and for averting those heavy judgments which our manifold provocations have most justly deserved?

Thus far we may be assured, that the call of the Lord of Hosts hath been distinctly and faithfully echoed from the throne. And lest, after all, we should turn a deaf ear to his voice, the Lord of Hosts hath written the same call upon the face of providence, in characters so legible, that they must be worse than blind who do not read and understand them.

The little cloud, like a man's hand, that arose a few years ago on the other side of the Atlantic, hath ever since been increasing both in size and in blackness.

Our envious and deceitful neighbors, who, by secret artifice, have endeavored from the beginning to keep the unhappy breach open between Great Britain and her colonies, have at length laid aside the mask, and are now straining every nerve to spread the desolations of war through the whole extent of the British empire.

The sword that was drawn for coercion abroad, now finds employment for self-defence at home; and the measures hitherto pursued have been so ineffectual, that after much expense of blood and treasure, we may say with the Jews in the days of Jeremiah, (chap. xiv. 19.) "We looked for peace, and there is no good; and for the time of healing, and behold trouble."

What shall we say to these things? Do they bear no impression of God's holy and righteous displeasure? "Will a lion roar in the forest, when he hath no prey? Will a young lion cry in his den, if he hath taken nothing? Can a bird fall in a snare upon the earth, where no gin is for him? Shall one take up a snare from the earth, and have taken nothing at all? Shall a trumpet be blown in the city, and the people not be afraid? Shall there be evil in a city, and the Lord hath not done it? The lion hath roared, who will not fear? The Lord God hath spoken, who can but prophecy?"

Our own wickedness is made to correct us, and our backslidings reprove us, that we may *know and see what an evil thing it is, and bitter, that we have forsaken the Lord our God.*

This, my brethren, is the primary aim of all God's corrections. He doth not afflict willingly, nor grieve the children of men; but when transgressors will not learn the malignity of sin by gentler means, then he causes them to feel the evil of it in the bitterness of affliction. Hence it appears, that temporal judgments are acts of mercy as well as of justice, especially when they are of such a nature as to bear the stamp and signature of those sins which are the cause of them. Till we discern the hand of God in the sufferings that befall us, we shall never have recourse to the true and the only effectual remedy. When public measures are defeated, we shall sometimes blame the contrivance, and at other times the execution; but still we shall look to the creature for help, and place our trust in the arm of flesh.

This was an express article of indictment against the Jews in the preceding context. They used every precaution to put their city into a proper state of defence. They inspected their magazines, they repaired the breaches in their walls, and provided large store of water for a siege. In all this they acted wisely, and did no more than was their duty. But herein lay their fault, (verse 11.) they relied upon the preparations for the safety of Jerusalem, and "*did not look unto the Maker thereof, neither had respect unto him that fashioned it long ago.*"

I have therefore endeavored to lead your attention to God himself, and to trace up all the penal evils we feel to the several instances of our criminal departure from him, as their true origin and source; and though perhaps I may have erred in the illustration of particulars, yet I cannot help thinking that the general truth will appear with sufficient evidence, that our own backslidings are reproving us, and that we ourselves have made the rod with which we are smitten.

By this time we may all see our concern in this subject, and the improvement we ought to make of it.

It is righteousness alone that exalteth a nation. Repentance towards God, flowing from faith in our Lord Jesus Christ, is the only effectual means for preventing the ruin of a sinful people. Without this we may obtain a temporary respite from punishment; but the clouds will return again after the rain; and all the while we are filling up the measure of our iniquity, the consumption is advancing, and every day we draw nearer and nearer to dissolution. Whereas, if we accept of the punishment of our iniquity, and put away from us those evil doings which provoke the Lord to jealousy, then may we hope that he will return to us in mercy, and rejoice over us to bless us and to do us good; according to that encouraging promise, (Jer. xviii. 7.) "At what instant I shall speak concerning a nation, and concerning a kingdom, to pluck up, and to pull down, and to destroy; if that nation, against which I have pronounced, turn from their evil, I also will repent of the evil that I thought to do unto them."

It is this which should always give check to any desponding thoughts. We have but ONE to please, ONE whose favor is desirable, and ONE who is most easily pleased; because he hath told us, without ambiguity, what will please him; and at the same time hath declared his readiness to aid our feeble endeavors, by working in us effectually both to will and to do of his good pleasure.

Let us then hearken to the call of the Lord God of Hosts. Let us, with weeping and mourning, return to him, from whom, alas! we have deeply revolted, and ask of him, this day, the spirit of repentance, and grace to walk in newness of life, by bringing forth fruits meet for repentance.

In this way only can we hope, that he who hath the hearts of all men in his hands, will give judgment to them who sit in judgment, and strength to those who turn the battle from the gate; and cause our eyes once more to see our Jerusalem a quiet habitation, a tabernacle that shall not be taken down, none of whose cords shall be broken, neither any of the stakes thereof ever removed. *Amen.*

SERMON LXI.

JOHN'S IMPORTANT COUNSEL.

REVELATION III. 18.—"I counsel thee to buy of ME gold tried in the fire, that thou mayest be rich; and white raiment, that thou mayest be clothed, and that the shame of thy nakedness do not appear: and anoint thine eyes with eye-salve, that thou mayest see."

BEFORE I enter upon the consideration of this gracious counsel, I conceive it may be of use to give you some account, *First*, of the person who gave the advice; and, *Secondly*, of those to whom it was addressed.

The person who gave the advice was our Lord Jesus Christ; that Wonderful Counsellor, and Prince of Peace, foretold by the prophet Isaiah, of the increase of whose government there shall be no end. Here he styles himself the Amen, the Faithful and true Witness: One whose word may be depended upon, who does not come and go, say and unsay, but who is always in one mind, without any variableness or shadow of turning. He is God's witness to the sons of men; and as he is perfectly acquainted with the Father, so he faithfully reports the Father's mind and will to us. His testimony is infallible; for as he cannot be deceived himself, so neither is he capable of deceiving others. I need scarcely observe to you the vast importance of this part of his character. Indeed without it, our faith, and consequently our hope and comfort, would be mere delusion; but blessed be God, the truth and faithfulness of this divine witness, doth infinitely remove from us every possible cause or ground of suspicion. Men may utter falsehoods through mistake and ignorance; or even when they know the truth, they may be induced, by selfish views, to conceal or disguise it. But neither of these grounds of distrust are applicable to our Lord. His knowledge is unlimited, and absolutely perfect; and his infinite fulness and self-sufficiency, raise him above all kinds of dissimulation or artifice. And probably this is the reason why he styles himself, (in the close of the 14th verse) the Beginning, or first Cause of the creation of God. He can have no dependence upon the workmanship of his own hands. As their goodness cannot profit him, neither can their malice hurt him; so that he can be under no temptation, either to overawe them with imaginary terrors, or to allure them with vain and flattering promises. Well then, the character of Counsellor is fair and untainted; and, if the advice he gives us is kind and obliging, there is no room to question the sincerity of his good-will. Here, therefore, my brethren, is one great point gained; and as I am afterwards to lay a considerable stress upon it, I beg you may attend to it in the mean time, and consider, as I go along, that the person who spoke in this passage, and in whose name I now speak to you, is the Faithful and True Witness, the independent Creator and Governor of the world.

Let us next inquire who the persons were to whom the advice or counsel was addressed. In general they were members of Christ's visible church, and inhabitants of the ancient city of Laodicea; it appears also from the description given of them, that with respect to their spiritual concerns, they were in a very degenerate and wretched condition. The first thing taken notice of is their lukewarmness and indifference—a temper which is peculiarly loathsome and offensive to Christ, and therefore he threatens to "*spew* them out of his mouth," that is, to testify his displeasure against them by some very awful and remarkable judgments. Their state is more fully represented in the verse preceding my text, where the Faithful and True Witness tells them that they were wretched, and miserable, and poor, and blind, and naked; and which prodigiously aggravated both their guilt and misery—they knew it not—they were insensible of it; though they might have known it, yet they would not. Such was their woful indifference, that they did not examine their spiritual condition, but took it for granted, and boasted of it, that they were rich, and increased with goods, and had need of nothing. And now judge, my brethren, whether these persons were worthy of any notice or regard, I mean in a way of mercy; for that they merited wrath, I suppose you will readily allow. Behold then, and admire the amazing grace and condescension of our Lord. Though the wickedness of the Laodiceans, aggravated by their pride and loathsome indifference, cried aloud for vengeance, and nothing but vengeance, yet, lo! he vouchsafes to counsel them as a friend!—O how encouraging may this be to those who are burdened with a sense of their guilt and pollution—who see their need of Christ, and pant and long for his great salvation. You say you are unworthy of his aid, and you are right when you say so; but such is his grace, as appears from this epistle, that the greatest unworthiness is no bar in the way of it. He not only counsels, but entreats those Laodiceans, whose condition was as bad as can well be imagined. "Behold," says he, in the 20th verse, "I stand at the door and knock; if any man hear my voice, and open the door, I will come in to him, and sup with him, and he with me." Here then is sufficient evidence, that there is mercy with Christ for the chief of sinners. This was his very errand, to seek and to save that which was lost. And therefore every soul that feels its misery has no reason to be discouraged, because of its unworthiness; on the contrary, this very temper lays it as it were in the way of his mercy; for though the Lord be high, yet hath he respect unto the lowly.—He resists the proud, but giveth grace to the humble.—Yea, he dwells with those who are of a contrite spirit, and that tremble at his word. The use I intend to make of this is to obviate an objection which frequently proves hurtful to newly converted sinners. They are tempted to think that their case does not admit of any hope; having dark and imperfect views of the grace of the gospel, they put away from themselves the sweetest and most condescending offers of mercy, supposing that they are not addressed to them, but to others whose guilt is less aggravated than theirs: but give me leave to assure you, in the name of the Faithful and True Witness, whose message I now bear, that the counsel I have read to you, and which I am farther to open, is directed to every soul within these walls, the vilest not excepted. Are you wretched, and miserable, and poor, and blind, and naked—hearken to the advice of your gracious Lord, an advice which he gives to every one of you in particular, as if he called you by your name:

"I counsel thee to buy of me gold tried in the fire, that thou mayest be rich; and white raiment, that thou mayest be clothed, and that the shame of thy nakedness do not appear; and anoint thine eyes with eye-salve, that thou mayest see."

It is needless to inquire very critically into the precise meaning of these figurative expressions. I reckon that every necessary blessing, even all the unsearchable riches of Christ, are comprehended in these three articles. It is sufficient to observe, that the supply here offered is exactly suited to the sinner's wants—that it is not scanty and penurious, but full and complete—and that all the parts of it are perfect in their kind. Let us dwell a little upon each of these heads.

I. Then, you will observe, that the supply here offered is exactly suited to the sinner's wants. As we come into the world we are poor bankrupt creatures. Adam had a vast stock put into his hands; but by his apostasy from God, he lost it for himself and for all his posterity; so that nothing is left that we can call our own, but guilt and misery. The image of God, which was the glory and riches of man in his first creation, is quite effaced; so that, as the apostle expresses it, "in us, that is, in our flesh, dwelleth no good thing." Well, then, to supply this woful defect, Christ here tells us that he hath gold to enrich us—even all divine and saving graces. The spirit was given to him without measure, to be communicated to his people. He is able not only to expel that corruption which hath got possession of our natures; but he can give us a new heart stamped with the image of God, and make us partakers of the divine nature. The truth of this is attested by the apostle John, from his own experience, (John i. 16.) where he says, "Of his fulness have all we received, and grace for grace."

Another branch of our misery is NAKEDNESS. We have nothing to cover us either from shame or hurt. We are exposed to the wrath of an holy, just and omnipotent God, who infinitely hates sin, and hath pledged his faithfulness, that he will not suffer it to pass unpunished. To relieve us in this case of extreme necessity, Christ hath raiment to clothe us, that the shame of our nakedness may not appear. He can spread his righteousness over us. He can sprinkle us with his atoning blood, so that the destroying angel, the minister of his Father's justice, shall have no power to hurt us: "For there is no condemnation to them who are in Christ Jesus—being justified by faith, we have peace with God, through our Lord Jesus Christ."

Again, we are BLIND creatures, having our understandings darkened, being alienated from the life of God through the ignorance that is in us.

To remedy this, our great physician hath eye-salve to anoint our eyes that we may see. By his Holy Spirit, he can dispel the thickest darkness, and diffuse heavenly light through the whole soul. "Ye were sometimes darkness," says Paul to the converted Ephesians, "but now are ye light in the Lord." In a word, something is to be found in Christ that exactly suits us in every case we can imagine. He hath bread for the hungry, water for the thirsty, wine for the faint, medicine for the sick; or, as the apostle beautifully expresseth it, "He is made of God unto his people, wisdom, and righteousness, and sanctification, and redemption." 1 Cor. i. 30.

II. It deserves our notice, that the supply here offered is not only such as we need, but likewise full and complete. A poor man may get an alms to keep him from perishing, a naked creature may get a rag to cover his nakedness, and to screen his body from the inclemency of the weather; but our bountiful Lord doth not deal with his people in such a sparing and niggardly manner. He gives them gold to enrich them—not merely to relieve their wants, to answer their pressing necessities —but to raise them above poverty. He advances them to a large and opulent estate. The raiment he clothes them with is fair and complete, so that the shame of their nakedness can no more be seen. He covers them from head to foot, spreads his whole sanctification over them, so that no part is left exposed to the sword of justice. They are made righteous by his righteousness imputed to them, and comely by his comeliness put upon them. And,

III. As this supply is suitable and full, so I farther observed to you, that all the parts of it are perfect in their kind. His gold is the most fine gold, gold tried in the fire, not only precious in itself, but thoroughly purged from all dross or alloy. His raiment is white, without spot or blemish; not only a covering, but an ornament to the soul.—His eye-salve has a sovereign and never-failing virtue. Other medicines may strengthen the eye, or recover a weak sight; but this cures blindness itself, and gives such vigor to the eye that is anointed with it, that the person can even look within the veil, and read his name written in the Lamb's book of life. And now let me ask you, What think ye of Christ? Is he not a gracious, as well as a faithful Witness? Are not his offers great, inconceivably great? and is not this counsel most kind and obliging?

But what is his counsel, and how does he direct us to obtain this full and all-sufficient supply? Let us hear his own words:

"I counsel thee," says he, "to buy it of me."

I frankly own to you, there is something in this expression which startles one at the first sight; but when we examine it more acutely, the difficulty vanishes. It is evident that the word *buy* cannot be taken in a strict and literal sense, unless we suppose it to have been said by way of ridicule; for the description of those to whom the advice was addressed necessarily implies that they had nothing to give. They were in the greatest extremity of misery and wretchedness, not only blind and naked, but poor, without money to buy either clothing or medicine. Where then could they find a price that bore any proportion to the blessings here spoken of? I think I could challenge the most sanguine advocate for merit to tell me what these people had to give, unless it was self-conceit, of which indeed it appears they had enough, and to spare; for poor and naked as they were, they boasted of great things, saying they were rich and increased with goods, and had need of nothing. Indeed I am of opinion, that this hint may help us to the meaning of the expression; for the very notion of buying, necessarily includes in it that something must be parted with, and as these Laodiceans had nothing to dispose of but their pride, our Saviour's advice might be intended to intimate this much to them, that in order to their receiving these invaluable blessings, it behoved them to forego their self-conceit in the first place, and then to come to him naked and empty as they were, under a deep and humble sense of their poverty and wretchedness, and on their knees to accept those offered mercies, as the free unmerited gifts of his bounty and grace. This accordingly is perfectly agreeable to other passages of Scripture, particularly to that gracious proclamation and call, (Isa. lv. 1.) to which the counsel here offered has a very near resemblance:—"Ho, every one that thirsteth, come ye to the waters, and he that hath no money, come ye, buy and eat; yea, come, buy wine and milk, without money and without price." Which last expression, "without price," seems to have been added, on purpose to guard against any wrong sense that might otherwise have been put upon the word *buying*. A person who wants money, may have other things of value to trade with, but here they are called to buy, not only without money, but without price; that is, in plain language, to buy and pay nothing, which is only another way of expressing the humble and thankful acceptance of a gift. It is even probable that our Saviour chose this rather than any other expression, to signify that their acceptance should not be rash and hasty, but deliberate and well advised; and at the same time to assure them, that upon their acceptance, these invaluable blessings should become as truly and irrevocably theirs, as if they had really bought them, and given a full and adequate price for them.

Thus have I opened the meaning of this counsel or advice—an advice seasonable at all times, and peculiarly adapted to the occasion of our present meeting. The character of those to whom it was originally addressed, would lead me to speak to proud self-justifiers, who, like the lukewarm Laodiceans, imagine themselves to be rich and increased with goods, and to stand in need of nothing. Might I stay accurately to examine your supposed righteousnesses, I think I could say several things to make you ashamed of them, and to convince you that they are all but filthy rags. But this would require more time than we have to spare. All I can do for you is to pray, and beg that others would pray, that God may pity you, and open your eyes.—I hope there are some now hearing me of a different character, to whom I reckon myself more immediately a debtor, I mean those whose eyes are so far opened, as to see that they are wretched, and miserable, and poor, and blind, and naked. It is to you, my dear friends, that our Saviour doth this day address the advice in my text:

"I counsel thee to buy of me gold tried in the fire, that thou mayest be rich; and white raiment, that thou mayest be clothed, and that the shame of thy nakedness do not appear; and anoint thine eyes with eye-salve, that thou mayest see."

What have you to object against this advice?—Are not these the very things you need? are they not exactly suited to your state and circumstances?—Would you not think yourselves bound to bless God eternally, for giving you such a rich and full supply? I think I may reasonably take all this for granted.—What discourages you then?—You say you are unworthy. I ask you, Where does Christ speak as if he supposed you to be worthy? Were this a secret known only to yourselves, you might indeed have cause to dread a discovery: but the Lord Jesus knew this before you knew it. Nay, if he had not told you of it, I dare venture to affirm you should never have found it out, I mean in this world, for death and judgment will clear up all mistakes. Why then do you make objections where Christ makes none?—Is his honor dearer to you than to himself?—Does he not know how to dispense his mercy till you have taught him? I charge you to beware of such presumptuous conceits. It is *because* you are poor, and blind, and naked, that he counsels you to come to him for the supplies here offered.

But does he not speak of buying; and what price can I offer him for such inestimable blessings? I have already told you what I take to be the meaning of that expression;—but as this objection is of a very deadly nature, and commonly proves one of the strongest bars in men's way to Christ, it is necessary to examine it with some more accuracy. And, first, I must ask those who make the objection, Are you really willing to take these blessings for nothing, if you can get them? Do not answer rashly, for I apprehend there is a secret deceit within you, that you are not aware of.—Say, would it not give you a mighty satisfaction, if you could discover something in yourselves that might entitle you to these blessings, or, at least, that might incline or dispose Christ to bestow them upon you? Would it not give you some courage, if you could shed more penitent tears for sin, if you felt more love for God and the Redeemer, or if you were more exact and blameless in your conduct and behavior? And are you not secretly displeased with yourselves, that you cannot attain to these things before you apply to Christ for his aid? If this is the case, allow me to put your objection in its proper form. It is not, as you apprehend, I have nothing to give to Christ as a price for his benefits; but I have not enough.—My stock is too small to buy such an inheritance; and till it is better improven, it is vain for me to hope that my offer can be accepted. Alas! brethren, it is plain from this, that pride is at the root of your objection, though it has artfully put on the form of humility; at the bottom, you are pleased with the notion of buying, and are only vexed that you have not enough to give. You secretly dream that, by diligence and good management, you may at length acquire something that may deserve the favorable regards of the Redeemer; and therefore, once for all, I must tell you, that, notwithstanding your mournful complaints of poverty, you are really far poorer than you suppose yourselves to be. You not only want a price in the mean time, but you shall never be able to find a price that bears the smallest proportion to the blessings you need; and Christ, who shed his blood to purchase these benefits, will never sell them below their value. The truth is, he does not intend to dispose of them in that way. Though he bought them at a high rate, he gives them away freely, and gives them only to those who, disclaiming all merit and worthiness in themselves, are willing to receive them merely as an alms, to which they neither have, nor can have, any title.

Let me therefore entreat you to come to him, poor and naked as you are. It is his own counsel, and, as I told you, he is the true and faithful Witness. You may depend upon his word, and shall never have cause to repent your following his advice. Come, then, O sinners, at his call, and believe it, that he is more willing to give you the blessings here spoken of, than you are or can be to ask them from him. You honor the truth of Christ when you obey his summons; whereas, you directly give him the lie, and call him a false and flattering witness, when, upon any pretence whatever, you keep at a distance from him, and question his readiness to perform what he hath promised. He not only counsels, but invites; he not only invites, but entreats; and to remove every ground of suspicion or jealousy, he adds his oath to his promise, and to both he superadds his seal, and is now ready to hold it out to you in the holy sacrament. Let me therefore, once more, beseech you to hearken to his advice. First come to himself by an humble faith, and then come and receive the New Testament in his blood.

As for you who have already been determined by grace to listen to the advice of this faithful Witness, I this day invite you, in his name, to come anew, and draw water out of the wells of salvation. For you, he hath again covered a table in the wilderness, and instituted this ordinance for your spiritual nourishment and growth in grace. You have formerly tasted that the Lord is gracious, he is now waiting to give you some farther experience of it. Come forward then with thankful hearts, and enlarged desires. Devise liberal things, for he is a liberal Giver. Open your mouths wide, and he will fill them abundantly. *Amen.*

SERMON LXII.

AWFUL DESTINY OF THE WICKED.

ECCLESIASTES VIII. 13.—"But it shall not be well with the wicked, neither shall he prolong his days, which are as a shadow, because he feareth not before GOD."

THE promiscuous distribution of good and evil, in the present life, has always tended to weaken the influence of moral and religious motives among mankind. Our minds are so framed, that pleasure or pain, immediately or soon to be experienced, affect them in a much stronger degree, than greater measures of either, removed by distance of future time. There is a prodigious difference between certainty, as the mere object of our understanding, and the strong impression produced by the consideration of those things which are not only certain, but near at hand. The former merely produces assent of the mind; the latter lays hold of the heart, and influences the conduct. Accordingly we find, that all who have aspired to the art of persuasion, in moral or religious discourses, have endeavored to heighten the influence of distant motives, by placing the objects of them in the strongest light. This may be done either directly, by representing their superior and infinite importance, or implicitly, by lessening our conceptions, and thereby lowering our solicitude, as to the intervening period.

This last is the method adopted by Solomon, in the passage with which the text is connected. In the preceding verse, he had expressed, in the strongest terms, the full assurance he had that it should finally be well with them that fear God. Many, indeed, in the present time, are the afflictions of the righteous. In the world, they are generally despised, and reviled, and persecuted. And what is the reason of this? Our Lord tells his disciples the reason: "If ye were of the world, the world would love his own; but because ye are not of the world, but I have chosen you out of the world, therefore the world hateth you." But what is the hatred, the calumny, or the persecution of the world, to those whose minds are raised above it, to an inheritance incorruptible, undefiled, and that fadeth not away; whose light affliction, which is but for a moment, works out an exceeding great and eternal weight of glory?

Let us now change the view. The sinner may do evil an hundred times, and as often prosper in his schemes of iniquity; yet, in the midst of all this outward success, he is still the object of pity and compassion, rather than of envy. To real happiness his heart is a stranger; he grasps at enjoyment, and embraces vanity; his days fly away as a shadow; they see no good; and he himself is fast hastening to those regions of darkness, where nothing is heard but the voice of fruitless lamentation, and everlasting despair.

This, it must be confessed, is a gloomy subject; but gloomy as it is, we must not forbear to press it on your attention. The same God who commands us to say to the righteous, It shall be well with him, commands us likewise to deliver this awful warning: "It shall not be well with the wicked, neither shall he prolong his days, which are as a shadow; because he feareth not before God."

But, before I proceed to illustrate the threatening in the text, there is a previous point to be settled, without which, all that I can say must have very little effect, and that is, who the wicked here spoken of are, who are the persons against whom this threatening is denounced?

Were I, in answer to this inquiry, to begin with describing those gross and flagitious crimes, which the natural conscience of every man abhors, I should only spend your time, and offend your ears to no purpose; for who is there in all the society of mankind, not to say in a Christian assembly, that will dispute the justice of this appellation, as applied to thieves and robbers, oppressors and murderers, blasphemers, false swearers, and open contemners of all laws, human and divine? I may safely presume on your assent, that characters such as these, so obnoxious even to human society, may properly be classed among the wicked, against whom the threatening of the text is denounced. I may even take it for granted, that the greater part of my audience will advance a step farther, and permit me to pass the same censure upon those who are guilty of the more prevailing sins of the present time, such as profane swearing, uncleanness, drunkenness, breach of the Lord's day, and habitual neglect of divine institutions. Thus far, I suppose, we are generally agreed. But if we consult the Scriptures, the only infallible rule of judging, we shall find that the term *wicked* is of a still more extensive signification, and comprehends a great many characters besides those already named. Of this I cannot give you a more convincing proof, than by referring you to that plain and instructive parable of the talents, (Matt. xxv. 14.) There we read of one who digged in the earth, and hid his lord's money, and at his return digged it up again, and restored it to him in the same state he got it. In this, according to the general style of judging, there seems to be nothing culpable. The man, though not profitably active, was at least harmless. He took nothing from his master's talent, neither did he put it to any bad use. But what character did his lord give him, when he came to call for his account? This you may read at the 26th verse. "His lord said unto him, Thou wicked and slothful servant;" and, in conformity with this character, he pronounces on him this awful sentence, "Cast ye the unprofitable servant into outer darkness, there shall be weeping and gnashing of teeth." Hence it appears, that not only the gross and flagitious transgressors of God's law, but even the slothful and careless, who neglect to improve the talents committed to them, are reckoned among the wicked, by the infallible Judge, in conformity with that decisive sentence of the apostle James, "To him that knoweth to do good, and doeth it not, to him it is sin." This at once undermines the foundation upon which thousands of deluded mortals build all their hopes of the divine favor and acceptance. In vain, O misguided men, will you plead at the great day, even though ye could prove that plea, that ye abused no talent bestowed on you—that you did harm to none of all God's works. Was it for this negative purpose only, do you think, that your Maker gave you a place in his world? Was it for this only, that he conferred the active powers of your nature; that he gave you reason to preside over these powers; and his word to guide that reason? Was it for this only that he placed you in a situation where activity is necessary for your own happiness, and for the happiness of all around you? Is it nothing that your being as a chasm in creation, where infinite wisdom intended that nothing should be void, nothing cumbersome nor unprofitable? The tree that bears no fruit, as well as that whose fruit is pernicious, is cut down and cast into the fire. In like manner, if your lives have not been fruitful in the works of righteousness, if they have not exhibited positive evidences of love to God, and benevolence to men, your abstinence from gross transgressions will be of no avail. You will not indeed be ranked with those who proclaim their sins as Sodom; but yet you will be numbered with the wicked, and with them expelled for ever from the presence of the Lord.

But what shall we say of those who are not only harmless, but also good and useful members of human society; decent in their conduct, upright in their dealings, beneficent and obliging to all around them? Of such persons we are certainly bound to speak and to think well. Where those good fruits appear, we ought to conclude, that the tree which produces them is good likewise. It is a bold and impious invasion of the divine prerogative to judge the hearts of others; and nothing can be more opposite to the spirit of Christianity, than to harbor any secret suspicion of men's inward tempers, when their conduct is proper, inoffensive, and useful.

But if the question be put in another shape, What ought these persons to think of themselves? the word of God obliges me to give another answer.

There we are taught to exercise a perpetual jealousy over ourselves, and to take no credit from particular acts of virtue, if our character be not entirely formed by those principles which it alone inspires. Of these, one of the most commanding is mentioned in the text itself. "It shall not be well with the wicked, *because he feareth not before God.*" Were all the combinations of language to be studied, it would be impossible to devise an expression more significant than this, or more calculated to discriminate the steady and commanding motives of virtue, from those which are unsound, accidental and fluctuating.

The openly profane fear not God at all. The unprofitable servant, who buries his talent in the ground, fears him as an austere master, and by that slavish fear is restrained from making the proper improvement of it. The man who aspires only to decency, and outward propriety of conduct, is actuated by a fear which respects sometimes God, sometimes the reproofs of conscience, but most frequently the opinion of his fellow men. In contradistinction to all these partial and inadequate principles, the truly good man *fears before God.* He dreads him not as an enemy, but, conscious of his inspection at all times, he dreads every thing that would make this thought a terror to him. To this decisive test I must therefore lead you. Is the authority of God become the great consideration to which you bend all your sentiments and conduct? Have you been led to renounce the maxims of the world, and the inclinations of nature, and to make the will of God the standard of all you do, regardless of present danger or advantage? Unless this be the habitual frame of your souls, all your seeming virtues are no better than dead works; ye are still in the bond of iniquity, and have every reason to tremble at the denunciation in the text: "It shall not be well with the wicked, neither shall he prolong his days, which are as a shadow, because he feareth not before God."

1*st.* It cannot be well with the wicked, because the consequences of their own conduct naturally involve misery. Independent of all the sanctions of the divine law, sin is in itself the destroyer of our happiness. There is so much slavery and distraction in obeying our corrupt passions, the consequences are so inconvenient and ruinous, that none ever followed such a course without a secret consciousness of fatal mistake. To be happy, it is necessary that we be at peace with ourselves. But how can the wicked have this peace? Their minds, torn by contending passions, are like the troubled sea, which cannot rest, whose waters cast up mire and dirt. They may indeed dethrone their reason, and trample on their conscience; but yet the voice of these degraded faculties will at times be heard, and even in their scenes of riot and frantic mirth, will, like the hand-writing on the wall of Belshazzar's palace, embitter all their joys. Many sins are destructive of bodily health, as well as of peace of mind. This is confessedly the case with sensuality and intemperance. Others expose men to dreadful hazards, weary them with incessant toils, and at last plunge them in infamy and ruin. "Come, say they, let us lay wait for blood; let us lurk privily for the innocent; let us swallow them up alive as the grave, and whole, as those that go down to the pit; we shall find all precious substance, we shall fill our houses with spoil." But behold the issue of these criminal projects. "They lay wait for their own blood; they lurk privily for their own lives. Knowest thou not this of old, since man was placed upon the earth, that the triumphing of the wicked is short, and the joy of the hypocrite but for a moment? They have sown vanity, and they shall reap the whirlwind."

2*dly.* It cannot be well with the wicked, because they are in a state of distance and alienation from God. The glorious attributes of his nature are to them objects of terror and dismay, and the secret wish of their hearts is, that there were no God. But there is a God, O sinner! a God who hateth wickedness, and who will destroy all the workers of iniquity. He hath bent his bow, and made it ready; he hath also prepared for them the instruments of death. But O how hopeless a warfare is it to contend with him! Who ever hardened himself against God and prospered? Is there any strong hold, where the enemies of his government may be safe? Go try the whole extent of creation. Ascend to heaven, and he is there in the brightness of his majesty. Go down to the regions of darkness, and he is there in the severity of his justice. Take the wings of the morning, and fly to the uttermost parts of the sea, even there his boundless dominion extends; even there his right hand shall hold thee a prisoner to his vengeance. Listen, O sinner, to the tremendous declaration of this omnipotent, omnipresent God. "I, even I, am he, and there is no God with me; I kill and I make alive, I wound and I heal, neither is there any that can deliver out of my hand; for I lift up my hand to heaven, and say, I live for ever. If I whet my glittering sword, and mine hand take hold on judgment, I will render vengeance to mine enemies, and will reward them that hate me. I will make mine arrows drunk with blood."

3dly. It cannot be well with the wicked, because they lie under the guilt of all the sins which they have ever committed. A dreadful load! One sin ruined myriads of beings superior to man; how shall they escape, then, who from their youth upwards have drunk iniquity even as the ox drinketh water? It is possible that you may soothe yourselves with the thought of having repented of the grosser sins with which your lives have been stained; you trust that these are forgiven, and presume that a merciful God will overlook the rest. But I must be allowed to inform you, that this is a rash and groundless thought. There is no such thing with God as partial forgiveness. If all your sins are not pardoned, not one of them is; and unless you have been renewed by the grace and Spirit of God, those sins you committed in your earliest years, are as much in force against you as those of the most recent date you can name. Conversion and pardon are inseparably connected; and it will ever remain a certain truth, that whom God justifies, them he also sanctifies. There is indeed no condemnation to them that are in Christ Jesus; but, on the other hand, these are such as walk not after the flesh, but after the Spirit: for if any man have not the Spirit of Christ, he is none of his.

4thly. It cannot be well with the wicked, because, while they remain in this state, nothing they do can please God. I mean not to affirm, that they cannot perform actions materially good, the substance of which is commanded by God. The morality of Christ's religion is so much accommodated to the interest of individuals, and to the good of society, that even they, who have no higher motives, may find it profitable to comply with some of its injunctions. Far less is it my meaning, that it would be better, or as good, for such persons to neglect or disobey these injunctions. But my meaning is, that there are so many defects, and so much unsoundness of motive in their best actions, that God can have no delight in them, such as he has in the obedience of his own people, who are reconciled to him by the great Mediator.

They cannot so far please God as to render their persons acceptable to him; nor have they any promise that this partial obedience of theirs shall be recompensed with any favor or reward. The truth of these observations is confirmed by a multitude of passages of Scripture. There we are told, that the thoughts of the wicked are abominable to him; that the ploughing of the wicked is sin; that the sacrifice of the wicked is an abomination; yea, he that turneth away his ear from hearing the law, even his prayer, saith Solomon, shall be an abomination unto God. And how can it be well with the man, whose whole life is a perpetual offence to the God that made him? Consider this, ye that now despise reproof, trample on the blood of Christ, and resist the motions of his Spirit. In vain do you rest on the favorable parts of your character, as a compensation for this ungrateful abuse of the divine goodness and long-suffering. In the sight of men, indeed, this balance may be of some avail to you; but God seeth not as man seeth. In his sight your whole character is depraved, and every part of your conduct offensive. I shall only add, in the

5th and *last* place, That if you die in this state, your perdition is inevitable. "Except a man be born again," saith our Lord, "he cannot see the kingdom of God." "Verily, verily, I say unto you, except ye be converted, and become as little children, ye cannot enter into the kingdom of heaven." These passages are plain and decisive; and I have selected them, among innumerable others to the same purpose, for this reason, that they were uttered by the firmest and tenderest friend of the human race, the truth of whose warnings we can have no reason to doubt.

In reviewing what has been said, the impression left is undoubtedly gloomy, and nothing but a sense of duty could have prevailed on me to deliver so harsh a message. But that watchman would be very unfaithful to his trust, who would not call the alarm of fire, because of the unpleasant sound it has in men's ears. I have not been sternly delivering truths in which I have no concern myself. We are all embarked in the voyage of life upon the same conditions. These conditions I have endeavored to set before you, according to that commandment of God, "Say ye to the righteous, it shall be well with him, for he shall eat the fruit of his doings; but woe to the wicked, it shall be ill with him, neither shall he prolong his days, which are as a shadow, because he feareth not before God." Knowing, therefore, the terrors of the Lord, I have been endeavoring to persuade you to fly from the wrath to come.

The way to escape all this misery is patent, even to the chief of sinners. The door of mercy is open. God is seated on a throne of grace, ready to receive every humble penitent; and this is his call to the sons of men, "Turn ye, turn ye, why will ye die?—Seek ye the Lord while he may be found, call upon him while he is near.—Let the wicked forsake his way, and the unrighteous man his thoughts, and let him return unto the Lord, and he will have mercy on him, and to our God, for he will abundantly pardon.—Incline your ear, and come unto me; hear, and your souls shall live,; and I will make with you an everlasting covenant, even the sure mercies of David." *Amen.*

SERMON LXIII.

CONSEQUENCES OF APOSTASY.

Revelation ii. 5.—"Remember from whence thou art fallen, and repent, and do the first works; or else I will come unto thee quickly, and remove thy candlestick out of his place, except thou repent."

These are the words of our Lord Jesus Christ to the church at Ephesus. They contain a call to repentance and reformation, with a severe and terrible threatening in case of disobedience. In the second and third verses, we have an acknowledgment of what was good in that church, "I know thy works, and thy labor, and thy patience, and how thou canst not bear them which are evil: and thou hast tried them which say they are apostles, and are not, and hast found them liars, and hast borne, and hast patience, and for my name's sake hast labored, and hast not fainted." Nevertheless, says he, in the 4th verse, "I have somewhat against thee, because thou hast left thy first love." Their affection was cooled, their zeal was abated, they were become more remiss and lukewarm in the duties of religion. Now, this our Saviour could not bear; he therefore calls them to remember their first estate, to consider their present degenerate condition, to mourn over it, and to rise from it by a speedy repentance and reformation. And to give this summons the greater efficacy, he threatens them with the removal of the gospel from them, if they did not repent: "I will come unto thee quickly, and remove thy candlestick out of his place, except thou repent."

Many useful observations might be made from this passage; as, *first*, that our Lord Jesus Christ takes special notice of those to whom the gospel is sent. His eyes are in every place, beholding the evil and the good; but he walks in the midst of the golden candlesticks, and carefully observes the improvement which men make of this precious light. This teaches us what manner of persons we ought to be. We are placed here, as it were, on a theatre, and act in the immediate view of our King and Judge. Yea, he hath in a manner intrusted us with his glory, and called the world to take notice of us, as the persons by whom he expects to be honored, and therefore our behavior cannot be indifferent to him. He may wink at others, but cannot wink at us. The husbandman is not dishonored by the unfruitfulness of a wild tree, upon which he has bestowed no culture; but the barrenness of what is planted in his garden, or inclosed field, reflects upon himself, and therefore he cannot be unconcerned about that, but must vindicate his honor upon it, by cutting it down, and casting it out as a cumberer of the ground.

Secondly. We may observe, that not only gross apostasy, but even the smallest decays among his people, are highly offensive unto him. This church had many good things among them, and after the commendation that was given them in the second and third verses, one would be ready to put the question, What lack they yet? But our Lord remarks the coldness of their hearts, and resents that inward and secret declension from their former love and zeal, and threatens them with swift destruction if they did not repent. O how does this magnify God's patience towards us! and what cause have we to tremble and be afraid of his judgments, seeing we have not only fallen from our first love, but by gross and open acts of enmity have made it extremely doubtful, whether there be any remains of love abiding with us at all? But, without insisting upon these, my design is, to consider this threatening separately by itself. And my method shall be,

I. To show that God may be provoked by the sins of a people, to remove the gospel from them.

II. I shall represent to you the terribleness of this judgment. And,

III. Direct you to the proper use of this awful subject.

In the Scriptures we have many comfortable promises of the church's stability: it is built upon a rock, and the gates of hell shall not prevail against it. It was Christ's promise to his apostles, "Lo, I am with you always, even unto the end of the world;" not with their persons, for these were soon to be removed out of the world by death, but with their doctrine, which was to endure throughout all generations; so that we have the fullest assurance, that the Zion of God, or the universal church, shall never perish; that the light of the gospel shall never be extinguished; but that the King of Zion shall always have subjects to serve him in some corner of the earth or other. But though the gospel shall never be removed out of the world altogether, yet it may be removed from particular places. The candlestick is a movable thing, and not an entailed inheritance.

The Jews are an eminent instance of this. Never was a nation so highly favored as they. To them pertained the adoption, and the glory, and the covenants, and the giving of the law, and the service of God, and the promises; theirs were the fathers, and of them, as concerning the flesh, Christ came, who is over all, God blessed for ever. They were God's chosen people, his peculiar treasure, his first born, and his spouse; for by these honorable titles were they long distinguished from the rest of the world. Nor were they only distinguished by titles, but actually blessed with all the privileges which these titles imported. God was indeed a father and husband unto them: he cherished them in his bosom, and employed his almighty power for their preservation. He conducted their arms, and dictated their laws; he formed their state, and was present among them by a visible glory, and established a method of correspondence, by which they might have constant access to him for counsel and direction in every case of difficulty. Never had any people such illustrious displays of the divine providence in their favor. Some nations have had a long tract of prosperity, a series of lucky accidents, as it were, by the help of which they have grown up to a very flourishing condition; but the various steps of their advancement were visible, and easy to be accounted for, and were nothing more extraordinary than a plentiful crop after a favorable seed-time and harvest, or the riches of a skilful and industrious merchant. But it was not so with the nation of the Jews; their prosperity was the admiration of all that beheld it, and forced them to acknowledge that the Lord was with them of a truth. God brought them out of Egypt by a high hand and an outstretched arm; the sea opened a passage for their retreat, and overwhelmed their enemies; bread was given them from heaven, so that man did eat angel's food; and the flinty rock yielded them water to quench their thirst. At the prayer of Joshua the sun stood still; and at the same time God slew his enemies before him with hail-stones from heaven, and gave his people a miraculous and complete victory over them. And after they were put in possession of the promised land, they did not grow up like other states; they were oftentimes brought so low that they seemed past recovery, and as often did God interpose for their relief; and the various changes they underwent were so sudden and surprising, as made it evident to themselves and all about them, that their affairs were conducted, not by the skill and strength of men, but by the immediate hand of God, who, by his irresistible power, governs all creatures and things, so that none can stay his hand, or say unto him, What doest thou? Yet, notwithstanding all these titles, and privileges, and providences, whereby God distinguished them in such a remarkable manner, they are now pulled up by the roots, abandoned by God, and despised among men. No spiritual dew falls upon those mountains of Gilboa. Those that were as pleasant to God as the grapes in the wilderness to a thirsty traveller, are now of as little regard as the heath or the bramble. Of a tender father he is become their enraged enemy; and flings vengeance down upon those heads which before he crowned with mercy. He caused the land in which he had planted them, by a series of miracles, to spew them out because of their sins; and now they wander as miserable vagabonds over the face of the world, a standing monument of God's righteous judgment, and a sad proof that spiritual privileges are not entailed to any nation; but that God may be provoked, by the sins of a people, to remove their candlestick out of his place, and punish them with darkness, who would not walk in the light of it whilst they enjoyed it.

The seven churches of Asia, mentioned in this and the following chapter, are another instance of this. These had their day, but are now benighted; the judgments threatened in these gracious epistles, which were directed to them, have been long ago inflicted. The banners of a blasphemous impostor have long triumphed over the standard of the gospel. Nor is the once famous church of Rome a great deal better; for though the gospel is still professed and honored by them in appearance, yet the light of it is so much obscured, and buried amidst the rubbish of idolatrous opinions and practices, that it is scarce discernible; and without breach of charity we may say of them, that God hath given them up to strong delusions to believe a lie; so that they have all the marks of a people whom God hath abandoned, though wrath be not as yet come upon them to the uttermost. By these examples we see that the gospel is not the inheritance of any particular people, but that it frequently has been, and therefore may still be forfeited, and that God may be provoked, by the sins of those who enjoy the light of it, to strip them of all their privileges, by removing their candlestick out of his place. Let us now proceed, in the

II. place, To consider the greatness of this punishment. And if we view it aright, we shall soon be convinced, that a more terrible judgment cannot be inflicted upon any people or nation. What can be more terrible than famine? Parents have been forced, against all the ties of natural affection, to devour their own children, and children to feed upon the flesh of their parents. The extremity of hunger hath reconciled very delicate people to things that are most loathsome and nauseous, carrion, dung, and vermin of all sorts; yet this is accounted a small judgment when compared with the other, (Amos viii. 11.) "Behold the days come, saith the Lord, that I will send a famine in the land, not a famine of bread, nor a thirst for water, but of hearing the word of the Lord." The want of spiritual food is so much worse than the want of natural food, as the soul is better than the body; the one makes the body weak, the other starves the soul, and leaves it both weak and wicked; the one may be a means to make us seek the Lord, but the other leaves us in gross darkness, without either help or hope. The gospel is the sun that enlightens the mind, the rain that waters the heart; it is that divine seed by which the quickening Spirit renews the soul, and implants a principle of spiritual life, which shall issue in a glorious and eternal one. By this our souls are refined, and our lusts consumed; without this, we can have no prospect of a world to come, nor any knowledge of the way that leads to it, for life and immortality are brought to light by the gospel, and by it only we are told, that God is in Christ reconciling the world to himself, not imputing their trespasses; and therefore the want of it must be the sum of all misery, and infinitely worse than any other calamity we can either feel or fear in this world. God may take notice of a people under the sharpest afflictions, but when he takes away his word, then he knows them no longer; then all gracious correspondence or intercourse is broken up. This, O this, is the very dregs of vengeance! Yea, when the gospel departs from a people, all other blessings commonly depart with it. This is the charter of all our privileges, both spiritual and temporal; and therefore in losing it we lose all that depends upon it, at least we forfeit our title; and any outward mercies that are continued with us, are only like food and raiment to a condemned criminal, which the King's clemency allows him till the fatal sentence be executed upon him.

The gospel is not only the glory, but the strength of a nation; when it departs, God ceases to be their protector. The flourishing condition of the seven churches soon withered when the candlestick was removed; and their deplorable and abject state ever since, even with respect to external enjoyments and worldly advantages, is a melancholy proof that the gospel does not take flight alone, but is attended with every other thing that contributes to the glory or happiness of a people.

Thus have I represented to you the terribleness of this judgment. And now I come to point out your concern in this subject, and to direct you to the proper improvement of it. And if these things be so, have not we in these lands great reason to fear, that our iniquities may provoke the Lord to inflict this punishment upon us? Are we better than Ephesus or the other churches of Asia? Are our privileges greater or better secured than theirs were? yet their candlestick has been long removed; and who dare affirm that ours may not be removed likewise? My brethren, I have no design to alarm you with groundless fears; but my duty as a watchman obliges me to blow the trumpet when I see danger approaching; and that I may give it a distinct sound, I shall briefly unfold to you the grounds of my apprehension of approaching danger in these following remarks: And,

1*st*. Is it not evident, that vice and immorality have grown up to an amazing height among us? Do not many proclaim their sins as Sodom, and hide them not? Yea, do not many glory in their shame, and count it their honor to excel in some branch of wickedness or other? I do not aggravate the charge; every one's observation must convince him of the truth of it. Now, what must be the fruit of this? Hear what God says by his prophet (Joel iii. 13.) "Put ye in the sickle, for the harvest is ripe, the press is full, the fats overflow; for their wickedness is great." I do not say we have just come this length, that we are already arrived at a fulness of iniquity; but surely we have for a long time been advancing towards it by very hasty steps. And this, I think, is one reasonable ground of fear.

2*dly*. Is there not a visible contempt of the blessed gospel? Are not the ordinances of religion slighted and despised? yea, is it not become fashionable among many, to reject the whole of Revelation as a cunningly devised fable, and to use all their influence to proselyte the more simple and unthinking to their opinion? Has not Deism, which began at court in King Charles II.'s reign, been still descending through all the inferior ranks, till now it has got low enough? And what does this presage? The Gadareans besought Christ to depart from their coasts, and got their request. The gospel is of too much worth to be always exposed to the injuries of men, and forced upon a people against their will. When children throw a precious jewel in the dirt, what can be expected, but that their father should take it from them, and lay it in another place, and punish them too for their folly and ingratitude? A

3*d* Sign of approaching danger is the small success which accompanies the preaching of the gospel, even among those who profess to believe it. How few converts are born into the church! Is it not visible, that numbers who attend upon ordinances are still lying in the gall of bitterness and the bond of iniquity? How few are seriously inquiring after the way to Zion, with their faces thitherward? And is not this too a presage of a departing gospel, when God ceases to pour oil into the lamp, to accompany the ordinances of religion with the influences of his Spirit? Surely we have reason to fear, that he intends to remove the candlestick to some other place, and to give it to those who will value it more, and make better use of it than we have done. A

4*th* Ground of fear is the present divided state of our church. Union is the strength of the religious, as well as of the civil society; for a house divided against itself cannot stand. It is a weighty saying of one upon this head, that when children fall out, and fight about the candle, the parents come and take it away, and leave them to decide their differences in the dark. We may justly fear that God will take away that light which we abuse in quarrelling, instead of walking and working by it. Add to all these, in the

5*th* place, The threatening aspect of divine Providence, the success of our enemies abroad, and the bold attempt, which is still carrying on, against our religion and liberties, at home, and then judge whether there be not sufficient grounds of fear. "Will a lion roar in the forest when he hath no prey? Will a young lion cry out of his den, if he have taken nothing? Can a bird fall in a snare upon the earth, where no gin is for him? Shall one take up a snare from the earth, and have taken nothing at all? Shall a trumpet be blown in the city, and the people not be afraid? Shall there be evil in a city, and the Lord hath not done it? The lion hath roared, who will not fear? the Lord God hath spoken, who can but prophesy?" My brethren, God has been speaking to us in a very awful manner for these six months past; and that we might not mistake his voice, most of the events that have fallen out in that space of time have been altogether surprising and unexpected. Our enemies themselves were amazed at their success, and ascribed it to the immediate hand of God, which favored their enterprise; and the hand of God has been no less remarkably displayed in our benign deliverance. The retreat of the rebels, immediately after a victory, without facing an army they had so lately overcome, was so contrary to the general opinion, that I believe the wisest heads were afraid of some cunning artifice, some deep laid plot, to draw our men into a snare, from which they should not easily escape. In a word, man's part of this whole affair has been so small and inconsiderable, that it is evidently the Lord's own doing; and though he has employed instruments both to distress and relieve us, yet he has done it in such a sovereign manner, that he seems to have used them upon no other design but only to convince us that he can work without them. I confess, my brethren, the care which God has taken to make himself observable in the conduct of these occurrences, is one of the principal grounds of my fears at this time; nor are my fears a whit lessened by the late favorable dispensation. I look upon it indeed as an intimation, that he who is a God of judgment is also a God of mercy; and that, notwithstanding all our past provocations, he is yet willing to be reconciled to us upon the terms of the gospel; and therefore I view it in the light of an encouragement to repentance, but not at all as a sign that God's anger is turned away from us, or a security that our danger is over. No, my brethren, the sun rose upon Sodom the morning of that very day in which it was consumed by fire from heaven. We have got a breathing time, a respite from judgment, but not a perfect deliverance; and if we do not improve the day of our visitation, this mixture of goodness with severity makes it only the more probable that the last exercise of God's patience is at hand, and that the things which belong to our peace are in the greatest danger of being hid from our eyes.

Thus then you see what grounds there are to fear, that the dreadful judgment threatened in the text may be inflicted upon us; and this, I hope, will dispose us all to listen to the exhortation here given us, "Remember, therefore, from whence thou art fallen, and repent, and do the first works."

This is the command of our Lord Jesus Christ, and the only way to prevent the ruin of a sinful people. The substance of this exhortation I have frequently pressed upon you, and therefore I shall not now enlarge upon it; and every thing I have just now delivered to you, may serve as motives to induce you to comply with it. The candlestick may be removed from you. This deprivation of the gospel is the most terrible of all God's judgments; and as our sins deserve it, so God by his providence has actually been threatening us with it. O then let us be awakened from our security, let us value the gospel dispensation, and improve it to the obtaining a gospel nature. Let us not loiter while the sun shines, lest we be benighted. It will not stand still at our pleasure, but will go its course according to the command of its Governor, and listens not to the follies of men, nor tarries for our delays. Let us then stir up ourselves to call upon our Lord, who is the Lord of Zion, and the protector and safeguard of our Jerusalem. Let us plead with him, as the disciples that were going to Emmaus, "Lord, abide with us, for the evening begins to come, and the day is far spent." Our Saviour did so, and gave them his blessing. He may do so with us likewise. He may return with a rich blessing to our land and church, and abide with us and our posterity till the day of glory break, and all the shadows fly away. *Amen.*

SERMON LXIV.

THE WORSHIP AND GLORY OF GOD.

2 CHRONICLES v. 13, 14.—"It came even to pass, as the trumpeters and singers were as one to make one sound to be heard in praising and thanking the LORD, and when they lift up their voice, with the trumpets and cymbals, and instruments of music, and praised the LORD, saying, For he is good, for his mercy endureth for ever, that then the house was filled with a cloud, even the house of the LORD: So that the priests could not stand to minister by reason of the cloud; for the glory of the LORD had filled the house of GOD."

THE day of Petecost excepted, when the Holy Ghost made a visible descent upon the apostles of our Lord, I look upon this to have been the brightest day of heaven upon earth that ever the church of God was favored with. It is impossible to conceive the joy, the wonder, the ecstasy of these devout worshippers, when they beheld the cloud, that well-known symbol of the Divine presence, and saw the temple filled with his glory. Solomon himself, as we learn from the 18th verse of the following chapter, was so overpowered with this extraordinary manifestation, that he made a sudden pause even after he had begun to pray; and, like one doubtful whether he should believe the testimony of his own senses, abruptly asks the question; "But will God in very deed dwell with men on the earth? Behold! heaven, and the heaven of heavens, cannot contain thee, how much less this house I have built!"

It appears, from the last chapter of the book of Exodus, that when the tabernacle was first erected in the wilderness, God was pleased to take visible possession of it in a way similar to what is here recorded; and the effects (though not precisely the same) were very much akin to those I have now read to you: For we are there told, that Moses, the man of God, was not able to enter into the tent of the congregation, because the cloud abode thereon, and the glory of the Lord had filled the tabernacle: But here the cloud not only filled the tabernacle, but the whole temple; and the Divine presence was displayed with such glory and majesty, that the priests who burnt incense at the golden altar, were obliged, at least for some time, to intermit the service. They could not stand to minister by reason of the cloud, for the glory of the Lord had filled the house of God.

I suppose I need scarcely observe to you, that such pompous and visible manifestations of the Divine presence are not to be expected in gospel days. The darkness of the former dispensation required those external aids, and rendered them not only desirable but useful and necessary; but now that the darkness is dispelled, and the dayspring from on high hath visited us; the great objects of faith being freed from the thick veil of types and shadows, penetrate the mind without the assistance of our bodily senses, and make a deeper and more lasting impression upon the believing soul than the most splendid scenes the eye could behold.

Zion's glory doth not now consist in outward pomp and magnificence, but in the spiritual though invisible presence of her King, according to his own gracious promise, "Lo, I am with you always, even unto the end of the world;" and "where two or three are gathered together in my name, there am I in the midst of them." When a divine power accompanies the ordinances of religion; when these waters of the sanctuary are impregnated with a healing and quickening virtue; when the souls of believers are enlightened and purified, revived and comforted, by the use of those means which Christ hath appointed, then is the temple filled with his glory; and there is no need of any visible cloud to convince the devout worshipper that his Lord is with him.

It has long been lamented, (would to God there was less cause for it,) that this gracious presence of our Redeemer is sensibly withdrawn from our public assemblies. We have heard with our ears, and our fathers have told us, what work the Lord did in their days, in the times of old; how his steps of Majesty have been seen in the sanctuary, and his arm revealed by its glorious effects, turning the disobedient to the wisdom of the just, enriching and beautifying the souls of his own people with righteousness, and peace, and joy in the Holy Ghost.

But, alas! How is the gold become dim, and the most fine gold changed? These blessed fruits of gospel ordinances are rarely to be seen in our day, and therefore is just ground for that mournful complaint, "The bellows are burnt, the lead is consumed of the fire, the founder melteth in vain; for the wicked are not plucked away from their wickedness." Few, comparatively speaking, are now converted by the means of grace. And even among the few who have a name to live, the decayed and languishing state of vital Christianity is too observable to need any proof or illustration.

To what cause shall we impute this? Is God's arm shortened that it cannot save; or is his ear heavy that he cannot hear? Is his mercy clean gone for ever? doth his promise fail for evermore? Hath the Lord forgotten to be gracious? Hath he in anger shut up his tender mercies? No, God is unchangeably the same, yesterday, to-day, and for ever, without any variableness or shadow of turning. He is the rock, his work is perfect, and all his ways are judgment; a God of truth and inviolable fidelity. The blame, my brethren, lies at our own door. Our iniquities have separated between us and our God, and withhold good things from us. We do not cry to him with our hearts; we do not stir up ourselves to call upon God; our prayers are cold and lifeless; our praises languish and die on our lips; we rush upon ordinances without any serious preparation, and are neither suitably concerned to obtain the Divine presence, nor duly affected when we miss it.

That this is too frequently the case cannot be denied. Our own observation and experience must convince us of the truth of it. But may I not be allowed to hope that some, nay that many, have come up to this solemnity with longing desires to behold and admire the beauty of the Lord, and to feel the power of his grace in the sanctuary? May I not hope, that there is a goodly number in this large assembly, who have been pleading, like Moses, in their secret retirements, "I beseech thee, O Lord, show me thy glory?"

Well, then, to such the passage I am now to discourse upon affords matter of useful and seasonable instruction, as it not only relates an extraordinary manifestation of the divine glory to his ancient church, but likewise informs us how the worshippers were employed at the time when that extraordinary manifestation was made. And I think the inference is perfectly just and natural, That if we desire and expect to share in their privilege, we ought, in so far as the difference of our circumstances will permit, to follow their example, and do what they did.

"It came even to pass, as the trumpeters and singers were as one, to make one sound to be heard in praising and thanking the Lord; and when they lift up their voice with the trumpets and cymbals, and instruments of music, and praised the Lord, saying, For he is good, for his mercy endureth for ever, that then the house was filled with a cloud, even the house of the Lord, so that the priests could not stand to minister by reason of the cloud; for the glory of the Lord had filled the house of God."

Where you may observe, in the

I. place, That the glory of God began to appear when the assembly were employed in praise and thanksgiving. This is a striking circumstance, and deserves our peculiar attention. Much time had been spent in solemn duties of another kind. Numerous and costly sacrifices had been offered up, as we read in the 6th verse of this chapter, even sheep and oxen that could not be told for multitudes. But these ritual parts of worship were all concluded before the cloud entered into the Temple. God delayed to honor them with this token of his favor till the spiritual and heavenly exercise of praise was begun. This is by far the most acceptable service we can be engaged in. "Whoso offereth praise," says God, "glorifieth me." David knew this when he said, (Psalm lxix. 30, 31, &c.) "I will praise the name of God with a song, and will magnify him with thanksgiving. This also will please the Lord better than ox or bullock that hath horn or hoof." Praise honors God, and therefore puts a distinguishing honor upon this duty. Prayer is an expression of our indigence and weakness. Thanksgiving expresseth our relish of the sweetness of benefits received; but praise rises above all selfish regards, and directly terminates on the greatness and amiableness of God himself. He loves our prayers, he loves our penitential tears and groans; but nothing pleases him so much as the cheerful adoration and praise of his people. Nay, penitential tears are no otherwise valuable than as they purge our eyes from the filth of sin, that we may behold more clearly the loveliness of God, and give him that glory which is due to his name. All the other duties of devotion are only means of preparation for this sublime exercise. The habitations of the blessed continually resound with the high praises of God. There the most perfect creatures, in their most perfect state, have this for their constant unwearied employment, "they rest not day nor night, saying, Holy, holy, holy, Lord God Almighty, which was, and is, and is to come."

We are too backward, my brethren, to this heavenly exercise, and perhaps that is one reason why we enjoy so little of heaven upon earth. Did we praise God more, he would give us greater cause to praise him; but this we seldom think of. We beg hard for relief when we feel our necessities; but alas, how slowly do we return to give glory to God. Let me therefore entreat you, in all your addresses to the throne of grace, to give praise and thanksgiving their due proportion. In days of humiliation, or in some special cases of distress, our sins and our dangers may have the greater share; but ordinarily, as much of our time and thoughts should be employed in the humble and thankful adoration of the divine greatness and goodness, as is spent in confessing our sins, or begging those supplies which our wants require. That excellent model of devotion which Christ hath left to his church lays a solid foundation for this remark. It both begins and ends with adoration; and of the six petitions which make up the body of the prayer, three directly relate to the advancement of God's glory. Nay, these three are first in order; and we are taught to pray that God's name may be hallowed, his kingdom come, and his will done on earth as it is in heaven, before we ask any thing for ourselves in particular. Would we then feel the divine presence, would we see the glory of God in his Sanctuary, let us address ourselves to this high and heavenly work. The occasion of our meeting gives us a fair invitation to it. The great object which this day presents to us is the Lamb of God which taketh away the sin of the world. We are to behold Christ in the holy sacrament, evidently set forth as crucified before our eyes. And can we refrain from adoration and praise, whilst we contemplate Him who is the brightness of his Father's glory, and the express image of his person? Should we not rejoice and give thanks, when we are called to commemorate the unspeakable gift of God to men? Every Lord's day bespeaks our praise and thanksgiving; but the peculiar language of a communion Sabbath is evidently this, "Let Israel rejoice in him that made him: Let the children of Zion be joyful in their King. Praise ye the Lord, for it is good to sing praises to our God; for it is pleasant, and praise is comely."

II. It deserves our notice, that the subject of praise, which God honored with this token of his acceptance, was his own goodness and everlasting mercy. And this, my brethren, is a most ecouraging circumstance; for it plainly enough tells us, that God is best pleased with our praises, when we adore and celebrate those perfections of his nature, which dispose him to pity the miserable, and have the kindest aspect towards the children of men. The song that the priests were singing when the cloud entered into the Temple, had none of that rhetorical pomp which a cold heart may borrow from a warm imagination; it consisted of a few plain but gracious words, "The Lord is good, and his mercy endureth for ever." And whilst they sung this plain and artless song, God made a sudden display of his glory, and caused them to feel the happy effects of that goodness which they praised. And shall not their success encourage us to follow their example? They adored and celebrated the divine goodness when the Ark was brought into the Temple, which was only a typical representation of the Messiah who was to come: And shall we need any solicitation to adopt their song, who know that the mercy promised to the fathers, the consolation of Israel, is already come? especially while we attend upon that sacred ordinance, which is both a solemn commemoration of his past sufferings, and a pledge of his return to complete our salvation. Here, indeed we have the brightest display of the goodness and everlasting mercy of God. "God so loved the world, that he gave his only begotten Son, that whosoever believeth in him might not perish, but have eternal life; for God sent his Son into the world, not to condemn the world, but that the world through him might be saved." Our great Redeemer is the liveliest image of infinite goodness, the messenger of the most unsearchable astonishing love, the perchaser of the most inestimable benefits that ever were revealed to the sons of men. "Greater love than this hath no man, that a man lay down his life for his friend; but God commendeth his love towards us, in that whilst we were yet sinners Christ died for us." Can we doubt of the divine goodness after this costly expression of it? "He that spared not his own Son, but delivered him up for us all, how shall he not with him also freely give us all things?" Behold, likewise, this adorable perfection shining through the whole of that gracious covenant, whereof this holy sacrament is the external seal. There you may see such sure, such great and wonderful mercies, freely given out to a world of sinners, as may remove all your suspicions of the divine goodness and mercy, and afford you constant matter of praise and thanksgiving. There you may see how unwilling God is that sinners should perish. There you may see an act of pardon and oblivion granted, upon the easy and reasonable condition of a believing, penitent, and thankful acceptance. The sins that men have been committing for many years together, their wilful, heinous, aggravated sins, you may there see pardoned by ascendant unwearied mercy; the enemies of God reconciled to him; condemned rebels saved from hell, nay, brought into his family, and made his sons. O what comfortable discoveries are these! The Old Testament saints saw them darkly through a veil, whereas we behold them with open face. God appears in his Son and covenant, to be not only good, but love itself. Let us then adore him in this amiable character; let us give him the glory of all his perfections; but especially let us praise him with thankful hearts, "because he is good, and his mercy endureth for ever." A

III. Circumstance in the text, which claims our attention, is the seriousness and fervor of this devout assembly. It is said, that they lifted up their voice, and praised the Lord. Here they exerted their whole strength and activity, as if they had been ambitious to spend themselves in this heavenly employment. Would we then this day obtain a token of the divine acceptance, let us learn from their example to seek it by a fervent and lively devotion. Great is the Lord, says David, and therefore greatly to be praised. Accordingly, when he enters upon this important duty, in Psalm ciii, he begins with a solemn address to his own soul, "Bless the Lord, O my soul, and all that is within me bless his holy name." The devotion of the soul is the soul of devotion; it is the praise and homage of the heart which God requires. If that is withheld, we have nothing else to offer him that is worthy his regard. We are commanded to love the Lord our God with all our heart, with all our soul, and with all our strength, and with all our mind; and what is the measure of our love, ought likewise to be the measure of our praise; for it is as impossible to exceed in the one as in the other. As we cannot love him too much, so neither can we praise him too highly. His greatness and his goodness infinitely surpass all that our minds can conceive, or our tongues express. But there is yet a

IV. Circumstance in the text, which deserves our particular notice upon this occasion, namely the harmony and unanimity of these ancient worshippers. "They were all as one, and made one sound to be heard in praising and thanking the Lord." The importance of this circumstance will appear in a stronger light, if we compare the passage now before us with that extraordinary manifestation on the day of Pentecost, which is related in the 2d chapter of the Acts of the Apostles. There we are told, that when the "apostles were all with one accord in one place, suddenly there came a sound from heaven, as of a rushing mighty wind, and it filled all the house where they were sitting." Every one will be sensible that there is a very striking resemblance between these two illustrious events; and I cannot help thinking, that the oneness and harmony of the worshippers, on both these occasions, is mentioned with peculiar emphasis, as a distinguishing characteristic of those religious assemblies which God delights to honor with his presence.

We are told in cxxxiiid Psalm, that where brethren dwell together in unity, there God commandeth the blessing; and our blessed Lord lays such stress upon unity of affection among his disciples, that he makes it an essential qualification of an acceptable worshipper; nay, he tells us, that where this is wanting, the person is disqualified for performing any service that is pleasing to God, (Matth. v. 23, 24.) "If thou bring thy gift to the altar, and there rememberest that thy brother hath aught against thee, leave there thy gift before the altar, and go thy way; first be reconciled to thy brother, and then come and offer thy gift." If this doctrine of brotherly love has not an obvious foundation in the text, yet I can hardly think I need make any apology for mentioning it, seeing it has a broad foundation in other passages of Scripture, and is strictly connected with the great ordinance before us. The sacrament of the supper is not only a solemn commemoration of our Saviour's death, and of his wonderful love to sinners of mankind, but was likewise intended to be a badge of love and union among his disciples. Of old, they who feasted upon the same sacrifice laid aside all enmity, and professed to be knit together in love and friendship. In like manner, all who partake of the great gospel sacrifice in the holy sacrament, are supposed to be members of one body, united under one head, our Lord Jesus Christ. "The cup of blessing which we bless," says the apostle, "is it not the communion of the blood of Christ? the bread which we break, is it not the communion of the body of Christ? for we being many are one bread and one body, for we are all partakers of that one bread." It would be monstrous to see one member of the natural body hurting and destroying another; the mouth devouring the hand, or the hand plucking out the eye. It is no less monstrous and unnatural for one member of Christ's mystical body to be at variance with another—to see those who partake of the table of the Lord, at the same time partaking of the table of devils, by entertaining hatred and malice in their hearts, by doing, or purposing to do, or even by wishing, any hurt to their brethren in Christ. Would we then obtain the divine presence and blessing on this solemn occasion? do we expect or desire that the King should sit at his own table this day, and impart to us the fruits of his favor and love, let us be one among ourselves; let every bitter passion be put away; and let us put on, as the elect of God, holy and beloved, bowels of mercy, kindness, humbleness of mind, meekness and long-suffering, forbearing one another, even as we look for forgiveness through the merits of Jesus, remitting to others their hundred pence, whilst we plead with God for the discharge of our ten thousand talents.

But the oneness here spoken of seems more immediately to respect their harmonious agreement in the great subject of their praise. They made one sound to be heard in praising and thanking the Lord, saying, "For he is good, and his mercy endureth for ever." And, when they thus concurred with heart and voice in extolling the goodness and mercy of God, "it came even to pass," says the sacred historian, "that the house was filled with a cloud, even the house of the Lord; so that the priests could not stand to minister by reason of the cloud: for the glory of the Lord had filled the house of God." That agreement in prayer has a mighty efficacy appears from the gracious promise of the Lord, (Matt. xviii. 19.) "Again, I say unto you, that if two of you shall agree, on earth, as touching any thing they shall ask, it shall be done for them of my Father which is in heaven." And my text affords a convincing proof, that agreement in praise has an equal efficacy to bring the glory of God into the assemblies of his people. We may at least take encouragement from it to make the experiment. We have been asking the divine presence by prayer; let us now go a little farther, and seek it in praise and thanksgiving. The EUCHARIST was the ancient name of the sacrament, which tells us that the sacramental devotions of the primitive church chiefly consisted in those laudable exercises I am now recommending; and certainly their example should have considerable weight with us.

Let none say, I am a guilty, depraved creature, and therefore groans, and tears, and sorrowful lamentations, become me better than the voice of praise; for if you are penitent, believing sinners, if, despairing of relief from any other quarter, you have fled to Christ, as your city of refuge, and taken sanctuary in his atoning blood and sacrifice,—praise is not only lawful, but highly becoming, nay, a necessary part of your present duty;—the design of your redemption, the tenor of the Gospel Covenant, the glorious privileges to which you stand entitled, loudly demand this grateful return. "We are built up," says Peter, "a spiritual house, an holy priesthood, to offer up spiritual sacrifices, acceptable to God by Jesus Christ." 1 Peter ii. 5. And that praise is one of these spiritual sacrifices appears from the 9th verse, "Ye are a chosen generation, a royal priesthood, an holy nation, a peculiar people, that ye should show forth the praises of Him who hath called you out of darkness into his marvellous light."

But alas! says one, what is all this to me? My harp must still hang upon the willows; for how shall I, a wretched captive, presume to sing the songs of Zion? No evidences of grace are legible in my heart. Grief and fear have so thoroughly possessed it, that the love of God can find no room. How then, or to what purpose, should I lift up my voice, whilst my soul is cast down and disquieted within me? Now, to such I would answer in general, that, let your case be as bad as you suppose it, yet still you have cause to bless the Lord. If you cannot thank him for his special grace, yet surely you ought to praise him for his unwearied patience, and these offers of mercy which are daily tendered unto you. Bless him that you are still on earth, in the land of hope, and not confined to the regions of everlasting despair.

But I must not stop here. Come forward into the light, thou dark, discouraged soul, and, in the presence of God, give a true and proper answer to these few questions. Thou complainest of the want of love to God, and thy complaints indeed show that thou hast no *delighting*, *enjoying* love: But answer me,

1*st*, Hast thou not a *desiring*, *seeking* love? A poor man who desires and seeks the world, shows his love to it as convincingly as the rich man who delights in it; —the tendency of the heart appears as truly in an anxious pursuit as in a delightful enjoyment. But, as the weakness of hope is frequently mistaken for the want of desire, I must ask you,

2*dly*, Do you not find a moaning, lamenting love? You show that you loved your friends by grieving for their death, as well as by delighting in them whilst they lived. If you heartily lament it, as your greatest unhappiness and loss, when you think that God doth cast you off, and that you are void of grace, and cannot serve and honor him as you would, this is an undoubted evidence that your hearts are not void of the love of God. Once more,

3*dly*, Would you not rather have a heart to love God than to have all the riches and pleasures in the world? Would it not comfort you more than any thing else, if you could be sure that he loveth you, and if you could perfectly love and obey him? If so, then know assuredly that it is not the want of love, but the want of assurance, that causeth thy dejection.

And therefore I charge thee, in the name of God, to render unto him that tribute of praise which is due. To be much employed in this heavenly duty, has an evident tendency to vanquish all hurtful doubts and fears;—by keeping the soul near to God, and within the warmth of his love and goodness;—by dissipating distrustful vexing thoughts, and diverting the mind to sweeter things;—by keeping off the tempter, who usually is least able to follow us when we are highest in the praises of our God and Saviour;—and especially by bringing out the evidences of our sincerity, while the chiefest graces are in exercise.

Praise brings comfort to the soul, as standing in the sunshine brings warmth to the body, or as the sight of a dear friend rejoices the heart, without any great reasoning or arguing in the case. Come then, my dear friends, and make the experiment. Obey that voice which proceedeth out of the throne, saying, "Praise our God, all ye his servants, and ye that fear him, both small and great." Let no voice be amissing on this solemn occasion, but let us all be as one, praising and thanking the Lord, while we commemorate his goodness and everlasting mercy; and then may we hope that he will grace our communion table with his presence, proclaim liberty to the captives, and the opening of the prison to them that are bound, and fill all the guests with the fatness of his house. *Amen.*

SERMON LXV.

MAN'S VIEW OF HIMSELF.

EZEKIEL xxxvi. 31.—"Then shall ye remember your own evil ways, and your doings that were not good, and shall loathe yourselves in your own sight for your iniquities and for your abominations."

THE Jews were at this time captives in Babylon, and so dispersed through that vast empire, that they said of themselves, in the language of despair, "Our bones are dried, and our hope is lost; we are cut off for our parts." Even the prophet himself looked on their case as so irrecoverable by human means, that, when God gave him a visionary representation of their state, by a valley covered with dry bones, and put the question to him, "Son of man, can these bones live?" his answer was, "O Lord God, thou knowest." With thee indeed all things are possible: Omnipotence may do this great thing; but whether it shall be done, or by what means it may come to pass, thou, O Lord God, and thou only knowest.

Thus abject and hopeless was the condition of the Jews, when God published his gracious design to take them from among the heathen, and to bring them back into their own land, (ver. 28.) "Ye shall dwell," saith he, "in the land that

I gave to your fathers; and ye shall be my people, and I will be your God. I will also save you from all your uncleannesses: and I will call for the corn, and will increase it, and lay no famine upon you. And I will multiply the fruit of the tree, and the increase of the field, that ye shall receive no more reproach of famine among the heathen." And then, even at this season of returning peace and plenty, at this season, which so often misleads and intoxicates the mind of man, "Then shall ye remember your own evil ways, and your doings that were not good, and shall loathe yourselves in your own sight, for your iniquities and for your abominations."

The account which we have of these penitents furnisheth us with some very important instructions with regard to the nature of true repentance, which I propose, in the *first* place, to illustrate; and then to recommend their example to your imitation. And the

1*st* Instruction which we obtain from this passage is, That true repentance is the gift of God, and the peculiar effect of his Holy Spirit. The course of Providence is indeed admirably adapted to reclaim the sinner from the error of his ways. Bitterness is written as with a sunbeam on the line of folly; and certain degrees of misery never fail to accompany our deviations from the path of duty. Yet so dead are men naturally in trespasses and sins, that nothing less than a divine power can render the best means of reformation effectual. Without this, judgments will harden rather than humble or reclaim the transgressor. We read of Ahaz, king of Judah, that in the time of his distress, he did trespass yet more against the Lord. And we are told in the book of Revelation, that the vials of wrath, which the angels shall pour out upon the men who have the mark of the beast, instead of leading them to repent and give glory to God, shall only cause them to blaspheme the name of God, who hath power over these plagues, and to curse the God of heaven, because of their pains and their sores. The calamities with which the Jews were visited in their captivity to the king of Babylon, were in like manner unproductive of any genuine repentance in that stiff-necked people. They had not only polluted their own land, but had also profaned the name of God among the heathen whither they went, and continued to do so, until He whom they had offended had pity on them for his own name's sake, and gave them a new heart and a new spirit, having taken away the stony heart out of their flesh, and given them a heart of flesh. A

2*d* Instruction which we derive from this passage is, That the grief and self-loathing of true penitents, do not flow so much from their feeling that sin is hurtful to themselves, as from the consideration of its own base nature, and especially of the ingratitude which it carries in it towards a kind and merciful God: For when were the Jews to remember their own evil ways? When were they to loathe themselves in their own sight for their iniquities and their abominations? Was it when they felt the rod, and lay under the feet of their cruel oppressors? No; it was when they should be delivered out of their hands, brought back to their own country, and enriched with the multiplied fruits of their trees, and the increase of their fields. *Then* were their sins to rise up in their remembrance, filling them with grief and shame, for having offended a Being of such transcendant goodness, and unmerited condescension.

Times of calamity do indeed often produce a temporary humiliation and repentance, which for a time resemble the real feelings of penitence; but self-love alone is at the bottom of the appearance. The man is wearied of the inconvenience, but not weaned from the love of sin. But true penitence hath its source in a nobler principle, and is rather the child of love than of fear. It is the melting of the soul at the fire of divine love; it is the relenting of the prodigal son, when his injured father runs forth to meet him; it is the tear of gratitude, which bursts from the condemned criminal, when a pardon from his offended sovereign is put into his hands. It appears, in the

3*d* place, from this passage, That the soul's conversion to God is the great introductory blessing which renders all other blessings valuable. This is evident from the order in which God arrangeth his promises to his captive people. He first engageth himself to take away the provoking cause of his anger, and then to put away his indignation, to receive them graciously, and to love them freely. The disease began within, and the cure must begin there likewise. Their captivity by men was the fruit of their voluntary captivity to sin, and therefore deliverance from sin must precede their deliverance from the hands of men. This God undertakes to perform by the powerful agency of his Holy Spirit. "A new heart," saith he, "will I give you, and a new spirit will I put within you, and I will take away the stony heart out of your flesh, and I will give you a heart of flesh; and I will put my Spirit within you, and cause you to walk in my statutes, and ye shall keep my judgments and do them," verses 26, 27. After which he gives the promise of temporal deliverance in the verses immediately preceding my text. And to show that this was no accidental arrangement, he declares with great solemnity, at the 33d verse, that in this very order he had meditated to dispense his mercy. "Thus saith the Lord God, in the day that I shall have cleansed you from all your iniquities, I will also cause you to dwell in the cities, and the wastes shall be builded."

These are the instructions which we may derive from this passage with regard to the nature of true repentance; and it is only to be added, although not expressly contained in the text, that as this great and valuable blessing cometh down from the Father of lights, who is the author of every good and perfect gift, it is therefore to be sought by our humble supplications and prayers: "For thus saith the Lord God," at the 37th verse of this chapter, "I will yet for this be inquired of by the house of Israel, to do it for them." God indeed is often found of those who seek him not. His powerful grace sometimes arrests the sinner in his mad career, while he is equally unmindful of God and of himself. But let none despise the use of means, because He who is almighty at times acts without them. It is our part to place ourselves in the way of his mercy, and to wait patiently at the pool until the angel trouble the waters, and communicate to them a healing virtue. It is our part to seek the Lord while he may be found, and to call upon him while he is near, having the certain assurance that he never said to any of the seed of Jacob, seek ye my face in vain. And this leads me to the

II. Thing proposed, which was to recommend the example of these penitents described in the texts to your imitation. In the

1*st* place, then, Let me call upon you to remember your ways. The neglect of serious consideration is the ruin of almost every soul that perisheth eternally. Hence it is that we continue in our sins, and that we relapse after having forsaken them; that we decline from our religious attainments, and being again entangled in the pollutions of this world, that our last state becomes worse than our first. All these evils flow from a thoughtless unreflecting life. A great part of mankind pass their days in a course of perpetual dissipation, without once reflecting on their actions, until the near view of an eternal world awakens them from this fatal security. Then, indeed, the case is extremely altered—then the remembrance of his ways forceth itself upon the sinner—then he sees his error, and laments his folly, and prays for mercy, and even asks the prayers of those whom once he derided as precise and fanatical. He would not reflect upon the great truths of religion while he might have done it to a good purpose. Now he reflects, and reflects at leisure; but it is a cruel leisure, for the fruits of it are perplexity and dismay.

God is represented, by the prophet Jeremiah, as putting this question, "Why is the people of Jerusalem slidden back with a perpetual backsliding? They hold fast deceit, they refuse to return." Jer. viii. 5. The answer is given in the following verse, "I hearkened and heard, but they spake not aright; no man repented him of his wickedness, saying, What have I done? The consequence of which was, "Every one turned to his course, as the horse rusheth into the battle." Whereas, did we seriously ask ourselves that important question, What have we done? we would soon discover so much guilt in our doings as to be compelled to ask ourselves another question, What shall I do to be saved?

Let me then prevail with you seriously and impartially to examine your past conduct. Consider what hath been the prevailing course of your life; and rest not satisfied with a general conviction that it hath been wrong, but labor to recollect as many passages of it as you can. Review all its different periods since you came to the years of understanding. Consider the various relations in which you have been placed, the special duties which arose from those relations, and the manner in which you have performed them. This will be a task displeasing indeed to the flesh, and mortifying to the natural pride of your hearts. But you must not hearken to these pernicious counsellors. The more they cry out, Forbear, the more resolutely must you persist. Charge your consciences with it as a religious duty, and implore the Holy Spirit of God to assist your endeavors. When by such means you have discovered your own evil ways, then proceed to consider attentively the nature and degree of that evil which is in them. Let it not suffice to know that you have been sinners, without pondering the dreadful malignity and demerit of sin. View it in its natural turpitude and deformity, as the plague and leprosy of the soul, which renders you loathsome and abominable in the sight of your Maker. View it as a daring act of rebellion against the most righteous authority, as the transgression of a law which is in all respects holy, just, and good; the precepts of which are not only reasonable in themselves, but also most kind and salutary to us. View it as the basest ingratitude towards your best and most unwearied benefactor. View it, above all, in the severity of the punishment which it deserves, exemplified in those mysterious and inconceivable sufferings which the Son of God underwent to expiate its guilt.

See here, O sinner, the awful demerit of thy transgressions. Thou wast doomed to the wrath of God, and to everlasting banishment from his presence; and thou wast not only incapable to deliver thyself by any works or sufferings of thy own, but all the angels in heaven could not have offered a price that would have ransomed thy perishing soul. None else could pay thy debt but the Son of God, and even he could pay it in no other way than by suffering the penalty which thou hadst incurred. O how hateful doth sin appear when viewed in this light! Adam's expulsion from paradise, the deluge of the ancient world, the burning of Sodom and Gomorrah, loudly proclaim its pernicious nature and heinous demerit. We feel it to be hurtful in the natural evils of sickness and pain to which it hath subjected us. Death, which is its wages, is an awful monitor of its malignant effects. It appears terrible in the worm that never dieth, and in that fire that is not quenched. But no where doth it appear so deformed and odious as in the sufferings and death of Christ; for how deep must that stain have been, which nothing could wash away but the blood of the Son of God! How deadly that disease which no other medicine could cure!

But as these considerations are applicable to all sins in common, it will be necessary, in order to your forming a just estimate of your own evil ways, to look more narrowly into the aggravating circumstances with which they have been attended.

Have not many of your transgressions been committed with knowledge and deliberation, nay, with artifice and cunning? Have they not cost you no small degrees of study, before those desires which lust conceived were accomplished in actual sin? Have you not courted temptation, and wearied yourselves with committing iniquity? Consider what degrees of resistance from your own minds you have vanquished; what obstacles in Providence you have overcome; what strivings of the Holy Spirit you have defeated in the course of your transgressions. Nay, have not some of your sins been still more aggravated by the breach of express vows and resolutions against them, often repeated with the greatest solemnity? Hide not your eyes from any of these aggravating circumstances which have attended your offences. Every sin which you wilfully cover, or extenuate, will thereby gain an invincible addition of strength. Every lust which you conceal in your bosom, will become a viper which one day will sting you to the heart. Every good disposition, which you magnify, shall languish and pine away; and those treasures of grace, with which the humble are enriched, shall be of no advantage to you, till you feel your poverty and wretchedness. Let me therefore call on you to exercise the

2d Branch of repentance, which is here exemplified to us, viz. Loathing yourselves in your own sight, for your iniquities and your abominations. And say, O sinner, is there not cause for this? Dost thou loathe that which is deformed and filthy? "We are all," saith the prophet Isaiah, "as an unclean thing, and all our righteousnesses are as filthy rags. The whole head is sick, and the whole heart faint. From the sole of the foot, even unto the head, there is no soundness in us, but wounds, and bruises, and putrefying sores." Thou art displeased with thine enemies who seek to injure thee; but where is there such an enemy as thou art to thyself? Men may wrong thee in thy temporal interests, but no man, nay, no created being, can ruin thy soul without thine own concurrence. It is thou, and none else, that hast wounded thy conscience, and thrown away thy peace, and exposed thy soul to everlasting misery. Thou abhorrest him who hath killed thy dearest friend; but where hadst thou ever such a friend as the Lord Jesus Christ, whom, by thy sins, thou hast crucified and slain? Thy sins brought him down from heaven to earth; thy sins subjected him to poverty, persecution, and reproach; thy sins involved him in conflicts dreadful and unutterable, nailed him to the cross, and laid him low in the grave. By thy sins thou hast often trampled on his blood, crucified him afresh, and put him to an open shame. Is there not cause then to loathe thyself in thy own sight for thine iniquities and for thine abominations? But as there are several counterfeits of this penitent disposition, it may be proper to mention a few of them, that you may have a clearer view of that self-loathing which I am desirous of recommending to you.

A man who, by his base, unworthy behavior, has forfeited the esteem of the world, may feel much inward shame and uneasiness on that account, which may be mistaken by others, and even by himself, for true humiliation. And yet, though he seem to loathe both himself and his sins, he doth neither truly, and there is nothing genuine or promising in this kind of remorse. If the world would be reconciled to him, he would soon be reconciled himself; for at bottom he hath no other quarrel with his sins, but that they happen to be disgraceful in the eyes of those whose esteem he would wish to preserve.

In like manner a natural conscience, irritated by some flagrant violation of the law of God, may severely sting the offender with shame and remorse. Yet when narrowly examined, this shame amounts to no more than a proud vexation, that he cannot think so well of himself as he would wish to do. If the exchange could be made, he would rather part with that conscience which gives him uneasiness, than with those sins which occasion its reproofs; and his only motive in condemning his sins is, that he may pacify that awful monitor. Nay, a man may advance a step farther, and make still nearer approaches to the gracious temper described in the text, without fully attaining it. He may see the baseness and deformity of sin, and be deeply afflicted at the remembrance of his multiplied transgressions, and yet, through ignorance of the inbred corruption of his nature, he may be far from loathing himself in the spirit of true penitence.

What a beast was I, may he say, to act in a manner so reproachful to my faculties? Had I not reason to direct me? Could I not have governed my will and affections? Was I not master of my own heart and ways? Thus he may complain, and seemingly condemn himself; but this self-condemning language is in truth the expression of reigning pride, even as none are more severe in blaming themselves for misconduct in their worldly affairs, than those who have the highest opinion of their ability to manage them aright.

In opposition to this, the truly convinced sinner sees himself to be all guilt, pollution, and weakness, destitute equally of righteousness and strength. He is led to see that corrupt fountain of inward enmity to God, which is manifested in the issues of his outward conduct. He is made sensible, that he "was conceived in sin, and brought forth in iniquity, and that in him, that is in his flesh, dwelleth no good thing." On these accounts he loathes himself in his own sight, not partially or occasionally only, for having acted a wrong part, which he supposes that by prudence he might have avoided, but universally as a degenerate and corrupted being. He can find nothing to be proud of, nothing that he can call his own, but guilt, disorder, and weakness. And under this conviction, he falls down before God, saying with Job, "I have heard of thee by the hearing of the ear, but now mine eye seeth thee, wherefore I abhor myself in dust and ashes."

This is that self-loathing which I now call upon you to exercise. And the necessity of it is apparent; for until you are brought thus low in your own estimation, you will never esteem the Lord Jesus Christ, who alone can save you from the wrath to come. Who is it that values a physician while he feels no disease, and hath no fears of death? Will any fly to Christ for refuge, who is not sensible that he stands in need of such a Saviour? No; they only who are perishing in their own apprehensions will welcome the tidings of a Redeemer, and look to him, as the stung Israelites looked to the brazen serpent, lying prostrate at his feet, and resigning themselves wholly to his disposal and government.

Let me then conclude with exhorting you to repair to that fountain which is opened for sin and for uncleanness, to that blood which can cleanse you from all sin. This is the proper use and improvement of all that hath been said. Here is a remedy for all your diseases, a full supply for all your wants. Here you will find gold tried in the fire, that you may be rich; and white raiment, that you may be clothed, and the shame of your nakedness do not appear. The Lord Jesus is a complete Saviour. Be your burden what it will, he is able to support it. His merit surpasseth your guilt by infinite degrees; and his victorious Spirit can subdue and mortify your most imperious lusts. Let what hath been said, then, lead you to him. Dwell on the consideration of your own vileness, till your self-confidence is entirely destroyed, and your hearts disposed to receive him as the unspeakable gift of God to man.

In this your Christianity doth consist, and on this your justification depends. This is the sum of your conversion, and the very soul of the new creature. Other things are only preparatives to this, or fruits that grow out of it. Christ is the end and fulfilling of the law, the substance of the gospel, the way to the Father, the help, the hope, the life of the believer. If you know not HIM, you know nothing; if you possess not HIM, you have nothing; and if you be out of HIM, you can do nothing that hath a promise of salvation. O then fly to him as your refuge and sanctuary, and commit your souls into his hands, that he may purify and form them for himself. Plead in the language of David, (Psal. li. 2.) "Wash me thoroughly from mine iniquity, and cleanse me from my sin. Purge me with hysop, and I shall be clean; wash me, and I shall be whiter than snow." And look by faith for the accomplishment of that promise, (Ezekiel xxxvi. 25.) "Then will I sprinkle clean water upon you, and ye shall be clean; from all your filthiness, and from all your idols, will I cleanse yon." *Amen.*

SERMON LXVI.

CHOICE BETWEEN INIQUITY AND AFFLICTION.

Job xxxvi. 21.—"Take heed; regard not iniquity; for this hast thou chosen rather than affliction."

These words were addressed to Job, who from the height of prosperity was suddenly plunged into the deepest and most complicated distress. They are the words of Elihu, the youngest, but by far the wisest and most candid of all Job's friends. The other three were indeed, as himself had styled them, miserable comforters. It was their belief, that adversity was in all cases a certain token of God's displeasure; and, upon this principle, they endeavored to persuade this excellent servant of God, that his whole religion was false and counterfeit, that divine justice had now laid hold of him, and that he was suffering the punishment of his hypocrisy and iniquity.

At length Elihu interposes; and moved with zeal for the honor of God, and with compassion to his friend, he unfolds the mysteries of Divine Providence, asserts and proves that affliction is designed for the trial of the good, as well as for the punishment of the bad, directs Job to the right improvement of his present distress, and comforts him with the prospect of a happy deliverance from it, as soon as his heart should be thoroughly moulded into a meek and patient submission to the will of his God. At the same time, he rebukes him with a becoming dignity for some rash and unadvised speeches which the severity of his other friends, and the sharpness of his own anguish, had drawn from him; and particularly cautions him in the passage before us, "Take heed; regard not iniquity; for this hast thou chosen rather than affliction."

The latter part of the text contains an heavy censure, for which some of Job's impatient wishes for relief had no doubt given too just occasion. But these expressions, uttered in his haste, he afterwards retracted, and finally came out from the furnace of affliction, like gold tried and refined by the fire.—What I propose, in discoursing on this subject, is to illustrate and prove the general proposition, that there can be no greater folly than to seek to escape from affliction by complying with the temptations of sin; or, in other words, that the smallest act of deliberate transgression is infinitely worse than the greatest calamity we can suffer in this life.

That the greater part of mankind are under the influence of the contrary opinion, may be too justly inferred from their practice. How many have recourse to sinful pleasures to relieve their inward distress? What unlawful methods do others use for acquiring the perishing riches or honors of this world? while, in order to evade suffering for righteousness sake, thousands make shipwreck of faith and a good conscience, through sinful compliances with the manners of the world, against the clear and deliberate conviction of their own minds. These things plainly show, that the subject I have chosen is of the highest importance; and if what may be said on it shall be so far blessed to any, as to render sin more odious, or affliction less formidable, I shall gain one of the noblest ends of my office, and we shall have reason to acknowledge, that our meeting together has been for the better and not for the worse.

In proof, then, of the general proposition, That there can be no greater folly than to choose sin rather than affliction, let it be observed,

I. That sin separates us from God, the only source of real felicity. That man is not sufficient to his own happiness, is a truth confirmed by the experience of all who have candidly attended to their own feelings. It is the consciousness of this insufficiency of the human mind for its own happiness, which makes men seek resources from abroad; which makes them fly to pleasures and amusements of various kinds, whose chief value consists in filling up the blanks of time, and diverting their uneasy reflections from their own internal poverty. But these are vain and deceitful refuges of lies. The want remains; and we have found out only the means of putting away the sense of it for a time. God alone can be the source of real happiness to an immortal soul, an adequate supply to all its faculties, an inexhaustible subject to its understanding, an everlasting object to its affections.

Sin bereaves the soul of man of this its only portion. "Behold," saith the Prophet, "God's hand is not shortened that it cannot save, neither is his ear heavy that it cannot hear; but your iniquities have separated between you and your God, and your sins have hid his face from you, that he will not hear." Affliction, on the other hand, instead of separating the soul from God, is often the means of bringing it nearer to him. Let a man be ever so poor, diseased, reproached, persecuted, still if he hold fast his integrity, if he be a real saint, he is near and dear to God. The eyes of the Lord are upon him, and his ears are open to his cry. The angel of the Lord encampeth round about him, and a guard of angels wait to carry his departing spirit into Abraham's bosom. Whereas sin renders us loathsome in the eyes of God. He is angry with the wicked every day; and even their prayers and sacrifices are an abomination to him. He hath bent his bow, and made it ready; he hath also prepared for him the instruments of death. God looks on them with abhorrence, and, when conscience is awake, they think of him with horror, and dare not come into his presence, knowing that he is a consuming fire to the workers of iniquity.

II. Affliction may not only consist with the love of a father, but may even be the fruit of it. "Whom the Lord loveth he chasteneth, and scourgeth every son whom he receiveth.—By this," saith the prophet Isaiah, speaking of affliction, "shall the iniquity of Jacob be purged, and this is all the fruit to take away sin." David could say, "It is good for me that I have been afflicted, that I might learn thy statutes. Before I was afflicted I went astray, but now I have kept thy word." A good man may even glory in tribulation, knowing that tribulation worketh patience, and patience experience, and experience hope, and hope maketh not ashamed, because the love of God is shed abroad in his heart by the Holy Ghost which is given unto him. But sin is always both evil in its own nature and pernicious in its effects. This contrast is very strikingly displayed by the apostle Paul. Of the one he speaks as a privilege, and a token for good to those who are exercised thereby. "Unto you," saith he, (writing to the Philippians, i. 29.) "it is given in the behalf of Christ, not only to believe on him, but also to suffer for his sake." But what doth he say concerning the other, (Rom. vii. 24.) "O wretched man that I am, who shall deliver me from the body of this death?" If any had ever reason to complain of the burden of affliction, Paul had more—"in labors more abundant, in stripes above measure, in prisons more frequent, in deaths oft." But in the midst of these sufferings, we never hear him crying out, Who shall deliver me from this unremitting distress? His inward corruption gave him greater pain than the evils of his outward condition; and his captivity to the law of sin was worse to him than prisons, and tortures, and death.

III. Sin is evil whether we feel it or not, and worst when we are most insensible of it. To be past feeling, in this respect, is the greatest curse we can possibly bring on ourselves; and the most desperate condition in which a human creature can be placed before his everlasting doom be pronounced, is when God saith of him, as he did of Ephraim of old, "He is joined to his idols, let him alone."

Affliction, on the other hand, though a bitter, is yet a salutary medicine; and though no chastening for the present seemeth to be joyous, but grievous, nevertheless afterwards it yieldeth the peaceable fruit of righteousness to them who are exercised thereby. Affliction is the discipline by which we are trained to glory, and honor, and virtue. If this world, indeed, were our only portion, there would be some reason, or at least some excuse, for choosing the pleasures of iniquity, rather than those sufferings which would embitter the short period of our existence in it. But the greatest error we can possibly fall into, is that of taking it for the place of our rest. To cure this fatal mistake, God visits us with afflictions. They are his messengers sent to teach us our true condition, what this world is, a fleeting scene of vanity and illusions; and what we ourselves are in it, pilgrims and strangers, hastening to another land of perpetual abode.

IV. In affliction we are commonly passive, but always active in sin. The one is left to our choice; the other is not. When we suffer in the cause of virtue, we are in the hand of our most faithful and everlasting friend; but when we sin in order to avoid suffering, we commit ourselves into the hands of that malicious, cunning, and eternal enemy, who goeth about seeking whom he may destroy. Affliction only hurts the body, but sin affects the health and well-being of that immortal principle, which is destined to survive the ruins of this earthly tabernacle, and to inherit happiness or misery for ever. Which leads me to observe, in the *last* place,

That the evil of affliction is of short duration, but that of sin perpetual. Weeping may endure for a time, but joy cometh in the morning; and these light afflictions, which are but for a moment, work out for us a far more exceeding and eternal weight of glory. Should they continue throughout our whole lives, yet even that is but a moment compared with eternity. The evil of sin, on the contrary, goes beyond the grave, and lasts as long as the soul itself, which it has polluted. The delight of it is soon gone, but the sting remains; the guilt and punishment of it pass with us into the other world, and there constitute the worm that never dieth, and the fire which is not quenched.

THESE observations may suffice to illustrate the general proposition, that there can be no greater folly than to seek to escape from affliction, by complying with the temptations to sin; or, in other words, that the smallest act of deliberate transgression is infinitely worse than the greatest calamity we can suffer in this life.

What hath been said, ought, in the 1*st* place, to serve for reproof to those who, so far from considering iniquity as more to be dreaded as a greater evil than affliction, will not refrain from their ungodly and vicious practices even when their sin proves their affliction. To many, alas! it seems to be as their meat and drink to obey the commands of sin, by fulfilling the lusts thereof. In vain hath the word of God and providence admonished them, that naught but bitterness is to be found in the path of folly. They still pursue that path, in defiance of their own experience, and weary themselves with committing iniquity. They break through all restraints, not only when an angel stands in the way, but where ruin, misery, and destruction, stare them broad in the face.

How many are to be seen bound with the cords of their own sins, from which they have neither the inclination nor power to free themselves? How many wasted and maimed by criminal indulgence? How many brought to poverty and rags, by riot and intemperance? "Who hath woe? who hath sorrow? who hath contentions? who hath wounds without cause? who hath redness of eyes? they that tarry long at the wine, they that go to seek mixed wine." Sin has had its martyrs as well as godliness, who, in premature old age, have been made to possess the transgressions of their youth, in all the bitter fruits of a body tortured with diseases, and a spirit wounded with remorse.

Let us then be warned, ere it be too late, against the fatal error referred to in the text; the preference of the momentary pleasures of sin, to the salutary discipline of affliction. Let us never allow ourselves to imagine, that any present pleasure or advantage of sin will compensate the dreadful evils which it carries in its train; but uniformly oppose to every such suggestion of a diseased mind, that important and solemn question which our Lord addressed to the multitude, "What shall it profit a man if he shall gain the whole world, and lose his own soul? or what shall a man give in exchange for his soul?"

2dly. Let us examine ourselves carefully, whether our judgment and choice have been rectified on this important point. What is it that affects us with the deepest concern and sorrow; the adverse events in providence, or the sins by which we have incurred the loss of the divine favor? When the hand of God lies heavy on us, what do we desire with the greatest earnestness? whether is it to have the trial sanctified, or to have it removed? What is the chief object of your ambition? Is it to grow in grace, and in conformity with the image of God? or is it to become great, and prosperous, and powerful in the world? Were God now to put wisdom or riches in our choice, as he once did to Solomon, would we determine as he did? or would we grasp at the riches, leaving it to age and experience to bring wisdom along with them in the ordinary supposed course of things? In what character does Christ appear most amiable to us, as a Saviour from punishment, or as a Saviour from sin? Finally, in what view does heaven appear most worthy of our desires and wishes; as a place of deliverance from suffering, or as a state of perfect freedom from sin and infirmity of every kind, where we shall be enabled to serve God with the entire affections and powers of our whole nature?

By these marks let us try the real state of our characters, that so we may not pass through life with a lie in our right hands; but knowing that we are of the truth, may assure our hearts before God, looking for his mercy unto eternal life. *Amen.*

SERMON LXVII.

THE SAINTS' PRESENT AND FUTURE HOME.

2 Corin. v. 1.—"For we know, that if our earthly house of this tabernacle were dissolved, we have a building of God, an house not made with hands, eternal in the heavens."

The prospect of a blessed immortality is one of the most powerful supports to the people of God, amidst all the trials of the present state; and therefore hope is compared to an anchor, which being cast within the veil, keeps the soul firm and unmoved, so that nothing from without can disturb its inward peace and tranquillity. This was the true foundation of that courage and constancy with which the apostles and primitive Christians endured and overcame the most grievous sufferings. Faith presented to their view a far more exceeding and eternal weight of glory; in comparison of which their present afflictions appeared so light and momentary, that they were incapable of giving them much pain or uneasiness, as the apostle more fully declares in the close of the preceding chapter. And being unwilling to leave such an agreeable subject, he further enlarges upon it in the words of my text: "For we know, that if our earthly house of this tabernacle were dissolved, we have a building of God, an house not made with hands, eternal in the heavens." Death itself can do us no real prejudice; on the contrary, we have reason to welcome it as a friend, because, when it beats down these tenements of clay in which we are lodged, or rather imprisoned upon earth, it only opens a passage for us into a far more commodious and lasting habitation, where we shall possess the greatest riches, the highest honors, and the most transporting pleasures, without intermission, and without end.

I. He compares the body to an earthly house, yea to a tabernacle or tent, which is still less durable, and more easily taken down; and therefore the dissolution of such a frail thing ought not to be reckoned a very great calamity. To this he opposes, in the

II. place, The glorious object of the Christian hope, which he calls a building of God, an house not made with hands, eternal in the heavens. And,

III. He expresses the firm persuasion which he had, in common with all true believers, of being admitted into that glorious and permanent dwelling-place, as soon as the earthly tabernacle should be dissolved.

Each of these particulars I shall briefly illustrate, and then direct you to the practical improvement of the whole.

I begin with the first of these heads, which respects our state and condition on earth. And in the description here given us, there are several things that deserve our notice.

1*st*. The body is called a house; and it may well get this name, on account of its curious frame and structure, all the parts of it being adjusted with the greatest exactness, insomuch that there is not one member redundant nor superfluous, nor any thing wanting that is necessary, either for ornament or use.

But it is principally with relation to the inward inhabitant that the body gets the name of a house in the text. It is a lodging fitted up for the soul to dwell in. It is the residence of an immortal spirit, and from thence it derives its chief honor and dignity. As God created this earth, before he made any of the creatures which were to inhabit it, and as the world was completely furnished with every thing necessary and desirable, before man, its intended sovereign, was introduced; so likewise, in the formation of man, God began with the body, and first completed the outward fabric, before he breathed into it a living soul. How foolish then are they who spend all their thoughts and cares upon the bodies, and overlook those immortal spirits within, for whose use and accommodation they were solely intended; especially when it is considered, in the

2*d* place, That the body was not only made for the service of the soul, but that it is likewise composed of the meanest materials, even that of the dust which we trample under foot. Upon this account the apostle calls it in the text, not merely a house, but an earthly house. Thus we are told, (Genesis ii. 7.) "that the Lord God formed man of the dust of the ground." None of us can claim an higher extraction. We may all say to corruption, Thou art my father, and to the worm, thou art my mother and my sister. And as the body is an earthly house with respect to its original, so it is constantly supported and repaired by that which grows out of the earth. "The king himself," says Solomon, "is served by the field;" yea, after a little time, we must all be reduced unto earth again. These bodies will shortly mix with the common clay. Dust we are, and unto dust we shall return. This, I confess, is a very humbling representation; but as it is true, it ought not to be slightly regarded by any of us; and young people, in a peculiar manner, may reap much advantage from it. You perhaps are strong and healthy, and, with respect to outward form, either have, or fancy you have, advantages beyond others. Come hither, then, and view yourselves in the glass of my text. Your bodies, in their highest perfection, are but earthly houses; and after all the pains you can take upon them, their beauty will shortly consume like the moth. If age do not wrinkle it, death will dissolve it. The comeliest body shall ere long be as loathsome as the dirt on the streets, and must be buried several years out of sight too, before it can be borne with as well. Need I tell you then, that the noble inhabitant within is by far most worthy of your care and attention. Here your labor can never be lost: for when the dust shall return to the earth as it was, the spirit shall return to God who gave it; it survives the ruins of this earthly tenement, and, if adorned while here with the beauties of holiness, it shall flourish eternally in the presence of God, in whose presence is fulness of joy, and at whose right hand are pleasures for evermore. Be persuaded, then, my dear friends, to make the improvement of your souls your principal study. They were made at first after the likeness of God, and herein consisted both their glory and felicity. Let this then be your highest ambition, your constant unwearied endeavor, to get this divine image re-instamped upon them, that being purged and refined from all your dross, you may become meet for the inheritance of the saints in light.

3*d*. It deserves our notice, that the apostle not only calls the body an earthly house, but the earthly house of a tabernacle, to make us still more sensible of its meanness and frailty. A tabernacle or tent, you know, is a very slender habitation—a few slight poles put in the ground, and a piece of canvas, or painted cloth, thrown over them; yet such is the body of a man, a fair but frail tenement, liable to be thrown down, or torn in pieces by every blast of wind. At any rate, we are told, in the

4*th* place, That these earthly tabernacles must at length be dissolved. Death will soon plant its batteries against them; this king of terrors will storm them with troops of pains and diseases, and shall in the issue so far prevail, as to dislodge the soul from the body, and throw down the house of clay, crumbling it into that dust from which it was taken. This is not a bye-law that binds only a few, but an universal royal statute that stands in force against the whole human race. "It is appointed for all men once to die," saith this apostle; hence the road to the grave is called the way of all the earth, and the grave itself is styled in Scripture, the house appointed for all living. Even the bodies of the saints, which have been the temples of the Holy Ghost, are subject to this awful decree; they too must be dissolved and see corruption; but with this material difference, that in due time they shall be raised up again in glory and incorruption. Nor shall their souls for any space be destitute of an habitation; for, as the apostle here informs us, "they have a building of God, an house not made with hands, eternal in the heavens." And this is the

II. Branch of the text, upon which I shall offer a few obvious remarks. I suppose you have already observed, that this figurative description of the future happy state of the saints, is conceived in terms of opposition to their present state of frailty and mortality. Once, indeed, the apostle calls the body a house, but he immediately explains his meaning, by calling it a tabernacle, a slender thing which is easily taken down, or moved out of its place; whereas their future abode is styled an house, without any diminishing epithet, a place of rest and safety, where they dwell with God the great Master of the family, and enjoy the sweetest communion with the Father of their spirits, and all those social pleasures which the company and conversation of their brethren and fellow-servants can be supposed to give them.

Our blessed Lord, in his last consolatory discourse to his disciples, made choice of the same similitude, as best adapted to dispel that gloom which was hanging over their minds. "In my Father's house," said he, "are many mansions; if it were not so, I would have told you. I go to prepare a place for you; and if I go and prepare a place for you, I will come again and receive you to myself, that where I am, there ye may be also." And is not this, my brethren, a delightful representation of the saints' felicity? Every word is full of melody. The very notion of an house or home is agreeable, especially to a poor pilgrim, who is tossed and persecuted in a malignant world, and perhaps, like his great Master, has not where to lay his head. But to what a height must our joy arise, when we hear that this is the house of God himself, the house of the Father of our Lord Jesus Christ, where we shall dwell with our dearest friend and benefactor, and have a place allotted us in those happy mansions which his blood hath purchased, and his infinite love hath prepared for us.

This house is farther described by the builder of it. The great God is the architect; and therefore we may be assured that nothing is wanting that can render it a fit habitation for his people. It is a house not made with hands; it was not built by any creature, neither was it formed out of any pre-existent matter, but created immediately by God himself. It is called his building by way of eminence. All things were made by him; but this was intended for the master-piece of his works, the brightest display of his creating power and goodness.

This house is farther described by its situation; it is a house in the heavens. The earth which we now inhabit is a valley of tears, a place of exile, a common inn as it were, where clean and unclean, saints and sinners, meet together, and are promiscuously entertained. Here the godly live as in a strange land, amidst the enemies of their Father and their King, where their righteous souls are vexed from day to day, with the unlawful deeds and filthy conversation of those among whom they are obliged to dwell. But heaven is a place of perfect purity, where there is nothing that defileth, nothing to hurt or destroy. None shall be able to ascend into that hill of God, none can dwell in that holy place, but such as have clean hands and pure hearts: who are washed, and sanctified, and justified, in the name of the Lord Jesus, and by the Spirit of our God. And,

Last of all, this house in the heavens is farther described and commended by its duration. It is not subject to decay or dissolution, it is an eternal house, an incorruptible inheritance, a kingdom that cannot be shaken. All other things shall wax old and perish, but this shall endure for ever and ever.

But who are the persons for whom this building of God is prepared; or how shall we know whether we belong to that happy number?—This, my brethren, is a most important inquiry, which I propose to make the subject of another discourse.

SERMON LXVIII.

THE SAINTS' PRESENT AND FUTURE HOME.

2 Cor. v. 1.—"For we know that if the earthly house of this tabernacle were dissolved, we have a building of God, an house not made with hands, eternal in the Heavens."

In the first part of this verse, the apostle compares the body to an earthly house, yea, to a tabernacle or tent, which is still less durable, and more easily taken down; and therefore the dissolution of such a frail thing ought not to be reckoned a very great calamity. To this he opposes the glorious object of the Christian hope, which he calls "a building of God, an house not made with hands, eternal in the heavens." At the same time expresses the firm persuasion which he had, in common with all true Christians, of being admitted into that glorious and permanent habitation, as soon as the earthly tabernacle should be dissolved. "We know." He does not say we think, or we hope so, but we are assured of it; we are firmly persuaded that this shall be our lot, as if we were already entered upon the possession of it. In handling this important branch of the subject, I propose, through divine aid,

I. To describe the persons for whom this building of God is prepared.

II. To inquire how, or by what means they come to know that they shall certainly possess it.

And then direct you to the practical improvement of the whole.

The Psalmist proposes a question in the 24th Psalm, which you must all be sensible deserves our most serious attention. "Who shall ascend into the hill of God, and who shall stand in his holy place?" This is the question which I am now going to answer; and as God enables me, I shall follow the light of his own word, and bring in nothing as a mark of the heirs of glory, but what is clearly expressed in the Scriptures of truth, that infallible rule by which we must all be judged at last.

1*st* then, We are taught that this building of God, this house in the heavens, is prepared for believers in Christ Jesus, and for them only, exclusive of all others. "This is the will of him that sent me," says our blessed Lord, (John vi. 40.) "that every one that seeth the Son, and believeth on him, may have everlasting life, and I will raise him up at the last day. He that believeth on the Son, hath everlasting life; he that believeth not the Son, shall not see life, but the wrath of God abideth on him." It is faith which unites us to the Lord Jesus Christ, who is the heir of all things; for, "to as many as receive him, to them gives he power to become the sons of God, even to them who believe on his name;"—and if once we are made sons, then are we likewise heirs, heirs of God, and joint heirs with Christ, and may confidently expect that inheritance which he hath purchased. By nature we are all children of wrath, and can look for nothing but judgment and fiery indignation, to devour us as adversaries; but immediately upon our believing on the Lord Jesus Christ, the great Mediator between God and man, we pass from death to life, God receives us into favor, adopts us into his family, and invests us with a title to all the privileges of children, of which this is the greatest and the best, that we shall dwell with him for ever in the building here spoken of, this house not made with hands, eternal in the heavens.

2*dly*. Another qualification by which the heirs of glory are distinguished, is this, that they are new creatures, born from above, born again of the Spirit of God. "If any man be in Christ, he is a new creature: old things are passed away, behold all things are become new." Whereas, "If any man have not the Spirit of Christ, he is none of his."—"Except a man be born again," saith the faithful and true Witness, "he cannot see the kingdom of God," (John iii. 3, and verse 5.) "Except a man be born of water and of the Spirit, he cannot enter into the kingdom of God." None but such as are born anew shall find access into this building of God, when death pulls down these earthly tabernacles. Heaven therefore is styled the inheritance of the saints in light. Nothing that is unclean can enter into that holy place. There must be a thorough change wrought in us before we can be admitted into the presence of God; for the Scriptures are peremptory on this head, that without holiness no man shall see God. Christ must be formed within us, before we can entertain the hope of glory. We only delude ourselves, if we look for happiness till our souls are renewed by the Spirit of God; for flesh and blood can never inherit the kingdom of heaven. A new heart must be given us, a new spirit must be put within us, before we can be fit for the sight and enjoyment of a holy God.

A partial reformation of manners will be of no avail—far less a mere abstinence from some grosser kinds of sin. The very frame and temper of our minds must be altered. Our corruptions must not only be restrained, but mortified. In a word, we must put off the whole old man, as the apostle beautifully expresses it, "and put on the new man, which after God is created in righteousness and true holiness."

3*d*. None shall dwell in this building of God, this house not made with hands, eternal in the heavens, but those who live as pilgrims and strangers upon the earth. If we seek the things which are above, where Christ sitteth on the right hand of God, then, and then only may we hope, that when he who is our life shall appear, we shall likewise appear with him in glory. It is one of the distinguishing characters of the wicked, that they mind earthly things. The children of God, on the other hand, have their conversation in heaven. They look upon that as their home, and view this world merely as a strange country, through which they must necessarily pass, before they can come to their Father's house. This heavenly temper is one of the most substantial evidences that are born from above; for every thing tends to the place of its original. And as it proves their divine birth, so it is likewise a certain pledge of their future glory; for God will never abandon his own offspring:—"If the Spirit of him that raised up Jesus from the dead dwell in us, he that raised up Christ from the dead, shall also quicken our mortal bodies, by his Spirit that dwelleth in us." He will certainly rebuild his own temples, and not suffer them to continue always under the ruins of death. I shall only add, in the

4*th* place, That a constant readiness to do good to all, especially to those who are of the household of faith, is another Scripture mark by which the heirs of glory are distinguished. This plainly appears from the account which our Saviour gives us of the process of the last judgment, (Matt. xxv. 34.) "Then shall the King say unto them upon his right hand, Come, ye blessed of my Father, inherit the kingdom prepared for you from the foundation of the world; for I was an hungered, and ye gave me meat; thirsty, and ye gave me drink; I was a stranger, and ye took me in; naked, and ye clothed me; I was sick, and ye visited me; I was in prison, and ye came unto me." Which he afterwards explains thus: "inasmuch as ye did it unto one of the least of these my brethren, ye have done it unto me." Upon this account, Paul exhorts Timothy, to "charge them that are rich in this world, to do good, to be rich in good works, ready to distribute, willing to communicate, laying up for themselves a good foundation against the time to come, that they may lay hold on eternal life." To the same purpose is that affectionate address of the apostle John, (1 John iii. 18, 19.) "My little children, let us not love in word, neither in tongue only, but in deed and in truth; and hereby we know that we are of the truth, and shall assure our hearts before him." Not that any thing done by us can merit a reward at the hand of God; for after we have done all, we are but unprofitable servants, we have done no more than was our duty; but these acts of obedience prove the sincerity of our faith and love. They are the genuine fruits of the new nature, and may lawfully be considered as evidences of our union with Christ, "who of God is made unto us wisdom, and righteousness, and sanctification, and redemption." Thus have I laid before you a few distinguishing characters of the heirs of glory. These are the persons for whom God hath prepared this glorious building whereof my text speaks, this house not made with hands, eternal in the heavens. And what I have said upon this head, will very much facilitate the

II. Inquiry proposed, namely, How, or by what means, the saints come to know that they shall certainly possess this glorious inheritance, when the earthly house of this tabernacle is dissolved.

Whatever proves our relation to Christ, at the same time proves our title to all the blessed fruits of his sufferings and death; for all the promises of God are in him, yea and amen. "He that spared not his own Son, but delivered him up for us all, how shall he not with him also freely give us all things." Whoever, then, can discover in himself those gracious qualifications which I formerly named, has a sufficient warrant to conclude that he is vitally united to the Lord Jesus Christ, and consequently an heir of that kingdom which he hath purchased. Thus Paul says of the primitive Christians, that "they took joyfully the spoiling of their goods, knowing in themselves that they had in heaven a better and enduring substance." They knew it in themselves; by looking inwards, they discovered such traces of the divine image, they felt such a supernatural life begun in their souls, as could be produced by no other agent than the Spirit of God, and might therefore be looked upon as a sure presage of their future glory. You see then how this assurance is commonly obtained. The Scriptures describe the persons who shall infallibly be saved. The Christian compares himself with this unerring rule; and finding that the essential characters agree to him, from thence he concludes the certainty of his own salvation.—He proceeds after this manner: God, who cannot lie, hath said, "He that believeth shall be saved;"—after the most serious and impartial examination, I find reason to conclude that by grace I have been enabled to believe—therefore I am persuaded that I shall be saved.

The first of these propositions is absolutely sure, having the truth and faithfulness of God for its foundation; the second, as it is a judgment or sentence of our own minds, must in its own nature be fallible, and hence it is that believers have not all of them an equal assurance of their salvation. Though they are all persuaded that he who believeth shall be saved, yet every one cannot say for himself, I am persuaded that I believe, and therefore I shall be saved. Before a person can say this there must be a farther work of the Spirit of God, even a divine light shining upon our faith and other graces, and making them visible to ourselves. We may derive good ground of hope from a strict and careful examination of our own temper and practice, but cannot arrive at a full assurance, till, as the apostle expresses it, (Rom. viii. 16.) "the Spirit himself bear witness with our spirits, that we are the sons of God." But when this divine Witness concurs with his testimony, irradiating his own workmanship within us, and discovering to our own minds such lineaments of the new creature, as plain evidence that we are born of God, then our assurance is full and complete; and we can joyfully say, with the apostle in the text, "We know, that if the earthly house of this tabernacle were dissolved, we have a building of God, an house not made with hands, eternal in the heavens." I now come to the practical improvement of the subject.

And, 1*st*. I must speak a few words to those who call themselves Deists. I know if you could you would stop our mouths, and bury the name of the Lord Jesus Christ; and yet I shall not cease to seek your good, and say from time to time what I can for your conviction. I seldom read the threatenings of the word, but I think of you with trembling; and I never read the comforts of it, but I think of you with pity. Pray, what assurance have you got of a happy eternity? In what house are you to take up your everlasting abode? Alas, every thing beyond the grave must be dark and fearful to you. You have no promise to build upon—no Mediator to take hold of—no atonement to plead—no covenant to depend upon. You know that God is just, and you know that you are sinners—thus far you can proceed in your own scheme with certainty; but I defy you to move one step farther upon sure ground. You cannot prove that God is reconcilable, far less can you tell upon what terms he will be reconciled to you; so that your causes of fear are real and certain, whereas your hopes are mere guesswork, having no other foundation than the doubtful conjectures of your own darkened minds. What will you do when you come to die? A Christian can say, "I know that my Redeemer liveth; and because he lives, I shall live also." But what will you be able to say, who have no Redeemer, no intercessor, into whose hands you can commit your departing spirits? who have nothing in your view but a tribunal of justice, a tribunal from which there is no appeal. Be entreated, my dear friends, to think of this in time. "Kiss the Son, lest he be angry, and ye perish from the way." If once his wrath begin to burn, then shall you find that they, and they only, are blessed who put their trust in him. But,

2*dly*. This comfortable subject doth principally direct me to speak to Christians; and I shall address my exhortation to you in the words of the apostle Peter, "Give all diligence to make your calling and election sure." That this assurance is attainable you have already heard. Let me then press you, by some motives, to seek after it. Consider how much it is for your present interest. O the joy to be assured of the favor of God! this is heart ease, this is the very rest and sabbath of the soul. How sweet and comfortable will the thoughts of a Saviour be to you, when once you can say, "My beloved is mine, and I am his." Then will it do thee good to view his wounds by the eye of faith, and to put, as it were, thy hand into his side, when thou canst call him, with Thomas, my Lord and my God. The holy Scriptures will then have a double relish. With what delight will you turn over this charter of your future inheritance, and ponder that exceeding and eternal weight of glory which you shall one day possess. With what holy boldness may you approach the throne of grace, when you can call God your reconciled Father! What would a despairing sinner, who feels the burden of guilt, and the foretastes of everlasting misery, give for such a privilege, especially in a dying hour. How will this sweeten the difficulties of obedience. It was this that kept the apostle from fainting, as we read in the close of the preceding chapter. What can quicken us more than to know, that after we have gone through a short life in this world, everlasting happiness shall be our portion in the next? Who would not mend his pace, who is assured that every step brings him nearer to heaven?

What a mighty cordial will this be, under the sharpest afflictions, to consider that God meaneth us no hurt, but, on the contrary, hath pledged his faithfulness, to make them all work together for our good? One who hath eternal life in the eye of his faith and hope, can look through tribulations, and see sunshine at the back of the darkest cloud.

And then, what comfort does it give in the hour of death? How miserable is the soul, that must be turned out of doors shiftless and harborless, and is not provided of an everlasting habitation, or a better place to go to; but assurance makes the soul to triumph over the grave, and take death cheerfully by the cold hand, and even long to be gone, and to be with Christ. Dark and doubting Christians may indeed shrink back, and be afraid of the exchange; but the assured soul desires to depart, and needs as much patience to live as other men do to die. Let us then, my brethren, press after this attainment, and not only seek to be in safety, but to know that we are so. And as it is a gift of God, let us, by humble and importunate prayer, ask it of him who giveth to all men liberally, and upbraideth not. And,

Last of all, Let those who have got this invaluable mercy, improve it for those purposes for which it was bestowed. "I will run the way of thy commandments," said the Psalmist, "when thou hast enlarged my heart." Make swift progress in the way of duty, if you desire the continuance of this comfortable privilege. Let it appear to all that your conversation is in heaven. Live above this world, and be daily "adding to your faith, virtue; and to virtue, knowledge; and to knowledge, temperance; and to temperance, patience; and to patience, godliness; and to godliness, brotherly kindness; and to brotherly kindness, charity:"—And then shall an entrance be administered unto you abundantly into the everlasting kingdom of our Lord and Saviour Jesus Christ, to whom be glory for ever. *Amen.*

SERMON LXIX.

Preached at the Celebration of the Lord's Supper.

GOD'S GREAT MANIFESTATION.

1 JOHN iv. 9.—"In this was manifested the love of GOD towards us, because that GOD sent his only begotten Son into the world, that we might live through him."

THE value of different truths, like that of all other objects, is to be estimated by the different degrees of their usefulness and importance. Judging by this rule, there are none which better deserve our attention, than those which relate to the character of the Supreme Being. If our ideas of him be different from what he really is, it is impossible that we can love him truly, or serve him with acceptance. There may be qualities in the imaginary being which we adore, utterly repugnant with the perfections of the true God; and the mode of worship by which we strive to please him, may of consequence be as absurd as the ideas which we entertain of his character. Various are the means which God hath provided for guiding us to the true knowledge of himself. The heavens declare his glory, and the firmament showeth his handy-works. The invisible things of him, even his eternal power and Godhead, are clearly seen, being perceived by the things which he hath made. His moral perfections may be learned from his general administration of the world, and especially from his conduct towards his rational creatures. Had we capacities sufficient to take a comprehensive view of all his works and ways, such a review would result in a full conviction, that righteousness and judgment are the habitation of his throne, and that mercy and truth continually go before him. But as we see only a small part of the great system which he is carrying on, and of consequence are liable to mistaken and partial conceptions, he hath been graciously pleased to rest his character on one great fact, which it is impossible to misunderstand. This fact the apostle places in our view in the passage before us. He is engaged in an argument for his favorite doctrine of universal benevolence. To enforce this doctrine, he reminds his readers of the love and benevolence of God, and of this he can find no other way to express his strong conceptions, than by denominating him love and goodness itself. "Beloved," saith he, at the 7th verse, "let us love one another, for love is of God, and every one that loveth is born of God, and knoweth God. He that loveth not, knoweth not God; for God is love." To prove this, he enters into no refined disquisitions, or abstract reasonings, on the divine nature. These, he knew, were but little adapted to the general apprehensions of mankind. He thinks it sufficient to appeal for a proof of it to that wonderful expedient which God devised for saving lost sinners. "In this," says he, "was manifested the love of God towards us, because that God sent his only begotten Son into the world, that we might live through him." These words then imply,

I. That the redemption of mankind was an act of the freest and most unmerited grace.

II. That it is a full demonstration of the unbounded love and goodness of God.

As these are truths of the greatest importance, and very properly suited to our meditation at this time, I will lay the evidence of them before you in as clear a manner as I can, and then conclude with an application of the subject.

I. then, The text implies, that the redemption of mankind was an act of the freest and most unmerited grace. God was under no obligation to provide a Saviour for his fallen creatures. Without any imputation on his justice, he might have left them to eat the fruit of their own doings, and to be filled with their own devices. He stood in no need of our services, nor could he be injured by our rebellion. Our perdition would have made no blank in his works, which his power could not have supplied in one moment. Man was indeed miserable enough to excite compassion; but he was deservedly so, and therefore compassion might have been restrained, and justice have had its course. He had left the station in which he was placed, insolently thrown off his dependence on his Maker, questioned his veracity, and dared his power. Nothing therefore but sovereign mercy could have interposed for his relief. But to make this point perfectly clear, let it be observed,

1*st*, That God's designs of mercy could not arise from his thinking the constitution he had made with Adam, as the head and representative of his posterity, severe and unrighteous. It is certain, on the contrary, that had it not been holy, just, and good, God could never have been the author of it; and if it was once righteous, no failure on the part of his creatures could alter its nature. There is no insinuation that God changed his opinion of that transaction, or that he hath ceased to consider man as justly condemned by the first covenant. In fact, the method of our recovery through Jesus Christ, contains a virtual ratification of the sentence by which we were condemned; for it hath appointed the second Adam to be the head of an elect world, that through the merit of his sufferings and death, mercy might be dispensed to the guilty, in a consistency with the rectitude of the divine nature, and the honor of his law.

2dly. God was not moved to provide a Saviour for his creatures, by any sense that his law was too strict in its demands for them to be able to obey. We find that the word of God still denounces a curse on every deviation from that perfect rule. There is no mitigation of the penalties annexed to disobedience. The law which requires perfect obedience is in full force. The exactions of justice are not in the least abated. How indeed is it possible that they could? for consider how the case stands. God is infinitely amiable and perfect; and what does he require of his creatures, but that they should love him with all the soul, strength, and heart, which he hath given them? Can this ever cease to be an obligation? What should make it cease? Nothing, but that God should become less amiable, that his perfection should fade, his goodness be exhausted, or his greatness impaired. On the other hand, what is it that he threatens to those who withdraw their hearts from him? Is it not the loss of his favor and friendship? Can either the obligation or penalty be accused of severity? Surely in this God does nothing unbecoming a wise and righteous governor. Nay, with reverence be it said, he could not do otherwise without denying himself. Is it conceivable that he should retract his word, that he should compound, like earthly creditors, for a part of what is owing to him; that he should depreciate the honor of his law, or dispense with the exactions of his justice? No; he hath said, and never will unsay it, "that the wages of sin is death;" but he hath purposed to display his compassion to fallen man, in a manner that should reconcile all his perfections. "And in this was manifested the love of God toward us, because that he hath sent his Son into the world, that we might live through him."

3dly. The inability to perform his duty, which man contracted by his fall, did not render his case in the least more deserving of compassion. This inability, as it proceeds entirely from the depravity of our tempers, and the enmity of our hearts, can only serve to render us more vile and odious in his sight. Had we indeed lost the affection of love altogether, had our natural powers been quite destroyed by the fall, our case might have moved compassion; but this case was not ours. The affection of love still remains, and we exert it with ardor and vivacity towards a variety of objects. Our natural powers, though impaired, are not destroyed, for we employ them successfully in our worldly concerns; so that our inability to love God, when translated in its true language, amounts just to this, that we love those things which are contrary to his nature so much, that it is impossible we can love him; and how this should extenuate our guilt, let those who plead it explain.

4thly. God was not moved to this act of unmerited grace by any foreknowledge he had that mankind would receive it with thankfulness. He foresaw, as appears by the prophetic writings, the ingratitude and contempt that would be poured upon his Son. He foresaw that he should be despised and rejected of men; that his person should be insulted, his name derided, his blood shed, and the calls of his grace rejected. All this was full in his eye when he laid the plan of our redemption; so that in all views, you see it was an act of the freest and most unmerited grace. It took its rise from no good in the creature, either existing or foreseen. Unmerited, unsolicited, and ill requited, the fountain of all this grace was in God himself; for his goodness is like himself, unsearchable. "His thoughts are not our thoughts, neither his ways our ways." I now proceed, in the

II. place, To show that the redemption of mankind is a full demonstration of the unbounded love and goodness of the Divine nature. "In this," saith the apostle, "was the love of God manifested towards us, because that God sent his only begotten Son into the world, that we might live through him." Consider then,

1st, The dignity of the person whom God sent on this gracious errand. Had he sent one of the meanest of his servants to sympathize with us in our forlorn state, it would have been an act of great condescension and goodness. Had he commissioned one of the least considerable of those spirits who surround his throne, to minister some relief to us in our miserable situation, with what gratitude ought we to have received such an instance of his compassionate regard. But who is this that cometh in the name of the Lord to save us? What are his rank, his titles, and dignity? Let a prophet declare: "Unto us a child is born, unto us a son is given, and his name shall be called Wonderful, Counsellor, the Mighty God, the everlasting Father, the Prince of peace." Let an evangelist declare: "The Word was made flesh, and tabernacled among us, and we beheld his glory, the glory as of the only begotten of the Father, full of grace and truth."—Let an apostle declare: "God who at sundry times, and in divers manners, spake to our fathers by the prophets, hath in these last days spoken to us by his Son from heaven—who is the brightness of his glory, and the express image of his person." Or if all these testimonies are insufficient, let it be declared by a voice from the excellent Majesty, "This is my beloved Son, hear ye him." Such was the person whom God sent to save us. "In this was manifested the love of God toward us, because that God sent his only begotten Son." But whither did he send this divine person? This is a

2*d* Circumstance that cannot fail to heighten our gratitude. He sent him into this lower world. He came from heaven to earth, from the throne to the footstool, from the bosom of his Father to this guilty and polluted world, which deserved to be visited with an executioner of justice, instead of an herald of peace. And in what circumstances did he appear on earth? Was it in the pomp of royalty, to receive the homage and services of his creatures? No; his life on earth was one continued scene of suffering. From his birth to his death he was a man of sorrows, and acquainted with grief. He was even so destitute of the common accommodations of life, that he said of himself, "The foxes have holes, and the birds of the air have nests, but the Son of man hath not where to lay his head." Yet these sufferings, though great, were light in comparison with what he afterwards underwent. The bitterest sorrows which the common lot of humanity knows, admit some intervals of ease and relief. At worst, the mind of man, in its most oppressed moments, anticipates the bright side of things; or, ignorant of futurity, feels but the weight of the present moment. But this consolation of human weakness, the prophetic mind of Jesus did not admit. He foresaw the approaching hour of suffering, and was fully aware of every bitter ingredient in the cup that was prepared for him to drink. He beheld the lowering cloud of darkness and distress. He knew the malice of his enemies, the perfidy of his betrayer, and the unfaithfulness of his friends. He saw the accursed tree, the torturing scourge, the piercing nails, the hour and the power of darkness.

Behold him in that unutterable conflict, which wrung from him those complaining accents, "My soul is exceeding sorrowful, even unto death." Behold him at his Father's footstool, offering up prayers and supplications, with strong crying and tears, unto him that was able to save him. Behold him going forth to meet his enemies; receiving the treacherous kiss; stretching forth his hands to the shackles; forsaken of all his friends; buffeted, scourged, and spit upon; at last nailed to a cross, and insulted, even in his expiring moments, with a derision of his woe. When you have beheld this complicated scene of anguish, say if there was ever sorrow like unto this sorrow; and yet far beyond all this must have been those mysterious feelings of the Son of God, when he cried out, "My God, my God, why hast thou forsaken me?"

Such was the treatment which the Son of God met with on earth, and which he was prepared to meet with for our sakes; and can we doubt, after this, of the love of God in sending him into the world? "Greater love than this hath no man, that a man lay down his life for his friend; but herein God commended his love towards us, in that while we were yet sinners, Christ died for us." Consider, in the

3*d* place, The gracious design on which he came into the world. It was, "that we might live through him." Life, you know, is the most important of blessings, and the foundation of all other enjoyments. To purchase life, we reckon no expense or loss too great. "Skin for skin, all that a man hath will he give for his life." But life, in Scripture language, is generally used to signify happiness in general, and in this sense it is to be understood in the text. It is here opposed to all that misery which we had brought upon ourselves by our apostasy from God. By nature we are dead in law, lying under a sentence of condemnation, the execution of which is only suspended by the brittle thread of life. We are also spiritually dead, alienated from the fountain of life and happiness, dead in trespasses and sins. To complete our miserable situation, we are liable to the second death, that awful death which subjects both soul and body to everlasting punishment in the world to come. Now, the death of Christ delivers us from all these evils. By him all who believe on his name are freed from condemnation, and obtain a right to live: "For Christ hath redeemed us from the curse of the law, being made a curse for us." Through him we also are made spiritually alive. "You hath he quickened," saith St. Paul to the Ephesians, "who were dead in trespasses and sins. The old man is crucified with Christ, that the body of sin might be destroyed, that henceforth we should not serve sin." To crown all, through him we have the gift of eternal life, being begotten again unto the lively hope of an inheritance incorruptible, undefiled, and that fadeth not away.

And is there now aught wanting to demonstrate the unbounded love and goodness of God? How warmly does Hezekiah speak! with what gratitude does he express himself on a few years being added to his natural life!—"The living, the living, they shall praise thee, as I do this day. The fathers to the children shall declare thy truth. Upon a stringed instrument will I praise thee, and upon the harp with a solemn sound." What then ought to be our feelings of gratitude! what ought to be our language of praise, to whom God hath granted length of days for evermore!

I have thus endeavored to show you that the redemption of mankind is an act of the freest grace; and that it is a full demonstration of the unbounded love and goodness of God.

From what hath been said, the first and most obvious inference is, our obligation to love that God who hath thus loved us. And is he not worthy of this affection in himself? Has the perfection of beauty and goodness no charms to move us, while with so much ardor we run after the faint traces of these qualities in creation? Especially what are our hearts made of, if they can resist the impression of a benefit so inestimable as I have been describing, conferred with a bounty that even prevented our requests. We value ourselves, we esteem others, for their grateful and affectionate feelings. We can hardly entertain any regard for a character in which we see no marks of sensibility. Shall this defect, then, excite our disapprobation in all cases, excepting in that where it is most glaring and odious? Shall we exert our affections with ardor on many inferior objects, and reserve none for him whose power made us, and whose goodness has made us happy? You excuse yourselves, perhaps, by saying, that your affections are engaged to your friends and benefactors, because they are objects of perception, and you have seen and conversed with them; whereas God is unseen and spiritual, so that your feelings with regard to him cannot be so lively. Is nothing then an object of your affections but what you have seen with your bodily eyes? Is it only the outward form of your friend that you love? Is it only the hand that confers the benefit, or the feet that move to serve you? Is it not rather the soul, the heart of your friend, that engages your love? even that kindness which never fails, that sincerity which you can always trust, that faithfulness on which you can at all times depend, that sympathy which makes your griefs and joys his own? Do you cease to love your friend after his body is laid in the dust? Sure I am, none who ever knew a friend will say so.

It is then the soul that engages affection—And is not the soul visible? Are you not as certain of the existence of God as you are of your own soul's existence, or the souls of those you converse with? True it is, that God is not to be discerned by our senses; but is he then afar off? Doth he not fill heaven and earth with his presence? Do not kindness, faithfulness, and sympathy, belong to his character, more than to any earthly friend? Who is it that hath said, "I will never leave thee, nor forsake thee?" Who is it that hath said, "Call upon me in the day of trouble, and I will deliver thee, and thou shalt glorify me?" Who is it that hath desired us to cast all our care upon him, because he careth for us? Who is it that hath said, "He that toucheth you, toucheth the apple of mine eye?" Say not, then, I cannot love God, because I have not seen him; say rather, if thou hast the heart to say so, I cannot love God, because that love is already engaged to his rival. I love the world too much, I love my sins too much, *i. e.*, I love his enemies too much to have any remaining affections to bestow on him. In the

2*d* place, We may infer from what hath been said, if God so loved us while we were enemies, how much more will he love us, now that we are reconciled to him by the death of his Son? There are but few points on which I am sanguine enough to think I could argue to the conviction of a person disposed to evade the force of evidence; yet if there is any, I think it is in proof of this sentiment of the apostle, "He that spared not his own Son, but gave him up to the death for us all, how shall he not with him also freely give us all things." Allow me that God has sent his only begotten Son into the world, that we might have life through him; and then say, is there another favor so costly that you should think it beyond the reach of his benevolence? You may perhaps say, that he hath already done so much, that you cannot conceive how he should do more. But I will ask you this, Why did he confer the first favor? Was it only to save appearances to his creatures? Do you conceive of it as of that constrained kind of benevolence which we sometimes see in the world—a man paying the debts of another, and then setting him adrift to do as he best can in the world? No; I will tell you what it rather resembles, if a resemblance to it can be found in this selfish world. It resembles a man taking up a helpless orphan. He at first clothes and feeds him; by and by, he conceives an attachment for him. Having done so much, he is unwilling to leave his work imperfect; he makes him worthy of his care, by instilling good principles into him. In time he adopts him into his family; at last he makes him his heir, and leaves him all he has. Whoever knows the human heart, knows that this is the natural progress of affection. He that gives, cherisheth his own benevolence by the gift; and to have conferred one favor, is a reason for continuing and adding others. I say not this, as if God's thoughts were to be measured by ours. I have a better warrant for using this comparison—"being confident," as an apostle has expressed it, "of this very thing, that he who hath begun a good work in you, will perform it until the day of Jesus Christ.—Behold what manner of love the Father hath bestowed upon us, that we should be called the sons of God—and if sons, then heirs, heirs of God, and joint heirs with Jesus Christ.—God commended his love towards us, in that while we were yet sinners, Christ died for us.—Much more, then, being now justified by his blood, we shall be saved from wrath through him: for if when we were enemies, we were reconciled to God by the death of his Son, much more, being reconciled, we shall be saved by his life."

But here, my brethren, I find the subject rising and widening beyond the reach of my thoughts, or feeble illustrations. "How great, O God, is that goodness which thou hast laid up for them that fear thee, which thou hast wrought for them that trust in thee, before the sons of men!"

One other inference from what hath been said we cannot omit, being the inference of the apostle himself in the context. "Beloved, if God so loved us, we ought also to love one another." I will not inquire whether this is an exhortation to universal benevolence, or an exhortation to Christians to love their brethren; certain it is, that the disciples of Christ are exhorted to both of these amiable dispositions. Of whom are we bold enough to say, that he may not be one of those for whom Christ died; that he may not become, through grace, one of the excellent ones of the earth? If thou art a vessel of mercy, consider who it was that filled thee; and may not the same fountain fill him—fill any of the race of Adam? Let your benevolence then extend to the whole of mankind: but let your love be special towards the household of faith. Love them for the image they bear—love them for the ties by which you are connected together. Let your love to them be fervent and active. Impart to them every assistance of friendship, especially of that friendship which regards the interests of their souls. Exhort one another daily, lest any of you be hardened through the deceitfulness of sin. Continue together in one accord, in prayer and supplication, forwarding one another in your way to Zion, and singing songs of comfort as you go along.

On the whole, you see how much the religion of Christ applies itself to the best affections of the human heart. To whom does it direct our worship?—To the God of love, the God who is love, and who manifested his love to us, in that he sent his only begotten Son into the world, that we might live through him. What doth it require of us, but that we should love him who first loved us; that we should yield ourselves to be his, and trust in him for all good things. Are ye willing? The pledges of the covenant are at hand, and may God seal them to your souls. *Amen.*

SERMON LXX.

Preached after the Celebration of the Lord's Supper.

THE ETHIOPIAN AND PHILIP.

ACTS VIII. 39. "——— and he went on his way rejoicing."

THE person of whom this account is given was a man of Ethiopia, who possessed a place of great trust and authority under the queen of that country. It appears from the history, that he was a proselyte to the Jewish religion; for he had come as far as Jerusalem to attend on the worship of the God of Israel. The manner of his conversion to Christianity, by the ministry of Philip the Evangelist, is circumstantially related in the preceding verses; and as there are several striking incidents in this passage of history, I shall point out a few of them which are chiefly remarkable.

1*st.* We are told, that when this officer of the Ethiopian queen was about to take his departure from Jerusalem, God sent his angel to Philip at Samaria, with a peremptory order to leave that place, and to travel southward till he should come upon the road that goeth down from Jerusalem to Gaza; which place he had no sooner reached, than lo, the illustrious stranger appears in his chariot, pursuing his journey to his own country.

2*dly.* It deserves our notice, that at the precise moment when Philip, by a divine impulse, ran to meet him, this devout proselyte was reading aloud a part of Isaiah's prophecy, which speaks plainly and directly concerning the Messiah The place of Scripture which he read was this: "He was led as a sheep to the slaughter, and like a lamb dumb before his shearer, so opened he not his mouth: In his humiliation his judgment was taken away, and who shall declare his generation? for his life is taken from the earth." Upon hearing these words, Philip accosted him with this question, "Understandest thou what thou readest?" The other ingenuously confessed that he did not; and having, with uncommon courtesy, taken the Evangelist up into his chariot, begged to be informed who the person was whom the prophet had in his eye. "Then," as we read in the 35th verse, "Philip opened his mouth, and began at the same Scripture, and preached unto him Jesus."

Thus both the preacher and his subject were very remarkably ordered in the providence of God; and, as might be expected from such favorable presages, the discourse was accompanied with the powerful influences of his grace: For upon their coming to a certain place where there was water, the new disciple, of his own accord, modestly signified his desire to be baptized, and after professing his faith in Christ, in these few but solemn words, "I believe that Jesus Christ is the Son of God,"—the chariot was stopt, and Philip went down with him into the water, and baptized him. A

3*d* Incident, no less remarkable than the former two, is recorded in the verse where my text lies. "When they were come up out of the water, the Spirit of the Lord caught away Philip, that the Eunuch saw him no more." How admirable, how perfect are the works of God! These two were brought together by the agency of an angel, and now they are parted asunder by a miracle, but a miracle of wisdom as well as of power. For this sudden and supernatural removal of the preacher, was a powerful confirmation of the doctrine which he taught, and had an obvious tendency to impress on the mind of the new convert this important truth, that although a man had been employed as the instrument of his conversion, yet the work itself was truly divine, and the glory of it due to God alone.

Accordingly we learn, from the latter part of the verse, that all these wonderful events had a most happy influence on his mind. He was transported with what he had seen, and heard, and experienced; his judgment approved the wise choice he had made, and he went on his way rejoicing. He went on his way, *i. e.*, he proceeded on his journey homeward. The new persuasion he had received into his mind did not mislead him into fanciful plans of action, inconsistent with, or perhaps opposite to, the duties of his station. No, he knew that the religion he had embraced, instead of releasing him from these duties, rather bound him to a more faithful and diligent performance of them. He therefore went on his way, and he rejoiced as he went. He felt his soul enriched with heavenly grace. He had now got a treasure which he could properly call his own, even that pearl of great price, with which all the treasures of Ethiopia were not worthy to be compared.

Your condition, my brethren, is in several respects similar to the condition of this man. He had solemnly avouched the Lord to be his God: You, with equal solemnity, have this day done the same. He had just received one seal of the covenant of grace: You, this day, have received the other. He had a long journey before him: Ye also are travellers through this wilderness, toward the promised land of rest. In these circumstances I think that, without apology, I may take occasion, from the words that have been read, to address you with a twofold exhortation:

I. To go on your way heavenward. And,

II. To rejoice as you go.

I TRUST I need hardly inform you, that the spiritual repast to which you have been this day admitted, is purely intended to strengthen you in your journey to the heavenly country. God sends us these grapes from the Canaan above, not to detain us in the wilderness, but to allure us out of it, and to make us hasten our steps towards that country of which they are the natural and spontaneous product. My first exhortation, therefore, is both seasonable and necessary—Arise and go forward. Many who mistake the nature of this ordinance, are very anxious and busy for a few days, in making a sort of formal preparation for it. Then their countenances are demure, and their steps are solemn, and their conversation is precise, and their attendance upon the most protracted services of devotion indefatigable; and this they call religion, and trust in its merit to absolve them from all the dishonest, worldly, uncharitable, and ungodly practices, of which they are guilty in the other periods of their time. But I trust, my brethren, that ye have not so learned Christ, and I trust that we, who are your spiritual guides, shall never encourage you in so fatal a delusion. I address you now, as the disciples and friends of Christ. I speak to you in his name; and that his authority may be the more unquestionable in the exhortation I am to give you, I shall deliver it in the very words which his own Spirit hath employed. "I beseech you, therefore, brethren, by the mercies of God, that ye present your bodies a living sacrifice, holy, acceptable unto God, which is your reasonable service." And beware of a sinful conformity to this world, "but be ye transformed by the renewing of your mind, that ye may prove what is that good, and acceptable, and perfect will of God.—As ye have this day received Christ Jesus the Lord, so walk ye in him," in a manner suitable to the vocation wherewith ye are called, with all lowliness and meekness, with long-suffering, forbearing one another in love, endeavoring to keep the unity of the Spirit in the bond of peace. Add to your faith, virtue; and to virtue, knowledge; and to knowledge, temperance; and to temperance, patience; and to patience, godliness; and to godliness, brotherly kindness; and to brotherly kindness, charity." Think not that ye "have already attained; but this one thing do ye, forgetting those things which are behind, and reaching forth unto those things which are before, press towards the mark, for the prize of the high calling of God in Christ Jesus.—And I beseech you, brethren, that every one of you do shew the same diligence, to the full assurance of hope unto the end; that ye be not slothful, but followers of them who through faith and patience do now inherit the promises.—Whatsoever things are true, whatsoever things are honest, whatsoever things are just, whatsoever things are pure, whatsoever things are lovely, whatsoever things are of good report, if there be any virtue, and if there be any praise, think on these things. —And let your path resemble that of the just—a shining light, that shineth more and more unto the perfect day.—Finally, my brethren, be strong in the Lord, and in the power of his might. Put on the whole armor of God, that ye may be able to stand against the wiles of the devil—having your loins girt about with truth, and having on the breastplate of righteousness, and your feet shod with the preparation of the gospel of peace; above all, taking the shield of faith, wherewith ye shall be able to quench all the fiery darts of the wicked. And take the helmet of salvation, and the sword of the Spirit, which is the word of God: Praying always with all prayer and supplication in the Spirit, and watching thereunto with all perseverance."

These few passages of Scripture, which speak to us directly as *soldiers* and *travellers*, who, under the conduct and tuition of the great Captain of Salvation, must force their way to the Zion above, fully express the meaning of my first exhortation; and as they are not my words, but the words of the living and true God, the divine authority with which they are marked must necessarily imply our obligation to obey them, and consequently give a greater weight to my present address than any arguments that I could possibly devise. Let me therefore once more repeat the exhortation, and call upon you to make progress in your Christian course. Let your present attainments, instead of satisfying you, only incite your zeal and ambition to rise still higher in the excellencies of the divine life. Carry ever in your minds, that the design of the solemn and instrumental duties of religion is to beget and strengthen those principles and habits of goodness in your souls, by which they will be gradually ripened for the life of heaven. Stir up your faith to behold him who is invisible, that you may walk before him in the light of the living, having no other anxiety but to do what he commands; no other ambition but to enjoy his favor now, and to receive his approbation at last. Let your meditation on those sufferings of the Redeemer, which ye have been showing forth to-day, instruct you what you are to expect in the present life, and how you ought to behave under all its trials and afflictions. Do not flatter yourselves with the prospect of uninterrupted ease, and unclouded enjoyment; but consider him who endured such contradiction of sinners against himself, when at any time ye are weary or faint in your minds; and study to know him in the power of his resurrection, and in the fellowship of his sufferings, being made conformable to his death. Exercise yourselves daily in mortifying the deeds of the body; in crucifying the flesh, with its affections and lusts; and in opposing your inclinations as often as they oppose your duty. Thus laboring to be examples of patience, meekness, contentment, and to come behind in no good thing to which you are called; go on in the strength of the Lord, making mention of his righteousness, even of his only: "And may the God of peace, that brought again from the dead our Lord Jesus, that great Shepherd of the sheep, through the blood of the everlasting covenant, make you perfect in every good work, to do his will, working in you that which is well-pleasing in his sight, through Jesus Christ, to whom be glory for ever and ever. Amen."

Having thus exhorted you to continue

your progress in the good ways of God, let me now exhort you, in the

II. place, To rejoice as you go on.

After all the comfortable topics that have been suggested to your meditation in the solemn service in which we have been engaged, it should be almost unnecessary to recall to your minds any of those copious sources of joy which belong to the redeemed of the Lord. Yet, lest there should be some mind so dark, some apprehension so slow, as to be at a loss in discovering its own comforts; I will mention in their order, a few of those that are most obvious and solid, and best fitted to fill the mind with peace and joy in believing. In the

1*st* place, then, If so be ye have tasted that the Lord is gracious, (and to those only who have had this experience do I speak) then rejoice that ye have passed from death to life, and that there is now no condemnation for them who are in Christ Jesus. Rejoice in that distinguishing grace which hath plucked you as brands from the burning, which hath brought up your soul from the grave, which hath kept you alive, that ye should not go down into the pit. Look around among your fellow-creatures, and behold the multitudes who walk in the broad way that leadeth to destruction, who go on headstrong and blindfold in the paths of folly, until their eyes are opened in the everlasting burnings. Then consider your own better choice and safer condition, and rejoice in that mercy which found you, when you were wandering from peace and happiness, which arrested you in your mad career, and brought you back to the Shepherd and Bishop of your souls. In the

2*d* place, Rejoice that you have not only passed from death to life, but are also advanced to the dearest and most intimate relation to all the Persons of the ever blessed Godhead. By your new birth ye are become the sons of God, members of Christ, and temples for the Holy Ghost. And what an overflowing source of consolation is this? Can there be any cause of fear or disquietude to those who dwell in the secret place of the Most High, and abide under the shadow of the Almighty? Can *they* want any good thing, of whom God hath taken the charge as his peculiar property, and for whom he provides as for his own? Is not his wisdom sufficient to guide you through all the perplexing paths of life? Is not his power sufficient to support you under every danger and difficulty? Is not his goodness sufficient to bestow on you all things richly to enjoy? In what shape, then, can any real evil assail you; or what imperfection can there be in your prospects of felicity? In the

3*d* place, Rejoice that God hath made with you an everlasting covenant, well ordered in all things and sure. He hath not only assured you, in general, of his good will and gracious purposes on your behalf; but hath also given you a variety of exceeding great and precious promises, so that there can be no possible exigence in your situation, in which you may not find a suitable and abundant relief, in these gracious assurances of a faithful God.

Were I to descend to particulars, it would be necessary for me to repeat the greater part of this sacred book, every page of which contains some reviving declaration of what God hath already done, or promised to do for his people. And "the words of God are pure words, like silver tried in a furnace of earth, purified seven times. He is the rock, his work is perfect, and all his ways are judgment; a God of truth, and without iniquity, just and right is he." Have not those, then, good cause to rejoice, who have such an ample charter put into their hands by the King of kings, a charter investing them with a full and unalterable right to every necessary blessing, even to all the unsearchable riches of Christ? In the

4*th* place, Rejoice that the life which is begun in you is an immortal principle that can never be extinguished. Ye are born again by the Spirit of God; and ye are kept by his mighty power, through faith unto salvation. United as you are to Christ, by a living faith, ye can never perish. His charge to preserve you is as strict and binding as his charge to redeem and renew you at first. Ye were given unto him from eternity by his heavenly Father, and will he not keep those whom the Father hath committed to him? Hear his own words: "All that the Father hath given me shall come to me, and him that cometh to me I will in nowise cast out." Christ formed in the heart of a true believer, resembles, in some measure, Christ incarnate in the world. The divine nature may be obscured for a season; it may, and probably will, have its season of humiliation; but though it may seem to die, yet it shall have its resurrection likewise, and afterwards its ascension into glory. This it was that enabled Paul to say, "I therefore run, not as uncertainly; so fight I, not as one that beateth the air." Perseverance is not only the duty, but the privilege also, of all who set themselves in good earnest to travel for heaven. And though the law of God obliges them, and their new nature inclines them, to work out their own salvation with fear and trembling, yet they have a far better security for their success than any efforts of their own. Omnipotence is their guardian: "the eternal God is their refuge, and underneath them his everlasting arms."

My brethren, time and strength would fail me, were I to attempt enumerating all the sources of joy which belong to the redeemed of the Lord. I trust, that in your own frequent meditation you revolve them, and that in your frequent addresses to the throne of grace, you commemorate them with thankful hearts before the God and Father of our Lord Jesus Christ. Do you not then express the joy and gratitude of your souls, for the benefit of your Redeemer's example, for the promised aids of his Spirit, for the assurance of his intercession, for the gracious appointment of him as the Judge of the world, for the access you now have by him to the throne of grace, for the means of communion with the Father of your spirits, and the pleasing fellowship of those who are travelling with you in the same road to the Zion above? Leaving these, then, to be revolved in your own minds, I will now only exhort you, in the

5*th* and *last* place, To rejoice in the hope of the glory of God. "Fear not, little flock," said the blessed Jesus, "for it is your Father's good pleasure to give you the kingdom." Ere long your trials and sufferings shall come to an end, and your light afflictions, which are but for a moment, shall be followed by an exceeding great and eternal weight of glory. At present we come from scenes of anxiety and vexation to keep our solemn feasts; and our wedding garments are stained with the pollution, or torn by the briers through which we travel. Even amidst our most sublime delights, we are conscious of a certain blank in our feelings, which reminds us that this is not our rest; but in the presence of God there is fulness of joy, and at his right hand are pleasures for evermore. The poor afflicted broken spirit, which now breathes in trouble as in its daily air, and scarcely knows any other rule for computing the periods of time, than by the revolutions of sorrows and disappointments, shall then be tuned to the high praises of God; and its love to him, who is the Lord of love, shall feel no bounds, and fear no end. O how the unveiled glory of God will then brighten many a face which is now darkened with grief, and stained with tears, and daily wears the hue of melancholy! There is not a sorrowful countenance in all the courts of Zion's King; their doubts and fears have dropped off with the veil of mortality, and sorrow and sighing have fled far away. Lift up your heads, then, ye that travel towards the heavenly Zion, and rejoice in the hope of the glory of God. It is not more certain that the sun doth shine in the firmament, than that ye shall live for ever in the heavenly Jerusalem, and join in the innumerable company about the throne, in the everlasting praise of your God and Redeemer. Then shall you understand the happiness of believers, and know better than I can tell you, what God did for your souls, when he called you out of darkness into his marvellous light.

Rejoice then in the Lord always, and again I say, rejoice. Let it appear, by the serenity of your countenance, and the alacrity of your steps, that your salvation is already begun, and that, though the fulness of your joys be reserved for another world, yet even in this you can remark, with a satisfaction unknown to the mere sons of earth, how sweet is the face of nature, how delicious are the fruits of the field. "Go your way, eat your bread with joy, and drink your wine with a merry heart, for God now accepteth your work." *Amen.*

SERMON LXXI.

ADVANTAGES UNIMPROVED.

Hebrews v. 12.—"For when for the time ye ought to be teachers, ye have need that one teach you again which be the first principles of the oracles of God; and are become such as have need of milk, and not of strong meat."

The apostle having, at the 10th verse, compared, in general terms, the priesthood of Jesus with that of Melchisedek, finds himself obliged to break off the argument, not from any defect of his own knowledge, but from the dulness of those to whom he wrote. Their minds were not as yet prepared for such sublime instruction, and that not owing to any natural infirmity, but merely to their neglect or misimprovement of the best advantages. "For when for the time ye ought to be teachers, ye have need that one teach you again which be the first principles of the oracles of God; and are become such as have need of milk, and not of strong meat." Accordingly, he tells them very plainly how disgracefully deficient they were in the improvement which might have been expected, from the time that they had been in the school of Christ. Instead of being in a capacity of teaching others, they were themselves in the lowest class of learners. Instead of making progress in the knowledge of divine truth, they had forgotten what they once possessed. Instead of growing to the stature of perfect men in Christ Jesus, they had shrunk again to the condition of babes, whose weak and tender organs must be nourished with the simplest food. Instead of expanding with a regular and solid growth, opening and enlarging their faculties, through disuse, had become so contracted as to refuse admittance to the plainest truths, much more to doctrines so deep and involved as those which he had begun to state. Such is the spirit of the apostle's reproof contained in the text: "For when for the time ye ought to be teachers, ye have need that one teach you again which be the first principles of the oracles of God; and are become such as have need of milk, and not of strong meat."

The case of the Hebrews, as represented in these words, is by no means singular. The neglect, at least the slow improvement of the means of knowledge, has not ceased to be a reproach in these latter days. Although blessed with the most abundant means of becoming wise unto salvation, how trifling are our attainments, how ill arranged are our religious ideas, how little established are we in the faith, and how ill qualified to give a good reason of the hope that is in us! Amidst all these infirmities, how disdainful are we often of common truths! how desirous to be gratified with novel speculations! how fantastical in our taste for religious instruction! I hope I may be allowed to offer some observations on these topics, without being supposed to aim at any peculiar censure, my sole design being to stir you up to further improvements, even to aspire to the wisdom of the perfect, and of those who, by reason of use, have their senses exercised to discern both good and evil.

The text naturally gives rise to the three following observations:

I. That all who are favored with the light of the gospel, shall be utterly inexcusable, if their improvements in knowledge do not bear a proportion to the time they have continued to enjoy it.

II. That those who are not careful to add to their knowledge, will be in great danger of losing what they have formerly acquired.

III. That without a proper acquaintance with the first plain principles of religion, men are unfit to receive doctrines of a higher and more speculative nature.

These observations I will confirm by some reasoning, and then make a practical application of the subject. The

I. observation was, That all who are favored with the light of the gospel, shall be utterly inexcusable, if their improvements in knowledge do not bear a proportion to the time they have continued to enjoy it.

This is one of those propositions which neither needs, nor will admit of much positive proof. There cannot be a plainer dictate of common sense, than what our Saviour hath taught us in these words: "Unto whomsoever much is given, of him the more shall be required." Every advantage bestowed on us by Providence is a trust, of which we must give an account hereafter. The advantages which tend to our improvement in heavenly wisdom, are a trust of the most important kind; and therefore the guilt of neglecting or abusing these must be of the deepest nature. But let us hear what may be said in opposition to this. Every objection that can be stated, may be resolved into one or other of these two—either that Christianity is not worthy of our study; or that, from its incomprehensible nature, it is impossible to make any considerable progress in the knowledge of it. To maintain the first of these, is in fact to deny the divinity of our holy religion; for certainly a revelation proceeding from infinite wisdom, with this merciful intention, to direct wandering sinners to everlasting and unspeakable felicity, must be allowed to deserve all the time and attention we can possibly bestow on it. As to the second objection, relating to the mysterious nature of Christianity, it must partly be admitted, but in no sense that will apply to the point in question. There are indeed doctrines taught in it far surpassing the extent of our understandings, which must be received with the obedience of faith, resting on this solid principle of reason, that they are revealed by him who cannot lie. But though there are deep and inscrutable mysteries in Christianity, it is far from being mysterious in all its parts. Its discoveries of the moral character of God, and of his gracious purposes toward the human race; its precepts, promises, and sanctions; and its general influence upon human conduct, present the noblest and most improving subject of contemplation, in which the faculties of man can be engaged. In these a well formed mind will taste a pleasure and satisfaction far beyond what all the treasures of science and philosophy can bestow. It is true, that even in this study, certain difficulties will at first be experienced; but shall it form an objection to the pursuit of heavenly wisdom, that it bears an analogy to every improvement of which the human mind is susceptible? Where is the valuable advantage that is to be acquired without patience, method, and application? Shall we expect to become masters of religious truth, with less diligence and application than we bestow on the most trifling science, or the meanest mechanic art? I mean not that it is either necessary or possible for every private Christian to attain a thorough knowledge of theology. The leisure and the capacities of men are so different, that an equal progress in divine knowledge cannot be supposed in every individual. This much, however, may be reasonably required and expected, that persons soliciting the outward privileges of religion, should know the great truths to which these privileges refer—should be able to tell what benefit they expect from them—should be able to show some fruit of all the instructions they receive. Yet how often is even this moderate expectation disappointed? How many are there to be found in this land of gospel light, almost as ignorant of Jesus and his religion, as those who never heard his name? How deep must be their shame, how heavy their condemnation, when at last it shall appear in what manner their time has been employed? This will stop the mouths of all ignorant Christians, and expose their vain apologies, when their consciences, awakened by the dawn of an everlasting day, shall reproach them with the hours, days, and months, in which they fatigued themselves with vice and folly, instead of studying how to become wise unto salvation. The

II. observation from the text was, That those who are not careful to add to their knowledge, are in danger of losing what they have already acquired.

This was the very case of the Hebrews. They had not been at due pains to increase their knowledge, in consequence of which neglect, they were even decayed in their former attainments. "Ye are *become* such," says the apostle, "as have need of milk, and not of strong meat." He does not say, Ye *are* still in the condition of babes; but ye are returned or shrunk back again to that condition, thereby plainly intimating that there had been a time when the case was otherwise with them

And as this proposition is well founded in the text, so it is sufficiently supported both by reason and experience. Our own observation, if we have not been extremely inattentive, cannot fail to furnish us with instances similar to what is here recorded. The truth is, a comprehensive knowledge of the whole, in all its connections, is the only security for the distinct knowledge, or remembrance of any one part. Nothing is so difficult as to retain the rudiments of any science, unless we pursue them to their proper use, and discover their subserviency to the general scheme to which they belong.

Let a man be introduced to the view of a complete piece of machinery, without being acquainted with the general purpose it is intended to accomplish; let him survey every part of it with the most minute attention, and labor to imprint the idea of each as deeply as possible in his mind; yet if he fall short of comprehending the intention of the whole, all that he has seen will be equally useless to himself and to mankind. His observations, unconnected with any leading principle, will float without method or application in his mind; or if they have any effect, it will be only to make him rash and petulant in hazarding opinions on a subject which he imperfectly understands.

Our pursuit of religious knowledge, under the disadvantages of our present dark and degenerate state, may be compared to a person swimming against the current, who has no other way to maintain his advantage but by pressing forward. Our faculties, by disuse, contract a rust, a disability either for discerning or pursuing those things that are excellent. Hence the apostle says, at the 14th verse, "Strong meat is for those who, by reason of use, have their senses exercised to discern between good and evil;" thereby intimating, that the mind must be kept in constant exercise, otherwise we may lose the faculty of distinguishing between things the most widely different. But this is not all: A person who stops short in his pursuit of religious truth, plainly discovers that he has lost that relish which alone imprints it in deep and lasting characters on the mind. It is well known how slowly we imbibe, and how quickly we forget, those parts of learning which we study with reluctance. No man will be careful to preserve a matter about which he is become indifferent, especially if this cannot be done without much labor and attention. Accordingly, it is never supposed in Scripture, that we should remit our application to make farther progress, through a lazy satisfaction with our present attainments. No saint ever set such an example of indolent self-contentment. "I count all things but loss," said the apostle Paul, "for the excellency of the knowledge of Christ Jesus my Lord; for whom I have suffered the loss of all things, and do count them but dung that I may win Christ, and be found in him, not having mine own righteousness which is of the law, but that which is through the faith of Christ, the righteousness which is of God by faith; that I may know him, and the power of his resurrection, and the fellowship of his sufferings, being made conformable unto his death; if by any means I might attain unto the resurrection of the dead: not as though I had already attained, either were already perfect; but I follow after, if that I may apprehend that for which also I am apprehended of Christ Jesus. Brethren, I count not myself to have apprehended; but this one thing I do, forgetting those things which are behind, and reaching forth unto those things which are before, I press toward the mark, for the prize of the high calling of God in Christ Jesus." The

III. and last observation from the text was, That without a proper acquaintance with the plain principles of religion, men are utterly unfit for receiving doctrines of a higher and more speculative nature.

This is the precise argument of the text, and needs only to be mentioned to force our assent. It is saying nothing more strange, than that a person, in order to be able to read, must first know letters; a proposition so plain and obvious, that it would be ridiculous to attempt a formal proof of it. The operations of grace, as well as those of nature, are, for the most part, gradual. Miraculous gifts indeed have been enjoyed, and miraculous progress hath been made in divine knowledge, beyond what the common use of means could have produced; but these have been rare instances for special purposes in Providence, and are by no means to be expected in the common course of things.

If, therefore, we aspire to eminent knowledge in religion, we must begin by cultivating distinct apprehensions of its first principles. Nothing has been of more prejudice to Christianity, than the premature indigested reasonings of novices, about its more speculative doctrines, before they have been well established in its great and fundamental articles. Hence have arisen all those odious names with which particular sects have stigmatized one another, while, in contending for the name of disciples, they have thrown away that badge of charity by which the true disciples of Christ are most effectually distinguished.

Justly, then, does the apostle say, that strong meat belongeth only to them who, by reason of use, have their senses exercised to discern between good and evil. The metaphor is highly proper and significant; for as strong meat, administered to a weak stomach, contributes only to increase its infirmity; in like manner the more difficult doctrines of Christianity, meeting with weak presumptuous understandings, have no other effect than to swell the natural vanity of the heart, which afterwards vents itself in words and behavior, equally dishonorable to God and offensive to man.

Having thus endeavored to confirm the observations which naturally arise from the text, it remains only to make a practical application of the subject.

In this application, the hearers of the gospel seem to have the first and principal concern. Ye have enjoyed this advantage from your earliest years. For the time, ye might have been teachers of others. Let us suppose that ye had attended as punctually upon instruction in any other science, would you not be ashamed, after ten or twenty years, to own you were as ignorant as the first month, and much more ashamed to have it thought that you were contented to be so? Let me ask how you would tolerate such carelessness and insensibility in your children, whom you educate at a great expense for the purposes of this world? Yet how do the cases differ? Much indeed in one respect; for a man may be happy without human learning, but without the knowledge of religion, you must be miserable for ever, and so much the more miserable for the neglect of the opportunities which you have enjoyed. Let me beseech you to bring this home to your minds. In all other subjects, you desire to be well informed. You would not prostitute your time to a ceremonial attendance of any other kind, without some solid and useful object. You would not give up four hours in every week, merely to hear words, without intending to derive some instruction from them. "Take heed then how ye hear." Be assured we do not speak in vain. Our defects indeed are many: we do not preach nor live as we ought to do—may God pardon and amend us; but we dispense the ordinances of God; and his word, though dispensed by weak unskilful hands, shall not return void, but shall accomplish the thing whereunto he sent it: it shall either be the savor of life unto life, or death unto death to your souls.

Again, ye have heard that they who are not careful to add to their knowledge are in danger of losing what they had formerly acquired. Beware then of resting satisfied with your present attainments, but follow on to know the Lord. Be assiduous to improve the advantages ye possess, for growing in grace, and in the knowledge of our Lord and Saviour Jesus Christ, that ye may walk worthy of God unto all pleasing, being fruitful in every good work, and increasing in the knowledge of God—Strengthened with all might, according to his glorious power; continuing in the faith, grounded and settled, and not moved from the hope of the gospel which ye have heard.

Once more, Ye have heard that, without a proper acquaintance with the plain principles of religion, men are unfit to receive doctrines of a higher and more speculative nature. Expect not, then, that we should study your amusement at the expense of your edification. There are persons, perhaps, who expect us to discuss some nice points in casuistry, or to clear up some controverted points in divinity; in short, who would take it kindly, if, dropping the common topics which have been long and much worn in the service of religion, we provided some fresh ones always for their entertainment. This may be very proper in its season, and, so far as it is fit, a faithful minister of Christ will not be wanting to their expectation; for he has gathered nothing in all the stores of divine knowledge of which he is not willing that they should partake. But in common, this indulgence is entirely out of place. The plainest and most practical truths are first of all to be inculcated. Many more stand in need of these than of novelties in speculation; and even of those who call out for such, many make the demand with a very bad grace. They might be amused, perhaps, with a curious discussion; but what if their sense of divine things be dead? What if they need to have their minds stimulated, and their consciences alarmed with the terrors of God's word? When our Lord was asked by a curious inquirer, if there were few that should be saved? instead of answering directly to the question, he addressed the person with a practical exhortation, "Strive to enter in at the strait gate; for many, I say unto you, shall seek to enter in, and shall not be able." If any of a similar character should attend our assemblies, let them not think it strange if we imitate so high an example, by preferring to impart to them the plainest and simplest, because the most necessary truths; especially as it cannot be doubted that the apostle's reproof in the text is still applicable to many hearers of the gospel:—"For when for the time ye ought to be teachers, ye have need that one teach you again which be the first principles of the oracles of God; and are become such as have need of milk, and not of strong meat." *Amen.*

SERMON LXXII.

DIVINE AND HUMAN AGENCY.

2 Cor. vi. 1.—"We then, as workers together with him, beseech you also, that ye receive not the grace of God in vain."

Nothing can be conceived more encouraging to creatures, in our feeble and depraved situation, than those views of the Supreme Being disclosed by the apostle in the concluding part of the former chapter. There God is represented in the characters of condescension and grace, so perfectly suited to our necessitous and guilty condition, as must render him the object of our supreme love and unreserved confidence.

The first question that will always occur to an awakened sinner, hath been expressed by the prophet Micah in these words: "Wherewith shall I come before the Lord, and bow myself before the High God?" And the only answer to this question, which an unenlightened mind can suggest, hath also been expressed by the same prophet, in the form of another question: "Shall I come before him with burnt-offerings, with calves of a year old? Will the Lord be pleased with thousands of rams, or with ten thousand rivers of oil? Shall I give my first born for my transgression, the fruit of my body for the sin of my soul?" A conscience alarmed with a sense of guilt, naturally represents the Most High as clothed with terrible majesty, as a God of vengeance, a stern unrelenting creditor, demanding payment even to the uttermost farthing. And however the advocates for the light of nature may boast of their discoveries, it may be pronounced impossible for unassisted reason, proceeding on sound principles, to discover any means whereby guilty creatures can hope to satisfy the justice, or regain the friendship of their Maker. All our knowledge, with regard to this subject, must flow from revelation alone. The sanctions of justice may indeed be comprehended by human reason; but justice demands inexorably the punishment of transgressors. Justice admits no claim for the exercise of mercy. Nay, more, mercy does not even come within the strict conception of legal administration, but is an act of pure prerogative having no other measure than the will of the sovereign. "And who knoweth the mind of the Lord, or who hath been his counsellor?" None else but the only begotten Son, who is in the bosom of the Father, and hath declared him unto us: and this is the name whereby he hath made him known, *God is love.*

What the apostle says, (chapter v. verse 18.) has a stronger signification than is commonly attended to. "All things are of God." It not only imports, that all things owe their existence to God, and are the effects of his creating power; but farther, that all the motives to exercise that power are of himself likewise. He finds them in his own perfect nature; and every exertion of power, whether for producing being or happiness to any of his creatures, is the spontaneous act of his essential goodness and benignity. Why did God create a world? No other answer can be given to this question, but that it was his sovereign pleasure so to do. No other reason, but the same sovereign pleasure can be assigned for man's existence on earth, with all the honors conferred on him at his first creation. And now that man hath forfeited these honors, and incurred the penalty annexed to his disobedience, whither shall he resort to find an inducement for his Creator showing him mercy? Can rebellion, outrageous unprovoked rebellion, furnish a motive to pity? Can deformity and pollution present any attractions of love? No; it is manifest, that after all our researches, we must finally have recourse to what God himself said to Moses of old, "I will be gracious to whom I will be gracious, and will show mercy on whom I will show mercy." Upon this principle the apostle proceeds in the passage I have quoted: "All things are of God," saith he, "who hath reconciled us to himself by Jesus Christ, and hath given to us the ministry of reconciliation, to wit, that God was in Christ, reconciling the world unto himself, not imputing their trespasses unto them." He it was who graciously spared those rebels whom his righteous vengeance might have crushed; and who, instead of requiring the fruit of our body for the sin of our soul, withheld not his own Son as the ransom of our transgressions, but gave him up to the death for us, that we might live through him. Having thus by his infinite wisdom, and self-moving goodness, opened a way for extending mercy to offenders, consistent with the honor of his perfections, he proceeds to complete the gracious plan, by sending forth some of the apostate race, as ambassadors for Christ, to beseech sinners in his own name, and in Christ's stead, to be reconciled to God. Paul was one of these chosen instruments; and accordingly he styles himself, in the text, "a worker together with God," and in this character beseecheth the Corinthians, in the most earnest manner, "not to receive the grace of God in vain."

The same exhortation I now address to you, deeming it peculiarly seasonable, in the near view we have of celebrating that solemn ordinance of our religion, in which the grace of God appears in all its lustre and glory. It seems unnecessary to employ many words in explaining the exhortation, its meaning being so clearly ascertained by the connection in which it stands, as to be obvious to every intelligent reader. All that is needful to be observed, is, that we are to look for the true import of the grace of God, which the apostle beseecheth the Corinthians not to receive in vain, in that ministry or word of reconciliation, which he had already said was committed to himself, and to his brethren in the apostleship. This plainly appears to consist of two parts.

1*st*. The declaration of an important fact, "God was in Christ reconciling the world unto himself." And,

2*dly*, An exhortation founded on this fact, "We pray you in Christ's stead be ye reconciled to God." Hence it is evident, that receiving the grace of God imports neither more nor less than believing the fact, and complying with the exhortation; and consequently every thing short of this is receiving the grace of God in vain. Without any further explanation, therefore, I shall now proceed to press the exhortation, by the most powerful arguments that I am able to present to your minds.

Let me beseech you, then, not to receive the grace of God in vain, by the consideration of the misery and abject bondage of your condition, while you continue thus perverse and ungrateful. I will not enter into any speculative disquisition with regard to the pretensions of natural religion. Whether those who never heard of the grace of God revealed in the gospel may yet be saved, by the efficacy of an unknown atonement, is a question with which we have little concern. I speak at present to those whose fate has nothing to do with the determination of this question. What say the Scriptures of truth with respect to them? "He that believeth on the Son hath life." Ponder what follows, "he that believeth not the Son shall not see life, but the wrath of God abideth on him." How awful are these words! "God is angry with the wicked every day. He hath bent his bow and made it ready; he hath also prepared for him the instruments of death." And O how hopeless a warfare is that which you have undertaken! Is there any that ever hardened himself against God and prospered? Is there any stronghold or lurking place, where the enemies of his government may be safe? Go, try the whole creation round. Ascend to heaven, and he is there in the brightness of his majesty. Go down to the regions of darkness, and he is there in the severity of his justice. Take the wings of the morning, and fly to the uttermost parts of the sea, even there his boundless dominion extends; even there his right hand shall hold thee a prisoner to his vengeance. Go, ask protection from the highest angel, and he will tell you that one sin ruined myriads of his companions; and how then should he protect you from the penalty of multiplied transgressions? And if so exalted a being cannot help you, what can you hope from any other part of the creation? "Surely in vain is salvation looked for from the hills and from the mountains." There is no other deliverer than this Jesus whom we preach. He is the alone surety that can pay all our debt; and even he can profit us nothing, till we receive him into our hearts by faith. Till that happy moment, the weight of all our sins lies on ourselves: and nothing but the brittle thread of life suspends us from sinking for ever into the pit where there is no hope.

But the prospect of impending misery is not the only circumstance that characterizeth your unhappy condition. Present bondage, distracting and disgraceful bondage, is no less a just description of your state. The enemy of God and man rules in your hearts, and by his imperious commands, all your inclinations and actions are swayed. It is possible, indeed, that this shameful slavery may be unknown to yourselves. You may flatter yourselves with a supposed liberty, and even boast of your freedom from those restraints to which the religious part of mankind are subject. But be assured this is no proof that your shackles are not real and binding. The tyrant to whom you are subject rules by deceit still more than by force; and all his artifices are used to blind the eyes of his prisoners. Nay, it may be asserted with confidence, that if you have not felt your chains, if you have not been conscious of a struggle in getting free of them, your redemption is not yet begun; for violence there must be, and violence that cannot but be felt ere the usurper of your liberty be dethroned. Such then is your unhappy and disgraceful condition, while ye receive the grace of God in vain. And let me remind you, that this is no painting of mine. I have only declared what the oracles of truth have pronounced; and to their sentence you must submit, or take the bold step of calling God a liar. In the

2d place, Let me beseech you not to receive the grace of God in vain, by the consideration of the happiness of those who give it a full and cordial reception. Every one of this happy number is justified from the guilt of all his iniquities; and say, whether you have well weighed the value even of this lowest privilege of believers? I am aware that thoughtless transgressors can have no conception of its importance; in their mad and desperate folly, they even make a mock at sin, and deride the fears of the contrite and penitent. But go ask the pardoned sinner what he thinks of the benefit of forgiveness. Hear the grateful accents of one who spoke from deep and thorough experience: "Blessed is he whose transgression is forgiven, whose sin is covered; blessed is the man to whom the Lord imputeth not iniquity:—For day and night thine hand was heavy on me, so that my moisture is turned into the drought of summer. O Lord my God, I cried unto thee, and thou hast healed me. Thou hast brought up my soul from the grave; thou hast kept me alive, that I should not go down into the pit; thou hast put off my sackcloth, and girded me with gladness. Therefore shall every one that is godly pray unto thee, in a time when thou mayest be found; and I will give thanks unto thee,

O Lord my God, for ever and ever." But this forgiveness, precious and invaluable as it is, is only the introductory blessing bestowed on those who give the grace of God a full and cordial reception. Being justified by faith, they have peace with God, and peace with their own conscience. The cause of enmity being removed, they are restored to friendship with their Maker. God is not ashamed to be called their Father, nor reluctant to bestow on them all the blessings and honors that pertain to his children. Hence the rapturous gratitude of the apostle John, too big for expression, and yet, by the very want of expression, more forcible than the most descriptive eloquence. "Beloved, now are we the sons of God; and it doth not yet appear what we shall be, but we know that when he shall appear we shall be like him, for we shall see him as he is." The meanest individual, nay, the most abandoned sinner that now hears me, may yet become an heir of God, and a joint heir with Christ, a king and priest unto God, and a pillar in the heavenly temple, never to be removed. Let your desires soar to the greatest height, stretch your imaginations to the utmost—yet the liberality of God will be still more unbounded. Much he hath promised to bestow on his people, and many similitudes he hath condescended to use, that their slow minds might be assisted in conceiving his bounty; but nowhere hath he said, this is all your portion, or beyond this no more is to be expected. No, his bounty will be an everlasting fountain, and benefits for ever shall nourish eternal gratitude in the bosoms of the redeemed. "For he that spared not his own Son, but gave him up to the death for us all, how shall he not with him also freely give us all things." Peruse the valedictory discourse of our Lord to his disciples, and learn from it what you may lawfully expect from a reconciled Father. All your prayers shall be heard. The Comforter, even the Holy Ghost, shall come into your hearts, and lead you into the knowledge of all truth. Ye shall be made fruitful in the works of righteousness. God himself shall make his abode with you. Ye shall be kept from the evil of the world while in it, and at last ye shall be where your exalted Redeemer is, to behold his glory, and to partake of his bliss.

And shall these considerations be still insufficient to determine your choice? O wonder not at the unbelieving Jews, who persecuted and slew the Lord of life. Let not your indignant sentiments rise at their injustice and cruelty. Their sin and folly were light compared with yours, who now reject his counsel and despise his grace. Their scorn was excited by his mean appearance, and they hid their faces from him, because disguised in the form of a servant. But I will tell you a thing more horrible and astonishing. The Son of God, clothed in all the mild glory of an exalted Saviour, and stretching forth his hands to bestow all the blessings purchased with his blood, is still despised and rejected. And thou, O impenitent sinner, art the man guilty of this contempt and ingratitude; yet, blessed be God, though you may justly be charged with this almost incredible guilt, I am still warranted to beseech you, in the

3*d* and *last* place, Not to receive the grace of God in vain, by the consideration of the riches of his long-suffering and forbearance. Long as his mercy has been insulted, it is still in your offer. I need not appeal to particular passages of Scripture to confirm this comfortable truth. It appears conspicuously through the whole tenor of revelation, every page of which contains the language of love and compassion to sinners. Review the history of Jesus, and after you have seen what he hath already done for our sakes, try if you can possibly question his goodwill. Did he condescend to be clothed with our mortal flesh, and will he disdain the entertainment of an affectionate and grateful heart? Did he bleed and die on the cross for our sins, and will he fail to perfect his work in our salvation? It was a powerful argument which the apostle Paul employed on a certain occasion with Agrippa, "Believest thou the Prophets?" So say I to you, Do you believe the history of your Saviour, as recorded by four evangelists? How do you read them? What was it that affected him with grief? was it not the hardness of men's hearts? What was it that drew tears from his compassionate eyes? was it not the view of

Jerusalem, that impenitent city, which knew not, or regarded not, the day of its merciful visitation? Nay, what was the errand on which he solemnly declared himself to be come into the world? was it not to "seek and to save them who were lost?" and O will ye counteract by your obstinate folly, all these gracious intentions on his part? Will ye persist in rejecting his grace, until ye have extorted vengeance and indignation from him whose heart is love? How dreadful, in that case, must your doom be! As ye love your souls, be warned in time against this desperate, this ruinous madness. The gracious call still resounds in your ears, "To-day, if ye will hear his voice, harden not your hearts." And we, as ambassadors, are still charged to "beseech you, in Christ's stead, be ye reconciled to God."

And now let me ask, what impression these plain and obvious remonstrances have made on your minds? What may be their effect, I cannot foretell. This I know, that could I hope to succeed better, I would with pleasure come down, and address each of you, even on my bended knees, obtesting you by every solemn, every tender argument, to fly from the wrath to come. I easily foresee the time when the remembrance of this offered grace shall either fill you with joy unutterable, or with fruitless and everlasting anguish. For whatever thoughtless sinners may imagine, no word of God shall ever return to him void, but shall accomplish the purpose for which he sends it. "We are a sweet savor to God," saith the apostle Paul, "in you that believe, and in you that perish; to the one we are the savor of life unto life, and to the other of death unto death." I am aware that pleadings of this kind are sometimes treated with ridicule; but the time is at hand when the scoffer shall be made sober. The view of death may do it—the day of judgment certainly will.

Now then is the accepted time. Now you may obtain an interest in this Saviour; and if you apply to him, as sure as God liveth, you shall find mercy. Thus far I can go, but one step farther I cannot proceed upon sure ground. I cannot promise you on any future time. If you reject the counsel of God now, I cannot assure even the youngest of you of another opportunity. Before to-morrow your doom may be fixed unalterably. May God enable you to profit by these instructions, and to his name be praise. *Amen.*

SERMON LXXIII.

THE IMPOSSIBILITY.

1 John ii. 15.—"Love not the world, neither the things that are in the world: If any man love the world, the love of the Father is not in him."

From these words I propose, by divine assistance,

I. To describe that excessive or sinful love of the world, from which the apostle here dissuades us.

II. To inquire wherein the malignity of this sin consists.

III. To lay before you a few symptoms of a worldly mind, and examine some of the apologies upon which men flatter themselves with being free of it. And,

IV. To enforce the exhortation, and give some directions how to get this undue affection towards earthly things mortified and subdued.

I. It will readily occur to you, that the exhortation is to be understood under certain restrictions. The place of his works which God has appointed us to inhabit, cannot in itself be supposed an object deserving our aversion or dislike. This would be to impeach the goodness of our Creator, and to tax his handiwork with imperfection. We may lawfully love the world, as it is the workmanship of God, and the mirror in which we behold the perfections of the invisible Creator. Creation is a large instructive volume, and the sense of every line is God. The proper use of all the creatures is to lead us upwards to him that made them, and to kindle in our souls the warmest gratitude to that unwearied Benefactor, who has provided so liberally for our comfort and happiness. They are naturally the means of supporting our bodies while we are employed in those duties which we owe to God, and they also enable us to supply the wants of others, to lessen the miseries, and to heighten the lawful joys of our fellow-creatures. On all these accounts we may and ought to value them as real blessings, which may be improved to the most important purposes.

But our love of the world becomes excessive and sinful, when we give it that room in our hearts which is only due to God; when it is desired for its own sake, as a sufficient portion independent of his favor and friendship. If the world will keep its due place, it may be valued and esteemed in that place; but if it usurp an higher station, and promise more than it is able to give, it must be rejected, as a deceiver, with abhorrence and contempt. When we seek after earthly things, merely that our inordinate desires may be gratified, that the pride of our hearts may be cherished, or our ambition attain its object; when we are not contented with our daily bread, and that portion of the good things of life which is sufficient to sustain us during our pilgrimage to a better country—then is our love of the world undue and excessive; and the more we desire it under such views, the worse, the more corrupted and estranged from the love of God, will our hearts become. This leads me,

II. To inquire wherein the malignity of this sin consists. This will be most effectually illustrated by considering how deeply it taints the whole character and principles of action.

There are sins which only engage particular faculties of our nature in their service. Thus the love of pleasure is chiefly seated in the senses and the imagination. While these are strongly agitated by a particular enticement, conscience may indeed be totally overpowered for a season, and the person be carried along by an headstrong irresistible impulse: But the moral faculties have afterwards leisure to resume their influence; reason is again at liberty to represent the pernicious consequences of transgression; and experience is always at hand, to convince the sinner how inconvenient and dangerous his forbidden pleasures are.

But no such checks are ready to occur to the man in whom the love of the world predominates. His sin is of deliberate choice, and engages the whole man in pursuit of its own ends. It is not an error about the means, it is not seeking a right end in a mistaken way; but it is pursuing a false and pernicious end, with care, anxiety, and self-approbation. Hence it is called in Scripture IDOLATRY, not from any resemblance it has to the outward act of falling down before stocks or stones, but because it entirely displaces our affections from their proper object, and leads them to the preference of an unjust and delusive rival. Hence it is asserted, by the apostle James, that "the friendship of the world is enmity to God." It is not merely a want of affection to our Maker, which more or less characterizes every sin; but it is an absolute opposition and hatred to him, so that, in the language of the text, "if any man love the world, the love of the Father is not in him."

From these considerations it is evident, that this sin stands as it were at the most remote distance from repentance. It overspreads the mind so entirely, as to leave in it no sound principle to withstand the progress of complete alienation from God. It resembles those diseases which do not attack one part of the body only, but which invade the whole constitution; and resembles such diseases in another respect also, that the person is seldom convinced of their reality, until the approach of a fatal termination renders it impossible for him longer to deceive himself.

This reasoning is confirmed by experience. No fault in the mind is in fact so rarely cured as a worldly disposition. Age and experience, which often bring a remedy with them for other follies, only confirm and increase the habits of an earthly mind. Even on the brink of the grave, when every other passion and desire has been extinguished, it has been known to occupy the departing spirit with an anxiety little, if it all inferior, to that which animated its most active pursuits.

Such is the peculiar malignity and dangerous nature of this sin. But as few will defend this criminal disposition directly, and as many who are enslaved by it are ready enough to join in generally condemning it, I proceed,

III. To lay before you a few symptoms of a worldly mind, and to examine some of the apologies upon which men flatter themselves with being free of it.

1*st*, then, We love the world plainly to excess, when we use any unlawful means to obtain its advantages. This is a mark which cannot well be controverted; and yet how many will it involve in the charge of a worldly mind! Prove yourselves, then, by this characteristic. Would any prospect of gain tempt you to cheat or dissemble? Will your consciences allow you to go beyond or defraud your neighbor, providing you can do it in a way so secret as to defy human discovery? Does it seem a light matter to you, to take advantage of the simplicity or ignorance of others in the course of business? If so, your minds are indeed deeply corrupted; and it is not regard to God or his law, but to your own credit and safety, which restrains you from the most flagrant acts of injustice. Such persons may assure themselves, without further examination, that the love of the Father is not in them, and that their hearts are wholly alienated from God: For, as the apostle to the Romans argues, "Know ye not, that to whom ye yield yourselves servants to obey, his servants ye are to whom ye obey, whether of sin unto death, or of obedience unto righteousness." And "no man can serve two masters; for either he will hate the one and love the other, or else he will hold to the one and despise the other; ye cannot serve God and Mammon."

2*dly*. We love the world to excess, when in the enjoyment of its good things we are ready to say, with the rich man represented in our Lord's parable, "Soul, take thine ease, thou hast goods laid up for many years, eat, drink, and be merry." Too much complacency, in what we possess, is no less an evidence of a worldly mind than an excessive desire of more. Examine yourselves, then, with regard to the source whence you derive your pleasures—from heaven or from earth—from the abundance of corn and wine, and oil, or from the light of God's reconciled countenance. Can you surrender yourselves to the relish of earthly enjoyments without any acknowledgment of him who bestows them? When riches increase, do you yield yourselves to the satisfactions arising from them, without considering the true state of your souls, whether they be growing in the favor of God, and in meetness for the heavenly inheritance? If so, the world has deceived you, and God has little room in your affections.

3*dly*. The world predominates in your hearts, when it engrosses the principal train of our thoughts; when it is the last idea that possesseth us when we lie down, and the first when we arise; when it distracts us in our attendance on the duties of religion, interrupts our devotion in prayer, diverts our attention in hearing, and fetters our minds in meditation. I mean not to assert, that every degree of influence which it has in these respects betrays its absolute ascendency over the mind; for who then could free himself of this charge? But when these worldly thoughts engross the mind by its own consent, when they make us grudge the time bestowed on religion, and eager to resume our earthly occupations, as soon as we have lulled our consciences with an unmeaning attendance on its ordinances—when, like the Jews of old, we say of the Sabbath, "what weariness! when will it be over, that we may sell corn?" This is not only a preferring of the world to God, but in reality a solemn mockery of him, not less provoking than open profanity itself. The

4*th* and *last* mark of a worldly mind which I shall mention, is unmercifulness to the poor. Those who have a large measure of temporal goods bestowed on them, ought certainly, in proportion to their abundance, contribute to the necessities of their fellow creatures.

This is evidently the design of Providence in permitting, or rather appointing, such extreme diversities of condition in the world. But too many of the opulent seem to think no such duty required of them. They flatter themselves that they do all that is incumbent on them in this respect, if, by the plenty of their tables the splendor of their dwellings, the sumptuousness of their equipage, and other articles of their luxury, they find employment for the poor by providing for their consumption. This, indeed, is an eventual benefit to society, but is far from absolving them from the obligation they owe to it, much less does it acquit them of their duty to him who favored them with such distinguished blessings: For what mark of gratitude to God is it, that we consume his bounty upon our own pleasures, although, in so doing, we cannot avoid distributing a part of it to our fellow creatures?

Such persons, whatever they may think of themselves, how remote soever they may think a worldly character from being applicable to them, are in fact deeply chargeable with it. Perhaps they even do give a part of their superfluity for the relief of their brethren, and estimating that by its proportion to what others give, and not to the extent of their own means, think themselves uncommonly bountiful. But this is a gross deception, and will be found so in the day when every false pretence shall be detected before the judgment-seat of Christ. Then shall they be found among those who loved the world, and in whose hearts the love of the Father had no place.

These symptoms, if properly attended to, may be of considerable use towards discovering the true state of your characters in this respect. But as the heart is deceitful, and as we are extremely prone to flatter ourselves that we are free of this criminal disposition, it may be proper to endeavor, before closing this head of discourse, to detect some of those false apologies upon which men flatter themselves that they are not chargeable with it.

One concludes thus in his own favor, because he is poor, and necessity obliges him to work for his daily bread. How (says he) should I be suspected of a criminal love to the world, when I possess so little of it, and can, by all my labor, procure so few of its advantages? But this is a very deceitful ground of reasoning. He who lacks riches, may love them as well as he who possesses them: And therefore if you be discontented with your state; if you envy those above you; if, in your habits of thought, you consider wealth and happiness as inseparable; and if your diligence to prepare for another world be not superior to your industry in endeavoring to obtain a share of this: the *world* is still your *idol*, "and the love of the Father is not in you."

Another flatters himself that he has no undue attachment to the world, because he does not project for himself any great or extensive acquisitions in it; very small matters would satisfy him, and a moderate competence is all that he desires. But if your hearts are more set on these supposed moderate matters than on the heavenly inheritance, you are still slaves to the world; and the more mean and inexcusable you are that your object is so trifling and inconsiderable.

Besides, this is a very indecisive mode of reasoning. He that engages to seek only a *competence*, takes on himself a very easy engagement, because he binds himself only to a condition which is to be ascertained by his own opinion. The most covetous man on earth may make the same profession, provided you leave him to be the judge of what that competency amounts to. Look above you to the superior ranks of society, and see whether their extensive possessions extinguish their desires for more. Is not the reverse the fact? The richest are often in as great necessity as the most indigent—as often, at least (and it is not seldom) as the imaginary wants created by luxury exceed their means of gratifying them. The decisive inquiry is not how much you desire, but for what ends you desire it.

A third conceives a favorable opinion of himself, because he uses no unlawful means to rise in the world. Now this is in so far good, and would to God we could all say as much for ourselves. But even this is not decisive in the point; for a man may love the world inordinately, who would neither steal nor rob, nor dissemble, in order to enrich himself. The fact is, that those who have a just and steady sense of their interest, find that these are by no means the best ways of advancing it.

A good character is so necessary to carrying on worldly business of any kind with success, that a *wise man in his generation* will be fair and honest in his dealings, from mere regard to his own advantage. But with all this prudential regard, coinciding with seeming virtue, his affections may be entirely placed on the world to the exclusion of things spiritual and everlasting; which is the very character described and condemned in the text.

But, saith a fourth, it is impossible that I should love the world to excess, for it is the very vice which I principally hate and condemn in others. But, alas! so do many thousands who are themselves abject slaves to the world, to the conviction of every person but themselves. It would indeed be utterly astonishing to observe, how keenly worldly men inveigh against the same dispositions in others, if this account of the appearance did not offer itself, viz., that the more they are rivals in this love, the more mutual jealousy and resentment must arise in their minds; or, to speak without any figure, the more covetous their neighbors are, the more they stand in the way to prevent their obtaining the emoluments they desire for themselves.

I will mention but one more pretence by which men deceive themselves in the respect we are considering, and that is the resolution of leaving their substance to charitable purposes when they die. But ah! what an absurd delusion is this, to offer their worldly possessions to God after they have abused them as they could, and can now retain them no longer. But upon this point I need not dwell longer; for although an abuse very common in former times, it is one with which the present age is not peculiarly chargeable. "Be not deceived then, God is not mocked. Whatsoever a man soweth, that shall he also reap. He that soweth to the flesh, shall of the flesh reap corruption; but he that soweth to the Spirit, shall of the Spirit reap life everlasting." *Amen.*

SERMON LXXIV.

THE IMPOSSIBILITY.

1 John ii. 15.—"Love not the world, neither the things that are in the world; if any man love the world, the love of the Father is not in him."

I have already described that excessive love of the world, from which the apostle here dissuades us, and represented to you the greatness and malignity of this sin. I also laid before you some symptoms of an earthly mind, and endeavored to detect the falsehood of those pretences, by which too many impose on their consciences, and flatter themselves that their love of the world is no greater than it ought to be. I now proceed to enforce the exhortation, and to offer a few directions for the help of those who are desirous of having their affections weaned from the world, that they may rise upwards to spiritual things. Consider then,

I. That this undue attachment to the world is absolutely inconsistent with the love of God. This is the apostle's argument in the text: "If any man love the world, the love of the Father is not in him." "No man," said our blessed Lord, "can serve two masters; for either he will hate the one and love the other, or else he will hold to the one and despise the other. Ye cannot serve God and Mammon." Hence covetous men are styled idolaters. They reject the true God, and substitute an idol in his room; they put the creature in place of the Creator, and make the gifts of his bounty, which should knit their hearts to him, the occasions of alienating their affections from him.

I am aware that worldly men are very unwilling to acknowledge this charge, and would be highly offended should any accuse them directly of hating the God that made them. There is something so monstrous and shocking in the idea of hatred and enmity against God, that it is scarcely to be supposed any thinking man can reconcile himself to it. But be assured this charge, however odious it may appear, will be made good against every worldly man at last; and, therefore, as you would avoid the shame of standing before the judgment-seat in such a character, labor to get your affections divorced from earthly things, and henceforth let God be supreme in your hearts. Consider,

II. That an immoderate love of the world is not less foolish than sinful. "All that is in the world," saith the apostle, in the verse following the text, "the lust of the flesh, the lust of the eye, and the pride of life, is not of the Father, but of the world. And the world passeth away, and the lust thereof." Many of its enjoyments are imaginary as well as transient. The pleasure and happiness we expect from them have no foundation in the nature of things, but depend entirely on a diseased corrupt fancy. If we look back to the history of mankind in all ages, the discontented and miserable will be as often found among the prosperous and affluent as among the poor and depressed conditions of life. Those situations which appear so desirable as objects of expectation, are often in experience found marvellously barren of real happiness. Whence does this arise? Is it not from the wise appointment of God, that nothing here below should satisfy the desires of an immortal creature? Vanity is, for this reason, engraved in deep and legible characters on all things below the sun; and he that pursues the good things of this world as his only portion, will inevitably find that the most fortunate experience of life will never amount to a solid happiness, in which the heart of man can find rest and satisfaction. "He that loveth silver shall not be satisfied with silver, nor he that loveth abundance with increase." Therefore said our Lord to the multitude, "Take heed, and beware of covetousness, for a man's life consisteth not in the abundance of the things which he possesseth."

Nature is easily satisfied; but when men create for themselves imaginary wants, they only provide an inexhaustible stock of solicitude and disappointment. The craving appetite will still be crying, Give, give; and in the fulness of their sufficiency they will be in want. What has the world ever done for its most devoted servants, that should make you desire it so greedily? Solomon went as far as any man ever did, both in the acquisition and enjoyment of earthly things, and in the conclusion passed this sentence on the review of all his experience, "Vanity of vanities, saith the Preacher, vanity of vanities; all is vanity and vexation of spirit." And have you discovered an art of extracting comfort from the creatures beyond what the wisest of men was able to do? What do you seriously expect from the world? Will it prevent or remove sickness? Will it ward off the stroke of death? or will it even administer any consolation to you at that trying season? Should one come to you on your death-bed, when your spirits are languishing, your hearts failing, and your bodies possessed with racking pain, and begin to console you by representing your vast acquisitions of wealth, would his words be reviving? Will it afford you any joy to contemplate those possessions, from which you are presently to be divorced for ever? You cannot think so. You must be sensible, that all things below the sun will prove miserable comforters in dying moments, and that the favor of God will then appear infinitely more desirable than ten thousand worlds. What infatuation then is it to set your hearts supremely on that which you know will appear most contemptible at last? Consider,

III. That as the love of the world to excess is sinful and foolish, so it is also pernicious and fatal. "They that will be rich," saith the apostle to Timothy, "fall into temptation, and a snare, and into many foolish and hurtful lusts, which drown men in destruction and perdition; for the love of money is the root of all evil."

It were an endless task to enumerate all the dismal effects of this sordid disposition. "From whence come wars and fightings?" saith the apostle James; "Come they not hence, even of your lusts which war in your members? Ye lust and have not; ye kill and desire to have, and cannot obtain." It is this which engenders strife and contention, and almost every evil work. It destroys the tranquillity of the person possessed by it; it incites him to trespass on the rights and enjoyments of others; and on both these accounts is often punished with remarkable judgments, even in the present life. How awful is that curse pronounced by the prophet Habakkuk! "Woe to him that coveteth an evil covetousness to his house, that he may set his nest on high, that he may be delivered from the power of evil. Thou hast consulted shame to thyself, and hast sinned against thy soul; for the stone shall cry out of the wall, and the beam out of the timber shall answer it." How dismal was the fate of Ananias and Sapphira! How horrible the end of Judas Iscariot! In both these instances the saying of the wise man, (Prov. i. 19.) was remarkably verified, "the greediness of gain taketh away the life of the owners thereof." But although they should escape in this world, yet they shall not escape the damnation of hell. Then shall they find that riches will not profit them in the day of God's wrath.

There is a striking passage to this purpose, (James v. 1.) "Go to now, ye rich men, weep and howl for your miseries that shall come upon you. Your riches are corrupted, and your garments are motheaten; your gold and silver is cankered, and the rust of them shall be a witness against you, and shall eat your flesh as it were fire. Ye have heaped treasures together for the last day." Such is the present wretchedness and the miserable portion at last of an earthly mind. Whereas,

IV. An heart disengaged from this excessive love of the world, would not only prevent all this misery, but likewise, give us the true relish of life, and make death itself easy and comfortable. Take away earthly things from a worldly man, and you take away his all; but the same things withdrawn from an heavenly minded Christian, do not annihilate his fund of happiness. When the streams of created comforts fail, he resorts to the fountain; when the creatures forsake him, he can rejoice in the Creator, and joy in the God of his salvation. The good things he possesseth have a peculiar relish, which earthly minds are incapable of feeling. He sees the bounty of God in every gift, and the faithfulness of his covenant in every comfort he enjoys. He, therefore, eats his bread with joy, and drinks his wine with a merry heart; and while he thus sits cheerfully at the feast which Providence has set before him, he fears not the intrusion of any unwelcome messenger to interrupt his peace. He is not afraid of evil tidings, his heart is fixed, trusting in the Lord. Prepared for all the vicissitudes of life, adversity can take nothing from him, which, in the discipline of his own mind, he has not resigned already. Nay, death itself, that presentiment so dreadful to the worldly mind, is to him, in a great measure, divested of its terrors: For he knows, "that if this earthly house of his tabernacle were dissolved, he has a building of God, an house not made with hands, eternal in the heavens."

Having thus endeavored to enforce the exhortation in the text, it only remains that I offer a few directions for the help of those who are desirous to have their affections weaned from the world, that they may rise upwards to spiritual things.

1*st.* Let us beware of receiving too flattering a picture of the world into our minds, or of expecting more from it than it is able to bestow. Let us correct our florid and gaudy expectations, and make a sober estimate of its real amount. For this purpose go sometimes to the house of mourning, rather than to the house of feasting. Behold there the untimely hand of death, taking away the desire of the eyes with a stroke, blasting the most virtuous joys of humanity, tearing asunder the dearest connections, demolishing the painted tapestry, and hanging up in its place the solemn sable and escutcheon.

Such objects, viewed with seriousness and attention, are far more profitable than the gilded scenes of mirth and gayety; they check that wantonness which is the growth of ease and prosperity, and lead us to reflect that this world is not our home, but a foreign land, in which our vexations and disappointments are designed to turn our views towards that higher and better state which we are destined to inherit.

2*dly.* Be very suspicious of a prosperous state, and fear the world more when it smiles than when it frowns. It is difficult to possess much of it, without loving it to excess. The great enemy of our souls is well aware of this, and therefore would give all his servants liberal portions in this world, were it in his power. This was his last effort in the train of temptations which he addressed to our Lord in the wilderness, and when this failed he immediately departed from him.

There is not a more salutary maxim in religious concerns, than always to suspect danger where we feel much delight. If our situation be such as entirely pleases our natural desires, it is high time to look well to the soul, and to set a strict guard on our heart, lest, by these pleasing enjoyments, they should be betrayed and alienated from God, who alone has a right to them.

3*dly.* Make a wise improvement of the afflictions with which you may at any time be visited. Beware of repining under them, or thinking them greater evils than they really are; but rather believe that they are graciously sent for the benefit of your souls, to mortify your inordinate affections to the present world. "Whom the Lord loveth he chasteneth."—Nay, the seasonable visitation of temporal calamities, is included in the tenor of that everlasting covenant, which is well ordered in all things and sure. Does the world then frown on you? Are you afflicted with poverty, sickness, pain, and reproach? Do relations grieve you? Do friends prove unfaithful? or are you bereaved of them by death? Neglect not so fair an opportunity of instruction, when you have experience itself to disgrace the pretensions of the world, and your very flesh is made to feel that it is both vain and vexatious. Remember that God has sent these rough messengers to bring you home to himself. Gratefully, then, comply with his call, and choose him for your portion, leaving the world to those who have no better sources of satisfaction.

4thly. Look forward to eternity, and take a serious view of that world, wherein you must dwell for ever, after you have spent a few more days and nights in this. Remember that heaven or hell must be your everlasting abode; and must it not be of the last importance to know which of these different states shall be your lot? Can that man spend his time and strength in the pursuit of trifles, who believes and who considers that he is hastening to appear before God in judgment, when his final state shall be allotted according to his present behavior? Must not the foresight of this awful trial disengage his mind from the world, and cure his anxiety about earthly things, by producing in him an anxiety about matters of infinitely greater consequence? "Let your moderation be known unto all men," saith the apostle; "THE LORD IS AT HAND." A more powerful argument could not be used. An habitual impression of this awful truth, that the Lord is at hand, that he standeth before the door, would effectually cure our feverish desires after earthly things, and awaken us to a deep concern about the interests of our precious and immortal souls.

Finally, let us be wise in time, and give the supreme affections of our hearts to God, who alone is worthy of them; imploring, for this purpose, the aid of his Holy Spirit, to enable us to comply with his own gracious expostulation, (Isa. lv. 2.) "Wherefore do ye spend money for that which is not bread, and your labor for that which satisfieth not? hearken diligently unto me, and eat ye that which is good, and let your soul delight itself in fatness. Incline your ear, and come unto me; hear, and your souls shall live; and I will make with you an everlasting covenant, even the sure mercies of David." *Amen.*

SERMONS

AND

EXPOSITORY LECTURES.

BY THE LATE

REV. JOHN LOGAN, F.R.S.,

OF EDINBURGH, SCOTLAND.

WITH AN INTRODUCTION, BY REV. D. D. WHEDON, D.D.

EDITED BY

"THE MINISTER'S LIBRARY ASSOCIATION."

SIXTH EDITION.

NEW YORK:

D. APPLETON AND COMPANY, 346 & 348 BROADWAY.

M.DCCC.LV.

CONTENTS.

INTRODUCTION.

By REV. D. D. WHEDON, D. D.

It is now about three quarters of a century since the following discourses were delivered by their eloquent and accomplished author in the ordinary routine of pulpit duty in one of the provincial towns of Scotland. Though he won thereby a deserved celebrity with a wide circle of friends and admirers, and enjoyed the personal intimacy of some of the most distinguished men of his native country, yet his name has not obtained a conspicuous place in the literary world; and even these sermons, on which his claim upon our notice principally depends, have been known and appreciated mainly by the comparatively few, even of professional readers, whose taste leads them into an extended perusal of pulpit literature. An American edition, published some fifty years ago, having long since been out of print, it is believed that a republication will be acceptable to our American public. We venture to present them not only as a choice model for the aspirant for professional excellence, but as a valuable addition to our religious literature, well calculated to exert a purifying influence upon the public mind, and fully entitled to take an honorable and permanent position in our libraries, as *a standard* SACRED CLASSIC.

JOHN LOGAN was born in the parish of Fulla, county of Mid-Lothian, in the year 1748. His parents belonged to that class of dissenters, who call themselves Burgher Seceders; and were distinguished for rectitude, benevolence and piety. As John exhibited, in addition to these qualities, early proofs of superior genius, his gratified parents fostered his love of learning, and resolved to educate him to the sacred profession. Having prepared at the parochial school, he entered the University of Edinburgh, where he formed a friendship with Dr. Robertson, which continued through life. The congeniality of genius cemented a friendship also between Logan and Michael Bruce, a young poet, whom premature death deprived of his fame. Logan paid to the deceased young poet the tribute of publishing his poems in a small volume, in which he inserted also some poems of his own, leaving the respective shares of the two a matter of doubt among the friends of both.

Having completed his theological course, and entered the ministry, Logan soon became celebrated for his eloquence, and received a unanimous call from the kirk-session, and incorporations of South Leith, to become one of the ministers of that church and parish ; and he was accordingly ordained in the year 1773. He discharged the duties of his ministerial office with steadiness and fidelity. His talents won the admiration and friendship of such men as Robertson and Blair. It was during his ministry at this place that the sermons forming the collection of this volume were preached.

The elegant taste and fervid genius of Logan looked with longing eyes to the attractive fields of general literature, poetry and belles-lettres. Having delivered, with much success, a course of Lectures on the Philosophy of History, his friends proposed him for that chair in the University, but without success, as that Professorship seems by custom to have been appropriated by the legal profession. He subsequently published the substance of his Lectures. He published at different times poems lyric, elegiac and dramatic. The same genius which shines so resplendently in his sermons, sheds its clear and beautiful light through his poems, but not with the same degree of splendor. An imagination pure and mild rather than intense ; a taste refined and perfect ; a sensibility alive to the gentler aspects of nature pervade his poems. Something of the excessive sensitiveness of the poet, too, we are sorry to say, resided in the personal character of Logan. The want of the full tide of literary success deeply impressed him with feelings of disappointment. Melancholy brooded over his spirit. Dissatisfaction arose between his parishioners and their pastor ; in anguish of heart he resigned the ministry, and devoted his few remaining days exclusively to literary pursuits. In the bloom of his years his health declined, and he closed his life December 25th, 1788. The tears of friends warmly attached to his memory mingled with the regrets of those from whom he had suffered, over the grave of the lamented Logan.

Two years after his death, in 1790, a volume of his sermons was given to the public under the inspection of Drs. Robertson, Blair & Hardy. A second volume followed in the following year. Both volumes attained a fourth edition in 1800. Several of his literary writings, we believe, have never been published. In regard to his secular productions, posterity will not change the verdict of his contemporaries. A measure of merit, a degree of beauty, a gentle attractivenesss, will be readily conceded them ; but amid the crowd of aspirants for the attention of the world, that mighty arbiter has no time to spend on secondary merit. Less and less are growing the chances of *respectable* poets. To a choice quire of superlative genuises alone, does a glutted and fastidious Public daily incline to confine its ear. For the gentle spirit of our friend as a poet then there is no hope. But why not be satisfied with the clustering honors that gather and must gather around the pulpit orator? Did he undervalue—we cannot believe it—or did he not anticipate, that while all his literary efforts would be abandoned to perish, the world would never let those sermons die? We shall not condemn him, that his sympathizing breast sighed at the thought of being forgotten by his fellow men; for even scripture promises it as a blessing to the just to be *held in everlasting remembrance.* But we seem to ourselves to wish that the despondencies that withered his life could have been cheered away with the presentiment, that though the memorials of himself which he wished to perpetuate, should perish, there were other memorials in which he less trusted, which should stand the test of time. Or rather that his soul might have listened to the voice of the divine spirit, teaching him wherein his great strength lay, and guiding him back to his lofty post of duty and honor, to put on a mightier manhood still, and raise still nobler monuments in the field of pulpit literature.

For our own part, we think a great sermon to be quite as noble an intellectual performance as a great poem. It is as great a genius that produces it. There are thousands we know to whom the name of *sermon* is a synonim with *tedium.* And as many thousands to whom poetry is just what the beauty of the starry firmament is to a herd of chewing kine—*nothing.* But a sermon just as truly as a poem, to gain our suffrage must not be *respectable.* And we aver it costs just as much genius to lift a sermon out of the *respectable* as it does a poem. We suppose the number of sermons delivered is immensely greater than that of poems written; and the immense mass of these are *respectable.* They must be so, and can afford to be so, for they are produced for plain, practical, homely use. And this utility is, in the more complimentary and the less complimentary sense of the term, *respectable.* And the very fact that of the immense number of sermons printed, so few survive their generation, fully proves that he who raises a sermon into an imperishable elevation, is greater than he who writes an immortal poem. Poorly do we think of an earthly immortality, such as men bestow on genius, compared with that immortality and eternal life which God bestows on goodness. Yet if the Saviour promised to the Mary who anointed him for his burial, that her alabaster box should be spoken of in all the world for a memorial of her, it may be in accordance with the great Master's purpose, that his servants, even in this world, shall have no cause to envy the monuments of the worldly great.

There are minds to whom the aspiration or endeavor after excellence in pulpit performance is esteemed an unhallowed ambition. To aim at a cultivation of the natural powers, to study the models, or practise the precepts of masters in that department, to form rules of criticism and apply that criticism to another's or own pulpit productions, in fine to construct a homiletic art, or accumulate a pulpit literature, is in their view, either in fact or in tendency, a vainglorious desecration of the sacred office, and a dishonor and dismissal of the Divine Spirit, by whose direct promptings alone the preacher should spontaneously speak. Now that there are dangers here, against which the preacher should carefully guard, we would not only concede, but most solemnly and warningly maintain. But our present purpose is to suggest to these mistaken consciences, that there is just as great a danger on the other side. He who would avoid an unholy ambition by discarding all endeavor after excellence, or would honor a divine aid, by abdicating the proper cultivation and energetic use of his own powers, will neither secure thereby his own higher holiness, nor attain the divine approbation on his own inertness. The danger also is that this prohibition of pulpit criticism and culture will produce an indolent presumption and a crude coarseness ; which will forfeit all power over an intellectual age by clothing religion in the garb of a repulsive fanaticism. The true rule on this subject is a plain one. A pious divine of the last century gave this striking advice to a young minister : "Prepare yourself as laboriously for preaching, as if there were no Holy Spirit ; and then fling yourself as fully upon Divine aid, as if you had made no preparation." This embraces the whole case. In his educational preparation, let the young minister labor, and in preparing her ministry let the church work, as if man must do all ; and pray then and trust, as if God would do all. This secures us equally from the Antinomianism of expecting God to honor our indolence ; and from the Pelagianism of setting up an independence of the Divine Spirit. It leaves us under the obligation to use all human appliances to secure excellence in the sacred profession. It opens wide the field for homiletic study, for criticism, model, and pulpit literature. It bids us use all these means in glad trust for the Divine blessing upon the whole. He who, in the engrossment of his preparations, forgets or loses that spirit of trust, loses, in fact, the deepest, richest, divinest delight in duty as well as the truest aid to his sacred eloquence. Let him never fear to shape his periods to the most finished perfection ; but let him never forget that, be his periods ever so rhetorically perfect, without that divine element impregnating them, they will not be divinely eloquent. The rhetorical round and sound will be there ; but there are tests by which he may sadly know, that the life and soul are wanting.

It is not the minister alone who is in danger of a dishonest forgetfulness of the bounden object of his efforts in the mere literature of his profession. The advocate may, as some most eminent advocates have done, most unjustly sacrifice the true interests of his client to the glory of a splendid oratorical performance. The Parliamentary debater often forgets the success of the measure he supports, in the acquirement of fame as an orator or place as a politician. The minister has an immortal soul for his client, and the attainment of salvation is the measure he supports. Either of the three may forget his cause and remember only himself. Yet it may be affirmed as a general truth that in all these departments, a literature, a critique, and models are the highest means of the most complete success. In rude times and in extraordinary emergencies, the natural orator of the backwoods may entrance the border jury, congregation or legislature, with a magic eloquence. But it is not in view of extraordinaries that we must make our ordinary provisions. Ordinarily, the entire arrangements of professional training are productive of the highest powers of performance. And with the cautions we have stated if our positions are correct, we may apply the principles of criticism as honestly and as purely, as keenly and as coolly, to the performances of the pulpit, as to those of the bar, or the senate—to the productions of the pencil or the chisel. We may analyze a sermon as we would a symmetrical piece of architecture or a finished poem. We may discuss what powers of mind are brought to bear in the performance; what faults are committed and excellencies attained ; and especially what effective adaptations it has for its purposes ; how well it is calculated to win attention, to fasten conviction, to stir up the deeper feelings of our nature.

Why should the children of light be less wise in their generation than the children of this world ? Against what an intellectual competition must the pulpit of the present day contend ! What a vivid polished spirit-stirring literature is starting up on every side, around us ! Almost every class of people are, now, readers ; and every class of readers are met, at every step, by the fascinating, stimulating, intoxicating aliment just suited to their tastes and appetites. From the yellow-covered twenty-five-cent pirate tale, engendered by the satanic press and hawked by the devil's colporteurs, through an incessant succession of periodicals,—newspaper, magazine and quarterly,—up to the sleek-coated novel, poem, history or travels ; there is a most formidable power of literature, all-alive and active, fresh from the perusal of which our congregations come to the presence of the pulpit. This literature is a rival with which the preacher is forced to compete. Nor has it any scruple or any difficulty to unite the most elaborate power of language to the most intense development of passion. It has, too, a class of most excitable passions, to which it can appeal, for which the pulpit can show no quarter. Yet, undismayed by this formidable array, let the preacher take on his armor of celestial proof, burnished with all the appliances of human diligence and skill. Knowing that from this war he has no retreat, let him learn, even from his foe, the policy of success ; and appropriate to a holy purpose that equipment, and those tactics, which may be as effective for good as for evil. Let him clothe himself with every possible accomplishment ; let him not hesitate to avail himself of all the precepts and all the models of the great masters ; let him appropriate all the advantages of natural and acquired elocution ; let him task the powers of language wherewith to clothe his conceptions ; and let him be assured that if his heart be warm, and his genius susceptible of a kindle, there are within his reach themes of beauty, sublimity and power, to fascinate, to thrill, to excite the deepest emotions of the heart, to arouse the utmost profound of the human soul.

And if mastery in any department is to be learned from the masters, to few masters of pulpit style in our language, can our ministry resort, superior to Logan. He possesses the power of so analyzing the topic he selects, as to present, with a natural, and even inartificial division, the varied phases of which it is susceptible, constructed into a symmetrical whole. He exhibits, in a rare degree, that imagination, which, under the law of truth, shapes powerful conceptions of eternal realities ; or unfolds in vivid colorings, the varied events, characters and sceneries so richly abounding in the volume of revelation. Though loving not the rugged paths of controversy, he firmly and faithfully expounds and applies to the conscience, heart, and life the great practical doctrines of our common Christianity. In the richness and range of his language, in the graceful swell of his ever varying periods, in the animated expansion of his climactic paragraphs, he satisfies the fancy : while in the chasteness and manliness of his style, in the purity of its diction, and the burnish of its texture, he may challenge the severest taste, and assert himself a place among the English classics. And the whole is so warmed and living with a deep devotional feeling, a rich and fervid zeal, as, coming most manifestly from the heart of the preacher, searches, pervades, and fills the heart of the hearer.

It may by some be thought that, in accordance somewhat with the lax theology of his time, the way of *faith* is not sufficiently developed, in his sermons. Yet he, certainly, belonged not to the school of pulpit moralists, who borrowed their text from Paul, and their sermon from Epictetus. Christ and his cross, heaven and hell, repentance and reformation, are his momentous themes. He may, like St. James, have *fused* the doctrine of faith into his system, rather than brought it out with genuine Pauline pungency. At the present day, when the preacher would bring the sinner to close quarters, and elicit from his soul the immediate act by which he consigns himself to Christ for salvation, he will perhaps find some exhibition of the doctrine of faith more explicit, than was usually found in the preaching of those times, necessary to his purpose.

The sermons of Logan are *eloquence*, purely within the central truths of the gospel; within the legitimate range of the pulpit; and within the comprehension of our ordinary congregations. We know not what was the style of Logan's delivery; but if the delivery was in any way commensurate with the composition, we know not how they could have failed of being most impressive. We know not how a people could well sit under such a ministry without being made better. We know not how men within reach, could fail to feel their steps attracted to such a ministry. We know not how such a ministry, spread over this and every other land, could fail of being a rich blessing, if not the saving of the world.

His is not so much that originality which startles us with the announcement of a new truth, as that more practical originality which invests established truths with new zest and freshness. Under his lucid touches, the rust of common-place disappears from that old truth, a new clearness beams upon it, a new beauty beams from it. Then a brighter lustre and a richer glow; then a more radiant glory and a blaze of splendor new and dazzling. Our attention is arrested; we are borne along on the tide of increasing interest; our feelings rise with the opening vistas; and we close the discourse, dissatisfied with its brevity, yet with hearts warmed, with views brightened, and with a grateful trust, that we are being made better Christians and better men. And, then, there is such a variety and spontaneousness as to make him seem inexhaustible. We learn to love the mind which was the ceaseless fountain of such beauty and power; and we drop a tear at the thought that his closing days were shaded with sorrow.

SERMONS.

SERMON I.

ON THE INFLUENCE OF RELIGIOUS INSTITUTIONS.

PSAL. XXVII. 4.—"One thing have I desired of the Lord, that will I seek after; that I may dwell in the house of the Lord all the days of my life, to behold the beauty of the Lord, and to inquire in his temple."

DAVID, the author of this psalm, is much celebrated in the sacred Scriptures. As a man, he was not without faults; but as a king, he shines with uncommon lustre. He distinguished himself in early youth, as the champion of his native land; in fighting the battles of Israel he became the hero of his age; and at last he ascended the throne, on which he sat with much splendor during many years. He was the founder of the Jewish monarchy. From being separate tribes, he made the Jews a nation. Their judge in peace, as well as their leader in war, he secured by his councils what he had gained by his arms, and gave to Judea a name and a renown among the kingdoms of the East. To the bravery of a warrior, and the wisdom of a statesman, he added what in all ages has been no less admired, the accomplishments of a poet or bard. "The sweet Psalmist of Israel" consecrated his harp to the praises of the Lord, and composed to it sacred strains, that have ministered to the improvement and to the devotion of succeeding times, till this day.

Notwithstanding all his other engagements, he found time for the exercises of religion; notwithstanding all the pleasures and honors of a throne, he found his chief happiness in the house of the Lord. "One thing have I desired of the Lord, that will I seek after, that I may dwell in the house of the Lord all the days of my life." Whenever his favorite subject presents itself, he takes fire, and speaks of it, not only with zeal, but with transport. "How amiable are thy tabernacles, O Lord of hosts! My soul longeth, yea, even fainteth for the courts of the Lord: my heart and my flesh cry out for the living God."

It becomes then a subject worthy of our attention, to inquire, *What there is* in the public institutions of religion, to have rendered them an object of so great importance to the king of Israel? This will appear, if we consider their influence on men, with respect to their religious capacity; with respect to their moral character; with respect to their political state; and with respect to their domestic life.

In the *first* place, let us consider the influence of religious institutions upon men, with respect to their *religious capacity*.

There are many qualities which we share in common with the inferior animals. In the acuteness of the external senses, some of them excel our species. They have a reason of their own; they make approaches to human intelligence, and are led by an instinct of nature to associate with one another. They have also their virtues, and exhibit such examples of affection, of industry, and of courage, as give lessons to mankind. But in all their actions they discover no sense of Deity, and no traces of religion. It was reserved to be the glory of man, that he alone should be admitted into the presence of his Creator, and be rendered capable of knowing and adoring the perfections of the Almighty. As piety is the distinguishing mark of the human race, a tendency to the exercise thereof is in some degree natural to the mind. When we look up to heaven, and behold the sun shining in glory, or the moon and the stars walking in brightness, untaught nature prompts us to adore Him that made them, to bow down and worship in the temple not made with hands. When we are surrounded by dangers on every side, overwhelmed with deep affliction, by the law of our nature we tend to some superior Being for safety and relief: or when we are surprised with a sudden flow of unexpected prosperity, spontaneously we lift up our eyes and hands to heaven, to pour forth the grateful effusions of the heart to our unseen Benefactor.

As there are principles, then, in human nature, which incline men to religion, and principles also which incline them to society, it would not have been extraordinary, if the combined influence of the religious and associating principles had been so strong as to have prompted men to have assembled in public, for the purposes of devotion, although no law had been given to that end. But it was not left to this. Among all the nations of the world, the public interested itself in the cause; the legislative authority interposed its sanction, and kings and lawgivers encouraged the propensity of the people to religion. It required no profound wisdom to foresee the manifold advantages that the public worship of a Deity would introduce among men. Accordingly temples were every where built, sacred ceremonies were instituted, an order of men was appointed to officiate in holy things, and certain days were set apart for the people to join in the celebration of divine worship. Indeed, as to the objects, and the manner of worship, little care was taken. The magistrate gave his authority to the current belief, though ever so absurd and ridiculous, and established that form of religion which the people were best disposed to receive. It was thought sufficient, if by public and solemn acts of piety, a sense of Deity, and feelings of religion, could be impressed, and frequently renewed in the minds of men. But in some nations this practice, so highly beneficial to mankind, was enjoyed by an authority superior to that of human governors. God himself, in the system of laws which he delivered to his ancient people, hallowed the seventh day, and appointed other festivals in which the people should assemble together in order to join in the services of the sanctuary. In what concerns the celebration of the Sabbath, Christianity confirms the Mosaic law. Our Saviour, whose practice ought to be a rule of life to Christians, attended upon the public worship in the Jewish synagogues; and the apostles followed his example, till by their labors in the ministry, they had gathered together, in one place, a sufficient number of converts to form a church. Then they constituted regular assemblies of Christians, they ordained proper persons to preside in the public worship, and both by their precept and example, recommended a constant attendance on these meetings of the faithful.

That there must be an established religion in every state, is a principle in which not only Christians, but infidels, have been agreed. In order that the public religion may be productive of any good effects, it is necessary that it make a deep impression upon the minds of the people. But if it were not for our assembling together on the Lord's day, for public worship, that form of Christianity which is established in this country would pehaps take too feeble a hold of the mind, to produce its proper effects. The Christian religion is very different from those systems of superstition which prevailed in the Pagan world. The Heathen religion had attractions for every feeling of the human frame. It contained every thing that could strike the senses, or please the imaginations of men. All the apparatus of false religion, which at once amuses and engages the mind, was exhibited; ceremonies, pompous festivals, costly sacrifices, were continually passing before the eyes of the worshipper. In the majesty of the temple, and the splendor of the worship, the Deity seemed to be present. Ancient superstition introduced the fine arts into her train, called the powers of genius to her aid, and employed the painter and the poet to hold out her charms to the world.

Very different was that religion of which Jesus Christ was the author. When the Son of God descended, he appeared not like the idols of the nations. The Christian religion is pure, spiritual, divine. It is the religion of the mind and the heart;

the worship of God, who is a spirit, in spirit and in truth. There is nothing here but the simplicity of truth and the majesty of reason to persuade the world. Man, however, is not a pure intelligence, and reason is not the only attribute of his nature. Were it not, therefore, for the mode of communication by discourse in public assemblies, Christianity, in its simplest form, could never be a popular religion. It might employ the leisure of philosophic men; it might operate its effect upon the few who are given to inquiry; but it never could engage the generality of mankind. They, who have not considered the subject, cannot possibly conceive the astonishing difference there is between written and spoken language; between the dead letter that appears to the eye, and the living voice that comes to the heart. The same discourse that in a popular assembly would raise the passions of the audience to the highest pitch; send it abroad in print, and it will often have no effect at all. Add to these, that it is to the meetings of the faithful, that the promise of the divine presence is made. In the gates of Zion, God delights to dwell; and when his disciples are gathered together, Jesus has promised to be in the midst of them. True piety indeed is not confined to the sanctuary. High is the pleasure, and great the benefit of private devotion. But sure I am, that they who have entered into the spirit, and tasted the pleasures, of devotion in secret, will not be thereby prevented from approaching to God in the ordinances of public worship. Society heightens every feeling, and improves every delight. All that charms the eye or the ear, or the imagination or the heart, is attended with double pleasure, when we share it in the company of others. In the presence of striking and exemplary piety, the careless worshipper will become devout, and the devout will become fervent. A holy emulation will rise in the bosoms of the faithful: the ardor will spread from breast to breast, and the passions of one inflame the passions of all. May I not appeal to your own experience, and ask, When you have been in the Spirit on the Lord's day, when the word of life was spoken from the heart to the heart, have you not felt that there was a divinity in virtue, have you not found yourselves as if translated from earth to heaven, and experienced the emotion of mind which the Patriarch felt, when he awoke from his dream, and cried out in rapture, "Surely the Lord is in this place! This is none other than the house of God, and this is the gate of heaven?"

Secondly, Let us view the effect of religious institutions upon men, with regard to their *moral character*.

Whatever brings men together, and connects them in society, has a tendency to civilize and improve them. Especially when they assemble together for such important purposes as the worship of a Deity, this will be the effect. There is something in the very idea of drawing nigh to God, that inspires virtue. When men accustomed to meet together as busy and as social creatures, assemble at stated times as rational and immortal beings, a sense of propriety will prompt them to act up to that high character. When the sons of God come to present themselves before the Lord, whatever is displeasing to God, and hostile to men, will vanish from their mind. The connection between such exercises of piety, and the practice of virtue, is nearer and more intimate than superficial reasoners are apt to imagine. There are indeed pretences to religion, without any virtue, as there are pretences to virtue without any religion; but whoever in reality possesses the fear of God, will be thereby determined to keep his commandments. It must be obvious at first view, that the sense of a Supreme Being, the inspector of human affairs, the patron of virtue, the avenger of sin, and the rewarder of righteousness, has a powerful tendency to strengthen moral obligation, to annex a new sanction to the laws, and to inspire purity into the manners of a people.

By the operation of such a principle, open violence will be restrained, and secret enmity will be checked. Society will assume a happier form, the insolence of the oppressor will be humbled, and the wild passions of the licentious be subdued. What the Scripture calls, "the power of the world to come," is felt strongly through every corner of this world. Heaven improves the earth, and the life which is to come, is a source of happiness to the life which now is. There are, indeed, I acknowledge, to the honor of the human kind, there are persons in the world who feel that the possession of good dispositions is their best reward, who would follow goodness for its own sake, and do their duty, because it is their duty, although there were neither rewards nor punishments to come. But I know as well, that the world is not composed of such persons. Men in general are governed by their passions, their interest, the prevailing bias of their minds; and whenever their passions, their interest, or the bias of their mind, stand in one scale, and their duty in the other, it is very evident where the balance will incline. To such persons you might declaim for ever to no purpose, on the beauty of virtue, and the harmony of a well governed mind; they hear you not; they are deaf to the voice of the moral charmer: nothing less than "Thus saith the Lord," will influence their conduct. The unjust judge in the parable represents and characterizes the great body of mankind; if they fear not God, neither will they regard men.

Thus, if the public institutions of religion were laid aside, private virtue would not long remain behind. Men in general have no principle of moral conduct but religion, and if that were taken away, they would work all impurity with greediness. whenever they could withdraw from the public eye. Human laws would often be of little avail, without a sense of divine legislation; and the sanctions of men have little force, unless they were enforced by the authority of God. There would then be no security for the public peace; the mutual confidence between man and man would be destroyed; the bond which keeps society together would be broken; oaths would become mere words of course, and an appeal to the Great God of Heaven no more regarded, than if he were an image of stone. Human life would be thrown into confusion, the safety of mankind would be endangered, and the moral world totter to its ruin, if such a pillar were to fall. And what is it that maintains and spreads religious principles in the world? What is it that keeps alive on the minds of the people, the fear of God and the belief of his providence? It is the public institutions of religion; it is the observance of the Lord's day; it is our assembling together in this place, for the celebration of divine worship. The people, in general, have no religious principles, and no rule of life, but what they learn here; and if these churches were once shut up, the hand of the civil magistrate would soon force them open, in order to reclaim the criminals that would thus be let loose upon the world.

In the *third* place, let us view the effect of religious institutions upon men, with regard to their *political state.*

The political systems that take place in the world, the facility with which the many are governed by the few, is one of the most wonderful things in the history of man. That mankind in all ages, and in all countries, should allow a few of their number to divide this globe among them; to appropriate to themselves the possessions, distinctions and honors, and leave nothing to the majority but burdens to bear, if we had not beheld it from the first, would have appeared one of the most astonishing of all events. Would it be at all suprising to hear a man struck with a sense of this state of things, complain thus: "Is nature unequal in the care of her children? A mother to some, and a stepmother to others? Has she appointed me to labor in the sweat of my brow, and another to riot in the fruit of my labors? No. The fault is not in nature. She has no favorites. She gives to all her sons an equal right to inherit the earth. The fault is in them who tamely bend their necks to the yoke, who kneel and kiss the rod which the haughty lord waves over their heads. It never surely was the will of Heaven, that the worthy should be scorned by the vile, and the brave be trampled upon by the coward. Cannot I then find a band of men as valiant and as determined as myself, to rectify these caprices of fortune, to vindicate the rights of nature, and restore mankind to their original inheritance? By doing violence at first, this usurpation on nature was made; and by a similar violence, nature requires that her reign be restored." What is it that prevents such a spirit as I have been now describing, from frequently breaking out? What prevents bloodshed and devastation, and all the evils of war? What prevents the world from being turned upside down? Nothing so much as the influence of religious principles upon the minds of men. Christianity gives honor to civil government, as being the ordinance of God, and enjoins subjection to the laws, under his own awful sanctions.

And not only by particular precepts, but by its secret and less visible influence, it prepares the minds of men for submission to lawful authority. When we meet together in this place, under the sanction of law, and under the protection of the civil magistrate, we are put in mind of our relation to the state and of our duty to the higher powers. *Fear God and honor the King*, have more than a local connection in Scripture.* Obedience to spiritual authority paves the way for subjection to the civil power. Hence wise legislators have, even on this account, favored the progress of religion: hence those who have attempted innovations in government, applied, in the first place, to the ministers of religion, and endeavored to gain the pulpit on their side. Julian, known by the name of the apostate, the most formidable enemy the Christians ever had, was so sensible of the influence and of the effects of preaching to the people, that he appointed a similar institution among the heathen.

"My son, fear thou the Lord and the King," (said the wisest of mankind), "and meddle not with them that are given to change." In confirmation, we may observe, that men, characterized as given to change, have either, from infidelity, not attended upon ordinances, or from enthusiasm, been above them: for, who have been innovators and disturbers? who have been the authors of seditions and rebellions? who have been the enemies of order and civil government, in many an age? a mixture of atheists and fanatics; two classes of men, who, though seemingly opposite, have been found in close bonds of union.

In the *fourth* and *last* place, we have to consider the influence of religious institutions upon men, with respect to *domestic life.*

It is chiefly on account of their domestic situation, that we can pronounce men happy or miserable. Here the pleasures are enjoyed which sweeten life; here the pains are felt which embitter our days. No uneasiness abroad will sit heavy on a man, when the pleasing reflection rises in his mind, that he has happiness at home: no enjoyment from without will give real and lasting satisfaction, when he knows that he has a curse in his own house.

It is no small advantage attending the institutions of divine worship, that they minister to the happiness of domestic life. A new bond will be added to the conjugal union, when those whom it connects walk to the House of God in company, take sweet counsel with one another, and set out jointly in the way that leads to life. Watered by the dews of heaven, which fall here, the olive plants will flourish round your table. What sacred sensations will fill the bosom of a parent, when, viewing his family sitting at the feet of Jesus, he says, in the fulness of a grateful heart, "Lord! behold me, and the children whom thou hast given me!"

There is a beauty, also, when the rich and the poor, when the high and the low, who seldom meet together on other occasions, assemble here in one place, one great family, in the presence of their common Lord, when they are stripped of every adventitious circumstance, and where virtue makes the only distinction among them. It is the image of those golden times when society began; it is the image of the state which is to come, when God shall be all in all.

Such are the effects of religious institutions upon men, with respect to their religious capacity, their moral character, their political state, and their domestic life.

Whoever, therefore, habitually absents himself from attending on public ordinances, has to answer for it to his God, to his neighbors, to his country, and to his family. He partakes with other men in their sins; he associates with the enemies of mankind; and does what in him lies, to undermine the basis of which the order and happiness of civil society is built. He teaches the false swearer to take the name

* See 1 Peter ii. 17.

of God in vain; he directs the midnight robber to his neighbor's house; and he delivers into the hand of the assassin a dagger, to shed innocent blood.

But, blessed be God! that, corrupted as the world is, there are not wanting instances of exemplary piety, in every station of life; not only in the middle, the lower, and the higher, but in the highest of all. While piety shines, as it now does, from the Throne; while it has the beam of Majesty to adorn it; let none of the subjects fail in copying the pattern: and while we meet together in this place, let us remember, that many who have worshipped, in times past, within these walls, are now in the Higher House, in the Church of the First-born, in the assembly of Angels, and in that Temple where the beatific presence of the Lord displays his glory, in a manner which it hath not entered into the heart of man to conceive.

SERMON II.

ON THE IMPORTANCE OF DEVOTION.

Rom. xii. 11.—"—— Fervent in spirit; serving the Lord."

The manners of mankind are perpetually varying. Two nations differ not more from one another, than the same nation differs from itself, at different periods of society. This change of customs and manners has given rise to two opinions, both of them generally received, and both of them founded on mistake. These are, that we are always improving upon our ancestors in art and in science, and always degenerating from them in religion and morals. When we talk of any work of ingenuity or of industry, composed or performed by our forefathers, from the highest liberal science, to the lowest mechanic art, if we allow it any praise at all, our panegyric runs in this style: "It is very well for the time in which it was done." On the other hand, we always allow our ancestors the preference in virtue. For these five thousand years past, the philosophers and moralists of every nation have extolled the times of antiquity, and decried the age in which they lived, as the worst that ever was known. "These wicked times;" "This degenerate age," are phrases that have rung in the public ear almost since the general deluge. The ages of antiquity are always ages of gold; the present always an age of iron.

The origin of these opinions I take to be this. As customs and manners are perpetually fluctuating, the reigning mode is always reckoned the best, because they have no other standard but fashion. But fashion is not the standard of morals. The hand of the Almighty hath written the moral law, the standard of virtue, upon the living tablets of every human heart. Here then the standard is fixed and eternal. Accordingly, as quite a different set of virtues and vices prevail in one age, from what prevail in another; as we are naturally disposed to bury the faults of our forefathers in oblivion; as we insensibly contract a veneration for whatever is great in antiquity; hence arises the opinion, that the virtues of a former age are greater than those of a following one. We think we degenerate from our fathers, because we differ from them. But were I to pronounce of the times in which we live, I would say that the present age is not inferior in virtue to the past. We have improved upon our ancestors in humanity, charity and benevolence; we have exchanged the rage and rancor of animals of prey, for the meek and gentle spirit of the dove. The gall of asps is transformed into the milk of human kindness. Great and enormous crimes are less frequent than they have been; we are better members of society, better neighbors, better friends than our ancestors were. People of different opinions and sects in religion, who some hundred years ago would have been putting one another to death, now live together in amity and peace.

Would to God I could carry on my panegyric, and add, that we are more religious and devout than our ancestors were, that our zeal for the honor of God, and the interests of religion, shines with a brighter lustre, and burns with a purer flame. But alas! my brethren, I must here change my strain. Your own eyes, your own hearts, will tell you the dismal truth. Is it not a deplorable fact, that instead of being fervent in spirit to serve the Lord, an indifference about religion almost universally prevails? The very face of seriousness is banished from society, and were it not for this day, on which we assemble together to worship the God of our fathers, the very form of godliness would be exterminated from the earth.

To induce you to the practice of devotion, it is proposed in the *first* place, To illustrate the importance and the advantage of serving the Lord; and, in the *second* place, To explain and to enforce, with a few arguments, the duty of serving the Lord with fervency of spirit.

In the *first* place, let us consider the importance and the advantage of serving the Lord.

We are urged to the practice of some virtues, by our strong sense of their inviolable obligation; we are allured to the love of others, by the high approbation of their native beauty, which arises in every well-disposed mind; we are engaged to the performance of others, by our experience of their utility and influence upon the public good. Piety is equally enforced in all these respects. Its obligation is indispensable; its beauty is supreme, and its utility is universal. It is not so much a single virtue, as a constellation of virtues. Here reverence, gratitude, faith, hope, love, concentre their rays, and shine with united glory. Whatsoever things are lovely, whatsoever things are pure, are honest, or of good report; if there be any merit, any praise in human action, piety comprehends the whole. There is not a disposition of the mind which is more noble in itself, or is attended with greater pleasure than piety. It is accompanied with such inward satisfaction, that the duty is sufficiently rewarded by the performance; and it hath such true grandeur in it, that when duly performed, it exalts us to a state but little lower than the angels. The most illiterate man, under the impressions of true devotion, and in the immediate acts of divine worship, contracts a greatness of mind that raises him above his equals. Thereby, says an admired ancient, we build a nobler temple to the Deity than creation can present.

Piety is adapted to the notions of happiness and chief good which all men entertain, although these notions were as various in themselves as the theories of philosophers have been about their object. If we are actuated by the mild and gentle affections, lovers of nature, willing to retire from the bustle of the world, and to steal through the vale of life with as little noise, and as much peace as possible, religion sanctifies our choice, and doubles all the joys of life with the peace of heaven. Are we lovers of society, delighting to enlarge the sphere of our acquaintance in the world, and to cultivate universal friendship with all ranks and degrees of men? Here too, religion befriends us, as it unites all men under one common interest, that of being probationers for eternity. Are we ambitious of fame and honor among men? This is indeed the universal passion. Nothing more distinguishes the nature of man, than this restless desire of rising above his fellows, of becoming famous, and acquiring a name. But it does not lie in the way of every one to rise in the world, by being advanced to honor and distinction, and commanding the applause of attending multitudes. Fame unbars the gates of her temple but to a chosen few; the candidate will infallibly meet with many a disappointment, and many a downfall, in climbing the steep ascent; but the paths of religion, that lead to glory, honor and immortality, are ever open and safe. By piety we already enjoy a reputation among the just, and the approbation of our own hearts, and have the certain expectation of that immortal honor which cometh from God only, who writes our name in the book of life. Hither let the man of the world turn, that he may find durable riches, more to be desired than gold and all earthly possessions. Here the man of pleasure may find a perpetual fund of enjoyment, in drinking of that stream which proceeds from the river of life; a stream whose fountain never fails, which has no sediment at bottom, and which runs for ever unmingled with the waters of bitterness.

Piety is the foundation of virtue and morality. True devotion strengthens our obligations to a holy life, and superadds a new motive to every social and civil duty. Upon an impartial observation of mankind, it will be found, that those men who are the most conscientious in the public and private exercises of divine worship, will be most diligent in performing the duties they owe to their neighbor, and in observing the rules of morality. Our holy religion lays us under strong obligations to duty; the spirit of Christianity dwelling in the heart, must of necessity inspire it with an ardent desire to perform whatever things are virtuous and praiseworthy; and the example of Jesus Christ, which the true Christian sets continually before his eyes, will engage him by all the laws of love, to walk as he also walked, who, according even to the testimony of his enemies, "did all things well." On the other hand, impiety and immorality naturally go together, as cause and effect. Who is it that is altogether corrupt, and a worker of iniquity? It is the fool, who hath said in his heart there is no God. When we read of the unjust judge in the Gospel, who feared not God, we naturally infer that he regarded not man. Under this particular, we may likewise take notice, that serving the Lord with sincere piety, is the most successful method of becoming publicly useful in the world. Man, fallen as he certainly is, is still a benevolent being. Formed for society, he delights in the exercise of his social qualities; he aspires to be eminently useful in the station in which he is placed, and is in his proper element, when he is dispensing happiness around him. The sympathetic emotions that rise in the bosom at the sight of an object in distress, the smile that wakens on the cheek, the tear that starts spontaneous from the eye, at the representation of scenes of human joy or sorrow, are indisputable indications of the benevolence of our nature. But the low station of many checks the benevolence of their hearts, and circumscribes it to a narrow sphere. Few have it in their power to become useful to their country, by contriving or effectuating public-spirited designs; few have it in their power to save their ountry from the miseries of war, by being its shield in the day of battle; few can act as the instruments of Providence, in bringing about national happiness. But all of us can be pious; and by serving the Lord with fervency of spirit, can become universally useful to our country and to the world. By piety, like the Prophets of old, we can shield our country from the wrath of heaven; we can interest Omnipotence on its side, and even derive blessings to ages unborn. A good man is the guardian angel of his country.

I shall only add on this head, that by serving the Lord here, we have an earnest and anticipation of the happiness of the heavenly state. It is a pleasant reflection, and well worthy of our most serious thought, that we are now entering upon a course of life that will be our employment through eternity. As man is a progressive being, gradually tending to perfection, it is a law of his nature, that he should endeavor to act, beforehand, the part to which he is destined in a higher state of being. The child, from his earliest years, anticipates in sport the employment of maturer age, loves to imitate the actions of men, and is pleased with the name. We are all of us children, with respect to our future existence; and should it not be as natural for him who is born from above, to act over the exercises and enjoyments of that state of being to which he is advancing? Piety is the beginning of heaven in the mind: here the sun faintly beams, as in the dubious twilight; there he shines forth in full meridian glory. What an inestimable privilege then is this, which God hath put into our power? A life sacred to piety, and to the observance of true and undefiled religion, introduces us beforehand into the world to come, and gives us an acquaintance with the state and society of the angels and blessed spirits who dwell in light.

I come now to the *second* thing proposed, which was, To explain that fervor of spirit so requisite in the exercises of devotion, and enforce it with a few arguments.

By fervor of spirit, in general, is meant an uncommon application of mind in the performance of any thing, a warmth bordering upon transport, that moves every spring of the heart, and carries all before it, to gain its end. So that by a fervency of spirit in serving the Lord, must be understood, an ardent and active desire of loving the Lord, of worshipping him in sincerity, and obeying his commands with all our heart, with all our soul, with all our mind, and with all our strength. It consists not in a few transient fits and starts of natural devotion, when we are in jeopardy, without help of man; neither is it a wild blaze of religious passion, that flashes and vanishes. Much less shall it be profaned by confounding it with those furies, *Enthusiasm* and *Superstition*, who would drench a country with innocent blood, under a pretence of serving the Lord. "Cursed be their anger, for it is fierce, and their wrath, for it is cruel. O my soul, enter not thou into their secret."

True fervor of spirit proceedeth from above. It is a beam from the Father of lights, pure and benign, which at once enlightens and warms the mind. It is a ray from the Sun of Righteousness, bright even at the beginning, and which shineth more and more unto the perfect day. It is a temper wrought into the heart by the Holy Spirit, compounded of love to God, and of zeal for his honor, attended with charity to man.

This fervor of mind, in its full extent, is one of the brightest ornaments of the Christian. It enters into the heart, and engages the whole man on the side of devotion; it gives a double measure of force and alacrity to that religion which before was sincere. In a word, it is to the spiritual life, what health is to the natural; it makes that spirited and cheerful, which otherwise would only breathe and move. Conscious that religion is his grand concern, the fervent Christian will set about the duties of it with suitable ardor and intenseness of mind. The passions and affections which God hath given man, as the springs of action, will in him be exerted to their noblest purpose, to inspire him with alacrity and cheerfulness in the ways of the Lord. He will be in pain till he has performed his duties of devotion, and labors of love, holding nothing too dear, which will procure to him that robe of holiness, which is beautiful in the eyes of heaven. He feels in his heart all the devout affections and desires so passionately described by the holy Psalmist, which we know not whether to admire most as beautiful strains of poetry, or raptures of devotion. "As the hart panteth after the water-brooks, so panteth my soul after thee, O God. My soul thirsteth for God, yea, the living God: when shall I come and appear before God? How amiable are thy tabernacles, O Lord of hosts! My soul longeth, yea fainteth, for the courts of the Lord. For, a day in thy courts is better than a thousand. The desire of my soul is to thee, O God, and to the remembrance of thy name. With my soul have I desired thee in the night, yea, with my spirit within me will I seek thee early. My soul waiteth for thee, O Lord, more than they that watch for the morning; yea, more than they that watch for the morning."

To engage us more effectually to the performance of this part of our duty, let us consider the general obligations we lie under, as rational creatures, to serve the Lord with fervency of spirit, and then the particular obligations that arise from Christianity.

And, in the *first* place, as the Almighty is the Creator of the world, and the Father of the human race, he is likewise their Preserver, and the Author of order and harmony in the universe.

In his Providence, he takes us, the children of men, into his particular tuition, in giving us, from his immediate hand, all things requisite for our subsistence, well-being and delight in this world, our well-ordered habitation; in making nature spontaneously unlock to us her hidden stores; in causing the wide creation, one way or other, to administer to our pleasures, as if heaven and earth contended which should be most liberal of their favors to happy man; and in fine, admitting us, above all the other inhabitants of our earth, into the plan of his creation, and making us spectators of that beauty, original and supreme, the image of himself, which he hath poured forth over all his works.

But when we consider his particular Providence, with respect to every one of us, our obligations will be infinitely heightened. Here we discern the finger of God. His goodness lent a favorable ear to all our feeble cries and complaints, when we were upon the breast; he guarded us from a thousand dangers and diseases which hung over our heads, and cut off more than one half of our equals in age. He hath led us, as it were, by the hand through the various stages of life, affording us many deliverances, and many tokens of his loving-kindness, which only ourselves and Heaven were privy to; and when all things in the world seemed to combine against us, he was a friend that never failed. Seeing then he upholds our existence, and is the parent of so many mercies, has he not, as our Supreme Benefactor, a title to the service of our whole lives, and to all the fervor of our spirits?

This will appear still more, in the *next* place, when we consider the superior obligations which we are laid under by Christianity. While many nations are sitting in darkness, and the shadow of death, on us hath the Sun of Righteousness arisen, in full glory. We are let into the mystery kept hid from ages. We have seen the Deity, in human form, descending upon earth, to teach the benighted nations the knowledge of salvation; to set a pattern of goodness and perfection for the world to imitate; and, by expiating the guilt of sin upon the cross, to finish our redemption. We have now a new and living way opened into the Heaven of Heavens, by the blood of Jesus. Life and immortality are brought to light, and promised to all who sincerely believe and obey the gospel. So that we may now rejoice with the Poet of Israel, "As the heaven is high above the earth, so great is the mercy of the Lord towards us; for as far as the east is from the west, so far hath he removed from us all our iniquities: he redeemeth our lives from destruction, and crowneth us with loving-kindness and tender mercies."

When we are obliged to any of our fellow-creatures for an important favor, what pleasure is it to a generous heart to be able to make the least return! If our benefactor be above us in his station in life, if he bestowed the favor without any solicitation on our part, and promises still to continue our friend, shall we not take every occasion of showing that we are not ungrateful, and search for opportunity of serving him, as for hid treasure? What thanks, what praises, what services, shall we not then render to our Supreme Benefactor, who hath translated us from the kingdom of darkness into the kingdom of his Son; who delivered up his Son unto the death for us, and with him freely gives us all things!

We have abundance of ardor and zeal in our temporal concerns. We rise early, and sit up late: we deny ourselves the pleasures and comforts of society: we forego our native country, and all the dear connections of early life: we traverse the whole terraqueous globe, expose ourselves to the mercy of winds and waves, and bear alternately the extremities of heat and cold: we breathe in the regions of infection and of death, to amass a few pieces of shining dust, whose acquisition costs us such sore trouble, and whose possession gives us so little happiness. Almighty God! shall we be thus fervent and zealous in every temporal, in every trivial concern, and remain cold and dead unto thee! If thus we continue, my brethren, the very heathens, issuing forth from their regions of darkness, will set up a tribunal, and call us before them. "The men of Nineveh shall rise up in judgment with us, and shall condemn us; because they repented at the preaching of Jonas, and behold a greater than Jonas is here! The Queen of the South shall rise up in judgment with us, and shall condemn us; for she came from the uttermost parts of the earth, to hear the wisdom of Solomon, and behold a greater than Solomon is here!"—"Verily, it shall be more tolerable for the land of Sodom and Gomorrah, in the day of judgment, than for our city."

Do ye consider, my brethren, the dignity and importance of that religion, to which your attachment is required? Do ye reflect, that this is the master-piece of infinite wisdom; that here the Almighty made bare his holy arm, and put forth all his strength? The introduction of this religion was the object of all the dispensations of the Deity upon earth. This is the centre in which terminates every line in the great circle of Providence. If one nation was victorious, and another put under the yoke; if war was commissioned to ravage and lay desolate the earth, or peace to make the joyful inhabitants sing beneath the vine; if kings were crowned, or were dethroned; if empires rose or fell, all was preparatory and subservient to this grand event. The monarchies which prevailed in the world, whether Assyrian, Persian, Grecian, or Roman, were erected as introductory to the Messiah, whose kingdom was to be without bounds, and whose reign was to be without end. That great image which the monarch of the east beheld in his dream, whose head was of gold, whose breast was of silver, whose thighs were of brass, and whose feet were of iron, was set up by Providence, to prepare the way for the Stone which was cut out without hands, which was destined to smite the image, become a great mountain, and fill the whole earth. All events, whether prosperous or adverse, whether malignant or benign, have co-operated towards the advancement of our religion. Saints have established it, by their lives: martyrs have confirmed it, by their deaths: hypocrites have added strength to it, by their dissimulation: tyrants have purified it, by their persecutions: infidels have corroborated it, by their opposition: the arrows of its enemies have served for its protection: the resistance which it has met with, from the combined wit and genius and malice of mankind, have brought forth those illustrious and immortal defences, which establish its truth upon the basis of demonstration.

Shall we not, then, reckon ourselves eternally indebted to the infinite goodness of God, and stir up all that is within us to bless his holy name? saying, in the language of true fervor of spirit, "We will praise thee, O God! we will praise thee with our whole heart! Our lives shall be thy sacrifice! We will adore thee in death, and through eternity."

God, from his throne in heaven, doth not behold an object more noble, and more worthy of his view, than a pious man; a man who, conscious of the dignity and immortality of his nature, employs himself with fervor and zeal, in those devout exercises which assimilate him to the Divinity: who, measuring time by his improvements in devotion and virtue, never loses a day. He is the favorite of Heaven. The arm of the Almighty is stretched out on his behalf. The Lord loves him, and keeps him, as the apple of his eye; he gives his angels charge concerning him, to preserve him in all his ways, lest at any time he should dash his foot against a stone. He delights to speak his praise in the assemblies of his saints and angels above: he writes his name in the book of his remembrance, and gives him the honorable title of the friend of God. He makes all things work together for his good in this world, and, in the dark vale of death, opens his eyes to discern the dawning of heavenly day. In fine, he holds his very ashes sacred; and, raising him up at the last day, carries him to his throne in heaven above, with the glorious company of the redeemed, to be made partaker of his own happiness.

These are thy palms, O Piety! Thine is the kingdom prepared above, thine the power with God and with man, and thine the crown of glory that fadeth not away.

SERMON III.

ON EARLY PIETY.

ECCLES. XII. 1.—"Remember now thy Creator in the days of thy youth."

WHEN Solomon, in early youth, had ascended the throne of Israel, the God of his fathers appeared to him in a dream. The Almighty was graciously pleased to condescend thus to visit his creature. He put in his offer all the pleasures of the world, and desired him to ask, and he should receive; to wish, and he should enjoy. The young king possessed a wisdom beyond his years, and a greatness above his crown. He did not ask to have his palace filled with the beauties of the east, to have his treasury stored with the gold of Ophir, or to wear the laurel of victory over the nations. He asked a greater boon than all these. "Give thy servant, O Lord," replied the wise prince, "Give thy servant wisdom and understanding." What he then made the object of his own choice, he recommends to you under another name, in the words of the text. "Remember now thy Creator in the days of thy youth."

This is the last chapter of the works

of Solomon, and these words may be regarded as his dying advice to the young. The philosophers of antiquity, who held out the lamp of wisdom to the heathen world, gave the same advice to their followers. But between them and Solomon, there is this remarkable difference. They, from the obscure retirement of the schools, declaimed against pleasures which they had never tasted, and affected to despise honors to which they never had it in their power to ascend. But Solomon, a great and powerful prince, in the pleasurable time of life, had in his own person tried the experiment. He made the tour of the sensual world. He went in quest of happiness through all the scenes of life. He extended his search over the broad and flowery way, as well as in the narrow path, as it should seem by a particular permission of Providence, to save the pains of future inquirers. Solomon acted the libertine upon a principle of inquiry. The result of his researches was, that all unlawful pursuits began with vanity, and ended in vexation of spirit, and that the true happiness of man, consisted in that understanding which teacheth us to depart from evil, and in that wisdom which instructeth us to fear the Lord.

It is common in Scripture, to express all the acts of devotion and virtue by some part or principle of religion, sometimes by wisdom and understanding; at other times by faith, love, the fear of God, walking with God, and many other phrases; all of which express the same meaning, and denote the whole economy of a religious life. So that remembering our Creator in the days of our youth, implies an early and an entire dedication of ourselves to the service of God.

In further discoursing upon these words, I shall enforce the exhortation in the text, and endeavor to persuade you to remember your Creator in the days of your youth, from the peculiar suitableness of religion to the early period of life. And in the *first* place, let me exhort you now in the days of youth, to remember your Creator, from your being as yet uncorrupted by the world.

Although both Scripture and experience testify that man is fallen, and that our nature is corrupted, yet it is equally certain that our earliest passions are on the side of virtue, and that the good seed springs before the tares. Malice and envy are yet strangers to your bosom. Covetousness, that root of evil, hath not yet sprung up in your heart; the selfish, the wrathful, and the licentious passions, have not yet obtained dominion over you. The modesty of nature, the great guardian of virtue, is not seduced from its post. You would blush, even in secret, to do a deed of dishonesty and shame. High sentiments of honor and of probity expand the soul. The color comes in our cheek at the smallest apprehension of blame; the ready lightning kindles in the eye at the least appearance of treachery and falsehood. Hence, says our Lord to his followers, Unless you become as a child; unless you assume the candor, the innocence and purity of children, you cannot enter into the kingdom of God. Therefore, whilst you are yet an offering fit for Heaven, present yourselves at his altar, devote yourselves to his service. How beautiful and becoming does it appear for young persons, newly arrived in this city of God, to remember the end for which they were sent into it, and to devote to their Maker's service the first and the best of their days? When they are in the prime of youth and of health, when the mind is untainted with actual guilt, and alive to every generous impression, to consecrate to religion the vernal flower of life? The virgin innocence of the mind is a sacrifice more acceptable to the Almighty, than if we should come before him with the cattle upon a thousand hills, and with ten thousand rivers of oil. If there be joy in heaven over a great and aged sinner that repenteth, how pleasing a spectacle will it be to God, to angels, and to the spirits of just men made perfect, to behold a person, in the critical season of life, acquit himself gloriously, and, despising the allurements, the deceitful and transitory pleasures of sin, choose for himself that better part which shall never be taken away!

Dare then, O young man, to remember thy Creator in the days of thy youth; have the courage to be good betimes. Beware of falling into the usual snare of the inexperienced; beware of thinking that you have time enough to be religious, and for that reason may defer the work of your salvation to maturer age, when, as you foolishly imagine, seriousness and sanctity will come of their own accord. In answer to this, let me ask you, my friends, How often have you observed time reform any one? Did time reform Saul? Did time reform Ahab? Did time reform Jezebel? On the contrary, did they not grow bolder in wickedness? You generally, indeed, observe a greater decency in maturer age. The ebullition of youth is then spent, its turbulence is over; but, too often, I am afraid, the wild passions have only given place to an external sobriety, whilst the heart is as far from God, and as carnal as ever. If you suspect this to be a hasty decision, examine what passes in the world. Do you not observe great part of men in the decline of life, as earthly-minded as before? The passion for pleasure has indeed abated, but the love of lucre, the most sordid of all passions, hath come into its place. If such persons have any regret for their past life, it is only because it *is past*. Even then they look with envy upon the gay and the flourishing state of the young. With what joy and triumph do they talk over the excesses of their early days, and seem to renew their age in the contemplation of their youthful follies? Alas, my friends, Is not God the Lord of all your time? Is there one of your days which doth not pertain to him? Why would you then take the flower of life, and make it an offering to the enemy of souls? Is your time too long, to be all employed in the service of God? Is the prime of your days too precious, to be devoted to Heaven? And will you only reserve to your Maker the refuse of life; the leavings of the world and the flesh? If you would speak it out, the language of your heart is this; that whilst you are good for any thing, you will mind the world and its pleasures; that you will crown yourselves with rose-buds, before they are withered, and let no flower of the spring pass away; but if at any time the world shall forsake you, if your passion for pleasure shall have left you, you will then seek the comforts of religion. Any part of your time, you think, is good enough for God; you will apply yourselves to the work of your salvation, when you are fit for nothing else; and when you cannot make a better of it, you will seek the kingdom of heaven.

Is it thus that ye requite the Lord, O people, foolish and unjust? Is this your gratitude to your Benefactor? Is this your love to your Father? Is this your kindness to your Friend? Whilst he now calls upon you in the sweetest language of heaven, "My son, give me thy heart," ought it not to be the natural movement of your heart, to answer with the good man of old, "With my soul have I desired thee in the night; with my spirit within me, will I seek thee early;"—"Whom have I in heaven but thee? and there is none in all the earth whom I desire beside thee."

In the *second* place, Let me exhort you to early piety, from the consideration of those evils which await you in your future days.

Now is your golden age. When the morning of life rejoices over your head, every thing around you puts on a smiling appearance. All nature wears a face of beauty, and is animated with a spirit of joy. You walk up and down in a new world; you crop the unblown flower, and drink the untasted spring. Full of spirit, and high in hope, you set out on the journey of life: visions of bliss present themselves to view: dreams of joy, with sweet delusion, amuse the vacant mind. You listen and accord to the song of hope, "To-morrow shall be as this day, and much more abundant." But ah! my friends, the flattering scene will not last. The spell is quickly broken, and the enchantment soon over. How hideous will life appear, when experience takes off the mask, and discovers the sad reality! Now thou hast no weariness to clog thy waking hours, and no care to disturb thy repose. But know, child of the earth, that thou art born to trouble, and that care, through every subsequent path of life, will haunt thee like a ghost. Health now sparkles in thine eye, the blood flows pure in thy veins, and thy spirits are gay as the morning: but alas! the time will come when diseases, a numerous and a direful train, will assail thy life; the time will come, when pale and ghastly, and stretched on a bed, "chastened with pain, and the multitude of thy bones with strong pain, thou wilt be ready to choose strangling and death rather than life."

You are now happy in your earthly companions. Friendship, which in the world is a feeble sentiment, with you is a strong passion. But shift the scene for a few years, and behold the man of thy right-hand become unto thee as an alien. Behold the friend of thy youth, who was one with thine own soul, striving to supplant thee, and laying snares for thy ruin! I mention not these things, my friends, to make you miserable before the time. God forbid that I should anticipate the evil day, unless I could arm you against it. Now remember your Creator, consecrate to him the early period of your days, and the light of his countenance will shine upon you through life. Amid all the changes of this fluctuating scene, you have a Friend that never fails. Then let the tempest beat, and the floods descend, you are safe and happy under the shelter of the Rock of ages.

Thirdly, The season of youth devoted to piety, will yield you a comfortable old age.

When the fire and spirit of youth are decayed; when sober age retires from the noise and bustle of a busy world, and loves to spend in peace the tranquil Sabbath of life, what joy will it afford to be able to look back with pleasure on the actions of other years! Worn out and weary of his pilgrimage, the traveller now entertains himself by recalling the times that are past, and recollecting the scenes of his early days. In particular, he now loves to recall the period of childhood and of youth, when he wandered up and down, a stranger to care and sorrow, and passed his days in innocence. Often does the fond idea recur; often the pleasant period return. It will add much, my friends, it will add much to the pleasures of the reflection, if you have it in your power to recall to mind that your early days were not only innocent, but useful, and devoted to the service of your Creator. To look back on a life, no season of which was spent in vain; to number up the days, the months, and the years, spent in the service of God, will be inward rapture, only to be felt. This will cause the evening of life to smile, and make your departure like a setting sun.

I shall conclude with one consideration, which I hope will have weight, and that is, if you seek God now in the days of youth, you are certain of success. Go out in the morning of youth, and you are sure to gather the manna of everlasting life. God himself will bend from his throne, and teach your spirits to approach unto him. They who seek him early shall find him, and shall be guarded from evil on his holy mountain.

SERMON IV.

ON THE IMPROVEMENT OF TIME.

Coloss. iv. 5.—"Redeeming the time."

Among those who have their time most at their own disposal, there prevails a maxim very different from that which is recommended in the text. The maxim of the world is, to spend time in idleness and folly, or, to speak in their own language, "to kill time" by dissipation and amusement. Life, which appears so short upon the whole, is nevertheless so long in particular parts, that vast numbers of men are overstocked with its days and hours; their time hangs heavy on their hands; they know not how to employ it, or what to make of themselves. As they have no fund of entertainment within, and for that reason, no happiness at home, they naturally look out for it abroad. Hence every pastime is greedily sought after, that can banish thought, and save them from their own company. Hence places of public entertainment are frequented, parties of pleasure are formed, plans of dissipation are concerted, and amusement, frivolous amusement, becomes the serious occupation of life. Only look around you into the world! Observe what policy and contrivance are continually put in practice by men, for pre-engaging every day in the week for one idleness or another; for doing nothing, or worse than nothing, and that with so much ingenuity and forecast, as scarce to leave an hour upon their hands to reproach them.

Such, my brethren, is the life of what is called the *world*, a repetition of the same childish conceptions, a perpetual round of the same trifling amusements. If you had been sent on earth to play the fool; if your pilgrimage through life were merely a jaunt of pleasure; it would be cruel and injurious to awaken you from the delusion. But as you profess to be Christians, and believe this life to be a state of moral discipline and probation for the next, it will be proper and seasonable to warn you of the folly of such a course, and to point out a nobler and a happier path, where at once you may see the world, and may adorn it; where at once you may improve your time, and enjoy life.

In order to this, I shall, in the *first* place, give you some directions for redeeming or improving the time; and, in the *second* place, set before you the obligations to the practice of this duty.

We begin with directions for redeeming the time. In the *first* place, treasure up in your memory a store of useful knowledge, as a proper foundation of employment to the mind.

It has been the complaint of discontented men in all ages, that life is a scene of dulness, not worth a wise man's care, where the same things come over and over like a tale that is told, which, however entertaining it may appear when it is new, yet, by frequent repetition, at last becomes tedious and insipid. The consequence of which has been, that many, viewing the picture in this disagreeable light, have been inclined to throw off all serious concern about their duty, to give themselves up to habits of indolence and languor, and to make no other use of their time, but to study how to trifle it away. True it is, indeed, that the days of many have thus been spent in vain; that their life has been a barren circle, within which they have been enchanted, going round and round, ever in motion, but never making any advances. But although many have made life a dull round of insignificant actions, yet no man had ever occasion to make it so. It is indeed so to the brutes, who soon arrive at that pitch of perfection which is allotted to their natures, where they must stop short without a possibility of going farther. Sense, which is their highest power, moves in a narrow sphere; its objects are few in number, and gross in kind, and therefore not only come more quickly round, but also grow more insipid at every revolution.

But man is endowed with nobler faculties, and is presented with nobler objects whereon to exercise and employ them. The contemplation of all divine truth to engage his understanding; the beauties of the natural and moral world to attract and captivate his affections; the power, the wisdom, and the goodness of God, manifested in the works of Creation, of Providence, and of Redemption, to exalt his admiration, and call forth all his praise. What employment can be more worthy of a rational being, or better adapted to the faculties of an immortal spirit, than thus to search out the order, the beauty, and the benevolence of nature, to trace the Everlasting in his works, and to mark the impression of his creating hand, yet recent on a beautiful world? Or if we turn our eyes towards the moral system, to observe a higher order of things, and a greater exertion of Divinity, in adjusting the plan of Providence, in bringing light from darkness, and good from evil, in causing the most unconnected and contrary events to co-operate to one great end, and making all to issue in the general good. Here is a noble path for a rational creature to travel in. Whilst day unto day thus teaches wisdom, night unto night will increase pleasure. The man who is thus trained up to the admiration of the works of God, and who has tasted the spirit of these sublime enjoyments, will not complain of the insignificance and languor of life. These studies will afford an occupation at all hours. They will make your own thoughts an entertainment to you, and open a fountain of happiness at home. They will diffuse somewhat of heaven over the mind; they will introduce you beforehand into the society of angels and blessed spirits above, and already prepare you to bear a part in that beautiful hymn of heaven, "Great and marvellous are thy works, Lord God Almighty; just and true are all thy ways, thou King of Saints."

Secondly, Have some end in view; some object to employ the mind, and call forth its latent powers.

In devising, or in executing a plan; in engaging in the whirl of active life, the soul seems to unfold its being, and to enjoy itself. Man is not like the soil on which he lives, which spends its powers in exercise, and requires repose, in order to recruit its wasted strength, and prepare it for new exertions. Activity is an essential attribute of mind. Its faculties exist only when they are exercised; it gains a new accession of strength from every new exertion, and the greater acquisitions it makes, it is enabled to make still greater. It is not a brook formed by the shower; it is a living fountain, which is for ever flowing, and yet for ever full. This will account for an observation that we have often occasion to make in life, that none have so little leisure as those who are entirely idle; that none complain so much of the want of time as those who have nothing to do. The fact is, they want that energy of soul which is requisite to every exertion, and that habit of activity which applies to every thing. Indolence unmans the faculties; impairs and debilitates the whole intellectual system. Those who, under its influence, become a kind of perpetual sleepers, degrade themselves from the honors of their nature, and are dead while they live. A habit of activity is a most valuable acquisition. He who is possessed of it, is fit for all events, and may be happy in every situation. This habit is only to be acquired by pursuing some great object that may agitate the mind. Think not that your labor may be spent in vain. Nothing is in vain that rouses the soul: nothing in vain that keeps the ethereal fire alive and glowing. The prospect of something coming forward; the pleasure and the pride which the mind takes in its own action, beget insensibly that habit of industry which will abide through life.

Thirdly, Set apart fixed and stated hours for the important duties of life.

It is the misfortune of great part of men, that they have no fixed plan of acting. They live *extempore*. They act at random. They are always led by instantaneous impulse, and are driven to and fro as inclination varies. Their life rolls on through a course of misspent time, and unconnected years, and appears upon review, like the path of a cloud in the air, which leaves no trace behind it. It was the custom of the great Alfred, one of the English kings, to divide the day into three parts, which he measured by the burning of tapers. One part he employed in the cares of the government; another part he dedicated to the cultivation of the liberal arts; the third he devoted to religion. It would be happy for you, my brethren, if, in this respect, you would imitate such an illustrious example. Let, at least, one part of your time be devoted to the service of God. When the morning ascends from the east, let it be your first care to offer up your earliest thoughts as incense to Heaven; to add your praises to the hymns and hosannas of the angels in light, and spirits of just men made perfect. When the shades of the night fall around you, let it be your constant care to implore the pardoning mercy of God for the errors of the past day, and to commit yourselves to the protection of His Providence who slumbers not nor sleeps. In particular, let this day, which is sacred to the memory of a Saviour's resurrection from the dead; which is a memorial of the full accomplishment of our redemption; let this day be set apart for holy contemplation on the wonders of redeeming love, on the height and depth and breadth and length of the love of Jesus to our race, which passeth all understanding; which prompted him to forego the glories of his divine nature for a time, to take upon him the robe of humanity, to lead a life of sorrows upon earth, and to suffer a cruel and ignominious, and an accursed death. Let us contemplate this amiable and divine love, till we are changed into the same image, and feel within ourselves an earnest and anticipation of that everlasting Sabbath of joy which is reserved for the righteous in the world to come, when time shall be no more.

In the *fourth* place, Endeavor to distinguish your days by some good deed.

As those who are intent to amass a for tune, attend to small sums, in like manner, if you would wish to improve your time, you must take care not to lose a day. Many are the ways, and frequent the occasions, which daily present themselves, of adding to your true happiness, of im proving your natures, and promoting the interests of society. You have all the world before you where to act, and the whole of human life as a theatre of virtue. Through the assistance of divine grace, conquer the excess of passion, correct some irregular desire, and obtain a victory over the vices that war against the soul. Let your goodness extend to society, and spread over the land, like the light of the morning. Can there be any employment so agreeable to a benevolent mind, and so congenial to the spirit of Christianity as to assuage the boisterous passions, and reconcile the jarring interests of men; to open the eye which prejudice has shut; to charm down the spirit of party, and to unite all your neighbors in one great family of love? Is not the employment god-like; is not the joy divine, to brighten up the face that was overcast with sadness; to wipe the tears from the cheek of sorrow; to turn the voice of mourning into the notes of joy; to make misery and woe vanish before us like darkness before the sun; to refresh with showers of blessings the dry and barren land wherein no water is, and, co-operating with a beneficent Providence, to watch for the happiness of the world? Where is there any one so destitute of the gifts of grace, of nature, and of fortune, as to have no mite to throw into the public treasury? He who cannot pretend to enlighten or reform the world, may instruct his ignorant, or comfort his afflicted neighbor: he who cannot communicate instruction, may give alms. If even these are not in your power, the gate of heaven is ever open; the throne of grace is ever accessible; and by your intercession with God, society may reap more benefit, than from the bounty of the opulent, or the labors of the learned. It was thus that Job improved his time, as we learn from his affecting complaint, when he reviewed the days of his prosperity: "O that I were as in months past, as in the days when God preserved me; as in the days of my youth, when the candle of the Lord shined upon my head, when the Almighty was yet with me, when my children were about me; when the ear heard me, then it blessed me, when the eye saw me, it gave witness to me, because I delivered the poor that cried, the fatherless, and him that had none to help him. I was eyes to the blind, feet was I to the lame: I was a father to the poor, and the cause which I knew not, I searched out. The stranger did not lodge in the street; I opened my doors to the traveller. The loins of the naked blessed me, and were warmed with the fleeces of my flock. The blessing of him that was ready to perish came upon me, and I caused the widow's heart to sing for joy."

In the *last* place, Accustom yourselves to frequent self-examination.

Call yourselves to an account at the close of the day. Inquire what you have been doing; whether you have lost a day or redeemed the time. Have you learned any useful truth? treasure it up in your heart, as a valuable acquisition; make it a principle of action, and bring it into life. Have you done a good deed? then enjoy the self-approving hour, and give thanks unto God for the pleasures of virtue, and the testimony of a good conscience. Have you been led astray by temptation; and overtaken in a fault? repent sincerely of your past transgression; implore the mercy of God, through the merits of Jesus Christ, and resolve, through divine grace, to be more guarded in the time to come. Did we, my brethren, thus make a study of a holy life; were we as much in earnest about improving the soul in piety and virtue, as we are about many trifling concerns, to what high degrees of sanctity might we ascend! How pleasant would it be at the close of any period of time, to look back on a life no season of which was spent in vain; to number up the days, the months, the years, that are marked with good deeds; to behold our youth, our manhood, and our age, as so many stages in our journey to the land of Emmanuel? This would inspire us with that peace of God which passeth all understanding. This would cheer the traveller in the decline of his days. His evening would be bright and pleasant, and his sun go down in glory. Life thus spent would make us triumph in death. Time thus improved would make us rejoice through all eternity.

I have thus given you some directions for the proper improvement of time. The second thing proposed, was to set before you the obligations to the practice of this duty, which I shall do by considering, in the *first* place, your nature as men, and, in the *second* place, your expectations as Christians.

In the *first* place, Let us consider our nature as men.

It is a study full of instruction to the curious or the pious mind, to contemplate the appearances in the universe, and trace the laws by which it is governed. All nature is busy and active. Something is ever coming forward in the creation; in the moral world, as well as in the natural, there is a design going on. The great purpose of nature in our system is to diffuse existence; to multiply all the forms of matter and classes of being. Every element is stored with inhabitants. Even the loneliest desert is populous, and putrefaction is pregnant with life. Worlds are inclosed in worlds, and systems of being going on, that escape the eye of sense.

Such is the plan of Providence in this inferior world. The order established at the first of time is still advancing. The divine Spirit, who at the beginning moved upon the face of the deep, and turned a chaos into a beautiful world, still continues to move, inform, and actuate the great machine. Nothing in nature is at rest: all is alive, all is in motion in the great system of God. Thou too, O man! art appointed to action. The love of occupation is strongly implanted in thy nature. One way or another, thou must be always employed. Woe to the man, who by his own folly is doomed to bear the pains and penalties of idleness. Rest is the void which mind abhors. An idle man is the most miserable of all the creatures of God. He falls upon a thousand schemes to fill up his hours, and rather than want employment, is contented to lie upon the torture of the mind, while the cards are shuffling, or the die is depending. The glory of our nature is founded upon exertions of activity. From the want of them, those in the more affluent stations of life, whose fortune is made at their birth, so often fail in attaining to the higher improvements and honors of their nature. Have you not, on the other hand, seen men, when business roused them from their usual indolence, when great occasion called them forth, discover a spirit to which they were strangers before, and display to the world abilities and virtues which seemed to be born with the occasion?

While there are so many splendid objects to allure the mind, why trust your character to be evolved by accident; why leave your glory in the power of fortune?

This activity is not only the source of our excellence, but also gives rise to our greatest enjoyments. Even the lower class of enjoyments, animal pleasures, are not only consistent with a life of activity, but also derive from it additional sweets. Hours of leisure, suppose hours of employment; they alone will relish the feast, who have felt the fatigues of the chase. But mere animal pleasures are not of themselves objects for a wise or a good man. Unless they are under the direction of taste; unless they have the accompaniments of elegance and grace; unless they promote friendship and social joy; unless they come at proper intervals, and have the additional heightening of being a relief from business, they soon pall upon the appetite, and disgust by repetition. Has sensuality a charm when thy friend is in danger, or thy country calls to arms? Who listens to the voice of the viol, when the trumpet sounds the alarm of battle? When the mind is struck with the grand and the sublime of human life, it disdains inferior things, and, kindling with the occasion, rejoices to put forth all its strength. Obstacles in the way only give additional ardor to the pursuit; and the prize appears then the most tempting to the view, when the ascent is arduous, and when the path is marked with blood. Hence that life is chosen, where incentives to action abound; hence serious engagements are the preferable objects of pursuit; hence the most animating occasions of life are calls to danger and hardship, not invitations to safety and ease; and hence man himself, in his highest excellence, is found to pine in the lap of repose, and to exult in the midst of alarms that seem to threaten his being. All the faculties of his frame engage him to action; the higher powers of the soul, as well as the softer feelings of the heart; wisdom and magnanimity, as well as pity and tenderness, carry a manifest reference to the arduous career he has to run, the difficulties with which he is destined to struggle, and the sorrows he is appointed to bear. Happiness to him is an exertion of soul. They know not what they say, who cry out, "Let us build tabernacles of rest." They mistake very much the nature of man, and go in quest of felicity to no purpose, who seek for it in what are called the enjoyments of life; who seek for it in a termination of labor and a period of repose. It is not in the calm scene; it is in the tempest; it is in the whirlwind; it is in the thunder that this Genius resides. When once you have discovered the bias of the mind; when once you have recognised your path in life; when once you have found out the object of the soul, you will bend to it alone; like an eagle when he has tasted the blood of his prey, who disdains the objects of his former pursuit, and follows on in his path through the heavens.

Thus have I set before you your obligations as men, to make a right use of life, and have shown you, from the principles of nature alone, without having recourse to Christianity, that the excellency and the happiness of man consists in a virtuous course of action, and in making a proper improvement of time. Let us now, in the *second* place, take in the considerations suggested by the Christian religion, and see what new obligations arise from it, to urge us to redeem the time.

It is the doctrine of revelation, then, that the present life is a state of probation for the life to come; that we are now training up for an everlasting existence; and that according to our works here, we shall be judged in a future world. According, therefore, as you now sow, hereafter you shall reap. The time is now passing that decides your fate for ever. The hours are at this instant on the wing, upon which eternity depends. In this view, let me exhort you to look back upon your past life. Call your former hours to an account. Ask them what report they have carried to heaven. Is there any thing in your life, to distinguish it from mere existence? Do you discern any thing but shadows in that mirror which remembrance holds up? Is the book of memory one vast blank, or blotted all over? If this be the case, and I am afraid it *is* the case with a great part of men, *what better* are *ye* than the animals of the field or the forest? Like you they sleep and they wake; like you they eat and they drink; like you they perform the various functions of nature. Alas! my brethren, did Almighty God create you after his own image, that you might sink that image to the resemblance of a beast? For, what have you done since you came into being, to distinguish yourselves from the brutes that perish? Have you glorified God in all your actions? Have you made your calling and election sure, by a lively faith in the Lord Jesus Christ, by repentance from dead works, and by universal purity of heart and life? Have you enriched your mind with the treasures of wisdom? Have you adorned your life with the beauties of holiness! Have you laid up many deeds of piety and charity, as a good foundation against the time to come? Unless you have done these things, you have done nothing. You have been blanks in the universe. You are as if you had never been. You have been fast asleep; nor has your sleep been the less sound, that you have dreamed you were awake.

I now call upon you to arise, or be for ever fallen. It is now high time to awake. Almighty God now calls upon you to finish the work which he hath given you to do. Glory and honor and immortality are set before you. Up then and be doing, and the Lord shall be with thee. With such views of your duty, and upon these principles of action, you will never join in the apology which some make for themselves, that the general tenor of their life is innocence, and that they have at least the negative merit to do no harm. Perhaps this account may be true; but let me ask such persons, Have you ever considered the parable of the master who called his servants to account? He delivered talents to each of them, according as he saw fit, with this charge, "Occupy till I come." The servant who received the one talent, was negligent and slothful. He wrapt up his talent in a napkin, and hid it in the earth. He thought he did well, if he secured the capital till his Lord's return. But the master received the talent with indignation. He cast the unprofitable servant into outer darkness, and condemned him to weeping and wailing and gnashing of teeth. The poor wretch was neither a thief nor a murderer. He had not wasted his Lord's goods. He had your plea, he had done no harm. But he was found guilty of idleness and sloth; he received his sentence, and was condemned to punishment. That which is the ground of your security, could not save him from condemnation.

But in good earnest, Do you no harm? Is it no harm to wander from the cradle to the grave, in a labyrinth of amusements, either vain or childish? Is it no harm to waste in dissipation and expensive pleasure, that wealth which might have saved an honest family from beggary and want? Is it no harm to squander in one continued round of vanity and folly, those precious hours on which your future happiness depends? If there be harm in human actions, *this* is harm. It is a criminal negligence which will turn the scale of your eternal doom.

To you, my younger friends, this duty recommends itself under the most interesting claims. You are now in that period, when time can be improved to the best advantage. With you, every hour of life is precious. The misimprovement of youthful days is more than the loss of time. It were of little consequence to throw away a few days from your life; but along with these, you cut off the substantial improvements, the real joys of maturer age. Figure to yourselves the loss which the year would sustain, if the spring were taken away; such a loss you sustain. No tears, nor lamentations, nor bitter upbraidings, will ever recall that golden period. The star sets, to rise no more; the flood rolls away, never to return.

Your own experience, my aged brethren, will urge the instant necessity of redeeming the time. Consider the fate that awaits you soon. A few steps will bring you to the threshold of that house which is appointed for all living. Man that is born of a woman is of few days. He cometh forth as a flower, and is cut down; he flieth as a shadow, and continueth not. By the unalterable law of nature, all things here hasten to an end. An irresistible rapidity hurries every thing to the abyss of eternity; to that awful abyss, to which all things go, and from which nothing returns. The great drama of life is perpetually going on. Age succeeds to age, and generation to generation. Not long ago, our fathers trod the path which their fathers had trodden before them; we have come into their room, and now supply their places. In a little time we must resign to another race, who in their turn also shall pass away, and give place to a new generation. The race of men, saith a Jewish writer, is like the leaves of the trees. They come forth in spring, and clothe the wood with robes of green. In autumn they wither; they fall; the winter wind scatters them on the earth. Another race comes in the season, and clothes the forest again.

Consider the world, my friends, as you saw it at first, and as you see it now. You have marked vicissitude and alteration in all human affairs. You have seen changes in almost every department of life. You have seen new ministers at the court, new judges on the bench, and new priests at the altar of the Lord. You have seen different kings upon the throne. You have seen peace and war, and war and peace again. How many of your equals in age have you survived? How many younger than you, have you carried to the grave? Year after year hath made a *blank* in the number of your friends. Your own country hath insensibly become a *strange* land, and a *new* world hath risen around you, before you perceived that the old had passed away. The same fate that hath taken your friends, awaits you. Even now the decree is gone forth. The king of terrors hath received his commission, and is now on his way. If you have misemployed your time, that talent which God hath put into your hand; if your life is marked with guilt or folly, how will you answer to your own heart at that awful hour? For previous to the general doom, Almighty God hath appointed *a day of judgment* in the *breast* of every man. The *last* hour is ordained to pass sentence on all the rest. The actions of your former life will there meet you again. How will you then answer at the bar of your own heart, when the collected crimes of a lengthened life, at *one view*, shall *flash* upon the mind; when the *ghosts* of your departed hours, of those hours which you have *murdered*, shall rise up in terrible array, and look you in the face? What would you then give for that time which you now throw away? What would the wretch who lies on a bed of agony, extended and groaning, who feels in his heart the poisoned arrow of death; who, looking back on his past life, turns aside from the view; who, looking forward to futurity, discerns no beam of hope to break that utter darkness which overwhelms him; what would he then give for those hours which you now despise, to make his peace with Heaven, and fit him for his passage into the world unknown? Remember, my friends, that this is no imaginary case; it is a case which may soon be your own. Be wise, therefore, while wisdom can avail, and save yourselves from the agony of repenting in bitterness of soul, when all repentance may be in vain.

To sum up all; my friends, the time is short. We are as guests in a strange land, who tarry but one night. We wander up and down in a place of graves. We read the epitaphs upon the tombs of the deceased. We shed a few tears over the ashes of the dead; and, in a little time, we need from our surviving friends the tears we paid to the memory of our friends departed.

Time is precious. The time is now passing that fixes our fate for ever. The hours are, at this instant on the wing, which carry along with them your eternal happiness or eternal misery.

Time is irrecoverable. The clock is wound up once for all; the hand is advancing, and, in a little time, it strikes your last hour.

SERMON V.

ON REVERENCE AND HOLY FEAR.

PSALM IV. 4.—"Stand in awe."

WHEN the Patriarch Jacob departed from his father's house, and entered on that state of pilgrimage, which only terminated with his life, he lighted on a certain place, where he tarried all the night. Agreeably to the simplicity of the ancient world, he laid himself down to rest on the open plain; without any pillow but a stone of the field; and without any covering but the curtains of heaven. A stranger he was to the elegance and luxury of after times, but he enjoyed pleasures of a higher kind. The God of his fathers was with him. In the patriarchal ages, before a public revelation was given to the world, the Deity frequently appeared to holy men in dreams, and visions of the night. Accordingly, Jacob, in his dream, beheld a ladder set upon the earth, the top of it reaching unto the heavens, and upon it the angels of God ascending and descending; and behold! the Lord stood above, and said, "I am the Lord God of Abraham, thy father, and the God of Isaac; the land whereon thou liest, to thee will I give it, and to thy seed; and thy seed shall be as the dust of the earth; thou shalt spread abroad to the east and to the west; to the south and to the north, and in thee, and in thy seed, shall all the families of the earth be blessed."

Did the Patriarch awake in a rapture of joy, when he had been thus so highly favored of the Lord? You shall hear: "And Jacob awaked out of his sleep, and he said, Surely the Lord is in this place, and I knew it not: and he was afraid, and said, How dreadful is this place! This is none other but the house of God, and this is the gate of heaven." Though he had ascended in the visions of God, and beheld scenes of glory which few are admitted to see; though he had received the most gracious promises of personal safety, of prosperous increase to his descendants, and of the Messiah who was to spring from his race, nevertheless an impression of reverence and awe was the last which remained upon his mind.

In like manner, my friends, although you have the near prospect of commemorating the most joyful event which signalizes the annals of time, yet if, at the approaching solemnity, God shall be in this place, you will experience that state of mind which the Patriarch was in when he awoke from his dream, and an impression of seriousness and awe will keep its hold of your hearts. There is a degree of reverence and holy fear which ever attends religion. Even when God manifests his mercy, it is, that he may be feared. Hence we are called to serve the Lord with fear, and rejoice before him with reverence. All objects make an impression upon the mind correspondent to their own nature. A beautiful object calls forth pleasing ideas, and excites a gay emotion. A grand object leaves upon the mind an impression of grandeur. In all sublime scenes, there is a mixture of the awful. The view of the skies by night; the moon moving in the brightness of her course; and the host of heaven in silent majesty performing their eternal rounds, strike an awe and adoration into the mind; we feel divinity present; we bow down and worship in the temple which the Most High God hath built with his hand, and hath filled with his presence. The presence of a respectable character raises a similar impression on the mind; and the man, who sets the Lord always before him, will feel his heart impressed with that mixture of seriousness and holy fear, which the Psalmist here recommends, when he says, "Stand in awe."

In further treating upon this subject, I shall, in the *first* place, point out the advantages of this seriousness and reverence which we ought to maintain upon our minds; and in the *second* place, show you the suitableness of this temper of mind to our present state.

The *first* thing proposed, is to point out the advantages of this seriousness and reverence which we ought to maintain upon our minds.

The great art of happiness consists in regulating, with propriety, the various offices of human life. To allow no duty to interfere with another; to prevent devotion from growing austere; and to restrain enjoyment from being criminal, is the mark of true wisdom, and of true piety. Every department of life is beautiful in its season. There is a time to be cheerful, and a time to be serious: an hour for solitude, and an hour for society. Providence hath appointed great part of our happiness to consist in society. We find, in every situation of life, that it is not good for us to be alone. Hence, civil society at first was instituted; hence, attachments are daily formed; and man is cemented to man by every feeling of nature, and every tie of the heart. But, as we abuse and corrupt every thing, the blessing of society is often turned into a curse. To innocent cheerfulness, a wanton levity succeeds, which banishes sober thought, and laughs at every thing that is serious. How often, in life, do we meet with the sons and daughters of folly, whose sole business is amusement; whose life is one continued scene of idleness and dissipation; everlasting triflers, whose volatile minds are perpetually on the wing, as if they had been sent to this earth merely to play the fool?

Not that I condemn cheerful society and innocent enjoyment. When God gives, let man enjoy. Let us drink from the fountain of joy, when we are sure there is no poison in the cup. But, my brethren, I must remind you, that but a narrow interval, often but a single step, lies between enjoyment and excess; between the voice of mirth, and the roar of riot; between innocent entertainment, and a loose and licentious indulgence. Look back on your past life, and tell me, O man! when was it that you felt yourself most strongly inclined to go astray? When was it that you found yourself seduced in thought, to wander from the paths of purity and uprightness? Was it not in the hour of levity and indulgence? Did not your heart betray you when your spirits were elevated; when you had banished sober recollection, and delivered yourself over to the delirium of excessive joy? Here then is the advantage of seriousness and reverence. It places a guard upon the heart. It keeps the world and its temptations at a due distance. It consecrates the mind in which it resides, as with the presence of the Deity. A heart thus impressed with the fear of God will not so readily be assaulted by the tempter; nor so easily yield to the temptation. An impure and profane guest will hardly venture upon hallowed ground, or dare to violate the sanctity of a temple. The presence of a good man is a check upon the turbulence and uproar of the giddy; they are inspired with a reverence for his character; they feel how awful goodness is, and restrain themselves from those indecent levities to which they are accustomed. If a regard for man has such influence upon the mind, what may the fear of God be supposed to have? The man who is possessed of this holy fear, sets the Lord always before him. He enters beforehand into heaven, and dwells in the presence of God. And canst thou, O man! defile the purity of heaven with the deeds of hell? Darest thou violate the law in the presence of the Lawgiver? Darest thou sin in the very face of thy Maker? Wilt thou make the Judge of all the earth the witness of thy wicked actions, the beholder of thy loose moments? No. In such a presence thou wilt banish all impure thoughts, and all unhallowed affections, like Moses at the burning bush, because the place whereon thou standest is holy ground.

Thus, of itself, this serious frame of mind is the guardian and the protector of religion; and it also associates with other virtues which belong to the Christian character. Those who are acquainted with the nature of the mind, know the influence and extent of association upon human life and manners. It is not a single quality that marks and characterizes a man; the virtues and the vices come in a train; it is the temper of the soul which is all in all in the conduct of human life. But to the temper and disposition here recommended, the most respectable attributes of the mind, and the most amiable qualities of the heart, are allied and peculiar.

In the first place, this serious frame of mind cherishes those higher virtues of the soul, which, in the emphatic language of the sacred Scripture, are called "the armor of God." In the solemn silence of the mind are formed those great resolutions which decide the fate of men; that magnanimity which rises superior to the events of life; that fortitude which bears up under the pressure of affliction; and that Christian heroism, which, neither moved with the threatenings of pain, nor with the blandishments of pleasure, holds on rejoicing to the end; are all of them but expressions of this character, varied and diversified according to the occurrences of life. They are the light, the giddy, and the volatile, who are the sport of caprice, or the prey of passion. Persons of such a character have no permanent principle of action; they are the sinners or the saints of accident; and assume every folly to which the fashion of the world gives its sanction. Very different is the serious man, who communes with his own heart. He follows not the multitude. He possesses that strenuous and steady mind, which walks by its own light, which holds its purpose to the last; that self-deciding spirit which is prepared to act, to suffer, or to die, as duty requires. Being thus, by the grace of God, the master of his own mind, he is above the world; and through prosperity or adversity, through life or death, goes forth conquering and to conquer. He is not guided by events like the giddy multitude, who fall into any form by the fortuitous concourse of accidents; but, imitating the providence of Heaven, he takes a direction of events, and makes the course of human affairs bend to his purposes, and terminate in his honor.

Further, this temper and disposition is no less favorable to the milder virtues of humanity. A serious mind is the companion of a feeling heart. It is akin to that virtuous sensibility, from which all the sympathetic emotions are derived; and readily associates with those good affections which constitute the most amiable part of our nature. The thoughtless and the dissipated are unconcerned spectators of human happiness or misery; they mar not their enjoyments by rushing into foreign woe; and are never so much in earnest, as to give a tear to the distresses of mankind. "They lie upon beds of ivory," saith the prophet; "they stretch themselves upon their couches; they chant to the sound of the viol; and they anoint themselves with the chief ointments: but they are not grieved for the affliction of their brethren." But he who feareth God will also regard man. The hour of incense has always been the hour of almsgiving. Whilst the heart is lifted up in devotion to God, the hands will be stretched out in beneficence to man. Think not, my friends, that these are duties of inferior importance, and not proper to be called up to your remembrance upon this occasion.

The ordinance which you are soon to celebrate, is the communion of saints, and the feast of love. The cup of blessing which we bless, saith the apostle, is it not the communion of the blood of Christ? The bread which we break, is it not the communion of the body of Christ? As we are all partakers of that one bread, so by that participation, we being many, become one body. Being thus the members of one body, the great law follows, which he afterwards lays down, that if one member suffers, all the members should suffer with it; and if one member rejoices, all the members should rejoice.

The *second* thing proposed, was to show you the suitableness of this temper of mind to our present state.

And, in the *first* place, it is suited to that dark and uncertain state of being in which we now live. Human life is not formed to answer those high expectations, which, in the era of youth and imagination, we are apt to entertain. When we first set out in life, we bid defiance to the evil day; we indulge ourselves in dreams and visions of romantic bliss; and fondly lay the scene of perfect and uninterrupted happiness for the time to come. But experience soon undeceives us. We awake, and find that it was but a dream. We make but few steps in life, without finding the world to be a turbulent scene; we soon experience the changes that await us, and feel the thorns of the wilderness wherein we dwell. Our hopes are frequently blasted in the bud; our designs are defeated in the very moment of expectation, and we meet with sorrow, and vexation, and disappointment, on all hands. There are lives besides our *own*, in which we are deeply interested; lives in which *our* happiness is placed, and on which our hopes depend. Just when we have laid a plan of happy life; when, after the experience of years, we have found out a few chosen friends, and have begun to enjoy that little circle in which we would wish to live and to die, an unexpected stroke disappoints our hopes, and lays all our schemes in the dust. When, after much labor and care, we have reared the goodly structure; when we have fenced it, as we fondly imagine, from every storm that blows, and indulge the pleasing hope, that it wlll always endure, an invisible hand interposes, and overturns it from the foundation. Who knoweth what awaits him in life? Who knoweth the changes through which he is destined to pass? Son of prosperity! Thou now lookest forth from thy high tower; thou now gloriest in thine excellence; thou sayest that thy mountain stands strong, and that thou art firm as the cedar of Lebanon—*But stand in awe.* Before the mighty God of Jacob, and by the blast of the breath of his nostrils, the mountain hath been overturned, and the cedar in Lebanon hath fallen like the leaf before the whirlwind. At this very moment of time, the wheel is in motion that reverses the lot of men; that brings the prosperous to the dust, and lays the mighty low. Now, O man! thou rejoicest in thy strength; but know, that for thee the bed of languishing is spread; pale, ghastly, and stretched on thy couch, thou shalt number the tedious hours, the restless days, the wearisome nights, that are appointed to thee, till thy soul shall be ready to "choose death rather than life." Thou now removest from thee the evil day, and sayest, in thy heart, thou shalt never see sorrow: but remember the changes of this mortal life; for thee the "cup of trembling" is prepared, and the wine of astonishment is poured "out." How often, in an instant, doth a hand unseen, shift the scene of the world? The calmest and the stillest hour precedes the whirlwind, and it hath thundered in the serenest sky. The monarch hath drawn the chariot of state, in which he was wont to ride in triumph, and the greatest who ever awed the world have moralized at the turn of the wheel.

In the *second* place, The propriety of this temper will appear, if we consider the scene that soon awaits us, and the awful change of being that we have to undergo. The sentence of the Lord is passed upon all flesh. Man, who art born of a woman! one day thou must die. The decree is gone forth, and the time appointed for its fulfilment is approaching fast. Short is the period which is allotted to mortal man. In a little time the scene changes, and the places that knew us shall know us no more. We bid an eternal adieu to all below the sun; we enter on a new state of being, and appear in the immediate presence of God. After death comes the judgment. Thou must answer, O man, to the Searcher of hearts, for the deeds done in the body. The actions of thy past life shall rise up to thy remembrance; the secrets of thy soul shall be disclosed; and thy eternal doom be fixed by God, the Judge of all. In thy last moments, thou *wilt be serious*, and *stand in awe*. The most thoughtless sinner will stand aghast, and the stoutest heart will tremble at that awful, that parting hour, when, to the closing eye, God appears, with as full conviction, as if the curtain between both worlds was withdrawn, and the Judge in very deed descended to his tribunal. How serious wilt thou be when surrounded by the sad circle of thy weeping friends, thou readest in their altered looks that thy hour is come; when cut off from all connection with mortality, thou takest thy last look of what thou heldest dear in life; when the cold sweat, the shivering limb, and the voice faltering in the throat, announce thy departure into the world unknown! What manner of persons ought we to be, who have such events awaiting us! Ought we not to stand in awe; to join trembling with our mirth; to commune with our hearts alone, and be still as in the presence of that God, before whose tribunal we have soon to appear?

In the *third* place, This frame of mind is peculiarly proper for you now, as a preparation for that solemnity which you are soon to celebrate. Holy is every ordinance of the Lord; but this is the holiest of all, and should inspire us with reverence and godly fear. You are to be engaged in the most solemn ordinance of our religion. You are to be employed in the most important work of your lives, to seal your vows in the faith of everlasting redemption. You are going to transact with the God of Glory, before whom ten thousand times ten thousand angels and archangels bow down and admire and adore. You are about to commemorate the most tremendous event which is to be found in the records of time; that scene which made the sun grow dark, and which the earth trembled to behold. God shows himself to be awful, even when he manifests his mercy, and causes all his goodness to pass before you. When he blesses men with the greatest testimony of his love, it is by smiting his own Son; when the gate of heaven is set open to the world, it is opened by *the blood of One who is higher than the heavens.* Whilst thou rejoicest therefore at the remembrance of thy redemption, think with wonder upon the ransom by which it is accomplished, and implore the assistance of the Divine spirit, that you may serve God acceptably, with reverence and godly fear.

SERMON VI.

ON DEATH.

Job xxx. 23.—"For I know that thou wilt bring me to death, and to the house appointed for all living."

This book of Job contains the history of a righteous man, fallen from the height of prosperity, into scenes of great distress. Almost every affliction which falls to the lot of mortal man embittered his life. His goods were taken away by robbers; his body was smitten by a loathsome and tormenting disease; his family was cut off, and all his company made desolate by a sudden stroke from heaven; his surviving friends proved miserable comforters, and, instead of relieving, added to his afflictions. His head was bare to every blast of adversity, and his heart bled with all the varieties of pain. In the course of his complaint, he utters the genuine voice of sorrow, and pours forth his soul in lamentation and woe. He sets before us the evil day; he shows us the dark side of things, and presents to view those shades in the picture of human life, which must one day meet our eye. From these calamities, he passes, by a natural transition, to the consideration of the last evil in human life: "I know that thou wilt bring me to death, and to the house appointed for all living."

Man is a serious being. There is a string in the heart which accords to the voice of sorrow, and impressions of grief take the strongest hold of the mind. There is a time when solitude has a charm; when cheerfulness gives place to melancholy; and when the house of mourning is better suited to the soul than the house of mirth. Even our amusements often partake of a serious turn. For the sake of amusement, we give our attention to histories of woe; we sit spectators to the scene of sorrow, and devote the hours to melancholy and to tears. And yet, by a strange perversion of mind, though we rush into foreign woe, and take delight in weeping for the fate of others, yet our own departure excites little attention or regard, notwithstanding the many warnings which tell us that here we have no continuing city. Although few weeks elapse without being marked with the funeral of a neighbor or a friend, we remain in a criminal indifference; the tear is soon dried upon our cheeks, and we muse upon the fate of our friends with unconcern. If, by removing the thought of death, men could remove the day of death, their conduct would admit of an excuse. But whether you think of it or not, death approaches, and the want of preparation will only serve to sharpen the sting, by the surprise with which it may strike.

Since we know then assuredly, that God will bring us to death, and to the house appointed for all living, let us consider, in the *first* place, the certainty of its approaching soon; *secondly*, the time and manner of its arrival; and, *thirdly*, the change which it introduces.

In the *first* place, let us consider the certainty of death's approaching soon.

All the works of nature, in this inferior system, seem only made to be destroyed. Man is not exempted. There is a principle of mortality in our frame, and, as if we were only born to die, the first step we take in life is a step to the grave. It was not always so. Adam came from the hands of his Creator perfect and immortal. The Almighty created man after his own image. He planted in his frame the seeds of eternal life, to grow and flourish through a succession of ages. This noble shoot, which the hand of the Most High had planted, was blasted by sin. When man became a sinner, he became mortal. The doom was pronounced, that, after few and evil days, he should return to the dust from whence he was taken. Since that time, as soon as our eyes open on the light, we come under the law of mortality, and the sentence of death is passed. In the morning of our day, we set out on our journey for eternity; thither we are all fast tending; and day and night we travel on without intermission. There is no standing still on this road. To this great rendezvous of the sons of Adam we are continually drawing nearer and nearer. Our life is for ever on the wing, although we mark not its flight. Our motion down the stream of time is so smooth and silent, that though we are for ever moving, we perceive it not, till we arrive at the ocean of eternity. Even now, death is doing his work. At this very moment of time, multitudes are stretched on that bed from which they shall rise no more. The blood is ceasing to flow; the breath is going out; and the spirit taking its departure for the world unknown.

When we look back on our former years, how many do we find who began the journey of life along with us, and promised to themselves long life and happy days, cut off in the midst of their career, and fallen at our side! They have but gone before us; one day we must follow. O man! who now rejoicest in the pride of life, and looking abroad, sayest in thy heart, thou shalt never see sorrow, for thee the bed of death is spread; the worm calls for thee to be her companion; thou must enter the dominions of the dead, and be gathered to the dust of thy fathers. If then death be certainly approaching fast, let us learn the true value of life. If death be at hand, then certainly time is precious. Now the day shines, and the Master calls us; in a little time the night cometh, when no man can work. Today, therefore, hear the voice which calls you to heaven. "Now is the accepted time; now is the day of salvation." Whatsoever thy hand findeth to do, do it with thy might; for there is no work, nor device, nor knowledge, nor wisdom in the grave, whither thou goest."

In the *second* place, we may consider the time and manner of the arrival of death.

Death is called in Scripture, *the land without any order*; and without any order the king of terrors makes his approaches in the world. The commission given from on high was, "Go into the world: Strike; strike so, that the dead may alarm the living." Hence it is, that we seldom see men running the full career of life; growing old among their children's children, and then falling asleep in the arms of nature, as in the embraces of a kind mother; coming to the grave like a shock of corn fully ripe; like flowers that shut up at the close of the day. Death walks through the world without any order. He delights to surprise, to give a shock to mankind. Hence, he leaves the wretched to prolong the line of their sorrows, and cuts off the fortunate in the midst of their career; he suffers the aged to survive himself, to outlive life, to stalk about the ghost of what he was, and aims his arrow at the heart of the young who puts the evil day far from him. He delights to see the feeble carrying the vigorous to the grave, and the father building the tomb of his children. Often when his approaches are least expected, he bursts at once upon the world, like an earthquake in the dead of night, or thunder in the serene sky. All ages and conditions he sweeps away without distinction; the young man just entering into life, high in hope, elated with joy, and promising to himself a length of years; the father of a family from the embraces of his wife and children; the man of the world, when his designs are ripening to execution, and the long expected crisis of enjoyment seems to approach. These and all others are hurried promiscuously off the stage, and laid without order in the common grave. Every path in the world leads to the tomb, and every hour in life hath been to some the last hour.

Without order too, is the manner of death's approach. The king of terrors wears a thousand forms; pains and diseases, a numerous and a direful train, compose his host. Marking out unhappy man for their prey, they attack the seat of life, or the seat of understanding; hurry him off the stage in an instant, or make him pine by slow degrees: blasting the bloom of life, or, waiting till the decline, according to the pathetic picture of Solomon, "They make the strong men bow themselves, and the keepers of the house tremble; make the grinders cease; bring the daughters of music low; darken the sun, and the moon, and the stars; scatter fears in the way, and make desire itself to fail, until the silver cord be loosed, and the golden bowl be broken, when the dust returns to the dust as it was, and the spirit ascends to God who gave it."

In the *third* place, We have to consider the change which death introduces.

Man was made after the image of God; and the human form divine, the seat of so many heavenly faculties, graces and virtues, exhibits a temple not unworthy of its Maker. Men in their collective capacity, and united as nations, have displayed a wide field of exertion and of glory. The globe hath been covered with monuments of their power, and the voice of history transmits their renown from one generation to another. But when we pass from the living world to the dead, what a sad picture do we behold! The fall and desolation of human nature; the ruins of man; the dust and ashes of many generations scattered over the earth. The high and the low; the mighty and the mean; the king and the cottager, lie blended together without any order. The worm is the companion, is the sister of him, who thought himself of a different species from the rest of mankind. A few feet of earth contain the ashes of him who conquered the globe; the shadows of the long night stretch over all alike; the monarch of disorder, the great leveller of mankind, lays all on the bed of clay in equal meanness. In the course of time, the land of desolation becomes still more desolate; the things that were, become as if they had never been; Babylon is a ruin, her heroes are dust; not a trace remains of the glory that shone over the earth, and not a stone to tell where the master of the world is laid. Such, in general, is the humiliating aspect of the tomb; but let us take a nearer view of the house appointed for all living. Man sets out in the morning of his day, high in hope, and elated with joy. The most important objects to him are the companions of his journey. They set out together in the career of life, and, after many mutual endearments, walk hand in hand through the paths of childhood and of youth. It is with a giddy recollection we look back on the past, when we consider the number and the value of those, whom unforeseen disaster and the hand of destiny have swept from our side. Alas! When the awful mandate comes from on high concerning men, to change the countenance, and to send them away, what sad spectacles do they become! The friends whom we knew, and valued, and loved; our companions in the path of life; the partners of our tender hours, with whom we took sweet counsel, and walked in company to the house of God, have passed to the land of forgetfulness, and have no more connection with the living world. Low lies the head that was once crowned with honor. Silent is the tongue to whose accents we surrendered the soul, and to whose language of friendship and affection we wished to listen for ever. Beamless is the eye, and closed in night, which looked serenity and sweetness and love. The face that was to us as the face of an angel, is mangled and deformed; the heart that glowed with the purest fire, and beat with best affections, is now become a clod of the valley.

But shall it always continue so? If a man die, shall he live again! There is hope of a tree if it be cut down; but man giveth up the ghost, and where is he? Has the breath of the Almighty, which animated his frame, vanished into the air? Is he who triumphed in the hope of immortality, inferior to the worm, his companion in the tomb? Will light never rise on the long night of the grave? Does the mighty flood that has swept away the nations and the ages, ebb to flow no more? Have the wise and the worthy; the pious and the pure; the generous and the just; the great and the good; the excellent ones of the earth, who, from age to age, have shone brighter than all the stars of heaven, withdrawn into the shade of annihilation, and set in darkness to rise no more? No. While "the dust returns to the earth as it was, the spirit thall return unto God who gave it." Life and immortality are brought to light by the Gospel of Christ. "We know, that if our earthly house of this tabernacle were dissolved, we have a building of God, an house not made with hands, eternal in the heavens."

The periods of human life passing away; the certainty of the dissolution which awaits us, and the frequent examples of mortality, which continually strike our view, lead us to reflect with seriousness upon the house appointed for all living. Death is the great teacher of mankind; the voice of wisdom comes from the tomb; reflections, which show us the vanity, will teach us the value of life. Such meditations are particularly suited to beings like us, who are subject to infirmities and defects. For such is the weakness of human nature in this imperfect state; such is the strength of temptation in this evil world, that frail man is often led astray before he is aware. The enemy of the soul attacks us in every quarter; approaches often under false colors, and tries every disguise, to deceive and to destroy. Vice often borders on virtue; the narrow path and the broad way lie so near, that it is difficult to distinguish them, so as to order our goings aright. Inadvertence may frequently betray; the impetuosity of passion may precipitate, and the gentleness of our own nature mislead us into steps fatal to our peace. I speak not of wicked men, who acknowledge no guide but their passions, and submit to no law but what one vice imposes upon another. I talk of the sincere and the good. The most watchful Christian has his unguarded moments; the most prudent man speaks unadvisedly with his lips, and the meekest lets the sun go down upon his wrath. Alas! Man in his best estate is altogether vanity, and always stands in need of the lesson from the tomb. "O that they were wise," said Moses, "that they understood this, that they would consider their latter end!"

SERMON VII.

ON THE CHRISTIAN'S VICTORY OVER DEATH.

1 Cor. xv. 55, 57.—"O death! Where is thy sting? O grave! Where is thy victory?—Thanks be to God who giveth us the victory, through our Lord Jesus Christ."

The Messiah is foretold in ancient prophecy, as a magnificent Conqueror. His victories were celebrated, and his triumphs were sung, long before the time of his appearance to Israel. "Who is this," saith the prophet Isaiah, pointing him out to the Old Testament Church, "Who is this that cometh from Edom; with dyed garments from Bozrah? This that is glorious in his apparel, travelling in the greatness of his strength?"—"I have set my King upon my holy hill of Zion. I shall give him the heathen for his inheritance, and the uttermost parts of the earth for his possession." As a Conqueror, he had to destroy the works of the great enemy of mankind; and to overcome death, the king of terrors.

The method of accomplishing this victory, was as surprising as the love which gave it birth. "Forasmuch as the children are partakers of flesh and blood, he himself likewise took part of the same, that through his own death, he might destroy him that had the power of death, that is the devil, and deliver them, who, through fear of death, were all their lifetime subject to bondage." Accordingly, his passion on the cross, which you have this day commemorated, was the very victory which he obtained. The hour in which he suffered, was also the hour in which he overcame. Then he bruised the head of the old serpent, who had seduced our first parents to rebel against their Maker; then he disarmed the king of terrors, who had usurped dominion over the nations; then triumphing over the legions of hell, and the powers of darkness, he made a show of them openly. Not for himself, but for us did he conquer. The Captain of our salvation fought, that we might overcome. He obtained the victory, that we may join in the triumphal song, as we now do, when we repeat these words of the apostle; "O death! where is thy sting? O grave! where is thy victory?"

It is the glory of the Christian religion, that it abounds with consolations under all the evils of life; nor is its benign influence confined to the course of life, but even extends to death itself. It delivers us from the agony of the last hour; sets us free from the fears which then perplex the timid; from the horrors which haunt the offender, though penitent, and from all the darkness which involves our mortal state. So complete is the victory we obtain, that Jesus Christ is said in Scripture to have *abolished* death.

The evils in death, from which Jesus Christ sets us free, are the following: in the *first* place, The doubts and fears that are apt to perplex the mind, from the uncertainty in which a future state is involved. *Secondly*, The apprehensions of wrath and forebodings of punishments, proceeding from the consciousness of sin. *Thirdly*, the fears that arise in the mind upon the awful transition from this world to the next.

In the *first* place, Jesus Christ gives us victory over death, by delivering us from the doubts and fears which arose in the minds of those who knew not the gospel, from the uncertainty in which a future state was involved.

Without Divine Revelation, men wandered in the dark with respect to an after life. Unassisted reason could give but imperfect information on this important article. Conjectures, in place of discoveries, presumptions, in place of demonstrations, were all that it could offer to the inquiring mind. The unenlightened eye could not clearly pierce the cloud which veiled futurity from mortal view. The light of nature reached little farther than the limits of this globe, and shed but a feeble ray upon the region beyond the grave. Hence, those heathen nations, of whom the apostle speaks, are described as *sorrowing* and *having no hope.* And whence could reason derive complete information, that there was a state of immortality beyond the grave? Consult with appearances in nature, and you find but few intimations of a future life. Destruction seems to be one of the great laws of the system. The various forms of life are indeed preserved; but while the species remains, the individual perishes. Every thing that you behold around you, bears the marks of mortality, and the symptoms of decay. He only who is, and was, and is to come, is without any variableness or shadow of turning. Every thing passes away. A great and mighty river, for ages and centuries, has been rolling on, and sweeping away all that ever lived, to the vast abyss of eternity. On that darkness light does not rise. From that unknown country none return. On that devouring deep, which has swallowed up every thing, no vestige appears of the things that were.

There are particular appearances also which might naturally excite an alarm for the future. The human machine is so constituted, that soul and body seem often to decay together. To the eye of sense, as the beast dies, so dies the man. Death seems to close the scene, and the grave to put a final period to the prospects of man. The words of Job beautifully express the anxiety of the mind on the subject. "If a man die, shall he live again? There is hope of a tree if it be cut down, that it will sprout again, and that the tender branch thereof will not cease. Though the root thereof wax old in the earth, and the stock thereof die in the ground; yet, through the scent of water it will bud, and bring forth boughs like a plant: but man dieth, and is cut off; man giveth up the ghost, and where is he? As the waters fail from the sea; as the flood decayeth and drieth up; so man lieth down, and riseth not; till the heavens be no more, they shall not awake, nor be raised out of their sleep." But what a dreadful prospect does annihilation present to the mind! To be an outcast from existence; to be blotted out from the book of life; to mingle with the dust, and be scattered over the earth, as if the breath of life had never animated our frame! Man cannot support the thought. Is the light which shone brighter than all the stars of heaven set in darkness, to rise no more? Are all the hopes of man come to this, to be taken into the councils of the Almighty; to be admitted to behold part of that plan of Providence which governs the world, and when his eyes are just opened, to read the book, to be shut for ever? If such were to be our state, we would be of all creatures the most miserable. The world appears a chaos without form, and void of order. From the throne of nature, God departs, and there appears a cruel and capricious being, who delights in death, and makes sport of human misery.

From this state of doubts and fears, we are delivered by the Gospel of Jesus. The message which he brought, was life and immortality. From the Star of Jacob, light shone even upon the shades of death. As a proof of immortality, he called back the departed spirit from the world unknown; as an earnest of the resurrection to a future life, he himself arose from the dead. When we contemplate the tomb of nature, we cry out, "Can these dry bones live?" When we contemplate the tomb of Jesus, we say, "Yes, they can live!" As he arose, we shall in like manner arise. In the tomb of nature, you see man return to the dust from whence he was taken. In the tomb of Jesus, you see man restored to life again. In the tomb of nature, you see the shades of death fall on the weary traveller, and the darkness of the long night close over his head. In the tomb of Jesus, you see light arise upon the shades of death, and the morning dawn upon the long night of the grave. On the tomb of nature, it is written, "Behold thy end, O man! Dust thou art, and unto dust thou shalt return. Thou, who now callest thyself the son of heaven, shall become one of the clods of the valley." On the tomb of Christ is written, "Thou diest, O man! but to live again. When dust returns to dust, the spirit shall return to God who gave it. I am the resurrection and the life; he that believeth in me, though he were dead, yet shall he live." From the tomb of nature, you hear a voice, "For ever silent is the land of forgetfulness? From the slumbers of the grave, shall we awake no more? Like the flowers of the field, shall we be as though we had never been?" From the tomb of Jesus, you hear, "Blessed are the dead that die in the Lord, thus saith the Spirit, for they rest from their labors, and pass into glory:—In my Father's house, there are many mansions; if it were not so, I would have told you: I go to prepare a place for you, and if I go away, I will come again, and take you unto myself, that where I am, there ye may be also."

Will not this assurance of a happy immortality, and a blessed resurrection, in a great measure remove the terror and the sting of death? May we not walk without dismay through the dark valley, when we are conducted by a beam from heaven? May we not endure the tossings of one stormy night, when it carries us to the shore that we long for? What cause have we to dread the messenger who brings us to our Father's house? Should not our fears about futurity abate, when we hear God addressing us with respect to death, as he did the Patriarch of old, upon going to Egypt, "Fear not to go down to the grave; I will go down with thee, and will bring thee up again."

Secondly, Our victory over death consists in our being delivered from the apprehensions of wrath, and forebodings of punishment, which arise in the mind from the consciousness of sin.

That there is a God who governs the world, the patron of righteousness, and the avenger of sin, is so manifest from the light of nature, that the belief of it has obtained among all nations. That it shall be well with the righteous, and ill with the wicked; that God will reward those who diligently seek him, and punish those who transgress his laws, is the principle upon which all religion is founded. But whether mercy be an attribute in the Divine nature to such an extent that God may be rendered propitious to those who rebel against his authority, and disobey his commandments, is an inquiry to which no satisfactory answer can be made. Many of the Divine attributes are conspicuous from the works of creation; the power, the wisdom, and the goodness of God, appear in creating the world; in superintending that world which he has made; in diffusing life wide over the system of things, and providing the means of happiness to all his creatures. But from no appearances in nature does it clearly follow, that the exercise of mercy to offenders is part of the plan by which the universe is governed. For any thing that we know from the light of nature, repentance alone may not be sufficient to procure the remission of sins; the tears of contrition may be unavailable to wash away the stains of a guilty life, and the Divine favor may be implored in vain by those who have become obnoxious to the Divine displeasure. If in the calm and serene hour of inquiry, man could find no consolation in such thoughts, how would he be overwhelmed with horror, when his mind was disordered with a sense of guilt? When remembrance brought his former life to view, when reflection pierced him to the heart, darkness would spread itself over his mind, Deity would appear an object of terror, and the spirit, wounded by remorse, would discern nothing but an offended Judge armed with thunders to punish the guilty. If, in the day of health and prosperity, these reflections were so powerful to embitter life, they would be a source of agony and despair when the last hour approached. When life flows according to our wishes, we may endeavor to conceal our sins, and shut our ears against the voice of conscience. But these artifices will avail little at the hour of death. Then things appear in their true colors. Then conscience tells the truth, and the mask is taken off from the man, when our sins at that hour pass before us in review. Guilty and polluted as we are, covered with confusion, How shall we appear at the judgment seat of God, and answer at the bar of eternal justice? How shall dust and ashes stand in the presence of that uncreated Glory, before which principalities and powers bow down, tremble, and adore? How shall guilty and self-condemned creatures appear before Him, in whose sight the heavens are not clean, and who chargeth his angels with folly? This is the sting of death. It is guilt that sharpens the spear of the king of terrors. But even in this view we have victory over death, through Jesus Christ our Lord. By his death upon the cross, an atonement was made for the sins of men. The wrath of God was averted from the world. A great plan of reconciliation is now unfolded in the gospel. Under the banner of the cross, pardon is proclaimed to returning penitents. They who accept the offers of mercy, and who fly for refuge to the hope set before them, are taken into favor; their sins are forgiven, and their names are written in the book of life. Over them death has no power. The king of terrors is transformed into an angel of peace, to waft them to their native country, where they long to be.

This, O Christian! the death of thy Redeemer, is thy strong consolation; thy effectual remedy against the fear of death. What evil can come nigh to him for whom Jesus died? Does the law which thou hast broken, denounce vengeance against thee? Behold that law fulfilled in the meritorious life of thy Redeemer. Does the sentence of wrath pronounced against the posterity of Adam sound in thine ears? Behold that sentence blotted out, that *handwriting*, as the apostle calls it, cancelled, nailed to thy Saviour's cross, and left there as a trophy of his victory. Art thou afraid that the cry of thy offences may rise to heaven, and reach the ears of justice? There is no place for it there; in room of it ascends the voice of that blood which speaketh better things than the blood of Abel. Does the enemy of mankind accuse thee at the judgment-seat? He is put to silence by thy Advocate and Intercessor at the right hand of thy Father. Does death appear to thee in a form of terror, and hold out his sting to alarm thy mind? His terror is removed, and his sting was pulled out by that hand, which, on mount Calvary, was fixed to the accursed tree. Art thou afraid that the arrows of divine wrath which smite the guilty, may be aimed at thy head? Before they can touch thee, they must pierce that body, which, in the symbols of divine institution, was this day held forth crucified among you, and which at the right hand of the Majesty in the heavens, is for ever presented in behalf of the redeemed. Well then may ye join in the triumphant song of the apostle, "O death! where is thy sting? O grave! where is thy victory?"

In the *third* place, Jesus Christ gives us victory over death, by yielding us consolation and relief under the fears that arise in the mind upon the awful transition from this world to the next.

Who ever left the precincts of mortality without casting a wishful look on what he left behind, and a trembling eye on the scene that is before him? Being formed by our Creator for enjoyments even in this life, we are endowed with a sensibility to the objects around us. We have affections, and we delight to indulge them: we have hearts, and we want to bestow them. Bad as the world is, we find in it objects of affection and attachment. Even in this waste and howling wilderness, there are spots of verdure and of beauty, of power to charm the mind and make us cry out, "It is good for us to be here." When, after the observation and experience of years, we have found out the objects of the soul, and met with minds congenial to our own, what pangs must it give to the heart, to think of parting for ever? We even contract an attachment to inanimate objects. The tree under whose shadow we have often sat; the fields where we have frequently strayed; the hill, the scene of contemplation, or the haunt of friendship, become objects of passion to the mind, and upon our leaving them, excite a temporary sorrow and regret. If these things can affect us with uneasiness, how great must be the affliction, when stretched on that bed from which we shall rise no more, and looking about for the last time on the sad circle of our weeping friends! How great must be the affliction, to dissolve at once all the attachments of life; to bid an eternal adieu to the friends whom we long have loved, and to part for ever with all that is dear below the sun! But let not the Christian be disconsolate. He parts with the objects of his affection, to meet them again; to meet them in a better world, where change never enters, and from whose blissful mansions sorrow flies away. At the resurrection of the just; in the great assembly of the sons of God, when all the family of heaven are gathered together, not one person shall be missing that was worthy of thy affection or esteem. And if among imperfect creatures, and in a troubled world, the kind, the tender, and the generous affections have such power to charm the heart, that even the tears which they occasion delight us, what joy unspeakable and glorious will they produce, when they exist in perfect minds, and are improved by the purity of the heavens!

Christianity also gives us consolation in the transition from this world to the next. Every change in life awakens anxiety; whatever is unknown, is the object of fear; no wonder then that it is awful and alarming to nature, to think of that time when the hour of our departure is at hand; when this animal frame shall be dissolved, and the mysterious bond between soul and body shall be broken. Even the visible effects of mortality are not without terror; to have no more a name among the living; to pass into the dominions of the dead; to have the worm for a companion, and a sister, are events at which nature shudders and starts back. But more awful still is the invisible scene, when the curtain between both worlds shall be drawn back, and the soul naked and disembodied appear in the presence of its Creator. Even under these thoughts, the comforts of Christianity may delight thy soul. Jesus, thy Saviour, has the keys of death; the abodes of the dead are part of his kingdom. He lay in the grave, and hallowed it for the repose of the just. Before our Lord ascended up on high, he said to his disciples, "I go to my Father and to your Father, to my God and to your God;" and when the time of your departure is at hand, you go to your Father and his Father, to your God and his God.

Enlightened by these discoveries, trusting to the merits of his Redeemer, and animated with the hope which is set before him, the Christian will depart with tranquillity and joy. To him the bed of death will not be a scene of terror, nor the last hour an hour of despair. There is a majesty in the death of the Christian. He partakes of the spirit of that world to which he is advancing, and he meets his latter end with a face that looks to the heavens.

SERMON VIII.

ON THE DOCTRINE OF A PARTICULAR PROVIDENCE.

PSALM XCVII. 1.—"The Lord reigneth, let the earth rejoice."

To thinking men, the universe presents a scene of wonders. They find themselves brought into the world, they know not how. If they look around them, they behold the earth clothed with an infinite variety of herbs and fruits, subservient to their use, or administering to their delight. If they look above them, they behold the host of heaven walking in brightness and in beauty; the sun ruling the day; the moon and the stars governing the night. If they attend to the course of nature, they behold with wonder the various revolutions of the year; the gradual return of the seasons, and the constant vicissitude of day and of night. Whilst thus they are employed, they behold in the heavens the glory of their Creator; they discover in the firmament the handiwork of Omnipotence, and they hear the voice that nature sends out to the ends of the earth, that all things are the workmanship of a supreme and intelligent Cause. As from these events they conclude the Almighty to be the Maker of the world; from the same events, they conclude that he is the Governor of the world which he hath made, and that Divine power is as requisite to preserve the order and harmony of the world now, as it was necessary to establish it at the first. But when experience unfolded to them the powers of natural bodies; when they saw machines contrived by human skill, exhibiting motions, and producing effects, similar to those which they observed in nature, by the impulse of matter upon matter; and when they saw these machines regularly exhibiting such motions, regularly producing such effects, although the head that contrived, and the hand that put them together, were removed from them; this raised an opinion, in some speculative minds, that the world resembled such machines; and that, as a clock will show the hour of the day, in virtue of its original frame and constitution, without any further interposition of the artificer that framed it, so nature, in virtue of its original frame and constitution, may and does produce every effect which we see around us, without any further interposition of its Divine Author.

This opinion is frequently mentioned and confuted in the Sacred Scriptures. Those men are condemned whose belief it was, that, in the course of human affairs, the Lord would not do good, neither would he do evil. Although I seldom choose to carry you through the barren and unpleasant fields of controversy, yet, as this question affects so deeply our religious comfort in this state, and our hopes of happiness in a future world, I shall consider it at large, and shall, in the *first* place, Show you the absurdity of that opinion which would exclude God from the government of the world. *Secondly*, Establish and confirm the doctrine of a *particular Providence*. *Thirdly*, Show you the grounds of joy arising to the world from such a Providence.

In the *first* place, I am to show the absurdity of that opinion which would exclude God from the government of the world.

It has been thought by some, "That the Creator of the universe formed the constitution of nature in such a manner at the beginning, as to stand in need of no succeeding change; that he established certain laws in the material and in the moral world, which uniformly and invariably take place, producing all the effects which he ever intended they should produce; as when an artist frames a machine for certain purposes, and for a limited duration, the effects which result from it spring not from the immediate direction and influence of the artist, but from the original frame and composition of the machine. Such is the opinion of those who hold what they call a *general Providence*. We, on the other hand, maintain, that "Almighty God, upon special occasions, directs and overrules the course of events, both in the natural and moral world, by an immediate influence, to answer the great designs of his universal government."

With respect to a general Providence, this mechanical system, this engine, by which some persons would throw out the superintending Providence of Heaven, is a creature of the brain. It is a mere presumption. It is by its own nature incapable of proof. From whence should the evidence arise? Art thou who excludest God from his works, intrusted with the secrets of heaven? Wert thou present when God laid the foundations of the world? Wert thou privy to his counsels? Or do you now see, or can you show, that original cause, or those original causes, established by God at the creation from which all the various effects in nature may be deduced, and into which they may mechanically be resolved? Can you show the immediate cause of lightning or of rain, or of any other phenomenon in nature, and from the immediate cause ascend to the second, from the second to the third, and so upward till you come to the last link of the chain, which hangs immediately upon the throne of God? This can be done in the works of art. An artist will show you the dependence of all the movements in a machine upon one another. And when you are as well acquainted with the facric of the world, as you may be with the structure of a machine, you may then speak of your chain of mechanical causes and effects. But, alas! the most improved philosophy can do no more but skim the surface of things; and in its progress from the immediate visible to the first invisible cause, at one or two removes, it finds its period, beyond which it cannot go.

Further, This mechanical system of governing the world without the immediate interposition of the Deity, undermines the foundation of all religious worship. When we pray for our daily bread, what do we ask but the blessing of God upon the earth, to yield her fruits in due season? When we ask the blessing of God upon our meals, what do we less than recognise his supreme power, and implore him to make the gifts of his Providence the means of our sustenance and refreshment? This disclaims every notion of natural causes and effects that shuts out God; it supposes his concurrence and co-operation directing all the operations of nature. Again, when we pray for the graces and virtues of the spiritual life, what do we ask but the Divine aid to strengthen the good dispositions he hath already given us, and so to direct and order the course of events, that we may be kept from temptation, or not be overcome when we are tempted? But this supposes the superintendence of God over us; supposes his interposition in human affairs; supposes his providence continually exerted in administering to the wants of his creatures, according as their circumstances require. If this account be just, then our worship is a reasonable service. But if these are vain words, then our worship also is vain. Then every one that goes into his closet to pray, goes only to act foolishly; then all the good and the pious, every where over the face of the whole earth, that are calling upon the Most High God, are as uselessly, as absurdly employed, as if they were falling down before a dumb idol, and paying their devotions to images of wood or stone.

Further still, this mechanical system, in a great measure, annihilates the moral perfections of the Divine nature. It places the Almighty in a state of indolence, which is inconsistent with every idea of perfection; it makes him an idle and unconcerned spectator of his own works, and represents him as beholding virtue and vice, the sinner and the saint, with an equal eye. There are many scenes in human life, at which, if we were present, it would be criminal for us not to take a part. Did we see the hands of the violent raised to shed innocent blood, and not rush to prevent the horrid deed; did we know the retreats of the robber and murderer, and not endeavor to bring them to public justice, we would be reckoned in part guilty of their crimes, as, by a criminal omission, we should endanger the peace of the public, and the interests of society. If we, being evil, would abhor such a character, shall we impute it, can we impute it, to Him who is infinite in goodness, and who is possessed of absolute perfection? To what purpose is God every where present, if he is not every where employed? Whereto serves infinite power, if it must be for ever dormant? Whereto serves infinite wisdom, if it is never to be exercised? To what purpose are the Divine goodness, and the Divine justice, if we only hear of their names? Are all the Attributes of the Godhead in vain? How false, how absurd, how blasphemous, is an opinion that would destroy every Divine perfection!

I have thus shown you the absurdity of that system which would exclude God from the government of the universe; and I am now, in the *second* place, to establish and confirm the doctrine of a particular Providence. This doctrine is founded both upon reason and the Scriptures.

Reason and true philosophy never attempt to separate God from his works. We must own him in the sky, to hold the planets in their respective orbits; we must own him in the earth; and in the seas, to keep them within their proper bounds, and we must own him through the whole system of nature, to support and maintain that gravitating force which gives consistency and stability to all material things. Reason tells us, that it is not probable that the Creator of the universe would forsake that world which he hath made; that it is not probable that a Being possessed of infinite perfection can be an idle and unconcerned spectator of his own works.

But our chief evidence for this doctrine rests upon revelation. Mankind obtained early notices of the Divine superintendence, by peculiar interpositions. In the history of the Old Testament, we have an account of the loss of Paradise by sin; of the banishment of Cain for the murder of his brother; of the translation of Enoch, as the reward of his righteousness; of the wickedness of the old world, and its destruction by the deluge, Noah and his family only excepted, who, by the eminence of his piety, found grace in the sight of God to become the father of the new world. When this new world revolted from God, and ran into idolatry, we see Abraham called out to be the head of a mighty nation, which grew up and flourished, by a series of the most wonderful providences; governed by laws of God's own appointment; with promises of protection and blessing, so long as they should be obedient, and threatenings of punishment and destruction, if they fell off to serve other gods; which in the event were punctually verified. This was a visible and standing evidence of a governing Providence. The doctrine was thus established upon a higher authority than reason, and upon better evidence than the light of nature. God revealed himself to men as the Governor of the world, the avenger of the wicked, and the protector of the good. But, although, in administering the affairs of the universe, the object of Providence should be to depress the bad and to favor the good; yet an exact retribution of rewards and punishments was none of the ends of his administration in this scene of things. This would have defeated the plan of his Providence, and superseded the necessity of a day of judgment. Nevertheless, he would frequently interpose to punish signal wickedness, or reward illustrious virtue. Thus, in the early ages of the world, he did often miraculously interpose, to let the nations understand that he took notice of their righteous or unrighteous deeds; that he had power to vindicate the honor of his laws; and to make examples whenever it was requisite, for the correction and reformation of men. Miraculous interpositions were not intended to be permanent or perpetual; yet the providence of God was not to cease. Accordingly, he took care to inform us, that what in the first ages he had done visibly and by miracles, he would do in the latter ages by the invisible direction of natural causes. The Scriptures are so full of this notion, that it would be endless to be particular. You may read the 28th chapter of Deuteronomy, where you will see all the powers of nature summoned as instruments in the hand of the Almighty, to execute the purposes of his will; where you behold them commissioned to favor the good with national prosperity, with domestic comforts, with safety from their enemies, with fruitful seasons, with a numerous offspring, and with an abundance of all blessings; commissioned to punish the wicked with national distress, with indigence, with slavery, with destructions, and molestations of every kind, by war, by famine, and by all sorts of diseases. From all which, the plain inference is this, That the most common and most familiar events, are under the direction of God, and by him are used as instruments, either for the hurt or for the good of men.

How this particular Providence operates, may, in some degree, be conceived by us. Man, in his limited sphere, can take some direction of natural causes. You can direct the element of fire either to warm or to consume; the elements of air and water to cherish and to annoy. Does not that power, then, in a more illustrious manner, belong to God? Is it not as easy for *Him*, think you, to give laws to the tempest, where to spend its force; to direct the meteor flying in the air, where to fall, and whom to consume? Are the elemental and subterraneous fires bound up? He can let them loose. Are they broken loose? He can collect them as in the hollow of his hand. And all this he performs, without unhinging the general system, and without any visible tokens to us, that he is at all concerned, though in truth he is the effective agent. In like manner, we may comprehend, in some measure, how God may direct, not only the motions of the inanimate and passive part of the creation, but also the determinations of free agents, to answer the purposes of his providence. The hearts of men are in the hand of the Lord, as much as the rivers of water. This does not in the least destroy the freedom of human actions. Every one knows that the acts of free agents are determined by circumstances; and these circumstances are always in the hand of God. The dispositions and resolutions of men are apt to vary, according to the different turn or flow of their spirits, or their different situations in life, as to health or sickness, strength or weakness, joy or sorrow; and by the direction of these, God may raise up enemies, or create friends, stir up war, or make peace. Take, as an instance, the history of Haman. That wicked man had long meditated the destruction of Mordecai the Jew, and rather than not satiate his vengeance upon him, would involve the whole Jewish nation in utter destruction. He at last obtained a decree, sentencing this whole people to the sword; and the day was fixed. In this crisis of their fate, how was the chosen nation to be delivered? Was God visibly and miraculously to interpose in favor of his own people? This he could have done; but he chose rather to act according to the ordinary train of second causes. He who giveth sleep to his beloved, withheld it from Ahasuerus, the monarch of Persia. In order to pass the night, he called for the records of his reign. There he found it written, that Mordecai had detected a conspiracy formed against the life of the king, and that he had never been rewarded for it. By this single circumstance, a sudden reverse took place. Mordecai was advanced to honor and rewards; the villany of Haman was detected; the decree fatal to the Jews was revoked; and the nation of the Jews was saved from instant destruction. In like manner, in the history of Joseph, and other histories of the Old Testament, you see the most familiar events made instruments in the hand of God to effect the purposes of his will.

There is then a particular Providence. The arm of the Almighty, reaching from heaven to earth, is continually employed. All things are full of God. In the regions of the air; in the bowels of the earth; and in the chambers of the sea, his power is felt. Every event in life is under his direction and control. Nothing is fortuitous or accidental. Let me caution you, however, against abusing this doctrine, by judging of the characters of persons from their outward circumstances. It is to be remembered, that the present life is not a state of recompense, but a state of trial; consequently, men are not dealt with in outward dispensations according to their true character. The goods of Nature and Providence are distributed indiscriminately among mankind. The sun shines, the rain falls, upon the just and the unjust. It is a dangerous error, therefore, to judge of moral character from external condition in life. This was the error of Job's friends; this the foundation of the censures they cast against this excellent person, and for which they were reproved. The intention of the book of Job is, to show the falseness of that supposition, by representing the incomprehensible Majesty of God, and the unsearchable nature of his works. Many instances in Scripture confirm the truth of this observation. Who, that saw David reduced to straits, wandering for refuge in the rocks and dens of the wilderness, would have believed him to be the prince whom God had chosen? Who, that beheld Nebuchadnezzar walking in his palace, surrounded with all the pomp and splendor of the east, would have believed him to be the objeet of Divine displeasure, and that the decree was gone out, that he was to be driven among the beasts? Who, that beheld our Lord in the form of a servant, would have believed that he was the Master of Nature?

I am, *lastly*, To deduce the practical consequences from the doctrine, by showing you the grounds of joy and consolation that it gives to the world.

In the *first* place, The doctrine of a superintending Providence yields us joy and consolation with respect to our lot in life. Many persons are accustomed to complain concerning their situation and circumstances in the world. Their desires and their fortune do not correspond; they think that they are misplaced by Providence, and look upon the lot of their neighbors as more eligible than their own. It is impossible, in the present system of things, that all men can be alike. Nature, through all her works, delights in variety. Though every flower is beautiful, and every star is glorious; yet one flower excelleth another in beauty, and one star exceedeth another in glory. There are also diversities in human life, and a beautiful subordination prevails amongst mankind. The Father of Spirits hath communicated himself to men in different degrees. But although all men cannot be alike; yet all men may enjoy a great measure of happiness. Every station in life possesses its comforts and advantages. In those comparisons you make of your life with that of others, when you would wish to exchange places with some of your more fortunate neighbors, do you not always find something in which you have the superiority? Is there not some talent of the mind, some quality of the heart, something where you think your strength lies, some one source of enjoyment, which you would wish still to retain? Is not this the testimony of nature, that you are happier in that path of life, than you would be in another? Wherever you are placed by Providence, the station appointed is the post of honor. A general, in the day of battle, marshals his army according as he sees proper, and distributes the posts of danger and importance, according to the courage and conduct of his soldiers. Your Commander knows your abilities better than you do yourselves; he prescribed to you the duty you have to execute; and he marked out the path in which you are to seek for honor and immortality. It is from your discharge of these offices assigned to you, that the happiness of your life, and the perfection of your character, are to arise. It is not from the sphere they hold in life, but from the lustre they cast around them in that sphere, that men rank in the Divine estimation, and figure in the annals of eternity. If, with five talents, you gain five more, or if, even with one talent, you gain another, you are as praiseworthy as he who, with ten talents, gaineth other ten talents.

Further, As in a kingdom, every highway leads to the capital; as in a circle, every line terminates in the centre; so, in the wide circle of nature, every line terminates in heaven; and every path in life conducts alike to the great city of God. The present state is intimately connected with the future; the life which we now lead, is an education for the life which is to come. If your mind were enlarged to comprehend all the connections and dependencies of things; if your eyes were opened to take in the whole of your immortal existence, you would then see and acknowledge, that Providence had assigned to you the very station you would have wished to fill; the very part you would have chosen to act. Trusting, therefore, in that God who presides over the universe; assured of that wisdom and goodness which direct the whole train of the Divine administrations, each of us may express our joy in the words of the Psalmist: "The lines have fallen to me in pleasant places: I have a goodly heritage: the Lord is the portion of mine inheritance; the Lord will command the blessing, even life for evermore."

In the *second* place, This doctrine will yield us consolation during the afflictions which we meet with in life. If we believed that the universe was a state of anarchy, confusion and uproar, that the Governor of the world was a cruel and malignant being, who made sport of human misery, and took pleasure in punishing his unhappy creatures, such a thought would overwhelm the mind; it would turn the gloom of adversity into the shadow of death, and mingle poison in the cup of bitterness which we are doomed to drink. But the Scriptures inform us, that the dark dispensations of Providence are part of that plan which has the good of the world for its object; take their rise from the goodness of our Father in heaven; are intended for the reformation and final blessedness of his children. The same word of life which says, "Blessed is the man whom thou choosest and makest approach unto thee," says also, "Blessed is the man whom thou chasteneth." So far from being marks of the Divine wrath, the afflictions of life are tokens of the Divine love. While heedless and unthinking we go astray, God interests himself in our favor, and sends these his messengers to bring us to himself. It is but a narrow and imperfect view we take of afflictions, when we consider them only as trials. They are not so much intended for the trial as for the cultivation of virtue. They are sent by Providence, to mortify your unruly passions; to wean you from the world; to prepare you for heaven. They are sent for the improvement of your nature; for the increase of your graces, and for the superabounding of your joy to all eternity. When under the afflicting hand of Heaven therefore, you are standing a candidate for immortality; you are singled out by Providence to exert the part of a christian, and you are called forth to exhibit to the world a pattern of the suffering virtues. He is but a novice in the school of Christ, who has not learned to suffer. The best affections of the heart, the noblest graces of the soul, the highest virtues of life, the offering that is most acceptable to Heaven, arise from the proper improvement of adversity. The blessed above, whom the Prophet saw arrayed in white before the throne, came out of great tribulation; the blessed above, whom he heard singing the song of Moses and the Lamb, learned the first notes of it on the bed of sorrow.

Such is the intention of afflictions which Providence sends, and even under these afflictions God is with his people. You are ever under the hand of a merciful Creator, who doth not afflict willingly, nor grieve the children of men. He knoweth your frame; he remembereth that you are but dust; he will afflict you no further than you are able to bear; and as your days are, he hath promised that your strength shall be. Nay, in all your afflictions he is present with you, and the hand that bruised you binds up the wound. Let not then your hearts be troubled. Bear up under the pressure of wo. Rejoice because the Lord reigneth, and exult in the language of the Prophet; "Although the fig-tree should not blossom, nor fruit be found in the vine; though the labor of the olive should fail, and the field should yield no meat; though the flocks should be cut off from the fold, and there shall be no herd in the stall, yet will I rejoice in the Lord, I will joy in the God of my salvation."

Thirdly, With respect to appearances of moral evil and disorder, it is afflicting to the mind to behold disorder in the universe of God: bad men often exalted, while the good man's lot is bitterness and pain: virtue depressed, and vice triumphant. He who caused light to arise out of darkness, and order and beauty to spring from chaos and confusion, can correct these irregularities. He not only restrains, and says, "Hitherto, and no further." He also overrules and makes the wrath of men to praise him. Hear how he gives commission, and sends Sennacherib against Israel, as a general sends a weapon of war. "O Assyrian, the rod of mine anger, I will send him against an hypocritical nation, and against the people of my wrath, to tread them down like the mire of the streets. Howbeit he meaneth not so, neither doth his heart think so;" that is, neither doth his heart think that he is a mere instrument in the hand of God. David was raised to the throne of Israel by those steps which his foes devised against him. The enemy of mankind, seducing our first parents, was the means of their being elevated to a greater degree of happiness and glory.

Lastly, With respect to our departure from this world, and entering upon a new state of being, we know that the time is appointed, when dust shall return unto dust, and the spirit unto God who gave it. But it is awful, it is alarming to nature, to call up the hour when the union between soul and body shall be dissolved; when our connection with all that we held dear in life shall be broken off; when we shall enter upon a new state of existence, and become inhabitants of the world unknown. But even then the providence of God will give us comfort. The Lord reigneth king for ever and ever. The dominions of the dead are a part of his kingdom; time and eternity, the world that now is, and the world that is to come, confess him for their Lord. When thou goest through the dark valley, he will go with thee: in the hour of dissolving nature, he will support thy spirit. Thou canst not go but where God is. Around thee is infinite love, and underneath thee are the everlasting arms.

SERMON IX.

ON CHARITY.

ISAIAH LVIII. 7.—"Deal thy bread to the hungry; —hide not thyself from thine own flesh."

WHY there are so many evils in the world, is a question that has been agitated ever since men felt them. As God is possessed of all perfections, he could have created the universe without evil. To him, revolving the plan of his creation, every benevolent system presented itself; how came it then to pass, that a Being, neither controlled in power, nor limited in wisdom, nor deficient in goodness, should create a world in which many evils are to be found, and much suffering to be endured? It becomes not us, with too presumptuous a curiosity, to assign the causes of the Divine conduct, or with too daring a hand, to draw aside the veil which covers the councils of the Almighty. But from this state of things, we see many good effects arise. That industry which keeps the world in motion; that society, which, by mutual wants, cements mankind together; and that charity, which is the bond of perfection, would neither have a place nor a name, but for the evils of human life. Thus the enjoyments of life are grafted upon its wants; from natural evil arises moral good, and the sufferings of some contribute to the happiness of all. Such being the state of human affairs, charity, or that disposition which leads us to supply the wants and alleviate the sufferings of unhappy men, as well as bear with their infirmities, must be a duty of capital importance. Accordingly it is enjoined in our holy religion, as being the chief of the virtues. There is no duty commanded in Scripture, on which so much stress is laid, as on the duty of charity. It is assigned as the test and criterion by which we are to distinguish the disciples of Jesus, and it will be selected at the great day, as being that part of the character which is most decisive of the life, and according to which the last sentence is to turn. Charity, in its most comprehensive sense, signifies that disposition of mind, which, from a regard and gratitude to God, leads to all the good in our power to man. Thus, it takes in a large circle, extending to all the virtues of the social, and many graces of the divine life. But as this would lead us into a wide field, all that I intend at present is, to consider that branch of charity which is called *Almsgiving;* and, in treating upon it, shall, in the *first* place, Show you how alms ought to be bestowed; and, *secondly*, Give exhortations to the practice of this duty.

The *first* thing proposed was, To show you what is the most proper method of bestowing charity. This inquiry is the more necessary, as, in the neighborhood of great cities, we are always surrounded by the needy and importunate, and it is often difficult to distinguish those who are proper objects of charity, from those who are not.

The best method of bestowing charity upon the healthy and the strong, is to give them employment: Almighty God created us all for industry and action. He never intended that any man upon the face of the earth should be idle. Accordingly, he hath placed us in a state which abounds with incentives to industry, and in which we must be active, in order to live. One half of the vices of men take their origin from idleness. He who has nothing to do, is an easy prey to the tempter. Men must have occupation of one kind or other. If they are not employed in useful and beneficial labors, they will engage in those which are pernicious and criminal. To support the indolent, therefore, to keep those idle who are able to work, is acting contrary to the intention of God, is doing an injury to society, which claims a right to the services of all its members, is defrauding real objects of charity of that which is their proper due, and is fostering a race of sluggards, to prey upon the vitals of a state. But he is a valuable member of society, and merits well of all mankind, who by devising means of employment for the industrious, delivers the public from a useless incumbrance, and makes those who would otherwise be the pests of society, useful subjects of the commonwealth. If it be merit, and no small merit it is, to improve the face of a country; to turn the desert into a fruitful field, and make the barren wastes break forth into singing; it is much more meritorious to cultivate the deserts in the moral world; to render those who might be otherwise pernicious members of society, happy in themselves, and beneficial to the state; to convert the talent that was wrapt up in a napkin into a public use; and by opening a new source of industry, make life and health to circulate through the whole political body. Such a person is a true patriot, and does more good to mankind, than all the heroes and man-destroyers, who fill the annals of history. The fame of the one is founded upon the numbers that he has slain; the glory of the other arises from the numbers that he preserves and makes happy.

Another act of charity, of equal importance, is to supply the wants of the really indigent and necessitous. If the industrious, with all their efforts, are not able to earn a competent livelihood; if the produce of their labor be not proportionable to the demands of a numerous family; then they are proper objects of your charity. Nor can there be conceived a more pitiable case, than that of those whose daily labor, after the utmost they can do, will not procure daily bread for themselves and their household. To consider a parent who has toiled the live-long day in hardship, who yet at night, instead of finding rest, shall find a pain more insupportable than all his fatigues abroad; the cravings of a numerous and helpless family, which he cannot satisfy; this is sufficient to give the most lively touches of compassion to every heart that is not past feeling. Nor can there be an exercise of charity better judged, than administering to the wants of those who are at the same time industrious and indigent.

Another class of men that demand our charity, is the aged and feeble, who, after a life of hard labor, after being worn out with the cares and business of life, are grown unfit for further business, and who add poverty to the other miseries of old age. What can be more worthy of us, than thus to contribute to their happiness, who have been once useful, and are still willing to be so; to allow them not to feel the want of those enjoyments, which they are not now able to procure; to be a staff to their declining days; to smooth the furrows in the faded cheek, and to make the winter of old age wear the aspect of spring?

Children also bereft of their parents, orphans cast upon the care of Providence, are signal objects of compassion. To act the part of a father to those upon whose helpless years no parent of their own ever smiled; to rear up the plant that was left alone to perish in the storm; to fence the tender bloom against the early blasts of vice; to watch and superintend its growth, till it flourishes and brings forth fruit: this is a noble and beneficial employment, well adapted to a generous mind. What can be more delightful than thus to train up the young to happiness and virtue; to conduct them with a safe but gentle hand, through the dangerous stages of infancy and youth; to give them, at an age when their minds are most susceptible of good impressions, early notices of religion, and render them useful members of society, who, if turned adrift, and left defenceless, would, without the extraordinary grace of God, become a burden and a nuisance to the world?

But there is a class of the unfortunate not yet mentioned, who are the greatest objects of all; those who, after having been accustomed to ease and plenty, are, by some unavoidable reverse of fortune, by no fault or folly of theirs, condemned to bear, what they are least able to bear, the galling load of poverty; who, after having been perhaps fathers to the fatherless, in the day of their prosperity, are now become the objects of that charity which they were wont so liberally to dispense. These persons plead the more strongly for our relief, because they are the least able to reveal their misery, and make their wants known. Let these, therefore, in a peculiar manner partake the bounty of the liberal and open hand. Let your goodness descend to them in secret, and, like the providence of Heaven, conceal the hand which sends them relief, that their blushes may be spared while their wants are supplied.

Concerning one class of the indigent, vagrants and common beggars, I have hitherto said nothing.

About these, your own observation and experience will enable you to judge. Some of them are real and deserving objects of your compassion. Of others, the greatest want is the want of industry and virtue.

The *second* thing proposed, was, To give exhortations to the practice of this duty. This duty is so agreeable to the common notions of mankind, that every one condemns the mean and sordid spirit of that wretch whom God has blessed with abundance, and consequently with the power of blessing others, and who is yet relentless to the cries of the poor and miserable. We look with contempt and abhorrence upon a man who is ever amassing riches, and never bestowing them; as greedy as the sea, and yet as barren as the shore. Numbers, it is true, think they have done enough in declaiming against the practice of such persons; for upon the great and the opulent they think the whole burden of this duty ought to rest; but for themselves, being somewhat of a lower class, they desire to be excused. Their circumstances, they say, are but just easy, to answer the demands of their family, and therefore they plead inability, and expect to be exempted from the performance of this duty. Before this excuse will be of any avail, it behooves them to consider whether they do not indulge themselves in expenses unsuitable to their rank and condition. Imaginary wants are boundless, and charity will never begin, if it be postponed till these have an end. Every man, whether rich or poor, is concerned in this duty, in proportion to his circumstances: and he that has little is as strictly bound to give something out of that little, as he that hath more is obliged to give more. What advantage was it to the poor widow, that she, by giving her one mite into the treasury, could exercise a nobler charity than all the rich had done! The smallest gift may be the greatest bounty.

The practice of this duty, therefore, is incumbent upon all. To the performance of it you are drawn by that pity and compassion which are implanted in the heart. Compassion is the call of our Father in heaven to us his children, to put us upon relieving our brethren in distress. This is an affection wisely interwoven in our frame by the Author of our nature, that whereas abstracted reason is too sedentary and remiss a counsellor, we might have a more instant and vigorous pleader in our own breasts to excite us to acts of charity. As far, indeed, as it is ingrafted in us, it is mere instinct; but when we cultivate and cherish it, till we love mercy; when we dwell upon every tender sentiment that opens our mind and enlarges our heart, then it becomes a virtue. Whosoever thou art whose heart is hardened and waxed gross, put thyself in the room of some poor unfriended wretch, beset perhaps with a large family, broken with misfortunes, and pining with poverty, whilst silent grief preys upon his vitals; in such a case, what wouldst thou think it reasonable thy rich neighbors should do? That, like the Priest and the Levite, they should look with an eye of indifference, and pass by on the other side; or like the good Samaritan, pour balm into thy wounded mind? Be thyself the judge! and whatever thou thinkest reasonable thy neighbors should do to thee, go thou and do likewise unto them.

Consider next the pleasure derived from benevolence. Mean and illiberal is the man whose soul the good of himself can entirely engross. True benevolence, extensive as the light of the sun, takes in all mankind. It is not indeed in your power to support all the indigent, incurable and aged; it is not in your power to train up in the paths of virtue many friendless and fatherless children: but if, so far as the compass of your power reaches, nothing is deprived of the influence of your bounty, and where your power falls short, you are cordially affected to see good works done by others, those charities which you could not do, will be placed to your account. To grasp thus the whole system of reasonable beings, with an overflowing love, is to possess the greatest of all earthly enjoyments, is to make approaches to the happiness of higher natures, and anticipate the joy of the world to come. For it is impossible that the man who, actuated by a principle of obedience to his Creator, has cherished each generous and liberal movement of the soul, with a head ever studious to contrive, a heart ever willing to promote, and hands ever ready to distribute to the good of his fellow-creatures, should notwithstanding be doomed to be an associate for ever with accursed spirits, in a place where benevolence never shed its kindly beams, but malice and anguish, and blackness of darkness, reign for ever and ever. No, the riches which we have given away will abide with us for ever. The same habit of love will accompany us to another world. The bud which hath opened here will blow into full expansion above, and beautify the paradise in the heavens.

SERMON X.

ON THE DANGER OF SMALL TRANSGRESSIONS.

MATTHEW v. 19.—"Whosoever therefore shall break one of these least commandments, and shall teach men so, he shall be called the least in the kingdom of heaven."

THE Roman Catholics divide sins into two classes, the venial and the mortal. In the first class, they include those slight offences which, as they say, are too inconsiderable to offend the Deity, and, in the second, those great and aggravated transgressions which expose men to the Divine vengeance in the world to come. Although this distinction, which overthrows the law of morality, is abjured by all Protestants, yet something like it is still retained by great numbers of men. What the Papists call venial sins, *they* call sins of infirmity, human failings, imperfections inseparable from men. And their own favorite vices, whatever they be, they call by these names. Cruel is the condition of the human kind, say they, and rigorous the spirit of the christian law, if we are to lie under such terrible restrictions; if breaking one of the least commandments shall exclude us from the kingdom of God. Will the Great Creator be offended by a few trivial transgressions; with little liberties, which serve only for amusement? If others take a general toleration, shall we not have an indulgence at particular times? If we are prohibited from turning back in the paths of virtue, may we not make a random excursion? If we are not allowed to taste the fruits, may we not at least crop the blossoms of the forbidden tree? While the waters of pleasure flow so near, and look so tempting, shall we not be permitted to taste and live? Will the Great Judge of the world condemn us to eternal punishment, for the indulgence of a wandering inclination, for the gratification of a sudden appetite, for a look, a word, or a thought?

As this is the apology of vice, which, at one time or another, all of you make to yourselves, I shall now show you the dangerous nature and fatal tendency of those offences you call *little sins*. And in entering upon the subject, Christians, I must observe to you, that the attempt to join together the joys of religion and the pleasures of sin, is altogether impracticable. The Divine law regulates the enjoyments as well as the business of life. You are never to forget one moment that you are Christians. The joys which you are allowed to partake of, are in the train of virtue. While you are pilgrims in the wilderness, if you return to Egypt again, you forfeit your title to the promised land. You have left the dominions of sin, you have come into another kingdom; and if now you revolt to the foe, you are guilty of treason, and may expect to meet with the punishment which treason deserves. How shall we distinguish then, you say, between the sins of infirmity, into which the best may fall, and the violation of those least commandments which exclude from the kingdom of God? I answer, The text makes the distinction. Sins of infirmity proceed from frailty and surprise. The temptation comes upon men unexpected; the foe meets them unprepared; and, in such cases, the most circumspect may be off their guard, and the best natures may fall. But those sins which exclude from the kingdom of God, are from deliberation and full consent of the mind. The persons who commit them, as the text says, "teach men so;" that is, they justify themselves in what they do, and sin upon a plan. Their evil intentions are not occasional and transient, but permanent and governing; they sleep and wake upon their bad designs, and carry them along in their going out and coming in; and thus forming evil habits, make their lives a system of iniquity. Whoever does so, though it be only in the violation of what he reckons the least commandment, shall be called least in the kingdom of heaven; that is, shall be excluded altogether from it.

It is proposed, at this time, to set before you the evil nature and dangerous tendency of the least transgressions. And, in the *first* place, it may be observed, that it is a series of little actions that marks the characters of men. Human life is not composed of great events, but of minute occurrences; and it is not from a man's extraordinary exertions, but from his ordinary conduct, that we form our judgment of his character. When a great event is transacting, a man is on his guard, he is prepared to act his part well, and often, on such occasions, in the hour of exhibition, he appears to the world a different person from what he really is. But in the series of little actions, in the detail of ordinary life, the turn of mind discovers itself, the temper unfolds, the character appears. It is then, when man is himself, the mask falls off, and the true countenance is displayed. Human life then, being a circle of petty transactions, and the temper of men being known from their conduct in little affairs, our character for virtue will depend on our performance of what the world calls the least of the commandments. This is not peculiar to virtue. What is it that constitutes the happiness of domestic life? Not the singular and uncommon situations, but the familiar and the ordinary: not the striking events that fly abroad in the mouths of the people, bnt the daily round of little things which are never mentioned. A miser may have a feast, and be a miser still; he only is a happy man who has his enjoyments every day. With very great talents, and without any remarkable vice, a man may become a most disagreeable member of society, by his neglect of the attentions and civilities, and decorum of life. In like manner, without being guilty of any enormous sin, by the habitual neglect of inferior duties, and by the practice of little offences, a man may sin unto death.

A good life is one of those pictures whose perfection arises from the nice and the minute strokes. It is not one blazing star, but the host of lesser lights, which forms the beauty of the heavens. In like manner, How does the great Judge at the last day decide the fate, and determine the characters of men? You reckon sins of omission but little sins, yet, on account of these, the sentence of everlasting condemnation is passed. Because ye gave no bread to the hungry, no water to the thirsty, and no raiment to the naked, relieved not the oppressed, and visited not the prisoner, therefore "depart into everlasting fire, prepared for the devil and his angels." In like manner he determines the character of the righteous, not from the striking and splendid virtues they exhibit to the world, but from the performance of the inferior duties of daily life: "Come ye blessed of my Father, inherit the kingdom prepared for you from the foundation of the world." Why? Is it for the splendid works of piety, for building temples to the Deity, or dying as martyrs to the Christian Faith? No. Men may build temples, without love to the Deity: they may die as martyrs, without real religion; but because ye have given food to the hungry, drink to the thirsty, and raiment to the naked; actions of life in which ye must have been sincere; because ye never expected that such actions would be heard of, and the practice of them grew so much into habit, that ye scarcely thought it a virtue to perform them.

Secondly, These little sins attack the authority of the Divine Legislator as much, or perhaps more, than great sins. Evil thoughts are as expressly prohibited in the Divine law as evil deeds. The same God who says, Thou shalt not kill, says also, Thou shalt not hate thy brother in thy heart. What sentiment must you entertain of the Majesty in the heavens, when his commands cannot restrain you from the commission of the least sin? Hath not God forbidden the impure desire and the malicious intention, as well as adultery and murder? And is it not as much his will that he should be obeyed in *those* commandments as in *these?* Have you a dispensation granted you to take the name of God in vain in common conversation, any more than you have to swear falsely before a civil magistrate? Have you more liberty allowed you to wound your neighbor's character than you have to shed his blood? No, the prohibition extends to the one as well as to the other. The same authority that forbids the action, forbids the desire. The same law which says, Thou shalt not steal, says also, Thou shalt not covet. But you say, that the indulgences you plead for, are with regard to things in their own nature indifferent. Alas! if you had proper ideas of a God possessed of infinite perfection, nothing that he commands or forbids would appear indifferent. To you it may appear a matter of little moment or concern, what the strain of your thoughts is, or how the tenor of your conversation runs; but when you learn that your thoughts are known in heaven, and that by your words you shall be justified or condemned, these assume a more serious form, and become of infinite importance. But if the things for which you beg an indulgence are in their own nature small, why do you not abstain from them? If the prophet had commanded you to do a great thing, you might have murmured against the precept; but when he only enjoins what you yourselves reckon a little thing, what pretence have you for a complaint? In place of being an excuse, this is an aggravation of your offence. With your own mouth you condemn yourself. Can there be a stronger proof of a degenerate nature and a stubborn mind, than this inclination to disobey your Creator, in things that you reckon of little consequence? What can show a heart hardened against God, and set against the heavens, so much as this refractory and rebellious disposition, which leads men to violate the majesty of the law, to insult the authority of the Lawgiver, to risk the vengeance of the Omnipotent, and to pour contempt on all the perfections of the Divine nature, rather than part with what they themselves reckon small and inconsiderable.

In the *third* place, You may contract as much guilt by breaking the least of the commandments, as by breaking the greatest of them. You start back, and are affrighted at the approach of great iniquity; the heart revolts from a temptation to flagrant sins; yet thousands of lesser sins, evil thoughts, malicious words, petty oaths, commodious lies, little deceits, you make no scruple to commit every day. But the guilt of such reiterated sins is as great, or greater, than that of any single sin. To hate your neighbor in your heart without cause, to take every opportunity of blasting his character, and defeating his designs, makes you as guilty in the Divine eye as if you had imbrued your hands in his blood. To use false weights, and a deceitful balance, is as criminal as a direct act of theft. He, who defrauds his neighbor daily in the course of his business, is a greater sinner before God, and a worse member of society, than he who once in his life robs on the highway. The frequency of these little sins makes the guilt great, and the danger extreme. The constant operation of evil deeds impairs the strength of the soul, and shakes the foundation on which virtue rests. Wave succeeding wave undermines the whole fabric of virtue, and makes the building of God to fall. The thorns, which at first could scarcely be seen, spread by degrees over the field, and choke the good seed. The locusts, which Moses brought over the land of Egypt, appeared at first a contemptible multitude; but in a little time, like a cloud, they darkened the air; as a mighty army, they covered the face of the earth; they devoured the herb of the field, the fruit of the tree, and every green thing, and turned what was formerly like the garden of Eden into a desolate wilderness. Thus these little sins increase as they advance; they blast where they enter; by degrees they make the spiritual life decay; they lay waste the new creation, and turn the intellectual world into a chaos, without form, and void of order. And yet we are not on our guard against them. It fareth with us as it did with the Israelites of old. We tremble more at one Goliath than at the whole army of the Philistines. One gross scandalous sin makes us recoil and start back; and yet we venture on the guilt of numberless smaller sins, without hesitation or remorse. What signifies it whether you die of many small wounds, or by one great wound? What great difference does it make, whether the devouring fire and the everlasting burnings are kindled by many sparks, or by one fire-brand? When God shall reckon up against you at the great day the many thousand malicious thoughts, slanderous words, deceits, oaths, imprecations, lies, that you have been guilty of, the account will be as dreadful, and the wrath as insupportable, as if atrocious crimes had stood upon the list.

In the *fourth* place, These little offences make life a chain and a continuation of sins, so that conversion becomes almost impossible. Often, upon the commission of a gross sin, a sober interval succeeds; serious reflection has its hour; sorrow and contrition of heart take their turn; then is the crisis of a man's character; and many improving this favorable opportunity, have risen greater from their fall. But if these little sins then come in; if between the commission of one gross sin and another, there intervenes a constant neglect of God, a hardness of heart, a vanity of imagination, and unfruitfulness of life, you stlll add to the number of your sins, and treasure up to yourselves wrath against the day of wrath. Such little sins fill up all the void spaces; so that, by this means, life becomes an uninterrupted and unbroken chain of iniquity. Thus you render yourselves incapable of reformation, and put yourselves out of the power of Divine grace. How is it possible that you can ever come within the reach of mercy? How can the voice of God reach your heart? He speaks to you in the majestic silence of his works; but you reckon it no sin at all to shut your ears against the voice which comes from heaven to earth, and reaches from one end of the world to the other. He speaks to you by the voice of his providence; but you reckon it of little moment to regard the doings of the Lord. He speaks to you in the holy Scriptures; but you reckon the precept to read these one of the least commandments. He speaks to you in the ordinances of his own institution, but alas! how many hold it a little sin to absent themselves from these altogether? And how many of those who attend, think it but a little sin to spend their time as unprofitably as if absent! He speaks to you with the still small voice; his Spirit whispers to your spirit. He seeks to enter in by your thoughts; but vanity, and folly, and vice, swarms of little sins, stop up the passage. Thus every corner of life is filled up. Every avenue to the heart is shut. You no where lie open to the impression of Divine grace, and the soul is so full, that there is no room for the Holy Spirit to enter.

In the *last* place, These lesser sins infallibly lead to greater. There is a fatal progress in vice. One sin naturally leads to another: the first step leads to the second, till, by degrees, you come to the bottom of the precipice. Deceit, duplicity, dissimulation in different matters, which many persons who maintain what is called a decent character, make no scruple to employ, have a tendency to render you insincere on more important occasions, and may gradually destroy your character of integrity altogether. He, who tells falsehoods for his own conveniency, will in the natural course of things, become a common liar.

The spirit of gaming perhaps you reckon a small sin. But whenever gaming is made a serious business, and the love of it becomes a passion, farewell to tranquillity and virtue. Then succeed days of vanity and nights of care; dissipation of life, corruption of manners, inattention to domestic affairs, arts of deceit, lying, cursing, and perjury. At a distance poverty, with contempt at her heels, and in the rear of all, despair bringing a halter in her hand.

Thus have I set before you the evil nature and the dangerous tendency of the least transgressions. And do you ask an indulgence in little sins, when you see how fatal they are? Do you still ask to make an excursion from the path of virtue? Such an excursion if you make you will fall in with the road to perdition. Do you still wish to taste the waters which unlawful pleasure presents to your eye? Taste them you may; but be assured that there is poison in the stream, and death in the cup. Alas! if we calmly indulge ourselves in the cool commission of the least sin, who knows *when* or *where* we shall stop? If once we yield to the temptation, in whose power is it to say, Hitherto shall I go, but no further? Many persons at their first setting out, would have trembled at the very *thought* of these sins, which in time, and by an easy transition, they have been brought to commit with boldness. The traitor consigned to eternal infamy, Judas Iscariot, who betrayed the Lord of glory, had at first only his covetousness to answer for. Fly, therefore, I beseech you, fly from the first approaches of sin. Guard your innocence, as you would guard your life. If you advance one step over the line which separates the way of life from the way of death, down you sink to the bottomless abyss. Come not then near the territories of perdition. Stand back, and survey the torrent which is now so mighty and overflowing, that it deluges the land, and you will find it to proceed from a small contemptible brook. Examine the conflagration that has laid a city in ashes, and you will find it to arise from a single spark.

SERMON XI.

ON THE DELIVERANCE FROM REMORSE.

HEB. XII. 24.—"The blood of sprinkling, which speaketh better things than that of Abel."

REASON and philosophy have applied their powers to external objects with wonderful success. They have traced the order of nature, and explained the elements of things. By observation and experience, they have ascertained the laws of the universe; they have counted the number of the stars; and following the footsteps of the Almighty, have discovered some of the great lines of that original plan according to which he created the world. But when they approach the region of spirit and intelligence, they stop short in their discoveries. The mind eludes its own search. The Author of our nature has cheked our career in such studies, to teach us that action and moral improvement, not speculation and inquiry, are the ends of our being. Accordingly, the moral part of our frame is the easiest understood. Having been placed here by Providence for great and noble purposes, virtue is the law of our nature. This being the great rule in the moral world, God has enforced it in various ways. He hath endowed us with a sense or faculty which, viewing actions in themselves, without regard to their consequences, approves or disapproves them. He hath endowed us with another sense, which passes sentence upon actions according to their consequences in society. He hath given us a third, which, removing human actions from life, and the world altogether, carries them to a higher tribunal. The first, which is the *moral sense*, belongs to us as individuals; is instinctive in all its operations; approves of virtue as being moral beauty; and disapproves of vice as being moral deformity. The second, which is the sense of *utility*, belongs to us as members of society, is directed in its operations by reason, and passes sentence upon actions according as they are favorable or pernicious to the public good. The third, which is *conscience*, belongs to us as subjects of the Divine government, is directed in its operations by the word of God, and considers human actions as connected with a future state of rewards and punishments. It is this which properly belongs to religion. Upon this faculty of conscience, the happiness or misery of mankind in a great measure depends. A good conscience is a continual feast, and proves a spring of joy amidst the greatest distresses. A conscience troubled with remorse or haunted with fear, is the greatest of all human evils. Accordingly, the Christian religion, which adapts itself to every state of our nature, and carries consolation to the mind in every distress, has presented to the weary and heavy laden sinner, "the blood of sprinkling, which speaketh better things than the blood of Abel." The meaning of which expression is this: as the blood of Abel, crying to Heaven for vengeance, filled the mind of Cain with horror, and as every sin is attended with remorse; so the blood of Jesus is of power to deliver the mind from this remorse, and restore peace of conscience to the true penitent.

In further treating upon this subject, I shall describe to you the nature of that remorse which is the companion of a guilty mind; and next the deliverance which the gospel gives us from it, by means of "the "blood of sprinkling." In the *first* place, then, Let us consider the nature of that remorse which is the companion of a guilty mind.

Almighty God having created man after his own image, intended him for moral excellence and perfection. Hence all his passions were originally set on the side of virtue, and all his faculties tended to heaven. Conscience is still the least corrupted of all the powers of the soul. It keeps a faithful register of our deeds, and passes impartial sentence upon them. It is appointed the judge of human life; is invested with authority and dominion over the whole man, and is armed with stings to punish the guilty. These are the sanctions and enforcements of that eternal law to which we are subjected. For even in our present fallen state, we are so framed by the Author of our nature, that moral evil can no more be committed than natural evil can be suffered, without anguish and disquiet. As pain follows the infliction of a wound, as certainly doth remorse attend the commission of sin. Conscience may be lulled asleep for a while, but it will one day vindicate its rights. It will seize the sinner in an hour when he is not aware; will blast him perhaps in the midst of his mirth, and put him to the torture of an accusing mind. For the truth of this observation, let me appeal to your own experience. Did you ever indulge a criminal passion, did you ever allow yourselves in any practice which you knew to be unlawful, without feeling an inward struggle and strong reluctance of mind before the attempt, and bitter pangs of remorse after the commission? Though no eye saw what you did; though you were sure that no mortal could discover it, did not shame and confusion secretly lay hold of you? Was not your own conscience instead of a thousand witnesses? Did it not plead with you face to face, and upbraid you for your transgressions? Have not some of you perhaps, at this instant, a sensible experience of the truths which I am now pressing upon you? In these days of retirement and self-examination, did you not feel the operation of that powerful principle? Did not your sins then rise up before you in sad remembrance? Has not the image of them pursued you into the house of God? And are not your minds now stung with some of that regret which followed the first commission?

My brethren, there is no escaping from a guilty mind. You can avoid some evils, by mingling in society; you can avoid others, by retiring into solitude; but this enemy, this tormentor within, is never to be avoided. If thou retirest into solitude, it will meet thee there and haunt thee like a ghost. If thou goest into society, it will go with thee; it will mar the entertainment, and dash the untasted cup from thy trembling hand. Whilst the sinner indulges his vain imagination; whilst he solaces himself with the prospect of pleasures rising upon pleasures never to have an end, and says to his soul, Be of good cheer, thou hast happiness laid up for many years, a voice comes to his heart that strikes him with sudden fear, and turns the vision of joy to a scene of horror. Whilst the proud and impious Belshazzar enjoys the feast with his princes, his concubines, and his wives; whilst he carouses in the consecrated vessels of the sanctuary; in a moment the scene changes; the handwriting on the wall turns the house of mirth into a house of mourning; the countenance of the king changes, and his knees smite one against another, whilst the Prophet, in awful accents, pronounces his doom; pronounces that his hour is come, and that his kingdom is departed from him.

It is in adversity that the pangs of conscience are most severely felt. When affliction humbles the native pride of the heart, and gives a man leisure to reflect upon his former ways, his past life rises up to view; having now no interest in the sins which he committed, they appear in all their native deformity, and fill his mind with anguish and remorse. Men date their misfortunes from their faults, and acknowledge their sin when they meet with the punishment. The sons of Jacob felt no remorse when they sold their brother to be a slave; they had delivered themselves from the foolish fear that he was one day to be greater than they; they congratulated themselves upon the mighty deliverance. But the very first misfortune which befell them, a little rough usage in a foreign land, awakened their guilty fears, and they said one to another, "We are verily guilty concerning our brother, in that we saw the anguish of his soul when he besought us, and we would not hear, *therefore* is this distress come upon us."

But that the prosperous sinner may not presume upon impunity from the lashes of a guilty mind, and to show you that no situation, however exempted from adversity, and that no station, however exalted, is proof against the horrors of remorse, I shall adduce two remarkable instances of persons who felt all the horrors of a guilty mind, without meeting with any judgments to awaken them. The first is that of Cain, referred to in the text. When the offering of Abel ascended acceptable and well-pleasing to God, Cain was seized with envy; from that moment he meditated vengeance against him, and at last imbrued his hands in the blood of his brother. There was then no law against murder; and if antecedent to law there is no original sense of right and wrong implanted in the mind; if conscience, as some affirm, was not a natural but an acquired power, the mind of Cain might have been at ease; he might have enjoyed the calm and the serenity of innocence. But when he was brought to the tribunal of conscience, was his mind at ease? Did he enjoy the calm and the serenity of innocence? No. He cried out in the bitterness of remorse, "My punishment is greater than I can bear." What punishment did he complain of? There was then no punishment denounced against murder, and the Lord expressly secured him from corporal punishment. But he had that within, to which all external punishments are light. He was extended on the rack of reflection, and he lay upon the torture of the mind. Hell was kindled within him, and he felt the first gnawings of the worm that never dies.

Another remarkable instance of the dominion of conscience, we have in the history of Herod. John the Baptist, the harbinger of our Lord, sojourned a while in the court of Herod. This faithful monitor spared not sin in the person of a king, but reproved him openly for his vices. Herod, although he disliked, yet he respected the Prophet, and feared the multitude, who believed in his doctrines.

But on Herod's birth-day, when the daughter of Herodias danced before him, he made a sudden vow, that he would grant her whatever she desired. Being instructed of her mother, she asked the head of John the Baptist. One of the common arts by which we deceive our consciences is to set one duty against another. Hence sin is generally committed under the appearance of some virtue, and hence the greatest crimes which have ever troubled the world, have been committed under the show of religion. Such was the crime which we are now considering. The observance of an oath has, among all nations, been regarded as a religious act; and here a fair opportunity offered itself to one who only waited for such an opportunity, to make religion triumph at the expense of virtue. If Herod had no inclination to destroy the Prophet, and no interest in his death, his conscience would have told him that murder was an atrocious crime, which no consideration could alleviate, nor excuse; it would have told him that vows, which it is unlawful to make, it is also unlawful to keep; but Herod was already a party in the cause; he determined to get rid of his enemy; he satisfied his conscience with some vain pretences, and gave orders to behead the Baptist. But were all his anxieties and sorrows buried with the Prophet? No: the grave of the Prophet was the grave of his peace. Neither the splendor of Majesty, nor the guards of state, nor the noise of battle, nor the shouts of victory, could drown the alarms of conscience. That mangled form was ever present to his eyes; the cry of blood was ever in his ears. Hence, when our Saviour appeared in a public character, and began to teach and to work miracles, Herod cried out, in the horrors of a guilty mind, "It is John the Baptist whom I slew; he is risen from the dead."

How great, my brethren, is the power and dominion of conscience! The Almighty appointed it his vicegerent in the world; he invested it with his own authority, and said, "Be thou a God unto man." Hence it has power over the course of time. It can recall the past; it can anticipate the future. It reaches beyond the limits of this globe; it visits the chambers of the grave; it reanimates the bodies of the dead; exerts a dominion over the invisible regions, and summons the inhabitants of the eternal world to haunt the slumbers, and shake the hearts, of the wicked. Tremble, then, O man! whosoever thou art, who art conscious to thyself of unrepented sins. Peace of mind thou shalt never enjoy. Repose, like a false friend, shall fly from thee. Thou shalt be driven from the presence of the Lord like Adam when he sinned, and be terrified when thou hearest his voice, as awful when it comes from within, as when it came from without. The spirit of a man may sustain his infirmity; but a spirit wounded by remorse who can bear?

The *second* thing proposed, was, to show you the deliverance which the Gospel gives us from remorse, by means of the "blood of sprinkling." This expression alludes to the ceremonial method of expiating sin under the Old Testament, by offering sacrifices, and sprinkling the blood of the victim upon the altar. But as this was in itself only typical of Christ, How welcome to the soul is the glad tidings of the Messiah, who did, what these sacrifices could not do,—actually save his people from their sins! By the atonement and blood of Christ, the sins of men have been completely expiated. It is the voice of the Gospel of Peace, "Take, eat, and live for ever." What relief will it give to the wounded mind, to hear of the blood of sprinkling, which speaketh better things than the blood of Abel! The Gospel being published to the world, and the offers of mercy through a Redeemer being made to all men, the sincere penitent accepts these offers, and flies for refuge to the hope set before him. Then Jesus saves his people from their sins, he heals the mind which was wounded by remorse, and bestows that peace which the world cannot give, and cannot take away. There is joy in heaven, we are told, over a sinner that repenteth, and the joy of the heavens is communicated to the returning penitent. When he beholds God reconciled to him in the face of his Son; when he hears, in secret, the blessed Jesus whispering in sweet strains to his heart, "Son, be of good cheer, thy sins are forgiven thee," he is filled with peace and with joy; with peace which passeth all understanding; with joy which is unspeakable and glorious. His sins being forgiven, he is accepted in the Beloved. He is an heir of immortality, and his name is written in heaven; to him is opened the fountain of life. He has a title to all the pleasures which are at God's right hand; to the treasures of heaven, and to the joys of eternity. He looks forward with a well-grounded hope, to that happy day, when he shall take possession of the inheritance on high; he anticipates the delights of the world to come, and breaks forth into strains of exultation, similar to those transports of assurance uttered by the apostle, "Who shall lay any thing to the charge of God's elect? It is God that justifieth; who is he that condemneth? It is Christ that died, yea, rather, that is risen again, and who now sitteth and intercedeth for us at God's right hand."

SERMON XII.

ON THE VALUE OF THE SOUL.

MARK VIII. 36.—"For what shall it profit a man, if he shall gain the whole world, and lose his own soul?"

THERE is not a person in this assembly, but who assents immediately to the truth of the maxim implied in the text. You all agree, that religion is the one thing needful, and that above all things you ought to seek the kingdom of God, and the righteousness thereof. But there is a wide difference between the assent of the mind to the truth of this principle, and that deep conviction of its importance, which, in Scripture, obtains the name of faith; sufficient to influence the heart, and to determine the life. A great part of mankind seem to have no steady belief that they are endowed with souls which are immortal; an eternity to come is with them merely a matter of speculation, and their faith in a future world has little more influence upon their lives, than their idea of a distant country, which they are never to see. Hence spiritual and eternal things are heard with little emotion or concern, while they are delivered in the house of God. Some can give themselves up to listlessness; and others soon lose all remembrance of what they have heard, in the next amusement, or in the news of the day. Even he who spoke as never man spake, and while he discoursed on points of such importance as the loss of the soul, had occasion often to take up the complaint, that in vain he stretched out his hands all day long to a disobedient people.

To call your contemplation, then, to these subjects, for they need no more but to be considered aright, in order to be felt, I shall endeavor to show you the value of the soul, from its native dignity, from its capacity of improvement, from its immortality, and from its unalterable state at death.

Let us consider then, in the *first* place. The native importance and dignity of the human soul. It is the mind chiefly that is the man. Our souls properly are ourselves. The bodily organs are the ministers of the mind; by these it sees and hears, and holds a correspondence with external things. It is by our souls that we hold our station in the scale of being; that we rank above the animal world, and claim alliance with superior and immortal natures. As the soul is superior to the body, so intellectual pleasures exceed the sensual; as heaven is higher than the earth, so the joys of a heavenly origin are superior to earthly enjoyments. I mean not in the common way, to depreciate temporal possessions, as being insignificant in themselves, and unworthy the cares or labors of a wise man. Such discourse is mere declamation; it is against nature, contrary to truth, and makes no impression at all. Let all the value be set upon wealth and temporal possessions which they deserve, as affording a defence from many evils to which poverty is liable; as ministering to the convenience, the consolation, and the enjoyment of life; as supporting a station with decency and dignity in the world, and as accompanied with an importance, by which a good man may find much pleasure arising to himself, and have the power of doing much good to his fellow-creatures; let all the value which reason allows, be set upon temporal acquisitions and enjoyments, still they are inferior to those of an intellectual and moral kind; still the maxim remains true, That he would be an infinite loser who should gain the whole world and lose his own soul. "Thou hast put more gladness into my heart," saith the Psalmist, "than worldly men know, when their corn, and their wine, and their oil abound." And do not your own feeling and experience bear witness to this truth? Who will not acknowledge that there is more excellence in wisdom, than in mere animal strength? Who will not own that there is more happiness in the improving conversation of the wise, than in the tumultuous uproar of the debauched and licentious? Are the rays of light as pleasant to the eye as the radiations of truth to the mind? Have sensual gratifications a charm for the soul, equal to intellectual and moral joys? While the former soon pall upon the appetite, are not the latter a perpetual feast? While the remembrance of the one is attended with no pleasure, is not the remembrance of the other a repetition of the enjoyment?

But great as the dignity of the human soul is, it may be still greater; for, in the *second* place, It possesses a capacity of improvement. This constitutes one essential difference between the intellectual and the material world. All material things soon reach the end of their progress, and arrive at a point beyond which they cannot go. Instinct grows apace, and the animal is soon complete in all its faculties and powers. Man ripens more slowly, because he ripens for immortality. Those enjoyments and pursuits of man also, which do not belong to him as an immortal being, come soon to their period. Amusement, when continued too long, becomes a fatigue. In pleasure there is a point, beyond which, if it be carried, it is a pleasure no more, it turns into pain. The pursuits of greatness too, are very limited, and the race of honor is soon run. After many a weary step, the votary of ambition finds that he has been running in a circle, and that he is come to the self-same point from which he set out. Mind, mind alone, contains in itself the principle of progression and improvement without end. There is no ultimate power in the progress of man: there is no termination to the career of an immortal spirit. The dominions of earthly greatness are circumscribed within narrow limits, and the hero has often wished for new countries to conquer: but the empire of the mind has no limit nor boundary; and we can never arrive at that period, where we may say, Hitherto can we go, but no further. Never have we learned so much, but we may learn more. Suppose life never so long, if the powers remain, new paths to science may be struck out, fresh accssions to knowledge may be made. And we know from experience, that the largest measure of knowledge proves no burden to the mind, nor weakens its powers; but that, on the contrary, the capacity enlarges with the acquisition, and that men, the more they have learned, the more apt they are to learn; the less is their labor, and the easier their progress.

Improvements in goodness keep pace with improvements in wisdom. Repeated acts of obedience grow into habit; the penitent is confirmed in righteousness, and he that is holy becomes holier still. From the fulness which is in God, he adds grace to grace. The day of small things shineth more and more; and that day is succeeded by no night. The pilgrims, who at first set out feeble and faint, grow vigorous as they advance, going forward from strength to strength; ascending from one degree of goodness to unother, they approach the everlasting hills, and, coming within the sphere of heaven, they inhale the spirit of their native region, they feel the attractions of the uncreated beauty, they receive a foretaste of the fruits of life, and with hearts already full of heaven, and with tongues already tuned to the songs above, they put on the brightness of angels, and enter into the mansions of paradise.

In the *third* place, The value of the soul will further appear, if we consider that it is immortal. All human things soon come to an end. Temporal possessions and earthly greatness have a short date. The world itself is for ever changing; the fashion thereof passes away, and he who knows it in one age, in the next would not know it again. How short-lived are the enjoyments of this mortal state! Although the flowers of transient joy, more hardy than the gourd of Jonah, may outlive the heat of the morning, and glow amid the blaze of noon, yet when the blast of evening comes, they are nipt and wither away. Ambition too has its day, and often a short one. Its votaries seem to be raised, but the more sensibly to feel their fall. The same whirlwind that snatches them up from the crowd, brings them down at even with tenfold fury. Not to mention these more violent revolutions, its natural period soon comes. He who runs the race of human glory, is lost in the very dust that is raised around him. And such is the sudden end of all terrestria' enjoyments, when, after the study and the labor of years, we have with much pains and care gathered together the requisites and materials of a happy life, and say to yourselves, "Soul, take thine ease, thou hast goods laid up for many years," the warning voice is heard, "Thou fool, this night thy soul shall be required of thee." So transient is the date, so short the day of power, and pleasure, and greatness! But wisdom never dies; but virtue is immortal. We have a higher life than that which beats in the pulse, and when the dust returns to the dust as it was, the spirit returns to God who gave it. It is indeed an awful, though a pleasing thought, that we have an eternity before us. When the sun shall be extinguished in eternal darkness, when the heavens shall be rolled together like a scroll, when the earth with all its works shall be dissolved, the soul shall survive the general wreck, and exult in the enjoyment of youth immortal! To think of an infinity of years of existence enduring beyond all the numbers which we can add together, beyond all the millions of ages which figures can comprehend, and that, when all this vast sum of duration is expended, our existence is but just beginning, is, indeed, beyond imagination to grasp. Never to come to an end, never to be nearer an end, is indeed amazing, overwhelming, and incomprehensible to the mind. But such is thine inheritance, O man! "Because I live," saith the Lord, "ye shall live also." Our duration shall be coeval with His years who sits upon the throne for ever; the Ancient of days, who is, and was, and is to come.

In the *last* place, To show you the value of the soul still more, after death its state is unalterable. This is our state of probation, and now is the time to fix the character for eternity. This is the spring-time of everlasting life; according as we now sow, hereafter we shall reap; on our present conduct, depends our happiness or misery for ever. There is neither repentance nor apostasy beyond the grave. The righteous can never fall away, and to the wicked there remaineth no more sacrifice for sin. From the judgment-seat of the Immutable, the voice is heard, "He that is righteous, let him be righteous still; and he that is unjust, let him be unjust still."

But even here, too, appears that goodness of God which is over all his works. For while we know not of any addition to the torments of the wicked, the happiness of the righteous shall be for ever on the increase. That capacity of improvement which we formerly ascribed to the soul, is a capacity of improvement without end. The progress which begins here, is carried on hereafter. Heaven is indeed the residence of the spirits of just men made perfect; but it is not to be imagined, that they are all at once advanced to a perfection which they shall not to eternity exceed. They will indeed find their state happy, when they are taken from this world; they will all be presented without spot or blemish in the presence of God, with exceeding joy; but still there is room left for their improvement in perfection and happiness. It cannot, indeed, be otherwise. For the more we know of the Divine perfections and works, our veneration and love of God will increase the more. Now, it is impossible that we can ever know so much of God and his works, but that we may know more. As our knowledge of God, therefore, and our views of the Divine glory will be enlarged without end, our love and admiration of him will also increase for ever. And in proportion to our love, our assimilation to the Divine nature, and our joy in the Lord, will be. What a prospect, O Christian, does this open up to thy mind! Here thou art at liberty to expatiate at large! Here is a noble field for thy contemplation! There is a time appointed when thou shalt occupy that station which is now occupied by the highest angel in heaven. Not that we shall overtake the angels in their course, or, in the career of immortality, press upon natures of a superior order; but that we shall make advances in moral perfections, and improve in the beauties of immortality. God shall behold his great family for ever brightening in holiness; for ever drawing nearer and nearer in likeness to himself. The river of their pleasures increases as it rolls. The fulness of their joy grows more and more full. Throughout all the ages of eternity, there is still a heaven which is to come; still a glory which is to be revealed.

If the soul then be of such infinite value, how inexpressibly great must the *loss* of it be! Over the mansions of utter darkness, the Scriptures draw a veil which does not authorize our conjectures. What is comprehended under these awful emblems, the worm that never dies, the fire that is not quenched, everlasting destruction from the presence of the Lord, and the glory of his power, we do not know. May the Almighty forbid, that any of us should ever know! But of this, the Scriptures assure us, that from these mansions there is no return; that the gates of the eternal world shut to open no more, and that when the soul is once lost, it is lost for ever and for ever!

SERMON XIII.

ON THE CELEBRATION OF THE LORD'S SUPPER.

PSALM XLIII. 4.—"I will go unto the altar of God, unto God my exceeding joy."

CHRISTIANS, as we are next Lord's day to go to the altar, and approach unto God, it may be proper for me now to explain the nature, and set before you the advantages, of such an approach.

The pleasures of devotion have been the theme of good men in all ages; and they are pleasures of such a kind as good men only can feel. In what I am now to say therefore, I must appeal to the heart, to the hearts of those who, in times past, have felt the joy of spiritual communion, and who will again feel that it is good still for them to draw nigh unto God.

This is the time when Jesus prepares a banquet for his friends; when the Spirit saith, Come; when the Church saith, Come; when he that is athirst is invited to come; and happy will it be when the friends of Jesus prepare to meet with their Lord, if those who have hitherto been strangers to the holy hill, shall be attracted with the beauty which is in true holiness, also to come and to take the waters of life freely. For thus runs the gracious promise of Heaven: "The strangers who join themselves to the Lord, to love him and to serve him, even them will I bring to my holy mountain, and make them "joyful in my house of prayer." In further treating on this subject, what I intend at present, is, in the *first* place, To explain the nature of that approach which the devout make to God; and, in the *second* place, Set before you the advantages which accompany such an approach.

I am, in the *first* place, then, To explain the nature of that approach which the devout make to God.

This earth is not the native region of that spirit which is in man. It finds not objects here congenial with its nature, nor a sphere adequate to its faculties. It wants room to expand to its full dimensions; to spread so wide, and stretch so far, and soar so high, as its immortal nature and unbounded capacity will admit. Descended from heaven, it aspires to heaven again. Created immortal, nothing that is mortal can satisfy its desires. Made after the image of God, it tends to that God whose lineaments it still bears. When we approach to God, therefore, we find objects suited to our nature, and engage in the employment for which the soul was made. Here we are at home in our Father's house. Here our spirits aspire to hold communion with the everlasting Spirit; and we tend to heaven with exceeding joy, as to our native country.

The sense of Deity is akin to the perception of beauty and the sensibility of taste. We are formed by the author of our nature to feel certain movements of mind at the sight of certain objects. Even inanimate things are not without their attractions. The flowers of the field have their beauty. Animal life rises in our regard. Rational excellence and moral perfection rank still higher in our esteem, and when expressed in action, and appearing in life, awake emotions of the noblest kind, and beget a pleasure which is supreme. Let any person of a right constituted mind place before his view a character of high eminence for generosity, fidelity, fortitude; let him see these virtues tried to the utmost, exerted in painful struggles, overcoming difficulties, and conquering in a glorious cause, and he will feel their effects in his admiring mind; he will be actuated with respect and love to such illustrious virtues. We account that faculty of the mind which gives us a relish for these pleasures, a perfection in our nature, and a high one; we look upon an insensibility to such enjoyments as a radical defect. Let us apply this principle to religion. Who can behold the vastness and magnificence of the works of God without emotion; and infinite perfection without wonder and awe? Can our thoughts be fixed upon infinite goodness and everlasting love, without affection and without gratitude? Can we behold Divinity in a form of flesh; the Son of God extended on the cross for the salvation of the world, and our hearts not burn within us with love to him who loved us unto the death? Can we behold the veil drawn aside from the invisible world, the heavens opened over our head, and the treasures of eternity displayed to view, and after all continue cold and dead; cold to the beauty of the heavens, dead to the love of immortality? Where there is any sensibility at all, where there are any affections that become humanity, they will be excited to their most lively exercise by the presence of spiritual and divine things.

Under the influence of these objects, and the impression of Deity, the devout enter into their chamber and shut the door; they turn aside their eyes from beholding vanity; they charge their passions to be silent, their minds to be still; and pour out their hearts to Him who made them, in all the fervency of prayer. Thus prepared to seek the Lord God of their fathers, they come to his temple to meet with him there. They are seized with a religious awe in the presence of the sanctuary, and approach to the altar wondering and adoring, as Moses to the burning bush, and as the High Priest of old to the holy of holies. They look beyond the externals of a sacrament, and, under the symbols in the communion, they discern the mysteries of redeeming love. Notwithstanding the veil with which a greater than Moses covers himself on this holy mountain, they behold his beauty, and cannot bear the brightness of his countenance. When they sit down with him at his table, they are sensible of his presence: while their hands receive the sacred symbols, their eyes behold the Lord of Glory. In the spirit of devotion, and on the wings of faith, they rise from earth to heaven; they pierce beyond the clouds, and enter within the veil. The everlasting doors are thrown open; the King of Glory appears upon his throne; Angels and Archangels cover themselves with their wings, and all the pillars of the firmament tremble.

But not to heaven is the Divinity confined. He fills the earth; he dwells with men. Look around you, and behold the marks of his presence, and the impression of his hand. In the gay and lovely scenes of nature, behold him in his beauty smiling on his works. In the grand and awful objects of creation, in the tempest, in the thunder, in the earthquake, behold him in the Majesty of Omnipotence. When, like the prophet who retired to the wilderness, you hear that voice which rends asunder the mountains, which breaks in pieces the rocks, and which shakes the pillars of the world, you hear behind it a still small voice, saying, "It is I, be not afraid."

Thus, good men see the Creator in his works; they have the Lord always before them. They know where they can find him, and can come nigh to his seat. They go forward and he is there, backward, and they perceive his footsteps; on the right hand his wonders are seen; on the left his goodness is felt. They cannot go but where he is. The Great Universe is the temple of the Deity, built by his hands, consecrated by his presence, bright with his glory.

The *second* thing proposed, was, To set before you the advantages which accompany this solemn approach to God, which are the following: there is honor in approaching to God, there is joy in approaching to God; there is consolation in approaching to God, there is preparation for heaven in approaching to God.

First, then, There is honor in approaching to God. The superiority of man to the animal world has been inferred from the structure and formation of his body. While the inferior animals, prone and grovelling, bend downwards to that earth which is their only element, man is formed with an erect figure, and with a countenance that looks to the heavens. His erect figure is given as the indication of an elevated mind, and the countenance that looks to the heavens is bestowed, in order to prepare us for the contemplation of what is great and glorious. With this formation of body, and with this tendency of mind, man feels that the earth is not his native region; he looks abroad over the whole extent of nature; he has an eye that glances from earth to heaven, and a mind, which, unconfined by space or time, seizes on eternity. The eye that glances from earth to heaven, the mind which seizes on eternity, draw the line between the intellectual and animal world. The beast of the field, indeed, beholds the face of the heavens; the bird of the air is cheered with the splendor of the sun; but man alone has the intellectual eye, which beholds in the heavens the handiwork of Omnipotence, and which traces in the sun the glory of its Creator. To him, high-favored of his Maker, a scene opens, unseen by the eye of sense; a new heaven and a new earth present themselves; the intellectual world discloses its rising wonders, and seen by his own light, in the majesty of moral perfection, God appears. It was reserved to be the glory of man, that he alone, of all the inhabitants of this lower world, should be admitted into the presence of his Creator, and hold intercourse with the Author of his being.

Accordingly, in the happy days of the human race, when the age of innocence lasted, and the Garden of Eden bloomed, there was an intercourse between heaven and earth, and God did dwell with man. Our first parents in Paradise were sensible of his presence; they heard his voice among the trees of the garden; they held converse with him face to face, and found that the chief honor of their nature consisted in drawing nigh to God. Nay, it is the happiness of higher natures, it is the glory of superior beings, of the principalities and powers in heaven, to dwell in the presence of their King, to worship at the throne of infinite perfection, and draw nearer and nearer to the fountain of all felicity. But this honor have all the saints. To thee, O Christian! it is given to hold communion with the Creator, and to become the friend of the Almighty. Truly your fellowship is with the Father, and his Son Jesus Christ. If it be great and honorable to be near the person and round the throne of an earthly king, how truly glorious are they whom the King of heaven delighteth to honor! No wonder then, that though exalted to the highest dignity which the world can bestow, the king of Israel was ambitious of higher still: "One thing have I desired of the Lord, that will I seek after, that I may dwell in the house of the Lord all the days of my life, to behold the beauty of the Lord, and to inquire in his temple."

Secondly, There is joy in approaching to God. "I will go to the altar of God, to God my exceeding joy." The idea of a perfect being is the most joyful subject of contemplation that can be presented to man. Moral qualities, even when they shine in a lesser degree, have a charm for the soul. The prospect of natural beauty is not more pleasant to the eye, than the contemplation of moral beauty to the mind. A great and good action, a striking instance of benevolence, of public spirit, of magnanimity, interests us strongly in behalf of the performer, and makes the heart glow with gratitude to him, although he be unknown. We take delight in placing before our eyes the illustrious characters that stand forth in history, wise legislators, unshaken patriots, public benefactors of mankind, or models of goodness in private life, whose virtues shone to the past, and shine to present times, whose lives were glorious to themselves, and beneficial to the world. If an imperfect copy gives so much satisfaction, how will we be affected at the contemplation of the great Original?

If a few faint traces and lineaments of goodness, scattered up and down, yield us so much pleasure, the pleasure will be supreme, when we contemplate His nature in whom every excellence, every moral perfection, all Divine attributes, reside as in their native seat, flow as from their eternal source, and ever operate as vital and immortal principles. For all created beauty is but a shadow of that beauty which is uncreated; all human excellence but an emanation of that excellence which is Divine; all finite perfection but a faint copy of perfections which are infinite; and all the traces of goodness to be found among men or angels, but a few faint rays from the Father of lights, the uncreated, unclouded and unsetting Sun of nature, who at first gave life to the universe, who kindled the vital flame which is still glowing, who supplies all the orbs of heaven with undiminished lustre, and whose single smile spreads joy over the moral world.

Thus, the very idea of a perfect Being is a source of high pleasure to the mind; but to us there is more implied in the idea of the Deity. For these perfections are not dormant in the Divine nature, they are perpetually employed for the happiness of man. This glorious Being is our Father and our Friend. He called us into being at first, to make us happy; he hath given us many proofs of his goodness, and he hath allowed us to hope for more. He is soon to give us an opportunity of commemorating the most signal display of his grace, his noblest gift to the children of men. And, if he spared not his own Son, but freely gave him up to the death for us all, may it not be depended upon, that with him he will give us all things? Entering into these ideas, and animated with this spirit, the pious man is never so much in his element, as when he is drawing nigh to God. The mind never makes nobler exertions, is never so conscious of its native grandeur and ancient dignity, as when holding high converse with its Creator: the heart never feels such unspeakable peace, as when it is fixed upon him who made it, as when its affections go out on the supreme beauty, as when it rests upon the Rock of ages, and is held within the circle of the everlasting arms.

Hence, the good men of old, in approaching to God, broke forth into the language of rapture, "As the hart panteth after the water-brook, so panteth my soul after thee, O Lord. O God, thou art my God, early will I seek thee. My soul thirsteth for thee. My flesh longeth for thee in a dry and parched land, wherein no water is; that I may see thy glory as I have seen it in the sanctuary. Because thy loving-kindness is better than life, my mouth shall praise thee with joyful lips. Surely we shall be satisfied with the goodness of thy house, and thou wilt give us to drink the river of thy pleasures.—Whom have we in the heavens but thee, and what is there upon the earth that we can desire beside thee? My flesh and heart shall fail, but thou art the strength of my heart, and my portion for ever."

Thirdly, There is consolation in approaching to God. Alas! in this world, afflictions so abound, that consolation is often our greatest good. In how few days of this mortal life do we not feel the want of a comforter? Ever since the introduction of sin into the earth, human life hath been a scene of misery. Man is born to trouble, and sore is the travel which is appointed to him under the sun. We come into the world the most forlorn of all beings; the voice of sorrow is heard from the birth; man sighs on through every path of future life; and the grave is the only place of refuge, where the weary are at rest. Sometimes, indeed, a gleam of joy intervenes, an interval of happiness takes place. Fond man indulges the favorable hour. Then we promise to ourselves the scenes of paradise; perpetual sunshine, and days without a cloud. But the brightness only shines to disappear; the cloud comes again, and we awake to our wonted anxiety and sorrow.

Not limited to our own personal woes we are doomed to suffer for sorrows not our own. We are not unconcerned spectators of human life. We are interested in every event that befalls our fellow men. Sympathy makes us feel the distresses of others, and the best affections of the heart become the sources of woe. How many deaths do we suffer in mourning over the friends that we have lost! While we lament their unhappy or untimely fate, we cut short the thread of our own days. The cords of love are broken, one after another; string after string is severed from the heart, till all our early attachments are dissolved, till our sad eyes have wept over every friend laid in the dust, and till we become lonely and wretched as we at first began.

Under these afflictions, and from these sorrows, devotion opens a retreat; the altar of God presents a place of refuge; the ear of the Eternal is open to thy cry; the arm of the Almighty is stretched out to relieve thee. There is a sanctuary where no evil can approach; there is an asylum where no enemy can enter. In the pavilion of his presence, God will hide thee in the time of trouble; in the secret of his tabernacle, he will cover thee in the day of danger. There the prisoners rest in peace, and hear not the voice of the oppressor. There are the small and the great, and the servant is free from his master. There the wicked cease from troubling, and the weary are at rest.

It is some consolation, it is some relief, to open our hearts to men, and tell our sorrows to a friend, who can give us no relief, but by mingling his tears with ours. What consolation, what relief will it then give to open our hearts, and tell our sorrows to that Friend above, who is ever gracious to hear, and ever mighty to save! To that friend who never fails; who is afflicted in all our afflictions, and who keeps us as the apple of his eye! Art thou therefore oppressed with the calamities of life; is thy head bowed down with affliction, or thy heart broken with sorrow? approach to the altar, go to God, present to him the prayer of thy heart, and he will send thee help from his holy hill.

Lastly, In approaching to God, there is preparation for heaven. The objects among which we are conversant, have a wonderful power over the mind. External things make such an impression within, that the character is often formed from the situation. The soul is assimilated to surrounding objects, and proportions itself to the sphere in which it moves. When employed in little and in low things, it is contracted; when occupied in earthly matters, it is debased; but acquires enlargement and elevation in the presence of what is grand and sublime. By daily converse with the world, and familiarity with material things, the soul is alienated from the life of God, and man, setting his affections on things below, becomes of the earth, earthy. But when we engage in the exercises of devotion, we counterwork the charm of material objects, we retire from the world and its temptations, and shut the door of the heart against every intruding guest that would disturb us in approaching to God. Standing upon holy ground, we put off unhallowed affections, and impure desires. From the presence of the Lord every sinful thought flies away. Our attention is turned from those things that would raise guilty passions in the mind. Pure and spiritual ideas are presented to view, and the perfections of Almighty God, are set before our eyes. When these are before us, our admiration of them will increase, our love to them will be kindled, and we will endeavor to resemble them in our own life. Thus, by approaching to God, we become like God. By devotion on earth, we anticipate the work of heaven. We join ourselves, beforehand, to the society of angels and blessed spirits above; we already enter on the delightful employment of eternity, and begin the song which is heard for ever around the throne of God.

Such, Christians! are the advantages of approaching to God, and encompassing the altar. And if, with pious affections, and a pure heart, we draw nigh unto God, God will draw nigh unto us. To the wide extent of his creation, to the great temple of heaven and earth, JEHOVAH prefers the heart of the pure and the pious. There he takes up his abode; where he delighteth to dwell. In the divine discourse which our Lord delivered to his diciples, the same night in which he was betrayed, there is a promise rich in consolation. "If a man love me, he will keep my words: and my Father will love him, and we will come and make our abode with him." While this promise sounds in your ears, I hope that your hearts correspond to the strain, and that you recall those precious hours when God manifested himself to you, so as he does not unto the world. When on former occasions, he sent his light and his truth;

when the fountain of living waters has been opened, and the voice came to your ears, "Drink, and live for ever;" Did you not feel emotions which came from no created source, and taste a joy which confessed its origin from heaven? Who can describe the blessedness of that time, when a present Deity is felt? It is the joy of heaven upon earth; the happiness of eternity in the moments of time.

SERMON XIV.

THE GOSPEL A SYSTEM OF SPIRITUAL JOY.

Luke ii. 10.—"Behold, I bring you good tidings of great joy."

The coming of the Messiah is always foretold in scripture as a period of joy and triumph. The Patriarchs rejoiced when they saw his day afar off. All the Prophets take fire at this great occasion, and rise into the strains of rapture when they describe the glory of the latter days, and the happiness of the Messiah's reign. In the most beautiful colors they paint its arrival as a new era of happy time, and as a general jubilee to the world. They represent it as accompanied with universal peace and prosperity; as effecting a renovation of nature, the return of innocence to earth, and the descent of God to dwell with men. "In those days the wilderness and the solitary place shall be glad; the desert shall rejoice and blossom like the rose. They shall blossom abundantly: and rejoice with joy and with singing. The glory of Lebanon shall be given unto it; the excellency of Carmel and of Sharon. The parched ground shall become a pool, and the dry land springs of water. In the wilderness shall waters break out, and streams in the desert. The light of the moon shall be as the light of the sun, and the light of the sun shall be sevenfold." When the heavens and the earth at first arose in beauty from the hands of the Creator, the morning stars sang together, and all the sons of God shouted for joy. In like manner, when these new heavens and this new earth appeared, all the angelic host broke forth into strains of gratulation, ascribing glory to God in the highest, peace on earth, and good-will towards fallen men.

Unhappily, the Jews, who were a gross and carnal people, misinterpreted the prophecies concerning the kingdom of the Messiah, took the magnificent style of prophecy for literal description, and fondly imagined that these glad tidings of great joy announced temporal and earthly blessings. They looked for no better a country than the land of Canaan, and expected no other redemption than to be redeemed from the Roman yoke. The veil is now taken off from the Prophets, and we discern the Gospel, not as meant to procure us possession of the earth, and dominion over the nations, but as intended to make us partakers of eternal life, and to give us an inheritance in the heavens, which is incorruptible, undefiled, and fadeth not away.

The Gospel, then, is a system of spiritual joy. And, in treating of it in this light, I shall, in the *first* place, consider it as a method of instruction, enlightening the darkness, and dispelling the ignorance of human nature: In the *second* place, As a plan of redemption from the guilt of sin: In the *third* place, As a scheme of comfort and relief during the afflictions of life; and, in the *fourth* place, As a system of consolation against the fear of death. Here are comprehended all the evils of human life; and if we find that the Gospel brings us relief from all of them, then it will appear to contain, indeed, "Good tidings of great joy."

I am to show you, then, in the *first* place, That, as a system of joy, Christianity enlightens the natural darkness of the mind, and gives us all requisite information concerning the truths necessary to our happiness.

Curiosity, or the desire of knowledge, is one of the earliest emotions of the human soul. No sooner does the mind arrive at the exercise of thought, than it proceeds to examine the objects around it, and to extend its researches wider and wider over the whole circuit of nature. One of the most obvious dictates of reason is the belief of a God. There are so many indications of wisdom and contrivance in the works of nature; such striking displays of order and beauty; such splendid demonstrations of a plan established, that an intelligent Mind is at once recognized, and a Deity, though invisible in himself, is every where seen in his works. Accordingly, all nations have agreed in acknowledging and worshipping a supreme Power, the Creator and Governor of all things. But although the light of nature reveals to us the existence of a God, it gives us no materials whereon to form an opinion concerning his attributes. A mixed dispensation of things seems to prevail in the world. There are many indications of goodness, but there are also many appearances of evil. Providence seems equally to favor the good and the bad. All things come alike to all, and there is one event to the righteous and to the wicked. Reason is at a loss what conclusion to draw from such contradictory appearances, and amidst the clouds and the darkness that surround the paths of the Almighty, cannot discern that justice and judgment are for ever the habitation of his throne. But a state of uncertainty and suspense, especially about an object of such great importance, is the most deplorable of all situations. To live and to die in ignorance and uncertainty, whether the Governor of the world be a tyrant or a friend, or whether we are under the misrule of hate, or the government of love, must sit heavy upon the candid and inquisitive mind, and give additional smart to all the sorrows which embitter human life. What beams of joy will break in upon such benighted minds, when the Sun of Righteousness appearing, scatters the clouds of ignorance and error, and lets in the pure light of heaven upon the darkness of the human condition? To make the discoveries of the Gospel to such persons, is to reveal to them a father and a friend. To discover that God is love; that he is a God in Christ reconciling the world unto himself; that he administers the affairs of the universe so as to issue in the general good; that he is for ever employing the attributes of his nature, his infinite wisdom, his boundless goodness, and his Almighty power, to favor the cause of righteousness, and to promote the happiness of the good throughout the whole creation. Such views of Deity as these fill the mind with joy and with consolation. The weary traveller has now got a shelter from the storm. He has found a sanctuary in the time of trouble; and he looks to the heavens *from whence cometh his aid.* The heart is fully at ease while it rests on him that made it, and reposes with perfect peace under the protection of the everlasting arms.

Further, Man in a state of nature is equally ignorant concerning himself. He finds himself here a stranger in a wide world, where the powers and operations of nature are very imperfectly known; where both the causes and the issues of things are wrapt up in much darkness, and where he can only form uncertain conjectures from whence he comes, for what purpose he was brought into being, and whither he is to go when he departs from hence. If he looks back to his origin, he is lost in uncertainty. Born to be at the head of the inferior creation, and to be the masterpiece of the Almighty in this lower world, he hath at the same time appetites and passions, the abuse of which degrades him below the level of the brutes that perish. His dignity and his meanness; the excellence of his frame, and the degeneracy of his nature; the elevation of his understanding, and the corruption of his heart, form a contrast which the philosophy of ages could never reconcile. How could such a creature come into the world? If he be the work of a wise and good being, whence come the seeds of evil that are latent in his heart? If he be the production of malignant beings, whence the seeds of goodness, and the lineaments of heaven, which, however obscured, are to be found in his frame? Whatever supposition we take, we are beset with insuperable difficulties. But, change the scene, and look forward to his future lot, and he is still more distressed and forlorn. He sees his friends and companions, one after another, continually disappearing. But whither do they go when they depart? Have they withdrawn into everlasting darkness, or do they still act in another scene? Is the beam of heaven for ever extinguished? Is the celestial fire which glowed in their hearts for ever quenched, and naught but ashes left to mingle with the earth, and be blown around the world?

Are their hopes limited to this life? Or, beyond the horizon which terminates their present prospects, does a more beautiful and a more perfect scene present itself, where the wicked shall cease from troubling, and where the weary shall be at rest? If we consult our affections, we shall be inclined to believe in a future state. Nature is loath to quit its hold. The heart still wishes to be kind to the friends whom once it loved. Imagination takes the hint, and indulges us with the pleasant hopes of one day meeting again the companions which we dropped in life. The perfections of the Deity also favor these wishes of nature. If God be infinitely wise and infinitely good, he would not have brought us into being only to see the light, and to depart for ever. Would a wise builder have erected such a noble structure, to last but for a moment? On the other hand, if we consult the analogy of nature, the horrors of annihilation surround us. The leaf that falls from the tree revives no more. The animal that mingles with the earth never rises to life again.

These doubts and horrors are now removed, and this darkness destroyed, by the gospel of Christ. No sooner did the day-spring arise from on high, but it became a light to lighten the Gentiles, and extended its radiance over the region and shadow of death. The nature of man is now unfolded, the origin of evil accounted for, and life and immortality brought to light. Our Saviour did not propose these doctrines as the controvertible opinions of a private man: he taught them with the authority of God. Of his peculiar doctrines he gave us a proof in kind. Did he teach that the dead were to arise? As an infallible confirmation of it, he himself arose from the dead. The good man need not now be in anxiety about his future existence. Come and behold the place where the Lord lay. Come and behold the place from which the Lord arose. You do not mourn as those who have no hope. You commit the bodies of your deceased friends to the grave in the hopes of a blessed resurrection. For we know that our Redeemer liveth, and we know that we shall in like manner revive. The sound of the last trumpet shall pierce even the caverns of the tomb; the dead shall hear the voice of the Son of God: the celestial fire shall again reanimate these ashes, and a glorious body spring forth from the bosom of corruption. What a source of consolation does this open to us in all the afflictions of life? Can that man despond and sink under the evils of life, who has the prospect of a blessed resurrection and a happy immortality?

It has been thus endeavored to show you the advantages that we derive from Christianity, in point of instruction. It was never my intention to exalt revelation at the expense of reason, or to establish Christianity upon the ruins of natural religion. The light of nature affords us many discoveries, and the religion of nature suggests many obligations to virtue. The heathens reasoned well concerning the existence of a supreme cause; from the things which are seen, they inferred his eternal power and Godhead, and gave many excellent lessons for the conduct of human life. But their discoveries had not the authority of uncontroverted truth, and their precepts wanted the obligation of laws. They were the private opinions of mere men, who had no commission to enact articles of faith, and who had no authority to establish laws for the conduct of human life. Their discoveries did not even carry conviction to their own minds. They doubted concerning points the most important and the most essential to the happiness of a rational mind. If, from the order and beauty of the natural world, they inferred the existence and the power of God; from the irregularities and evils of the moral world, they were led to doubt concerning his wisdom and goodness. The immortality of the soul was rather the object of their wishes, than of their firm belief. The law of nature, amidst the multiplicity of vicious and criminal customs, was almost totally obliterated. The sense of moral good and evil, amidst the universal degeneracy and depravity of manners, was in danger of being altogether lost. So general, so gross was the darkness which long involved the nations, so deep and thick did the cloud sit over the moral world, that the wisest of the ancient philosophers thought it was a necessary step in the Deity, in order to ascertain his perfections, and vindicate his ways to men, that a prophet should descend from heaven, clothed with a divine commission, to make a revelation of the Divine will.

But they labored under a difficulty still more dreadful than ignorance, that was, a sense of guilt. This leads us to the *second* head of discourse, To consider the gospel as a plan of redemption from the guilt of sin.

When the sins of a criminal life rose up before them, horror of conscience overwhelmed them. Unenlightened nature presented nothing to their eye but an offended Judge, arrayed in all his terrors. The violated law called aloud for reparation. Justice unsheathed her flaming sword. The mercy of the Judge was altogether unknown. All was darkness and dismay, without one beam of hope. It was in this dreadful dilemma that, in order to appease the wrath of the incensed Deity, they had recourse to sacrifices and to the shedding of so much blood. It was this that drove them to violate the strongest and most sacred laws of nature; drove them to torture their own flesh before the shrine of the offended God, and terrible to tell, drove them—drove the tender parent to take his son, his first-born son, and, with his own trembling hands, to shed his blood as a ransom for his soul! The grand inquiry of the heathen world was that with which the prophet Micah introduces the king of Moab, "Wherewith shall I come before the Lord, and bow myself before the High God?"

As a sense of moral good and evil is implanted in the mind, and as a principle of conscience, condemning sin and approving righteousness, is universally felt, we see and we feel, by sad experience, that all men have sinned, have come short of the glory of God, and that, without an atonement, there could be neither joy nor peace in the heart of man.

Further, It was necessary that, in this atonement, provision should be made for delivering men from the state of degeneracy and imperfection, that they might not again fall into deadly sin, and stand in need of a new atonement. In consequence of that original corruption derived to us from our first parents, our nature is degenerated, and our moral abilities impaired so, that no man can yield perfect obedience to the law of God. It would therefore be of little consequence to blot out our transgressions for the time past, unless we were also to be delivered from the dominion of sin in the time to come. To be always falling into sin, to be always standing in need of new acts of indemnity and forgiveness, is neither consistent with the dignity of the divine government, nor with the perfection of a rational and immortal nature. Accordingly, the great atonement proposed in the gospel, not only provides for our redemption from the wrath to come, but also for our restoration to the image of God. From the cross of Christ, virtue flows to the world, and healing to the nations. In consequence of his sufferings and death, our Saviour is now ascended to the right hand of the Majesty in the heavens, to administer the affairs of his kingdom, and dispense the treasures of the new covenant. He retains our nature, and represents our persons in the presence of God, and makes intercession with the Father in our behalf. He sends down his sanctifying Spirit to repair the ruins of our nature; to create in us the clean heart; to renew within us the right spirit; to lead us on from grace to grace, and from strength to strength, till we perfect holiness in the fear of the Lord. Having thus recovered the original honor of our frame, and being restored to the image of God, he translates us to the mansions of immortality above, where these good tidings of great joy are a subject of praise amidst an innumerable company of angels, and the spirits of just men made perfect.

We proceed to the *third* general head of discourse, To consider the gospel as a scheme of comfort and relief during the afflictions of life.

Ever since the introduction of sin into the world, human life hath been a scene of misery. Man that is born of a woman is of few days; and few as they are, they are full of trouble. He is doomed to suffer from the womb. When he comes into the world, he enters on a state of pain; and from the cradle to the grave, his life is a pilgrimage of sorrow. Where is the kingdom; where is the city; where is the family; where is the individual that is exempted from affliction? It enters the palaces of the great, as well as the cottages of the low; it invades the throne of the king, as well as the hut of the peasant; and scarce are the sanctuaries and the altars of the Lord asylums against its approach. The calamities of life are always great; but when the mind is under the impression of melancholy, and bleeds from recent sorrow, then are they felt in extreme. The cloud sits deep upon the face of things; the prospect before us is dark and lurid; and the mind, if not supported, would sink under its woes. It is the great excellence, my brethren, of the Christian religion, that it abounds with consolations in all the evils of life. To the upright, says the Scripture, light shall arise in the midst of darkness. Those who are weary and heavy laden with their woes, if they come to Christ, he will give them rest.

The first consolation which the gospel proposes to us, is, That there is a particular Providence which watches over human affairs. It is part of the glad tidings revealed to us in the gospel, that the Lord God omnipotent reigneth; that although his throne be in the heavens, and though the heaven of heavens cannot contain him, yet he condescends to visit the earth, to take up his abode and dwell with men. He who counts the number of the stars, numbers also the hairs of our head; a sparrow cannot fall to the ground without the will of our heavenly Father. The most ordinary, as well as the most casual events, are under the direction of that arm which reaches from heaven to earth. Ever watching over the world, there is an eye above, which slumbers not nor sleeps. The archer may draw the bow at a venture; but the arrow is directed by an higher hand. This will administer relief to the mind in all the afflictions of life. Trusting to the providence of God, the devout mind will rest in hope, and break forth into joy, "The Lord reigneth, let the earth be glad; the Lord reigneth, let the multitude of the isles rejoice. His kingdom ruleth over all, and he will make all things co-operate for the good of those who love him." Shall not I therefore trust in him who is ever present to help me in time of need? Are not these perfections, which are equal to the government of the whole system of nature, more than sufficient to direct my little concerns? My God is a present help in time of trouble. He is not far off when grief is near, nor like an absent friend to the distressed. Let the darkness of the tempest surround me; let the winds blow, and the waves rage, I have an interest in the Ruler of the storm; I have an interest in him who can say to the winds "cease," and to the waves "be still."

In the next place, afflictions take their rise, not from the wrath, but from the love of God. Did we believe that the world was governed by a malignant being, who made sport of human misery, and took a malicious pleasure in punishing his creatures; did we consider ourselves as under the dominion of hatred, as objects of the Divine vengeance, and pursued by the Almighty as victims devoted to perdition, such thoughts would make us miserable indeed. They would sharpen the arrows of adversity, and mingle poison into the bitter cup which we are doomed to drink. Then might we cry out with Job, in the hour of despair, "I will speak in the anguish of my spirit, I will complain in the bitterness of my soul. The terrors of the Lord set themselves in array against me. The arrows of the Almighty are within me, the poison whereof drinketh up my spirit. Why hast thou set me as a mark against thee? My soul chooseth strangling and death rather than life." These doubts and terrors are now removed. Fear not, O man! who strugglest under the adversities of life, I bring you good tidings of great joy; the afflictions which thou endurest are not the stripes of an hard master, who seeks thy destruction; they are the chastisements of a kind father, who punishes only to reform. The God of love has no pleasure in the misery, or in the death of his creatures. His eye overflows with pity whilst his hand is lifted up to strike. Whilst he bruises, he binds up the wound. This surely will administer consolations to the wounded in mind, and speak peace to the broken in heart, when they reflect that the evils in their lot are a part of His providence, who doth not afflict willingly, nor grieve the children of men that they are not marks of his wrath, but indications of his love.

Further, as a consolation to the afflicted and distressed, Christianity assures us, that the various occurrences in human life are not accidental, nor detached events, but parts of a great plan that was concerted in the councils of Heaven before the world began, and is going on from age to age. If the moral world were a chaos without form, and void of order; if every event in life was separate, unconnected and final, men, under the pressure of affliction, would often have occasion to complain. But, when we take in the discoveries of revelation, and behold a general order of things established, and a great plan going on; when we consider that every particular event is a part of the great system of Providence, and conduces to form a perfect whole; when we call to mind that no part of our life is an ultimate event, but has a reference to a future state, and is only the means to an end, we will acquiesce in the established order of nature, and follow on, active and cheerful, wherever we are called by Providence. In the early part of our life, when we are under the discipline of a master, we are instructed in arts, and trained to exercises, of which we knew not then the meaning, nor the use. This life is but the infancy of our being, and a state of moral discipline for a better world; let us not therefore be surprised or murmur, if many things fall out which seem adverse to our present good. When the Christian considers that the sufferings of the present life are connected with the enjoyments of heaven, and with the improvements of eternity, the unfavorable and hostile appearances of this world will vanish from his view. Familiarized to this grand and magnificent system of things, he will not complain concerning the conduct of Providence, nor think the universe in confusion when he is in disorder. He does not look upon himself, as self-love would suggest, as a whole separated and detached from every other part of nature; he regards himself in the light in which he imagines the great Spirit of the world regards him. He enters into the sentiments of the Divine Being, and considers himself as a particle, as an atom in an infinite system, which must and ought to be disposed of according to the good and the conveniency of the whole.

Lastly, As a ground of joyful consolation to the distressed, let me remind you, that afflictions are not only requisite parts of our education for heaven, but that they are also necessary means of our improvement in the virtues and graces of the divine life. Adapted to the progressive and probationary state of fallen man, the administration of Providence assumes a variety of forms. Light and shade, the sunshine of prosperity, and the storm of adversity, succeed each other, and checker the scene of human life. In this mixed dispensation of suffering and enjoyment, the wisdom of Providence shines conspicuous. Were we always to be favored with the smile of prosperity, and the candle of the Lord ever to shine upon our head, we would be apt to grow intoxicated with pride, to prove ungrateful to the Author of our being, and reserve to ourselves some part of that incense which we ought to burn upon his altars. On the other hand, were we always to be under the cloud of adversity, were Providence for ever to frown upon our designs, we would be ready to resign ourselves to despair, and cry out with the good men of old, "Is the mercy of Heaven clean gone? Will he be favorable no more?" This mixed dispensation of Providence is not only most favorable to religion, but is also best adapted to the nature of man. Man is made for suffering as well as for action. There are many principles in the human frame, many faculties of the mind, and many qualities of the heart, which would lie for ever latent, were they not called forth to action by the adversities of life. Man was never destined by his Maker to slumber on the couch of repose, and to bask in the sunny season: he was appointed to labor and to action; to struggle with the tempest; to weather the winter of affliction; to encounter peril; to endure pain, and by Christian magnanimity and heroism, by patience, by perseverance and invincible vigor, to reach the crown of glory which is reserved on high for all the sons of God. The afflictions of life present an occasion for this spirit to exert itself, and for these graces to appear. If there were no adversities in human life, the scene of action would be limited, the career of virtue would be shortened, and a wide field of moral glory be lost to the world. Had we no trials in our lot, what need were there for the exercise of patience and resignation to the Divine will, which form such a striking part of the Christian character? Had we no afflictions to encounter, and no evils to fear, what occasion would there be for that strength of mind which enables us to brave the dangers of life, to bid defiance to the evil day, and to repose, at all times, firm and unshaken, upon the arm of the Almighty? Were there no dangers to combat, why should we take unto ourselves the whole armor of God, the sword of the Spirit, the shield of faith, and the helmet of salvation? Not only does adversity present the occasion of spiritual improvement, but has also in every age produced an host of saints, who, clothed with this divine armor, have fought the good fight, and have come forth conquerors. You have recorded to you the faith of Abraham; you have recorded the meekness of Moses; you have recorded the patience of Job; but had it not been for the trials which they underwent, the dangers they had to combat, and the distresses they had to bear, their glory might have perished, and their names been lost in oblivion. As the nightingale, it is said, when bereft of her young, fills the woods with the music of woe, and from the impulse of sorrow, warbles her sweetest strains; so, from the wounded mind, and from the broken spirit, the fervor of devotion, and the eloquence of prayer, come up with such pathetic memorial before the throne, that the Divine ear listens delighted. True religion, true virtue, brightens in distress; she emerges from the deep with tenfold radiance, and never shines with such transcendent, such triumphant, such immortal beauty, as when wandering through the darkness of an eclipse. You see then, that in these paths you are in the company of the good, and are encompassed with a cloud of witnesses. You are not left alone to climb the arduous ascent. On these mountains, the feet of patriarchs, the feet of prophets, and the feet of martyrs, have trod. On these mountains, a greater than patriarchs, than prophets, than martyrs appeared.

The *fourth* and *last* thing proposed, was, To consider Christianity as affording a joyful consolation against the fear of death.

Many and various are the evils to which human life is subjected. To finish the mighty sum of them, and to make the scene end with pain, as it began with sorrow, comes the evil of death. The king of terrors, with his black train of attendants, even when seen at a distance, makes the firmest knee to shake, and the stoutest heart to tremble; and, when exerting his influences upon feeble minds, and assisted by the power of the imagination, has kept multitudes all their days under the cloud of melancholy, and under subjection to bondage. It is the great excellence of the Christian Religion, that as it affords consolation in all the evils of life, so it also provides a remedy against the fear of death. Hence the prophet, looking forward unto the days of the Messiah, breaks out into these strains of exultation: "I will redeem them from death: I will ransom them from the power of the grave: O death, I will be thy plague: O grave, I will be thy destruction." Hence says the Apostle Paul, "Forasmuch as the children were partakers of flesh and blood, he himself also took part of the same, that he might destroy him that had the power of death, that is the devil, and deliver them who, through fear of death, were all their lifetime subject to bondage."

The evils attending death to men, in a state of nature, are manifold.

One of these is the uncertainty of our future destination. Reason gives us little information concerning the state of the soul when it departs from the body. We see the body mingle with its kindred elements, and return to the dust from whence it was taken. But what becomes of the soul? Does it too cease to exist, and vanish into air? Or does it still live and act in another scene? Here we are lost in conjectures and uncertainty. We see the traveller involved in the cloud of night, but we know not assuredly of any morning that awaits him. The ocean spreads before us vast and dark, but we know not with certainty if it will waft us to any shore. What a disconsolate situation of mind is this! Afflicted with the view of our past life; tormented with present pain; and hovering over an abyss from which we are uncertain if we shall ever emerge! To pass for ever into the dominion of darkness; to go we know not where! Lost in these doubts, troubled with the fears of futurity, the Roman Emperor addressed his departing soul: "O my soul, thou art leaving thy once loved haunts, thy former companions, and thy wonted joys; but into what unknown regions and dark abodes art thou now going? Alas! thou canst not tell!" These doubts and perplexities are now removed by the coming of Christ. When the Sun of Righteousness rose in our region, it dispelled the shadows of the everlasting evening; it poured its radiance upon the path of immortality, and brought full to view the scenes of the invisible world. The future scenes of happiness and glory are not only discovered by the gospel of Jesus, but are set before our eyes. In the inspired oracles, we hear the voice of the archangel and the trump of God; we see the dead arising from their graves; a mighty army of saints and martyrs springing with joy from dust and corruption. We see Jesus upon the throne, and the faithful at his right hand. We hear the happy sentence pronounced upon them, "Come ye blessed of my Father, inherit the kingdom prepared for you before the foundations of the world were laid." We see them with palms of victory in their hands, and with crowns of glory on their heads, ascendingus on high with their Lord, and sitting down with him upon his throne.

Another evil attending on death is the sense of our sins and transgressions, which then rising up to our memory in black colors, overwhelm us with horror of mind. But to those who receive the privileges of Christianity, the bed of death will not be a scene of terror. With a faith which overcometh the world, they give up their souls into the hands of him who made them. "I have indeed sinned, most merciful Father, against Heaven and in thy sight. Mine iniquities compass me about. I am covered with confusion, and condemn myself, and often have been afraid lest thy judgment should confirm the sentence of my own heart. But thou art merciful and gracious. Thou hast no pleasure in death. I am unworthy of the least of all thy mercies. But worthy is the Lamb that was slain, to receive blessing and glory and honor and power. In his death I see the price of my redemption. In his life I see the path which leads to immortality. In his resurrection I see the proof of my own, and evidence of my immortal existence. I have accepted the offers of thy mercy, and have endeavored to walk worthy of the vocation wherewith I was called. With whatever failings I may have been encompassed, thou knowest that it has been the study of my life to approve myself to thee, and to obtain the testimony of a good conscience. Trusting to thy mercy, and relying on the merits of my Redeemer, Father of all, I come to thee! With the joy of the Patriarch, I follow thy call into the land unknown."

Thus, my brethren, I have endeavored to set before you some of the joyful consolations derived from the Gospel of Jesus; consolations which not only serve to support and animate us under the afflictions of this present life, but which also enter within the veil, and constitute our happiness through everlasting ages. But before I conclude, regard to my duty prompts me to warn and admonish you, that though the glad tidings of the Gospel are proclaimed to all, yet the consolations which they contain are not intended for, and are not conferred upon, all who hear the Gospel. It is only they who believe, who repent, who reform, that will ever reap any solid advantage from the Christian religion. The profession of Christianity will avail us nothing. It will avail us nothing to say that we have faith. We may easily deceive ourselves, and make a lively imagination pass for a strong faith. But unless our faith purify the heart, unless it work by love, unless it produce the fruits of righteousness, it is no better than the faith of the devils, who believe and tremble. Let me therefore persuade you, never so much as in thought, to separate ideas of faith and morality; of belief in Christianity and a good life. If you make the attempt, you are undone for ever.

SERMON XV.

ON THE DANGER OF DELAYING REPENTANCE.

2 Cor. vi. 2.—"Behold, now is the accepted time; behold, now is the day of salvation."

There is not a man upon the earth but who has some sense of religion upon his mind, and intends one day or another to work out his salvation. When we look into the world, we find that all men are just about to reform. However loose in their principles, however profligate in their lives, they seriously purpose to amend their conduct, and the sinner of to-day resolves to be a saint to-morrow. Seeing then that all men are so favorably disposed towards religion; seeing that all men are in earnest one day to repent; how does it come to pass that so many men never repent; that such multitudes live and die in their sins? It is because they delay their repentance; it is because they put off the day of salvation; because they begin not a course of reformation, but are only *about* to reform. This infatuation is not confined to the inexperience of our early years, it extends through every period of life. In this the hoary head is no wiser than the youth of yesterday; and the same lying spirit that deceived us at twenty, is believed at threescore and ten. In this, experience does not make us wise, and when we buy instruction it avails us not. The fool, who, wanting to cross the river, lay down on its bank till the waters all ran by, is but a just emblem of that man who delays his repentance from time to time, who is always purposing but never performing, and who, neither warned by the past, nor alarmed for the future, purposes on to the last, and dies the same. Such is the life which numbers of men lead in the world, spending the prime and vigor of their life in vain pursuits; letting all their religion evaporate in empty resolutions, till, in an hour in which they are not aware, the warning is given. At midnight is the cry made, and when they seek to enter in with the bridegroom, the door is shut!

That you may understand the expressions made use of in the text, I must recall to your remembrance, that in the language of Scripture, the period of our probation is called a time, a season, or a day. There is an accepted time, there is a season of merciful visitation, there is a day of grace, which, if we let slip, the night cometh, in which no man can work, in which we shall grope for the wall like the blind, in which we shall stumble at noon-day as in the night, and be in desolate places as dead men. This does not arise from a defect of mercy in God, from a defect of merit in Christ, or from a defect of grace in the Holy Spirit; it arises from ourselves and from the nature of things. Almighty God hath appointed this life to be our state of probation. He hath set apart a time to fix the character for eternity. When, therefore, by repeated acts and by long habits, this everlasting character is fixed, no alteration can succeed. To give an instance that may have occurred to the observation of you all; you have seen, or you have heard of, criminals who have been trained up from their youth in the practice of vice, who have advanced from less to greater crimes, who have been punished according to law, who have been imprisoned, who have been banished, who have returned from banishment, and for greater crimes have been condemned to die, who from some artifice or incident have escaped in the critical moment, and who, instead of being reformed by all these punishments, have fallen into the same crimes again, and even grown bolder in wickedness. There have indeed been instances of great sinners who have turned penitents, and been good Christians; but it is much to be questioned if there be any such instance among those who have been *long* sinners, who have committed iniquity, not by fits and starts, but upon a fixed and determined plan, who have spent in the service of sin all the fire of youth and coolness of age.

Having explained to you the meaning of the phrase used in the text, before proceeding further, take next a view of life, and you will see, that a great part of men let slip the accepted time and day of salvation, till it be too late. It is the happiness of most men in countries where the Christian religion is professed, to receive a good education, and to be trained up from their youth in the principles of religion, and in the practice of virtue. But when this period of discipline is over, when a man sits out in life, and becomes his own master, he frequently becomes a different person in that different state, and looks upon the good habits of his youth as some of those childish things which he ought now to put away. If his education has been severe and rigorous; if his parents restrained in him that gayety of heart and flow of the spirits which is the portion of youth; if he pined in his closet, whilst his equals in age frequented those entertainments which can be enjoyed with innocence, he then generally goes to the other extreme, and plunges with a precipitant step into all the follies and vices of the age. The prisoner having got loose, grows wild and extravagant. Being formerly shut up, he now wants to know the world; and, in order to this, ventures on forbidden paths, resigns the reins of conduct to inclination, and gives a loose to all his desires. Having found his former principles to be inconsistent with the enjoyment of life, he confounds his early prejudices with true piety; for which cause he throws off religion altogether; he becomes a patron and defender of vice; he laughs at every thing that is serious; and perhaps out of contempt to this day, in which we assemble together to worship the God of our fathers; out of contempt to the sacred rites of his country, which all wise heathens have revered; out of contempt to the venerable institutions of our holy religion, spends this day in dissipation and profaneness, and open impiety.

But, not to draw the character with such black stains, let us suppose men at that period passing their days in folly rather than in vice, at the head of every idle scheme, first in every fashionable amusement, and as the Scripture happily expresseth it, "walking in vain show." Behold them making amusement one of the cares of life; spending those precious hours, which no dower can ever recall, which no future labor can ever compensate, spending those precious hours in vanity and folly, whilst all along they forget the business of their salvation, and are no more affected with the prospect of a world to come, than with a tale that is told. But whilst thus they dance round in a circle of folly; whilst they solace themselves with the prospect of pleasures rising upon pleasures, never to have an end, and say in secret to their souls, "To-morrow shall be as this day, and much more abundant;" whilst, like the foolish virgins, they slumber and sleep in the arms of this Delilah, at midnight is the cry made, O man, thy hour is come! And the trembling soul takes its departure unawares and unprepared to God the Judge of all!

To guard you against the fatal error which has undone its thousands, allow me to recommend to your practice the necessity of instant repentance and reformation. In the *first* place, No time is so proper as the present; *secondly*, If you delay, your reformation will be difficult; *thirdly*, If you delay long, it may become altogether impossible.

In the *first* place then, There is no time so proper as the present.

The prodigal son exhibits to us a scene which we often see realized in life. A young man, who had been educated in the paths of virtue, declining from these paths, and going astray into forbidden ground, from the fond expectation of meeting with some strange, vast, unknown happiness in the gratification of sensual desire. In the course of this unhallowed pilgrimage, he gives loose reins to his mind, he indulges every wandering inclination, he denies himself nothing that his heart wishes for. At last he comes to himself, he sees the folly of his ways, he repents, he resolves, he amends. Such a change of life we can easily conceive. In his former situation, he knew not what he did, he was transported by passion, he went headlong down the torrent. But when once he began to reflect, he found that that was the critical moment of life, which, if he had neglected, his return would have been more difficult. In his former situation, he went forward in the path which seemed right in his own eyes, without looking back. He did not act against the admonitions of conscience, he did not think at all. But if, after his eyes were opened to discern the state of wretchedness and guilt into which he had fallen; if, after this, he had returned to folly again, it would have been much more difficult to restore him by repentance. Let this then be your conduct; whenever you come to the knowledge of your sins, whenever you perceive any thing amiss in your lives, seize the favorable moment, as the proper time to reform.

What is it, I beseech you, that you do by delaying? You allow corruption time to strengthen and fortify itself; you give temptation double force, by yielding to it, not from suprise, but with deliberate consent; you weaken the power of conscience, that check which God appointed to you in your evil courses; and, with your own hand, you throw obstacles in the way of your conversion. You now see you are sinful and undone; you now resolve to repent and amend; you are now setting out in the path which leadeth to life; you are not far from the kingdom of God. But if you resolve and perform not; if, when you are once engaged, you draw back; you then fly off from the path of life to the way of destruction; you throw yourself farther from the kingdom of God than if you had never set out. At once, then, at once make your escape from the allurements of sin; break the chains by which you are held; cut off all the avenues and approaches to the sin that besets you; give no time to the enemies of your soul to collect their strength; by faith and repentance now enter on the way that opens into the heavens; when you say, with sincere purpose of heart, "I will arise and go to my Father," in that moment arise and go to thy Father; *now* is the accepted time, *now* is the day of salvation.

In the *second* place, By delaying, your conversion will become extremely difficult.

Thou sayest, O man! that thou wilt repent in some future period of time; but thou knowest not the danger of such a resolution. It is amazing to think with what ease we can impose upon ourselves. In spite of all his boasted wisdom, man is more simple than the beast of the field. Do you consider, my friends, that delaying from day to day, and from year to year, that postponing the work of your salvation to some future period of time, is little better than a fixed determination that you will never begin it at all? Do you reflect, that the time to come, if it ever comes, will be the same to you *then*, that the present time is to you *now?* There will occur the same difficulties to deter you, the same pleasures to allure you, the same dangers to terrify you. Objects will then be as present, and strike the senses as strongly as ever; and the time of reformation will still be to-morrow. Nay, it will then be more difficult to be saved than it is now. You will have more sins to repent of; more bad habits to subdue; a more corrupted nature to put off. It is a remarkable fact, and deserves your most serious attention, that, among all the conversions recorded in Scripture, there is not one of a sinner who delayed his repentance. Among all the returning penitents there mentioned, there is not one in the situation of a Christian, who daily hears the Gospel without its having any effect upon his life. Zaccheus, upon hearing Jesus Christ proclaim the glad tidings of salvation, yielded to the influences of that grace to which he had hitherto been a stranger, and surrendered himself to a call which had never been made before. The apostles, in the course of their ministry, converted Jews and Gentiles. They converted the Jews, by proposing to them an idea, which was new to them, the Lord of glory, whom they with wicked hands had crucified and slain. They converted the Gentiles, by working miracles in proof of their divine commission, and by preaching the doctrines of salvation to them, which they had never heard before.

But what new methods can we attempt with *you?* Is there any motive to repentance which hath not already been urged upon you? Is there one avenue to the heart which has not already been tried, and which has not already been tried in vain? Shall we address ourselves to your conscience, to give you the alarm? But alas! you have often heard its voice, you have often disregarded its voice, and by efforts too successful, have lulled it into a profound sleep. Shall we address ourselves to your hopes, by describing to you the joys of heaven, the rivers of pleasures which are at God's right hand, the happiness of the blessed, the triumphs of eternity? All these have been already presented to your eyes, and to all these you have preferred the enjoyments of an hour. You have sold your birth-right to immortality for a sordid gratification, and you now only mind earthly things. Shall we endeavor to alarm your fears, by setting before you the horrors of hell, the worm that never dies, the fire that is never quenched, everlasting destruction from the presence of the Lord and the glory of his power? These have been traced out to you an hundred times, and you have learned the fatal art of freeing yourselves from the fears of them. Shall we implore you by the grace of the Gospel, and by the tender mercies of the God of Peace? But alas! you have undervalued his mercy, you have turned his grace into wantonness. Shall we set before you the image of a Saviour dying on the cross for the redemption of the world? But alas! a crucified Redeemer hath been often preached to you, the memorial of his sacrifice hath been renewed in your sight, and after all you have counted his blood as a common thing, you have looked upon the Son of God suffering on the cross with as much unconcern as the Jews of old, when they cried out, "Away with him, away with him!"

In the *third* place, By long delaying, your conversion may become altogether impossible.

Habit, says the proverb, is a second nature; and indeed it is stronger than the first. At first, we easily take the bend, and are moulded by the hands of the master; but this nature of our own making is proof against alteration. The Ethiopian may as soon change his skin, and the leopard his spots; the tormented in hell may as soon revisit the earth; as those who have been long accustomed to do evil, may learn to do well. Such is the wise appointment of Heaven to deter sinners from delaying their repentance. When the evil principle hath corrupted the whole capacity of the mind; when sin, by its frequency and its duration, is woven into the very essence of the soul, and is become part of ourselves; when the sense of moral good and evil is almost totally extinct; when conscience is seared as with a hot iron; when the heart is so hard that the arrows of the Almighty cannot pierce it; and when, by a long course of crimes, we have become what the Scripture most emphatically calls, "vessels of wrath fitted for destruction;"—then we have filled up the measure of our sins; then Almighty God swears in his wrath that we shall not enter into his rest; then there remaineth no more sacrifice for sin, but a fearful looking for wrath, and indignation which shall devour the adversary. Almighty God, weary of bearing with the sins of men, delivers them over to a reprobate mind, when, like Pharaoh, they survive only as monuments of wrath; when, like Esau, they cannot find a place for repentance, although they seek it carefully with tears; when, like the foolish virgins, they come knocking, but the door of mercy is for ever shut.

Further, Let me remind you, my brethren, that if you repent not now, perhaps you will not have another opportunity. You say you will repent in some future period of time; but are you sure of arriving at that period of time? Have you one hour in your hand? Have you one minute at your disposal? Boast not thyself of to-morrow. Thou knowest not what a day may bring forth. Before to-morrow, multitudes shall be in another world. Art thou sure that thou art not of the number? Man knoweth not his time. As the fishes that are taken in an evil net, as the birds that are caught in the snare, so are the sons of men snared in an evil hour. Can you recall to mind none of your companions, none of the partners of your follies and your sins, cut off in an unconverted state, cut off perhaps in the midst of an unfinished debauch, and hurried, with all their transgressions on their head, to give in their account to God the Judge of all? Could I show you the state which they are now in; could an angel from heaven unbar the gates of the everlasting prison; could you discern the late companions of your wanton hours overwhelmed with torment and despair; could you hear the cry of their torment which ascendeth up for ever and ever; could you hear them upbraiding you as the partners of their crimes, and accusing you as in some measure the cause of their damnation!—Great God! how would your hair stand on end! how would your heart die within you! how would conscience fix all its stings, and remorse, awaking a new hell within you, torment you before the time! Had a like untimely fate snatched *you* away *then*, where had you been *now?* And is this the improvement which you make of that longer day of grace with which Heaven has been pleased to favor you? Is this the return you make to the Divine goodness for prolonging your lives, and indulging you with a longer day of repentance? Have you in good earnest determined within yourself that you will weary out the longsuffering of God, and force destruction from his reluctant hand?

I beseech, I implore you, my brethren, in the bonds of friendship, and in the bowels of the Lord; by the tender mercies of the God of Peace; by the dying love of a crucified Redeemer; by the precious promises and awful threatenings of the Gospel; by all your hopes of heaven and fears of hell; by the worth of your immortal souls, and by all that is dear to men; I conjure you to accept of the offers of mercy, and fly from the wrath to come. "Behold now is the accepted time, behold now is the day of salvation." All the treasures of heaven are now opening to you; the blood of Christ is now speaking for the remission of your sins; the church on earth stretches out its arms to receive you; the spirits of just men made perfect are eager to enroll you amongst the number of the blessed; the angels and archangels are waiting to break out into new alleluiahs of joy on your return; the whole Trinity is now employed in your behalf; God the Father, God the Son, and God the Holy Spirit, at this instant call upon you, weary and heavy laden, to come unto them that ye may have rest unto your souls!

SERMON XVI.

ON THE PARABLE OF THE PRODIGAL SON.

LUKE XV. 18.—"I will arise and go to my Father."

THE parable of the prodigal son is one of the most beautiful and affecting pieces of composition which is any where to be found. The occasion on which it was spoken, and the persons to whom it was addressed, are well known to you. Dropping therefore what was peculiar at the first narration, I shall consider it as representing in general the return of sinners to God by true repentance.

Such a return is not a single act in the Christian life; it is the habitual duty of every man who is subject to infirmities and defects. For such is the weakness of human nature in this imperfect state, such is the strength of temptation in this evil world, that frail man is often led astray before he is aware. Alas! in our best estate we are but returning penitents; and to the last hour of this mortal life we stand in need of amendment.

We may observe the following steps in the return of the prodigal to his father's house; *first*, His restoration to a better mind, by means of consideration. "When he came to himself, he said, How many hired servants of my father's have bread enough, and to spare!" *Second*, Ingenuous sorrow for sin, accompanied with faith in the Divine mercy. "Father, I have sinned against Heaven and before thee." *Third*, A resolution to return to a sense of duty. "I will arise and go to my father." And, *fourth*, His immediate performance of that resolution. "And he arose and came to his father."

First, His restoration to a better mind by means of consideration. "He came to himself."

With great propriety is this expression used; for a wicked man is *beside himself.* Madness, saith Solomon, is in the heart of the sinner. As madness is a disease of the rational powers, so is vice of the moral. Sin, in like manner, unhinges the whole frame of the moral being, tinges with its baleful colors every sentiment of the heart, and presents to view a spectacle more melancholy still, a being, made after the image of God, sinking that image into the resemblance of a brute, or the character of a fiend. Mad, however, as such persons are, they are not always so. Sin cannot always keep its ground. The evil principle has its hour of weakness and decline. There is no man uniformly wicked. The exertion is too strong to last for ever. Nature does not afford strength and spirits sufficient to keep a man always in energy. The most abandoned have fits and starts of soberness and recollection. There are lucid intervals in the life of every person. At such a time is the crisis of a man's character. At such a time the prodigal son came to his right mind. At once the spell wa sbroken and the enchantment dissolved. He is amazed, he is confounded to find himself degraded from the rational character; cast down to the herd of inferior animals; making one at the feast where the vilest of brutes were his associates and companions. Then the false colors with which fancy had gilded his life, vanish away. The flattering ideas which imagination and passion presented to his mind, disappear in a moment. Disenchanted from the delusions of the great deceiver, what he esteemed to be the garden of Eden, he finds to be a desolate wilderness. "Then he came to himself."

You know that when a man recovers from a fit of lunacy, and is restored to his reason, the mind annihilates the lurid interval, forgets the events of such a state like a dream, and resumes the train of ideas it had pursued in its sound state. Thus, the penitent in the parable, awaking as from a dream, recovering as from a delirium, transports himself into the time past, his former life recurs to his mind, his father's house rises to view, he recalls the first of his days before he went astray. Happy days of early innocence and early piety, before remorse had embittered his hours, or vice corrupted his heart! Happy days! when the morning arose in peace, and the evening went down in innocence; when no action of the past day disturbed his slumbers by night; when no reflection on the riots of the night threw a cloud over the succeeding day; when he was at peace with his own heart; when conscience was on his side; when reflection was a friend; when memory presented only welcome images to the mind; when, under the wings of paternal care, he was blessed in his going out and coming in; when his father's eye met his with approbation and delight.

Having veiwed the picture, he compares it with his present situation. Sad contrast! By his own folly, a vagabond in a foreign land; banished from all that he valued and held dear; cut off from the joys of his better days; languishing out life under the most abject form of misery; pining under poverty; sunk into servitude; feeding swine, and himself desiring to partake with them in their husks; miserable without, but more miserable within; a spirit wounded by remorse, a heart torn by reflection of itself, an accusing conscience, which told him that he merited his fate, and which held up to him his past life in its blackest colors of folly and guilt. Astonished at himself, startled at his own image, which, in its true colors, he had never seen before, he was ashamed of his conduct, and came to a better mind. Such were the effects of consideration, and such will ever be the effects of consideration to those who duly exercise it. Why does the sinner go forward in the error of his ways? Because he does not consider. "Hear, O heavens; give ear, O earth: the ox knoweth his owner, and the ass his master's crib; but my people do not consider." Consider your ways, is the voice which God addresses to mankind in every age; and unless you consider, the calls of the gospel and the offers of grace are made to no purpose. The world which is to come has no existence to you but what you give it yourselves; the eternity that is before you, the happiness of heaven and the pains of hell, are no more than dreams, unless you realize them to yourselves, unless you give them their full force, by bringing them home to the heart. When a man reviews the error of his ways, nothing is wanting to a further reformation but reflection and thought. Think, and the work is done. "I have considered my ways," saith the Psalmist. What was the consequence? "I turned my feet unto thy testimonies."

The *second* step in the return of the prodigal, is ingenuous sorrow for sin, accompanied with faith in the Divine mercy. "Father, I have sinned against Heaven and before thee."

We are formed by the Author of our being to feel contrition for the offences we commit. This pungent sense of infirmities, this penitential sorrow for errors and defects, is a beauty in the nature of man. It is an indication that the sense of excellence exists in its full vigor, and the mark of a nature that is not only improvable, but that also is making improvements. When a man seriously considers that the tenor of his life has been irregular and disorderly; that much of his time has been misemployed, and great part of it spent altogether in vain; that he has walked in a vain show, unprofitable to himself or others, an idler upon the earth, a cumberer of the ground; that by his negligence and perversion of his powers he has been lost to the world which is to come, has marred the beauty of his immortal spirit, and stopped short in the race which conducts to glory, honor, and immortality; when he further considers that his offences have extended to his fellow-men, that by his conduct he has been the cause of misery to others, has disturbed the peace of society, done an injury to the innocent, such reflections in a heart that is not altogether callous, will awaken contrition and sorrow.

This penitential sorrow will be increased when he considers against whom he has offended; that he has sinned against infinite goodness and saving mercy and tender love; that he has resisted the efforts of that arm that was lifted up to save him; that he has rebelled against the God who made, and the Saviour who redeemed him. This is one of the characteristics of true repentance. The penitent does not mourn for his sins as being ruinous to himself so much as for their being offensive to God. The returning prodigal, in the address he makes to his Father, dwells, not upon the misery he had brought upon himself, upon the ruin to his character, his fortune and his expectations in life. "I have sinned against Heaven and in thy sight." What grieves me most is, that I have offended thee; that I have sinned against goodness unspeakable; against that goodness to which I am indebted for the care of my infant years; against that goodness to which I owe my preservation; against him who visited me while I was flying from his presence; who supported my powers while they were employed against him. It is my Benefactor whom I have offended; it is my best Friend that I have injured; it is my Father himself against whom I have risen in arms.

This sorrow for sin is accompanied with faith in the Divine mercy. To wicked men laboring under the agonies of a guilty mind, the Deity appears an object of terror. They figure to themselves an angry tyrant, with his thunder in his hand delighting to punish and destroy. Like Adam when he had sinned, they are afraid, and flee from the presence of the Lord. But from the mind of the penitent these terrors vanish, and God appears, not as a cruel and malignant power, but as the best of beings, the Father of mercies and the Friend of men, as a God in Christ reconciling the world unto himself. Encouraged by these declarations, the penitent trusts to the Divine goodness, and flies for refuge to the hope set before him. It is the wicked man only that despairs. Horrors of conscience and forebodings of wrath affright and overwhelm the sons of reprobation. Such horrors felt Cain and Judas Iscariot. But the penitent never despairs. He sinks indeed in his own eyes, and throws himself prostrate on the ground, but still throws himself at the footstool of mercy, not without the faith and the hope that he will be taken into favor. The language of his soul is, "Though I am cast out of thy sight, yet will I look again to thy holy temple. I will arise and go to my Father, for though I have offended him, he is a Father still. He now sits upon a throne of mercy, and holds a sceptre of grace. At thy tribunal former offenders have been forgiven, and former sinners have been taken into favor. To thy ears the cry of the penitent has never ascended in vain. Thou art ever nigh to all who call upon thee in sincerity of heart. When we tend to thee, at the first step of our return, thou stretchest out thy hand to receive us." So different is that repentance which is unto life from the sorrow of the world which worketh death. Different as the look of melancholy upon the face of the virtuous mourner, is from the unkindly glow which burns the cheek of shame: different as the tender tears which a good man sheds for his friends, are from those bitter drops which fall from the malefactor at the place of execution.

The *third* step is a resolution to return to a sense of duty. "I will arise."

Without determined purposes of amendment, contrition is unavailing and ineffectual. The Deity is not delighted with the sufferings of man. Sorrow for sin is so far pleasing, as it softens the heart, and makes it better. It is the resolution of amendment, the purposes pointed to reformation, that make the broken heart and the contrite spirit an acceptable sacrifice; such is the nature of true repentance; it flows not so much from the sense of danger as from the love of goodness.

In true repentance, there is not only a change of mind, but a change of life. When the day-spring from on high arises on him who is in darkness, when God says, Let there be light, the scales fall from his eyes, a new world breaks upon his sight, futurity becomes present, and invisible things are seen; then first he beholds the beauty which is in holiness, and tastes the joy which flows from returning virtue. In that happy hour he forms the pious purpose, and seals the sacred vow to be holy for ever. Then he prefers the peace which flows from virtue, and the joy which arises from a good conscience, to every consideration. Then the servants of God appear to him the only happy men, and he would rather rank with the meanest of these, than enjoy the riches of many wicked. "Great God, withhold from me what thou pleasest, but give me to enjoy the approbation of my own mind, and thy favor. I would rather be the humblest of thy sons than dwell in the tents of wickedness." None shall enter into the New Jerusalem, and sit down at the right hand of the Father, but they who prefer the testimony of a good conscience, the smiles of Heaven, and the sentence of the just, to all the treasures of the world.

Had the penitent not been in earnest, false shame might have prevented or retarded his return. Conscious of guilt, and covered with confusion, how shall he appear before his friends and acquaintance? "I know (might he have said) the malice of an ill-judging and injurious world. The sins which are blotted out from the book of God's remembrance are not forgotten by them. Let me fly rather to the uttermost parts of the earth, retire to the wilderness untrodden by the foot of man, and hide me in the shades which the beams of the sun never pierced, than be exposed to the scorn and contumely and reproach of all around me."

But the penitent was determined and immovable. * * *

[*The rest of the MS. was not legible.*]

SERMON XVII.

THE SPIRIT WHICH IS OF GOD AND THE SPIRIT OF THE WORLD DESCRIBED.

I. CORINTHIANS II. 12.—"Now we have received, not the spirit of the world, but the spirit which is of God."

THERE are two characters which, in Sacred Scripture, are set in perpetual opposition, the man of the earth, and the citizen of heaven. The first character pertains to that class of men, who, whatever speculative opinions they entertain, yet, in practice, consider this life as their only state of being. A person of this character centres all his regards in himself; confines his views entirely to this world, and, pursuing avarice, ambition, or sensual pleasure, makes these the sole objects of pursuit. Good dispositions he may possess, but he exercises them only when they are subservient to his purposes. Virtues also he may cultivate, not for their own sake, but for the temporal advantages they bring along with them. The citizen of heaven moves in a nobler sphere. He does not indeed affect the character of sanctity, by neglecting his temporal concerns. He looks upon the maxim of David, as inspired wisdom. "If thou art wise thou art wise for thyself." But although he has his temporal interest in his eye, he has a higher interest in his heart. What is necessary, what is useful, will often be a subject of attention; but what is generous, what is lovely, what is honorable, what is praise-worthy, become the chief objects of pursuit. He cultivates good dispositions from a sense of their beauty, previous to his experience of their utility; he esteems the possession of virtue more than the earthly rewards it procures; he lives in a constant discharge of the duties of life in this state, and with a well-grounded faith, and an animating hope, looks forward to a better world, and a higher state of being.

These two characters, which divide all mankind, are always represented in Scripture as inconsistent and incompatible with each other. It is impossible, says our Lord, at one and the same time to serve God and to serve Mammon. If any man love the world, says the apostle John, the love of the Father is not in him. The principles that actuate these characters are represented in the text as two spirits opposite to one another, the spirit of the world, and the spirit which is of God. The spirit of any thing is that vital principle which sets it agoing; which keeps it in motion; which gives it its form and distinguishing qualities. The spirit of the world is that principle which gives a determination to the character, and a form to the life, of the man of the earth. The spirit which is of God is that vital principle which gives a determination to the character, and a form to the life, of the citizen of heaven. One of these spirits actuates all mankind. While therefore I represent the striking lineaments in these opposite characters, take this along with you, that I am describing a character which is your own: a character which either raises to eminence, or sinks down to debasement.

In the *first* place, then, The spirit of the world is mean and grovelling; the spirit which is of God is noble and elevated. The man of the earth, making himself the object of all his actions, and having his own interest perpetually in view, conducts his life by maxims of utility alone. This being the point to which he constantly steers, this being the line from which he never deviates, he puts a value on every thing precisely as it is calculated to accomplish his purposes. Accordingly, to gain his end, he descends to the lowest and the vilest means; he gives up the manly, the spirited, and the honorable part of life; he makes a sacrifice of fame, and character, and dignity, and turns himself into all the forms of meanness, and baseness, and prostration. The Prophet Isaiah, with infinite spirit, derides the idols of the heathen world. "A man," saith he, "planteth a tree, and the rain doth nourish it; he heweth him down cedars, and taketh the cypress and the oak; and of the tree which he planted he maketh to himself a god. The carpenter stretcheth out his rule, he marketh it out with a line; he fashioneth it with planes, and maketh it after the figure of a man; and then he worshippeth it as a god. Part thereof he burneth in the fire, with a part thereof he maketh bread, and with the residue he maketh a god." Similar to this is the creation of these earthly gods. Read the pages of their history, and behold them rising to divinity by compliance, by servility, by humiliating meanness, and the darkest debasements. How dishonorable often is that path which conducts to earthly grandeur; and how mean a creature frequently is he whom the world calls a great man! So low and grovelling is the spirit of the world.

It is a spirit of a different kind that animates the citizen of heaven. He is born from above; he derives his descent from the everlasting Father, and he retains a conscious sense of his divine original. Hence, Christians, in Scripture, are called "noble;" are called the "excellent ones of the earth." It is unworthy of their celestial descent, it is unbecoming their new nature, to stoop to the meanness of vice. The citizen of heaven scorns the vile arts, and the low cunning, employed by the man of the earth. He condescends indeed to every gentle office of kindness and humanity. But there is a difference between condescending and descending from the dignity of character. From that he never descends. He himself ever feels, and he makes others feel too, that he walks in a path which leads to greatness, and supports a character which is forming for heaven. Such is the difference between the spirit of the world, and the spirit which is of God. Suppleness, servility, abject submission, disgrace the one; dignity, elevation, independence, exalt the other. The one is a serpent, smooth, insinuating, creeping on the ground, and licking the dust: the other is an eagle, that towers aloft in the higher regions of the air, and moves rejoicing in his path through the heavens.

In the *second* place, The spirit of the world is a spirit of falsehood, dissimulation and hypocrisy; the spirit of God is a spirit of truth, sincerity and openness. The life which the man of the earth leads is a scene of imposture and delusion. Show without substance; appearance without reality; professions of friendship which signify nothing, and promises which are never meant to be performed, fill up a life which is all outside. With him the face is not the index of the mind, nor the tongue the interpreter of the heart. There is a lie in his right hand. He is perpetually acting a part, and under a mask he goes about deceiving the world. He turns himself into a variety of shapes; he changes as circumstances change; he goes through all the forms of dissimulation, and puts off one disguise to put on another. He does not hesitate to counterfeit religion when it serves a turn, and to act the saint in order to gain his ends. Hence the spirit of the world hath often passed for the spirit which is of God, and Satan under this disguise hath been mistaken for an angel of light. Such is the spirit of the world.

The spirit which is of God is a spirit of truth, sincerity and openness. The citizen of heaven esteems truth as sacred, and holds sincerity to be the first of the virtues. He has no secret doctrines to communicate. He needs no chosen confidents to whom he may impart his favorite notions; no private conventicles where he may disseminate his opinions. What he avows to God he avows to man. He expresseth with his tongue what he thinketh with his heart. He will not indeed improperly publish truths; he will not prostitute what is pure and holy; he will not, as the Scripture says, throw pearls before swine; but neither will he on any occasion, partake with swine in their husks. He is what he appears to be. Arrayed in the simple majesty of truth, he seeks no other covering. Supported by the consciousness of rectitude, he holds fast his integrity as he would guard his life. Such is the difference between these characters. The man of the earth turns aside to the crooked paths and insidious mazes of dissimulation; the citizen of heaven moves along in the onward track of integrity and honor. The spirit of the world seeks concealment and the darkness and the shade; the spirit which is of God loves the light, becomes the light, adorns the light.

Thirdly, The spirit of the world is a timid spirit; the spirit which is of God is a bold and manly spirit. Actuated by selfish principles, and pursuing his own interest, the man of the earth is afraid to offend. He accommodates himself to the manners that prevail, and courts the favor of the world by the most insinuating of all kinds of flattery, by following its example. He is a mere creature of the times; a mirror to reflect every vice of the vicious, and every vanity of the vain. His sole desire is to please. If he speak truths, they are pleasing truths. He dares not risk the disapprobation of a fool, and would rather offend against the laws of Heaven than give offence to his neighbor. To sinners he appears as a sinner, to saints he appears as a saint. In the literal sense he becomes all things to all men, without aspiring to that faith which would set him above the world, or to that spirit which would enable him to assert the dignity of the rational character. He is timid because he has reason to be so. Wickedness, condemned by its own vileness, is timorous, and forecasteth grievous things. There is a dignity in virtue which keeps him at a distance; he feels how awful goodness is; and in the presence of a virtuous man, he shrinks into his own insignificance.

On the other hand, the righteous is bold as a lion. "I fear my God, and I have no other fear," is the language of his heart. With God for his protector, and with innocence for his shield, he walks through the world with an erect posture, and with a face that looks upwards. He despises a fool, though he were possessed of all the gold of Ophir and scorns a vile man, though a minister of state. The voice of the world is to him as a sounding brass or tinkling cymbal. The applauses or the censures of the high or the low affect him not. Like distant thunder, they vibrate on his ear, but come not to his heart. To him his own mind is the whole world. There sits the judge of his actions, and he appeals to no other tribunal upon the earth. He possesses the spirit which rests upon itself. He walks by his own light, he determines upon his own deeds. Supported by the consciousness of innocence, and acting with all the force of Providence on his side, he has nothing to fear; knows that he can no more be hurt by the rumors of the idle, impious, and hypocritical, than the heavens can be set on fire by the sparkles that arise into the air, and that die in the moment they ascend. Animated with this spirit, the feeble become strong in the Lord. The apostles who on former occasions had been weak and timid, whom the voice of a woman frightened into apostasy, who deserted their Master in his deepest distress, and hid themselves from the fury of the multitude; these apostles no sooner felt the impulse of this Spirit, than they appeared openly in the midst of Jerusalem, published the resurrection of Jesus to those priests and elders who had condemned him to death, and discovered a boldness and magnanimity, a spirit and intrepidity, which shook the councils of the Jewish nation, and made the kings of the earth to tremble on their thrones.

In the *last* place, The spirit of the world is an interested spirit; the spirit which is of God is a generous spirit. The man of the earth has no feeling but for himself. His own interest is his only object; he never loses sight of this; this is his all; every line of his conduct centres in this point. He has a design in every thing he does. As the Prophet Malachi says, "He will not shut the doors for naught." He deliberates not whether an action will do good, but whether it will do good to him. That generosity of sentiment which expands the soul; that charming sensibility of heart which makes us glow for the good and weep for the woes of others; that Christian charity which comprehends in its wide circle all our brethren of mankind; that diffusive benevolence reduced to a principle of action which makes the human nature approach to the Divine, he considers as the dreams of a visionary head, as the figments of a romantic mind that knows not the world.

But the spirit which is of God is as generous as the spirit of the world is sordid. One of the chief duties in the spiritual life is to deny self. Christianity is founded upon the most astonishing instance of generosity and love that ever was exhibited to the world; and they have no pretensions to the Christian character who feel not the truth of what their master said, "That it is more blessed to give than to receive." This is not comprehended by worldly men, and the more worldly and wicked they are, the more it is incomprehensible. "Does Job serve God for naught?" said the first accuser of the just. Yes, thou accursed spirit! he serves God for naught. Thy votaries serve thee for lucre and profit and filthy mammon; but the children of God serve him from reverence and love. Rewarded indeed they shall be in heaven, while thine are to be tormented, and by thyself, in hell; but they account that to be a sufficient reward which they have even here in their own hearts, the consciousness and the applauses of generosity.

SERMON XVIII.

ON THE INFLUENCE OF THE HOLY SPIRIT.

LUKE XI. 13.—" —— How much more shall your heavenly Father give the Holy Spirit to them that ask him!"

IN the beginning of this chapter, our Lord prescribed to his disciples a pattern of prayer. He discovered the Deity to them under the tender name of a Father; and he taught them to approach the throne of Grace with the affection and the confidence of children. To encourage them still more to practise this duty, he assures them of success upon their perseverance in devotion; and to impress his instructions in the strongest manner upon their minds, he delivers a parable to them, which he concludes with these words: "Ask, and it shall be given you; seek, and ye shall find; knock, and it shall be opened unto you. For every one that asketh, receiveth; and he that seeketh, findeth; and to him that knocketh, it shall be opened. If a son shall ask bread of any of you that is a father, will he give him a stone? or if he ask a fish, will he for a fish give him a serpent? or if he shall ask an egg, will he offer him a scorpion? If ye then, being evil, know how to give good gifts unto your children, how much more shall your heavenly Father give the Holy Spirit to them that ask him?" As if he had said, "I have told you that God is your Father; that his ear is ever open to your cry, and that his hand is ever stretched out in your behalf. You that are fathers can judge of the paternal affection. If you see a child in distress, will your bowels of compassion be shut against him? When he utters the voice of sorrow, will you turn a deaf ear to his complaint? Will you refuse to stretch out the hand to save him from the pit, and instead of relieving him, push him down into destruction? There is no father so barbarous, and no heart so cruel. If you, then, evil and corrupted as you are; if, clothed as you are with human frailties and infirmities, you know how to give good gifts unto your children; if the workings of nature, and the yearnings of paternal affection, prompt you to perform good offices, how much more will the infinite benevolence of the Deity prompt him to bless all his offspring, and open his bountiful hand to the whole family of heaven and earth! As the Most High God who inhabiteth eternity, excels his meanest creature, the being of a day, so far doth the infinite benignity and everlasting love of your Father in heaven exceed the fondest affection of an earthly parent."

In further discoursing to you upon this subject, I shall explain what is meant by giving the Holy Spirit.

Perhaps these words may refer to the extraordinary effusion of the Holy Ghost upon the apostles on the day of Pentecost, when they received the gift of tongues, and were endued with the power of working miracles. Though these words may include this meaning, yet they chiefly refer to the ordinary influence of the Divine Spirit, which extends to every generation; which is the principle of the spiritual life within us, and continues with the faithful in all ages. Reason and revelation concur in assuring us, that the great Creator hath never withdrawn himself from his works. Above us, around us, and within us, God is seen, God is felt. The vast universe is one great temple which he fills with his presence. As he is ever present in the world, he is ever employed. The hand that at first stretched out the heavens, still supports the pillars of the firmament. The breath which kindled the vital heat of nature, still keeps the flame alive and glowing; God still acts through all his works, preserving and upholding the whole system of things, and carrying forward the designs of infinite wisdom and goodness. His providence is a continued exertion of creating power. As he is employed in the material, he acts also upon the moral world. The Father of spirits communicates himself to holy men, enlightens their understandings with divine knowledge; by secret ways, at once strengthens and ravishes the mind, and fills them with a conscious sense of his own presence. Hence the wisest among the heathens, guided only by the light of nature, acknowledged the necessity of supernatural aids, and taught that nothing great or good could be performed without the influence of a divine Spirit. But as this doctrine hath been by some denied altogether, and by others involved in mysticism and absurdity, it will be proper to give you that just and rational account of it which the Scripture authorizes.

There is hardly any one thing of which mankind may be made more sensible from their own experience, than the necessity of divine aids. For alas! the balance in human nature, between reason and appetite, between the powers of the mind, and the inclinations arising from the body, is in a great degree lost. There may be, and there once was, a more harmonious temperament in the human frame. The rational part of our nature was better enlightened and more vigorous; the passions and appetites of the animal part moved under its control. But that state of innocence is no more. Our nature is now degenerated; we find a law in the members warring against the law of the mind. This disorder of our frame is more and more increased by those false notions of happiness which we are apt to imbibe, and by the many bad examples among which we pass our early years, insomuch, that by the time that we are grown up to the full power and exercise of reason, we find ourselves brought under the dominion of sensual and wicked inclinations. How then shall we recover our liberty? How shall we regain the original rectitude of our nature, and obtain a victory over the vices which war against the soul? Is nature, such as it now is, sufficient for these things? Is reason alone an equal match for the passions and desires of the heart, broke loose from all their restraints, authorized by custom, and inflamed by example? Can we cease to do evil and learn to do well, purely of ourselves, and be able to turn the stream of our affections from sensible and earthly things, to objects worthy of the choice and pursuit of a reasonable nature? Can we, in short, convert ourselves by our own strength, and turn from the power of Satan unto the living God? Are we sufficient for these things?

We are not. When we would do good, evil is present with us; the sensual part of our nature obtains dominion over the rational; we are chained down to the earth, while we attempt to soar to the heavens. Here, therefore, God hath graciously interposed for our recovery. As he sent his Son into the world to redeem us from the guilt of sin and the curse of the law, he gives us his Holy Spirit to deliver us from the dominion of sin, and to translate us from the bondage of Satan into the family of Heaven, and the glorious liberty of the children of God. Hence he is said to work in us both to will and to do that which is his good pleasure. We are said to receive the Spirit, and our bodies are styled the temples of the Holy Ghost.

Concerning this Spirit given to those that ask him, I observe, in the *first* place, that his influence is consistent with the freedom of a reasonable being. The assistance which we receive from above, both in our first conversion from sin, and through the whole course of a religious life, are entirely rational, and have only a persuasive and moral influence. They do not resemble the inspiration of the prophets of old, which was sudden and violent, and overpowered the mind; which superseded the use of reason, and suspended for a while the exercise of the natural faculties. The prophets were but the instruments of the Spirit, but we work together with God. The grace of Heaven does not take away the powers of the mind, but exalts them. It does not destroy the natural liberty of the mind, it makes us free indeed. If a man loses his free agency he ceases to be a man. He is a machine, and is acted upon. In opposition to this, God is said in Scripture, to draw us with the cords of love, and with the bands of a man: that is, in such a manner as is most consistent with freedom of choice, and agreeable to the constitution of a reasonable nature. Reason being the noblest faculty of the human frame, it first partakes the influence of the divine Spirit. Its views are enlarged to take in the system of divine truth, and its power is increased to govern the whole man. These divine aids extend to the heart and the affections, place them on proper objects, and give them their noblest joys. In short, they take in the whole of the Christian life. They inspire good resolutions and purposes of new obedience; they carry us on, and encourage us in the ways of righteousness; they render the practice of our duty easy and delightful, and bring us at last to the enjoyment of uninterrupted and everlasting happiness.

Thus you see, that the influence of the divine Spirit is in a way agreeable to the frame of human nature, gentle and persuasive; not controlling or obstructing the use of reason, but by the use of reason influencing the will, moderating the affections, and regulating the whole conversation. It is no argument against the reality of such divine aids, that they are not distinguishable from the operation of our own minds, and that we feel them not in a sensible and striking manner. How difficult is it in our own character to distinguish what is natural from what is acquired; to distinguish between the natural treasures of the mind, and those foreign stores which she imports from education.

The Spirit of God acts in such a manner as is most agreeable to the faculties of the mind. It is in this manner also, that God acts in the material world. Whatever is done in the heavens, or in the earth, or in the sea, is brought about by divine Providence. Yet all that chain of causes and effects, from the lowest up to the throne of God, we call by the name of the course of nature. But what is this? The course of nature is the energy of God.

In the *second* place, I observe, concerning the influence of the Spirit, that its reality is only known by its operation and effect upon our lives. "Marvel not," said our Lord to Nicodemus, "that I said unto you, Thou must be born again. The wind bloweth where it listeth, and thou hearest the sound thereof, but canst not tell whence it cometh, and whither it goeth. So is every one that is born of the Spirit." That is, as if he had said, the influences of the Spirit are indeed imperceptible to sense, and cannot be distinguished in the precise moment of their operation, but they are visible and certain in their effects, and in the fruits which they produce. A life of obedience and holiness, therefore, is the proof, and the only proof, that the Spirit dwells in us. The fruit of the Spirit, say the Scriptures, is goodness and righteousness and truth. The fruit of the Spirit is love, joy, peace, long-suffering, gentleness, meekness, and temperance. The life, then, my friends, the life is the criterion and test by which we shall know if we are born of the Spirit. There are indeed other marks, easier attained, which some people have found out to themselves. A light within, a call from heaven, a secret voice, and an extraordinary impulse, these are often the effects not of a divine fervor, but of a weak understanding and a wild imagination, and often of something worse, even of arrant hypocrisy and unblushing impudence. These indeed are the marks of a spirit which hath often appeared in the world, but which is very different from the Spirit of God. These are the symptoms of that intolerant and persecuting spirit, the offspring of darkness and of demons, which, excepting a few favorites, pursues the human race with unrelenting hatred in this world, and consigns them over to eternal pains in the next. This is a spirit which hath slain its thousands. Fire and sword mark its approach; its steps are in the blood of the just, and it shakes the rod of extermination over the affrighted earth. But the Spirit of God is the Spirit of love. It fills us with affection and benevolence towards all our brethren of mankind. For he that dwelleth in love, dwelleth in God, and God dwelleth in him.

This doctrine of the Spirit dwelling in us, and assisting us to perform good works, furnisheth a strong argument for humility. Why boastest thou, O man? What hast thou which thou hast not received? From God descendeth every good and every perfect gift. We can do nothing of ourselves, not even so much as to think a good thought. It is by the grace of God that we are what we are. He graciously accepts of our sincere endeavors to please him; and at last rewards those services, which by his grace he enables us to perform. Let us therefore be sensible of our own imperfections, and give all the praise to him. Let this stir us up to activity in our Christian course. The proper use and improvement of this doctrine is not to sit still and take our rest, because God gives us his Holy Spirit, but relying on the assistance of his Spirit to move forwards in our Christian race. Seeing God worketh in you, therefore work out your salvation. Up therefore and be doing, seeing the Lord is with you. You not only act with the force of Providence on your side; you have not only the Captain of Salvation fighting with you; but you have also his Spirit within you, leading you on to victory.

In the *last* place, Let us express our gratitude and praise to this divine Guest, who vouchsafes to be our guide and our comforter; let us be careful not to grieve and offend him by wicked actions, lest he withdraw himself from us; and let us always remember, that he who is a pure and holy Spirit, cannot dwell in polluted hearts, and in temples that are not his own.

SERMON XIX.

ON RELIGIOUS RETIREMENT.

Isaiah xxvi. 20.—"Come my people, enter thou into thy chambers, and shut thy doors about thee."

Without viewing these words in connection with what goes before or follows after, I shall consider them as containing an exhortation to religious retirement. Man was intended by his Creator for society. All the powers of his frame, the faculties of his mind, and the qualities of his heart, lead him to the social state as the state of his nature. But although man was made for action, he was also intended for contemplation. There is a time when solitude hath a charm for the soul; when weary of the world, its follies and its cares, we love to be alone, to enter into our chamber, to shut the door about us, and in silence to commune with our heart. Such a retirement, when devoted to pious purposes, is highly useful to man, and most acceptable to God. Hence the holy men are represented in Scripture as giving themselves to meditation; hence Jesus Christ himself is described as sending the multitude away, and going apart to the mountain.

An opinion once prevailed in the world, and in many parts of it still prevails, that all virtue consisted in such a retreat; that the perfection of the Christian life consisted in retiring from the world altogether, in withdrawing from human converse, in shutting ourselves up in the solitude of a cell, and passing our days in barren and unprofitable speculation. Such notions of a holy life have no foundation in the word of God. Moses and the prophets, Jesus and the apostles themselves, acted a part in public life, and enjoin their disciples not to withdraw from the world, but to go about doing good; not to wrap up their talent in a napkin, but to improve it by their industry; not to put their light under a bushel, but to make it shine before men. The retreat, therefore, which scripture recommends, is temporary, and not total; it is not the retreat of a monk to his cell, or a hermit to his cave; but of men living in the world, going out of it for a time, to return with greater improvement. To retire at times into the closet for these purposes, is of general obligation upon all Christians. To induce you, therefore, to the practice of this duty, I shall now show you the advantages which thereby you may expect to reap.

The advantages attending religious retirement are these: it takes off the impression which the neighborhood of evil example has a tendency to make upon the mind; it is favorable for fixing pious purposes in the mind, and strengthening our habits of virtue; it brings us to the knowledge of ourselves; it opens a source of new and better entertainment than we meet with in the world.

In the *first* place, Religious retirement takes off the impression which the neighborhood of evil example has a tendency to make upon the mind. The world, my friends, is not in general a school of virtue, it is often the scene of vanity and vice. Corrupted manners, vicious deeds, evil communications, surround us on every side. From our first entrance into life, we become spectators of the vicious, and witnesses to the commission of sin. This presence of the wicked lessens our natural horror at a crime, it renders the idea of vice familiar to the mind, and insensibly lulls asleep that guarded circumspection which ought always to be awake. Besides this contagion of evil example, the unhappy proneness of men to imitate the manners of those with whom they live, adds strength to the temptations of the world. Our favorable opinion of the person extends to the action he commits, and by our fatal fondness of imitation, we do what we see done. Our way then in the world lies through snares and precipices; we see and we hear at the peril of our souls. The contagion in which we live, transfuses itself into our own minds. How often is the purity of the closet lost amid the pollution of the world! The good resolutions of the morning give way to bustle and business, or to the career of pleasure, and the day that began with innocence and devotion, ends in vanity and vice. Temptations in every form assault your innocence, and the adversary of your soul is for ever on the watch. One false step may send you to the bottom of the precipice. One word spoken in passion, hath given rise to quarrels that have lasted through life. A single glance of envy, of revenge, or of impure desire, hath raised a conflagration which could only be quenched by blood. To avoid the pollution with which the world is infected, to keep off the intrusion of vain and sinful thoughts, enter into thy chamber, and shut thy doors around thee. There the wicked cease from troubling, there the man who is wearied of the world is at rest. There the glare of external objects disappears, and the chains that bound you to the world are broken. There you shut out the strife of tongues, the impertinences of the idle, the lies of the vain, the scandal of the malicious, the slanders of the defamer, and all that world of iniquity which proceeds from the tongue. In this asylum thy safety dwells. To thy holy retreat, an impure guest dares not approach. Enjoying the blessed calm and serenity of thy own mind, thou hearest the tempest raging around thee and spending its strength; the objects of sense being removed, the appetites which they excited, depart along with them. The scene being shifted, and the actors gone, the passions which they raised die away.

In the *second* place, This devout retirement is favorable for fixing pious purposes in the mind, and strengthening our habits of virtue. We are so formed by the Author of our nature, that the material objects with which we are surrounded raise ideas in us, and make impressions upon us merely by their own nature, and without any assistance from ourselves. There are motions in the body which are involuntary and spontaneous, and there are impressions in the mind which are as much out of our power. At the presence of certain objects, we feel certain passions whether we will or not; we cannot command the emotions which arise in the mind; on many occasions we are merely passive to the influence of external things. When imminent danger threatens, or the shriek of jeopardy is heard, the heart throbs, the blood takes the alarm, and the spirits are agitated without our direction or consent. As the nature of the plant is affected by the soil where it grows; as the nature of the animal is affected by the pasture where he ranges; so the character of the man who never thinks, who never retires into himself, arises from the mode of life in which he is engaged. His mind is in subjection to the objects which surround him. He passes from object to object as the scene changes before him, and he is delivered over from passion to passion according to the events which vary his life. Thus in society we are in a great measure governed by accidents, and the mind is passive to the impressions which it receives.

But in solitude we are in a *world of our own.* We can call up what ideas, and converse with what objects we please. We can say to one desire, "Go," and to another, "Come." Dazzled no longer with the false glitter of the world, we open our eyes to the beauties of that better country which is a heavenly one; stunned no more with the noise of folly, we can listen in silence to the still small voice. Escaped from the broad way, we set out on the narrow path. That is the place, and then is the time to seal the useful truth, and to fix the pious purpose. Then you can best recollect your native strength, and stir up the grace of God which is in you. Then at leisure you can reflect by what temptations you were formerly foiled, that you may guard against them in the time to come; foreseeing the evil day, you will look out for the best support when it comes; and putting on the whole armor of God, you will be able to resist the fiery darts of the evil one, and to go forth conquering and to conquer. By these means the good thoughts which were scattered up and down your life will be collected together, and settle in a fixed purpose of new obedience. The various rays thus converging into one, will kindle into a fervent flame.

In the *third* place, By means of religious retirement, thou wilt be brought to the knowledge of thyself. This is a part of our superiority to the other creatures, that we are not confined to present objects, that we can extend our view beyond the province of sense, and turn our attention wherever we please, throughout the whole system of nature. The mind can arrest itself in its motion, and become the object of its own contemplation. The noblest of sciences is to know ourselves. But however useful and important this study is, there is none with which we are so little acquainted. Delighting to wander abroad, and familiar every where, you are strangers at home, strangers to your own character, strangers to your own heart, strangers to all that is most important for a rational creature to know. You give your thoughts to wander through the whole world; on the wings of imagination you fly from pole to pole; but you never descend into yourself. For what reason art thou so averse to know thyself? Because thou art afraid of losing thine own good opinion; because thou wantest to impose upon thyself, and then to impose upon the world. For this cause, thou darest not appeal to thine own mind, thou darest not meet thy heart alone. Thou avoidest the light, lest thine evil deeds should be made manifest. Thou fliest from the God within, as Adam when he had fallen, fled from the Lord, because thou art afraid. What can be more suspicious than for reasonable creatures to decline the bar of reason? What can be more shameful than for those who have an understanding, not to be able or willing to give an account of their actions to themselves? What can be more reproachful than for men to allow themselves in a course of life, which they have not the courage or the confidence to reflect upon?

Sinner! deal plainly with thyself. If thou wert not ashamed of thyself, Why, in the name of the all-knowing God, shouldst thou decline conversing with thyself? If all were well at home, what should make thee so fond of rambling abroad, and losing the remembrance of thyself in a crowd of vain amusements? Here, here is the cause of thy love of noise and hurry, and tumult and dissipation, and perpetual diversions: thy aim is by this means to escape from thyself, to employ and divert thy mind, that it may not be forced upon such an ungrateful subject. Yet, here wisdom begins. Thou never canst ascend to the knowledge of Him, whom to know is life eternal, without knowing thyself; and thou canst never know thyself, without retiring from the world, without stripping off whatever is artificial about thee, without throwing off the veil which thou wearest before men, and devoting thy secret hours to serious consideration. Enter then into thy chamber, shut the doors about thee, commune with thine own heart, be still, say with the Psalmist, "Search and try me, O Lord; see if there be any evil way in me, and lead me in the way everlasting."

In the *fourth* place, Retirement and meditation will open a source of new and better entertainment than you meet with in the world. You will soon find that the world does not perform what it promises. The circle of earthly enjoyments is narrow and circumscribed, the career of sensual pleasure is soon run, and when the novelty is over, the charm is gone. Who has not felt the satiety and weariness of the king of Israel, when he cried out, "All is vanity and vexation of spirit!" Unhappy is the man who in these cases has nothing within him to console him under his disappointment. Miserable is the man who has no resources within himself, who cannot enjoy his own company, who depends for happiness upon the next amusement, or the news of the day.

But the wise man had treasures within himself. He has a spring shut up, and a fountain sealed. The hour of solitude is the hour of meditation. He communes with his heart alone. He reviews the actions of his past life. He corrects what is amiss. He rejoices in what is right, and wiser by experience, lays the plan of his future life. The great and the noble, the wise and the learned, the pious and the good, have been lovers of serious retirement. On this field the patriot forms his schemes, the philosopher pursues his discoveries, the saint improves himself in wisdom and goodness. Solitude is the hallowed ground which religion in every age has adopted as its own. There her sacred inspiration is felt, and her holy mysteries elevate the soul; there devotion lifts up the voice: there falls the tear of contrition; there the heart pours itself forth before Him who made, and Him who redeemed it. Apart from men, you live with Nature and converse with God.

SERMON XX.

ON THE UNHAPPY STATE OF THE WICKED.

ISAIAH LVII.21.—"There is no peace, saith my God, to the wicked."

It is universally agreed that the works of creation demonstrate the being and the attributes of the Deity. The invisible things of God, even his eternal power, his unerring wisdom and his infinite goodness, are every where legible throughout the great book of Nature. It is very astonishing, however, that many persons who from the *creation* of the world infer the existence and perfections of the Deity, should, from the *government* of the world, infer the necessity of a day of judgment to rectify the course of Providence, and vindicate the ways of God. The works of God must certainly be uniform and of a piece. According to the representations of Sacred Scripture, the day of judgment was not appointed to account for the conduct of Providence, but to pass sentence on the actions of men. All the administrations of God are conducted with supreme wisdom and goodness. He is forever employing the power of his providence to favor the cause of righteousness, and to diffuse happiness over the world. When the blessed above sing the wonders of creating power, and cry out, "Great and marvellous are thy works, Lord God Almighty;" they also add, "Just and true are all thy ways, thou King of saints." If the Almighty is possessed of infinite perfection; if, as the Scriptures assert, he loveth righteousness and hateth iniquity, we may naturally infer it to be one of his eternal decrees, that righteousness and happiness, that sin and misery, must be inseparable in the course of things.

Notwithstanding the force of the arguments that prove this truth, opinions pretty generally prevail to the contrary. Many persons are of opinion that the wicked man has more enjoyment in life than the good man has, that virtue exposes us to many evils, and that if it were not for a future state, Christians would be of all men the most miserable. The origin of this opinion it is not difficult to unfold. It is natural for men to judge of the course of things, by what happens in their own lot. When we are in a prosperous situation, when the candle of the Lord shineth upon our heads, all nature puts on a face of beauty and wears a smiling appearance. But, when adversity and a train of afflictions come in their turn, the eye of the impatient sufferer tinctures every thing around him with its own baleful colors. To his disordered mind, darkness seems to involve the system of nature, malignant demons to usurp the sceptre of Providence, and invade the throne of God. Hence the many complaints of good and holy men in sacred writ, that the righteous were cut off from the earth, whilst the wicked flourished like a green bay-tree. But these were not the maxims which governed their lives, they were only sudden exclamations made in the moments of impatience under distress. The universal voice of Scripture is expressly on the other side. "Say ye to the wicked, It shall be ill with him; say ye to the righteous, It shall be well with him. There is no peace, saith my God, to the wicked. Great peace have they who love the laws of the Lord."

In further treating upon this subject, I shall endeavor to show you, that there is no peace or happiness to the wicked, whether you consider him as a subject of the divine government, as a member of society, or as an individual.

In the *first* place, then, Let us consider the wicked in his religious capacity as a subject of the divine government.

Religion is the distinguishing quality of our nature, and is one of the strongest features that marks the human character. As it is our distinguishing quality, so it possesses such extensive influence, that however overlooked by superficial inquirers, it has given rise to more revolutions in human society, and to more changes in human manners, than any one cause whatever. View mankind in every situation, from the earliest state of barbarity, down through all the successive periods of civilization, till they degenerate to barbarity again, and you will find them influenced strongly by the awe of superior spirits, or the dread of infernal fiends. In the heathen world, where mankind had no divine revelation, but followed the impulse of nature alone, religion was often the basis of the civil government. Among all classes of men, the sacrifices, the ceremonies and the worship of the gods were held in the highest reverence. Judge what a strong hold religion must have taken of the human heart, when, instigated by horror of conscience, the blinded wretch has submitted to torture his own flesh before the shrine of the incensed Deity, and the fond father has been driven to offer up with his own hands his first-born for his transgression, and the fruit of his body for the sin of his soul. It is possible to shake off the reverence, but not the dread, of a Deity. Amid the gay circle of his companions, in the hour of riot and dissipation, the fool may say in his heart that there is no God; but his conscience will meet him when he is alone, and tell him that he is a liar. Heaven will avenge its quarrel on his head. Judge then, my brethren, how miserable it must be for a being made after the image of God, thus to have his glory turned into shame. How dismal must the situation be for a subject of the divine government to consider himself as acting upon a plan to counteract the decrees of God, to defeat the designs of eternal Providence, to deface in himself the image and the lineaments of heaven, to maintain a state of enmity and war with his Creator, and to associate with the infernal spirits, whose abode is darkness and whose portion is despair!

Reflections upon such a state will give its full measure to the cup of trembling. Was not Belshazzar, the impious king of Babylon, a striking instance of what I am now saying? This monarch made a feast to a thousand of his lords, and assembled his princes, his concubines and his wives. In order to increase the festivity, he sent for the consecrated vessels which his father Nebuchadnezzar had taken from the temple of Jerusalem, and in these vessels, which were holy to the Lord, he made libations to his vain idols, and in his heart bade defiance to the God of Israel. But, whilst thus he defied the living God, forth came the fingers of a man's hand, and on the wall, which had lately resounded with joy, wrote the sentence of his fate! In a moment his countenance was changed, his whole frame shook, and his knees smote one against another, whilst the prophet in awful accents denounced his doom: "O man, thy kingdom is departing from thee!" Although Providence should not now particularly interpose to punish thee, O guilty man! yet the sentence of thy doom is written in thy heart, and there is a prophet within, who upon the commission of crimes will tell thee, that for these the kingdom of heaven is departed from thee.

In the *second* place, As wickedness makes a man miserable in his religious character, so does it also in his social.

However corrupted men may be in their lives, their moral sentiments are just and right; that is, although from an immoderate self-love we may excuse wickedness in ourselves, yet such is the force of conscience within, so deeply rooted in the mind is the eternal difference' between good and evil, that by the very frame of our natures, we abhor wickedness in others. When we are conversant in the world, or give our attention to a story that is a faithful picture of human manners, from the impulse of natural feeling, we attach ourselves to the side of innocence, we take part with the virtuous hero, and consider his enemies as our own. There is no vice but what tends to make a man contemptible or odious to society. Against the greater and more atrocious crimes, the sword of the law is forever drawn, and its stroke is death. Other vices which come not under the cognizance of the laws, either have ways of punishing themselves, or are marked with public infamy. Pride makes every affront a torment, and puts a man's happiness in the power of every fool he meets with. The envious man is literally his own tormentor, and preys upon his own bowels. The drunkard exposes himself to the derision of mankind, and falls into follies that cover him with shame in his sober hours. Does not a habit of intoxication deprive a man of all sense of decency, indispose him for the business of life, and render him a sorrow to all his friends? Will the atheist conciliate the love of men by showing us that he possesses not the fear of God? Is not the miser pointed at with the finger of scorn, and doomed to the double curse of hoarding and guarding? Is not a liar universally odious, and does he not prepossess us against him even when he speaks truth? Do not fraud and dishonesty mar a man's fortune, ruin his reputation, and hinder his success in life?

In truth, my brethren, there is not a sin but what one way or other is punished in this life. We often err egregiously by not attending to the distinction between happiness and the means of happiness. Power, riches and prosperity, those means of happiness and sources of enjoyment, in the course of providence are sometimes conferred upon the worst of men. Such persons possess the good things of life, but they do not enjoy them. They have the means of happiness, but they have not happiness itself. A wicked man can never be happy. It is the firm decree of Heaven, eternal and unchangeable as JEHOVAH himself, that misery must ever attend on guilt, that when sin enters, happiness takes its departure. There is no such thing in nature, my brethren, there is no such thing in nature, as a vicious or unlawful pleasure. What we generally call such, are pleasures in themselves lawful, procured by wrong means, or enjoyed in a wrong way; procured by injustice, or enjoyed with intemperance; and surely neither injustice nor intemperance have any charm for the mind; and unless we are framed with a very uncommon temper of mind and body, injustice will be hurtful to the one, and intemperance fatal to the other. Unruly desires, and bad passions, the gratification of which is sometimes called pleasure, are the source of almost all the miseries in human life. When once indulged, they rage for repeated gratification, and subject us, at all times, to their clamors and importunity. When they are gratified, if they give any joy, it is the joy of fiends, the joy of the tormented, a joy which is purchased at the expense of a good conscience, which rises on the ruins of the public peace, and proceeds from the miseries of our fellow-creatures. The forbidden fruit proves to be the apples of Sodom and the grapes of Gomorrah. One deed of shame is succeeded by years of penitence and pain. A single indulgence of wrath has raised a conflagration which neither the force of friendship, nor length of time, nor the vehemence of intercession, could mitigate or appease, and which could only be quenched by the effusion of human blood. One drop from the cup of this powerful sorceress, has turned the living stream of joy into waters of bitterness. "There is no peace, saith my God, to the wicked."

If a wicked man could be happy, Who might have been so happy as Haman? Raised from an inferior station to great riches and power, exalted above his rivals, and above the princes of the empire, favorite and prime minister to the greatest monarch in the world. But with all these advantages on his side, and under all these smiles of fortune, his happiness was destroyed by the want of a bow, usual to those of his station, from one of the porters of the palace. Enraged with this neglect, this vain great man cried out in the pang of disappointment, "All this availeth me nothing, so long as I see Mordecai sitting at the king's gate." This seeming affront sat deep on his mind. He meditated revenge. A single victim could not satisfy his malice. He wanted to have a glutting vengeance. He resolved, for this purpose, to involve thousands in destruction, and to make a whole nation fall a sacrifice to the indulgence of his mean-spirited pride. But, as it generally happens, his wickedness proves his ruin, and he erected the gallows on which he himself was doomed to be hanged!

In the *third* place, If we consider man as an individual, we shall see a further confirmation of the truth contained in the text, "That there is no peace to the wicked."

In order to strengthen the obligations to virtue, Almighty God hath rendered the practise of sin fatal to our peace as individuals, as well as pernicious to our interests as members of society. From the sinner God withdraws his favor and the light of his countenance. How dark will that mind be, which no beam from the Father of lights ever visits! How joyless that heart which the spirit of life never animates! When sin entered into paradise, the angels of God forsook the place. So from the soul that is polluted with guilt, peace and joy and hope, those good angels, vanish and depart. What succeeds to this family of heaven? Confusion, shame, remorse, despair.

Cætera desunt.

SERMON XXI.

ON OBEDIENCE TO THE DIVINE LAW.

PSALM LXXXVIII. 1.—"Give ear, O my people, to my law."

THIS is the call which God addressed to his ancient people, and which at sundry times and in divers manners he addresses to the world. It is the voice of the Almighty to mankind in every age. His voice all nature hears, and his law all nature obeys. The sun moves in the path marked out to him by his Creator; the moon keeps her appointed course, and the host of heaven proceed from age to age in their original beauty. The seasons know their time, and the earth obeys the law impressed upon it at first. The elements confess their Lord; the tempest hears his voice, and the sea submits to the mandate which said, "Hitherto shalt thou come, and no farther; here shall thy waves be staid." The orders of celestial spirits, the principalities and powers of heaven, obey the command of their King, minister to the purposes of his providence, and in acts of goodness, or on errands of mercy, perform his pleasure.

Throughout all nature, one being alone is deaf to the voice and disobedient to the command of God, that is, the *sinner*. He alone has departed from his sphere, has rebelled against the law of his nature, and rejected the universal dominion of the Deity in the universe. To recall him from this rebellious state, to replace him in his original station, and restore him again to the kingdom of God, is the end of true religion. For this purpose Moses and the prophets were inspired, Jesus and the apostles were sent. For this purpose the heaven was opened, the Almighty appeared, and the voice uttered to the world, "Give ear, my people, to my law."

Your obligation to obey this law will appear, if you consider that it is the law of your nature, that it is the law of heaven, that it is the law of society, and the law of happiness.

In the *first* place, It is the law of your nature.

When God created man, he did not leave him to act at random, or to live in a state of anarchy. He gave him a law, the emanation of eternal wisdom and the transcript of Divine perfection. The same fingers that upon Mount Sinai wrote the commandments upon tables of stone, had written them beforehand upon the living tables of the human heart. The foundation of morality is laid deep in human nature; its principles result from the constitution of our frame; and its authority will be supreme, while there is a mind to discern, or a heart to feel, or a conscience to judge. Darkness is not more different from light, nor bitter from sweet, than good is from evil, and virtue from vice. You are no more masters of the emotions that rise in the mind, than of the sensations which rise in the body. You can no more give the law to internal nature than to external nature. You may as well call the sun to come down from the firmament, as aim to extingish the light of heaven which shines in the breast. Inferior animals are incapable of morality. They have no law but instinct; they are left to obey the call of appetite, and to follow blindly the prevailing impulse. But it is not so with man. Reason is his law; and the dictate of virtue is the dictate of nature. The question with him is not, what is the call of appetite? but, what is the voice of reason? Not what is the prevailing impulse? but, what is the impulse which ought to prevail?

If, therefore, you disown the obligation of this law, you renounce your nature and unman yourself. If you claim an exemption from the authority of reason and sentiment and conscience; if you take the license to indulge every appetite and every passion without restraint or control; you may;—but first come down from your rank in the scale of being; break off all intercourse with rational creatures; depart from the society of men; go to your equals; herd with the animals of the field, and eat grass with the brutes that perish: there display humanity degraded: exhibit thyself a monument of folly and guilt, to be pointed at by the hand of scorn, and to be shunned like the pestilence. If ever, like the Monarch of Babylon, thou shalt rise from thy degraded state; if ever thine understanding shall return, and thou shalt be able to lift up thine eyes to heaven, like him thou wilt praise and extol and glorify the King of heaven, and give ear to that law which he promulgates to the armies in heaven and to the inhabitants of the earth.

In the *second* place, Your obligation to obey this law will further appear when you consider that it is the law of Heaven.

It comes to you not only recommended by your own authority, but it comes enforced by a higher authority, that of God himself. The appearances of the Almighty to confirm the law, the prophets and the gospel, were made for the instruction and improvement of those who saw them, and are recorded for the instruction and improvement of those who read them. The mighty God, even the Lord, hath spoken, and called the earth from the rising of the sun to where he goeth down. The first promulgation of the law was from Mount Sinai. To strike a rude and barbarous people, to reclaim a perverse and obstinate generation, it was requisite that the arm of power should be stretched out, and that the majesty of terror should be displayed. Accordingly, when the law was given from Sinai, there was blackness and darkness and tempest; there were thunders and lightnings and a thick cloud upon the mount; and when Moses brought the people from the camp to meet with God, they trembled as one man; and hill Sinai was altogether on a flame, and the smoke thereof went up as the smoke of a furnace, for the Lord descended upon it in fire, and the mountain quaked; and when the voice of the trumpet sounded long, and waxed louder and louder, God called Moses up to the top of the mount, and gave the law.

The same precepts that were given upon Mount Sinai, Jesus Christ came to confirm and to extend. At his first public appearance, in his sermon on the mount, he republished, restored and perfected the law. The new dispensation indeed was different from the old. The God of Abraham dwelt in darkness, and was clothed with terror. The God and Father of our Lord Jesus Christ dwells in the light, and is clothed with grace. Miracles of power confirmed the one; miracles of grace distinguished the other. We come not to Mount Sinai, but to Mount Zion. At the publishing of the gospel no fire descended, no thunders rolled; at the publishing of the gospel, when our Saviour, being baptized, entered upon his ministry, the heaven was opened over his head, the Spirit descended upon him in the form of a dove, the messenger of peace, and a voice came from the overshadowing cloud, " This is my beloved Son in whom I am well pleased." Revelation then concurs with reason in establishing the law, and to the voice of nature is added the voice of God. Such an authority you will not despise. You will not join with the impious king of Egypt, who hardened his heart, and said, " Who is the Lord that I should obey his voice?"

In the *third* place, Our obligation to obey the law will be further manifest, when we consider that it is the law of society.

That righteousness exalteth a nation, and that vice is not only a reproach but also a depression to any people, are truths so universally received as to require no confirmation. All lawgivers in all ages have thought so, and made it their object to cultivate justice and temperance and fortitude and industry, conscious that public virtue is the source of public happiness. Philosophers and moralists have been of the same opinion; and have taught, with one consent, that the good morals of the people were the stability of the government, and the true source of public prosperity. Practice and experience have confirmed the truth of these speculations. If we consult the history of the most renowned nations that have made a figure in the world, we shall find that they rose to greatness by virtue, and sunk into contempt through vice; that they obtained dominion by their temperance and probity of manners, and a serious regard to religion, and when they grew dissolute, corrupted and profane, they became slaves to their neighbors, whom they were no longer worthy to govern. Public depravity paves the way for public ruin. When the health and vigor of the political constitution is broken, it is hastening to its decline. When internal symptoms of weakness appear, the least external violence will accomplish its dissolution.

It is a duty, then, which we owe to society and to our country, to observe the rules of righteousness; for in order to be good members of society and true patriots, we must be virtuous men.

To show your obligation to give ear to this law, let us, in the *last* place, consider that it is the law of happiness.

This, in some measure, follows from what has been already said; for if virtue be necessary to the happiness of public societies, it is also necessary to the happiness of private families and of private men, unless we can suppose the body politic to be flourishing, while every individual is in misery and distress. In consulting for others, all agree that virtue leads to happiness; but if for others, why not for you? When you consult for them, you have no passions to darken your understanding and perplex your judgment. When you consider with coolness and with candor, the observation and experience that all of us have had occasion to make, it will be sufficient to convince you, that the law of the Lord is truly favorable to the interests and friendly to the happiness of man; that it corresponds to the just dictates of the mind, and consults the best affections of the heart. What does it forbid? Desires, passions and vices, from which for our own sakes we should abstain, though there was no such prohibition. It forbids the gratification of desires which would lead us to ruin; the indulgence of passions which are the troubles of human life, and the source of our greatest misery; the commission of vices which waken remorse, and deliver us up to the tormentors. What does the law of the Lord command? What is lovely and pure and praise-worthy; what tends to make men peaceable, gentle, humane, merciful, benevolent and happy.

SERMON XXII.

ON JESUS CHRIST DYING FOR SINNERS.

ROMANS v. 7, 8.—"For scarcely for a righteous man will one die; yet peradventure for a good man some would even dare to die. But God commendeth his love toward us, in that, while we were yet sinners, Christ died for us."

THE Apostle Paul, the author of this epistle, was bred at the feet of Gamaliel, and instructed in all the learning of the Jews. To his Hebrew literature he superadded the erudition of the Gentiles; for we find him in his epistles quoting their celebrated authors, and alluding to their remarkable customs and the events in their history. These verses which I have now read, carry an illusion and reference to a distinction of characters which prevailed among the Jews, and to some illustrious actions performed by the Romans, to whom he addressed this epistle.

The Jews distinguished men with respect to their characters, into sinners, just men, and good men. Sinners are those who violate the laws of God and man, who disturb the public peace, and are bad members of society. A just man is one who does no injury to his neighbor, who pays his debts, who conforms to the letter of the law, and who is not deficient in any of the great duties of life. A good man is one who goes farther; who is not only innocent but useful, who is not only decent but exemplary, who is generous, beneficent, public-spirited; who sacrifices his ease, his pleasure, his safety, and, when his country calls for it, who sacrifices his life for the public good. Such was the character of this apostle himself. In order to propagate the Christian religion among the nations, the greatest blessing of God to the world, in order to diffuse the knowledge of this religion, he gave up all that was dear in life, undertook long and hazardous journeys, exposed himself to the dangers of the deep, to the chains of captivity, to the sword of the persecutor, to the derision and hatred of Jews and Gentiles. Accordingly, he met with this return, which he here mentions as being sometimes made to superior goodness; for we read in the sixteenth chapter of this epistle, that he found persons who for his life would have laid down their own.

The apostle also in these verses alludes to some illustrious actions performed by the Romans, to whom he addresses this epistle. The love of their country was the darling passion of that great people. All the soul went out in this generous ardor, and every private affection flowed in the channel of the public welfare. Judge what a strong hold it must have taken of the heart, when it glowed even in the female breast; when the wife encouraged the husband, and the mother exhorted the son, to die for their country. It was a principle in the breast of every Roman, that he owed his life to his country. This being the spirit of the people, gave birth to many illustrious and heroic actions. The spirit of patriotism glowed among the people for many ages of the republic; one hero sprung from the ashes of another; and great men arose from age to age, who devoted themselves to death for the public good. These being the most celebrated actions in the history of mankind, the apostle here compares them with the death of Jesus Christ. Following the train of thought suggested by the apostle, I shall show you the infinite superiority of that love which prompted Jesus to die for the sins of the world, to that patriotism which prompted the heroes and great men of old to die for their friends or for their country.

In the *first* place, then, Those who devoted themselves to death for their friends or their country, submitted to a fate which they must one day have suffered. But Jesus Christ, who is the true God and possesseth eternal life, submitted to death for our redemption.

We are all born mortal creatures. Sprung from the dust, we return to the dust again. The sentence of the Lord is passed upon all flesh, and there is no exemption from the law of mortality. We know not how soon our last hour may come. The darts of death are continually on the wing; the arrow of destruction flieth by night, and smiteth at noon-day; victims are daily falling at our right hand and at our left, and we know not how soon we too may fall a sacrifice. He, therefore, who exposes himself to danger, or devotes himself to death for the good of others, only anticipates the evil day, only resigns a life which he must soon part with, and submits to a doom which sooner or later he must lay his account to endure. But Jesus Christ was the King eternal and immortal. His outgoings were from everlasting, and he is God blessed forever. He would have remained happy in himself, happy in the contemplation and enjoyment of his own perfections, happy in the administration and government of the moral world, though he had never cast an eye of pity upon mortal man. He would have inherited the praises of eternity though man had never been redeemed. Yet for our sakes he left the glories of the heavens, he veiled his Divinity in a form of flesh, he took our nature with all its infirmities upon him, he submitted to every affliction which embitters human life, and he suffered an excrutiating, an ignominious and an accursed death. For the salvation and the happiness of the world which he had made, the King of kings appeared in the form of a servant, and the Lord of life was crucified at Jerusalem. A crown of thorns was put on that head where the diadem of nature was wont to sit. Where is the deed of human virtue that can stand in comparison with this meritorious exertion of the Divine benevolence? All the perfection of created nature fades before it, and is but a foil to set off the brightness of redeeming love.

In the *second* place, Those, among the sons of men who devoted themselves to death for the good of others, made the sacrifice for their friends, for those by whom they were beloved; but Jesus died for his enemies.

We are united to our friends by the strongest ties of affection, we are interested in all that befalls them, and adopt their joys or their sorrows. Long habits of attachment, and a mutual intercourse of good offices, draw close the cords of friendship, and make them twine with every string of life. Hence we are fellow-sufferers with our friends in distress, we are afflicted in all their afflictions, so that suffering a great temporal evil for them, is in reality removing a load from our own minds. Thus strongly are we attached to our friends, nor is the charm less which binds us to the community. The sacred name of country, strikes us with veneration; we feel an enthusiasm for our native land; when it is in danger, hardships are cheerfully undergone, and death scarce appears an evil in such a glorious cause. Such inducements there are to him who dies for his friends or his country. But Jesus died for the redemption of his enemies, for those who threw off their allegiance to him, who rebelled against his authority, and rose up in arms against their benefactor. Their groans would never have reached his ear, nor afflicted his heart, had he not graciously inclined to sympathize. The misery of mankind would never have disturbed the happiness of the Divine nature, would never have thrown a cloud over the serenity of the heavens, nor made a pause in the alleluiahs of the blessed, had he not chosen to bear their sorrows. It was unmerited goodness, it was sovereign mercy, it was pure benevolence, it was love truly divine, that moved him to interpose in our behalf. He saw the race of men on the very brink of destruction, he saw the bottomless pit just opening to swallow them up, and in the moment of danger, the Redeemer appeared, gracious to pity, mighty to save. A cloud had long been gathering over the nations, the hand of the Omnipotent was stretched out in wrath, the thunder of his power was ready to burst over a devoted world; when the Patron and the intercessor of the human race stepped in, and stayed the avenging arm with the words of mercy; "Lo I come to do thy will. Sacrifice and burnt-offerings thou dost not desire. On me let thine anger fall. Let me die that these may live."

In the *third* place, He who dies a martyr for the public good, departs with honor; but Jesus made his departure with ignominy and shame.

It is honorable, it is glorious, to die for the public good. He who falls a martyr to the happiness of mankind, is supported by the native fortitude of the soul, is carried forward by the consciousness of a good cause, is encouraged with the admiration and applause of the world, and becomes famous to all succeeding times. To him the temple of fame spontaneous opens its gate, his name is repeated with applause, honors are paid to his memory, and he is the heir of perpetual praise. Circumstances of such a nature take away the terror of death. The secret consciousness of a great soul, the approach of an event which is so glorious in itself, and so beneficial to the world, the anticipation of the praises of succeeding times, exalt the man, and fill him with the elevation and magnanimity of virtue. Few enjoyments in life can be compared with a death so glorious. But Jesus Christ submitted to the ignominious death of the cross. The greatest trial and exercise of virtue, is when an innocent man submits to the imputation of a crime that others may be free from the punishment. This our Lord did. In his life he was branded with the blackest names, and accused of the most flagitious crimes; branded with the name of publican and sinner, accused of associating with the profligate, and of being in compact with the powers of darkness. But at his latter end, in a peculiar manner, he endured the shame. He was betrayed like an impostor by one of his own disciples, apprehended like a robber by a band of soldiers, led like a malefactor through the streets of Jerusalem, nailed like a murderer to the accursed tree, and in the sight of Israel died the death of a traitor and a slave, that he might atone for the real guilt of men. In all these respects the merit of Jesus was infinitely superior to the heroism of men. As the heavens are higher than the earth, as the Most High God excels the offspring of the dust, so much superior was his love to their beneficence.

To conclude, Let me ask you, my brethren, what impression does the love of Jesus make upon your hearts, what influence does it exert upon your lives? They whose minds are dazzled with the idea of false glory, with arms and conquests and fields of battle, and triumphal processions and songs of victory, may not be disposed to relish those acts of heroism which have nothing of the sword in them. But to the mind that is freed from vulgar prejudice, and acquainted with true glory, the triumphs of Jesus will appear the greater that they are the triumphs of peace, that they were not obtained at the expense of slaughtered thousands, nor erected on the ruin of nations, but rose on the basis of general happiness, and everlasting life to all good men.

Are you then actuated with a proper sense of gratitude to this Captain of our salvation? The temporal hero and deliverer is received with a tribute of applause; every heart beats with admiration, and every tongue is vocal in his praise. Let us also celebrate the Prince of Peace, the Redeemer of our fallen race, who delivered us from everlasting wrath, and opened a way to the heavens by the blood of his cross. Beautified with his salvation, let us rejoice in the Saviour, saying with the apostle, "God forbid that I should glory, save in the cross of Jesus Christ." Let us also love Him who first loved us. Let us give the chief place in our hearts to that Divine Friend of mankind, whose affection to us was stronger than death.

SERMON XXIII.

ON THE CHARACTER OF THE RIGHTEOUS.

PROVERBS XII. 26.—"The righteous is more excellent than his neighbor."

THE sentiments of men concerning virtue, and their own particular practice, form a very strange and striking contrast. Notwithstanding their own irregular or imperfect conduct, a general feeling, with regard to morality, pervades the human species. Philosophers have differed about the origin of moral distinctions, and delivered various theories concerning virtue; but the people who judge from their feelings, have no system but one; and whenever right and wrong become the subject of decision, if the fact be fully explained, the voice of mankind is uniform and constant.

Without this moral sense or sentiment, the question with regard to virtue had never been started at all, nor exercised the ingenuity of the greatest and best spirits in every age of the world. For, independent of the national religions, men arose among the heathens who strove to improve or reform their countrymen, the lights of one age shone to another, the great and the good not only left their example, but lifted up their voice to ages which were to come.

Religion gives its powerful sanction to the maxims of morality, and this volume was written to republish that law which is engraven on the heart.

The book from which these words are taken, was the work of a great king who sometimes left the throne to adorn it the more, and, retiring from the splendid follies of a court, consecrated his hours to the benefit of all posterity. It was addressed by Solomon to his son, and contains such ideas of religion, and urges such motives to virtue, as are most effectual with the young, representing them as the perfection of human nature, and the true excellence of man. "The righteous (says he) is more excellent than his neighbor." With great propriety is this picture set before the young; for the love of excellence is natural to the youthful mind. What is manly, what is generous, what is honorable, are then the objects of admiration and pursuit; fired with noble emulation, each ingenuous disciple aspires to be more excellent than his neighbor.

The objections against a holy life have proceeded on maxims directly contrary to the text. The inducements to vice, which have been powerful in all ages, are the same that were presented by the tempter to our first parents. Wisdom was promised, "Ye shall be wise to know good and evil;" the attractions of ambition were presented, "Ye shall be as gods;" the allurements of pleasure were added, and the forbidden fruit recommended as "good for food and pleasant to the eye." If in opposition to these it shall be shown, that the righteous man is wiser, and greater, and happier, than his neighbor, the objections against religion will be removed, the ways of Providence will be vindicated, and virtue established upon an everlasting foundation.

In the *first* place, The righteous man is wiser than his neighbor.

There is no part of his nature in which man is so earnest to excel, and so jealous of a defect, as his understanding. Men will give up any part of their frame sooner than this; they will subscribe to many infirmities and errors, they will confess a want of temper, and the proper government of their passions, they will even admit deviations with regard to the lesser moralities, but never yield the smallest iota in what respects their intellectual abilities.

No wonder that man is jealous of his understanding, for it is his prerogative and his glory. This draws the line between the animal and the intellectual world, ascertains our rank in the scale of being, and not only raises us above inferior creatures, but makes us approach to a nature which is divine. This enters into the foundation of character, for without intellectual abilities, moral qualities cannot subsist, and a good heart will go wrong without the guidance of a good understanding. Without the direction and the government of wisdom, courage degenerates into rashness, justice hardens into rigor, and benevolence becomes an indiscriminate good nature, or a blamable facility of manners. Where then is wisdom to be found, and what is the path of understanding? If you will trust the dictates of religion and reason, to be virtuous is to be wise. The testimony of all who have gone before you, confirms the decision. In opposition, however, to the voice of religion, of reason, and of mankind, there are multitudes in every age who reckon themselves more excellent than their neighbors, by trespassing against the laws which all ages have counted sacred, the younger by the pursuit of criminal gratification, the old by habits of deceit and fraud.

The early period of life is frequently a season of delusion. When youth scatters its blandishments, and the song of pleasure is heard, "Let us crown ourselves with rose-buds before they are withered, and let no flower of the spring pass away;" the inexperienced and the unwary listen to the sound, and surrender themselves to the enchantment. Not satisfied with those just and masculine joys which nature offers and virtue consecrates, they rush into the excesses of unlawful pleasure: not satisfied with those fruits bordering the path of virtue, which they may taste and live, they put forth their hand to the forbidden tree. One criminal indulgence lays the foundation for another, till sinful pleasure becomes a pursuit that employs all the faculties, and absorbs all the time of its votaries.

There is no moderation nor government in vice. Desires that are innocent may be indulged with innocence; pleasures that are pure may pe pursued with purity, and the round of guiltless delights may be made without encroaching on the great duties of life. But guilty pleasures become the masters and tyrants of the mind; when these lords acquire dominion, they bring all the thoughts into captivity, and rule with unlimited and despotic sway.

Look around you. Consider the fate of your equals in age, who have been swept away, not by the hand of time, but by the scythe of intemperance, and involved in the shade of death. Contemplate that cloud which vests the invisible world, where their mansion is fixed for ever. When the sons of the Siren call you to the banquet of vice, stop in the midst of this career, pause on the brink, look down, and while yet one throb belongs to virtue, turn back from the verge of destruction. Think of the joyful morning that rises after victory over sin, reflection thy friend, memory stored with pleasant images, thy thoughts like good angels announcing peace and presaging joy.

Or, if that will not suffice, turn to the shades of the picture, and behold the ruin that false pleasure introduces into human nature. Behold a rational being arrested in his course. A character that might have shone in public and in private life, cast into the shades of oblivion; a name that might have been uttered with a tear, and left as an inheritance to a race to come, consigned to the roll of infamy. All that is great in human nature sacrificed at the shrine of sensual pleasure in this world, and the candidate for immortality in the next, plunged into the irremediable gulf of folly, dissipation and endless misery.

Cætera desunt.

SERMON XXIV.

RELIGION AN ANTIDOTE TO THE DANGERS AND TEMPTATIONS OF THE WORLD.

DANIEL xi. 32.—"The people that do know their God shall be strong."

THE follies and vices which disfigure human life, do not always proceed from a principle of depravity. The thoroughly abandoned, who sin from forethought and contrivance, who commit iniquity upon a fixed plan, and who are wicked merely from a love of wickedness, I hope and believe are not a numerous class. The indiscretions and vices into which men fall, I am apt to imagine proceed often from a weakness of mind rather than from a badness of heart. There is a certain feebleness in the springs of actions, a facility of disposition, a silliness of soul, which marks the character, and runs through the life of many men, as pernicious to them in the conduct of life, as a principle of actual depravity could be. Persons of this class, properly speaking, sustain no character at all. They assert not the rights of an independent being, they make no original efforts of mind, but patiently surrender themselves to accident, to be guided by events, and to be fashioned by those with whom they live. They have not strength of mind to stand alone, they dare not walk in a path unless it is beaten. Feebleness, fluctuation, timidity, irresolution, fill up the period of their insignificant days, and often betray them into crimes as well as indiscretions. This weakness of the mind is not only pernicious but criminal. There are mental defects that are inconsistent with a state of virtue. The Sacred Scriptures never draw the line of distinction between intellectual and moral qualities, but prescribe both as requisite to form the character of the righteous man. Hence a sound mind, as well as a good heart is mentioned as an ingredient in the character of a saint. Hence, in the sacred books, religion and virtue go under the name of *wisdom*, vice and wickedness under the name of *folly*. Hence intellectual qualities become the subject of divine precept, and we are called upon to be wise and to be strong, as well as to be holy and to be pure. In opposition to the feeble-minded, it is said in the text, that they who know their God, or are truly religious, are strong. Religion, when rightly understood, and virtue, when properly practised, give nerves and vigor to the mind, infuse into the soul a secret strength, and, presenting a future world to our faith, make us superior to the dangers and temptations of the present.

To show what this strength is, I shall set before you some of the most remarkable scenes in human life in which the feeble-minded give way, and in which they who know their God are strong. This strength then, inspired into the mind by the knowledge of God, makes us superior to the opinion and fashion of the world, superior to the difficulties and dangers of the world, superior to the pleasures and temptations of the world, and superior to desponding fears at our departure from the world.

In the *first* place, It makes us superior to the opinion and fashion of the world.

To sustain an amiable character so as to be beloved by those with whom we live, to maintain a sacred regard to the approbation of the wise and good, and to follow those things which are of good report, when at the same time they are pure and lovely and honorable, is the duty of every honest man. But unhappily the bulk of the world is not composed of the wise and the good; religion and virtue are not always in the fashion; to fix the rule of life, therefore, by the public approbation or dislike, is to make the standard of morality uncertain and variable. According to this doctrine, the Christian life would be the work of mere caprice, there would be a fashion in morals as well as in dress, and what is virtue, or vice in one age or country, would not be so in another. In such critical cases, when truth is to be defended, or integrity to be held fast against the current of popular opinion, the feeble-minded are apt to make shipwreck of the faith. The feeble-minded man rests not upon himself, he has nothing within to support him, he thinks, and acts, and lives by the opinion of others. "What will the world say?" is the question that he puts to himself on all occasions. Thou fool! look inwards, thine own heart will tell thee more than all the world. This pusillanimous deference to the opinion of others, this criminal compliance to the public voice, will make you lose your all, your soul.

Hence, in certain companies, men are ashamed of their religion. They lend a pleased ear to arguments that shake the foundations of their faith: they join in the laugh that is raised at the expense of all that they hold sacred and venerable, and themselves assume the spirit, and speak the words of profaneness, while the heart often secretly agonizes for the liberties of the tongue. In opposition to such characters, the man who is truly religious, performs his duty through bad report as well as through good. The applause of such fools as make a mock at sin, he despises. His standard of moral conduct, is his own conscience well informed by the word of God. He knows that the fashion of the world passeth away, and vice or folly is not recommended to him by being practised by others. He remembers the words of his Master, "Whosoever shall be ashamed of me, of him shall the Son of man be ashamed." He dares to be singular and good: "Though all men forsake thee, yet will not I."

In the *second* place, This strength inspired by true religion, makes us superior to the difficulties and dangers we meet with in the world.

The feeble-minded man is intimidated upon the slightest occasion: he starts at difficulties, and shrinks from dangers, whenever they present themselves. Happy to catch at any subterfuge, he finds or makes a thousand obstacles to the discharge of his duty; and when any thing great is to be done, there is "a lion in the way." What infinite mischief has this pusillanimity done in the world! How often has the best and most generous cause been lost by the weakness of its defenders! How often have the most innocent and worthy characters suffered by the shameful cowardice of their friends! How often have men purchased an inglorious ease, an infamous tranquillity, at the expense of character and conscience, and every thing great and good!

Very different is the character of him who is strong in the Lord. When he is assured he is in the right path, he sees no obstacles in the way. Nothing is difficult to a determined mind. Through the divine aid, resolution is omnipotent. To the unwearied efforts of persevering courage, art and nature have yielded: and there is a ladder by which the heavens may be scaled. Through Christ strengthening him, the man of God can do all things No appearance of difficulty, no form of danger, no face of death, terrifies him from doing his duty. He gives up his possessions, his country, his parents, his friends, his wife and children, his own life also, rather than desert the post of honor assigned to him by Providence. "None of these things move me," saith an apostle, "neither account I my life dear unto myself, so that I may finish my course with joy. What mean you to weep, and to break my heart? For I am willing not to be bound only, but to die at Jerusalem, for the name of the Lord Jesus."

This was not the vain boast of men who were brave when the day of battle was distant, and who in the midst of tranquillity, talked of despising danger. It was the speech of one who acted what he spoke. To the confirmation of it, we can adduce a cloud of witnesses, an host of martyrs, multitudes of all nations, and ages, and conditions, for whom the flames of the tormentor were kindled to no purpose; against whom the sword of persecution was drawn in vain; who held fast their integrity, though they knew death to be the consequence, and followed their Redeemer in a path that was marked with blood. Among these martyrs, doubtless there were many who naturally were as feeble, and flexible, and timorous, as any of you are: but when they were inspired with this hidden strength, and were supported by the everlasting arms, the timorous waxed valiant, and the feeble became strong in the Lord.

Cœtera desunt.

SERMON XXV.

THE DANGER OF FOLLOWING A MULTITUDE TO DO EVIL.

Exod. xxiii. 2.—"Thou shalt not follow a multitude to do evil."

Imitation is one of the great characteristics of the human species. As the passion for society is strong in the breasts of all rational creatures, the gratification of it is sought after as one of the highest enjoyments of life. The same passion that impels us to society, impels us to take part with our companions in their interests and inclinations. Insensibly and without thought we fall into their customs and their manners; we adopt their sentiments, their passions, and even their foibles, and follow the same course as if we were actuated by the same spirit. This principle appears in children even in the infant state. From their earliest years they love to mimic whatever strikes the organs of sense; and soon as the young idea begins to shoot, and the embryo of the manly character to appear, they form themselves insensibly upon the model of their parents, and the persons with whom they converse. To this, and not to any fancied physical cause, is owing that strong and striking resemblance, which we frequently find between the parents and the offspring; a resemblance as remarkable in the temper and character, as in the features of the face.

This principle is not confined to individuals, it extends to nations. There is a national character, a national spirit, and even a national mode of thinking, down the current of which we are insensibly carried. When any novelty, any improvement in art or in science, makes its appearance in a nation, it flies from man to man, and from place to place by a kind of contagion, till it has overspread the whole country. So powerful is sympathy, and the love of imitation among men: and thus are our minds framed by the hand of our Maker, to accord with those of others; like the strings of musical instruments in unison, when one is struck, the rest correspond to the impression, vibrate in the same key, and sound the same note. As this principle is implanted in us by the Author of our nature, it must no doubt be intended for great and important purposes. It serves to strengthen the bonds of society, to promote friendship and love, and is the aptest and most successful means, not only to teach wisdom and goodness, but also to inspire them.

But as all principles have their unfavorable and vicious extreme, to which they may be carried, so likewise hath this. Here, therefore, hath the Almighty interposed, and set bounds to it which it ought not to pass, and on the farthest verge of innocence hath engraven this inscription, "Hitherto shalt thou come, and no farther; here shall the progress of thy imitation be stayed;" or, as it is expressed in the words of our text, "Thou shalt not imitate men in their wickedness; thou shalt not follow a multitude to do evil."

In further treating on this subject, I shall, in the *first* place, endeavor to show you by what means we are to keep ourselves from following a multitude to do evil; and, in the *second* place, adduce some arguments that urge the necessity of this duty.

The *first* thing proposed, was to show you by what means we are to guard ourselves from the multitude that do evil.

And, in the *first* place, In order to this, let us be early and firmly established in the principles of our holy faith. When we look about us into life, and behold how many persons enter into the world, without having their minds instructed, or their hearts established in the great principles of virtue and religion, we cannot be surprised that they go astray on occasion of the first temptation, and follow the multitude to do evil. Perhaps they have acquired some general knowledge of Christianity, but their knowledge of it is merely speculative, has played around the head, but has not reached the heart. Accordingly, as mere speculation is utterly unfit to combat the strength of passion, and the violence of temptation, they soon fall off and sink into all the corruptions of the world around them. This course of life is well described in the beautiful parable of the sower and the seed.—"Behold a sower went forth to sow; and as he sowed, some seeds fell upon the stony places, where they had not much earth, and forthwith they sprung up, because they had no deepness of earth; and when the sun was up they were scorched, and because they had no root, they withered away." That is, they had received the knowledge of the Christian religion, but they had not attained to that true faith, which is not barely an assent of the understanding to speculative truth, but which is also a principle of action which purifies the heart, works by love, and regulates the whole conversation.

It is education chiefly that forms the human character; and it is a virtuous and religious education that forms the character of the Christian. The mind, at that early and innocent period, being untainted with actual guilt, and all alive to every generous impression, bends without labor to the force of instruction; is easily formed to all the beauties of holiness, and by frequent and repeated acts, acquires habits of devotion and virtue. The principles that are then imbibed, and the habits that are then acquired, although they may be sometimes shaken and weakened by the contagion of evil example, are seldom or never entirely obliterated. When the good seed is thus sown, we have the promise of Almighty God, that he will grant it the increase, and cause it to spring up into everlasting life. When the Christian doctrines are thus received, not merely as articles of belief, but also as principles of action, through the blessing of God, they will attain the ascendant over the unruly passions, and exert such an entire influence over the mind, as will enable it to resist temptation, and to come off triumphant. When the good foundation is thus laid, the winds may arise, and the rains may descend; the tempest may blow and beat upon the house, but the foundation of the structure shall not fail, for it rests upon a rock.

Next, In order to preserve our innocence and integrity uncorrupted from the world, let us beware with what company we associate. Evil communication corrupts good manners. It is not indeed always in our power to avoid falling into the company of the wicked, but it is always in our power not to make such persons our confidants and companions. It is the grand secret of life, both with respect to virtue and happpines, to select good and worthy persons to be our friends and companions; such persons with whom we would not only wish to live, but also desire to die. Such persons whom we would not only choose to be the companions of our careless hours, but also the partners of our enjoyments through all eternity.

There is something in the friendship and familiarity of good men, extremely great and honorable to human nature; and there are some considerations in Christianity that carry these to their highest perfection. The great commandment of our Lord to his followers, was to love one another. In the holy sacrament of the supper, we are united together in such intimate bonds of union, as to become members of one body. We have one faith, one hope, one baptism, one Lord, the Father of all, one Saviour who died for the sins of the world, one Spirit who dwells in the hearts of the faithful. We are fellow heirs of the same grace of life, fellow expectants of the same heavenly rewards.

Under these considerations, the friendship of good men would be attended with the most beneficial effects. They would support each other in the temptations and afflictions of life, and by quickening each other's diligence, provoke one another to love and to good works. Such associations of good and worthy persons, in times of public degeneracy and corruption, are spoken of in Scripture with the highest honor. "Then they that feared the Lord, spake often one to another, and the Lord hearkened and heard it; and a book of remembrance was written before him for them that feared the Lord, and that thought upon his name. And they shall be mine, saith the Lord of Hosts, in that day when I make up my jewels; and I will spare them as a man spareth his own son that serveth him."

Further, In order to keep ourselves unspotted from the world, let us acquire firmness and fortitude of mind. There is no principle in human nature that is attended with a train of more dreadful consequences, than that facility of manners, that simplicity of disposition, that weakness of soul, which is easily persuaded from its resolution, to comply with every proposal. This good nature, as it is falsely called, is the worst nature in the world, and is the occasion of more calamities, and of more crimes, than the actual inclination to wickedness. To oppose the actual vicious inclination, Almighty God hath indued us with an understanding to discern its evil, and with a conscience to check its progress; but this pernicious feebleness of mind has the appearance of sociableness and of virtue, and, by that appearance, deceives us to our ruin.

Persons of such a character make no original efforts of mind. They seem born to enlist under a leader, and are the sinners or the saints of accident. Fortitude of mind, and strength of resolution, are requisite for every purpose of human life. In particular, they are necessary to keep us from the contagion of evil example. Let us be cautious in laying down resolutions: let us be cautious in concerting plans of action: but when we have once resolved, let us be immutable. When we have chosen our path, let us hold on, though the temptations of life should beset us on one hand, and the terrors of death on the other, not suffering the commotions of the world, nor even the changes of nature, to shake or to disturb the more steadfast purpose of our souls. The most valuable of all possessions is a strenuous and steady mind, a self-deciding spirit, prepared to act, to suffer, or to die, as occasion requires.

This is not an ideal character, which exists only in description. God hath never wanted his thousands who have not bowed the knee to the idols of the world. We can reckon up a venerable company of Patriarchs, and a sacred society of Prophets, a holy fellowship of Apostles, an innumerable army of Martyrs and Confessors, who were found faithful in the midst of the faithless, who approved themselves the sons of God without rebuke, in the midst of an evil and profane generation, and having received the recompence of reward, are now sitting on thrones, and singing hosannas in the heavens.

The contemplation of their lives should animate us to run the race that is set before us, with the same alacrity and zeal. Did we frequently and seriously call up to our remembrance, the lives and the virtues of those who are now inheriting the promises; did we, by faith and contemplation, represent to our minds those unseen rewards of which they are now in possession, we should feel our hearts burn within us; with zeal and emulation, we would inhale a portion of the same divine spirit, and beholding as in a glass reflected, their virtues and victories, we would be changed into the same image, from glory to glory, as by the Spirit of the living God.

Cœtera desunt.

N. B. The Sermon which was delivered in its finished state, by the Author, from this Text, was much admired by his hearers. The above is only a part of it, and a first copy.

SERMON XXVI.

ON LOVE OF OUR COUNTRY.

Psalm cxxii. 6.—"Pray for the peace of Jerusalem."

Fellow-citizens, we now assemble, in obedience to the command of our Sovereign, to pray for the peace of Jerusalem, and for the prosperity of those that love her. Loyalty to our king, and love to our country, are the passions which ought to animate us on this day.* That attachment which good citizens bear to their country, has ever been esteemed a virtue of the highest class. Not to mention the Greeks and Romans, the history of the Israelites, with which you are better acquainted, presents us with grand and striking instances of patriotism and public spirit. They never mention the names of Zion and Jerusalem, without gladness and rapture. The words which I have now read to you, seem to have come from the heart, and breathe this spirit in the most lively manner.

During their captivity, when they sat by the rivers of Babylon, the Jews

* Upon a fast-day during the American war.

thought upon Zion and wept. When they prayed to heaven, they turned their faces towards Jerusalem. At their return from captivity, they are described as halting on a hill, over which they had to march, taking a fond look of Judea, from which they had been banished so long; bursting into tears at the view, weeping as they went forward, at the recognizance of their ancient country, and their native land. Our Saviour, who was a pattern of all goodness, set us an example of this virtue. He loved his country, and uttered that celebrated exclamation of patriotism, " O Jerusalem, Jerusalem, How often would I have gathered thee, as a hen gathereth her brood under her wings."

As we now meet to pray for the peace or welfare of our Jerusalem, (for in the language of Scripture, peace is put for all kinds of prosperity,) I shall endeavor to show you at this time, wherein the public welfare consists.

It consists in the national liberty, the national wealth and industry, the national defence, and the national character.

The *first* ingredient in the public happiness is liberty; a privilege invaluable, but frequently misunderstood, and still more frequently abused. Absolute liberty to do what we please, is absolute power. If one alone, or a few possess this, the rest are in slavery; if all have it, the whole must be in confusion. In order to prevent mutual encroachments, and ascertain each person's claims, liberty must be secured by a constitution, and guarded by law. In the state of nature, men are not only free, but independent; among the wandering tribes of savages, none claim authority over others; but as such a state cannot subsist long, whenever men enter into formed society, they give up some of their natural rights, in order to preserve the rest: they no longer wield the sword of justice themselves; it is given to the magistrate; they intrust their property to the laws, and their protection to the king.

Still, however, that is the happiest form of government, which best secures the natural rights of men. It is here that the British constitution triumphs. Possessing advantages which no other form of government ever possessed, it stands forth the envy of the neighboring nations, and a pattern to succeeding times. Liberty is the birthright of every Briton. That grand charter of Nature to her children is established and confirmed by law. The constitution, like the providence of Heaven, extends its gracious regards to all: while it protects the poor in the possession of their legal rights, it checks the insolence of the great, and sets bounds to the prerogative of majesty itself, saying to the king, "Thus far, and no farther, does thy power extend." All the members of the state are represented in the great council of the nation, and have a voice in the legislature; the subjects are taxed by their own consent. There is no despotic or discretionary power in any part of the constitution. No action must be deemed a crime, but what the laws have plainly determined to be such; no crime must be imputed to a man, but from a legal proof before his judges; and these judges must be his fellow-subjects and his peers, who are obliged, by their own interest, to have a watchful eye over encroachments and violence. "We must ever admire, as a masterpiece of political wisdom, and as the key-stone of civil liberty, that statute which forces the secrets of every prison to be revealed, the cause of every commitment to be declared, and the person of the accused to be produced, that he may claim his enlargement, or his trial, within a limited time." By these means, Great Britain hath become what ancient patriots wished, a government of laws, and not of men. Highly favored nation and happy people, if they knew their felicity, and did not upon occasions, by their own fault, turn the greatest of civil blessings into a curse!

In the *second* place, The national welfare consists in the national industry and wealth. It is a vulgar error to suppose that the greatness of a nation depends upon the number of its inhabitants. It is not the number of the people, but their being usefully employed, that adds to the true grandeur and felicity of a state. A nation is a great family, where every member has a sphere marked out and a part to perform, and which, if it abounds with the idle, must fall to ruin. "Men crowd where the situation is tempting, and multiply according to the means of subsistence." Present the proper objects; let the mechanic arts be cultivated; let manufactures abound, and commerce flourish; and citizens will come from the east and from the west, and from the south and from the north. Every thing in the world is purchased by labor and by industry.

Our passions and desires are the causes of labor and industry. When a nation introduces manufactures and commerce, new desires are created, and new passions raised; men increase the enjoyments, and refine upon the pleasures of life. Not satisfied with what is *necessary*, which is a vague term, and has a reference to the fancy, and to the habit of living, they look out for what is comfortable, what is elegant, and what is delicate in life. In order to supply these recent wants, the possessor of land, the manufacturer, and the merchant, redouble their labor and attention. Thus new industry is excited, greater numbers of men are employed, the grandeur of the sovereign, and the happiness of the state, come to coincide. By this means, a stock of labor comes to be laid up for public use.

Trade and industry are in reality nothing but a stock of labor, which, in times of peace and tranquillity, are employed for the ease and satisfaction of individuals; but in the exigencies of state, may in part be turned to public advantage. The cultivation of these arts is favored, and forwarded in our country, by that security which we enjoy. What every man has is his own. The voice of the oppressor is never heard in our streets. The hand of rapacious power is never stretched out to rob the industrious of the fruit of his labor.

Thirdly, The public welfare consists in the national defence. The police of every well-modelled state has a reference to war and to national safety. The legislator of Sparta, one of the most famous of the ancient republics, thought that nations were by nature in a state of hostility; he took his measures accordingly, and observing that all the possessions of the vanquished pertain to the victor, he held it ridiculous to propose any benefit to his country, before he had provided that it should not be conquered. A most necessary provision; for unless a state be sufficient for its own defence, it must fall an easy prey to every invader. It was the intention of nature, that nations, as well as men, should guard themselves. Hence lessons of war are delivered in sacred Scripture, and principles of emulation and dissension are strongly implanted in the soul of man. Human nature has no part of its character, of which more striking examples are given in every part of the globe. What is it that stirs in the breasts of ordinary men when the enemies of their country are named? Whence are the prejudices that subsist between different provinces and villages of the same empire and territory? What is it that excites one half of the nations of Europe against the other? The statesman may explain this conduct upon motives of national jealousy and caution; but the people have dislikes and antipathies, which proceed from sentiment, not from reasoning. Among them the materials of war and dissension are laid without the direction of government, and sparks are ready on every occasion to kindle into a flame.

This being the disposition of the people, happy is that institution which prevails in a part of this island,* of putting arms into the hands of the people, of making every citizen a soldier in his turn, and by this means having a force at hand to rise in arms at any sudden emergency. When such a system of military arrangements takes place, the prosperity of a state becomes independent of single men; there is a wisdom which never dies, and a valor which is immortal. A state may hire troops, but valor is not to be bought; the wealth of a nation will procure soldiers to fight its battles, but let it not be forgotten, that the possessions of the fearful are easily seized, that a timorous multitude falls into rout of itself. Ramparts may be erected, and the implements of war may be furnished, by a pacific people; but let it be remembered as an eternal truth, that there is no rampart which is impregnable to valor, that arms are only of consequence when they are in the hands of the brave, and that the only price of freedom is the blood of the free. When an ancient Spartan was asked, what

* Originally published before the institution of the Scottish Militia.

was the wall of his city? he pointed to a band of brave men; a defence more permanent and more effectual than the rock and the cement with which other cities are fortified.

Lastly, The public welfare consists in the national character. That righteousness exalteth a nation, and that vice is not only a reproach, but also a depression to any people, are truths so universally received, as to require little confirmation. All lawgivers in all ages have thought so, and made it their object to cultivate justice and temperance, and fortitude and industry, conscious that public virtue is the source of public happiness. Philosophers and moralists have been of the same opinion, and have taught, with one consent, that the morality of the people was the stability of the government, and the true source of public prosperity. Practice and experience have confirmed the truth of these speculations. If we consult the history of the most renowned nations that have made a figure in the world, we shall find, that they rose to greatness by virtue, and sunk to nothing by vice; that they obtained dominion by their temperance, their probity of manners, and a serious regard to religion; and that when they grew dissolute, corrupted and profane, they became slaves to their neighbors, whom they were no longer worthy to govern. Public depravity paves the way for public ruin. When the health and vigor of the political constitution is broken, it is hastening to its decline. When internal symptoms of weakness appear, the least external violence will accomplish its dissolution. Besides the natural tendency of virtue to make nations great and happy, if we have just notions of divine Providence, if we believe that the perfections of God are at all concerned in human affairs, virtuous nations will be his peculiar care, and under his immediate protection; he will counsel their counsellors, cover their armies in the day of battle, and crown them with victory and peace.

SERMON XXVII.

ON DEATH.

Hebrews ix. 27.—"It is appointed to men once to die; but after this the judgment."

Death is the conclusion of all events; of all that ever have been, and of all that ever will be. The schemes of the base, the plots of the ambitious, the projects of the visionary, the studies of the learned, all terminate here. However different the paths be that we take in life, they all lead to the grave. Whilst, therefore, we make death the subject of contemplation, and meditate upon the house which is appointed for all living, let us take this thought along with us, that we shall bear a part in those scenes which we now describe, and that we are meditating on a fate which will one day be our own.

In the *first* place, Let us consider death as an event, the period of which is uncertain.

In the days when Noah entered into the ark, they did eat, they drank, they married, they were given in marriage; and the flood came, and destroyed them all. On the day that Lot went out of Sodom, they did eat, they drank, they bought, they sold, they planted, they builded; and it rained fire and brimstone from heaven, and destroyed them all. As it was in the days of Noah and in the days of Lot, even thus, my friends, shall it be to you when the day of death cometh. In the present state of things, the soul of man is blind to futurity. Surrounded with material objects, and occupied in present affairs, we make these the sole objects of attention; we find in them the only sources of attachment, and overlook those spiritual and distant events on which our future life and happiness depend. Hence, we are always surprised with our latter end, and the day of the Lord cometh like a thief in the night. No instruction can make us so wise as to consider our latter end; no warning can incite us to set our houses in order, that we may die; and no example give the alarm so strong, as to set us on serious preparation for meeting with God. Void of thought, and careless of futurity, we live on from day to day, like the victim that plays and dances before that altar where its blood is to be shed. Even after the longest life, and under the most lingering sickness, death comes unexpected; the arrow is still unseen that strikes through the heart.

This is not peculiar to a few men; it describes a general character, and is exemplified in all the classes of life. This infatuation does not arise from ignorance. You all know that death is certain; you all know that it is generally unexpected. You assent to every thing that we can say upon this head, that there is no action of life, but what may lead to its end, and no moment of time but what may be your last. You need not be informed, that death spares no age; your own observation presents you with many instances of persons cut off in all periods of life. In that churchyard you see graves of every length; on those monuments of mortality, you read the histories of the promising boy, of the blooming youth, of the man in middle life, and of the hoary head, mingled together in sad assemblage amongst the abodes of the dead. You can reckon up instances of persons cut off in a sudden and unexpected manner; of a Herod who was struck amidst the applauses of the people; of a Jezebel who was thrown headlong from that window where she had prepared to display herself to the people; of a Belshazzar who was slain at a banquet, when he was carousing with his princes, his concubines, and his wives; and of a Holophernes, who met his fate surrounded with his army, and crowned with victory and fame.

With all these in your memory, you act as if you were *immortal*. Even the death of those who fall around us, and before our eyes, affects us not with serious concern. One person opposed us in a favorite object, and we rejoice at his decease; another stood in our way to preferment and power; the death of a third opens to us a prospect of rising to wealth and fortune: we profit not by all these lessons of mortality; the voice from the tomb sends us back to the world, and from the very ashes of the dead there comes a fire that rekindles our earthly desires. We look upon all our neighbors as mortal; we form schemes to ourselves upon their decease, but forget all the while that we ourselves are to die. O foolish and infatuated race, will you always continue deaf to the voice of wisdom? Will neither the instructions of the living, nor the warnings of the dead, induce you to serious thoughts? Will you continue to lengthen your prospects, when perhaps you stand upon the very verge of life; and can you enjoy the feast, when the sword hangs over your head, by a single hair? Who knoweth what a day may bring forth? The morning has smiled upon multitudes, who before the evening have slept the sleep of death. Who knoweth how soon you may be hurried to the judgment-seat of God? The ears which hear these sayings may soon be shut for ever; and the heart which now throbs at the thought, may, in a little time, be mingled with the clods of the valley. Some who last Lord's day worshipped within these walls, are now gone to the eternal world, and God only knows how soon some of us may follow.

Seeing then that life is so uncertain, that the thread thereof breaks at every blast, let me exhort you to set apart some time for serious meditation upon your mortality. Let it be on some solemn occasion, in the silent hour of night, when deep sleep falleth on man, when midnight closeth awful all the world, and naught in nature is awake but God and thee: there, in deep and solemn meditation, think over the terrors of that house which is appointed for all living, and with the ancient patriarch, say to corruption, Thou art my father, and to the worm, Thou art my mother and my sister. Ask seriously at your own heart, "Should these eyes never open upon the light of another day; should the awful mandate issue forth from the Almighty Arbiter of life and death,—This night, this night thy soul shall be required of thee;" could you, without fear and trembling, face the tribunal of God, the Judge of all? If frighted nature starts back and trembles at the thought of instant dissolution, make your former life pass before you in review, compare it with the law of God: if your former mispent time comes up before you in sad remembrance; if your past transgressions stare you in the face, and point to the lake that burneth with fire and brimstone, instantly and without delay, whilst the gate of heaven is yet open, whilst the throne of mercy is yet accessible, prostrate yourselves before God in deep humility and abasement, mourn over the sins of your past life in bitterness of soul, believe in a crucified Redeemer, who died for the sins of the world, implore compassion and forgiveness from the Father of mercies, through the merits of Jesus Christ. Thus continue fervent in prayer and supplication, and in the exercise of faith and repentance; give not sleep to your eyes nor slumber to your eyelids, till you have made your peace with God, till you feel within yourselves that peace which passeth all understanding, that joy which is unspeakable and glorious. Thus continue at solemn and stated occasions, to consider your latter end, till death shall grow familiar to your mind, till the grave shall gradually lose its terrors, and the Sun of Righteousness arise upon you in full glory.

In the *second* place, Let me remind you, that a good life is the best preparation for death. You may lay it down as a maxim confirmed by universal experience, that every man dies as he lives; and it is by the general tenor of the life, not a particular frame of mind at the hour of death, that we are to be judged at the tribunal of God. It is a dangerous mistake which prevails amongst men, that it is sufficient for their eternal happiness, if they feel some serious emotions at their latter end. If your life has been wicked, what will it avail you, that on your death-bed you have been actuated with sorrow for your offences? Judas Iscariot felt such a sorrow when he went to his own place. Late conversions are not to be trusted to, and death-bed repentances are generally nothing more than the first gnawing of the worm that shall never die. Suppose death to halt a little, the sick person recovers, washes his couch with floods of penitential tears, a thousand vows of amendment are made; but if repentance lasts no longer than sickness, the disease and the devotion go off together; the man returns to walk in his former ways.

Be blameless, therefore, and harmless in the general tenor of your life. Keep a conscience void of offence towards God and towards man. Let not the sun go down upon one unrepented sin. Make it your business every night to review the actions of the foregoing day. If, through the frailty of nature, or the force of temptation, you have sinned against God, prostrate yourselves before the throne of grace, and ask pardon through Christ. As you would not wish to yourselves distress and anguish and tribulation at the day of death; as you would not wish to bring down your gray hairs with sorrow to the grave; beware of persisting in a course of unrepented sin.

Notwithstanding, however, of the utility of such meditations, there is no subject on which we are so reluctant to fix our attention as our mortality. We shift from one speculation, and from one pursuit to another; we give our thoughts to wander through immensity, but cautiously avoid this theme which touches us so near; but this is the point where wisdom begins. We can never live as we ought, till we have learned how to die. I mean not by this, that we should make death the constant subject of our meditation, and have funerals always passing before our eyes. This would withdraw us from life altogether; would indispose us even for its business and its enjoyments; but although we cannot always employ ourselves in such meditations, let us at times give this subject its full weight; that certainly merits some place in our thought which is the great close of our being here. It is awful, indeed, I acknowledge, my friends, to make approaches to the mansions of the dead; it is melancholy to think upon the fall of this goodly structure, which was built by the hand of the Most High; but fall it assuredly must. The present moment hastens us on to our last hour. Let us therefore prepare for an event which we cannot avoid. We may learn some lessons from the tomb, which will avail us through all eternity.

In the *third* place, I shall consider death as becoming present to us, and endeavor to give you that view of it, which you will one day have.

None, indeed, ever returned from the invisible world to describe the bed of death, and tell us the agonies of the last hour. But up to that hour we can trace the man, and survey him stretched upon the bed from which he is to rise no more. A death-bed discovers the real character of men; dissimulation is then at an end. At the close of the scene, the mask drops off, and the man appears in his true colors. Then, then, often for the first time, a man turns a serious eye upon himself; cut off from all connection with the living world; bidding adieu for ever to all below the sun; entering within the dominions of the dead, and about to appear before the judgment-seat of God; surounded by the sad circle of his friends and attendants, he reads in their trembling looks, that all is over with him, that his hour is come; then the illusion vanishes that was spread upon all earthly things; then the past rises up, often rises in bitter remembrance; then the future rushes upon his view with all its dark and unknown terrors; then the sense of Deity revives, which, however disguised, lies at the bottom of every heart; then conscience, rising up in majesty supreme, holds out such a picture of the eternal world, as convinces the most unbelieving mind; convinces him that a future state is not the dictate of a wild imagination, is not the figment of priests and lawgivers, to terrify the ignorant, and keep the people in awe; he sees and feels that it is an awful reality. When the time of his departure is announced by the cold sweat and the shivering limbs, and the voice faltering in the throat, he casts a last look, perhaps a sad one, on all that he leaves behind. Then the whole creation fades from his view, the world seems to be dissolved, and, to the closing eye, nothing appears but God alone; that God, before whose tribunal he is summoned to appear.

If this fate shall one day be ours, what manner of persons ought we now to be? At that hour, the very best shall wish that they had been better, and after all the preparation that we have made, we shall wish that we had made more. Let this thought have its influence in determining us to the choice of objects which we pursue, and the course of life which we embrace. The greatest part of mankind, having no fixed or certain plan of life, have no choice in the objects which present themselves, but give the loose rein to a wandering inclination, and follow on without thinking, where accident points the way. Here, therefore, let us often pause and seriously ask ourselves, Is the course of life which I am now engaged in, of such a nature that it will bear a review upon the bed of death? Are the motives of my present conduct, and the reasons which now determine me to action, so strong and well founded, that I could plead them in my defence at the bar of eternal justice? If that is not the case, consider and be wise before it is too late. Why should you vex yourselves in vain? Why should you pass your time in such a manner, as to make its end bitter? Why will you treasure up to yourselves anguish and remorse and tribulation, and make no other use of the present time, but to embitter your last hour? Be consistent with yourselves. You cannot live the life of the wicked, and die the death of the righteous. Let, therefore, your course of action be of that kind, that draws no repentance after it; then shall your path in life be like the morning light, which shineth more and more unto the perfect day.

Having thus set out, and made progress in the ways of righteousness, you will look forward with joy. This will cause the evening of your days to smile, and the stream of life to run clear to the last. Let this consideration moderate our attachment to earthly things. What profit hath a man in that sore travel to which he is appointed under the sun? Why should we vex ourselves in vain, deny ourselves to the enjoyments of life, withdraw sleep from our eyes, and peace from our minds? Why should we add to the evils of life, and carry about with us a burden to the grave? Even with a view to present tranquillity and enjoyment, this is folly of the first magnitude; but, when we take in the consideration of a future life, it is worse than folly, it is sin. If we are entirely immersed in the concerns of this world; if earthly things occupy and engross our whole attention, what shall we do when God taketh away the soul? How will the closing eye contemplate the pomp and glitter of life, the evil of avarice, the bustling of ambition, and all this circle of vanity to which we are now enchanted? Use this world, therefore, as not abusing it; let not the business or the pleasures of it take hold of your heart, make them not essential to your happiness, sit loose to them, remember that the fashion of this world passeth away, and that death soon puts a period to the scene, which no wise man would wish to last for ever.

In the *fourth* place, By making the thought of death present to us, regulate our conduct with respect to the friendships which we form, and concerning the animosities which we entertain.

Affection and friendship are the best and most valuable part of human nature. The heart of man wishes to be kind, and looks around for objects. This fund of generous love is often misapplied; this favorable bias of humanity is often perverted; sometimes by that general and indiscriminate good nature which looks upon all men as alike; sometimes by frivolous attachments, founded upon a conformity of trifling dispositions; and sometimes by a more criminal alliance, by a partnership in iniquity. In the course of business, indeed, we must converse with persons of all kinds. No man has the choice of the companies into which he may fall; but every man has the choice of the friends with whom he cultivates more intimate connections. In forming these connections, therefore, let us look forward to the time when they shall be dissolved, and let us live only with such persons with whom we would desire to die.

This thought should also check us in the animosities which we are apt to entertain. In the present state of things, where men think so differently, where opposite passions are felt, and interfering interests occur, dissensions will naturally arise. And, where men have not the aid of philosophy to restrain, or the influence of divine grace to subdue their passions, these will often be attended with dismal effects. From this root proceeds the wormwood which embitters the cup of human life. But when the blood begins to cool, when the passions grow calmer, and reason reassumes its office, greater moderation will prevail; things will appear in a different light; honest and candid men will then look back with pain upon those excesses to which they have been carried by the impetuosity of passion. However some men choose to live, all men would wish to die at peace with their neighbors; there is no enmity in the grave; there is no discord in the house which is appointed for all living: there friends and foes rest together in peace, and the ashes of those who were mortal enemies, mingle together in friendly alliance. Let us, therefore, now cultivate those benevolent dispositions to all men, and live in those habits with our neighbors, which we would wish to prevail in us at the hour of death.

These exhortations, my young friends, I address particularly to you. You are apt to reckon yourselves privileged from death; you put the evil day far off; you promise to yourselves a length of happy days, and think that melancholy reflections upon mortality are ill suited to the bloom of your years, and the gayety of your spirits. "Let the old," you say, "think upon death; let those who are drawing nigh to the grave, prepare for that better world to which they are advancing; but sure it is the duty of the young and the gay to make the most of life." True; and in order to make the most of life, you must conquer the fear of death. The king of terrors, when not subdued, is the most formidable of all foes. In every path of life he will meet you, and haunt you like a ghost: even at the banquet his form will appear; he will blast you in the midst of your joy, and turn the house of mirth into a house of mourning. Trust not, O man, to thy youth, nor presume upon impunity from the destroyer. How often, when the tree puts forth buds, and spreads its blossoms to the sun, does the wind of the desert come and blast the hopes of the year! The widow of Nain wept over her son, who died, fair in the prime of life; and many a parent hath followed his child to the grave, crying with bitter lamentation, "Would to God that I had died for thee, my son! my son!" Your own experience may enforce this truth. None who now hear me, but have seen their equals in age cut off, and younger than they laid in the grave. As, therefore, you are always in danger, be always on your guard. Instead of filling you with gloom and melancholy, this is the true way to prevent them. Having subdued the last enemy, you have none other to fear. Adopted into the family of God, interested in the merits of Christ, entitled to the glories of immortality, you go forward through life and death, conquering and to conquer. Then all things are yours; death is a passage to a better life, and the gate to immortality.

Much more is it incumbent on you, my aged friends, to consider your latter end. Why stand you here all the day idle? Consider how vain, and foolish, and sinful, it is to be forming schemes of long life, when you are within the threshold of the house of death? Consider how terrible will be the hour, if you have never thought of death till you come to die; like Jonah, to be awakened from a sound sleep, and to be cast into the ocean. Look into life, behold a young generation rising around you, and you yourselves left alone in a new world. Look into the records of mortality, into the repositories of the dead, and hear your equals in age calling to you from the tomb, and warning you to prepare for that fate which is theirs to-day, and may be yours to-morrow. Embrace, therefore, the opportunities of grace which you now enjoy. Whilst the Prince of Peace extends the golden sceptre, kiss the Son, lest he be angry, and ye perish from his presence. Be wise, and consider your end that is so near.

SERMON XXVIII.

THE CHRISTIAN LIFE A LIFE OF EASE AND PLEASURE.

MATTHEW XI. 30.—"My yoke is easy and my burden is light."

JESUS hath lately been addressing to you the gracious invitation which here he gives to penitent sinners. With his invitation you have testified your compliance. Last Lord's day you confessed at these tables, that you were weary and heavy laden with the yoke of the world; that you came to Jesus in hopes of finding rest to your souls; and that you were resolved to learn of him, and to take his yoke upon you. The good confession, my friends, which you then witnessed, the happy choice which you then made, you will never have cause to repent. The world, indeed, will represent religion to you as a heavy burden and a galling yoke; but I assure you, upon the authority of Jesus Christ, and upon the testimony of all his disciples, that his yoke is easy, and his burden is light; that his commandments are not grievous, and the ways he points out to his followers, are ways of pleasantness and paths of peace.

The ease and pleasure of the Christian life, is to be the subject of the present discourse. But, before I enter upon it, I have one observation to make, which is, That in order to taste the joys of religion, we must have been accustomed to its government, and made advances in the divine life. We can never have a taste for any pursuit till we be acquainted with it: we can never enter into the spirit of any science, till that science be familiar to us. To those who have long engaged in a course of wickedness, the duties of religion will at first be grievous and irksome, because they oppose strong prejudices and confirmed habits of vice. But when these bad habits are removed, and good ones are contracted, when a man acquires the temper, and enters into the spirit of religion, he then feels the joy which a stranger intermeddles not with. Give a musical instrument to an unskilful person, we hear nothing but harshness and discord from every string: the artist alone makes music and harmony accompany all the motions of his hand. Religion is an art, and like an art is to be learned before it be understood.

In the *first* place, The Christian life is a life of ease and pleasure, on account of the principle from which the Christian acts.

The Christian is not a slave who obeys from compulsion, nor a servant who works for hire; he is a son who acts from ingenuous affection and filial love. When the Christian contemplates the goodness, and tender mercies, and loving-kindness of God, particularly his inexpressible love in the Redemption of the world by Christ Jesus, he is constrained to new obedience by the most powerful of all ties, by the cords of love, and the bands of a man; thus reasoning, and thus feeling, that if one died for all, then they which are alive ought not to live to themselves, but to him who died for them. Gratitude to a benefactor, affection to a father, love to a friend, all concur to form the principle of evangelical obedience, and to strengthen the cord that is not easily broken. Love, then, is the principle of the Christian life: love, the most generous passion that glows in the breast of man, the most active principle that works in the human frame, the key that unlocks every finer feeling of the heart, the spring that puts in motion every power of the soul. Pleasant are the labors of love. Short is the path and cheerful the journey when the heart goes along. A determined mind, enamored of the object it pursues, removes mountains, and makes the crooked path straight: the fire cannot extinguish, nor the waters quench its force; it reigns supreme in the heart, and diffuses a gayety over every path of life. By its influence labor is rendered easy, and duty becomes a delight.

In the *second* place, The ease and pleasure of the Christian life will appear if we consider the assistance we receive from above.

"Work out your salvation; for it is God that worketh within you every good work and word." There are difficulties in the Christian life: I have no intention to deceive you, my friends; you will often find it difficult to act the proper part; to maintain a conscience void of offence towards God and towards man; to keep your passions within the bounds of reason; to subdue your irregular inclinations to the obedience of faith, and to hold fast your integrity uncorrupted amid the temptations of the world. These and many other difficulties will beset you in running the Christian race. But let me remind you, that one half of the pleasures of human life arise from overcoming difficulties; and to overcome these difficulties which surround us, God bestows the influence of his Holy Spirit. The Lord is ever nigh to them who call upon him in the sincerity of their heart. To those who wait at the salutary stream, an angel descends to stir the waters. God never said to the seed of Jacob, Seek ye my face in vain. He never neglected the prayer that came from the heart. He never forsook the man that put his trust in him.

If you were left to climb the arduous ascent, by your own strength alone, then the Christian life would neither be easy nor pleasant; then you might sit down in despair of ever attaining the top. But whatever duties God calls you to, he gives you abilities to perform them. According as your days are, he hath promised that your strength shall be. His grace is sufficient for us; his strength is made perfect in our weakness. No, my friends, God hath never withdrawn himself from the world. The Father of spirits is ever present with his rational offspring; he knows their frame, he helps their infirmities, assists their graces, strengthens their powers, and makes perfect what concerns them. He assists the feeble, he revives the languishing, he supports the strong. He aids the efforts of the captive, who endeavors to break loose from the fetters that hold him; he favors the ascent of the devout mind, that with the confidence of faith rises to himself, and he forwards the pilgrim, journeying to his native country. The good husbandman superintends the vine which his own right hand planted. He waters his vineyard with dews from heaven, and breathes ethereal influence on those trees of righteousness that shall adorn the paradise of God.

Hast thou not felt him, O Christian! restraining thy evil inclinations, suggesting holy thoughts, kindling heavenly affections, and drawing thee to thy duty with a hand unseen? Hast thou not felt him as a Spirit within thy spirit, imparting secret strength, animating thy frame as with new life, actuating thy faculties, purifying thy passions, begetting in thee an abhorrence of sin and a love of righteousness, and making all thy graces shine out with fresh beauty? How easy and delightful then will the Christian life be, when you have divine aids to strengthen, support, and assist? It is God himself who is on your side, it is God himself who works with you; his wisdom is your guide, his arm is your support; his Spirit is your strength; you lose your own insufficiency in the fulness of infinite perfection.

In the *third* place, It will appear, that the Christian life is easy and pleasant, if we consider the encouragements the good man receives.

The good man waits not for all his happiness till he come to heaven: he hath treasures in hand, as well as possessions in hope: he hath a portion in the life that now is, as well as in that which is to come. There is a sense of moral good and evil implanted in the mind; a principle of conscience which condemns us when we do ill, and applauds us when we do well. This principle is the chief foundation of our happiness, and gives rise to the greatest pleasures and the greatest pains in human life. By means of this moral sense, there is no peace to the wicked. Inward struggles, strong reluctance and aversion of mind, precede the commission of sin. Sin, when committed, is followed by guilty blushes, alarming fears, terrible reviews, startling prospects, and remorse, with all its hideous train. Against the sinner, his own heart rises up in judgment to condemn him; the terrors of the Lord set themselves in array agsinst him; a fire not blown consumes him. "There is no peace to the wicked." The foundations of peace are subverted in his mind; he is at enmity with himself; he is at enmity with his fellow-creatures; he is at enmity with God. It is *not so* with those that take upon them the yoke of Christ. When pure religion forms the temper, and governs the life, all is peaceful and serene; the man is then in his proper element; the soul is in a state of health and vigor; there is a beautiful correspondence between the heart and the life; all is serene without, all is tranquil within. Delivered from the anxieties that perplex, and from the terrors that overwhelm the guilty man, the Christian resigns himself to peace and joy, conscious that he possesses a temper of mind which is acceptable to God, and leads a life which is useful to men. In the heart of such a man there is a blessed calmness and tranquillity, like that of the highest heavens.

But there is more than a calmness and tranquillity. The air may be calm and tranquil, when the day is dark; the sea may be smooth, when there is mist upon the waves; the sky may be tranquil when it is overcast with clouds: but the pious and virtuous mind resembles a sky that is not only calm, but bright; resembles a sea that is not only smooth, but serene; resembles an unclouded sky, beautiful with the rising sun. There are joys in the Christian life, unknown to transgressors: there is a spring shut up, and a fountain sealed, that refreshes the city of God; there are secret consolations reserved for the just; there are silent pleasures that flow into the pious mind; there is a still small voice that comes to the pure in heart, and bids them be of good cheer; there is an inward peace of God that passeth all understanding; there is a joy in the Holy Ghost, resulting from the well-grounded hope of a happy immortality, that is unspeakable and glorious.

When the heart is thus pure, it becomes the temple of the Deity; and, as a temple is consecrated with the presence of God; "If a man love me, and keep my words, my Father will love him, and we will come and make our abode with him." Who can describe the joy of those happy moments, when a present Deity is felt, when God manifests himself to his people, so as he does not to the world, when our fellowship is with the Father and with his Son Jesus Christ? Then a foretaste of immortality is given, the joys of the blessed are let down, and heaven descends to men.

In the *fourth* and last place, The ease and pleasure of the Christian life will appear, if we consider the joyful prospect that is set before us.

The Christian has joys in this life; but he is not confined to these. His hopes do not terminate with life; they extend beyond the grave. Death puts a final period to the happiness of the wicked man; but it is then that the happiness of the righteous man begins. We are assured in Sacred Scripture, that there is a kingdom prepared for the righteous from the foundation of the world, when they shall enter into rest from all their labors, and sufferings, and sorrows of this mortal life; when they shall enter into a state where no ignorance shall cloud the understanding, and no vice pervert the will; where nothing but love shall possess the soul, and nothing but gratitude employ the tongue; where they shall be admitted to an innumerable company of angels, and to the general assembly and church of the First-born; where they shall see Jesus at the right hand of the Father, and shall sit down with him upon his throne; where they shall be admitted into the presence of God, shall behold him face to face, and be changed into the same image, from glory to glory; that glory which eye hath not seen, nor ear heard, nor has it entered into the heart of man to conceive.

To conclude, It may be observed, that it hath been the fate of Christianity in all ages, to suffer more from its friends than from its enemies. Attacks from the enemies of our faith have generally proved subservient to its propagation and success; but the misrepresentations and injuries of its friends have often wounded it in a vital part. One of the greatest of these misrepresentations, and one of the most flagrant injuries that ever was done to religion, was to represent it as a burdensome service; as a grievous and a galling yoke, to which no man would submit, but from the terror of eternal punishment. What adds to the injury, this has sometimes been done by persons of real seriousness, who, unhappily possessed of a gloomy imagination, and who, probably, in some period of their days, having been guilty of crimes, have been so deeply affected with remorse and contrition, that they have continued all their lifetime subject to bondage. But blessed be God, my friends, that such unfavorable and forbidding delineations of religion have no foundation in truth. In these volumes, Christians are called upon to rejoice evermore. Religion promises happiness to us in the life which now is, as well as in the life which is to come. The Wisdom that is from above, is represented as having length of days in her right hand, and in her left hand riches and honor. The prophets and apostles ransack heaven and earth for images to express the joys of the just. They bring together the most beautiful and most delightful objects in the whole compass of nature, and introduce the inanimate parts of the creation as joining in the happiness of the good; the hills and the mountains breaking forth into singing, and all the trees of the wood shouting for joy. All concurs to prove the truth in the text, "My yoke is easy, and my burden is light."

SERMON XXIX.

THE EXPEDIENCY OF JESUS CHRIST APPEARING IN A SUFFERING STATE.

HEBREWS II. 10.—"For it became him, for whom are all things, and by whom are all things, in bringing many sons unto glory, to make the Captain of their salvation perfect through sufferings."

WHEN Christianity was first published to the world, the earliest objection that was raised against it, arose from the low and suffering state in which its Author appeared. It was a stumbling-block to the Jews, and seemed foolishness to the Greeks, that a prophet sent from heaven to enlighten and reform the world, should lead a life of indigence and obscurity, and make his exit with ignominy and with pain.

If we consider the character and prevailing opinions of the Jews and the Greeks at the time when our Saviour appeared, we shall see the reason of the unfavorable reception which they gave to his doctrines. The Jews had been the favorite people of God. By signs and miracles, and mighty works, he had delivered them from a state of slavery in Egypt, had conducted them through the wilderness, and at last given them a settlement in the promised land. The arm of the Lord was made bare in their behalf, the sea was divided to make way for them, and the waters stood as a wall on their right hand and on their left. During their wanderings through the wilderness, a pillar of fire conducted them by night, and a pillar of cloud by day. Manna descended to them from heaven, and water sprung from the flinty rock. Accustomed to these great and marvellous exertions of the Divine power, in the days of the Messiah they expected still greater and more marvellous. If a God was to descend, they looked for him in the whirlwind, they looked for him in the thunder, they looked for him in the earthquake, and when the still small voice came, it was neither heard nor regarded. Besides this, they had imbibed false notions concerning the Messiah, and the nature of his kingdom. They misinterpreted the ancient oracles, which foretold his coming; they took the magnificent style of prophecy for literal description, and, in place of a spiritual Saviour, expected a temporal prince. Accordingly, at the time when our Saviour appeared, the whole nation was intoxicated with the idea of a triumphant conqueror, who was to deliver them from the Roman yoke, to erect an universal monarchy on earth, and to make Zion the seat of empire, and capital of the world. To persons under the influence of these prejudices, a suffering Messiah was a stone of stumbling, and a rock of offence.

A different set of prejudices prevailed in Greece. The Greeks were an ingenious and an active people. Situated in a fortunate climate, and blessed with the highest degree of liberty which mankind can enjoy, they bent their genius to the cultivation of the arts. Smitten with the love of wisdom, they gave up their paternal estates to attend the school of philosophy. They journeyed from region to region, and traversed the world, to bring home fresh accessions of knowledge, and new improvements in the arts. Under these favorable circumstances, Greece arose to fame, and beheld an age of glory, which is unrivalled in the records of history. The ideas of virtue and of merit amongst any nation are founded upon the splendid examples with which their history abounds, and upon a perfection in those arts which they cultivate, and in which they excel. The Greeks excelled in the arts to which the imagination gives birth, as well as in the sciences, which reason brings to maturity, and their history abounded with the most splendid instances of public spirit, of heroic friendship, and of intrepid valor. Dazzled with the lustre of these arts, and with the glory of these virtues, they fixed the standard of excellence by them, and had no admiration to bestow upon the humble Prophet of Nazareth, and the mortifying doctrines of the cross. As they had been a stumbling-block to the Jews, to the Greeks they seemed foolishness.

It is then a subject worthy of our contemplation, to inquire into the reasons that might move Almighty God, thus, in direct opposition to the prejudices and expectations of both Jews and Greeks, to appoint the Captain of our salvation to be made perfect by a state of sufferings. It is hence proposed to show the expediency and propriety of appointing such a Captain of our salvation. This will appear, from considering our blessed Saviour in these four capital views of his character: as the founder of a new religion, as a pattern of all perfection, as a priest who was to make atonement, and a king who was to be crowned with glory.

In the *first* place, If we consider our Saviour as the author of a new religion, his appearance in a suffering state frees his religion from an objection which applies with full force to every other religion in the world.

Amongst all the nations whose history we have recorded, the laws gave birth to the religion. The public faith was modelled by the sovereign authority, and established by the sovereign power. The prince was also the prophet. The religion which he established, was such as suited the genius of the people, the nature of the climate, or the views of the sovereign; and, in short, was nothing more than a mere engine of civil government. When we take a view of Christianity, a different scene presents itself. Here we see a religion published by a person, obscure and unknown, amongst a nation hated and despised to a proverb, one day to become the religion of the world, and to be propagated by the efforts of a few illiterate fishermen, who had to combat against the prejudices of the Jews, the superstition of the Gentiles, the wisdom of the philosophers, the power of armies and of kings, the ancient systems of religion established over the whole world, and the combined wit and genius and malice of all mankind.

Had our Saviour appeared in the pomp of a temporal prince, as the Jews expected him; had he appeared in the character of a great philosopher, as the Greeks would have wished him, often had we heard of his power and of his policy, and been told, that our religion was more nearly allied to this world than to the other. But when we hear the Author of our faith declaring from the beginning, that he must suffer many things in his life, and be put to an ignominious and tormenting death; when we hear him forewarning his disciples, that they were to meet with the same fate, these suspicions must for ever vanish from our mind. Thus our religion stands clear of an objection, from which nothing, perhaps, could have purged it, but the blood of its divine Author.

In the *second* place, If we consider our Saviour as a pattern of virtue and all perfection, the expediency of his appearing in a suffering state will further be evident.

One great end of our Saviour's coming into the world was to set us an example, that we might follow his steps. But, unless his life had been diversified with sufferings, the utility of his example had been in a great measure defeated. What we generally call a perfect character, is a cold insipid object, that does not interest mankind. Were it possible for nature to realize the man of virtue, as drawn by those who misrepresent the Stoic philosophy; a man without the feelings of nature, and the weaknesses of humanity, proof against the influence of passion, and the attacks of pain; we would turn aside from such a caricature of humanity, and exclude the faultless monster from the number of our species. No example can make any impression upon the minds of man, but the example of men of like passions with themselves. Let us suppose, that the life of an angel were exhibited to the world, it might afford a pleasant subject of contemplation. But the question would naturally arise, What is this to me? This does not belong to my nature; I discover here no traces of my own character, no features of humanity. On the other hand, to set up an imperfect example for our imitation, would be attended with still worse consequences. We know, from the instances of the saints recorded in Scripture, how apt men are to quote their imperfections as an excuse for themselves, and by copying after these, come short of that perfection to which they might have arrived.

Both these defects are remedied in the example of Jesus of Nazareth. His example is perfect, and, at the same time, has all that effect upon us which the example of one of our brethren would have had. When we behold the man Christ Jesus involved in distresses similar to our own, clothed with all the innocent infirmities of our nature, and groaning like ourselves under the sinless miseries of life, we are touched with the feelings of his infirmities and his pains; our passions take part with the illustrious sufferer, and we behold him in some measure brought down to our own level. It is from these shades that this picture derives its beauty, derives its effect upon the world, and that, notwithstanding the glory that surrounds it, we recognize our own image, we trace the features and the lineaments of humanity, and by these, are drawn to copy after such an illustrious pattern of excellence and perfection.

The suffering state in which our Lord appeared, not only conduced to the efficacy of his example, but also to its more extensive utility, by presenting an ample theatre for the sublimest virtues to appear. It is observed by an historian, in relating the life of Cyrus the Great, that there was one circumstance wanting to the glory of that illustrious prince; and that was, the having his virtue tried by some sudden reverse of fortune, and struggling for a time under some grievous calamity. The observation is just. Men are made for suffering as well as for action. Many faculties of our frame; the most respectable attributes of the mind, as well as the most amiable qualities of the heart; carry a manifest reference to the state of adversity, to the dangers which we are destined to combat, and the distresses we are appointed to bear. Had the Greeks consulted their own writers, they would have given them proper information on this head. To approve a man thoroughly virtuous, said one of the sages, he must be tortured, he must be bound, he must be scourged, and having suffered all evils, must be impaled or crucified.

Who are the personages in history that we admire the most? Those who have suffered some signal distress, and from a host of evils have come forth conquerors. If we look into civil history, need I call up to your remembrance the patriots of Greece, the heroes of Rome; the wise, the great, and the good, of every age, who grew illustrious as they grew distressed, and in the darkest hour of adversity shone out with unwonted and meridian splendor. If we look into sacred history, we shall find that the good and holy men, who are there pointed out as patterns to the world, like the Captain of their salvation, were made perfect through suffering. The most illustrious names that are recorded in the book of life, the patriarchs of the ancient world, the prophets of the Jewish state, the martyrs of the Christian church are witnesses on record of this important truth, that the most honorable laurels are gathered in the vale of tears, and that the crown of glory sits brightest on the brows of those who have gained it with their blood. Jesus of Nazareth, too, was appointed to learn obedience by the things that he suffered. All the virtues of adversity shone forth in his life. The patience that acquiesces with cheerfulness, in all the appointments of Providence, the magnanimity which triumphs over an enemy by forgiveness, the charity which prays for its persecutors, are striking and conspicuous parts of his character. But we injure his merit as a sufferer, if we consider it only as breaking out in single and occasional acts of virtue. His sufferings themselves, his condescending to become a victim for the sins of men, and to die for the happiness of the world, is an infinite exertion of benevolence that admits of no comparison, that is transcendent and meritorious. The consideration of this, more than the circumstances of his departure, more than the rocks which were rent, than the sun which was darkened, than the dead which arose, had we been present at the scene, should have made us cry out with the centurion, " Surely this man was the Son of God."

In the *third* place, If we consider our Saviour as a priest, who was to make an atonement for the sins of men, the expediency of his making this atonement by his sufferings and death, will be manifest. It is one of the doctrines revealed in the New Testament, that the Son of God was the Creator of the world. As therefore he was our immediate Creator, and as his design in our creation was defeated by sin, there was an evident propriety that he himself should interpose in our behalf, and retrieve the affairs of a world, which he had created with his own hands. But it is evident, at first sight, that redemption is a greater work than creation; that it requires a more powerful exertion to recover a world lying in wickedness, to happiness and virtue, than to create it at first in a state of innocence. In the work of redemption, therefore, it was expedient that there should be a brighter display of the divine perfections, and a greater exertion of benevolence than was exhibited in the work of creation. Now, if God, without a satisfaction by sufferings, and by a mere act of indemnity, had blotted out the sins of the world, such a display of the divine attributes would not have been given. But by the Son of God's appearing in our nature, and suffering the punishment which was due to our sins, a scene is presented, on which the angels desire to look. This, in the language of Scripture, was the glory that excelleth; here the Almighty made bare his holy arm, and gave testimony to the nations what was in the power of a God to effectuate. Hereby all the perfections of the divine nature were glorified. That immaculate purity, which cannot look upon sin, and that astonishing love, which could not behold the ruin of a sinner, were awfully displayed. The majesty of the divine government was sustained, and the rigor of the law was fulfilled, justice was satisfied, mercy without restraint, and without measure, flowed upon the children of men. In short, more glory redounded to God, and greater benevolence was made manifest to men, than when the morning stars sung together at the birth of nature, and all the sons of God shouted for joy.

In the *last* place, If we consider our Saviour in that state of glory to which he is now ascended, the propriety of his being made perfect by sufferings will more fully appear. Because he humbled himself, and became obedient unto death, therefore hath God highly exalted him, hath given him a name above every name, and committed to him all power in heaven and in earth. By the appointment of Providence, suffering hath ever been the path to honor. Ought not Christ, therefore, also to have suffered, and to enter into his glory? As, upon earth, he submitted to the lowest degree of abasement, and appeared in the form of a servant, he is now in heaven, exalted to the highest pinnacle of honor, and appears in the form of God. As, in his state of humiliation, he was poor, and had not where to lay his head, he is now the Lord of nature, and inherits the treasures of heaven and of earth. Instead of the mock title of King of the Jews, which they wrote upon his cross, he is now in very deed the King of kings, and the Lord of lords. Instead of the crown of thorns, which pierced and wounded his blessed head, he is now for ever encircled with a crown of glory.

What dignity does it reflect upon all our race, that one who wears our likeness, who is not ashamed to call us brethren, now sits upon the throne of Nature, now holds in his hand the sceptre of Providence, and exercises uncontrolled dominion over the visible and invisible worlds! What abundant consolation will it administer to Christians in all their afflictions, what openings of joy will it let down into the vale of tears, when we recollect that the Governor of the world is a God who partakes of our own nature, who, in the days of his humanity, had a fellow feeling of all our wants; who, like ourselves, was a man of sorrows, and acquainted with grief; who, by consequence, will be more apt to sympathize with his fellow-sufferers, and to send relief to those sorrows of which he himself bore a part.

SERMON XXX.

Preached at the celebration of the Sacrament of the Lord's Supper.

ON GLORYING IN THE CROSS OF CHRIST.

GALATIANS VI. 14.—"God forbid that I should glory, save in the cross of our Lord Jesus Christ."

"MY ways are not as your ways, and my thoughts are not as your thoughts," said the Lord to the Old Testament church. And never, surely, did the Eternal Wisdom so disappoint the expectations and blast the hopes of men, as by the cross of our Lord Jesus Christ. Had men been consulted concerning the state in which it was most proper for the Messiah to appear, they would have introduced him into the world with all the circumstances of external pomp and splendor; they would have put into his hand the sceptre of dominion over the nations, and subjected to his kingdom all the people of the earth, from the rising to the setting of the sun. A Messiah, whose glory should not strike the senses, whose kingdom was not to be of this world, who was to be made perfect through sufferings, who was to triumph by humiliation, who was to become victorious by a shameful death, and in whose humiliation, and sufferings, and cross, the world was to glory; that was an idea which never presented itself to their minds, and which, if it had presented itself, would have been immediately rejected, as having no form nor comeliness, for which it could have been desired; yet, such was the method contrived by Infinite Wisdom to accomplish the redemption of the world. One great end of all the divine dispensations, has been to humble and confound the *pride* of man. It was pride that at first introduced moral evil into the world. It was pride that tempted the angels to rebel against their Maker, that brought them down from the mansions of light, to the abodes of darkness and despair. It was pride that tempted our first parents to disobey the divine commandment. The language of their apostasy was, "I will ascend into the heavens, I will rise above the height of the clouds, I will exalt my throne above the stars of God, I will be like the Most High." Pride, although not made for man in his best estate, hath not forsaken him in his worst. Even the fall did not efface the strong impression from his mind. As if he had continued the same noble being he came from the hands of his Creator; as if he had been still the happy lord of the inferior world, he retained the consciousness of his original excellence, when that excellence was no more; he surrendered himself to delusions which flattered his vain mind; he tried new paths to elevation and worldly greatness; he even appropriated to himself the attributes of the divinity, and, possessed with the madness of ambition, arrogated to himself those honors which are due to God only. Hence the world deified mortal men, worshipped as its creators those to whom it had lately given birth, and adored as mortal and divine the human creatures whose death it had beheld.

As man fell by pride, it was the appointment of Heaven that he should rise by humility. This doctrine was early delivered to the world. God testified by his prophets, that he knew the proud afar off; that the proud in heart was an abomination to him, but that he would hear the cry of the humble; that though he dwelt in the high and holy place, he would dwell also with that man who was of a humble and contrite spirit. But more than instructions were requisite to reform the sentiments, and change the spirit, of a world which had been so much intoxicated with dreams of earthly greatness, and so long enchanted with spectacles of human glory. Accordingly it pleased God, in the fulness of time, to send forth his own Son into the world, in fashion as a man, in the form of a servant, to become obedient unto death, even the death of the cross, and hath appointed all Christians to glory in his cross, nay, to glory in nothing else. "God forbid that I should glory, save in the cross of our Lord Jesus Christ."

These words might give occasion to many useful discourses. All that I intend at present is, to show you by what means we are to glory in the cross of Christ.

In the *first* place, then, We are to glory in the cross of Christ, by frequently meditating upon the circumstances of his death and passion.

The human actions and events in which we glory, become often the objects of contemplation; they present themselves spontaneously to the mind, and become the favorite ideas of the soul. We turn them on all sides, we view them in every light, we delight in them, we dwell upon them, we make them our meditation day and night. Surely, then, it becomes us to revolve often in our mind this great mystery of godliness, God manifested in the flesh, and dying on a cross for the salvation of the world. The angels in heaven, as we are told in Scripture, desired with earnest eyes to look into the sufferings of Jesus; much more should we make the sufferings of Jesus the object of our meditation, for he took not on him the nature of angels, but of the seed of Abraham.

Call up to thy mind, then, O Christian! the doleful circumstances of thy Saviour's passion, the sad variety of sorrows which he suffered, the torment of body and agony of mind which he underwent, the cruel, the ignominious, and accursed death which he endured. Make these things present to thy mind, till the blended emotions of contrition and sorrow, of awe and wonder, of joy and pleasure, of gratitude and love, take possession of thy heart. "Can you not watch with me one hour?" said our Lord to his disciples, when he entered into his agony. "Can you not watch with me one hour?" saith our Lord to his disciples in every age, when they are about to renew the memorials of his death and passion. Agreeably to his dying charge, accompany thy Redeemer, O Christian! in the last scene of his sufferings. Look to him with such a lively sense and feeling of his sorrows, till, like Paul, thou art crucified with Christ. While all nature is thrown into disorder, while the rocks are rent, and the dead arise, wilt thou continue unmoved? Wilt thou continue harder than the rocks, and more insensible than the ashes of the dead? No; while thou thus musest, holy affections will be kindled, and the heavenly fire will burn; from the altar which was erected on the hill of Calvary, a living ember will touch thy lips, and purify thy heart.

In the *second* place, We are to glory in the cross of Christ, by giving his death that rank in our estimation, and that place in our affections, which its importance requires.

When we glory in any thing to an extraordinary degree, we prefer it to all others, we give it the chief place in our heart, and rest our happiness in a great measure upon it. And thus it becomes us to glory in the cross of Christ; thus it becomes us to prefer it to all things, to give it the highest place in our heart, and to rest our eternal happiness on it alone. The manifestation of the Son of God is, in all regards, the most wonderful of the divine works, and to us in particular is the most important event that distinguishes the annals of time. His death upon the cross was the most splendid part of his mediatorial office; the most illustrious instance of his love to men, and the most meritorious act of his obedience to God. By his death, the wrath of God was averted from the world, and the atonement requisite for the sins of men was made. By his death the glories of the Godhead shone out with new lustre, the majesty of the moral law was not only sustained, but rendered illustrious, and a dignity was reflected on virtue which it had never known before. To his death we are indebted for the pardon of our sins, for adoption into the family of Heaven, and for our hopes of a happy immortality in the future world. His death upon the cross quenched the fire of hell, and set open the gate of heaven for a repenting world to enter in.

In the cross of Christ, therefore, we do not glory aright, if we admire only the circle of virtue which shone out in his suffering state; if we admire only the patience with which he submitted to all the appointments of Providence, the fortitude with which he encountered all the dangers of life, the magnanimity which induced him to forgive his enemies, the charity which prompted him to pray for those who had bound him to the accursed tree, and that noble principle of love to mankind, the spring of all his undertakings as our Redeemer. This merit we must do more than admire; upon it we must rest as the ground of our acceptance with God, and the foundation of our title to eternal life. The blessed above ascribe their salvation not to their own righteousness, but to the merits of their Redeemer; "Unto him that loved us," is the strain of their song, "Unto him that loved us unto the death, and washed us from our sins in his own blood, be praise and honor and blessing." "These are they," said the angel to the apostle John, "who have come out of great tribulation; they have washed their robes, and made them white in the blood of the Lamb, therefore are they before the throne."

Our virtues are insufficient to procure our acceptance with God, or merit a title to happiness in the life to come. Even man, in his state of innocence, could not pretend to have merit with his Creator. By the law of his nature he was bound to render obedience to that God from whom he received his being, and to whom he owed his preservation. The moral law was the law of his being. When he had done his best, he did no more than was his duty. If man, then, in a state of innocence, could not claim the crown of heavenly glory, as the reward of personal merit, shall man in a state of guilt pretend to have merit with a holy God, with whom evil cannot dwell, and who is of purer eyes than to behold iniquity? Supposing the day of judgment arrived, where is the man that durst face the tribunal of the Almighty, and demand one of the thrones of heaven upon the footing of personal righteousness? The most arrogant presumption durst not aspire so high. But, blessed be God, that though we are unworthy, yet worthy is the Lamb that was slain, to receive blessing, and honor, and praise, because he hath redeemed us by his blood, and hath given us a right to sit down with him upon his throne. To fallen man the cross is the tree of life; there grow the fruits which are for the healing of the nations; fruits, which, if we take and eat, we shall live for ever.

In the *third* place, We are to glory in the cross of Christ, by commemorating his death in the holy sacrament.

Those events in which a nation glories

the most, those events which restored or secured to them their liberties, from which they begin an era of happy time, are commemorated with a laudable spirit of joy. A day is set apart, that the memory of such glorious deeds may be transmitted down to posterity, and that the names of those who distinguished themselves on the occasion, as patriots or as heroes, may receive a just tribute of praise from all succeeding times. Agreeably to this, the Christian church hath in all ages set apart certain times to keep in remembrance this most important event, the death and passion of our Redeemer. It was the commandment of our Lord himself; it was his commandment, given in that night in which he was betrayed; it was his last commandment to his disciples, "Do this in remembrance of me." And surely the disciple who loves his Lord, will be cautious how he disregards his dying charge.. There are, indeed, persons in the world, who bear the Christian name, and who, notwithstanding, never join in this solemn ordinance. Although they were baptized into the faith of Jesus, and have never publicly renounced Christianity, yet, instead of glorying in the cross, they seem to be ashamed of it, and testify plainly to the world, that they pay no regard to the dying charge of their Lord, and that they would blush to be seen at a communion-table. How such persons can reconcile their conduct to any sense of duty, to any idea of Christianity, is beyond my capacity to discover. Sure I am, if they have any conscience, if they have any reflection, if they have any feeling at all, it will interrupt their peace of mind in life, it will shut up the chief avenues to comfort in their last moments, and prevent that tranquillity and fulness of joy which is then the portion of the Christian, to think that they have lived in the wilful neglect and contempt of an express injunction of their Lord, and may have, in some degree, incurred the guilt of those whom the apostle declares to have trodden under foot the Son of God, and to have counted the blood of the covenant wherewith they might have been sanctified, an unholy thing.

You say you are unfit to approach the table of the Lord. Let me ask you, Are you fit to *die?* Do you think it more solemn, more awful, to witness a good confession at these tables, than to appear before the judgment-seat of God? Do you think, that they ought to be received to the society of the blessed above, who never joined themselves to the communion of the saints below? Do you think that Jesus will admit those to sit down with him on his throne in heaven, who were ashamed to sit down with him at his table on earth? What is, then, I beseech you, in the holy sacrament, to banish any decent and good man from these tables? We sit down at the table of the Lord, to give thanks unto God for his inestimable love in the redemption of the world; to express our regard and gratitude to our Redeemer, who loved us unto the death; to unite ourselves to all the faithful and the good, as being members of the same body, and to bind ourselves by solemn vows to the practice of whatever is amiable and excellent and praiseworthy. And if there be any man so void of gratitude and love to God his Creator, and to Jesus Christ his Redeemer, as to be averse to acknowledge the favors he has received; if there be any man so dead to the feelings of the heart, to benevolence and love, as to have no bowels of love for his brethren of mankind; if there be any man so lost to the sense of virtue, and to the beauty of holiness, as to see no charms, to feel no attractions, in those things which are lovely, and pure, and honest, and of good report; then, indeed, he is unfit to sit down at the table of the Lord, he has neither portion nor lot in this matter; he is also unfit to join with Christians in any religious duty; nay, he is unfit to perform a decent part as a member of civil society.

I address these things to those who absent themselves from this ordinance, from a wilful disregard. To those who are restrained by their unhappy fears and scruples, I speak in a different language, and such persons I can assure, that they who, after serious, and diligent, and mature preparation, still think themselves unworthy, are not the least acceptable guests at the table of the Lord. Do you feel a grateful sense of the love of Jesus to mankind, particularly that amazing act of his love, in giving his life as a ransom for the world? Have you such a value for the covenant established by your Saviour's blood, that you are resolved to accept of it with gratitude, and adhere to it with all your soul? Have you such a regard to holiness and universal goodness, that you determine to lead decent, and pious, and exemplary lives? If you have these, come to express that gratitude, to accept that covenant, and to seal those vows at the foot of the cross. Jesus breaks not the bruised reed, nor quenches the smoking flax. The humility of the heart will not banish the Eternal Spirit from taking up his residence with you.

In the *fourth* and *last* place, We are to glory in the cross of Christ, by living to those purposes and for those ends for which Jesus died.

We glory in the Reformation from Popery, when we maintain and defend that pure religion which was then established. We glory in the Revolution, when we support the rights and maintain the liberties which were secured to us at that memorable period: and, in like manner, we glory in the cross of Christ, when we fulfil the intention, and answer the purpose for which Jesus died. Jesus died, that he might redeem us from all iniquity, and purify us unto himself a peculiar people, zealous of good works. In this view, Christians, your whole life is glorying in the cross of Christ. When you suppress the motions of irregular desire, when you conquer the excess of passion, and subdue the vices which war against the soul, you are glorying in the cross of Christ; for he, upon the cross, crucified these your enemies, and died that you might be delivered out of their hands. When you check in yourselves the spirit of animosity, when your heart relents towards him against whom your wrath was kindled, when you forego resentment, forgive an injury, and hold out the ready hand of reconciliation to your offending brother, you are glorying in the cross of Christ; for he, upon the cross, displayed a most amazing instance of forgiveness, in praying for those who brought him to that accursed death. When your heart expands with benevolence to mankind; when you feed the hungry, clothe the naked, and rescue the oppressed; when you feel the distresses of your unhappy brethren and relieve them, or give a tear to the distresses you cannot relieve, you are glorying in the cross of Christ; for he, upon the cross, exhibited a most illustrious instance of benevolence, in giving his life for the happiness of the world. When you yield to the sweet impulse of natural affection, when you indulge the tender sensibilities of the heart, when you cultivate the spirit of a generous friendship, and join in the endearing offices of social life, you are glorying in the cross of Christ; for he, upon the cross, gave us a most amiable display of these virtues. One of his last acts on earth was an act of natural affection and friendship; from the cross he recommended his mother to the care of the friend whom he loved.

In short, whenever you make advances in the divine life, and add to your faith virtue, and to virtue, patience, and temperance, and brotherly kindness, and charity; whenever you do a good deed, whenever you think a good thought, you are glorying in the cross of Christ; for he, upon the cross, perfected this character, and finished the pattern of universal goodness for the world to study, to imitate, and to admire.

SERMON XXXI.

Preached at the celebration of the Sacrament of the Lord's Supper.

ON THE SALVATION OF MAN BEING ACCOMPLISHED.

John xix. 30.—"It is finished."

These are the last words of Jesus. The words which he uttered when his hour was come; when in the presence of a great assembly, he breathed out his soul in agony upon the cross. It was ordered by the providence of God, that as Jesus by his death was the Saviour of the world, he should die publicly, when all Israel, from Dan to Beersheba, were assembled at Jerusalem.

There is something grand and awful in assembled multitudes of men, especially when convened on any great occasion, such as to pass sentence of life and death. In that silence of the mind, that awful pause of thought, the human genius is agitated strongly; it labors in expectation, and fills up the dreadful interval with emotions of terror and astonishment. When, therefore, at this period, all Judea was present to celebrate the paschal solemnity; when the great council of the nation, the chief priests, the scribes and the elders, convened in Sanhedrim, added dignity to the multitude; when Pilate the Governor of Judea, and Herod the Tetrarch of Galilee, with their attending armies, displayed the grandeur of the Roman empire, and sustained the majesty of the masters of the world; when all these were assembled at the time of the death and crucifixion of a Prophet of the Lord, how great would be the agitations of the multitude! What astonishing ideas would strike the mind, when they heard the expiring Prophet cry out, "It is finished!" When in a moment they saw that the face of nature was changed; when they felt the earthquake which shook the nations; when they were struck with the darkness which veiled the sun; when they were surrounded with the inhabitants of the eternal world who arose from their graves, would not they then think, indeed, that all was finished, that the last hour of nature was come, and that the world was departing with its Creator?

Never from the time that the idea of creation rose in the Divine Mind, did an hour revolve that labored with such vast events. To this great point of view, as to the deciding hour in the annals of time, as to the crisis of the moral world, all the preceding ages looked forward, and all succeeding ages looked back. The grand question was now deciding, Whether happiness or misery should finally triumph in the universe of God? From this event the powers of hell dated the rise or fall of their dominion. The fate of the creation was now weighing in the scales. All eternity rested upon this hour.

Whilst we are now assembled to commemorate these great events, and to renew the memorials of thy death and passion, be present with us most blessed Jesus! May we behold thy face, not as it was then covered with anguish and tears, but smiling upon us with heavenly complacence! Fill our hearts with love to thee, and lead us joyfully up into thine holy altar!

"It is finished," said our Lord when he expired upon the cross. What was then finished? The following events. God had early manifested to the fathers his purpose of grace to redeem the world. He chose a peculiar people from whom the Redeemer was to descend, and appointed a dispensation of religion to prepare the world for his appearance. By the death of Jesus, this ancient dispensation was finished.

Jesus Christ, foretold by all the prophets, had now appeared unto Israel. As the Prophet of the world, he published a new religion which he adorned by his life, which he confirmed by his miracles, and which he had now sealed with his blood. By the death on the cross, his mission to the Jews, as the Author of a new religion, was finished.

From the beginning of the world, God had appointed sacrifices to make atonement for sin. These could not by any virtue of their own propitiate the Deity, or purify the soul from pollution. A more perfect sacrifice, therefore, was necessary in order to atone the divine wrath. By the death of Jesus, this atonement was finished. Jesus Christ, thus constituted the Prophet of the world, and the Priest who was to make atonement for the sins of men, was to be made perfect through suffering. By the appointment of Providence, he was to suffer before he entered into his glory. By his death on the cross, these sufferings were finished.

That is; the Old Testament dispensation was finished, the mission of Christ to Israel, as the Author of a new religion, was finished, the atonement requisite for the world was finished, and the sufferings of the Messiah were finished.

In the *first* place, then, The ancient dispensation which had been erected, and the plan of Providence which had been carrying on to introduce the time of the Messiah, were now finished.

When our first parents had broken the covenant of innocence, had forfeited their title to immortality, and exposed themselves to the sanction of the violated law, the judge descended to pronounce their sentence. But along with the terrors of the Judge he mingled also the grace of the

Saviour; and when he pronounced their doom, he comforted them with the hopes of mercy. He discovered to them his benevolent design of redeeming the world by a Mediator who was to interpose in their behalf, and gave them the gracious promise, that the seed of the woman should bruise the head of the serpent. Thus no sooner had man fallen, than the Redeemer was promised who was to repair the ruins of his fall. In the following ages, the providence of God seems to have been entirely occupied in preparing the world for this great event. If he manifests himself to the patriarchs, it is to show them the day of the Messiah afar off; if he inspires the prophets, it is to foretell his appearance; if he chooses a peculiar people, it is to render them the depositaries of the promises concerning his coming; if he appoints sacrifices, ceremonies, and religious rites, it is to trace beforehand the history of the Messiah. Do you read of the blood of the paschal lamb, which being sprinkled on the doors of the Israelites, secured them from the destroying angel? It was a figure of Jesus Christ, the Lamb slain from the foundation of the world, who, as our passover, was sacrificed to deliver us from eternal death. Do you read of a rock, which being smitten, furnished waters to a great people? That rock, says Paul, was a figure of Christ, from whom proceed fountains of living waters springing up into everlasting life. Do you read of a brazen serpent lifted up in the wilderness which cured the Israelites? It was a type of the Son of man, who was lifted upon the cross for the salvation of the world. In short, the whole legal economy, the whole system of Levitical worship was intended to prefigure, and to introduce a better dispensation.

The plan of Providence which had been carrying on to prepare the world for this great event, was not confined to the Jewish nation; it extended over the whole earth. This was the great end of all the designs of the Deity, and furnishes the key to all the divine dispensations. "If empires rose or fell; if war divided, or peace united the nations; if learning civilized their manners, or philosophy enlarged their views, all was, by the secret decree of Heaven, made to ripen the world for that *fulness of time* when Christ was to publish the whole counsel of God." What a magnificent conception, my friends, does it give us of the divine government, when we behold the princes, the kings, and the masters of the world, entering one after another upon the stage of time, to prepare the way of the King of kings!

If, in the Gentile world, a plan was carrying on to prepare the nations for the coming of the Messiah, among the chosen people a dispensation was erected to typify and prefigure the great events of his life. The economy which was established, the sacrifices which were appointed, the ceremonies in their church, and the events in their history, all concurred to this great end. Do you read of a continual burnt-offering? It was a type of him who through the eternal Spirit offered up himself a sacrifice without spot unto God. Do you read of the paschal lamb? It was a type of that Lamb which was slain from the foundation of the world. The law only paved the way to the gospel. Moses and the prophets were but the harbingers of the Messiah. This ancient dispensation was now come to a close: and when our Saviour on the cross cried out, *It is finished*, "the law ceased, the gospel commenced."

In the *second* place, The mission of Christ to Israel as the author of a new religion was finished.

God had never left the nations without a witness of himself. In the early ages of the world he sent forth his light and his truth. He manifested himself to the fathers, and taught them the knowledge of the true religion. From time to time righteous men were raised up, and a succession of prophets and of martyrs was carried on, whose lives and doctrines distinguish and adorn the several ages of the world. One nation was chosen above the rest, to whom the living oracles was committed. The particular revelations which had been delivered in the patriarchal ages, the various rays from the Father of lights which had been scattered over the earth, were here collected, and shone out with new splendor. Nevertheless, though God was the Author of this dispensation, though he himself was the King of Jeshurun, and a Lawgiver to Israel, the economy which he established among his own people, was not intended to be immutable, or make the comers thereunto perfect. It is one of the great laws by which this world is governed, that no perfection of any kind is attained of a sudden. There is a rise and a progress in the works of nature. This holds in all the productions of the natural, and in all the improvements of the moral world. This also seems to have regulated the divine conduct with respect to the dispensations of grace.

"The light of religion was not poured upon the world all at once, and with its full splendor; the obscurity of the dawn went before the brightness of the noonday. The will of God was at first made known by revelations, useful indeed, but dark and mysterious. To these succeeded others more clear and perfect. In proportion as the situation of the world rendered it necessary, the Almighty was pleased further to open and unfold his gracious scheme." The light increased as it shone. Star after star arose to enlighten and bless the earth, till the day-spring from on high appeared. As in the early period of our days the instructions which we receive look forward to manhood, and the various steps we take conduct us to future life; so in this infancy of the church, a dispensation took place which was only intended to introduce a better. Every thing in the Jewish dispensation testified that it was not intended to last for ever. The presence of God circumscribed to one nation, the place of acceptable worship confined to Jerusalem, the numerous rites and burdensome ceremonies of the Mosaic law, the typical and shadowy nature of the whole dispensation, showed that it was nothing more than a temporary institution, appointed to introduce a most perfect worship, and to prepare the world for a new dispensation, which was to comprehend every nation of the earth, and to extend through all the ages of the world.

Accordingly Moses, the Jewish legislator, after he had established their government and formed their laws, tells them that another prophet should arise among them, and deliver a new revelation: "Thus saith the Lord, I will raise up a prophet to you from among your brethren; I will put my words in his mouth; him shall ye hear in all things." Accordingly, the Old Testament church never rested upon any revelation which was made to them, but always looked forward to the promised era when the great Prophet should arise, who was to fill Zion with judgment and righteousness.

As the Old Testament economy, in its bets estate, was but a temporary institution, in the progress of time it was greatly corrupted. After the return from the Babylonish captivity, there was a strange degeneracy among the people of God! The spirit of prophecy ceased, and the intercourse between heaven and earth was shut up. The Jews had been at all times remarkably prone to superstition and idolatry. Neither the instructions of their lawgiver, nor the thunders of Sinai, nor the sword of the heathen, nor the chains of captivity, could cure them of this perverse spirit. The true prophets had always endeavored to lead them from the observance of those precepts which were "not good, of those statutes by which a man could not live;" but in the decline of the Jewish nation, their public teachers, the Scribes and Pharisees, accommodated themselves to the prejudices of the people. They collected the various rites and traditions of antiquity, and formed them into a regular system of superstition. They explained away the sense and spirit of the Sacred Scriptures. They had recourse to what they called the oral law, never committed to writing, but delivered, as they pretended, to Moses, and from his time handed down by tradition from age to age. By this they subverted the moral law, and made the word of God of none effect by their traditions.

If the situation of the Jews called thus loudly for reformation, what might be expected in the Gentile world? If such was done in the green tree, what would be done in the dry? They were without God, and without hope in the world. Their religion consisted entirely of superstitious observances, and had no connection with virtue: their worship was a system of abominable rites; their temples were haunts of lewdness and impiety; their gods were monsters of cruelty, rage, and all the vile passions which disgrace humanity. The doctrine of the soul's immortality, which had been but obscurely revealed to the Jews, was only a conjecture among the heathens. Their wise men saw the evil, but could not discover the remedy. They confessed their own ignorance, and with humble expectation looked for a prophet of the Lord, to make a revelation of the divine will to man.

Whilst thus the people wandered in gross darkness, whilst the cloud sat deep over the moral world, at last the groans of the nations reached the ears of mercy; the voice of nature mourning for her children, was heard in heaven. He who dwelleth there, rose from his throne. The Almighty rose in mercy, and sent his Son to be a light to lighten the Gentiles, and to be the glory of his people Israel. The Sun of Righteousness arising in our region, dispelled the darkness which involved the nations, revealed all the heavens to mortal view, and poured its radiance upon the path of immortality. The great Prophet discovered the mystery which had been kept hid from ages. He declared the whole counsel of God. He spoke as never man spake, and he lived as never man lived. His mission from God he proved by performing miracles and works which God only could perform; to these he constantly appealed as a testimony from heaven, and as the finger of God witnessing in his behalf. Accordingly, when the high-priest asked him, Art thou the Christ, the Son of God? he answered nothing. Had his disciples been standing by, they might have replied, What need is there for the inquiry? You who have the key of knowledge, search the Scriptures, inquire at Moses and the prophets who foretold and described his coming. Inquire at John the Baptist, whom you held to be a prophet, and who pointed him out to the people as the sent of God. Inquire at the companions and witnesses of his life, if an impostor had ever so many works of innocence and sanctity. Inquire at the lost sheep of Israel whom he brought back to the path of life. Inquire at the multi. tude whom he fed with a few loaves. Inquire at the blind whom he restored to sight. Inquire at the dumb, who now speak his praise. Inquire at the diseased whom he raised from the bed of affliction. Inquire at the dead whom he raised from their graves. Inquire at the seas and tempests which heard and obeyed the voice of their master. Inquire at the heavens, which thrice opened over his head, to publish to the world that he was the beloved of the Father. And if these suffice you not, inquire at hell itself, and receive the testimony of the devils whom he dispossessed,—That he was "the holy one of God."

Having thus confirmed his doctrine by his miracles; having adorned it by his life, it only remained that he should seal it with his blood. And when now he bowed the head upon the cross, his mission to Israel as the Author of this new revelation was finished.

In the *third* place, The atonement which was requisite for the sins of the world was finished.

As Almighty God created the world, he claims the right of taking it under the superintendency and direction of his providence. In order to attain the ends of his administration, he acts upon a fixed plan, and according to wise and righteous laws. If there were no fixed plan of Providence, and no system of laws to govern the world, the order of society would soon be subverted, the happiness of the human race would be destroyed, and the earth be reduced to one vast scene of anarchy, confusion and uproar. That these laws may have their full effect, they must be guarded with the terrors of a penal sanction, and when violated be put in execution, in order to intimidate offenders, and prevent transgression in the time to come. The Judge of all the earth would not do right unless he executed his righteous laws, and punished those crimes which tended to the subversion of order, and extinction of happiness in human society. If men, then, throwing off their allegiance to Heaven, violate his righteous laws, and expose themselves to his wrath and vengeance, justice requires that they be punished for their sins, and the honor of the Godhead is pledged for the fulfilment of the threatening denounced against sin. But all of us have thus incurred the divine displeasure, and become obnoxious to the sanction of the moral law. Our first parents disobeyed the divine commandments, broke the covenant of innocence, and involved us, their posterity, in the ruins of the fall. We have added innumerable transgressions of our own to that original apostasy. We have neglected the good which it was in our power to perform, and committed the evil from which God commanded us to abstain. We have sinned against the clearest light; in opposition to the greatest goodness, and in the face of direct threatening, times and ways without number we have exposed ourselves to the wrath of God.

But it is one of the most obvious dictates of reason, that punishment must ever attend on wickedness, that the soul which sinneth ought to die. But if sin be thus severely punished, if sinners be dealt with according to the maxims of rigorous and unrelenting justice, What shall become of the human race? Here lay the difficulty that stood in the way of our redemption. If, on the one hand, sin was forgiven without satisfaction, and the sinner taken into favor upon every new application for mercy, such an undistinguishing exercise of lenity, such a facility of forgiveness, would only serve to embolden offenders and multiply crimes. If, on the other hand, rigorous justice held the balance, if the thunderbolt was aimed at the head of every offender, the race of men must perish from the earth. Hence, the Divine Being is introduced in Scripture, as deliberating with himself, as being straitened how to reconcile the seemingly jarring attributes of mercy and justice, and how to make the happiness of men accord with the honor of his laws. "How shall I give thee up, Ephraim? How shall I deliver thee, O Israel? How shall I make thee as Admah? How shall I set thee as Zeboim? Mine heart is turned within me, my repentings are kindled together." Herein appears the wisdom of that plan concerted for our redemption, through the sacrifice of Christ, by which these seemingly jarring attributes are reconciled, in which mercy and truth meet together, righteousness and peace kiss each other. Hence, in that eucharistic hymn which the angels, at the nativity of our Lord, sung to the shepherds, when they ascribed glory to God in the highest, they also proclaimed peace upon earth, and good will towards fallen man. By this atonement, all the perfections of the Deity were glorified. That immaculate purity which cannot look upon sin, and that astonishing love which could not behold the ruin of the sinner, were awfully displayed. The majesty of the divine government was sustained, the honor of the law was vindicated, justice, in its rigor, was satisfied, mercy without measure and without restraint flowed upon the children of men. The gate of the heavenly paradise was set open wide to a returning world, the angel with the flaming sword, who guarded the tree of life, was removed, and a voice heard from the throne of mercy, "Take, eat, and live for ever."

As this doctrine concerning the atonement and sacrifice of Jesus Christ, is one of the fundamental articles of our holy faith, God, in the course of his providence, had prepared the world for its belief and reception. A sense of guilt lying upon the mind, and the fear of punishment from that Judge, who will render to every man according to his works, drove the sinner to some expedient for atoning the wrath of an offended Deity. It is very extraordinary, that among all the people of the world, the method of making atonement for sin was invariably the same. All the nations of antiquity, that are to be found in the records of history, all the modern nations whom recent discoveries have brought within the sphere of our knowledge, however they may have differed in customs and manners, have universally and invariably agreed in making atonement for sin by offering sacrifices to the Deity. This fact is the more extraordinary, as such a method of propitiation is not founded on nature, is not the dictate of reason, nor the result of any feelings of the human frame. If we consult with reason, reason will tell us, that the Deity can never take any pleasure in the tortures or in the blood of innocent animals; reason will tell us that it is impossible that the blood of bulls and goats, or the ashes of a heifer can avail to satisfy the divine justice, or purify the soul from sin. A practice therefore so universal, not founded on nature, nor deducible from reason, can be accounted for no otherwise, but by considering it as the remains of those ancient traditions delivered to the descendants of Noah, and by them handed down to succeeding ages. Here we cannot but admire the wisdom and watchful care of Providence, that whilst many other traditions perished in the course of time, and are in the gulf of oblivion, this was kept entire all over the world, in order to prepare the nations for the reception of Christianity, which establishes the capital doctrines of an atonement for sin upon a sacrifice.

Not only were sacrifices in general use among the heathen, but also, among the most celebrated nations of antiquity, illustrious personages had arisen, who, inspired with generous patriotism, had, in cases of danger and calamity, devoted themselves to certain death, to save their country. These self-devoted heroes, these martyrs to the good of mankind, were held in admiration by their countrymen, first in the song of praise, and highest in the temple of fame. After the publication of Christianity, it was no difficult task to transfer the praise and veneration which was paid to these temporal deliverers, to that Divine Lover of mankind, and Redeemer of our race, who offered up himself a sacrifice for our sins, and died for the happiness of the world. Hence the atonement requisite for the sins of the world was finished.

In the *fourth* place, The sufferings of the Messiah were now finished, and naught but glory was to follow.

It seemed expedient to Infinite Wisdom, to set up the Son as head over the great family of God. It was in this capacity that he created the earth: for it is one of the doctrines revealed to us in the New Testament, that the Son of God was the Creator of the world. As he, therefore, was our immediate Creator, and as his intent in our creation was defeated by sin, there was an evident propriety, that he himself should interpose in our behalf. The fall of man was the loss of so many subjects to Christ, their natural Lord, in virtue of his having created them. Redeeming them, was recovering them again, was re-establishing his power over his own works. In the epistle to the Colossians, the apostle Paul runs a parallel between the relation in which Christ stands towards us as our Creator, and the new relation he acquired in virtue of his redemption. In the first view, he styles him the image of the invisible God, the first-born of every creature; for by him were all things created, and by him all things consist. In the second view, he calls him the head of the body, the church, the beginning, the first-born from the dead, that in all things he might have the pre-eminence. "For it pleased the Father that in him should all fulness dwell, and having made peace by the blood of his cross, by him to reconcile all things to himself."

The scheme of thought which runs through the passage, seems to be this, that as we owed to Christ our first life, it was also expedient that we should owe to him our second; that, as he was the head of the creation, and made all things, so when God thought fit to redeem the world, it pleased him that Christ should also be the head of this new work, the first-born from the dead himself, and the giver of life to every believer. This much we collect from the apostle's reasoning, and plainly discern, that the pre-eminence of Christ, as head of the Church, is connected with his pre-eminence as head of the creation, and his being set over the great family of God. Jesus Christ, thus constituted the Redeemer of mankind, and the Captain of our salvation in the discharge of his office, was to be made perfect through sufferings.

In the present state of humanity, the character cannot be complete without the virtues of adversity. We are made for suffering, as well as for action; there are many principles in the human frame, many faculties of the mind, many qualities of the heart, which would be for ever latent, were they not called forth to action by danger and distress. There is a hidden greatness in the mind of man, which afflictions alone can bring to light. When we are bereft of all human help; when heaven seems to forsake us, and the earth to fail beneath our feet, it is then that the soul asserts her native strength, summons all her virtue to her aid, and exhibits to heaven and earth an object worthy of their contemplation and regard. Afflictions thus supported by patience, thus surmounted by fortitude, give the last finishing to the heroic and the virtuous character. Thus the vale of tears is the theatre of human glory; that dark cloud presents the scene for all the beauties in the bow of virtue to appear. Moral grandeur, like the sun, is brighter in the day of the storm, and never is so truly sublime, as when struggling through the darkness of an eclipse.

SERMON XXXII.

Preached at the celebration of the Sacrament of the Lord's Supper.

JESUS CHRIST THE RESURRECTION AND THE LIFE.

JOHN XI. 25.—"I am the Resurrection and the Life."

"I SAW in the right hand of him that sat on the throne," said the Prophet of the New Testament,—"I saw in the right hand of him that sat on the throne, a book written within and on the backside, sealed with seven seals. And I saw a strong angel proclaim with a loud voice, Who is worthy to open the book, and to loose the seals thereof? And no man in heaven, nor in earth, neither under the earth, was able to open the book, neither to look thereon. And I wept much, because no man was found worthy to open, and to read the book, neither to look thereon. And one of the elders said unto me, Weep not. Behold, the Lion of the tribe of Juda, the root of David, hath prevailed to open the book, and to loose the seven seals thereof."

In this mysterious manner, the apostle, who ascended in the visions of God, and saw into past and future time, represents the restoration of mankind to life. When man had fallen from his state of innocence, and all flesh had corrupted their ways, Almighty God, with eyes that for ever overflow with love, looked down upon the earth. He beheld the world; not as he had beheld it at first, when the morning stars sang together, when all the sons of God shouted for joy, and when he himself pronounced that all was fair and good; that very world he now beheld involved in confusion and uproar; the original state of things marred; the order of nature destroyed; the laws of Heaven overturned; his once beautiful and happy creation defaced and laid in ruins. He beheld his rational offspring, whom he had adorned with his own image, whom he had appointed to immortality, fallen from their primitive innocence, debased with ignorance, depraved with guilt, subjected to vanity, and appointed to dissolution. Following the footsteps of sin, which had thus laid waste his works, he beheld *death* advancing with swift steps; extending his dominion over the nations, and shaking his dart in triumph over a subjected world. He saw, he pitied, and he saved.

Although offended with the guilty race, he would not cast them off for ever. His time of visitation was a time of love. In mercy to mankind he devised a scheme for our restoration and recovery. But man was not now, as in innocence, in a condition to treat with God by himself. Between sinful dust and ashes, and infinite purity, there could be no communication. A Mediator, therefore, was requisite to make peace between heaven and earth, and where was such a Mediator to be found?

Accordingly, at the declaration of the gracious purpose of God, for the future happiness of the world, when the book of life sealed with its seven seals was brought forth, a strong angel proclaimed with a loud voice, "Who is worthy to take the book, and to open the seals thereof?" Who is worthy to mediate between an offended God and guilty man; to unfold the secret purpose of the Most High, and to give life to a world that is dead? There was silence in heaven, and silence in heaven there might have been for ever; but in that moment of mercy, the crisis of our fate, the Son of God interposed; "I am the resurrection and the life, by me shall the world live. I will forsake these mansions of glory, and dwell with men. They who now wander in darkness, I will bring to light, and life, and immortality; they are now under sentence of death; that sentence shall be executed on me, and I will purchase for them life everlasting; they have now gone astray into the paths of perdition, I will point out to them the way that leads to the heavens."

In this manner did Jesus Christ become the resurrection and the life. As the Prophet of the world, he gave us the assurance of life and immortality; as the Priest of the world, he purchased for us life and immortality; and as the King of the world, he set before us the path that leads to life and immortality.

In the *first* place, then, as the Prophet of the world, he gave us assurance of life and immortality.

Curiosity, or the desire of knowledge, is one of the earliest and one of the strongest emotions of the human soul. No sooner does the mind arrive at maturity, but it proceeds to examine the objects around it, and to extend its researches wider and wider over the whole circuit of creation. With peculiar earnestness man turns his attention to his own nature, and becomes the object of his own contemplation. But here clouds and darkness surround him. He perceives himself a stranger in a wide world, where the plan of nature is very imperfectly known, where the system of things is involved in much obscurity, and where the Author of the universe is a God who hideth himself. Life appears to him as an intermediate state, but he is ignorant of what was before it, and is as ignorant of what is to come after it He observes symptoms of decay and marks of mortality on all the productions of nature, the human race not exempted from the general law. He sees his friends and companions, one after another, perpetually disappearing; he sees mankind, generation after generation, passing away; passing to that awful abyss to which every thing goes, and from which nothing returns. But whither do they go when they depart? Have they withdrawn into everlasting darkness? Or do they still act in another scene? We see the body incorporate with its kindred elements, and return to the dust from whence it was taken. But what becomes of the soul? Does it, too, cease to exist? Is the beam of heaven for ever extinguished? Is the celestial fire which glowed in the heart for ever quenched? Or beyond the horizon which terminates our present prospect, does a more beautiful and perfect scene present itself, where the tears shall be wiped from the eyes of the mourner, where the wicked shall cease from troubling, and the weary be at rest?

If we consult our affections, we shall be inclined to believe in a future state. Nature is loth to quit its hold. The heart still wishes to be kind to the friends whom once it loved. Imagination takes the hint, and indulges us with the pleasing hope of one day meeting again with the companions whom we dropt in life. The perfections of the Deity favor these wishes of nature. If God be infinitely wise and infinitely good, he would not have brought us into being only to see the light and to depart for ever. Would a wise builder have erected such a noble fabric to last but for a moment? On the other hand, if we consult the analogy of nature, the horrors of annihilation surround us. All the works of nature seem only made to be destroyed. The leaf that falls from the tree revives no more. The animal that mingles with the earth never rises to life again. Appearances also make against us. The mind seems to depend much upon the body. The temper of the one arises from the state of the other. When the external senses decay, the faculties of the soul are impaired. When the blood ceases to flow, the spirit evaporates, the last stroke of the pulse seems to put a final period to the whole man.

Between these fears and these wishes of nature, no conclusion can be drawn. After the maturest investigation, and deepest reasoning, all that we arrive at is uncertainty. We see the traveller involved in the cloud of night, but we know not of any morning that awaits him. The ocean spreads before us vast and dark and awful, but we know not if it will waft us to any shore. What a disconsolate situation is this to a serious inquiring mind? These thoughts would perplex us at all times, but if they affect us with anxiety in the gay and smiling scenes of life, how will they overwhelm us with horror, when our feet stumble on the dark mountains, and the shadows of the everlasting evening begin to close over our head? In that hour of terror and dismay, how shall the wretched man support himself, who knows not the hope of immortality? Afflicted with the view of his past life, tormented with present pain, and hovering over an abyss from which we know not if we shall ever emerge, How must it embitter the last hour, and mingle despair with the pangs of dissolution, to think on our bidding adieu to the living world; to go perhaps for ever into the dominion of darkness, into the region of shadows, into the land of forgetfulness, where, for any thing we can tell, we shall be as though we had never been! To such persons, the end of life must be insupportable. Their setting sun goes down in a cloud, and the long night closes over their head in its darkest and deepest shade.

But when the Sun of Righteousness arose in our region, it dispelled the shadows of the everlasting evening; revealed all the heavens to mortal view, and poured its radiance upon the path of immortality. Our Saviour did not propose his doctrines as controvertible opinions, he confirmed them by proofs and miracles. Did he teach the immortality of the soul, and the resurrection of the body? As an infallible confirmation of these doctrines, he himself arose from the grave, and being the first-born from the dead himself, he gives life to the world. The good man need not now live in a state of anxiety about his future existence, or mourn for his deceased friends as those who have no hope. We know that our Redeemer liveth; we know that we shall in like manner revive.

There is a time appointed, when the year of the redeemed shall come; when the everlasting morning shall dawn; when the voice of the Son of God shall pierce the caverns of the tomb; shall be heard over the dominions of the dead; shall reanimate the ashes of all that ever lived upon the earth, and raise a glorious and immortal army from the bosom of corruption.

In the name, and by the authority of Him who was once dead, but is now alive, and lives for evermore, I am this day to give you the bread of life, and deliver into your hand the pledges of immortality. It is the voice which Jesus this day addresses to you from these tables, "I am the resurrection and the life. He that believeth in me shall never die."

In the *second* place, Jesus Christ as the Priest of the world, purchased for us life and immortality.

When man came from the hands of his Creator he was innocent, and therefore happy and immortal. For although, in the present degenerate state of human nature, the imperfect virtue of good men neither insures their happiness here, nor merits an everlasting reward hereafter, yet if we suppose them in a state of innocence or confirmed goodness, we can neither set bounds to their enjoyments or their existence. The ideas of perfection and felicity are inseparable; wherever pure virtue is, it is in paradise; all good beings throughout the universe are happy. Righteousness is by its own title, immortal. The spring of innocence and the fountain of life, for ever mingle their streams.

Accordingly, as the world when it was first created, contained in it no principles of decay, so man, its noblest inhabitant, harbored in his nature no seeds of dissolution. The world, if it had not been cursed, had moved on in its original beauty, fresh, in undecaying vigor, and fair with perpetual youth; and man, if he had never fallen, would only have exchanged an earthly paradise for a heavenly one. For, as we are told, God created not death, and there was no poison of destruction in the world which he made. Immortality was a part of his image, which he conferred upon our first parents. Amid the garden of Eden a tree arose, the sacramental pledge of life, and sign of immortality to man. And if man had never fallen by tasting of its fruits, he would have lived for ever. But, by the fall, death entered into the world. On the day that man became a sinner he died. The man who was made after the image of God, died; the man who was created immortal, died; and there remained a lifeless form, a guilty and a mortal creature, doomed to earn his bread with the sweat of his brow, to drag out a threescore and ten years of wretchedness and pain, and then to return to the dust from which he was taken.

How art thou fallen from heaven, son of the morning! How is the gold become dim, and the most fine gold changed! The celestial spirits, appointed the guardians of Eden, knew our first parents no longer, they recollected no traces of original innocence in a form so fallen. They discerned none of the lineaments of heaven in a face so clouded with guilt. They drove out the man; drove him out from the garden of Eden, where he had access to the tree of life; drove him out from the society of all those good beings who were at once happy and obedient; drove him out from the presence of the Lord, with which, in paradise, he had been often blessed.

Behold him now in his fallen state! Behold, O man! and mourn over this image. Fallen from the dignity of his nature, and in ruins; the beauty of innocence defaced; the splendor of heaven obscured; cut off from the career of glory and immortality; his name erased from the book of life, no more to claim alliance with the Father of spirits, no more to rank among those happy sons of God, who present themselves before the Lord; no more to behold His countenance in bliss, in whose presence there is fulness of joy, and at whose right hand there are pleasures for evermore! Such was the state into which man was brought by the fall; the sentence of death passed upon him; the gate of heaven shut against him; the wrath of an offended God hung over his head. To persons in this state, what consolation would it bring, to hear of an immortality beyond the grave, if it was to be an immortality of misery and torment? To hear of heaven, and be cast down to hell; to be told of the rivers of pleasure, which are at God's right hand, while they were doomed to drink the unmingled cup of his wrath!

But the Great Restorer of our race, the Redeemer of mankind, not only as a Prophet, discovered to us a future state, but also as a Priest purchased for us eternal happiness in that future state. It was the guilt of our sins that shut the gate of heaven against us, that subjected us to the wrath of God, and to misery in the world to come. But Jesus Christ, as our Surety and Redeemer, fulfilled that law which we had broken; endured that wrath which we had deserved; made an atonement for those sins which we had committed; and by the righteousness of his life, by the efficacy of his sufferings, by the merit of his death, he satisfied the justice of God; he blotted out the sins of the world; he abolished death; he purchased life; he quenched the fire of hell, and opened the heavens for the righteous to enter in. Thus, what the first Adam, the man of the earth, had lost, the second Adam, the Lord from heaven, restored again. By the sacrifice of himself, which we are this day to commemorate, he ransomed us from destruction; by his death upon the cross, of which we are this day to renew the memorials, he purchased the life of the world.

Yes, O Christian! the ransom was paid. While thousands of rams, and ten thousand rivers of oil were insufficient, a price of higher value was given; while the blood of bulls, and of goats, and the cattle upon a thousand hills, were unavailable, a sacrifice of greater efficacy was offered up. The fund of heaven was exhausted; the treasures of eternity were bestowed; the blood of the Son of God was shed upon the cross—Yes, O Christian! the ransom was paid. Liberal to you is the divine benignity; free to you the blessing of life flows. But the anguish which thy Redeemer felt, when his soul was exceeding sorrowful, even unto death; the groans which he uttered; the tears which he shed; the fears which came upon him in the hour of darkness; his bloody sweat during his agony in the garden; the earnest prayer which he offered up, that the cup of wrath might pass from him for a time; his complaint of dereliction upon the cross, when he cried, "My God, my God, why hast thou forsaken me?" These testify at what a price the blessing was bought. Yes, O Christian! the ransom was paid. When this awful event was transacting; when the great hour of sacrifice was solemnizing, astonishment seized the world. All nature labored in expectation, when the eternal life of her children was procuring. An earthquake rent asunder the rocks, and shook the earth from its foundations. The sun, beyond the course of nature, suffered eclipse in the heavens; unusual darkness, at noon, overspread the nations; the invisible world, through all its mansions, felt that

tremendous hour. The dead arose from the grave. With astonishment the host of heaven looked down. Man alone, for whom these wonders were wrought, man alone was an unconcerned spectator of the event.—Yes, O Christian ! the ransom was paid. Behold the victim led to the sacrifice, patient, uncomplaining, marking the way with his own blood. Who is it they drag like a murderer to Mount Calvary ? Who is it they are stretching on a cross, and nailing to the accursed tree ? Prince of life ! Lord of glory ! Saviour of men ! Great High Priest of the world ! we cannot call upon thee to come down from the cross, for thou art now purchas-
the eternal life for us !—Yes, O Christian !
ing ransom was paid. The sacrifice which was offered up, was accepted by God. Jesus, before he bowed upon the cross, cried out, "It is finished." As a full confirmation that the merit of his sacrifice was available to purchase everlasting life, he rose from the dead on the third day, and is now ascended up on high, to take possession of those heavens he hath purchased for his people, and is now preparing a place for them in those mansions, which are in his Father's house.

In the *third* place, as the King of the world, he sets before us the path that leads to life eternal.

Having, as a Prophet, opened up a future world to mortal view; having, as a Priest, purchased life eternal in that future world, as a King he marks out the way by which we may ascend to take possession of that eternal life which he hath purchased for us. The gate of heaven is set open, by his blood; but they alone who walk in the path which he hath appointed shall enter in. You come to these tables, not only to receive instruction from Jesus as a Prophet, not only to profess your faith in him as a Priest, but also to recognize his authority as a Legislator, and to vow obedience to him as a King.

One of his first appearances on earth was in his legislative capacity. One of the first acts of his ministry was to publish a system of laws for regulating the life of his disciples. Moses is celebrated for having been faithful in his house, and for having ordered every thing in his tabernacle, according to the pattern showed him in the mount. No less faithful in his house was the Prophet like unto Moses, the Minister of the true tabernacle which the Lord pitched, and not man. He hath given us the purest and most effective precepts, for the regulation of our life. He hath pointed out our duty in every instance with such clearness, that he that runneth may read. The King of that future world which he hath purchased by his death, hath made the path that leads to it, not only plain but luminous.

It shall come to pass in those days, saith the prophet Isaiah (describing the times of the Messiah), that the "eyes of the blind shall be opened, the ears of the deaf shall be unstopped; the lame shall leap as an hart, and the tongue of the dumb shall sing. For in the wilderness shall waters break out, and streams in the desert.—And a highway shall be there, and it shall be called the way of holiness; the unclean shall not pass over it; but the redeemed shall walk there, and wayfaring men, though fools, shall not err therein." Such is the perfection of the Christian law; such the purity of those morals which Jesus delivered; such the beauty of the Gospel, as a rule of life, as to have gained the love and admiration of many who have disbelieved its doctrines. But he gave them a still higher lustre by his example. The perfection of the Christian law, the purity of those morals which Jesus delivered, the beauty of the Gospel, as a rule of life, appear nowhere to such advantage, as in the life of our Lord. There you contemplate holiness, not as a dead letter, but as a living form; substantial, present, speaking to the world. He trode before you the path that leads to heaven. It is pointed out by his precepts; it is marked by his example; it is consecrated by his blood.

Would you learn what virtue is, would you be in love with virtue, would you practise virtue, contemplate the life of Jesus; study the life of Jesus; imitate the life of Jesus. He to whom the Jews preferred a robber and a murderer, was fairer in his life than the sons of men, and purer in his heart than the angels of God. That head which they crowned with thorns, was ever intent on benevolent deeds, and at that very moment of time meditated their good. Those feet which they bound to the cross, went about on errands of mercy. Those hands which they nailed to the accursed tree, were lifted up in devotion to God, or stretched out in beneficence to men. Jesus, through his whole life, marked out the path which leads to the heavens. Walk in that path, Christians! You shall arrive at heaven; and be of that happy number, who are to inhabit the mansions prepared for you, by Him who is "the resurrection and the life."

SERMON XXXIII.

ON THE SUFFERINGS OF JESUS CHRIST.

LUKE XXII. 44.—"And being in an agony."

THE agony of our Lord in the garden, and his complaints upon the cross, are the most extraordinary parts of his life. A dread of those sufferings which he was to undergo, appears to have made a strong impression upon his mind. Forebodings of them frequently disturbed his repose, and overwhelmed his spirits. Many days before his passion, he cried out, "Now am I troubled, and what shall I say? Father save me from this hour." It was probably with a view to console his mind in such a dejected state, that he was transfigured; that he re-assumed the glory which he had with the Father before the foundation of the world, and was favored with the presence of Moses and Elias from the mansions of immortality; for, as we are informed by the Evangelist, they talked of that decease which he was to accomplish at Jerusalem. Magnanimity in all its exertions was a conspicuous part of his character. He who walked upon the water, who slept in tranquillity amid the storm, and who encountered the foe of mankind in the desert, cannot be accused of a defect in courage. When a band of soldiers, with Judas at their head, came to apprehend him, and inquired for Jesus of Nazareth, he said unto them, "I am he," and by the dignity of his demeanor, struck them with awe. When he was accused by the chief priests and elders before the judgment-seat of Pilate, with that majestic silence which is sometimes the best expression of fortitude, he answered not a word. Nay, when he underwent the severest of his bodily sufferings upon the cross, he endured them with a tranquillity, a firmness, and magnanimity, which display a mind truly great and undaunted. How, therefore, on some other occasions, his spirit was overwhelmed, is a subject worthy of our inquiry at all times. More particularly on this day, when we have assembled together to renew the memorial of his death upon the cross, and to recall the remembrance of all his sufferings.

In further discoursing upon this subject, I shall, in the *first* place, set before you the account which is given of his sufferings: and, *secondly*, endeavor to assign the causes of them.

In the *first* place, I am to set before you the account which is given of his sufferings.

That night in which he was betrayed, the Saviour of the world went into the garden of Gethsemane and ascended the mountain of Olives, as he was wont to do. This had been his accustomed retreat from the world; here was the hallowed ground to which he retired for prayer and contemplation; here he had often spent the night in intercourse with Heaven. He was accompanied by Peter, James, and John, the very same disciples who had been the witnesses of his glorious transfiguration, when Moses and Elias had appeared to him, and a voice had come from the overshadowing cloud, "This is my beloved Son, in whom I am well pleased." What a different scene now presented itself! the rays of glory shone no more; the Divine presence was withdrawn; the voice from heaven ceased; that time was now come, which is so emphatically called *the hour and power of darkness.*

He had lately partaken of the passover with his disciples; that passover which, with so much earnestness, he had desired to eat; he had instituted the holy sacrament of the supper; he had delivered those divine discourses recorded in the Gospel of John; he had warned them against deserting him in the hour of temptation; he had selected three of them to attend him in his sorrows: nevertheless, even these three, thus favored, thus honored, thus warned, forgat all that had been said and done, and unconcerned sunk into sleep. He was left alone to endure the bitterness of that hour.

The severity of his sufferings in the garden, the anguish and the horror which then overwhelmed him, appear from the strong colors in which they are drawn by the sacred writers. They speak of his sorrow, "My soul is exceeding sorrowful, even unto death." They speak of his agony, that is, the most inexpressible torment of mind: "And being in an agony." They speak of his fears: "He was heard in that he feared." They speak of his cries and his tears: "He offered up prayers and supplications with strong crying and tears." They speak of the prodigious effects his agony had upon his body: "His sweat was as it were great drops of blood." They speak of the desire he had to withdraw from his sufferings for a time: "Father, if it be possible, let this cup pass from me."

They who are acquainted with the style of the Holy Evangelists, know how remarkable they are for simplicity of narrative. They make use of no oratorial arts to interest the passions of their readers, they affect no threatenings or embellishments of eloquence, but place the plain action before our view, devoid of all ornament whatever. Historians contemporary to the events which they record, and who beheld the actions which they describe, usually give free vent to their passions in relating the occurrences of their history, and enter with the zeal of parties upon the various subjects which engage their attention. The sacred writers, on the other hand, lay aside every thing that looks like passion or party zeal; they relate events not like men who were interested in the facts which they describe; not like men who had acted a part in the history they write; not even with the ordinary emotions of spectators, but with all the simplicity, and conciseness, and brevity, of an evidence in a court of justice. The torments which our Saviour endured in the garden, therefore, must have been great and amazing, when the sacred writers clothe them with all the circumstances of terror, and paint them in all the colors of distress. What shall we say, then, to account for this dejection which our Lord felt, and for this desire which he expressed to be saved from his sufferings? In the ordinary course of human affairs, an innocent man of common fortitude, resigns himself with acquiescence to his fate; his integrity supports him; a good cause and a good conscience carry him onwards through life and death, undaunted and undismayed. Hence, many illustrious and virtuous men in the heathen world, supported by the native fortitude of the human mind, poured contempt upon all the forms of death, and departed with magnanimity and with glory. If a man who had only innocence to support him, might thus acquiesce in his doom, one whose sufferings were to be publicly useful, whose death was to be glorious to himself, and beneficial to the world, might rejoice in the midst of his sufferings, and exult in the prospect of death. In the early times of the Christian Church, the first disciples followed their Lord in a path that was marked with blood; persons of all ranks, of all ages, and of both sexes, braved the rage of the enemy, the sword of the persecutor, the fire of the tormentor, became candidates for the crown of martyrdom, and with triumph embraced that very form of death at which our Lord, to appearance, now trembled and stood aghast.

This leads us to the *second* thing proposed, which was to account for these appearances; to assign the causes of our Lord's peculiar sufferings. In general, then, there were circumstances in the passion of our Lord, of a singular kind, fully adequate to produce the effects here mentioned. What these were, will appear when we consider that our Lord died in a state where he was abandoned by his friends, and by mankind; that he died in a state of ignominy; and that he died in a state, where, after suffering an agony of spirit, he was at last forsaken by his Father in heaven. While the two former of these can hardly be paralleled in all their circumstances, the last is entirely peculiar to our Lord, and constitutes the chief branch of his sufferings.

First, He died in a state where he was abandoned by his friends and by mankind.

From the beginning he found the world against him. He came unto his own, and his own received him not. He was to be made perfect through sufferings, and many were the distresses which wrung his heart, before the decease which he accomplished at Jerusalem. This was the severest of all, from the manifold terrors that were now combined together. He had not only to carry his own cross, to have his head crowned with thorns, to be derided and buffeted, to be extended upon the accursed tree, to suffer the scourge, the nails, and the spear. All this he was superior to; but to be abandoned by his friends, and by all mankind, at the very time he was suffering for their sakes, was the peculiar and forlorn fate of the Saviour of the world.

The presence of our friends, in the hour of trial, gives a secret strength to the mind; it affords a melancholy pleasure to die among those with whom we lived. But this consolation our Saviour had not. He had chosen twelve friends to be the partners of his life, and the companions of his death. One of these betrayed him, another denied him; all forsook him and fled.

It is some relief to the unhappy sufferer, to have the passions of the spectators on his side; from their sympathy he derives courage, and the pain that is felt by many is alleviated to the one who suffers.

But the high and the low, the Jew and the Heathen, entered into the conspiracy against Christ. The priests and elders accused him. The High Priest cried out, "He is guilty of death." Pilate, his judge, though conscious of his innocence, though he washed his hands from the guilt of his death, ordered him to be scourged, and allowed him to be crucified. The people, with a frantic ardor, sought his death. That very people who, a few days before, upon his triumphal entry into Jerusalem, had strewed the way with palm-branches, and cried out, "Hosanna to the Son of David;" that very people, such is the giddiness of the multitude, now cried out, "Crucify him, crucify him." Thus, in his sorrows, he stood by himself, a wretched individual without a friend. When the Shepherd was smitten, the sheep were scattered abroad. He trode the wine-press alone. Of the people there were none with him. When he died for all, he was pitied by none.

In the *second* place, He died in a state of ignominy. The death of the cross was not only painful and tormenting, but ignominious also, and accursed. A death that was never inflicted upon free men, but reserved for slaves and malefactors, for the basest and the vilest of the human kind. There is implanted in the mind of man a strong abhorrence of shame and disgrace. The sense of ignominy is more pungent in a noble nature, than the feeling of pain. To want the appearance of innocence, while, at the same time, we preserve the reality; to lie under the imputation of heinous crimes; to die the death of a criminal, and leave the world with an indelible stain upon our name and memory, is one of the sorest trials that virtue can meet with upon earth. Yet even this our Lord had to suffer. He had to endure the cross, and submit to the shame. It was foretold by the Prophet, that he should be "numbered among transgressors." And although he was holy, harmless, undefiled, and separate from sinners, yet he was impeached of the highest crimes: not only as a violator of the divine law, in breaking the Sabbath, and frequenting the company of sinners, but also as an impostor, deluding the people; as a blasphemer, assuming to himself the prerogatives of God; and as a seditious person, perverting the nation, usurping royal authority, and forbidding to give tribute to Cæsar. "If he had not been a malefactor," said the Jews to Pilate, "we should not have delivered him up to thee." The resentment of such a situation our Lord felt strongly, and discovered in that remarkable speech, "Are ye come against me as against a thief, with swords and with staves?" Thus, our Lord was not only a sufferer, but in appearance a criminal: he had not only to endure the pain, but the ignominy of the cross; not only to be wounded and tormented, but also to be mocked, reviled, and scorned by the vilest of mankind. Then were fulfilled the words of the mystical Prophet, "I am a reproach of men, and despised of the people. All they that see me, laugh me to scorn: they shoot out the lip, they shake the head, saying, He trusted on the Lord, that he would deliver him: let him deliver him, seeing he delighted in him." There is not a circumstance in the history of mankind so ignominious, and to an ingenuous nature so tormenting, as the following, which is recorded by the Evangelists. Pilate said, "Shall I release Jesus?" "They all cried, Not this man, but Barabbas. Now Barabbas was a robber."

There is a misapprehension into which we are apt to fall, in considering the sufferings of Jesus Christ. Whenever he appears before our eyes, the splendor of his Divinity overcomes the mind, and in the Lord of Glory the man of sorrows is forgotten. But, my friends, you are to remember that as God is by his nature incapable of pain or sorrow, in all scenes of distress, the *Divinity* withdrew, that the *Humanity* might suffer. Yes, Christians, the man Christ Jesus was like one of ourselves, as encompassed with the same infirmities, and subjected to the same distresses; as accessible to sorrow, and as sensible of ignominy and pain.

Thirdly, Our Lord died in a state, where, after undergoing an agony of spirit, he was at last forsaken by his Father in heaven. The presence of God, and the aids of his Holy Spirit, have always been the consolation of good men in their afflictions. They experienced the fulfilment of these promises, "As thy days are, so shall thy strength be. When thou goest through the waters I will go with thee, and through the rivers, they shall not overflow thee. Our fathers trusted in thee," saith the Psalmist, "they trusted, and thou didst deliver them." But in the sufferings endured by the Redeemer in the garden, and on the cross, God departed from him, and the Divine presence was withdrawn.

Christians! what an hour was that, which our Saviour passed in the garden of Gethsemane! In the time of his passion, his torments succeeded one another. He was not at the same time betrayed, mocked, scourged, crowned with thorns, pierced with a spear, extended on a cross, and forsaken by his Father; but here all these torments rose before him at once: all his pains were united together: what he was to endure in succession, now crowded into one moment, and his soul was overcome. At this time, too, the powers of darkness, it should seem, were permitted to work upon his imagination, to disturb his Spirit, and make the vale through which he was to pass, appear more dark and gloomy.

Add to this, that our Saviour having now come to the close of his public life, his whole mediatorial undertaking presented itself to his view; his eye ran over the history of that race which he came to save from the beginning to the end of time; he had a feeling of all the misery, and a sense of all the guilt of men. If he looked back into past times, what did he behold? The earth a field of blood, a vale of tears, a theatre of crimes. If he cast his eyes upon that one in which he lived, what did he behold? That nation to whom he was sent, rejecting the counsel of God against themselves, imprecating his blood to be upon them and their children, and bringing upon themselves such a desolation as has not happened to any other people. When he looked forward to succeeding ages, what did he behold? He saw that the wickedness of men was to continue and abound, to erect a Golgotha in every age, and by obstinate impenitence, to crucify afresh the Son of God. He saw that in his blessed name, and under the banners of his cross, the most atrocious crimes were to be committed, the sword of persecution to be drawn, the best blood of the earth to be shed, and the noblest spirits that ever graced the world to be cut off; he saw that for many of the human race all the efforts of saving mercy were to be defeated; that his death was to be of no avail; that his blood was to be shed in vain; that his agonies were to be lost, and that it had been happy for them, if he had never been born. He saw that he was to be wounded in the house of his friends; that his name was to be blasphemed among his own followers; that he was to be dishonored by the wicked lives of those who called themselves his disciples; that one man was to prefer the gains of iniquity, another the blandishments of pleasure, a third the indulgence of malicious desire, and all of you, at times, the gratification of your favorite passion, to the tender mercies of the God of peace, and the dying love of a crucified Redeemer. While the hour revolved that spread forth all these things before his eyes, we need not wonder that he began to be in agony, and that he sweated as it were great drops of blood.

On the cross that agony returned, and was redoubled. Judge of what he felt, by the expressions of the Prophet in the mystical psalm, "My God, my God, why hast thou forsaken me, why art thou so far from helping me, and from the words of my roaring? O my God, I cry in the day-time, but thou hearest not, and in the night-season I am not silent. Our fathers trusted in thee; they trusted, and thou didst deliver them. But I am a worm, and no man, a reproach of men, and despised of the people. I am poured out like water. My heart is melted like wax in the midst of my bowels; thou hast brought me to the dust of death."

This constituted what the ancient church called the *unknown sufferings* of Christ. In the cup which the Father gave him to drink, there was something sharper than the vinegar, and more bitter than the gall. The darkness which at that time covered the face of the earth, was but a faint emblem of that blacker cloud which overwhelmed his soul. What the degree of these unknown sufferings was, how they were inflicted, or how they were sustained, we cannot tell. But the complaint of dereliction which the Saviour then uttered, the sense which all nature had of its Creator rising in wrath, when the earth trembled, the rocks were rent asunder, and the grave gave up its dead, testify that they were such as God only could inflict, and the Son of God only could sustain.

Never was there sorrow like unto this sorrow wherewith the Lord now chastened him in the day of the fierceness of his anger. Upon his agony in the garden, an angel from heaven strengthened him. But in this hour, when he bore the sins of his people, when the pangs of death took hold of him, when the sorrows of hell encompassed him; in this hour of unutterable woe, where were the heavenly messengers, and where was the countenance of his Father, which used to comfort him, and to smile upon him? Alas! from his Father proceeded those very sufferings, the severest of all which he was now experiencing. From him came the cup of trembling, which he was now doomed to drink, and the vials of vengeance which were now poured upon his head. Abandoned and smitten, and overwhelmed, he cried out, "My God, my God! why hast *thou* forsaken me?"

The measure of his woe was now full: the sufferings of Christ were completed. Before he bowed the head and yielded up the ghost, he looked up to the heavens, and saw the darkness disappearing from before the throne of God. Filled with celestial satisfaction, "Father," said he, "into thy hands I now commit my spirit." There was but one pang more. The last cloud was vanishing from the sky, and all was to be serene for ever.

From such a subject, Christians, what sentiments arise in your breasts and what reflections ought we to conclude with? How is the condition of our Redeemer now changed! From a scene of terror and distress, he is exalted to the right hand of the Majesty in the heavens. As the sun broke out from the eclipse which it then suffered, so did the light of his Father's countenance upon his soul. Shame, and sorrow, and suffering, were succeeded by glory, and victory, and triumph.

What consolation does not this yield to Christians in all their afflictions! The high-priest under the Law was taken from among men, that he might have compassion on the ignorant, and on those who were out of the way; for that he himself was also compassed with infirmity. So likewise "we have not a high-priest who cannot be touched with the feeling of our infirmities, but was in all points tempted like as we are, but without sin." "It behoved him to be made like unto his brethren, that he might be a merciful and faithful high-priest, in things pertaining to God, to make reconciliation for the sins of the people: for in that he himself hath suffered, being tempted, he is able to succor them that are tempted."

I shall conclude with another reflection. Persons of humane and compassionate feelings, when they hear the account of their Saviour's sufferings, are apt to be moved with pity for his distresses, and to be actuated with indignation against his enemies. But these passions, in the present case, my brethren, are misapplied. 'Weep not for me, ye daughters of Jerusalem," said our Lord, when in the midst of his sufferings. These sufferings were not intended to excite the sighs of sensibility, and the tears of distress. Sympathy is not the proper return for his love. His sufferings are the objects of your faith, and ought to awaken your gratitude. Neither vent your wrath against the enemies and the crucifiers of your Saviour. Look inwards, O man! search thine own bosom: there dwell the murderers of thy Lord. Thy sins, thy crimes, thine unhallowed desires and unmortified passions were the actors in that dreadful scene. The Jews and Romans were but instruments in *their* hands: but the feeble executioners of that wrath which *they* provoked and drew down. On these, therefore, exhaust thy vengeance: bring forth those enemies of thy Saviour, and slay them before his eyes.

How will it affect the mind with contrition and godly sorrow, when, on this solemn occasion, you call up your past sins to your remembrance! How will it grieve you to think, as one by one they pass before you in review, that each of them added a pang to your Saviour's agony, and formed the bitter ingredients of that cup which he drank! Will not this consideration break your covenant with death, and disannul your agreement with hell? Can you ever again cherish those sins in your heart, which not only crucified the Lord of glory upon Mount Calvary, but which even now crucify him afresh, and put him to open shame?

But, Christians, I hope better things of you. On this occasion, let me beseech you, by the sufferings of your crucified Redeemer, to break off your iniquities by repentance. Resolve sincerely, by the grace of God, to live no longer in sin. Finally, implore the assistance of the Divine Spirit, to renew your wills, and purify your souls. Then may ye rejoice in this the day of your solemnity, and be welcome guests at the table of the Lord. Then shall ye be joyfully invited to the marriage-supper of the Lamb. Then shall Jesus manifest himself to you in the breaking of bread. He shall say unto your souls, "Be of good cheer, thy sins are forgiven thee;" and inspire into you the well-grounded hope of sitting down with him at his table above, where in his presence ye shall rejoice for evermore. Which may God grant, and to his name be the praise!—Let us pray.

10

SERMON XXXIV.

ON THE RESURRECTION OF JESUS CHRIST.

MATTHEW XXVIII. 6.—"Come, see the place where the Lord lay."

WHEN our Saviour expired upon the cross, the cause of Christianity seemed to be lost. Rejected by that nation to whom he was sent, condemned under the forms of a legal trial, and crucified as a malefactor before all the people, an effectual bar seemed to have been put for ever to all his designs. It then seemed that all was over. A people whom their prophets taught to look for a king, did not look for him to come down from a cross; a nation who expected the appearance of a Messiah, did not expect him to appear from the grave. His followers were few in number, and feeble in spirit. Although he had frequently foretold his death, the idea of a temporal prince was so strong in their minds, that they could not reconcile themselves to the thought of a suffering Saviour; and though he had also on various occasions foretold his resurrection, they were so much under the power of prejudices, deeply rooted, that they either did not understand, or did not believe, his predictions. When he was apprehended by a band of soldiers, they forsook him and fled; they had not courage to attend him in the last hour of his life; to go with him to the tribunal and to the cross: afar off only, they followed with their eyes, and beheld with tears, him whom they expected to behold no more. Then they gave up all for lost. The sun, which was soon after darkened by a preternatural eclipse, and the rock which was rent asunder by an earthquake, appeared to be the sad tokens of a glory that had departed, and of a kingdom that was to be no more.

Dark and dismal were the shades of that night which descended on the Saviour's tomb: the hearts of the disciples were troubled, and their Comforter was gone.

All the scenes of their past lives, the miracles they had seen, the discourses they had heard, the hopes they had entertained, were like a dream; they abandoned themselves to despair, and, as we learn from the evangelist Luke, they were about to leave Jerusalem, and betake themselves to their old employments.

While the enemies of Jesus triumphed, and his friends lamented, the counsels of heaven were executing, and the operation of the Almighty was going forward. We read in the Gospel of Matthew—"In the end of the Sabbath, as it began to dawn towards the first day of the week, came Mary Magdalene, and the other Mary, to see the sepulchre. And behold, there was a great earthquake; for the angel of the Lord descended from heaven, and came and rolled back the stone from the door, and sat upon it. His countenance was like lightning, and his raiment white as snow. And for fear of him, the keepers did shake, and became as dead men. And the angel answered and said unto the women, Fear not ye: For I know that ye seek Jesus, which was crucified. He is not here: For he is risen, as he said: Come, see the place where the Lord lay."

The nativity of our Lord had been announced by an angel to the shepherds of Bethlehem. "While they were abiding in the field, and keeping watch over their flocks by night, Lo, the angel of the Lord came unto them, and the glory of the Lord shone round about them; and the angel said unto them, Fear not, for behold I bring unto you glad tidings of great joy, which shall be unto all people; for unto you is born this day, in the city of David, a Saviour, which is Christ the Lord." In like manner, his second nativity, his resurrection to a new life, was here announced by an angel. What emotions would arise in the minds of these ministers of heaven, who had attended him through his life, we cannot tell: this only we know, that "into these things they desire to look." Much more then doth it become us to contemplate the life and death and resurrection of our Lord; for he took not on him the nature of angels, but of the seed of Abraham. Christians! you have this day beheld your Saviour set forth crucified among you; let us now contemplate him as arising from the dead, and appearing in glory: you have already sat at the foot of the cross, and I hope reaped benefit from the commemoration of your Redeemer's passion; let me now carry you to the tomb, to behold "the place where the Lord lay."

Behold then, in the *first* place, in the resurrection of your Lord, the proof that the redemption of the world is accomplished.

Our salvation is every where ascribed in Scripture, to the death and passion of our Saviour. As our great High Priest, he made an atonement for the sins of the world upon the cross; his death was our redemption, and his blood the ransom that was paid for the soul: but his resurrection was the proof, that the sacrifice which he offered up was accepted by God, and that the price which he paid, was available for our recovery. By his suffering unto death, we were freed from condemnation; but our freedom was not made manifest till he arose from the grave. His resurrection then is the basis of the whole Christian institution, and the ground of our faith and of our hope in him. That Christ appeared on earth as a Great Prophet; that he passed his days in instructing and reforming the world; and that after a life of eminent and exemplary goodness, he died the death of a malefactor, was common to him and others, whom God had raised up to be the lights of the world, and patterns to mankind. Thus the prophets of old were persecuted and destroyed by sundry kinds of death; thus the martyrs, since the time of our Lord, were cut off in a cruel and ignominious manner: but in *their* deaths there was no expiation for sin; the blood of the prophets and of the martyrs spoke no such language; their blood cried, indeed, to heaven—not for mercy, but for vengeance against a guilty world. If Christ had died like one of them, and been heard of no more, how should we have believed that his death had atoned to the penitent, for all the blood that had been shed from the foundation of the world? How should we have believed that the whole earth had obtained remission of sin from God, by destroying one prophet more? Although he had declared, that he was to be offered up as a sacrifice, and to give his life a ransom for many, if he had never appeared again, How should we have known that the sacrifice was accepted, or that the ransom was paid? The natural conclusion then to be drawn was, that his labors had been in vain. Then might we have said with the disciples, who were going to Emmaus, "We trusted that it had been He who was to have redeemed Israel;" but now all our hopes are buried in his grave. When he burst the bands of death, and rose victorious from the tomb, then it was manifest to all, that he had finished the work which the Father gave him to do. For if he had not accomplished his undertaking, and expiated the sins of the world, he had never been released from the prison of the grave. When he arose, therefore, and brought back with him the pardon which he had sealed with his blood; when, instead of executing wrath upon his enemies, he sent again the offer of peace and reconciliation, and took upon himself to be their intercessor, as he had already been their sacrifice, what room was there to doubt of the efficacy of his death, the efficacy of which was so undeniably confirmed by his resurrection?

Here, therefore, we hail the completion of that plan by which the world was to be redeemed; here we rejoice over the finishing of the new heavens and new earth, wherein righteousness is to dwell, and come to the close of the celestial song, which ascribed glory to God in the highest, peace upon the earth, and good will towards men. Now we may join in the triumphant language of the apostle, "It is God that justifieth, Who is he that condemneth? It is Christ that died, yea rather that is risen, who is even at the right hand of God, who also maketh intercession for us." As if he had said, "Who can condemn those whom God hath justified, and for whom Christ hath died? Our great High Priest hath now offered up the sacrifice which was requisite for the redemption of the world. The wrath of God is atoned; the guilt of sin is taken away; peace is made between God and man; and there is joy in heaven over the world of the redeemed." That this sacrifice was acceptable and meritorious in the sight of God, he hath testified unto all men, by raising his Son from the dead, by exalting him to his own right hand, and committing to him the sceptre of Providence, to rule and govern for the good of his Church.

In the *second* place, Christians, behold your Saviour at his resurrection, entering into his glory.

His first appearance was not distinguished by marks of greatness or splendor. The wise men who came from the east to worship the King of the Jews, expected not to find him a babe at Bethlehem, lying in a manger. Descended of humble parents, and born in a mean condition, he passed his early life in obscurity, and in the labors of poverty. What the Prophet calls the "stem from Jesse," was, at its first appearance, but a root out of a dry ground; it had no form nor comeliness, for which it could have been desired. Hitherto it had been only unknown and obscure; and at the time of his appearing unto Israel, he was a man of sorrows, and acquainted with grief. But even while he stood forth in the power of the Lord, and confirmed his mission by the miracles which he wrought, the opposition to him increased, and every act of charity he did to others, became a new source of misery to himself. During this time in which he went about doing good to all the sons of men, he had not where to lay his head. When he cast out devils, he was immediately charged with being in league with the prince of them. When he sat with publicans and sinners, he was called a glutton and a wine-bibber. When he healed the sick of their infirmities, and forgave their sins, then was he called a blasphemer, and an encroacher on the prerogative of God. When he restored the withered hand, and cured the blind or the lame on the Sabbath-day, then is he no longer fit to live. These were such offences as nothing but his death could expiate. And to death at last they brought him. He is betrayed by one of his own disciples, and carried to judgment. He is charged with the most opprobrious crimes. In cruel sport they pay him the mock honors of a prince; they crown him with thorns; they put a reed into his hand; they bow the knee before him, and, with profane and impious derision, cry, "Hail, King of the Jews." And that nothing might be wanting, to show how much he was despised and rejected of men, the question was put between him and a murderer, which should be released; and with one voice, the people answered, "Release unto us Barabbas." He was then nailed to the accursed tree, and died the death of a malefactor.

And is this the Messiah whom the Jews expected, and whom the prophets had foretold? Is this He, concerning whom Isaiah had prophesied, "Unto us a Son is born, unto us a Child is given, and his name shall be called Wonderful, Counsellor, the Mighty God, the everlasting Father, the Prince of Peace?" Is this he who was to raise up the tabernacle of David; who was to repair the desolations of many ages; who was to sit upon the throne of Zion, extend his dominion from sea to sea, and from the river to the ends of the earth? Yes, it is he! But, as the Scriptures foretold, he must suffer before he enter into his glory. Hence, saith the same prophet, when he shall be stricken for the transgression of the people, and make his soul an offering for sin, then he shall prolong his days, and the pleasure of the Lord shall prosper in his hand. At his resurrection, the prophesies of the Old Testament are understood, and the scandal of the cross is wiped away. The history of the man of sorrows ends, and the Lord of Glory appears. A brighter train of years begins, and a new era of happy time revolves. From the cloud which had concealed him long, he now issues forth in the beauties of immortality; from the veil which had obscured him in the days of his flesh, the splendor of his divinity now shines forth; celestial rays circle and distinguish his head; and he appears to be the Son of God with power, when he comes in triumph from the tomb, having subdued the powers of death, and leading captivity captive. He now sees the travail of his soul, and is satisfied; he enters on the joy that was set before him; and has all power committed to him in heaven and in earth.

In the *third* place, Christians, behold in the resurrection of your Lord, your nature restored to its original dignity.

Man was at first made after the image of God, clothed with the robe of innocence, and crowned with the honors of immortality. There was no discord among the principles of his frame; no darkness in his mind, and no disorder in his heart. Happy and harmonious was the temper of his soul. Order, the great law of heaven, was also the law of man. He had a paradise without, and a fairer paradise within. But by his disobedience and fall he became a different person: his nature was degraded, and his dignity was lost. He who was the Lord of the inferior world, and was invested with dominion over the works of nature, was now sunk into a state little superior to the beasts that perish. This change was the death of the man whom God had created; the divine life was no more; the image of God lay buried under the ruins of iniquity. Hence the human form in Scripture is called a "body of death;" and the world is said to be "dead in trespasses and sins." But as by man came death, by man came also the resurrection to life. As in Adam all die, so in Christ all are made alive. "The creature was made subject to vanity, not willingly." We consented not to the degradation of our nature; and he who subjected us in hope hath restored us again. Christ rose as the representative of all his people; as the Leader of an innumerable multitude who shall follow him into the heavens. Hence we are said in Scripture to be begotten again by the resurrection of Christ from the dead; to be made alive with Christ; to be risen with him; and sit with him in heavenly places. Here then you behold your nature rising anew from the tomb of Christ; fair as when it first came from the hands of the Creator, when he saw his own image, and pronounced it good. Here you behold it rising with additional honor; made at first a little lower than the angels, it was assumed by one who was greater than they, and is now dignified in heaven by him before whose throne the angels of God worship.

In the *last* place, Christians, behold in

the resurrection of Christ, the proof and the earnest of your own resurrection.

Our Saviour not only taught the immortality of the soul, but also the resurrection of the body. This doctrine was new to the world, and contrary to the observation of mankind; for there is nothing in the whole compass of nature, that yields a similitude to dust and ashes rising up again into organised bodies, and to perpetual life. It required therefore a proof of a particular kind, which it obtained; for as a proof that the dead were to arise, our Saviour arose from the dead. Hence God is said to have given assurance to all men of the general resurrection, by raising his Son from the dead. This subject is handled professedly, and at great length, by the apostle Paul, in a most eloquent discourse to the Corinthians, part of which I shall now read to you. 1 Cor. xv. 20, 21, 22, 23. "But now is Christ risen from the dead, and became the first fruits of them that slept. For since by man came death, by man came also the resurrection of the dead. For as in Adam all die, even so in Christ shall all be made alive. But every man in his own order: Christ the first-fruits; afterwards they that are Christ's, at his coming."

In the times of the apostle, this doctrine was more felt than it is now; a strong impression of immortality did then animate the disciples of Jesus. From whence, but from this doctrine, proceeded the zeal and spirit of the primitive Christians, who embraced the religion of Jesus at the expense of all that was dear, and at the peril of their lives. The sword of the persecutor had no terrors, when they saw it succeeded by a crown of glory. When they looked on the shore of bliss and immortality, they trembled not, though they knew they had to swim through a sea of blood. Even when death was before their eyes, their hearts sprung with joy, and their hopes began to bloom. Not the frown of the tyrant, nor the face of the king of terrors, nor the executioner that thirsted for blood, could rob them of their peace. They looked upon these as messengers sent by Providence, to carry them to that better world where their hearts longed to be. This was the armor by which the saints and martyrs overcame the world; by which they triumphed over pain, and ignominy, and death, and looked upon fires and racks, and gibbets, upon every engine of torture, and every form of dissolution, as so many doors opening into the kingdom of glory. They were invincible, because they knew they were immortal.

From the doctrines which have been now laid down, let us conclude with some inferences and reflections.

Christians, you are the disciples of a risen Redeemer. As we glory in his cross and passion, let us also rejoice in his resurrection. The disciples were glad when they saw their Lord restored to life again; and the first Christians considered it as such a joyful event, that they used to greet one another with this salutation, "Christ is risen." He who was once dead, is now alive, and lives for evermore. He hath removed the terror and the sting of death; he hath hallowed the grave as a place of rest for all his followers, and risen as the Forerunner of the faithful, who shall rise to eternal life. He left the vestments of mortality behind him. Death hath no more dominion. And if ye be risen with Christ, put off the old man and his affections; let sin have no more dominion over you; walk in newness of life. As you have set out in the paths of righteousness, continue your course therein. Religion was not intended for extraordinary occasions. Holiness is not a robe which you can put off and on at pleasure. You must never lay aside the wedding garment. Transient emotions which you may now feel, will not change the heart. Starts and sallies of goodness which you may now experience, will not form the character. The temper of the mind, and the tenor of the life are all in all. When religion and virtue have been matured by time, and grown into habit, then we can pronounce them to be sincere and genuine. Let him that is righteous then, be righteous still. Let him that is holy, be holy still. Let the spirit of this day accompany you all the days of your lives. Carry into the world, into the business and into the pleasures of the world, the purity of this ordinance, the dispositions you now feel, and the purposes you now form. Be faithful unto death, and God will give you the crown of life. Further, As ye have gained the victory over death, through our Lord Jesus Christ, therefore be assured, that a life of faith and duty will effectually conduct you to happiness. "Therefore, my beloved brethren, be ye steadfast, immovable, always abounding in the work of the Lord, forasmuch as ye know that your labor is not in vain in the Lord." Miserable indeed would be the condition of the human kind; feeble would be our efforts, and few our attainments, if after a well-ordered life, we were obliged to sit down with the sad confession, that virtue was but an empty name; that we had cleansed our hands in vain, and purified our hearts to no purpose. But, Christians, our labor shall not be in vain; our works of faith and love, our exertions of magnanimity, our efforts of patience in the cause of goodness; the tender offices of humanity, charity, and pity, that we have performed, the kind dispositions that we have cherished or improved, the upright intentions which we have maintained, even the silent aspirations of a good heart, the warm wishes of the benevolent, for the happiness of the human kind, are now well-pleasing in the sight of God. We know, even from our own experience, that there is a reward for the righteous. Never have we done a good deed, but we have obtained the gratulations of our own conscience, and enjoyed the triumph of the mind.

Let the wicked call upon the mountains to overwhelm, and the rocks to hide them in the day of the Lord. Let infidels look for the shades of annihilation to conceal them, and the curtains of the dark night to be drawn around them for ever. Better prospects are presented to us. The hope of immortality is set before us, and heaven opens its everlasting gates to receive us to its mansions.

Because of this our heart is glad, and our glory rejoiceth. The Everlasting Father will not leave us in the grave, nor suffer his holy ones to see corruption. He hath shewed us the path of life. In his presence there is fulness of joy, and at his right hand there are pleasures for evermore. Know then thyself, O man! Make thyself acquainted with thy future state. Enter early, my brethren, upon your eternal life; and now think, and act, and live, as the heirs of immortality. Implore the Divine goodness to give you the spirit of that better country to which you tend, and to bless you with a foretaste of the joys which are to come. And in the strength of Heaven, go forth from this assembly, immortal; go forth into the world, the sons of God, the heirs of heaven, candidates for a crown of glory which fadeth not away. Then you will have good cause to remember this day, as one of the days of the right hand of the Most High, and to endless ages you will bless the time when you retired from the vanities of the world, and learned to meditate at your Saviour's tomb.

Now may the God of peace, who brought again from the dead our Lord Jesus, that great Shepherd of the sheep, make you perfect in every good work, to do his will, working in you that which is well-pleasing in his sight, through Jesus Christ; to whom be glory for ever and ever. *Amen.*

SERMON XXXV.

ON A LIFE OF PROGRESSIVE VIRTUE.

PROVERBS IV. 18.—"The path of the just is as the shining light, that shineth more and more unto the perfect day."

HUMAN life has been often compared to a journey, for this as well as for other reasons, that we are always making progress in our way. In whatever path we set out, there is no standing still. Evil men wax worse and worse: the corruptions of their nature gather strength: the vices which they have contracted grow into habit; the evil principle is for ever on the increase, till having attained the ascendent over the whole man, it subjects him entirely to its own power, the willing and obedient servant of sin. Good men, on the other hand, make advances in the paths of righteousness. The grace of God, which is given unto them, lies not dormant. The better mind with which they are endowed, incites them to virtue; the new nature which they have put on, pants after perfection. They give all diligence to add to their faith virtue, and to virtue temperance, and to temperance brotherly-kindness, and to brotherly-kindness charity; until, having abounded in every good work, they perfect holiness in the fear of the Lord. Such a life is here called the *path of the just.* By the just in Scripture, are not meant those who merely abstain from doing unjust and injurious things to their neighbors. The just man is he who possesses that sincerity of heart, and that integrity of the whole life, which God requires of man.

The life of such a man is here compared to the light of the morning. Nothing in nature is more lovely than the light. When the Spirit began to move upon the face of the deep, light was the first effect of his creating power; and when the six days' work was finished, light, collected and centred in the sun, continued to be the grandest and most beautiful work of nature; so grand and beautiful, that among many of the heathen nations it was worshipped as the visible divinity of the world. What light is to the face of external nature, the beauty of holiness is to the soul. It is the brighest ornament of an immortal spirit; it throws a glory over all the faculties of man; and forms that robe of beauty with which *they* shine, who walk in *white* before the throne of God.

But it is chiefly on account of its progressive nature, that the path of the just is here compared to the shining light. In order to illustrate this, I shall, in the *first* place, show you how we shall know if we have made progress in the paths of righteousness. *Secondly*, give you some directions how to make farther progress. *Thirdly*, exhort you to a life of progressive virtue.

I am first, then, to show how we shall know if we have made progress in the paths of righteousness.

In the *first* place, Let me ask you, are you sensible of your faults and imperfections? The first indication of wisdom is to confess our ignorance, and the first step to virtue is to be sensible of our own imperfections. The novice in science is puffed up with his early discoveries; when the first ray of wisdom is let in upon his mind, he thinks that by it he can see and know all things; deeper views and maturer reflection convince him how little he knows. In like manner, he knows little of religion, and has been but a short time in the school of Christ, who is blind to his own imperfections. Our fall from innocence was by pride, and we must rise by humility. "He that humbleth himself shall be exalted," is the doctrine which our Lord delivered upon all occasions. Till we feel our own weakness, we can never be strong in the Lord; we never can rise in the Divine sight, till we sink in our own estimation. We often meet with persons in life, who talk very strangely upon this subject. They tell us that they are as good as ever they expect to be; that in looking back upon their past life, they see nothing done which they would wish undone; and that if they were to begin life anew, they would act precisely as they have acted. Concerning such persons, we may safely pronounce that they have made but little progress in the path of the just. They are strangers to their own hearts, and have not proper ideas of the Divine law. They measure the law of God by the laws of men, and think that if their external conduct is blameless, they have acted their part well; not considering that the law of God extends to the heart, and punishes for the omission of duty as well as for the commission of sin. Such errors the Pharisees taught of old; and such notions of duty Paul had imbibed before his conversion to Christianity. "After the straitest sect of our religion," says he, "I lived a Pharisee; touching the law, blameless. I was alive without the law once:" That is, when I did not know the law in its true sense, I thought myself alive and a saint. The Pharisaical doctrines in which he had been educated, taught him that God required no more than a conformity of the external behavior to the letter of the law. But when he discovered that the Divine law extended to the heart, when thus in its power, the commandment came, "sin revived and I died;" then I saw myself to be a sinner, and died to the self-conceit which I formerly entertained.

Secondly, Let me ask you what is the strength of your attachment to the cause of righteousness? As you are sensible of your faults, and have seen the deformity of sin, are you enamored with the beauty of holiness? Do you desire nothing more earnestly than to put on the graces of the Gospel, and be conformed to the image of God? Men will never imitate what they do not love; if then you are not lovers of goodness and virtue, you never will be good and virtuous. So long as they keep to generals, men may easily deceive themselves. Let us then come to particulars, and let me ask you with what regard and estimation you view those patterns of piety which you see exhibited in life. Are the good and righteous, to you the *excellent ones* of the earth? The wise do not proportion their respect to men according to the rank they hold, or the name they bear in the world. It is the character of the just man, as drawn in Scripture, that he scorneth the vile, however exalted, and honoreth them that fear the Lord, however depressed. Do you then scorn the vile man, with all his attributes of rank and wealth and power? Do you despise the rich, the noble, the right honorable villain, and choose for your companion the righteous man, although he has not where to lay his head? Could you sit down with virtue in her cell, contented with her homely fare, with her poor abode, and look down with a generous contempt upon the splendid roof, where luxury and guilt lead on the festive hours? When you behold the wicked great in power, and flourishing like a green bay-tree, does your heart revolt from giving him that homage which the favors of Mammon never fail to extort from the venal multitude; and can you say, in the sincerity of your heart, "I would not exchange the peace of my own mind for the wealth of the world? Whatever thou art pleased to give, Father Almighty, may I possess it with honor: The world approaches to thine altar, and bends before thy throne for temporal blessings; the prayer of my heart is, *Lord, lift up on me the light of thy countenance.*"

Thirdly, Let me ask you, are your resolutions as firm, and your application as vigorous now, as when you first set out in the spiritual life? There are times in which all men are serious,—in which the most obdurate minds feel impressions of religion, and in which persons of the most abandoned character form resolutions of amendment. With all the zeal of new converts, they set about a thorough reformation. They wonder how they have been so long blind to their true interest; they mourn over the time that they have lost in vain, or in sinful pursuits, and now seem fully determined to follow religion as the one thing needful. With many, this course continues not long; the first new object engages their attention, and turns them aside from the path of the just. But true religion, my friends, does not consist in such fits and starts of devotion; in random resolutions, made in the fervor of zeal; in the wavering, desultory, and inconsistent conduct which marks the character of multitudes in the world. He alone is a good man who perseveres in goodness. When the vernal year begins, and the shower of summer descends, all nature bursts into vegetable life; the noxious weeds rival the trees among which they grow; but these sudden growths as suddenly disappear; while favored by the influences of heaven, the trees arise to their full stature, and bring forth their fruit in season. Are you then as much in earnest now, as when your first love to God began to bring forth the fruits of righteousness? Without this undiminished ardor, without these unremitting efforts, you never will run the race set before you, so as to finish your course with joy. At the same time, I must take notice, that as you advance in years, all the passions will gradually cool. When, therefore, the fervor of youth has subsided, and mature age hath given a sober cast to the temper, you will not feel that degree of ardor in your devotions which you experienced in your early years. Many serious persons have been alarmed at this appearance, not considering that it was the effect of their constitution, and not a mark of apostasy from God. But your devotion will continue as sincere, though not so inflamed, as before, and religion will be as effectual as ever in the regulation of your life; like a mighty river, before it terminates its course in the ocean, it rolls with greater calmness, but at the same time with a greater strength, than when it arose from its source.

Fourthly, Another mark of increasing grace is, when you obey the Divine commandments from affection and love. They who, from the fear of hell, put on a form of religion for a time, find it to be a hard and a painful service. They are out of their place, when they strike into the path of the just; they consider religion as a heavy burden, which they would not bear but from necessity, and look upon the duties of the Christian life, as so many tasks which they have to perform. Whoever entertains such notions of religion, will not rise to high attainments in righteousness. The passions and affections are the powerful springs of action in the soul; and unless these are put in motion, the machine will move heavily along. He alone will make progress in the path of the just, who is drawn by the cords of love. Pleasant are the labors of love; and sweet is the precept when the duty pleases. The yoke is easy, and the burden light, when the heart goes along. The Christian is not a slave who obeys from compulsion, or a servant who works for hire; he is a son who acts from filial affection, and is happiest when he obeys. The love of Christ alone constraineth him. The beauty of holiness allureth him: though rewards and punishments were set aside, he would follow religion and virtue for their own sake, and do his duty, because therein he found his happiness. Do you then, my friends, feel this affection, this passion for righteousness? Can you say with the Psalmist, "How do I love thy laws, O Lord? They are my meditation all the day. More to be desired they are than gold, than much fine gold; sweeter than honey from the honeycomb."

I now come to the *second* thing proposed, to give you some directions how to make further progress in the path of the just.

In the *first* place, then, in order to this, make a serious business of a holy life. There are many persons in the world who give a sanction to piety by their example, but who feel very little of its power. They think religion an exceedingly decent thing; they see it patronized by all wise men, and they know it to be necessary for the purposes of society. For these reasons they follow the faith, and conform to the usages of their fathers: they pay a proper respect to the institutions of the Church; and they attend upon the ordinances of Divine worship with all the marks of external reverence. So far their conduct is not only decent, but laudable. But if they go no farther than this; if they confine their sanctity to these walls; if they think that they have done their duty, when they have complied with the external ceremonies of the Church, and have adopted this as the easiest and most compendious method of being religious; the religion of such persons is rather a kind of good manners than real devotion. The true Christian will not be deficient in his attention to the externals of religion; but he will not rest there; he will attend upon the ordinances of public worship, not because it is the custom of the country, but because it is his duty to God; and he will observe the institutions of Christianity, not from complaisance to established usages, but from a sincere desire of making progress in righteousness. We must make piety more than a matter of form; we must make a study of a holy life, in order to advance from strength to strength, in the ways of the Lord: it is with religion, my friends, as with the other pursuits of life. In those arts where success depends upon genius and industry, unless a man have an enthusiasm for his own profession, unless he follow it from choice, and prefer it to all others, he will never rise to eminence and fame. In like manner, unless a man have an attachment of the heart to the cause of virtue; unless he be fervent in spirit to serve the Lord; unless he prefer a good conscience to everything upon earth, he will never obtain that crown of glory which is reserved for the righteous. In his journey through life the pilgrim may turn aside to behold a beautiful scene, or enjoy a passing delight; but he will never forget that his chief object is his journey to the promised land.

In order to attain eminence in the arts just mentioned, the candidate devotes his best and happiest years; lives laborious days and restless nights; makes a sacrifice of ease, and health, and social joy; and at last consoles himself by the triumphant prospect of lying down upon the bed of fame, and living to future ages. If, then, studies of inferior importance become such a serious concern; if the desire of an imaginary immortality has such power over the mind; will this noblest of studies, the science of being good, have no attractions for the soul? Will this passion for a real immortality have no power over the heart? Under the influence of this principle, will not every one who has the faith of a Christian, or the feelings of a man, join with the apostle, "Yea, doubtless, I count all things but loss, for the excellency of the knowledge of Christ Jesus my Lord,—that I may know him, and the power of his resurrection and the fellowship of his sufferings, being made conformable to his death, if by any means I may attain to the resurrection of the dead." Under the influence of these principles, will not every person who desires to make advances in the path of the just, adopt also the resolution of Job, "While my breath is in me, and the Spirit of God is in my nostrils, my lips shall not speak wickedness, nor my tongue utter deceit; till I die I will not remove mine integrity from me: my righteousness I hold fast, and will not let it go; my heart shall not reproach me so long as I live."

In the *second* place, in order to make progress in the path of the just, you must never rest satisfied with any degrees of holiness or virtue which you attain. The law of the spiritual life is to aim at perfection: the intention of Christianity is that we may stand perfect and complete in all the will of God. "As he who hath called you is holy, be ye holy in all manner of conversation." Absolutely perfect, indeed, we can never become in this life; but we must be always aspiring and endeavoring after perfection. There is no end of your journey till you come to heaven; there is no place by the way where you are to expect a termination from labor, or a period of repose. It is not uncommon to hear persons express themselves in terms of great indifference about the higher attainments in sanctity and virtue. They seem to be much afraid of being better than their neighbors; they have no ambition, they say, to be saints; they do not desire to rank among the very best; and they would be content with the lowest place in heaven. Happy, beyond all controversy, shall he be, who shall obtain a place, though the lowest, in the heavenly mansions; but for men to mark out to themselves boundaries in the path of virtue, beyond which they are resolved not to go; for men, with impious presumption, to cut out to themselves just such a portion of duty as they think will entitle them to an inestimable reward; this is undervaluing the pearl of great price; it is sacrificing the riches of the Divine goodness to their own indolence; it is doing despite to that Spirit of grace which might have been a powerful principle of advancing holiness in the heart. Had he to whom in the parable ten talents were given, gained no more than he to whom five were given, can you think that he would have obtained the title, and received the reward of a good and faithful servant? No, but of a slothful and unprofitable one, who had not improved aright the deposit of his Master. What saith the apostle upon this subject? "Brethren, I count not myself to have apprehended;" to have already attained perfection; "but this one thing I do; forgetting the things which are behind, and reaching forth unto those things which are before, I press toward the mark, for the prize of the high calling of God in Christ Jesus."

"Forgetting the things that are behind," saith the apostle. What things had this apostle to forget? He had to forget his labors in the course of his apostolical functions, his unwearied zeal, his unremitting industry in discharging the trust committed to him; his perilous journeys and voyages over the greatest part of the known world, to propagate the religion of Jesus; the many noted persons he converted by his ministry; the many flourishing churches he erected in the course of his travels; the many famous nations he brought over to the Christian Faith;—he had to forget what of all things the best men pride themselves most in, the persecutions which he suffered for the sake of the Lord; the imprisonments which he endured, the wounds which he received, and the stripes which he bore as a witness of truth, and a preacher of righteousness; —he had to forget that he was not behind the very chiefest apostles; the many miracles which he wrought; the frequent revelations that were made to him;—he had to forget that, in the vision of God, he had ascended into the third heaven, and was admitted to scenes, the beauties and the joys of which, eye hath not seen, ear hath not heard, and the heart of man cannot conceive. If, notwithstanding such a high degree of grace and favor; if, after a life of such extraordinary piety, this apostle forgot the things which were behind, and reaching forth to the things which were before, pressed toward the mark, for the prize of the high calling of God in Christ Jesus; where is the man who can pretend to say, "I am already as perfect as I can ever expect to be?" Where is the man who is entitled to set a boundary to himself in the path of righteousness, saying, "Hitherto shall I go, but no further?"

In the *third* place, in order to make progress in the path of the just, be always employed in the improvement of your souls. There is no standing still in the path of heaven. Your evil habits, those cords that hold you in captivity to sin, you may not perhaps be able to cast away at once; but through the Divine grace, you will insensibly weaken, and at last break them asunder. Your inclinations that may have taken a wrong bent, you may counteract, and at last recover to their original rectitude. Where nature favors a particular exertion, or habit has formed you to a particular virtue, the one you may cherish, the other you may cultivate; upon both the fruits of righteousness will grow. Afterwards, be still attending to the culture of the soul, and meditating improvements, by calling forth graces that have not yet made their appearance, and bringing forward to perfection those that have. Thus will your minds resemble those trees, in which, at one and the same time, we behold some fruits arrived at full maturity; some half advanced and others just formed in the opening blossom. By cultivating these graces in the soul, you will not only have an earnest, but also an image of heaven. The trees which thus grow up by the rivers of water, which bring forth their fruit in their season, and whose leaves continue ever green, shall be transplanted to happier climes, to adorn the paradise of God.

In the *fourth* and *last* place, in order to make your endeavors effectual, you must abound in prayer to God for the assistance of his Holy Spirit. "No man becomes good without the Divine influence. No man can rise above the infirmities of nature unless aided by God. He inspires great and noble purposes. In every good man God resides. The strength which renders a man superior to all those things which the people either hope or dread, descends from him. So lofty a structure cannot stand unsupported by the Divinity." These, my friends, are the words of a heathen, and express a doctrine equally agreeable to reason and to revelation. In consequence of our corrupted nature, we are unable of ourselves to produce the virtues and graces of the Divine life. But we are not left without a remedy. In the gospel of Jesus Christ, aids are promised from above, to repair the ruins of our nature, and to restore the powers of the soul: God hath not forsaken the earth: as at the first of days, the Divine Spirit is still moving over the world to produce life. The Lord is ever nigh to them who call upon him in the sincerity of their heart. While we strive against sin, we may safely expect that the Divinity will strive with us, and impart that strength and power which will at last make us more than conquerors. As he who continues in wicked devices shall be sure to find Satan standing at his right hand, so he who begins a good life, shall find God befriending him with secret aid. He will assist the spirit that is struggling to break loose from the bonds of its captivity; he will aid the flight of the soul that is taking wing to the celestial mansions; he will support our feeble frame under the trials and conflicts to which we are appointed, and lead us on from grace to grace, till we appear in Zion above. "They that wait upon the Lord shall renew their strength; they shall mount up as on eagle's wings: they shall run and not be weary; they shall walk and not be faint."

I come now to the *last* thing proposed, to exhort you to a life of progressive virtue.

In the *first* place, then, it is your duty

to make progress in the ways of righteousness. In your sanctification, you are enabled more and more to die unto sin and live unto righteousness. It is not enough that you continue steadfast and immovable; you must also abound in the work of the Lord, if you expect your labors to be attended with success. It is not sufficient that you *continue* in well-doing; you must also grow in grace, and increase with all the increase of God. This progressive nature of righteousness is implied in all the figures and images by which a good life is represented in Sacred Scripture. It is compared to the least of all seeds, which waxes to a great tree, and spreads out its branches, and fills the earth. It is compared to the morning light, at first faintly dawning over the mountains, by degrees enlightening the face of the earth, ascending higher and higher in the heavens, and shining more and more unto the perfect day. We are said to be here at the school of Christ; and in order to attain the character of good disciples, we must not only retain what we have acquired, but also add to the acquisitions we have made. The Christian life is represented as a warfare, and in this warfare we shall never gain the victory, unless we not only maintain the ground we have got, but also gain upon the foe. It is represented as a race set before us, and in running it we must continually press forward, or we shall never gain the prize. Every degree of grace which you receive, and every pitch of virtue to which you attain, is a talent for which you are accountable; a talent, which if you only retain, but not improve, you will receive the doom of a slothful and wicked servant, and be cast into outer darkness. The Christian life is a life of continued exertion. At every stage in our pilgrimage on earth, new scenes will open; new situations will present themselves; and new paths to glory will be struck out. The sphere of action varies continually. We have, one while, to support adversity; another while, to adorn prosperity; sometimes to approve ourselves to God in solitude; at other times, to cause our light to shine before men in society. Different situations in the world, and different periods of life, require the exercise of different virtues. What is accepted from the young soldier will not be excused in the veteran; what is an "ornament of grace" to the youthful brow, will not be a "crown of glory" to the hoary head.

Secondly, Let me exhort you to this life of progressive virtue, from the pleasing consideration that you will be successful in the attempt. In the pursuit of human honors and rewards, the successful candidates are few. In a race many run, but one only gains the prize. But here all who run may obtain. In the career of human glory, time and chance happen unto all, and many are disappointed. "The race is not always to the swift, nor the battle to the strong; nor riches to men of understanding; nor favor to men of skill." There is a concurrence of circumstances required to raise a man to reputation; and when these circumstances concur, if the moment of opportunity be not embraced, the field of glory may be lost for ever. In human life there is a favorable hour which never returns, and a call to fame which is repeated no more: even in its best estate, men ought to lay their account with disappointment and vexation. What thou hast set thy heart upon from thy youth; what has been the aim of all thy labors; what has been the object of thy whole life, accident, artifice, ignorance, villany, caprice, may give to another whom thou knowest not. When thy ambition is all on fire; in the utmost ardor of expectation, in the very moment when thou stretchest out thy hand to grasp the prize, fortune may snatch it from thy reach for ever. Nay, thou mayest have the mortification to see others rise upon thy ruins, to see thyself made a step to the ambition of thy rival, and thy endeavors rendered the means of advancing him to the top of the wheel, while thou continuest low.

In the pursuits of ambition or avarice, you may be disappointed; but if by a progressive state of righteousness, you seek for glory and honor and immortality, I in the name of God assure you of success. Never was the gate of mercy shut against the true penitent; never was the prayer of the faithful rejected in the temple of heaven; never did the incense of a good life ascend without acceptance on high.

Liberal and unrestricted is the Divine benignity: free to all the fountain flows. There is no angel with a flaming sword to keep you from the tree of life. At this moment of time, there is a voice from Heaven calling to you, "Come up hither." And if you are obedient to the call, God assists you with the aid of his Spirit; he lifts up the hands that hang down; he strengthens the feeble knees, and perfects his strength in your weakness. You are not left alone to climb the arduous ascent. God is with you, who never suffers the spirit which rests on him to fail; nor the man who seeks his favor, to seek it in vain. Your success in the path of the just will not only be pleasing to yourselves, but also to all around you. In the struggles of human ambition, the triumph of one arises upon the sorrows of another; many are disappointed when one obtains the prize. But in the path of the just, there is emulation without envy, triumph without disappointment. The success of one increases the happiness of all. The influence of such an event is not confined to the earth: it is communicated to all good beings; it adds to the harmony of the Heavens; and is the occasion of new hosannas among the innumerable company of angels and spirits of just men made perfect, who rejoice over the sinner that repenteth.

Thirdly, Let me exhort you to make advances in the path of righteousness, from the beauty and the pleasantness of such a progress. Whatever difficulties may have attended your first entrance upon the path of the just, they will vanish by degrees; the steepness of the mountain will lessen as you ascend; the path, in which you have been accustomed to walk, will grow more and more beautiful; and the celestial mansions, to which you tend, will brighten with new splendor, the nearer that you approach them. In other affairs, continued exertion may occasion lassitude and fatigue. Labor may be carried to such an excess as to debilitate the body. The pursuits of knowledge may be carried so far as to impair the mind; but neither the organs of the body, nor the faculties of the soul, can be endangered by the practice of religion. On the contrary, this practice strengthens the powers of action. Adding virtue to virtue is adding strength to strength; and the greater acquisitions we make, we are enabled to make still greater.' How pleasant will it be to mark the soul thus moving forward in the brightness of its course! In the spring, who does not love to mark the progress of nature; the flower unfolding into beauty, the fruit coming forward to maturity, the fields advancing to the pride of harvest, and the months revolving into the perfect year? Who does not love in the human species, to observe the progress to maturity; the infant by degrees growing up to man; the young idea beginning to shoot, and the embryo character beginning to unfold? But if these things affect us with delight: if the prospect of external nature in its progress, if the flower unfolding unto beauty, if the fruit coming forward to maturity, if the infant by degrees growing up to man, and the embryo character beginning to unfold, affect us with pleasurable sensations, how much greater delight will it afford to observe the progress of this new creation, the growth of the soul in the graces of the divine life, good resolutions ripening into good actions, good actions leading to confirmed habits of virtue, and the new nature advancing from the first lineaments of virtue to the full beauties of holiness! These are pictures that time will not take away. While the animal spirits fail, and the joys which depend upon the liveliness of the passions decline with years, the solid comforts of a holy life, the delights of virtue and a good conscience, will be a new source of happiness in old age, and have a charm for the end of life. As the stream flows pleasantest when it approaches the ocean; as the flowers send up their sweetest odors at the close of the day; as the sun appears with greatest beauty in his going down; so at the end of his career, the virtues and graces of a good man's life come before him with the most blessed remembrance, and impart a joy which he never felt before. Over all the moments of life, religion scatters her favors, but reserves her best, her choicest, her divinest blessings for the last hour.

In the *last* place, Let me exhort you to this progressive state of virtue, from the pleasant consideration that it has no period. There are limits and boundaries set to all human affairs. There is an ultimate point in the progress, beyond which they never go, and from which they return in a contrary direction. The flower blossoms but to fade, and all terrestrial glory shines to disappear. Human life has its decline as well as its maturity; from a certain period the external senses begin to decay, and the faculties of the mind to be impaired, till dust returns unto dust. Nations have their day. States and kingdoms are mortal like their founders. When they have arived at the zenith of their glory, from that moment they begin to decline; the bright day is succeeded by a long night of darkness, ignorance, and barbarity. But in the progress of the mind to intellectual and moral perfection, there is no period set. Beyond these heavens the perfection and happiness of the just is carrying on; is carrying on, but shall never come to a close. God shall behold his creation for ever beautifying in his eyes; for ever drawing nearer to himself, yet still infinitely distant from the fountain of all goodness. There is not in religion a more joyful and triumphant consideration than this perpetual progress which the soul makes to the perfection of its nature, without ever arriving at its ultimate period. Here truth has the advantage of fable. No fiction, however bold, presents to us a conception so elevating and astonishing, as this interminable line of heavenly excellence. To look upon the glorified spirit as going on from strength to strength; adding virtue to virtue, and knowledge to knowledge; making approaches to goodness which is infinite; for ever adorning the Heavens with new beauties, and brightening in the splendors of moral glory through all the ages of eternity,—has something in it so transcendent and ineffable, as to satisfy the most unbounded ambition of an immortal spirit. Christian! does not thy heart glow at the thought, that there is a time marked out in the annals of Heaven, when thou shalt be what the angels now are; when thou shalt shine with that glory in which principalities and powers now appear; and when, in the full communion of the Most High, thou shalt see him as he is?

The oak, whose top ascends into the heavens, and which covers the mountains with its shade, was once an acorn, contemptible to the sight; the philosopher, whose views extend from one end of nature to the other, was once a speechless infant hanging at the breast; the glorified spirits who now stand nearest to the throne of God, were once like you. To you, as to them, the Heavens are open; the way is marked out; the reward is prepared. On what you do, on what you now do, all depends.

SERMON XXXVI.

ON REPENTANCE.

Acts xvii. 30.—"And the times of this ignorance God winked at; but now commandeth all men everywhere to repent."

This is part of a sermon which the apostle Paul delivered at Athens. The Athenians were the most ingenious and most illustrious people of Greece. Situated in a happy climate, and blessed with the highest degree of liberty which mankind can enjoy, they bent their genius to the cultivation of the sciences and arts. These they carried to such a pitch of perfection, as gained the palm from the contending world, and has attracted the eyes and admiration of all succeeding ages. But to show the darkness and the ignorance of the human mind when not enlightened by the wisdom which cometh from above, as soon as they turned themselves to religion, they displayed nothing but their own absurdities and follies. In place of a rational and liberal form of religion, a gross and stupid idolatry universally prevailed; in place of the true God, they bowed the knee to a dumb idol; and instead of the worship of the heart, consecrated to his service impure and profane observances. Zealous to destroy this fabric of superstition, the apostle Paul, rising in the midst of an assembly that was convened on the hill of Mars, reproved those masters of science, those lights of the Heathen world, with the boldness and the majesty of an apostle of the Lord. "Ye men of Athens, I perceive that in all things ye are too superstitious;—the times of this ignorance God winked at; but now commandeth all men everywhere to repent."

Repentance towards God is the great and leading duty enjoined both in the Old and in the New Testament. Along with every revelation of the Divine will, along with every new commission to prophets and holy men to preach this Divine will, the duty of repentance is alway inculcated in the strongest terms. The Patriarch Noah preached repentance to the world before the flood. John the Baptist began his public ministry by preaching the doctrine of repentance. "Except ye repent, ye shall perish," was the awful denunciation of our Lord. And his apostles constantly began or ended their sermons with exhortations to this duty. This message, so often delivered to the world, I now address to you; and demand your serious attention to this most important subject. And, in further treating upon it, I shall, in the *first* place, Explain to you the nature of repentance; and *secondly*, Lay before you the motives which ought to influence your minds to the practice of this duty.

The *first* thing proposed, was, To explain the nature of true repentance.

Repentance unto life, as it is well defined in that excellent summary of theology, the Shorter Catechism, is "a saving grace, whereby a sinner, out of a true sense of his sin, and apprehension of the mercy of God in Christ, doth, with grief and hatred of his sin, turn from it unto God, with full purpose of, and endeavor after, new obedience." According to this definition, repentance includes, *first*, A true sense of sin; *secondly*, Grief and hatred of sin; *thirdly*, Apprehension of the mercy of God in Christ, the forsaking of sin, and endeavoring after new obedience.

First, A true sense of sin. This must be the ground-work of all the rest, because it is impossible to hate what we do not feel. It is impossible to conceive a hatred and aversion against a thing of which we are not sensible, or to flee from a danger of which we have no apprehension. Where there is no sense of sin, therefore, there can be no repentance. Accordingly the Pharisee, who trusted in himself that he was righteous, was too proud, even when he was praying to God, to confess any guilt of his own. "God, I thank thee," says he, "that I am not as other men are." He was conscious, it seems, of no sin, though inwardly full of rottenness and hypocrisy. Such insensibility is a certain sign of a hardened and impenitent heart, and can proceed from nothing but a gross and conceited ignorance, a wretched inconsideration, or a long continuance in sin, that has rendered the conscience callous and past feeling. This first step of repentance supposes the sinner, in the first place, to be feelingly affected with a sense of his sins; to have his mind enlightened and his conscience awakened by the word of God; to be convinced from thence of the irregularity of his ways, and their contrariety to the holiness of the Divine nature; to labor under the load of his guilt; and in the consciousness of his own ill deserving, to be ready to sink under the number and the weight of his transgressions. Such were the sentiments of David's heart, and such the confession of his tongue. "I acknowledge my transgressions; my sin is ever before me; mine iniquities are gone over my head; as a burden they are too heavy for me." This sense of sin is often accompanied with the emotions of fear. For when the sinner, already convicted in his own conscience, begins to reflect upon his past life, and at the same time to look up to God whom he has offended, and forwards to eternity, upon the brink of which he daily stands shivering; what a spectacle of terror must this be to a man who has been long spiritually blind, and whose eyes are but just opened to see this startling scene! And behold, behind him a formidable troop of sins; sins red as crimson, and numberless as the sand upon the seashore! Above a holy and a just God, the Judge of the world, armed with the thunders of his wrath! Before him the infernal world disclosing all its horrors, and ready to swallow him up in perdition! Doubtless the terrors of the Lord, when thus set in array against a self-condemned sinner, will fill him with fear and dismay, especially when he considers that God is greater than his heart, and knoweth all things.

The *second* step of repentance, is being affected with a grief and hatred of sin. The former was a selfish feeling; this is a generous passion. The former respects sin as ruinous to the sinner; this regards it as offensive to God. When the penitent is already affected with a deep sense of the danger of his sin, how will it wound his mind, and pierce him to the heart, to consider that he has not only been long an enemy to himself, but also an enemy to God; to consider that he has trespassed so far upon infinite goodness; that he has dallied so long with infinite justice; that he has misspent the precious talents committed to him of Heaven; that he has abused the faculties of his immortal soul; that he has been defacing the image of God his maker; and that with his own hands he has been excluding himself from happiness, from heaven, and from the presence of the Lord. These, and such alarming thoughts, pierce to the dividing asunder of soul and spirit; enough to constrain the sorrowful penitent to lift up his eyes in the midst of his torment, and to cry out with Job in the bitterness of his soul, "I have sinned, and what shall I answer to thee, O thou Preserver of men? Alas! the arrows of the Almighty are within me! the poison of them drinketh up my spirit. But what grieves me most is, that I have offended thee, the Author of my life, and the Preserver of my being; that I have sinned against so much goodness, and provoked such tender mercy. Mine iniquities deserve thy wrath and vengeance. But thy goodness reacheth from heaven to earth. Thy mercy, like thyself, is infinite. Let this remorse which I now feel, be the only punishment of my sin; and let me not be finally delivered over to the tormentors. This I request and pray on account of the merit of my Redeemer. His righteousness is all-sufficient and meritorious. By it may I obtain favor and acceptance with thee, and be translated from the kingdom of darkness into the kingdom of God."

The *third* step in repentance towards God, is an apprehension of the mercy of God in Christ, and a forsaking of sin. This is properly an act of faith. Faith and repentance are twin graces of the soul, and can never be separated. True repentance includes faith, and true faith includes repentance. The mercy of God through a Redeemer being proclaimed in the Gospel, and a new and living way to the holiest of all being set open by the blood of Jesus, the true penitent flies for refuge to the hope set before him, and lays hold on eternal life. He forsakes his sins, and walks in newness of life. He begins with alacrity to run the race set before him, and feels, to his blessed experience, that the ways of wisdom are ways of pleasantness, and that her paths are peace. This is the crowning act of true repentance, and the test of its sincerity. That is not true repentance, when the sinner, after feeling some compunctions of mind, some touches of remorse, forms a few feeble resolutions, which he breaks at the first approach of temptation. He is not a true penitent, who, after mourning over his old sins, begins a new course of wickedness. This is only changing one sin for another. A man who has spent his youth in profusion and extravagance, may devote his riper years to avarice and the cares of the world. Such a person is indeed a different man, but he is not a penitent. In like manner, a person who has been at the head of the follies and the vices of the world, who has taken the lead in all fashionable and criminal gratifications, may grow tired of such a course of life, as human nature will tire of every thing: Such a person may take a fit of devotion, and rush into a variety of gloomy superstitions and severities; but this is not true repentance. This is only passing from one error to another. This is only giving a different direction to your passions. Repentance must effect a thorough change, or it is no repentance at all. Neither is he a true penitent who, after being affected with remorse for sin, falls into the same course again; who is always sinning and always repenting; and who goes on in a sad circle of making resolutions, and breaking them as soon as they are made. True repentance is repentance from dead works to serve the living God. It consists in confessing and forsaking our sins. It consists in denying ungodliness and worldly lusts, and abounding in the fruits of righteousness unto eternal life.

I do not mean by this, that any man in this life is altogether free from sin. Imperfections cleave to the best. Who can say that he has made his hands clean, or his heart pure? Good men oftentimes may be off their guard; they may be surprised in the hour of temptation, and be overtaken in a fault; but they will never sin upon a plan; they will never make a system of iniquity; they will not deliberately concert plots of wickedness upon their beds, and rise up to execute with warmth what they have contrived with coolness. The grace of God does not act by fits and starts; is not a transient but an abiding principle. The Christian is fixed and immoveable, and abounding in the work of the Lord. He is not of those apostates, mentioned by the apostle Jude, who resemble the morning clouds, that are ever varying their form, and are carried about with every wind: who resemble wandering stars, to whom is reserved the blackness of darkness for ever. But he advances from strength to strength: his path is like the light of the morning, which shineth more and more unto the perfect day.

There is one other part of repentance which I have not yet mentioned, and which merits your serious attention; that is, making restitution and reparation, as far as lies in your power, for the evils you have done. "If I have wronged any man," said Zaccheus when he repented, "lo I restore him fourfold." Have you wronged any man in his property? Have you taken away his goods? Make restitution. Have you wronged any man in his reputation? Have you taken away his good name? Make reparation: confess that you were a defamer: confess that you were a liar. Have you offended and injured any one? Ask his forgiveness. Let no false shame hinder you from doing your duty. You have good cause to be ashamed. Be always ashamed to offend; but never blush for your returning virtue. Let no false shame, therefore, no foolish obstinacy, no pride of heart, prevent you from a thorough reformation. Better be exposed to shame here, than be doomed hereafter to everlasting pains.

The *second* thing proposed, was, To lay before you the motives to repentance.

And, in the *first* place, The superior light and information derived to the world by the Christian religion, concerning the rule of righteousness according to which we ought to conduct our lives, suggests a strong motive and inducement to repentance. God indeed never left himself without a witness in the world. He made the firmament bright with his glory, and commanded the heavens with all their host to declare his handiwork. With his own finger he inscribed the laws of justice and of virtue upon the heart of man. Attentive to this voice of God within, and assisted by those impressions of Divinity without, the moral teachers among the Gentiles struck out many useful discoveries, and taught many valuable lessons of wisdom to the world. They wandered not in the dark concerning the essentials of natural religion. They were not ignorant of the chief duties of life. The invisible things of God, even his eternal power and Godhead, they discovered by the works of creation; and having the law of nature written in their hearts, they were a law unto themselves. But the defect which they labored under, was the want of authority to enforce the discoveries which they made, and the want of a proper sanction to the rules of life which they established. When keen and violent, the passions of men push them forward; they will not be restrained by the voice of reason and philosophy. On these occasions, men will reply to such an instructor, "Who gave thee a commission to teach and reform the world? Did the voice of heaven come to thine ears? Who invested thee vith authority and dominion over the mind? Who appointed thee instructor of the nations, and legislator of the moral world?" The heathen teachers could pretend to no such authority. But Jesus of Nazareth was invested with a divine commission. He descended from heaven to teach the will of God upon earth. He performed miracles in confirmation of his religion. He set the seal of heaven to the doctrines which he taught, and guarded the laws which he established with the sanction of rewards and punishments. Such was the difference betwixt a human teacher and a prophet of the Lord; and such ought to be the difference betwixt the lives of heathens and the conduct of Christians. What signifies the superior excellency of your religion, unless its superiority appear in your life? What avails the light to you, if ye continue to walk in darkness? Unless ye repent, it had been better for you that the kingdom of God had never come amongst you. If ye still walk in the region and shadow of death, it had been better that the Day-spring from on high had never risen over your benighted land. The heathens shall rise up in judgment against you, and shall condemn you. It shall be more tolerable in the day of judgment for the inhabitants of Sodom and Gomorrah, those cities of sin, those monuments of the vengeance of God to all succeeding times; it shall be more tolerable for these, than for those wicked Christians, who have disregarded the voice which spoke from heaven; who have profaned that blessed name by which they were called; and who, by their obstinacy and impenitence, have counted the blood of the covenant wherewith they were sanctified an unholy thing.

A *second* motive and encouragement to repentance, is the hope and prospect of success. Before the introduction of Christianity, when the world lay in darkness as well as in wickedness, a sense of guilt burdening the conscience, and a dread of future punishment as consequent upon that guilt, drove the nations to a variety of expedients, in order to avert the vengeance of Heaven, and make an atonement for their sins. Hence various rites and ceremonies were instituted. Hence so many sacrifices were offered up, and so much blood was shed. Reason indeed could have told them that these means were unavailable, that the blood of bulls and of goats, and the ashes of a heifer, could never take away sin. But reason could not assure them that any other means, that even their repentance, would be effectual to that end. Here Revelation steps in to our aid. The Gospel assures us, that the wrath of God is not only averted from men, that he is not only reconciled, but also that he is a God in Christ reconciling the world unto himself. The gate of mercy is set open by the blood of Jesus; and an inheritance that is incorruptible, undefiled, and that fadeth not away, is promised to all those who sincerely repent of their sins, to all who believe and obey the Gospel. He that confesseth and returneth shall find mercy. The sacrifices of God are a broken heart and a contrite spirit; a broken and a contrite heart the Lord will not despise. "Thus saith the high and lofty One that inhabiteth eternity, whose name is Holy, I dwell in the high and holy place; with him also that is of an humble and a contrite spirit, and who trembleth at my word." Seeing then that the favor of God, and all the blessings of the new covenant, are promised to true repentance, will you by your impenitence and unbelief cut yourselves off from these blessings? When such strong consolation is offered, will you not fly for refuge to the hope set before you? When heaven is opened for your reception, will you refuse to enter in? When the fruits of the tree of life are presented to you, will you not put forth your hand, and take and eat, and live for ever?

A *third* motive to repentance is the assistance of the Spirit, which the Gospel offers. Christianity is called the ministration of the Spirit. The effusion of the Holy Ghost on the day of Pentecost upon the apostles, which enabled them to speak all languages, and to work miracles, was extraordinary, and intended to cease with that age. But the heavenly Comforter still abides with all the disciples of Christ, to guide them into all truth, and incline them to the practice of every duty. The prophet Zechariah, foretelling the glory of the latter days, or times of the Messiah, says, "It shall come to pass in those days, that I will pour out upon the house of David, and upon the inhabitants of Jerusalem, the Spirit of grace and of supplication, and they shall look upon me whom they have pierced, and they shall mourn and be in bitterness." The Spirit of grace and of supplication, then, poured out abundantly, shall impress men with sorrow and contrition for their sins; shall incline them to renounce their former sinful ways, to repent of their past transgressions, and to walk in newness of life. This operation of the Divine Spirit upon the mind, does not impel men to action by mechanical influence, and obstruct the exercise of their natural powers. The grace of God does not turn a man into a machine. It draws him, as the Scripture happily expresses it, with the cords of love, and with the bands of a man. It acts in such a manner as is adapted to the powers of a rational being, and to the liberty of a free agent. When such gracious aids are offered to us, when the Spirit of God strives in order to reclaim and reform us, it must be a high aggravation of our wickedness to resist his operations, and by our hardness and impenitence of heart, to treasure up wrath against the day of wrath, and revelation of the righteous judgment of God. What more could the good husbandman have done to his vineyard than he has done? He calls upon you to repentance by the voice of nature; he calls you by the voice of reason; he calls you by the voice of providence; he calls you by the voice which spake from heaven. He sends down his Holy Spirit to second these Divine calls, to help your infirmities, to enlighten your darkness, to strengthen your feeble powers, and to work in you both to will and to do that which is his good pleasure. Not only does he prepare the crown of glory, but he also assists you to fight the good fight, and to finish your course, that you may obtain that crown. Not only does he open the heavens to receive you, but he also stretches out his hands to conduct you thither. And if, after all, you resist his Holy Spirit; if you counterwork his saving plan; if you defeat the efforts of mercy, the labors of Heaven used for your recovery, your guilt is upon your own head, your ruin is owing to yourselves, with your own hand you push yourselves over the brink into the pit of utter perdition.

In the *fourth* place, as an inducement to repentance, consider the cross of Christ, who suffered the punishment due to our sins. How great must be the evil of sin, and how strong the obligation for us to repent of our sins, when such a sacrifice was required in order to expiate our guilt, and atone the wrath of Heaven! Burnt offerings, thousands of rams, and ten thousands of rivers of oil, the first-born offered up for the transgression, the fruit of the body for the sin of the soul, could not suffice. The Lamb of God could alone take away the sin of the world. Look then on him whom thou hast pierced, and mourn. Every groan that he utters, every tear that he sheds, every drop of blood that he pours, calls thee to repentance. View him stretched out on the cross, groaning under the pains of death, inclining his blessed head, and addressing his last words to you, "Sinners, behold your Saviour! behold him who was persecuted by Satan and by wicked men; behold him who was forsaken by God; behold this head which was crowned with thorns; behold these hands which were nailed to the tree; behold this side which was wounded with the spear; behold the blood that flows from every part; sinner, it was shed for you." Canst thou, O man! behold that scene without emotion? Canst thou continue impenitent in the practice of those sins, which brought thy Saviour to that painful and ignominious death?

Lastly, It is another motive to repentance, that God "has appointed a day in the which he will judge the world," as is mentioned in the verse following the text. That the soul of man survives the body, that there is a state of rewards and punishments beyond the grave, has been the general belief among all nations. Testimonies of this truth everywhere abound. Whether we turn to the east or to the west; whether we consult the history of ancient or of modern times; whether we listen to the accounts of the old world or of the new, we are presented with proofs and evidences of this important doctrine. How this opinion came to be so general, as to form an article in the popular creed of all nations, is a question of some difficulty. To those who have no guide but the light of nature, and who have no supernatural aids to assist the efforts of their own understanding, the arguments on both sides seem to be so equally balanced, that upon principles of reasoning, it is almost impossible to come to any determination. But, in all inquiries concerning human nature, we ought to attend to the heart more than to the understanding. Man is oftener guided by sentiment and feeling than by abstract reasoning. Almighty God hath endowed us with a sense of moral good and evil. He hath placed within us a principle of conscience, which passeth judgment upon human actions, approving the good, and condemning the bad. This tells us, that in the Divine administration it ought to be well with the righteous, and ill with the wicked. In confirmation of this, we see that, by the original appointment of Heaven, and in the daily course of Providence, there is no peace to the wicked, and that they have great peace who love the law of the Lord. At the same time, we frequently observe in the course of human affairs, that the lot of the wicked falls to the righteous. We see many instances in life of good men depressed, and bad men exalted; of vice holding a sceptre, and virtue pining in chains. How often have we seen the best of men reduced to eat the bread of sorrow, and to drink the waters of affliction, whilst the worthless and the infamous have rioted in the abundance of life, and enjoyed what their hearts could wish! When such scenes are presented to our eyes, our heart rises within us. Shall it always continue thus, we say within ourselves, shall it always continue thus in a world that is governed by God? Shall oppressed righteousness never be taken into the protection of Providence, and triumphant wickedness never fall under his censure? Shall the cry of the innocent, of the oppressed, and of the persecuted, never reach the throne of justice? Are the wrongs and grievances of the good and the righteous, never to be redressed? Is wickedness finally to triumph over oppressed virtue; to triumph over the laws of nature; to triumph over the providence of Heaven? Will the time never come when the Almighty shall rise from his throne to adjust and rectify the affairs of the moral world? If not in this, certainly in some future state, he will assume the part of a Judge, to reward the just, and to take vengeance upon the wicked.

All this has at last been fully revealed. It was reserved to the Divine Prophet, who came from the bosom of the Father to bring life and immortality to light by his Gospel. He taught that God had appointed a day in which he was to judge the world; that the dead were to be raised, and all that ever lived upon the earth to appear at his tribunal. Of this doctrine he gave assurance unto all men by his own resurrection from the dead; and as surely as he arose, shall we at the time appointed arise. When the mystery of God is finished, the last trumpet will sound. The voice of the Son of God will pierce the caverns of the tomb, will be heard over the kingdoms of the dead, will reanimate the ashes of thousands of generations, and sist an assembled world at the seat of judgment. By the unalterable appointment of Heaven, every thing has its period. The cedar of Lebanon fades away like the leaf upon its top. Lebanon itself decays in the course of years. States and empires have their day, like mortal man. Limits are set to time, and the world has its last hour. A few generations more having passed away, the day comes which God hath appointed to judge the world; the great day for which all other days have revolved. When this period approaches, heaven opens wide its everlasting doors, and behold the Judge comes forth! He comes in the glory of his Father; in the effulgence of unveiled Divinity he comes, attended with all the host of heaven! Before him the harbinger of his appearance, the destroying angel of nature, descends, clothed with a cloud, having his face like the sun, and his feet like pillars of fire. He sets his right foot upon the sea, and his left foot upon the earth; he lifts up his hand to heaven, and swears "by him that liveth for ever and ever, that time shall be no more!" As the doom of nature is denounced, the thunders of heaven for the last time utter their voices: the laws of nature are dissolved; the stars fall from the firmament; the moon is turned into blood; and that sun, whose beams you now behold, sinks in the darkness of eternal night; the earth hears its last sentence, and shakes to the centre; the four corners of the world hear it; all that are alive hear it; all the dead hear it, and live; from the presence of their Creator, the heavens depart like a scroll rolling itself together; the earth vanishes, and there is no place found for it; every mountain and every island is fled; creation fades away, to give place to uncreated glory; the great tribunal is erected; the books are opened; the Judge descends; the world is assembled; the sentence is pronounced; the sentence is executed: down to the prison of darkness and despair, the habitation of unquenchable and everlasting fire, the wicked are driven, where, bound in chains, they feel the torment of the worm that never dies, and suffer in the flames of the lake whose smoke ascendeth up for ever and ever;

whilst, enthroned in glory above, and adorned with the beauties of immortality, the righteous ascend with their Lord, and approaching to the fountain of life, partake of those pleasures at the right hand of God, which shall occupy and animate the praises of eternity.

Let me now ask you, my brethren, do you believe what you have now heard? Do you believe that there is a judgment to come, and that each of you shall bear a part in that tremendous scene? I appeal to a witness that cannot lie. I appeal to your own conduct. Do you live and act in such a manner as becomes those who have one day to answer for their lives and their actions? Is your conversation in heaven, from whence you look for the Saviour and the Judge? Are your loins girt about, your lamps burning, and you yourselves like unto men who wait for the coming of their Lord? Were the general judgment to begin, were these heavens to open, and the sign of the Son of Man to appear overhead, could you face his tribunal? Could you lift up your heads with confidence and joy amidst the ruins of nature, and the crash of a dissolving world? If not, I call upon you to repent, and to reform your lives. You are still under the administration of grace, and have the hope of glory set before you. Heaven and immortality are in your offer. God graciously calls you to repentance and newness of life. The Spirit helps your infirmities, and strives to conquer the stubbornness of your spirits. But he will not always thus wait to be gracious. Your day of grace does not last for ever. If mercy reclaims you not, you are delivered over to the hand of justice. If you reject the golden sceptre when it is held out to you, a rod of iron succeeds, to destroy the children of disobedience. Repent you must, in one form or other. If your sins affect you not with sorrow and contrition here, they will fill you with unavailable remorse and despair hereafter. You must either be affected with the kindly emotions of that repentance which is unto life, or be tormented with the stings of the worm that never dies.

Knowing these terrors, we endeavor to persuade men. Happy for men, if they would endeavor to be persuaded! If these things, my brethren, which you have been now hearing, be true; if it be true that we shall be raised up at the last day; that the day of judgment shall as surely arise as this morning arose, in obedience to laws which can no more fail to bring it forth than the sun could this morning refuse to arise at the command of its Creator; if it be true that all of us who are here assembled shall be assembled again around the judgment-seat of God; if it be true that this is our only state of probation, and that life and death are now in our choice, that heaven and hell are now set before us; if these things be true, (and true they are, otherwise this book is a collection of fables,) if these things be true,—then, O my brethren, what manner of persons ought we to be!—then, O my God, what manner of persons ought we to be!

SERMON XXXVII.

ON THE VIRTUE OF MEEKNESS.

MATTHEW v. 5.—"Blessed are the meek, for they shall inherit the earth."

THEY mistake the nature of the Christian religion very much, who consider it as separate and detached from the commerce of the world. Instead of forming a distinct profession, it is intimately connected with life; it respects men as acting in society, and contains regulations for their conduct and behavior in such a state. It takes in the whole of human life, and is intended to influence us when we are in the house, and in the field, as well as when we are in the church or in the closet. It instructs men in their duty to their neighbors, as well as in their duty to God: It is our companion in the scene of business as well as in the House of Prayer; and while it inculcates the weightier matters of the law, faith, judgment, and mercy, it neglects not the ornament of a meek and quiet spirit, which in the sight of God is of great price. All that refinement which polishes the mind; all that gentleness of manners which sweetens the intercourse of human society, which political philosophers consider as the effects of wise legislation and good government; all the virtues of domestic life, are lessons which are taught in the Christian school. The wisdom that cometh from above is "gentle." The fruit of the Spirit is "meekness." As the sun, although he regulates the seasons, leads on the year, and dispenses light and life to all the planetary worlds, yet disdains not to raise and to beautify the flower which opens in his beam: so the Christian religion, though chiefly intended to teach us the knowledge of salvation, and be our guide to happiness on high, yet also regulates our conversation in the world, extends its benign influence to the circle of society, and diffuses its blessed fruits in the path of domestic life.

In farther treating upon this subject, I shall, in the *first* place, describe to you the character of meekness which is here recommended; and, in the *second* place, show you the happiness with which it is attended.—I am, in the *first* place, then, to describe to you the character of meekness which is here recommended.

Every virtue, whether of natural or revealed religion, is situated between some vices or defects, which, though essentially different, yet bear some resemblance to the virtue they counterfeit; on account of which resemblance they obtain its name, and impose upon those who labor under the want of discernment. This meekness which is here recommended, is not at all the same with the courtesy of manners which is learned in the school of the world. That is but a superficial accomplishment, and often proceeds from a hollowness of heart. It is also quite different from constitutional facility, that undeciding state of the mind which easily bends to every proposal; that is a weakness, and not a virtue. Neither does it at all resemble that tame and passive temper which patiently bears insults and submits to injuries; that is a want of spirit, and argues a cowardly mind. This meekness is a Christian grace wrought in us by the Holy Spirit: it is a stream from the fountain of all excellence. A good temper, a good education, and just views of religion, must concur in forming this blessed state of the mind. It becomes a principle which influences the whole life. Though consistent in all its operations with boldness and with spirit, yet its chief characteristics are goodness, and gentleness, and long suffering. It looks with candor upon all; often condescends to the prejudices of the weak, and often forgives the error of the foolish.

But to give you a more particular view of it, we may place it in three capital lights, as it respects our general behavior, our conduct to our enemies, and our conduct to our friends.

With respect to his general behavior, the meek man looks upon all his neighbors with a candid eye. The two great maxims on which he proceeds, are, not to give offence, and not to take offence. He enters not with the keenness of passion into the contentions of violent men; he keeps aloof from the contagion of party madness, and feels not the little passions which agitate little minds. He wishes, and he studies, to allay the angry passions of the contending; to moderate the fierceness of the implacable; to reconcile his neighbors to one another; and, as far as lies in his power, to make all mankind one great family of friends. He will not indeed descend one step from the dignity of his character; nor will he sacrifice the dictates of his own conscience to any consideration whatever. But those points of obstinacy, which the world are apt to call points of honor, he will freely and cheerfully give up for the good of society. He loves to live in peace with all mankind; but this desire too has its limits. He will keep no terms with those who keep no terms with virtue. A villain, of whatever station, of whatever religious profession, he detests as abomination. Thus you see, that though softness, and gentleness, and forbearance, and long-suffering, are the chief characteristics of this virtue, yet at the same time it is very consistent with exertions of spirit. When it acts, it acts with vigor and decision. Moses, who has the testimony of the Divine Spirit, that he was the meekest man upon the face of the earth, yet when occasion presented itself, felt the influence of an elevated temper, and slew the Egyptian who was wounding his countryman. A meeker than Moses, even our Lord himself, though gentle and beneficent to all the sons of men, yet when the worldly-minded Jews profaned the Temple, he was moved with just indignation, and drove the impious from the House of God. Nothing is often more calm and serene than the face of the heavens; but when guilt provokes the vengeance of the Most High, *forth comes the thunder* to blast the devoted head.

Such is the influence of meekness on our general behavior. It ought also to regulate our conduct to our enemies. There is no principle which more strongly operates in human nature than the law of retaliation. This appears from the laws of all nations in the early state, which always ordained a punishment similar to the offence; eye for eye, tooth for tooth, and life for life. This appears also from our own feelings; when an injury is done us, we naturally long for revenge.' Our heart tells us, that the person offending ought to suffer for the offence, and that the hand of him who was injured must return the blow. Such are the dictates of the natural temper. But pursue this principle to its full extent, and you will see where it will end. One man commits an action which is injurious to you; you feel yourself aggrieved, and seek revenge. If you then retaliate upon him, he thinks he has received a new injury, which he also seeks to revenge; and thus a foundation is laid for reciprocal animosities without end. Did this principle and this practice become general, the earth would be a field of battle, life would be a scene of bloodshed, and hostilities would be immortal. Legislative wisdom hath provided a remedy for these disorders and for this havoc which would be made of the human species. The right of private vengeance, which every man is born with, by common consent, and for the public good, is resigned into the hands of the civil magistrate. But there are many things which come not under the jurisdiction of the laws, and the cognziance of the magistrate, which tend to disturb the public peace, and set mankind at variance. Private animosities and little quarrels often rise, which might be productive of great disorder and detriment to society. Here, therefore, where legislative wisdom fails, religion steps in and checks the desire of vengeance, by enjoining that meekness of spirit which disposes not to retaliate, but to forgive. He, therefore, who possesses this spirit, will not answer a fool according to his folly. He will not depart from his usual maxims of conduct, because another has behaved improperly. Because his neighbor has been guilty of one piece of folly, he will not reckon that an inducement for him to be guilty of another. He will regulate his conduct by the standard of virtue which is within, and not by the behavior of those around him. Accordingly, instead of harboring animosities against those who have done him ill offices, he will be disposed to return good for evil; remembering that our Lord adds at the conclusion of this chapter, "I say unto you, love your enemies, that ye may be the children of your Father which is in Heaven; for he maketh the sun to rise on the evil and on the good, and sendeth rain on the just and on the unjust."

This meekness ought also to appear in

our conduct towards our friends. In the present state of things, where human nature is so frail, where the very best have their weak side, and where so many events happen, which give occasion to the passions of men to show themselves, there is great scope for the exercise of meekness and moderation. The faults of mankind, in general, present a most unpleasant spectacle; but the failings of those we love, of those on whom we have conferred obligations, are apt to fill us with disgust and aversion. If it had been an enemy who had done this, I could have borne it. I would have expected no better; but thou, O my familiar friend, how shall I forgive thee? Such, at the time, is the language of nature. But better views, and more mature reflection, will teach us to throw a veil over those infirmities which are inseparable from the best natures, and to frame an excuse for those errors, which proceed not from a bad heart.

In all these instances of meekness, Jesus of Nazareth left us an example, that we should follow his steps. In his general behavior, he was meek and lowly, and condescending. He went about doing good, and received testimony from his enemies, that "he did all things well." To the errors of his friends, he was mild and gentle. When, moved by false zeal, in which they are still followed by many who have the assurance to call themselves his disciples, they besought him to cause fire to descend from heaven, and consume a city which believed not in his doctrines; all the rebuke he administered was, "Ye know not what manner of spirit ye are of; the Son of Man came not to destroy men's lives, but to save them." When he suffered his agony in the garden, in the hour and in the power of darkness, when he besought his disciples to watch with him in this dreadful scene, and when, instead of giving him comfort, they sunk unconcerned into sleep; instead of reproving them with severity, as their conduct deserved, he himself sought for an excuse for them: "The spirit indeed is willing, but the flesh is weak." Though he was the friend of all mankind, yet he had enemies who sought his life. "I have done," said he, "many good deeds among you, for which of these do you stone me?" And when, after persecuting him in his life, they brought him to the accursed death of the cross, his last words were, "Father forgive them, for they know not what they do." Go thou! and do likewise.

The *second* thing proposed was, to show the happiness annexed to this character, expressed here by "inheriting the earth." The meek are not indeed always to be great and opulent. Happiness, God be praised, is not annexed, and is not confined, to the superior stations of life. There is a great difference between possessing the good things of life, and enjoying them. Whatever be his rank in life, the meek man bids the fairest chance for enjoying its advantages. A proud and passionate man, puts his happiness in the power of every fool he meets with. A failure in duty or affection from a friend, want of respect from a dependant, and a thousand little circumstances, which a candid man would overlook, disturb his repose. He is perpetually on the fret, and his life is one scene of anxiety after another. On the other hand, the meek is not disturbed by the transactions of this scene of vanity. He is disposed to be pleased at all events. Instead of repining at the success of those around him, he rejoices in their prosperity, and is thus happy in the happiness of all his neighbors. Such are the blessed effects of meekness on the character. This beam from heaven kindles joy within the mind; it spreads a serenity over the countenance, and diffuses a kind of sunshine over the whole life. It puts us out of the power of accidents. It keeps the world at a due distance. It is armor to the mind, and keeps off the arrows of wrath. It preserves a sanctuary within, calm and holy, which nothing can disturb. Safe and happy in this asylum, you smile at the madness of the multitude. You hear the tempest raging around, and spending its strength in vain. As this virtue contributes to our happiness here, so it is also the best preparation for the happiness which is above. It is the very temper of the heavens. It is the disposition of the saints in light, and angels in glory; of that blessed society of friends who rejoice in the presence of God, and who, in mutual love, and joint hosannas of praise, enjoy the ages of eternity.

To conclude: There is hardly a duty enjoined in the whole book of God, on which more stress seems often to be laid, than this virtue of meekness. "The Lord loveth the meek.—The meek will he beautify with his salvation.—He arises to save the meek of the earth." Christ was sent to preach "glad tidings to the meek." Upon this our Lord rests his own character: "Learn of me, for I am meek." In the epistles of Paul, there is a remarkable expression: "I beseech you by the meekness and the gentleness of Christ." The Holy Ghost, too, is called "the Spirit of Meekness." Implore then, O Christian! the assistance of the Divine Spirit, that he may endow you with this virtue, and that you may show in your life the meekness of wisdom.

L E C T U R E S.

LECTURE I.

THE CONDITION OF THE GOOD MAN AND THE BAD MAN DESCRIBED.

PSALM I.

1 Blessed is the man that walketh not in the counsel of the ungodly, nor standeth in the way of sinners, nor sitteth in the seat of the scornful.
2 But his delight is in the law of the Lord, and in his law doth he meditate day and night.
3 And he shall be like a tree planted by the rivers of water, that bringeth forth his fruit in his season; his leaf also shall not wither, and whatsoever he doth shall prosper.
4 The ungodly are not so: but are like the chaff which the wind driveth away.
5 Therefore the ungodly shall not stand in the judgment, nor sinners in the congregation of the righteous.
6 For the Lord knoweth the way of the righteous: but the way of the ungodly shall perish.

CHRISTIANS and Brethren! The most critical period of human life is when we set out into the world. Frequently the first step is decisive. The young adventurer, set free from the authority of parents and of guardians, becomes his own master, and follows his own inclination. It is then that he begins to form his character; and the character that is then formed generally lasts through life. Mankind for the most part continue in the same path in which they set out. The passions of youth may resign to the passions of age, and one set of vices or of virtues give place to those of a similar kind; but seldom does the formed character undergo an essential change. Our first steps ought therefore to be ordered with the greatest care and deliberation, as upon them, in a great measure, depends not only our present, but also our eternal happiness.

It was with a design to direct us in this important period, that the Psalm before us was written; in which the practice of righteousness is recommended, not only from the advantages attending it in this life, and in that which is to come, but likewise from the pernicious tendency of sin to embitter our earthly enjoyments, and to render us unqualified for inheriting the joys of heaven. The gradual deviation of a sinner from the onward path of virtue, till he is inextricably bewildered in the insidious mazes and winding ways of iniquity, are here most beautifully described.

The first step in reality, though it be the second in the description, is, *He standeth in the way of sinners.* Frequenting the company of the wicked is a certain introduction to a life of wickedness. Mankind are oftener led astray by the company of the profligate than by their own depraved inclinations. This unhappy bias to associate with the profane arises from two causes, which operate powerfully on the minds of inexperienced youth. The first is that vigorousness and austerity which some gloomy-minded Christians attach to their religion. There are many persons of such an unhappy constitution, as to indulge themselves in perpetual moroseness and melancholy. Those sons of sorrow turn every house into a house of mourning, and behave in life as if it were one of their principles, that mirth was made for reprobates, and cheerfulness of heart denied to all those who have the best title to be cheerful. My brethren, there is no connection; God and nature have established no connection, between sanctity of character and severity of manners. To rejoice evermore, is not only the privilege, but is also the duty of a Christian. A cheerful temper is a perpetual hymn to the Divinity. A gloomy cast of mind is not only a certain source of misery and discontent, but is really in itself sinful, by deterring others from a holy life, by representing religion in an unfavorable and forbidding light, as if it conjured up a spirit to darken the face of the heavens and the earth, to trouble the peace and the harmony of nature, and to banish gladness from the circle of human society. Very opposite is the conduct of the votaries of vice. To betray unwary innocence into their snares, they put on the masks of mirth; they counterfeit gladness amidst the horrors of guilt, and borrow the accents of pleasure, and the air of joy. "Let us crown ourselves with rosebuds," say they, "let us crown ourselves with rosebuds before they be withered, let no flower of the spring pass away, let us devote the present moments to joy, and give thought and care to the winds." By their flattery and fair speeches, too often are the innocent ensnared. They mark the fair attire, and the smiles upon the cheek of the deceiver, Sensual pleasure; but they discern not, till too late, the pains, the diseases, and the destruction that follows in her train. They discern not that her steps lead down to the grave, and that her bower is an antechamber to hell.

There is a second cause which has often been known to make men associate with the profane, and that is, an opinion that wickedness, particularly some kinds of it, are manly and becoming; that dissoluteness, infidelity, and blasphemy, are indications of a sprightly and strong mind. By the most unhappy of all associations, they join together the ideas of religion and dulness; and if they have a good opinion of a man's faith and his morals, they are led to have a very bad one of his understanding. This opinion, although it has gained ground where it might not have been expected, is without foundation in nature or in fact. Some instances there may have been of great men who have been irregular; but the experiences of ages is on the other side. Those who have shone in all ages as the lights of the world; the most celebrated names that are recorded in the annals of fame; legislators, the founders of states, and the fathers of their country, on whom succeeding ages have looked back with filial reverence; patriots, the guardians of the laws, who have stemmed the torrent of corruption in every age; heroes, the saviors of their country, who have returned victorious from the field of battle, or more than victorious, who have died for their country; philosophers, who have opened the book of nature, and explained the wonders of almighty power; bards, who have sung the praises of virtue and of virtuous men, whose strains carry them down to immortality; with a few exceptions, have been uniformly on the side of goodness, and have been as distinguished in the temple of virtue as they were illustrious in the temple of fame. It was one of the maxims which governed their lives, that there is nothing in nature which can compensate wickedness; that although the rewards and punishments, which influence illiberal and ungenerous minds, were set aside; that although the thunders of the Almighty were hushed, and the gates of paradise were open no more, they would follow religion and virtue for their own sake, and co-operate with eternal Providence in perpetual endeavors to favor the good, to depress the bad, and to promote the happiness of the whole creation.

The second stage in the perversion of a sinner, is *walking after the counsel of the ungodly*. It is a maxim established by the sad experience of ages, that evil communication corrupts good manners. The power of nature and of conscience, and the influence of a religious education, may, for a while, withstand the shock, but these gradually will be overpowered, and yield to the impetuosity of the torrent. Hence follow the painful struggles between reason and the senses, between conscience and inclination, which constitute a state of the utmost misery and torment. Such persons, when they are carousing in the gay circle of their acquaintance, when the blood is warm, and the spirits high, will then go all lengths with their fellow-debauchees, and give a loose to every wanton and every wicked desire. But when the fumes of intoxication have forsaken the aching head; when the calm forenoon hour of reflection comes, then conscience, faithful to its trust, summons them to her awful bar, fills them with confusion and remorse, and condemns them to the severest of all tortures, to be extended on the rack of reflection, to lie upon the torture of the mind. This is a state in which great part of mankind live and die. They have as much corruption as to lead them to the commission of new sins, and as much religion as to awaken in them remorse for these sins. They repent of their old vicious pleasures, and at the same time are laying plans for new ones, and make their lives one continued course of sinning and repenting, of transgression and remorse.

The third and last stage of impiety is *sitting in the chair of the scorner*, or laughing at all religion and virtue. This is a pitch of diabolical attainment, to which few arrive. It requires a double portion of the infernal spirit, and a long experience in the mystery of iniquity, to become callous to every sense of religion, of virtue, and of honor; to throw off the authority of nature, of conscience, and of God; to overleap the barrier of laws divine and human; and to endeavor to wrest the bolt from the red right hand of the Omnipotent. Difficult as the achievement is, we see it sometimes effected. We have seen persons who have gloried in their shame, and boasted of being vicious for the sake of vice. Such characters are monsters in the moral world. Figure to yourselves, my brethren, the anguish, the horror, the misery, the damnation, such a person must endure, who must consider himself in a state of enmity with heaven and with earth; who has no pleasant reflections from the past, no peace in the present, no hopes from the future; who must consider himself as a solitary being in the world; who has no friends without to pour balm in the cup of bitterness he is doomed to drink; who has no friend above to comfort him, when there is none to help; and who has naught within him to compensate for the irreparable and irredeemable loss. Such a person is as miserable as he is wicked. He is insensible to every emotion of friendship; he is lost to all sense of honor; he is seared to every feeling of virtue.

In the class of those who sit in the chair of the scorner, we may include the whole race of infidels, who misemploy the engines of reason or of ridicule to overthrow the Christian religion. Were the dispute concerning a system of speculative opinions, which of themselves were of no importance to the happiness of mankind, it would be uncharitable to include them all under this censure. But on the Christian religion, not only the happiness but the virtue of mankind depends. It is an undoubted fact, that religion is the strongest principle of virtue with all men, and with nine-tenths of mankind is the only principle of virtue. Any attempt therefore to destroy it, must be considered as an attempt against the happiness and against the virtue of the human kind. If the heathen philosophers did not attempt to subvert the false religion of their country, but, on the contrary, gave it the sanction of their example, because, bad as it was, it had considerable influence on the manners of the people, and was better than no religion at all, what shame, what contempt, what infamy, ought they to incur, who endeavor to overthrow a religion which contains the noblest ideas of the Deity, and the purest system of morals, that ever were taught upon earth? He is a traitor to his country; he is a traitor to the human kind; he is a traitor to heaven, who abuses the talents that God has given him, in impious attempts to wage war against Heaven, and to undermine that system of religion, which, of all things, is the best adapted to promote the happiness and the perfection of the human kind. Blessed then is the man who hath not brought himself into this sinful and miserable state, who hath held fast his innocence and integrity in the midst of a degenerate world; or if, in some unguarded hour, he hath been betrayed into an imprudent step, or overtaken in a fault, hath made ample amends for his folly by a life of penitence and of piety.

VERSE 2. *His delight is in the law of the Lord.* He makes religion and virtue the grand business of his life, and his business becomes his delight. He does not take it up occasionally, and by fits and starts, it is his employment *day and night.* In the morning he riseth with the sun, and joins with the choir of angels and archangels in celebrating the great Creator. He looks around him with a pious pleasure on the living landscape which the hand of the Almighty hath drawn for his delight, and he adores that benevolent power who makes all nature beauty to his eye, and music to his ear; but he has a fairer prospect within, than nature can furnish without, and the still small voice of conscience whispers peace to his heart in sweeter strains than all the music of the morning, which hails him on every side. With a cheerful and a grateful heart, he contemplates the wonders of creating bounty, he recollects the instances of preserving goodness, and he traces the annals of redeeming love. He looks through the veil of created things, and raises his thoughts from this world to that state of happiness and immortality which is reserved for the spirits of just men made perfect. His religion does not consist in contemplation alone. He goeth about doing good. He instructs the ignorant in the light that leads to heaven; he pours the balm of consolation into the wounded mind; and he wipes the tears from the cheeks of the distressed. He distinguishes every day with some good, some memorable deed; and he retires to rest with that inward, serene, and heartfelt joy, that sober certainty of bliss, which is only to be found in a life of holiness and piety.

VERSE 3. *And he shall be like a tree planted by the rivers of water, that bringeth forth his fruit in his season; his leaf also shall not wither, and whatsoever he doth shall prosper.* A tree planted by the rivers of water, is a beautiful object in all nations; but to the Jews, who lived in a hot country, and were scorched with the heat of the sun, it was an object both of signal beauty and of signal utility, by affording them a shadow from the heat. Hence, when they describe mankind in their happiest state, they represent them as sitting under their vines and their fig-trees. This allusion expresseth well the flourishing state of the righteous man. Planted in the garden of his God, and watered with the dew of heaven, his leaf is ever green, and he brings forth the fruits of righteousness in due season. His goodness is liberal and unconfined and his beneficence is shared promiscuously by friends and foes. He is clothed with righteousness, and his judgment is a robe and a diadem. The ear that hears him blesseth, and the eye that sees him gives witness to him, because he delivereth the poor, the fatherless, and them that have none to help. He is eyes to the blind. He is feet to the lame. The loins of the naked bless him. The blessing of him that is ready to perish comes upon him, and he causes the widow's heart to sing for joy.

All he doth shall prosper well. Among the Jews, to whom this Psalm was addressed, this held invariably true. There was a particular dispensation of providence exercised towards that people, distributing temporal rewards to righteousness, and temporal punishments to sin. In the ordinary course of providence now, this does not always hold. Success and disappointment are administered variously to the sons of men. But still, in all his endeavors, the good man bids the fairest for success. While he acts in character, he will attempt nothing but what is just and honorable in itself, or beneficial to the interests of society; he will always have the good wishes of mankind on his side. And although he should sometimes be disappointed, the consciousness of his good intentions will keep his mind at ease, and his faith in the good providence of his heavenly Father will fill him with a contentment and peace of mind, that is a stranger to the breast of the wicked man, even when he obtains his wishes.

VERSE 4. *The ungodly are not so: But are like the chaff which the wind driveth away.* The Psalmist hits upon the distinguishing feature in the character of a wicked man. He never acts upon a plan. He lives and acts at random. He has no rule for his life but the veerings of passion. Present gratification being his only object, different and contrary passions solicit him at the same time. One appetite saith unto him, Go, and he goeth, another says, Come, and he cometh. The slave of sense, and the sport of passion, he is driven to and fro like the chaff before the whirlwind, and his life is one continued scene of levity, inconsistency and folly.

VERSES 5. and 6. *Therefore the ungodly shall not stand in the judgment, nor sinners in the congregation of the righteous.—For the Lord knoweth the way of the righteous: But the way of the ungod-*

ly shall perish. The miseries which the wicked endure here, are but the beginning of their sorrows. That God, whose grace they abused, whose mercy they undervalued, and whose power they despised, is now their awful and inexorable Judge. The wicked have no cause to complain of the sentence that is passed upon them. They have brought it upon their own heads. They have been the instruments of their own ruin. They have brought themselves into a situation in which it is impossible for them to be happy. Let us suppose them to be admitted into the company of the blessed, their situation would be still deplorable. They would pine in the mansions of bliss, and search for heaven in the midst of paradise. We may venture to say, that it is even impossible for Omnipotence to make a wicked man happy; it implies an express contradiction. They have put themselves out of the reach of divine mercy, and become what the Scripture most emphatically calls, "Vessels of wrath fitted for destruction." "Therefore they shall not stand in the judgment." The poor and distressed, whom they refused to relieve, the widow and the fatherless whom they oppressed, the innocent whom they injured, the unhappy wretches whom, by their artifices, they betrayed into the paths of destruction, shall rise up and witness against them. Their own hearts will condemn them. The final sentence is pronounced, they are driven from the presence of the Lord, they are cast into outer darkness, where the worm dieth not, where the fire is never quenched, and it had been happy for them that they had never been born.

I shall conclude with one reflection. You see, my brethren, from what has been said, that a life of wickedness is gradual and progressive. One criminal indulgence lays the foundation for another, till, by degrees, the whole superstructure of iniquity is complete. When the sinner has once put forth his hand to the forbidden fruit, and thinks that he can taste and live, he returns with greater and greater avidity to repeat his crimes, till the poison spreads through all his veins, and all the balm of Gilead be ineffectual for his cure. Fly therefore, I call upon you in the name of Heaven, fly, from the approaching foe. Guard your innocence as you would guard your life. If you advance one step over the verge of virtue, unless the grace of heaven interpose, down you sink to the bottomless abyss. Come not then near the territories of danger. Stand back. One sin indulged, gathers strength and abounds; it increases, it multiplies, it familiarizes itself with our frame, and introduces its whole brood of infernal inmates, worse than pestilence, famine, or sword.

LECTURE II.

ON THE DEDICATION OF THE TEMPLE.

PSALM XXIV. 1—7.

1 The earth is the Lord's, and the fulness thereof; the world and they that dwell therein.
2 For he hath founded it upon the seas, and established it upon the floods.
3 Who shall ascend into the hill of the Lord? and who shall stand in his holy place?
4 He that hath clean hands, and a pure heart; who hath not lift up his soul unto vanity, nor sworn deceitfully.
5 He shall receive the blessing from the Lord, and righteousness from the God of his salvation.
6 This is the generation of them that seek him, that seek thy face, O Jacob. Selah.
7 Lift up your heads, O ye gates, and be ye lift up, ye everlasting doors, and the King of glory shall come in.

THIS Psalm was composed when David removed the ark of the covenant from the house of Obededom to Jerusalem. But though it was composed for that occasion, it is evident, from the latter part of it, that it was ultimately intended for that more illustrious event, when Solomon transferred the ark from the tabernacle into the temple which he had built. As David was not only the poet, but also the Prophet of God, he foresaw the future events of the Church, by the inspiration of the Divine Spirit; and by the same inspiration, he composed songs and pieces of music adapted to these events. These he committed to Asaph, Hemon, and Jeduthun, the prefects of sacred poetry, to be sung as opportunities required.

The occasion of this psalm is one of the grandest and most illustrious that any where occurs in history. Solomon, by the divine direction, had now finished the temple, that superb monument of oriental magnificence and glory, which drew the princes of neighboring nations to come and contemplate. The feast of tabernacles, the most solemn and most frequented of the Jewish festivals, was now at hand. All the tribes of Israel, from Dan to Beersheba, were now assembled at Jerusalem to the feast. It was then that Solomon proceeded to dedicate the temple, and to fix the ark in its appointed place. The procession to the temple was grand and triumphant. Solomon, arrayed in all his glory, attended with the elders of Israel, and the heads of the tribes went before; after him marched the priests in their sacerdotal robes, bearing the ark; to them succeeded the four thousand sacred musicians, clothed in white robes, and divided into classes, some of them singing with the voice, others playing upon harps and trumpets, and psalteries and cymbals, and other instruments of music; behind them followed the whole congregation, with palms in their hands, rejoicing and wondering. Solomon had, on this occasion, made an oblation of twenty-two thousand oxen, and one hundred and twenty thousand sheep, of which the Almighty testified his approbation and acceptance, by causing the sacred fire to come down anew from heaven, and consume the sacrifice. The Priests and Levites, as they went along, sprinkled the ground with the blood of the victims, and perfumed the air with frankincense and sweet odors. This, with the fumes of incense which rose in clouds from the altars, had diffused such a potent perfume through the air, that people at a distance reflected on the breath they drew as a celestial influence, and regarded the strains of harmony which they heard, as something more than mortal; actually imagining that the God of the Hebrews had descended from his heaven to take possession of the temple which they had dedicated to his service. Nor were they mistaken. For after the priests had carried the ark into the holy of holies, had placed it between the cherubims, and had reverently withdrawn, the cloud of divine glory descended and rested upon the house. The Shechinah or divine presence took up its abode in the most holy place. Animated by this sublime occasion, the Psalmist begins his ode with celebrating the dominion of the Deity over this vast universe, and all its inhabitants, and setting forth their entire subjection to his power and providence.

VERSE 1. and 2. *The earth is the Lord's, and the fulness thereof; the world, and they that dwell therein.—For he hath founded it upon the seas, and established it upon the floods.* David ascertains the sovereignty of God over the world, and its subjection to him, from his having created it at first; from his having established it upon the seas, and founded it upon the floods. By this he opposes the skeptics and infidels of those times, who withdrew nature from the Divinity, and denied the interposition of Providence in human affairs; by this he distinguishes the God whom he adored, from the idols of the Gentiles around him, who were confined to one part or province of nature: by this he endeavors to inspire the Jews with gratitude and love to their God and King, who chose them from among all the nations whom he governs by his providence, to be his favorite people, the object of his particular providence, and peculiar loving-kindness. The Psalmist next determines where that God whose perfections he had been describing was to be worshipped, and which of his worshippers were to be the objects of his favor and approbation.

VERSE 3. *Who shall ascend into the hill of the Lord? and who shall stand in his holy place?* It was usual among the Jews to add the name of God to any thing that was great, that was wonderful, and of which they would give us a high idea. Lofty cedars in Scripture, are called the trees of the Lord: high hills are called the mountains of God: wine, on account of its generous, joyous, and exhilarating qualities, is said to cheer the heart of God and man. In this place, the phrase is not to be taken in its usual sense. By the hill of God, is here meant the hill of Zion, which the Almighty had chosen to be the place of his worship, and where he had commanded his temple to be built. Near the same tract of ground there were three hills. Zion, where the city and castle of David stood; Moriah, where the temple was built, and Calvary, where our Saviour was crucified; but these, for the most part, went under the general name of Zion. By the phrases of ascending into the hill of God, and standing in his holy place, the Psalmist would point out the persons who are to be admitted to worship God in his temple here, and in consequence of that, to be received into the temple of his glory above, and to dwell for ever with the Lord. We have the character and qualities of these persons expressed in the following verse.

VERSE 4. *He that hath clean hands, and a pure heart; who hath not lifted up his soul unto vanity, nor sworn deceitfully.* It is very observable, that in ascertaining the qualifications of the citizens of the spiritual Jerusalem, the Psalmist does not so much as mention the external observances, the costly and laborious rites of the ceremonial law, in which the Israelites generally prided themselves, but dwells alone on the great and essential duties of morality, which are of universal and eternal obligation. The fond affection and attachment of the Jews to the rites and ceremonies of the Mosaic law, so as to neglect other duties, is the more remarkable, as God, by the mouth of his Prophets, frequently declared that he had no pleasure in them, calling them precepts which were not good, and statutes by which a man could not live. In the fiftieth Psalm, we have an express declaration to this purpose; "Hear, O my people, and I will speak; O Israel, and I will testify against thee: I am God, even thy God. I will not reprove thee for thy sacrifices, or for thy burnt-offerings, to have been continually before me. I will take no bullock out of thy house, nor he-goats out of thy folds. For every beast of the forest is mine, and the cattle upon a thousand hills. I know all the fowls of the mountains: and the wild beasts of the field are mine. If I were hungry, I would not tell thee, for the world is mine, and the fulness thereof. Will I eat the flesh of bulls, or drink the blood of goats? Offer unto God thanksgiving, and pay thy vows unto the Most High, and call upon me in the day of trouble, and I will deliver thee, and thou shalt glorify me." The qualifications here required are those of the heart and the life, "Clean hands and a pure heart." It is not enough that we wash our hands in innocence before men, we must be pure in heart before the eyes of infinite perfection. True religion is the religion of the heart; it is a principle dwelling in the mind, that extends its influence through the whole man, and regulates the life. Unless our religion enter into the heart, we have no religion at all. The form of godliness is insufficient and unavailing without the power thereof. We can never attain to the true beauties of holiness, unless, like the king's daughter, we be all glorious within. On the other hand, when clean hands and a pure heart are united in the same person; when a conversation without blame, and a conscience void of offence, coincide, they are in the sight of God of great price. A life sacred to devotion and virtue, sacred to the practice of truth and undefiled religion, joined to a heart, pure, pious, and benevolent, constitute an offering more acceptable at the altars of the Most High God, than whole hecatombs of burnt-offerings, and a thousand hills of frankincense in a flame.

By *lifting up the soul unto vanity*, the Psalmist means making riches and honor, those vanities of the world, the object of our affection and pursuit; saying to the gold, thou art our trust, or to the most fine gold, thou art our confidence. Or it may mean the worshipping of idols, which, in Scripture, go under the denomination of vanity, as in Jeremiah, "Are there any among the vanities of the Gentiles that can cause rain?" *Swearing deceitfully*, includes all manner of perjury. This vice is always represented in Scripture in the most dreadful colors. He that sweareth falsely, and he that feareth an oath, is an equivalent term for the wicked and the righteous. As an oath is the greatest pledge of veracity, and the end of all strife, general and customary violations of it must have the most pernicious effect upon society. Such a practice would entirely banish religious principles from the world; it would dissolve the bands of society, it would shake the fundamental pillars of mutual trust and confidence among men, and destroy the security arising from the laws themselves. For human laws and human sanctions cannot extend to numberless cases in which the safety of mankind is essentially concerned. They would prove but feeble and ineffectual means of preserving the order and peace of society, if there were no checks upon men, from the sense of divine legislation; if no belief of divine rewards and punishments came in aid of what human rewards and punishments so imperfectly provide for. We have in the next verse, the rewards promised to the persons possessed of these qualifications.

VERSE 5. *He shall receive the blessing from the Lord, even righteousness from the God of his salvation.* This alludes to the appointed custom of the Jewish priests, who, on solemn and stated occasions, were wont to bless the people. Their form of blessing we have prescribed in Numbers vi. 22. "And the Lord spake unto Moses, saying, Speak unto Aaron and unto his sons saying, On this wise shall ye bless the people of Israel, the Lord bless thee and keep thee; the Lord make his face to shine upon thee, and be gracious unto thee; the Lord lift up his countenance upon thee, and give thee peace." But as the priest was a fallible creature, his blessing might be indiscriminately bestowed, and fail of its effect. But the person who hath clean hands and a pure heart, who hath not lift up his soul unto vanity, nor sworn deceitfully, shall receive the blessing from God himself, whose favor is better than life, and whose blessing maketh rich, and addeth no sorrow. These blessings are summed up in the eighty-fourth Psalm, "The Lord God is a sun and shield; the Lord will give grace and glory; no good thing will he withhold from them that walk uprightly." *Righteousness from the God of our salvation,* may either mean the reward of righteousness, as the word in Scripture is frequently put for the reward; or it may mean kindness, mercy, and the benefits from righteousness, as in 1 Sam. xii. 7. "Now therefore stand still, that I may reason with you before the Lord, of all the righteousnesses of the Lord, which he did to you and your fathers:" where it is evident, from what follows, that by righteousnesses of the Lord, he means the deliverance that God had wrought for them.

VERSE 6. *This is the generation of them that seek him, that seek thy face, O Jacob,* or, *O God of Jacob,* as it might better be rendered. This is the generation, who, in obedience to the commandments of God, and in the methods of his appointment, seek his face, that is, his favor and friendship, and to whom he never said, "Seek ye my face in vain."

Animated by his subject, the Psalmist proceeds to higher strains, and, in the sublime spirit of eastern poetry, calls upon the gates of the temple to open and admit the triumphal procession.

VERSE 7. *Lift up your heads, O ye gates, and be ye lift up, ye everlasting doors, and the King of glory shall come in.* To illustrate this part of the Psalm, we must take a short view of the Hebrew psalmody. The Psalms of David are of various kinds. Some of them are dramatic, having speakers introduced making a kind of musical dialogue. Of this the ninety-first psalm is a remarkable instance. In the first verse, the high priest, rising up, declares the happiness of him who putteth his trust in the Almighty. In the second verse, David himself, or one of the singers, representing the faithful among the Jews, declares his faith and confidence in God. From the third to the fourteenth, the ode was performed by the sacred singers, both with the voice and instruments of music. The three last verses were spoken by the high-priest alone in the character of God Almighty.

Many of the Psalms are intended to be sung by two divisions of the sacred singers, the chorus and the semichorus. Such is the Psalm before us. Every verse is divided into two members, exactly of the same length, and generally representing the same thought, expressed in a different manner. "The earth is the Lord's and the fulness thereof;—the world and they that dwell therein." When we come to the seventh, the verse is evidently altered. The verses are not divided into two members as before, and for a very good reason. The semichorus asked the question, and the chorus made the reply. Apostrophes, or addresses to inanimate nature, are among the boldest figures in poetry, and when properly introduced, as in this place, are in the highest manner productive of beauty. The simple thought, when stripped of its poetical ornaments, is no more than this: When the priests had carried the ark to the temple, Solomon ordered

12

the gates to be thrown open to admit the ark. How much this thought is improved, when embellished by the fine imagination of the singer of Israel, and clothed in all the graces of poetry, let persons of the smallest critical discernment judge. In short, the passage is too well known, and too beautiful, to need or admit of any illustration. Like the meridian sun, it shines in its own light, and to endeavor to adorn it, were wasteful and ridiculous excess.

As we are assured by an authority that cannot err, that the ceremonies of the Jewish law were a figure of good things to come, and as the ark has been considered as a type of our Saviour, it is highly probable, that its introduction into the temple prefigured to the faithful among the Jews, that solemn and triumphant period when our Saviour ascended into the heaven of heavens, to take possession of the glory which he had with the Father before the world was.

LECTURE III.

ON THE PARABLE OF THE RICH MAN AND LAZARUS.

LUKE XVI. 19—31.

19 There was a certain rich man, who was clothed in purple and fine linen, and fared sumptuously every day.

20 And there was a certain beggar named Lazarus, who was laid at his gate, full of sores.

21 And desiring to be fed with the crumbs which fell from the rich man's table: moreover, the dogs came and licked his sores.

22 And it came to pass that the beggar died, and was carried by the angels into Abraham's bosom: the rich man also died, and was buried.

23 And in hell he lift up his eyes, being in torments, and seeth Abraham afar off, and Lazarus in his bosom.

24 And he cried, and said, Father Abraham, have mercy on me. and send Lazarus, that he may dip the tip of his finger in water, and cool my tongue; for I am tormented in this flame.

25 But Abraham said, Son, remember that thou in thy lifetime receivedst thy good things, and likewise Lazarus evil things: but now he is comforted, and thou art tormented.

26 And besides all this, between us and you there is a great gulf fixed: so that they who would pass from hence to you, cannot; neither can they pass to us, that would come from thence.

27 Then he said, I pray thee therefore, father, that thou wouldst send him to my father's house:

28 For I have five brethren; that he may testify unto them, lest they also come into this place of torment.

29 Abraham saith unto him, They have Moses and the prophets; let them hear them.

30 And he said, Nay, father Abraham: but if one went unto them from the dead, they will repent.

31 And he said unto him, If they hear not Moses and the prophets, neither will they be persuaded though one rose from the dead.

THE method of instruction by parables, was much in use among the eastern nations. Both physical and moral causes contributed to introduce and to support this custom. The people of the east have always been more under the government of the imagination and fancy, than the nations of the north. They use the liveliest and the boldest figures of speech in their ordinary conversation; and their writings are all in the manner as well as in the spirit of poetry. What the influence of the climate made natural, the form of their government rendered necessary. As the form of their government has always been despotic and tyrannical, they were afraid to speak out their sentiments with openness and with freedom. Truth durst not approach the throne, nor appear in public.

Such was the origin of parables. This method of instruction possesses many advantages. It is obvious to all capacities, and has a charm for every hearer. It is well adapted to strike the fancy; it interests the passions, and thus makes a deeper and more lasting impression than mere moral instruction could convey. It likewise possesses one advantage peculiar to itself. It makes a man his own instructor. When the parable is told, we ourselves draw the moral, and make the application. Observations and reflections that we make ourselves, are of more avail to us in the conduct of life, than any instruction we can learn from others.

The parable now before us contains many useful and important lessons. We have here represented two characters not uncommon in the world; a rich man, who enjoyed the pleasures and the luxuries of life, and a poor beggar, who lived and who died in poverty and in distress. This man was a signal object of pity. He was a beggar, and he was full of sores. Notwithstanding this double call to sympathy and compassion, the heart of the rich man was hardened against him. All the advantage he reaped from lying at the great man's gate, was, that his dogs, who had more feeling than their master, came and licked his sores. Nevertheless this rich man was not a miser. He was not a niggard of the gifts of Providence. He enjoyed life. He was arrayed in purple, which, in those days, was the vestment of kings. Hospitality presided in his hall, and luxury reigned at his table. He made sumptuous entertainments for his friends, and he made them every day. He seems to have been one of that class of men, and a very numerous class they are, and very frequently to be found in life, who are very hospitable to those who do not want, but very unfriendly to those that do; who prepare rich and splendid entertainments for those tribes of flatterers and sycophants who always crowd the mansions of the great, and at the same time have nothing to spare to a real object of distress. However, he acted very agreeably to the principles of his sect; for, as we learn from the sequel, he was a Sadducee, or what in our days we call an infidel, that is, one who has no religion at all. He did not believe in the immortality of the soul. He did not believe that there was either a heaven or a hell. Accordingly, he endeavored to make the most of this life, and acted up to the maxims of his sect, "Let us eat and drink, for to-morrow we shall die."

Learn hence the folly and the danger of endeavoring to establish virtue upon any foundation but that of true religion. People may tell us that social affection is the law of our being; they may talk of virtue being its own reward; they may sing the praises of disinterested benevolence; but if you take away the rewards and punishments of the world to come, you set the greatest part of mankind free from every moral obligation, and open a door to universal depravity and corruption of manners. If the beauty of virtue is laid in one scale, and interest in the other, it will not be difficult to determine to which side the balance will incline.

The accusations of conscience will be little regarded, unless they are considered as an earnest of the worm that never dies. Take away the doctrine of a world to come, and you make this world a scene of universal depravity and open wickedness.

At first view we would be apt to wonder at the ways of Heaven, and perhaps tempted in our minds to arraign the conduct of Providence, in crowning this worthless and wicked man with wealth and prosperity, whilst all that diversified the good man's lot was scene after scene of poverty and pain. But let us suspend our judgment. We see but one link in the great chain of Providence. We live but in the infancy of being. The great drama of life is but begun. When the catastrophe is brought about, when the curtain between both worlds is undrawn, the morn will arise that will light the Almighty's footsteps in the deep, and pour full day upon all the paths of his providence.

VERSE 22. *And it came to pass that the beggar died.* He died, and all his miseries died with him. He whom this rich man would have disdained to have considered as his fellow-creature, had a company of angels sent down to transport him to the regions of the blessed, to the bosom of Abraham, where all his sorrows had an end, and the tears were for ever wiped from his eyes. Let the needy and the oppressed take consolation from this salutary doctrine. With God there is no respect of persons. Let it be the great business of your lives to be rich in faith and in good works, and to lay up treasures in heaven, and then you may rejoice in hope, that though you have nothing here, yet yours is the kingdom of God.

VERSE 23. to 26. inclusive. Before our Saviour's incarnation, the Greek language had made its way into Judea. Along with the language of the Greeks, their opinions in philosophy, and the fictions of their poetry, had been introduced, and made part of the popular belief. This part of the parable which we have now read, is evidently founded upon the fictions of the Grecian poets concerning the state of departed souls. They, as well as our Lord in this parable, represent the abodes of the blessed as lying contiguous to the regions of the damned, and separated only by a great impassable river, or deep gulf, in such a manner, that the ghosts could talk with one another from its opposite banks. In the parable, souls, whose bodies were buried, know each other, and converse together, as if they had been embodied. In like manner, the heathens introduce departed souls as talking together, and represent them as having pains and pleasures analogous to what we feel in this life; and they thought that the shades of the dead had an exact resemblance to their bodies. The parable says, that the souls of wicked men are tormented in flames; the Grecian poets tell us, that they lie in a river of fire, where they suffer the same torments they would have suffered while alive, had their bodies been burnt. From this account, therefore, we are to draw no inferences concerning the real nature of heaven or of hell. A parable is no more than an instructive fable or tale, and the only thing to be regarded in it is the moral that it conveys. We cannot therefore conclude from this parable, that there is material fire in hell, or that the abodes of the blessed and the regions of the damned are contiguous to one another. The word of God gives us no materials wherein we can make a description either of hell or heaven. It was never the intention of scripture to satisfy our curiosity, but to influence our practice, and for that purpose to awake our hopes and our fears, by representing the one as being the region of the greatest torment, and the other as the scene of unmingled and everlasting joy.

The rich man died, and was buried. We read not of the burial of the poor man. He would be thrown into a common grave, and mingled with vulgar and obscure dust. But the rich man was buried with pomp and with splendor. Crowds of mercenary mourners would attend his funeral, and venal tears be shed upon his tomb. Every amiable and every respectable quality would be ascribed to him by those ready flatterers, who have always a character at hand for the deceased of quality. But, insensible to this incense, *in hell he lift up his eyes.* How astonishing and how awful must it be, my brethren, for a person who believes not in a future state, to receive his first conviction from the flames of the lake which burneth for ever, and from the gnawings of the worm that never dies. The request of the rich man is very remarkable. He does not acknowledge the justness of his punishment, nor confess the greatness of his sins. He does not show any remorse of mind for the offences he had committed against God, for the injuries he had done to society, or for the ruin he had brought upon his own soul. He had no sorrow for sin, he had only a feeling of pain. He did not want to be delivered from his guilt, but only from punishment. But such had been his character in this world. The fact is, my brethren, we retain the same dispositions hereafter, that we cultivate here. It is utterly impossible, that the mere separation of the soul from matter, can make any alteration upon the essential qualities of the soul. We carry to the other world the same qualities, the same temper of mind, and the same character, that we have on earth. What manner of persons doth it become us then to be. As we now sow, hereafter we reap. Our heaven or our hell is already begun within us. The worm that never dies hath already begun to gnaw the heart of the wicked; and the good man hath already begun those hymns and hosannas of praise which shall employ him through eternity.

Son, remember that thou in thy lifetime receivedst thy good things. This answer of the Patriarch is remarkable for mildness. When a person by his imprudence and folly hath involved himself in a scene of distress, there is nothing more common than for those who visit him at such a time, to upbraid him with his bypast conduct in the severest manner, and to administer rebukes with acrimony and bitterness. Instead of giving their assistance to extricate him from his distresses, those miserable comforters push them deeper into the pit, and take a cruel pleasure in adding affliction to the afflicted, conscious that whilst they are insulting over their unfortunate brother, they are paying encomiums to their own superior prudence and discretion. This rich man had brought himself into the last of evils, into an evil that admitted of no remedy, by his own wickedness. Yet Abraham did not address him in this severe and insulting language. He calls him *son*, his descendant according to the flesh. The good Patriarch wanted not to add to the horrors of hell. The spirit of rage and rancor never gains admittance into the bosoms of the blessed. This shows us how different the meek, the gentle, and the benevolent temper is from that cruel and merciless zeal which often passeth for it upon earth.

His own petition being refused, the rich man now applies for his relations. VERSE 27. *Then he said, I pray thee therefore, father, that thou wouldst send him to my father's house.* Let no wicked man boast himself of possessing some virtues amid the number of his crimes. You see there is even some goodness in hell. The rich man retained still some affection for his brethren, and had a desire for their conversion. Though they had been partakers with him in his sins, he did not want them to be partakers of his punishment. The repetition of the request shows he was in earnest.

VERSE 31. *Neither will they be persuaded, though one rose from the dead.* As this is a point of great consequence, it requires to be illustrated at some length. Let us suppose, that in order to convince a person of the immortality of his soul, Almighty God sent one of his deceased friends, either in his unembodied state, or with the same body he had in life. As no person would require such a proof, but one who was very much addicted to skepticism, it is very probable, that even then his doubts would not be removed. He might say, this may be an impostor, perhaps this may be some evil spirit who has assumed the shape of my deceased friend.

But let us suppose that these doubts are removed, that he is convinced of the reality of the apparition, and the truth of a future state. Let us then see what effect it would have upon his life. He goes into company. He tells the story of the apparition to his companions. They hear it with derision and ridicule, and consider him as a visionary enthusiast, disturbed in his imagination. As the experience of all mankind is against him, and the laws appear to be fixed for ever, of no intercourse between this world and the next, in whatever companies he tells it, it meets with the same treatment, and all the effect of the apparition is, that it makes every one to conclude him to be beside himself. You all know how difficult it is to remain single in opinion against the whole world. It is still harder to become the object of laughter and ridicule; so that with these difficulties in his way, it is ten to one but he falls in with the opinion of the world, and believes the apparition to have been the phantom of his own fancy. That this is not a mere conjecture, but what would really happen, appears from undoubted matter of fact, that did really happen. You remember the history of Saul. When the Lord would not answer him by his prophets, he went in quest of a woman who had a familiar spirit. She raised up to him an apparition, which he believed to be the ghost of Samuel the prophet. The apparition assured him that his kingdom was departing from him, and that he had only one day longer to live. What effect had this upon the king? Did he repent of his sins? At first he was sore afraid, and was melancholy; but through the persuasion of his attendants, he soon resumed his joy; and, on the morrow after the battle was lost, in order to fulfil the prophecy of the devil, he proceeded to commit the most deliberate crime that can be perpetrated by man: he raised impious hands against his life, and plunged his sword in his own breast.

The fact is, my brethren, mankind are not always in a mood to be convinced. In spite of speculative opinion, men act from their passions, and bad passions will always produce bad actions, to the end of the world. The reluctance of mankind to assent to evidence, when it makes against their preconceived opinion, is remarkably apparent in the reception the Jews gave to our Saviour. All the prophecies concerning the Messiah were fulfilled in him. He appeared in the world in the precise time predicted for the coming of the Messiah; he was descended of the lineage of David; he was born in the city of Bethlehem. A prophet went before him in the spirit and power of Elias. He performed miracles and mighty works, which no man could perform. But after all these proofs, after all these miracles, the Jews, who expected their Messiah to be a temporal Prince, still demanded more evidence. "Show us," said they, "a sign from heaven." A sign from heaven they obtained. Now, in the presence of multitudes, a voice came from heaven, the voice of the Eternal, piercing the clouds, and proclaiming aloud, "This is my beloved Son!" Were they then convinced? No: they persecuted him with reproaches in his life, and at last brought him to an ignominious death. And when they had nailed him to the accursed tree, they still affirmed they would believe on him on proper evidence. "Let him come down from the cross, and we will believe on him." If he had come down from the cross, the redemption of mankind would have been defeated, as it was to be accomplished by his death; but he did more than come down from the cross. He rose from the dead. Did they then believe on him? No: they charged the soldiers who brought them the news of his resurrection, to give out that his disciples stole him away while they slept. Well then may we adopt the maxim of the Patriarch Abraham, and affirm, That if ye believe not Moses and the Prophets; if ye believe not Christ and his Apostles; ye will not be persuaded *though one rose from the dead.*

LECTURE IV.

ON THE PARABLE OF THE FOOLISH VIRGINS.

MATTHEW XXV. 1—10.

1 Then shall the kingdom of heaven be likened unto ten virgins, which took their lamps, and went forth to meet the bridegroom.
2 And five of them were wise, and five were foolish.
3 They that were foolish took their lamps, and took no oil with them:
4 But the wise took oil in their vessels with their lamps.
5 While the bridegroom tarried, they all slumbered and slept.
6 And at midnight there was a cry made, Behold, the bridegroom cometh; go ye out to meet him.
7 Then all those virgins arose, and trimmed their lamps.
8 And the foolish said unto the wise, Give us of your oil, for our lamps are gone out.
9 But the wise answered, saying, Not so; lest there be not enough for us and you: but go ye rather to them that sell, and buy for yourselves.
10 And while they went to buy, the bridegroom came; and they that were ready, went in with him to the marriage; and the door was shut.

IN a former lecture, I explained to you the nature, the origin, and the use of parables. They were the common vehicles of instruction among the oriental nations. The wisdom of the east loved to go adorned with flowers and with figures, and by means of the imagination to make its way to the heart. This mode of instruction was frequently honored by our Lord's adopting it. Accommodating himself to the practice of the east, and to the manners of the Jews, he wrapt up his wisdom in this veil, and delivered his doctrines to the people in parables. As men are much under the guidance of the external senses, and strongly impressed by the material objects around them, he who knew what was in man, and who laid hold of every avenue to the human heart, frequently addressed himself to this part of our frame. He spiritualizes the whole system of nature, he turns the most common and familiar occurrences of life into vehicles of Divine truth, and in the gentlest and most insinuating manner, leads us from earth to heaven.

In the parable which I have now read, the kingdom of Heaven, or dispensation of the Gospel, is likened to a marriage solemnity. On such occasions it was a custom among the Jews, that the bridegroom, in company with his friends, came late in the night to the house of the bride, where, upon a signal given, she and her bridemaids went out in procession to light him into the house, with great ceremony and splendor. It is said that *five of these virgins were wise, and that five of them were foolish.* I explained to you, on a former occasion, that, in a parable, we are not to apply particular expressions, but to consider the intention and design upon the whole. If we understood and applied this expression literally, we should be led to conclude that, under the New Testament, the number of the good and of the bad was equal. But to settle this point, to ascertain the number of those who are to be saved, and of those who are to be damned, was not the intention of our Lord in the parable. For, by the same way of arguing, we might infer from the parable of the talents, which immediately follows this, that the number of the good was double the number of the wicked, as there were two faithful servants who improved the talents committed to them, for one slothful servant who wrapt up his in a napkin; and in the parable of the marriage supper, in the foregoing chapter, amongst all the number of the guests who were called to the feast, there was only one who wanted the wedding garment: only from this general scheme of thought which runs through all our Lord's parables, from their being always framed with a view to the charitable side, we may safely draw two conclusions. In the *first* place, Let us always form a favorable judgment concerning the character and state of those who are externally decent, whether they agree or differ from us in opinion; and, if we do err, let us err on the side of charity. There are a set of men to be found in the world, who are remarkably fond of passing sentence and judgment upon the external state of their neighbors, and in passing this judgment, they attend not so much to the general tenor of life, and integrity of conduct, as to the system of doctrines which a man believes, and the sect or party in which he arranges himself. Unless you believe in every point precisely as they do, down you go in their estimation.

Rash and profane mortal, who gave thee a commission to fix the mark of election and reprobation upon men? Did Almighty God depute thee to draw the line betwixt the kingdom of darkness and the kingdom of light, to fill the heavens, and to people hell? We are astonished, and stand aghast at the boldness and impiety of the Roman Pontiff, who pretends to open and to shut the gate of mercy, and who arrogates to himself the keys of the kingdom of heaven. And yet thou who accusest him, art thyself equally guilty. Thou rushest unto the throne of the Eternal, and darest to direct the thunders of the Divine vengeance. Thou prescribest bounds to the mercy of the Omnipotent, and sayest to his saving grace, "Hitherto shalt thou come, and no farther." Vile worm! dost thou not tremble at thine own impiety? Fall prostrate in the dust. Shrink into thine own insignificance.' Let thy time be employed in working out thine own salvation, rather than in dealing of damnation to thy neighbors.

At the same time, though I condemn this rage which some men discover to condemn their neighbors, as, in my opinion, entirely inconsistent with the genius of the Gospel, and the spirit of Christianity, nevertheless I would not go into their extreme, and pass the same sentence on them which they pass upon others. To pass a judgment upon characters is a difficult task, and requires a very delicate hand. We ought to distinguish what flows from a narrowness of mind, from what flows from a badness of heart. We ought to make great allowances for the prejudices of education. If a man be educated in the belief, that none are to be saved but those who believe every article of that system which he embraces; if his judgment concerning the characters of men rest not upon the goodness of their lives, but upon the soundness of their belief, such a man's charity must be narrow and constrained. And this may sometimes be owing, not to the badness of his nature, but to the badness of his religious principles. And I have sometimes seen such persons, though I must acknowledge very rarely, striving and struggling to get the better of their system; the heart and the affections true to Christianity, whilst the mind was enslaved by the prejudices of education.

Verse 3. *They that were foolish took their lamps, and took no oil with them.* The foolish virgins seemed at first to resemble the wise, and shone out for a while with the same lustre. They made the same profession and appearance at first. Themselves were awake, and their lamps were burning. But they had no supply for the future. Their goodness was like the morning cloud, and soon vanished away. They had no real religion in the heart. They wanted that inward principle of grace, which can alone enable us to stand fast in the Lord. They were not rooted and grounded in the faith. They had no steady principles of conduct, nor settled habits of action. Like the seed which was sown in the stony ground, they forthwith sprang up, because they had no deepness of earth, and when the sun arose they withered away.

But the wise took oil in their vessels with their lamps. They sought and obtained the influences of the Divine Spirit to abide with them through life. They made a serious business of religion. They laid up a store of useful knowledge. They acted upon fixed and steady principles, and acquired habits of religion and virtue. They kept the heart well, knowing that out of it are the issues of life. They looked forwards to the time to come; they provided against the evil day, and extended their view to take in all the temptations and afflictions of human life.

Verse 5. *While the bridegroom tarried, they all slumbered and slept.* Whether we interpret this coming of the bridegroom, to be the second coming of our Lord to judge the world, or whether we apply it to our appearance before his tribunal at death, is a subject of no consequence; the material point to be considered is, that while the bridegroom tarried, all of them, the wise as well as the foolish virgins, slumbered and slept. The wise grew remiss and careless, and the spiritual life declined within them. The foolish virgins returned again to foolishness, and because the Lord delayed, because sentence against an evil work was not speedily executed, were fully bent to do evil. Seeing then that the wise virgins slumbered as well as the foolish; seeing that good men, as well as bad men, may fall into sin; a question, a very serious one, naturally arises: how shall we distinguish between those temporary relaxations in the Christian race, into which a good man may fall, from the final apostasy of the wicked; how shall we distinguish between the sins of infirmity, into which the best men may fall, from those sins which are unto death? And to this I beg your attention, as one of the most important subjects which can ever occupy your thoughts. In order to decide this question, Let me ask you, in the *first* place, What was the nature of your relapse into sin? There are times in which all men feel religious impressions and devout dispositions of mind. The seed is sown in stony places, as well as on the good ground. The influences of heaven descend on the barren desert, as well as on the field which is to be fruitful. On such occasions, the seed which was sown on the stony places will spring up for a time, and the barren desert will seem to bloom. To speak without a figure, the Spirit of God in one manner or another, in his common or in his special influences, descends upon all men. After such times of refreshing, the saint of a day, as well as the persevering Christian, will receive the word with gladness, and set about a thorough reformation. And as both of them receive the word with gladness, so both of them are subject to sin. Yet they are not alike in their errors. The sinner having no real principle at bottom, having no fixed plan of life, and but doing every thing by fits and starts, may, at the first approach of temptation, advance with swift steps to ruin. But the true Christian, laying his account to meet with hardships and temptations, prepares against them, and will not wholly fall off. The coward may at once desert his post, and fly from the banners of the Captain of salvation, to the standard of the prince of darkness: but the good soldier of Jesus will make head against the enemy; he will encounter his spiritual foe; he may be foiled for a moment, but he will never be subdued.

In the *second* place, Let me ask you, what is the state of your mind during these relapses? Are you in total subjection to the sins which have dominion over you? Is your conscience lulled in a profound sleep? Do you roll iniquity like a sweet morsel under your tongue? Do you find the ways of sin to be ways of pleasantness, and all her paths to be peace? Is your bondage sweet, and are the chains of your captivity become pleasant to you? Then I pronounce that there are no symptoms of spiritual life within you; then your sleep is unto death. But, on the other hand, is the dominion which sin has over you, against the bent of your soul? Whilst you sleep, does your heart wake? During your captivity, is your face towards Jerusalem? Do you lament the deceitfulness of your heart, the feebleness of your resolutions, and your own impotence to save yourself? Do you strive to burst asunder the bands which detain you? Then there is hope in Israel concerning you.

In the *third* place, Let me ask you, what is the nature of the sins into which you fall? Are they contrived beforehand, deliberate? Do you commit them with coolness and with consideration? Or are you led astray on a sudden by the strength of temptation, and power of prevailing passion? The best of men are subject to the impulse of passion; may yield to the strength of temptation, and be overtaken in a fault. But he is a wicked man who sins upon a plan; who makes a system of iniquity; who contrives scenes of mischief upon his bed, and who rises to execute with ardor what he has contrived with coolness. If the sun goes down upon thy wrath, or any other bad passion; if day unto day uttereth speech of your evil deeds; if night after night findeth you in the service of sin, then you are a sinner indeed, then you are in the gall of bitterness and in the bond of iniquity.

Let me ask again, What are the sins that most easily beset you? The sins of men may be divided into two classes.

The one kind flows from a good principle wrong directed, from the perversion and abuse of laudable inclinations; the other kind flows from evil principles and a bad heart. Of the latter kind, are malice, envy, treachery, cruelty, malignity, deceit, and hypocrisy. These indicate a mind which neither fears God nor regards man. The best Christians will at times fall into sins; but they will never harbor in their heart the dark offspring of hell. They may have the failings and the faults of men; but they will never have the crimes of devils, nor the spirit of the damned.

VERSE 6. *At midnight there was a cry heard.* At midnight, the hour of silence and repose, when the operations of nature seemed to stand still, and all things were at rest, when there was no expectation of any event, then was the cry heard, then was the alarm given—*Behold the bridegroom cometh, go ye out to meet him!* And indeed, my brethren, it often happens, that our last hour comes unexpected. When we are busied in some favorite scheme, when we are laying a scene of happiness which we expect will last for years, the awful voice comes, " This night thy soul shall be required of thee." I mention not this as if I thought it one of the evils of life. If we are prepared to die, a sudden death must be the most agreeable of all. The servant who is doing his duty, will be agreeably surprised at an unexpected visit from his master. The soldier whose arms are crowned with conquest, would be happy if his prince should suddenly come to be the witness of his victory.

VERSE 7. *Then all those virgins arose, and trimmed their lamps.* Their lamps were not gone out, though they were not burning bright. They soon arose and trimmed them, to meet the bridegroom. A good man is always habitually prepared for death. He has an interest in the righteousness of his Redeemer, which purchased life and immortality to men; and he is possessed of those good and holy dispositions which fit us for the inheritance of the saints in light. Such a person is ever in a state of preparation to meet with his Lord.

VERSE 8. *And the foolish virgins said unto the wise, Give us of your oil.* Mark here, my brethren, the triumph of religion. Wicked men at the last envy the state and the happiness of the good, and desire to partake in it. There is a time coming when those who scoff at religion, and laugh at every thing that is serious, will gladly say to those humble and contrite ones whom they now despise, " Give us of your oil." " Let us die the death of the righteous; let our last end be like his." " Would to God our souls were in your souls' place." Feeble and ineffectual wishes! which discover their misery, but which cannot save them from it.

VERSE 9. *Lest there be not enough for us and you.* There are no works of supererogation. After we have done all, we are unprofitable servants; and though we were perfect, we can assign no part of our righteousness to you: "*go to those that sell.*" Go to the ordinances of Divine appointment; improve those means of grace which you formerly despised; break off your sins by repentance; who knows if it be yet too late?—*Cætera desunt.*

LECTURE V.

ON THE TRANSFIGURATION OF JESUS CHRIST.

LUKE IX. 28—36.

28 And it came to pass, about an eight days after these sayings, he took Peter, and John, and James, and went up into a mountain to pray.
29 And as he prayed, the fashion of his countenance was altered, and his raiment was white and glistering.
30 And behold, there talked with him two men, which were Moses and Elias;
31 Who appeared in glory, and spoke of his decease which he should accomplish at Jerusalem.
32 But Peter, and they that were with him, were heavy with sleep: and when they were awake, they saw his glory, and the two men that stood with him.
33 And it came to pass, as they departed from him, Peter said unto Jesus, Master, it is good for us to be here; and let us make three tabernacles, one for thee, and one for Moses, and one for Elias: not knowing what he said.
34 While he thus spake, there came a cloud, and overshadowed them: and they feared as they entered into the cloud.
35 And there came a voice out of the cloud, saying, This is my beloved Son, hear him.
36 And when the voice was past, Jesus was found alone: and they kept it close, and told no man in those days any of those things which they had seen.

IN these verses, we have an account of a very remarkable event. Our Saviour having foretold his sufferings and death, in order to keep alive the faith and hopes of his disciples, who would be apt to despair under that mournful event, also foretold them, that some of their own number, before their departure, should behold him coming in his kingdom. "But I tell you of a truth, there be some standing here, which shall not taste of death till they see the kingdom of God."

As an accomplishment of this prediction, he takes his three favorite disciples, Peter, James, and John, and having carried them to an high mountain, was transfigured before their eyes, that he might give them some idea of the glory of that kingdom to which he was afterwards to ascend. The mountain here mentioned, by tradition, is Tabor, a hill of great beauty, and, according to Josephus, very high.

Many magnificent events in the Divine dispensations, have been transacted on hills. It was on mount Sinai that God descended to give the law: it was on the hill of Moriah that he commanded Isaac to be sacrificed: it was on the hill of Zion that he ordered the temple to be built: from the mount of Olives, Christ was wont to send up his prayers to Heaven; and on the mount Tabor he was transfigured, and appeared in glory to his disciples. This is founded upon nature. There is an air of grandeur in a lofty mountain, that loses itself in the heavens, and casteth its shadow into distant lands, which accords with the natural greatness of the soul, and awakens a feeling that is highly favorable to devotion. The grandeur, the awfulness, the silence, and the solitude of the scene, assist sentiments of religious adoration. Remote from man, and exalted above the turbulence of the inferior world, we breathe celestial air, we feel divinity more present, and bow down and worship in the temple not made with hands. Hence men, actuated by their natural feelings, and under the impressions of religious awe, have so often been guided to erect their temples upon hills, and to consecrate to the Deity such places as those, on which he had appeared, and where his footsteps were seen.

We are told, that our Saviour went up to this mountain to pray. Christ began all his great works with prayer to Heaven. Before he entered on his public ministry, he retired into the wilderness, and devoted forty days to contemplation and prayer. When he was about to suffer his last agony, he went and prayed in the garden. And here, when he enters upon his transfiguration, he went up to a mountain to pray. Illustrious example of piety and devotion! worthy the study and imitation of the world. If the eternal Son of God, the Mediator between God and man, who had no errors to be corrected, who had no sins to be forgiven, and who had few wants to be relieved, if he entered upon no important work without prayer to Heaven, if he spent whole nights in the fervor of devotion, shall men, shall feeble, indigent, and sinful men, dare to attempt works of importance, or rush into scenes of danger, without lifting up their eyes and hearts to Heaven, and imploring the protection and assistance of Providence? And yet it is to be dreaded that there are many persons who go under the name of Christians, who live in the constant and habitual neglect of this duty, who go out and come in, who rise up and lie down, without once bending the knee to the God of Heaven, and who, unless on this returning day, when they join in the public devotions of the Church, never acknowledge their dependence upon God. Far be such conduct from you, my brethren.

Peter, James, and John, were also chosen as the witnesses of our Saviour's agony. If they rejoiced with him on mount Tabor, they also suffered with him in the garden of Gethsemane. And indeed it seems to be one of the general laws by which this world is governed, that those who have the highest enjoyments should also have the deepest afflictions. Providence has wisely balanced human affairs, and set the day of prosperity against the day of adversity. The most enchanting hopes give rise to the most mortifying disappointments; the most transporting enjoyments end in the cruelest lassitude and disgust; and the highest honor is succeeded by the lowest disgrace. The same lively passions and fine feelings that give the greatest relish to prosperity, give also the severest smart to the wounds of adversity.

The transfiguration itself is next related. The evangelists seem to vie with one another in describing the glories of this scene. During this period, we are told, *the fashion of his countenance was altered; his face did shine as the sun, and his raiment was white as the snow.* When Moses received the law upon mount Sinai, his countenance shone in such a manner that the Israelites could not behold him. But a greater than Moses was here; and he was invested with greater majesty. The splendor of his Divinity shone through the veil with which it was clouded; he re-assumed some rays of that glory which he had with the Father before the world was; and he stood confessed the Son of the living God.

To heighten the grandeur and the solemnity of the scene, Moses, the giver of the law, and Elias, the greatest among the Prophets, descended from heaven, and conferred with him concerning his kingdom. It is usual for the chief ministers of a kingdom to resign the seals and badges of their authority to their successors in office. Thus, Moses and Elias, who had been the ministers of the kingdom of God under the Old Testament, the one representing the law, the other representing the prophets, resigned their authority to Jesus Christ, who was to reign for ever and ever. Had we, my brethren, been present on the mount of transfiguration, been spectators of this wonderful scene; had we beheld the glorified spirits of Moses and Elias, arrayed in the robes of heaven, and adorned with the beauties of immortality; had we beheld the Son of the Most High clothed with uncreated light, and appearing in the glories of Divinity unveiled; had we heard the voice of the Almighty proclaiming from the overshadowing cloud, *This is my beloved Son, hear him;* would we not have been thrown into that delightful amazement of soul that trance and ecstasy of spiritual joy, which the disciples were in when they cried out, not knowing what they said, *Lord, it is good for us to be here; let us build three tabernacles, one for thee, one for Moses, and one for Elias!*

The evangelist tells us, that the disciples were heavy with sleep, or rather heavy as with sleep; and Mark says that they were sore afraid. From comparing them together, it appears to have been a rapture and an astonishment that suspended all the powers of the soul, with a stillness similar to sleep. The sublime appearances which they saw struck a sudden terror into their minds, and occasioned that ecstasy of soul which holy men were generally in when they were favored with the visions of God. Moses and Elias were properly chosen as messengers to our Saviour, and witnesses of his transfiguration, as both of them were eminent types of Christ, acceptable to God for their faith and holiness, and admired by the Jews their countrymen, for the miracles which they had performed. Both of them were admitted to conference with God in Horeb; both of them had fasted forty days; both of them had divided the waters; they had been both the messengers of God to Kings; and as they were marvellous in their lives, so there was something extraordinary and miraculous in both their departures. Moses died at the commandment of the Lord, and was buried in a place which no man knew. Elias, without seeing death, was translated to heaven in a chariot of fire.

When this celestial triumvirate had assembled, what was the topic of their conversation? Did their discourse run upon the fate of empires and the fall of kings? Did they converse about the progress of the human genius, about the improvements of society, the inventions of art, and the discoveries of science? Did they talk of the glories of that heaven from which they had descended, or attempt a description of those mansions above, whose beauty eye hath not seen, and whose joys ear hath not heard? No, my brethren, an event greater than all these engaged their attention. *They talked of that decease or departure which our divine Redeemer was to accomplish at Jerusalem.* The prospect of suffering an ignominious and an accursed death, had always appeared to our Saviour a circumstance of distress, and filled him with dismal forebodings of mind. As the event drew nearer, these forebodings increased. The prospect of being forsaken, denied, and betrayed by his friends; of being mocked and tortured and crucified by his enemies; the terrors of the hour and power of darkness; the agony in the garden; the horrors of the cross; the assault of devils and wicked spirits; and, far above all, the hiding of his Father's countenance, and drinking the cup of the wrath of God; these were circumstances of tremendous suffering, sufficient to have overwhelmed his human nature with horror and despair.

But as an angel was sent to comfort him in the garden, so here two illustrious saints descended from heaven to allay the terrors of that decease which he was to accomplish at Jerusalem. They might represent his passion to him as entering into the councils of heaven before the world began; as the hope and expectation of all the patriarchs and prophets and righteous men under the law; as the accomplishment of all the prophecies delivered to the Old Testament Church; as the fulfilment of all the types and prefigurations of the Mosaic institution; as the consummation of the legal economy, and period of the Jewish Church; and as the commencement of a new age and higher order of events. They might place it before his eyes as confirming his doctrine from above; as magnifying the law and making it honorable; as rendering glory to God in the highest, and restoring peace on earth, and good-will towards men; as conquering the principalities and powers of darkness, and setting open the gates of paradise for all the faithful to enter in. They might set it before his eyes as the means of overthrowing the kingdom of Satan; as diffusing light and life and salvation through the world; as uniting the nations in the bonds of charity and love; as being the great theme to the Church universal under the New Testament; as affording a subject for new hymns and anthems to the heavenly host; as reaching beyond the circle of time, and drawing hosannas of praise from the heirs of immortality, through the round of everlasting ages. These considerations would comfort our Redeemer under the forebodings of his passion; and the prospect of the joy that was set before him would animate and strengthen him to endure the cross, to despise the shame, and to finish the work which the Father gave him to do.

Seeing then that the death and passion of our Saviour is an event of such infinite importance, let us, my brethren, make it the theme of our praise, and the subject of our contemplation. Let us frequently call to mind that scene which mount Calvary beheld, the sufferings that our Saviour there endured, the groans that he uttered, and the blood that he shed on our behalf. Let us dwell on that marvellous love which moved him to undergo such unutterable agonies, till we feel its transforming power and efficacy, and are changed into the same image from glory to glory: that so the cross of Christ, which was to the Jews a stumbling-block, and to the Greeks foolishness, may become to us the wisdom and the power of God.

VERSE 36. *And they kept it close, and told no man.* Though they were so highly favored of their Lord, allowed to behold him in the glories of his future kingdom, and to hold converse with two illustrious messengers from the mansions above, nevertheless they made no merit of the preference that was shown them, and even concealed from the world that they were distinguished from the rest of the apostles. Such, my brethren, is the uniform conduct of good Christians. The manifestations of heaven only inspire them with humility. He is but a novice in the school of Christianity, who is puffed up by any privileges which he has attained. Greater degrees of grace, and higher attainments in virtue, banish all self-conceit and spiritual pride. This holds in other matters as well as in religion. The pretender always outdoes the real character. The actor always exceeds nature, and goes beyond the life. In friendship, those who have least of the reality, have generally most of the appearance and pretence. Men of the greatest talents and abilities appear in conversation but like other men; whilst fools and coxcombs assume those airs of superiority, and that tone of solemn pedantry, which amazes the ignorant. This holds even in infidelity itself. Those wretches, who set their mouths against the heavens, and profess open impiety, are generally hypocrites in wickedness, who believe and tremble when alone, and are in the horrors whenever they are left in the dark.

Beware therefore of a form of religion without the power thereof. The voice of true piety is not heard in the streets. She sounds no trumpet before her, affects no appearances, and lays claim to no distinctions. Those persons are always to be suspected who covet the public eye; who make a show of their sanctity, and who endeavor to dazzle the world with the pomp and the parade of godliness. Let men discover your piety and virtue; do not you discover them yourselves. There is all the difference in the world betwixt being exemplary and being ostentatious. When the angels descended of old, they were in form and appearance like men; but when the devil appeared, he transformed himself into an angel of light.

www.ingramcontent.com/pod-product-compliance
Lightning Source LLC
LaVergne TN
LVHW021104110826
845150LV00001B/164

* 9 7 8 1 4 2 5 5 6 5 3 4 3 *